17183

DOCUMENTS ON
GERMAN FOREIGN POLICY
1918–1945

FROM THE ARCHIVES OF THE
GERMAN FOREIGN MINISTRY

UNITED STATES
GOVERNMENT PRINTING OFFICE
WASHINGTON : 1950

DEPARTMENT OF STATE

Publication 3838

For sale by the
Superintendent of Documents
Government Printing Office
Washington 25, D. C.
Price $3.25 (Buckram)

BOARD OF EDITORS[1]

DOCUMENTS ON GERMAN FOREIGN POLICY
1918–1945

SERIES D (1937–1945)

VOLUME III

GERMANY AND THE SPANISH CIVIL WAR
1936–1939

CONTENTS

GENERAL INTRODUCTION

In June 1946 the British Foreign Office and the United States Department of State agreed to publish jointly documents from captured archives of the German Foreign Ministry and the Reich Chancellery. Although the captured archives go back to the year 1867, it was decided to limit the present publication to papers relating to the years after 1918, since the object of the publication was "to establish the record of German foreign policy preceding and during World War II." The editorial work was to be performed "on the basis of the highest scholarly objectivity." The editors were to have complete independence in the selection and editing of the documents. Publication was to begin and be concluded as soon as possible. Each Government was "free to publish separately any portion of the documents."[1] In April 1947 the French Government, having requested the right to participate in the project, accepted the terms of this agreement.

The three Governments realized the unique nature of the enterprise. Captured enemy documents had been published in the past, and especially by the Germans themselves, but only documents which supported a propaganda thesis. Never had three victorious powers set out to establish the full record of the diplomacy of a vanquished power from captured archives "on the basis of the highest scholarly objectivity."

The editors wish to state at the outset that they have not only been permitted, but enjoined, to make their selection on this basis alone. In the selection of documents for publication, and in the editing of the documents, the editors have had complete freedom. No effort has been made at any time by any of the participating Governments to influence their work. The editors, therefore, accept complete responsibility for the volumes as published.

II

The archives of the German Foreign Ministry came into Anglo-American custody partly as a result of planning, partly by accident, but chiefly through the incomplete execution of orders to destroy the most important portions. During hostilities, the Allied military forces were instructed to keep close watch for enemy archives, and

---

[1] It was in accordance with this provision that the Department of State, in January 1948, published the volume of documents entitled *Nazi-Soviet Relations, 1939–1941.*

teams of experts were assembled behind the lines so that the examination of captured documents might begin without delay. In April 1945 units of the United States First Army discovered more than 300 tons of Foreign Ministry papers in various storage places in the Harz Mountains. The Anglo-American experts were immediately summoned. They located other parts of the archives in the Harz Mountains and Thuringia. Their most important discoveries were a box containing memoranda summarizing conversations of Hitler and Ribbentrop with foreign statesmen, and a quantity of German microfilm which, when made into continuous rolls and printed at the Air Ministry in London, was found to record some 10,000 pages of the working files of the Foreign Minister (*Büro RAM*).

Under the supervision of the Anglo-American experts, the captured archives were assembled at Marburg Castle, in the American zone of Germany. Later the collection was moved to Berlin. Finally, in the summer of 1948, the archives were moved to England, where they are to remain until conditions in Germany become more stable. Between 1945 and 1948 the collection was augmented by many tons of Reich Chancellery documents and other smaller collections.

III

When the Foreign Ministry archives were captured in April 1945, the question was considered whether they had been deliberately placed in the path of the Anglo-American armies and spurious documents added to the collection, with the purpose of sowing discord among the enemies of Germany. Documentary evidence and interrogation of surviving German officials have completely dispelled these suspicions. Actually, the German Government made efforts to prevent the capture of the documents, both by moving them from place to place and by ordering the destruction of the files for the Nazi period only a few days before the arrival of the American First Army.

The dispersal of the archives began in 1943, when the air attacks on German cities had become intense. It was then decided to keep only a skeleton staff and the current files of the Foreign Ministry in Berlin; the rest of the staff with their files were moved to less vulnerable parts of Germany. Most went to Krummhübel, a resort in the Riesengebirge, but some branch offices were sent as far away as Lake Constance. The archives were also dispersed to castles in the Harz and south and east of Berlin. In the summer and autumn of 1944 the Soviet advance enforced the transfer of those archives which had been stored south and east of Berlin to the Harz region. Orders were given for the destruction of the non-essential secret documents at Krummhübel and for the removal of the remainder to Thuringia. It is impossible to determine with precision what was destroyed by accident or design in the hurried movement which followed. It is known that these transfers were not entirely completed before the arrival of Soviet troops. Only in the early months of 1945, therefore, were the Foreign Ministry archives concentrated in the west.

By spring the German armies were in full retreat. Early in April 1945 the evacuation center at Meisdorf received a list of categories of documents which were to be prepared for destruction. These included all important files for the Nazi period. On April 10 an order was received by telephone to commence immediately the destruction of these categories. When the American troops arrived a few days later, only a small fraction had actually been destroyed.

IV

Including the accessions received since April 1945, the captured documents now in the joint custody of the United States Department of State and the British Foreign Office weigh about 400 tons. The tens of thousands of bundlés of papers have been repeatedly packed, moved by train, truck, or plane, and then unpacked and shelved. The packing, the moving, the unpacking, and the shelving were done hurriedly, under war conditions. Until the contents of every bundle in the collection have been examined, therefore, it will not be possible to be certain that the selection for publication has been made from all the surviving documents on a particular problem or year.

An analysis of the files in Anglo-American custody is appended to volumes I (p. 1177) and II (p. 1021) of this series. A summary of this analysis reveals the following situation: For the years from 1867 to 1920 the collection seems complete; there are gaps in the files dealing with 1920–1936, but they appear to be relatively unimportant. Thereafter, the gaps become increasingly a problem. Fortunately many copies were made of most documents, and it is possible to find enough papers in other files to fill in the significant lines of the picture. This or that document may be lost completely, but other documents give the essential material. That is not always true, but until 1940 it is usually true. After 1940, and until 1943, one is continually reminded of a half-finished picture: the outlines are obvious; some parts are completed with minute detail; other parts are only sketched in; there are blank spaces. From 1943 the materials are fragmentary, but peculiarly valuable because there is so little other evidence on these years.

The most important defect of the captured archives for the period from 1936 is the absence of the registers and journals in which were recorded the departmental file number and the distribution of each paper, with a summary of its contents. The captured Foreign Ministry archives are not a single, coherently organized file of the Ministry as a whole. They are the working files of officials, such as the Foreign Minister and the State Secretary; of parts of the Ministry, such as those of the Political Department and the Legal Department. The documents in these captured files are arranged so as to facilitate the work of these individual departments and officials: sometimes the arrangement is alphabetical (by countries, by subjects, or by individuals), sometimes it is chronological, sometimes it is topical. Sometimes secret papers are segregated; sometimes they are not. The captured documents do not, therefore, constitute a central Ministerial file, and there is no uniform filing system. There is no place where, for instance, all the telegrams from the Embassy in London may be found. Ten or twenty copies of one telegram may be found in various files; the only surviving copy of another telegram may be found in the file of another mission abroad to which it was sent for information (bearing the departmental file number, and not the telegram number given in London); occasionally no copy can be found.

Theoretically, the registers and journals could be reconstructed by collating the surviving files, but the resources for this gigantic task are not available. As their work in the Foreign Ministry archives progresses, the editors are learning from experience which departments, individuals, and missions abroad were likely to receive copies of papers, and where the papers were likely to be filed. Beginning with series D, volume III, it is possible to make a clear distinction between papers which are not printed because unimportant, and papers not printed because not found. In volumes I and II of series D it was not possible to make this distinction with confidence, so the footnote "Not printed" was used for both categories of omission.

Some of the documents missing from the Foreign Ministry archives are in the possession of the Soviet Government, but the extent of its collection is not known. Beginning in June 1946 the Soviet Government published several volumes of German Foreign Ministry documents. Usually, but not always, other copies of these documents are in the Foreign Ministry files, together with other much more voluminous material on the same subject.

V

The editors learned only by trial and error the limitations of the available material and the difficulties inherent in exploiting disordered and incomplete archives. The filming of the Foreign Ministry archives, begun in 1945 by American and British experts for intelligence purposes, and continued by historians representing the three Governments participating in the publication of these records, will facilitate scholarly investigation in the future. More than a million pages of the most important documents for the years from 1914 to 1945 have by now been preserved on microfilm.

At the outset, the selection of documents for publication was made from these microfilms by historians working in London, Paris, and Washington. It was found, however, that this method was too cumbersome, and all except the final selection is now made by an international team of American, British, and French historians working on the original files. In the work of the tripartite team, and in the periodic conferences of the editors-in-chief, the international character of historical scholarship is convincingly demonstrated.

VI

In selecting documents for publication the fundamental test has been their value for an understanding of German foreign policy. Since the German estimate of the policy of other powers was one of the most important factors shaping German policy, these estimates have been included. They should, of course, be viewed with caution. Very often German diplomats wrote what they thought would please Hitler. Even those who wished to convey unpleasant truths used language which would carry conviction to the Nazi Party leaders.

Even so far as German foreign policy is concerned it is necessary to remember the peculiar characteristics of Nazi diplomacy. A large proportion of the officials in the Foreign Ministry and of the German representatives abroad were career diplomats who were kept at their posts only because Hitler found them indispensable. He did not trust them, sometimes with reason, and he often kept them in ignorance of his intentions. The attentive reader will frequently see evidence of this situation and will realize that their reports and instructions do not always reflect the actual policy of the Reich.

Two categories of evidence which bulk large in the archives of the German Foreign Ministry find little place in these volumes: the press summary and the intelligence report. Undoubtedly a minute examination of the material in the press summaries and of the rumor and gossip set down in tens of thousands of reports by confidential agents will some day yield results of significance for an understanding of German policy. But such an examination requires study of all the evidence, and all the evidence would fill hundreds of volumes. This is true also of the analyses produced by the prolific and imaginative members of Ribbentrop's private information service, the *Dienststelle Ribbentrop*. The editors have agreed, therefore, that press summaries, intelligence reports, and the analyses prepared in the *Dienststelle Ribbentrop* will be included only where there is clear evidence that they directly influenced German policy.

Even after excluding all but a few examples from this material, the sheer mass of evidence presents baffling problems. In this age of shorthand and the typewriter, documents grow in number and length.

Bismarck's conversations were usually summarized in a few hundred words; the summaries of Hitler's conversations often run to thousands of words. When Embassy reports are dictated, a lengthy report requires less thought and time than a brief report. The editors have often been tempted to summarize, or to print excerpts, but they have decided to do neither. Except in a few cases, which are clearly indicated, every document has been printed without omissions or alterations. In every case, too, significant material such as file numbers and marginal comments have been included. Where there is no important difference between the preliminary draft and the dispatch as sent, the latter has been preferred; where there are differences, they have been described. To save space the telegraphic summary has been used if it includes all essential points; otherwise, the detailed report has been used; if the telegraphic summary is not complete, but action was taken before the report was received, both the telegram and the report are printed.

The order in which documents should be presented in a collection such as this has long been a disputed subject among historians. The editors agreed that documents should be grouped by topics, but within each topic they are presented in the chronological order in which they originated. In this volume the Spanish Civil War is considered a single topic, and the chronological order of the documents has been followed. It should be borne in mind that a report from a mission abroad might be received after action had been taken in Berlin, although the report bears an earlier date than the document recording the action. Where the date of receipt in Berlin can be determined, it is given. Each document is preceded by an editorial heading and by reference to the serial number of the film and the frame number on the film.[2] A list of film serial numbers is appended to each volume, showing the description of the corresponding German Foreign Ministry file; this permits identification of the location in the archives of the copy of the document published. As each volume is published, the pertinent films will be made available for study by scholars so that the specialist may be able to fill in the details of the record.

Because the immediate origins of the Second World War, and the course of the war, are of most immediate interest and of most obvious importance, the editors have decided to begin their work with the fourth series (D). This series will include documents dating from 1936 or 1937, the starting point depending on the topic, and continuing through the war. The three series of volumes to be published subsequently will include the documents for the earlier years.

---

[2] For an explanation of these terms, see appendix II.

VII

After the joint selection of documents to be included in a volume is completed, the task of preparing the editorial notes is entrusted to the editors in one of the three capitals, subject to review by the other editors. Similarly, the task of preparing the English translation is divided by volumes, or sections of a volume. Each volume will contain a statement on responsibility for the notes and translations.

Translation from the German presents peculiar difficulties, particularly since, under Hitler, there was no one style of diplomatic German, as there had been under Bismarck. Some of the writers use "Nazi German," which conveys only a foggy impression in German and translates into completely opaque English. The translation is therefore often inelegant, but the editors believe that where the meaning is clear in German the English can be understood. In general, they have preferred to sacrifice grace to precision. Paraphrase has been used only where the German is clear but exact translation resulted in ambiguity.

The parallel series in German, giving the original text of the documents, will enable those interested to check the translation.

In printing the translated version of the documents the editors have not aimed at giving a facsimile reproduction of the German original as regards arrangement and spacing. All important notes and marginalia are, however, included either in the text or as footnotes, the only exception being purely routine notations.

The editorial notes have been kept to the minimum necessary for the factual elucidation of the text. They do not attempt interpretation except where this is necessary to establish the date or identity of a document. No attempt is made to correct German reports by reference to other sources, even when the German reports present a false or one-sided picture. It is as a source-book for the study of history, and not as a finished interpretation of history, that these documents are presented.

VII

After the final selection of the documents to be included in a volume is completed, the task of preparing the edited text is entrusted to one of the three typists, subject to review by the editor-in-chief. Similarly, the task of translating the English transla-tion. Similarly, the task of assigning of a volume. Each volume will contain a translation responsibility for the notes and typescript. Translation from the German has its peculiar difficul-ties, since under Hitler there was no normal loss of diplomatic Ger-man, as there had been in her literature. Some of the writers use "Next German," which sometimes gets a freer expression in learned and transcision into quaintly modern English. The translation is literatum from German but the editor believes that where the mean-ing in German can be understood. In general, the ... have preferred the original when in possession. Paraphrase has been used only where the German is clear but exact translation re-sulted in stilted style.

The parallel expression in texts giving the original text of the docu-ment will assist those interested in the free translation.

In printing the translated version of the documents the editors have not aimed at giving a facsimile reproduction of the German containing every misprint and meaning. All important notes and marginalia in the originals were included either in the text or in foot-notes, the early omission being purely a matter of notations.

The editorial efforts have been kept to the minimum necessary for the factual elucidation of the text. They do not attempt importa-tion except where it seems necessary to establish the date or identity of a document. No attempt is made to correct German reports by reference to other sources even when the German reports present a false or one-sided picture. It is as a source-book for the study of history and not as a finished interpretation of history, that these documents are presented.

PREFACE TO VOLUME III, SERIES D

The documents printed in this volume have been selected by the British, French, and United States editors acting jointly. The translations were made in the Division of Language Services of the Department of State and reviewed by the British and United States editors, who are also responsible jointly for the editorial notes and footnotes.

Although series D of this publication is, in general, intended to provide knowledge of German foreign policy from the autumn of 1937 to the end of World War II in 1945, a volume dealing with the policy pursued by Germany during the Spanish Civil War logically begins in July 1936, when the Civil War broke out. It extends to July 1939.

The documents first make clear the German attitude toward the revolt against the Spanish Government by certain generals, pass on to the appeal of General Franco to Hitler for assistance, which was conveyed by a German businessman, Johannes Bernhardt, and then indicate Hitler's reply; they also describe the organization of the Spanish trading company Hisma, and its German counterpart Rowak, to promote the exchange of German military supplies for Spanish raw materials and concessions. Other subjects illustrated are the beginnings of German military aid to the Franco regime, the recognition of that Government by Germany, and the proposals for securing the non-intervention of the powers in the Spanish conflict. After these issues, the documents deal with the alleged attacks on German naval vessels off the coasts of Spain and with the Nyon conference of September 1937, which met to consider the attacks on merchant vessels by submarines.

It is clear from the documents that relations were not always smooth between the Germans and their Italian allies in Spain and that the Germans exerted extreme pressure on the Franco regime in order to be assured of economic advantages, especially mining concessions, in Spain after a Franco victory. The documents also indicate that the Germans were not always satisfied with General Franco's attitude, particularly during the Munich crisis of September 1938, and that they did not feel fully assured of Franco's victory until the final Catalonian offensive of the Nationalists which began late in December 1938.

For the final period of the Civil War, the documents are concerned with German efforts to secure repayment for assistance, Spanish ad-

XVII

herence to the Anti-Comintern Pact, the victory celebration of the Condor Legion, and the failure of arrangements for the widely heralded meeting of Göring and Franco.

In spite of its obvious interest it has not been possible, from lack of space, to cover fully the extended negotiations in which Germany had a part by reason of membership in the Non-Intervention Committee, though numerous documents have been printed. Some further information on these negotiations has been supplied in editorial notes.

ANALYTICAL LIST OF DOCUMENTS

Chapter I. The First Phase: July 19–November 18, 1936—Continued

CHAPTER I. THE FIRST PHASE: JULY 19–NOVEMBER 18, 1936—Continued

CHAPTER I. THE FIRST PHASE: JULY 19–NOVEMBER 18, 1936—Continued

CHAPTER I. THE FIRST PHASE: JULY 19–NOVEMBER 18, 1930—Continued

CHAPTER I. THE FIRST PHASE: JULY 19–NOVEMBER 18, 1936—Continued

CHAPTER I. THE FIRST PHASE: JULY 19–NOVEMBER 18, 1936—Continued

CHAPTER II. GERMAN RECOGNITION OF THE FRANCO REGIME, AND ITS RESULTS;
NOVEMBER 18, 1936–MARCH 20, 1937—Continued

Chapter II. German Recognition of the Franco Regime, and Its Results;
November 18, 1936–March 20, 1937—Continued

CHAPTER III. GERMAN-NATIONALIST TIES STRENGTHENED; THE MARCH AND JULY
PROTOCOLS: MARCH 20–JULY 16, 1937—Continued

CHAPTER III. GERMAN-NATIONALIST TIES STRENGTHENED; THE MARCH AND JULY
PROTOCOLS: MARCH 20–JULY 16, 1937—Continued

CHAPTER III. GERMAN-NATIONALIST TIES STRENGTHENED; THE MARCH AND JULY
PROTOCOLS: MARCH 20–JULY 16, 1937—Continued

CHAPTER III. GERMAN-NATIONALIST TIES STRENGTHENED; THE MARCH AND JULY
PROTOCOLS: MARCH 20–JULY 16, 1937—Continued

CHAPTER III. GERMAN-NATIONALIST TIES STRENGTHENED; THE MARCH AND JULY
PROTOCOLS: MARCH 20–JULY 16, 1937—Continued

CHAPTER IV. THE POWERS AND NON-INTERVENTION: JULY 19–NOVEMBER 1, 1937—Continued

CHAPTER IV. THE POWERS AND NON-INTERVENTION: JULY 19–NOVEMBER 1, 1937—Continued

CHAPTER IV. THE POWERS AND NON-INTERVENTION: JULY 19–NOVEMBER 1, 1937—Continued

CHAPTER IV. THE POWERS AND NON-INTERVENTION: JULY 19–NOVEMBER 1,
1937—Continued

CHAPTER V. GERMAN ECONOMIC PRESSURE ON FRANCO: NOVEMBER 4, 1937–
MARCH 10, 1938—Continued

CHAPTER VI. CONTINUED AID TO FRANCO AND NEGOTIATIONS FOR A TREATY:
MARCH 16–DECEMBER 19, 1938—Continued

CHAPTER VI. CONTINUED AID TO FRANCO AND NEGOTIATIONS FOR A TREATY: MARCH 16–DECEMBER 19, 1938—Continued

CHAPTER VI. CONTINUED AID TO FRANCO AND NEGOTIATIONS FOR A TREATY:
MARCH 16–DECEMBER 19, 1938—Continued

CHAPTER VI. CONTINUED AID TO FRANCO AND NEGOTIATIONS FOR A TREATY:
MARCH 16–DECEMBER 19, 1938—Continued

CHAPTER VII. THE CATALONIAN CAMPAIGN AND THE END OF THE WAR:
DECEMBER 23, 1938–MARCH 31, 1939—Continued

CHAPTER VIII. GERMAN WITHDRAWAL FROM SPAIN: APRIL 2–JULY 8, 1939—Con.

CHAPTER VIII. GERMAN WITHDRAWAL FROM SPAIN: APRIL 2–JULY 8, 1939—Con.

CHAPTER VIII. GERMAN WITHDRAWAL FROM SPAIN: APRIL 2–JULY 8, 1939—Con.

CHAPTER VIII. GERMAN WITHDRAWAL FROM SPAIN: APRIL 2–JULY 8, 1939—Con.

CHAPTER I

THE FIRST PHASE
JULY 19–NOVEMBER 18, 1936

[EDITORS' NOTE. Following preliminary outbreaks, full-scale revolt spread over Spain on July 18 and 19, 1936. The revolt had no acknowledged leader; in the early days there were several officers with regional authority, notably General Franco in southwestern Spain, General Queipo de Llano in Seville, and General Mola in northern Spain. On July 25 a Junta was organized at Burgos. General Franco became a member of the Junta early in August, and on October 1 he became commander in chief of the Nationalist Army and assumed the title of Chief of the Spanish State.

The documents examined in the archives of the German Foreign Ministry do not disclose evidence of German assistance to the Spanish rebels prior to the outbreak of hostilities.[1] From interrogations and other captured enemy documents it appears that Hitler promised assistance within a few days after the outbreak of the revolt. About July 22, 1936, Franco sent a German businessman resident in Morocco, Johannes Bernhardt, and the local Nazi Ortsgruppenleiter, Adolf Langenheim, to Germany by air to request planes and other assistance,

---

[1] There may be noted, however, the following passage in a private letter of July 6, 1936, from Secretary of Legation von Bülow to the German Counselor of Embassy in Spain, Voelckers (47/31583–85) : ". . . Solely for your information, in case the people involved should approach you too, I inform you further at Dumont's urging that the latter had a visit from a certain Walter Wagner some time ago. Wagner told a highly romantic story, according to which Wagner's father-in-law, a Herr Fehndrich, whom you presumably know, together with a Spaniard by the name of Torroba, allegedly is negotiating here with a certain Herr Feltjen, an airplane manufacturer. The negotiations concern weapons for the Spanish Fascists which were to be delivered to Spain by a German submarine. The Ortsgruppenleiter in Barcelona is supposed to have approved the plan. The whole thing probably amounts to some big gunrunning deal, if only because, as I have heard from friends of mine elsewhere, Herr Feltjen is said to ply this laudable trade most zealously. Here, we have all kept our hands off the matter, of course, and indicated to the gentlemen that the Foreign Ministry has not the slightest interest in it. It may be, however, that they will approach you as well, and that you will hear something more about the matter. In such a case, I should be grateful if you would inform my successor, Sandro Dörnberg. The latter will step into my shoes July 15, since I am going to Sofia around the middle of the month as successor to Prince Schaumburg. . . ."

1

and through the agency of the Auslandsorganisation they quickly were admitted to the presence of Hitler and Göring.[2]

Promises of assistance were obtained and there was established for the conduct of the necessary operations the firm Hisma, Ltda., a contraction of Compañía Hispano-Marroquí de Transportes, in which Herr Bernhardt quickly won a powerful position. As early as August 2, 1936, Hisma began the transport of rebel troops from Morocco to Spain, and the firm was soon active in many fields of Spanish economic life. Another company, Rowak (Rohstoffe-und-Waren-Einkaufsgesellschaft), was organized with Göring's assistance to handle the German end of the economic cooperation with the rebels. Eventually, in 1937, when Bernhardt's expanding interests had resulted in the formation of other Spanish companies, these were grouped within a new holding company, the Sociedad Financiera Industrial Ltda. (Sofindus). These three names—Hisma, Rowak, and Sofindus—will recur in the documents printed in this volume.]

---

[2] An account of these events appears in a document of the Präsidialkanzlei of the Führer and Chancellor dated July 5, 1939, entitled "Recommendations for Decorations in Connection with the Conclusion of the Spanish Civil War." In recommending decorations for two members of the Auslandsorganisation, Dr. Wolfgang Kraneck and Robert Fischer, the document reviews the course of events at the end of July 1936:

"At that time Herr Langenheim and Herr Bernhardt, Party comrades of the Auslandsorganisation of the NSDAP, arrived in Berlin from Spain with a letter from General Franco to the Führer. After Gauleiter Bohle had been informed, a long conference took place with the Führer's Deputy, who as a result directed that the letter should be delivered to the Führer immediately by several Party comrades. At the direction of the Führer's Deputy, Herren Langenheim and Bernhardt were accompanied by Herren Burbach, Dr. Kraneck, and Fischer, who were at that time Amtsleiter on the staff of the Auslandsorganisation and who, by virtue of their duties, were in a position to give an opinion on questions which might arise.

"The first interview with the Führer, on which occasion the letter was delivered, took place in Bayreuth in the late evening of the same day, after the Führer's return from the theater. Immediately thereafter the Führer summoned Field Marshal Göring, the then War Minister Colonel General von Blomberg, and an admiral who was present in Bayreuth. That night support for the Generalissimo was agreed to in principle, while additional details were worked out during the course of the following day.

"This train of events, and particularly the fact that the support came about through the efforts of the leadership of the Auslandsorganisation, is little known and should even today be treated confidentially."

No. 1

654/256243

The Chargé d'Affaires in Spain to the Foreign Ministry

Telegram

No. 119 of July 19   SAN SEBASTIÁN, July 19, 1936—2 : 00 p.m.
Received July 24—12 : 05 p.m.
Pol. III 290.

With reference to our report No. 2530 [1] of July 15 to the Foreign Ministry.

Beginning yesterday, the expected military revolts have broken out all over Spain. In so far as it is possible to verify reports in spite of the blocking of all postal, telephone, and rail traffic, the movement began with the uprising of the Foreign Legion in Morocco, which attempted a landing at Málaga as well. At the same time there were local revolts of the garrisons at Madrid, Barcelona, Seville, Granada, Burgos, Pamplona, San Sebastián, etc. The Government ordered the men released from allegiance to their officers, had the officers arrested with the help of police and workers' militia, and announced over the radio that it was in control of the situation. The extent of the losses is not known so far; martial law has been declared. The Marxist unions, in accordance with an appeal by the Government, today announced a general strike.

The radio announced reorganization of the Government under Martínez Barrio with Azcarate as Minister for Foreign Affairs and Barcia as Minister of the Interior. [2]

VOELCKERS

---

[1] Not printed (654/256250–57). It was an analysis of conditions in Spain following the death of Calvo Sotelo during the night of July 12–13; it contained, however, only a vague allusion to the possibility of revolt. The report was received in Berlin on July 26.

[2] Marginal note: "The telegram of July 19 received here today, July 24, has been superseded by events. File. D[umont] July 24."

No. 2

4793/E236218

The Consul at Tetuán to the Foreign Ministry

Telegram

No. 5 of July 22   TANGIER, July 22, 1936—8 : 58 p.m.
Received July 23, 1936—1 : 45 a.m.
Po. I 960 g.

Lieutenant Colonel Beigbeder has asked me to forward the following very secret dispatch:

"For Military Attaché General Kühlental:[1]

"General Franco and Lieutenant Colonel Beigbeder send greetings to their friend, the honorable General Kühlental, inform him of the new Nationalist Spanish Government, and request that he send ten troop-transport planes with maximum seating capacity through private German firms.

"Transfer by air with German crews to any airfield in Spanish Morocco. The contract will be signed afterwards.

"Very urgent! On the word of General Franco and Spain."

For the Consul:
WEGENER

---

[1] Military Attaché of the German Embassy in France, also accredited to Portugal.

No. 3

654/256241–42

The Ambassador in France to the Foreign Ministry

Telegram

No. 370 of July 23   PARIS, July 23, 1936.
Received July 23—9 : 35 a.m.
Pol. III 277.

I have learned in strict confidence that the French Government declared itself prepared to supply the Spanish Government with considerable amounts of war matériel during the next few days. Approximately 30 bombers, several thousand bombs, a considerable number of 75-millimeter guns, etc., are involved. At the outbreak of the revolt the Government's enemies supposedly destroyed the majority of the planes at the Madrid airport. On the other hand Franco is supposedly trying to buy 12 bombers, since he has only a small number of planes at his disposal.

Franco's situation is likely to deteriorate decisively especially as the result of the supplying of bombers to the Government.[1]

WELCZECK

---

[1] Marginal note: "At 7 : 00 p.m. Count Welczeck reported by telephone that a member of the Cabinet had expressly confirmed to him the fact reported above.

"Herr von Dörnberg personally took the above telegram to Herr Schellert in the War Ministry and informed him of the supplementary telephone report. Moreover, at the instruction of Ministerialdirektor Dieckhoff, I informed the Embassy at London by telephone that we had learned from Paris 'from a fully reliable source' that the French Government had 'declared itself prepared . . . .'

"I was only able to reach Chancellor [Kanzler—title of a clerical official] Achilles, who took down the conversation, including the supplementary report and the statement that Ministerialdirektor Dieckhoff asks Prince Bismarck to take up this matter with the Foreign Office as soon as possible.

"Any further distribution is superfluous—at least at the moment—since today's evening papers have already reported the news of the delivery of French weapons and planes to Spain (compare the enclosed D[eutsche] A[llgemeine] Z[eitung] of July 23, evening edition). D[umont] July 23."

No. 4

3207/697819–23

The Embassy in Spain to the Foreign Ministry

Telegram

Md 9/23   MADRID, July 23, 1936.
Sent July 24—12 : 30 p.m.

From many reports, some of them contradictory, there emerges the following picture of the political and military situation:

The east coast from Barcelona to Cartagena and the strip of land which is bounded on the north by Guadalajara and the Guadarrama and Gredos Mountains, and on the south by Jaén and Badajoz, are in Government hands. The entire south, with Seville, Córdoba, and Granada, and the north, with Salamanca, Ávila, Segovia, Valladolid, León, Burgos, Saragossa, and Lérida, are in the hands of the rebels. The Government is striving to add to its territory through military operations toward the north and south. Aside from Madrid, the Government has been successful so far in Alcalá de Henares, Guadalajara, Toledo, and Barcelona. At the present time an operation is in progress against Albacete.

In appraising the prospects of success of the opposing sides, the following should be taken into account:

A. The Government has the advantage of the inner line, possession of the central governmental machinery with unified leadership and with the bank of issue and the gold reserve of the Bank of Spain; in the Guardia Civil it possesses the best troops in Spain, in addition to the Guardia de Asalto and the Red Militia; the latter, while of little military value, is filled with fanaticism.

Disadvantageous for the Government are the comparative barrenness and lack of depth of the strip of land it controls, which can lead to shortages of food and war matériel if the fight lasts for any length of time; in addition, the small number of trained officers, since most of these revolted or have already been taken prisoner.

B. The rebels. Their advantage consists in the greater expanse of the area controlled by them, containing the greater part of Spain's natural resources and armament industries; furthermore, they have on their side the greater part of the regular Army, almost the entire officer corps, among them a number of capable generals, and, finally, the entire Moroccan Army of approximately 40,000 men, among them troops experienced in warfare.

Disadvantageous for the rebels are the lack of geographical and organizational cohesion, and the great distances, but above all the opposition within the lower strata of the population of the abovementioned cities and of parts of the country population, as well as opposition within the governmental machinery of the federal and local administrations in the rebel-occupied area. Lastly, they lack ideological unity and objectives. The monarchy, which fell because of internal decay, offers no attractive slogan and is considered synonymous with reaction by the broad masses of the Spanish people. The close connection between monarchism and Fascism, coupled with the lack of both a real leader and a social program appealing to broad circles, has not permitted Fascism to develop into a national movement. The combat value of the regular Spanish Army, with the exception of the Moroccan troops, is slight.

C. So far the combat actions all present the same picture. The rebels occupied the public buildings, churches, barracks, etc., and defended them with rifles and machine guns. The Government attacked with light and medium artillery and planes, through whose action the buildings occupied by the rebels became untenable within a few hours. If the rebels continue their previous combat tactics, the Government is assured of further successes. If, however, the rebels are able to set in motion against Madrid a large army equipped with close-combat and long-range weapons and planes, the picture would change considerably.

D. Prospects. From Government circles I hear that the Government expects the fighting to continue for more than two weeks. Among the things to be considered are the great distances, the hot summer, the little-developed railroad network, and the small progress made in motorizing the Spanish Army, for which a good network of roads is actually available. The Government troops and especially the Red Militia have motorized themselves by confiscating most of the private cars in Madrid. Probably a quick decision is possible only through a quick thrust from the north, where the rebels, in Segovia and Ávila, are only about one hundred kilometers from Madrid. Whether they possess sufficient forces for this is not clear.

It is probable that the present Civil War will be of long duration, with correspondingly heavy loss of life and property. Already there have been heavy losses in valuable art treasures. Without military necessity and only because of Communist fanaticism, numerous churches have been destroyed in Madrid since the beginning of the revolt, among them some of the largest and most beautiful; likewise, the Cathedral of Alcalá de Henares, filled with valuable art treasures, and the Alcázar in Toledo. The further advance of the Red Militia to the south and the north is endangering much of the country's most valuable art.

Both sides picture optimistically the prospects of victory. Nothing is known here concerning the real mood of the rebel leadership. Government circles here are very apprehensive. The formation of an authorized government in Valencia for the provinces of Valencia, Alicante, Castellón, Cuenca, Albacete, and Murcia under the leadership of Martínez Barrio, the Speaker of the Cortes, which was announced in the official gazette here, gives the impression of preparing a retreat position in case the capital should fall into rebel hands. The consequences of a Government victory would be very grave for internal and foreign affairs. Domestically they would insure Marxist control of Spain for a long time, with danger of a Spanish Soviet regime. As regards foreign policy, Spain, ideologically and materially, would become closely allied to the Franco-Russian bloc.

The effects of such a development on German-Spanish relations and on the Germans in Spain would be very serious.

An opposite development would result in case of a victory of the monarchist-Fascist rebels.

SCHWENDEMANN

No. 5

4793/E236219

The Foreign Ministry to the War Ministry, Foreign Department

IMMEDIATE BERLIN, July 24, 1936.
zu Pol. I 960 g.

Drafting Officer: Counselor of Legation von Kamphoevener.

The following telegram,[1] apparently sent at the instance of the former Spanish Military Attaché in Berlin, has just been received from Tangier, from Kanzler Wegener, who is in charge of the German Consulate in Tetuán during the absence of the German Consul, now on leave:

(Insert here the whole telegram)

In the view of the Foreign Ministry compliance with the Spanish request is out of the question at this time.

By direction:
DIECKHOFF

---

[1] Document No. 2, p. 3.

No. 6

4793/E236222

The Consulate at Tetuán to the Foreign Ministry

Telegram

No. 6 of July 23 TANGIER, July 24, 1936—4:15 p.m.
Received July 24—8:05 p.m.

With reference to my telegram No. 5 of July 22.

The Lufthansa plane D–APOK seized yesterday by the Spanish Nationalist Government at Palmas brought General Orgaz to Tetuán today. It is under orders to take a Spanish Air Force officer and the German citizens Langenheim and Bernhardt via Marseille to Berlin, if possible, in order to deliver two letters from General Franco to the Führer and Chancellor and the Air Minister.

WEGENER

No. 7

654/256249

The Consulate at Tetuán to the Foreign Ministry

Telegram

No. 7 of July 24   TANGIER, July 24, 1936—4 : 15 p.m.
                                          Received July 24—8 : 05 p.m.
                                                              Pol. III 327.

With reference to my telegram No. 6 of July 23.

During today's conversation with General Franco I handed him a written protest against the confiscation and utilization of German planes.

Freedom of movement and protection of all German official agencies in case of danger were promised. In addition Franco told me the following:

The Nationalist uprising was necessary in order to anticipate a Soviet dictatorship, which was already prepared. The advance in Spain was slowed up by unexpected opposition.

A Nationalist Government had been set up at Burgos under General Cabanellas. The provinces of Málaga, Almería, Valencia, Catalonia, and Huelva were still in the hands of the previous Government. There was great slaughter in the first two of the provinces mentioned.

France had promised the Madrid Government 25 planes and 12,000 bombs. Negotiations to prevent their delivery had been initiated. The General considered the situation favorable.

WEGENER

No. 8

4793/E236223

The Chargé d'Affaires in Portugal to the Foreign Ministry

Telegram

No. 51 of July 24   LISBON, July 24, 1936—8 : 45 p.m.
                                          Received July 24—10 : 45 p.m.
                                                              Pol. I 1005 g.

Grote, commissioner for the Reich Airplane Industry Association, has requested that the following be transmitted:

"For Killinger. Marquis Quintanar, who is here on instructions from the headquarters of the Spanish military regime at Burgos, inquired today whether we were willing in principle to deliver matériel promptly. I consider that it would be advisable to agree, in view of the effect on the Portuguese, too, although no concrete proposals have been received so far."

Please send telegraphic instruction.

DU MOULIN

No. 9

1629/389437–39

The Consul at Tetuán to the Foreign Ministry

No. 1050/Pol. XI

TETUÁN, July 25, 1936.
Pol. III 647.

Subject: The Nationalist uprising under General Franco.

The efforts of Azaña's Spanish Government to disrupt the Army have caused the greatest unrest in military circles. For this reason it cannot cause surprise that these circles were intent upon eliminating the Spanish Leftist Government. The preparations for the planned military revolt have been in progress for some time; what had not been decided, however, was the time for starting the revolt. After the Rightist military faction learned that Soviet ships had arrived in Spanish harbors with arms and ammunition for an uprising planned by the Communists, they believed that they should no longer delay the military uprising.

The uprising, therefore, broke out in the Spanish zone of Morocco during the night of July 17. The leader of the movement is General Franco, who was transferred to Las Palmas after the formation of Azaña's Leftist Government. General Franco arrived in Tetuán from Las Palmas by plane the morning of July 18 and took over control in the Spanish zone. He has credit for building up the Tercio (Foreign Legion), whose founder is General Milan d'Astrée.

If one considers that the greater part of the population of the cities of Ceuta and Melilla in Spanish North Africa is composed of very Leftist elements, which would have been armed if the Nationalist movement had become known in time, it must be considered fortunate that General Franco's preparations for the revolt were made so accurately that his troops were able to occupy the entire Spanish zone almost without bloodshed. Only a few persons were wounded in Tetuán, where the Air Force wanted to resist. They detached the gasoline tanks and let them drop to the ground, putting the planes here out of commission for several days. In addition, two officers were killed in Larache following General Franco's proclamation. The guilty soldiers have in the meantime been shot, after court-martial proceedings. The revolutionary government immediately declared a state of war, and all military buildings, the electric plant, the banks, and the food stores are under military guard. Military patrols are likewise guarding the approaches to the city. Strict military surveillance is also being maintained at several points along the roads leading to Ceuta and Tangier.

Following General Franco's proclamation, the workers immediately went on strike. Natives who were willing to work were prevented by their Spanish co-workers from returning to their jobs. Work in the stores and on building construction was resumed a few days ago. No further incidents of any kind took place while work was resumed.

The revolutionary government immediately had all known Communists arrested. Then it proceeded to arrest the Freemasons, whose register was found in the lodge. On this occasion the symbols of Freemasonry which were found were taken to the police. Since the police facilities are too small to hold the many prisoners, most of them have already been transferred to a concentration camp in the vicinity of Tetuán, where they are camping in tents.

Attempts of a number of speculators to increase food prices were prevented by the levying of heavy fines. Thus the best-known food store in Tetuán was fined 100,000 pesetas (approximately 3,500 reichsmarks). Smaller fines were levied on a number of Jewish stores.

Further reports will follow.

For the Consul:
WEGENER

No. 10

629/251742–43

Memorandum by the Director of the Political Department

BERLIN, July 25, 1936.
Pol. III 492.

I should like to make the following comment on the attached letter from Count Welczeck:[1]

There arrived in Berlin yesterday by Lufthansa plane at Tempelhof two officers of the Spanish rebels bearing instructions of General Franco to negotiate with our authorities for the purchase of planes and war materials.

The plane had been stationed in the Canary Islands and was confiscated there by the rebels allegedly for this purpose. It reached here by way of Spanish Morocco, Seville, and Marseille. The two officers brought a letter from General Franco to the Führer and Chan-

---

[1] Not found.

cellor,[2] which they delivered today at the Auslandsorganisation together with a letter of recommendation from the Ortsgruppe at Ceuta.

The War Ministry had already approached us in this matter yesterday. We agree with the War Ministry that the officers should not be received by any official military authorities; I arranged rather that they first be given a comradely reception here as guests of the Lufthansa. Today I likewise strongly advised Gauleiter Bohle, who telephoned me in this matter, against bringing the two officers into contact with official Party authorities and against promoting their plans here in any way. The Auslandsorganisation will therefore confine itself to receiving the letters and, if indicated, transmitting the one addressed to the Führer.

In my opinion it is absolutely necessary that at this stage German governmental and Party authorities continue to refrain from any contact with the two officers. Arms deliveries to the rebels would become known very soon (*Liberté* has already carried such reports). Especially would there be serious consequences for the situation of the German colonies in Spain and that of the German merchant and naval vessels there if it became known now that we are making deliveries to the rebels.[3] Likewise the idea which has appeared in some quarters, that German plane deliveries could be made by way of a third country and camouflaged, seems to me impracticable and should not be furthered.

It is another question, of course, whether Franco's representatives should reach agreements here now for the period following a possible assumption of power. In any case, all governmental authorities should remain completely aloof for the present on this point also.[4]

DIECKHOFF

---

[2] Not found. The letter is apparently the one referred to by Hitler in his speech of June 6, 1939, when he said that he decided in July 1936 to respond to Franco's appeal for help.

[3] Marginal note in Neurath's handwriting: "Correct."

[4] Marginal note in Neurath's handwriting: "Yes."

No. 11

3207/697824–29

The Embassy in Spain to the Foreign Ministry

Telegram

Md 16/25   MADRID, July 25, 1936.
Sent July 26—3 : 20 a.m.

On the basis of the latest reports, the situation described in telegram 9/23 [1] can be further defined as follows:

A. In Government hands are the following: the northern coast, with Gijón, Santander, Bilbao, and San Sebastián, as well as the

---

[1] Document No. 4, p. 5.

passes across the Cantabrian Mountains; further, the entire Mediterranean coast from the French border as far as Gibraltar, with Barcelona, Tarragona, Castellón, Alicante, Murcia, Cartagena, Almería, and Málaga, and on the Atlantic coast Huelva; in the interior of the country the cities of Lérida, Cuenca, Guadalajara, Alcalá de Henares, Madrid, probably Toledo, Cáceres, and Badajoz.

The rebels are in control in all of Spanish Morocco; in the south in Cádiz, Seville, Granada, and Córdoba; in the north along the coast in La Coruña, Pontevedra, Vigo, Oviedo, Salamanca, León, Palencia, Valladolid, Burgos, Pamplona, and Saragossa, Vitoria, Lagroño, Huesca, Iaca, and also in Albacete in central Spain.

The Government is continuing its tactics, described in the previous telegram, of attacking with superior weapons individual cities occupied by the rebels. At the present time Albacete, Saragossa, Oviedo, and Seville are under attack. The attack is simultaneously carried out from the outside by troops and artillery brought up in motor vehicles of all kinds, and from the inside by masses of workers in the attacked cities themselves. The capture of Albacete, Oviedo, and Seville seems to be imminent.

The rebels, on the other hand, show much less striking power. While they have so far developed no perceptible activity in the south, where they have at their disposal a strong and effective army in Morocco, in the north General Mola has begun the advance on Madrid from Old Castile via Ávila-Segovia and the passes of the Guadarrama Mountains. During the last few days there has been heavy fighting at the mountain passes and in the valleys leading down to New Castile. The Government threw all available forces into the threatened mountain line, from which the thunder of the cannons reechoed as far as Madrid. It succeeded in pushing back the enemy, in winning the passes, and in threatening Ávila and Segovia. If the rebels are unable to commit strong new forces, they are in danger of being strangled gradually from the south via Ávila and Segovia, from the west up the Ebro Valley via Saragossa, and from the north from the coastal provinces which are held by the Government.

The inactivity of the rebels in the south can be explained as follows: In the first place, the Navy for the most part is evidently loyal to the Government; use of the Moroccan Army, and thus of the strongest reserve of military power, on the mainland was therefore limited to the troops which were able to cross the Strait during the first few days. Secondly, opposition by the broad masses of the population in both city and country is very great. In Seville the workers' sector was never conquered by the rebels. Rebel troops are inactivated as a result of this opposition.

The development of the situation since the beginning of the revolt consequently shows distinctly increasing strength and progress on the part of the Government and standstill and retrogression on the part of the rebels, whose only large offensive across the Guadarrama Mountains in the direction of Madrid bogged down and pulled back, mainly because the advance of the rebels from the south did not develop and the Government was able to throw all available forces against the attackers from the north. Thus the military situation in general has become considerably more favorable for the Government.

The relative strength of the opponents from the standpoint of morale and propaganda, as described in the previous telegram, has likewise continued to develop in favor of the Government. The latter boasts of a program which appeals to the broad masses of the people: defense of the Republic, liberty, progress, fight against political and social reaction. Its proponents are politicians well versed in all the ways of demagoguery, propaganda, and rhetoric, who handle the radio and the press consistently and ably, and who are able to exert a strong influence on a population which is 45 percent illiterate, far behind the rest of Europe in its development, and for which the democratic phraseology is still attractive. Its opponents are generals who have neither an understanding of these arts nor a clear and compelling program, except perhaps for the slogan of the fight against Communism. This relative strength in the propaganda field also affects military matters. The members of the Red Militia are filled with a fanatical combat fervor and fight with exceptional valor, with corresponding losses. These, however, are easily replaced from the masses of the population, while the rebels, who have only their troops at their disposal, are generally lacking such reserves.

Unless something unforeseen happens, it is hardly to be expected that in view of all this the military revolt can succeed, but the fighting will probably continue for some time. I have the impression that the real situation is not generally recognized in Germany and that the German radio, especially, represents it as too favorable for the rebels. This is done probably under the influence of rebel transmitters, which, however, are reliable only to a limited extent. I have on several occasions definitely observed grossly incorrect reports by these transmitters. I advise instructions for the orientation of press and radio.

SCHWENDEMANN

July 25

P. S. Albacete was captured this afternoon by Government troops.

No. 12

4793/E236224

The Chargé d'Affaires in Portugal to the Foreign Ministry

Telegram

URGENT   LISBON, July 26, 1936—11 : 05 p.m.
No. 53 of July 26   Received July 27—1 : 30 a.m.
                                                              Pol. I 1006 g.

With reference to my telegram No. 51 of July 24.

The commissioner for the Reich [Airplane Industry] Association requests that the following be transmitted to Killinger:

"The following concrete proposals have now been received from the Provisional Government of the military at Burgos: Appealing to our common anti-Communist interest, we request the earliest possible delivery to Saragossa or Burgos of at least ten Junkers transports, and, if at all possible, up to twenty bombers also—if necessary, through a private Portuguese sales contract, in which case planes first making an emergency landing at Burgos would receive instructions from the buyer that all the planes be left in Burgos against payment in Seville. I can vouch for British agreement to a similar proposal on transport planes. The Spaniards insist that the Genoa-Burgos route is also possible, since the Italians allegedly are also delivering. The above negotiations took place at the private residence of the adjutant of the Portuguese President. At least some kind of an answer is requested immediately."

DU MOULIN

No.13

4793/E236225

Memorandum by the Head of Political Division III

BERLIN, July 28, 1936.

Herr Lewinski of the Reich Airplane Industry Association inquired by telephone on the afternoon of July 27, whether no telegrams for the Reich Association had been received from its Lisbon representative. I asked Herr Lewinski to see me on the forenoon of July 28.

After consulting with Ministerialdirektor Dieckhoff, I gave Herr Lewinski the two telegraphic reports Pol. I 1005 g and Pol. I 1006 g,[1] in the modified versions shown in the annex hereto.[2] After reading the two telegrams, he expressed serious misgivings and viewed the possibility of complying with the Spanish wishes for deliveries as very problematic.

In reply to his question regarding our attitude, I told him that the Foreign Ministry could not but warn against such deliveries because

---

[1] Documents Nos. 8 and 12, p. 8 and *supra*.
[2] Annex not found.

they were hardly likely to remain secret and public knowledge of the deliveries might have the worst repercussions for the Germans in Spain. Herr Lewinski stated that he would get in touch with the Air Ministry.

DUMONT

No. 14

3371/E010617–18

The Chargé d'Affaires in Portugal to the Foreign Ministry

Telegram

No. 57 of July 28   [LISBON,] July 28[, 1936]—8 : 00 p.m.

1. The Consulate at Seville today transmitted the following urgent request of General Queipo de Llano : [1]

He needs at once 10 large and 5 small planes, or in any case at least 3 large planes for transporting troops and bombs, and 3 fast ones. In order to avoid being compromised he proposed that the planes be sent singly—but as quickly as possible—in the Lufthansa mail service via Seville or Las Palmas, where they could then be confiscated by the military authorities as surety for payment. I request telegraphic instructions for Grote.

This proposal is entirely independent of the requests from Burgos (telegraphic report No. 53 of July 26).

2. The General stated that several Italian planes have already arrived in Morocco with Italian pilots who nominally joined the Spanish Foreign Legion. Four three-engine Fokker planes ordered in England are supposed to arrive today in Lisbon for further flight to Seville. A telegraphic report of their arrival will follow.

DU MOULIN

---

[1] The request, as explained in a long letter of July 27 transmitted by the Consulate (3371/E010615–16), resulted from fear that the French might interfere with the journey of an envoy of General Franco bearing a letter to Hitler and Göring if he proceeded to Berlin via Marseille. General Queipo de Llano's request apparently summarized the letter from Franco to Hitler and Göring, which has not been found in the Foreign Ministry archives.

No. 15

660/257062

The Embassy in Spain to the Foreign Ministry

Telegram

VERY URGENT   MADRID, July 29, 1936—8 : 23 p.m.
No. 44 of July 29   Received July 30—8 : 25 a.m.
                                         Pol. III 482.

The State Secretary of the Foreign Ministry, Ureña, just called on me at the Embassy and informed me as follows : The Spanish Government had heard of the arrival in Tetuán of the first Fokker plane, which was part of a rather large shipment from Germany made available to the rebels. In view of the enormity of this report the Republican Government did not dare to believe it but requested an official communication from the Reich Government. I request instruction.[1]

SCHWENDEMANN

---

[1] Marginal note in Dumont's handwriting: "Dörnberg has delivered one copy to the Air Ministry. On instructions from D[?] the telegram is not to be answered."

No. 16

4446/E086263

The Consulate at Tetuán to the Foreign Ministry

Telegram

No. 11 of July 29   TANGIER, July 29, 1936.
Pol. III 493.

For transmission to Colonel General Göring:

"In accordance with instructions I report the following: I had a conversation with General Franco. The future Nationalist Government of Spain has been organized in the form of a directorate of the three Generals, Franco, Queipo de Llano, and Mola, with General Franco presiding. Our view of future German commercial, cultural, and military relations with Spain conforms fully with General Franco's desires and intentions.

Heil Hitler!   LANGENHEIM"[1]

WEGENER

---

[1] Ortsgruppenleiter of the NSDAP in the local German community.

No. 17

1819/415899

The Ambassador in France to the Foreign Ministry

Telegram

CONFIDENTIAL   PARIS, July 30, 1936—1 : 00 p.m.
No. 400

Regarding the question of arms deliveries to the Spanish Government, the following statement was made to the Embassy by the Press Department at the Quai d'Orsay: No arms deliveries had ever been made, and they had furthermore been denied officially and formally. In this connection reference was made to the denial circulated by the Agence Fournier, which was reported by DNB. The phraseology used there, that France would not intervene, was entirely clear and could refer only to arms deliveries. When the question had arisen for the French Government, the Foreign Ministry had been consulted. The latter had taken the stand that, while arms deliveries were quite permissible from the viewpoint of international law, they would be contradictory to the tradition of French diplomacy not to support civil war [*ne pas alimenter guerre civile*]. Thereupon the Government had decided on non-delivery and had strictly adhered to this decision. It was different with private deliveries of fuel and civilian planes, which could not be prevented.

As I reported earlier, I have no doubt that at first war matériel from France was delivered to the Spanish Government. At the end of last week this question was the topic of a lengthy Cabinet discussion, during which the Radical-Socialist Ministers, especially, expressed grave misgivings. Since then the Government would seem to have been exercising greater restraint, and above all the greatest caution. However, even the statements of the Press Department to the Embassy indicate that military support of the Spanish Government has still not been abandoned by any means.

WELCZECK

No. 18

1819/415900

The Ambassador in France to the Foreign Ministry

Telegram

SECRET   PARIS, July 31, 1936—9 : 25 p.m.
No. 413

Reports in the press this evening that the Italian planes which crashed in French Morocco were military airplanes are correct, as I hear confidentially from a good source. The preliminary report on the investigation started by General Denain is said to indicate that these are Savoia-Marchetti planes of an older type, with their military markings painted over but still partly recognizable. The crews are said to have carried regular Italian Army passes. While the officers allegedly asserted that the delivery had been at the order of an unnamed private firm, a sergeant is said to have admitted that the planes had taken off on orders from the Italian commander of a military airport in Sardinia for delivery to Franco.

WELCZECK

No. 19

1819/415925–27

The Embassy in Great Britain to the Foreign Ministry

A 3065   LONDON, July 31, 1936.

Subject: British anxiety over developments in Spain.

In the last few days a growing anxiety over future developments in Spain, in particular with regard to their effect on the general international situation in Europe, has been observable in conversations and to some extent also in the British press. It is feared that a critical deterioration in relations between France and Italy might result if France should in any way support the Spanish Government, and Italy the so-called rebels. These apprehensions are fed by constant rumors or reports regarding deliveries of French airplanes to the Spanish Government, and Italian planes as well as war matériel to Spanish Morocco. French and Italian denials of such deliveries are, to be sure, reported in the press but do not contribute materially toward allaying fears of international complications.

I hear from a reliable source that in the Foreign Office they are particularly concerned about developments in the Tangier Zone, which is under international control. They are worried about how this international administration is to work without friction when part of the higher-ranking Spanish officials are on the side of the rebels, part of the large Spanish population is pro-Communist, the French officials range themselves on the side of the Spanish Government, and the Italian officials on the side of the rebels. These administrative difficulties have apparently already had their effect in connection with the presence of Spanish Government warships in the harbor of Tangier. The rebels in Morocco threaten an invasion of the Zone if the warships do not leave the harbor; the French desire that the warships remain in the harbor, the Italians that the ships leave the harbor. The latter, I was told, is also the desire of the British, but they do not say so expressly because they hope to avoid complications.

Also, from the standpoint of British interests alone, they are watching with anxiety the course of the Civil War in Spain and the prospects of its ending. A Government victory is not desired in very large sections of the British population, because such a victory would mean a strengthening of Communism, which the British hate but which, unfortunately, they often underestimate. But they also see dangers for the interests of England in a victory by the rebels, above all for her Mediterranean interests. It is feared that a government formed by the Spanish rebels would seek the closest ties with Italy and that such a government might grant naval bases for the Italian fleet, for example on the Balearic Islands or in the port of Ceuta, which is opposite the harbor of Gibraltar.

In the greater part of the British press the anxiety finds relatively little expression, since the treatment of events in Spain is overshadowed in the press by the hostile attitude of these newspapers toward a so-called Fascist dictatorship, while, apparently, the opposite of such a dictatorship is regarded as a symbol of freedom and democracy.

The diplomatic correspondent of the *Morning Post*, in considering the situation in Spain, takes the view that these events and the general insecurity in the international situation attending them might lead to a postponement of the meeting of the Five Power Conference.[1] A clipping from the *Morning Post* of July 31 containing these statements is enclosed.[2]

BIELFELD

---

[1] The proposed meeting of the five Locarno Powers (Great Britain, France, Belgium, Italy, and Germany) to negotiate a new agreement to take the place of the Locarno Agreement and to deal with the situation created by the German occupation of the Rhineland in March 1936.

[2] Not reprinted.

No. 20

168/132369

Memorandum by the Head of the European Section of the Political Department

BERLIN, July 31, 1936.

The Portuguese Minister called on me today and asked for information about the German point of view on events in Spain.   I told him that the reports available in the Foreign Ministry contained nothing essentially new as compared with the reports in the press, and that we were not able to foretell how events in Spain would end.   We had, of course, serious misgivings that Bolshevist conditions might develop in Spain.

When he asked about the German stand on the internal events in Spain, I told the Minister that the German Government strictly believed in the principle of non-intervention in internal Spanish events. Senhor da Veiga Simões said that this corresponded to the viewpoint of his Government also; he mentioned that from earlier times and as the result of the latest events, approximately 100,000 Spanish refugees were in Portugal, who belonged preponderantly to the Right, but who might, after all, also contain Communist elements.   In Portugal herself there existed no popular sentiment at all for Communism, as was confirmed by the elections.   Nevertheless the Government was, of course, concerned about the neighboring events.   Partial mobilization had taken place; there were 4,000 men at the Spanish frontier.

WOERMANN

No. 21

665/257365

The Embassy in Spain to the Foreign Ministry

Telegram

No. 64 of August 1   MADRID, August 1, 1936—2 : 05 p.m.
                                            Received August 1—6 : 20 p.m.
                                                            Pol. III 578.

Sturm, the delegate here of the Airplane Industry Association, was summoned to the Prime Minister's office today, where Foreign Minister Barcia informed him as follows:

The Government urgently desires to purchase pursuit planes and bombers that are not too heavy, as well as aerial bombs of 50 and 100 kilos.   An offer on these, as well as on all . . . (group garbled) or quick deliveries of combat and aviation matériel, is requested.   Payment as specified by the supplier, possibly even in gold.   Barcia stressed the extreme urgency of the matter.   Sturm was requested by Barcia to use the code of the Embassy.   The Airplane Industry Association has therefore not been informed.

SCHWENDEMANN

No. 22

3162/674280–81

Memorandum by the Head of Political Division III

BERLIN, August 1, 1936.
Pol. III 595.

The Spaniard, Marquis de Portago, called on me today with the enclosed letter [1] addressed to the Foreign Minister concerning notification of the military government in Burgos.   Marquis de Portago, whom I happen to know personally from Biarritz as the nephew of the former Spanish Ambassador to Paris, Count Molina, called himself the envoy of General Mola.   He asked me whether he could be given an acknowledgment of the letter.   I told him that I regretted not being able to fulfill his wish.   We maintained official relations with the Spanish Government in Madrid and therefore could not enter into relations with the military regime, as long as the former was still in power.   The question of special sympathy or dislike for one or the other of the combatants did not enter in at all.   We had our Chargé d'Affaires stationed in Madrid with the Government there and could therefore not take any other stand, if only—aside from

---

[1] This letter does not accompany the file copy of the memorandum.

considerations of principle—in the interest of protecting the thousands of Germans in Spain.

Marquis de Portago completely understood this point of view and did not press his request any further.

He told me that General Franco and the military leaders had not wanted the military movement to get under way until two weeks later. After Deputy Calvo Sotelo [2] was assassinated, however, it had no longer been possible to delay matters. The opposition which the military had encountered was, to be sure, much greater than they had imagined; nevertheless they were absolutely sure of final victory, since the members of the Government had no leaders among the military and at the present time the mob, whose heroic deeds did not go beyond lootings and murder, was dominant everywhere in Spain where the military was not in control. This condition might unfortunately last a considerable time, but not too long, and must necessarily evoke a reaction in favor of the military. If only they had sufficient planes and if possible two submarines, the victory would be speeded up considerably. Marquis de Portago told me this only in passing, without asking any question. I therefore had no reason to comment on the subject.

DUMONT

---

[2] José Calvo Sotelo, monarchist politician, killed during the night of July 12–13, 1936, in the course of political disorders preceding the outbreak of the Civil War.

No. 23

665/257366

The Embassy in Spain to the Foreign Ministry

Telegram

No. 66 of August 1   MADRID, August 2, 1936—2:45 a.m.
                                      Received August 2—7:15 a.m.
                                      Pol. III 650.

With reference to my telegraphic report 58.[1]

The military situation as described in telegraphic report 59 [2] has developed further in favor of the rebels, who are displaying great and often successful activity in the south and north. Statements from those in authority on both sides, as well as the impression of the general situation, indicate the decisive importance of the Air Force. That the Government here, which is under radical Leftist influence, is appealing to us is indicative of its situation. Since we have no

---

[1] Not printed (4687/E225449).
[2] Not printed (3207/697834–35).

interest in the victory of the Government here, the delivery of war matériel should not be considered, nor a flat refusal either, but rather dilatory handling, such as reference to industry being occupied with German orders, long delivery periods, etc.[3]

SCHWENDEMANN

[3] Marginal note in Dumont's handwriting: "Madrid has received telegraphic instruction regarding telegrams 64 [document No. 21, p. 20] and 66. The War Ministry has been informed by means of carbon copies. Aug. 4."

No. 24

1819/415901–04

The Ambassador in France to the Foreign Ministry

A 3274   PARIS, August 2, 1936.

Subject: Events in Spain and their effects on European politics.

The slow pace of the bloody events in Spain and the fact that the great European powers are taking sides in favor of one or the other of the combatants fill the French Government with serious concern. They fear that through this taking of sides blocs will necessarily be created in which the powers, according to their sympathies, will support either the Spanish Government or the rebels so intensively, that, in spite of all attempts at camouflage, even the semblance of a neutral attitude can no longer be preserved. In this manner the flames fed in Spain would finally be bound to turn into a European conflagration. Since the French, in spite of all denials, undoubtedly preceded the others in delivering war matériel, it is understandable that they are somewhat uneasy, in view of the consequences of their action. It is frequently pointed out also that Spain once before had given occasion for a war between Germany and France.

It is obvious that after a victory of the Nationalists—as the rebels are wont to call themselves—their relations with present-day France would probably be very cool, but very cordial with us and Italy. The Popular Front Government consequently fears that in case of a European war a Fascist Spain might be on the side of France's enemies, not only with its sympathies but perhaps even actively, while a Spanish Leftist government, if only out of gratitude for the assistance given it, would offer the French an alliance. Therefore one counts no longer as heretofore on Spain's neutrality in case of a European conflict, but on her active participation on one side or the other. Thus an important credit or debit would be entered on France's military balance sheet. The more intensively and unplatonically France's interest in the course of events in Spain is expressed, the louder does the Government preach maintenance of the strictest neutrality.

Insofar as it can be done unobtrusively, investigations concerning the extent and type of war matériel delivered since the beginning of the Civil War are being made here by our Spanish friends from the Fascist camp, and I should like to mention in this connection that the delivery of civilian planes, gasoline, and mazut is termed permissible under international law by the French Government. The reason given for delivering bombs and ammunition would probably be that an earlier order was being filled.

If I may permit myself an opinion on developments in Spain on the basis of my long-standing familiarity with Spanish psychology, I would assume that, after having armed the mob, the Government even now is no longer master of the situation in most places—perhaps with the exception of Madrid and its vicinity—and that after a Government victory its Anarchist allies will present it with an account which will spell final ruin for the country. It should therefore be taken into consideration that, aside from the Government and the rebels, a third power has come into being composed of the armed mob and the Anarchist militia, which are still allied for the time being with the Madrid Government.

I mention this in case the idea should be advanced from some quarter of initiating mediation proceedings between the combatants in order to put an end to the unparalleled slaughter, and in order to prevent the Spanish conflagration from becoming a serious problem for European politics. Certainly a government which took the initiative in this matter and was successful would earn the gratitude not only of many Spaniards but of the entire world. However, in spite of the rumors current here that both parties are tired of the bloodshed, I fail to see any possibility at the present time for bringing about a settlement among the Spaniards, who are always so averse to compromises, now that the bloody events have progressed this far. It appears, therefore, that one of the two parties will first have to be entirely beaten, which can still take months, according to the statements of Indalecio Prieto.

If, however, contrary to expectations, combat weariness should be manifested on both sides after all, thus preparing the ground for a settlement, we might do well to consider being the first to take up this idea of mediation which I have mentioned. Germany could then perhaps propose that she, together with Britain, Italy, and France, invite the combatants to stop hostilities, promising strictest neutrality and assuring the Spanish people moral and economic aid in reconstruction.

This action would definitely be in our interest and would be advisable if it is to be feared that the rebels might lose. Otherwise only a complete defeat of the Left—which, after sizable deliveries of war matériel, especially planes, to the rebels does not appear at all out of the question, according to the information available to me—could make possible the formation of a Fascist dictatorship, which alone, in view of what has happened, can in my opinion pacify the country.

WELCZECK

No. 25

1819/415905–08

The Ambassador in France to the Director of the Political Department

PARIS, August 2, 1936.

DEAR DIECKHOFF: As an old Spanish hand, I have just set down very hurriedly in a political report [1]—perhaps somewhat exceeding my authority—my thoughts concerning the effects of the events in Spain on European politics and the stand which we should take. Developments in Spain appear to me to become increasingly important for Europe the longer they last.

It is somewhat embarrassing for me that all emissaries of the rebels and many old Spanish friends come to call on me here in order to give me information and to implore help of me for their fellow fighters. Even when I am absolutely certain of their reliability I tell them that I cannot concern myself with these things and direct them to the Nationalist Committee which has been established here, to which belong the former Spanish military and naval attachés, who were relieved of their duties at their own request. Since these are friends of our military and naval attachés, respectively, the connection is established. Our unofficial liaison is Captain [*Kapitän*] Lietzmann, who meets with his former Spanish colleague, but, of course, only at constantly changing neutral places, using all possible precautions, in order to avoid compromising a member of the Embassy. Also, I have been giving him the secret material which has been brought me by my Spanish friends, especially concerning French arms deliveries, so that he can send it on to Canaris. Thus with today's courier he is sending Canaris a report from a very well-informed source, the content of which interests us too, as proof of French arms deliveries to the Spanish Government. I did tell Lietzmann to ask Canaris to send us a copy of the report, which is in Spanish, but perhaps you

---

[1] Document No. 24, *supra*.

could nevertheless remind Canaris to send you a copy; the report is interesting from several points of view.

The day before yesterday Danielson had lunch with me; he is my former Swedish colleague in Madrid. Azaña returned his credentials because of the dislike for the Spanish Leftist Government which Danielson—and still more his wife—expressed somewhat too freely even before the outbreak of civil war [*schon früher*]. Danielson, by the way, is a very quiet, sensible man, and he has been my friend for many years. He just came from Portugal, where he was likewise accredited and where, because of his departure from Madrid, he had to submit his letter of recall. Salazar told him confidentially that he planned to support the Spanish Rightists with all available means—the Spanish Committee here even asserts that he promised intervention by the Portuguese Army in case of a setback on the rebels' western front— since the bolshevization of Spain would be a serious danger to Portugal. Unfortunately he had only a few planes ready for action which could be armed as bombers. Perhaps our Chargé d'Affaires in Portugal knows more about this.

Unless the rebels soon receive at least the same number of planes and bombs as the French have delivered to the Spanish Government, I fear that they will not be able to hold out. On the other hand the rebels claim to be able to dispose within two weeks of the Government's militia, who are mostly untrained and frequently recruited against their will. After the conquest and pacification of the rest of Spain, they intend to block off Catalonia first of all by a customs border, and they hope in this manner to obtain a surrender to their Rightist Government in Madrid within a few months.

My Spanish friends who live in Hendaye and St. Jean de Luz tell me that French Ambassador Herbette and his wife, who have always sympathized with the Communists and who live in the border town of Fuenterrabía, are said to be doing some lively gun-running with two automobiles. During the last week Madame Herbette is supposed to have driven her car from Fuenterrabía, where she has her own villa, to San Sebastián as many as five times in one day. As soon as the rebels have advanced close enough to this road near Oyarzun, they are planning to stop and search her car.

Since the courier is leaving, I must close; I only want to add that I tell everybody very openly and truthfully that many Spaniards come to see me, asking me to institute a search for their relatives, and that unfortunately I have to refuse to do so in most cases.

With German greeting, Heil Hitler!

Ever yours,
WELCZECK

No. 26

3371/E010621

The Chargé d'Affaires in Portugal to the Foreign Ministry

Telegram

No. 63 of August 3   [Lisbon,] August 3[, 1936]—8 : 00 p.m.

With reference to my telegram No. 61 of August 1.[1]

Grote requests that the following be transmitted to the proper authorities:

"For fear that liaison with Marquis Guadalquivir might not function, Nicolás Franco, the General's brother, was established here (Calçada de Sacramento 14) under a Portuguese cover-name (Aurelio Fernando Aguila[r]) as procurement supervisor. He urgently requests earliest possible quotation of price and date for 10,000 simple gas masks affording protection against all gases.

"In addition to Linares Rivas' order of day before yesterday, a request has been made for three Junkers mechanics."

I request telegraphic instructions for Grote.

Du Moulin

---

[1] Not printed (3371/E010622).

No. 27

4446/E086275-80

The Consul at Tetuán to the Foreign Ministry

No. 1099/Pol. XI   Tetuán, August 3, 1936.
                                    Received August 8.
                                    Pol. III 884.

Subject: Visit to Ceuta by a squadron composed of the pocket battleship [*Panzerschiff*] *Deutschland* and the torpedo boat *Luchs*. Admiral Carls' visit with General Franco.

At about nine o'clock this morning I was informed by a military authority in Ceuta of the arrival of two German warships and was requested to come to Ceuta at once. I had the message transmitted by telephone to the local Ortsgruppenleiter, Herr Langenheim, as well as to his deputy, the businessman Johannes Bernhardt, for their information, and, after changing clothes, left at once for Ceuta in my own car.

Spanish and Moroccan troops as well as members of the Foreign Legion had been called out and were already assembled at the pier in Ceuta, in order to give a ceremonious welcome to the squadron commander, Admiral Carls, upon his debarkation. In the meantime I learned that a number of Germans had already gone aboard the *Deutschland* and had returned to shore without awaiting my arrival.

Since the squadron commander's launch was expected at any moment, I waited for him on the pier and reported to him immediately upon his arrival. He was accompanied, aside from his military entourage, by Secretary of Legation Fischer of the German Embassy at Madrid.

After introductions had been made on both sides, the Admiral inspected the assembled troops in the presence of the town commandant of Ceuta and the officers accompanying him, to the strains of the German national anthem. Many spectators of this unexpected event, especially the Spanish Blue Shirts (Falange), spontaneously gave the Admiral the German greeting. With a "Long Live Spain," which was answered with a "Long Live Germany" and partly with "Heil Hitler," the Admiral and his entourage then took leave of the Spanish officers, the assembled troops, and the numerous spectators. In two waiting automobiles, in which Admiral Carls and his entourage as well as Secretary of Legation Fischer and the undersigned consular officer seated themselves, the trip to Tetuán (the capital of the Spanish protectorate) was begun.

The main square of Tetuán, Plaza de España, in which the local High Commissioner's office is situated, was crowded with people as the result of the troops assembled there to receive the squadron commander. Here, too, Admiral Carls was greeted with the German national anthem played by Moroccan troops and proceeded at once to the High Commissioner's office for a long talk with General Franco. Following the audience General Franco kept as luncheon guests the squadron commander and his entourage, as well as the German citizens present at the High Commissioner's office—Ortsgruppenleiter Langenheim, Party Member J. Bernhardt, Secretary of Legation Fischer, and myself. On the Spanish side there were General Franco's Army and Navy staff officers; the Chief of Asuntos Indígenas,[1] Colonel Beigbeder; the Chief of the Diplomatic Cabinet, Temes; and a gentleman from Protocol. After lunch I had a short official talk with the squadron commander and his staff officer, whereupon Admiral Carls took cordial leave of General Franco. Franco replied equally cordially in his quiet and deliberate manner and expressed his thanks above all for the moral support which Germany and her Führer, by sending the German squadron, had shown for his efforts to overcome Communism in Spain. The "Viva España" which the squadron commander called to the Spanish officers assembled in the vestibule as he left the High Commissioner's office was enthusiastically answered with shouts of "Viva Alemania" and "Viva Hitler." Thereupon the Admiral and his companions began the return trip to Ceuta in the waiting automobiles.

---

[1] The Department of Native Affairs.

The unexpected visit of a German squadron aroused the greatest joy among the Germans in Ceuta and Tetuán and has given them courage and strength for possible difficult times in the future. For now they all know that in case of renewed dangers they can count on the strong and effective protection of the homeland. It may be pointed out in this connection that no German warship has entered Moroccan harbors for 20 years.

In addition, however—and this is probably the most important politically—the unexpected appearance of the German warships in Ceuta and the visit of the squadron commander to Tetuán made the greatest possible impression on all groups of the population, especially on the Moors. I have reported separately that a considerable portion of the Jews here are of a different opinion. The visit is considered direct support of the Nationalist uprising of General Franco, who, in his own words, would like to be looked upon not only as the savior of Spain but also as the savior of Europe from the spread of Communism. I may mention further that the squadron commander and the officers accompanying him were greeted very cordially by a large part of the population, too, wherever they were seen.

Admiral Carls thought that he would be able to comply with my suggestion of also sending a ship of his squadron to the Germans in Melilla, who had been frightened by the shelling of Melilla, and that he would be able to do so within the next week.

For the Consul:
WEGENER

Postscript of August 4, 1936: As I was just informed after finishing the above report, 250 members of the crews of the German warships were the guests of the city of Ceuta yesterday afternoon at the invitation of the town commandant. The population, restaurants, postcard venders, etc., were instructed not to ask any money from the German sailors for meals or purchases.

For the Consul:
WEGENER

No. 28

3207/697839

The Chargé d'Affaires in Spain to the Foreign Ministry

Telegram

No. 87 of August 4   MADRID, August 4, 1936—midnight.

With reference to No. 57 of August 3.[1]

Today Sturm was again repeatedly urged by the Government to give a clear reply. The Government will no longer condone further

---

[1] Not printed (4687/E225483).

delay. In case of categorical refusal it must be expected that the matter mentioned in telegraphic reports 29/28 [2] and 44/29,[3] which is used for general agitation against Germans, may perhaps at some time be used by the Government as a motive for confiscating Lufthansa commercial planes or for taking other reprisals. Under these circumstances Sturm has proposed to the Government that they send a representative to Berlin to negotiate concerning the purchase of civilian planes.

VOELCKERS

[2] Not printed (4687/E225409).
[3] Document No. 15, p. 15.

No. 29

1758/404697–98

Memorandum by the Foreign Minister

BERLIN, August 4, 1936.
Pol. III 757.

The French Ambassador called on me this morning and asked me in the name of his Government whether Germany was prepared to take part in a joint declaration of the interested powers regarding non-intervention in the internal affairs of Spain. His Government had already conferred with England and Italy and received assent of a general nature from the former.[1]

I told the Ambassador that the German Government itself did not actually need to make a declaration of neutrality since we naturally did not intervene in Spanish internal political affairs and disputes. We were prepared, however, to participate in a discussion aimed at preventing the extension of the Spanish Civil War to Europe, and for this purpose to discuss the possibility of actually preventing intervention by foreign powers. A necessary condition was that all the interested countries, particularly the Soviet Republic, should join in such an agreement.

At this point I called the Ambassador's attention to the fact that there had first been intervention by the French through deliveries of airplanes and arms. To his objection that we, too, had supplied airplanes, I replied that it was an old principle, as long as no international agreements existed, to place no obstacles in the way of trade in war matériel with foreign governments or rebels. As he knew, this principle was upheld especially by the British Government.

[1] On Aug. 1 the French Government had appealed to the British and Italian Governments to act quickly in concerting an "arrangement for non-intervention in Spain." The French had announced simultaneously that, in view of the amount of supplies being sent to the rebels, they were considering the possibility of changing their decision not to supply the Spanish Government.

The Ambassador also referred to the fact that a German Junkers plane had had to land in Morocco in French territory, and he was afraid that under certain circumstances such slight causes might give rise to dangerous complications. I told the Ambassador that, if planes had been delivered to the Nationalist Spanish Government in Morocco by a German firm, these planes had from the moment of purchase become Spanish property. Besides, I must again and again point to the French deliveries to Spain.

v. NEURATH

No. 30

1758/404705–06

The Ambassador in Italy to the Foreign Ministry

Telegram

No. 132 of August 6   ROME (QUIRINAL), August 6, 1936—6 : 05 p.m.
Received August 6—9 : 50 p.m.
Pol. III 827.

With reference to telegram No. 167 [1] and the telephone conversation of August 6 with the Foreign Minister.

After I had ascertained yesterday that the Italian reply to the French initiative was imminent and that the basic view was essentially in agreement with ours, I spoke today with Foreign Minister Ciano himself. He had just previously received the French Ambassador and informed him orally of the Italian position. Regarding the substance I refer to the long-distance telephone conversation; the communiqué is being published today.

Ciano added that the general situation was beginning to take on a menacing aspect. The Soviets and the French were unreservedly supporting the Spanish Government, which in reality hardly existed any longer but was entirely in the hands of the Communists. At the same time the French and Soviet newspapers were reviling Italy and Germany most scurrilously, the Radek article being especially characteristic. The rebels in Spain were summarily termed Fascists or National Socialists. Italy was, like Germany, opposed to the formation of blocs but the French-Russian behavior was driving Europe directly to a split between Communists and anti-Communists. At any rate the greatest vigilance and closest collaboration between Germany and Italy were necessary in order to avert dangers that were arising. I referred to the decisive importance that the British attitude necessarily had; unfortunately, it was to be noted that so far it lacked a clear orientation. Ciano agreed but said he was not very optimistic in

---

[1] Not printed (4796/E236694–95).

that respect. At any rate it was right that the military of the two countries, also, should come to agreement for all contingencies, and fortunately this was already under way. As far as Italy was concerned, she was entirely available, if Germany should have any wishes in implementing her defense measures for any eventuality.

As to the Italian view, he had left the French Ambassador no room for doubt. On first impulse the Ambassador had declared with regard to section 2 of the Italian reply that France could not accept this point—to which he had replied that he did not know in what respect, since France was not being mentioned at all. Chambrun, whom I saw between the two conversations, seemed little satisfied with the answer and said that the Italians had, to be sure, accepted, but as usual only in principle.

Ciano further mentioned that he had asked the Russian Ambassador to see the Under Secretary of State, in order to make clear to him the Italian opinion of the tone of the Soviet press.

In the ensuing conversation with Under Secretary of State Bastianini, the latter supplemented these remarks by stating that the situation of the troops in the north was obviously difficult because of lack of war matériel—which was all the more regrettable since General Mola was the most competent of the commanders. While the troops in the south were better supplied, the transportation of matériel to the troops in the north was difficult. A certain possibility was offered by the small bay in the Gulf of Biscay. The French contention that on the one side was the legitimate Government, on the other the insurgents, was not tenable, since actually on the Government side there was no authority but only Red terror. A few days ago a Spanish torpedo boat flying the Red flag without the national insignia of Spain had entered the French port of St. Jean de Luz and stayed there unmolested.

HASSELL

No. 31

666/257386–87

Memorandum by the Director of the Political Department for the Foreign Minister

BERLIN, August 6, 1936.
zu Pol. III 763.

On several occasions during the last few days members of the diplomatic corps told me that the Italian stand in favor of the rebels in Spain—aside from the ideological elements involved—could be explained by the existence of a secret agreement between Mussolini and Primo [de] Rivera. This agreement, which concerned mutual cooperation in case of an Italo-French war (utilization of the Balearic Islands as a naval base for Italy, prevention of transports of French colonial troops, etc.), later had been revoked by the Republican Government. Mussolini now was hoping to be able to renew this treaty with a Nationalist government in Spain. Paris was aware of this intention and on this account, aside from ideological and other reasons, was strongly supporting the Republican Government in Spain.

Our files do not show anything definite about the alleged secret treaty between Mussolini and Primo [de] Rivera, as may be seen from the enclosed memorandum.

DIECKHOFF

[Enclosure]

BERLIN, August 5, 1936.
e.o. Pol. III 763.

The Spanish-Italian treaty of August 7, 1926, conforms to the usual agreements and arbitration treaties. The reports and memoranda on this subject which are in our files all indicate that the significance of the treaty should not be overestimated and that Mussolini's expectations of concluding a political and military alliance with Spain had not been fulfilled. Article 13 of the treaty contains a neutrality clause which corresponds to the one in our treaty with Russia.

In subsequent years rumors appeared several times concerning secret agreements between Primo de Rivera and Mussolini on the utilization of the Balearic Islands as a naval base. Use of Mahón harbor on Minorca by the Italian fleet has been particularly mentioned.

Our Embassy in Madrid regularly termed these reports highly unlikely and consistently took the stand that Primo de Rivera attached great importance to friendly relations with Italy, to be sure, but wanted to avoid commitments which might be directed against France.

Submitted herewith to Ministerialdirektor Dieckhoff for his information.

DUMONT

No. 32

1758/404699–700

Memorandum by the Foreign Minister

RM 628   BERLIN, August 7, 1936.

The French Ambassador came to see me again today and, following up the statements he had made on the 4th and the promise then made to him in principle that proposals which might be made would be studied, handed me the enclosed draft [1] of a declaration by which the interested countries are to obligate themselves not to give any aid to the parties fighting for power in Spain.

I first told the Ambassador we would study this proposal thoroughly and later inform him of our decision and of any wishes we might have. At the same time, however, I called his attention to the fact that the execution of the measures proposed would encounter extremely great difficulties. Unless all countries joined in such a declaration, there was danger that support of the contending parties in Spain would in the future take place in roundabout ways. Thus, a blockade of Spain might be necessary, with all its attendant consequences, among other things the need for searching foreign ships. I also called the Ambassador's attention to the fact that even if the Russian Government gave its assent, the Comintern, according to past experience, would not adhere to it, and that a unilateral support of the Reds in Spain would therefore result. The Ambassador conceded the difficulties but said it would still mean considerable progress if at least the principal states of Europe decided on an arms embargo. The danger that the conflagration would spread from Spain was extremely great, unless everything was done to confine it to its starting place.

I then asked the Ambassador what replies the governments queried by the French Government had given so far. He said that the British, Dutch, Belgian, Polish, Czechoslovak, and Soviet Russian Governments had replied affirmatively in principle, adding that I knew the reply of the Italian Government and its counterquestions.

When the Ambassador then began to speak of the delivery of airplanes and war matériel by Germany to the rebel generals, I pointed out to him that it would probably be better not to bring up this subject, for I was in a position to prove to him that the chief support of the parties of the Left in Spain, especially the Communists, came from the French. This went so far that French Cabinet members admitted the fact openly and even wanted the aid stepped up. Under these circumstances I even had certain doubts as to whether the proposal of the French Government for issuing a general ban on aid was intended seriously. The Ambassador protested against this suspicion and stated that precisely by such a measure his Government also intended to bind any Cabinet members who might be dissenting.

BARON V. NEURATH

---

[1] Not printed (1758/404703–04). The draft declaration called for the renunciation of all direct or indirect traffic with Spain in war matériel and airplanes, including goods already contracted for, and for an exchange of information on steps taken to see that these measures were carried out.

No. 33

629/251772

The Ambassador in France to the Foreign Ministry

Telegram

URGENT   PARIS, August 8, 1936.
No. 447 of August 8   Pol. III 901.

Please transmit at once to Rear Admiral Canaris at the War Ministry the following report from the agent known to him [*bekannten Gewährsmann*].

WELCZECK

The northern group under Mola continues to be optimistic. However, in the long run there will be a shortage of rifle ammunition. Mola requests that 10,000,000 cartridges for the Spanish Mauser rifle be sent at once to La Coruña if at all possible.

Since reliable communication with Franco does not always seem assured at the present time, Mola requests that Franco's agent in Berlin be informed of the above; he can also report on the caliber and on the Spanish Mauser rifle. Messerschmidt can also give information concerning the latter.

SEYDEL

No. 34

3416/E015744–45

Memorandum by the Foreign Minister

RM 630   BERLIN, August 8, 1936.

The British Ambassador called on me this morning and read me a telegram from his Government, in which he was instructed to give his warmest support to the step taken by the French Government to bring about an agreement regarding non-intervention in the internal affairs of Spain. The British Government, he said, had already approved the French proposal in the form in which it was transmitted to us.

I replied to the Ambassador that we were at present carefully examining our reply. One had to realize that it was easy to make such an agreement on paper, but extraordinarily difficult to carry it out in practice. First of all we had to demand that all countries that had a large arms and munitions industry of their own participate in the agreement, among them, therefore, the United States, Sweden, and Switzerland. Moreover, I had to point out to him, as I had done yesterday to the French Ambassador, the doubts we entertained with regard to the assent of the Russian Government to the non-intervention agreement. It was generally known that the Comintern paid no heed to the international obligations of the Soviet Russian Government. Also it was perhaps possible to prevent an importation of arms and munitions by sea, but it would be difficult to close effectively the long frontier between France and Spain, even with the best intentions on the part of the French Government.

The Ambassador admitted the correctness of these objections but declared again how important it was, in the opinion of his Government, at least to make the attempt to localize the conflagration in Spain by acceding to the non-intervention agreement proposed by the French Government. He therefore asked that we give our assent as soon as possible.

BARON VON NEURATH

No. 35

1758/404707–08

The Ambassador in France to the Foreign Ministry

Telegram

URGENT
No. 454 of August 10

PARIS, August 10, 1936.
Received August 10—9 : 35 p.m.
Pol. III 987.

Delbos asked me to call on him today in order to tell me in the name of his Government how much the German Government's understanding reception of the French neutrality proposal had been appreciated and how much importance was attached to German-French collaboration in isolating the Spanish conflagration. France would see in this collaboration a favorable omen for future negotiations on the questions of concern to our nations, the settlement of which was, no doubt, very much desired by both Governments. For the rest, he could inform me that the Soviet Government had given an affirmative answer at noon today.

I replied that the sympathetic reception of the French step augured favorably for the future. I firmly believed that we did not intend to obstruct the realization of the French plan. Speaking only in a personal capacity, however, it seemed important to me that small countries with munitions industries of their own should also be included, to which Delbos agreed. I stated further that France as a border country was in a privileged position and that export of arms, as well as the movement of volunteers over the passes of the Pyrenees, would probably be hard for the Government to control. Last year, on the occasion of a trip to the Catalonian Pyrenees, I had been able to convince myself at first hand of the extensive arms smuggling in favor of the Spanish Popular Front. Delbos stated that the French frontier guards had received the strictest instructions to put a stop to all smuggling of arms. When the French Government issued solemn declarations, it also observed them and saw to it that they were strictly complied with.   Incidentally, nothing but airplanes had so far been supplied to the Spanish Government.   In the course of the conversation Delbos also spoke of the possibility of mediation after acceptance of the neutrality proposal by all parties concerned.   At this time, however, such ideas seemed to him premature.

WELCZECK

No. 36

629/251840

The Ambassador in the United States to the Foreign Ministry

No. 1044   WASHINGTON, D. C., August 11, 1936.
                                                        zu Pol. III 1587.

With reference to my telegraphic report No. 200 of August 7.[1]
Subject: Disorders in Spain.

Submitted herewith is a collection of American press comments [2] on the Spanish disorders and on Germany's alleged intentions to intervene.

The extent of the agitation directed against Germany on this score is shown by the great number of protesting telegrams that the Embassy has been receiving in the last few days from pacifist and Communist organizations.   An assortment of such telegrams is also enclosed.[2]

LUTHER

[1] Not printed (629/251768).
[2] Not reprinted.

No. 37

3174/682354–55

Memorandum by the Head of Political Division III

BERLIN, August 12, 1936.
Pol. III 3554.

On the afternoon of August 12, the Foreign Minister instructed me to telephone the French Ambassador, M. François-Poncet, and to tell him that the rumors and suspicions which he had reported to Minister Woermann by telephone, to the effect that the German Government was pursuing dilatory tactics with respect to the French arms embargo declaration, were without any foundation.   We would have been ready to agree to the declaration in principle if the Spanish Government had not created an incident by seizing a Junkers airplane intended to evacuate Germans from Spain, and by interning the crew.   As long as the Spanish Government did not comply with our just demand that it surrender the airplane—which was strictly a transport plane—and release the crew, we felt compelled to withold our reply.

M. François-Poncet thanked me for the message and asked me also to inform our Ambassador in Paris, Count Welczeck, as soon as possible. For he knew that the Quai d'Orsay and also the French Foreign Minister, M. Delbos himself, were somewhat annoyed at our reserve thus far, and they were beginning to suspect that we did not *wish* to reply for certain reasons. He himself would in any case inform his Government of my telephone call.

I thereupon called the Ambassador, Count Welczeck, and gave him the same message as M. François-Poncet. Count Welczeck told me he would make use of this information in authoritative quarters.

DUMONT

[EDITORS' NOTE. On August 9 a Junkers plane made a brief landing at Madrid and then later in the day came down again at Badajoz, where it was detained by the Spanish authorities, along with the crew. Informed of this by telephone, the German Government instructed its Chargé d'Affaires in Madrid to demand the release of the plane and crew (4446/E086283–84). When the Spanish Government did not agree to this, the Director of the Political Department of the Foreign Ministry, Dieckhoff, declared on August 10 that Germany would have to consider a break in relations if the demand was not complied with by the Spanish Government (3207/697855–56, 4446/E086285). The Chargé d'Affaires was evidently unable on August 11 to obtain any satisfaction, for on August 13 he was instructed to raise the issue again with the Spanish Foreign Ministry and make clear that Germany regarded the situation as "extraordinarily serious" (629/251968). Since he could obtain from the State Secretary only a promise to refer the matter to the Spanish Government (629/251790), the Chargé d'Affaires drafted the following document, No. 38.]

No. 38

3207/697868–69

Note from the Embassy in Spain to the Spanish Foreign Minister

August 13, 1936.

EXCELLENCY: With reference to the conversation which I had the honor of having on August 11 with you and His Excellency the Prime Minister, I beg to inform Your Excellency on behalf of my Government of the following:

The German Government expects the immediate release of the transport plane D–AMIM, which made an emergency landing in Spanish territory on August 9 and was held by the Spanish Government, as well as the immediate release of the crew interned by the Spanish authorities.

Should the Government of the Spanish Republic fail to comply with this justified demand, the German Government would feel obliged to resort to the most serious measures.

Accept, Excellency, etc.[1]

---

[1] Marginal notes in Voelckers' handwriting: "Approved by Dumont by telephone" and "Delivered by the Counselor of Embassy in person.   Aug. 14."

No. 39

47/31652

The Consul at Seville to the Foreign Ministry

SECRET   SEVILLE, August 14, 1936.
                                              Pol. I 1440 g.

The Germans who came to Seville in order to deliver certain materials to Spain were, of course, immediately and unmistakably recognized here as Germans, in their white uniforms and white Olympic caps, and wherever they appeared in the streets of Seville great ovations were accorded them.   When I consulted Herr Lindner here, the latter had to admit this fact and concede that of course these uniforms were really bound to attract the attention of the public and of all foreign press correspondents, some of whom, of course, even have access to the airport.   It is manifest, therefore, what our people are doing here.

The Italian fliers who came here appeared in the uniforms of officers of the Spanish Foreign Legion, and so no one took notice of them, although six Caproni bombers were temporarily at the Seville airport at the same time.

I assume that this matter has meanwhile been taken up with the proper authorities in Berlin, but I for my part do not wish to fail to point out that, because of the way it has been handled, it has long since been impossible to keep the enterprise secret.

                                              DRAEGER

No. 40

1758/404717–19

The Chargé d'Affaires in Italy to the Foreign Ministry

3854   ROME, August 14, 1936.
                                         Received August 15.
                                              Pol. III 1269.

Subject: Italy and the events in Spain.

In the field of foreign policy everything else is overshadowed here at the present time by the events in Spain.   Developments there, and their effects, concerning which the newspapers publish columns of reports every day, are followed with the greatest attention. The Italian stand, insofar as partiality for one or the other of the combatants is concerned, was clear from the very beginning. Italy sympathizes unreservedly with the rebels and tries to support them in their fight as much as possible. The press consistently takes the part of the rebels, and there can be little doubt that Italy is supplying them with weapons and ammunition. I hear that picked men, among them militia officers, have gone to Spain as volunteers.

The situation is considered so serious here because victory for the Spanish Government is regarded as the equivalent of a victory for Communism. Such a development is abhorred in Italy for ideological reasons, but it also seems highly undesirable for political reasons to Italy in particular, since the Italians believe that it would finally result in strengthening the position of France and Russia in the Mediterranean at the expense of Italy. Furthermore, it is feared that Bolshevism, once it had taken hold in Spain, might also spread beyond her frontiers.

While Italy thus is anxiously hoping for a rebel victory, she is endeavoring, on the other hand, not to aggravate the international situation. This explains her stand in the question of the non-intervention agreement proposed by France. The Italians are convinced that, once the agreement has been signed, Italian arms deliveries will no longer be possible, in contrast to French deliveries, which are difficult to control, and they therefore feel at a disadvantage as compared with France, whom they mistrust. However, they do not want to be the ones to obstruct the agreement. Italy will therefore presumably join in signing a non-intervention agreement. She is trying, however, to delay its actual conclusion, in order to be able to continue arms deliveries to General Franco as long as possible. That is why she is asking the familiar questions and making her counterproposals, which, of course, also have the purpose of making it exceedingly difficult— in particular for France and Russia—to continue supporting the Government party in case a convention is concluded.

There are bitter complaints here about the British stand. As I have heard from a reliable source, Count Ciano made the statement that the British Foreign Office believed that if the Spanish Government won it would be able to master Communism. England was making the same mistake with regard to Spain that she made at the time of Kerenski with regard to Russia. In addition, it was not possible to eradicate the suspicion in England that Italy had concluded an agreement with General Franco concerning the cession of territory in Spanish Morocco, a suspicion which had been spread by France. He

(Ciano) had had the rumor denied, with the argument that Italy would have to desire a Communist victory if she actually had such intentions, since only then would such disintegration occur in Spain that cession of territory would be possible. All his attempts, however, had remained unsuccessful; British distrust of Italy was too strong (cf. in this connection the London Embassy's report of July 31, A 3065,[1] transmitted to us together with the instruction of August 7, Pol. III 655[2]).

PLESSEN

---

[1] Document No. 19, p. 17.
[2] Not printed (4796/E236693).

No. 41

47/31611

The Ambassador in France to the Foreign Ministry

Telegram

URGENT   PARIS, August 15, 1936.
No. 471 of August 15   Received August 15—2:45 p.m.
                                                   Pol. I 1249 g.

Please transmit at once to Admiral Canaris at the War Ministry through secure channels the following report from the agent known to him.

WELCZECK

1. General Mola has just communicated the following through a special agent:

(*a*) Liaison [*Verbindung*] with Franco is still not satisfactory.
(*b*) The northern group is most urgently in need of planes (particularly fighters), bombs, rifle and machine-gun ammunition, hand grenades, and side arms.   Most of all, ammunition is needed.
(*c*) The point of destination for all supplies is La Coruña.

2. In my opinion, supplies for the northern group are especially urgent at present, since thus far the southern group has been supplied exclusively.
I am more and more of the impression that it is extremely urgent to dispatch an expert at once to appraise on the spot the question of supplies for the northern and southern groups.   The place for him to report with the northern group: Pamplona, Colonel Solchaga at the Comandancia General, Noain Airport.
3. General Mola's representative is waiting here for decision on points 1 and 2.

SEYDEL

No. 42

3207/697870–73

The Chargé d'Affaires in Spain to the Foreign Ministry

Telegram

No. 170 of August 15   MADRID, August 15, 1936—midnight.

Reference 149 of August 13 [1] and report of August 14, 770–3.[2]

1. At today's diplomatic session the French Chargé d'Affaires told me he had been instructed by his Government to put pressure on the Spanish Government to comply with our demand, for France was greatly interested in settling this matter in order not to delay the signing of the neutrality agreement. He added that he had already conferred twice with the Foreign Minister, and he was accurately informed about every phase. [*Deleted:* When I asked him in extreme astonishment how he happened to know about this matter, he replied that the Spanish Foreign Minister himself had informed him of it.] [3]

2. Half an hour after this conversation, the State Secretary invited me to the Foreign Ministry in order to give me a reply to my last *démarche*, referred to above. He said that the Council of Ministers had decided last evening to give me a written reply. He was instructed to inform me even now of its substance. The decision was as follows:

(*a*) The crew of the airplane will be surrendered to the Embassy;

(*b*) The airplane, which had been flown without permission, had to be detained by the Government. The latter obligated itself not to use it. Should the German Government oppose this provision, the Spanish Government was prepared to submit the matter to a court of arbitration;

(*c*) At the request of the German Government the plane could be sealed by the Embassy and be kept in its name at the Barajas (Madrid) Airport.

The Spanish text of the decision will follow by air mail.

I told the State Secretary at once that points (*b*) and (*c*) were not acceptable and strongly demanded the immediate release of the airplane, against which there could be no other complaint than that in making a short intermediate landing in Madrid it had overlooked a prescribed customs formality. The State Secretary replied that point (*b*) of the decision had been taken in order to insure that the plane would not fly to Seville—whereupon I reminded him that the

---

[1] Not printed (3207/697866–67).
[2] Not printed (5076/E292416–17).
[3] The copy used is from the Madrid Embassy file; it was handwritten and amended by Voelckers.

plane had had orders to evacuate refugees. Visibly embarrassed, the State Secretary said finally that he had to bring up my point of view once more before the Council of Ministers, convening this evening. In response to my question he assured me that the decision relative to release of the crew would be unaffected. In conclusion I asked him to expedite the matter, for the German Government was losing patience and the Spanish Government, which had already been protracting the matter for six days, had only itself to blame for the consequences. [*Deleted:* Finally I expressed to the State Secretary my very great surprise that the Minister should have raised the issue with a foreign government; I had to report this to my Government and reserve all further decisions.]

3. The whole crew will be taken to the Embassy at 6 p. m.

4. The French Chargé d'Affaires, who had meanwhile spoken with the Foreign Minister again, called on me in the evening. He said that the Minister had told him the decision of the Council of Ministers was the utmost concession that the Government could obtain from the Red committees controlling it. The Government had the very best intentions but could not prevail, and it feared that if it gave up the airplane acts of sabotage or reprisals would follow, if nothing worse. In view of the desperate situation of the Government, the Frenchman recommended that we yield and warned us against going too far. I did not commit myself in any way.

5. France's intervention is in accordance with France's interest in supporting the Government. Our interest is the opposite.

VOELCKERS

No. 43

47/31612–14

The Ambassador in France to the Foreign Ministry

Telegram

VERY URGENT PARIS, August 16, 1936.
VERY SECRET Received August 16—1 : 55 p.m.
No. 472 of August 16 Pol. I 1250 g.

Please convey to Admiral Canaris at the War Ministry, through the quickest secure and reliable channels, the following agent's report.

WELCZECK

With reference to yesterday's telegram.[1]

A conversation on Saturday, August 15, with Count Rojas, hitherto Spanish Minister at Tangier, who arrived in Paris on a mission for Franco, revealed the following picture:

1. Franco and the Nationalist Government at Burgos are in urgent and immediate need of obtaining through the firm here [*hiesige*

---

[1] Document No. 41, p. 40.

Firma] all details known about assistance rendered by France and other countries to the Red Spanish Government with regard to matériel, finances, and personnel. Without detailed information, I am not in a position to comply with their request. Everything I have learned here I have sent there. I urgently request that by Tuesday's courier all the requested material be sent, if possible in Spanish translation, including material from the Foreign Ministry.

2. On this occasion I again recommend a concentration of forces.

In the last few weeks there have been numerous unwelcome messengers, coming partly from Franco, partly from Mola, and partly on their own initiative. I warned especially against various uncoordinated excursions to Berlin as being unnecessary and dangerous.

3. As desirable as unified direct contact of the fighting troops with Berlin may seem, I nevertheless consider it desirable, at least at present, to make use of the firm here, especially in view of the lack of time that is almost always clearly apparent. A reliable telegraphic report will be sent after inspection of the material. This presupposes close contact by special courier, for which I am personally available. The present situation is disadvantageous.

4. The victory at Estremadura has outwardly established contact between the northern and the southern group, as well as contact with Lisbon. The Commander in Chief is definitely Franco.

5. I stress the latter point since recurrent rumors of rivalry between the generals are absurd, particularly since both of them, and everyone else, know that everything is at stake.

6. The external contact established between Franco and Mola does not preclude careful observance of the needs of both groups, particularly since the most important centers of the armament industry are still in Red hands. I have the definite impression that we must help here for obvious reasons. With the best intentions Franco will not be able to forego considerable supplies for the southern group, particularly since the capture of Málaga and later of Cartagena, which will further check the Red forces and, above all, safeguard communications to the rear, is a *conditio sine qua non* in view of the situation in Andalusia, which has always been infested with Communism.

On the other hand, Mola's need for the speedy delivery of matériel, reported a number of times, is reiterated; at the same time on both fronts, the desire for antiaircraft guns has recently become more apparent than heretofore.

Reports made to date with respect to matériel and local appraisal by experts thus still hold good.

La Coruña is stressed as the new point of destination because of the saving in time, because of the protection afforded there by the Spanish Nationalist naval forces, and because possible danger from the Red Front navy in the south is thus avoided.

7. I learned today from a friendly neutral source that England allegedly delivered to the Spanish Red Front Government aviation matériel valued at many thousands of pounds. Hitherto the press has spoken of two planes for Madrid and four for Franco. I shall report Monday if the suspicion is confirmed. Personally I am skeptical concerning the complete transfer of Franco's troops and supplies from Morocco. At the very least, I consider it essential that preparation be made for one or more plausible submarine attacks.

SEYDEL

No. 44

47/31618

The Ambassador in France to the Foreign Ministry

Telegram

VERY SECRET   PARIS, August 17, 1936.
VERY URGENT   Received August 17—1 : 30 p.m.
No. 474 of August 17   Pol. I 1280 g.

Please transmit the following agent's report to Admiral Canaris at the War Ministry.

WELCZECK

I hear from a reliable source, V 110, that the transfer of French volunteers to the Spanish Red Militia began a few days ago in small groups.

One hundred to 170 men are being transferred per day, a total of about 30,000 in all. Most of them are trained reservists. I suggest informing the Foreign Ministry in connection with the question of the neutrality declaration.

SEYDEL

No. 45

168/132356–58

Note to the French Embassy

BERLIN, August 17, 1936.
Pol. III 1300 Ang. 1.

EXCELLENCY: In reply to the *note verbale* of August 16 [1] handed me today by Your Excellency, by which you informed me of the agreement between the French Government and His Britannic Majesty's Government concerning the attitude toward events in Spain, I have the honor to inform you as follows in the name of the German Government:

The German Government, in accordance with the declaration of the French Government contained in the note of the 15th from the French Minister of Foreign Affairs to His Britannic Majesty's Ambassador at Paris, is, for its part, also prepared:

1) to prohibit the direct and indirect exportation, reexportation, and transit of arms, munitions, and war matériel, as well as airplanes,

---

[1] Transmitting an exchange of declarations by which the British and French Governments agreed to prohibit the export of war matériel to Spain as soon as similar declarations were made by the Governments of Germany, Italy, Portugal, and the U.S.S.R. (168/132359–63).

assembled or unassembled, and warships, to Spain, the Spanish possessions, and the Spanish zone of Morocco;

2) to apply this prohibition to all contracts in process of being fulfilled; and

3) to inform the other participating governments of all measures being taken to carry out this prohibition.

The German Government makes the execution of the foregoing measures subject to:

(*a*) the release of the German transport plane still being detained in Madrid by the Spanish Government; and

(*b*) a similar obligation not only by the governments mentioned in the note of the French Minister of Foreign Affairs of August 15, but also by the governments of other countries that to an appreciable extent possess industries for the production of articles affected by the prohibition, said obligation to include delivery by private firms or persons.

In order to ascertain whether the condition under (*b*) above is complied with, the German Government would be grateful to the French Government for information as to which other governments, besides His Britannic Majesty's Government, have already joined, or will join, in the declaration of the French Government.

The German Government would, moreover, like to point out that in its opinion it would be highly desirable if the governments concerned extended their measures to prevent the departure of persons who have volunteered for the fighting taking place in the areas in question.

Please accept, Excellency, the expression of my highest consideration.

BARON VON NEURATH

No. 46

168/132346–48

Memorandum by the Acting State Secretary [1]

BERLIN, August 19, 1936.

The French Ambassador called on me this afternoon and by direction of his Government informed me as follows:

From reports that the French Government had received from Madrid, the Spanish Government had promised not to use the confiscated German airplane, but to seal it and leave it at a Madrid airport at the disposal of the German Embassy. Should the German Government not accept this suggested solution, the Spanish Government was prepared to submit the question of the airplane to a court of

---

[1] Dieckhoff was appointed Acting State Secretary on Aug. 11.

arbitration.   The French Government was extremely desirous, as M. François-Poncet stated very earnestly and emphatically, that the German Government accept one of these two solutions and thus clear the path for the entry into force of the proposed arms embargo.   The matter was urgent and important, and the French Government believed that in view of the cooperativeness of the Spanish Government in the matter of the airplane, the German Government should also adopt a conciliatory attitude.

As far as the question of the arms embargo was concerned, M. François-Poncet said that he could assure me in the name of his Government that in France an official authorization was always required for the exportation of arms, etc., so that there was a complete guaranty that private deliveries would also be prevented.   As far as the replies of the individual states were concerned, Italy had at first made the demand that collections of money and recruiting of volunteers be forbidden too; the French Government hoped, however, that in the negotiations with the Italian Government it would succeed in having this condition weakened to a wish.   The Russian reply was in the affirmative, except that the Russians refused to accept the proposed preamble, since the wording of the preamble, referring to the two parties in Spain in the same terms, did not seem right to them.   The Portuguese Government had assented.   The Belgian and Czechoslovak Governments had for the time being given their oral assent; their written assent was to be expected shortly.   The Swiss Government had declared that although it could not join, it would carry out the embargo through an independent arrangement.   As far as the Government of the United States was concerned, it had indicated in Paris that it would observe the strictest neutrality.

I thanked the Ambassador for the information but emphatically called his attention to the fact that we could not depart from our demand for the complete release of the confiscated airplane.   I would naturally inform the Foreign Minister at once of his *démarche*, but I did not believe that the situation could change as long as the airplane was not released.   I pointed out in this connection that the situation had recently become still more acute through the stopping of a German merchant ship on the high seas by a Madrid warship—an incident that we considered extremely serious.

The British Chargé d'Affaires, who also called here somewhat later in the afternoon, by direction of his Government made substantially the same statements as M. François-Poncet and insisted very strongly that we yield in the matter of the airplane and thus clear the path for the entry into force of the arms embargo.

DIECKHOFF

No. 47

1758/404743–44

·*The Chargé d'Affaires in Italy to the Foreign Ministry*

3990   ROME, August 20, 1936.
                                                Received August 22.
                                                Pol. III 1565.

With reference to report 3854 of August 14.

Subject: Convention regarding non-intervention in Spain.

Our reply to the French *note verbale*—informing us of the agreement between the French and the British Governments as to their attitude toward events in Spain—has, I am reliably informed, caused great satisfaction in the Foreign Ministry here; it fits perfectly into the policy followed here, since it makes possible a further delay in the conclusions of the proposed non-intervention agreement.

This still seems to be the goal of present Italian endeavors. Although the opinion is held that a convention will finally materialize, there is a desire to postpone it as long as possible. The present conversations with France are being conducted in this sense by the Italians. They revolve principally around the question of the recruiting of volunteers, public collections of money, and the practicability of carrying out the obligations that the individual governments would have to undertake. Italy is afraid that democratic France does not have at its disposal the same means as "totalitarian" Italy of putting obligations it has assumed into practical effect—a concern that Count Ciano has apparently expressed in all clarity to the French Ambassador.

PLESSEN

No. 48

168/132343–45

The Acting State Secretary to Various German Missions Abroad

Draft Telegram

BERLIN, August 20, 1936.

To all the missions listed in telegraphic instruction No. Pol. III 1190 of August 14, 1936.[1]

Telegraphic instruction No. . . .

For the orientation of your conversations:

We take it for granted that our attitude on the French-British arms embargo agreement is known from the DNB communiqué. From this

---

[1] Not printed (1758/404715–16). The addressees included all missions in Europe and the Embassy in the United States.

it is evident that settlement, in the sense demanded by us, of the airplane incident created by the Spanish Government is one of the conditions on which the German Government has declared itself ready to assent to the agreement.

The Spanish Government has settled the airplane incident only to the extent of releasing the crew. It is still detaining the plane. It is willing to declare only that it will not use the plane; that, if necessary, it will submit the matter to a court of arbitration and in the meantime seal the plane and leave it at the Madrid airport. Since the facts of the case are beyond question and since there is no doubt that the plane is a civilian plane, consent to compromise proposals is out of the question. The German Government insists, on the contrary, on its justified demand for release.[2]

The Spanish Government meanwhile has created a new incident, the effects of which are apt to influence our subsequent attitude on the question of the embargo, too. After the Spanish Government by decrees first declared the Moroccan coast and the Protectorate zone and then all the Spanish areas occupied by the rebels, including the coast, to be war zones, Spanish warships in two cases recently prevented German ships in the ports of Spanish Morocco from discharging their cargoes, and in one case even fired upon a German ship in port without reason and without warning. The German Government has protested very sharply against this interference with its legitimate shipping. Now a Spanish cruiser has fired on the German steamer *Kamerun* on the high seas, 7½ miles from the coast, forced her to follow, and had her searched by armed soldiers. The German Government through its Chargé d'Affaires in Madrid has declared very sharply that it fully maintains its former protests against interference with German shipping and does not recognize war-zone declarations. In accordance with instructions the Chargé d'Affaires said that the German Government would hold the Spanish Government responsible for all consequences of a repetition of similar incidents, and that German warships have received orders to protect German ships outside Spanish waters with all the means at their command against interference contrary to international law. In accordance with their orders, the commanders of the *Admiral Scheer* and the cruiser *Köln* have informed the chiefs of the Spanish Government Navy that naval forces had been instructed to oppose with force every unjustified act of force.

DIECKHOFF

---

[2] The Spanish Government, instead of surrendering the plane, proposed that the matter be referred to the Permanent Court of International Justice (4686/E225316–17). In October the German Government again asserted that the plane was not a military plane but was privately owned; it again demanded the immediate release of the plane (168/132230–31). The matter was taken up in the Non-Intervention Committee (1759/404987–90), but before anything was decided the plane was destroyed in an air attack on Madrid (4686/E 225354–55).

No. 49

1758/404739–40

The Ambassador in France to the Foreign Ministry

Telegram

No. 482 of August 20   PARIS, August 21, 1936.
                                   Received August 21—10 : 00 a.m.
                                                    Pol. III 1469.

I have been reliably informed by the Quai d'Orsay that Blum and Delbos are extremely worried about the delay in the final assent of Germany and Italy. Both have clearly realized that the Spanish question holds serious dangers for France, in both domestic and foreign policy.

The military successes of the rebels have given rise, not only in the Popular Front but also in the widest possible circles, to growing anxiety and nervousness over a probable Fascist victory in Spain, an increase in power of Fascist governments, and France's being wedged in between countries with similar regimes—regimes hated by France. Complete anarchization of Spain is regarded as the lesser evil.

Within the Cabinet the moderate members, particularly Blum and Delbos, believe they will be able to prevail against the interventionist members, steeped in the Popular Front ideology, only if they can find support very soon in an international obligation regarding an arms embargo. If the arms embargo does not materialize within the next few days, Blum and Delbos fear that they can no longer resist the growing domestic political pressure and that they will have to give unlimited support to the Spanish Government. The deliveries and the stream of Red Front volunteers to Spain would then assume such proportions that consequences for foreign policy would be incalculable.

Delbos believes that the arms embargo can prevent the battle between the Fascist and anti-Fascist powers from being fought to a finish on Spanish soil; it would at least preclude official participation of governments, since continued deliveries of arms would then take on such a fraudulent character that no government could admit responsibility for them.

On the basis of thoroughly reliable information from various camps here I have become convinced that postponement of final assent to the arms embargo must work to the disadvantage of the rebels, since, from considerations of geography alone, deliveries from countries which sympathize with them could not compete with French support. The Madrid Government, recognizing this situation, seems intent on sabotaging the creation of an arms embargo by showing itself uncompromising with regard to the German demand for the release of the airplane, despite earnest representations by the French.

WELCZECK

No. 50

168/132335–39

Memorandum by the Acting State Secretary

BERLIN, August 22, 1936.

Admiral Raeder called me on the telephone yesterday evening and very urgently asked for a conference with me. I therefore called on him at 9:30 a. m. today and, at his request, discussed with him the state of affairs in Spain and the general situation connected with Spain. Herr Raeder gave me a copy of a memorandum which he had given the Führer's Adjutant, Lieutenant Colonel Hossbach, for transmittal to Berchtesgaden and which Herr Hossbach will submit to the Führer there today.

I told the Admiral that by and large we judged the situation in Spain as he did, and that I thought that the most urgent necessity was to have Germany join the arms embargo soon; I had already expressed this opinion by telephone and by letter to Foreign Minister Baron von Neurath yesterday.

DIECKHOFF

[Annex]

1) In the opinion of A.[1] it is absolutely necessary to achieve clarity as to German political aims in Spain in order to take the proper military and political measures and to protect ourselves against surprises for which we are not prepared or organized at present.

2) The present military and political situation is appraised as follows:

(*a*) Military group:

Under good military leadership; numerically weak, for it lacks support among the broad masses. At present united in the common fight against Communism, which does not mean, though, that the aims of the military group may be identified with those of National Socialism. Fighting on the side of the military group are various political parties with various aims—including parties such as the Clericals, Monarchists, etc., which can by no means be called Fascist.

Since the military group is consequently limited in military power, particularly because the greater part of the air and naval forces are fighting on the side of the Government, it is not to be expected that the Franco Government can hold out for long, even after outward successes, without large-scale support from the outside.

---

[1] Probably a reference to the *Abteilung Ausland* (Foreign Department) in the War Ministry.

(b) The Madrid Government:

The Madrid Government, which at this writing is still officially recognized, is composed, politically, not only of the radical Leftist parties, but also of liberal middle-class circles and of the opponents of the parties which at present are fighting on the side of Franco—for example, the anti-Clericals and anti-Monarchists. Also fighting on the side of the Government are the Spanish separatists, who themselves are not at all Communist, as for example the Catalans and the Basques. Undoubtedly the Communist and radical wing has the upper hand at present within the Government front. On the other hand, however, this does not mean—at least not yet—that the Government can be called Communist as such. The military situation of the Government must be called not unfavorable. On the one hand there is available to it the great manpower of the working population; on the other hand, it still undoubtedly has trained military personnel which certainly includes part of the regular Army, the Navy, and the Air Force. Finally, it is also being supported by neighboring France to an extent which, for reasons of geography alone, the support that Franco receives cannot even remotely counterbalance. From the whole attitude of the Spanish Government toward our *démarche* it is evident that it does not by any means consider itself very weak. It can undoubtedly also base its resistance on the consciousness of its military strength, which in the long run is superior, and on the support from neighboring France and other countries.

3) The present situation can be briefly characterized. We and Italy are supporting Franco as far as our sympathies are concerned but are not in a position as regards matériel and personnel to send him enough aid to make him a match for the other side in the long run. On the other hand, we are daily taking a sterner attitude toward the Government, which is still recognized—an attitude which, under certain circumstances, may very suddenly lead to a break, at least in diplomatic relations. The Spanish Government assumes in advance that we have this intention and even says as much to the Chargé d'Affaires. There is no telling, however, what the political consequences of such a break in political relations would be, particularly since this break may under certain circumstances even be initiated not by our side but by the other side. Such a break undoubtedly would almost immediately bring about the danger of very rapidly spreading complications in Europe. We must expect that not only France and Russia but England as well will support the Spanish Government and that in the last analysis even Portugal can do nothing against the desire of England. Therefore, if we wish to continue with our previous course, we must also quite definitely prepare ourselves militarily and

politically for the consequences.   This means, on the one hand, support for Franco to an extent very different from heretofore and, on the other hand, the definite preparation of our naval forces and probably the rest of the Wehrmacht, too, for coming military conflicts. For the Navy this would then mean strengthening naval forces now in Spain with more equipment—submarines, for example—and quite generally preparing to distribute our forces in such a way that warlike developments can be met.   If the decision is reached, however, that a break in relations and the possibility of war are to be avoided under all circumstances, the only thing that remains for us is to rule out all sentiment in our Spanish policy and, unless we see the possibility of giving Franco the considerable forces needed to assure his victory, to display an impartial attitude more strongly than heretofore, both in our propaganda and in our conduct.   It can by no means be in the interest of a sane German policy to stake valuable German matériel and forces on a cause which, when all is said and done, cannot be helped to victory anyway.

4. A. considers it necessary that such a clarification of the political course in the case of Spain be obtained from the Führer, and as soon as possible, in order that the proper political and military measures can be started in the direction then laid down.   A decision in this question is especially important for the naval forces, since almost the whole German fleet is at present in Spanish waters.

No. 51

629/251826

The Ambassador in the Soviet Union to the Foreign Ministry

Telegram

URGENT   Moscow, August 22, 1936.
No. 116 of August 22   Pol. III 1529.

With reference to your No. 82 of August 17.[1]

I had already protested to Krestinsky [2] a few days ago against the false and senseless accusations in the Soviet press against the German Government, German warships, etc., in the Spanish question.   After Litvinov returned from his leave and took charge, I repeated my protest to him yesterday in the most energetic terms and extended it to the outrageous editorial that appeared in the *Journal de Moscou* on August 18.   I pointed out to Litvinov that the agitation of the

---

[1] Not printed (629/251793).   It repeated the complaints of the German Chargé d'Affaires in Madrid against the tone of Moscow radio broadcasts to Spain and instructed Schulenburg to make a strong protest.

[2] Nikolay Nikolayevich Krestinsky, Vice Commissar for Foreign Affairs.

Moscow transmitter against our Chargé d'Affaires and Party members in Madrid, who are in a most difficult situation anyway, endangered the lives of our people. Did he want to assume responsibility for this? At first, Litvinov hid behind the plea that he was familiar neither with the radio broadcasts in question nor with the article in the *Journal de Moscou* and that the broadcast presumably involved only a repetition of the statements of foreign newspapers. I replied that he who spreads obviously untrue and dangerous reports is just as guilty as the originator. Litvinov then asserted that it was difficult to restrain the Soviet press, since the German press unceasingly attacked the Soviet Union and had done so in the Spanish question in the most trenchant manner. I pointed out that Soviet propaganda had recently broken all records.

The conversation was in part quite lively, but Litvinov finally promised to heed our complaints and to put an end to excesses of Soviet propaganda.

SCHULENBURG

No. 52

47/31636

The Chargé d'Affaires in Portugal to the Foreign Ministry

Telegram

SECRET   LISBON, August 22, 1936—6 : 25 p.m.
No. 92 of August 22   Received August 22—8 : 55 p.m.
Pol. I 1396 g.

1. After the steamships *Kamerun* and *Wigbert* arrived in Lisbon, the material was sent on most smoothly through the agency of Herr Bernhardt (Hisma).[1] Prime Minister Salazar removed all difficulties within a very short time by his personal initiative and *personal* handling of details. He entrusted former Minister of Commerce Ramires with the project.

2. The reports regarding the military situation are as follows: The original plan of the rebels to direct the principal thrust from Córdoba northwards appears to have encountered difficulties, and therefore the greatest emphasis is now placed on the advance of the Badajoz–Tagus Valley–Toledo column. In addition, strong forces of Moroccan troops have been dispatched to Burgos for an advance over the Sierra de Guadarrama. This plan is not to be carried out, however, until the arrival of white troops from Toledo. The conduct of the Tercio in the latest battles has been outstanding.

DU MOULIN

---

[1] See Editors' Note, p. 1.

No. 53

3369/E010569-73

The Chargé d'Affaires in Portugal to the Foreign Ministry

CONFIDENTIAL   LISBON, August 22, 1936.
No. 2469   Sent by air courier August 23.

Subject: Portugal's attitude toward the Spanish Civil War.

In Portugal the outbreak of the Spanish Civil War confronted the Government with grave decisions. Although everything remained quiet in the country itself and the few stirrings of radical groups could very quickly be silenced by energetic measures without attracting any attention, it still had to be taken into account that there are numerous hidden Communists in Portugal who are waiting for the victory of the extremists in Spain. At the same time, the preparedness of the Portuguese Army, whose rearmament has been delayed all too long, is considered so unsatisfactory that the opinion is quite generally held here that two months after a defeat of the Spanish Nationalist Army, Portugal would go Communist. The possibility of exorcising this danger by assuming a more neutral attitude and attempting to win the sympathy of Red Spain for any eventuality appeared absurd and fruitless for Portugal from the beginning; the pan-Iberian tendencies of the Spanish extremist parties made it altogether unlikely that they would have a conciliatory attitude toward Portugal, who, moreover, was following a sharply anti-Communist course.

On the other hand, it had to be realized here that taking the part of the rebels meant staking everything on one card and bringing conflict closer in case of Red victory. The decision was made particularly difficult by the fact that the British ally by no means encouraged a policy in line with the interests of Portugal, but on the contrary tried by all manner of remonstrances to get her to follow a different course. I have confirmed recently that England went so far as to threaten that her obligations as an ally should by no means be taken for granted in the event of a conflict with a Red Spain provoked by Portugal's attitude. To be sure, according to available reports it appears rather doubtful whether Britain has offered the Portuguese Government adequate guaranties in case it should assume a strictly neutral attitude toward the Azaña Government.

In this situation Portugal decided to protect her own interests; her Government determined on the clear policy of complete support for the rebels as far as it was possible to do so and maintain the semblance of formal neutrality, and it has consistently adhered to this policy.

This decision, extremely difficult as it was to carry out, could never have been taken, of course, if the political structure of the country had not placed the Government in the hands of a leader who is aware of his responsibilities and who has the courage of his convictions: Prime Minister Salazar. By his authoritarian influence he made the entire Portuguese press serve the cause of propaganda for the Spanish Nationalist revolution. He facilitates the acquisition of all kinds of war matériel by the revolutionaries, as I have had the honor of pointing out in Embassy reports. In so doing, he unhesitatingly discharges unreliable customs officials and himself supervises the measures which are in the interest of the revolutionaries. I hear from the most reliable source that he even permitted a munitions shipment of the revolutionaries en route from Seville to Burgos to pass through Portuguese territory, before the capture of Badajoz established communication between the northern and southern armies, seeing to it that the shipment was expedited as much as possible (cf. also telegraphic report No. 92 of August 22, 1936, from the Legation).

He reserved the greatest possible freedom of action for himself by the wording of the answering note to the Anglo-French proposal for a neutrality pact. When the Spanish Ambassador protested to the Foreign Ministry here that members of the Government Militia who crossed the Portuguese boundary were immediately placed in a concentration camp, while officers of the Nationalist Army at all times had free entry into Portugal, he received the reply that Communism was outlawed in Portugal and that the Portuguese Government was therefore not in a position to grant Communists from foreign countries freedom of movement in Portugal.

Since Portugal in pursuing this policy is acting in pronounced opposition to her British ally, it is natural that popular sympathy in Portugal should, as a result of the situation created by the Spanish Civil War, turn sharply away not only from France but also from England—whose prestige, moreover, has suffered through the outcome of the Italo-Abyssinian conflict—and that public opinion is inclined toward the countries that favor the Spanish revolutionaries. There are thus numerous evidences of admiration for our Führer and respect for the new Germany in Portugal today, and there is no doubt that our reputation here has been greatly enhanced. Under these circumstances the question arises whether one might not take advantage of this favorable sentiment by prompt and generous action with regard to participating in the rearmament program of the Portuguese armed forces, in case the execution of this program should now be accelerated. We should bear in mind that the Italians, who suffered a great deal of damage in this field at the time of the sanctions, have lately been very active here.

Furthermore, I do not wish to neglect pointing out that conditions are particularly favorable for having one of our warships now in Spanish waters visit Lisbon, perhaps after completion of her operations, since there is a great deal of sympathy here for our naval forces operating in Spain. However, it should be remembered that a large part of the German colony in Lisbon is away till the middle of October and that there is therefore comparatively little to offer the crew.

COUNT DU MOULIN

No. 54

168/132334

Note to the French Embassy

BERLIN, August 24, 1936.

EXCELLENCY: Pursuant to the letter which Foreign Minister Baron von Neurath sent to you on August 17 regarding our attitude toward events in Spain, I have the honor to inform you of the following by direction of the German Government:

The German Government has noted with satisfaction that the other governments concerned have also adhered to the declaration proposed by the French Government. It has now decided to put into effect immediately the measures contemplated for Germany in that declaration. In making this decision, despite the fact that it has not yet been possible to conclude the discussions with the Spanish Government regarding the release of the German transport plane, the German Government was guided by the desire to do everything possible on its part to hasten the conclusion of the contemplated international agreement. The German Government is hopeful that the other governments concerned will now do all that is necessary, insofar as this has not already been done, to carry out effectively the measures agreed upon.

Accept, Excellency, the assurances of my highest consideration.

DIECKHOFF

No. 55

168/132329

The Foreign Minister to the Acting State Secretary (Excerpt)[1]

STRICTLY CONFIDENTIAL BERLIN, August 24, 1936.

• • • • • • •

Furthermore, I have convinced the Führer that we now cannot wait any longer to join the neutrality declaration, if we do not wish to be suspected of sabotaging the whole matter. That is why I telephoned

---

[1] The complete text of this letter has not been found. Copies of this excerpt were sent on Aug. 25 to the Director of the Legal Department (Gaus) and to the Acting Director of the Political Department (Weizsäcker).

you. I considered it necessary to inform the French Ambassador today, since tomorrow the Führer will announce the introduction of two-year military service. It seemed to me that it would be well for us at least to make known our desire to cooperate on the neutrality question before this announcement, which naturally will again occasion unfriendly comments in France, and probably also in England.

. . . .

No. 56

1758/404753–55

The Chargé d'Affaires in Great Britain to the Foreign Ministry

[Telegram]

No. 175 of August 25   LONDON, August 25, 1936.

Pol. III 1686.

Today I called on the Acting Under Secretary in the Foreign Office, Sir Alexander Cadogan, in order to inform myself upon returning from my leave regarding the view entertained here on the Spanish crisis. Sir Alexander has been taking the place of Sir Robert Vansittart since the latter started his vacation. Vansittart will resume his post at the beginning of September.

First we discussed the question of the arms embargo, and Sir Alexander expressed great satisfaction at yesterday's decision of the German Government to place a ban on the export of arms. Since all of the countries approached had now come out for the declaration of such an embargo, the international situation had doubtless been considerably calmed. At the moment conversations were taking place between the French and British Governments regarding the proposal made by Italy that a commission be appointed to supervise the execution of the arms embargo. Since it might no doubt be safely assumed that sooner or later accusations would be made against one country or another as having violated the arms embargo, it seemed desirable to the British Government to appoint such a commission of the powers concerned, and it had therefore expressed its agreement with this proposal in Paris.

To my question whether there was any truth in the press reports that a step was being planned by several powers to exhort the belligerents in Spain to declare a truce, Cadogan replied that in this form the reports were not in accordance with the facts. On the other hand, at the instance of Argentina, the chiefs of missions assembled at Hendaye had suggested that a humanitarian appeal be addressed to the warring parties in Spain, and he had just informed Ambassador Chilton that the British Government declared itself in agreement with this proposal.   He assumed that our Chargé d'Affaires in Madrid knew about the plan.

With regard to the military situation within Spain, Cadogan said that it was not possible for the Foreign Office to obtain a clear picture of the situation from the reports at hand.   They were, to be sure, in radio communication with the Chargé d'Affaires in Madrid via the British warships in Spanish waters, but the reports coming in were so contradictory that they made it impossible to form a clear opinion. Thus, for example, they had received reports to the effect that in the areas occupied by the military group the whole population was on the side of the military, while other equally reliable reports claimed the exact opposite.   At the moment both parties apparently had their teeth so deep in each other that an early decision was hardly to be expected, and even if one of the parties should be victorious he could not imagine how Spain could be restored to order in the near future. General Franco was a good soldier, to be sure, but no politician, and as far as he knew the military group did not possess any politicians at all.   If the parties of the Left were victorious, however, constant Communist disorders would have to be expected.

To my question as to how the British Government had reacted to the war-zone declaration by the Spanish Government, Cadogan replied that the Foreign Office had sent the Madrid Government a note in which it stated that it could not recognize the blockade proclaimed by the Spanish Government.   In practice, however, this British non-recognition of the blockade referred only to the open sea.   Within the three-mile limit the Spanish Government could probably take the stand that it had the right to stop ships.   At any rate, the British Government had notified British ships that they should avoid the three-mile zone as much as possible, and particularly the ports declared closed by the Spanish Government.

BISMARCK

No. 57

4446/E086328

The Chargé d'Affaires in Spain to the Foreign Ministry

Telegram

SECRET   MADRID, August 27, 1936—1 : 50 p.m.
No. 263 of August 27   Received August 28—1 : 15 a.m.
                                                            Pol. III 1782.

This morning Junkers 52's made an air attack on Madrid and dropped bombs on the airports.

It is reported that leaflets were dropped demanding that the local garrison surrender within three days; otherwise the capital would be bombed systematically.

Please arrange that at least as long as Lufthansa traffic is maintained no Junkers planes raid Madrid.

VOELCKERS

No. 58

3371/E010624

Memorandum by the Chargé d'Affaires in Portugal

SECRET   LISBON, August 27, 1936.
                                                        e. o. No. 2548.

The economic expert of the NSDAP, Herr Vollmer, called on me today and informed me that he had received a request from Spain to pass on an order for 2,000 aerial bombs (1,000 each of the 85-kilogram and the 50-kilogram types). Delivery could be made through Holland, which had not joined the pact. I called his attention to the fact that Spain must route such orders through a central office, without commenting further on the situation created by Germany's joining the neutrality pact.

He wanted to find out more about the matter.

D[U MOULIN]

No. 59

47/31659–60

The Acting State Secretary to the Ambassador in France

Telegram[1]

No. 373   BERLIN, August 27, 1936—12:45 p.m.
                                                        zu Pol. I 1459 g.

DEAR WELCZECK: The reports concerning the events in Spain which are being forwarded by the Embassy to the Foreign Ministry and are meant for the War Ministry must be treated as particularly secret. Although there are no indications of any kind that our cipher system is unreliable, we consider it advisable in any case to be still more careful than before in these very secret matters. I should therefore like to ask you not to continue sending the reports in question by telegram, but rather in cipher by courier. If the courier connections are not frequent enough, they should be increased.

In very urgent cases, in which a great deal depends on rapid transmittal, the telegraphic method may still be used in the future. I should be grateful, however, if in such cases the telegrams were worded with particular caution.

With cordial greetings and Heil Hitler!

Yours,
DIECKHOFF

---

[1] This document was prepared for dispatch by post and then sent as a telegram.

No. 60

1758/404780–81

The Chargé d'Affaires in Italy to the Foreign Ministry

3990 II
ROME, August 28, 1936.
Received August 29.
Pol. III 1904.

With reference to my report of August 20, 3990.[1]

Subject: Non-intervention in Spain.

The reply of the Italian Government to the last French *note verbale* concerning non-intervention in Spain was made sooner than was to be expected. Until shortly before the reply became known, the impression was that the conversations with the French Ambassador were progressing but slowly. I believe that even the French Embassy was surprised by the reply.

I have reported by telegram concerning the reasons which were supposedly decisive for the Italian Government in replying to the French proposal (cf. telegraphic report no. 136 of August 21 [2]). For one thing, Italy did not wish to appear as the one preventing the agreement from being concluded; in addition, as I deduce from a remark which Under Secretary of State Bastianini made to me, another important consideration for the Italian Government was that it is after all doubtful whether in Spain the Government party or the party of General Franco would gain more benefit from a further delay in concluding the non-intervention agreement. Signor Bastianini informed me that the Italian Ambassador was told in Berlin that a further delay would work in favor of the Government party—an argument which he fully understands.

That the Italian Government has attempted, by the way its reply has been formulated, to reserve far-reaching freedom of action for all contingencies is just as obvious as that it does not intend to abide by the declaration anyway.

I have heard, however, that the prohibition on exporting weapons to Spain is to be expected some time today.

PLESSEN

---

[1] Not printed (1758/404743–44).
[2] Not printed (1758/404741–42).

No. 61

4793/E236234

The Chargé d'Affaires in Portugal to the Foreign Ministry

SECRET
No. 2567

LISBON, August 28, 1936.
Received August 31.
Pol. I 1447 g.

Subject: Representative of the AGK.

Herr Eberhard Messerschmidt has arrived here as the representative of the Export Cartel for War Matériel with instructions to proceed to Seville. Since Herr Messerschmidt was recommended by an associate of Rear Admiral Canaris, the Legation assisted him in continuing his journey to Seville.

DU MOULIN

No. 62

629/251876–77

The Chargé d'Affaires in Spain to the Foreign Ministry

[Telegram]

No. 280 of August 29

MADRID, August 29, 1936.
Pol. III 1880.

With reference to my No. 278 [276] of August 28.[1]

1. Last night at 12 o'clock there was another air attack on Madrid by a Junkers 52 [*durch Ju 52*] escorted by two fighter planes. Four heavy bombs were dropped on the War Ministry, falling in the garden and at the entrance. There was considerable property damage, and several persons were killed. Five more bombs were dropped on the Barajas airfield.

2. The planes dropped new leaflets, which announce that Madrid will be destroyed in reprisal for the Government's gas and bomb attacks on open cities, and exhort the population to drive out the Government.

3. A Spanish Lufthansa mechanic, who was placed on the highest tower of the city in the immediate vicinity of the War Ministry at night as a listening post because of his exact knowledge of Junkers planes and of the sound of their motors, told a German Lufthansa mechanic that he had determined definitely that a Junkers plane was involved in the attack; the technique of the attack had been quite un-Spanish, which indicated that the crew was probably German, and bomb splinters showed their German origin.

---

[1] Not printed (629/251875).

[4.] Today's newspapers carry an increasing number of reports concerning German support of the rebels and increasing attacks on Germany. The leading Anarchist newspaper claims that there are German Junkers planes with German crews in Seville.

5. From various sides I get reports on the aroused feeling of the Leftist population here against Germany, and on threats against the Embassy.

6. Referring to paragraph 2, great damage and loss of life are probable if the night air attacks are repeated regularly, considering that there are almost no air defenses in Madrid.

7. A sudden outbreak of popular feeling against everything German is then certain to occur.

8. Under these circumstances further maintenance of Lufthansa traffic can no longer be justified. The same applies to a further stay of the remainder of the German colony and the Embassy. The Government has refused my request, repeatedly expressed during the last few days, to restore the former reliable Embassy guard. As a matter of fact, the hitherto unified police force no longer exists; all units have been infiltrated by members of the Red Militia since the day before yesterday, on the basis of a new decree. As a consequence the Embassy guard is in the hands of the Anarchist-Communist Militia.

VOELCKERS

No. 63

1758/404778–79

The Ambassador in the Soviet Union to the Foreign Ministry

[Telegram]

No. 121 of August 29   Moscow, August 29, 1936.
                                        Pol. III 1893.

With reference to your No. 92 of August 27.[1]

I protested to Litvinov today concerning the *Izvestiya* article of August 26, as directed. Litvinov replied that the Moscow radio station had not made a personal attack against our Chargé d'Affaires in Madrid but had only repeated reports current in British newspapers accusing German Government and Party officials in general of taking the part of the rebels. To my objection that broadcasts by Radio Moscow in the Spanish language were more dangerous than statements in British newspapers, which no one in Spain reads, Litvinov replied that the reports in the *Manchester Guardian* had surely

---

[1] Not printed (5195/E307473). On Aug. 26 the German Chargé d'Affaires in Spain requested that new representations be made in Moscow against "the inflammatory campaign against Germany" being conducted by the Moscow radio (telegram No. 261, 629/251863).

been repeated in the Spanish Government papers, and Radio Moscow had thus not brought up anything new.

Litvinov went on to explain that any Soviet propaganda against Germany regarding the Spanish matter was merely a reply to German propaganda, which continually sought to make the Soviet Union responsible for events in Spain. I vigorously denied this assumption. Litvinov declared that both he and the Soviet Government deplored the continual propaganda war between Germany and the Soviet Union and that they were far from desiring a deterioration in the relations between the two countries. He could assure us that Soviet propaganda would cease immediately if Germany would stop constantly attacking the Soviet Union. He feared, however, that the impending Party rally would bring a new high point in German anti-Soviet propaganda.

I then protested vigorously against the defamation of the Führer and Chancellor in the Kharkov newspaper (see report A 1801 of August 27,[2] which will follow by courier) and the slandering of Minister Goebbels in *Izvestiya* (see my telegram No. 117 of August 28 [2]) and reminded Litvinov of his promise to refrain from personal slander. He replied that instructions to the Soviet press to abstain from libelous personal attacks were still in force. He would see that both papers were reminded of that fact.

SCHULENBURG

[2] Not found.

No. 64

168/132318–21

The Acting State Secretary to the Foreign Minister

BERLIN, August 29, 1936.

MY DEAR MINISTER: Shortly after our telephone conversation today regarding the French proposal for supervision of the non-intervention obligations with regard to Spain, M. François-Poncet telephoned and, on the basis of a conversation I had with him yesterday, gave Herr von Bargen [1] some supplementary information concerning the French plan.[2] What M. François-Poncet said was: According to the reports he had received from Paris meanwhile, the duties of the committee were more modest than he had assumed. The committee was intended primarily to afford the participating governments the opportunity of maintaining constant touch with each other on the subject of the arms embargo. Furthermore, it was meant to serve the purpose of enabling the governments to inform one another of the decisions made in the

---

[1] Dr. von Bargen of the office of the State Secretary.

[2] The French plan for a committee to supervise the working of the non-intervention declarations was contained in *notes verbales* dated Aug. 27 and 28 (168/132323–26). The notes were published and are adequately summarized in this and the following documents.

various countries in carrying out the arms embargo and possibly to adjust these decisions to one another.   There was no intention of appointing special delegates for this purpose; it would be sufficient if the chiefs of missions or a member of the embassy or legation in London were assigned to this committee.   It would probably develop from the work of the committee that detailed complaints, too, would have to be examined.

In the light of these explanations I again looked over the text of the two French notes of August 27 and 28 together with Gaus, Weizsäcker, and Woermann.   We felt that it would be very difficult and on the other hand perhaps unnecessary to assume a completely negative attitude toward the matter.   Besides, although we have still received no reply from Rome to our inquiry, Italy herself in her first note brought up the question of supervision of the non-intervention obligations, and I was just informed by Welczeck that the Italian Chargé d'Affaires in Paris had told him that Italy was in favor of the plan, provided the conversations of the Ambassadors were held in London and not in Paris.   Thus we would probably be quite alone in our negative attitude.

Moreover, I hardly believe that the plan could really entail any serious danger for us.   The word "control" does not appear in the French note; according to François-Poncet's explanation, too, what was involved was primarily an exchange of information and a coordination.   We ourselves, after all, can play a part in seeing that this London arrangement does not develop into a permanent political agency which might make trouble for us; and in this we can secure Italian and British support, too.

Naturally, we have to count on complaints of all kinds being brought up in London regarding failure to observe the obligation not to intervene, but we cannot avoid such complaints in any case.   It can, in fact, only be agreeable to us if the center of gravity, which after all has thus far been in Paris because of the French initiative, is transferred to London.   I also consider it self-evident that past grievances can no longer be brought up; at any rate, we could withhold our cooperation to that extent.   It may doubtless also be assumed that the French Government, which has, of course, done very much more to support one of the two sides than any other country, is not interested in discussing the past.

If you agree with this reasoning, a reply might be sent to the French Embassy stating, roughly, that the German Government is prepared to take part in a continuous exchange of ideas in London regarding the implementation of the declarations made by the various powers in this question and that it has instructed the German Chargé d'Affaires in London accordingly.   It was taken for granted that the Chargé d'Affaires might at any time be represented by another member of the Embassy.

Incidentally, M. François-Poncet also asked Herr von Bargen whether we agreed to the publication of our note replying to the French embargo proposal and of our present proposals regarding the London committee. I believe there are no particular objections, if we accept the new proposal. If we do not, Germany's negative attitude on the entire question and a deviation from the attitude we assumed in our first reply would probably be rather too apparent to the public.

I should be very grateful to you if you could let me know by Monday morning whether you agree with this mode of procedure.

Please accept, my dear Minister, my most sincere regards.

DIECKHOFF

No. 65

1758/404772–73

The Acting Director of the Political Department to Various German Missions Abroad [1]

Telegram

No. . . . BERLIN, August 31, 1936—5 : 30 p.m.
zu Pol. III 1848, 1849 II.

The French Embassy here has handed us two notes, in which it is suggested, with reference to article 3 of the declaration concerning the arms embargo against Spain, that a committee be established in London for the purpose of collecting all information pertaining to the measures taken and investigating the practical possibilities for carrying out the provisions of the above-mentioned declaration.

In article 3 of the arms embargo declaration the participating governments declare that they are willing to inform one another of all measures which they take to carry out the arms embargo.

The French Embassy has been given the following reply:

"The German Government does not consider it necessary or advisable to establish a formal committee. For its part, it would deem it adequate and appropriate, and would agree, if the individual governments were simply to inform the British Government of the measures they take to implement the above-mentioned declaration. Similarly, all suggestions made by the various governments on the question of the arms embargo could be centralized in London and passed on by the British Government to the different diplomatic missions accredited there."

---

[1] This circular instruction was addressed to all German diplomatic missions in Europe, the Embassies in the United States, Japan, and Turkey, and the Consulates General at Geneva and Barcelona.

For your personal information:

The reason for this attitude of ours is uneasiness lest the committee suggested by the French Government might gradually develop into an agency of extended competence with control functions.

WEIZSÄCKER

No. 66

1758/404774–76

Memorandum by the Acting State Secretary

BERLIN, September 1, 1936.
e. o. Pol. III 1849 a.

The French Ambassador called on me today before going to Vichy for several weeks for a cure. He first expressed his great regret that in yesterday's note [1] we had responded in such a negative manner to the French invitation to establish an embargo committee in London. I told the Ambassador that we did take a negative stand on the question of the committee, and for obvious reasons. But we were quite willing to attain, in the manner we suggested in our note, the objective desired by the French Government of exchanging information concerning the embargo measures taken by the various governments, and of exchanging suggestions by the governments on the question of the arms embargo. We were not in any way evading a reasonable, constant exchange of views on the questions connected with the embargo but simply did not find the suggested idea of a formal committee promising. Then the Ambassador made a few more remarks to the effect that this note would have an unfavorable effect on the outside world and would probably be interpreted as proving that, although Germany had joined the embargo, she was now unwilling to cooperate in seeing it applied; such criticism would be all the more likely in the outside world since our joining the agreement had been interpreted almost everywhere as merely a defense measure for lessening the impression of the announcement of two-year compulsory military service, which was made on the same day. I answered M. François-Poncet that one is never safe from malicious interpretations but that in the present case these interpretations were false and we rejected them categorically. I repeated that we had no intention whatever of evading a constant exchange of views on the execution of the embargo, but that we merely found the form which the French Government had suggested impractical. To his question whether we would agree to publication of our two letters on the embargo question as well as our *note verbale* of yesterday on the question of the committee, I replied in the affirmative.[2]

---

[1] For substance of the German reply see the preceding document.
[2] Marginal note in Neurath's handwriting, referring to the first paragraph: "Our collaboration will depend on the way the committee works."

The Ambassador then turned to the problem of negotiations for the Western Pact [3] and asked about our attitude. I told him that we were willing, as in the past, to take part in the diplomatic preparatory work for the Five Power Conference; according to what we had heard from our Chargé d'Affaires in London, the British Government would approach the four powers in the near future and in this way the preparatory discussions would presumably get under way. M. François-Poncet was particularly interested in hearing whether we were willing to go to the conference and negotiate on the first points on the agenda without bringing up the fifth point, or whether we wanted to force the French Government now, in advance, expressly to renounce the fifth point, that is, the ties in the East. In other words, did the German Government take the stand that it was possible to start out by negotiating on a Western Pact, leaving the Eastern questions open? Or did it demand from the very first that France renounce her Eastern ties, before Germany would enter into a discussion concerning a Western Pact? If Germany followed the first course, he believed he could say that the Franco-Russian ties would gradually cool, particularly since they had never been popular with a large sector of the French people; we would then attain our objective slowly but surely. If, on the other hand, we should apply pressure to the French Government now and demand that it give up the Russian alliance, the French Government could only refuse to do so. In a long discourse M. François-Poncet tried to convince me of the rightness of the one alternative and the wrongness of the other, emphasizing solemnly during the course of his statements that there were no special military ties between France and the Soviet Union. I limited myself to telling the Ambassador that he had to realize that in Germany people had grown even more conscious of the Russian danger during the last few months than they had been formerly, and that the Franco-Russian pact was indeed considered still more serious than before. I did not go into his question as to which of the two courses Germany would take with regard to the French Government.[4]

DIECKHOFF

---

[3] The proposed meeting of the five Locarno Powers (Great Britain, France, Belgium, Italy, and Germany) to negotiate a new agreement to take the place of the Locarno Agreement and to deal with the situation created by the German occupation of the Rhineland in March 1936. Representatives of Great Britain, France, and Belgium met in London on July 23, 1936, and issued a communiqué containing five conclusions and suggesting an early meeting of the Locarno Powers. An invitation was extended to Germany and Italy and was accepted by the German Government on July 31. Questions relating to the agenda of the proposed conference were the subject of extended negotiations through diplomatic channels during August and September 1936.

[4] Marginal note in Neurath's handwriting: "In my opinion we, for our part, do not need to bring up the question of the Soviet-French alliance, but can first negotiate concerning the Western Pact."

No. 67

47/31694

The Ambassador in France to the Acting State Secretary

PARIS, September 2, 1936.
Pol. I 1643 g.

With reference to your telegram No. 384 of September 1, 1936.[1]

DEAR DIECKHOFF: In my opinion the French will suspend their deliveries to the Spanish Red Front only if the British put strong pressure upon the Government here. The key to this is therefore in London. I believe that England fears victory for Franco principally because she assumes that, in gratitude for the support he received, he will give the Italians advantages of some kind in the Mediterranean. One should therefore take advantage of the presence of my friend Almazán [2] to extract from Franco a statement to the effect that British interests in the Mediterranean will suffer no diminution after a victory by the White Front, in case England is willing and is in a position to exert so strong a pressure upon the French that French support of the Spanish Red Front ceases immediately. Only if the British speak seriously with the French will Blum and Delbos succeed in holding their colleagues in check.

In this connection I would also like to remind you of the Mannesmann properties in Spanish Morocco, taken over at one time by the Reich; as such the titles to them have no validity under Moroccan law but might be recognized by Franco as a return service.

In haste, as the courier is just leaving.

Heil Hitler! [3]

Yours,

H. WELCZECK

---

[1] Not printed (4796/E236697).
[2] On Aug. 31 Welczeck had been informed in a telegram from Dieckhoff that Almazán would proceed from Rome to Berlin and wished to speak with Welczeck, Göring, and Hitler on questions of "the highest international importance" (47/31667).
[3] Marginal note: "I hear by telephone from Plessen that Almazán has returned to Spain and is not coming to Berlin. D[umont]. Sept. 12."

No. 68

168/132310–11

Memorandum by the Acting State Secretary

BERLIN, September 2, 1936

The British Chargé d'Affaires called on me today and, at the direction of his Government, expressed the "earnest hope" that the German Government would reconsider its negative answer in the question of the establishment of a committee for Spanish arms embargo questions. Mr. Newton stated that all the other powers had acceded to the French proposal and that Germany was the only country that had raised objections. There was no question of setting up the committee in London as an independent body which would have to make decisions or whose jurisdiction might later be extended in any way; it was a question only of organizing loosely the diplomatic representatives of the interested powers accredited in London. The British Government itself by no means intended to go beyond this and to create a new international organ but was really confining itself to making available a meeting place for the joint conferences which, would take place from time to time. The committee was not to have the task either of exercising control powers or of making majority decisions or the like. It was impossible to see how a certain amount of coordination, which after all was necessary, could be achieved other than by the proposed method; Germany, too, in the opinion of the British Government, had an interest in this, for she could, for example, bring up for discussion the proposal which she had already made that the influx of volunteers to Spain also be suppressed. At any rate the British Government declined to create a sort of clearing-house for the execution of the embargo declaration in accordance with our counterproposal; this involved a great deal of red tape and a great loss of time and would also place the British Government in a position which involved more responsibility than the British Government wished to assume in this matter.

I once again explained to Mr. Newton all our objections to the establishment of a commission but told him that his statements as to the nature and procedure of the work of the committee had given us a clearer picture than we had been able to obtain before and that we would therefore consider the matter once more.

DIECKHOFF

No. 69

1758/404817

Memorandum by the Acting Director of the Political Department

BERLIN, September 3, 1936.
Pol. III 2302.

The French Chargé d'Affaires, M. Lamarle, called on me today in order to revert once more to the matter of the arms embargo committee.

He said that the French Government was particularly interested in a speedy and practical handling of matters and had no preference for any particular procedure; it would, however, be very desirable that an agreement be reached as soon as possible regarding procedure. Fourteen or fifteen countries had, as I knew, already acceded.

M. Lamarle, who clearly implied that the committee and its powers had been a British rather than a French invention, said that no difficulties would be raised in Paris if we were able to make some sort of practical proposal, corresponding to German interests, for the procedure and functions of the proposed central office. As his personal idea M. Lamarle proposed that it might perhaps even suffice to set up an office (regarding whose composition he said nothing) within the Foreign Office in London and to achieve through its mediation the necessary exchange of information and opinion without any formal sessions, or even any sessions at all, of the diplomatic corps.

I promised the Chargé d'Affaires that I would transmit his suggestions, which strike a somewhat more cooperative note than what we have been offered so far; however, I called M. Lamarle's attention to the fact that in our note of August 31 we had already mentioned what in our opinion was materially necessary and had really expected new suggestions concerning a procedure that would suit us to come from the French and the British.[1]

WEIZSÄCKER

---

[1] Marginal note in Neurath's handwriting: "What matters is to define exactly the powers of the committee."

No. 70

1758/404812–15

The Minister in Portugal to the Foreign Ministry

No. 2666   LISBON, September 4, 1936.
                                                       Received September 7.
                                                       Pol. III 2281.

Subject: Conversation with the Portuguese Foreign Minister.

Today, during my first conversation with the Portuguese Foreign Minister since my return, it was easy to see the change that has taken place in the political atmosphere in Portugal since the outbreak of the Spanish Civil War. Senhor Armindo Monteiro, who with all natural respect for Germany and her reconstruction nevertheless strongly inclined toward England in the past and at the same time desired for himself the post of Minister to Paris, admitted today quite candidly that he simply did not understand the British policy and called France her own gravedigger.

He described the developments of recent weeks in particular detail: how Portugal had been asked to take part in the general embargo and how at first there had been no desire to understand the special position of his country. Portugal touched directly on the conflagration in

Spain, and whereas, for instance, they would still have a great deal of time in London to theorize about further measures, Portugal might possibly long since have been forced to take immediate action because of direct dangers. Therefore he had asked first about the guaranties which could be given to Portugal in case of her agreement. By way of reply, he had been referred to the League of Nations Covenant; this suggestion he, remembering the poor Negus, had declined with thanks—as Portugal's official representative on the League of Nations Council stated ironically. Finally Portugal had set the familiar conditions, which had been accepted.

Then the question of the London control commission had been raised. There, too, Portugal's interest was quite different from that of the countries situated farther away. For instance, one could not possibly demand of him that he agree to having Russians or other representatives of Marxist states carry out any sort of control along the Portuguese border. Thus, before agreeing to the creation of a new commission, he must know what the commission controlled and how it was to exercise its control. Basically he was against such a commission, just as Germany was, and he only wished to avoid being accused later of having obstructed a solution of the situation.

Both the Foreign Minister and Secretary General de Sampayo, whom I called on afterwards, were exceedingly indignant about a *Berliner Tageblatt* dispatch from London, not yet published here, according to which the Portuguese position in the embargo question could be traced to remonstrances which the British Ambassador here made to the Foreign Ministry in Lisbon. This statement had already called forth a sharp retort by the Portuguese Minister in Berlin, who pointed out that evidently Germany had not understood the true significance of the Portuguese declaration of acceptance, which after all had almost been changed to the opposite by the reservations appended to it. He had arranged for the *Berliner Tageblatt* to give further explanations in the near future regarding the true Portuguese position. One can understand that the Portuguese Government is bitter at having its attitude misunderstood. After all, it can point with pride to the fact that in the struggle for order and culture, in which in the last analysis the existence of its own country is at stake, it has acted independently of foreign influences and has heard few kind words for its attitude from its British protector.

Aside from these political statements, Minister Monteiro could not speak gratefully enough about the friendly reception which the Portuguese athletes and the Portuguese State Youth Organization had been accorded during the Olympic Games. He was particularly grateful that, by invitation of the Hitlerjugend after the Olympic Games, the State Youth had had the opportunity during their trip through Germany to become acquainted with our institutions and our discipline; for it was above all up to them to make use some day of what they had seen in building the new Portugal.

HUENE

P. S.:   LISBON, September 5, 1936.

The morning papers of September 5 published the text of the Portuguese reply in the question of Portuguese participation in the London control commission. I have the honor to append a clipping of the Portuguese text.[1]

HUENE

---

[1] Not reprinted.

No. 71

1758/404801–04

Memorandum by the Director of the Legal Department

BERLIN, September 4, 1936.
Pol. III 2270.

The British Chargé d'Affaires called on me this afternoon in order to continue the conversation on the London arms embargo committee. He gave me confidentially a copy of the telegram which he had sent to London on the basis of his last conversation with Herr Dieckhoff (enclosure 1) and also a copy of the instruction which was sent to him today from London in reply (enclosure 2).

Mr. Newton stated that surely this instruction now removed all difficulties for us. The British Government considered it of the greatest importance to clear up the whole matter before the week end, and all that was still lacking was the agreement of the German Government.

When I asked whether the other governments involved agreed with the British view of the character of the committee, he answered that of course he could speak formally only for his Government but that the understanding between our two Governments afforded sufficient guaranty that the work of the committee would not expand in an undesirable manner. Moreover, the Foreign Office had communicated with the French Embassy in London, which had stated that it agreed with the instruction sent to him; it had only made a slight reservation with regard to the statement of Herr Dieckhoff that the question of volunteers participating in the Spanish fighting might be included under the authority of the committee, since the French Embassy doubted whether a strict prohibition in this respect could be issued in France.

Mr. Newton made special reference, moreover, to the second paragraph of his instruction, in which it is stressed that we retain full freedom to express our views in the committee concerning its functions and its duration.

I told Mr. Newton that I could not, of course, give him a final answer today. I would report on the matter as soon as possible and then get in touch with him again. However, that would probably not be possible before Saturday noon.

In conclusion he repeated his request for the greatest possible speed.

GAUS

[Enclosure 1] [1]

Herr Dieckhoff has just informed me that the question of German participation in the proposed Committee has been further considered, but before a final answer can be given, the German Government wish to be more precisely informed as to the Committee's functions and scope, that is to say, what will be the nature of its terms of reference.

Without being able to make any definite promise, Herr Dieckhoff gave me the impression that the answer of the German Government would be favourable if they could be assured that the functions of the Committee would be confined solely to matters directly concerned with the Spanish arms embargo, such as the exchange of information regarding measures for its enforcement, of views as to the execution and efficacy of these measures, and the consideration of suggestions for further measures, e. g. the control of volunteers.

The German misgivings originally felt, that the powers of the Committee might develop in a manner which they would think undesirable, had been strongly confirmed by articles in the French press by Madame Tabouis and by a leader headed "A Gap to Fill" in the *Times* of September 2nd, to the last three lines of which Herr Dieckhoff drew my particular attention. I gathered that if there were any question of the Committee developing on these lines, Germany would refuse to take part. Herr Dieckhoff said he noted that the Portuguese Government seemed to entertain the same uncertainty and misgivings as the German Government.

[Enclosure 2] [1]

You may assure German Government that it is intention of His Majesty's Government that functions of Committee should be confined to matters directly concerned with embargo on arms for Spain as described in paragraph 2 of your telegram under reference. His Majesty's Government fully appreciate that there would be danger in ventilating delicate questions in Committee or in entrusting to it tasks which fall outside immediate problems of arms embargo.

You are correct in saying that Committee itself will be able to settle most convenient method of working and that in any case German

---

[1] The file copy of this document is in English.

representative will retain full liberty to express views of his Government as to Committee's functions and duration. Essential thing is to secure an early preliminary meeting of Committee at which all Governments will be represented and in which scope of future discussions can be amicably worked out and defined.

You should therefore express earnest hope of His Majesty's Government that in the light of these explanations German Government will now agree to establishment of proposed Committee and at once appoint their representative.

No. 72

1758/404807–08

Memorandum by the Director of the Legal Department

BERLIN, September 5, 1936.
Pol. III 2272.

According to the instructions which the Foreign Minister gave me by telephone this morning, I informed the British Chargé d'Affaires orally this noon that on the basis of his declarations yesterday we were willing to take part in the London arms embargo committee. Prince Bismarck would receive the corresponding authorization today. I emphasized once more that the latest assurances of the British Government were decisive for our attitude with respect to the committee and that if necessary we would have recourse to them.

Purely personally, I pointed out to Mr. Newton that in my opinion it made a misleading impression when the committee was always referred to as "control committee"; to the newspaper reader it could very easily appear as if one were thinking of sending military experts into the various countries for some sort of control activity. The words "control commission" had very bad associations in Germany. Mr. Newton shared this opinion and said that he also considered it proper to name the committee according to its real character and that he would work toward having this done.

I then informed Mr. Newton that our agreement would be made known for the first time in the Sunday morning newspapers, in a very general and brief manner. He agreed entirely with our communiqué, which I read to him, and will do what he can to see that our agreement is not published in London either before Sunday morning.

Mr. Newton finally asked whether we did not wish to inform the French Chargé d'Affaires also; I told him that this was already provided for and would be done directly after his visit. However, we would limit ourselves to an oral statement to the French, too, which Mr. Newton entirely approved.

GAUS

No. 73

1758/404800

Memorandum by the Director of the Legal Department

BERLIN, September 5, 1936.
e. o. Pol. III 2191.

When I telephoned the Italian Chargé d'Affaires to tell him of our accession to the London committee, he asked if he might call on me in person, since he also had a communication to make to me.

During the visit I informed Count Magistrati of the latest developments and told him confidentially that Prince Bismarck had received instructions to keep in touch with Signor Grandi regarding committee questions. Count Magistrati welcomed this very much.

He in turn told me about a secret instruction to Grandi to do his best to give the committee's entire activity a purely platonic character and to call attention to the many reports regarding support of the Red Party by certain countries. In particular, he was to make suitable use of the available reports concerning shipments of arms by the Mexican Government.

GAUS

168/132303–305

No. 74

The Director of the Legal Department to the Embassy in Great Britain [1]

Telegram

IMMEDIATE
VERY URGENT
No. 210

BERLIN, September 5, 1936.
zu Pol. III 2078.

Two days after the dispatch of our note to the French Embassy in the question of the London arms embargo committee, the British Chargé d'Affaires called and urgently requested, at the direction of his Government, that the German Government reconsider its attitude on the question; all other powers had acceded to the French proposal, at least in principle, and only Germany had raised objections. He asserted in this connection that the London committee was not contemplated as an independent body which would make decisions; it was a question only of organizing loosely diplomatic representatives of the interested powers accredited in London. The committee was to exercise no control powers and make no majority decisions.

---

[1] The telegram was repeated for information to the German Embassies in France and Italy and the Legation in Portugal.

The Chargé d'Affaires was told in reply that his statements relative to the committee's functions made it possible for us to reconsider the matter. It was essential, aside from the views he presented, that the activity of the committee remain confined to questions relating to the arms embargo, such as the obtaining of reports, exchange of opinions on measures of execution, effective organization of the embargo, and the presentation of proposals such as the ban on the recruitment of volunteers. The body must not assume a permanent character and must not be entrusted with other problems, either now or later. The committee itself must regulate its methods of operation, and the German representative must have complete freedom to express his views regarding the duties and the duration of the committee.

The Chargé d'Affaires reported in this vein, as is evident from the exchange of telegrams with his Government which were submitted by him very confidentially; the British Government acceded to our wishes and observed that it would be dangerous if the committee discussed delicate questions outside the scope of the Spanish arms embargo. A copy of the exchange of telegrams will follow by air mail.

Under these circumstances we informed the British and French Chargés d'Affaires here orally today that we would have our Chargé d'Affaires in London represent us in the committee. I therefore ask that you accept the invitation, should you be called upon to participate. Please govern your attitude by the above-mentioned views, which I sum up to the effect that the committee must not be a decision-making body nor assume a permanent character. It must regulate its own methods of operation, confine its discussions to execution of the arms embargo and questions directly connected therewith, such as the recruiting of volunteers and the collection of money, and by no means permit discussion of other problems. Basically, this involves a simplified diplomatic procedure, so that the individual representatives would have to obtain instructions from their governments every time that positive proposals, that is, proposals exceeding the mere exchange of information, are to be discussed. I suggest that special contact be established with the Italian and Portuguese representatives.

Should you be approached regarding our measures for putting the arms embargo into effect, please refer to the war matériel law of November 6, 1935, which makes the export of munitions and war matériel subject to special permit. In the application of this law, the necessary measures for preventing the exportation and transit of arms and war matériel, including airplanes, to Spain were taken through administrative channels, in accordance with the embargo declaration.

The press announcement will not be made until Sunday morning.

GAUS

No. 75

168/132302

Memorandum by the Head of the European Section of the Political Department

BERLIN, September 6, 1936.

The French Chargé d'Affaires called me on the telephone early this morning and informed me that late Saturday evening he had received from the Quai d'Orsay the following reply to our communication on the embargo question, with instructions to transmit it to us:

"We accept for our part the proposal presented by Mr. Newton. We do not insist on the adoption of an express formula of control. However, we expect to find in the practical functioning of the committee every guaranty for the application of the restrictions which we ourselves decree."

M. Lamarle stressed that this signified an *acceptance* of the British formula, a fact which Paris had emphasized particularly, and that the last sentence contained nothing surprising but seemed almost obvious.

It was evident from the conversation, without its being explicitly discussed, that the French Government does not expect a counter reply.

WOERMANN

No. 76

3369/E010576–77

Memorandum by the Head of the European Section of the Political Department

BERLIN, September 7, 1936.

The Portuguese Minister called on me today and informed me that, according to the telegraphic communications he had received from his Government on September 5, Portugal will not take part in the London embargo committee as long as some preliminary questions are not clarified. The principal issue involved was that the other powers agree to the Portuguese reservations, particularly to the intensification of the embargo by a ban on additional volunteers, on the collection of money, etc.

Press reports that Portugal would join the committee without fulfillment of these conditions were false.

In strict confidence the Minister added that Portugal found it necessary to take an extremely reserved attitude, since she considered her position with regard to Spain as extremely dangerous. The present Spanish Prime Minister, Caballero, had declared before assuming power that in case of a Government victory three cities would be punished, namely Burgos, Seville, and Lisbon.   Even aside from this, the Portuguese Government feared either a direct invasion by the Spanish Army or an invasion by uncontrolled bands.   It had to reserve its freedom of action against these eventualities.   In all these statements it was not quite clear how much was in the Minister's instructions and how much he added on his own.

Finally the Minister mentioned that on the occasion of a session of the Committee of Three in London at the end of June [1] the Portuguese Foreign Minister had asked Eden whether Britain would consider a conflict with Spain grounds for appealing to the alliance. Mr. Eden had given an evasive answer.

WOERMANN

---

[1] Altered to read "July" in the original.   The reference is to the meeting of representatives of Great Britain, France, and Belgium in London on July 23, 1936.

No. 77

3371/E010626

The Director of the Legal Department to the Legation in Portugal

Telegram

No. 127 of September 7   BERLIN, September 7, 1936—2 : 00 p.m.
                                          Received September 7—5 : 30 p.m.

At the request of the Portuguese Government, the German ship *Usaramo* was unable to discharge a "certain" cargo in the port of Lisbon and must return to the northern coast of Spain.   According to information received by the Navy, the Portuguese Government acted under British pressure.   I request a telegraphic report as to whether, in your judgment, we must count on a change in the Portuguese attitude under British influence.

GAUS

No. 78

168/132295–300

The Head of the European Section of the Political Department to the Chargé d'Affaires in Great Britain

BERLIN, September 8, 1936.

DEAR PRINCE BISMARCK : We here are very conscious of the fact that you will have a quite difficult role to play in the so-called "embargo committee."   From your last visit to Germany you are, of course, sufficiently informed regarding the background factors in the German attitude.   It is certain, I suppose, that hardly one of the countries represented in the committee has a clear conscience in the question of supporting one party or the other.   I am sending you herewith the material available at the present time on the support given the Reds by various governments.[1] This material, however, is still quite incomplete, and you will continue to receive more information on the subject.

We are of the opinion here that it would be inexpedient for us to begin with attacks on France or other countries on this score. However, should attacks be made upon Germany, you must naturally be prepared to counterattack. Moreover, it appears that the Italians, also, are well prepared in this respect, as may be seen from the memorandum of a conversation between Herr Gaus and Count Magistrati, a copy of which is enclosed.[2] In case such attacks take place, we consider it expedient that you let the Italians make the first move; we deem it expedient in any case that you maintain close contact with Signor Grandi in this question, as we have already pointed out in telegram No. 210 of September 5.

As for the rest, it is quite difficult at the outset to supplement those telegraphic instructions, the quintessence of which is that you obtain instructions before making any statements which might bind the German Government. During the Nuremberg days it will, of course, be rather difficult for you to receive instructions on important questions quickly. The Foreign Minister will arrive in Nuremberg Wednesday afternoon; Herr Gaus and Herr Dieckhoff will be there from tonight on. I am leaving Wednesday night for Nuremberg. From Wednesday evening until the end of the Party rally, Herr von Weizsäcker will be back in Berlin.

I think there is a possibility that the French Government may press for the conclusion of a formal treaty on the embargo question. In this case it would be important that the embargo declaration be supplemented by addenda, for instance such as have been suggested by Italy, Portugal, and also by us (question of volunteers). The way things are, however, we are not interested now in taking the initiative to bring the question of volunteers to the fore. Should it be necessary for you at one of the meetings of the committee to take a stand on the question of supplementing the present embargo declaration, there would be no objection, however, to your bringing up the question of volunteers, even without previous additional instructions. In that case, you also could support suggestions by other powers intended to prohibit any unneutral support. Even in this question, however, it would be preferable if you would first request instructions, if only to comply with our basic conception of the nature of the committee.

Significant for the question of unneutral support going beyond the French text of the embargo declaration is the attitude of the French

---

[1] Unsigned marginal note: "Follows under separate cover with instruction Pol. III 2245."
[2] Document No. 73, p. 75.

Government toward the transport of troops and matériel from the Spanish Irún front to other parts of Spain through French territory. Count Welczeck broached this question to the Political Director at the Quai d'Orsay, M. Bargeton, who termed it a matter of course that such support should be permitted. The essence of the problem is naturally not touched by such a purely formalistic standpoint, since this behavior, after all, amounts to support for the Reds. If you consider it expedient to bring this point up for discussion, we would ask you to make such a suggestion to the Foreign Ministry beforehand.

Beyond that it is difficult to give you supplementary instructions to telegram No. 210.[3] I should merely like to inform you confidentially, as an illustration of the state of affairs, that there are currents here which are pressing for a severance of diplomatic relations with the present Spanish Government; this might then perhaps lead automatically to a recognition of the Burgos Government. For the present, however, we in the Foreign Ministry see no advantage in such a course.

I now revert once more to the question, already discussed above, concerning recriminations for neutrality violations by the individual powers. From the purely formal standpoint, such recriminations could naturally be made retroactively only to the date when the individual powers obligated themselves to take embargo measures. A date after which such recriminations can be brought up for discussion will probably be agreed on in the London committee. Naturally we should prefer to have this date set as late as possible. You are aware of the fact that our embargo declaration is dated August 17. For the rest, your duty on this point, too, would be confined to receiving such communications and transmitting them to Berlin.

Finally, I enclose a memorandum [4] regarding a communication of the French Government, which the French Chargé d'Affaires sent me last Sunday. The text of this declaration, which is drafted very carefully, makes it seem possible that the French, too, are contemplating some sort of positive control measures for the conduct of the individual powers. We consider it a matter of course that we cannot permit an international control in our own country or over German shipping on the high seas and in Spanish ports. Nor could I imagine that the French would be ready to permit international control at the Spanish-French frontier, a fact which would dispose of the control idea once and for all. Nor can we quite imagine here what other "guaranties" could be demanded and given for execution of the embargo declarations. At any rate, this is a period in which no promises of any kind could be considered under any circumstances without previous instruction.

[3] Document No. 74, p. 75.
[4] Document No. 75, p. 77.

There is another point that is not yet quite clear to me. Our note of August 17 contains the *si omnes* clause. It should probably be the first task of the committee to determine, at the outset, which powers are participating, what the individual powers have pledged themselves to do, and on what date this obligation begins.

With cordial greetings and Heil Hitler!

As ever,

WOERMANN

[EDITORS' NOTE. With a few exceptions, all documents relating to discussions in the Non-Intervention Committee from September 9 to December 4, 1936, have been omitted, because they add nothing of importance to what was reported in the press at the time and summarized in such readily available accounts as the *Survey of International Affairs, 1937* (vol. II, The International Repercussions of the War in Spain, London, 1938). During September the committee discussions centered around problems of organization and procedure. At the end of September Lord Plymouth, British Under Secretary for Foreign Affairs, replaced W. S. Morrison as chairman of the committee. Francis Hemming was chosen secretary. On September 14 a chairman's subcommittee was created to care for routine matters and to prepare material for consideration by the committee. Representatives of the Belgian, British, Czechoslovak, French, German, Italian, Soviet, and Swedish Governments sat in the subcommittee; on September 28 a Portuguese member was added.

On October 6, 1936, the British Government directed the attention of the committee to a dossier drawn up by the Spanish Government to support charges of German, Italian, and Portuguese aid to Franco. The Soviet representative at once proposed that a commission be sent to examine the situation on the Spanish-Portuguese frontier, and on October 7, in a note to the chairman, the Soviet Government stated that unless violations of the non-intervention agreement ceased, the U.S.S.R. would not be bound by the provisions of that agreement. A series of angry sessions ensued, with charges and countercharges of breach of the agreement. By November 10 the committee had decided that these charges were unproved.

On November 12, 1936, a British plan to control the shipment of war materials by sea and land to both Spanish factions, which had been discussed in the chairman's subcommittee since October 24, was submitted to the committee. In the debates which followed, the representatives of Germany, Italy, and Portugal insisted that air traffic also be controlled. On December 2, however, the committee, with Portugal abstaining, agreed that the plan for land and sea control should be presented to the two Spanish factions with a request for their approval.]

No. 79

168/132291–94

The Chargé d'Affaires in Great Britain to the Foreign Ministry

Airgram

No. 184 of September 9   LONDON, September 9, 1936.

Received September 10—8 : 35 a.m.

With reference to telegraphic instruction No. 210.[1]

At noon today the first meeting of the London arms embargo committee took place in the Locarno Room of the Foreign Office, and I participated as instructed. In addition to the British Delegation, headed by Mr. Morrison, Parliamentary Financial Secretary to the Treasury, and including Lord Cranborne, the meeting was attended by the accredited representatives of all the European countries which had been invited by the French Government to take part in the committee. Besides Germany and England, the following powers were represented: Albania, Austria, Belgium, Bulgaria, Czechoslovakia, Denmark, Estonia, Finland, France, Greece, Hungary, Ireland, Italy, Latvia, Lithuania, Luxembourg, Norway, Poland, Rumania, Soviet Russia, Sweden, Turkey, and Yugoslavia. Non-European nations were not represented, nor was Switzerland, which, as the chairman announced, had not, because of her policy of neutrality, acceded to the French proposal for an arms embargo but issued her own ban on the exporting of arms.

Morrison opened the meeting by reading a letter from the British Foreign Secretary, who was sick and therefore could not attend, in which the latter wished the committee complete success in its work. Morrison himself expressed the same wish. The French Ambassador then replied, thanked the nations present for responding to the French proposal, and likewise expressed the hope that the committee would accomplish practical and effective work. Following this he moved that Morrison be elected chairman of the committee, and this was done unanimously.

Thereupon Morrison again took the floor and asked the committee to decide whether the sessions were to be public or secret. The committee decided unanimously in favor of secret sessions. On the basis of this decision Morrison asked the members of the committee to exercise as much restraint as possible toward the press and proposed that at the end of each session a communiqué, jointly agreed upon, should be issued. The proposal was adopted. Then Morrison announced that the Portuguese Government had informed him that it could not take part in the deliberations of the committee until the latter's functions were more clearly defined. The British Government only yesterday

---

[1] Document No. 74, p. 75.

had made earnest representations to the Portuguese Government, urging that it participate in the work of the committee, and he could only hope that Portugal would soon see her way clear to take part.

Proceeding to the practical work of the committee, Morrison then proposed that all the replies made by the various powers to the French Government's proposal for an arms embargo be collected and published jointly as one document. The French Ambassador replied that the French Government was already preparing such a document in the form of a White Book and that he expected to have copies at his disposal by this afternoon. I asked the French Ambassador, next to whom I was sitting, whether the reply of the German Government would be contained in the White Book he had mentioned, since I did not know whether the German Government had approved of the publication of its note. The Ambassador was not in a position to answer my question, so when Morrison asked whether all the representatives were agreeable to the proposal, I declared that I would first have to obtain instruction from my Government in regard to the publication of the German reply to the French Government. (In the meantime I have ascertained from Minister Woermann by telephone that the French Government was given permission to publish the German note of August 17 in the White Book, and I have already informed the secretariat of the committee.)

Morrison then proposed that the committee be given the following name: International Committee for the Application of Non-Intervention in Spain. The proposal was adopted unanimously.

As the next point to be considered, Morrison proposed that all the powers should as soon as possible give the secretariat of the committee a copy of the text of the pertinent laws or decrees by which the arms embargo had been put into force in the various countries. When these texts were received, they would first be circulated among the members of the committee and then perhaps also be published. At the request of the Italian Ambassador it was determined that with regard to this question, too, the various committee members should first obtain the consent of their Governments.

Finally, the committee took up the text of the communiqué to be given the press; at this point, in particular the question of when the next meeting of the committee was to take place provoked lively discussion. As Morrison took the view that the next meeting should not be held until at least the greater part of the necessary legal material mentioned above had been obtained, an agreement was finally reached to express in general terms the committee's hope of meeting again as soon as possible but to leave the exact date to the chairman.

The English text of the communiqué is as follows:

"After a general discussion of the scope of the work of the committee it was proposed that the several delegations should, as soon as possible, furnish the committee with particulars regarding the legislative and other steps taken by their respective countries to give effect to the agreement for non-intervention.

"It was agreed that this proposal should be referred to the Governments represented on the committee for their consideration.

"The committee expressed the wish to meet again as soon as possible. A second meeting will accordingly be summoned by the chairman as soon as, in his judgment, sufficient material has been received for the purpose."

Today's meeting left the impression that with France and England, the two powers principally interested in the committee, it is not so much a question of taking actual steps immediately as of pacifying the aroused feelings of the Leftist parties in both countries by the very establishment of such a committee. In particular during my conversation today with Vansittart in regard to another matter, I had the feeling that the British Government hoped to ease the domestic political situation for the French Premier by the establishment of the committee.

I should like to be informed whether the administrative measures taken with reference to the war-matériel law for the purpose of preventing the export and transit of weapons, etc., to Spain were issued in the form of a special decree; if so, I should like to be sent a copy of the decree in question for transmittal to the secretariat of the committee.

BISMARCK

No. 80

4793/E236273, E236327–33

The Minister in Portugal to the Foreign Ministry

SECRET   LISBON, September 11, 1936.
No. 2797   Received September 14.
                                    Pol. I 1728 g.

Subject: Forwarding of a report by the representative of the AGK.

I have the honor to transmit the enclosed copy of a report by Herr Messerschmidt, the representative in Spain of the Export Cartel for War Matériel, which he submitted here expressly for forwarding to the Foreign Ministry. In view of their political implications it would appear necessary to clarify the proposals outlined on pages 6 and 7.[1] The Legation remained entirely noncommittal vis-à-vis the author and promised transmittal to the Foreign Ministry.

Herr Messerschmidt intends to get in touch with the procurement agency of the Burgos Mission in Lisbon (Fernandes Aguilar), but

---

[1] See pp. 88 and 89.

merely, as he stressed explicitly, by way of placing himself at its disposal. In the event that business openings should develop from this contact, he will ask Berlin for instructions.[2]

HUENE

[Enclosure]

LISBON, September 8, 1936.

REPORT ON MY TRIP TO LISBON, SEVILLE, CÁCERES, AND RETURN TO LISBON BETWEEN AUGUST 27 AND SEPTEMBER 8, 1936

Immediately on arrival in Lisbon I got in touch with the "Hisma" organization and through personal acquaintance with several of the Hisma men was able even while in Lisbon to form an approximate picture of the course we had adopted.

I then flew in a Hisma plane to Seville, where, on August 28, I had a talk with Herr Bernhardt, the head of Hisma, which prompted me to write my letter of August 29 to "Ino." I stated in that letter that all the deliveries made by us are officially monopolized by Hisma, so that in consequence there are no business opportunities for the Reich Industry Association and that all I can do is to place myself at the disposal of Hisma.[3]

Since, however, Herr Bernhardt had nothing for me to do at the moment as the representative of the industry because, as he put it, no business note must be injected into our aid program on any account, I occupied myself with gaining a picture of the general situation through first-hand observation.

To this end I first paid a visit to the Pirotécnica artillery factory in Seville, where I saw the deputy director, Lieutenant Colonel José Sánchez. He told me that the factory undertook no purchases whatever because the initiative was exclusively with headquarters, where procurement was handled directly with Hisma. However, there was a commission in Lisbon, also believed to be abundantly provided with foreign exchange, which engaged in the purchasing of materials. The head of that commission was Aguilar. As I learned here in Lisbon, he is Franco's brother Nicolás (a naval officer) and acts here under that alias.

Next I went by one of the first available flights to the headquarters at Cáceres, where I had an opportunity to talk for almost an hour with General Franco and the chief of aviation, General Kindelan.

---

[2] According to handwritten notations by Ripken and Dörnberg on the original of this document, a carbon copy was referred to General von Wilberg of the Air Ministry on Sept. 17 with the request that it be returned. On the carbon copy there appears the following comment, possibly in the hand of General von Wilberg: "Who allowed M. to go to Spain in the first place? I did *not* want it." The other marginal comments noted in the body of the document are in the same hand.

[3] Marginal note: "Yes, correct."

I put myself in touch also with the military head of Hisma, Herr von Scheele, to whom I was introduced by Herr Schottky.

The conversation with Señor Kindelan was not very productive. He was generally very optimistic and anticipated that Madrid would be taken in four or five days. That would have been yesterday or the day before. He praised the activity of the German fliers although, as I was aware, there had on that very day been a certain tension between him and Herr von Scheele because the German pursuit fliers considered the use of the HE–51 planes on the Saragossa front inadvisable in view of the fact that the very modern French Bréguet pursuit planes with far superior speed were operating there and the HE–51 planes would probably have been lost in an unequal combat with them. General Kindelan therefore demanded that Herr von Scheele turn over the planes to him so that he could use them with Spanish fliers. Being convinced that the Spanish pilots would not be able to fly these planes and that they would crack up even before getting into action, Herr von Scheele refused and was able to straighten out this unpleasant episode only after a long conference with General Franco.

For the rest, I discovered that there is some bad feeling between the military head of Hisma and its administrative head, Herr Bernhardt, because Herr Bernhardt considers himself the director general and insists on keeping all strings in his hands, thus making it difficult for the military head to maintain direct contact with Franco. It is obvious that Herr Bernhardt has tailored the whole organization to fit his personal pattern. It was only after considerable effort that Herr von Scheele succeeded in establishing direct contact with General Franco, and his first problem was to dissipate Franco's erroneous conception that he was an employee of Herr Bernhardt.[4]

My conversation with General Franco dealt primarily with general political ideas because, in view of the fact that the Hisma organization was already in existence, I had to avoid any business subjects and merely expressed the readiness of our industry to place itself at his disposal.

I asked Franco's opinion as to whether it was not to be feared that the long duration of the Civil War might cause the enthusiasm of the population in the areas occupied by the Nationalists to wane and change direction. He replied that he did not entertain such apprehensions because in the areas which were White today the movement was actually supported by popular sentiment, while in the areas which he had conquered by force measures had been taken to suppress any Communist movement.

---

[4] Marginal note: "No, not correct."

I then said to him that it was probably easier to conquer a country by force of arms than the soul of the people and asked whether he did not anticipate certain difficulties in later introducing an idea among the people from above. He replied that he did not conceive this to be his task; rather, as a soldier, he had felt it his duty to prevent the Bolshevization of Spain. The Red Government had systematically destroyed the Army in order to give Bolshevism a free hand. He had taken the very last opportunity to make an attempt, with the remnant of the dependable Army, to insure the national unity of the country. If this attempt achieved success, he would help any national movement supported by the mass of the people to assume the government of the country and would place himself with the Army in the service of that movement.

I then asked him whether he did not deem it necessary to carry out a reform of the Church, for it had been demonstrated time and again that large sections of the people obviously felt an intense hatred for the Church. He answered that, in his opinion, this hatred was artificially inculcated by Russia; the overwhelming majority of the Spanish people were attached to the Catholic faith and this spiritual support was also indispensable to them. Besides, the greater portion of the clergy were themselves totally impoverished, and, as he saw it, his task consisted only in inducing the wealthy leaders of the Church to make great sacrifices now for the national cause, and in seeing to it that they would have no opportunity in the future of enriching themselves unduly. I then asked him what his view was regarding the role that the Catholic party, the "Ceda," would play in the future, because we, in Germany, had as a rule not been able to understand the policy of Gil Robles, the party chief, especially since he had strengthened the political influence of the Church again to a considerable degree. He replied that of course he, too, was in no way in agreement with this policy and that there was no question but that the Ceda would have to disappear. For all practical purposes it did not even now exist any longer.

As regards the military situation, the General was for more cautious in his statements than General Kindelan had been and emphasized that we were still in the midst of the struggle. He had no doubt that Madrid would be taken sooner or later despite the very stiff resistance of the French, but afterwards the war against Catalonia would still cause much trouble because France was the actual ruler of Catalonia,[5] as had already become very painfully apparent on the Saragossa front. He even had definite proof that French naval and artillery officers were active on naval vessels of Red Spain.

[5] Marginal note: " ? "

This was in substance my talk with General Franco; it is apparent from it that his political ideas are quite sensible and matter of fact. Whether he will succeed in starting a genuine popular movement through the Spanish Fascist Party, the Falange, remains to be seen. At the moment one has the impression that the members of the Falangist militia themselves have no real aims and ideas; rather, they seem to be young people for whom mainly it is good sport to play with firearms and to round up Communists and Socialists. For the rest, they rely on our efforts and the courage of the Moroccans, who fight at the front.

As regards the policy of Hisma or, rather, the personal policy of Herr Bernhardt, who looks upon himself as the Führer's delegate to Franco, I should say that there is doubtless room also for other opinions. It cannot be denied that he took the initiative since he happened to be at Tetuán at the moment and was there informed of Franco's wishes, and it must be conceded that he displayed great energy and zeal in getting the implementation of the aid program under way.[6] It is also true that at first it was necessary to act without any negotiating. But it should not be overlooked that we must demand some value in return for our gifts. Schottky indeed very rightly recognized that fact and induced Franco, over Herr Bernhardt's opposition, to make deliveries of copper to us to begin with. However, we must look ahead to our future interests, and I believe that now, while Franco is still under a certain pressure, is the moment for getting pledges from him with respect to our future economic and perhaps even political influence. For otherwise there is no doubt but that England or Italy, with an eye to preserving their influence, will turn up at the last moment and pose as the real moving spirits.

Thus, for instance, now would be the moment to assure ourselves of a basic treaty [Rahmenvertrag], as contemplated earlier, which would lay down for a number of years to come what raw materials Spain is to deliver to us and to what extent Spain must buy manufactured goods from us. I am sure that Franco would be willing in every respect to conclude such an agreement, provided that Herr Bernhardt is now prepared to give up his role of Santa Claus and demand value in return for our gifts. Herr Bernhardt's opposition to such a policy is founded primarily on his wish to ingratiate himself personally with Franco by coming to him only with presents. That Franco would comply with reasonable demands is demonstrated by the prompt success of Schottky's negotiations for copper.[7]

---

[6] Marginal note: "Yes."
[7] Marginal note: "?"

As I have heard, Herr Eltze [8] is to come here soon upon the request of the Lisbon Legation, and I believe it would be profitable if he were to go also to Franco in order to formulate with him the future return payments. It would be desirable to have the demands we plan to make carefully studied and fixed beforehand in Berlin.

The purpose of my trip to Lisbon was to exchange ideas with the Legation here on the subject of the above questions and to get in touch with the Aguilar commission with a view to ascertaining whether the Export Cartel for War Matériel could do business through that channel. Now, to be sure, after I have found out who Aguilar is, I shall have to consider further whether such a step is advisable. I plan to go from here to Valladolid for the purpose of forming an idea there of the feeling in Mola's headquarters, without, of course, pursuing any business or political objectives. It goes without saying that everything must remain concentrated in Franco's hands so that there may be a leader who can hold everything together. My trip to Valladolid is purely for information. If there are any instructions for me, please forward them for the time being to the Legation in Lisbon.

With German greeting,
MESSERSCHMIDT

---

[8] Director general of the AGK.

No. 81

682/259012

The Consul General at Barcelona to the Foreign Ministry

[Telegram]

No. 120 of September 15   BARCELONA, September 16, 1936.

Pol. III 2606.

With reference to my telegram No. 104 of September 9.[1]

I have learned from a reliable source that thirty-seven airplanes, seven of them already assembled, were landed by the Russians in a small Spanish harbor about a week ago. Thirty Russian aviators disguised as members of the International Red Cross arrived here likewise. The Portuguese Embassy in Madrid is said to have been looted yesterday in revenge for the non-participation of Portugal in the London conference. As the code had been left behind in Madrid by the Portuguese Chargé d'Affaires, the Portuguese Consul General here fears that the Embassy might be compromised.

Recently four shipments of gold valued at 70, 170, 59, and 45 million pesetas were sent from here to France by plane. España, the Spanish Minister of the Interior, is said to have accompanied three of

---

[1] Not printed (4797/E 236706).

these shipments personally. Yesterday two French planes without any marks of identification landed here. In order to deceive the Military [i. e. the rebels], they were painted here with the Spanish colors; planes of the Government usually have red stripes.

KÖCHER

No. 82

1758/404855–56

The Acting State Secretary to the Embassy in Great Britain

Telegram

No. 219   BERLIN, September 18, 1936—10 : 25 p.m.

e. o. Pol. III 2707.

Drafting Officer: Counselor of Legation Dumont.

According to information received from the Portuguese Minister here, the British and French diplomatic representatives in Lisbon again took a vigorous step on September 16 regarding Portugal's participation in the embargo committee. In the absence of the Foreign Minister, the Secretary General categorically rejected participation by Portugal. As we have learned from Attolico,[1] the French are increasing their pressure on Portugal by threatening to bring up the question of extending the arms embargo to Portugal. Léger[2] revealed this to the Italian Ambassador in Paris, who received instruction from Ciano to inform the French Government that the Italian Government had no intention whatsoever of participating in any such action against Portugal.

I request that in line with your previous attitude you continue to reject any discussion on the subject of extending the embargo to Portugal, as being outside the competence of the committee. Regarding the question of Portugal's participation in the committee, I request that you maintain complete reserve and exert no influence whatsoever on the Portuguese representative.

I would consider the adoption of rules of procedure based on article 29 of the draft arms traffic agreement a source of danger. You are requested to advocate the view that, since the committee is intended to handle complaints, a business procedure modeled after the League of Nations document is out of the question.

DIECKHOFF

---

[1] Italian Ambassador in Germany.
[2] Secretary General of the French Ministry of Foreign Affairs.

No. 83

4793/E236275

The War Minister to the Foreign Ministry

SECRET   BERLIN, September 21, 1936.

Abw. Nr. 4075/9.36 III Luft geh.

Subject: Messerschmidt.

Reference: None.

Attention of Herr von Dörnberg.

The Intelligence Department finds it necessary to call in Messerschmidt's report of September 8, 1936,[1] on his trip to Lisbon, etc., and also requests transmittal of any copies that you may have.

By direction:
BÄMLER

---

[1] Enclosure to document No. 80, p. 85.

No. 84

1758/404866–67

The Acting Director of the Political Department to the Embassy in Italy

Telegram

No. 215   BERLIN, September 21, 1936—2:25 p.m.
zu Pol. III 2718.

Drafting Officer: Counselor of Legation Dumont.

With reference to telegraphic instruction No. 213.[1]
The London Embassy telegraphed as follows on September 18:[2]

The position of Portugal is to be discussed at the next session of the subcommittee on Tuesday. Meanwhile the committee members are to ascertain the attitude of their respective governments. "In case the Portuguese Government persists in its refusal to participate in the committee—and according to the information the Portuguese Chargé d'Affaires gave me today it is very unlikely that the Portuguese Government will take part—I should in all probability be in an isolated position if I merely continued to limit myself to declaring that the committee would exceed its authority if it concerned itself at all with Portugal. While the Italian Ambassador expressed agreement with my view when I objected during the first session of the subcommittee, he did not express himself on this matter today but on the contrary energetically stressed before the committee the necessity of Portugal's participation. In a private conversation with me,

---

[1] The text of this telegram was the same as that of No. 219 to the Embassy in Great Britain, document No. 82.
[2] Telegram No. 189, not printed (1758/404864–65).

Grandi vigorously expressed his displeasure at the Portuguese attitude and asked me whether the German Government did not wish to remonstrate with the Portuguese Government in Lisbon to this effect. An additional factor in the situation is Morrison's statement that if Portugal continued her negative attitude it would in the long run be impossible not to deal with the Portuguese problem in the committee. The task of the committee was to bring about coordination among all the powers participating in the arms embargo, and since Portugal was one of these powers they would have to be in a position to discuss her position in case Portugal herself refused to be represented on the committee." (End of the telegram from London.)

I intend to uphold the instruction given London yesterday. Please request the Government there to give Grandi instructions similar to ours regarding the question of Portugal's participation in the arms embargo committee.

WEIZSÄCKER [3]

[3] This telegram appears to have been prepared for Dieckhoff's signature, but a marginal notation by Weizsäcker, Sept. 19, reads as follows: "If it should be impossible to get in touch with the State Secretary today, please send the telegram over my signature."

No. 85

1758/404885–86

Memorandum by the Acting State Secretary

BERLIN, September 22, 1936.

Pol. III 3017.

The Italian Chargé d'Affaires called on me this afternoon and informed me first of all that he had received word from Rome to the effect that participation by Italy in the deliberations of the League of Nations Assembly was out of the question as long as the problem of Abyssinia's participation remained unsettled. Count Magistrati then inquired about the status of the negotiations regarding a Western Pact, and I sketched for him in outline the contents of the British memorandum.[1] During the late afternoon he telephoned and said that he had just been informed by the Palazzo Chigi that the British memorandum had made a predominantly "negative" impression in Rome, since it looked as if England wanted to conclude a pact without Italy. He had been instructed to inform us of this. I limited myself to listening to this message and to saying that we had not yet concluded our own study of the matter but would communicate with the Italian Government when we had.

Regarding the arms embargo against Spain, Count Magistrati developed the thesis that during the first weeks of the Civil War, when

[1] The reference is to the British memorandum of Sept. 18, 1936, to Belgium, France, Germany, and Italy concerning preparations for a conference of the Locarno powers and proposing that such a conference meet in October.

the Nationalist forces had been practically without weapons, Germany and Italy had had no interest in a strict enforcement of the arms embargo against Spain.   Now, however, when the Nationalist forces were well supplied and, on the other hand, the Madrid Government lacked war matériel, the situation had changed, and Germany and Italy now were very much interested in having the embargo strictly enforced. The attitude of the Italian representative in London, who insisted upon strict enforcement of the embargo and upon control measures, was based on these considerations.   These tactics furthermore had the advantage of placing the Blum Government in a difficult position in relation to its extreme elements, which were clamoring for support of the Madrid Government, and had the additional advantage of putting the blame for the imminent collapse of the Madrid Government, in the eyes of the Leftists in Spain, on the French Government, which had neglected to help in time.   I avoided entering into these deductions and limited myself to stating that we had, as was known, declared an embargo and were therefore enforcing it, and that our Chargé d'Affaires in London had been instructed to maintain contact as much as possible with Ambassador Grandi concerning all questions brought before the embargo committee.

DIECKHOFF

No. 86

3174/682348

The Chargé d'Affaires in Italy to the Foreign Ministry

Telegram

ROME (QUIRINAL), September 22, 1936—6 : 15 p.m.
Received September 22—8 : 30 p.m.
No. 164 of September 22 Pol. III 2883.

With reference to your telegram of September 21, No. 215.

Your instruction has been carried out.   According to a communication from the Political Director, Grandi thereupon received instructions by telephone repeating those already given him under the date of September 14.   These contain the following directives for his conduct in the committee: "Italy refuses to exert any sort of pressure on Portugal for participation in the committee.   Italy would not think of extending the arms embargo to Portugal.   Portugal is a sovereign state, and she alone should have the right to decide her conduct."

In the course of the conversation, the Director mentioned that the participation of Portugal naturally was desirable per se.

PLESSEN

No. 87

690/259764–69

The Chargé d'Affaires in Spain to the Head of the European Section of the Political Department

ALICANTE, September 23, 1936.
Pol. III 3790.

DEAR WOERMANN : Many thanks for your letter,[1] which I was very glad to receive.

I should like to try to contribute toward your evaluation of the chances in the present bull fight, insofar as this can be done from the field of observation open to me. As one who is acquainted with this country, I know that one must beware of making predictions here even in normal times, since politics and temperament often take logic-defying leaps. You will have to draw your own conclusions, since you know more about things concerning which I only learn bits now and then in a roundabout manner.

In Spanish revolutions the organization of the revolt for the most part does not come off very well. That is particularly true of revolts by the Right. Either they start off before the word is given, or part of the conspirators make themselves scarce at the last minute.

Evidently such was the case this time also.

The assassination of Deputy Calvo Sotelo in Madrid had hastened the decision to take countermeasures. The defection of the Navy was then the first serious upset in Franco's calculations. This was a disastrous failure in organization; it jeopardized the whole plan, needlessly sacrificed the garrisons in the large cities, which were standing by and waiting in vain for orders, and above all wasted valuable time. Only the success and acclaim which Mola enjoyed in the north at this critical time made it possible to continue.

After bringing the troops over from Africa, Franco won two important victories, at Badajoz and at Irún. The former brought about the junction of the southern and the northern armies, and the latter cut communications with France in the northwest and won an outlet to the sea.

Two months have gone by since it started. This time has presented the Government with many opportunities. It has known how to popularize the war throughout the country by its propaganda and to call on the whole Marxist world for its defense.

The powerful effort which the Government, despite many crises, has put forth by recruiting a volunteer People's Army with the assistance of the well-organized trade unions deserves wide recognition; at the same time it indicates the enormity of the social problem which, having

---

[1] Not found.

developed through the centuries as a result of the sins of the landed nobility and the Church, now presses for a decision. The settlement of the social question in Spain would have to be the most important item in the program of any White Government if, in case of a Franco victory, anything really permanent is to be achieved.

The military value of the People's Militias originally was nil according to our standards. For example, when you see the new, large army of volunteers now in process of formation, who are being sent to Madrid in squads, there given a short period of training, then handed Mexican or Russian guns and sent to a sector of the front, you cannot help feeling that these troops are cannon fodder when facing a well-trained army. What they lack in training they are supposed to make up in numbers. Since they have killed all their officers, and their leaders are immediately shot from behind in case of defeat, they are completely lacking in discipline and unified leadership. In the face of technically superior attack they do not stand their ground. I have been told that a few aerial bombs, a little artillery fire, or a few tanks have had such a demoralizing effect that whole battalions turned and ran for miles and could not be driven forward again. The Militia members recruited in the Province of Madrid, along the southeastern coast, and in Andalusia may be able to carry out an occasional patrol, but they are not dependable and are fundamentally cowardly. The North Castilians, the Catalans, and the Basques are much more dangerous opponents. In spite of all the attempts made, it has not been possible to determine the number of Government troops at the front around Madrid. They are relieved every week and change continually. But the great number of recently procured rifles, running into the hundreds of thousands, gives an approximate indication.

In my opinion the Government wants to prepare for a large-scale operation with the new equipment. Enormous shipments of war matériel reach the eastern harbors by sea and are immediately moved on to Madrid; this includes particularly planes, artillery, antiaircraft guns, machine guns, and motorcycles. It is also said to include tanks. Thanks to this abundant modern equipment, for which foreign instructors are available, the People's Army is acquiring an entirely new appearance.

If Franco has hitherto been able to advance only at a very slow pace, it must be expected that his army will not be able to cope with this new matériel unless he can employ something equivalent. His hesitant advance is extraordinary. His troops are evidently few in number. On a long front they are bound to be wasted in isolated encounters. The military forces in the north are not yet available. Junction with the troops in the south is not yet complete, and his right flank remains dangling in midair. It is incomprehensible why he does not cut the sole railway connection between Madrid and the Levant, which carries the big troop and ammunition transports. Demolition of the railroad bridge at Aranjuez would suffice to cut connections with Barcelona, Valencia, Alicante, and Cartagena. After overcoming considerable difficulties of terrain west and south of Madrid, Franco is now in the open plain where he should be able to advance easily. Every day lost brings the Government an abundance of new war matériel. Ultimately, superiority in matériel will be decisive. In view of the situation, Franco needs principally tanks and planes.

Whether the Government will be able to go over to the offensive at this time in order to free itself from threatening encirclement will depend solely on whether the White troops continue to dally. If the circle around Madrid is closed and the Government is forced to fall back to the last fortified line of defense prepared 25 kilometers outside of Madrid, then Franco's game is won, for this city of a million inhabitants cannot endure a siege.

The food shortage in Madrid is very great even now. There are no stocks on hand to speak of. Every incoming train carrying provisions is seized by the Anarchists in Madrid for themselves. Cutting the water supply by capturing the fortified positions at the Somosierra (north of Madrid), where the great dams are located, would spell the immediate end of Madrid.

The Anarchists are playing their own game. They control Catalonia and Valencia completely and are on the point of seizing Alicante and Cartagena. Their headquarters, which were temporarily located in Madrid, have been moved back to Barcelona. In Madrid they are actually in the majority, since their own armed units have remained behind in the rear area while the Socialists and Communists are up at the front. Most of the murders and the pillaging in Madrid are to be attributed to them. The Government is helpless in the face of this situation. At the present moment a serious crisis has again arisen, the outcome of which is still in doubt. In view of the military situation, all possible efforts are being made by the Government, aided by the Russian Ambassador, to satisfy the Anarchists. If Largo Caballero is able to win out now, and if he can keep the enemy out of Madrid, then the settlement of internal differences between the Communists and the Anarchists can be left to the future. If, however, Franco's advance cannot be stopped, the Government probably will attempt to flee to Valencia at the decisive moment and leave the fate of Madrid to the Anarchists, who will complete their work of destruction there as the hyenas of the battlefield or—come to terms with the White forces.

Morale in Madrid is very low. The people are despairing. The workers are already saying that the Government has betrayed them.

The Government itself is under the control of the Anarchists. Only Largo Caballero is still holding his own, and continuing the fight in all directions. Acting Foreign Minister Giner de los Ríos very pessimistically told me the day before yesterday in Madrid: "When you come to Madrid again, you will find here nothing but stones and corpses; we shall be buried under the ruins of the city."

The Government's protest against us, Italy, and Portugal, as well as the dispatch of notes to all the governments, is obviously designed for the benefit of Geneva. Such a step was to be expected. It will be an easy matter for us to counter with the list of the deliveries made to the Spanish Government. I do not believe in the possibility of a new world war, although it would of course suit the Spaniards, in order to relieve their situation, to turn the struggle between the two great ideologies now being waged by Spaniards on Spanish soil into a general European conflict. The Russian Jews know exactly how much they can risk. Still, the attitude of the Spanish Government, which as late as the middle of August was panic-stricken when we threatened to break off relations, has changed materially since the active intervention of Russia.

With cordial greetings to you and all your colleagues,

Heil Hitler!

Yours,

VOELCKERS

No. 88

1810/414343–48

The Chargé d'Affaires in the Soviet Union to the Foreign Ministry

A 2036   Moscow, September 28, 1936.

With reference to our report No. A 1953 of September 14.[1]

Subject: Agitation in the Soviet Union for support of the Spanish Popular Front Government.

The campaign for support of the "Spanish people," which refers here to the followers of the Madrid Popular Front Government exclusively, lately received new impetus in the Soviet Union. This was done systematically and from above, but the impression was to be created that a spontaneous movement was involved, originating among the workers. A further propagandistic effect was evidently expected from the fact that the initiative was assigned to a group of women workers. The choice fell to the Moscow Tryokhgorka Textile Factory, which has been given preference before on occasions involving

---

[1] Not printed (1810/414320).

manifestations of loyalty for domestic consumption and demonstrations of class struggle for foreign consumption.   This group launched the slogan which was largely meant to make a favorable impression on humanitarian-minded circles abroad: "Assistance to the women and children of heroic Spain." *Pravda* on September 12 published an "open letter" from the women workers of Tryokhgorka, requesting gifts of money for the above-mentioned purpose.   The agitation was carried out by the unions in the usual manner: The appeal originating in one factory was followed by the usual statements of "spontaneous" approval and emulation on the part of other factories; resolutions by assemblies and stirring appeals of individuals appeared in the press; this was followed by meetings of the women workers and employees of entire cities.

It was conspicuous that, the well-known slowness of Soviet organizational measures notwithstanding, the Soviet steamer *Neva* was able to leave Odessa for Alicante as early as September 19 with 2,000 tons of food, which supposedly had been paid for with the donations received in the meantime.   According to a report of the Central Council of Trade Unions of the Soviet Union in *Pravda* on September 22, the steamer *Neva* carried a cargo of 30,000 pood [2] of butter, 95,000 pood of sugar, 17,000 pood of canned goods, 18,000 pood of margarine, and 12,000 pood of confections; no account of the cost was given. It was announced, however, that the total sum of gifts collected by September 20 "for the women and children of Republican Spain" amounted to more than 7,000,000 rubles.

After the collection of money carried on in the name of women's aid had run its course, the propaganda campaign was extended to the male workers and employees.   The signal for this was given in *Pravda* on September 22, and it fell to the lot of the Stalin Automobile Factory at Moscow to come out with a suitable resolution.   During the last week the same machinery as had previously been obligatory for the women—prescribed factory resolutions, letters to the papers, and assemblies—went into operation for the male part of the wage-earning population.   The general meeting for factory delegations from all Moscow was set for the starting day, September 24, at the Dynamo Stadium; the procedure in the other large cities, for example in Leningrad, was organized along similar lines.   Aside from high-sounding announcements concerning the "solidarity of the workers" of the Soviet Union with the Spanish people, who are "fighting heroically against brutal Fascism," in which attacks on non-Spanish "Fascists," especially Germany, were by no means lacking, the usual

---

[2] One pood=36.113 pounds.

Byzantine homages, which can hardly be surpassed any more, were paid to Stalin. This offered another opportunity for anti-Fascist tirades and for condemnation of Trotskyites and Zinovievites. In practice the campaign, which was carried on with great noise in the papers and with much outward ado, but without any genuine participation by the population, was aimed at having each worker and employee sacrifice one quarter of a day's wages each month until further notice for the benefit of food assistance for "Republican" Spain.

Side by side with the above-mentioned campaign, biased reports were printed about the progress of the Civil War in Spain, in which the followers of the Madrid Government were glorified in every way and the opposing party was reviled and accused of every atrocity imaginable.

During the past week, growing concern about the military situation of Madrid was manifested; after the defense maneuver of flooding the old bed of the Alberche River, the reports on this subject again became more optimistic.

The campaign against the "Fascist" states of Italy, Germany, and Portugal, suspected of helping the Spanish Nationalists, continued unchanged. This included, among others, the reports made during recent days concerning the negotiations of a London "commission" which had taken it upon itself "to investigate German and Italian intervention in events in Spain." According to the reports of the Soviet press, a number of well-known pro-Soviet and anti-Fascist personages were on this committee, as for example Miss Rathbone, Pritt, Noel-Baker, and others. After statements by all sorts of "witnesses" and "agents" of the committee, who presented "evidence" of "intervention" by Germany and Italy, had been reported from London for several days, a Tass dispatch from London of September 25 (*Izvestiya*, September 27) stated that the sessions of the committee had been "postponed for an indefinite period."

Taken together, the symptoms of the Soviet campaign with regard to Spain, as manifested in the press campaign described above and in domestic propaganda, do not permit the conclusion that the Soviet Government is preparing an open change of its previous conduct in the non-intervention question. It has neither announced any such change of itself nor even admitted the expression of such a desire. The Soviet press rather was content with ridding itself of the responsibility for the arms embargo, which is disadvantageous to Madrid, by a sympathetic reception of Del Vayo's protests, by ill-disguised criticism of Delbos' statements in Geneva about non-intervention policy, and by other statements, while the gifts of food are meant to prove to public opinion that the Soviet Union is doing what it can. Therefore it has also been announced that a new food ship, the *Kuban*, is already being equipped.

To what extent the Soviets are rendering more than "humanitarian" assistance remains an open question. There are, to be sure, reports of such other assistance (compare telegraphic report No. 134 of September 26 [3]) but so far no confirmation. Certain conclusions may be drawn from the following report: An expert foreign observer has noted that in the Black Sea harbor of Novorossiisk access to the harbor area has been more severely restricted since the summer months. The old entrance permits have been annulled and replaced by new ones. The same observer felt he had grounds for assuming that there was more than food in the heavy crates composing the cargo of the *Neva*, which left Odessa for Spain. So far, however, it has been impossible to obtain reliable proof of violation of the arms embargo by the Soviet Government.

Since the wide expanse of the Soviet Union, the position of her harbors, and the well-known Soviet system of surveillance and of restricted areas greatly facilitate any camouflage maneuvers, it is quite naturally extremely difficult to obtain such information.

v. TIPPELSKIRCH

---

[3] Not printed (1810/414334–35). It summarized reports of shipments from Odessa to Spain.

No. 89

1810/414361

The Chargé d'Affaires in Spain to the Foreign Ministry

[Telegram]

No. 399 of September 29   ALICANTE, September 29, 1936.
Pol. III 3172.

On September 25 the Russian steamer *Neva*, announced as a food ship, arrived here; according to an Italian report the ship on its western trip passed through the Bosporus on September 21, together with the steamer *Volga*.

The steamer carried a letter to the Civil Governor, but no other papers, and unloaded at night directly into freight cars and trucks with the harbor closed off. According to a report from a harbor official, so far 1,200 bales of buckskin for uniforms have been unloaded, 1,360 crates (approximately 125 centimeters long) labeled "stockfish" in Spanish and containing rifles, and over 4,000 crates marked "pressed meats" in German and containing ammunition.

I shall try to obtain further proof.

The *Volga* is said to be at Valencia.

VOELCKERS

No. 90

3207/697894–95

The Chargé d'Affaires in Spain to the Foreign Ministry

Telegram [1]

No. 407 of September 30   ALICANTE, September 30, 1936.

According to the latest information, the military and political situation in and around Madrid is as follows:

The encirclement of the capital by the White troops is proceeding slowly but systematically from four directions:

1) From the northeast toward Guadalajara.

2) From the north, from the Somosierra. This column has already seized the Madrid waterworks and thus could cut off the water supply.

3) From the west, from San Martín de Valdeiglesias, in order to roll back the Reds who have regained a foothold in the north and in El Escorial.

4) From the southwest, from Toledo.

The capture of Toledo represents a great strategic victory. It is assumed that Franco will first bring up his fourth column in the Navalcarnero-Illescas area and then turn right and capture Aranjuez, thus closing the gap in the southeast.

The increasing pressure of the encirclement is already beginning to weaken the power of resistance of the Madrid Government, the defense forces, and the people. The Government and the different parties are at variance regarding the question of defense. The President, whose wife is supposed to have gone aboard a British destroyer at Alicante, and who himself is reported to have arranged for asylum in the French or Argentine Embassy, urged the Prime Minister in vain to surrender the capital. Prieto urged the same thing in a violent discussion that led to blows, during which he was allegedly wounded or even arrested. Five Ministers failed to attend yesterday's meeting of the Council of Ministers. The press published a Government statement which seeks to excuse their absence as necessary because of activities outside of Madrid. It is assumed, however, that they have fled.

The Prime Minister continues to favor defending the capital to the last, for which purpose preparations such as the digging of trenches and the erection of barricades and artillery emplacements are in evidence in many places.

The attitude of the Anarchists, who continue to refuse to join the Government, is not clear.

---

[1] Transmitted via OKM to the Foreign Ministry.

The approach of White troops and the reaction against the Red rule of force are encouraging supporters of the Right to make plans for revolt and resistance within Madrid. A supposed statement by Franco is being circulated, according to which he answered the question as to which of his four columns would capture Madrid first by saying that it would be the fifth column waiting in the city.

Thus the unified, consistently executed advance of the Military is opposed by a divided Government, threatened on the one hand by Anarchists and on the other by resurgent Rightists at the seat of the Government itself. The report that the Government is preparing a withdrawal position in Alicante, where numerous members of the families of the Ministers have already arrived and where an airport is being built, is therefore credible.

The fall of Madrid is certain. It must not be assumed, however, that the Civil War will definitely be decided thereby, although it is considered possible that the resistance of Catalonia can be broken by economic isolation.

VOELCKERS

No. 91

1819/415965

The Chargé d'Affaires in France to the Foreign Ministry

STRICTLY CONFIDENTIAL   PARIS, October 1, 1936.
A 4378   Sent October 2.

Subject: Statements of the Burgos Government against the export of gold by the Madrid Government.

With reference to my report of September 30, A 4303.[1]

Another memorandum, which is enclosed,[2] was sent to the Embassy by the Burgos Government with the request that it be submitted to the Foreign Ministry. It was sent through the same channels as the one enclosed with my last report. The memorandum deals with the export of gold by the Madrid Government.

The Burgos Government asked that the attention of the German Government be called very particularly to the danger that the Madrid Government would either spend all the remaining Spanish gold during the fighting or else take it to France. This would not only make it exceedingly difficult for the new Spanish Government to rehabilitate the country but would also make it impossible for it to enter into any sort of fruitful financial and commercial relations with friendly countries.

It was also pointed out strictly confidentially that, when explaining

---

[1] Not printed (1819/415960–64).
[2] Enclosure not printed (1819/415966–67).

these dangers in France, the representatives of the Burgos Government were not finding a hearing even in the Rightist circles friendly to them. Evidently the desire to see as much of the Spanish gold as possible brought to France predominates among them too.

The Burgos Government emphatically requests the German Government to investigate how these dangers could be countered and if possible also to communicate with the British Government on this score.

FORSTER

No. 92

629/251946–47

The Acting State Secretary to the Legation in Portugal

Draft Telegram

BERLIN, October 3, 1936.
zu Pol. III 3275 III.

Drafting Officer: Counselor of Legation Dumont.

General Franco has sent the following telegram to the Führer and Chancellor:

"Upon assuming the leadership of the Spanish State and the office of Generalissimo of the Nationalist troops, I have the honor to convey my warmest wishes to Your Excellency as chief of the great German nation for the well-being of Your Excellency and the prosperity of the noble nation with which we are united by so many bonds of sincere friendship and deep gratitude."

Please dispatch Du Moulin to Franco with instructions to express to him orally the thanks of the Führer and of the German nation for his friendly wishes; the Führer's most sincere congratulations on his assumption of power and designation as Generalissimo and his best wishes for the further success of the work of liberation undertaken by Franco; and admiration for the heroic conduct of the Spanish Army and of the Spanish population loyal to Franco. In carrying out this commission please explain that the Führer refrained from giving a telegraphic or written reply to the telegram because the world might have considered this to mean recognition of the Nationalist Government, but that recognition at the present moment would compromise our work in Spain and therefore serve neither Franco nor Germany's interest.

For your confidential information only: We have asked Rome to proceed in like manner and do not intend to accord *de facto* recognition until the Nationalist troops have taken Madrid.

DIECKHOFF

No. 93

4793/E236274

An Official of Political Division I to the Minister in Portugal

BERLIN, October 3, 1936.

DEAR BARON HUENE: At the request of Baron Weizsäcker I should like to ask you to send to this office the drafts and accompanying papers for your report of September 11—No. 2797/36—subject: forwarding of a report by the representative of the Export Cartel for War Matériel. Particular importance is attached to any copies that you may have of Herr Messerschmidt's report of September 8.

For your personal information I wish to add that by higher orders the entire correspondence in this matter is to be placed in an especially secret category.

With the request to extend my best regards to Baroness von Huene, I remain, with cordial greetings and

Heil Hitler!

As ever,

VON DÖRNBERG

No. 94

629/251956

The Minister in Portugal to the Foreign Ministry

Telegram

SECRET   LISBON, October 8, 1936—2 : 54 p.m.
No. 171 of October 8   Received October 8—5 : 00 p.m.
                                          Pol. III 3487.

With reference to your telegram No. 181 of October 3 [1] (Pol. III 3275 III) and my telegram No. 169 of October 5. [2]

Du Moulin has returned from Salamanca, Franco's new headquarters. He carried out the instructions.

General Franco expressed his heartfelt thanks for the Führer's gesture and complete admiration for him and the new Germany. He expressed the hope soon to be able to hoist his banner beside the banner of civilization that the Führer had raised. He asked that his thanks be conveyed for the valuable moral and material help thus far given. Franco showed the greatest understanding for the statement contained in the next-to-last paragraph of the telegraphic instruction.

A written report will follow by air mail.

HUENE

---

[1] Document No. 92, p. 103.
[2] Not printed (4796/E236699).

No. 95

1819/415974

The Acting Director of the Political Department to the Embassy in France

BERLIN, October 8, 1936.
Pol. III 3477.

For your confidential information.

In conversations with Mussolini, the Ambassador at Rome stated that, should Madrid fall, the Führer was inclined to recognize the Nationalist Government *de facto* if an agreement was reached with Italy on a similar procedure. Portuguese collaboration was desirable but not a condition. Mussolini assented and said that the Italian standpoint was essentially that, in the event of the capture of Madrid, Italy and Germany should come to an agreement as to the form in which sympathy and formal or factual recognition could be expressed to the Nationalist Government. The dispatching of ambassadors to Madrid could also be considered.

WEIZSÄCKER

No. 96

47/31707–11

The Minister in Portugal to the Foreign Ministry

SECRET   LISBON, October 10, 1936.
No. 3141   Received October 12.
                                          Pol. I 2034 g.

With reference to telegraphic instruction No. 181 of October 3, 1936 (Pol. III 3275).[1]

Subject: Trip of Counselor of Legation Count Du Moulin to Spain.

I have the honor to enclose a memorandum by Counselor of Legation Count Du Moulin regarding the trip he made to General Franco as directed in the above-mentioned instruction.

VON HUENE

[Enclosure]

MEMORANDUM

SECRET   LISBON, October 8, 1936.

1. On the basis of the orders in instruction No. 181 of October 3, I visited General Franco on October 6 at his headquarters, which

---

[1] Document No. 92, p. 103.

were transferred to Salamanca on that day. The Burgos mission here had Secretary of Legation Marquis de Villa Urrutia, who is working with the mission, accompany me in order to facilitate as prompt a reception as possible in Salamanca and to cope with possible difficulties during the trip, which was made by automobile.

General Franco set the reception for the afternoon of the day of my arrival. Franco had just arrived in Salamanca and was living in the palace of the Archbishop, who had placed it at his disposal. He received me in the presence of his Chef de Cabinet, after I had been introduced by the Chief of Protocol of the former Foreign Ministry. I carried out my commission by repeating word for word the statement prescribed in the instruction. Franco first answered with a speech the essential contents of which were reported in telegram No. 171 of October 8, and followed it with a long conversation. Then he invited me to a small dinner party, which was also attended by the highest ranking German flier present, as well as by General Kindelan [2] and Franco's immediate associates. During my stay I was the guest of General Franco. Until my arrival no diplomatic representatives of foreign countries had called on Franco since he was designated Chief of State.

2. From the conversations with General Franco and his brother, Nicolás Aurelio, the following is noteworthy:

General Franco showed great understanding for the fact that we are not yet recognizing the Burgos Government. He understood perfectly that it was much easier for us to furnish aid to the extent done heretofore as long as the possibilities of support were not hampered by international complications. The cordiality with which Franco expressed his veneration for the Führer and Chancellor and his sympathy for Germany, and the decided friendliness of my reception, permitted not even a moment of doubt as to the sincerity of his attitude toward us.

He was very optimistic with regard to the military situation and was counting on taking Madrid in the near future, without, however, committing himself by mentioning a date. The superiority of the Nationalist Army over the Marxists was obvious, he said. During the advance from Badajoz to Toledo the Reds had lost 16,000 verified dead alone. In the same period the White Army had lost, including those wounded, only 1,600 men. Particularly the machine guns, and to a lesser extent the artillery, accounted for the enormous losses of the Reds.

---

[2] Of General Franco's Air Force.

At the moment stress was being laid principally on a "unification of ideas" within the White Front. Marxist propaganda had tried to create the impression, in foreign countries, too, that after a victory by the Nationalist Government the former privileges of the nobility and the Church would be restored. This was not intended in the slightest, and there should be no doubts on this score. The question of the monarchy was by no means acute; whether at some later time an effort would be made to return Spain to monarchist rule again was not being discussed at present. It was absolutely necessary to work toward creating a common ideology among the co-fighters for liberation: the Army, the Fascists, and the monarchist organizations, as well as the Catholic CEDA. But it would be necessary to proceed with kid gloves. It had been necessary to fix the main lines for the future government at this time; this was much easier to do prior to the occupation of Madrid, since now, in the middle of the undecided fight, no resistance was to be expected. For this reason, too, the designation of Franco as Chief of State had been accelerated. From intimations, I gathered that a conference with German agencies had not been without influence in this decision.

Evidently it is intended that Franco's brother, Nicolás Aurelio, heretofore chief of the so-called Office for Procurement of Materials in Portugal, remain with the Generalissimo as Secretary General. He is an untiring worker, who performed his task in Portugal with the greatest skill and energy. I hear consistently that he possesses great influence with General Franco, who, too much occupied in the past by purely military tasks, has had little time for decisions in the field of internal policy. Aurelio Franco will play a very important role particularly in formulating the internal policy of the new Spain, whereas old General Cabanellas will probably retire from his present post very soon. Aurelio Franco is a great friend of Germany and is very grateful to us for saving his family (cf. telegram No. 124 of September 5[3]). We will probably have a valuable ally in him in the future, too.

Among statements of general interest there should also be mentioned General Franco's remark that the expectations which had been placed on the air arm in fighting warships had not been entirely fulfilled. A warship could at best be sunk only by bombs dropped from a very low altitude.

Count Du Moulin

---

[3] Not printed (681/258946).

No. 97

1759/404964–68

The Ambassador in the Soviet Union to the Foreign Ministry

A 2132   Moscow, October 12, 1936.
                                                  Received October 14.
                                                     Pol. III 3682.

Subject: The Soviet Union's action in the question of non-intervention
  in Spain.

The step of the Soviet Government on October 7 in the London
Non-Intervention Committee [1] was foreshadowed by a number of circumstances. Even when the Soviet Government joined the arms
embargo affecting Spain, this was done to the accompaniment of
criticism in the Soviet press. "It must be frankly stated," wrote
Izvestiya on August 26, "that a declaration of neutrality in the face
of such events as are taking place in Spain is not our idea." This
was a hint that, as was reported in diplomatic circles here, the arms
embargo was submitted to the Soviet Government in August as a
finished Anglo-French project—something which annoyed Litvinov.
But the August 26 issue of *Izvestiya* immediately criticized the principle of the non-intervention agreement too, and the agreement was
further discredited in the Soviet press by the constantly repeated
assertion that it was "not being observed by the Fascist states of Italy,
Germany, and Portugal." For a time, the same diplomatic considerations which had prompted the U.S.S.R. to join the arms embargo in
August continued to act as a restraining influence. The prime consideration then had been the desire to respect the precarious position
of the French Government and to remain in accord with the British
Government. However, as the position of the Madrid Government
deteriorated, the influence of different forces, growing out of the
basically revolutionary orientation of the Soviet Union, became ever
stronger.

In accordance with this basic orientation of Soviet policy and in
consideration of the situation of the Madrid Government, which was
becoming hopeless and about which Del Vayo probably informed
Litvinov sufficiently in Geneva, Moscow now felt forced to come
to the aid of the Madrid Government by a new action. In addition,
unrest and confusion have spread among the ranks of the Soviet
followers abroad as the result of the Trotskyite trials; also, the reproach that Moscow is leaving the Spanish proletariat in the lurch for
opportunistic reasons is causing all the more serious difficulties for
foreign Communist leaders loyal to Stalin. It is understandable,

---

[1] Threatening to withdraw from the Non-Intervention Committee unless violation of the agreement ceased. See Editors' Note, p. 81.

then, that the Soviet Government felt impelled "to do something." Another contributory factor, according to a version current here, is the fact that Thorez,[2] after approaching the French Government in vain for help for Madrid, later tried to move Moscow to take action.

As regards the timing of the Soviet action, the situation which arose in Geneva in the meantime probably played a part. The last session of the League of Nations evidently did not bring the expected success to Litvinov's anti-German policy of encirclement and to his attempts at disrupting the Western Pact; besides, he has still other reasons to be dissatisfied with France and England. As a result he felt less impelled now than before to afford particular consideration to France and England. If difficulties for the Five Power Conference should also develop out of the Spanish question, this can only be agreeable to Soviet policy.

Concerning the effect which can be expected from the Soviet action in London on October 7, the diplomatic corps here feels that for the time being the Soviet Union is less intent on destroying the non-intervention agreement than on forcing France and England to see that the agreement is observed by other countries. On the other hand, the diplomatic corps is of the opinion that the Soviet Union would not be sorry if the embargo were to break down. The French suggest that the Soviet Government is merely interested in obtaining a certain satisfaction in London which would permit it to save face. In any case everyone is agreed that the intended propaganda effect constitutes a very important feature of the Soviet action.

It is obvious that it is a maneuver calculated for its propaganda effect; the lack of any thorough substantiation of the accusation contained in the Soviet declaration of October 7 and the absence of a concrete proposal for further procedure, along with the most extreme threats to withdraw, reveal clearly that the Russians were in a hurry to create a definite agitation.

The comments which appeared in the Moscow newspapers after the London attack fit in with this supposition. They expand broadly on the propaganda side of the subject and emphasize the merits of the Soviet *démarche*, which has now "turned a bright spotlight on the true situation"; at the same time one is given to understand that the matter is not yet finished. In this sense an editorial article in *Izvestiya*, for instance, directs particularly violent attacks against Grandi, Italy's representative on the Non-Intervention Committee, because he had tried with the help of "formal tricks" to prevent an investigation of the "criminal acts" taking place at the Spanish-Portuguese border. *Izvestiya* declares it should not be permitted that ["] clear, unrefuted accusations which admit no misconstruction of

---

[2] Maurice Thorez, French Communist leader and Deputy.

any kind," such as the Soviet representative had brought against Portugal, Italy, and Germany, should be drowned "in the murky tide of formal procedure."

Pravda expresses itself similarly. It also censures the Non-Intervention Committee, as such, for not offering sufficient opposition to the representatives of the "Fascist states"; rather there had been obvious tendencies to bury the Soviet protest under procedural difficulties. The attitude of the Soviet Union remained unchanged, however. She demanded that the violations of the non-intervention agreement cease and that the Non-Intervention Committee resort to effective measures in this direction.

In summary it can be said that the Soviet Union, through the *démarche* in the London Non-Intervention Commission, has at any rate abandoned the zigzag course which she has used heretofore and has started on a new tack. In undertaking such a diplomatic step she has now committed herself to a different type of conduct which will probably prescribe for her a more active attitude in the future, too, a fact which must result in new tensions.

SCHULENBURG

No. 98

3176/682858

Minute by an Official of the Economic Policy Department

BERLIN, October 13, 1936.

On the occasion of a discussion of the exchange of goods with Majorca, I have just heard from the Reich Foreign Exchange Control Agency (Reichsbankrat Ludwig) that there, too, the Burgos Government has suggested the sending of a representative for negotiations on a trade and clearing agreement. This wish was advanced by Videl, the Spaniard introduced at the Foreign Ministry by Minister Schmidt (Ret.).

The wish was said to be based on the fact that the military regime did not have at its disposal enough officials experienced in economic questions and was therefore helpless in its dealings with the German firms. A certain mistrust of businessmen by the military was making it more difficult to resume commercial relations, despite the great interest which the Burgos Government basically had in doing so.

The Economics Ministry is of the opinion that a general arrangement should be made soon and a representative sent. Ministerialdirektor Sarnow has already been asked to work on the matter.

Herewith submitted to Ministerialdirektor Ritter.

SABATH

Copies to Counselors of Legation Benzler and Dumont.

No. 99

3176/682859–60

Minute by the Director of the Economic Policy Department

BERLIN, October 15, 1936.

With regard to the negotiations with Spain I have determined the following:

Minister President Colonel General Göring complained to Minister Hess a short time ago that he had no adequate personnel to handle deliveries of goods to and imports from Spain. Minister Hess thereupon said that he could have the entire personnel of the Auslandsorganisation for this purpose, and he named in particular Major von Jackwitz [1] in this connection. Minister President Colonel General Göring then asked Herr von Jackwitz whether he had sufficient personnel for this purpose and whether he could begin tomorrow. Jackwitz had answered yes to both questions. Herr von Jackwitz, who was heretofore detailed by the Auslandsorganisation to the Keppler [2] Economic Staff, has given up this position and is now directly under Minister President Colonel General Göring. The Finance Ministry is supposed already to have granted the necessary funds for Herr von Jackwitz. He will shortly occupy twelve rooms in Columbus House.

Furthermore, the Auslandsorganisation is already concerned with Spanish affairs through the director of the Economic Agency of the Auslandsorganisation in Tetuán, whose name is Bernhardt. As a result of his stay in Morocco, Bernhardt has close connections with General Franco from former times and is now being employed a great deal by General Franco.

To be submitted to: The Foreign Minister, Ministerialdirektor Dieckhoff, Minister von Weizsäcker, Herr Benzler, Herr Sabath, Ambassador von Stohrer.

RITTER

---

[1] More correctly Jagwitz. This was Eberhard von Jagwitz of the Auslandsorganisation, leading figure in the organization of Rowak, later Under State Secretary in the Economics Ministry.
[2] Dr. Wilhelm Keppler was the Führer's Commissioner [*Beauftragter*] for Economic Affairs.

No. 100

690/259758–61

The Chargé d'Affaires in Spain to the Acting Director of the Political Department

ALICANTE, October 16, 1936.

DEAR HERR VON WEIZSÄCKER: The report received today from Cartagena from the torpedo boat *Luchs* concerning the unloading of 50 four-man tanks with trained crews from a Russian steamer—the report has been confirmed by the British, according to a radiogram from the *Deutschland*—will not only be a welcome addition to the arms embargo list; as a substantiated single case in addition to many other reports which are more or less difficult to confirm, it shows the enormous contribution in war matériel and manpower which Russia is constantly putting at the disposal of the Spanish Government. Russia is directing Spanish policy, which—in both internal and foreign affairs—has consciously gone over to a policy of attack since the arrival of Rosenberg.[1] Russia even seems to be able to master the Anarchist problem. She directs the press propaganda, which is developing into increasingly provocative agitation against us. Russia is mobilizing international Marxism in its entirety and has adopted a threatening tone in London. Just as we, in making our first decisions and in consistently executing them, were clear about the real issues, so, obviously, is Russian diplomacy fully aware of what this is really all about. Nevertheless I do not believe that the Russians can risk open military intervention, in other words that there is danger of a European conflict. England does not want such a conflict, and France, with divided feelings as to Spanish events, with the definite expectation that Germany and Italy would be in the opposite camp, and with the allegiance of several of her allies uncertain, will think twice before resorting to the *ultima ratio*.[2]

As for England, we have made the interesting observation that she is supplying the Whites with ammunition via Gibraltar and that the British cruiser commander here has recently been supplying us with information on Russian arms deliveries to the Red Government, which he certainly would not do without instructions.

The development of the military situation, which for about three weeks has been stagnating or showing the Reds in a dangerous advance on some sectors of the front, as in Oviedo, gives cause for reflection. If the Whites are advancing so slowly in spite of their present superior equipment and discipline, it is to be feared that the large amount of Russian aid in arms and manpower will further delay their progress or even stop it altogether.

The conclusions to be drawn by the other participants in the Spanish game are obvious: the Russian stake forces them to increase their own, probably also with regard to manpower, since one cannot wait until the technique of handling new equipment has been learned.

In addition, however, careful study must be given the question whether the utilization of the matériel delivered can be left entirely to the recipients, as has evidently been the case in the past, or whether

---

[1] The Soviet Ambassador in Spain.
[2] On Oct. 10 (telegram No. 431), Voelckers argued that the Spanish and Soviet Governments were trying to precipitate a general war (4446/E086361).

they must not be aided in their strategic planning and the tactical execution thereof; whoever gives such valuable assistance can also demand control over its use. It is obvious that, in so doing, feelings must not be hurt. This could be assured by the choice of liaison personnel familiar with the language and the country. I should be glad to make suggestions in this regard.

I am not of the opinion, by the way, that we can expect an early end to the Spanish disorders, for, although the capture of Madrid would be an important step ahead, it would not mean that the final goal had been reached.

With many cordial greetings and Heil Hitler!

VOELCKERS

No. 101

3176/682861–63

Minute by an Official of the Economic Policy Department

SECRET BERLIN, October 16, 1936.

e. o. W II WE

Subject: Trade with the territory occupied by the Burgos Government.

I have heard the following from the Economics Ministry:

The Economics Ministry had intended to send Reichsbankrat Ludwig to Burgos and Seville for the purpose of a general regulation of trade. He was supposed to leave today by plane. In the last few days, however, the Economics Ministry had received reports according to which negotiations with the Burgos Government for the same purpose are already supposed to have been begun by another agency. State Secretary Posse [1] thereupon made inquiry of State Secretary Körner [2] by letter. On the basis of this inquiry a discussion took place yesterday afternoon between State Secretary Posse and State Secretary Körner, in the course of which Herr Posse received more detailed information.

At the instigation of Minister President Colonel General Göring, a corporation by the name of Rovag [*Rowak*] has been formed in Germany, while a corresponding company called Hisma (with German participation in the person of Bernhardt) has been created in Seville.[3] The purpose of the companies is to regulate the trade in *raw materials*. It is supposedly not intended to extend their activities to other commodities. The activities of these companies also will not extend to the Balearic and the Canary Islands. Both companies have a monopoly of purchases and sales. If, for example, a German exporter wishes to deliver to Spain, he has to sell to Rowak, which then resells

---

[1] State Secretary in the Economics Ministry.
[2] State Secretary in the Four Year Plan.
[3] See also Editors' Note, p. 1.

to Hisma. The Finance Ministry has extended Rowak a credit of 3 million reichsmarks to begin with. Hisma is said to have obtained Spanish credits. Approximately twenty men from Jackwitz' organization went to Madrid recently to get the business going.

A fleet of ships has been assembled. Further arrangements for providing protection have been made with the Naval Command.

After the conference between the two state secretaries, conversations were initiated between the Jackwitz organization and the Economics Ministry (yesterday and today), in which an agreement was reached on technical procedure under the foreign exchange regulations. These conversations are being continued.

The Economics Ministry would have preferred it if its own plans could have been realized. After having been confronted with an accomplished fact, however, it will await further developments and take no steps on its own initiative for the present, particularly since the specific promise has been given that the measures which have now been initiated are to be only temporary.

SABATH

No. 102

47/31721–22

The Chargé d'Affaires in Spain to the Foreign Ministry

Telegram

No. 441 of October 16   ALICANTE, October 17, 1936.
Received October 17—10 : 00 a.m.
Pol. I 2125 g.

For the State Secretary personally.

On October 13 . . . (group garbled) Acting Consul von Knobloch reappeared here in the company of two Spaniards. He said that, in agreement with Franco, he had been authorized by the Spanish Fascist Party to arrange a meeting with the Civil Governor here on a German or an Argentine warship and, by means of a bribe consisting of an unlimited sum, to induce him to liberate the Fascist leader, Primo, who is imprisoned here. If this attempt at liberation is not successful within 4 days, forcible liberation by a thousand armed Fascists was being planned; their arrival here on merchant ships escorted by two White cruisers was already arranged.

Before the arrival of Knobloch, the Embassy had already begun an attempt at liberation through the Anarchist Alpha, the only real authority here, an attempt which offers perhaps the only possible hope of getting prisoners out alive.

After extensive deliberations on the *Deutschland*, during which Knobloch was interrogated regarding details of the plans and their unrealistic nature was revealed, Admiral Carls, who was under instructions from the OKM to reach a decision in agreement with the Foreign Ministry, decided as follows with my approval:

1. An attempt to bribe the Governor seems hopeless in view of the latter's Leftist attitude, and particularly because he could by no means release prisoners alive without or in opposition to the Anarchists who supervise the jail. The attempt would therefore only result in the death of the prisoner.

2. Forcible liberation which, with the right preparation and execution would in itself stand a good chance of success, offers little prospect of releasing the prisoner alive; he is guarded by specially detailed Anarchists.

3. Therefore the efforts initiated by the Embassy should be continued, and only if they are unsuccessful should the question of forcible liberation, to be carried out by no one but Spaniards, again be considered.

Knobloch has now . . . (group garbled) a new plan of liberation through the mediation of the Italian, Serisi, on the . . . (group garbled) of Primo's Italian citizenship, and then have his extradition demanded by Italy. This plan, too, . . . (two groups garbled) capable of endangering the life of the prisoner.

Knobloch alleges that the liberation of Primo is a vital question for Spanish Fascism, which must bring about a National Socialist revolution of the Spanish people now, during the Civil War, since otherwise, after victory, reactionary elements such as the Clerical-Military Party and the Carlists would hinder Franco in the execution of his . . . (group garbled) program. This is allegedly also the opinion of authoritative Party circles in Germany.

Admiral Carls refused to accede to such plans before victory because they jeopardized victory and were not worthy of credence, since he and the Embassy were without instructions. I took the same attitude. I call attention to the fact that the plans of Knobloch, who cannot go ashore himself and wants to use the machinery of the Embassy, would endanger the work of the Embassy even if they were successfully carried out. An attempt at forcible liberation would make the further stay of the Embassy here questionable.

I request instructions on the following:

1. Whether the alleged plan for a National Socialist revolution actually has the approval of authoritative German agencies.

2. Whether the liberation of Primo is so important that it should be given priority over the work of the Embassy.[1]

VOELCKERS

---

[1] For the reply to these inquiries see documents Nos. 104 and 108, pp. 116 and 120. Primo de Rivera was executed at Alicante on Nov. 20, 1936.

No. 103

168/132212–13

Minute by the Director of the Economic Policy Department

BERLIN, October 17, 1936.

Today I found a memorandum to the effect that Field Marshal von Blomberg had telephoned in my absence.   When I called back and was informed that the Field Marshal could not be reached today or tomorrow, I telephoned General Wilberg and asked him what Field Marshal von Blomberg had wanted.   General Wilberg told me that he had merely wanted to call my attention once again to the following two points, namely:

1. Until recently it had been the task of General Warlimont to represent, as it were, the German Government in relation to the Burgos Government.   That could no longer be done now for the reasons stated.   Therefore he considered it necessary that the Foreign Ministry now appoint a suitable person to be sent to Burgos for the purpose of representing the entire German Government.

I replied to General Wilberg that I had already communicated this viewpoint to the Foreign Minister.

2. If this person could not be Herr von Stohrer, as General Wilberg could understand, it must not on the other hand be a young secretary of legation.   That would not suffice for the Burgos Government and would also place the representatives of our Defense Ministry there in an undesirable position.   The man should, in fact, be a quasi "chargé d'affaires."

I told General Wilberg that the person we were considering if the occasion should arise had exactly this attribute of a quasi chargé d'affaires.   He was satisfied with this.

To be submitted to: The Foreign Minister, Ministerialdirektor Gaus, Ministerialdirektor Prüfer, Minister von Weizsäcker.

RITTER

No. 104

47/31723

The Acting Director of the Political Department to the Embassy in Spain (at Alicante)

Telegram

No. 77   BERLIN, October 19, 1936—7: 50 p.m.

zu Pol. I 2125 g.

With reference to your telegraphic report No. 441.[1]

I agree with the attitude which, in agreement with Admiral Carls,

---

[1] Document No. 102, p. 114.

you proposed taking in the question of liberation. Further instructions follow with regard to question 1 of your telegraphic report.

WEIZSÄCKER

[EDITORS' NOTE. In the collection of Count Ciano's papers published under the title *L'Europa verso la catastrofe* ([Milan], 1948), pp. 87–99 (English translation: *Ciano's Diplomatic Papers*, edited by Malcolm Muggeridge, London, 1948, pp. 52–60), there are summaries of Ciano's conversation with Neurath in Berlin on October 21, and with Hitler at Berchtesgaden on October 24. In both conversations there was agreement that military assistance should be given to insure the capture of Madrid and that Franco should be recognized after the capture of Madrid. Hitler and Ciano asserted that their Governments had no territorial ambitions in Spain. No record of these conversations has been found in the archives of the German Foreign Ministry.]

No. 105

1819/415980–83

The Ambassador in France to the Foreign Ministry

A 4673
PARIS, October 22, 1936.
Sent October 30.

Subject: Question of the recognition of the new Spanish Government and of a possible independent Catalonian Government by France.

With reference to report A 4404 of October 8.[1]

Numerous reports which I have received corroborate the impression that the French Government considers the question whether and when it should recognize the new Spanish Government and a possible independent Catalonian Government as a difficult problem to be treated with great caution, concerning the solution of which it cannot make any decision at the present time.

It is generally believed here that Germany, Italy, and Portugal will publicly recognize the Nationalist Government in one form or another immediately after the fall of Madrid. It is a known fact that French Rightist circles have for some time been advocating the view that France must assume the same attitude in order not to take a back seat completely and in order to regain the ground lost thus far in relation to the new Spain. One will not be mistaken in assuming that similar viewpoints also play a part in the considerations of the French Government, especially of the Quai d'Orsay. Opposing them, how-

---

[1] Not printed (1819/415969).

ever, are weighty scruples, especially with regard to domestic policy. The animosity not only of the Communists but also of the entire Popular Front against the Nationalist Government in Spain continues to be strong. Even the well-known interview of General Franco in the *Echo de Paris*, in which he expressed his sympathies for France, cannot have decreased this animosity, since he spoke expressly against the French Popular Front and stated that it did not represent the real France. Under these circumstances a report from an excellent source appears to me to be significant, according to which the question was considered in the Cabinet to be so difficult that an open discussion regarding it had thus far been avoided. No one could predict at the moment what the Government would decide to do.

From another side it is pointed out that, quite apart from the domestic opposition of the French Popular Front circles, the French Government would certainly not announce recognition if it did not receive definite assurances in return. In this connection the question of recognizing Catalonia as an independent state was discussed. The fact was stressed that it would be very difficult for France to bargain with regard to recognition on the one hand of the Nationalist Government and on the other of an independent Catalonian Government. It was certain, to be sure, that in case a Catalonian state was proclaimed the French Popular Front Government would be strongly inclined, for psychological and political reasons, to support such a government, even if the career diplomats in the Quai d'Orsay had scruples. It was to be feared, however, that the Nationalist Spanish Government would regard this as an announcement of hostility toward it, which would render worthless the simultaneous formal recognition accorded it by France. But the French Government was certainly well aware that even if an independent Catalonian state was proclaimed Franco would still rule by far the greater part of Spain, and France would have a much longer common boundary with Nationalist Spain. In addition, although a close connection between France and Catalonia appeared desirable, to be sure, the fact that Catalonia would probably be dependent on Moscow might also give France cause for concern.

The above-mentioned viewpoints make it quite likely that even after the fall of Madrid the French Government will make no quick decisions but will first wait and see what attitude the other governments assume. Should the former Spanish Government continue the fight in the east, as is likely, particularly from Barcelona, then the French Government could allege that it was adhering to its carefully defined policy of non-intervention. At any rate, I understand that in circles close to the Government the view is expressed even now that the capture of Madrid in itself would not affect the status of the so-called "legal" Spanish Government. The question of possible recognition of an independent Catalonia could not confront France until it was brought up by the Spanish rump Government. However, it should be pointed out that this sort of juridical reasoning might easily be outstripped by events.

On the whole it must be remembered that the treatment of the Spanish question confronts France with such unpleasant problems and such great difficulties that there is less indication of a definite direction here than in any other department of foreign policy. The conflict between material interests and the great variety of interpretations placed upon them by the various authoritative groups are so great that it appears utterly impossible to make any predictions whatsoever. Thus, for example, a Spaniard close to the Nationalist Government, who has always been very well informed and who has very good connections with both the Right and the Left in France, assured me positively that the French Government would recognize the new Spanish Government immediately after the fall of Madrid. In view of the above analysis I for my part feel unable to confirm this assumption. Personally I believe that the French Government, given the lack of resolution which it has shown particularly in the Spanish problem, is more likely to allow actual developments to overtake it and determine its course of action.

WELCZECK

No. 106

1759/404997

Memorandum by the Foreign Minister

RM 764   BERLIN, October 23, 1936.
                                          e. o. Pol. III 4038.

On the basis of the reports from England regarding the possible withdrawal of Soviet Russia from the embargo committee in London, I discussed with Ciano yesterday evening and this morning the attitude to be taken by us in this case. Count Ciano shared the opinion I expressed that if this should happen we should first wait and see what the attitude of the British and French would be. At any rate we should not make any hasty decisions leading to immediate announcement of our withdrawal.[1]

BARON V. NEURATH

---

[1] See Editors' Note, p. 81.

No. 107

1810/414411

The Ambassador in the Soviet Union to the Foreign Ministry

No. A 2244 Moscow, October 26, 1936.

Subject: Soviet deliveries to Spain.

The German Consulate in Odessa reported the following by telegram on October 24:

"The ocean liner *Transbalt*, said to have arrived here from Holland and Spain, left Odessa again on about October 20. I now learn from a person close to the ship personnel that the cargo consists of arms with timber and food on top and is destined for Spain; also that the crew of the ship refused to expedite the cargo and was completely replaced by Party members. There were on the docks approximately 200 new 2-ton trucks of Soviet make, dark green in color and without any markings; the steamer is supposed to have taken all or part of this freight aboard, too.

"According to a report in *Krasni Krim*, the *Kuban* arrived in Kerch harbor from Alicante on October 15, took on a cargo of cast iron for Belgium, and left 'for abroad' on October 17. Aboard and ashore, meetings took place on behalf of Spain. The *Kuban* arrived here on October 20 to take on further cargo, having come directly from Alicante, according to the report of the Odessa paper."

By direction:
VON TIPPELSKIRCH

No. 108

47/31724

The Acting Director of the Political Department to the Embassy in Spain

Telegram

No. 84 BERLIN, October 26, 1936—7:35 p.m.

With reference to your telegraphic report No. 441.[1]

For your confidential information: There is no question of any authorization of Knobloch by the Party to work there toward a National Socialist revolution in Spain.

WEIZSÄCKER

---

[1] Document No. 102, p. 114.

No. 109

696/260477–79

The Foreign Minister to the Embassy in Italy

Telegram

No. 268 of October 26   BERLIN, October 27, 1936—6 : 50 p.m.
                                      e. o. Pol. III 4281.

The military progress of the Nationalists in Spain has been so great that one can count on the capture of Madrid in the course of this week or the next. It would therefore be advisable for us, in accordance with the agreement just made in Berlin, to adjust the details of our procedure regarding recognition of Franco's Government with that of the Italian Government in advance.

After the capture of Madrid we intend to have General Franco informed, probably via our Legation in Lisbon, that we propose to accord him *de facto* recognition and to send a German representative [*Beauftragte*] to his headquarters for the purpose of looking after our interests. Insofar as necessary we would publicly justify this step on the grounds that General Franco had actually seized the territory and power in the greater part of Spain to such an extent that the situation demanded a representation of German interests with his Government.

Our diplomatic mission to the former Madrid Government would then presumably be quietly withdrawn.

Even beyond that, however, the consular representatives in the areas not yet under Franco's control are to remain at their posts as long as possible.

After the withdrawal of the German Embassy from Alicante we would presumably inform the Madrid Government's representation in Berlin that we were now discontinuing further official intercourse with it.

Later, when *de jure* recognition is accorded, we shall appoint a regular chargé d'affaires to the Franco Government and issue the declaration contemplated in the office memorandum of October 23 [1] under number 4 regarding the principle of non-intervention, etc.

Please discuss this outline of our procedure with the Government there, continuing to treat the discussions as purely preparatory for the time being.

Please send a telegraphic report regarding Italy's plans.

v. N[EURATH]

---

[1] Not found.

No. 110

696/260504

The Ambassador in Italy to the Foreign Ministry

Telegram

No. 215 of October 28   ROME, October 28, 1936—3 : 30 p.m.
                                         Received October 28—7 : 20 p.m.

With reference to your telegrams Nos. 268 [1] and 269.[2]

For the Foreign Minister personally.

Today I informed Ciano of the contents of telegram No. 268, whereupon he said that he agreed in principle. To be sure, at first glance he could not understand why only a representative was to be appointed at first and a chargé d'affaires not until later. Might it not be better to extend formal recognition immediately after the capture of Madrid? However, Italy would in any case do nothing without coming to an agreement with us in advance; and he would get in touch with us tomorrow after conferring with his advisers regarding the procedure proposed by us. Ciano declared that he knew nothing whatever about the alleged approach of 400,000 Russians by the sea route. He asked me, however, to inform the German Government that Italy had instituted an observation service between Sicily and Africa, for the present without orders to take action, of course, but merely to observe the Russian transports.

Finally, Ciano once again confirmed the fact that Italy is finishing [*fertig macht*] two submarines for the Nationalists.

HASSELL

---
[1] Document No. 109, p. 121.
[2] Not found.

No. 111

696/260503

The Ambassador in Italy to the Foreign Ministry

Telegram

No. 219 of October 29   ROME, October 29, 1936—9 : 25 p.m.
                                         Received October 29—11 : 45 p.m.

With reference to my telegram No. 215 of October 28.

By direction of Ciano, Ministerial Director Buti [1] informed Plessen today as follows: The Italian Government is of the opinion that Germany and Italy should take a more decisive stand.

1. If matters were delayed until the occupation of Madrid, then, in the opinion of the Italian Government, not "representatives" but chargés d'affaires should be sent, and the diplomatic representatives to the former Madrid Government should be withdrawn simultaneously and without further ado. This procedure could be justified

---
[1] Gino Buti, Director General of the Department of European and Mediterranean Affairs in the Italian Ministry of Foreign Affairs.

on the grounds that Madrid had fallen, that the Red Government was consequently fugitive, and that its control was confined to a part of Spain. It would be dangerous to recognize the Nationalist Government and not to withdraw the former representatives, since this could be interpreted as though Italy and Germany in a certain sense recognized the simultaneous existence of two governments.

2. Since the occupation of Madrid might perhaps be delayed, the Italian Government was of the opinion that open relations with the Nationalist Government of Burgos should be established at once. For this purpose "delegates of the German and Italian Governments to the Nationalist Government in Burgos" should be appointed, who would be replaced by chargés d'affaires after the fall of Madrid. In this case the former diplomatic representative could perhaps be withdrawn simultaneously with the appointment of the delegates.

The Italian Ambassador in Berlin has instructions to discuss the matter there in the above vein and to report on Germany's stand.

HASSELL

No. 112

47/31748

The Consul General at Barcelona to the Foreign Ministry

Telegram

No. 178 of October 29 BARCELONA, October 29, 1936—8 : 40 p.m.
Received October 29—11 : 45 p.m.

For the War Ministry.

Crienitz Grünkohl reports through an entirely reliable agent the arrival in Cartagena of twenty Russian planes (single-seater fighters and bombers) with Russian crews, including mechanics and fitters. The speed of the planes is said to be 500 kilometers per hour. The Russians, rejecting assistance and collaboration with the Spanish Government, are working isolated by themselves on their own airport. A tank with a speed of 60 kilometers was also delivered. To expedite their work the Russians have brought along their own automobiles, both trucks and passenger cars. The Russians reject collaboration with the Spanish Government because this has previously proved unsatisfactory.

KÖCHER

No. 113

701/261139–43

The Foreign Minister to the Ambassador in Italy

BERLIN, October 30, 1936.

DEAR HASSELL: Herewith I am sending you a copy of an instruction which the War Minister, after consultation with me, issued today for Admiral Canaris, who has already returned to Spain, as well as for Lieutenant General Sperrle, who is leaving for Spain tomorrow via Rome.[1]

In reply to your telegram No. 219 [2] let me state that, if possible, we want to insist as heretofore on not recognizing the Burgos Government until the conquest of Madrid has been accomplished. We do not deem it expedient to send "delegates" or "agents" to Burgos beforehand, if for no other reason than that General Franco might thereby possibly be confirmed in his delaying tactics. Therefore, when Attolico presents himself here, we shall tell him that we insist on the previous agreement (joint recognition of the Burgos Government immediately after the fall of Madrid) and that we, too, shall then immediately send a chargé d'affaires to the Burgos Government. That we will at the same moment break off relations with the previous Spanish Government by withdrawing our Embassy from Alicante as well as by informing the Spanish Embassy here that its activity is ended, is a matter of course and was never intended otherwise.

With best wishes,

Yours,
NEURATH

[Enclosure]

BERLIN, October 30, 1936.

To: Admiral Canaris,
　　Lieutenant General Sperrle,
　　Foreign Ministry (for Rome), with the request for parallel instructions.

The following point of view is to be expressed most emphatically to General Franco:

1. In view of possible increased Russian help for Red Spain, the German Government does not consider the combat tactics hitherto employed by White Spain, in ground fighting as well as in aerial combat, promising of success. Continued adherence to this hesitant and routine procedure (failure to exploit the present favorable ground and air situation, scattered employment of the Air Force) is even endangering what has been gained so far.

The quick occupation of Madrid is of decisive political importance, since the recognition of the White Government by Germany and Italy will take place then, and only then will the basis for far-reaching aid be established.

---

[1] Marginal note in Hassell's handwriting: "According to Lieutenant General Sp[errle], the Prince of Hesse has also arrived here in the same matter. He has meanwhile communicated with me."

[2] Document No. 111, p. 122.

2. Conditions for greater support of the Air Force are:

(*a*) Leadership of the German units in Spain will be in the hands of a German commander; he will be the *sole* adviser to General Franco in questions pertaining to the German Air Force corps and is responsible *only* to General Franco personally for all his measures. Outwardly, Spanish leadership will be maintained.

(*b*) Integration of all German pilots, antiaircraft and air communication units, and their rear echelons at present in Spain into the German Air Force corps to be formed according to the above paragraph (*a*).

(*c*) Protection of the German air bases through adequate ground forces, which are to be reinforced if necessary.

(*d*) More systematic and active conduct of the war with regard to ground and aerial operations and with regard to cooperation between the two for the purpose of quick occupation of the harbors important for Russian supplies.

3. On the condition that General Franco recognizes these demands without reservations, a further activation of German aid is envisaged.

See annex.

Annex

It is planned to send the following German military units:

One bomber group
One fighter group
One long-range reconnaissance squadron
One flight of short-range reconnaissance planes
Two signal companies
Two operating companies
Three heavy antiaircraft batteries
Two searchlight platoons

No. 114

630/252084

The Foreign Minister to the Spanish Chargé d'Affaires [1] (*Draft Note* [2])

BERLIN, November . . ., 1936.

MR. CHARGÉ D'AFFAIRES: By order of the German Government I have the honor to inform you as follows:

Since General Franco has captured the Spanish capital of Madrid, and control over the greater part of Spanish territory has thus passed into the hands of his Government, the German Government has decided to appoint an official representative to the Government of Gen-

---

[1] José Rovira Armengol.
[2] Marginal note: "Cessat [canceled]. File, Dec. 8, D[umont]."

eral Franco in order to look after German interests. The new German Chargé d'Affaires will proceed immediately to the seat of General Franco's Government. The former Chargé d'Affaires in Alicante has been recalled.

Accordingly, the German Government considers your diplomatic activity in Germany terminated.

Accept, Mr. Chargé, the assurance of my highest consideration.

BARON VON NEURATH

No. 115

1810/414474

The Ambassador in Turkey to the Foreign Ministry

[Telegram]

VERY SECRET   ISTANBUL, November 6, 1936.

No. 16 of November 6

With reference to your inquiry I have learned reliably of the following shipments: October 22, on the *Karl Lepin*, Russian, Odessa to Alicante, 20 trucks and tanks, 4 cannons, 500 tons of ammunition, 1,000 tons of food; October 22, on the *Transbalt*, Russian, Odessa to Cartagena and Barcelona, 40 trucks, 12 tanks, 10 cannons; October 23, on the *Shahter*, Russian, Odessa to Alicante and Barcelona, 6 trucks, 8 cannons, 500 tons of ammunition, 2,000 tons of grain; October 24, on the *Kuban*, Odessa to Barcelona, 2,500 tons of grain, 1,200 tons of food; October 25, on the *Varlaam Avasanov*, Russian, Odessa to Barcelona, 8,500 [tons] of Diesel oil; October 25, the *Aldecca*, Spanish, Barcelona to Nikolayev, for the account of the Spanish Government; October 25, the *Cabo Palo*, Barcelona to Odessa, the same; October 27, on the *Kurak*, Russian, the Black Sea to Barcelona and Alicante, 40 trucks, 12 armored cars, 6 cannons, 4 planes, 700 tons of ammunition, 1,500 tons of food; October 28, on the *Blagoyev*, Russian, Black Sea to Cartagena and Alicante, 20 trucks, 8 cannons, 4 tanks, 500 tons of war matériel, 150 tons of clothing, 1,500 tons of grain; October 31, on the *Komsomol*, Black Sea to Barcelona, 50 trucks, 5 planes, 8 tanks, 2,000 tons of war matériel and ammunition, 1,000 tons of food, 100 tons of medicines.

November 3, the *Darro* and the *Segarra*, both Spanish; November 4, the *Georg Dimitrov* left Alicante with 17 Spanish soldiers, 3 of them wounded and 3 of them women disguised as soldiers; these were put ashore at Istanbul and sent on to Odessa on the *Jan Rudzudak* the same day. Further names of ships, the cargo of which could not be ascertained, will follow.

KELLER

No. 116

4446/E086392–93

The Ambassador in France to the Foreign Ministry

Telegram

No. 666 of November 10   PARIS, November 10, 1936.
Received November 10—10 : 45 p.m.
Pol. III 4743.

With reference to the written instruction of November 7, Pol. III 4475 I. [1]

I agree that Azaña's remark concerning a possible Spanish declaration of war on Germany and Italy is probably not serious from the standpoint of foreign policy. The report of the Italian Embassy in Paris that France will not march if the Soviet Republic or Spain should provoke a war is in my opinion quite accurate. The Blum Government itself neither desires, nor is in a position to contemplate, any but a defensive war; furthermore, it must reckon with the basic attitude of the people, who, just as during the Abyssinian war, now have an extremely negative attitude in the case of Spain.

It is another question whether and to what extent the Blum Government, under the pressure of the Second and Third Internationals, recently has been considering the idea of relaxing its non-intervention obligation to a great extent. In this connection Red resistance in Madrid, which is continuing and which can hardly be explained from a purely military standpoint, seems remarkable. A well-informed foreign diplomat in Madrid, who visited me here before the start of Franco's general Madrid offensive, said at the time that the Red Militia was disorganized and unable to put up vigorous military resistance. The stiffening of the Reds which has occurred subsequently seems attributable to moral and material support from outside, mainly from Soviet Russia but possibly also from France. What would fit in with the latter is Blum's statement—not fully released to the press—made during his well-known speech before the National Council of the Socialist Party on November 8—to the effect that if there was a change in British public opinion the French Government might alter its position on the question of non-intervention in agreement with the British Government. What would fit in, too, is the National Council's acceptance of the ambiguous resolution in which Blum was urged, in cooperation with England, to apply the policy desired by the Second International. An article on the Spanish question by the Socialist leader, Bracke, in the *Populaire* of November 8, according to which there would be no neutrality and no blockade for France and which speaks of "*perfectionnement et redressement*" of the policy of the Government, seems to have the same implications.

WELCZECK

[1] Not printed (698/260643–44).

No. 117

1819/415997

The Head of Political Division III to the Embassy in France

Telegram

No. 488 of November 11   BERLIN, November 11, 1936.

For your information.   Voelckers wires:

"It has been ascertained that all purchases of war matériel from Russia are made through the agency of the Soviet Embassy in Paris."

DUMONT

No. 118

1810/414470

The Chargé d'Affaires in the Soviet Union to the Foreign Ministry

Telegram

No. 169 of November 13   Moscow, November 13, 1936—5 : 00 p.m.

The German Consulate at Odessa wired on November 12:

A ship of about 4,000 tons, grey in color, lay in the Odessa roadstead without a flag from November 4 to 8; the name was made illegible; she loaded and unloaded at night; this might have been the Spanish ship spoken of in the instruction of the Foreign Ministry of October 21, No. 768.[1]

Since yesterday, a white foreign ship, whose name is also not recognizable, has been lying at the furthermost berth.

Saturday morning a ship—recently from Nikolayev—arrived.

Of late increasingly strong guard (Navy) has been kept on the harbor, and there have been no reports in the newspapers concerning "food" ships.

Foreign newspaper reports concerning the shipment of Soviet Russian war matériel by means of Greek ships seem to be confirmed. The *Nitsa* and the *Memas* are lying here.

TIPPELSKIRCH

---

[1] Not found.

No. 119

4446/E086397

The Foreign Ministry to the Embassy in Italy

[BERLIN, November 16, 1936.] [1]
Pol. III 4916.

Please inform the Italian Government this evening of the following:

---

[1] Marginal note: "Transmitted by telephone to Herr Plessen (Rome Embassy) on November 16 at 5 : 30 p.m. in accordance with instructions. D[umont]."

In view of recent developments in Spain, and particularly in view of the new blockade order of the Red Government, which seeks to stop German ship traffic to White ports, we do not consider it right to wait until the fall of Madrid to recognize the Franco Government. Rather, we intend to declare recognition sooner, if possible even tomorrow (Tuesday), to announce the dispatch of a Chargé d'Affaires to Franco, and to withdraw the present Chargé d'Affaires at Alicante as well as the Consul General at Barcelona.

Please ask the Italian Government whether it is willing to take similar measures.

No. 120

1810/414478–80

The Consul at Odessa to the Embassy in the Soviet Union [1]

CONFIDENTIAL   ODESSA, November 16, 1936.

Subject: Shipments to Spain.

With reference to our previous report of November 12.[2]

While up to about the middle of October almost all Soviet newspapers published reports of the arrival and departure of so-called "food" ships, the press has been entirely silent on the subject since. In this consular district, the last news of this kind was carried by the Simferopol *Krasny Krim* of October 21, which reported the arrival of the steamer *Neva* in Alicante (October 18) and the departure of the steamer *Syryanin* from Barcelona for Odessa (also on October 18). Actually, however, shipments are continuing undiminished.

The following ships bound for Spain have been in the harbor of Odessa in the last two weeks:

1. *Syryanin*
2. *Voikov*
3. *Uralless*
4. *Sysran*, according to newspaper reports, a freighter which was built at the Ordzhonikidze (Nikolayev ?) factory, has just gone into service and took on its first partial cargo at Kherson.
5. *Neva;* this ship supposedly took on grain, among other things, for Alicante some time ago but brought it back here.
6. Two previously reported ships, presumably foreign, whose names cannot be ascertained. Both ships were loaded and unloaded mainly at night under particularly strong guard. It is a likely surmise, therefore, that Spanish gold or other valuables were unloaded. As a matter of fact, a figure was quoted to me on the amount of this gold,

---

[1] A notation on the Embassy copy of this report shows that it was received in Moscow on Nov. 19 and dispatched to Berlin on Nov. 20.
[2] See document No. 118, p. 128.

namely, 70 tons.[3] The report comes from a reliable person who is close to shipping circles, and can therefore be considered true. One of the two ships is still being loaded. There are unusually large crates among the cargo.

7. Three or four other Soviet steamers, whose names could not be ascertained either.

8. The Greek steamer *Nitsa*, which has already been reported. (The Greek steamer *Memas* is still here at the moment and is taking on oil cake; she is therefore probably not bound for Spain.)

The above list can make no claim to being complete, since it is particularly difficult to get information here. It might be remarked further that the information obtained so far has been confined almost exclusively to Odessa. It is still more difficult to obtain information concerning the other Soviet Black Sea ports belonging to this consular district. Up to now it has been possible to report the arrival of only one Spanish steamer in Nikolayev. Another Spanish ship is supposed to have arrived in Novorossiisk some time ago, but in both cases no details are known. The Consulate has reason to suppose that the Black Sea ports such as Nikolayev, Kherson, Sevastopol, Kerch, etc., are as important for shipments to Spain as Odessa. The transport of troops, in particular, probably took place and is still taking place from those ports, since up to now nothing has become known concerning such transports from Odessa.

Concerning the steamer *Transbalt*, which put out to sea around October 20, I was told that the wives of the seamen employed on this steamer learned nothing of the fate of the steamer for a long time, and that a number of them energetically demanded information from the responsible port authority. The desired information was not given them, however; they were told that they had to wait and be silent. But the women insisted on their demands. It was not until they were threatened with immediate arrest that they retreated.

The anxiety concerning the fate of the seamen on the *Transbalt* can be attributed on the one hand to the steamer herself, because she is old and has long been in need of repairs, but on the other hand also to the dangerous cargo, which consisted of tanks and ammunition and because of which it was feared that there might be encounters with Nationalist ships.

For the Consul:

AURICHS

---

[3] Unsigned marginal note: "70, 000
                                               2, 800
                                            ———————
                                            56, 000,000
                                            140, 000
                                            ———————
                                            196, 000,000
                                        196 million RM !"

No. 121

168/132137–38

Memorandum by the Head of Political Division III

BERLIN, November 17, 1936.
e. o. Pol. III 4895.

Plessen, of the Embassy at Rome, telephoned me at 1:15 and told me the following at the direction of Ambassador von Hassell:

Mussolini agreed to the recognition of the Franco Government. This very day he would send Franco a communication to this effect, would appoint a Chargé d'Affaires to him, and would recall the previous Chargé d'Affaires from Alicante. He only wanted to know definitely whether our decision would stand. I told Plessen that I could not give him an answer by telephone as yet, since there would be a decisive conference with the military this afternoon.

Thereupon Herr von Hassell came to the telephone. At his request I connected him with the Foreign Minister. The Foreign Minister told Ambassador von Hassell that our reply could hardly be made before 7 o'clock tonight. It might therefore be advisable for the Italian Government to wait until tonight before giving its instructions.

Plessen further asked me whether we intended to recall our Consul General in Barcelona at once. The Italians were rather inclined to leave the Consul General there until further notice. I told Plessen that we considered Köcher's position so dangerous that we had planned his immediate recall in case Franco was recognized. The Foreign Minister repeated this to Herr von Hassell.

At 1:35 Plessen telephoned me once more and told me that Herr von Hassell had informed the Under Secretary of State in the Italian Foreign Ministry of our decision. The latter asked to be informed of our final reply at 7 o'clock if possible. He recommended preparation of a short communiqué now which should be given to the press this evening.

He further suggested that we should come to a decision as to what was to be done with the naval vessels which were in the Red ports at the present time.

DUMONT

No. 122

168/132155

The Foreign Minister to the Legation in Portugal

Telegram

URGENT   BERLIN, November 17, 1936.
No. 227   Pol. III 4921 (Angabe).

Please send Du Moulin to Franco with the greatest possible speed and inform the latter of the following decision of the German Government, which will be published here on Wednesday, November 18, at 6 p.m.

Since the Government of General Franco has taken possession of the greater part of the Spanish national territory, and since developments of the past weeks have shown more and more clearly that no responsible governmental authority can be said to exist any longer in the rest of Spain, the German Government has decided to recognize the Government of General Franco and to appoint a Chargé d'Affaires to it for the purpose of taking up diplomatic relations. The new German Chargé d'Affaires will proceed immediately to the seat of General Franco's Government. The former German Chargé d'Affaires in Alicante has been recalled. The Chargé d'Affaires of the former Spanish Government left Berlin early in November on his own initiative. End of the DNB report.

Please inform Franco further that we shall soon name a Chargé d'Affaires.

Please inform the Portuguese Government simultaneously of the above decision of the German Government, which was taken in agreement with the Italian Government, and urge a similar procedure. Report by wire.

NEURATH

No. 123

168/132156–57

The Acting State Secretary to German Diplomatic Missions (except the Embassies in Italy and Spain and the Legation in Portugal) and the Consulate at Geneva

Telegram

BERLIN, November 17, 1936.
Pol. III 5436.

On Wednesday, November 18, at 6 p.m. Berlin time, and in agreement with the Italian Government, we shall announce recognition of the Franco Government and recall our former Chargé d'Affaires from Alicante. We have decided on this step even before the complete occupation of Madrid, since the Franco Government has uncontested control over the greater part of Spanish territory, and since no responsible governmental authority can be said to exist any longer in the rest of Spain.   The experiences of recent days have shown to an ever-increasing degree that conditions in the areas not occupied by Franco are completely anarchic.   The present Spanish Government has not only been unable to prevent the worst acts of violence against Germans and their property, but in reply to our constantly repeated protests it had to admit itself that it lacked the means of control necessary to take effective steps.   In this connection the unpunished murders of a number of Germans, the looting of numerous German homes, destruction of German property, and the unwarranted arrests of German citizens should be recalled especially.   Please emphasize in all conversations there that the sole factor preventing anarchy in Spain is undoubtedly the Franco Government and that the elements still opposing him are directed by orders from Moscow.

DIECKHOFF

No. 124

4446/E086400

Memorandum by the Head of Political Division III

BERLIN, November 18, 1936.
Pol. III 4988.

At 1: 15 o'clock Ambassador von Hassell telephoned to say that Foreign Minister Count Ciano would follow our procedure on all points in the question of recognizing General Franco's Government.

DUMONT

CHAPTER II

GERMAN RECOGNITION OF THE FRANCO REGIME, AND ITS RESULTS
NOVEMBER 18, 1936–MARCH 20, 1937

No. 125

696/260525

Memorandum by the Foreign Minister

November 18 [,1936.]

This afternoon in my presence the Führer received General Faupel (Ret.) and instructed him to represent the Reich as Chargé d'Affaires to the Government of General Franco. At the desire of the Führer, Faupel is to take with him from here one man for propaganda and one for questions of organization of the Falangists. Faupel will first get in touch with the Führer's Deputy with regard to the persons who could be considered for these posts. No definite date has been set for the departure of General Faupel; possibly he will leave around the middle of next week if he has completed his preparations by then.[1]

I instructed General Faupel first to get in touch with Director Prüfer (funds and that part of the personnel which will be furnished by the Foreign Ministry). I request that he now be given the opportunity to inform himself on the situation in Spain, the embargo committee, etc. Concerning military matters, General Faupel will establish contact with the War Minister. Faupel is not to concern himself with military matters, but he must naturally be currently informed about everything, by the military, too. His task consists essentially in advising General Franco upon request, in representing our interests with him, and in informing us of developments.

v. N[EURATH]

---

[1] The German diplomatic mission established by General Faupel upon his arrival in Spain was known as the "German Diplomatic Representation to the Spanish Nationalist Government" (*Deutsche diplomatische Vertretung bei der spanischen Nationalregierung*). It usually appears in the documents as the "Embassy."

134

No. 126

1819/416008–10

The Ambassador in France to the Foreign Ministry

Telegram

SECRET   PARIS, November 21, 1936—11:45 a.m.

No. 687

The French Government and public opinion were prepared for German and Italian recognition of the Franco Government directly after the capture of Madrid. Recognition at the present moment, on the other hand, was a surprise which has increased the uneasiness and distrust here, in view of the familiar difficulties in the Spanish problem, the uncertainty and indecision as to how to cope with them, and the strong internal differences created thereby.

It appears from some comments in the press and particularly from private statements that recognition is welcomed in principle in anti-Communist Rightist circles because they see in it a strengthening of the Franco Government and a weakening of the Red Government— and therefore of the Communist danger. Approval is accorded mainly for reasons of French domestic policy; possible international consequences are viewed with doubts and not without anxiety even in these circles.

Leftist circles are naturally coming out unequivocally against recognition. They conclude that the Franco Government, which supposedly has no support among the people and can maintain itself only with the bayonets of the Moroccans and the Foreign Legion, is faring badly. Germany and Italy had realized this, and recognition amounted to a declaration of full military support without further regard for non-intervention obligations. Anxiety concerning military measures on the part of Germany and Italy extends far beyond Leftist circles. It is thought that this step, taken before the capture of Madrid, shows that Germany and Italy now not only wish to draw the logical conclusion from an accomplished fact but are determined to control developments on their own. In this connection there is a special significance in the question of Catalonia, where acute danger of a general conflict is being evoked on the one hand by the Red Government's declaration of a war zone and on the other by the alleged intention of Germany and Italy to cut off Russian and other supplies to the Red Government.

All eyes are focused upon England. The need for the closest Anglo-French accord is again being very strongly emphasized. There are discernible in many places, particularly on the Left, doubt and anxiety as to whether the British Government, in view of conflicting British interests, is determined and is in a position to find and adhere to a line that might help France out of difficulties that are hard to solve. In this connection Eden's statement that other powers had violated the non-intervention agreement to a greater extent than Germany and Italy has not been well received.

The widespread mistrust is increased by the fact that the recognition coincides with the German step in the question of repudiating the internationalization of German rivers and with the reports concerning a German-Japanese-Italian agreement. There is a growing feeling that a storm is looming higher and higher on the international horizon. This feeling is deliberately nurtured by the Left to create bad blood against Germany in order to arouse British public opinion in particular, by pointing to our alleged plans for forming an anti-Communist war bloc and to the resultant danger to world peace.

Nevertheless, by far the greater part of public opinion here still clings to the non-intervention agreement in accordance with popular sentiment, which shrinks from being drawn into war because of Spain; this agreement, as numerous newspapers are trying to prove, remains valid even after recognition of Franco. It is noteworthy that some big newspapers are discussing the question of a later recognition of the White Government and are rather taking a position in favor of it.

For the attitude of the Government, I refer to the report of the Havas Special Service which I transmitted to you in telegraphic report No. 682 [1] and which is confirmed by other information I have received. Of particular interest here is the reference to the security measures of the French Navy, which are also being discussed in several newspapers. Their purpose is supposed to be to safeguard traffic with Spanish ports, particularly on the eastern coast, in order, it is said, merely to protect French citizens and French property. Some newspapers report that the French Government, together with the British Government, wishes to obtain from Franco a safety zone for ships under the French and British flags.[2]

WELCZECK

[1] Not printed (4798/E236712–14).
[2] On Nov. 21 (telegram No. 339), the German Embassy in Washington reported that the American press regarded the recognition of Franco by Germany and Italy as "a step on the road toward the outbreak of the long-expected hostilities in Europe" (1819/416016–17).

No. 127

168/132121

Memorandum by the Director of the Press Department

BERLIN, November 23, 1936.

According to a communication from the Ministry for Public Enlightenment and Propaganda, the Führer and Chancellor has ordered that the belligerents in the Spanish Civil War be designated as follows:

(*a*) The Spanish Nationalist Government.

(*b*) The Spanish Bolshevists.

ASCHMANN

No. 128

1819/416027–30

The Embassy in Spain (at Seville) to the Foreign Ministry

[Telegram]

No. 557 of November 23   SEVILLE, November 24, 1936.

With reference to our No. 556 of November 21.[1]

Reception of the Embassy by officials and population was decidedly friendly and cordial, from the point of disembarkation, Sanlúcar, to Seville. Here the German Embassy, and the Italian Embassy that arrived on the same day, were cordially received by the commanding general, Queipo de Llano, the national and municipal authorities, the population, and the press. Yesterday evening a great demonstration of friendship was held by the population in the square before the city hall, which was festively illuminated, and a banquet followed.

First impressions of the situation in White Spain:

1. Queipo de Llano, who took Seville for the military in July with one hundred and fifty men, is apparently a determined, energetic personality with political ability. He is very popular with the people, whom he knows how to captivate in daily radio addresses. He has a remarkable understanding of propaganda.

2. The external aspect of city, country, and population is very different from that of Red Spain; this has both its positive and its negative sides.

(*a*) On the positive side: Social order, discipline, security, and tradition are maintained. Military and civil authorities function unimpeded by the interference of the irresponsible forces which have local power everywhere in Red Spain. The country gives the impression of peace and complete tranquillity.

(*b*) On the negative side: The importance and gravity of the war has thus far obviously not been recognized and experienced by the masses and by the majority of the ruling class. Opinion is optimistic and frivolous. Willingness to serve, accordingly, is entirely inadequate and falls far below that on the Red side, where mobilization of the people for war has progressed much further. Whereas the Red Government weeks ago decreed militarization of the male population between 20 and 45 years of age, no similar measures were taken here; they are allegedly being studied. Accordingly

---

[1] Not printed (696/260531).

the number of fighters at the front is completely insufficient, as is that of reserves in training.

3. While with the Reds divergent political groups have come to terms, here sharp differences have arisen between the Fascist Falange and the monarchist-clerical Requetés. Revolutionary tendencies in the working population are suppressed by energetic measures, to be sure, but are not eliminated. There is also rivalry among the leading generals. Whereas the Reds have an extensive Communist social and economic program, there is no corresponding program here for the solution of social questions, which are at the root of the Civil War. The same is true with respect to propagandizing and mobilizing large strata of the population, which is being done effectively on the Red side under Russian leadership, but here only in a very rudimentary way, with really wretched press conditions.

4. The military situation is not very satisfactory. Operations have been conducted to date principally with shock troops of Moroccans and Foreign Legionnaires. These are in danger of wearing themselves out before Madrid even if they succeed in capturing the capital. The difficulty of taking Madrid is obviously underestimated. The Red Government's announcement that Madrid would fall into White hands only as a field of ruin and carnage threatens to become a reality. On other fronts there is only weak protection for the troops, so that a surprise attack by the Reds at another point would necessarily lead to a dangerous situation.

5. The principal goal of our endeavors here should therefore be to see to it that mobilization and employment of the population are expedited. This is of primary importance because the necessity of crushing Bolshevism here, come what may, would force us to make up the deficit with German blood, if not enough Spaniards were employed.

6. Even in leading Government circles the opinion is already fairly prevalent that the war is not being fought in the interest of Spain but is a showdown between Fascism and Bolshevism on Spanish soil. This is a rather dangerous obstacle in the way of continued German-Spanish collaboration.

7. The economic problems seem no less difficult than the political and military ones. It is urgently necessary to study the questions of how our deliveries are to be paid for and how our economic interests will be safeguarded and indemnification will be made after the war is over. The war will result in serious financial and economic exhaustion of the countries [sic] and in widespread destruction. The export possibilities, especially for the raw materials in which we are principally interested, are relatively small, considering the volume of our deliveries, which will greatly increase in the course of a probable long war, and considering the extent . . . (group garbled) requirements

after the war, and can probably be increased only by investing considerable capital. The danger that countries strong in capital will get ahead of us by granting credits after the war should not be lightly dismissed.

There is already an Italian economic commission in Salamanca, and negotiations with the British in San Sebastián are allegedly impending.

Address of the Embassy: Embajada Alemana, Hotel Andalucía Palace.

VOELCKERS

No. 129

1819/416032

The Ambassador in Italy to the Foreign Ministry

[Telegram]

No. 264 of November 25　　　　　　　ROME, November 25, 1936.

In a conversation Mussolini expressed himself as greatly dissatisfied with the achievements of the Spanish Nationalists. They were obviously lacking in offensive spirit and also in personal bravery. There were evidently very few real men in Spain. This was all the more regrettable since a very serious decision was at stake. I pointed to the necessity for the Nationalists to obtain naval supremacy along the Mediterranean coast; he emphasized this point in stressing that events in Spain furnished interesting proof of the decisive importance of ruling the seas. Therefore Germany and Italy, since they had said "a", now must go on to "b". To an Italian he described the European situation, and particularly Germany's relations with Russia, as strained to the breaking point.

HASSELL

No. 130

168/132074

The Ambassador in Italy to the Foreign Ministry

Telegram

No. 266 of November 27　　　　ROME, November 27, 1936—2:15 p.m.
　　　　　　　　　　　　　　Received November 27—5:30 p.m.

1. Ciano informed me yesterday evening that he was sending Anfuso,[1] who had just returned, again to Franco. In view of the situation in Spain, Italy was determined to send to Spain a whole division of Black Shirts, of whom 4,000 men were already organized in four battalions; but first Italy had to have certain guaranties as to the

---

[1] Filippo Anfuso, of the Italian diplomatic service.

future course of Spanish policy.   Anfuso would therefore submit a written statement to Franco in which Franco was to obligate himself to conduct future Spanish policy in the Mediterranean in harmony with that of Italy, of course without Italy's making territorial demands; but the transit of French native troops through Spanish territory, for example, must be barred.   Spain also was to obligate herself to build certain airports.   He would communicate further details to me in a few days.

In yesterday's conversation Mussolini confirmed to me his intention to keep to his course unswervingly in the Spanish question.   To be sure, one was tempted to say with Faust: "Cursed above all be patience"; he was certain of gradual success, however.   Moreover, after the naval review that went off splendidly yesterday he expressed the conviction that the Italian fleet was in the best possible condition today and was in the process of constant organic development.

2. Ciano informed me that upon final consideration Grandi had been sent back to London without the agreement [2] having been put into written form after all.   The matter was therefore still in a nebulous preliminary stage, so to speak.

HASSELL

[2] A reference presumably to the negotiations which resulted in the Anglo-Italian agreement of Jan. 2, 1937. See Editors' Note, p. 199.

No. 131

1819/416020–22

The Chargé d'Affaires in Great Britain to the Foreign Ministry

A 4674   LONDON, November 27, 1936.
                                                                                Pol. III 5323.

With reference to telegraphic instruction No. 302 of November 25 [1] and to our telegraphic report No. 274 of November 26.[2]

Subject: Attitude of England on the Spanish Civil War.

The British Government's declaration that for the time being it would not recognize the parties in the conflict in Spain as "belligerents" often is construed incorrectly, in my opinion.   As is shown by the whole behavior of England in the Non-Intervention Committee and also recently toward the Franco Government in the question of a safety zone in the harbor of Barcelona, the British Government recognizes both parties as parties in a civil war but not as belligerents in the sense of the rules of war, in which connection doubtless only the rules of naval warfare are meant.   This means that in principle England concedes to both parties the right, within their sovereign

[1] Not printed (4796/E236701).
[2] Not printed (4796/E236702).

territory and including the three-mile zone, to engage in military operations, but that the parties should not have the right to exercise the rights on the high seas that appertain to a country at war, particularly not the right of blockade and the right of seizure, including the right to stop and search. This view closely corresponds to the one that we took with respect to the Spanish Leftist Government, at any rate before we recognized the Franco Government.

According to reports which I have not yet been able to verify, there was for a time a tendency in the Cabinet to go a step further and concede to both warring parties belligerent rights in the sense of the rules of war. This tendency originated in the attempt to keep England out of any conflicts, so far as this can possibly be done. This, however, is exactly the policy of the whole Cabinet. It was therefore mainly a question of which of the two alternatives would offer less possibility of conflicts.

A practical exception to the concession that both parties may engage in military operations within their sovereign territory is the above-mentioned British demand for safety zones, that is, for harbor zones in which British ships are not exposed to bombardment. Such safety zones for British ships were already in existence in a considerable number of Spanish ports, but not in Barcelona. According to the reports available today, the Franco Government has now complied with this British request.

It is evident from the whole attitude of the British Government and from the debates in the House of Commons that British policy aims at effecting a settlement in order to prevent England and other powers as well from becoming embroiled in a war as a result of the complications in Spain. The British attitude in the embargo committee is also aimed in this direction. As is known, both Italian Ambassador Grandi and Soviet Russian Ambassador Maisky made long political speeches in the committee which served to aggravate the situation. As I have heard, the Foreign Secretary himself expressed disapproval of the fact that the chairman of the embargo committee, Lord Plymouth, permitted such debates at all and gave him instructions to prevent this in the future. The former committee chairman, Morrison, now Minister of Agriculture, also deprecated in private conversations this manner of conducting the negotiations and added that he would never have permitted it. The ruling that all questions of principle should, even more than heretofore, first be discussed in the subcommittee also serves to relieve the embargo committee of possibilities of political conflict.

I know from statements made in an authoritative British quarter that the British Government sees in the embargo committee a useful means of avoiding possibilities of conflict and that it is therefore encouraging as dilatory action as possible on the part of the committee. At the same time, the existence of the committee offers the Government a comfortable shield against Parliamentary pressure.

For the rest, the situation in Spain continues to be followed here with the greatest attention and anxiety. Regarding today's Cabinet session, I refer to my telegram No. 278.[3]

WOERMANN

---

[3] Not printed (3359/E009527).

No. 132

696/260527–28

Minute by an Official of the Economic Policy Department

CONFIDENTIAL   BERLIN, November 27, 1936.
                                              W II WE.
                                           zu Pol. III 5058.

On November 26 General Faupel inquired of Ministerialdirektor Ritter about economic relations with Spain. Counselor of Legation Sabath took part in the conversation.

Ministerialdirektor Ritter gave General Faupel a short memorandum regarding present actual and legal commercial relations with Spain, with three statistical tables on the development of trade in the last few years and on the most important German export and import items.

General Faupel stated that he had received instructions from the Führer to concern himself particularly with the extension of commercial relations between Germany and Spain and to utilize the present favorable moment so that England, which was well provided with capital [*kapitalkräftige*], would not take the market away from us at a later stage.

Ministerialdirektor Ritter declared that we should try to regulate trade within a larger framework. The Rowak and Hisma organizations, which had been useful and advantageous in a transitional period, would not be able in the long run to meet the demands of trade between the two countries. As anticipated, we had to give thought to changing over the activities of these two companies to commercial trade under government regulation. Nothing could be said at present regarding the time when conversations on reorganization of trade and particularly of payments could be opened. He proposed waiting until General Faupel had informed himself to some extent in Spain. For the present, the Commercial Attaché of the Madrid Embassy, Herr Enge, was at his disposal. It was contemplated, however, to place at the disposal of the Embassy shortly an official experienced in commercial policy.

General Faupel's attention was called to Taverno, the Spanish economic expert of the Burgos Government, who is known to us from the last economic negotiations.

General Faupel agreed with the statements of Ministerialdirektor Ritter. He was glad to have in Enge an economic expert familiar with the country. He intended to keep the staff of the Embassy as small as possible for the time being, since a rather large number of people were traveling with him to Spain as it was, and he first wanted to obtain on the spot a general idea of the problems and of the personnel required.

Herewith respectfully submitted to the Political Department.

SABATH

No. 133

168/132075–76

The Ambassador in Italy to the Foreign Ministry

Telegram

ROME (QUIRINAL), November 28, 1936—10 : 25 p.m.
No. 275 of November 28   Received November 29—2 : 30 a.m.

In continuation of a conversation which I had with Ciano yesterday on the Spanish affair, his Chef de Cabinet, at his direction, today let me read the text of the agreement which Anfuso presumably will propose to Franco today as the basis for further support. As soon as the agreement was signed I would be given the final text; Franco would be told that we were informed. In the preamble the draft expresses the mutual determination to fight Communism and defend the social order and then proceeds to enumerate approximately the following points: a promise of further aid until the Government has been stabilized in the entire European and colonial territory of Spain; political cooperation between the two Governments and agreement on their respective policies, especially in the western Mediterranean; the territories of neither country may be permitted to serve an enemy as a base or transit route. Article 16 of the League of Nations is politically dangerous and must be eliminated or completely changed; the parties to the agreement may not support collective measures against the other party decided on by the League of Nations on the basis of this article but will maintain benevolent neutrality in every respect and will afford the other party every assistance with regard to material supplies as well as air service, etc.; the contracting parties will not enter into agreements with any other state which run counter to the above; existing agreements of this type are null and void; the two parties assure one another preferred delivery of raw materials; through a revision of existing agreements, trade relations are to be made as favorable as possible for both countries.

I called attention to the far-reaching character of the proposed agreement and to the fact that Germany was aiding Spain just as Italy was, which would, of course, have to be taken into consideration. The Chef de Cabinet said that went without saying; that was why Germany was being informed of the negotiations. Naturally Germany could enter into a similar agreement, since the Italo-Spanish . . . (group missing) was not exclusive in character with regard to us, but was only a safeguard to keep the influence of other countries from spreading in Spain.

HASSELL

No. 134

4446/E086466–67

Memorandum by the Deputy Director of the Cultural Policy Department

BERLIN, November 28, 1936.
Pol. III 5621.

Today the Reverend Dr. Gerhard Ohlemüller, Secretary General of the Protestant World Council, called on me. He stated that the reports received by the Protestant World Council concerning the situation of the Protestant ministers in the territory occupied by General Franco were extremely alarming. Twenty Evangelical ministers had already been shot. He asked whether the German Government might take steps with General Franco in order to avoid further oppression of the Protestant Church. I told Herr Ohlemüller that intervention in this question seemed to me extraordinarily difficult, so long as there was no reliable information that the Protestant ministers had not been active on the side of the Popular Front.

According to my information, most Protestant ministers at present were active adherents of the Popular Front for reasons which had to do with restraining the dominant influence of Catholicism. Dr. Ohlemüller confirmed this. I then suggested to him that he go, not as a German, but as the Secretary General of the Protestant World Council, to the Spanish Chargé d'Affaires here and explain that it would make a very good impression in Protestant circles if the Protestant Church and its servants were spared, and ask him to transmit to his Government this request of the Protestant World Council.

I told him he should send me a report concerning this visit with the Spanish Chargé d'Affaires, and I would pass it on to our envoy in Salamanca.

In the afternoon Bishop Heckel of the Foreign Department of the Evangelical Church called on me, also with the request to intervene in the matter of the fate of the Protestant ministers in Spain. I gave Bishop Heckel the same answer, but at his request granted that Oberkirchenrat Krummacher might join Dr. Ohlemüller in calling on the Spanish Chargé d'Affaires in order to express the same plea in the name of German Protestantism. (The Fliedner Foundation in Madrid is on a Protestant basis. Fliedner and several of his sons are still German citizens.)

Submitted to Minister Stieve and the State Secretary. Forwarded to Political Division III.[1]

TWARDOWSKI

---

[1] Marginal note: "Pol. III. Please append the file concerning Protestant ministers and activities in Spain which we sent to Salamanca recently. D[umont]. Dec. 3." This may refer to a memorandum of Oct. 20, 1936, not printed (4446/E086369–72), which summarized reports of the persecution of Protestants in Spain and requested an investigation; no reply to the request has been found.

No. 135

168/132113–14

Minute by the Acting Director of the Political Department

BERLIN, November 28, 1936.

The present Italian Chargé d'Affaires, Zamboni, made an appointment to see me today, saying that he had urgent instructions from Rome. Signor Zamboni opened the conversation by stating that he merely wanted to inquire as to the "German view of the situation in Spain." The somewhat ponderous way in which Signor Zamboni worded his statements, however, clearly betrayed a doubt regarding the lucky star under which the Franco Government has been fighting thus far.

I gave Signor Zamboni some information concerning the reports we have received on the status of the military operations and then told him the following:

1. It was clear that the conflict must remain localized on Spanish territory.

2. It must be admitted that time was not in our favor in Spain and that Franco would have to make all possible haste in order to bring his action to a successful conclusion.

3. Having said "a", one must go on to "b".

I added that, to my knowledge, the Head of the Italian Government was also of this opinion, which was all the more understandable since after all vital Italian interests were involved. Signor Zamboni did not deny this but intimated that there was a slight doubt in his mind as to whether we were backing the affair with as much enthusiasm as seemed desirable in Italy. He concluded the conversation by saying that he had really only come because it was good to have as thorough an exchange of views as possible regarding the reports coming in from Spain.

I do not know Signor Zamboni well enough to judge to what extent he based his statements upon instructions from Rome and to what extent he expressed his own ideas.

WEIZSÄCKER

No. 136

701/261292–93

The Ambassador in Italy to the Foreign Ministry

Telegram

No. 281 of December 1   ROME, December 1, 1936—1 : 30 a.m.

1. Ciano just informed me by personal order of the Head of the Government that on Sunday, December 6, a conference would be held with Mussolini presiding, at which Ciano as well as General Roatta and the Chiefs of Staff of the Army, Navy, Air Force, and Militia would be present, in order to discuss thoroughly the action in Spain and to determine further energetic and systematic procedure. The Head of the Government would appreciate having a military representative of the German War Ministry who understands Italian and, if we consider it advisable, also the corresponding representatives of the Air Force and the Navy attend the conference as observers, in order to be precisely informed as to its subject matter and possibly also to make suggestions or give information. Please send telegraphic instructions tomorrow if possible as to the participants and the date of their arrival. I suggest that you consider whether a high officer, if sent, should be assisted by the Wehrmacht attachés here as needed.[1]

2. Today Ciano handed me the original text of the Italo-Spanish agreement, which has been signed; it could have undergone only unimportant changes, about which we would be informed after Anfuso's return. The agreement was, of course, strictly secret and known only to very few persons. Upon a remark from me he expressly emphasized that the agreement naturally had no exclusive character with regard to Germany; Italy's special viewpoint was solely with regard to the Mediterranean. The text will follow tomorrow through safe channels.

HASSELL

---

[1] No report on this conference has been found ; there is mention of one decision reached at the conference in document No. 151, p. 165.

No. 137

701/261146–53

The Ambassador in Italy to the Foreign Ministry

SECRET   ROME, December 1, 1936.
5618   Sent December 2.

With reference to my previous report of December 1, No. 281.

Subject: Italo-Spanish agreement.

I submit herewith the Italo-Spanish agreement in Italian and in German translation.   Please treat it as strictly secret.

HASSELL

[Enclosure]

PROTOCOL [1]

SECRET

The Fascist Government and the Spanish Nationalist Government, united in the common fight against Communism, which at this moment is threatening the peace and security of Europe more than ever, and animated by the desire to strengthen and to develop their relations with one another and to contribute with all their might to the social and political stability of the European nations, have proceeded, through their respective representatives in Rome and in Burgos, to a thorough examination of the questions of interest to the two countries and have come, in mutual accord, to the following conclusions:

1. The Fascist Government will continue to lend the Spanish Nationalist Government its support and assistance for the maintenance of Spanish independence and integrity, both on the continent and in the colonies, and for the reestablishment of the internal social and political order.   The technical agencies of the two countries will continue to maintain contact with one another for this purpose.

2. The Fascist Government and the Spanish Nationalist Government, convinced of the advantages for the two countries and for Europe's social and political order of close collaboration between themselves, will maintain contact with one another and will consult one another about all problems concerning the two countries, especially about the problems of the western Mediterranean, concerning which they will act in agreement and will afford one another reciprocal aid for the effective protection of their respective interests.

3. Each of the two Governments obligates itself not to participate in any way in coalitions or agreements of powers which might be di-

---

[1] Translated from the Italian.

rected against the other party, and not to join directly or indirectly in military, economic, or financial measures of any kind which are directed against the other party. Especially they obligate themselves not to permit their respective territories, harbors, and territorial waters to be used for operations directed against one of them, or for the preparation of such operations, or to permit passage of supplies or troops of a third power. For this purpose the two Governments obligate themselves to regard as null and void any commitments which they may have entered into previously and which are in contradiction to the clauses of the present protocol, and to suspend any execution of such commitments which may have been initiated.

4. The Fascist Government and the Spanish Nationalist Government agree that article 16 of the League of Nations Covenant, as it is at present formulated and as it has recently been interpreted and applied, contains grave dangers for peace and should either be revoked or basically changed. In any case, and beginning with this moment, as soon as one of the two countries should become involved in a conflict with one or several other powers, or collective measures of a military, economic, or financial nature should be applied against it, the other country obligates itself to adopt toward it an attitude of benevolent neutrality and to assure it all the supplies which it might need, as well as all facilities for the use of harbors, airlines, railroads, transit routes, and *traffico di rimbalzo* [transshipment? return traffic?].[2]

5. For this purpose the two Governments recognize the advantage of determining even in peacetime the methods of utilizing their economic resources—and especially their raw materials—and of using their means of transportation. The technical agencies of the two countries will make the necessary agreements for this purpose as soon as possible.

6. The Fascist Government and the Spanish Nationalist Government recognize the possibility and the advantage for both countries of intensifying as much as possible the economic relations of all kinds existing between them, and the respective sea and air communications. For this purpose, they assure each other, in view of their special ties of friendship, all possible preferential treatment with regard to goods, merchant shipping, and their respective civil aviation.

The two Governments will as soon as possible revise in this sense the agreements existing between the two countries with regard to trade and to sea and air navigation.

In witness whereof the present protocol is signed.[3]

---

[2] The German translation also uses the Italian term at this point and adds a translator's note reading as follows: "An exact translation is not possible at the moment."

[3] No signatures appear on the file copy.

No. 138

168/132100

The Chief of the Armed Forces Office in the War Ministry to the Acting Director of the Political Department

BERLIN, December 2, 1936.

DEAR HERR VON WEIZSÄCKER: Lieutenant Colonel Scheller has reported to me concerning the conference with you on November 30, particularly concerning your suggestion of a practical way to increase even further the cooperation between the Foreign Ministry and the War Ministry in the Spanish question.

However, the means which you suggest, namely, that the Wehrmacht send a representative of each of its three branches to you for periodic conferences, does not seem to me the most appropriate. For, after all, the purpose of such conferences should and must be to bring military measures into harmony with aims of the political leadership, in a word, to create unity between military strategy and diplomacy. In my opinion, however, this aim would not be reached if the unified stand of the political authorities which you represent were confronted by three opinions, which might differ in some cases, on the part of the branches of Wehrmacht leadership.

The more expedient way, I feel, would be to have a representative of the OKW call on you, either at regular intervals or—and this might be even better—at any time when needed. I myself would be glad to be at your disposal on more important occasions, and Lieutenant Colonel Scheller as my representative on others, to come to the Foreign Ministry at any time desired. I believe that this would best serve both parties and our common objectives.[1]

Heil Hitler!

Yours,

KEITEL

---

[1] Marginal note: "Concur, but with possible participation of specialists from the branches of the Wehrmacht. W[eizsäcker]. Dec. 3."

No. 139

701/261291

The Acting State Secretary to the Embassy in Italy

Telegram

CONFIDENTIAL   BERLIN, December 2, 1936—12:35 p.m.
No. 316 of December 2   Received December 2—12:45 p.m.

With reference to your telegram No. 281 of December 1.

For the Ambassador personally. To be deciphered by him personally.

1. Field Marshal von Blomberg is sending Admiral Canaris.

2. We reserve our position with regard to the agreement reported in your telegram No. 275.[1]

DIECKHOFF [2]

---

[1] Document No. 133, p. 143.
[2] Marginal note: "Ciano informed by telephone. H[assell]. Dec. 2."

[EDITORS' NOTE. On December 2, 1936, the Non-Intervention Committee agreed, the Portuguese delegate abstaining, to submit to the rival factions in Spain the plan for the control of shipments to Spain which had been under discussion since October. The plan called for international control over the land frontiers and the seaports of Spain. On the same day, the committee instructed the chairman's subcommittee to examine the possibility of prohibiting the entrance of volunteers into Spain. The question of volunteers had become acute as a result of rumors that organized bodies of troops were being dispatched to the assistance of Franco by Italy and Germany.]

No. 140

168/132101–02

The Acting Director of the Political Department to the Embassy in Great Britain

Draft Telegram

BERLIN, December 3, 1936.
zu Pol. III 5413 und 5418.

Drafting Officer: Counselor of Legation Dumont.

With reference to the telephone call by Kordt and your telegraphic report No. 284.[1]

Please state the following with regard to the question of volunteers for Spain:

1. The German Government, as is known, suggested at the time of the discussions concerning the arms embargo that participation by foreign volunteers in the Spanish Civil War be prevented by appropriate measures of the governments concerned. (Cf. the letter of August 17 sent by the German Foreign Minister to the French Ambassador in Berlin.[2])

2. This suggestion failed because of the opposition of other governments.

3. Whether and in what numbers German volunteers are in Spain at the present time cannot be ascertained from here.

---

[1] Not printed (4797/E236708–09).
[2] Document No. 45, p. 44.

4. Reports are available concerning constant participation in the Spanish Civil War by volunteers from many countries, including France and England.

5. Should the question be put directly whether the governments are willing to prevent the participation of additional volunteers in the future, you should state that the German Government, in accordance with the stand it has taken in the question from the very beginning, is prepared to accede to any proposal which gives promise of success. Such a proposal would have to include all the governments represented in the embargo committee, would have to be effective, and its execution would have to be supervised.

WEIZSÄCKER

No. 141

168/132097–99

The Acting Director of the Political Department to the Embassy in Italy

Draft Telegram

URGENT   BERLIN, December 5, 1936.
SECRET   zu Pol. III. . . .

The French and British Ambassadors made separate *démarches* with the Foreign Minister today, leaving memoranda with almost identical texts.[1] In these it is stated that the purpose of the *démarches* was to induce the powers especially interested jointly to seek new methods of eliminating the existing Spanish crisis. The French and British Governments call upon the other four Governments who were handed the same *démarche*, namely the German, Italian, Portuguese, and Russian Governments, to announce together with them their firm determination to refrain from any direct or indirect action which might result in foreign intervention in Spain. The six Governments should then without delay examine in the London committee the feasibility of establishing an effective control over all shipments of war matériel. For the purpose of reestablishing peace in Spain, these Governments should join in a common action in order, with the help of an offer to mediate, to induce Spain to cease hostilities, thereby putting her in a position to voice the will of her people. If this was accepted in principle, the six Governments should consult in order to determine the form of the planned mediation. For the time being the entire mediation proposal is to be handled as strictly confidential. A similar step has been taken with the Italian, Portuguese, and Russian Governments.

---

[1] Neurath's summary of his conversation with the British and French Ambassadors is printed as document No. 146, p. 156.

The Foreign Minister told the two Ambassadors that the complications which had developed in Spain could in no way be blamed on the German Government. It was a well-known fact that the latter had proposed some time ago that indirect intervention be stopped in addition to direct intervention. If large numbers of foreign volunteers were now participating in the fighting in Spain, the responsibility rested on powers other than Germany.

As for the plan to approach the Spanish combatants with a mediation proposal, the following should be said: By recognizing Franco, the German Government as well as the Italian wanted to indicate that the guaranty for the reestablishment of orderly and settled conditions in Spain lay in the person of Franco as opposed to the Bolshevist and Anarchist elements of the opposition. One could not rightly expect General Franco to place himself on an equal footing with those elements of unrest and to make contact with them in order to reestablish orderly conditions.

The Foreign Minister, however, termed the above remarks a provisional answer and reserved a thorough study and reply for later. On the basis of the full text of the *démarche*, which is probably available in Rome, and the above information, please get in touch with the Italian Government at once, determine that Government's stand, and report it by telegram.

WEIZSÄCKER

No. 142

168/132094–96

The Foreign Minister to the Embassy in Italy

Telegram

URGENT   BERLIN, December 5, 1936.
SECRET   Pol. III 5580.
No. 323

For the Ambassador personally.

The agreement which the Italian Government concluded with the Government of General Franco is evidently a political and economic agreement of considerable scope. By accepting it Franco, whose hands are tied at the present time, becomes dependent on Italy in the future to an extent which precludes similar agreements with third powers, including Germany. Remarks like those Ciano made to you, that the agreement was not of an exclusive nature, must therefore be considered meaningless. In view of the close interrelationship between German and Italian policy in the Spanish crisis and after the Berlin conversations with Ciano, it would have been the duty of the Italian Government to consult us before concluding an agreement of such proportions. Naturally we are reserving all rights with regard to the demands we shall make of Franco, which are preponderantly of a commercial character.

Thus, although we have cause to be highly surprised by the Italian procedure in view of the above, we are, after all, not blind to realities, and we recognize that Italian interests in Spain go further than ours, if only for geographic reasons. In the Spanish conflict Germany has predominantly the negative goal of not permitting the Iberian Peninsula to come under Bolshevist domination, which would involve the danger of its spreading to the rest of western Europe. The existence of a greater Italian interest is clearly expressed in the Italian agreement with Franco and will therefore also have to be reflected in the amount of aid to be furnished by Italy. I gather from your telegram No. 275 [1] that the Italian Government is determined to furnish this aid. A gradual readjustment in the relative strength of German and Italian aid will follow as a matter of course. So far they have been on an equal basis. In the future, provision should be made for reducing German participation as compared with that of the Italians, in accordance with natural interests and local conditions. Admiral Canaris, who is now en route there, will inform you on the details of this matter.

Without going into detail on this last point, please make your statements conform with our provisional stand outlined here; do not, however, take any special initiative.

NEURATH

---

[1] Document No. 133, p. 143.

No. 143

1819/416054–55

Memorandum by the Acting State Secretary

BERLIN, December 5, 1936.

The American Ambassador called on me today and expressed his grave concern about the general situation. He had had word from Washington, too, that they viewed the European situation with great concern and were reckoning with the possibility of war. Great influence was being exerted on President Roosevelt from many sides, especially by the peace organizations and the churches, to present the world with a proposal for limiting armaments or for disarming, and it was to be expected—Mr. Dodd intimated that he had been informed to this effect by the State Department—that a resolution to this effect might be debated even now, during the present conference in Buenos Aires. I told the Ambassador that I did not quite see why people in America were so particularly worried. Certainly the Spanish situation contained many elements of risk, but this was due only to Russia's outrageous violation of the embargo. Germany would place no great hopes on a big disarmament conference, in view of the experience gained in Geneva; on the other hand, the German stand in the disarmament question, so far as I knew, was still the same as that laid down in the Führer's speech of May 21, 1935.

The Ambassador then brought up the following: The American Government had learned from Rome and Latin America that a secret agreement had recently been concluded between the Italian Government and the Government of General Franco, whereby Franco granted the Italian Government far-reaching privileges in the future. If Franco won and this agreement went into force for all of Spain, Spain's sovereignty would be at an end; Spain would, as it were, assume Albania's position and be under a kind of Italian suzerainty. The Latin American countries, which had so far been much in sympathy with Franco, were watching this development with concern; the force of tradition played a part in this (Spain, the mother country). The Ambassador asked whether we had any knowledge of this agreement. I answered Mr. Dodd that I knew nothing about it. He knew, of course, that during Count Ciano's visit to Berlin the integrity of the national and colonial territory of Spain had been recognized explicitly by the Italian Government. Under these circumstances his information seemed improbable to me.

DIECKHOFF

No. 144

168/132070

The Chargé d'Affaires in Spain to the Foreign Ministry

Telegram

VERY SECRET　　　　　　　　　SALAMANCA, December 5, 1936—9:15 p.m.
No. 581 of December 5　　　　　Received December 6—4:35 a.m.

With reference to events here—for the State Secretary personally.

On the basis of detailed conferences and personal observations I report as follows concerning the military situation, in agreement with Sperrle and Funck:[1] Red resistance in and around Madrid has stiffened. It is now no longer possible to capture the city in house-to-house fighting. It is unlikely that the Reds can be driven out of Madrid solely by air raids. It is, of course, altogether possible to surround the city from both sides, but there is no prospect of success with the troops available at the present time. Extensive conscription of able-bodied men and constant substantial shipments of armaments on the side of the Reds, as well as the presence of French and probably

---

[1] Lieutenant Colonel von Funck, Military Attaché of the German Embassy in Spain.

also Czech officers, whom the Reds apparently obey willingly, make it appear possible that sizable Red offensive operations will take place in the near future.

Franco's best troops are committed in an unfavorable position in Madrid. If they were withdrawn from their present positions it would mean giving up the city, which Franco does not want to do. We are now faced with the decision either to leave Spain to herself or to throw in additional forces, making very definite demands on our part, in order to prevent Bolshevism from taking hold first in half and later in all of Spain. If the decision is made in favor of the latter alternative, then one strong German and one strong Italian division would be required. Even though preparations should be most thorough, deployment should be speeded up as much as possible, since right now these troops, with their superior training and leadership, can still gain a quick and decisive victory, which may no longer be possible a few months later, even with still stronger forces. Training personnel would have to be sent at once.

At the same time, White troops should be conscripted, armed, and trained under our guidance with the greatest energy, and arms deliveries for the Reds stopped with all means internationally acceptable. Similar deliberations are going on among the Italians.

FAUPEL

No. 145

F3/0252–53

Memorandum by the Acting State Secretary

[Undated]

Referring to telegram No. 581 of December 5 from Salamanca:

Even if we should be in a position to send forces to Spain, in the strength suggested by General Faupel, the following objections would nevertheless speak against doing so:

1. *Technical objections:* It will be next to impossible to transport such a force, for which a large number of ships would be required and which would have to be escorted by German naval vessels all the way to Spain, past England and France, without being observed and without risking complications.

At any rate it will then no longer be possible to adhere to the embargo agreement.

2. *Political objections:*

(*a*) If the situation in Spain is really as General Faupel describes it, and a satisfactory solution can be obtained only by sending Italian and German forces, we must expect that the entire burden of the Civil War will then fall upon us and Italy. We will have to assume the entire odium of carrying on the war (requisitioning, destruction, suppression of the population, etc.) and will thereby probably soon arouse the public opinion of the whole country against ourselves. We and the Italians will then assume the role of the French in 1809, which has not been forgotten by the entire Spanish people even today.

(*b*) It seems hardly imaginable that two foreign divisions could bring the war to a victorious conclusion for Franco. I believe that a much greater force would be needed for this. However that may be, it is extremely improbable that the entire world would look on quietly while Germany and Italy took over the leadership of the Civil War against Spain, especially when the sympathies of the greater part of the world are by no means on Franco's side. In this connection I call attention to the statement of the American Ambassador concerning a secret agreement between Italy and Franco,[1] which, he said, was having an irritating effect even on the Latin Americans, who sympathize with Franco.

In summary, I believe that an urgent warning should be given not to follow General Faupel's proposal. If Italy, who for many reasons is primarily interested, considers intervention necessary and possible, let her intervene, although there are also considerable objections even against this; Germany should not permit herself to be drawn deeper into the Spanish enterprise.

DIECKHOFF

---

[1] See document No. 143, p. 153.

No. 146

168/132084–85

Memorandum by the Foreign Minister

RM 880   BERLIN, December 7, 1936.

On the morning of December 5 the French and British Ambassadors called on me jointly, in order in the name of their Governments to submit suggestions concerning an intensification of the non-intervention measures. Both Ambassadors, without asking me, had on the previous evening asked to see the Führer and Chancellor for an urgent *démarche*. The Führer had declined the audience and had referred the gentlemen to me. I requested both Ambassadors in the future to make their *démarches* with the Foreign Minister, who was the proper authority in these matters.

The *aide-mémoire* handed me by the two Ambassadors are identical in text and contain three points:

1. The demand that non-intervention in Spanish affairs be observed;
2. A control over possible aid to the Spanish combatants;
3. A proposal for possible mediation between the combatants.

[1.] I called the attention of the gentlemen first of all to the fact that we, as well as the Italians, had demanded as early as August that the non-intervention obligations of the countries participating in the London committee should include measures preventing volunteers from aiding the Spanish combatants. This demand had at that time been rejected by the French and British Governments as not enforceable. It was astonishing that now, with thousands of French, Belgian, Czech, and Russian volunteers fighting on the side of the Reds in Spain, this demand was suddenly being made in those quarters which had refused to ban the participation of volunteers. We had the greatest interest, as did Britain and France, in seeing that the conflagration in Spain did not spread to the rest of Europe. On the other hand, however, we did not conceal the fact that our sympathies were on the side of the General's party. Presumably the bloodshed in Spain could long since have been halted if the British and French Governments had not placed themselves behind what we considered the Bolshevist-Anarchist hordes. We had already stated repeatedly that we would not tolerate the establishment of a new Bolshevist center in Spain because of the danger which this involved for all of Europe. I doubted that it would be possible to withdraw from Spain the volunteer troops fighting on both sides. We would carefully study the proposal of the French and British Governments, however, and would revert to it later.

2. As for control measures, this matter, as well as the possibility of putting them into practice, was already being discussed by experts in the Non-Intervention Committee in London. It might be advisable to await the outcome of these discussions.

3. We were, of course, willing to help end the Civil War in Spain as quickly as possible. Now that passions had been whipped up to fever pitch in months of fighting, however, and the resentment on both sides was enormous as a result of the fighting methods, shooting of hostages, arson, and persecution of political enemies, I could not quite imagine that a platonic desire for reconciliation expressed by the powers to the combatants could be successful. The proposal to hold elections in Spain at the present time seemed entirely absurd to me. I also did not know how they should be carried out if they were really to give a picture of the intentions of the Spanish people.

Finally I told the two Ambassadors that I would report the entire matter to the Führer and Chancellor and would then inform them of our decision.

BARON V. NEURATH

No. 147

3253/E000569–70

The Ambassador in Great Britain to the Foreign Ministry

[Telegram]

SECRET   LONDON, December 8, 1936.
No. 299 of December 8   Pol. III 5746.

For the Führer and Chancellor and the Foreign Minister.

Today Eden gave me a copy of the memorandum presented by the British Ambassador in Berlin, with a proposal for mediation in Spain by the six powers. At the same time he referred with special earnestness to . . . (one group apparently missing) of a European war on a small scale getting under way in Spain. I told Eden I was convinced that my Government would collaborate in all attempts to prevent the situation in Spain from becoming a source of danger, but at the present it considered one of the greatest dangers to be the establishment of a Communist state in Spain. Eden thereupon declared that he did not desire the establishment of a Communist state either.

In reply to my question as to how Eden envisaged the practical execution of the mediation proposal, he admitted that this involved extraordinary difficulties. In his opinion, the first step would be a joint declaration by the six powers of their intention to mediate. Then both parties should be called upon to conclude an armistice. At the same time the dispatch of a commission to Spain might be considered. In reply to my question regarding its composition, Eden said it might perhaps consist of representatives of the three Mediterranean powers: England, France, and Italy. I put in here as my personal opinion, without taking a stand on the proposal, that the matter would have to be handled by the powers chiefly concerned. After the conclusion of an armistice, Eden hopes that a government could be set up composed of men who had kept out of the present struggle, an idea that had been given him, he said, by an adherent of Franco in London. I did not leave Eden in doubt as to my conception of the enormous difficulties of such an undertaking. Eden himself was very skeptical of the possibility of putting it into practice.

On Wednesday I shall see Grandi; I shall discuss the matter with him and then report further.

In reply to my question as to the British attitude in the coming meeting of the Council [1] Eden said that the British representative, Lord Cranborne, had received instructions to keep the matter within

---

[1] On Nov. 27, 1936, the Spanish Government requested a meeting of the Council of the League of Nations to consider the Spanish situation. The Council was summoned to meet on Dec. 10; on Dec. 12 a resolution was adopted commending the recent Anglo-French effort to strengthen the effectiveness of the non-intervention agreement.

a small compass in Geneva. He expects some resolution calling for the cessation of all attempts at intervention. Perhaps the memorandum presented in the six capitals would facilitate such a resolution at Geneva. In reply to my question whether it was intended to refer the matter back to the Non-Intervention Committee, Eden said that would depend on the course of the discussions in Geneva.[2]

RIBBENTROP

---

[2] Marginal note: "Our reply has meanwhile been sent. D[umont]. Dec. 14."

No. 148

F3/0241

The Chargé d'Affaires in Spain to the Foreign Minister

STRICTLY SECRET   SALAMANCA, December 10, 1936.
Sa. 102

I enclose a report on the military situation and the measures to be taken, with two carbon copies. I respectfully request that one carbon copy each be given to the Führer's Deputy and Field Marshal von Blomberg.

FAUPEL

[Enclosure]

F3/0243–51

STRICTLY CONFIDENTIAL   SALAMANCA, December 10, 1936.
Sa. 102

ESTIMATE OF THE MILITARY SITUATION AND SUGGESTIONS AS TO THE MEASURES TO BE TAKEN

After arriving at Salamanca on November 28 by air, I used the first 48 hours to get as clear a picture of the situation as possible, by countless conversations with Germans, Italians, and Spaniards.

When, on November 30, I had my first full discussion with General Franco, I asked him how he visualized the further course of operations, particularly the continuance of the attack on Madrid, which even then was completely stalled. Franco gave me an explanation lasting about half an hour, the gist of which could be compressed into one sentence: "I will take Madrid; then all of Spain, including Catalonia, will fall into my hands more or less without a fight."

That was an estimate of the situation that I cannot call anything but frivolous. According to everything that I hear, General Franco personally is a ruthlessly brave soldier, with a strong feeling of responsibility, a man who is likable from the very first because of his open and decent character, but whose military training and experience do not fit him for the direction of operations on their present scale. His sense of responsibility and his accomplishment up to the penetration of Madrid deserve the fullest recognition. For judging him fairly, one must consider that the whole Army, and the officer corps in particular, has been systematically broken up and contaminated during recent years by the Leftist governments. At the beginning of the conflict the essential military offices (General Staff, War Ministry, Military Geographic Institute with all maps) were in Red Spain, particularly in Madrid and Barcelona, as were numerous depots and arsenals, all signal units, and the majority of the officer corps. Some of the officers were murdered, and some cast into prison. Some are still in hiding in Red territory, and others are in the ranks of the Reds, so that, aside from the troops in Morocco, Franco did not have a single usable military unit available but only the wreck of an army. Hence the endless difficulties of making useful soldiers out of hundreds of thousands of men.

Franco owes the successes of the first few weeks to the fact that his Moroccan troops were not opposed by anything of equal quality, and also to the fact that there was no systematic military command on the Red side. But the situation has changed greatly, particularly in the course of the last 4 to 6 weeks. The Reds have received much greater reinforcements in men and matériel than have the Whites. The influx of Communists from every country under the sun continues without interruption. According to the reports available here, some 47,000 rifles for the Reds have arrived in the last 4½ weeks alone. They are also receiving far more supplies of other types than Germany, together with Italy, is making available to the Whites. I quite agree with the Italian general here when he says that time is working in favor of the Reds.

According to the figures available here, the Whites can be estimated at 180,000 to 200,000 men at present, and the Reds at perhaps 200,000 to 230,000 men. Among the very numerous Russian, French, and Czech training personnel there are officers of high rank who have begun systematic training behind the front. On the side of the Whites, far too little has been done in this particular field. Of course, the great bulk of the foreign instructors among the Reds have to struggle with the same language difficulties in dealing with the Spaniards as do those among the Whites. But still the French instructors can train the thousands of Frenchmen and Belgians in their own language, just as is the case with the Russian officers and the Russian enlisted men.

The front is more than 2,000 kilometers long and is, of course, only very thinly held. If either of the two opponents succeeds in forming a strong combat unit of 15,000 to 30,000 men, for example, he can break through the enemy's front and thus bring about a turn of events that will decide the war. At present, the Reds' prospects of success in this respect are better and are improving from week to week, as things now stand. I am therefore urging Franco first of all to build up behind the front a sufficiently strong reserve that can be moved by trucks.

The following measures are also needed:

1. A uniform and adequate supply of arms and ammunition absolutely must be insured. I have requested of Franco that he report his average monthly requirements to us 3 or 4 months in advance. No matter how desirable it may be to have as much as possible purchased in Germany, it must be clear in our minds that the most important thing is the winning of the war. Thus if Germany is actually unable to supply what is necessary, even with the greatest exertions, that must be made known here as quickly as possible and without ambiguity, so that Franco will be in a position to order the needed arms, ammunition, etc., in some other country, before it is too late.

I have told Franco that sharp orders for the better care of equipment, rifles and machine guns in particular, must be given to the troops here at the same time. However, in view of the complete lack of training, we can expect only very slow improvement in this respect.

2. The training of Army officers, non-commissioned officers, and enlisted men is very poor. That of the Falangist militia can hardly be said to exist. However, I have convinced myself both at the front and by inspection of Falangists that a large part of the men are willing, and that something can be made of them with the right measures. I therefore request most urgently that as many Spanish-speaking officers and non-commissioned officers as possible be found. Even those who have not had any military service for years but have the ability to teach men how to fire while standing, kneeling, and lying, how to jump and crawl, how to dig trenches, and other elementary things, can perform excellent service here. At the urgent wish of the head of the whole Falange, and in agreement with General Franco, I therefore request that Major (reserve list) von Issendorf of the Cavalry Inspectorate be made available and dispatched at once to direct the training of the Falange in all Spain. I likewise ask that Major von Frantzius (Ret.) (who can be reached through the Ibero-Amerikanisches Institut, Berlin S. 2, Breitestr. 37) be sent out at once to command an infantry training unit, and also, if possible, Major Sibor (Ret.) (whose address can be obtained from the Auslandsorganisation) to direct the training of the signal units and supervise the signal equipment used.

There is also urgent need of a senior officer who gets along well with Spaniards and can speak the language, to function as liaison officer with the divisions at the front, which urgently require supervision and from which clear reports cannot be obtained at all. I should therefore be very grateful if Lieutenant Colonel von Doering (at present Commandant of the Horst Wessel Squadron) could be detailed here for several months for this purpose. All the men mentioned above have worked for long periods in South America and meet the conditions necessary for the rapid success of the work. Every other officer who has served as instructor in South America is urgently desired, unless he has defects of some kind.

3. The most important measure, on which victory or defeat in the campaign primarily depends, is the dispatch of an effective unit, trained especially in the combined use of arms, which can be employed to make a break-through before the enemy does. Franco, by the reports he has received during the past few days, has grasped the seriousness of the situation; during our last interview (see my telegram No. 592 of December 9 [1]) he asked that one German and one Italian division be placed at his disposal as soon as possible. I explained to him that such a unit could, of course, only be under German command, which he understood. According to what the Italian Chargé d'Affaires told me yesterday, General Ruata [sic] is now negotiating in Rome about the dispatch of stronger Italian forces.

A decisive success can be attained if these units can be brought up so as to make the push in January, and if, as must be possible, approximately a division of Spanish troops can by that time be in condition to serve as the center column of the three assault columns to be formed, and to keep pace fairly well with the German and Italian troops. Every week of time that is lost, however, means making this task harder. If this plan does not succeed, a long war of position is likely to ensue, or, if it does not, it must be expected that the Reds, who are constantly growing stronger in personnel and supplies, will gain the upper hand within the foreseeable future and that all Spain will become a Soviet republic.

From here I cannot judge how the dispatch of a division can be made acceptable from the standpoint of foreign policy. However, the decision must be made quickly, and as soon as that has been done the vanguard of the personnel, which should be ample, must be dispatched at once.

In view of these proposals, I may perhaps be accused of meddling in things which are outside my present sphere of activity. I will gladly bear that reproach and its consequences if we succeed in winning the war. In view of the very serious situation here, it is not a question of administrative jurisdiction but only of the quickest possible action. Whenever and wherever I intervene, it is done in such a way that the work of Sperrle, Funck, etc., is not interfered with, but rather supported. Because of the tremendously long front, all of them have so much to do in performing their duties and supervising the units under them that they gratefully welcome any help coming from me. Any friction between us is out of the question.

FAUPEL

---

[1] Not found.

No. 149

3253/E000559

The Ambassador in Italy to the Foreign Ministry

Telegram

SECRET · · · · · · · · · · · · · · · · · ROME, December 11, 1936—9:10 p.m.
No. 297 of December 11 · · · · · · · Received December 12—1:00 a.m.

Buti informed von Plessen today, with a request that it be treated as strictly confidential, that in a conversation with Grandi, Eden had proposed to limit action regarding Spain to the three Mediterranean powers primarily interested: England, France, and Italy, leaving out Germany and Russia. Grandi was being directed to decline the proposal, on the ground that Italy considered Germany an essential element for maintaining European peace. Besides, the proposal came too late, since Italy had already established liaison with Germany. Buti added that the latter statement was made for reasons of courtesy. The Italian Ambassador in Berlin had been instructed to notify the German Government, calling attention to the friendly nature of the Italian reply as regards Germany.[1]

HASSELL

---

[1] Marginal note: "Attolico told me the same thing today. I told him that I did not entirely understand what Eden was aiming at with this proposal. At any rate, in a committee together with England and France, Italy would always be in the minority. D[ieckhoff]. Dec. 12."

No. 150

1819/416040–42

The Chargé d'Affaires in France to the Foreign Ministry

Telegram

No. 755 · · · · · · · · · · · · · · · · · · · PARIS, December 11, 1936—9:45 p.m.

The Foreign Minister asked me to call on him today so that he could give me an explanation of the Anglo-French mediation project.

By way of introduction he stated that he wanted to emphasize to me, too, the great interest which the action merited, in the opinion of the French Government. It appeared to him significant not only because of its real purpose but, beyond that, because of the prospect for improving the general atmosphere in Europe and German-French relations in particular. Joint action by the Great Powers might, if it attained its immediate goal, at the same time form a point of departure for further German-French collaboration, in which case many questions of interest to Germany could be handled with good results.

Of course, the work of mediation could not be executed all at once. In his opinion, the first stage was complete agreement on non-intervention, which must naturally extend to volunteers also. The second stage would be to bring about an armistice, which would automatically eliminate the danger of war in Europe. In that way the time and calm necessary for the third stage, that is, the future settlement of conditions in Spain, would be provided. At present, exact ideas on that score could not yet be formed; perhaps some form of support or control of the provisional government by other European states could be considered, with the will of the people being determined subsequently in some way. The settlement of these questions appeared to him entirely possible, once an armistice had restored tranquillity. In the whole action, the French Government considered German collaboration of decisive importance, as it had demonstrated by the fact that, out of consideration for Germany, the proposal for mediation did not involve the League of Nations.

German collaboration would be all the more valuable, since Germany did not border on Spain, as France did, and felt the heat of the conflagration less. (This remark, not elucidated further, might perhaps mean that France, as a neighbor to both parties, would like to keep herself more in the background for the time being and have the practical execution begin with the influence of Germany and Italy on Franco and of Russia on the Reds.) The main thing now was complete non-intervention, which would cause the conflagration to die out. The Civil War was in the main being carried on by both sides with foreign troops only (Moors, members of the Foreign Legion, Italians, Germans, Russians, as well as Frenchmen and Italian and German exiles). If this was stopped, the war, so to speak, would end of itself. In reply to my question whether he believed that the Spaniards, whose passions had after all been aroused to the highest degree, were inclined to cease hostilities, Delbos answered that the passions still existed, to be sure, but that the time seemed to him not unfavorable for intervention; fatigue was evident on both sides, operations were bound to be rendered more difficult by the winter, etc.

Delbos then once more emphatically expressed the view that successful mediation would create a favorable atmosphere for a more general discussion and for German-French collaboration. He knew that Germany had definite wishes and needs; he mentioned by way of example the questions of raw materials, colonies, and credit. When Delbos in this connection touched on the favorable course of Schacht's visit,[1] I asked him what he thought of the present status of those negotiations. He replied that the French Government was still of

---

[1] Concerning Schacht's visit to Paris, see also vol. I, document No. 83, pp. 136–137.

the same opinion as at that time, but he believed that the continuance of the negotiations depended on the improvement of the general atmosphere. After the settlement of the Spanish crisis we could, as he repeated several times, discuss all questions affecting Germany.

Delbos did not mention the problem of disarmament.

The report in the *Paris-Soir*, which has just appeared, to the effect that I stated the German position is, of course, not correct. I did not commit myself; nor did the Foreign Minister address any questions to me.

FORSTER

No. 151

395/212439

Memorandum by the Acting State Secretary

BERLIN, December 11, 1936.

The Italian Ambassador, who visited me today for another reason, asked whether it was correct that General Franco had told our Chargé d'Affaires a few days ago that he urgently needed at least one German and one Italian division. I told the Ambassador that, while we had received word that General Franco had expressed the desire to see the foreign forces in Spain strengthened, I thought that this had been outdated by the conference with Canaris in Rome on December 6. During this conference, as he doubtless knew, it had been agreed to refrain from sending complete units to Spain.

I purposely did not go into the question whether Franco's cry for help which General Faupel reported in his telegram [1] came before or after the conference in Rome on December 6.

DIECKHOFF

---

[1] Document No. 144, p. 154.

No. 152

1819/416062–63

Memorandum to the British and French Embassies

BERLIN, December 12, 1936.

The German Government has the honor to reply as follows to the memoranda of His Majesty's Government and the French Government of December 5 [1] concerning the situation in Spain:

1. The German Government naturally shares the desire of the two

---

[1] Not printed here. For substance, see document No. 146, p. 156.

Governments to see orderly, peaceful conditions restored in Spain as soon as possible, and especially to eliminate the danger of having the conflagration spread to the rest of Europe. It is prepared to support all measures which are truly adapted to serving this purpose, which all European governments which love order and are concerned with securing the peace must have at heart.

2. As regards the proposal of the two Governments to strengthen the agreement on non-intervention in the Spanish troubles and to make it effective through further agreements, the German Government feels bound to point out that from the very beginning, for instance, in its note of August 17, 1936, it advocated extending the agreements which were to be reached to prevent the departure of volunteers for the fighting in Spain. It regretted exceedingly that at that time other governments were unable to reach such a decision, a fact which doubtless contributed substantially to aggravating the situation in Spain. It must unfortunately appear rather doubtful whether the general prohibition of any direct or indirect intervention can still lead to the desired result under the conditions prevailing today. Considering the well-known role which alien elements have played and still are playing to an increasing degree in unleashing anarchic actions in Spain, this needs no further explanation. However, the German Government continues to be willing to participate in all discussions held in the London committee on how this state of affairs might be changed and how the control of any future agreements might be effectively carried out. It is of the opinion, however, that prohibition of direct or indirect intervention should be treated as one single problem.

3. The idea of putting an end to the fighting in Spain by means of joint mediation by the powers concerned certainly deserves full sympathy in itself. However, the German Government has already shown by its recognition of the Nationalist Government that it sees no other factor in Spain besides this Government which could still claim to represent the Spanish people. The party opposing this Nationalist Government, moreover, by its whole method of fighting, the murder of political opponents, shooting of hostages, arson, and other atrocities, has whipped up passions to fever pitch. A reconciliation with this party seems hardly conceivable, if only because of the obvious predominant tendency to anarchy. The German Government is unable to see how there could be any question of holding an orderly plebiscite in Spain in view of this state of affairs. Nevertheless, if the other governments believe they can make workable, concrete proposals for mediation, it will willingly cooperate in examining and implementing them.

No. 153

3253/E000564

The Acting Director of the Political Department to the Embassy in Italy

Telegram

No. 333   BERLIN, December 14, 1936—5 : 30 p.m.
                                             zu Pol. III 5699.

Drafting Officer: Counselor of Legation Dumont.

In connection with the discussion in the embargo committee of the problem of indirect intervention, the idea of granting priority to the question of volunteers arose. The German Government, in accordance with the position it has taken from the outset, unconditionally advocates the extension of the embargo measures to the question of volunteers, but it is of the opinion that the problem of indirect intervention at the present stage must be considered as a whole, or that at least the question of financial support, which is of equal importance in strengthening the belligerents, should be settled simultaneously. You are requested to advocate such a procedure there. The Italian representative in London has thus far, probably for tactical reasons mainly, placed the question of volunteers in the foreground. Report by wire.

WEIZSÄCKER

No. 154

1819/416045–47

The Ambassador in France to the Foreign Ministry

Teleprinter

VERY URGENT   PARIS, December 15, 1936—11 : 00 p.m.
No. 769

During a rather lengthy conversation with Blum yesterday I asked the Premier his opinion on the method of procedure in the Spanish question. Blum said first that it was truly a wonder—probably for the most part attributable to the non-intervention pact—that the Spanish conflagration had thus far been kept under control; it would, however, really be playing with fire if every effort was not made to prevent the continuation of the struggle of ideologies in the Spanish arena. To begin with, any influx of combatants and war matériel had to be more effectively prevented than heretofore. In London suitable ways and means to achieve this had been found; these, to be sure, were expensive "fire insurance" but cheaper nevertheless than a world conflagration. In order to show the good will of France, he was even considering the idea of putting the French Pyrenees border under international control. Since there were already indications of battle weariness on both sides, he believed that if the conflagration was effectively isolated, it would die out of itself—which I questioned.

The second phase should consist in an attempt to exert influence on the belligerents and bring about an armistice. It was to be expected that Franco would rather listen to us and the Italians, while his enemies would prefer the advice of the French, the Russians, and the British.

As far as the pacification of Spain and the regulation of her internal affairs were concerned, there was probably nothing else to do but first of all establish an international administration and expel all foreigners who had entered the country during the last few years. After the country had been completely pacified, one would have to consider arranging a plebiscite in order to let the Spaniards choose their own form of government.

Halting the entry of combatants and war matériel, as the first step, necessitated the utmost speed in order to prevent either of the two sides from trying in the meantime to gain advantages.

The Premier did not enter into any discussion of our note of reply,[1] the positive nature of which I stressed, since he stated that he had not yet examined its text; nor did he enter into any discussion of my detailed objections to his plan, giving as his reason in the latter case that my stay of more than ten years in Spain made me too much of an expert as compared with him.

W[ELCZEC]K

---

[1] Document No. 152, p. 165.

No. 155

F3/0242

The Foreign Minister to the War Minister

BERLIN, December 15, 1936.

DEAR HERR VON BLOMBERG: I am sending you herewith a carbon copy of a report by General Faupel,[1] and I hope that we shall have an opportunity to discuss it soon. I should like to state right now that under no circumstances do I consider it feasible to send a complete division, as General Faupel desires, especially at the present time, when particularly strenuous attempts are being made by the Great Powers to limit the conflict and to bring about mediation.

Heil Hitler,

Yours,[2]

---

[1] Document No. 148, p. 159.
[2] File copy not signed, but endorsed "Sent Dec. 15."

No. 156

701/261323–25

The Ambassador in Italy to the Foreign Ministry

Telegram

SECRET   ROME, December 17, 1936.

No. 304 of December 17

For the Foreign Minister personally.

During yesterday's conversation Mussolini stated that the latest reports from Spain sounded somewhat better; nevertheless, the situation was not very satisfactory. I informed him of General Faupel's impressions, which interested him very much, and I outlined measures of assistance which in Faupel's opinion were particularly important for Franco, especially arms deliveries and instructors. Mussolini declared that he fully understood why Field Marshal von Blomberg did not wish to send any complete units; however, in view of the unsatisfactory situation he had decided to send 3,000 Black Shirts with their equipment tomorrow from Gaeta to Cádiz by a large ship of the South American service. I inquired whether the Black Shirts would be sent into action as units or with Spanish cadres. Mussolini replied: as independent columns. I pointed out the decisive importance of naval supremacy in the Mediterranean not only for cutting off Soviet Russian deliveries, but also for the moral effect. Mussolini agreed completely, even if, as he said, reports regarding deliveries of matériel were perhaps somewhat exaggerated; seven submarines were active there now, but unfortunately Red warships did not come out in the open any more. For carrying out the entire action he attached decisive importance to intensive, systematic, intimate cooperation between the army commands, and particularly between the naval commands—the latter precisely because of the necessity of a blockade, which I had rightly emphasized. I asked Mussolini whether during the current Anglo-Italian discussions the British had brought up the question of the Spanish troubles, to which he replied in the negative. The British had always shown a strong tendency to extend the agreement to France and other Mediterranean powers—something which he had unequivocally declined to do.

Without making any commitment, I held out the prospect that on his return trip General Faupel would, if possible, call on Mussolini.

HASSELL

No. 157

168/132045–50

The Ambassador in Italy to the Foreign Ministry

5855

ROME, December 18, 1936.
Received December 19.
Pol. IV 5360.

POLITICAL REPORT [1]

Subject: The Spanish troubles and German-Italian policy.

In January 1935 the agreements between Mussolini and Laval marked a low ebb in German-Italian relations. In January 1936 Mussolini executed his change of front on the Austrian question. Between these two dates, as the primary basis for the German-Italian *rapprochement*, lay the Abyssinian operation and the policy which Germany, on the one hand, and England and France, on the other, adopted toward the conflict. July 11, 1936,[2] brought the conclusion of the Berlin-Vienna agreement, and in November the agreements made with Ciano at Berlin and at Berchtesgaden sealed the restoration of German-Italian relations.

Meanwhile a new factor came into play: the Spanish troubles. They caused a sudden increase in the warmth of German-Italian cooperation. Rome's policy on this question chilled Italian relations with Russia, hence resulted in a *rapprochement* with Japan and further deterioration of relations with "pink" France. The opposition to England, however, faded into the background somewhat; it appeared that the first successful attempt at an understanding was in progress; at the same time, particularly after the Abyssinian conflict, Italy put forth a strong effort to capture the sympathy of the United States. In the midst of these tendencies, her relations with Germany, complemented or flanked by her relations with Austria and Hungary, today appear as the keystone of Italian foreign policy.

It is useful to call to mind the elements that are decisive for maintaining this Italian course, both as to the purely material, as it were physical, power of resistance, and as to "morale," i.e. the question of dependability. Two aspects are particularly important today in this connection: in the first place, a series of events indicating a stronger solidarity among the so-called Western powers, including the United States, vis-à-vis German-Italian cooperation and, above all, vis-à-vis Germany. In this regard, report No. 353 1/12 of December 2 from the German Embassy in Washington (instruction of December 5,

---

[1] On Dec. 25, 1936, copies of this report were sent to other German missions for their information (1819/416090–95).
[2] See vol. I, pp. 278 ff.

W VIIIa N.A. 1598 II) and Roosevelt's speech in Buenos Aires [3] are of importance. The second aspect concerns the possibilities and dangers that might arise because of further developments in Spain.

Conscious and concentrated cooperation by the three Western democracies with a view to forcing the "Fascist" states, as disturbers of the peace, to "come to their senses," and above all to force Germany to submit to their economic directives, would undoubtedly bring into the field material forces far superior to ours, particularly so if Eastern Bolshevism gave aid to Western capitalism. Of course, the threatening attitude of Japan forms a bastion on the other side, but its value is problematical and at any rate is not sufficient to restore the balance. The pressure, and under certain circumstances even the threatening pressure of such cooperation, might be very effective, all the more so with Italy, since attempts would presumably be made to draw that country away from us by means of alluring promises, including promises in the financial field. On the other hand, Germany and Italy do have two factors working in their favor—factors which we have learned to appreciate highly, especially in the last few years: common fundamental principles as to their form of government, and the superiority of this form of government in a political struggle because of its capacity for making quick and courageous decisions. However, the balance of power remains unfavorable enough.

It goes without saying that Germany is doing everything she can to prevent such an acute political antithesis in world affairs. That is the reason for the rejection of all bloc politics and for the strenuous attempts to arrive at an understanding with England and if possible also with France. We desire an understanding with the West, though not in the form of "being forced to our knees," but, on the contrary, as an equal partner. Mussolini, too, has repeatedly rejected bloc politics; the attempt which he is currently making to bury the hatchet with England has already been mentioned, as has his unmistakable desire for a *rapprochement* with the United States.

But it remains an open question what attitude the other side will take and whether it will not shortly try again to draw Italy over to itself in accordance with the motto, "divide and rule."

In this connection the Spanish matter in my opinion acquires particular importance.

The interests of Germany and Italy in the Spanish troubles coincide to the extent that both countries are seeking to prevent a victory of Bolshevism in Spain or Catalonia. However, while Germany is not

---

[3] For President Roosevelt's speech at the opening session of the Buenos Aires conference on Dec. 1, 1936, see *Report of the Delegation of the United States of America to the Inter-American Conference for the Maintenance of Peace, Buenos Aires, Argentina, December 1–23, 1936* (United States Government Printing Office, Washington, 1937), pp. 77–81. The report from the German Embassy in Washington has not been found.

pursuing any immediate diplomatic interests in Spain beyond this, the efforts of Rome undoubtedly extend toward having Spain fall in line with its Mediterranean policy, or at least toward preventing political cooperation between Spain on the one hand and France and/or England on the other.   The means used for this purpose are: immediate support of Franco; a foothold on the Balearic Islands, which will presumably not be evacuated voluntarily unless a central Spanish government friendly to Italy is set up; political commitment of Franco to Italy; and a close tie between Fascism and the new system of government to be established in Spain.

The entire Spanish operation has undoubtedly developed somewhat differently and more dangerously than was at first expected; above all, the Spaniards themselves have proved to be very unsatisfactory political and military material.   The possibility of failure or a bad outcome for the Nationalists cannot be dismissed and must be taken into account.   In a moment of pessimistic anger Ciano said to me recently: "I fear that these Nationalists may possibly agree to 'mediation,' and then some day the Spanish rallying cry may be, 'Out with the foreigners!' "

For the time being, however, such sentiments are only of an academic nature.   The Italians, having said "a", are still determined to go on to "b" and to do everything on their part to bring the "White" cause to a successful conclusion.

In connection with the general policy indicated above, Germany has in my opinion every reason for being gratified if Italy continues to interest herself deeply in the Spanish affair.   The role played by the Spanish conflict as regards Italy's relations with France and England could be similar to that of the Abyssinian conflict, bringing out clearly the actual, opposing interests of the powers and thus preventing Italy from being drawn into the net of the Western powers and used for their machinations.   The struggle for dominant political influence in Spain lays bare the natural opposition between Italy and France; at the same time the position of Italy as a power in the western Mediterranean comes into competition with that of Britain.   All the more clearly will Italy recognize the advisability of confronting the Western powers shoulder to shoulder with Germany—particularly when considering the desirability of a future general understanding between Western and Central Europe on the basis of complete equality. In my opinion the guiding principle for us arising out of this situation is that we should let Italy take the lead in her Spanish policy, but that we ought simultaneously to accompany this policy with so much active good will as to avoid a development which might be prejudicial to Germany's direct or indirect interests, whether it be in the form of a defeat for Nationalist Spain or in the nature of a direct Anglo-Italian understanding in case of further stagnation in the fighting.   We surely have no reason for jealousy if Fascism takes the fore in the thorny task of creating a political and social content behind the hitherto purely military and negatively anti-Red label. Anyone who knows the Spaniards and Spanish conditions will regard with a good deal of skepticism and also concern for future German-Spanish relations (perhaps even for German-Italian cooperation) any attempt to transplant National Socialism to Spain with German methods and German personnel. It will be easier for Latin Fascism, which is politically more formalistic; a certain aversion to the Italians on the part of the Spaniards, and their resentment against foreign leadership in general, may prove to be a hindrance, but that is a matter for the Italians to cope with. We must deem it desirable if there is created south of France a factor which, freed from Bolshevism and removed from the hegemony of the Western powers but on the other hand allied with Italy, makes the French and British stop to think—a factor opposing the transit of French troops from Africa and one which in the economic field takes our needs fully into consideration.

HASSELL

No. 158

2128/463508–09

The Ambassador in Italy to the Foreign Ministry

Telegram

SECRET   ROME, December 20, 1936.
No. 306 of December 20   Sent December 21—10 : 30 a.m.

For the Foreign Minister.

Ciano informed me this evening that Mussolini would send a group of bombers to Spain, in view of the German message as to the difficulty of sending additional planes. 3,000 Black Shirts with artillery had left, and 3,000 more were being made ready; if necessary an additional division would be sent, since it was absolutely necessary to force a victory. For this purpose the speedy training of Spanish brigades by Italians and Germans, as agreed upon, was important. The arrangement made here of concentrating the Spanish affairs in the Foreign Ministry under a diplomatic chief with military consultants had proved very successful; a similar procedure on our part would in his opinion greatly facilitate cooperation.

Since the British were concerned about the Balearic Islands, the so-called Count Rossi [1] (actually Buonacorsi) was being called here from Palma. But the flight personnel and Rossi's deputy, Margottini, would remain there; besides, Rossi would be sent to Seville in the near future, where he could be very effective because of the legend surrounding him, and from where he could return to Palma at any

---

[1] Italian commanding officer in the Balearic Islands.

time, if necessary.   Evacuation of the Balearic Islands was, of course, feasible only after the Nationalist Government was firmly established in all of Spain.

HASSELL

No. 159

1819/416096–101

The Ambassador in the Soviet Union to the Foreign Ministry

No. A 2692   Moscow, December 21, 1936.
                                                    Pol. III 5928.

With reference to your telegram No. 136 of December 14, 1936,[1] and our report No. A 2300 of November 2, 1936.[2]

Subject: Meagerness of information to be gleaned from the Soviet press with regard to Soviet intervention in Spain.

One would look in vain in the Soviet press for any material to prove *direct* intervention by the Soviet Union in the Spanish Civil War, in particular since orders have obviously gone out that not a word is to appear in the Soviet newspapers regarding the sending of war matériel, military instructors, and active combatants from the U.S.S.R. to Spain.   Since the Soviet press not only is strictly bound by instructions from the competent central authorities but—with the exception of *Izvestiya* and *Pravda*—receives politically important material only in final form from Tass, indiscretions are practically eliminated.

As for *indirect* intervention of the U.S.S.R. in domestic Spanish affairs three periods may be distinguished in the outward form of such intervention and thus its reflection in the press.

The first period comprises the time up to the adherence of the Soviet Union to the non-intervention agreement—August 23—and a short time after that.   In this period we have the first great demonstrations of sympathy and the solidarity meetings, at which it was decided to give moral and material support to "the Spanish people fighting for their freedom," and at which financial contributions were requested. By August 6 the proceeds of these collections were reported to be 12,145,000 rubles; on that day the All-Union Central Council of Trade Unions requested the Soviet State Bank to place the equivalent of this sum "at the disposal of the Spanish Government, in the name of Giral, the Prime Minister of the Spanish Republic," in French francs, i.e. 36,435,000 francs.

---

[1] Not printed (1810/414505).
[2] Not printed (1810/414441–46).

After the beginning of the negotiations regarding the adherence of the Soviet Union to the Non-Intervention Committee and after this adherence had taken place on August 23, Soviet material aid was for a time no longer mentioned officially; the dominant tone in the press was merely the propaganda carried on by word and picture in favor of the "Reds" and against the "Fascists" and their protectors (Italy, Germany, and Portugal).

The second period began early in September, when through numerous noisy meetings a drive for contributions was once again undertaken under the pretense of "rendering aid to the women and children" of "Republican Spain." By the end of September this had gone so far that—on the basis of allegedly "spontaneous" and "voluntary" decisions of workers—wage deductions up to ¼ of a day's pay were withheld in all factories. It is a known fact that from September 18 to October 21 several Soviet merchantmen (*Neva, Kuban, Syryanin*, and *Turksib*) were outfitted in Odessa or Leningrad with the funds raised in this manner and sent to Barcelona or Alicante with cargoes allegedly consisting only of foodstuffs or articles of clothing. On September 21 and October 2, 11, and 27, the newspapers published the report of the All-Union Central Council of Trade Unions on the total amount, as of those dates, of the contributions collected since September; on October 27, this total amount was said to be 47,595,318 rubles; after that time no more of these reports were made. A detailed accounting of the expenditure of the donations was never published. One learned only what quantities of goods had been transported by the food ships and paid for out of the funds donated. Whether the funds donated were all used for this or not, or whether the money was perhaps used for other purposes as well, the All-Union Central Council of Trade Unions did not say.

During the period since the end of October, which constitutes the third period, the Soviet press made no more reports regarding meetings and collections of donations. The intensity of the journalistic propaganda during this most recent period, on the other hand, reached its highest point thus far.

In this connection it must of course not be overlooked that, however unscrupulous this propaganda is in its choice of means, the Soviet press in its political statements regarding the Spanish question only repeats—not in form, but in substance—the statements made by Stalin, Kalinin, Molotov, and Litvinov in Moscow and by the representatives of the Soviet Government on the Non-Intervention Committee in London. To the extent that an undisguised fundamental bias in favor of the Reds in Spain has been expressed by these "authorities," it also appears in the Soviet press; the same is true with regard to the well-known objections of the Soviet Government to the policy of non-intervention, to which Moscow has acceded only reluctantly and with reservations.

Everything intended for the public is kept within this prescribed framework. With regard to Spain they speak of "sympathy," "solidarity," "support," "assistance," and also of "moral and material aid"; but this represents the limit established for anything that becomes public knowledge.

Thus far there has been only one instance—and not a very important one—when this limit was exceeded. At the Congress of Soviets, Delegate Khromushin, spokesman for the collectivized farmers in the Don Cossack region, said: "We are prepared to proceed to Spain at any moment to defend the Spanish revolution and to assist the Spanish people against the Fascist barbarians." Characteristically, however, these words by Khromushin were left out of the newspaper reports on the Congress, and the foreign correspondents who had heard them were forbidden by the censor of the Commissariat for Foreign Affairs to report them.

The press reports from Spain are colored in the same manner. The "heroic deeds" of the Reds are extolled daily; the "International Brigade" gets full recognition; Soviet propaganda outdoes itself in disseminating stories of atrocities by the "Spanish Fascists" and accusing Germany and Italy of acting in Spain as "interventionists," "imperialists," "annexationists," and "instigators" of a new world war. Every indication of Soviet intervention in Spain, however, is concealed; indeed, even the material in support of the accusations brought against the U.S.S.R. in the London Non-Intervention Committee was scarcely touched upon at the time and was dismissed as "groundless," "trifling," etc.

The following may be said in summary: The facts regarding the demonstrations of sympathy, the collection of money, and the so-called food shipments for Red Spain are well known. Any support beyond this is carefully concealed from the public and kept secret. The forms in which the "anti-Fascist" hate propaganda appears are frequently unprecedented and indicate not only a monstrous brutalization but also the intention to arouse in the people an intensely hostile attitude toward Germany and Italy in particular.

Samples of press reports of this kind are more adapted to characterizing the state of mind here than to proving direct Soviet intervention in Spain. I shall, however, collect a number of comments by the press, which may perhaps be a suitable framework for concrete accusations of Soviet intervention in Spain based on other material.

I may add that the press will be watched closely in the future along the lines indicated in your telegraphic instruction.

COUNT VON DER SCHULENBURG

No. 160

1819/416069-70

The Ambassador in France to the Foreign Ministry

Telegram

VERY URGENT   PARIS, December 22, 1936—9 : 10 p.m.
No. 785

Major Loriot, Chief of the Deuxième Bureau of the General Staff of the Air Force, who is known to the Embassy as a calm man, told Ritter yesterday, with the request that the information be passed on to Freyberg,[1] that a special consultation of the Premier, the Minister of Foreign Affairs, and the three Ministers of National Defense had been held on the Spanish question yesterday, and he declared that in view of the landings of German troops—landings which had already taken place and additional landings which were still being planned—the situation was extremely serious and dangerous (*situation extrêmement sérieuse et dangereuse*). If the landing of troops continued, a general war would be unavoidable. Besides, he added, we probably did not know as yet that the Italians had given their pledge to the British to withdraw from Spain in exchange for *de facto* recognition of Italian sovereignty in Abyssinia.

This statement corresponds with the rumors which have cropped up everywhere here, particularly during the last few days. They are generally believed and, strangely enough, lead to the feeling that war is imminent. This time the mood is only incompletely reflected in statements and commentaries in the press, as reported by DNB. The remarks on the seriousness of the situation evidently come directly from leading political circles, including members of the Cabinet. They are believed also in the diplomatic corps. A friend of mine who is chief of a mission told me that the French Government claimed to be entirely certain of its case, since its informant had been an eye witness of the debarkations in Cádiz. Let me add in strict confidence that Viénot [2] invited a member of the Embassy with whom he is on friendly terms to his office and pointed out to him most emphatically the danger of the situation.

I have everywhere denied most sharply the reports on landings of troops and have instructed the members of the Embassy to do the same. I shall do the same with Delbos, who has invited me to call on him Wednesday afternoon at 4 o'clock, French time, doubtless in order to discuss this same question with me.

In line with his statements to Forster, the Foreign Minister is likely to ask me whether we are willing to work jointly toward creat-

---

[1] Colonel Baron von Freyberg-Elsenberg-Almendingen, Air Attaché of the German Embassy in France.
[2] Pierre Viénot, Under Secretary of State for Foreign Affairs.

ing an atmosphere favorable to a more general discussion by stricter non-intervention, cessation of hostilities, and pacification of the country. I should therefore be obliged for immediate instructions as to my answer.

WELCZECK

No. 161

2128/463511–12

The Ambassador in Italy to the Foreign Ministry

Telegram

SECRET   ROME, December 23, 1936.

No. 308 of December 23

For the Foreign Minister.

1. Ciano informed me last night that, with the arrival of the first 3,000 Black Shirts in Cádiz, another 3,000 would leave during the next few days, as I had already been told. According to his information the progress made by the Nationalists was slight, to be sure, but the disintegration of the Red party was increasing, and Soviet deliveries had greatly diminished as the result of measures taken at sea.

2. Ciano then stressed once more the communication transmitted yesterday at his direction (telegram No. 307 of December 22 [1]); he thought it important to reiterate to me, too, that friendship with Germany would continue to be the backbone of Italian policy. He did not believe it possible for either Italy or Germany to reach an understanding with the present French Government, the policy and authority of which he did not trust. If a nationalist government should come to power in France, the situation might change; then Italy could perhaps make herself useful in the direction of German-French understanding.

HASSELL

---

[1] Not found.

No. 162

1819/416071

The Head of the Extra-European Section of the Political Department to the Embassy in France

Telegram

VERY URGENT   BERLIN, December 23, 1936.

No. 566 of December 23

With reference to your telegram No. 785 of December 22.

In case Delbos should make statements of that kind, the Führer and Chancellor wishes you to express surprise at hearing such unjustified accusations from a Government which was being attacked daily by its own press for breaking the non-intervention agreement. You are also surprised that these accusations, which you personally could reject as entirely unjustified, had not been submitted to the London committee, where they belonged. Otherwise please restrict yourself to listening to the statements made.

ERDMANNSDORFF [1]

[1] Presumably in charge of Spanish affairs during the Christmas holidays.

No. 163

3176/682874–75

The Director of the Economic Policy Department to the Embassy in Spain

Telegram

VERY URGENT   BERLIN, December 23, 1936.
No. 155   W II WE 4914.

Drafting Officer: Counselor of Legation Sabath.

1. The German-Spanish trade agreement of March 9, 1936, expires on December 31 but will be considered as extended for one year if both parties reach an agreement on that point by the end of the year. It can then be denounced on a month's notice by the end of any quarter of a calendar year. There is no time limit on the payment agreement of December 21, 1934, and it therefore remains in effect beyond December 31.

2. Lest we find ourselves without a treaty covering commercial transactions, please propose at once to the Spanish Government the extension of the trade agreement—for only three months, however, because of changed conditions. At the same time we propose that both parties consider taking up negotiations by April 1 on adapting the trade agreement to present conditions. This preliminary treaty should express the readiness of both parties to give trade relations with each other as favorable a form as possible and to assure preference in the supply of those goods which are of special interest to them.

A like reciprocal preferential agreement is said to have been made between Spain and Italy.

3. The payment agreement will presumably not require any essential changes, so that we will not need to mention it in the preliminary treaty. In case the Spanish Government wishes changes, however, the Embassy is authorized to pledge that we are willing to adapt the payment agreement to changed conditions.

Please report by wire.

RITTER

No. 164

1819/416072-75

The Ambassador in France to the Foreign Ministry

Telegram

URGENT   PARIS, December 24, 1936.
No. 794

With reference to our telegraphic report No. 755.[1]

Delbos invited me to call on him yesterday evening and asked me whether I had received instructions with regard to his proposals made to our Chargé d'Affaires some two weeks ago. I answered in the negative, referring to our note of reply which had gone out in the meantime.[2] Delbos pointed out that his communications referred not only to the Spanish question but over and above that—after joint work on this peace project—to all the questions of interest to us. As far back as 1919, he had spoken up boldly for *rapprochement* and understanding with Germany; being a farmer's son, he belonged to the middle classes, and as such he believed that he could speak for almost the entire French people in conveying the honest desire to reach—now or never—an understanding with Germany. Nor did England, under the circumstances, want to bar the door to Germany's wishes with respect to colonies, raw materials, and loans; and as to America, he knew that she desired nothing more ardently than German-French understanding in order that she could give her gold and her raw materials to a pacified Europe.

The Foreign Minister formulated his proposal as follows: We should have raw materials, colonies, and loans, in return for which the only compensation required of us was *peace*. In reply to my question as to what he understood by peace, and how he thought it would be brought about, Delbos answered that the peace which he had in mind must be basically different in form and substance from the present state of affairs, in which everything was governed by mistrust. It could be attained only by deeds, not by declarations. The most important prerequisite was the creation of an atmosphere of peace, without which the tender little plant of understanding could not thrive. One of the prime requirements was a disarmament of minds, not of armies. In order to attain this, what was discussed within a country was far more important than what was said for the benefit of the outside world. So long as we, whose press legislation gave us entirely different powers from those of the French Government, continued to represent France in our newspapers as a decadent

---

[1] Document No. 150, p. 163.
[2] Document No. 152, p. 165.

country, disintegrating more and more and standing on the verge of Bolshevism, an understanding would be impossible. But unfortunately the German newspapers snapped up every false report of the French opposition press without criticism and provided their editorials with headings as distorted as they were insulting. There was still much to be said as to how disarmament in speech and writing could be attained on either side. First of all, good will would have to be shown.

If Germany wished to rejoin the concert of Europe—and here one did not immediately have to think of the League of Nations or of such utopias as general disarmament—and was willing to observe the standards customary in the past in the life and association of nations, the door for successful negotiations was open. It would be futile, however, to try to pick out and propagandize our individual wishes.

He would suggest the following as the *modus procedendi:*

1. Collaboration in isolating and extinguishing the Spanish conflagration.

2. Creation of an atmosphere conducive to peace.

3. Discussion and satisfaction of Germany's wishes and, at the same time, settlement of the Locarno question.

4. Limitation of armaments.

The Spanish question appeared to him to be the most acute, for the sending of further troop transports would necessarily lead to war.

In reply to my question as to the origin of the stories which were current everywhere concerning landings of complete units of German volunteers in Cádiz, Delbos replied that he could only tell me that a short time ago a French delegation which sympathized strongly with the Franco Government had been in Saragossa and had seen almost none but German troops there marching and drilling in complete units. The possibility of a massing of German troops in a country with which France had an open border made many French patriots uneasy and probably gave rise to these and other stories, considering the nervousness which had prevailed for some time in public opinion. France had a *vital* interest in the shape of things in Spain for a variety of reasons, not least because of traffic with Africa. This was not true with us to the same extent, even though our anxiety regarding a Communist victory in Spain was comprehensible and justified. Consequently France could not permit the fate of this neighbor country to be decisively influenced, even determined, by another power, no matter whether the latter sympathized with the Right or with the Left. For the purpose of damming this influence as much as possible, France and England could find no more effective means for the time being than strict international control of the Spanish border and ways of access. France would even go so far as to permit a control of her garrisons and flying fields, her munitions factories, and other installations, on condition, of course, that this was done everywhere. Unfortunately, the course of the discussions in the London committee so far had not been very promising; recently there had even been the peculiar case of Germany and Russia making similar proposals.

Delbos said nothing of a proposal for mediation, but he did speak again and again of the urgent necessity for not pouring more oil on the Spanish fire at this time. He firmly hoped that we could see this necessity.

The objective way in which Delbos treated the Spanish problem, his understanding treatment of German ideological interests in the developments in the Iberian Peninsula, and his avoidance of any criticism of our action in Spain were certainly based on the intention of avoiding anything which might offend us. The calm and decisive tone adopted by Delbos contrasted sharply with the downright hysterical nervousness that has been evident among the public here for several days and has started crack-brained rumors circulating regarding the inevitability of a war, simultaneous military attacks on France from the east and the south being planned by Germany, etc. On the other hand, he told me in the most serious way that continuance of the "ideological warfare" in Spain must inevitably lead to a world war.

I gained the following impression from the conversation:

1. Liquidation of the Spanish problem to avoid the acute danger of war is in the foreground here.

2. France wants to be given proof that we are willing to collaborate in the creation of an atmosphere conducive to peace in Europe and are willing to desist from arbitrary methods.

3. Thereupon, France earnestly desires to negotiate with us regarding our wishes. But, in her opinion, this can be done only through a general conversation aiming at the complete settlement of all pending problems.

4. France appears to have British and also American approval of this general plan.

Delbos asked me for an answer as soon as I had received instructions from my Government.

Bastid,[3] with whom I conferred today regarding the new request for foreign exchange for the exposition, also expressed the hope that political questions might be settled; this would be of the greatest importance for economic negotiations.[4]

WELCZECK

---

[3] Paul Bastid, French Minister of Commerce.

[4] A personal letter of Dec. 26, 1936, from Welczeck to Neurath, amplifying this telegram and urging the necessity for negotiations with France, is translated in *Documents and Materials Relating to the Eve of the Second World War* (Moscow, 1948), vol. II, pp. 217–225. No copy of this letter has been found in the archives of the German Foreign Ministry.

No. 165

137/128256–58

Note from the British Embassy [1]

URGENT   BERLIN, December 26th, 1936.
No. 413
(523/240/36)

His Majesty's Ambassador has the honour, under instructions from His Majesty's Principal Secretary of State for Foreign Affairs, to make the following communication to His Excellency the Minister for Foreign Affairs.

2. For some time past His Majesty's Government in the United Kingdom have observed with growing concern the increasing number of foreigners entering Spain for the purpose of taking part in the civil war in that country. In their opinion this development constitutes a grave danger to the peace of Europe, and they therefore consider that it is of the utmost importance that steps should be taken by the Governments represented on the Non-Intervention Committee to put an immediate stop to the departure from their respective countries of their nationals with a view to their taking service with either of the parties in Spain.

3. At a meeting of the Non-Intervention Committee on December 4th the United Kingdom representative made an appeal in this sense, as a result of which all the representatives undertook on December 9th to ask their respective Governments to agree to extend the Non-Intervention Agreement to cover indirect as well as direct intervention and, as a first step, that this extension should cover the question of "volunteers".

4. From the start the German, Italian and Portuguese Governments have taken the line that the question of volunteers forms only a part of the more general one of indirect intervention and that all aspects of this latter question, especially the problem of financial assistance, should be dealt with together. It was, however, hoped that they might nevertheless agree to a discussion of the question of volunteers first, on the understanding that the other aspects of the problem would also be examined as soon as possible.

5. At a meeting held on December 22nd the Earl of Plymouth again stressed the importance which His Majesty's Government attached to this question and the urgency with which they consider it should be dealt with. He then proposed that, in order to put a stop to the present situation, each Government should be asked to take itself the action necessary to prevent the departure of its nationals to take part in the

---

[1] The file copy is in English.

war in Spain, and that the date of enforcement of the prohibition should be January 4th. In reply to this suggestion the representative of the Union of Socialist Soviet Republics [2] said that he could not agree to any such prohibition until a system of control was actually in operation. This would clearly entail considerable further delay and thus defer the opportunity which the present proposal offers to the participating Governments of giving fresh proof of their determination to make the operation of the Non-Intervention Agreement more effective.

6. This step on the part of the Soviet representative made it possible for the German and Italian representatives to insist on the appointment of a technical sub-committee to examine the matter in further detail.

7. In these circumstances His Majesty's Government in the United Kingdom have come to the conclusion that no further progress can be made in the Committee and they have therefore instructed His Majesty's Ambassador to take the matter up immediately with the German Government.

8. Sir Eric Phipps has been directed to urge once more the view already put forward by Lord Plymouth to the Committee that this question is by far the most important and urgent of all those arising out of the war in Spain with which the Governments are faced. The problem involved covers all forms of recruiting as well as volunteering for service in Spain, whether by groups or individually. It is therefore in the opinion of His Majesty's Government vital, if serious international complications are to be avoided, that steps should be taken without further delay to put a stop to this increasing flow of foreign nationals to Spain. His Majesty's Government therefore earnestly hope that the German Government will agree to take such legislative or other appropriate action as may be necessary to prevent their nationals leaving their territory in order to take service with either party in Spain. Sir Eric Phipps has the honour to add that His Majesty's Government are confident that the German Government will agree that such measures should be taken with the utmost possible speed and that they will be glad to learn whether the Government of the Reich will be prepared to put this prohibition into effect on a date early in January to be fixed by agreement with the other participating Governments, in order to ensure simultaneous action.

9. A similar communication is being addressed to the Italian, Portuguese and Union of Socialist Soviet Republics' Governments by His Majesty's Ambassadors in the capitals concerned.

---

[2] This word order appears in the original of this document and of several which follow.

No. 166

137/128254–55

Aide-Mémoire from the French Embassy [1]

BERLIN, December 26, 1936.
Pol. III 5977.

By order of his Government, the Ambassador of France has the honor to bring to the knowledge of the Government of the Reich the following communication:

1) On December 5 last, the Government of the Republic, in agreement with the British Government, proposed to the Government of the Reich that the principle and practice of non-intervention in the affairs of Spain should be strengthened by resorting, if necessary, to the establishment of an effective control.[2]

On December 12 the Government of the Reich declared that with certain reservations it was prepared to examine constructively the concrete proposals which might be submitted to it.[3] Since then the London committee has been making every effort to draw up a plan in the sense desired. The French representative on this committee has had occasion to declare the adherence of the Government of the Republic to the extension of the non-intervention agreement so as to prohibit as far as possible direct or indirect interference in Spanish affairs.

2) At the present time the most urgent problem is undoubtedly that of the volunteers. If measures are not taken, there is danger that the increase in the number of nationals of different countries of Europe facing each other in Spain will give the Civil War in the Peninsula more and more the character of an international conflict, and most serious complications are to be feared.

3) However, it has not been possible to reach agreement in the London committee on the necessity of examining this problem before, and independently of, any other problem relative to direct or indirect interference—the German, Italian, and Portuguese representatives maintaining that this is only part of the more general problem of indirect intervention, all the aspects of which should be studied at the same time, and the representative of the U.S.S.R. making any prohibition dependent on the effective enforcement of a system of control.

As a result of this double opposition, the whole question is in a state of suspense.

4) The position of the French Government is very clear; for it is prepared on the one hand to examine the problem of indirect interference as a whole and on the other hand it fully appreciates the importance of control. But in either case difficulties are encountered which cannot very quickly be overcome.

[1] Translated from a copy in French.
[2] See documents Nos. 141 and 146, pp. 151 and 156.
[3] See document No. 152, p. 165.

Under these conditions the Government of the Republic, in agreement with the British Government, considers that the problem of volunteers requires an immediate solution.

For its part, it is immediately prepared, on the formal condition that the other Governments make the same decision, to extend the non-intervention agreement so as to prohibit the recruitment in any form, the shipment or transit, in groups or individually, across its territory, of all persons planning to participate in the Spanish Civil War.

5) The Government of the Republic inquires whether the Government of the Reich is prepared on its part to take all legislative or other measures which would be necessary for this purpose. It calls the full attention of the German Government to the predominant importance and the urgency of the question. It hopes firmly that these measures may be taken as rapidly as possible so that the prohibition may enter into force at the beginning of January, on a date to be fixed by agreement among the various Governments concerned in order that their action may be simultaneous.

The same request has been made of the Governments in Lisbon, Moscow, and Rome.

No. 167

137/128259–63

Memorandum by the Director of the Legal Department

BERLIN, December 26, 1936.

At noon today, directly after the French *aide-mémoire* [1] on the question of prohibiting volunteers from leaving for Spain had been received, the French Ambassador called on me in order, as he expressed it, to explain more exactly the purpose of this step by his Government. He stated in great detail that this step should not be considered alone, but only in connection with the other aims of French policy, as M. Delbos had recently outlined them to Count Welczeck. The important thing now was, by a joint effort, to remove the very acute danger that had arisen in Spain, thus clearing the way for a discussion of other problems (the question of colonies; economic questions). In this connection the Ambassador also endeavored to give the reasons why the discussions between President Schacht and M. Blum had not shown any further results. Aside from questions of currency, which had at first required a great deal of attention from his Government, it had above all else been the negative influence of the Communist wing of the French parliamentary majority that had stood in the way of continued discussions. But now the French Government had mastered the radical Leftist tendencies of Parliament and was in a position to pursue a more positive policy aiming at an understanding with Ger-

---

[1] Document No. 166, *supra*.

many.   For that reason the problem brought up in the *aide-mémoire* was so important and so urgent.   Negotiations in the London committee appeared to have come to a complete standstill; in the meantime the situation in Spain, where there were evidently many more foreigners than Spaniards opposing each other, was becoming more serious every day.

I replied to the Ambassador that I would immediately inform the Foreign Minister of the *aide-mémoire* and of his oral representations and that today I could only give him my opinion, which was, of course, entirely personal.   It was after all known to him that German Government circles had been much surprised by the cessation of the Schacht-Blum discussions, which had appeared so promising at first.   As the Ambassador had admitted himself, the fault was entirely with the French, and if I was not mistaken there were also other grounds, in addition to those cited by him, such as certain conversations between French and British statesmen, for example.   But at this time I, for my part, could not and did not wish to go more deeply into this general topic.   On the other hand, I considered it necessary to make a few quite frank remarks regarding the *aide-mémoire* on the question of volunteers.   There would certainly be great surprise in Germany at this new step based upon Anglo-French agreement. After Germany and, in a similar way, Italy also had at one time spoken with great emphasis in favor of an immediate ban on the departure of volunteers for Spain, and after the French and British Governments had been unable to bring themselves to decide at that time on such a ban, they were now approaching Germany with a joint formal *démarche*, just as if Germany had been remiss in some way and was to blame for the presence of so many foreign elements in Spain as depicted by him, the Ambassador.   That was after all quite a peculiar distortion of the actual facts.   The Anglo-French step was all the more astonishing, since to my knowledge the question mentioned in the *aide-mémoire* was under full discussion in the London committee. Ambassador von Ribbentrop and Minister Woermann had reported orally within the last few days to the German authorities on the status of the matter.   According to their reports, two special subcommittees had been established in London, one for the question of volunteers, and the second for the other questions connected with indirect intervention.   Both subcommittees were to begin their consultations as early as December 31.   I said that I could not understand what factual reason there was, under these circumstances, for separate action by the French and British Governments.   In addition I must point out, with respect to the problem of volunteers itself, that this problem had assumed an entirely different aspect in consequence of the developments in Spain, and was now much more difficult than it had been several months ago, at the time of the first

non-intervention agreements.   It was a well-known fact, after all, that
the fight against the Nationalist movement of General Franco had
been inspired from the beginning by emissaries from Moscow and had
been carried on to an ever increasing degree by Communist elements
from all countries, and in particular from France.   Personally, I
thought it rather doubtful whether it would still be a truly neutral
and equitable measure if the door were to be closed at this late date,
when the Red portion of Spain was entirely controlled by foreign
Communist and Anarchist elements.   Even so, as he would recall, the
German Government in its reply to the earlier Anglo-French step
at the beginning of December had declared itself willing, in principle, to participate in a factual discussion of the problem.   However,
we were aware of the great difficulties, which were not the fault of
Germany, and would therefore not consider it justified if an attempt
were now made, so to speak, to force us to commit ourselves and then
to appear in default.

The Ambassador replied that there was no thought of placing the
blame on Germany.   In the *aide-mémoire* his Government was merely
asking a question.   If Germany now quickly answered the question in
the affirmative and then the Russians nevertheless continued their
support of Red Spain, the whole international situation would assume
a different aspect.   The negotiations in the London committee appeared to have come to a complete standstill.   The new *démarche* had
been made for that reason alone; it was addressed not only to Germany but also to Italy and Soviet Russia.   If in France they had not
been willing earlier to approve a ban on the departure of volunteers,
this was to be attributed to the fact that the problem had not been
considered sufficiently important to undertake such an interference
with personal freedom of movement by way of legislation.   But,
contrary to expectations, matters had now become so serious that
they were determined to undertake such interference, provided all
others joined.

When the Ambassador intimated in this connection, even though
cautiously, that according to the reports received by his Government
very considerable German forces were in Spain fighting on the side
of Franco and that these volunteers had a very special character, in
that they evidently came from German military formations, I interrupted him and said it was a good thing that such allusions and
accusations were not contained in the text of the official *aide-mémoire*.
In view of the reports published in the French press itself regarding
extensive violations of the non-intervention agreement by France, we
could by no means grant the French Government the right to cast
any aspersions on Germany.   As to the various addressees of the

démarche, by the way, it was not made any more palatable for us by having Germany and Italy placed on the same footing with Moscow. He could certainly understand that.

In reply the Ambassador said that it was better now to put aside all questions of blame and everything that had happened in the past and simply to set our eyes on the goal of banishing by joint action the danger threatening us from Spain. Germany should not make the mistake now with which we had so often reproached the French Government, and not entirely wrongly—that is, the mistake of allowing a good opportunity to go by. I, for my part, closed the conversation by repeating that I would immediately inform the Foreign Minister of the *aide-mémoire* and the course of our conversation. The Foreign Minister was keeping in constant touch with the Foreign Ministry even during his absence from Berlin.

GAUS

No. 168

4078/E068900

The Embassy in Spain to the Foreign Ministry

Telegram

No. 620 of December 27   SALAMANCA, December 27, 1936—6 : 00 p.m.
Received December 28—12 : 10 a.m.
Pol. III 5996.

Franco has complained strongly to the Italian Chargé d'Affaires about the Pope's attitude toward the Nationalist Government. The diplomatic representative of the Nationalist Government had suggested to the Pope that he publicly take a stand against cooperation of the Catholic Basque Nationalists with the Reds, in order to contribute toward a Basque withdrawal from the fighting, which Franco is hoping for. The Pope had refused. All he had finally agreed to was a statement in the sense of a general condemnation of cooperation of Catholics with Bolshevism. However, he had expressed himself very pessimistically on Franco's prospects for success and had complained sharply about the execution of Basque Catholic priests by White troops. In Franco's opinion the Pope's unfavorable attitude toward the Nationalist Government can be attributed to the influence of the Bishop of Vitoria, since that bishop is a Basque. Franco therefore intends to send two bishops who are sympathetic with him to Rome for the purpose of enlightening the Vatican.

I have learned from another source that Franco has lively hopes at present that the Basques will give up the fight and that the northern Red front will collapse.

SCHWENDEMANN

No. 169

1819/416076–78

*The Ambassador in France to the Head of the Extra-European Section
of the Political Department*

PARIS, December 28, 1936.

DEAR HERR VON ERDMANNSDORFF: On the 10th of this month I left
the Foreign Ministry with the impression that we would gradually
get out of Spain, or at any rate would not send any more troops there.
The Delbos proposal to place a close cordon around Spain and to
refrain from any further military support, in close cooperation with
the French—a prelude, as it were, to an epoch of peace and understanding—therefore struck me as an especially fortunate coincidence.
I hoped that I would be able to give Delbos some indication to this
effect during my interview set for December 23, and I therefore made
a previous telegraphic inquiry as to how I should react if Delbos
should ask about our readiness to engage in such cooperation. However, I received no guidance on this point in the instruction of December 23, No. 566. From the directive in the closing sentence that I
should not commit myself, it could even be deduced that we intend to
increase our military operations in Spain.

At any rate the interview with M. Delbos took place somewhat
differently and more peaceably than I was bound to fear would be
the case, according to all indications. He took great pains not to let
his statements be influenced by the general excitement prevailing here
and limited himself to setting forth to me once more the ideas pro-
pounded to Herr Forster: French mediation and the hopes that might
arise from such mediation in the future, hopes affecting German-
French relations, too. The purpose of my communication, however,
is to point out once more the gravity of the situation, which cannot be
dispelled by the calm tone of the latest statements of the Foreign
Minister. A nervousness prevails in political circles here such as
has probably not existed since the end of the war. The word "war"
is in the air. I have no doubt that the French Government will not
be able to resist much longer the pressure that is being exerted on it
by all parties and will very soon be compelled to demand a plain
answer to the basic questions which M. Delbos asked us two weeks
ago in his interview with Herr Forster.[1]

With best regards and

Heil Hitler!

Yours,
WELCZECK

---

[1] See document No. 150, p. 163.

No. 170

701/261316–17

The Ambassador in Italy to the Foreign Ministry

Telegram

SECRET   ROME, December 29, 1936.
No. 310 of December 29

For the Foreign Minister.

By direction of Mussolini, who is still absent from Rome, Ciano asked me today to report to the Führer that on Sunday, January 10, Mussolini intended to hold another staff discussion on further action in Spain and was requesting German participation.

As it would be a question this time of bringing about a real decision in Spain and consequently of forming important resolves, Mussolini would appreciate it if Admiral Canaris or any one else sent in his place or along with him would come with full powers, and not as an observer, as had been the case the last time. In reply to my question whether he could indicate the topics to me in greater detail, he replied that what was at issue was the general problem of further action in Spain; besides, there were still 12 days left in which to prepare the discussion.

I have informed Ciano in the sense of telegram No. 344 of December 27.[1]

Ciano also informed me of the departure of a second expedition of 3,000 Black Shirts, which I have already reported, and also the earlier dispatch of about 1,500 specialists, who would be followed shortly by a group of specialists of about the same strength, with technical equipment.

HASSELL

---

[1] Not printed (3365/E010323–24).

No. 171

701/261250–52

The Ambassador in Italy to the Foreign Ministry

Telegram

No. 311 of December 29   ROME, December 29, 1936—7 : 00 p.m.

With reference to your telegram No. 345 of December 28.[1]

Today I discussed with Ciano the handling of the Anglo-French step regarding the prevention of the influx of volunteers and informed

---

[1] Not printed (701/261246–49). The telegram summarized the British and French notes of Dec. 26 and the conversation of Gaus with François-Poncet on Dec. 26.

him of the content of Gaus's provisional verbal reply. Ciano said that the French Chargé d'Affaires had delivered no note, but had only made oral statements, with express reference to a *pro memoria* to be delivered by the British Ambassador—another proof of the closeness of Anglo-French cooperation. In reply to my reference to the systematic Anglo-French press campaign with the aim of making Germany and Italy suspicious of each other and in particular of representing Germany as the real driving force in Spain, Ciano correctly emphasized that at his direction the Italian press had repelled these attempts very sharply. In view of this state of affairs he considered it desirable that this time the German and Italian replies either be identical in text, or at any rate correspond exactly in their essential content. He would instruct the Ministry to work out a draft and would show this to me tomorrow or the day after. He had replied to the British and French representatives that, if he understood their step correctly, England and France were now proposing what they had refused when Germany and Italy suggested it in August.

He was of the opinion that this step should be answered quite promptly, particularly so in view of the crafty British and French tactics. He thought that our reply should first of all tell the whole world what he had stated to the two diplomats, that is, Germany's and Italy's action at the very start, and the failure of the other side in this matter. Secondly, we should promise cooperation on condition that all states concerned participate and that effective supervision of their methods be worked out through the Non-Intervention Committee. Thus his basic tendency was toward a quick and positive-sounding reply, which would make it possible to gain more time.

HASSELL

No. 172

3253/E000640

The Chargé d'Affaires in Spain to the Foreign Ministry

Telegram

No. 625 of December 30   SALAMANCA, December 30, 1936—6 : 00 p.m.
Received December 30—8 : 40 p.m.
Pol. III 6068.

The Italian Chargé d'Affaires informs me that 3,000 Black Shirts, who recently landed in Cádiz and whose arms are in transit, are being sent into action in battalion units under Italian officers but in the uniform of the Spanish Foreign Legion. The arrival of another 3,000 Italians is impending.

FAUPEL

No. 173

1819/416086–88

The Ambassador in France to the Foreign Ministry

Telegram

VERY URGENT   PARIS, December 30, 1936—12 noon.

No. 802

With reference to our telegraphic report No. 794 of December 24.

The fact of our rearmament, the desire of the entire French people for peace and quiet, and the hope for economic consolidation and hence internal political tranquillity in case of a German-French *rapprochement* have brought about the present willingness of the French Government to come to an understanding for the purpose of cooperating with us in the Spanish question and restoring an atmosphere of confidence.

Blum and Delbos, who, against the wish of their radical Leftist colleagues in the Cabinet, were able to prevent the dispatch of a strong Red Front army at the beginning of the Franco rebellion only through the conclusion of the non-intervention pact, have now, despite the sharpest opposition from the same side and the most intensive counter-efforts by the Soviet mission here, undertaken the attempt to reach an understanding with Germany. It is worthy of note that it is the Popular Front Government which, in spite of its anti-National Socialist attitude and in spite of what it considers repeated violations of French treaty rights, makes an offer and undertakes what is allegedly a final attempt to reach an understanding with Germany. The disregard of prestige politics can be explained in part as follows: After the latest British assurances France feels strong, and the Anglo-Italian agreement has had a reassuring effect here; her intensive rearmament and her present defense measures seem to guarantee her a certain security; and the danger of a Communist overthrow is no longer acute.

Dilatory tactics in our reply would give the radical Leftist and Soviet propaganda new material for agitation against Blum and Delbos; a rejection would possibly lead to the fall of the Cabinet and in any case would bring to naught any possibility of an understanding in the foreseeable future.

WELCZECK

No. 174

1819/416089

The Foreign Minister to the Embassy in France

Telegram

No. 585 of December 30   BERLIN, December 30, 1936.
                                          Received December 30.

For the Ambassador personally.

The questions touched upon by Delbos in your conversation with him on December 24 [*23*][1] are now being given careful study. An instruction for your reply will be sent to you as soon as possible.

As far as the Spanish question is concerned, a reply to the *démarche* made here by the French and British Governments will be forthcoming in the next few days after an understanding with the Italians. I wish to point out, moreover, that in the last few years the Führer has repeatedly made far-reaching offers to come to an understanding with France, without ever receiving any reply to them. If M. Delbos insists on an early statement of the German position with regard to his proposals, which are after all vague, I request that you point this out to him. We have no intention of becoming infected with the almost hysterical nervousness of the French Government.

NEURATH

---

[1] See document No. 164, p. 180.

No. 175

701/261253–57

The Director of the Legal Department to the Embassy in Italy

Telegram

No. 350 of December 30   BERLIN, December 30, 1936—11 : 25 p.m.
                                       Received December 31—12 : 30 a.m.

With reference to your telegram No. 311.[1]

The Führer and the Foreign Minister are in complete agreement with Ciano's view that the German and Italian replies should either be identical in text or at any rate correspond exactly in their essential substance. Likewise, they are of the opinion that the reply should be made as soon as possible. We for our part propose the following reply:

"1. The German Government must first express its astonishment that the British Government and the French Government have considered it necessary a second time to make a separate direct appeal outside the procedure of the London Non-Intervention Committee to other governments represented on this committee. The question of

---

[1] Document No. 171, p. 191.

prohibiting participation of foreign volunteers in the fighting in Spain, which is the subject of this appeal, is at present under consideration in the London committee. It is not conceivable how these deliberations could be benefited by such a method of separate diplomatic action by individual governments. If, however, the procedure in the committee for discussing the Spanish affair is considered inadequate or unsuitable, it would be in the interest of clarity and uniformity in the handling of these questions to dispense altogether with a continuance of the committee procedure.

"2. The German Government must protest against the impression created by the new step of the British and French Governments, that the problem of the foreign volunteers in the Spanish Civil War is to be laid at Germany's door, or even that she has failed to recognize it. I therefore state once more that it was the German Government and the Italian Government which from the beginning demanded a ban on the participation of volunteers in the fighting in Spain and that it was the British Goverment and the French Government, on the other hand, which rejected such a ban.

"3. The original position of the British and French Governments in this question could only be explained as indicating that the two Governments did not wish to see in the influx of volunteers any inadmissible intervention in Spanish affairs. If the two Governments now take a different attitude, the German Government must seriously ask itself whether this change of attitude at the present time is not tantamount to open favoring of the elements hostile to the Spanish Nationalist Government. Now that the stream of Soviet Russian, French, British, Czechoslovak, and Belgian volunteers has been pouring into Bolshevist Spain unhindered for months, and after the press campaign which has now suddenly begun against the further entry of volunteers, it is really difficult to dispel the impression that the ban decreed will only benefit the Bolshevist party in Spain, which now is sufficiently bolstered with foreign volunteers.

"4. However, since the German Government has advocated the checking of the influx of volunteers into Spain, it is still willing to support all measures serving this end. But it must lay down the condition that all back doors for direct or indirect intervention in the Spanish conflict now be closed once and for all. Therefore it makes the measures to be taken by it subject to the condition that in the London committee

"(a) the other powers concerned decide to adopt the same measures;

"(b) the solution of other problems connected with indirect intervention also be undertaken immediately; and

"(c) all governments concerned adopt absolutely effective, locally enforced control measures for the embargoes to be agreed upon.

"The best solution of the problem of volunteers in the opinion of the German Government, however, would be to remove from Spain without exception all non-Spanish participants in the fighting. The German Government therefore proposes that the London committee make a study immediately of how such a measure could be effectively carried out. It is prepared for its part to cooperate therein in every respect."

Conclusion of the draft of our reply.

For your information: I also wish to remark that the wording of our draft is based on the personal order of the Führer and that it would therefore be desirable if the Italians concurred in it without any extensive change. Attolico will be informed here tomorrow morning.

Please get in touch with Count Ciano immediately.

GAUS

No. 176

701/261258–60

The Ambassador in Italy to the Foreign Ministry

Telegram

No. 316 of December 31   ROME, December 31, 1936.

With reference to your telegram No. 350 of December 30.

After I had given Pietromarchi,[1] who called on me at 10 o'clock this morning, the Italian text of our draft reply and commented on it, Ciano asked me to see him today at 6:30 p. m. The result of the conversation is as follows:

Ciano also had a draft of his own drawn up, which he gave me and discussed with me along with the German draft. In substance, Ciano's draft, which is being mailed to Attolico today, is not much different from the German, but the text is naturally quite different, all the more so since it contains a historical section documenting the Italian attitude in the question of volunteers, a section which Ciano considers particularly important. Ciano also believes that for tactical reasons the German draft might be formulated in a somewhat more conciliatory way, though he fully agrees that a negative attitude should be taken. The actual differences, which, however, are merely a question of tactics, are as follows: Point (1) of the German reply, concerning the contradiction between treatment by the committee on the one hand and Anglo-French separate initiative on the other, is lacking in the Italian reply at present. Ciano is willing, however, to insert something of this sort. With regard to point (3) Ciano objects to the second paragraph, namely, the mentioning of the influx of volunteers of various nationalities. This sentence invited the obvious retort that there were also numerous German and Italian exiles. Regarding point (4) Ciano suggests a positive formulation of the idea under (*b*), that is, Italy was willing to prevent the influx of volunteers but expected a subsequent solution of other questions; otherwise, she reserved the right to declare herself free of the obligation assumed. Finally, Ciano has strong objections to the proposal for removing all non-Spaniards from Spain. Since the offer was, of course, entirely

---

[1] Luca Pietromarchi of the office of the Chef de Cabinet of the Italian Minister of Foreign Affairs.

impracticable, it would be evaluated as such, i. e. as not meant seriously; on the other hand, if it were taken literally, an embarrassing situation might result.   Ciano asks that these points be studied and that I then be authorized to work with him to reconcile the two texts as much as possible, on the basis of their agreement in substance.   There was no objection to abandoning the idea of completely identical texts if we agreed on submitting them at the same time and on stressing the fact that our two Governments had come to an agreement beforehand.

With regard to the time, Ciano declared that he had to revise his opinion and request that the answer not be submitted before the middle of next week.   The reason was that certain measures now in progress, which are mentioned in my telegram No. 310 of December 29, require somewhat more time than originally planned and, besides, are to be further reinforced.

HASSELL

No. 177

137/128250–51

Memorandum by the Foreign Minister

RM 933   BERLIN, December 31, 1936.

This morning I had the French and British Ambassadors call, and spoke to them separately as follows: In my absence they had made a joint *démarche* with regard to the question of volunteers in the Spanish Civil War.   They would soon receive our reply to this *démarche*, and just as they had made this *démarche* jointly, our answer would be made jointly with the Italian Government.   I wished to remark even at this time—without, however, going into detail—that this *démarche* had caused considerable surprise among us.   They would learn the reasons in the reply.   I, at any rate, had received the impression that this sudden zeal for halting the influx of volunteers to Spain could only be explained by the fact that their Governments were of the opinion that the Reds in Spain now had a sufficient lead as a result of the stream of Communist elements that had been pouring in for months, and that they feared to lose this lead again as a result of the increase of volunteers on the side of Franco.   Under certain conditions—important among which were the effective surveillance and isolation of Spain—we were nevertheless prepared to join in all measures which could serve the goal, also desired by us, of localizing the Spanish conflagration.   However, I had to declare in all seriousness, and with the request that my statements be reported verbatim to their Governments, that we would in no case tolerate the establishment of a Soviet Communist government in Spain.   Under certain circumstances we would even prevent this by force.   The British and French Governments had to decide definitely whether they wished to lend their support to such a Soviet Communist government. The responsibility for the consequences would then be theirs.

While the French Ambassador repeated the statements he had previously made to Director Gaus concerning the attitude of his Government, Sir Eric Phipps confined himself to listening to my statement.

BARON V. NEURATH

No. 178

3253/E000646

Memorandum by the Head of the Extra-European Section of the Political Department

BERLIN, December 31, 1936.
e. o. Pol. III 42.

The First Secretary of the American Embassy, Mr. Lee, called on me and on instructions from his Government read to me a communication by the American Department of State.

According to this communication, the American Government was unable to reject the application of the Robert Cuse firm to ship airplanes and engines to Bilbao in the amount of $2,775,000, since the joint resolution of Congress called for an embargo on the shipment of weapons and war matériel to belligerent nations only and did not apply to the case of civil war. During the Spanish conflict the American Government had received many applications from exporters with regard to the shipment of war matériel to Spain. For patriotic reasons, however, they had all, with the exception of the aforesaid firm, given up their plans, in view of the non-intervention policy of the American Government.

The State Department, which sincerely regrets the contravention of the non-intervention policy of the American Government in the present case, further states that most of the planes intended for export in this case are not new and first have to be repaired, so that their shipment cannot begin in less than two months and cannot be completed in less than six months.

V. ERDMANNSDORFF

No. 179

1819/416080

The Head of the Extra-European Section of the Political Department to the Ambassador in France

BERLIN, December 31, 1936.

MY DEAR COUNT WELCZECK: Before the office closes I just wish, very hastily, to thank you so much for your interesting letter of the 28th.

I reciprocate your friendly New Year wishes with all my heart for
you and your family.

The note in reply to the British and the French is still being worked
out with the Italians. I need not go any further into its content
(fundamental agreement expressed in blunt form), since you will
undoubtedly have it before you when Hempel brings you this letter.

For the rest, the inclination here seems to be not to go beyond the
scope of the aid given thus far and to let the Italians take the lead;
they have a still greater interest in the course of developments.

With best wishes and Heil Hitler,

Sincerely yours,
ERDMANNSDORFF

[EDITORS' NOTE. On December 31, 1936, notes were exchanged between the British Ambassador in Rome and Count Ciano. Sir Eric
Drummond's note requested formal confirmation of the repeated assurances that Italy did not intend to impair the territorial integrity of
Spain. Ciano's note stated that, "so far as Italy is concerned, the
integrity of the present territories of Spain shall in all circumstances
remain intact and unmodified." On January 2, 1937, an Anglo-Italian
declaration was signed "concerning assurances with regard to the
Mediterranean." By one clause of the declaration the two Governments disclaimed "any desire to modify" the territorial *status quo* in
the Mediterranean.]

No. 180

3176/682876–77

The Chargé d'Affaires in Spain to the Foreign Ministry

Sa. 10–322   SALAMANCA, January 1, 1937.

With reference to our telegraphic report No. 629 of December 31.[1]
Subject: Protocol concerning the extension of the agreement on
    German-Spanish trade.

I am enclosing the German and Spanish texts of the protocol, announced in the above-mentioned telegraphic report, concerning the
extension of the agreement on German-Spanish trade.

The Government here has expressed the wish to begin negotiations
soon for adapting the trade agreement to present conditions and to
conduct them here or in Burgos. I was told that for technical reasons it was hardly possible to send a Spanish commission to Berlin.
Since most of the persons that could be considered for such negotiations were in the territory of the Red Government at the outbreak

---

[1] Not printed (3176/682878).

of the Civil War and either were killed or are working on the side of the Reds, the Nationalist Government has at its disposal only a limited number of persons with the necessary qualifications for handling economic and financial questions.

I should appreciate a communication stating when a commission could be sent here.

An opinion on the subject matter of the negotiations is reserved.

For the Chargé d'Affaires:
SCHWENDEMANN

[Enclosure]

PROTOCOL

The Government of the German Reich and the Spanish Nationalist Government have agreed as follows:

The agreement of March 9, 1936, on German-Spanish trade is extended in its present form until March 31, 1937.

For the purpose of adapting the trade agreement to present conditions, negotiations between the two parties shall be started as soon as possible and not later than April 1, 1937.

There is agreement in principle that the commercial relations between the two countries shall henceforth be conducted on as favorable a basis as possible, and that preference in supplying such goods as are of special interest to the two parties shall be mutually guaranteed.

Done in duplicate at Salamanca in the German and Spanish languages on December 31, 1936.

For the Government of the German Reich:
FAUPEL

For the Spanish Nationalist Government:
F. SERRAT

No. 181

3253/E000652-53

The Chargé d'Affaires in Spain to the Foreign Ministry

Sa. 3–324
A 221

SALAMANCA, January 2, 1937.
Received January 6.
Pol. III 71.

The diplomatic Chef de Cabinet to the Generalissimo, Sangroniz, spoke to me today about the attitude of the British toward the Franco Government. He told me that the British Ambassador, Chilton, who is accredited to the Red Government and has been staying at St. Jean de Luz ever since the sojourn of the diplomatic corps at San Sebastián during the summer, was maintaining active diplomatic intercourse with the Franco Government. Notes and telegrams came from him every day. Eden's statements in his last important speech in the House of Commons on the Spanish question had been communicated in advance to the Nationalist Government. The speech had been delivered in the House of Commons at 3 o'clock in the afternoon, and by about 10 o'clock in the morning the Government here had already received a long telegram on its contents from Ambassador Chilton. The commercial attaché of the British Embassy, Mr. Pack, was frequently in Burgos and Salamanca in order to discuss economic questions.

With reference to the Anglo-French *démarche* in Berlin, Rome, Lisbon, and Moscow regarding the inclusion of volunteers in the non-intervention agreement, Sangroniz remarked that the British had undoubtedly joined in this step at the instance of the French without being very serious about it themselves.

However, Sangroniz is of the opinion that a Franco victory and the building up of an authoritarian and militarily strong Spain would be extremely displeasing to France. France would then be in the same position as at the time of Charles V, when Germany, Italy, and Spain had been united against her.

For the Chargé d'Affaires:
SCHWENDEMANN

No. 182

47/31862–64

Memorandum of Political Division I

January 3, 1937.
zu Pol. I 234 g.

Lieutenant Commander Schubert of the Supreme Command of the Navy called on me today and told me that the Supreme Command of the Navy intended to take sterner measures with regard to the release of the rest of the cargo of the steamer *Palos*, as well as of the Spanish passenger, which has thus far been refused.[1]

A report on this was to be made to the War Minister tomorrow morning, and his consent was to be requested for the following radio message to be sent by the commander of the armored cruisers in Spanish waters to the Red Spanish commander in Bilbao:

---

[1] On Dec. 24, 1936, the German steamer *Palos* was seized by naval forces of the Spanish Government. The ship was released, but part of the cargo and a Spanish passenger were retained. In January 1937 German naval forces seized three Spanish ships. When the demand for the release of the cargo and passenger was not complied with, these ships were given to the Spanish rebels.

"Since, despite repeated demands, no amends for the violation of German sovereignty have been made by release of the passenger and the remaining cargo of the steamer *Palos*, the German Government is forced to take sterner measures, unless the passenger and the remaining cargo have been released by noon of . . . ."

Among the sterner measures contemplated, which are not to be announced in the meantime, are:

1. Extension of the raids already carried out to include Red Spanish steamers in convoy;

2. Measures against the Red Spanish naval forces on the north coast of Spain;

3. Possible bombardment of a Red Spanish port.

A period of three days is contemplated before resorting to these measures.

Concerning the question whether the bombardment of a Red Spanish port was also to be proposed to the War Minister as a sterner measure, Lieutenant Commander Schubert told me that the position of the Supreme Command of the Navy was not yet completely clear.

By this confidential communication regarding its plans the Supreme Command of the Navy intends to make it possible for the Foreign Ministry to give an opinion even before the plans are submitted to the War Minister. Lieutenant Commander Schubert asked me to inform the Supreme Command of the Navy by 11:00 a.m. Monday, if possible, of the Foreign Ministry's attitude toward the proposed measures. No written opinion is expected.

Lieutenant Commander Schubert told me in this connection that as early as December 20, 1936, the German steamer *Pluton* was stopped by a Red Spanish warship on the high sea near the northern coast of Spain by a shot fired across her bow and was forced to head for Bilbao. After the *Pluton* had followed this course for two hours, she was released by the warship without any explanation and continued her voyage to Vigo. Not until December 28, supposedly, did the captain of the *Pluton*, in the course of a conversation, inform the German Consul there of the incident. The Supreme Command of the Navy, Commander Schubert told me, was not informed until today.[2]

RIPKEN

---

[2] A handwritten note attached to the memorandum reads as follows: "To be submitted immediately to the Foreign Minister. This involves the very serious question whether we wish to proceed to direct military action, as the Navy plans to do, or whether we will be satisfied with continuing, on a *larger* scale, the present raids on shipping. The proposed communication (ultimatum) to the Red commanders in Bilbao seems to me unobjectionable *per se*, since it does not state what the sterner measures are to consist in. Gaus. Jan. 3."

A note in Neurath's handwriting reads as follows: "I agree to the ultimatum, but not to the bombardment of a Spanish port." A note in another hand reads as follows: "Ministerialdirektor Gaus informed on Jan. 4."

No. 183

47/31865–66

Memorandum by the Director of the Legal Department

BERLIN, January 4, 1937.
Pol. I 235 g.

On the basis of the instructions which I received from the Foreign Minister by telephone this morning, I telephoned Admiral Marschall [1] at about 11 : 00 o'clock and, since I could not reach him, called General Keitel to tell him that the Foreign Minister agreed to the proposed ultimatum to the Red authorities in Bilbao, but that he had serious objections to the measures planned by the Navy at the expiry of this ultimatum. I based my objections, above all, on the fact that the consequences of the measures planned could not be disregarded. If they were unsuccessful and we did not then wish to withdraw, we would have to go further and further. A feasible way, on the other hand, was to continue intensively with the raids on shipping until we had captured enough tonnage. We could then regard this tonnage as a pawn, would not need to continue with the measures, but could state that we would part with this pawn only if our demands were met.

General Keitel was very grateful for the information and told me that our views coincided with those of the Field Marshal,[2] and that appropriate instructions to the Navy were already in preparation; he would keep me informed.

After the talk with General Keitel I also informed Admiral Marschall, who confirmed to me the statements made by General Keitel.

At about 12 : 30 General Keitel called me once more to tell me that a draft of the order to our naval forces had just been prepared; he would send it to me during the afternoon; the draft fully conformed with the standpoint of the Foreign Ministry.

GAUS

---

[1] Chief of the Operations Division of the Supreme Command of the Navy.
[2] Field Marshal von Blomberg, the War Minister.

No. 184

3253/E000657

Note from the British Embassy [1]

No. 5
(4/13/37)

BERLIN, 6th January, 1937.

His Majesty's Ambassador has the honour, under instructions from His Majesty's Principal Secretary of State for Foreign Affairs, to

---

[1] The original of this document is in English.

refer to his note No. 413 of December 26th [2] and to make the following communication to His Excellency the Minister for Foreign Affairs.

2. Sir Eric Phipps has been instructed to request urgently that a reply may be given by the end of this week at the latest to his note referred to above. His Majesty's Government in the United Kingdom, who view the continued flow of volunteers to Spain with increasing concern, are making a similar request to the Italian Government.

3. Sir Eric Phipps is instructed to repeat that His Majesty's Government are prepared to take such legislative or other appropriate action as may be necessary to prevent their nationals leaving their territory in order to take service with either party in Spain, as soon as a similar undertaking is given by the other participating Governments. The French Government have made it plain in a communication to the Non-Intervention Committee that they are also prepared to do this.

4. His Majesty's Government cannot but take the gravest view of any further prolongation of the present circumstances in which so-called "volunteers" continue to flow in organised contingents into the affected areas of Spain. Time is therefore the essence of this dangerous problem and for that purpose it is essential that no further time should be lost by any delay in any quarter.

[2] Document No. 165, p. 183.

No. 185

1819/416128–29

Memorandum by the Director of the Legal Department

BERLIN, January 6, 1937
Pol. III 118.

The British Ambassador called on me this morning and handed me the enclosed note.[1] At the same time he stressed orally that his Government was extremely anxious to obtain a speedy reply to the Anglo-French *démarche* in the question of volunteers.

I called the attention of the Ambassador to the fact that the Foreign Minister, after all, had as early as December 31 informed him exactly about our intentions, revealing both the approximate date of our reply and its general substance. I could therefore not see the necessity for this new *démarche*. If we replied in the next few days, which we had planned to do until now, it might appear to the public as if we were acting under British pressure. If only for this reason, I considered this superfluous reminder regrettable.

[1] Document No. 184, *supra*.

Sir Eric replied that there could naturally be no talk of pressure. England's interest was the purely objective one of wishing to see the problem of the volunteers speedily solved. The Foreign Minister had promised during the conversation on New Year's Eve that our answer would be given by January 4. Several days had now passed since this deadline. Since there were continual reports of new transports of volunteers (he did not mention any country), London was very anxious to get a reply by the end of the week. A corresponding British *démarche* was being made in Rome.

I replied that the Foreign Minister had not, to my knowledge, committed himself to any definite date for our reply; moreover, there was not such a great difference between the 4th and the 7th as to sound an alarm on that account. I did not wish again to go into the problem itself, since the Foreign Minister had already told him what was necessary, and our reply would contain the rest. This reply could probably be given him as early as tomorrow. But I did not commit myself to this date, and also indicated that I did not know whether the new British step might make renewed consideration necessary here.

GAUS

No. 186

8369/E010581–82

The Chargé d'Affaires in Great Britain to the Foreign Ministry

[Telegram]

No. 10 of January 7   LONDON, January 7, 1937.

Eden asked me to call on him this afternoon in order to tell me the following, with the request that I transmit the information to the German Government: He was under the impression that the Anglo-Italian agreements [1] could be misconstrued in Germany to mean that since their conclusion England was less interested in putting the ban on volunteers into immediate effect. The contrary was the case. Since the signing of the Mediterranean pact, England's attitude on the question of volunteers had rather stiffened considerably as a result of the numbers flocking to both Spanish parties. He had just spoken with Baldwin, who had expressed to him his grave anxiety with regard to the European situation because of the influx of volunteers to Spain.

I replied that I had not drawn this conclusion and did not believe that the German Government construed the Anglo-Italian pact in this way, and I asked him how he had arrived at this opinion. Eden thereupon read to me the report of the *Times* correspondent in Berlin

---

[1] Of Dec. 29, 1936, and Jan. 2, 1937. See Editors' Note, p. 199.

in the issue of January 7, according to which Germany had been encouraged in her attitudes by the Mediterranean pact, and the Italian declaration regarding the Balearic Islands had been construed "in some German circles" to mean that England would be more apt to condone intervention in Spain as a result of Italy's renunciation of territorial demands. England, however, desired neither a Fascist nor a Communist Spain. Taking up this thread I said that this statement seemed important to me; I inferred from it that England, too, would not tolerate a Communist Spain. Eden replied that England wished to see such a government in Spain as the Spanish people themselves desired, and he was firmly convinced that the Spaniards desired neither Fascism nor Communism.

I further asked Eden, who had received the French Ambassador before me, whether he spoke to France in the same terms on the question of volunteers in which he spoke to Germany. The influx of volunteers from France was, after all, well known. Eden admitted this and said that he spoke to France in the same terms. The difference was, however, that France had given her promise immediately to stop the stream of volunteers provided that all other powers acted accordingly; Germany, however, had not given this promise. I pointed out that the German reply to the Anglo-French step was to be expected forthwith.

WOERMANN

No. 187

643/254221–22

The Chargé d' Affaires in Spain to the Foreign Ministry

Sa. 3–360   SALAMANCA, January 7, 1937.
                                                    Pol. III 160.

Subject: Situation report.

Since I reported orally in Berlin on December 17, 1936, the military situation has improved. First, at Christmas time an advance was made east of Córdoba, which ended a few days ago, and which resulted in considerable losses for the Reds and the capture of numerous trucks and guns, among them two 10.5 batteries, as well as other matériel. The territory gained is 30 to 40 kilometers in depth and comprises an area of approximately 1,500 square kilometers.

General Queipo de Llano, the commander of the southern army (headquarters in Seville) told me that there are rather large stores of olive oil in the captured territory. On the assumption that this information is correct I have taken steps to obtain these stores of olive oil for us.

A further improvement in the military situation may be seen in the arrival of considerable Italian reinforcements. When I was in Seville five days ago, 4,000 Black Shirts had already arrived; according to General Queipo de Llano, another 2,000 were en route from Italy and so was their equipment. He expected that these 6,000 men would be ready for action in one or two weeks.

The arrival of the first German instructors, who immediately started their work of training the Falange units, likewise resulted in improving morale. Since we have anticipated the Italians in this field, and Spain's future depends on the ideas held by the Falangists, I consider that cooperation with the Falangists holds certain possibilities for the future.

Altogether approximately 50 German instructors can be expected to arrive in the course of the next 6 weeks, most of whom were active in Spain until a few months ago as merchants, etc., and who will now have the opportunity of reestablishing themselves here in their former occupations as soon as the situation permits.

The information which I was able to give General Franco yesterday concerning German matériel in prospect was not without effect. It seems to me advisable to take advantage of the favorable atmosphere thus created to conclude agreements of a political and economic nature as soon as possible. A suitable point of departure for the latter is provided by the protocol on the extension of the German-Spanish trade agreement of December 31, 1936, a copy of which has already been transmitted.[1] The very close personal relations of the director of Hisma, Herr Bernhardt, with General Franco and with his brother Nicolás Franco, who has the powers of a prime minister, should be utilized for the economic agreements.

The gratitude and joy over German aid is currently finding expression in a variety of ways. Streets are named "Alemania"; German flags can frequently be seen together with those of Italy and Portugal; I am receiving letters of thanks with hundreds of signatures from entire towns and villages. When I am asked by a military governor or commander to inspect a troop detachment or a Falangist unit, or something of the sort, as happens occasionally, I am usually greeted with cries of "Viva Alemania" and "Viva el Führer."

FAUPEL

---

[1] Document No. 180, p. 199.

No. 188

3253/E000696–99

The Chargé d'Affaires in the United States to the Foreign Ministry

No. 31   WASHINGTON, D. C., January 7, 1937.
                                                    Received January 26.
                                                         Pol. III 446.

With reference to our report No. 2 of January 4.[1]

Subject: Deliveries of American war matériel to the Socialist Govment in Spain and activity of American fliers.

Enclosed I have the honor to submit more newspaper reports,[2] concerning the shipment of war matériel, particularly of planes, to the Socialist Government in Spain. Immediately after the opening of Congress, as has already been reported, a joint resolution was introduced in the Senate providing for a ban on all deliveries of war matériel to Spain and also to third countries, in case delivery to Spain is intended. This resolution was passed unanimously in the Senate, and in the House of Representatives with one dissenting vote. The text of the resolution[3] is enclosed. Meanwhile the firm of Mr. Cuse[4] in great haste had loaded planes and other war matériel on the Spanish ship *Mar Cantábrico* lying in the harbor of New York, and a race reminiscent of a detective story started between the parties interested in this cargo of arms and the Congress. Because of a technical error made in the Senate, the resolution could not enter into force before the 8th. On the afternoon of the 6th the *Mar Cantábrico* consequently left the three-mile zone, and thus the territorial limits of the United States, without interference. We still lack details on the connections between the firm of Vimalert and Amtorg, that is to say, the Soviet Government. No great significance should be attributed in this connection to the denial issued by Ambassador Troyanovsky here.

The airplane purchases made by the Ambassador of the Spanish Leftist Government in Mexico through an agent in San Francisco, who likewise received his license from the State Department, have been confirmed. The list of purchases made by him is enclosed.[5] The Mexican Government, on the other hand, as the State Department announced, had pledged itself to prohibit the reexport of war matériel purchased in the United States.

---

[1] Not printed (3253/E000666–69).
[2] Not reprinted.
[3] 50 Stat. 3.
[4] Robert Cuse was a representative of the Vimalert Company of Jersey City, New Jersey, which had been acting as agent for the Spanish Government in connection with the airplanes shipped in the *Mar Cantábrico.*
[5] Not printed (5067/E292197/1).

Finally, the publications of the Department of Commerce show that in the last 6 months a considerable number of airplanes have been sold to the Central American countries.

Because of the impossibility of preventing the export of war matériel for Spain until the new embargo law is enacted, the State Department was in a very embarrassing position because it had to expose itself to the reproach of seriously disturbing the efforts of the European powers to prevent further intervention in the Spanish Civil War. This confusion in the State Department is said to explain the contradictions in which that Department has become involved in the last few days. For example:

1. In the note to the powers in which it explained the granting of the license to Cuse, the State Department asserted that the planes and engines would not be ready for shipment for several months.[6] This assertion has already been refuted by the sailing of the *Mar Cantábrico* on the 6th of this month with a portion of the shipment in question.

2. The State Department denied that the planes sold to Central American countries in the last few months have been or would be exported to Europe. This is contradicted, among other things, by the published reports of exports of American war matériel from Mexico.

3. It was stated in an official American quarter that no American planes of any kind were being used in the Spanish Civil War. This claim, too, was proved to be false by the reports of the American fliers who have reported the use of Douglas and Curtiss planes.

I also enclose two more very illuminating reports by the American transoceanic flier, Acosta, who served on the Spanish front for the Leftist Government, as well as some reports of American correspondents regarding the participation of German Communists on the side of the Spanish Socialists, which give a detailed picture of the dominant role played by Russian officers and Russian fliers in the Spanish Civil War.[7] The Hearst press has, moreover, published material on the recruiting activity of agents of the Spanish Socialists among the fliers here. I also enclose this.[7]

Finally, I enclose some newspaper clippings regarding the activities of the Ambassador of the Socialist Spanish Government here, De los Ríos, who, in the last few days especially, has again been making intensive efforts to win over public opinion in the United States for the Spanish Socialists.[7]

THOMSEN

---

[6] See document No. 178, p. 198.
[7] Not reprinted.

No. 189

3253/E000654

Memorandum by the Director of the Legal Department [1]

BERLIN, January 7, 1937.

Count Magistrati called on me at 11 : 30 today in order to inform me of what he had heard in Rome about the British *démarche* of yesterday. From this it was evident first of all that the Italian Government sees no reason for altering the present arrangements (delivery of the reply on January 7, at 6 : 00 p.m.). From the oral reply which Count Ciano made to the British Ambassador in Rome regarding the *démarche*, and which Count Magistrati read to me, it is particularly noteworthy that Count Ciano did not deny the transports of Italian Black Shirts. He told the Ambassador that the stream of Italian volunteers was pouring into Spain without pressure from the Government. Italian youth, because of its convictions, was resolved to fight Bolshevism in Spain even without pressure from the Government; it would continue to do so as long as the stream of volunteers to Spain was not finally stopped by all countries concerned.

I gave Count Magistrati a copy of our reply and our communiqué.

GAUS

---

[1] This memorandum was directed to the Foreign Minister and the Political Department of the Foreign Ministry.

No. 190

1819/416123–26

Memorandum to the British Embassy

BERLIN, January 7, 1937.
Pol. III 119.

MY DEAR AMBASSADOR: By direction of the Foreign Minister, Baron von Neurath, I have the honor to send Your Excellency herewith a memorandum containing the reply to your note of December 26, 1936.[1]

The text of the German memorandum will be published in the Friday morning papers.

Baron von Neurath, to whom I transmitted the note which Your Excellency handed me yesterday,[2] also asked me to inform you in this connection that this new step had surprised him very much. After the detailed statements which he made to you on December 31, he was of the opinion that there was no need for such a reminder to the German Government.

With the expression of my highest esteem, I am, most respectfully yours,

GAUS

---

[1] Document No. 165, p. 183.
[2] Document No. 184, p. 203.

[Enclosure]

MEMORANDUM

January 7, 1937.

zu Pol. III 119.

The German Foreign Minister has the honor in the name of the German Government to reply as follows to the note of His Excellency, His Britannic Majesty's Ambassador, dated December 26, 1936:

1. The German Government must first express its astonishment that the British Government and the French Government have considered it necessary a second time to make a separate direct appeal outside the procedure of the London Non-Intervention Committee to the other governments represented on this committee. The question of prohibiting participation of foreign volunteers in the fighting in Spain, which is the subject of this appeal, is at present under consideration in the London committee. It is not conceivable how these deliberations could be benefited by such a method of separate diplomatic action by individual governments. If, however, the procedure in the committee for discussing the Spanish affair is considered inadequate or unsuitable, it would be in the interest of clarity and uniformity in the handling of these questions to dispense altogether with a continuance of the committee procedure.

2. The German Government must protest against the impression created by the new step of the British and French Governments, that the problem of the foreign volunteers in the Spanish Civil War is to be laid at Germany's door, or even that she has failed to recognize it. It therefore states once more that it was the German Government and the Italian Government which from the beginning demanded a ban on the departure of volunteer participants to the fighting in Spain and that it was the British Government and the French Government, on the other hand, which rejected such a ban.

3. The original position of the British and French Governments in this question could only be explained as indicating that the two Governments did not wish to see in the influx of volunteers any inadmissible intervention in Spanish affairs. If the two Governments now take a different attitude, the German Government must seriously ask itself whether the proposed ban would not at the present time in effect result in discrimination in favor of the forces fighting the Nationalist Spanish Government. Now that the stream of Bolshevist elements has been pouring in unhindered for months, it is really difficult to dispel the impression that the ban would now benefit only the Bolshevist party in Spain, which is obviously amply bolstered with foreign volunteers.

4. However, since from the very beginning the German Government has advocated the checking of the influx of volunteers into Spain, it is still willing to support all measures serving this end. It must at the same time, however, express the expectation that now all possibilities for direct or indirect intervention in the Spanish conflict be eliminated once and for all. Therefore it makes its approval conditional upon the following:

(*a*) The other powers concerned decide to adopt the same attitude;
(*b*) The solution of other problems connected with indirect intervention also be undertaken immediately; and
(*c*) All governments concerned adopt absolutely effective, locally enforced control measures for the embargoes to be agreed upon.

The German Government will instruct its representative in the London committee to conduct further negotiations on this basis. Should it be impossible to reach an agreement regarding the prevention of the other forms of indirect intervention, the German Government would have to reserve the right to reexamine its attitude on the question of volunteers, too.

The best solution of the problem of volunteers, in the opinion of the German Government, would be achieved if it were possible to remove from Spain all non-Spanish participants in the fighting, including political agitators and propagandists, and thus restore the condition of August of last year. The German Government would welcome it if the London committee would at once take under consideration how such a measure could be effectively carried out. It is prepared for its part to cooperate therein in every respect.

No. 191

1819/416113–16

The Ambassador in France to the Foreign Minister

PARIS, January 8, 1937.

DEAR BARON NEURATH: Understandably, developments in Spain are the center of interest here, and every conversation revolves around the question of the quickest way to put out the conflagration raging there. In view of my more than ten years of activity in Madrid, and since it is known in diplomatic and financial circles here that I was correct in predicting the fall of the monarchy as well as the systematic undermining activity of the Russian and German Communists in Spain aiming at the establishment of a Soviet republic on the Iberian Peninsula, I enjoy the reputation here of being somewhat of an authority on all matters pertaining to Spain; I have even been asked repeatedly by Government officials such as the Premier and the Foreign Minister to give my opinion. Consequently, I am also in a position to pick to pieces the basic views and deductions which obviously stem from the reports of Ambassador Herbette,[1] a follower of the Soviet line, whose views, while completely erroneous, still predominate here. Except for the observations I made in Spain, as far as present occurrences are concerned I unfortunately have at my disposal only Spanish sources and reports from the Italian Embassy. As for our present experiences on the side of the Nationalists, I am dependent on sketchy

---

[1] Jean Herbette, French Ambassador to Spain.

reports by German journalists passing through here. Even if our experiences are for the most part not suitable for transmittal, it would still be enlightening for me to know about them, since I often talk to Frenchmen fighting in Franco's ranks who are aware of everything going on there. It would at least be desirable if I had enough information to be able to refute the concrete figures regarding our latest troop transports given me by members of the French Government, such as those recently provided by Viénot. A simple denial is not enough, as you know. But if one says nothing at all, one is considered either a know-nothing or a secretive person. The principle followed by the Italians of conceding a part and representing this as being an answer to the French assistance is undoubtedly more effective. But in order to be able to do this one must at least be informed of what can be denied and what might more profitably be ignored. Just because the French regard me as being the best expert on Spain and because my words often fall on fertile soil, I could be effective here in an enlightening and pacifying capacity.

When Minister Chautemps, State Secretaries Viénot and De Tessan,[2] as well as other political figures, dined with me last night, the various possibilities for a solution of the Spanish question were discussed in detail. On this as on numerous other occasions I sought to make clear to the French how misleading and impracticable their proposals were and to reduce them to absurdity. Thus one constantly hears Frenchmen and Englishmen make the demand, which is not feasible in practice, that both Fascism and Communism be eliminated from Spain, since the Spaniards are suited to neither of these two doctrines. Spain should be left to the Spaniards, a plebiscite should be held, and other such utopian ideas. Most of these theorizers are not aware that even in peacetime there were very few Spaniards who favored a middle-of-the-road policy; most of them were either Red or White, but not pink as the Popular Front desires. If the middle-of-the-road policy was scarcely known before Franco's uprising, how could it be achieved after months and months of murdering! Another error is the opinion that the victory of the allegedly "Fascist" General Franco means the victory and definite establishment of Germany and Italy in Spain. I told the French that the Don Quixote type was practically extinct in Spain and that the character of Sancho Panza was the dominant type. When the Moor has served his purpose, he is usually told to go. Any Spanish government, even a Fascist government, would necessarily have to maintain correct relations with France and would have to have money for the reconstruction of the country. Loans could be had only

---

[2] Camille Chautemps, Minister of State, Pierre Viénot, Under Secretary of State in the Ministry of Foreign Affairs, and François de Tessan, Under Secretary of State in the Presidency of the Council, in the Cabinet of Léon Blum.

in America, France, and England; but one generally maintained good relations with money lenders, and for this reason alone it would be madness to believe that Italy, let alone Germany, would be permitted to set up a permanent base of operations in Spain. Every intelligent Frenchman should prefer the victory of Franco to Bolshevist chaos; there was no compromise solution.

The dispatch of an international expeditionary corps to Spain, an idea which had cropped up here, might, in view of the well-known xenophobia on the part of the Spaniards, perhaps lead to temporary agreement between Reds and Whites for a common struggle against the foreign occupation troops; but no other kind of agreement appeared possible to me.

In all the conversations I have had with Frenchmen, and with Englishmen, too, their complete ignorance of the Spanish mind and their helplessness as regards the solution of the problem have constantly been apparent.

In the event that we decide to continue military commitments in Spain, I urgently recommend that a calming statement be issued, approximately along the lines taken by the article which appeared in the *Börsenzeitung* some time ago.

With the most sincere greetings and Heil Hitler, I remain

WELCZECK

No. 192

47/31857–58

The Chargé d'Affaires in Spain to the Foreign Ministry

Telegram

STRICTLY SECRET   SALAMANCA, January 9, 1937—11 : 00 p.m.
No. 16 of January 9   Received January 10—5 : 40 a.m.
                                                                Pol. I 221 g.

For the Foreign Minister and the State Secretary personally.

On African soil and in Melilla there is a unit of German volunteers, namely, a squadron of seven seaplanes. Melilla, however, is not a part of the Spanish zone of Morocco, but an old Spanish possession, to which the Morocco agreement, so far as is known here, does not apply.

To what extent there are individual German volunteers in the Spanish Foreign Legion is not known. But the French *démarche* [1] can

---

[1] Rumors of German military activity in Spanish Morocco spread in December 1936. Early in January 1937, French troops were concentrated along the border of the French zone of Morocco, and on Jan. 9 the attention of the authorities of Spanish Morocco was directed to the promise given in the French-Spanish convention of Nov. 27, 1912, not to alienate rights in the Spanish sphere of influence in Morocco.

hardly apply to them. The latter apparently either was motivated by false reports or else is an intimidation maneuver.[2]

FAUPEL

---

[2] Marginal note in Neurath's handwriting: "Telegraph Welczeck. He should energetically dispel the fears of the French. There are no German volunteers of any kind in the Morocco zone."

Marginal note in Dumont's handwriting: "Superseded by the arrangement made at the Foreign Minister's New Year's reception. Count Welczeck has been informed by telegram. Jan. 16."

No. 193

1819/416117–18

The Ambassador in France to the Head of the Extra-European Section of the Political Department

PARIS, January 9, 1937.

DEAR HERR VON ERDMANNSDORFF: I should like to add a few points to yesterday's telegraphic report [1] about my conversation with Léger regarding an allegedly projected landing of German volunteer units in Spanish Morocco. Léger spoke very earnestly and impressively, but contrary to his usual habit was obviously striving to be as conciliatory in form as possible.

Then Léger in a few short words gave me his first impression of the German note of reply—François-Poncet had reported its main points to him over the telephone. The harsh polemical tone of the note—in paragraph No. 3 bad faith had even been imputed—unfortunately was in strong contrast to the conciliatory spirit which the French Government had been attempting to create—so far in vain—by means of the familiar announcements made to me by the Premier and the Foreign Minister. Besides, the tone of the note was in vivid contrast to the words with which our Foreign Minister had ended his conversation with Ambassador François-Poncet on December 31, when he had said that he confidently hoped that Spain, instead of being an apple of discord as hitherto, would shortly develop into a bond of conciliation and agreement. I replied to Léger that our note had been sent independently of the conciliatory step by the French Government. The reply to that step had yet to be made. The more thoroughly and energetically one proceeded with the settlement of the Spanish affair—and this required some plain speaking—the sooner the points of difference could be eliminated and the way opened for an agreement on the question. As a matter of fact this was the purpose of the note. In my opinion the note was thoroughly positive in tone; this, after all, was the one thing that really mattered. Léger conceded in general that I was right and only criticized the demand for a complete settle-

---

[1] Not found.

ment, which in his opinion was not feasible; surely one ought first to try to achieve what was possible, and not allow things to fail because of a demand for "all or nothing." I told Léger that the coarse meshes of the net which had thus far been thrown around Spain, in particular the loopholes on the side of the Pyrenees, had brought such a hypocritical spirit into the negotiations that the sooner this spirit was eliminated the better it would be for achieving practical results.

I consider the note very good. The French should be told the truth without reservations, something which I often do here in an even more unmistakable manner, without making myself particularly unpopular so far, to my knowledge. What I did not understand was why the month of August was mentioned in the note, for part of the French Red Front guardsmen were mobilized for Spain long before that and the principal ringleaders have been in Spain since the beginning of the year 1936.

With the most cordial greetings and Heil Hitler, I remain,

Sincerely yours,

WELCZECK

No. 194

3206/697689–91

Note from the British Embassy [1]

No. 13   BERLIN, January 10th, 1937.
(4/32/37)

His Majesty's Ambassador has the honour, under instructions from His Majesty's Principal Secretary of State for Foreign Affairs, to make the following communication to His Excellency the Minister for Foreign Affairs.

1. From the tenour of the replies now received to their communication to the Governments of Germany, Italy, Portugal and the Union of Socialist Soviet Republics of December 24th last, His Majesty's Government in the United Kingdom are happy to note that there is in principle general agreement among the Powers mainly concerned that immediate measures should be taken to stop the inflow of foreign volunteers into Spain. Indeed some of the replies indicate that certain Governments would have readily taken such action at an earlier stage. It is now generally stipulated that these measures should be simultaneously taken by all the participating Governments, that the whole problem of dealing with indirect forms of intervention in Spain is also actively pursued forthwith, and that there is established an efficient and effective system of control.

2. As regards the establishment of a system of control, the Governments are aware that the Non-Intervention Committee has elaborated a detailed scheme for supervision at Spanish ports and on the land frontiers of Spain and that this scheme is at present being con-

---

[1] The file copy of this document is in English.

sidered by the two parties in Spain. It appears to His Majesty's Government that this scheme could without difficulty be extended to cover the arrival in Spain, both by land and by sea, of volunteers and military personnel as well as of war material. Such an extension might indeed render the scheme more acceptable to the two parties in Spain than it may be in its present limited form.

3. His Majesty's Government recognise that this scheme, which provides for supervision, can only be made into a satisfactory guarantee of a genuine application of the agreement, provided all participating Governments are willing loyally and wholeheartedly to carry out their undertakings. They are encouraged by the reception which their previous communication has met with to believe these conditions will in fact prevail and that consequently the Non-Intervention Committee's present scheme, suitably adapted, may be sufficient for the purposes envisaged. Nevertheless they note that the Governments in their replies refer in various terms to the establishment of a system of rigid control of supplies to Spain. They would be glad to learn whether the Governments have in mind any particular methods or forms of control other than that described above. They are ready to consider with the utmost urgency any suggestions which may be put forward to this end. They would also be glad to consider any detailed proposals for the control of other forms of indirect intervention and would be ready for an early discussion by the Committee on Non-Intervention of any such proposals submitted to it.

4. In the meantime His Majesty's Government are themselves of opinion that the general desire expressed in the replies received from the other Governments for the exclusion of foreign volunteers and military personnel from Spain would warrant the immediate adoption by each Government within their own territories of the prohibitory measures required for that purpose, even in advance of the establishment of a complete system of control for Spain.

5. As evidence of their sincere desire to reach international agreement at once on this aspect of indirect intervention in Spain His Majesty's Government are spontaneously and without further delay issuing a public notice in which attention is drawn to the fact that it is an offence punishable under the Foreign Enlistment Act for British subjects to accept or agree to any commission or engagement in the forces of either side or for any person to recruit volunteers in the United Kingdom for service in Spain.

6. It is in the hope of receiving a favourable response to the above suggestions that His Majesty's Government propose to communicate to the London Committee on Non-Intervention the exchanges of views which have taken place since their communication of December 24th last, with the replies of the German Government and other Governments to their present communication, with the request that, in the event of these replies expressing agreement to this suggestion the Committee should then fix a date on which the prohibitory measures referred to above should be simultaneously put into operation.

7. His Majesty's Government desire in this connection to explain that in addressing their communication of December 24th last on the subject of the inflow of foreign volunteers into Spain, direct to the Governments of Germany, Portugal, Italy and the Union of Socialist Soviet Republics His Majesty's Government in the United Kingdom were impressed by the gravity of the situation which had developed

and were convinced that it was in the general interest imperative that immediate decisions should be taken by the Powers mainly concerned to concert remedial measures.

8. In taking this step His Majesty's Government had no wish or intention to interfere with the activities of the Committee on Non-Intervention established in London. On the contrary it was from a desire to facilitate and expedite the task of that Committee that they addressed themselves to the four Powers direct in the hope that by taking a lead on the particular issues raised by the Governments mainly concerned they might assist the other Governments represented on the Committee to arrive at speedier conclusions.

9. His Majesty's Ambassador has the honour, in making the above communication to Baron von Neurath, to request that His Excellency will be so good as to favour him with a very early reply.

10. A similar communication is being addressed to the French, Italian, Portuguese and Union of Socialist Soviet Republics' Governments by His Majesty's Representatives in the capitals concerned.

No. 195

643/254223–24

Memorandum by the Foreign Minister

RM 11   BERLIN, January 11, 1937.
                                              Pol. III 170 a.

The French Ambassador, who is leaving for Paris this evening, called on me this afternoon. He told me that when he spoke about the alleged aims of Germany in Spanish Morocco at the reception in the Presidential Palace this morning, the Führer categorically stated that Germany had no territorial or political aspirations whatsoever either in Spain or in Morocco. The Ambassador thereupon declared that the French Government did not intend to alter existing conditions in Morocco, which meant that it would not encroach in any way upon Spanish sovereignty. He, Poncet, had immediately telephoned the Führer's statement, which was exceedingly important, to M. Delbos, who had expressed his very great satisfaction with it. It would help considerably to calm public opinion in France if the Führer's statement could be published. At the same time his own statement regarding the absence of any French designs whatsoever against Spanish Morocco could also be published.

The Ambassador asked if I had any objections to such publication. I replied that if publication would help to allay the hysterical nervousness in France, which was gradually assuming dangerous proportions, then I had no objections whatsoever. Moreover, the Führer's statement merely confirmed the view which we had repeatedly emphasized, and which we had expressed to him, too. I reminded the Ambassador of the conversation which I had had with him recently, on December 31, when I had told him exactly the same thing. The Ambassador then replied that I had not, however, said anything about Spanish Morocco, but only about Spain.   I told him that Spanish Morocco had not been an issue at all at that time.

M. Poncet said that he wished to get in touch with M. Delbos once more to have him confirm that publication of the sentence pertaining to Spanish Morocco was satisfactory to him.   Some time later M. Poncet called me back on the telephone and informed me that M. Delbos had given his consent to the intended publication.   M. Poncet would, however, appreciate also having this statement reprinted by the German press.   I told him that I would try to have this done.

BARON V. NEURATH

No. 196

1534/374403–04

The Chargé d'Affaires in Spain to the Foreign Ministry

Telegram

No. 21 of January 12   SALAMANCA, January 12, 1937—7:20 p.m.
Received January 13—6:00 a.m.

With reference to our telegraphic report No. 629 of December 31 [1] and written report 322 S A 10 of January 1.

As is known there, the Italians have begun to commit a strong military force during the last few days.   Its effect on the military situation will make itself felt as soon as the troops are completely assembled. Because of the tremendous significance of the conduct of the war for the political attitude of the Nationalist Government, it is to be expected that the Italian commitment will result in a further increase in Italy's political influence, while, on the other hand, the Nationalist Government's dependence on us will decrease.   The fear cannot be dismissed that our political influence, which heretofore was on a par with the Italian, will fall to second place.

For this reason it would seem to be to our interest to conclude negotiations about economic and compensation questions before this development has become clearly apparent.   I suggest therefore that a delegation be sent here speedily for negotiations.[2]

FAUPEL

---

[1] Not printed (3176/682878).
[2] A note appended to this document, which is from the files of the Reich Chancellery, reads as follows:
"1. The Führer desires that the suggestion at the end of the telegram be acted on as soon as possible.
2. I have informed the Foreign Minister.
3. Respectfully submitted to:
   a. Ministerialdirektor Wienstein
   b. Ministerial Counselor Röhrecke
for their information.   Berlin, Jan. 15, 1937
4. To be filed.   L[ammers]"

No. 197

701/261170–71

The Foreign Minister to the Embassy in Italy

Telegram

URGENT   BERLIN, January 12, 1937—9 : 10 p.m.
No. 11 of January 12   Received January 12—9 : 40 p.m.

I request that you communicate as soon as possible with Count Ciano regarding a reply to the last British note on the question of volunteers.[1]

We believe we should not delay our reply but should send it by about the end of this week. We should, in our opinion, state that we are prepared in principle to prohibit by law any Germans from leaving for Spain for military or other participation in the Civil War, making reference to our note of January 7.[2] First there would have to be a binding agreement, however, among the powers represented on the London committee regarding the substance of the ban and the date when it is to become effective. We would, moreover, demand that the powers concerned, including the two Spanish parties, agree that the control measures intended for the Spanish land and sea frontiers also be extended to the entry of volunteers. The control measures would also have to be put into actual operation not too long after the exit ban goes into effect. Finally, we would stress that we insist on the proposal made at the end of our note of January 7 concerning the withdrawal of all non-Spanish participants, and that we would soon submit a concrete proposal to this effect in the London committee.

General Göring has been informed of the above-mentioned guiding principles but will not include the subject of a reply to the British note in his negotiations.[3]

NEURATH

---

[1] Document No. 194, p. 216.
[2] Document No. 190, p. 210.
[3] Göring arrived in Rome on Jan. 13. His visit was made the occasion for public statements on the solidarity of the Rome-Berlin Axis. As Göring did not report on the discussion in Rome through the German Embassy (see document No. 203, p. 225), little information on these discussions has been found in the archives of the German Foreign Ministry.

No. 198

47/31860

The Ambassador in Italy to the Foreign Ministry

Telegram

SECRET
No. 8 of January 12

ROME, January 13, 1937—3 : 05 a.m.
Received January 13—6 : 30 a.m.
Pol. I 229 g.

For the Foreign Minister.

Ciano informed me today that in transmitting the second note concerning the volunteers the British Ambassador had . . . (group garbled) the desire that Italy, even before giving her official reply, take measures on her own forbidding additional volunteers to leave the country. Ciano had declined to do so, referring to the continuous flow across the French borders for the purpose of further reinforcing the 45,000 Red volunteers already there.[1]

He thought the further tactics should be to delay the reply for another few days, because on January 14 an additional 4,000 men will be shipped; in addition, a new division, or 9,000 combat troops plus 4,000 other personnel, will be ready between January 22 and January 25. He then said that the text of the reply should be agreed upon by our two Governments, as was done last time. The main emphasis should be placed on the working out in advance of an effective control system on the basis of the committee's old draft, and on reaching agreement among all participating governments regarding the simultaneous entry into force of the ban on volunteers.

Within 10 days to 2 weeks the Italian forces are to carry out a surprise offensive against Málaga, which will be the general base of further operations on the part of Italy and will be important for shortening the front.

Through the mediation of the Vatican negotiations are being carried on in the north with the Basque separatists at Bilbao.

HASSELL

---

[1] An account of this conversation is given in *L'Europa verso la catastrofe*, pp. 124–125 (*Ciano's Diplomatic Papers*, pp. 78–80).

No. 199

47/31859

The Chargé d'Affaires in Spain to the Foreign Ministry

Telegram

STRICTLY SECRET   SALAMANCA, January 13, 1937—7 : 45 p.m.
No. 23 of January 12   Received January 14—12 : 40 a.m.
                                                        Pol. I 228 g.

For the Foreign Minister and the State Secretary personally.

In the last few days large contingents of Italian volunteers with equipment, particularly heavy artillery, have landed in Cádiz. When the Italian general assumes his duties, these troops will be organized into a division. The men and the officers are volunteers, about half of them being veterans of the Ethiopian campaign. The strength of the contingent was determined not by previous agreement with Franco but according to independent Italian estimates.

FAUPEL

No. 200

137/128218–19

Memorandum by the Foreign Minister

RM 16   BERLIN, January 13, 1937.

The Italian Ambassador, who called on me today to discuss various matters, also showed me a telegram from Rome concerning the tentative position of the Italian Government regarding the last British note. (The telegram corroborates telegram No. 8 from Ambassador von Hassell.[1]) Signor Attolico repeatedly endeavors to induce us to send larger troop contingents to Spain. I told him clearly today that we were not prepared to do this, because we considered that such a step would seriously endanger the larger European situation. Unless we wanted to accept the risk of war, we would have to realize that the time was drawing near when we would have to abandon any further support of Franco. In the last note to the British we had therefore agreed in principle to an understanding regarding the question of volunteers, and we now had to take a definite position regarding the second note. It was perhaps possible to delay taking a definite stand for a few days more, and naturally we would not only have to demand actual control measures and simultaneous enforcement of the embargo on volunteers, but we would also have to adhere to it. The Ambassador suggested that in the reply to the British note the demand be made that the French first

---

[1] Document No. 198, p. 221.

take effective measures to stop the stream of volunteers. I told him that I considered it more advisable to demand the simultaneous entry into force of the embargo on volunteers, since the French would probably reject acting ahead of others just as we and the Italians would.

Furthermore, I informed the Ambassador of the instruction sent by us to Hassell last night.[2]

BARON V. NEURATH

[2] Document No. 197, p. 220.

No. 201

3376/E011159–61

The Chargé d'Affaires in France to the Foreign Ministry

[Telegram]

No. 38 of January 14   PARIS, January 14, 1937.

With reference to your No. 17 of January 12.[1]

In regard to the background of the most recent French *démarche* regarding Morocco and the hate campaign against Germany in the French press, I received from several frequently well-informed sources the following strictly confidential account of events, which I think is generally accurate: On Thursday, January 7, during the absence of Blum and Delbos, alarming reports came to Viénot from Resident-General Noguès in Rabat regarding an alleged German penetration into Spanish Morocco. Viénot got in touch with Blum by telephone and received instructions to take immediate steps. This resulted in Léger's *démarche* with Count Welczeck at 7:00 p.m. In that *démarche* the emphasis was not on allegedly accomplished facts but rather on a warning. Simultaneously, Corbin was requested to inform the British Government and to ask that it support France in case of further developments. Vansittart, who received Corbin, had agreed to energetic measures in case the reports transmitted by the French Government should prove correct. To be sure, Eden later did not entirely uphold the Under Secretary. In addition, Viénot decided to play the matter up considerably in the press, in spite of certain doubts expressed by Léger and Comert.[2] Consequently, the French journalists at the daily evening conferences had been given details about the reports of a German penetration into Morocco, which was already supposed to have taken place, and the press was mobilized against Germany.

On the basis of investigations then made on the spot, not only the

[1] Not found.
[2] Pierre Comert, Chief of Press and Foreign Service in the French Ministry of Foreign Affairs.

Foreign Minister, who had in the meantime returned to Paris, but also the journalists were convinced that the press campaign had far overshot its mark. In recognition of this, no full-scale counterattack against the German retort issued by DNB was undertaken. The German tactics of repaying in kind rather met with a certain amount of understanding. On the other hand, the reference in the DNB announcement to the attitude of French Rightist circles was a help to the instigators of the press campaign, forcing the Rightist papers to swing fully into line in a common front. Indeed, as seen from here, this reference is regrettable. Although the very great differences between Right and Left, especially in the Spanish question, represent a factor which we should watch carefully and, if there is the opportunity, take advantage of, every appeal to these differences publicly in Germany is interpreted as interference in French domestic affairs on the part of Germany, an interference which everybody here rejects. When the facts of the case had been ascertained and the Führer had made his statement to the French Ambassador, the originators of the press campaign had the ground cut from under them. They now attempted to tell the journalists, who felt that they had been made fools of, that the press campaign was a success in that it had shown that in the face of an allegedly imminent German attack the entire public opinion of France, including Rightist circles, was uniformly closing ranks behind the Government, enabling it to prevent further developments by sounding an alarm. Nevertheless dissatisfaction with the mistaken press campaign is said to linger in the minds of many of the journalists who were forced to follow this line outwardly. The same opinion regarding the press campaign is also likely to be held by the statesmen responsible for foreign policy. As the reports of the Embassy show, the principal line followed in the foreign policy of Blum and Delbos is to convince Germany and world public opinion that France will not put up with any more *faits accomplis* by Germany. Since Morocco is known to be a particularly sensitive spot for France, the alarming reports from there had induced the Government all the more readily to demonstrate this determination by a practical example, even though it did not completely believe them. In this connection the intention of responsible statesmen is likely to have been more clearly expressed in Léger's statements than in the press campaign. It appears to me to be perfectly credible that the patent excesses and provocations against Germany in the press campaign went too far for the leading statesmen, even if they were pleased with the unanimous attitude of the press. The decidedly favorable reception which, I understand, the Government accorded the Führer and Chancellor's statement is in line with this.

FORSTER

No. 202

701/261162–63

The Foreign Minister to the Embassy in Italy

Telegram

No. 15 of January 14   BERLIN, January 14[, 1937]—5 : 44 p.m.
                               Received January 14—6 : 45 p.m.

Attolico informed us here yesterday that the Italians had received
from Franco the draft of the reply which Franco intended to make
to the control plans submitted to him by the London committee for his
consideration. According to this, Franco intends to reject control
fundamentally and finally, giving as his reason that it would mean an
intolerable limitation of sovereignty for the Nationalist movement
and that it would favor the Red Army exclusively.

We consider such a purely negative reply very questionable. It
would immediately cause the entire work of the London committee to
fail, but above all it would expose us and the Italians to the reproach
that, while for external consumption we were saying "yes," we had
induced Franco to say "no." As things stand, the matter is very
important because the question of control measures might under certain circumstances form the point of departure for a solution of the
Spanish problem. Consequently, the matter is most intimately related
to the conversations going on there at the present time. We would
therefore consider it advisable that Franco, on the contrary, should
agree to control in principle but should stipulate certain plausible
conditions whose implementation would mean a gain in time. A condition that might be considered is that control would only be acceptable if it covered all forms of foreign intervention, particularly volunteers, since otherwise it would work exclusively in favor of the Red
Army. Please discuss the matter there immediately and inform
Göring.

NEURATH

No. 203

43/28735

Memorandum of the Dienststelle Ribbentrop [1]

BERLIN, January 15, 1937.

According to a remark of Baron von Weizsäcker of the Foreign
Ministry (on Thursday, January 14), the Spanish enterprise is to be

---

[1] This report is in the files of the Dienststelle Ribbentrop. The material assembled by this private information service of the Ambassador was usually, as in
this case, presented in memoranda by its head, Rudolf Likus.

abandoned. It is only a question of drawing Germany out of the affair gracefully, that is, without loss of prestige.

On the same matter there is a report from Göring's immediate entourage: The decision on further German involvement in Spain will be made in Rome. Colonel General Göring in his conversations with Mussolini will clarify the Spanish problem with respect to the risk Germany and Italy are willing to assume. Upon this depends whether and how the involvement in Spain is to be extended. In his conversation with Mussolini, Göring will state that under no circumstances will Germany tolerate a Red Spain. In addition, there will be a firm decision on everything which the two countries will undertake from now on through their representatives on the London Non-Intervention Committee.

My informant hears further on this, that the Führer and Göring agreed that the German answer to the last Anglo-French note would be made after Göring had reported on his Italian journey.

LIKUS

No. 204

137/128212

The Ambassador in Italy to the Foreign Ministry

Telegram

SECRET   ROME, January 15, 1937—6 : 00 p.m.
No. 12 of January 15   Received January 15—8 : 20 p.m.

For the Foreign Minister.

Colonel General Göring will himself report on the course of the discussions thus far and their further progress. As far as the political aspect is concerned, leaving aside military matters, the following should be said now about the situation: Since there is agreement that the last effort to help Franco should be made by January 31—with Germany supplying matériel only—it appears advisable to accord dilatory treatment to the British note until then. To be specific, replies should be worked out in about four or five days on the basis of the views already agreed upon, but containing a remark to the effect that England had not accepted the idea of general evacuation advanced by Germany and Italy and was now being asked to comment on it. Ciano added that in the further course of the discussions the question could be asked whether the conditions essential for assured control had been created; this would certainly not be the case, since Franco—and perhaps Valencia too—rejected control.

I then discussed the contents of your telegram No. 15 of yesterday with Mussolini as well as with Ciano and also with General Göring. The Italians agree with us that a fundamental and final rejection of control by Franco is tactically inadvisable. The Italian Chargé d'Affaires at Salamanca will be instructed to try to bring about a reply in line with the above-mentioned telegraphic instruction.

HASSELL

No. 205

2938/569697–98

The Director of the Political Department to the Embassy in Spain

Telegram

No. 25   BERLIN, January 15, 1937—10 : 15 p.m.

W II WE 341/37 II.

Drafting Officer: Counselor of Legation Dumont.

We should be grateful to receive information on the agreements regarding the Rio Tinto mines.[1] We hear from the Army Economic Planning Staff [*Wehrwirtschaftsstab*] that it is a question of agreements between Franco, the British, and us, placing 40 percent of the total output of the mines confiscated by Franco at the disposal of the British, and 60 percent at our disposal. Of this amount we are supposedly obligated to give 20 percent to Franco. According to other reports disseminated by the British press, official investigations undertaken by the British had revealed that products of the Rio Tinto Company and the Sulphur and Copper Company of Glasgow had been confiscated by the Franco Government and resold to German manufacturers. The British companies had, however, received compensation from the Spanish Government for the products which were requisitioned. This compensation would not be paid at the black-market rate of exchange for pesetas (100 pesetas=one pound) but at the official rate (42 pesetas=one pound). Nevertheless, the British companies had requested their Government not to interfere. Evidently they were by no means so dissatisfied with the present treatment of the matter as the press indicated.

WEIZSÄCKER

---

[1] On Jan. 13 Woermann reported that "the alleged confiscation of the Rio Tinto mines for the benefit of copper exports to Germany" had led to a lengthy discussion in the main subcommittee of the Non-Intervention Committee. Woermann requested information on the subject (2938/569695–96).

No. 206

3176/682895–96

The Director of the Economic Policy Department to the Embassy in Spain

Telegram

No. 26   BERLIN, January 16, 1937.
                                                  W II WE 335 I.

With reference to your telegraphic report No. 21 [1] and written report Sa. III 360 of January 7.

1. Conclusion of an agreement of a political nature is out of the question for the present.[2]   On the other hand, we are entirely of your opinion, that negotiation for a commercial agreement should be started as soon as possible.

2. The preliminary work will be speeded up and the economic delegation is expected to leave by plane at the end of next week, so that negotiations can begin there about Monday, January 25.   Please make sure that by that date the Spanish negotiators will also be available for negotiations on a full-time basis, so that the German delegation need not stay there too long.   Please wire whether the negotiations will take place in Salamanca or in Burgos.

3. The leader of the German economic delegation will again be Geheimrat Wucher, who has for many years headed the delegations to Spain.   Two or three representatives of the ministries concerned, as well as a representative of Rowak, either Herr von Jagwitz or Herr Bethke,[3] will be members of the delegation.   These appointments and the composition of the delegation are based on agreements with State Secretary Körner.   Naturally the delegation is counting on the closest collaboration of Herr Bernhardt.

4. Please wire, because of preparations here, what is meant by the "compensation question" in telegraphic report No. 21.   Does this refer to payment for German deliveries to date or compensation for damage sustained by Reich Germans in Spain in connection with the disorders?

5. Please report at once concerning the status of the negotiations or agreements between the Nationalist Government and Italy and England on economic questions and matters of compensation.   What agreement was reached with England regarding the duty on coal?   It would be very desirable if the full text of such agreements could be dispatched by air mail.

                                                                    RITTER

---

[1] Document No. 196, p. 219.
[2] The first draft of this sentence reads as follows: "For the time being, we withhold an instruction as to whether negotiations leading toward an agreement of a political nature are to be initiated, either now or in the near future."
[3] Friedrich Bethke, director of Rowak and department head in the Economics Ministry.

No. 207

47/31868–69

The Chargé d'Affaires in Spain to the Foreign Ministry

SECRET   SALAMANCA, January 18, 1937.

Sa. 3–459   Received January 22.

              Pol. I 338 g.

Subject: Report on the general situation.

According to a statement by Mancini, about 20,000 Italians with two battalions of heavy artillery and 1,800 trucks are to be ready for action by the end of January in the vicinity of Seville. As a result of this prompt and powerful assistance the crisis that existed in December may be regarded as definitely overcome. Our latest deliveries cannot take effect until much later since the units to be equipped with them must first be trained and organized. On the whole, the prospects of military success are far more favorable now. Nevertheless, even if operations proceed smoothly, months will probably still pass before the borders of Catalonia proper are reached.

Mancini told me that Italy had thus far put about 800 million lire into the Spanish enterprise; he anticipated an additional 200 million lire. I am reporting these figures with all due reservations. Furthermore, Mancini states that in return for this Italy has thus far got virtually nothing out of Spain. If this is true, we have obtained far more in this respect through Hisma.

In internal politics the Carlists and other monarchist groups have in the last few weeks drawn closer to the Government and a certain coolness has set in between the Government and the Falange; this, however, is to be overcome. The Government believes at present that by taking over part of the Falange program it can carry out social reforms even without the Falange itself. This is possible. But it is not possible without the cooperation of the Falange to imbue the Spanish workers, especially those in the Red territory to be reconquered, with national and really practicable social ideas and to win them over to the new state. For that reason collaboration between the Government and the Falange is still indispensable.

The enclosed minute gives a few indications of the view prevailing among the Carlists.[1]

              FAUPEL

---

[1] Not printed (47/31870–71). The minute summarized a conversation between four Carlist leaders and Faupel. The Carlists affirmed their sympathy for Nazi Germany and their recognition of the necessity for social reform is Spain.

No. 208

2938/569699

The Chargé d'Affaires in Spain to the Foreign Ministry

Telegram

No. 34 of January 20   SALAMANCA, January 20, 1937—8 : 00 p.m.
Received January 21—4 : 30 a.m.
W II WE 519 a.

With reference to telegraphic instruction No. 25 of January 15.

The Nationalist Government assures us that the information regarding agreements on the Rio Tinto mines is incorrect. The arrangement proposed by the British on the basis indicated was flatly rejected by Spain for the reason that the company is an enterprise under Spanish law. The Spanish Government explicitly reserved for itself full freedom of action in distributing the production of Rio Tinto. Hisma has a written promise from the Franco Government that it will receive up to 60 percent of the production at the rate of 42 pesetas to one pound sterling. It can be expected that a final contract will be concluded in the very near future. Hisma requests that for the present we do not interfere in the negotiations.

FAUPEL

[EDITORS' NOTE. In *L'Europa verso la catastrofe*, pp. 126–142 (*Ciano's Diplomatic Papers*, pp. 80–91), there is a summary of the conversation of Göring, Mussolini, and Ciano in Rome, on January 23, 1937. On Spain, there was agreement that, since Franco had now been amply supplied with men and arms, Germany and Italy should support the British proposal to prohibit the entrance of volunteers into Spain. There was also agreement that the Spanish Civil War must not lead to a general European war. Although the summary as printed is signed by the German interpreter, Paul Otto Schmidt, no copy has been found in the archives of the German Foreign Ministry.]

No. 209

47/31878

The Chargé d'Affaires in Spain to the Foreign Ministry

Telegram

No. 57 of January 24   SALAMANCA, January 25, 1937.
Received January 25—3 : 20 p.m.
Pol. I 394 g.

For the Foreign Minister personally and the State Secretary personally.

The memorandum agreed upon in Rome regarding the extent and duration of German and Italian assistance for the Nationalist Government was given Franco yesterday by Ciano's Chef de Cabinet, Anfuso. The text of the memorandum will leave by courier tomorrow.[1]

Franco will comment on it this evening. I shall wire again when I learn what his comment is.

FAUPEL

---

[1] Not found.

No. 210

47/31886

The Chargé d'Affaires in Spain to the Foreign Ministry

Telegram

No. 61 of January 25   SALAMANCA, January 25, 1937—11 : 55 p.m.
Received January 26—12 : 15 a.m.
Pol. I 455 g.

For the Foreign Minister and the State Secretary personally.

With reference to my telegraphic report No. 57 of the 24th.

The Nationalist Government replied with a detailed note to the German-Italian memorandum mentioned in the previous telegram. After some introductory remarks regarding the difficulty of effective control and the need of the Nationalist forces for arms and war matériel, the latter are enumerated in detail. These demands, which exceed the concessions made in the German-Italian memorandum, are addressed partly to Italy, but chiefly to us. A translation of the list [1] left with today's courier in a private letter to Ministerialdirektor Dieckhoff.

FAUPEL

---

[1] Not found.

No. 211

47/31889–90

The Chargé d'Affaires in Spain to the Foreign Ministry

Telegram

No. 62 of January 26   SALAMANCA, January 26, 1937.
Received January 27—10 : 45 a.m.
Pol. I 475 g.

For the Foreign Minister and the State Secretary personally.

With reference to my telegraphic report No. 61 of the 25th.

The note of the Nationalist Government mentioned at the beginning of the previous telegram reads as follows:

"The Government of General Franco has studied the note of the German and Italian Governments and thanks both nations for their sympathy and aid, also for their decision to increase this aid in order to achieve an early victory which will restore peace to Spain, and the principles and order of western civilization which she is defending.

"The Nationalist Army will shun no efforts to bring the work it has begun to a speedy conclusion. The Nationalist Government therefore submits to the Italian and the German Governments the following considerations, which serve on the one hand to clarify its international position respecting the probability of a control of supplies and on the other hand to show the situation in which the Army finds itself on account of this probability and its indispensable requirements for a successful continuation of the campaign. The form that the control is to take is unknown. In its replies to the British note the Nationalist Government formulated its standpoint in terms of a rejection of the control proposal transmitted by England and a refusal to have it put into effect in the territory of the Nationalist Government.

"This control could not cut off the supplies being delivered to our enemy, since it would apply only to those states which agreed to it. There are countries, however, which have not agreed, among them Mexico; she has sold her flag and made her ships, including warships, available for contraband en route to the Red zone, and she undoubtedly intends to continue this traffic. Thus the governments of the nations which have given us their friendship and the honor of recognition will surely realize that, if the control is carried out, incidents will result which in the present situation our enemies desire, as their propaganda proves, in the hope of prolonging the Spanish Civil War."

The further text of the note, except for the addition given below and insignificant changes, is identical with the list of requirements of the Nationalist Government sent by Franco to General Sander, which left by courier yesterday as annex 3 of report Sa. 13–544/37 [1] in a private letter to Ministerialdirektor Dieckhoff. The only significant change is the proposal that Italy and Germany, in case one of them cannot supply all the matériel which he asks for in his note, agree on portioning the delivery between themselves to the best of their ability.

FAUPEL

---

[1] Not found.

No. 212

3253/E000705–07

The Foreign Minister to the Embassy in Great Britain

Telegram

No. 32   BERLIN, January 26, 1937—9 : 35 p.m.

Brücklmeier [1] will deliver oral instructions on the Spanish question. For your guidance in the discussions at the next committee meeting: We assume that at the next session a position will first be taken on the replies of Franco and the Red Government to the question,

---

[1] A secretary in the London Embassy.

whether they agreed to a plan for control within Spain. On the basis of Franco's note particularly, a plan for control within Spain is probably out of the question, but let the other powers take the lead in finding this out. In case an appeal should be directed to us and Italy to use our influence with Franco again, please reply that you would have to transmit the proposal to Berlin for a decision.

As far as control outside Spain is concerned, we and the Italians are pursuing the intention of putting through a control that is effective in every respect, to go into force some time after the middle of February, but not earlier than February 10. You will, however, give strong emphasis even now to the German desire for establishment of a control that is effective in every respect.

On the subject of the control plans before the committee, please state in very general terms that we are willing to participate in the control. In order to facilitate a decision and expedite the matter as much as possible, we are prepared to join in any form of control generally approved in the committee, on the condition that it is set up effectively and on a parity basis and does not extend to German sovereign territory. With respect to the naval patrol, therefore, we reject any activity by agents in German ports.

We realize that in the case of control outside Spain the Portuguese problem can cause difficulties. If any influence is again to be exerted on Portugal to induce her to permit control on Portuguese territory, we should like to leave this mainly to England. Should a proposal be made to include Portugal in the naval patrol, you will state that you have to transmit the proposal to your Government. Please keep in close touch with Grandi on all these questions.

There are no objections to agreeing to the measures against financial support as proposed in document 261.[2] Settlement of the gold question[3] in the manner desired by us is not an absolute prerequisite for this.

NEURATH

---

[2] Of the Non-Intervention Committee.
[3] That is, the use of the gold reserve of the Bank of Spain by the Madrid Government. See document No. 221, p. 243.

No. 213

47/31895–99

Memorandum by an Official of Political Division I

BERLIN, January 26, 1937.
e. o. Pol. I 731 g.

Admiral Canaris, Director of the Intelligence Department [*Abt. Abwehr*] in the War Ministry, summoned me today on an urgent matter. A White Spaniard was with him by the name of Augusto Miranda, who is staying in Berlin (Eden Hotel) at the moment, and whom Admiral Canaris has known well for a long time. Señor Miranda is the successor of the Spanish flier, De la Cierva, who was killed in an accident and who had been commissioned by General Franco to go to London and promote arms purchases from there. Señor Miranda now has the same task.

Señor Miranda stated as follows:

Herr Bernhardt of Hisma called on General Franco a few days ago and told him that all the foreign exchange which is available to General Franco must be placed at the disposal of Herr Bernhardt or Hisma. In view of the extraordinary services that Germany had rendered General Franco in the past, this demand was not unreasonable. In his statement, which had made a very strong impression upon General Franco, Herr Bernhardt gave him to understand that he was acting in a semiofficial capacity.

Shortly after this conversation with Herr Bernhardt, General Franco summoned his brother, Nicolás Franco, and Señor Miranda to discuss Bernhardt's demand with them. Both gentlemen had opposed meeting this demand. General Franco had not wished to reject it outright, however, and had directed his brother Nicolás to speak with General Faupel. General Faupel had supported the demands of Herr Bernhardt in principle and had shielded him in every way. He had, nevertheless, reserved a final opinion.

So much for "the facts," as Señor Miranda expressed it. Señor Miranda explained briefly to Admiral Canaris and me why Nicolás Franco and he (Miranda) were opposed to granting Bernhardt's demands. Señor Miranda pointed out that the value of the German deliveries was entirely disproportionate to the foreign exchange at General Franco's disposal. If the Germans wished to insist on the surrender of this foreign exchange, it would be possible to apply it only in small part to deliveries of matériel from Germany, and it would be lost in the general reckoning. If General Franco, however, could dispose of his foreign exchange as before, then he was in a position through his representative to buy additional arms and matériel in all sorts of places. He wished to point out further that Bernhardt was not an arms dealer, whereas the Spaniards whom Franco had charged with this task had been in the arms business for years. An attempt had been made once before to put through an arms transaction directly with Bernhardt, but the result had been as unsatisfactory as it could possibly have been. Working from London, he, Miranda, purchased arms everywhere and was in touch with the best-known arms dealers in Holland, Germany, etc. He had, for instance, concluded various transactions with the well-known German arms dealer, Veltgens, which had been executed concurrently with the regular German deliveries. He also had to point out that the foreign exchange at General Franco's disposal had been supplied almost exclusively by Spanish patriots and friends of the Spanish cause, who would not understand it if their money were used to give Herr Bernhardt a monopoly position in foreign-exchange questions. Señor Miranda added further that in his opinion Herr Bernhardt was extremely unpopular in all leading Spanish circles.

Señor Miranda made his statement in an entirely composed and restrained manner. He did not make a bad impression personally. Miranda is ready to repeat his statements in the Foreign Ministry at any time. Admiral Canaris leaves it entirely to the Foreign Ministry to evaluate these statements.

Herewith respectfully submitted to Minister Baron von Weizsäcker.[1]

DÖRNBERG

---

[1] Marginal note: "State Secretary Körner considers the information improbable. He will have a further report sent us. W[eizsäcker]. Jan. 27."

An appended memorandum reads as follows:

"I discussed the matter today with Herr Bernhardt. It developed that Miranda's statements do contain a germ of truth, to be sure, but in the main are not correct.

"Bernhardt told me the following about it:

"Germany had made the deliveries to Spain in the last half year almost entirely without payment. So far as any payment was made at all, it was made in goods. Only in exceptional cases was a relatively small amount of foreign exchange given. It should be stated at the same time, however, that the Franco Government was paying other countries in foreign exchange with the relatively small means at its disposal. Señor Miranda, in particular, had in the past carried on these transactions involving cash payments in foreign exchange. Bernhardt had recently requested that if the Franco Government could make payments in foreign exchange, this be done exclusively in favor of Germany. He gave as a particular reason for this that after the last large deliveries to Spain it was no longer necessary for General Franco to procure any additional supplies at all from other countries. The reason given formerly, which had had a certain validity, was that the Franco Government had been forced to obtain deliveries from other countries also, where something was to be had only in return for foreign exchange; this reason has, in Bernhardt's opinion, disappeared entirely, in consequence of the last large German delivery. He therefore considered it right and just that Franco pay Germany the little foreign exchange that he can use for this purpose.

"This seems to me quite justified. The main thing is to present it properly to Señor Franco. I definitely have the impression that Herr Bernhardt made his justified demand in a form that cannot give offense to Señor Franco. So far as I was able to clarify the matter in the conversation with Bernhardt, it is largely a question of a certain business jealousy on the part of Señor Miranda, regarding whom, moreover, Herr Bernhardt said nothing unfavorable.

R[itter]
January 28, 1937"

These two interviews were described to the German diplomatic mission at Salamanca in an instruction of Feb. 16 signed by Dumont (47/31900–03) which concluded, "I would be grateful if you would speak to General Franco on this matter in a suitable fashion and inform him of Bernhardt's statements."

No. 214

47/31887

The Chargé d'Affaires in Spain to the Foreign Ministry

Telegram

URGENT   SALAMANCA, January 27, 1937—10: 00 p.m.
No. 67 of January 27   Received January 28—12: 30 a.m.
                                                          Pol. I 456 g.

For the Foreign Minister and the State Secretary personally.

At the request of Anfuso and Mancini I called on Franco last evening with them.   To the question as to which portion of the extensive deliveries requested by him on the basis of the German-Italian memorandum was especially urgent, Franco answered that all the matériel he was now requesting was urgently necessary in order to bring the war to a successful conclusion.   Anfuso remarked that the German and Italian experts, on whose judgments the decisions in Rome were based, were of the opinion that Franco could end the war with the matériel promised in the German-Italian memorandum.   Franco replied that he was trying with all his might to win the war, but that the German-Italian experts' estimates of the requirements for the coming months, in particular of explosives for the production of artillery shells and aircraft bombs, had been much too low.

Franco declared himself in agreement with the plan for a joint German-Italian general staff.   Mancini proposed a general staff of some five German and five Italian officers, with each of these groups under the command of an experienced colonel.   Franco agreed to this.

It is my personal opinion that this German-Italian general staff is absolutely necessary in order to assure the necessary influence on operations and their expert execution.   I take the liberty of suggesting Colonel Knauer (Ret.), as head of the German general staff group. In the World War he was chief of staff of a corps and until a year ago was adviser to the Chilean General Staff.

Knauer was especially successful in Chile because of his tact, his great calmness, his expert knowledge, and his mastery of the Spanish language.   Knauer's son is a flier here.

Please transmit the above telegram to General Göring also.

                                                                    FAUPEL

No. 215

3372/E010652–53

The Foreign Minister to the Embassy in Spain

Telegram

No. 51 of January 28   [BERLIN, January 28, 1937.]
Received January 28—9 : 00 p.m.

The text of our note [1] on the question of volunteers handed to the British Ambassador on Monday follows by air mail. The contents of the note are based on German-Italian agreement. Minister President Göring's visit to Rome strengthened the basis of our common policy with Italy. This is expressed, on the one hand, by the similar line of thought in both notes, on the other, by the joint letter of the Minister President and Mussolini [2] with which you are familiar.

In agreement with the War Ministry, I should like to observe for your information that deliberations have not yet been concluded on the question whether a shipment can be made, in excess of the delivery contemplated in the above letter.

Our attitude on the question of control corresponds in every respect to the line of argument laid down in our note of reply. The German Government does in fact desire to participate in as effective a control as possible, and to cut Spain off from imports after it is established. Accordingly, the German representative in the Non-Intervention Committee has been instructed as follows :

"As far as control outside Spain is concerned, we and the Italians are pursuing the intention of putting through a control that is effective in every respect, to go into force possibly some time after the middle of February, but not earlier than February 10. You will, however, give strong emphasis even now to the German desire for establishment of a control that is effective in every respect.

"On the subject of the control plans before the committee, please state in very general terms that we are willing to participate in the control. In order to facilitate a decision and expedite the matter as much as possible, we are prepared to join in any form of control generally approved in the committee, on the condition that it is set up effectively and on a parity basis and does not extend to German sovereign territory. With respect to control at sea, therefore, we reject any activity by agents in German ports."

---

[1] The German and Italian replies, delivered Jan. 25, declared that the two Governments had already introduced legislation enabling them to prohibit the departure of volunteers and that they were prepared to put the measures into effect simultaneously with the other powers as soon as the general lines of an adequate system of control had been agreed upon ; they referred again to their proposal that the withdrawal of volunteers already in Spain should be considered. The text of the German note is printed in *Dokumente der deutschen Politik*, vol. V (5th ed., 1942), p. 107.

[2] Not found.

In this instruction we have assumed that control inside Spain is out of the question on the basis of the replies of Franco and the Red Government.

It would be of interest here to learn what considerations, in your opinion, led Franco to give so negative a reply after the Italians had advised him to take a more positive stand.

Please report by wire.

NEURATH

No. 216

3372/E010654-55

The Chargé d'Affaires in Spain to the Foreign Ministry

Telegram

No. 82 of January 30   SALAMANCA, January 30, 1937.

With reference to telegraphic instruction No. 51 of January 28.

The Nationalist Government denies that it gave a negative reply in the question of control. In the first reply it had put four questions. Of these only one had been answered. In the second reply it had stressed the failure to answer the other three questions, as well as the significance of the common border between France and Red Spain for the question of control, but had not expressed a refusal in principle. The question of sovereignty, which would be affected by the control, was decisive. But how could the Nationalist Government reach agreements with England regarding a control that would represent a substantial curtailment of its sovereignty, without England's having recognized the bearer of this sovereignty as such?

The Nationalist Government has evidently handled the question of control on the one hand within the framework of its efforts to obtain recognition by other powers, and on the other in the consciousness that it cannot bring the war to a successful conclusion without constant imports of arms and munitions from abroad. The latter conception is again expressed in the supplementary requests called forth by the German-Italian memorandum.

FAUPEL

No. 217

3253/E000718-21

The Acting State Secretary to the Legation in Portugal

Telegram

No. 17   BERLIN, February 2, 1937—11:30 p.m.

Pol. III 549.

The British Ambassador, on instructions of his Government, sent the Foreign Ministry a note on January 31 transmitting to us a copy of an instruction that the British Ambassador at Lisbon was to carry out with the Portuguese Government. The note states that the British Ambassador at Lisbon had been asked to make serious but friendly representations in conversation with the Portuguese Prime Minister in the sense of the above-mentioned instruction, with the request for an early and favorable reply to the Non-Intervention Committee. The British Ambassador was directed to propose to the German Government that it instruct its representative at Lisbon to make similar representations to the Portuguese Government. A similar proposal was being made through the British representatives at Paris and Rome to the French and Italian Governments.

The instruction sent the British Ambassador at Lisbon first of all points out that it has appeared necessary to shift the intended control measures pertaining to Spain to areas outside Spain. After a detailed account of the last proposal, it is stated that this proposal had been submitted on January 29 to the chairman of the subcommittee and that there had been general agreement in the subcommittee to support it in principle. The Portuguese representative had on former occasions personally expressed the view of his Government that it would not be in a position to agree to control within Portuguese territory, since this would be incompatible with the prestige of his country. At the last session of the subcommittee he had repeated this, his personal opinion, without, however, committing his Government. It would be extremely deplorable from every standpoint if Portugal should refuse to accept the control, particularly since the proposal provides that the agents of the committee would possess no authority of any kind over Portuguese officials, but would confine themselves to transmitting reports to the committee. France and England had given their consent to control within their territories contiguous to Spain, and the British Government could not understand why the Portuguese Government objected in any way to giving its consent. In case Portugal refused, the only alternative was to include Portugal in the sea blockade, which, as was well known, would be most undesirable to the Portuguese Government. Such an inclusion of Portugal was naturally not up for discussion yet today. In any case, however, if the Portuguese Government persisted in its attitude, it would have to assume full responsibility before world opinion for the collapse of the non-intervention policy which would result from its refusal.

So much for the British instruction to Lisbon.

On the basis of the above-mentioned British *démarche* with me, please call on the Portuguese Foreign Minister to inform him of the development and to tell him that the German Government joins the British in its desire to obtain Portugal's consent to the control but does not wish to put any pressure upon the Portuguese Government in this question.   Nevertheless, please let it be understood that we, too, would consider it desirable if the Portuguese Government could see its way clear to withdraw its objections to control.   Before making your *démarche*, please consult with the Italian Ambassador, since a similar procedure has been agreed upon here with the Italian Ambassador.

Please report [1] by wire.

DIECKHOFF

---

[1] The German Minister in Portugal reported in telegram No. 14 of Feb. 5, 1937 (3253/E000728), that the Portuguese Government rejected controls on land but had no objections to the other proposals of the Non-Intervention Committee.

No. 218

3176/682916–17

Memorandum by an Official of the Economic Policy Department

BERLIN, February 4, 1937.

Mr. J. M. Magowan of the Commercial Department of the British Embassy here called on me today and took up the following matter.

The Rio Tinto Company, a British company, had reported to the British Government that the Nationalist Government in Spain had confiscated certain quantities of the output of their copper mines in Rio Tinto; namely,

1. 2,120 tons of "copper precipitate" [1] (*Zementkupfer?*) [2] which, after seizure on September 13 of last year, had been shipped to Germany from a Spanish port on the S. S. *Girgenti;* further,

2. Five hundred tons of copper precipitate, which had already been confiscated but was still lying in the port of Huelva.

The Rio Tinto Company was lodging a claim against the German Government, either

(*a*) to return the quantity shipped to Germany, or

(*b*) to deliver a like amount, or

(*c*) to pay in pounds sterling for the quantity shipped.

The British Government was presenting and supporting the claim of the Rio Tinto Company because the seizure constituted an illegal act, in which the German Government was involved through acceptance of the copper confiscated.

The total output of copper precipitate from the Rio Tinto mines in Spain, apart from Spain's own requirements, had thus far gone to the refineries of the Rio Tinto Company in Port Talbot, South Wales; new supplies were not to be had, and actually the refineries had

---

[1] The quoted passage is in English in the original.
[2] Thus in the original.

had no deliveries from Spain since October 15, 1936, so that closing of the plants was to be expected. The refineries were an important element of the British economy, and it would make an unfavorable impression if closing were attributed to "circumstances beyond our control," for which Germany was partly responsible.

Mr. Magowan also stated in support of the claim that the Rio Tinto Company had for 60 years (except for the interruption during the war) enjoyed the most friendly relations with the German concerns interested, the I. G. Farben A.G.-Duisburger-Kupferhütte, the Ertel-Bieber-Hamburger Kupferhütte, and the Metallgesellschaft, and that in the mutual interest these relations should by all means not be disturbed. He also pointed out that both the British and German companies were members of the European Pyrites Cooporation [sic], the copper pyrites association in which all companies had thus far collaborated in a friendly way.

Finally he asked for a statement on the German attitude toward the claim and at the same time hinted that the Rio Tinto Company was ready to enter into direct negotiations with the German governmental agencies or firms concerned.

I confined myself to receiving Mr. Magowan's representations and promised him that the matter would be studied and that he would be informed.

RÜTER

No. 219

3253/E000723–25

The Acting State Secretary to the Embassy in Great Britain

Telegram

No. 47   BERLIN, February 6, 1937—5 : 05 p.m.
zu Pol. III 6338.

Drafting Officer : Counselor of Legation Dumont.

In discussing control plans you will advocate the following principles:

The introduction of land control and sea control may not be staggered. On the contrary, it is absolutely necessary that they enter into force at the same time.

The War Ministry, which has just completed final examination of document 285,[1] has the impression that land control is less effective than sea control. We must, however, strive with every possible means for as complete as possible a closing of the Pyrenees border. We request, therefore, that you again emphasize the necessity for effective-

---

[1] Of the Non-Intervention Committee.

ness in the land control and propose that this be assured by increasing the number of agents and control posts.[2]

For the rest, you will emphasize in principle that the different types of control by land, sea, and air form a unified whole. In order not to delay the execution of agreements already achieved, you will at the present moment not insist that the air-control plan also be put into force at the same time. In any case, however, the discussion of air control is to be resumed and kept alive.

For your information: To demand that land and sea control be made dependent on air control is not contemplated for the following reasons: In the first place an air-control plan is difficult to carry out outside Spain. In addition, air control is less important than land control and sea control. Finally, by such a condition we should jeopardize not only the implementation of the land and sea control but also the prohibition against the influx of volunteers. We should thereby run the risk of being made responsible if the solution of the problem, advanced by all sides and also by ourselves and now about to be accepted, should at the last minute be delayed or even collapse entirely.[3]

DIECKHOFF

---

[2] This text was substituted for the original version of the paragraph which read as follows: "Land and sea control must, moreover, be equally effective. The impression here is that land control is less effective than sea control. A considerable increase in the number of land control posts should therefore be demanded, reference being made to the fact that the main traffic in smuggling goes on particularly along the French-Spanish border and volunteers are streaming to Spain principally by this route."

[3] Footnote in Weizsäcker's handwriting: "A conference with Lieutenant Colonel Scheller on February 5 formed the basis for this instruction."

Marginal note in another hand: "A copy has been sent to the War Ministry. Feb. 8."

No. 220

701/261191–93

The Ambassador in Italy to the Foreign Ministry

Telegram

SECRET   ROME, February 8, 1937—8:30 p.m.

No. 38 of February 8

With reference to my telegram No. 36 of February 7.[1]

For the Foreign Minister.

During his conversation with me today Ciano received an official report from the Italian command in Málaga of the capture of the city, and he relayed it at once by telephone to the Duce, who announced the promotion of Roatta to General of Division. Ciano expressed great optimism with regard to the further progress of the operations, since the capture of Málaga had been accomplished by only nine battalions and with only slight losses. Twenty-seven more battalions, as well

---

[1] Not printed (4446/E086509–10).

as the Littoria Division, which was en route, were available. The moral effect of this success must be reinforced immediately by a further advance beginning in the direction of Almería in order then as soon as possible to launch an offensive northeast of Madrid toward Teruel and Valencia. He was now convinced of final success, particularly as the enemy was in a state of advanced disintegration. Mussolini would quite approve if the German press, not at once but in the next few days, quite casually and unobtrusively mentioned the participation of Italian volunteers in the operations.

After I had informed Ciano, in accordance with telegram No. 32 of February 6,[2] of our instructions with regard to the control plan, to which he offered no objections, Ciano read me a telegraphic instruction to Grandi which he had just written regarding Italy's basic stand in the further discussion of the questions of control and volunteers. After describing the favorable military situation and predicting final success, Ciano instructs Grandi to continue to take a positive stand on the questions of control and volunteers, since all essential shipments had been completed in the last few days. On the other hand, the idea of evacuating all foreigners, which had been supported by both Italy and Germany for tactical reasons but was now apparently being taken up by England as a countermove against them, naturally was now entirely unacceptable to Italy; resistance could not be open, but only through sabotage in the form of delay, etc. The Portuguese stand (your telegram 31 of February 6 [3]) was known to Ciano.

Concerning the Ambassador at Salamanca, Ciano declared that the appointment had been unavoidable, since the Chargé d'Affaires was personally completely inadequate. The matter was in his opinion not basic, so that if we preferred we could simply retain our Chargé d'Affaires. The Ambassador had been instructed to keep entirely in the background; at the present stage Roatta was the decisive authority.

HASSELL

---

[2] Telegram No. 32 of Feb. 6 repeated to Rome the contents of telegram No. 47 of that date to London, document No. 219, p. 241.
[3] Not printed (701/261161).

No. 221

1819/416143

The Ambassador [1] in Spain to the Foreign Ministry

Sa. 10–883   SALAMANCA, February 21, 1937.
Pol. III 1067.

Subject: French policy toward Spain.

In yesterday's conversation General Franco told me that the French Foreign Minister had tried, through an intermediary, to initiate con-

---

[1] General Faupel was named Ambassador on Feb. 11.

versations with the Nationalist Government for the purpose of resuming commercial relations. This intermediary was a French consul who was known to be sympathetic to Nationalist Spain. He had been told by the Spanish that, as long as men and matériel for the Reds came over the French border, a resumption of commercial relations was not to be thought of.

I indicated to General Franco that the French had, above all, to be told that any attempt to restore commercial relations was futile as long as the gold of the Bank of Spain taken to France by the Reds was not returned to the Nationalist Government. He told me that he had also taken this viewpoint into consideration. I shall, however, once more call the attention of Franco, as well as his brother Nicolás, the person primarily responsible for handling economic and financial questions, to this point or have someone else do it. The new Italian Ambassador is also working in this direction.

General Franco also informed me that the French General Staff had prepared a situation report—evidently on the basis of reports from agents in Seville—and submitted it to the French Government. The report pointed out that the prospects of military success for the Reds were exactly nil at present.

For the rest, General Franco went into French policy in general and also mentioned the fact that France was pursuing a decidedly Leftist policy in Catalonia, while in the particularist but conservative Basque provinces of the north, with the help of a portion of the clergy, it was pursuing an opposite policy, but always one aimed at weakening Nationalist Spain.

FAUPEL

No. 222

4446/E086518

The Ambassador in Spain to the Foreign Ministry

Telegram

No. 118 of February 23   SALAMANCA, February 23, 1937.
Pol. III 949.

Although steps in the same sense have already been taken with General Sander, Generalissimo Franco again pointed out to me too the necessity that all the matériel promised arrive by March 6.

FAUPEL

No. 223

3176/682939-44

Memorandum by an Official of the Economic Policy Department

W II WE 1334 BERLIN, February 23, 1937.

([For] conference of principal officials February 26 on German-Spanish economic relations.)

A. *Legal situation.*

German-Spanish economic relations are regulated by the following treaties:

    (*a*) The commercial treaty of May 7, 1926;

    (*b*) The commodity agreement of March 9, 1936;

    (*c*) The payments agreement of December 31, 1934.

Theoretically these agreements also hold good in relation to the Spanish Nationalist Government. The commodity agreement, which expired on December 31, 1936, was extended to March 31, 1937, by agreement with the Nationalist Government. The payments agreement exists practically only on paper, since it does not function for lack of special implementation agreements.

B. *Present situation.*

Trade and payments are at present conducted through the Hisma company in Seville and the Rowak company in Berlin, established by the Auslandsorganisation at the instance of Minister President Colonel General Göring. These companies have a virtual monopoly. To be sure, other commercial firms can also transact business, but for lack of other agreements between the two Governments this can only be handled through the clearing accounts of Hisma and Rowak. The firms must pay a commission to these two companies.

1. Arguments in favor of *retaining* the present arrangements are as follows:

    (*a*) The undeniable success of Rowak/Hisma, which have succeeded through their relations with General Franco in placing Germany ahead of all other countries in Spanish trade and in directing the raw materials available in Spain primarily to Germany.

    (*b*) To guarantee the delivery of Spanish raw materials to Germany requires steady pressure on the Franco Government, which would rather sell these raw materials to other countries against foreign exchange. Rowak/Hisma have at their disposal suitable means of pressure through special deliveries which they are able to make to the Franco Government.

    (*c*) Through the special deliveries that Germany has made to Spain, such a large credit balance has accrued in favor of Germany that it will take a very long time to liquidate it by deliveries of Spanish merchandise or by German participation in Spanish enterprises. For this reason there is no great interest in increasing this credit balance further by possible additional German exports.

2. Arguments in favor of *changing* the present arrangements are as follows:

(*a*) The understandable desire of German trade for a restoration of normal commercial relations and terms of payment, that is to say, the possibility of transactions independent of Rowak/Hisma without paying commissions to them;

(*b*) The desire not to let long-standing commercial relations be disrupted;

(*c*) The favorable situation for our commercial policy. The Franco Government is at present dependent on the special German deliveries and therefore presumably is more prepared to make concessions than somewhat later on, after the termination of military operations.

(*d*) A number of other countries (England, Italy) have meanwhile already concluded clearing agreements with the Nationalist Government.

(*e*) The State Technical Commission in Burgos at the beginning of February expressly proposed to the Embassy in Salamanca that a clearing procedure be established (through the opening of an Aski account [1]).

(*f*) In the exchange of notes regarding the extension of the commodity agreement, it is provided that by April 1 of this year at the latest a new commodity agreement is to be concluded. Such an agreement, without a simultaneously concluded clearing agreement, would remain on paper.

C. From a commercial policy standpoint, the present monopoly of Rowak/Hisma would necessarily continue if a new payments agreement is *not* concluded but would be abolished as soon as an accord is reached on a new payments agreement. Rowak/Hisma therefore understandably oppose the conclusion of such a payments agreement and in this are supported by General Göring, to whom Herr von Jagwitz has reported on these questions. On the other hand, President Schacht of the Reichsbank is insisting very vigorously upon the conclusion of a payments agreement. The Finance Ministry and the Food Ministry have thus far sided with him (although now the Food Ministry seems prepared to reconcile itself to the present arrangement). The Foreign Ministry has taken the stand that, as long as abnormal conditions in Spain continue, the privileged position of

---

[1] A blocked mark account.

Rowak/Hisma is justified, and has therefore in the main been in agreement with General Göring.

It must now be decided in the conference of principal officials whether a payments agreement is to be concluded or not. There is unanimity, moreover, that Rowak/Hisma are not to be excluded in the conclusion of such an agreement. The question is, whether a privileged position (no monopoly, however) could perhaps continue to be given them within the framework of a payments agreement, possibly with regard to some products that are especially vital to Germany (ores).

D. The initiative for undertaking negotiations came from Herr Faupel.

There is unanimity that negotiations can be conducted with the Franco Government on an improvement of the commercial treaty; on an extension and possibly on improvement of the commodity agreement; on the unfreezing of old German credits dating back to the time before the uprising; and also, in principle, on the question of the form in which the claims arising from the special deliveries by Germany can be liquidated.

Accordingly it would also have to be decided whether, in case the conclusion of a clearing agreement is rejected, a German delegation should nevertheless be dispatched to Spain for negotiations on the other questions mentioned above. Unity obtains regarding the composition of this delegation (Head: Ministerial Counselor Wucher, Finance Ministry). It is possible that President Schacht of the Reichsbank might raise objections to granting Rowak a representative as agreed upon between Ministerialdirektor Ritter and State Secretary Körner.

Should the dispatching of a delegation be rejected, then, in accordance with a suggestion made by Ambassador Faupel, there might be considered the sending, solely for information purposes, of a representative of the Reich Foreign Exchange Control Agency, who would first examine the pertinent problems locally.

BENZLER

No. 224

3206/697700

The Chargé d'Affaires in Great Britain to the Foreign Ministry

[Telegram]

No. 115 of February 27   LONDON, February 27, 1937.
                                          Pol. III 1014.

The reversal by the Soviet Union yesterday on the question of participating in control of the Spanish seas can probably be explained principally by the fact that the Soviet Union feared that she was not up to the tasks in the Biscay zone and saw herself faced by a solid front opposed to allocating her another zone.[1] The Italians were firmly determined not to admit the Russians into the Mediterranean. In private conversations the French clearly indicated that they were opposed to surveillance of Morocco by Soviet ships; the British stated in the meeting that they did not want Soviet Russian ships in the vicinity of Gibraltar; and we declared that we did not wish to be given a zone adjacent to the Soviet Union's. Incidentally, it is inferred here that the Soviet Union from the very beginning did not wish to participate and that she had been interested only in recognition of the principle. I do not believe this version to be correct, for then there would have been no efforts to secure another zone. The Soviet attitude is generally treated ironically by the public here. I call attention further to our previous reports according to which Germany did not definitely consent to the Soviet Union's participation.

WOERMANN

---

[1] The reference is to the proposed establishment of an international high-seas naval patrol, with definite portions of the high seas off the Spanish coast being assigned to each of the four powers for naval patrol.

No. 225

3253/E000748

The Chargé d'Affaires in Great Britain to the Foreign Ministry

Telegram

No. 125 of March 2

LONDON, March 2, 1937—7:59 p.m.
Received March 2—10:45 p.m.
Pol. III 1076.

With reference to our No. 123 of March 1.[1]

On the initiative of the Italian Chargé d'Affaires I have agreed with him on the following tactics for the further handling of the withdrawal of volunteers from Spain:

In the first place we shall, as we already did in the last session, argue the thesis that all non-intervention questions still pending must now be dealt with simultaneously, meaning, in addition to the withdrawal of volunteers, the question of financial support, including the gold question, and the question of foreign agitators.

In the second place attention will then be called to the difficulties arising out of the problem of the withdrawal of volunteers. In this connection it will be brought out that without the cooperation of both parties in Spain success is not possible, especially on account of the naturalization of foreign volunteers by the Red Government and the necessity of control in Spain itself.

In view of the original German initiative in this question and the

---

[1] Not printed (4906/E255212).

preponderance of Italian interest in a dilatory handling of it, I told the Italian Chargé d'Affaires that the Italians would have to take the main responsibility for such handling, but that they would get full support from us.

We agreed further that a committee resolution to be made public on the subject of withdrawal should not be too strongly worded and that it should require not withdrawal itself but only an examination of the question.

WOERMANN

No. 226

3253/E000749–51

The Foreign Minister to the Embassy in Great Britain

Telegram

VERY URGENT

BERLIN, March 4, 1937—9 : 30 p.m.

No. 82

zu Pol. III 1076 I.

With reference to your telegram 125.[1]

We assent in principle to the tactics which you and the Italian Chargé d'Affaires have agreed upon for dealing further with the withdrawal of volunteers from Spain. In your statements, however, please emphasize at all times that the proposal for withdrawing volunteers is of German origin, that our view in this matter has not changed, and that we still favor furthering the matter in every way. Outwardly please describe the difficulties of the question as far as possible in a form which implies that the solution would, of course, have to be all inclusive and on a basis of parity. It could then be pointed out in this connection that considerable numbers of volunteers on the Red side have been naturalized. Furthermore, simultaneous treatment of other forms of indirect intervention must be required. In this connection please point out that in our note of January 7 [2] we made our agreement to the ban on volunteers dependent, among other points, on having the solution of other questions connected with indirect intervention also taken up at once, since the German Government would otherwise have to reconsider its stand even on the question of volunteers.

Please adopt this attitude also when conferring on the committee's resolution planned for publication, which was mentioned in the last paragraph of telegram No. 125.

For your own information I point out that we expect that after the control measures have been introduced the question of withdrawing volunteers from Spain will be emphasized to an increasing extent by the British and the French. Therefore, we must proceed with

---

[1] Document No. 225, *supra.*
[2] Document No. 190, p. 210.

great caution so that we do not fall into noticeable contradiction with our attitude up to now and so that the very great practical difficulties, which doubtless will arise of themselves, will develop so as not to bring the problem to a premature solution contrary to our interests. What is involved in all this, therefore, is more a question of terminology, while in the matter itself, of course, we shall proceed in conformity with the Italians.

The Embassy at Rome has been instructed to explain our stand to the Italian Government and to urge that similar terminology be used. In any case, as you have already stated to the Chargé d'Affaires, we want to leave the main burden of the delaying tactics to the Italians but actually support them in this in every way.

NEURATH

No. 227

3253/E000755

The Ambassador in Italy to the Foreign Ministry

Telegram

No. 63 of March 5   ROME (QUIRINAL) March 5, 1937—6:45 p.m.
Received March 5—9:45 p.m.
Pol. III 1079 a.

For the Foreign Minister.

1. Ciano informed me today that the assembling of three divisions northeast of Madrid will be concluded tomorrow; the Sigüenza offensive will begin on March 8 provided the weather is tolerable. Roatta appraises the general situation as favorable.

2. Since the British have once again brought up in the London Non-Intervention Committee the idea of withdrawing all volunteers, he repeats the request that the German representative be instructed to sabotage it. Ciano added that behind the British move there was presumably the ulterior motive of obtaining from Italy a guaranty to withdraw following the conclusion of peace, if withdrawal now should prove impractical. This was what England was really interested in.

Telegram No. 55 of March 4,[1] which has just arrived, was not available at the time of the conference. I had the impression that Ciano was somewhat concerned because of the tactics of the German Chargé d'Affaires. I shall make an additional statement of the German views.

HASSELL

---

[1] Telegram No. 55 of Mar. 4 to Rome, not printed (3253/E000751), repeated the contents of telegram No. 125 of Mar. 2 from London (Document No. 225, p. 248) and telegram No. 82 of Mar. 4 to London (Document No. 226, *supra*) and added, "Please inform Ciano accordingly and make clear to him the meaning of our instruction."

No. 228

3253/E000761

The Acting State Secretary to the Embassy in Great Britain

Telegram

No. 88 of March 6   BERLIN, March 6, 1937—6 : 30 p.m.

zu Pol. III 1150.

The Embassy at Salamanca telegraphs:

"According to a Trans-Ocean [1] report of March 3, the blockade is expected to become effective two weeks after the previous deadline. Franco told me that such a delay was exceptionally disadvantageous for him."

At the next opportunity which offers, please press for an early application of the control measures, and telegraph the probable date of their entry into force.[2]

DIECKHOFF

---

[1] The Trans-Ocean agency was the semiofficial foreign news agency.
[2] On the same day the Foreign Ministry telegraphed the Embassy in Spain as No. 89 of Mar. 6 (3253/E000761–62) : "The reasons for the delay in putting the control measures into force are technical, the still unclarified question of costs, and the transfer difficulties of various countries. Reports up to now indicate a two-week delay must actually be anticipated. The London Embassy has been instructed to press for early action, and to telegraph the probable date on which the control measures will go into force. Bismarck."

No. 229

701/261197–98

The Ambassador in Italy to the Foreign Ministry

Telegram

SECRET   ROME, March 10, 1937—10 : 30 p.m.

No. 71 of March 10

For the Foreign Minister.

Ciano, on whom I called today just as he received the latest telegraphic reports from the theater of war in Spain, expressed his satisfaction with the progress of operations, especially as so far only one of the four divisions has actually been under fire. He hopes to force a decision now, although the difficulties are not inconsiderable, since the Red party, realizing that the decisive moment has arrived, is committing all its forces. In addition, the weather and the road demolitions are hindrances, and finally the Spanish troops are advancing only very slowly. Today the Italians met with fierce resistance. Losses were not inconsiderable. The opponents were principally Russians. A telegraphic report from the Italian Supreme Command, which just arrived and which I saw, sounds confident and terms the morale and bearing of the troops excellent. Ciano added that he had assumed the direction of affairs himself, including the military aspects; he was in constant communication, of course, with the Duce, who left today for Tripoli, but he himself was foregoing the Tripoli journey in view of the situation.

HASSELL

No. 230

701/261199–200

The Ambassador in Italy to the Foreign Ministry

Telegram

SECRET   ROME, March 17, 1937.

No. 78 of March 17

For the Foreign Minister.

During today's conversation Ciano was obviously preoccupied with the expectation of strong resistance, especially in the air, from the Red enemy, as well as with the failure of the Spanish columns at Guadalajara; he confirmed that General Liuzzi of the Militia had been killed and that the division in action had lost approximately 1,500 men in killed and wounded. A small Italian detachment had been trapped by Red Italian émigrés, captured, and interrogated, especially as to whether they were volunteers or were under orders, and some had admitted the latter. The action of the Valencia Government at Geneva was not to be taken too seriously, however. He would no longer send large numbers of men to Spain, but only a few to replace losses, as well as replacement matériel of all kinds, especially planes and chemical warfare supplies, the latter with instructions that they be used only if absolutely necessary. Deliveries for the Reds seemed to be continuing in considerable quantities, and new decisions might become necessary if this persisted.

In spite of the stubborn resistance mentioned, the military situation did not give cause for concern; a new offensive was at the present time being discussed by Franco, Roatta, and Sperrle and would begin in a few days.

HASSELL

No. 231

3176/682951–53

Minute by the Director of the Economic Policy Department

CONFIDENTIAL   BERLIN, March 17, 1937.

On Monday, March 15, I discussed the present situation in Spain with Herr von Jagwitz. He told me the following concerning the course of the conference of principal officials some time ago:

When he was called into the conference, Colonel General Göring first of all asked him to explain alleged unjustified claims for commissions made by the Rowak organization. Rowak and Hisma are said to have claimed commissions for transactions in which they did not participate, namely, for the well-known ship purchase. He (Jagwitz) had had the impression that this question was put to him on the basis of a document which was in the hands of Herr von Neurath. Since he was not informed of the matter, he had asked that he be given details. He would investigate the matter. It was agreed that any excessive commissions should be cut.

He had then presented the substance of his memorandum of February 10, 1937, and its annexes.[1] His proposal was accepted unanimously. Specifically it was decided not to conclude a trade agreement or a clearing agreement for current business at the present time. President Schacht himself had fully agreed with the proposal.

Herr von Jagwitz also told me the following concerning his views on further procedure. The various attempts by private persons to make private clearing settlements with Spain had not worked out satisfactorily. Especially with regard to timber and hides it had been evident that bids made by private German individuals on the basis of private settlement resulted only in increased prices and reserve on the part of the Spanish sellers. He therefore favored preventing any private settlements with Spain until further notice. With regard to wool, for example, where the supervisory agency was working in harmony with him, purchases were going surprisingly well.

The Spanish Government's *note verbale* five weeks ago, in which Spain requested that a commodity and clearing agreement be concluded, can be explained according to his information or his conjectures by the private and unauthorized initiative of Herr Ullmann of the Deutsche Überseeische Bank. Herr Ullmann, who wishes to bring the Deutsche Überseeische Bank into the Spanish business again, had used the Junta bureaucracy as a tool and in this manner brought about the Spanish *note verbale*.

Concerning the composition of the delegation, I told Herr von Jagwitz that I considered it hardly acceptable for the Economics Ministry that no one from there was included. If he excluded Herr Kölfen,[2] it would presumably only lead to a controversy between the Ministers. Jagwitz said that he would agree to any other gentleman from the Economics Ministry. He did not, however, consider it advisable to take along Herr Kölfen, not because of personal objections, but because of his attitude in the matter. (Moreover, as he told me

---

[1] Not printed (3176/682930–34).
[2] Hans Kölfen, Ministerial Counselor in the Economics Ministry.

confidentially, President Schacht had made a statement to Ambassador Faupel, from which the latter had gathered that President Schacht himself did not wish to send Herr Kölfen.)

Concerning the tactics of the delegation, Jagwitz said that he considered it advisable for the delegation to prepare for only a short stay and to avoid attracting particular attention in Spain. The agreement would have to be put through in one stroke, if necessary by immediate intervention with Franco. The Junta should not be given any opportunity to intervene decisively.

Jagwitz also repeated what he had said earlier, that any agreement should be signed only after the full text had been submitted to General Göring and had been approved by him.

To be submitted to Pol. III, Herr Benzler, and Herr Sabath for their *confidential* information.

RITTER

No. 232

3373/E010782

The Ambassador in Spain to the Foreign Ministry

Telegram

No. 156 of March 18   SALAMANCA, March 18, 1937.
                                    Received March 18—11 : 10 p.m.
                                              Pol. III 1409 a.

For the State Secretary personally.

During yesterday's conversation Mancini informed me of the following statement by Mussolini : Italy would strictly adhere to the London agreement concerning the ban on volunteers for Spain. As soon as he could establish, however, that another country was violating this agreement, he, for his part, would send General Franco 100 Italians for every man put at the disposal of the Reds.

FAUPEL

No. 233

3373/E010791

Memorandum by the Foreign Minister

RM 206   BERLIN, March 20, 1937.
                                         e. o. Pol. III 1459.

The British Ambassador appealed to me today to abandon our opposition to the separate treatment of the question of the withdrawal of volunteers from Spain and that of the Spanish gold. I replied to him that we had to insist that these questions be treated together.

If the British Government could prevail on the Russians to give up their objection to the discussion of the gold question, we should have no objection to the discussion of the question of volunteers next Monday.   No decisions on these questions could be made anyway, so long as control was not effective.   I also called the Ambassador's attention to the increase reported to us in the deliveries to the Red Spaniards from Russia.

BARON V. NEURATH

CHAPTER III

GERMAN-NATIONALIST TIES STRENGTHENED:
THE MARCH AND JULY PROTOCOLS
MARCH 20–JULY 16, 1937

No. 234

136/73560–61

Protocol

TOP SECRET   SALAMANCA, March 20, 1937.
                                                    zu Pol. I 1648 g Rs.

The German Government and the Spanish Nationalist Government,
convinced that the progressive development of the friendly relations
existing between them serves the welfare of the German and the Spanish peoples and will be an important factor for the maintenance of
European peace, which is close to both their hearts,

are agreed in their desire to lay down even now the guiding principles for their future relations, and for this purpose have come to an
understanding on the following points:

1. Both Governments will constantly consult with one another on
the measures necessary to defend their countries against the threatening dangers of Communism.

2. Both Governments will constantly maintain contact with one
another in order to inform each other concerning questions of international policy which affect their joint interests.

3. Neither of the two Governments will participate in treaties or
other agreements with third powers which are aimed either directly
or indirectly against the other country.

4. In case one of the two countries should be attacked by a third
power, the Government of the other country will avoid everything
that might serve to the advantage of the attacker or the disadvantage
of the attacked.

5. Both Governments are agreed in their desire to intensify the
economic relations between their countries as much as possible. In
this manner they reaffirm their purpose that the two countries shall
henceforth cooperate with and supplement one another in economic
matters in every way.

6. Both Governments will treat this protocol, which becomes effective at once, as secret until further notice. At the proper time, they will regulate their political, economic, and cultural relations in detail by special agreements in accordance with the principles laid down above.

Done in duplicate in the German and Spanish languages.

For the German Government:

FAUPEL

For the Spanish Nationalist Government:

FRANCISCO FRANCO

No. 235

3373/E010801–02

The Ambassador in France to the Foreign Ministry

Telegram

VERY URGENT
No. 180 of March 25

PARIS, March 25, 1937.
Received March 25—6 : 20 p.m.
Pol. III 1527.

The Foreign Minister requested me to call on him yesterday evening, and informed me of the following:

The attitude of Italy at the last meeting of the London Non-Intervention Committee, in which Grandi stated that the question of the withdrawal of Italian volunteers from Spain could not be discussed and declared that the volunteers would not leave Spanish soil before Franco had won complete and final victory, was such a flagrant violation of the basis and the spirit of previous agreements that France considered it a serious danger to the peace. Viewed from the standpoint of reciprocity, France had at least as much right to intervene in Spain as Italy, and could not permit Italy to usurp in the most obvious manner the right to decide the fate of Spain, at the same time completely disregarding the interests of this neighboring country. France would show Mussolini that she would not allow herself to be treated in this cavalier manner, as if she were a second-rate state. A matter of such importance could not be dealt with by the Non-Intervention Committee in London alone, which was competent for technical details, but, in view of the gravity of the situation, would also have to be brought up for discussion through the usual diplomatic channels.

In France and also in Germany the agreement had been punctiliously and faithfully observed since February 20, while in spite of Ciano's and Cerruti's [1] denials there was indisputable evidence of the fact that Italy had broken her word. The presence of complete units of active Italian troops in uniform under the command of their officers had been

---

[1] Vittorio Cerruti, Italian Ambassador in France.

875667—50—VOL. III——23

confirmed by eyewitnesses; also, the Fascist Grand Council had congratulated the Italian troops, although, to be sure, the reason for this was hardly understandable after the capture of Málaga.

France had gone to the very limit of tolerance in the face of this inadmissible behavior on the part of Italy, but she could permit such cavalier treatment no longer. The French Government did not request that we exert pressure on our Italian friends, but that we join with those powers which demanded of Italy the same strict observance of obligations entered into as was required of all the other participants. Thus it was not a question of mediation but of a joint appeal for good faith in observing an agreement. In the course of the discussion we also spoke in a general way of the practical implementation of the plan, which I termed impossible, as far as the Reds were concerned, because of lack of authority. Delbos replied that reciprocity was, of course, essential, and, if this should prove impossible for the Left, then those on the Right would have to be granted the same privilege. In no case, however, should it be permissible for one of the partners to reject implementation bluntly from the very start and thereby violate the very concept of non-intervention.[2]

WELCZECK

[2] Marginal note: "Please send telegraphic instructions to W., pointing out that the Italians and the Germans were the very ones who had for a long time been demanding withdrawal of volunteers, and that, in spite of agreements, volunteers are still going to Spain from France. We consider indignation rather inappropriate. Naturally we would keep to our agreements and we were convinced that the Italians were also keeping to theirs. Neurath. Mar. 28." Such an instruction was sent to the Embassy in France as telegram No. 96 of Mar. 31 (3373/E010803-04).

No. 236

3373/E010805-07

The Ambassador in Italy to the Foreign Ministry

Telegram

No. 81 of March 25

ROME, March 25, 1937—11:25 p.m.
Received March 26—3:20 a.m.
Pol. III 1530.

Following my return from Berlin I had a long conversation with Mussolini today, from which the following is worthy of note:

1. Secret, for the Foreign Minister.

Mussolini showed great agitation on account of events in Spain and ill-concealed dissatisfaction with Italian achievements. To be sure, he emphasized again and again that from a military viewpoint the reverse [1] suffered was inconsequential, that the situation had already been reestablished, and that a resumption of the offensive could be expected in a few weeks. However, he admitted the highly unfavor-

[1] At Guadalajara.

able psychological effect of the reverse. When I emphasized, referring to a similar statement by Göring, that the psychological effect would readily be dissipated by a new victory, he agreed enthusiastically. Following my remark that I had found the Führer and everybody else in Berlin convinced of Mussolini's firm determination to force a victory, he exclaimed with an expression of utmost resolution that there was no doubt as to that; he had had the Italian command in Spain informed that none of them should return home alive unless they achieved victory. He added that there was no question of sending out more troops; those on hand had to suffice, and there would be replacement only of commanders, subordinate commanders, and equipment. He answered affirmatively my question whether this stand might not change if the other side sent troops; however, their procedure was different and consisted in a trickle of single individuals and small groups. He said that the main cause for the failure was inexperience in the use of motorized troops. If they advanced too quickly and later met with strong resistance before reserves had been brought up, a fatal situation resulted with the motorized units immobilized and clogging the roads. (Pariani, the Chief of the General Staff, with whom I spoke later, explained this likewise and said that one might state paradoxically that with motorized columns it was almost more important to prepare their withdrawal than their commitment.) Mussolini added that the military should give the greatest attention to dangerous combined attacks of tanks and planes, which in this case had proved disastrous to the Italians. French direction had been unmistakably evident on the side of the Reds in their whole tactical procedure. In conclusion Mussolini stated that militarily the set-back was of no real importance and would be made up for without delay, but this would require that the Spaniards, who had hardly fired a shot during the decisive days, would not again fail to do their share.

Under Secretary of State Bastianini spoke to me earlier about the French attempts to separate Germany from Italy by applauding her greater reserve in contrast to Italy's conduct, and to disinterest her in the Spanish affair. I told him that following my Berlin conversations I had to term such conduct on the part of Germany as entirely out of the question.—End of the secret part.

2. During the discussion of the general political situation I called attention to the importance of the impending agreement with Yugoslavia,[2] which would not fail to have an effect especially on France and the Little Entente. Mussolini agreed and termed the agreement a

---

[2] The reference is to the Pact of Belgrade, between Italy and Yugoslavia, signed on Mar. 25, 1937, by which the signatories pledged themselves to respect their common land and sea frontiers, not to have recourse to war as an instrument of national policy in their mutual relations, and not to support on their territory activities directed against the other. A translation of its text may be found in *Documents on International Affairs, 1937* (London, 1939), p. 302.

chemical solvent in international affairs, adding that Blum would long since have been overthrown if international Jewry were not supporting him. In reply to my question whether difficulties were still to be expected in Belgrade, Mussolini declared that he would not send his Foreign Minister to a foreign capital unless he were sure of being on safe ground. Concerning the contents of the agreement he further remarked that Italy was abolishing once and for all support of the Crotian émigrés, since it had proved pointless over a period of 8 years. Albania could now feel doubly secure, since her independence was guaranteed both by Italy and by Yugoslavia. We then spoke about Hungary's concern because of our policy and that of Italy in the southeast, and we agreed that both countries would continue friendly relations with Hungary and that the present German and Italian policies in the Danube area would in the long run be to the advantage of Hungary.

3. I informed Mussolini as to the German motives for sending Field Marshal von Blomberg to the coronation,[3] at the same time mentioning Blomberg's scheduled visit to Italy. Mussolini raised no objections to the German decision.

4. I then reported to Mussolini on the method which General Göring wanted to adopt with regard to economic agreements of a military nature, namely, to have preliminary discussions by experts and a basic discussion by himself during his next stay in Rome. Mussolini agreed and stated, pointing to a sizable document lying before him, that he was constantly dealing with this question; the Italian situation with regard to many raw materials was more favorable than was supposed and would improve further through systematic action. To my question whether it was possible to assist Germany with grain he stated that this was possible in good years; gradually Libyan grain was also assuming importance.

HASSELL

---

[3] Field Marshal von Blomberg was chief German representative at the coronation of King George VI in London. He visited Italy shortly thereafter.

No. 237

701/261201

The Ambassador in Italy to the Foreign Ministry

Telegram

No. 82 of March 27   ROME, March 27, 1937.

With reference to your telegram No. 75 of March 25.[1]

State Secretary Bastianini told me in strict confidence that Grandi's sharp declaration to the effect that the Italian volunteers would remain

---

[1] Not printed (701/261202). The telegram instructed Hassell to ascertain Italian views on the further withdrawal of volunteers, so that Germany could adapt her attitude accordingly.

in Spain had been a surprise here, since it exceeded his instructions. They were waiting now for Grandi's reply to a telegram sent him. With this reservation he could state today that it was not Italy's intention flatly to oppose a discussion of withdrawal of volunteers but merely to gain time and not to take up the actual discussion of the matter, if possible, before the set-back at Guadalajara had been made good.   To begin with, the gold question could serve to delay matters. Furthermore, he had caused references to be made in the Italian press to the inefficacy of control measures in the face of the Red influx. The establishment of the special committee should not be opposed in principle, however, since it was precisely in a special committee that dilatory tactics could best be carried on later.   A convincing argument was, for example, a reference to the fact that the authoritarian governments were probably in a position to effect the withdrawal of their volunteers, but the other governments would find it difficult. Moreover, reference should be made to the necessity of insuring that equal numbers of Red and White volunteers would depart simultaneously.

A further telegraphic report follows.

HASSELL

No. 238

701/261211–12

The Ambassador in Italy to the Foreign Ministry

Telegram

SECRET   ROME, March 29, 1937.
No. 84 of March 29   Sent March 30.

With reference to my telegram No. 82 of March 27.

For the Foreign Minister.

Today Ciano read to me the personal instruction which Mussolini sent Grandi Friday, laying down the Italian viewpoint in final form. It stated that *actual* withdrawal of the Italian volunteers was out of the question until the set-back at Guadalajara, which was not very significant militarily but was awkward politically, had been made good.   Mussolini was not entirely opposed in principle to a withdrawal of the volunteers after he had obtained his revenge, especially in view of certain Spanish currents of opinion which deserved notice; in any case, however, an equal number of Whites and Reds should be withdrawn.   *Tactically* it was not expedient to assume the odium of refusing to withdraw.   It would be better to consent to turn the matter over to a subcommittee and to continue the tactics of sabotage and delay there.   Ciano commented on the instruction to the effect that Mussolini considered the possibility of a withdrawal of volunteers very unlikely in the foreseeable future, but, apart from the above-mentioned tactical aspect of the question, he did not altogether exclude the possibility of a situation in which a withdrawal of volunteers might be more advantageous to the Whites than to the Reds, and also might forestall the development in Spain of an antiforeign tendency. He expressly stressed that at the present time there was no dissension whatsoever between the Italians and the Spaniards but that certain underground currents against foreigners should be kept under observation. For the present the goal would continue to be a military victory in order to wipe out the defeat. For this purpose, officers, matériel, weapons, and airplanes would be sent, perhaps also four submarines, although without crews, and Franco had been informed to this effect.

As compared with previous statements, there was unmistakably a slight undertone of possible resignation both in Mussolini's instruction and in Ciano's words with regard to future developments in Spain after they had succeeded in avenging their defeat.

HASSELL

No. 239

3373/E010811–14

The Ambassador in Great Britain to the Foreign Ministry

Telegram

No. 189 of March 30   LONDON, March 30, 1937—4 : 57 p.m.
                                       Received March 30—9 : 00 p.m.
                                       Pol. III 1619

With reference to my telegram No. 181.[1]

For the Führer and Chancellor and the Foreign Minister personally.
The situation as viewed from the Non-Intervention Committee:

1. The supervision and control of the Spanish land and sea frontiers will probably go into effect the middle of April, since it will not be possible for the control agents, ships, etc., to be at the designated places or for the legal measures which have been prepared to enter into force in the various countries before that time. The effectiveness of the supervision depends upon the smooth functioning of the control scheme, which is still untested in practice and is limited by the fact that air supervision is impossible and that various questions such as the participation of non-European states in the control scheme, as well as several other questions which have been reported on, still await solution in the Non-Intervention Committee. Nevertheless, it can probably be expected that the sending of war matériel and volunteers by land and sea on any large scale will gradually become more and more difficult, so that the two combatants will soon be mainly de-

---

[1] Not printed (3373/E010799–800).

pendent upon themselves, a fact which should be taken into consideration in evaluating the entire situation. To what extent it will be possible to send reinforcements by air, however, cannot be judged from here.

2. The question of the withdrawal of non-Spanish volunteers from Spain could be solved, according to our view here, only with the approval of the Spanish Government and the Spanish Bolshevists, and thereafter by the employment, at great expense, of a strong international police force. Since this approval is problematical—refusal by Franco at least is assured . . . (group evidently garbled)—an evacuation does not appear feasible. This opinion, as already reported, is apparently shared by the British Government.

The blunt Italian refusal even to discuss the question of withdrawing non-Spanish volunteers is, according to Grandi's statement after the session in question, to be attributed principally to the fact that they do not wish to discuss the question of withdrawal at the present time on account of the Italians fighting in Spain, and even more to the fact that the Italian Government considered a drastic action necessary in the face of the reports of the Italian defeat in Spain (comparisons with Caporetto by British press and radio). But the Italians also appear to object in principle to discussing the question of the withdrawal of volunteers.

I supported Grandi in a suitable manner during the committee meeting while avoiding any fundamental stand on the new Italian attitude in this question, and I prevented the sensationally exaggerated statements made by the Ambassadors of France [2] and Soviet Russia [3] for propaganda purposes from being included in the communiqué. By thus preventing the publication of the really serious declarations of the above-mentioned Ambassadors, a deterioration of the international situation has been avoided, whereas, as appears from the world press, Italy has nevertheless achieved her desired drastic press reaction.

It seems as if Grandi was somewhat carried away by the provocation of the Soviet Ambassador. Grandi had been told, as reported earlier, that his Government would, if necessary, declare that the question of the withdrawal of volunteers was not ripe for discussion at the present time; he had told me nothing in advance regarding his sharp manner of procedure. This little Hussar-sortie of the Italians in a not very vital question came off without damaging the joint front in favor of Franco.

3. Now the problem is how the question of volunteers is to be handled further in the Non-Intervention Committee.

---

[2] Charles Corbin.
[3] Ivan Maisky.

The general military situation in Spain, which cannot be evaluated from here, would seem to be decisive in this matter. The question is: Will Franco, in view of the present military position in Spain, and assuming that it will hardly be possible to send any further troop contingents in the foreseeable future, be able to master the situation? If this question is answered in the affirmative, the following possibilities exist for our attitude in the Non-Intervention Committee in order to prevent the evacuation of non-Spanish volunteers:

(1) The German Government supports the Italian stand and declares that it also does not deem it opportune to discuss this question at the present time (one might for example cite the technical impracticability as a reason), or

(2) Germany continues to support her proposal for an evacuation, in the certainty that the committee will in any case eventually recognize the impossibility of carrying out such a withdrawal of volunteers.

To support the present Italian viewpoint would in my opinion involve a certain aggravation of the situation. I do not foresee any real danger in this procedure as such. This opinion is supported by Lord Plymouth's personal statement, already reported, and by the attitude of the British press over the week end. Nevertheless, such procedure seems unnecessary, if the same goal can be achieved by the second course without, in this case, exposing ourselves to any blame before world opinion for the failure of the evacuation.

I request instructions on how to proceed further. If my opinion is shared in Berlin, then a suitable agreement with Rome on further procedure would be advisable and a correspondingly clear instruction from Rome to Grandi would be necessary. This should not be difficult to bring about, since Grandi told me after the meeting that he does not believe that the refusal to submit the question to a committee of experts represents the final position of his Government.

4. Matters are different, however, if the military situation in Spain must be so assessed that Franco cannot achieve victory without further large-scale reinforcements of men and matériel. In this case we would have to pursue fundamentally new tactics in the committee, particularly with regard to implementation of the plan of supervision, and also in the treatment of the gaps still found in the supervision.

Particularly the latter should be improved to keep open certain possibilities for further reinforcement measures, so that, although not much can be changed at the present stage in the implementation of the plan for supervision, we could negotiate in a decidedly dilatory manner here in the future. This question is also important for normal reinforcements.

If this is to be done, please send instructions to that effect after agreement is reached with the Italians.

5. It is not easy to answer the question how England and France would react if further Italian measures to send reinforcements should become known. I consider incorrect the Swedish Minister's remark to me that France would certainly send divisions to Spain if Mussolini sent additional troops there. I believe that France would do nothing without the approval of England. England, however, would see grave danger of a European war in such a development, which she, in her need for peace, does not desire. The attitude of the representatives of the Entente over the week end supports the correctness of this line of reasoning. Since France, however, will not undertake any serious measures without the approval of England, I believe that, although possible further Italian support of Franco by sending new troops would indeed sharpen the tension, no irremediable situation would arise in view of British efforts to reach a settlement. It would be important, however, for reinforcements to be sent as cautiously and gradually as possible.

The next session on the question of withdrawing volunteers has not yet been scheduled, but it will probably not take place before . . . (group evidently garbled) April 8. I should be grateful for information concerning the situation in Spain and our intentions.

RIBBENTROP

No. 240

3373/E010815–17

The Acting State Secretary to the Embassy in Great Britain

Telegram

IMMEDIATE   BERLIN, April 1, 1937—8 : 50 p.m.
SECRET   zu Pol. III 1619.
No. 127

Drafting Officer : Counselor of Legation Dumont.

For the Ambassador. With reference to your 189.[1]

According to reports from our Embassy in Rome the attitude of the Italian Government is as follows :

A withdrawal of the Italian volunteers was for all practical purposes out of the question before the defeat at Guadalajara had been made good. The defeat was of no great military importance, to be sure, but on the other hand it had had unfavorable psychological and political reactions which had to be stamped out by a military victory.

Tactically it was not expedient, however, to refuse to discuss the

---

[1] Document No. 239, *supra.*

question of volunteers, if only so as not to incur the odium of having prevented a solution of the problem. Rather, it was advisable to agree to submit the matter to a technical subcommittee where difficulties would develop of themselves. Not until later, after successful revenge, could a situation arise necessitating a change in these tactics, especially if a withdrawal of volunteers were more advantageous to the Whites than to the Reds and also if a hostile tendency toward foreigners should develop in Spain. Even though there was no dissension at the present time between the Italians and the Spaniards, there did exist nevertheless certain undercurrents against foreigners.

The next goal would, in any case, be a military victory to wipe out the defeat. The situation had already been restored and the resumption of the offensive was to be expected shortly.

The Italian Government has sent Grandi instructions in accordance with this viewpoint. Please adjust your attitude to that of the Italians.

DIECKHOFF

No. 241

701/261213

The Ambassador in Italy to the Foreign Ministry

Telegram

SECRET   ROME, April 9, 1937.
No. 95 of April 9

For the Foreign Minister.

Ciano informed me today that the situation in Spain was satisfactory thus far; the offensive at Bilbao was proceeding quite well. The evident lack of matériel would have to be remedied. The most unpleasant fact which had appeared recently was the marked inferiority of the Nationalist Air Force. Italy was therefore sending 72 fighter planes, of which the first squadron of 24 had already arrived. An estimated 50 German bombers were urgently desired to supplement these.

Ciano added that General Roatta had been recalled and in his place General Bastico, formerly a corps commander in East Africa and recently a corps commander in Alessandria, had been appointed commander of the Italian forces. General Terruzzi, the former head of the militia, was being placed under his command as leader of all the Black Shirts.

HASSELL

No. 242

4078/E068914

The Ambassador in Italy to the Foreign Ministry

Telegram

No. 97 of April 9   ROME, April 9, 1937.
                                           Pol. III 1756.

I spoke to Ciano today about the sharp policy of the Vatican toward the Third Reich and its incomprehensible weakness in Spain, for example, as well as its obvious lack of influence among Catholic Basques. Ciano replied that the Vatican had lost a great deal of ground in Spain. With regard to Germany he had told the Nuncio here [1] recently that he did not understand the Vatican's policy toward Germany, which was the only country, together with Italy, actively combating Communism. The question was also important for Italy, since the hostile attitude of the Vatican toward Italy's friend, Germany, also constituted a burden for Italian policy.

                                                         HASSELL

---

[1] Mgr. Francesco Borongini Duca.

No. 243

4446/E086526–31

The Ambassador in Spain to the Foreign Ministry

Sa. 3–1420   SALAMANCA, April 14, 1937.
                                      Received April 20.
                                         zu Pol. III 1931.

Subject: Domestic policy and the reform program; the future form of government; military questions.

On April 11 I had a conference with General Franco lasting more than two hours, in the course of which he expressed his views on some questions of domestic policy, the future form of government, and the military situation.

Franco's starting point was that even before the outbreak of fighting the conviction had prevailed in wide circles in Spain that the country was not making any progress with the old parliamentary system. The Falange, which in its ideas leaned heavily on the National Socialist and Fascist model, had only a year ago been very weak numerically. Only after the beginning of the Nationalist movement led by Franco had the Falange, with considerable assistance from Nationalist-minded officers, obtained a great number of adherents and thereby its present importance. But after the death of José Antonio Primo de Rivera, regarding whose death there is in Franco's opinion no doubt, the Falange lacked a real leader. Young Primo de Rivera, although he had as yet had little experience, had been a leader because of his intelligence and energy. His successor, Hedilla, was a completely honest person, but by no means equal to the demands imposed on the leader of the Falange. Hedilla was surrounded by a whole crowd of ambitious young persons who influenced him instead of being influenced and led by him.

As for the leaders of the monarchist parties, Franco spoke against Falconde in particular. Immediately before the beginning of the Nationalist movement last year Falconde had told General Mola that the Requetés [1] would participate only if definite promises were given to him, Falconde, that the monarchy would be restored. Mola had rejected this very sharply and demanded that the promises already given by the Requetés to participate in the fight against the Marxist Government be kept. The same Falconde had not long ago taken a number of measures for the reintroduction of the monarchy, which he, Franco, could not but regard as directed against him and his Government. He had thereupon summoned the most prominent leaders of the Requetés, who had told him that they in no wise approved of Falconde's conduct. Franco told me that he had then been on the point of deciding to have Falconde executed immediately for high treason but had refrained from doing so since that would have produced a bad impression among the Requetés at the front, who were fighting bravely there. He had therefore confined himself to banishing Falconde from the country within 48 hours. The latter was now in Portugal.

There negotiations had recently taken place between the Falange and the Traditionalists for the purpose of merging the two parties. On this occasion, too, the question of the monarchy had been placed in the foreground by the Traditionalists. The negotiations had not led to any tangible result. Hedilla, the leader of the Falange, had said afterward that he had known of these negotiations but did not approve of them, a fact which Franco very properly called proof of Hedilla's lack of qualities of leadership.

Franco intended more than a month ago to make a public announcement of his reform program. General Queipo de Llano had advised him at that time to wait and come forward with a proclamation at the fall of Madrid, which was assumed to be imminent. Now that the capture of Madrid was not to be expected for the present, Franco had decided to announce his reform program in the near future.

Regarding his attitude toward the Falange and the monarchist parties, Franco told me that he wished to fuse these groups into one party, the leadership of which he himself would assume. To my objection that the leadership of a party would take up a very great deal

---

[1] The Requetés were the combatant section of the Traditionalists, or Carlists.

of his time and would hardly be possible in addition to the conduct of military operations and other governmental affairs, Franco replied that he, as head of the new unity party, intended to form a Junta, probably consisting of four representatives of the Falange and two representatives of the monarchist groups. The core of the unity party would be formed by the Falange, which had the soundest program and the greatest following in the country.

I discussed this development yesterday with our Landesgruppenleiter and the representative of the Fascio at the Italian Embassy; the latter, not inaccurately, described the situation in these words: "Franco is a leader without a party, the Falange a party without a leader." If in his attempt to bring the parties together Franco should meet with opposition from the Falange, we and the Italians are agreed that, in spite of all our inclination toward the Falange and its sound tendencies, we must support Franco, who after all intends to make the program of the Falange the basis of his internal policy. The realization of the most urgently needed social reforms is possible only with Franco, not in opposition to him.

I then directed the conversation with Franco to the rumor which has been circulating here for several weeks regarding an impending regency, the purpose of which was said to be keeping open a place for a king or a candidate for the throne. Franco told me that for Spain the return to the monarchy was absolutely out of the question for the foreseeable future. He would consider it wrong, however, to adopt measures or provisions which were calculated to block the road to a monarchy even for a later date. Only after completion of the reconstruction of Spain, which would take a long time, could one consider whether a certain continuity could not be established by a reintroduction of the monarchy. It was entirely premature, however, to occupy oneself seriously with this question now.

Taking up the military situation, Franco said, among other things, that the set-back of the Italians on the Guadalajara front could be explained mainly by the fact that while General Mancini was in Salamanca on the day in question in order to report to him—Franco—the Chief of the Italian General Staff, acting as Mancini's deputy, had prematurely given the order for all the Italian forces to withdraw on account of the disorganization that had occurred in part of the troops in the front line. To me this statement by Franco proves that the very clever Mancini is now making the Chief of his General Staff the scapegoat in the eyes of the Spaniards in order to save at least something of the very severely shattered prestige of his troops. Mancini himself told me as early as March 17, that is, the day before the set-back at Brihuega, that the training and composition of his units, especially of the officer corps, were bad and not equal to continuing the Guadalajara offensive. It is by no means, therefore, merely a question of failure on the part of the Chief of the Italian General Staff.

Franco told me further that he had commissioned one of his best officers, General Orgaz, to supervise all the training behind the front; he then spoke of the very good results of the first training course conducted by Major von Issendorff (Reserve List), which had just been concluded. Franco told me in this connection that he considered it desirable to make use of the Germans' broad training experience, for the officer-candidate courses given in Burgos, for example. It also seemed desirable to him that General Orgaz should be assisted in problems of training by a man like Colonel von Knauer, who had at his command such broad experience and linguistic knowledge. This recognition by General Franco is very much to be welcomed, for it touches one of the very basic reasons why, apart from Málaga, virtually nothing has been achieved in the military field during the last five months. Without expert combat training of the Spanish troops behind the front, the war cannot be won.

FAUPEL

No. 244

1819/416187–88

The Ambassador in Spain to the Foreign Ministry

Sa. 3–1421   SALAMANCA, April 14, 1937.
Received April 21.
Pol. II 1156.

With reference to my telegraphic report No. 124 of April 3.[1]

Subject: Laval's offer to Franco to collaborate against Communism.

In continuation of the above-mentioned telegraphic report, I submit the text and translation of a confidential memorandum sent me by the Director of the Diplomatic Cabinet of the Chief of State and Generalissimo regarding the conversation of an agent of Franco with the former French Premier Laval.

Franco told me today that he had so far not defined his position with respect to Laval's wishes; before doing so he wished to learn what backing Laval had.

FAUPEL

[Enclosure] [2]

STRICTLY CONFIDENTIAL   SALAMANCA, April 13, 1937.

The French ex-Minister, P. Laval, through the intermediary of a person related to him and in his confidence, caused to be conveyed to

---

[1] Notation in handwriting: "Should read No. 194 of April 13. Has not yet reached the office." Neither No. 124 nor No. 194 has been found.

[2] The original of this document is in Spanish.

His Excellency, General Franco, the desire that a confidant of the latter might meet with him in order to discuss with him matters of great importance connected with the Nationalist cause in Spain. M. Laval, in expressing this wish, stated himself to be in favor of the Nationalists.

The conversation took place and the French statesman brought out the serious internal situation in France and the imminence of a Communist movement in that country, and stated that he was in touch with Doriot,[3] Colonel La Rocque,[4] and Marshal Pétain. He also stated that toward the end of July or the beginning of August, when France had to ask for credit, it was expected that the financial world would refuse to grant a loan and that the Blum Government would fall. M. Laval was of the opinion that the salvation of France lay in a Pétain government and that the Marshal was determined to assume this responsibility, but that President Blum, whom he compared to Alcalá Zamora, and with whom they were secretly working to this end, did not seem inclined to accept it.

M. Laval hopes that, should the occasion arise, regardless of irreparable damage and local successes of Communism, he will be able to save France through a Nationalist movement. He announces that he is going to carry out an intense propaganda in our favor, and he wanted His Excellency, the Generalissimo, informed. He offered to send journalists who, since they belong to the Left, could work on our side in Spain, and he asked that we accept the offer of an extremely high-powered radio station which, if set up in San Sebastián at the disposal of the Spanish Government, could conduct great propaganda in France in favor of the Spanish Nationalist cause. M. Laval seems very depressed over his treaty with Russia, which he now finds dangerous for his country.

In view of the international character of this note and the trustworthiness of its source, it would seem of interest to pass it on to our friends.

---

[3] Jacques Doriot, leader of the French Popular Party (PPF).
[4] Former leader of the Croix de Feu, later of the French Social Party, active in semi-Fascist movements.

No. 245

2938/569711–12

Memorandum by an Official of the Economic Policy Department

BERLIN, April 16, 1937.
zu W II WE 2586.

Subject: Rio Tinto mines (northwest of Seville).

The matter of ore purchases from the Rio Tinto mines first engaged the attention of the German Government through negotiations in the

Non-Intervention Committee. At the session of January 12, Sweden's representative asserted that gold exports could not be discussed without at the same time prohibiting the confiscation of copper exports in favor of Germany.

To our inquiry, the Embassy at Salamanca reported on January 20 [1] that the Spanish Government reserved to itself complete freedom of action with respect to distribution of the production of the Rio Tinto mines. Hisma had the written promise of the Franco Government for 60 percent of the production.

On February 4 Magowan, a member of the commercial section of the British Embassy, submitted a demand of the British Government for indemnification for the 2,120 tons of copper precipitate purchased by Hisma, and possibly for another 500 tons already confiscated.[2] The British Government demanded restitution in kind or by delivery of ores or a cash indemnity in English pounds.

The matter was particularly unpleasant for the British Government because the copper refineries in the areas of unemployment in South Wales had had to be shut down.

After consultation with the proper authorities, Mr. Magowan was informed on February 8 that the matter did not concern the German Government because purely private transactions were involved. It would nevertheless be willing to follow the pending negotiations in a sympathetic manner.

In fact, a representative of Rowak intended to go to London to negotiate with Copper, Tharsis, and Peronel, the three companies interested in the export of copper ores from Spain.

On February 24 Mr. Magowan again appeared at the Foreign Ministry. He repeated his demand, denying the legality of the German standpoint. We also adhered to our point of view.

The negotiations between Rowak and I. G. Farben Industrie, on the German side, and the three British companies regarding the purchases of copper ores have not yet come to an end. It is intended to bring them to a close in the very near future. These negotiations, however, are concerned mainly with the utilization of pyrites.

The Rio Tinto is a company under Spanish law with predominantly British capital.

SABATH

---

[1] Document No. 208, p. 230.
[2] Document No. 218, p. 240.

No. 246

3373/E010849–51

Memorandum by the Head of Political Division III

CONFIDENTIAL   BERLIN, April 21, 1937.
                                               Pol. III 1939 a.

Subject: Conference of the Foreign Minister in Rome with regard to
    Spain (Pol. IV 2043).

Military:

The next goal of the Italians is a military success to wipe out the
defeat of Guadalajara.   The necessary preparations have been and are
being made.

Diplomatic:

The effectiveness of the control plan put into force on the night of
April 19 remains to be seen.   In any case, it is probably in the German
and Italian interest to supply our Embassies in London with material
regarding any violations by the other states of the embargo on volunteers and arms, particularly for the period after February 21 and
after April 19, 1937, so that in case of an accusation against Germany
or Italy by other states we can proceed at once to counterattack in
the committee.

Should the reports on the smuggling of arms and volunteers
along the Pyrenees border continue, it may be desirable to work
together with the Italians in the committee for a strengthening of controls at the French-Spanish border.

The question of the withdrawal of volunteers:

We are in agreement with the Italians on the following line of
policy:

A withdrawal is out of the question at present.   However, it is not
expedient from a tactical standpoint to refuse to discuss the question,
particularly since the difficulties in the way of a solution of the problem
will make themselves felt in the special committee that is now occupied
with the matter.   The Italians are therefore interested only in gaining time, and do not wish to start a real discussion, if possible, until
after the defeat at Guadalajara has been made good.   As a means of
delay a reference to the slow progress of the negotiations on the gold
question is perhaps suitable.   After they have succeeded in squaring
accounts the Italians will have no objection to a factual discussion
of the question of volunteers in the special committee.   They would
not even oppose a withdrawal of the volunteers under certain circumstances and at the proper moment, as Herr von Hassell wires, if, for
me that he believed the new British King was not entirely in accord

Reds, or in case of growing hostility to foreigners. Even though there is no bad feeling between the Italians and the Spaniards at present, there are nevertheless certain undercurrents against foreigners.

D[UMONT]

No. 247

47/31963–68

The Ambassador in Spain to the Foreign Ministry

STRICTLY SECRET

Sa. 3–1504

SALAMANCA, April 21, 1937.
Received April 26.
Pol. I 2104 g.

With reference to telegraphic report No. 212 of April 21.[1]

Subject: Conference with Mancini regarding the internal political and military situation.

Today General Mancini called on me by instruction of General Doria, the new Commander in Chief of the Italian troops, who was prevented from coming in person for a conference. He began by informing me that the purpose of his visit was to discuss the following questions:

1. The internal political situation.
2. The general military situation.
3. Can Bilbao still be taken by Franco or not?

In response to my question, Mancini first explained his own situation by saying that he did not have a clearly defined assignment at the moment. There were the following possibilities for him: either to take over command of several Italian divisions, that is, an army corps under the general supervision of General Doria; or to become military adviser or Chief of Staff to General Doria, who is in command of all the Italian troops; or, finally, to assume the post of first Italian adviser to General Franco.

With regard to the first of the three above-mentioned questions, I told Mancini that by the measures of the last few days[2] Franco had undoubtedly made great progress toward achieving internal political unity, even though, on the other hand, all sorts of opposition, precisely with regard to these measures, was still to be expected. Mancini was of the same opinion.

In the discussion of the second question, Mancini took the view that the war could no longer be won if it continued to be waged in its present form. General Franco should now be told plainly, therefore, that he had to adopt certain measures proposed to him or else dispense with further help from Italy and also Germany. These measures to be

---

[1] Not found.
[2] On Apr. 19 General Franco decreed the amalgamation of the Falange and the Traditionalist parties.

proposed to Franco should be such that, in the first place, Germans and Italians would be granted a decisive influence upon operations, and, in the second place, new units would be organized and trained behind the front with the assistance and under the decisive supervision of German and Italian officers. Mancini thus formulates the same demands that I advocated 4 weeks ago in Berlin and which, insofar as they concern the training of assault troops, Lieutenant Colonel von Funck recently also supported.

To my question whether his statements simply represented his personal opinion, Mancini replied that he was giving me the views of General Doria and all the important Italian officers in Spain.

With regard to the third question, concerning Bilbao, Mancini said that in his opinion the offensive had bogged down. I agreed, replying that unless something quite unforeseen occurred, I also no longer counted on the capture of Bilbao. Mancini continued that Franco had asked the Italians to give him the Littoria Division for the attack on Bilbao, in addition to the 14 battalions and 7 artillery sections already placed at his disposal. The Italian Supreme Command was therefore considering whether this request of Franco's should be granted, but they judged the situation to be such that even if the Littoria Division were committed Bilbao could hardly be taken now, since the Reds had had several weeks in which to concentrate their forces on the northern front and fortify new positions.

Regarding the Italian troops and their combat readiness, Mancini informed me that the Littoria Division would be ready for attack in approximately 1 week. The other Italian units had been formed into 2 militia divisions and the Francisi group, which was not much smaller than a division. Besides, the Italian Supreme Command still commanded the 2 brigades which had been organized since the beginning of February, *Flechas Negras* and *Flechas Azules*, staffed with Italian officers and non-commissioned officers. Each of these brigades, which had had a training period of some 6 weeks before being committed, had some 150 Italian officers and 300 Italian non-commissioned officers; in all, each brigade had 1,500 Italians, including the Italian specialists (radio operators, etc.).

To restore the full combat strength of the Italian divisions which had been depleted on the Guadalajara front, numerous officers had been sent home and replaced by more suitable ones; likewise, some 3,000 of the troops had been sent home, and another 3,000 had been sent back to the support area, so that the fighting quality of the militia divisions had been improved. One thing that the battles at Guadalajara had proved, Mancini said, was that a war simply could not be won with an insufficiently trained militia. I can only add here that the Italians should have known this 3 months ago.

He asserted that the militia divisions would need some 3 weeks more before they would be ready to be committed in an attack. Since I had estimated that approximately 2 months would be needed for rehabilitating the Italian divisions after the reverses north of Guadalajara, my estimate of that time coincides with Mancini's present statements.

Mancini continued to the effect that as soon as the Italian divisions were completely rehabilitated, thought would be given to committing them as complete units.

He then spoke of the rumor, which I had heard some time ago in a hardly credible form, to the effect that the Basque Government had made General Franco a peace proposal several weeks ago on condition that the Basques be promised a certain amount of autonomy and due consideration for the Basque language in the schools. A new proposal had now been made to Franco to the effect that Basque leaders be assured of freedom to leave Spain and the Basque people be promised that their lives would be spared even if they had participated in the fighting. These proposals had been made by persons who were probably not to be taken seriously. In the event that Franco acceded to the last-mentioned conditions, the Basques desired the guaranty of a neutral government. Franco rejected this last demand and, in addition, took the stand that he would win Bilbao in about 2 weeks by an attack and without negotiations. Mancini and I agreed that this hope of Franco's had very little foundation. Mancini suggested that we could propose to Franco, in case he did not grant the guaranties of a neutral government, that the safety of the Basque population be assured by having the conquered territory, in particular Bilbao, occupied first of all by the Italian and German troops which were on the northern front. Mancini added that since the Nationalist troops had shot a large number of people after the capture of Málaga, the desire of the Basques for such a guaranty was very understandable. I pointed out to Mancini that even to negotiate with the Basque Government in the sense of his proposal would mean officially admitting the presence of German and Italian units. Mancini answered that naturally only volunteer units should be mentioned, and the guaranty would have to be made by the commanders of these units. I should like to remark on this proposal of Mancini that it would also have the disadvantage of tying up German and Italian troops for a considerable time solely for the purpose of occupying Bilbao and other places. Aside from this, I do not believe that Franco would be quick to accept such a proposal.

I intend to inform myself further on the whole Basque question tomorrow in a conference with Franco.

FAUPEL

No. 248

3373/E010885–89

The Ambassador in Spain to the Foreign Ministry

Sa. 3–1600   SALAMANCA, May 1, 1937.
                                              Received May 10.
                                              Pol. III 2297.

Subject: Development of the internal political situation.

The last few days have led to a temporary, severe tension in the internal situation.

Through the *Gobernadores Civiles* (corresponding to our Regierungspräsident or Oberregierungspräsident), thereby circumventing Hedilla, Franco had sent the *Jefes Provinciales* (corresponding to our Gauleiters) the command that in future they were to follow only orders given by him, Franco. In this manner Hedilla was eliminated from his own party. He answered this measure of Franco with a telegram to the Gauleiters to obey the instructions of the Chief of State only if they came through him, Hedilla. As Franco at the same time became convinced that Hedilla had told him untruths in various previous conversations, and since he received other news which made the situation more serious, the Chief of State had Hedilla and 20 other leading Falangists arrested. The decisive factor seems to have been, as Franco told me, that a young Falangist from one of the provincial capitals reported to headquarters, naming witnesses, that the local Gauleiter had ordered his subordinate leaders immediately to initiate strong propaganda against Franco.

Franco told me a few days ago that he was determined, since he was fighting a war, to nip in the bud any action directed against him and his Government by shooting the guilty parties.

Both sides are to blame for this momentary deterioration in the situation. Franco overlooked the fact that one can, to be sure, make one brigade out of two regiments by an order, but that the merging and fusing of two parties takes some time even if, as in this case, their social programs are very similar. Franco therefore had to give Hedilla the time and the opportunity partly to integrate the numerically much weaker Requetés and partly, insofar as that was not possible, to eliminate them. On the other hand, Hedilla, under pressure from his subordinates, who accused him of treason toward the party, sent the above-mentioned telegram to the *Jefes Provinciales*, which meant open rebellion against Franco.

I again urgently advised the Chief of State to calm the excited feelings in certain parts of the Falange by hastening the announcement of certain social measures, or at least by the immediate institution of commissions for the early discussion of such measures. I gave him a number of written or printed documents, among others a Spanish translation of our "Law Regulating National Labor", and informed him that we could also put at his disposal this or that specialist for social legislation, etc., if he liked. Franco thanked me and, like his brother Nicolás, promised to make use of the documents supplied him. With a reference to the inadequate propaganda in White Spain, I also recommended to Franco that he not only announce his social decrees in the *Official Gazette* and just once in the press, but make them generally known and therefore more effective through repetition over the radio and in newspaper articles.

Signor Danzi, the very young and extremely active leader of the local Fascio, some days ago gave General Franco or his brother a draft made by him, Danzi, of a constitution leaning heavily on the Italian model. From statements which Franco made to me, I do not believe that he will consider adopting this draft. In the present situation, it is not, after all, a question of the proclamation of an artificially constructed constitution, but of the immediate announcement and execution of social reforms which would bring relief to the very poorest of the population and bring the Falangists the certainty that their party program will be executed.

Franco has assured me again and again that he intends to do this. But as questions of social legislation are somewhat out of his personal province, and as he has hitherto had no suitable advisers around him in this field and is, in addition, fully occupied with the military command and with foreign policy and economic questions, the social measures are getting started only very gradually. The best thing Franco could do would be to put into immediate effect some of the proposals for reform which have already been prepared by the Falange, partly with German collaboration, and make use of suitable representatives of the Falange itself for this purpose.

In the final analysis the internal difficulties at the moment can be traced to the lack of large-scale military victories. What the effect of such victories is upon general morale could best be observed on the occasion of the capture of Málaga. The Bilbao offensive, too, which has now been going on for 5 weeks, from the very first day suffered from faulty preparation, mistakes of the commanders, and wholly insufficient training of the troops. Action upon these points is the nucleus of the military problem, which is the foundation for a solution of the whole Spanish problem. The second requirement is the introduction and realistic execution of social reforms. Without these even the military victory could not lead to final pacification of the country; on the contrary, sooner or later a new revolution would follow. Franco also realizes this clearly. Therefore, with his cleverness and energy, it is to be expected that he will, in spite of some resistance, fulfill the promise, made to me several times, of putting into effect the social program of the Falange.

There is no doubt that [after] a war won because of our intervention a Spain socially ordered and economically reconstructed with our help will in the future be not only a very important source of raw materials for us, but also a faithful friend for a long time to come; for the result of these events of the last year has been that there is hardly a politically conscious Spaniard who has not recognized that France and England always want a weak Spain and only we are interested in a strong Spain.

FAUPEL

No. 249

3373/E010877–78

The State Secretary to the Embassy in Spain

Telegram

No. 151   BERLIN, May 4, 1937.
                                   zu Pol. III 2200.

Drafting Officer: Counselor of Legation Dr. Dumont.

In yesterday's debate in the British House of Commons on the incidents in Guernica, accusations against Germany were again made.[1] Eden answered evasively, but ordered the British Ambassador and the Consul in Bilbao to report and promised Commons a further answer before the Whitsuntide adjournment.

Our Ambassador in London wires: "From various quarters the Embassy is receiving communications making German fliers responsible for the bombardment of Guernica, in spite of our denials. In private conversations Franco's denial is still given prominence and is construed to mean that Franco indirectly admits the attack was made by German fliers. The debate in Commons could perhaps be taken as a basis for inducing Franco now to issue an energetic and sharp denial which could not be equivocally construed."

Please induce Franco to issue an immediate and energetic denial. Our press has rejected the false British reports, by using material meanwhile received which proves destruction of the city by the Bolshevists.

MACKENSEN

---

[1] The destructive bombing of the Basque town of Guernica on Apr. 26, 1937, was alleged to have been carried out by German fliers in the service of the Spanish Nationalists.

No. 250

3373/E010880–81

The State Secretary to the Embassy in Great Britain

Telegram

VERY URGENT   BERLIN, May 5, 1937.
No. 173   zu Pol. III 2213.

Drafting Officer: Counselor of Legation Dr. Dumont.

With reference to your 257.[1]

Please explain, in line with your previous policy, that we do not consider the committee competent for the British proposal [, which changes the idea of non-intervention into the opposite].[2] Nevertheless, we are prepared, on purely humanitarian grounds, to participate in the projected appeal. In doing so, we take it for granted that no precedent would be created, and this should be expressly stated in the resolution. Another condition for our participation is the omission of even indirect reference to the Guernica incidents and of any propagandistic presentation (No. 1 and 2 at the end of your telegraphic report). With regard to Red atrocities I refer you to the report of Radio Salamanca, which was sent by special delivery today. It is left to your discretion to use it as the course of the discussion indicates.

We are also entirely in agreement with the action suggested in No. 4 but request that this demand should not in the end be made a *conditio sine qua non.*[3]

Along with the War Ministry, we are of the opinion that an attitude of rejection in principle is not to be recommended if only because, by a completely intransigent attitude, we would run the danger of being made responsible by the governments and by world opinion for the failure of a humanitarian action. Moreover, difficulties will probably arise of themselves in practice, primarily because agreement by the combatants as to open cities, etc., could hardly be brought about.

MACKENSEN

---

[1] Not printed (4906/E255214–17).

[2] The bracketed passage was deleted from Dumont's draft. The British proposal was that the Non-Intervention Committee should appeal to both combatants to abstain from bombing open towns.

[3] The telegram from London had suggested that, to insure that no precedent would be set, it might be insisted that the appeal be issued in the name of the governments represented on the committee and not by the committee as such.

No. 251

3373/E010883

The Ambassador in Spain to the Foreign Ministry

Telegram

No. 237 of May 5   SALAMANCA, May 5, 1937.
                                        Received May 6—3 : 45 a.m.
                                                Pol. III 2238.

Answer to telegraphic instruction 151.[1]

The denial agreed upon with Franco regarding Guernica has not been issued.   On April 29 and April 30 the Nationalist Government's press bureau [issued] dispatches in the form of an article regarding the burning of Guernica.   These were also given to foreign press representatives.   In the sharpest terms they reject as lies and slander the Basque Government's report regarding the alleged destruction of the city by German fliers.   The interpretation that this denial indirectly admits a German plane attack is malicious and unsupported by the text of the denial.   A translation of some of the important passages of the denial of April 29 follows:

"Guernica was destroyed with fire and gasoline.   It was set afire and reduced to ruins by the Red hordes in the criminal service of Aguirre, the President of the Basque Republic.   Aguirre planned the destruction of Guernica with the devilish intention of laying the blame before the enemy's door and producing a storm of indignation among the already conquered and demoralized Basques."

The text of the two denials follows.

I request instructions in case a new denial by the Nationalist Government is considered necessary.

                                                FAUPEL

───────────

[1] Document No. 249, p. 279.

No. 252

3373/E010890–92

The Ambassador in Spain to the Foreign Ministry

Sa. 3–1698   SALAMANCA, May 5, 1937.
                                                Received May 10.
                                                Pol. III 2298.

Subject: Franco's stand on the internal and external situation.   Reports on Laval.

In yesterday's conversation Franco informed me that he had received in all some 60,000 telegrams of congratulation and approval from the whole country in response to his decree on the merging of the Falange and the Requetés.   Investigations so far had shown that

Hedilla was heavily compromised.   The instruction issued by the *Jefe Provincial* in Zamora to the leaders of the Falange there to create opposition and propaganda against Franco was also to be traced to Hedilla's order.   Meanwhile, on Sunday, May 2, 22 Falangist leaders had visited him, Franco, in order to declare to him once more that the Falange was putting itself unreservedly under his orders.   Since its social order also corresponded to the desires of the Requetés, and since the latter had clearly recognized that the idea of a monarchy could not even be discussed for the time being and for a long time to come, he, Franco, believed that the process of merging the Falangists and the Requetés could now be carried out without any particular difficulties. Franco stated that he was convinced that the tension of recent days had thereby been overcome.   This view is essentially in accord with the reports which I have received from various quarters.

I then told Franco that abroad one occasionally hears the opinion that, in view of the long duration of the Civil War, both sides might finally be exhausted and consequently a compromise between White and Red might occur.   Franco rejected any idea of a compromise as completely impossible, stating that the war would under all circumstances be fought to a final decision.

To my question whether he knew anything new about Laval, Franco answered that his last reports were to the effect that a *rapprochement* between Laval and Lebrun, the President of the French Republic, had been set in motion.   The latter had realized that, as long as Blum was Premier, France would be drawn more and more into the wake of Communism.   Laval seemed to be succeeding in winning not only the Right but also parts of the Left to his views.   On the basis of the reports he had received, Franco considered it not impossible that Laval would one day become Premier.

As regards British policy, Franco had received news by way of Portuguese Foreign Minister Monteiro,[1] who, having returned from London a few days ago, had communicated his observations there to former Portuguese Minister Ramírez, a friend and confidant of Franco.   Monteiro, and therefore Franco, too, is of the opinion that lately they are particularly intent in England on dissuading Germany principally, but Italy too, from their present Spanish policy and on separating them from Nationalist Spain.

Going into the development of relations with Portugal, Franco asserted that when he was still in Seville in the fall of last year the Portuguese Government had promised him it would break off relations with Red Spain and recognize his, Franco's, regime, as soon as all the Spanish territory along the Portuguese border was in Franco's hands. Nevertheless, recognition by the Portuguese had not occurred after

---

[1] Armindo Monteiro was actually Portuguese Ambassador to Great Britain.

the Spanish border territory had been cleared of Reds by Franco. The Portuguese Government had told him at that time that, being under strong pressure from England, it regretted its inability to announce the recognition promised, but that Portugal would nevertheless support Spain with all its means, because a Red Spain would inevitably result in a Red Portugal. The firm conviction that the fate of Portugal in this respect was dependent upon the result of the Civil War in Spain was still decisive today for the attitude of the Portuguese Government. Franco also mentioned that he had reports that 6 million francs had been put at the disposal of agents in France by the Reds in order to provoke disorders in Portugal.

FAUPEL

No. 253

137/128159–60

The Ambassador in Great Britain to the Foreign Ministry

Telegram

URGENT   LONDON, May 6, 1937—4:24 p.m.
No. 261 of May 6   Received May 6—6:00 p.m.

For the Führer and Chancellor and the Foreign Minister.

In yesterday's conversation with Eden regarding the Guernica incident, he declared that the British Government had not yet been able to form a final judgment regarding the matter, since reports thus far had been conflicting. In reply to my question as to what reports he actually had regarding alleged participation of German fliers, Eden could only refer to the British newspaper reports. I, on the other hand, stoutly defended the familiar German viewpoint. I asked Eden whether he was prepared to publish a communiqué regarding my step in this matter, as he had in the matter of false reports regarding the Non-Intervention Committee. Eden stated that, in view of the fact that the question was not yet fully clarified and there was a debate in Parliament on the subject, he wished to refrain from doing so; he had no objection of any kind, however, to my making a suitable statement to the press. I therefore gave the Press Association such a report. For the text, I refer to the DNB dispatch. Both Eden's communication to the press regarding my step with respect to false press reports concerning the Non-Intervention Committee and my statement regarding the Guernica incident were given satisfactory publicity by almost the entire press. Only the *Daily Herald* and the *News Chronicle* add remarks that weaken their effect.

During the conversation, Eden asked me casually whether Germany would agree to an international investigation of the incident. I stated that I wished to obtain the views of my Government on this point, and I request the earliest possible instructions. Possibly a proposal would have to be made by Belgium to extend the investigation to Red atrocities, more specifically to concrete instances of recent occurrence, if possible. In any case, I request such material at once. A note from the Red Spanish Government demanding an international investigation was received at the Foreign Office yesterday. It is to be expected that the Russians will bring up this demand in the committee as soon as possible.

RIBBENTROP

No. 254

1819/416200–04

The Ambassador in Spain to the Foreign Ministry

Sa. 3–1740   SALAMANCA, May 11, 1937.
                                             Received May 19.
                                             Pol. III 2453.

Subject: Is a compromise conceivable between the Whites and the Reds? The elimination of Hedilla. The strong influence of the attorney, Serrano Suñer. Franco's views on England. Disorders in Barcelona.

The idea of a conciliation of the two warring parties in Spain, namely, the Whites and the Reds, has recently received frequent mention in German oral and written discussion. As I mentioned in my report of May 5—Sa. 3–1698—General Franco rejects even the remotest possibility of such a solution. On the side of the Reds, Alvarez del Vayo recently told a special reporter of the *Temps* that after so much blood had been shed he considered impossible any mediation between the two parties, as suggested by Mr. Churchill. The fact is that hundreds of thousands of Spanish families have suffered the loss of close relatives by murder or military execution and that this has given rise to an implacable hatred, which has developed in part into a thirst for revenge. The possibilities of conciliation are therefore so slight that we can by no means posit them as a factor in political calculations of any kind.

But if, despite all this, we assume that both sides would be exhausted after a few months more of fighting—which is not to be assumed from the duration of former Spanish civil wars—or that external political pressure upon both Whites and Reds should lead to an armistice and later to a peace of some kind, what would then be the result? Sooner or later there would have to be elections. Since Red propaganda in Spain, however, is at present undoubtedly far more clever and effective than that of the Whites and since, moreover, Red propaganda would have the support of the Marxists, Jews, and

Freemasons of the entire world, these elections would necessarily lead to the formation of a government the political composition of which can, of course, by no means be predicted in detail but which would certainly be decidedly Leftist, openly anti-German, and anti-National-Socialist. This development would then shake the authoritarian Government in Portugal and probably bring its fall. A Spanish government launched in this way would sympathize with Russia and all the countries in which so-called "Popular Front" governments have been formed. We cannot therefore have the slightest interest in a compromise solution in Spain. The fight must under all circumstances be carried on to the victory of General Franco.

As far as the internal political situation in White Spain is concerned, it is becoming more and more apparent that Hedilla is finished for the time being. He is still under detention on the ground that he will have to account for his conduct in court, and it does not seem that he has sufficient support in the Falange to effect his immediate release. Franco told me a few weeks ago that he was considering sending Hedilla to Germany and Italy for a few months in order that he might learn something there and later on apply his experience to social reconstruction here in Spain. Franco seems for the present to have given up this idea, which had the support of the Italian Chief of Propaganda, Danzi.

On the other hand, the attorney, Serrano Suñer, has come more and more into the foreground in recent weeks. He is the husband of a sister of General Franco's wife. Not until February did Serrano Suñer flee from Madrid, where he was held prisoner by the Reds in constant danger of his life. Although he formerly belonged to the Acción Católica, he told me he had been one of the closest confidants of José Antonio Primo de Rivera and intended to safeguard the latter's political heritage. Serrano Suñer, who evidently has strong influence with Franco in internal political affairs, brought away with him from the prisons of Madrid a burning hatred for the Reds, having witnessed numerous murders. He is convinced of the need for fundamental social reforms and is determined, in collaboration with and by order of his brother-in-law, to carry out the program of the Falange, the organization of which he wishes to see preserved, since the spirit of the Falange must permeate the State. (See report of May 8, Sa. 3–1734.[1]) Serrano Suñer assured me that he had from early youth been a confirmed friend of Germany. Even at school during the World War he had had scuffles with the pro-French students.

In my last conversation with Franco on the 7th, the latter informed me that he believed the new British King was not entirely in accord

---

[1] Not printed (4905/E255205–08).

with the policy of his Cabinet. There were also a great number of British naval officers whose sympathies were on the side of Franco and who repudiated the policy of their own Government, as was evident again and again from occasional statements they made.

England had encouraged the Basque Government a few months ago to continue its resistance to Franco. If England now suddenly came out so strongly for the removal of women and children from Bilbao, there was, in his, Franco's, opinion, a very material reason for this. There were several ships in the harbor of Bilbao belonging to a Spanish company with British capital. England was therefore using the opportunity to get these ships out of the port with the women and children being evacuated, and so to save the ships for her own use.

As for the disorders in Barcelona, Franco informed me that the street fighting had been started by his agents. As Nicolás Franco further told me, they had in all some 13 agents in Barcelona. One of these had given the information a considerable time ago that the tension between the Anarchists and Communists was so great in Barcelona that he would guarantee to cause fighting to break out there. The Generalissimo told me that he had not at first placed· confidence in the statements of this agent but had then had them checked by others, who had confirmed them. He had intended at first not to make use of this possibility until a military operation against Catalonia was begun. Since the Reds, however, had recently attacked at Teruel in order to relieve the Euzkadi [2] Government, he had judged the present moment to be right for the outbreak of disorders in Barcelona. Actually the agent had succeeded, within a few days of receiving such instructions, in having street shooting started by three or four persons, and this had then produced the desired success.

FAUPEL

---

[2] Basque.

No. 255

1819/416191

The State Secretary to the Embassy in France

Telegram

No. 185 of May 13   BERLIN, May 13, 1937.

For strictly confidential information.

In conversation with the Foreign Minister,[1] Mussolini expressed himself on the Spanish question to the effect that both Italy and Germany had now made enough sacrifices for Franco and he intended to inform

---

[1] Neurath had visited Rome from May 4 to 6, 1937.

Franco at the beginning of June that he would withdraw the Italian militia if the war were not being prosecuted more energetically by that time.   He was of the opinion that Franco could still be victorious if he followed German and Italian advice, particularly as to the formation of reserves.

Mussolini promised the Foreign Minister that he would get in touch with us before taking the step he planned with respect to Franco.

MACKENSEN

No. 256

3176/682989–94

The Director of the Economic Policy Department to the Embassy in Spain

Telegram

No. 168

BERLIN, May 13, 1937.
e.o. W II WE 3282.

I. For confidential use of the Embassy only, regarding the view at present taken here of the economic negotiations.

We have gathered from oral reports of the delegation that the Junta, including Nicolás Franco, insists strongly upon the conclusion of the clearing agreement.   Nevertheless, for the reasons given below, we should like at least at present to hold to the instructions issued by the ministerial conference here on February 26.[1]   Therefore the *démarche* with General Franco, contemplated at the time and so far postponed, is now to be undertaken in order to make clear whether the demand of the Junta really has the full backing of General Franco. Only if this proves to be the case, that is, if General Franco also insists on a clearing agreement, would we be prepared to conclude at most a partial clearing agreement covering regular, current trade; at the same time, however, we must have a guaranty that the big transactions in raw materials and essential foods are reserved to Hisma and Rowak as hitherto.

II. We therefore request the Ambassador personally to tell General Franco the following:

The negotiations of the delegations had so far not progressed with the rapidity we expected and desired, because there was a fundamental difference of opinion between the two delegations as to whether a clearing agreement should be concluded so soon for the regular, current trade.   The conception of the German Government is different on this point from that of the Spanish delegation, but not because of any possibly selfish interest on the part of Germany.   We believed, on the contrary, that it would also be better for the Spanish National

---

[1] Document No. 223, p. 245.

Government, and particularly for Franco's Government, to give up a clearing agreement at present, for the following two reasons.

As the first reason we would recall that the Hisma-Rowak machinery was set up earlier primarily to insure that the possibilities for procuring German goods of any kind might be utilized by one person only, namely, General Franco. We therefore regarded Hisma-Rowak not as a merely German organization but also as a confidential and control agency of General Franco. We believed that this fundamental idea had been correct in the past and that it still was. We did not, to be sure, wish to deny that even under a clearing agreement both the competent Spanish and German authorities could function according to the general directive at present in effect. We should not, however, deceive ourselves into thinking that with the introduction, if only a partial one, of free trade, the individual transactions could any longer be controlled and directed as surely as has thus far been the case.

The second reason is the following: There had thus far been complete and friendly agreement that if Germany, on the one hand, rendered assistance to Nationalist Spain in every way possible, she should, on the other hand, also receive something in return within the scope of Spain's potentialities, and specifically through the procurement of essential raw materials and foods. The German Government was pleased to acknowledge that General Franco had, on the whole, faithfully observed this friendly arrangement, even if at times temporary difficulties had been experienced with subordinate Spanish officials. There also the Hisma-Rowak machinery had rendered good service. If now through a clearing agreement countless small channels for private trade were opened up, in addition to the large and safe channel of Rowak-Hisma, we feared that the unified procurement of raw materials and essential foodstuffs from Spain would no longer be assured in the same way. This, too, was of interest not to Germany alone, but also to Spain. Although we did not wish to make our procurement of raw materials strictly a condition for our services to General Franco, the latter would nevertheless admit that in view of our own limited potentialities our services to him were to a certain extent dependent on our essential imports from Spain. I therefore request that you call General Franco's attention particularly to the fact that in the past few months it was only the preferential use of the proceeds of Spanish exports through Hisma-Rowak which made it possible to finance an important part of the Spanish orders for war matériel in Germany.

We knew very well that Hisma-Rowak was not very popular with Spanish exporters and importers. We could report, moreover, that the same was true of the German exporters and importers. They, too, assailed the present monopolistic position of Hisma-Rowak. From the private business standpoint of these interests, this was to a certain degree comprehensible. In our opinion, however, General Franco and we should, at least for the present, reject the one-sided views of such special interests.

Before the German Government took a final position on the desire of the Spanish delegation, it was anxious to present its own views frankly to General Franco and to ascertain whether he insisted on the present attitude of the Spanish delegation on this main issue.

III. We are anxious that this talk with General Franco take place in a very friendly spirit, and that in particular everything be avoided that might give him the impression that undue pressure is being exerted.

In case General Franco decides to reverse the stand of the Spanish delegation on this question, in other words, if he does not now insist on the conclusion of a clearing agreement, please request him to give strict and binding instructions to his delegation in this sense so that the negotiations can be quickly concluded at one stroke upon the return of the German delegation.

Should General Franco, however, support the Spanish delegation and insist that a clearing agreement be concluded even under the present conditions, please confine yourself to saying that you will report this to Berlin for further decision by the Reich Government.

We are anxious for a very early clarification of the situation. We therefore request that you make the *démarche* as soon as possible.

RITTER

No. 257

3366/E010337

The Ambassador in Great Britain to the Foreign Ministry

Telegram

URGENT   LONDON, May 15, 1937—6:12 p.m.
No. 274 of May 15   Received May 15—7:40 p.m.
                                          Pol. III 2415.

For the Führer and Chancellor.

Eden spoke with the Field Marshal [1] and me concerning the intention of the British Government to work for a cessation of hostilities in Spain. His plan was not yet ready. In no case did he wish to surprise other governments with it. On the contrary, the matter was to be prepared through diplomatic channels.

RIBBENTROP

---

[1] Field Marshal von Blomberg.

No. 258

137/128158

Memorandum by the State Secretary

BERLIN, May 15, 1937.

State Secretary Lammers has informed me by telephone that the Führer and Chancellor had expressed himself on the subject of telegram No. 261 of May 6, from London, to the effect that he expected the Foreign Ministry to emphasize in the instruction to London that the investigation of a single military action was entirely outside the bounds of possibility and that such an investigation therefore had to be flatly rejected. If an investigation could be considered at all, it would have to apply to all incidents.

I replied to State Secretary Lammers that our instructions had conformed to the ideas of the Führer and in agreement with the War Ministry we had taken the stand that an investigation of the Guernica case was to be rejected under all circumstances.

VON MACKENSEN

No. 259

3206/697705

The Ambassador in Italy to the Foreign Ministry

Telegram

No. 127 of May 16   ROME (QUIRINAL), May 16, 1937—1 : 30 p.m.
Received May 16—3 : 30 p.m.
Pol. IV 2507.

Ciano informed me yesterday evening that the British Ambassador had visited him and on instructions of his Government had taken up discussion of a kind of truce. He, Ciano, will make a report to the Head of the Government at once. I had the impression that Ciano is inclined to be conciliatory.

HASSELL

No. 260

3206/697706–07

The British Ambassador to the Foreign Minister [1]

BERLIN, 17th May, 1937.

DEAR BARON VON NEURATH: His Britannic Majesty's Government have, as Your Excellency is aware, invited the London Non-Intervention Committee to consider the question of reaching an agreement whereby the foreign volunteers in Spain can be withdrawn. In order to deal with this problem the technical Advisory Sub-committee has

---

[1] This document is in English in the original.

undertaken to prepare a report embodying its recommendations for submission to the Committee for early consideration. Inasmuch as the participating Governments have signified their readiness to submit the practical issues involved to the consideration of the sub-committee, His Majesty's Government trust that it may be assumed that they are favourable to this proposal.

2. In these circumstances I have been instructed to enquire whether the German Government, in anticipation of the formulation of a practical scheme for withdrawal of foreign volunteers, would be prepared to join His Majesty's Government and the other participating Powers in approaching both parties in Spain, with a view to inducing them to agree to an armistice on all fronts for a period of time sufficient to enable the withdrawal of volunteers to be arranged.

3. I am directed to explain in this connection that His Majesty's Government feel that, since the arrangements for the withdrawal of foreign volunteers could scarcely be carried out, except with the utmost difficulty, in the midst of active hostilities, the only prospect of success lies in making an appeal of this nature to the contending parties before the application of any agreed practical scheme.

4. As these instructions have reached me in the midst of the Whitsuntide holidays and as His Majesty's Government are most anxious that their proposal should receive early and favourable consideration, I venture to write you this letter direct. I am, however, ready to come and discuss this matter with Your Excellency whenever you may so desire.

5. I would add that His Majesty's Representatives at Paris, Rome, Lisbon and Moscow have been similarly instructed to enquire the views of the Governments to which they are accredited.

Yours sincerely,
N. M. HENDERSON

No. 261

1819/416211

The Ambassador in Italy to the Foreign Ministry

Telegram

No. 129 of May 19   ROME (QUIRINAL), May 19, 1937—6 : 25 p.m.
Received May 19—9 : 00 p.m.

State Secretary Bastianini informed me today, in Ciano's absence, of the British *note verbale* [1] with regard to bringing about an armistice in Spain even before discussion in the subcommittee on the question of withdrawing volunteers. Attolico was ordered to get in touch with the German Government. The Italian Government had replied to

---

[1] For the British communication presented in Berlin, see document No. 260, *supra*.

the note that in its opinion the suggested new tack was inadmissible; on the contrary, the discussion of the problem in the subcommittee first had to run its course as agreed.   Bastianini regards the British note as a move to reach a compromise in Spain in accordance with the old British aim of preventing a victory of Fascism under all circumstances; he said the reorganization of the Government in Valencia, with a tendency more to the Right, pointed in the same direction.

Private reports which I have received from Spanish circles here confirm the existence of lively British efforts, supported by the Vatican, to bring about an anti-Fascist settlement of the Civil War.   In this connection the name of Gil Robles, who is supposedly in Portugal, was mentioned to me.

HASSELL

No. 262

3366/E010341–42

Memorandum by the Foreign Minister

RM 361   BERLIN, May 21, 1937.
                                              Pol. III 2534.

The British Ambassador called on me today to discuss the question of an armistice proposal to the two parties in Spain which was raised in his communication of May 17.   He told me that Mr. Eden attached great importance to obtaining our opinion prior to his departure for Geneva.   I told the Ambassador the following:

We welcomed any measure, of course, which was capable of putting an end to bloodshed in Spain.   On the other hand, however, it appeared most unlikely to us that the armistice proposal would be accepted by the combatants at the present time.   According to a report received today from our Ambassador to Franco, matters had not yet reached the stage where the parties were ready for an armistice. Embitterment was still too great, and neither side was as yet exhausted.   Under these circumstances it appeared more advisable to us first to pursue further in the subcommittee of the London Non-Intervention Committee the question of evacuating volunteers.   Once a method was found whereby the difficulties of evacuating volunteers could be handled further with prospects of success, then an armistice proposal coupled with such an evacuation proposal would certainly have more chance of succeeding than the mere advice to reach an armistice.   We also did not know what was to be done if the fighting parties rejected the joint proposal of the powers.   Would England then, perhaps, wish to employ military coercion?

The Ambassador stated that it also appeared more advisable to him first to discuss the evacuation question further, and he would inform his Government in this sense yet today.

BARON V. NEURATH

No. 263

3176/682995

The Ambassador in Spain to the Foreign Ministry

Telegram

No. 268 of May 21   SALAMANCA, May 21, 1937.
Received May 22—12: 10 a.m.

Franco made the statement yesterday that he did not attach any importance to a clearing agreement. The members of the Spanish commission, whom he had allowed complete freedom so far, had gone too far in their efforts toward concluding a clearing agreement and had already realized this themselves. He, Franco, attached the greatest importance to strengthening German-Spanish friendship, in the economic sphere as well, through signing the planned agreements, provided, of course, they complied with Spanish law, as had already been discussed in detail in the sessions of the delegations.

I propose that the German commission leave for Burgos at once for the purpose of concluding the negotiations. Please wire the departure date as soon as possible so that the members of the Spanish commission can be called together in time. I recommend that the German commission be authorized at their own discretion to show the Junta some concessions, provided, needless to say, that the entire delivery of raw materials is fully guaranteed.

FAUPEL

No. 264

3366/E010368–70

The Ambassador in Spain to the Foreign Ministry

Sa. 3–1867   SALAMANCA, May 23, 1937.
Received May 27.
Pol. III 2615.

Subject: Franco's stand on the British armistice proposal, the Pope's encyclical, and the German answer.

Yesterday I had a long conversation with General Franco, concerning which I have already reported separately in communications No. Sa. 3–1790/37,[1] No. Sa. 3–1856/37,[2] and No. Sa. 10 (Beiakt) 1866/37,[1] insofar as it dealt with French plans for attacking Morocco, the wishes of the German Embassy in London, and the economic negotiations now in progress.

---

[1] Not found.
[2] Not printed (3374/E010908–09).

Concerning the British armistice proposal (cf. my telegrams No. 274 [3] and No. 277 [4] of May 23), Franco most decisively rejected any such possibility.   The consequences of such an armistice and of a subsequent peace would in the final analysis be the equivalent of a complete defeat for White Spain.   He and all Nationalist Spaniards would rather die than place the fate of Spain once more in the hands of a Red or a democratic government.   The present fight must and would lead to a rebirth of Spain.

To my question whether he believed that Red Spain would accept the armistice proposal, Franco replied that he thought this quite possible, since the entire action had originated with Prieto.   The latter, a few weeks ago when the fighting broke out inside Barcelona, had had a conference with Blum in Paris, which had led to an inquiry of the North American Government whether it was willing to act as mediator.   The United States had twice rejected this request.   Prieto had evidently intimated that Franco probably would also accept mediation. In view of the internal difficulties of the Valencia Government Prieto saw no solution other than an armistice.   Franco's own internal and military situation was so favorable that he had no reason whatsoever to consider an armistice.

On the basis of prospective iron-ore deliveries England had advanced large sums to the Bilbao Government in order to enable it to continue resistance.   England feared an early fall of Bilbao and consequently the loss of the sums advanced to the Euzkadi Government. Therefore England had the greatest interest in a quick armistice with a view to preventing the capture of Bilbao.

Several men who have the reputation of being especially friendly to the Vatican have recently appeared in Franco's entourage, especially in the Delegación para Prensa y Propaganda; I mentioned this to Franco.   I obtained the impression that he had no move planned in this matter.   Nevertheless I shall keep this question especially in mind.

In the course of the conversation we came to speak of the Pope's last encyclical and the answer given by Germany.[5]   I told Franco that no government aware of its duties and its dignity could tolerate such interference in its internal affairs.   I reminded him that those very Spanish rulers under whom the country experienced its greatest prosperity, such as Charles V and Philip II, had forbidden any encroachment by the Popes and, on the contrary, had imposed their will on them, while in the periods of Spain's greatest weakness interference

---

[3] Not printed (1819/416206).
[4] Not printed (1819/416207).
[5] The encyclical, *Mit brennender Sorge*, issued Mar. 14, 1937, and read in Catholic churches in Germany on Mar. 21.   For documents concerning the encyclical and the controversy following its issuance see vol. I, ch. VI, pp. 932 ff.

by the Vatican had been the strongest. Franco remarked that this applied also to the present. The Pope was indeed recognized as the highest religious authority in Spain, but any interference by the Vatican in internal Spanish affairs had to be rejected. He, Franco, also had to fight against the Vatican in this respect. With regard to the encyclical just mentioned, he had recently instructed the Archbishop of Toledo that no mention should be made in Spain of the encyclical and the German answer. He wanted by this means to cut off at the source any criticism directed against Germany.

FAUPEL

No. 265

3414/E015735

Memorandum by the Foreign Minister

RM 371 BERLIN, May 24, 1937.
e. o. Pol. III 2549 a.

The Spanish Chargé d'Affaires called on me today to report at General Franco's direction that he had sent a lengthy note to Ambassador Faupel yesterday, setting down his stand on the British armistice proposal. General Franco requests that the British proposal not be accepted, since it would only serve the interests of the Reds.

I told the Chargé d'Affaires that we had received the British suggestion and had already answered it to the effect that, in spite of all readiness to contribute to the pacification of Spain, we did not consider the conclusion of an armistice practicable at the present time. I added that it would be extraordinarily effective for the psychological and military situation in Spain if the attack on Bilbao were continued energetically. The Chargé d'Affaires stated that he had already meant to report to General Franco in this sense on his own but that he would also inform him of my statements.

BARON V. NEURATH

No. 266

3176/682996–97

The Director of the Economic Policy Department to the Embassy
in Spain

Telegram

No. 185 BERLIN, May 26, 1937.

With reference to your No. 268.[1] zu W II WE 3619.
We are very glad that through your démarche and through Franco's decision the stand hitherto adopted by the German delega-

---

[1] Document No. 263, p. 293.

tion has been fully justified and its position for further negotiations strengthened.

Although after Franco's decision it would still be possible to reject a clearing agreement entirely, we have nevertheless resolved, pending a final decision, to follow the advice of the Ambassador and make certain concessions to the Junta. The German delegation is at present engaged here in working out the details for such concessions, i.e. for a limited clearing agreement. As soon as this formula is approved here by the agencies concerned, the delegation will once more leave for Burgos. As far as can be seen at the present time the departure will take place at the end of next week, so that the German delegation will be available for continuing the negotiations in Burgos at the beginning of the following week.

We would consider it a mistake if the other side were informed at the present time that we intend to make certain concessions. Concessions to the Junta can be used with greater tactical effect if for the time being the Junta remains under the pressure of the strict and binding order which we hope Franco has issued in the meantime, and if the concessions are then offered spontaneously by the German delegation. The German delegation will then also be in a better position to keep these concessions within the limits desired by Germany.

Therefore please use the above only for your own information for the time being and confine yourself to communicating to the other side that the German delegation will probably be available again at the beginning of week after next.

RITTER

No. 267

424/217427–28

The Foreign Minister to the Embassy in Great Britain

Telegram en Clair

[No. 216]   BERLIN, May 30, 1937.

After Red airplanes bombed British, German, and Italian ships lying in the harbor of Majorca a few days ago and killed six officers on an Italian ship, German ships were forbidden to remain in the harbor any longer. On Saturday, May 29, 1937, the pocket battleship *Deutschland* was lying in the roadstead of Iviza. The ship belongs to the forces assigned to the international sea patrol. In spite of this, the pocket battleship was suddenly bombed between 6 and 7 p.m. by two planes of the Red Valencia Government in a gliding attack. Since the ship was off duty, the crew was in the unprotected crew's quarters forward. One of the Red bombs hit in the midst of the enlisted men's mess, just as in the recent attack on the Italian ship the officers' mess was hit. The result of this criminal attack was that 20 were killed and 73 wounded. A second bomb hit the side deck but caused only slight damage there. The ship, which is fully operative, sailed to Gibraltar to put the wounded ashore. The ship had not fired on the airplanes.

Since the Red Valencia Government was twice warned by the Non-Intervention Committee and the German Government against further attacks on the ships engaged in the international patrol, this new criminal attack on the German ship compels the German Government to take measures of which it will immediately inform the Non-Intervention Committee.

NEURATH

No. 268

424/217429

The Foreign Minister to the Embassy in Great Britain

Telegram

BERLIN, MAY 30, 1937.

Continuation of telegram No. 216.[1]

Please take the floor at once at the beginning of Monday's session of the Non-Intervention Committee and make known the facts reported in the preceding telegram.

Then, after you have referred to the previous incidents discussed in the committee on Friday and to the warning given by the committee to the Spanish parties, I request that you make the following statement:

The Reich Government will henceforth not participate in the patrol or in the deliberations of the Non-Intervention Committee until it obtains a positive guaranty against a repetition of such incidents. The Reich Government will of course determine as it sees fit the measures to be taken against the Red tyrants in reply to the incredibly treacherous attack. Moreover, it has instructed its warships to ward off by armed action any Red Spanish plane or warship that may approach while this state of affairs continues.

NEURATH

---

[1] Document No. 267, *supra*.

No. 269

424/217434

Memorandum by the Foreign Minister

RM 390   BERLIN, May 31, 1937.

I asked the Italian Ambassador to call on me today and informed him of the steps which we have instituted in the London Non-Intervention Committee because of the attack on the pocket battleship

Deutschland. I also told him that in addition we had ordered reprisals on our own initiative; I did not tell him, however, where they would take place and what they would be.

Upon the Ambassador's inquiry whether we wished that the Italians also withdraw from the Non-Intervention Committee, I told him that, on the contrary, it was our wish that they remain in the committee.

BARON V. NEURATH

No. 270

424/217435–36

Memorandum by the Foreign Minister

RM 391   BERLIN, May 31, 1937.

The French Ambassador, who returned from Paris this morning, paid me an urgent call and expressed his sincere regret concerning the German sailors killed on the pocket battleship *Deutschland.* He then inquired about the details of the incident. I gave him an account of the events and also informed him of the military and diplomatic steps taken by us. I emphasized especially that the incident was closed by the bombardment of the fortified harbor of Almería in reprisal for the unprovoked attack by the Red air forces. We would expect, however, that now the other powers concerned would take energetic steps to prevent a recurrence of such incidents and to bring the Red rulers in Valencia to their senses. As long as this was not done we would no longer participate in the sessions of the Non-Intervention Committee. On the French Ambassador's question as to what sort of action I anticipated from the Non-Intervention Committee, I told him that I could imagine, for example, that the powers represented on the Non-Intervention Committee might decide to take concerted military action at once against that side undertaking to attack patrol vessels or personnel engaged in the patrol service, and that this decision might be communicated at once to both Spanish parties.

I also pointed out to the French Ambassador that we had displayed exceptional restraint in carrying out reprisals for the outrageous attack, and that I expected that this restraint would be recognized as such and taken into account in further actions of the French Government with regard to events in Spain. The Ambassador confirmed the fact that our military action had been kept within extremely moderate limits.

BARON V. NEURATH

No. 271 •

424/217450

Memorandum by the Foreign Minister

RM 392   BERLIN, May 31, 1937.

I asked the British Ambassador to call on me this morning and informed him of the events at Iviza.   At the same time I informed him of the steps we have taken in the Non-Intervention Committee and of the military action against Almería.   The Ambassador was extremely upset by the incident and emphasized again and again that by our action we should nevertheless not do the Reds the favor of expanding the conflict in Spain into a world war.   I told him that this depended to a great extent on the attitude of the British Government, and I urged him to make his Government realize clearly the seriousness of the situation and to report the expectation which I expressed that the British Government would now change its previous benevolent attitude toward the Red rulers in Valencia.

BARON V. NEURATH

No. 272

424/217443-44

Memorandum by an Official of the Foreign Minister's Secretariat

BERLIN, May 31, 1937—5:15 p.m.

The Italian Ambassador just called on me and told me the following for transmission to the Foreign Minister:

The Foreign Minister had informed him earlier in the day that we did not wish a withdrawal from the Non-Intervention Committee; that, on the contrary, we were interested in Italy's remaining in the committee.   Mussolini had considered this idea from all sides but with all regard for the supporting arguments had made a different decision. In this he had been prompted primarily by the consideration that in this situation, where the actual circumstances in the case of both Germany and Italy were identical, the reaction of the two powers should not be different. This would only evoke rumors of a divergence in the views of the two countries, in other words, would result in the opposite of what we were trying to achieve. We would not have an especially strong position, nor would we preserve for ourselves the possibility of further influencing the committee, but would rather be weakened by the nonsensical talk which would result as to the divergence of our political views.   Therefore he had telephoned to London around midday and had instructed Ambassador Grandi to tell the chairman of the Non-Intervention Committee the following:

1. Italian ships would be withdrawn from the patrol.

2. He, the Ambassador, would no longer participate in the meetings of the Non-Intervention Committee.

These measures would continue until a sufficient safeguard for the Italian patrol units had been provided by the committee.

The fact that the Italian step was not taken until this time would be explained by stating that the succession of Italian[1] and German incidents proved that the Red rulers were acting according to a premeditated plan, and that consequently the incidents which had occurred so far were calculated attacks which could be followed by others.

The Italian Ambassador then asked me how the French and British Ambassadors, who had been received this morning after him, had reacted to the announcement by the Foreign Minister. The Foreign Minister, I told him, had answered the French Ambassador's question as to how possible action by the Non-Intervention Committee was envisaged, by stating that the desired effect might be achieved, for example, by announcing the intention of taking concerted action against a future aggressor, and by making this known at once to the warring parties.

Respectfully submitted to the Foreign Minister.

v. Kotze

---

[1] The reference is to the incident of May 24, 1937, when the Italian cruiser *Barletta* was struck by a bomb in the course of an air raid against Palma de Mallorca.

No. 273

424/217431–33

Memorandum by the Deputy Director of the Political Department

Berlin, May 31, 1937.

Herr Woermann just telephoned me after his visit with Eden and told me the following about the conversation:

Eden had first expressed to him his deep sympathy over the loss of German lives in the attack on the *Deutschland*. Then Mr. Eden had stated that he had just heard through the British Admiralty that German naval vessels had bombarded the harbor of Almería this morning. He considered this measure too extreme; as a result a very dangerous situation had arisen. Italy and England, who likewise had lost lives through bombs dropped on naval vessels, had been in a situation similar to that of Germany. Neither of these two countries, however, had resorted to such reprisals.

Eden then asked whether the German Government or the captain of the German warship had communicated with the Red Government prior to the bombardment of Almería. Woermann replied that the situation was different in the case of the *Deutschland*. The German representative on the Non-Intervention Committee had repeatedly warned against attacks by Red planes and naval forces on German warships, and the matter had been discussed as late as at the last session of the Non-Intervention Committee. Furthermore, the captain of the warship *Admiral Scheer* had issued a radio warning to all forces in the Mediterranean. Also factually the case of the *Deutschland* was different, for it involved a *premeditated* attack on a German warship.

Eden replied that he was not familiar with the details of the episode but expressed the urgent hope that the German Government would not go further.

Herr Woermann had then informed Mr. Eden of the note which the German Ambassador in London will present to the chairman of the Non-Intervention Committee this afternoon.

I telephoned Ambassador Hassell and gave him the text of the communiqué concerning the bombardment of Almería, the reinforcement of the German naval forces, and the German stand with regard to the Non-Intervention Committee. Herr von Hassell said that he had spoken with Count Ciano this morning and that the latter had asked him for information, since the Italian Government intended to act in conformity with the German stand.

I also transmitted to our consul in Geneva the text of the three communiqués mentioned. Herr Krauel confirmed that Señor del Vayo had told the press that he would request a meeting of the League of Nations Council.

BISMARCK

P. S.   In the meantime Herr Krauel telephoned me once more and told me that the first reaction to the German communiqué, which had now become known in Geneva, was that Del Vayo had taken the communiqué to the Secretary General and to the Russian Assistant Secretary, General Sokolny. The following interpretation was being disseminated as the result of this conversation:

The German communiqué left no doubt as to the German attitude. Therefore they would propose in Geneva that the League of Nations Council be called to London, and that Germany and Italy be requested to participate in this session of the Council.

BISMARCK

No. 274

3357/E009341–43

The Ambassador in the United States to the Foreign Ministry

Telegram

URGENT   WASHINGTON, May 31, 1937—5 : 25 a.m.
SECRET   Received June 1—3 : 30 a.m.
No. 137 of May 31   Pol. III 2765.

For the Foreign Minister.

Mr. Hull today urgently requested me to call on him at his hotel and spoke to me with visible anxiety about the Spanish situation. He first expressed his heartfelt sympathy for those who had been killed and wounded on the *Deutschland*, then went into the details of the Iviza incident, mentioned the bombardment of Almería, expressed the hope that it might not be necessary for us to take further action, and concluded with a friendly, rather vaguely phrased statement to the effect that Germany could presumably be counted on to continue doing everything possible to preserve the peace.

I first explained to the Secretary of State that it was only in response to the urging of the other powers that we had permitted units of our fleet to participate in the patrol of the Spanish coasts; these ships were performing a difficult international task there in the interest of localizing the Spanish Civil War as far as possible. If attacks were now made on these ships by planes of the Valencia Government, the action was downright criminal. The attack on the *Deutschland* was the third assault of this kind, since both a British and an Italian ship had recently been attacked in the same manner. It was all the more criminal since the *Deutschland* had been lying peacefully in the harbor, resting from patrol duty; the crew had been eating in the mess. No shot had been fired by the Germans; the attack by the planes had been entirely unprovoked. The result of this outrageous attack had been 23 dead and more than 80 wounded German sailors. As for the bombardment of Almería, I had no official report on it, but it was evidently the natural German counteraction against the attack on our ship. Whether we would take still further action, I did not know; that would presumably be determined chiefly by the attitude of Valencia. Our further participation in the activities of the Non-Intervention Committee and in the coastal patrol would also probably depend on this attitude, since we could not continue exposing our ships and men to such attacks without some guaranty. That the German Government would do nothing to increase the tension, unless it should be absolutely compelled to do so, was self-evident and hardly needed any proof, in view of everything that the Secretary of State knew about our attitude in the

Spanish question—a remark with which Mr. Hull immediately agreed. The further developments depended less, in my opinion, on Germany than on the attitude of the Non-Intervention Committee and, naturally, on the attitude of the Government in Valencia. As far as the latter was concerned, however, I had considerable doubt whether it even wished to contribute at all toward lessening the tension; in the very difficult situation in which it found itself, militarily and politically, it was probably more interested in complicating matters, and in the last analysis this was very likely the reason for these air attacks . . . (group garbled) warships.

DIECKHOFF

No. 275

3357/E009351

The Consul at Geneva to the Foreign Ministry

Telegram

No. 50 of June 1
GENEVA, June 1, 1937—10 : 20 p.m.
Received June 2—1 : 10 a.m.
Pol. III 2773.

The Spanish-Russian attempt to convene the Council of the League of Nations because of the German reprisals for the air attack on the pocket battleship *Deutschland* has failed completely. Litvinov and Del Vayo left Geneva this afternoon.

As is known from the telephone report from the consulate, a strong disposition to convene the League of Nations Council in London prevailed all day Monday in local circles of the League of Nations and of the delegations, under the impression of the shelling of Almería and the misrepresentation of this incident in the world press, influenced as it is by the sensational Spanish-Communist propaganda sent out from Geneva. Under the influence of Litvinov and Sokolin, Del Vayo submitted to the Secretary General as early as Monday evening a draft of the proposal to convene. However, British opposition set in immediately, and the matter was postponed until Tuesday. Meanwhile, an understanding was reached between London and Paris to the effect that the convening of the League of Nations Council was not advisable. Today Litvinov and Del Vayo bowed to this Anglo-French decision.

The fact that the League of Nations Council was not convened is generally interpreted here as a defeat of Spanish-Russian designs, and Popular Front sympathizers in League of Nations circles consider it a reverse. The idea that the Red air attack on Majorca and Iviza was a Bolshevik attempt to arrest the increasing decline of tension in the Spanish question is generally gaining ground and has found expression in the local press.   Reference is made particularly to the editorial in the *Journal de Genève* of June 2, No. 148.

KRAUEL

No. 276

3357/E009364

The Ambassador in the United States to the Foreign Ministry

Telegram

CONFIDENTIAL   WASHINGTON, June 2, 1937—5 : 53 p.m.
No. 144 of June 2   Received June 3—1 : 55 a.m.
Pol. III 2820.

Yesterday (Monday was a holiday [1]) General Bötticher [2] had an opportunity to speak with leading Army and Navy authorities. He gave an exact description of the incidents at Iviza and Almería, emphasizing in particular that the German pocket battleship had the right to anchor off Iviza, that she lay there peaceably, and did not fire a shot either before or after the airplane attack. This information was very enlightening to the Army and the Navy in the face of the propaganda according to which the German ship opened fire first and had no right to anchor off Iviza. In view of the widely circulated suspicion that Germany acted irresponsibly and that she had warlike intentions, Bötticher spoke of the need for immediate reprisals, for which there was full understanding when the true facts of the case were explained. Of particular importance was the explanation that our measures were directed against a fortified city, since propaganda here . . . (group incomplete) that the shelling was a particularly harsh measure against the population. A well-informed person from the General Staff stated confidentially that there were exceedingly bad reports concerning the Red Government and conditions in Red Spain. In the armed forces they regard the situation and . . . (group garbled) in part authoritative assertions of certain American political figures calmly ; they do not believe the newspaper reports that a threat of war exists, and they say they would be grateful for any more detailed information. A reassuring influence emanates from the armed forces, which has all the more political effect the less it is evident to the public. For this reason, and also because of the valuable position of confidence which Bötticher possesses personally, please treat this telegram as confidential. Request transmission to the War Ministry.

DIECKHOFF

---

[1] May 31, following Memorial Day, May 30, which fell on Sunday.
[2] Military and Air Attaché of the German Embassy in Washington.

No. 277

307/188440–41

The British Ambassador to the Foreign Minister [1]

VERY URGENT BERLIN, 3rd June 1937.

MY DEAR REICHSMINISTER: I have received the enclosed telegram from His Majesty's Principal Secretary of State for Foreign Affairs in regard to the guarantees necessary to enable Germany to resume participation in Non-Intervention Committee and Spanish patrol.

May I communicate the text of His Majesty's Government's proposal in this form so that Your Excellency may consider it in the first place? When you have done so I should be grateful if you would summon me to call on you.

If the German and Italian Governments agree to the proposal, His Majesty's Government would at once approach the two Spanish parties on the lines indicated.

Yours sincerely,
NEVILE HENDERSON

[Enclosure]

In view of the deplorable incidents involving serious loss of life on the German man-of-war "Deutschland" and the Italian man-of-war "Barletta" and the narrow escape from similar injury of their own and other ships taking part in the patrol scheme, His Majesty's Government in the United Kingdom have been carefully considering what guarantees are necessary in order to ensure the future safe operation of the non-intervention patrol scheme and to prevent a recurrence of the recent attacks on foreign shipping engaged in that task. They have come to the conclusion that the following arrangements should be adequate to give security to such shipping against the dangers which have been shown to exist in the present situation.

(*a*) That the two parties should be asked to give a solemn assurance that they will respect foreign warships on the high seas and elsewhere and will take steps to see that their naval and air forces implement this assurance.

(*b*) That in order to avoid accidental attacks or damage to foreign warships undertaking the patrol when lying in the ports of either party, the two parties should be asked to designate safety zones in any Spanish ports which may be agreed as necessary for use as refuelling bases for such ships.

(*c*) That the two parties should be informed that failure to implement these assurance [*sic*] and any interference with ships employed

---

[1] This document is in English in the original.

in patrolling duties will in future form the subject of consultation between all four countries on the situation thus created.

They trust such guarantees would enable the German Government and the Italian Government to renew their participation in the patrol and the work of the London Committee.

No. 278

307/188443

The Supreme Command of the Navy to the Foreign Ministry

SECRET   BERLIN W. 35, June 4, 1937.
A I 6279 Sp.   zu Pol. III 2904.

Subject: Guaranties for the resumption of German participation in the activities of the Non-Intervention Committee and the Spanish Naval Patrol.

The changes proposed by the Supreme Command in the British Government's proposals are incorporated in the following new draft; the passages changed or added are underscored.[1]

The proposed changes communicated by telephone to Counselor of Embassy Prince Bismarck through Lieutenant Commander Wagner are herewith confirmed.

"1. That the two parties should be asked to give a solemn assurance that they will respect foreign warships on the high seas and elsewhere—in other words also in the Spanish territorial waters of both parties—and will take steps to see that their naval and air forces implement this assurance. 'Respect' is to be understood: neither to attack nor to approach in a manner suggesting an attack.

"2. That in order to avoid accidental attacks or damage to foreign warships undertaking the patrol when lying in the ports of either party, the two parties should be asked to designate safety zones in any Spanish ports which may be agreed as necessary for use as refueling bases for such ships.

"3. That any infraction of the foresaid assurances will be regarded as concern of all 4 powers who, irrespective of any immediate defensive measures considered necessary by the directly concerned power, will immediately seek agreement among themselves concerning the steps to be taken concertedly."[2]

By direction:
MARSCHALL

Note: Paragraph 3 corresponds to the change proposed by the Foreign Ministry.

---

[1] Underscoring, which is lacking in this copy of the document, was supplied by comparison with document No. 277.

[2] The English translation of this paragraph is one apparently prepared by the Germans themselves. It was found on a separate sheet carrying the number Pol. III 2904, Annex IV (307/188444).

No. 279

307/188445

Memorandum by the Foreign Minister

RM 406   BERLIN, June 4, 1937.

This evening I handed the British Ambassador the changes proposed by us in the British proposals presented yesterday concerning the guaranty question. The Ambassador told me he had expected that we would raise objections to the phrasing of paragraph (*c*) of the British draft and had himself prepared a changed draft.[1] This draft corresponded in its content to our counterproposal but did not contain the German reservation about freedom of action. On the other hand, however, it did contain at the end the proposal for concerted action.

The Ambassador promised to send our counterproposal to London at once. He believed that the proposal would be accepted subject to some changes in style.

BARON V. NEURATH

---

[1] No copy of the British revision referred to here has been identified in the files of the Foreign Ministry.

No. 280

3357/E009378

Memorandum by the Director of the Legal Department

BERLIN, June 7, 1937.
Pol. III 2966.

I informed the Italian Ambassador this morning of the new British formula accepted yesterday by the Foreign Minister concerning the guaranties to be provided for the patrol vessels.

Signor Attolico appeared somewhat annoyed. The Foreign Minister had informed him yesterday by letter that he had had another conversation with the British Ambassador, which concerned several formal points. He, Attolico, therefore could not have assumed from this that the British had proposed a formula that was altered in substance and that we had accepted it. In actual fact the new British formula departed very essentially from our proposal. The words "irrespective of any immediate defensive measures considered necessary" could and would be universally interpreted as meaning that we had abandoned our basic stand with regard to the Almería incident.

I tried to talk the Ambassador out of this. He did, indeed, concede that the matter should, after all, make no difference to his Government, since Almería concerned only us. His dissatisfaction could probably be explained primarily by the fact that he had transmitted information to Rome yesterday which was not entirely accurate.

Shortly after his visit Signor Attolico sent me, without any accompanying note, the enclosed copy of an Italian *pro memoria* of June 5.[1]

GAUS

---

[1] Not printed (4907/E255236/1–2).

No. 281

860/285700–01

The State Secretary to the Legation in Yugoslavia

Telegram

VERY SECRET   BERLIN, June 8, 1937.

No. 59 of June 8

For the Foreign Minister personally.[1]

On the occasion of his visit today in regard to the Iviza affair, Sir Nevile [Henderson] repeated the British Government's invitation to the Foreign Minister for June 23 or 24 and expressed the hope that the Foreign Minister could accept the invitation and arrive in London either on Wednesday evening, which the British Government preferred, or early on the 24th. The British Government hoped that Baroness Neurath, who, like the Foreign Minister, had left countless friends in London, would accompany him. The topics of conversation envisaged were the situation in Spain and the general European situation, with particular reference to Anglo-German relations. Under no circumstances were there to be any sort of negotiations.

For the press announcement of the visit, which should be made simultaneously at a time to be agreed upon, the British Government proposes the following text:

"Baron von Neurath will visit London on June 24th as the official guest of His Majesty's Government. No negotiations are under consideration but it is hoped that visit will offer an opportunity for an exchange of views [on Spanish problem and] on [other] matters of common interest to the two countries." [2]

The final communiqué on the visit would be completed at the proper time in London, and to obtain the widest attention it should if possible be published in London's Saturday papers, which are more important there than the Sunday newspapers.

Sir Nevile asked me to transmit this to the Foreign Minister immediately.

Concerning the proposed text of the press announcement I noticed the absence of any emphasis on the fact that the invitation comes from the British Government. Sir Nevile was of a different opinion, since in England to be a "guest" means to be "invited." Any particular

---

[1] Neurath was in Belgrade from June 7 to 9, 1937.
[2] This paragraph appears in English in the original. The words in brackets have been stricken through in this copy.

emphasis on the Spanish question as the subject of discussion is in my opinion inexpedient because of the sensational effect to be expected from it. Reference to a *tour d'horizon* would probably be sufficient.

Please send instructions, also with regard to preparing the Italians in time, which will no doubt be necessary.

MACKENSEN

No. 282

307/188429–30

Memorandum by the Head of Political Division III

BERLIN, June 8, 1937.

Lieutenant [*Kapitänleutnant*] Neubauer called on me today and submitted to me for my confidential information a memorandum circulated internally in the War Ministry, Foreign Department [*Abtlg. Ausland*], concerning the status of the guaranty question. It included the proposed change given the Foreign Minister on June 6 by British Ambassador Henderson and carried the notation, "The Reich Foreign Minister has agreed to this proposed change in the name of the Cabinet."

Herr Neubauer argued that we had hereby definitely renounced our right to reprisals. He based his conclusion on an inaccurate statement in the memorandum concerning the significance of the British proposal ("henceforth only defensive measures are possible").

After consulting Ministerialdirektor von Weizsäcker I explained to Herr Neubauer:

1. The matter was still in a state of flux; the texts thus far should be considered provisional; the final wording would be settled later in London. On this point I could show him telegram No. 319 [1] just arrived from London, which stated that on June 8 Eden would propose in the three capitals that the details be discussed in London between him and the Ambassadors of Germany, France, and Italy.

2. The proposal made it clear that in case of a repetition of an incident like that at Iviza the attacked ship might, of course, take immediate defensive measures.

3. There was no doubt that in case the four powers patrolling the seas should not reach an immediate understanding the attacked power would recover freedom of action, i.e. the right also to proceed alone.

Herr Neubauer stated that he was interested to learn this interpretation of the Foreign Ministry; he would report it to his superiors. He insisted, however, that this was still a change in our original stand, which provided for the right to take *immediate* measures of reprisal.

DUMONT

---

[1] Not printed (3357/E009377).

No. 283

307/188431-32

Memorandum by the State Secretary

BERLIN, June 8, 1937.

The British Ambassador called on me this afternoon to inform me, on the basis of the original of the instruction sent him from London, which he read to me in translation, how the British Government believes the question of our resuming participation in the Non-Intervention Committee should be handled further. According to this the three Ambassadors of Germany, Italy, and France are to meet with Eden as soon as possible in order to agree, on the basis of the opinions now available from the various Governments, on the final text of the statement which is to be sent to the two Spanish parties. This last, the Ambassador confirmed, is to be done through the British Government. He emphasized that the expression, "Non-Intervention Committee," was not mentioned anywhere in the entire instruction, and thus shared my opinion that the Non-Intervention Committee should merely be informed at a given time.

In reply to my question whether the changes suggested by the Foreign Minister in paragraphs 1 and 2 had been given consideration, Sir Nevile [Henderson] stated that he had reported them to London and that Eden had taken cognizance of them. He added that this implied nothing as to the final version, since, after all, it was this which was now to be determined. At this juncture I expressed the hope that the final text of paragraph 3 would appear in a form which would permit no doubt concerning the view expressed to him by the Foreign Minister, who had stated explicitly that the change proposed by the British and accepted by him on Sunday had only formal significance. The Ambassador confirmed this summary of the content of his conversation on Sunday and expressed the opinion that paragraph 3 would also be put into final form during the impending conference.

I called the Ambassador's attention to the fact that Herr von Ribbentrop was at present absent from London, as was known, but that I believed he was expected back there within the next few days. If he was actually to return in the next few days, I thought it well to postpone the conference of Ambassadors until Herr von Ribbentrop was again in London. Sir Nevile expressed his agreement.

I then established contact with Herr von Ribbentrop through Count Dürckheim and learned that he would be flying back to London some time tomorrow; he requested, however, that the conference be called for the day after tomorrow if possible, and then only in the afternoon, since he first had to get in touch with our friends.

I informed the British Ambassador of the above by telephone, and he promised to communicate with London as soon as possible so that the joint conference might not be started before Thursday afternoon.

MACKENSEN

No. 284

860/285703–04

The British Ambassador to the State Secretary [1]

PERSONAL AND URGENT   June 9, 1937.

DEAR SECRETARY OF STATE: May I emphasize to you the fact that it is particularly desirable that no hints be given out on the proposed visit of the Foreign Minister to London before the official communiqué is published. Indeed, such an indiscretion could bring the entire purpose of the visit to naught.

For this reason it is so very important to agree immediately on the various details of which I informed you yesterday, in order that the official invitation may be issued as soon as possible.

Mr. Eden has requested me to transmit the above to your Government. I am doing so, although I am convinced that you already completely share this point of view.

Yours sincerely,

NEVILE HENDERSON

---

[1] This letter is in handwriting on stationery of the British Embassy in Berlin. It is in German except for the phrases at the beginning and end.

No. 285

307/188420–22

Memorandum by the Director of the Legal Department

BERLIN, June 9, 1937.

This morning Ambassador von Ribbentrop telephoned me in order to inquire immediately before his departure for London about the status of the negotiations concerning the guaranties against a repetition of the Iviza incident. He had just spoken by telephone with Herr Woermann, who, however, had not been able to give him any definite information. I told Herr von Ribbentrop that all the material had been sent to the Embassy in London and that it would surely be there upon his arrival.

We then discussed the various formulas, and it appeared advisable to continue the discussion orally with the help of the texts. I gave Herr von Ribbentrop copies of the British proposals, our counterproposal, and the telegraphic instruction sent to London today. [1]

---

[1] Not printed (307/188424–26).

Herr von Ribbentrop first thought that, after all, the last British proposal represented a great change in substance compared to our counterproposal, since it allowed individual control powers only the right to immediate defensive measures, but excluded measures of reprisal like the Almería action. He did not believe that it was the Führer's intention to have our hands tied to this extent. I then explained in the sense of the instruction to London that the last British formula did not exclude, but only delayed, an Almería action. That, however, conformed to the logic of the situation. It would be a contradiction if the power directly affected by an attack on the one hand demanded concerted action by the other control powers but, on the other hand, simultaneously claimed the right to act alone; one could only choose the one or the other. Naturally the power immediately affected did not have to wait long to see whether agreement was reached with the other powers, but regained its freedom of action after only a brief lapse of time, commensurate with the circumstances.

Herr von Ribbentrop conceded this in principle but wondered if it were not advisable to append to the formula an express statement to the effect that, in case no immediate agreement was reached between the control powers, it was left to any one of them to take the measures it thought necessary. I told him that I personally believed this unnecessary but not really objectionable. It would probably have to depend on the course of the Ambassadors' conference with Eden whether and in what form such a proposal could be made. Perhaps it would even suffice to state orally in the conference the idea of the addendum as a self-evident interpretation of the formula.

GAUS

No. 286

3366/E010376

The Ambassador in Spain to the Foreign Ministry

Telegram

VERY URGENT   SALAMANCA, June 9, 1937—9:30 p.m.
No. 300 of June 9   Received June 9—11:45 p.m.
                                                      Pol. III 3012.

Hedilla, leader of the Falange, and three other Falangists, who have been imprisoned for about 6 weeks, have been sentenced to death by a military court whose impartiality is very doubtful. The sentence means a victory of the circles opposing the Falange and thorough social reform—circles which have influenced Franco increasingly of late. In a friendly conversation I pointed out that the shooting of Hedilla, the only real representative of the workers, will make a very bad impression and that it is dangerous to create martyrs in the present situation.

In case Berlin shares my apprehensions concerning the situation which would be created if Hedilla were shot, please authorize me if necessary to inform Franco by official order of the Reich Government, approximately as follows:

"Without taking any stand with regard to the court proceedings and the sentence of Hedilla, the Reich Government takes the liberty of pointing out in a friendly way that the execution of Hedilla and his comrades at this time appears for political and social reasons to be a doubtful step."

Request telegraphic instructions.

FAUPEL

No. 287

860/285705

The Foreign Minister to the State Secretary

Telegram

No. 41 of June 9   SOFIA,[1] June 9, 1937—11:30 p.m.
                                                           Received June 10—1:15 a.m.

For the State Secretary personally.
With reference to telegram No. 59 of June 8, 1937 to Belgrade.[2]

For myself, I am prepared to arrive in London on the evening of June 23. The decision as to whether my wife will accompany me cannot be made before my return to Berlin.

The press announcement of the visit: In the English text[3] please omit "Spanish problem,"[4] and after "opportunity for an exchange of views"[4] add "on matters of common interest for the two countries."[4]

Please inform the Italian Government now through Herr von Hassell of the invitation to visit London and its acceptance, and add that the visit also appears useful for the purpose of advancing Anglo-Italian relations.

Please tell Henderson that the visit will be possible only on condition that the question of the guaranty after the Iviza incident has been settled in a manner satisfactory to us.

NEURATH
RUEMELIN [5]

---

[1] Neurath arrived in Sofia from Belgrade on June 9.
[2] Document No. 281, p. 308.
[3] There appears in the file (860/285708) the text of a statement in English reading as follows: "Baron von Neurath will visit London on June 24th as the official guest of His Majesty's Government. No negotiations are under consideration but it is hoped that visit will offer an opportunity for an exchange of views on matters of common interest to the two countries." Notation by Mackensen: "Given today to Sir Nevile."
[4] The quoted passages are in English in the original.
[5] German Minister in Bulgaria.

No. 288

860/285714

Memorandum by the State Secretary

BERLIN, June 10, 1937.

On the basis of telegram No. 41,[1] which I received today, I asked the British Ambassador to call on me this morning and informed him in the sense of the instructions. Sir Nevile [Henderson] once more stressed that in order to avoid indiscretions, which were always to be feared, the British Government attached importance to having an early announcement of the visit made in the press. He had no objection to the change in the text which I had proposed and did not believe that his Government would have any either. Since we had made a satisfactory settlement of the Iviza incident a prerequisite for the visit, this set the earliest possible date for the announcement.

I told the Ambassador that I welcomed a delay of several days if only because I had to make sure that the Führer and Chancellor was informed of the plan for the trip and approved of it before the announcement appeared in the press. Sir Nevile replied that he had been told by the Foreign Minister personally that the Führer had already declared that he was in agreement with the idea of the trip in principle, and that this concern was therefore groundless, especially since he knew that Herr von Ribbentrop, whom Eden had taken into his confidence regarding the trip, had also been with the Führer in the meantime.

Sir Nevile will immediately report the content of our discussion to London by telegram.

MACKENSEN

[1] Document No. 287, *supra*.

No. 289

395/212397

Memorandum by the State Secretary

BERLIN, June 10, 1937.

During today's conversation with the British Ambassador in regard to another matter, the conversation also came around to Eden's discussion today with the three Ambassadors. Sir Nevile [Henderson] said that in his opinion the further procedure would be that, after an agreement had been achieved, the British Government would send word to that effect without delay to both Spanish parties. It was not a matter of asking their agreement, but merely of notifying them of the measures which the four Great Powers participating in the naval patrols had decided to undertake in case of any new incidents. He assumed that after this declaration had been made to both Spanish parties, Germany and Italy would immediately resume their places at the council table in the Non-Intervention Committee.

I told him that this was also my personal opinion.

He seemed to be somewhat worried about a newspaper report which he had found somewhere today, to the effect that the Non-Intervention Committee was supposed to deal with the question between the time the agreement was reached by the four Great Powers and the notification of the Spanish parties. He personally considered such an interpretation misleading, and he believed that his Government would share this judgment. He expressed himself somewhat uncertainly with regard to the results expected from today's discussion with the Ambassadors, since he had been told nothing officially in the last few days regarding the attitude of the British Government, and he was still groping in the dark regarding the French standpoint, also, even though he had had several conversations with François-Poncet.

MACKENSEN

No. 290

860/285711–12

The British Ambassador to the State Secretary [1]

PERSONAL AND URGENT June 10, 1937.

DEAR STATE SECRETARY: Since I saw you this morning I have received another telegram from Mr. Eden in which he expresses the wish that the communiqué be published within the next few days in order to prevent the circulation of any untimely reports (regarding the settlement of the Spanish question).

Baron von Neurath's prerequisite will prolong the uncertainty and will certainly be incomprehensible to my Government. It seems so important to me to insure a favorable atmosphere that I have not yet telegraphed to London.

Could you wire a request to the Foreign Minister that he abandon this condition, or at least ask the Chancellor if he insists on it? It would be so much simpler and so much more agreeable to my Government to answer immediately that everything is agreed upon and that the communiqué can be published Saturday, for example, with the text proposed by Baron von Neurath.

I am very much afraid that otherwise the reply will produce an unfavorable impression in London.

---

[1] This letter is in handwriting on stationery of the British Embassy in Berlin. It is in German except for the phrases at the beginning and end.

Perhaps it will be possible for you to give me your reply this afternoon.

Yours sincerely,
NEVILE HENDERSON

Please forgive haste and bad German.

No. 291

860/285713

Memorandum by the State Secretary

BERLIN, June 10, 1937.

I informed Herr von Kotze [1] by telephone of the contents of the letter [2] which I just received from the British Ambassador, and I ascertained that the Foreign Minister shares my opinion that the announcement of the trip to London *can* be made only when the Iviza question has been settled. I shall inform the British Ambassador, whom I shall see at his reception, to that effect.

v. MACKENSEN

---

[1] Of the Secretariat of the Foreign Minister.
[2] Document No. 290, *supra.*

No. 292

860/285706

The State Secretary to the Foreign Minister

Draft Letter [1]

BERLIN, June 10, 1937.

I enclose the carbon copies of my memoranda on my discussion with the British Ambassador today and on the conversation with Kotze.[2] Sir Nevile's letter of today, of which I enclose a copy,[3] is incomprehensible to me, since we would get into an extremely unpleasant situation if, contrary to expectations, the Iviza incident should not be cleared up by the time of your departure for London and the trip should be given up. I shall now speak with him in this sense at his official reception.

From the conversation with Kotze I gathered that the time for the announcement depends solely on the Iviza incident, that it will not be necessary for the Führer to concern himself again with the trip before the announcement is made.

I enclose a joint greeting from today's luncheon with Chinese Finance Minister Kung, which took place in the same sort of tropical heat as did the dinner given by Schacht yesterday.

---

[1] This draft addressed to Baron von Neurath at Budapest was typed with indications that the salutation and conclusion were to be added by hand and was marked to be sent by special courier.
[2] Documents Nos. 288 and 289, p. 314, and document No. 291, *supra.*
[3] Document No. 290, p. 315.

No. 293

33/25322

The Ambassador in Great Britain to the Foreign Ministry

Telegram

No. 323 of June 10   LONDON, June 10, 1937—6 : 50 p.m.
                                      Received June 10—8 : 45 p.m.

With reference to my telegraphic report No. 317 of June 5.[1]

For the Führer and Chancellor personally.

During today's conference I informed Eden that I had discussed with the Führer and the Foreign Minister the question of the latter's visit to London. The suggestion was welcomed in Berlin, and I myself also thought it would be very useful. The Foreign Minister was in principle prepared to come to London in the near future. The question had been considered whether it would not be practical to agree in advance on an outline of the principal topics for discussion. Eden said that in addition to the Spanish question the general international situation could be considered for discussion. When I referred to the colonial question, Eden became somewhat hesitant but was willing to think the matter over. We agreed to discuss it again in a few days.

RIBBENTROP

---

[1] Not found.

No. 294

3357/E009380–81

The Ambassador in Great Britain to the Foreign Ministry

Telegram

No. 324 of June 10   LONDON, June 10, 1937—11 : 08 p.m.
                                      Received June 11—2 : 30 a.m.
                                      Pol. III 2979 a.

For the Führer and Chancellor and the Foreign Minister.

I called on Eden today in order to speak with him about the progress of the Spanish question. We discussed the following points :

1. As is known there from the press, the Soviet Russians have addressed a note to the chairman of the Non-Intervention Committee which deals with the *Deutschland* incident and, among other things, objects to the fact that negotiations were conducted among the four powers. Eden is not prepared to yield to the Russian wishes in this matter. I hear that the chairman of the Non-Intervention Committee has in the meantime already given the Russian Ambassador a negative reply.

2. I pointed out to Eden that the formula for consultation agreed upon in Berlin was to be understood to the effect that although, in

the event of further incidents, an immediate consultation among these four powers would take place, the right to take isolated counteraction would naturally revert to any individual power if consultation did not lead to agreement within a reasonable time. Eden evaded a clear stand on this and said that it could be discussed in the proposed conference of the four powers. Obviously his view hitherto was that the obligation to consult should tie the hands of the four powers with respect to isolated action. I left him in no doubt regarding our view, and I shall assert it in the proper form in the coming conferences.

3. The French Ambassador has addressed a note to Eden, in which it is proposed, among other things, that ships of the supervisory powers take neutral observers on board and in which the old French plan for increasing the number of the control powers in the sense of a joint fleet is again taken up.

Eden told me that the British Government still adhered to the four-power plan; on the other hand the Admiralty, after its original objections, was no longer opposed to taking a neutral observer on board. With reference to this I said, speaking generally, that I could not believe this plan would be accepted by us. I would consider the question, however. In the meantime the French Ambassador has told me that these questions are not to be discussed at the present stage, but only after acceptance by the Spanish parties of the guaranty proposals.

4. I then turned the conversation again to the question of press coverage and handed Eden a note in which a statement is requested from the British Government on how press indiscretions and distorted press reports may be avoided in the future. In this connection I suggested that Eden call a press conference in order to discuss the question there and also that the Non-Intervention Committee obtain an official of the Foreign Office as its own press officer. Eden received both these suggestions in a friendly spirit.

5. Eden's conference with me and the two other Ambassadors will presumably be held on Friday.

RIBBENTROP

No. 295

3357/E009379

The Ambassador in the Soviet Union to the Foreign Ministry

Telegram

No. 103 of June 10

Moscow, June 10, 1937—7:25 p.m.
Received June 10—8:45 p.m.
Pol. III 2974.

Comments in the press here on the letter sent by Soviet Ambassador Maisky to the Non-Intervention Committee on June 8 about the

Deutschland incident and the negotiations connected therewith show annoyance at the fact that the negotiations concerning the return of Germany and Italy to the Non-Intervention Committee and measures for safeguarding the patrol vessels had been carried on by Britain together with France, Germany, and Italy, without the participation of the Non-Intervention Committee and especially without the participation of the Soviet Union. With great concern the *Journal de Moscou* of June 8 and *Izvestiya* of June 10 try to represent the British proposal for consultation among the four powers participating in the naval patrol in case of an attack on the patrol vessels, and for possible joint defensive measures, as a revival of the idea of the four-power pact of which the aggressor powers dreamed. The *Journal de Moscou* severely criticizes the British efforts to settle the incident and, on the other hand, praises the French stand. Without even obtaining the views of other members of the Non-Intervention Committee, the British Government had thought it necessary to make proposals to Germany and Italy. France, on the other hand, condemned the idea of a four-power pact, as was apparent from Delbos' statements to press representatives, and insisted on the incontestable right of the Non-Intervention Committee to put the control agreement into effect.

Izvestiya states that an end should be put to the attempts of Fascist interventionists to capitalize on the Almería incident. This can best be achieved by again conducting the negotiations in the London committee, and publicly, too, with all powers represented on the committee participating.

SCHULENBURG

No. 296

3366/E010377

The State Secretary to the Embassy in Spain

Telegram

URGENT   BERLIN, June 10, 1937.
No. 213   zu Pol. III 3012.

With reference to your telegram No. 300.[1]

Your proposal to make a statement to Franco in the name of the Reich Government would involve increased responsibility with regard to internal political developments in Spain. I therefore request that you let the matter rest with the friendly remark you have already made to Franco concerning the effect of the possible execution of Hedilla.[2]

MACKENSEN

---

[1] Document No. 286, p. 312.
[2] Unsigned marginal note: "Such a reply to Faupel seems advisable also by reason of further instructions envisaged."

No. 297

47/32252

Memorandum by the Director of the Economic Policy Department

CONFIDENTIAL   BERLIN, June 10, 1937.
                                                e. o. Pol. I 4076 g.

General Wilberg told me the following today in the course of a conversation on a different subject:

A survey made in his department had disclosed that the total claims amounted to only about 150 million RM.

This total consists of the following:

1. Deliveries before November 7   43 million RM
2. Deliveries through Rowak-Hisma   52   ”   ”
3. Total value of other deliveries up to the end of
    May   55   ”   ”

If the deliveries are continued, there will be an additional 5 or 6 million RM monthly. However, these new current deliveries will be paid in cash, in so far as possible.

                                                        RITTER

No. 298

860/285717

The State Secretary to the Embassy in Great Britain

Telegram

VERY SECRET   BERLIN, June 11, 1937.
No. 241   RM 431.

For the Ambassador personally.

At the direction of the Foreign Minister I have informed the British Ambassador that Baron Neurath is prepared to arrive in London on the evening of the 23rd, and I added, as instructed, that the visit will be possible only on condition that the question of the guaranty after the Iviza incident has been settled in a manner satisfactory to us.

                                                        MACKENSEN

No. 299

3357/E009382

The Minister Counselor of Embassy in Great Britain to the Foreign Ministry

Telegram

VERY URGENT   London, June 11, 1937—9 : 36 p.m.
No. 325 of June 11   Received June 11—11 : 30 p.m.
                                     Pol. III 2991.

The conferences of the three Ambassadors with Eden have almost resulted in an agreement on the text of the statement to be sent to Franco. In addition, there was discussion on the text of a protocol of the meeting, which is to be published and is to make clear that in case consultation does not lead to a satisfactory result within a reasonable time, there will arise for each of the participating powers a new situation with regard to which it reserves its stand. This formulation was chosen in order to put into a form which would also be acceptable to the two other powers the German and Italian desire for freedom of action in case consultation should fail.

The conferences will be continued Saturday morning in the expectation of reaching a final accord.

As to the question of when the Non-Intervention Committee is to be brought into the matter, no accord has been achieved as yet. This also will be discussed further tomorrow.

WOERMANN

No. 300

860/285716

Memorandum by the State Secretary

BERLIN, June 11, 1937.

During today's telephone conversation with the Foreign Minister in Sofia I asked his opinion as to when we ought to return to the Non-Intervention Committee, i.e. whether this should be done, as Sir Nevile [Henderson] and I think, though Attolico does not share this view entirely, as soon as the British Government has notified the two Spanish parties of the formula of agreement of the four naval powers, or not until the reply from the Spanish parties has arrived. The Foreign Minister declared that in his opinion the return should be made as soon as agreement had been reached in London and the results had been communicated to the two Spanish parties.

The Foreign Minister added that this would also be the time when the condition for his London visit could be considered as met. He agrees that information for Herr von Hassell in the sense of his tele-gram of yesterday [1] be delayed somewhat longer, so that the period between the orientation of Herr von Hassell and the publication of the British invitation is not too long in view of the need for discretion.

v. MACKENSEN

---

[1] Document No 287, p. 313.

No. 301

3176/683012–13

Memorandum by the Director of the Economic Policy Department

BERLIN, June 11, 1937.

MEMORANDUM OF A CONFERENCE WITH MINISTER PRESIDENT GÖRING IN THE PRESENCE OF RITTER, JAGWITZ, AND BETHKE

Although Minister President Göring today upheld his opinion that free trade should be given consideration in view of the future, he believed that just at this moment the monopolistic position of Rowak-Hisma should not be weakened. He stated as the reason for this that if Bilbao was captured, the question of dividing between Germany and England the iron ore stored and forwarded there would become of immediate concern. To deal with this he needed to have Rowak-Hisma in a strong position with regard to Franco, the Junta, and free enterprise. All concessions which it will be possible to make to Spain in any field should therefore still be retained.

Regarding the impending continuation of the negotiations, Minis-ter President Göring is therefore of the opinion that no clearing agree-ment should be offered or discussed at the present time, reference being made in this matter to Franco's decision. Only such matters as can be settled should be negotiated to the end. With regard to a clearing agreement it should only be stated that the German Government has taken sympathetic cognizance of the earlier wishes of the Junta in this respect. It is likewise of the opinion that at a given time, perhaps soon, a clearing agreement on a limited basis should be considered. In view of the present special situation, however, it does not believe the time for this has yet come. In particular, Minister President Göring did not want the question of the rate of exchange (the fixed Spanish rate or that of the London quotations), a question which has so far not been clarified in our own discussions, to be touched upon. He feared that those Spanish circles which have for some time been advocating devaluation might use this against Franco's policy, which is intended to avoid anything that might be interpreted as deflation or inflation.

RITTER

No. 302

3357/E009383

The State Secretary to the Embassy in Great Britain

Telegram

No. 246   BERLIN, June 12, 1937,
                                                    zu Pol. III 2991 I.

For your information:
The Foreign Minister is of the opinion that the moment for our resuming participation in the Non-Intervention Committee will have arrived as soon as the guaranty formula to be agreed upon by the four naval patrol powers has been definitely accepted by them.
Same text to Rome.

MACKENSEN

No. 303

860/285719–21

The State Secretary to the Legation in Hungary

Telegram

VERY SECRET   BERLIN, June 12, 1937.
No. 52

For the Foreign Minister personally.[1]
The British Ambassador just called on me again in order to inform me of the following at the personal request of Eden, whose instruction he read aloud to me:
Eden regretted exceedingly that the visit had suddenly been made to depend on a settlement of the Iviza incident and reminded us that the first suggestion for the visit had been made precisely in connection with a settlement of this incident. Nor had the Foreign Minister set this condition later but had made the time of the visit dependent first upon the completion of his Balkan trip and then on sounding out the Führer's opinion, and had finally designated the time between June 21 and 28 as convenient for the trip, without mentioning the condition which was now being advanced. Eden deplored the present standpoint all the more since the danger of indiscretions continued to make it extremely desirable to announce the visit as soon as possible. The Ambassador went on to read from the instruction that Eden did not understand why the Spanish question should not be taken up in the London discussions. I replied by pointing out to the Ambassador that this impression was completely mistaken and that of course the Foreign Minister was prepared to discuss this question, too. He had

---

[1] Neurath was in Budapest from June 11 to June 14.

merely not wished to place particular emphasis on it in the communiqué, in order to prevent misinterpretations. Sir Nevile agreed with me immediately and said he would correct Eden's wrong impression, but he stressed that, if only in view of possible questions in Parliament, Eden would like very much to have the communiqué mention the Spanish question, which, after all, was the most important one at the present moment. He proposed adding the final words: "particularly the Spanish problem" to the draft which we had given him. He hoped that the Foreign Minister would have no objections to this.

Sir Nevile, who energetically supported Eden's wishes, and pointed out that the Foreign Minister had so far treated the question of the invitation in a more dilatory fashion than Eden had expected, urgently requested that I give him a speedy reply, in order that the announcement might be made on Tuesday, if possible—even if, contrary to his expectations, the Iviza incident had not been finally settled by that time. England and Germany were in agreement, and that was, after all, decisive for his request that the condition be withdrawn. I promised the Ambassador the greatest possible speed but added that there could scarcely be a reply before tomorrow—Sunday evening.

MACKENSEN

860/285718

[Annex]

Baron von Neurath will visit London on June 24th as the official guest of His Majesty's Government. No negotiations are under consideration but it is hoped that the visit will offer an opportunity for an exchange of views on matters of common interest to the two countries, particularly the Spanish problem.[2]

---

[2] This document is in English in the original. The last four words were added in handwriting. A notation in Mackensen's hand reads: "Handed to me by the British Ambassador."

No. 304

307/188405-07

The Minister Counselor of Embassy in Great Britain to the Foreign Ministry

Telegram

URGENT   London, June 12, 1937—10:30 p.m.
No. 326 of June 12   Received June 13—12:05 a.m.
                                                      Pol. III 3008.

With reference to our telegram No. 325.[1]

---

[1] Document No. 299, p. 321.

I. The comparatively long duration of the four-power conference on the Spanish question was due, on the one hand, to the German and Italian desire to make it clear that if the consultation failed the powers would regain freedom of action and, on the other hand, to the French effort to obtain a text which cannot be construed as an advance sanctioning of measures of force. Not for a moment was there any difference of opinion concerning the principle that the powers had freedom of action in case consultation failed. For the French and to a certain extent also for the British the question was rather one of wording, out of consideration for their parliaments. The last two paragraphs of part II of the decision (beginning with the words "the four powers further") were added at the request of the French. They appeared acceptable from the German standpoint, also, since they clearly express the solidarity of the four powers in the *Deutschland* case as well as in the future work of the committee. The French Ambassador stated explicitly that France no longer insisted on her earlier proposal that an international fleet be organized with a unified high command, but tried stubbornly to have it stipulated in this agreement that the ships of the four powers should take neutral observers aboard. Our Ambassador and Grandi said that they would submit the proposal to their Governments but at the same time expressed strong objections to it. The French Ambassador, for his part, will shortly submit concrete proposals. Our Ambassador brought up for discussion the possibility of providing the naval vessels of the patrol powers with uniform markings for recognition by planes.

II. The following further procedure was agreed upon:

Part I of the four-power proposals will be communicated today by the British Government to the chairman of the Non-Intervention Committee, who will inform all non-intervention powers of the text, although no request will be made to call the committee together. It is believed possible, however, that such a request will be made by the Soviet Union. Independently of the action of the committee, the British Government will transmit the text to the Spanish Government. The time has been left open, but transmittal is to take place no later than Tuesday morning.

III. Eden asked whether Germany and Italy were prepared to return to the committee as soon as the communication had been transmitted to the Spanish parties. Our Ambassador stated at this point that the condition on which Germany had made her return dependent in the note of May 31 was still not fulfilled with this communication to the Spanish parties. Rather, reentry was possible only after the Spanish parties had accepted the proposals, it being understood that acceptance of only sections (*a*) and (*b*) and not of section (*c*) of part

I was necessary. Moreover, the Ambassador pointed out that assurance would also have to be given that no debates about the past would be started in the committee; this referred especially to Almería. Furthermore, the Ambassador called attention in this connection to the necessity of practical measures for dealing with the press. Eden promised to discuss with Lord Plymouth the proposals which the Ambassador had made earlier.

IV. It appeared doubtful to Eden whether the Valencia Government would accept the proposals at once. It would be all the more important that Franco consent quickly. Grandi promised to direct a request to this effect to the Italian Government. Please also approach Franco from Berlin.

V. The texts are not being released in the press today, but there was agreement that it would be informed in broad outline, which we have done from here as regards the German press.

WOERMANN

No. 305

307/188402–04

The Minister Counselor of Embassy in Great Britain to the Foreign Ministry

Telegram

No. 327 of June 12   LONDON, June 12, 1937.
                                        Received June 13—12:55 a.m.
                                        Pol. III 3009.

Conversations of the German, French, and Italian Ambassadors with Eden were continued this morning and this afternoon and were brought to a conclusion.

The decisions of the four powers are divided into two parts: The first contains the three familiar points that are to be communicated to the Spanish parties, in which connection (*c*) has undergone some revision as compared to the text with which Berlin is familiar; the second part contains an agreement of the four powers among themselves; it will not be communicated to the Spanish parties but will be given to the press when the communication to the Spanish parties is handed over at the beginning of next week. The text of part I is as follows: [1]

"(*a*) That the two parties should be asked to give a specific assurance that they will respect foreign warships on the high seas and elsewhere and will take steps to see that their naval and air forces give effect to this assurance.

(*b*) That in order to avoid accidental attacks on or damage to foreign warships participating in the patrol when lying in the ports

---

[1] The quoted text is in English in the original.

of either party the two parties should be asked to come to an agreement with the four powers upon a list of Spanish ports to be made available for use as bases for their patrol ships and upon a definition of the safety zones which should be established in those ports.

(c) That the two parties should be informed that any infraction of the aforesaid assurances or any attack upon foreign warships responsible for the naval patrol will be regarded by the four powers participating in the control as a matter of common concern and that the four powers irrespective of any immediate measures of self-defence considered necessary by the forces of the power actually attacked will immediately seek agreement among themselves concerning steps to be taken in concert, taking into consideration the views which the government concerned is naturally entitled to express as to further appropriate measures."

End of part I.

Part II has the following text: [2]

"In agreeing to the text of the communication to the two Spanish parties it was generally understood under (c), that the four powers undertook to meet as quickly as possible for the purpose of consultation in regard to the appropriate steps to be taken to meet the situation. It was also generally agreed that every effort would be made by all the four powers to reach a satisfactory agreement as a result of such consultations. In the event, however, of failure to reach agreement within a space of time appropriate to the circumstances of each case, it was understood that a new situation would be created for each of the four powers concerned in regard to which they must reserve their respective attitudes; the four powers further agreed that it was their joint objective to create the maximum international confidence, both in the efficacy and in the impartiality of the patrol system. They desired to emphasize its neutral and international character; they accordingly declared themselves ready to submit without delay for the examination of the Non-Intervention Committee practical proposals to realise this objective."

End of part II.

WOERMANN

---

[2] The quoted text is in English in the original.

No. 306

860/285726–27

The Ambassador in Italy to the Foreign Ministry

Telegram

No. 155 of June 12   ROME, June 12, 1937—10 : 45 p.m.
Received June 13—3 : 30 a.m.

Mussolini, in his discussion with me today, expressed lively satisfaction at Blomberg's visit [1] and inquired about his impressions, which I described to him in general terms on the basis of conversations with

---

[1] Blomberg visited Rome and Naples from June 2 to June 7.

the Field Marshal. Mussolini then began to speak in detail, and often vehemently, about relations with England. The pivot of future world policy was the relationship of Germany and Italy with England, for France was approaching a severe social crisis and was an unimportant factor at the present time. Russia appeared to be nearing a severe convulsion; the development of a state of chaos there would be the most desirable solution for us. As far as England was concerned, it would be dangerous if people in Germany gave themselves over to illusions which were being systematically nourished by England in the present situation in order to separate Berlin and Rome. He himself had no more earnest desire than an understanding with England, for which, however, unfortunately the state of mind there was evidently not yet ripe. This understanding had to be a comprehensive one and had to begin with the recognition of the Empire,[2] continue with clarification of other African questions between the British and Italian colonies, and be concluded with an understanding regarding the Mediterranean. I said that a recognition of the Empire as the first prerequisite would still be difficult for England to swallow for the present but that otherwise the difficulties were perhaps not insurmountable, since I doubted that there was any spirit of revenge in England. As far as we were concerned, we shared the desire for an understanding with England, and I considered the Berlin-Rome Axis a particularly sound basis for it. Mussolini replied that he shared the latter view; the only correct principle for both of us was: no understanding between Berlin and London without Rome, and no London-Rome understanding without Berlin. But England had in fact not yet recognized and accepted the situation today; whether this was called a spirit of revenge or not, at any rate England considered that she had lost the first round on points but had not been knocked out, and she had her eye on the second round. He, Mussolini, knew that public opinion in England was against Italy at present and in particular against him personally more than ever before, and more than in Government circles. The man in the street regarded him as a dangerous bulldog. I replied that this attitude, which, moreover, was really a compliment, was a delayed effect of Eden's policy, to which Mussolini replied that then it would have to be the task of sensible British statesmen to do away with such ideas among the British people by well-considered speeches. England need not delude herself; if her armaments were strengthened considerably by 1940, Italy's would be, too, especially in the air and on the sea, as well as by the organization of a very strong native army

---

[2] i. e. the Italian Empire.

in Africa. Perhaps England still underestimated the potential effectiveness of Italian aviators and the importance of the fortification of Pantelleria. It would be a struggle between lion and leopard, in the course of which the leopard might be defeated in the end, but the lion would be severely wounded. He, Mussolini, did not prefer a struggle but rather an understanding, and indeed on the basis of German-Italian cooperation, the intrinsic, logical necessity of which England appeared to underestimate; but he had to prepare for the possibility of a struggle.

HASSELL

No. 307

860/285723

The Foreign Minister to the State Secretary

Telegram

VERY URGENT — BUDAPEST, June 13, 1937—1 : 50 p.m.
VERY SECRET — Received June 13—4 : 00 p.m.
No. 32 of June 13

For the State Secretary personally.

I have no objection to the addition of the final words "particularly the Spanish problem" to the British communiqué. Since I am not oriented regarding the progress of the London negotiations on the Iviza incident and in particular do not know whether the British have expressed any opinion at all on our counterproposal, I have no way of judging what difficulties stand in the way of a final settlement. I required from the beginning that at least an agreement in principle on our terms be reached before my departure for London. I do not intend to concern myself with the Iviza incident in London; please inform Henderson of this. I expect the British Government to state its position on our proposal by tomorrow afternoon. I shall not give a final reply to the invitation until then.

Since the projected trip to London has already become known, as I gather from an utterance of Kanya,[1] we shall now have to inform the Italians at once. Please instruct Hassell accordingly. Notification of Attolico is advisable only when the trip has finally been decided upon.

I shall telephone from Leinfelden [2] between 5 and 6 o'clock tomorrow.

NEURATH

---

[1] Hungarian Minister of Foreign Affairs.
[2] Neurath's residence in Württemberg.

No. 308

860/285725

The Foreign Minister to the State Secretary

Telegram

BUDAPEST, June 13, 1937—2 : 37 p.m.
Received June 13—3 : 35 p.m.

For the State Secretary personally.

I am leaving for Leinfelden by air tomorrow after a conference with the Führer. The accompanying plane will arrive in Berlin about 12 noon. Please order the Ministry's baggage truck there.

NEURATH

No. 309

860/285722

The State Secretary to the Embassy in Italy

Telegram

VERY SECRET   BERLIN, June 13, 1937.
No. 175 of June 13

For the Ambassador personally.

The Foreign Minister requests that you inform the Italian Government, pointing out the necessity of strictly confidential treatment for the time being, that he intends to accept an official invitation to London, probably during the last week of this month. He will do so, of course, only on condition that the question of a guaranty after the Iviza incident has been settled in a manner satisfactory to us. The Foreign Minister requests that in informing the Italian Government you add that the visit would also appear to be useful in promoting better Anglo-Italian relations.

MACKENSEN

No. 310

860/285724

Memorandum by the State Secretary

BERLIN, June 13, 1937.

I informed the British Ambassador this evening—by telephone, since he was at Hoppegarten—that the Foreign Minister had no objection to the addition of the final words, "particularly the Spanish problem." [1]

---

[1] See document No. 307, p. 329.

Although I could refer over the telephone only to the addition of the proposed four last words, the Ambassador understood the message and said he would transmit it to London at once.

I have not yet made use of the rest of the telegram, since a personal meeting was not possible; I merely informed him that I thought I could give him a final answer tomorrow afternoon. If, as is to be expected, the Iviza affair is so far cleared up in the course of tomorrow that there is "an agreement in principle on our terms" (cf. the Foreign Minister's telegram), it probably will not be necessary to argue with the British on whether such a demand was made from the beginning.

According to instructions, Ambassador von Hassell was informed this very evening by telegram.

MACKENSEN

No. 311

3357/E009391

The Ambassador in Great Britain to the Foreign Ministry

Telegram

URGENT　　　　　　　　　　　　LONDON, June 14, 1937—4:48 p.m.
No. 330 of June 14　　　　　　　　Received June 14—6:00 p.m.
　　　　　　　　　　　　　　　　　　　　Pol. III 3103.

For the Führer and Chancellor and the Foreign Minister.

With reference to telegraphic instruction No. 246.[1]

The telegraphic instruction according to which we are again to participate in the Non-Intervention Committee as soon as the guaranty formula has been definitively accepted by the control powers did not arrive here until after the conclusion of the four-power discussions. As appears from telegraphic report No. 326,[2] section III, I personally expressed the opinion in those discussions [*dort*] on Saturday that, in view of the text of the note of May 31, we could consider reentering only when the Spanish parties had in principle accepted sections (*a*) and (*b*) of the four-power agreement. In so doing I indicated that this did not mean that there would have to be agreement on all details in the question of the safety zones. If we should return to the committee today, an ambiguous and difficult position for us would arise there. We must take into account the possibility that the Valencia authorities will accept the proposals only with modifications. Thus it is already reported in the British press today that the Valencia Government is expressly demanding the exclusion of the right of reprisals.

---

[1] Document No. 302, p. 323.
[2] Document No. 304, p. 324.

We would therefore probably have to expect that Maisky will raise the question of Almería, which according to your instructions might result in our withdrawing again.   In my opinion, the . . . (group missing) resulting from the reply of the Spanish sides must be awaited, in order to avoid discussions of this matter in the committee during our participation.

RIBBENTROP

No. 312

3357/E009387

The Director of the Political Department to the Embassy in Spain [1]

Telegram

No. 218   BERLIN, June 14, 1937.
                                                  zu Pol. III 3009 II.

With reference to telegraphic instruction No. 216 of the 13th.[2]

The text of the London decisions, which was sent to you by wire yesterday, meets the demands of the German Government in all essential points.   We assume that Franco has meanwhile been requested by the British Government to comply with points (*a*) and (*b*).[3]   Please urge Franco to give an affirmative reply.

WEIZSÄCKER

---

[1] On the same day the contents of this telegram were repeated to Rome as No. 177.
[2] Not printed (4907/E255237–43).
[3] See document No. 305, p. 326.

No. 313

860/285734–35

Memorandum by the State Secretary

BERLIN, June 14, 1937.

The Foreign Minister shares my view that the condition he attached to acceptance of the British invitation has been fulfilled by the agreement reached in London between the four great naval powers, and he authorizes me to inform the British Ambassador to that effect.   As soon as the official invitation of the British Government has been received, the announcement may be made in the manner we have contemplated.   The agreement with the British Ambassador must insure that this announcement will be made simultaneously in London and in Berlin.

The Foreign Minister requests that the British Ambassador be reminded that the official functions during the visit are to be kept within the narrowest limits possible.   He intends, therefore, to take with him only Herr von Kotze and a secretary, who has not yet been named. The question whether Frau von Neurath will go along on the trip will have to remain open at the present time but will be settled soon.

The Foreign Minister fully agrees that in addition to the information already given to Herr von Hassell he should be sent another telegram [1] which would enable him to dispel Mussolini's worries as much as possible. I gave only a short sketch of the content of the telegram but received authorization to have it sent this evening; I promised the Foreign Minister, however, that he would get a carbon copy together with the dispatch which is still to go off to him today.

v. MACKENSEN

[1] Document No. 319, p. 338.

No. 314

424/217495

Memorandum by the State Secretary

BERLIN, June 14, 1937.

In today's telephone conversation I pointed out to the Foreign Minister that contrary to our instructions, which arrived too late in London, Ambassador von Ribbentrop, without consulting Berlin but perhaps after conferring with Obersalzberg, had taken the position in the Ambassadors' discussions with Eden that before resuming work in the Non-Intervention Committee we had to wait for the replies of the two Spanish parties. The Foreign Minister said he agreed that we should not intervene from here now; he himself could not understand the view advocated in London, for it went beyond our original intentions, according to which we had only demanded agreement among the four great naval powers on the future guaranty measures. If the Spanish Red Party should reply in the negative, this in itself would be a reason for the four great naval powers to meet for a conference to discuss further measures.

The Foreign Minister reserves the right, if necessary, to obtain a decision in line with the view advocated by him from the Führer and Chancellor.

v. MACKENSEN

No. 315

860/285736

Memorandum by the State Secretary

BERLIN, June 14, 1937.

I received the British Ambassador this evening and informed him that the Foreign Minister considered the condition which he had attached to his acceptance of the invitation of the British Government to be fulfilled, now that the four great naval powers had come to an agreement in London. The Ambassador thanked me warmly for this information, which he said he would transmit to Eden immediately. We agreed that the delivery of the official invitation, which should take place as quickly as possible, was of purely formal significance, hence did not affect the time of the announcement. We agreed further that in view of indiscretions to be feared—which, I indicated to the Ambassador, had already occurred—the announcement should be made as soon as possible. Mr. Henderson thought that the time of day (7 p.m.) was already too far advanced to make certain that he would be able to communicate with London. Since the announcement absolutely must be made in Berlin and in London at the same time, we agreed that it is to be made in both places on Wednesday morning and that he will inform me sometime tomorrow that the time fixed has been accepted in London.

I then told him about the Foreign Minister's wish that all official functions be restricted to a minimum. He said he would also transmit this to London immediately.

In regard to the question whether Baroness Neurath would go along, I promised to give him further information, and I added that, furthermore, in keeping with the character of the trip, the Foreign Minister would restrict the number of people accompanying him as much as possible.

v. MACKENSEN

No. 316

860/285737

Memorandum by the State Secretary

BERLIN, June 14, 1937.

The British Ambassador telephoned again about 8 p.m. to inform me that thus far he had been able to get in touch only with an under secretary in London. He had, however, asked him to inform Mr. Eden's private secretary of the call, so that he hoped to be able to settle the matter early tomorrow.

The Ambassador will telephone me sometime tomorrow forenoon.

v. MACKENSEN

No. 317

860/285728–33

Memorandum by the Director of the Political Department

BERLIN, June 14, 1937.

I submit herewith a memorandum for the Foreign Minister's visit to London as a framework for the conversation; at certain points it should be elaborated either orally or in writing.

Submitted to the State Secretary.

WEIZSÄCKER

[Enclosure]

An Anglo-German conversation at the present time at British invitation can have positive advantages. Anglo-German relations may be improved several degrees without injury to our other relations (especially with Italy) and may perhaps also be given a direction toward continuing improvement.

To be sure, it will still take a long time for England to become accustomed to the Third Reich. England can in no case be induced in the foreseeable future to go further than to take a middle road between France and Germany.

The conversation might be thought of as taking something like the following course:

1. *German introduction:* Mutual relations leave something to be desired. But there is no reason why there should not be an essential improvement.

(*a*) We do not desire war, not even between third states. The world has nothing to fear from our armaments.

(*b*) We desire improvement in our living conditions and our supply of raw materials by peaceful means, without perceptible prejudice to England. We are not disturbing any vital British interests.

(*c*) We are carrying on our struggle against Communism defensively and only on our own territory.

(*d*) Divergent ideologies ought not to constitute any hindrance for a realistic British policy.

2. *German grievances:* We encounter British resistance everywhere, even where in our opinion no real British interests are involved. The attitude of the British press.

If England would leave us alone where German interests are predominant and British interests are not affected, and if she would take our raw-materials situation seriously and help us to improve it, Anglo-German cooperation in the interest of preserving peace would be assured.

3. *British grievances:* Alleged threat to peace seen in German Eastern policy toward Czechoslovakia, Austria, and Russia; German-Japanese agreements; German-Italian bloc policy; the division of Europe into two ideological groups; rejection of international cooperation, and self-isolation.

4. *Possibilities of improvement in Anglo-German relations:* No planned introduction of a new era in Anglo-German relations; instead, a gradual *rapprochement* through practical cooperation.

(*a*) Western Pact.[1] In case of its failure, agreements to respect the Belgian and perhaps [*eventuell*] the Dutch boundary.

German readiness to meet for consultation with the other three Locarno Great Powers, if critical situations should arise between these powers. In case of necessity, the circle of consulting powers could be enlarged.

(*b*) Declaration of mutual willingness to enter into an agreement for the limitation of armaments as soon as that appears to be internationally expedient.

(*c*) Investigation by a bilateral commission of German needs for a raw-materials area.

(*d*) German guaranty not to pursue an anti-British policy in the Far East.

British assurance to render as much assistance as necessary to ease tension in Germany's relations with her Eastern neighbors, the Balkan states, and in the Baltic.

(*e*) In Spain, continuation of the non-intervention and blockade policy. Joint exploration of the possibilities of bringing the Spanish war to an end.

(*f*) Anglo-French and German-Italian relations are not to be affected by points (*a*) to (*e*).

5. In a final communiqué pledges or agreements arising under No. 4 (*a*), paragraph 1; 4 (*b*); 4 (*c*); and 4 (*e*) might be set down in writing.

---

[1] For documents relating to the Western Pact, see series C.

No. 318

860/285738–39

Memorandum by the State Secretary

BERLIN, June 14, 1937.

I asked the Italian Ambassador to call on me this evening in order to inform him of the approaching trip of the Foreign Minister to London and request that the information be treated as confidential until a public announcement is made. Signor Attolico obviously had no knowledge of the impending visit, but he displayed remarkably little surprise and was by no means unfavorably impressed. I expounded to him approximately the same ideas as those which formed the basis for our telegram to Ambassador von Hassell. Signor Attolico declared that from his point of view he could only welcome it if the trip was made. He had always advocated the viewpoint that a *rapprochement* with England was desirable. We were living, so to speak, in a historic age, or rather in a period of transition, in which we would have to make up our minds whether we wished to reach a general European *rapprochement*, or retain our former policy of dividing Europe into different camps and head directly for another war. Thus, anyone who was of the same opinion as he could only welcome the projected trip. To my question whether his Government, especially the Duce, shared his view in all its implications, the Ambassador replied that that could not be said. Mussolini regarded such a policy with very great reserve; this in turn could be explained by the undoubtedly anti-Italian operation of British policy, which was apparent from day to day. On the one hand, England—through Eden, who was thoroughly unreliable in his attitude—assured everyone who would listen, for instance, at the Coronation recently, Blomberg, van Zeeland,[1] and even the Papal representative,[2] that the case of Abyssinia was settled as far as England was concerned and that no one was contemplating revenge or anything evil against Italy. In reality, however, things were entirely different. Even the British activity which could recently be observed in the Danube area was to be charged to this account. He, the Ambassador himself, would not, however, permit himself to be diverted from his effort to work for a policy of general *rapprochement*, even if in so doing he encountered contrary views in Rome. How very anxious he was also for a settlement with England, I had probably been able to observe recently at his first dinner for me, at which he had intentionally brought together the new British Ambassador, General von Blomberg, and me.

When the Ambassador later brought up the subject of a Western Pact, I requested him to reserve a conversation on this for some later time, since I had not yet done more than take a superficial glance at the note which had been handed to us. The Ambassador said that this was agreeable to him and added that, as a confirmed supporter of the Locarno idea, he could only welcome the new note on the Western Pact.

v. MACKENSEN

---

[1] Belgian Prime Minister.
[2] Mgr. Giuseppe Pizzardo.

No. 319

860/285740–42

The Foreign Minister to the Embassy in Italy

Telegram [1]

URGENT   BERLIN, June 14, 1937.

No. [176] [2]   e.o. RM 427.

With reference to your telegram No. 155 [3] and our No. 175.[4]

As far as the invitation of the British Government is concerned, I myself was surprised by it and do not consider it quite timely. It is evident, however, that I could not decline without violating the requirements of courtesy.

On the matter itself, I should like to make the following remarks:

I have the impression that Mussolini at the time of his conversation with you on June 12 already knew about the official invitation of the British Government. Mussolini's statements indicate some concern that an Anglo-German understanding is taking shape, by which the recent success of German-Italian cooperation might suffer. I do not share this concern. I fully approve the point of view you presented to Mussolini, in particular the opinion that the Rome-Berlin Axis cannot fail to have a restraining influence on England. Mussolini may rest assured that we fully approve of the principle that there shall be no understanding between Berlin and London without Rome, and no understanding between Rome and London without Berlin, and that I shall, of course, act in accordance with this principle on my trip.

I offer no opinion as to which policy, the Italian or the German, is being more strenuously opposed by England at the present time, in particular whether British armaments are directed more against Italy or more against us. But, particularly if Mussolini fears preparation for a second round between England and Italy, it should be a matter of importance to him to see Anglo-German relations improved several degrees, if possible to the extent that we can present our common German-Italian viewpoints in London with a certain prospect of being heard.

There can be no question of any planned introduction of a new era in Anglo-German relations. The subjects which London will bring up during my visit are: the general European political situation, and Spain as its most critical point.

---

[1] Marginal note: "To be dispatched immediately over the signature of the Foreign Minister. Mackensen."
[2] Another copy (33/25338–39) bears the telegram number.
[3] Document No. 306, p. 327.
[4] Document No. 309, p. 330.

What other problems I for my part may bring up, I shall have to reserve until after my study of the material at hand on my return to Berlin. I should, however, be grateful for any suggestions made by Italy, and especially for any information as to what Mussolini's wishes are regarding the treatment of the Spanish question and the problem of a Western Pact.

NEURATH

No. 320

860/285743–44

The Ambassador in Italy to the Foreign Ministry

Telegram

No. 157 of June 14   ROME (QUIRINAL), June 14, 1937—11 : 35 p.m.
Received June 15—4 : 20 a.m.

With reference to your telegram No. 175 of June 13.

As instructed, I today informed Ciano very confidentially of the contemplated visit of the Foreign Minister to London, stressing in particular the last sentence of the instruction. Ciano showed himself very much taken aback by the communication and did not conceal that it was an unwelcome surprise here. In the present situation, and as Anglo-Italian relations stood, the trip would seem strange to Italian public opinion and would be systematically interpreted in the world press as a sign of weakening of the Berlin-Rome Axis. I answered that this was possible but was not a decisive consideration; in the final analysis it was not a question of the interpretation by the opposition, but a question of facts. And the information given the Italian Government showed how these facts were to be evaluated. Furthermore, it was a question of British initiative, namely an official invitation, which really could not very well be declined. Finally, however, the Head of the Government himself had stated to me the day before yesterday that Italy also desired an understanding with England. Ciano replied that naturally he had no thought whatever of passing judgment on German conduct with regard to the invitation. He merely deplored the unfavorable effect on world public opinion which would surely set in for both of us. As far as an agreement between Rome and London was concerned, it was probably more correct to say that "Italy was prepared for it" rather than that "Italy desired it." For the time being, however, the non-recognition of the Empire stood between England and Italy. Above all, however, the Head of the Government had also stressed in his conversation with me that the Berlin-London road should not be taken without Rome, nor the Rome-London road without Berlin. But the visit of Herr von Neurath at the present moment would not be interpreted in this sense. I replied that the visit of the Foreign Minister to London by no means indicated an intention on the part of Germany to come to an agreement with London apart from Rome. I hoped that Ciano would not retain that impression either. At any rate, I would report his concern to Berlin, and undoubtedly everything possible would be done by us on this occasion, too, to take into account the cooperation between Berlin and Rome. Ciano stated that he would report to the Duce, who was away; but the Duce's reaction would undoubtedly be the same as his. He then inquired whether there was any sort of agenda for the London visit, whether any agreements were planned, and so forth. I answered that I believed it was merely a question for the time being of the invitation and its acceptance in principle. But in any event the Italian Government would be kept completely informed in regard to the matter.

Please send me instructions with regard to the proposed factual content of the London discussions as soon as it is known, and authorize me to inform the Italian Government and to receive any requests it may make.

HASSELL

No. 321

307/188414

Memorandum by the State Secretary

BERLIN, June 15, 1937.

The Italian Ambassador telephoned at noon today and requested that he be informed regarding our position as to the date on which we would resume work in the Non-Intervention Committee. I replied to Signor Attolico that the Foreign Minister, and hence the Reich Government, took the position that the agreement reached in London among the four Great Powers participating in the naval patrol was sufficient to clear the way for our early return to the Non-Intervention Committee. To be sure, the German Ambassador in London had expressed his personal view at the Ambassadors' conference that we had to wait for a satisfactory answer from both sides in Spain before we reentered. We intended to have the Ambassador withdraw this purely personal viewpoint and inform Eden of the position of the Reich Government outlined above.

The Italian Ambassador remarked that Ambassador Grandi had been instructed to declare, after agreement was reached among the four great naval powers, i.e. now, that the time had come for Italy to return to the Non-Intervention Committee.

MACKENSEN

No. 322

860/285751

Memorandum by the State Secretary

BERLIN, June 15, 1937.

The British Ambassador telephoned at 1:30 p.m. today to inform me that the question of the publication of the communiqué regarding the Foreign Minister's trip to London had been satisfactorily settled and that, accordingly, the report would appear tomorrow morning in the British press.

I pointed out to the Ambassador that we were desisting from the radio announcement, which would otherwise ordinarily have been made at 10 p.m. the previous evening, and it was expected that London would do likewise.[1]

MACKENSEN

---

[1] There appears in the file (860/285750) the following copy of the English text of the communiqué as received from the British Embassy: "Text of Communiqué to be issued in London in morning newspapers of 16th June. Baron von Neurath will visit London on 23rd June as the official guest of His Majesty's Government. No negotiations are under consideration but it is hoped that the visit will offer an opportunity for an exchange of views on matters of common interest to the two countries and particularly the Spanish problem." For the earlier text, see document No. 303, p. 324.

Also in the file (860/285746) is the text of the proposed DNB statement: "DNB for Wednesday morning papers (but not radio): Minister for Foreign Affairs von Neurath will leave for London on June 23 at the official invitation of the British Government. No negotiations are contemplated, but it is to be expected that the visit will provide opportunity for an exchange of views regarding questions of common interest to the two countries, particularly in regard to the Spanish question." The paper bears a marginal note indicating that a copy was sent to the British Ambassador.

No. 323

860/285748–49

The Ambassador in Great Britain to the Foreign Ministry

Telegram

No. 332 of June 15

LONDON, June 15, 1937—4:12 p.m.
Received June 15—5:30 p.m.

For the Foreign Minister personally.

On the occasion of a meeting with Eden I mentioned the impending visit of the Foreign Minister and asked him if he had already formed an idea of the questions to be discussed. Eden answered that he had informed the Foreign Minister that he thought it right in announcing the visit to speak not of negotiations, but only of a friendly exchange of views regarding questions of interest to both nations.

The Foreign Minister had declined to have any mention made of a discussion of the Spanish question, which Eden had proposed; the Foreign Minister had, furthermore, told him that he could not discuss a Western Pact. I replied to Eden that I also considered it wrong to mention Spain, since that might arouse among the public and in other nations hopes impossible of fulfillment, and incorrect . . . (group garbled) might be made. Eden said that he had now ordered that a study be made of what subjects might be discussed. The German condition for the visit, that the question of the Spanish guaranty be settled by then to the satisfaction of all parties, would, it was hoped, soon be fulfilled.

In this conversation I felt again how disadvantageous it is when the Embassy is not kept currently informed of such discussions between the Ministry and the British Embassy in Berlin. After first hearing of the fact of the British Government's invitation to the Foreign Minister last week from Eden—after Berlin's reaction already had been received here—I now also learned from Eden for the first time the particulars of the negotiations held in Berlin concerning the details of the Foreign Minister's visit. The impression which this must make is injurious to our policy. Eden wishes to discuss with me again within the next few days the program for the Foreign Minister's visit. I shall then transmit Eden's ideas. Please inform me whether any further discussions regarding the questions to be considered during the visit are to be held in Berlin. In that case, it is necessary that I be kept currently oriented for my conversations with Eden. If it is desired that further preliminary preparations be made by the Embassy here, I request that I be informed of your intentions. Double-track operation [*Doppelgleisigkeit*] should by all means be avoided.

RIBBENTROP

No. 324

307/188412–13

Memorandum by the State Secretary

BERLIN, June 15, 1937.

Ambassador von Ribbentrop telephoned from London at 6: 30 p.m. and inquired what attitude he was to take henceforth on the question of the date for resuming our work in the Non-Intervention Committee. Our telegram with the decision of the Foreign Minister [1] had unfortunately reached him only after he—in a purely personal capacity—had taken a different position on the question at the meeting of the Ambassadors. I replied that the Foreign Minister had told me again yesterday that the view stated in our telegram still stood. We had already been on the point of informing him to that effect, since Ambassador Attolico asked me the same questions on the tele-

---

[1] Document No. 302, p. 323.

phone at noon today [2] and added that the Italian Government took the position that the way was clear for an immediate return to the Non-Intervention Committee. Herr von Ribbentrop thought that it would not be difficult for him, in accordance with the wishes of the Foreign Minister, to clarify the position he had hitherto maintained personally and not without reservation, especially since he had also just been informed of the Italian position by Grandi.

With regard to the time for announcing the return to the Non-Intervention Committee, Herr von Ribbentrop suggested tomorrow morning's papers. Pointing out that the communiqué on the Foreign Minister's trip to London was expected in the same papers and that the time was very short for insuring a simultaneous announcement in Rome, I suggested to him that it seemed to me better to make the announcement in tomorrow evening's papers. He wanted to get in touch with Grandi immediately and will call me again afterward.

MACKENSEN

[2] Document No. 321, p. 340.

No. 325

860/285752

Memorandum by the State Secretary

BERLIN, June 15, 1937.

During today's telephone conversation about another matter Herr von Ribbentrop mentioned that according to his information the British Government intended to release the communiqué regarding the Foreign Minister's visit as early as 10 o'clock this evening. I replied that this was contrary to the agreement between Mr. Henderson and me; I had expressly told him that, in deference to his wish to have the announcement made jointly tomorrow morning, we were desisting from transmitting the announcement to the radio stations (for broadcast at 10 o'clock tonight), which was otherwise customary here. Herr von Ribbentrop promised to take steps to see that the British Government also did not make the announcement before tomorrow morning.

MACKENSEN

No. 326

307/188410–11

Memorandum by the State Secretary

BERLIN, June 15, 1937.

Ambassador von Ribbentrop telephoned again at 7:05 p.m. and reported that he had agreed with Ambassador Grandi, who in the meantime had conferred with Rome, that they will both announce the resumption of their work in the Non-Intervention Committee in separate letters to be handed to Eden tomorrow.   In tomorrow's *evening papers* a corresponding announcement is to be made, the content to be about as follows: "Since the representatives of the four Great Powers participating in the naval patrol have agreed on the measures, etc., the German representative has now resumed his work in the Non-Intervention Committee."

I arranged with Herr von Ribbentrop that a similar announcement in Rome is to be secured exclusively via Grandi, whom he will inform to this effect.

Herr von Ribbentrop then touched upon the question of the resumption of control activities by the Navy.   I told him that Herr von Weizsäcker had just been in touch with the Navy about this and had informed them of the latest status of the matter.   Herr von Ribbentrop raised the question whether the resumption of control activities was also to be mentioned in the communiqué.   Since neither of us had at hand the text of the announcement with which we had suspended our activity in the Non-Intervention Committee, we left this question open for the time being.   He will examine whether any mention in the communiqué is necessary and only in that case will he send me another report.   Otherwise we will limit the communiqué to the statement that the German representative has resumed his activity.

MACKENSEN

No. 327

860/285745

Memorandum by the Deputy Director of the Political Department

BERLIN, June 15, 1937.

Counselor of Embassy von Plessen [1] telephoned me this morning in order to inform me that our telegram No. 176 [2] (containing the long instruction to Ambassador von Hassell for explaining the London visit) and the Rome Embassy's telegram No. 157 [3] (a report of yesterday's discussion with Count Ciano) had crossed.   In order to avoid further crossings Ambassador von Hassell intended to wait until a reply to his telegram No. 157 had been received before carrying out the instruction contained in telegram No. 176.   After consulting with Ministerialdirektor von Weizsäcker, I called Herr von Plessen on the telephone again and informed him that no reply would be given by us to telegram No. 157 from Rome.   It was a matter of very great importance to us that Ambassador von Hassell should carry out the

---

[1] Of the German Embassy in Italy.
[2] Document No. 319, p. 338.
[3] Document No. 320, p. 339.

instruction contained in telegram No. 176 today. Herr von Plessen replied that this would be done, not with Mussolini, to be sure, but with Ciano, since the former was not in Rome.

v. BISMARCK

No. 328

860/285758–60

Memorandum by the State Secretary

BERLIN, June 16, 1937

The Italian Ambassador called on me this forenoon by appointment. It developed that his request for a discussion was due to a desire to give vent in agitated terms to the annoyance caused by the notification, much too late in his opinion, to the Italian Government of the Foreign Minister's London visit. He also believed that he deserved our confidence to the extent that we could at least have advised him to this effect in advance in a few words, so that he would have been in a position to make the proper preparations in Rome in order to avoid a shock such as the Duce had in fact now suffered. I interjected the remark that this shock had perhaps not been so violent as he represented it to be; for we had received the impression, from a conversation between Hassell and Mussolini about Anglo-Italian relations, that Mussolini had already known for some time of the plans for the visit. The Ambassador replied that the content of this conversation was known to him. It had, however, come about for an entirely different reason, and he gave his word of honor that the Duce did not know anything about the plans for the trip at that time. It was rather that Field Marshal von Blomberg had taken up with Mussolini the subject of Anglo-Italian relations and related to the Duce what he had heard in London during his stay there at the Coronation with regard to England's real attitude toward Italy. This had given the Duce the occasion to set forth his own ideas, and he had then repeated these ideas to Herr von Hassell in order to be sure that they reached the German Government in the right form. But he had had no inkling at that time of the impending visit of the Foreign Minister to London.

The Ambassador then harped at considerable length on the emphasis given the Spanish question in our communiqué; he characterized it as particularly serious, since it was interpreted by the world at large and, as he had already been able to note, also in all journalistic circles here, as indicating Germany's intention to dispose of the Spanish affair with England, possibly even against the wishes of Italy. This was certainly only an impression, which in no way corresponded to the true state of affairs, but this impression was now definitely there and could easily have been avoided.

I tried to calm the Ambassador as best I could and explained to him why it was not possible to inform the Italian Government sooner, and in so doing I also stressed the fact that not even Field Marshal von Blomberg had been informed in advance, precisely because the whole matter had not reached the point of decision until the very last few days. The Ambassador requested urgently that if it was at all possible he be received personally by the Foreign Minister tomorrow forenoon, even if only for a few minutes, in order that he might then obtain direct confirmation of what Hassell, on instructions from us, had already said in Rome and I had already told him here in regard to this. His desire to quiet as quickly as possible the excitement which had undoubtedly been aroused in Rome was surely understandable enough to justify his request.

On leaving, the Ambassador spoke to me again about Lord Plymouth's recent stay in Berlin. He showed me the short telegram from Ciano relating thereto, which he also interpreted as an indication of nervousness in Rome. I answered that I could give him information from a most reliable source regarding Lord Plymouth's visit. Sir Nevile Henderson himself on the occasion of his reception recently told me that he had to go to the station immediately afterward to meet Lord Plymouth, who was returning to England from a visit to the Baltic states. Lord Plymouth would then have supper with him, and some two and a half hours later would be accompanied by him to the *Nord Express*. That was the entire Berlin visit of Lord Plymouth, who had made no contact whatever with any German officials.[1]

MACKENSEN

---

[1] Unsigned marginal note: "Ambassador Attolico will call on the Foreign Minister tomorrow at 12 noon."

No. 329

860/285761

The Ambassador in Italy to the Foreign Ministry

Telegram

No. 160 of June 14   ROME (QUIRINAL), June 16, 1937—2:15 p.m.
                                        Received June 16—5:10 p.m.

With reference to your telegram No. 176 of June 14.

I explained to Ciano today the points of view contained in the telegram and requested communication of any Italian suggestions and desires, particularly relating to the Spanish question and the problem of a Western Pact. Ciano, who in the meantime had got in touch with the absent Head of the Government and had received an informative report from Attolico, declared that the Italians realized that as things stood the British invitation could not very well be refused. He was very glad to take note of my statements regarding the nature of the meeting as well as German fidelity to the Rome-Berlin Axis and agreement with the principle: no understanding between Berlin and London without Rome, or between Rome and London without Berlin. As far as Anglo-Italian relations were concerned, he requested that, in line with my recent conversations with the Head of the Government and with him, the Foreign Minister stress in London that Italy in no wise sought a conflict with England, but, on the contrary, was fully prepared for an improvement in relations, indeed for a friendly development of them. The "gentlemen's agreement" of January had remained nebulous because the most decisive point of all, namely, the recognition of the Empire, had been avoided. Thus, an understanding with England would be very welcome to Italy, provided it was an understanding that included all essential points, to which, above all, belonged recognition of the Empire. He reserved the statement of any further suggestions and desires until he had spoken with the Head of the Government. In regard to Spain, it could be said even now that Italy did not consider mediation practicable, especially since it would surely be rejected by Franco as well as by the Reds. As for the Western Pact, Italy adhered to the viewpoint set forth in her note and could not discern any essential progress in the French note; the language was, to be sure, somewhat more accommodating, but in the essential points, in particular the role of the League of Nations, there was no change.

HASSELL

No. 330

860/285753–54

The State Secretary to the Embassy in Great Britain

Draft Telegram

URGENT!   BERLIN, June 16. 1937
PRIORITY!

For the Ambassador personally.

With reference to your telegram No. 332.[1]

For the sake of certainty I should like to recapitulate as follows the information I conveyed by telephone this morning:

The statements made to you by Eden regarding the preparations for the Foreign Minister's visit to London are inaccurate in several details. There have been no negotiations with the British Ambassador here regarding the subjects and the problems of the impending discussions in London.   Thus far we have discussed only the communiqué, which

---

[1] Document No. 323, p. 341.

has meanwhile been published; in this connection the Foreign Minister finally agreed, in deference to the special wish of the British, that the Spanish question also be mentioned. Concerning a Western Pact, it was stated only incidentally that no "negotiations" for such a pact could be undertaken during the Foreign Minister's visit, especially since the Foreign Minister intends to take only one or two men from his immediate staff with him to London.

It has not yet been decided what subjects the Foreign Minister for his part will bring up in London. The Foreign Minister returns to Berlin on the 17th and has reserved further decisions. If you send your suggestions here by that time, the Foreign Minister will surely welcome them. Whether the Foreign Minister will then send London a list of subjects for his visit, and through what channels, he has not yet announced.

Another communication, from an instruction sent to Hassell,[2] is sent separately for your information.

MACKENSEN

---

[2] Document No. 319, p. 338.

No. 331

307/188408

Memorandum by the Director of the Political Department

BERLIN, June 16, 1937.

Admiral [*Generaladmiral*] Raeder just told me the following on the telephone:

So long as there is no satisfactory answer from Red Spain to point (*a*) of the latest London agreement,[1] the conditions for the return of the German ships to the ranks of the naval-patrol powers were not fulfilled. A settlement regarding point (*b*) would also first have to be found.

Regarding point (*b*) (safety zones), Admiral Raeder said he would not object if agreements on this took a longer time, presumably a few weeks.

With regard to point (*a*) we agreed that in the light of the strong attitude taken by the Admiral the exact date when the German ships would join in the naval patrol would still be discussed between the Foreign Ministry and the Navy. For Admiral Raeder believed that sufficient guaranties against the real danger of attacks on our ships could and must be obtained through an assurance from Red Spain, while I gave chief emphasis to the political act of satisfaction of the German demands by the London agreements and stated that any real danger to our ships thereafter was not very great.

---

[1] See Document No. 305, p. 326.

The word of the Red Spanish Government, which otherwise does not exist as far as we are concerned, is certainly not so important for the actual safety of German ships as are the consequences which would follow in the event of a repetition of occurrences à la Iviza. Consultation with the War Ministry will, however, still be necessary.

WEIZSÄCKER

No. 332

3357/E009395

Memorandum by the State Secretary

BERLIN, June 16, 1937.
e.o. Pol. III 3139.

General Keitel telephoned me this noon to state, by way of supplement to the conversation between Herr von Weizsäcker and the Commander in Chief of the Navy, that on the basis of Herr von Weizsäcker's statements Admiral Raeder expressed to Field Marshal von Blomberg grave objections to immediate resumption by Germany of participation in the naval patrol of Spanish waters. General Keitel suggests that the communiqué concerning the resumption of our participation in the Non-Intervention Committee be so formulated that the question whether and when the German warships would resume their patrol activity would remain open. I replied to the General that our communication to the Non-Intervention Committee at this time, when in our opinion the conditions for our resumption of participation have been met, could not undertake to qualify our cooperation, but we could at will determine the moment at which we desired once more actually to participate in the control measures. In my opinion we must as a matter of course also resume active participation in the naval patrol within a very short time, if only because the arguments of the Commander in Chief of the Navy, who wants to have certain guaranties granted in advance by the Reds, apply, after all, to all four Great Powers; in any case, I believe we must, in the interest of the prestige of our Navy, by no means allow the Italians to resume active participation in the naval patrol before we do. I proposed that the question be made the subject of a discussion between the Foreign Minister, who will return tomorrow, and Field Marshal von Blomberg, whereby I proceeded on the assumption that according to the statements made by Admiral Raeder the Navy is technically in a position to resume its activity at any moment.

V. MACKENSEN

No. 333

860/285773–75

Memorandum for the Foreign Minister [1]

[ca. June 16, 1937.]

PROPOSALS FOR A DISCUSSION OF THE SPANISH PROBLEM ON THE OCCASION OF THE IMPENDING VISIT OF THE REICH FOREIGN MINISTER TO THE BRITISH FOREIGN SECRETARY IN LONDON

I.

It may be taken for granted that after the return of Germany and Italy to the Non-Intervention Committee and the resumption of patrol activities by the two navies, the British Government will attach the greatest importance to the question of the withdrawal of volunteers. This demand, which was raised by Germany at the beginning of the year, has since that time repeatedly been the subject of deliberations in the Non-Intervention Committee. While at the beginning the British and French Governments paid little attention to the problem, a change in attitude has been noticeable since last March, particularly on the part of the British. In repeated public statements the British Government designated this as the most important problem requiring solution at the present time. The Italian attitude has not been entirely unequivocal. Whereas Grandi declared in the Non-Intervention Committee that Italy would never withdraw her volunteers prior to a victory, Mussolini gave the Reich Foreign Minister to understand during the latter's last visit to Rome [2] that he was determined to withdraw his militia during the summer even without obtaining a prestige success.

As the problem stands now, a subcommittee set up for this purpose has worked out a plan for the withdrawal of volunteers, and this has been submitted to the participating governments for consideration. On account of the temporary withdrawal of Germany and Italy from the Non-Intervention Committee no stand has yet been taken on this project by the various governments. The opinion of the War Ministry which we requested has not yet been received, but an attempt will be made to obtain it before the departure of the Foreign Minister.

Pending receipt of this military opinion, the project in itself appears to be technically practicable. To this extent there will be involved primarily a political decision as to whether Germany and Italy—with whom we naturally must act in conformity in this problem—declare their approval of the evacuation. The consent of both

---

[1] Copies of this memorandum, which is unsigned, were also directed to the State Secretary and the Director of the Political Department.

[2] May 3–5, 1937. For documents regarding this visit, see series C.

Spanish parties is required, of course. From the German point of view, the question of cost will also have to be taken particularly into consideration, since the proposal provides that Germany must contribute £ 300,000.

The question ought to be considered whether, after consulting with the Italian Government, Germany should perhaps propose that the problem first be orally discussed at a conference between representatives of the four Western powers, that is, the powers which actively participate in the naval patrol.[3]

II.

Should it be possible to bring about such conferences, it is conceivable that, from these conferences on the withdrawal of volunteers, conferences on other questions related to the Spanish problem might also develop, particularly the bringing about of peace.

[3] Unsigned marginal note: "Superseded."

No. 334

860/285762

The Ambassador in Great Britain to the Foreign Ministry

Telegram

No. 336 of June 16   LONDON, June 16, 1937—10 : 15 p.m.
                                       Received June 17—12 :45 a.m.

For the Führer and Chancellor and the Foreign Minister.

Eden informed me today that he was holding the dates June 24 and 25 open for the conversations and suggested having the first meeting at 10 : 30 a.m. on June 24.

Eden again stressed that the conversations were principally for the purpose of obtaining a general view of the European situation. In regard to the details of the program, Eden will confer further with the proper British authorities and will probably inform me about these on Friday. The only individual subjects he mentioned were the question of a Western Pact—in connection with which there is agreement with Berlin that it is to be discussed only in general outline—and the Spanish question. The plan for the withdrawal of volunteers is very much in the foreground. Eden apparently did not yet have any practical proposals for it, and he expressed the hope that the Germans could perhaps make suggestions in this regard.

In the course of the conversation I interjected into the discussion a word regarding the colonial question, whereupon Eden expressed the opinion that there would be no objections to an exchange of views on this question also.

RIBBENTROP

No. 335

3357/E009394

The Ambassador in Spain to the Foreign Ministry

Telegram

No. 307 of June 16   SALAMANCA, June 17, 1937—12 : 30 a.m.
Received June 17—2 : 45 a.m.
Pol. III 3122.

With reference to your telegram No. 218.[1]

The Chief of the Diplomatic Cabinet stated orally that an affirmative reply by the Franco Government to the London decisions could be expected.

FAUPEL

---

[1] Document No. 312, p. 332.

No. 336

3176/683019–20

Memorandum by an Official of the Economic Policy Department

BERLIN, June 17, 1937.
W II WE 4167.

CONFERENCE AT THE FOREIGN MINISTRY ON JUNE 15, 1937—11 : 00 A.M.
Subject: Shipments to Red Spanish territory.

Participants in addition to the Foreign Ministry:
Representatives of the Economics Ministry,
the Food Ministry,
the Clearing Office.

The Economics Ministry reported that it had received numerous requests for shipments of goods to Red Spain. Payment for the goods would be made in foreign exchange. The Economics Ministry wanted to hear the opinions of the other agencies as to whether, in view of the situation with regard to foreign exchange, exports to Red Spain could not be approved in all cases in which it was certain that they would not lead to a strengthening of its powers of resistance. The requests for export licenses came mainly from German firms which wished to provide their branches in Red Spain materials absolutely essential for their continued operation. The Economics Ministry can make no estimates of the amounts involved.

The participating agency representatives were of the unanimous opinion that from a purely economic point of view an export license could be granted if it is established that:

1. The goods to be exported would not strengthen Red Spain's powers of resistance. The Economics Ministry and the War Ministry

would have to decide on this basis which goods could be approved for export;

2. Payment in foreign exchange is assured;

3. The goods are not transported on German ships and, whenever possible, are sent through a third country, so that Germany will not appear as the exporting country.

The War Ministry (Commander Koch) stated that from its standpoint there would be no objections to such an arrangement.

The decision is predominantly of a political nature. Therefore respectfully submitted to Pol. II with a request for an opinion as to whether there exist political objections to transactions of the type described above.

SABATH

No. 337

860/285763

Memorandum by the State Secretary

BERLIN, June 17, 1937.

The British Ambassador informs me that the following is the program scheduled for the visit of the Foreign Minister to London:

Thursday, June 24: Lunch with a very small circle at Mr. Eden's.
Friday, June 25: At 11:30 a. m., an audience with the King; later lunch together with a small circle at the Prime Minister's; on the evening of the same day, an official dinner given by the British Government.

I ascertained, and thereupon informed the British Ambassador, that this program is agreeable to the Foreign Minister. At the special request of the Foreign Minister I have asked the British Ambassador to arrange for a reception of the Foreign Minister by Queen Mary, if she is in London at that time. In this matter Henderson will today get in touch directly with Queen Mary's private secretary.

V. MACKENSEN

No. 338

3357/E009398

The Minister Counselor of Embassy in Great Britain to the Foreign Ministry

[Telegram]

No. 340 of June 18   LONDON, June 18, 1937.
Pol. III 3163.

Before today's session of the Non-Intervention Committee the German and Italian Ambassadors had requested Lord Plymouth to prevent any discussion of the past in the committee meeting and to point out the consequences which might otherwise arise. Lord Plymouth successfully used his influence on the Soviet Ambassador to this end. In order to avoid any discussion of the past the chairman also refrained from welcoming Germany and Italy after they resumed work in the committee.

The German press has been requested by us to refrain from publishing the text of the humanization appeal, since after the Iviza incident Germany has no interest in it. The German press should therefore limit itself to reporting the fact that according to all indications the humanization appeal . . .[1]

WOERMANN

---

[1] Footnote in the original: "One word apparently missing."

No. 339

3357/E009399–401

The Foreign Minister to the Embassies in Great Britain, France, and Italy

URGENT!   [June 19, 1937.]
e.o. Pol. III 3168.

1) Telephone message to the German Embassy, London.

Please transmit the following communication to the British Foreign Secretary this morning:

"By order of my Government I have the honor to inform Your Excellency as follows: (insert paragraphs enclosed in parentheses in the annex).

"In informing His Majesty's Government of the above, the German Government requests that it induce the four Governments participating in the agreement of June 12 to come to an immediate understanding on the joint measures to be taken. The German Government observes at once that it is not willing to permit such attacks on its ships to pass unnoticed.

"In the interest of expediting matters, I have at the same time informed the French and the Italian Ambassadors in London accordingly."

End of the note.

In accordance with the concluding paragraph of the note, I request that you send a copy of the note at once to the two Ambassadors mentioned.

In the discussions which should be started immediately, please propose as one of the measures to be taken that both Spanish parties be asked to give up all their submarines and have them interned in the harbor of Gibraltar. Rome and Paris are being notified simultaneously from here.[1]

NEURATH

---

[1] Marginal note: "Office memorandum: I have carried out the instruction on 1 as directed. Marchtaler, June 19."

2) Telephone message to the German Embassy, Paris.

I have just instructed Ambassador von Ribbentrop as follows:

(insert text of 1)

End of instruction to London.
Please inform the Government there without delay.

3) Telephone message to the German Embassy, Rome.

I have just instructed Ambassador von Ribbentrop as follows:

(insert text of 1)

End of instruction to London.
Please inform the Government there without delay.

[Annex]

SPANISH-BOLSHEVIST SUBMARINES FIRED TORPEDOES AT CRUISER *Leipzig* ON JUNE 15 AND JUNE 18

THE CRUISER IS UNDAMAGED

A new and unprecedented provocation on the part of the Bolshevist incendiaries.

(On June 15 the rumor was circulated in certain circles abroad that the *Leipzig* had been torpedoed and sunk.

Actually, the captain of the *Leipzig* reported that three torpedoes had been fired at the ship north of Oran the morning of June 15, one being fired at 9:25, one at 9:26, and one at 9:58 a.m. The course of the torpedoes was traced by sound detectors.

But since the *Leipzig*, as is now known, was not hit, it seemed advisable before taking further steps first to trace the rumors which reported the torpedoing, in spite of the fact that, on the part of Germany, the incident was kept secret for the time being.

The confirmation arising out of the agreement of these rumors with the captain's report was further strengthened by a new incident on June 18. For that day, at 3:37 p.m., a fourth submarine attack was indisputably established by the cruiser *Leipzig*. The torpedo track was seen plainly by several reliable observers. One of the torpedoes was clearly traced by the cruiser's sound detectors as it passed across her bow. This fourth attack, too, missed the ship.

It will be up to the four powers now to take measures appropriate to the circumstances in accordance with the agreements made.

The German Government is, in any case, not inclined to stand by and watch the torpedoing attempts of Spanish-Bolshevist submarine pirates until perhaps a hit is scored after all.)

Ambassador von Ribbentrop this morning in all urgency informed the representatives of the three other powers participating in the naval patrol of the occurrence.

At midnight the Führer returned by plane from Godesberg on the Rhine to Berlin.

No. 340

307/188401

Memorandum by the Director of the Political Department

BERLIN, June 19, 1937.

Ambassador Attolico told me today that Rome still considered it right to have the Italian ships join the naval patrol again immediately, for

1. This had already been promised in London;

2. It would probably come to this in the end anyhow, and consequently it was better not to stand on ceremony any longer; and

3. The Italian Government had a material interest in the patrol of its zone.

I replied to the Ambassador that these considerations were somewhat outdated by certain new occurrences in the western Mediterranean. I then informed Attolico of our instruction today to Herr von Ribbentrop and Herr von Hassell with regard to the *Leipzig* incident, whereupon Attolico for his part also stated that his argument was not of any present interest.

WEIZSÄCKER

No. 341

3242/712294–97

The Ambassador in Great Britain to the Foreign Ministry

Telegram

VERY URGENT   LONDON, June 19, 1937—11 : 23 p.m.
No. 343 of June 19   Received June 20—2 : 15 a.m.

For the Führer and Chancellor and the Foreign Minister.[1]

Before today's four-power conference I had a discussion with Grandi, which revealed that he was entirely disinclined to any thought of steps vis-à-vis *both* Spanish parties, since there was no occasion for it. To the proposal for interning the Spanish submarine fleet at Gibraltar he also had the objection, from the Italian point of view, that this would too greatly increase British prestige. He told me frankly that despite all our community of interests, even on this question, he could not support me in this demand.

---

[1] Marginal note: "Submitted to the Führer. v. N[eurath]. June 20."

On the basis of the discussion with Grandi I then made the following proposal at the four-power meeting:

1. An immediate joint naval demonstration by the four powers off Valencia; I emphasized that this mild form was proposed since there had been no loss of life.

2. Surrender of the submarines of the Valencia Government to the four control powers.

[3.] A stern warning to the Valencia Government that any further attack would result in immediate military reprisals by the four powers.

In my introductory statements I referred to the extreme seriousness of the situation, among other things, and emphasized that immediate and drastic steps by the four powers were necessary in order to prevent further and still more serious incidents.

The French Ambassador summed up his position as follows: He had no desire to question the report of the captain of the *Leipzig*. However, France was being requested to take steps that were directed against the Government with which she sympathized. This required that the facts of the case be very clearly ascertained for French public opinion. He requested detailed clarification of the following points:

(*a*) The exact position of the warship off Oran.

(*b*) Where and in what form were the reports concerning the *Leipzig* spread on June 15 by "certain foreign circles"?

I referred the French Ambassador to the statement in the German morning papers on June 16. He requested information in addition as to whether the reports were carried in the foreign press.

He stated further that personally he would have to inform himself regarding the technical possibilities of determining submarine attacks by sound detectors, etc., in which connection he emphasized again that this did not signify any doubt as to the captain's report.

On the whole the French Ambassador's attitude, though not negative, was very reserved.

Grandi supported my statement to the fullest extent without directly endorsing the three proposals.

Grandi just telephoned me that Ciano fully accepts our points.

Eden stated first of all that he would have to consult his cabinet colleagues. A report which he had from the Admiralty fully confirmed that the account of the captain of the *Leipzig* corresponded to the technical possibilities. However, the Admiralty had no reports for the last few weeks of the presence of Spanish submarines in the Mediterranean. I pointed to the report of June 11 by the Bilbao radio regarding a new Red submarine flotilla in the Mediterranean and its announced object of sinking all German and Italian ships. Eden admitted that a very serious situation had arisen and that prompt action was required. He mentioned in this connection that at the moment the most important political problem was the withdrawal of the volunteers, since the conflict in Spain had become so bitter only as a result of foreign intervention. He mentioned further that the proposal for neutral observers on the patrol ships should be carried out all the more quickly.

It was agreed that those participating in the discussion should report immediately to their Governments regarding my proposals and that not later than Monday, at an hour still to be fixed, another conference should take place. Eden will also hand the Spanish Chargé d'Affaires [2] a copy of the note and point out to him the seriousness of the charge being made against his Government. It is naturally understood that the action of the four powers on the basis of the agreement of June 12 is not dependent on receipt of a Spanish opinion. Eden will use the opportunity to obtain an answer from the Valencia Government to the four-power proposal.

From the attitude of the representatives it appears that there is, to be sure, willingness to do something, but also difficulty in finding a common line. I repeatedly insisted that an understanding must be reached on Monday in order not to create the impression that the agreement of June 12 would lead only to endless debates. Now, in this first consultation, the four powers had to show whether the agreement was of any value or was only paper. Against the Bolshevists, who only desired to push Europe toward involvement in war, only the most drastic methods were of any avail. I regard it as urgently desirable that pressure also be brought to bear directly from Berlin on the French Government. I request instructions for the Monday conference as to what Berlin considers the minimum demand.

Regarding the substance of the deliberations, in particular the details of the proposals made by me, it was agreed to maintain secrecy. The agreed communiqué was transmitted by DNB.

RIBBENTROP

[2] Señor A. Cruz Marín.

No. 342

3357/E009407–09

The Foreign Minister to the Embassy in Great Britain

Telegram

URGENT   BERLIN, June 20, 1937—6: 50 p.m.
No. 257   Pol. III   3199 Ang. I.

With reference to your telegram No. 343.[1]

I am in complete agreement with the language you used on Saturday afternoon in the four-power meeting.

[1] Document No. 341, *supra*.

For the reply to the questions raised by the French Ambassador a special instruction follows. Count Welczeck has been instructed, in accordance with your suggestion, to exert influence on the French Government. I myself have already done the same through François-Poncet.

To achieve our demands it would still seem desirable here to propose to the four control powers the surrender of the Salamanca Government's submarines also. I have instructed Herr von Hassell to bring influence to bear on the Italian Government to this effect, and remarked in that connection that we do not insist on Gibraltar as the port of internment but would agree to any other suitable place of internment.

If nothing should come of the surrender of the submarines, the naval demonstration suggested by you must under all circumstances be insisted upon. If this too is not attainable, I request that in the conference on Monday you ascertain the maximum on which the agreement of all four powers can be obtained, so that we may obtain a corresponding decision by the Führer. Whether this maximum will then appear sufficient to the Führer and Chancellor, is a question that must be reserved.

In general I wish to remark:

If in further discussions the official report of our commander with regard to what actually happened in the torpedo attacks should be doubted, such doubt should be most sharply rejected. You may make it clear that if such doubt should persist, you would be compelled to leave the conference.

You have our full approval in opposing with the utmost resolution any delay in a joint decision, since this would only be interpreted by the leaders of Red Spain as a sign of weakness and as an encouragement to new provocations. The interest of the common non-intervention policy absolutely requires an immediate decision.

NEURATH

No. 343

1877/424262–63

The Ambassador in Great Britain to the Foreign Ministry

Telephone Message

LONDON, June 21, 1937—6 : 00 p.m.
Pol. III 3224.[1]

At the four-power conference today Grandi and I adhered to our standpoint as instructed.

The British and French standpoints, which are in agreement, can be summarized as follows so far:

---

[1] This number appears on another copy (307/188358–59).

1. The immediate launching of an investigation directed at both Spanish parties. According to the statements of Eden and Corbin this does not mean that German reports are doubted, but even the Germans had not proved the nationality of the attacking submarines. In any case the accused Red Government, which through its Chargé d'Affaires here denies any responsibility and has offered to submit to investigation, must be given an opportunity to defend itself.

2. An immediate joint inquiry as to how all of the patrol ships could be accorded greater security; Eden suggested in this connection that both parties could be approached on the subject of abolishing submarine warfare or even interning the submarines.

3. An immediate sharp warning to both parties that in case of future attacks immediate concerted action would be taken if adequate satisfaction were not given immediately. The French Ambassador added that action must be limited to purely military objects.

With the support of Grandi I termed the Anglo-French proposals entirely inadequate, as instructed, and said that an immediate demonstration by the joint fleets before Valencia was the minimum of solidarity to be shown, a standpoint which Grandi also took. Eden and Corbin maintained a reserved attitude. After further insistence on our part it was decided that the representatives would inform their Governments of the stand taken by the two sides at the present time. A new conference was then set for this evening at 9 p.m. at Eden's suggestion.

Following upon this telephone message, the Ambassador would like to discuss the situation with the Foreign Minister over the telephone. It is requested that this message be transmitted to the Foreign Minister at once. The Ambassador will call the Foreign Minister himself in about a quarter of an hour and give him additional information on the situation and the further procedure.

No. 344

3242/712252

Memorandum by the Foreign Minister

RM 469   BERLIN, June 21, 1937.

Result of the conference between the Führer, Field Marshal von Blomberg, Admiral Raeder, and me on the subjects discussed in today's four-power conference:[1]

The demand under point 1 of the telephone message from London at 6 p.m. is to be rejected as impractical. At the head of our demands will be placed:

---

[1] Marginal Note: "Ambassador von Ribbentrop has been informed by me, v. N[eurath], June 21."

1. The naval demonstration;
2. An immediate, sharp warning to both sides;
3. Among the measures for safeguarding the patrol ships, the internment of submarines and suspension of submarine warfare are to be demanded but without attaching decisive importance thereto.

Any proposals that may be made by the other side for preventing a repetition [of the incident] should be reported here by tomorrow morning.

The next conference will be at 9:30 tomorrow morning in the Führer's office.

v. N[EURATH]

No. 345

3242/712291

Memorandum by the Head of Political Division III

BERLIN, June 21, 1937.
Pol. III 3204.

Herr Forster informed me by telephone from Paris as follows:
In the French press great prominence was being given to a denial which had been broadcast by the Stuttgart radio at 10 p.m. on June 15. This denial was as follows:

"The rumors concerning an attack by Red naval forces on the *Leipzig*, which have been circulated by part of the foreign press, are entirely without foundation. These reports are of sinister origin and must be characterized as malicious fabrications. The captain of the *Leipzig* reported upon inquiry by the naval command that everything is well on board and that the *Leipzig* has not been involved in any incident."

Herr Forster suggested that this denial broadcast by the Stuttgart radio might be corrected by the press.

Captain [*Kapitän*] Wagner, to whom I reported this, said that the denial had in fact been made at the instance of the Navy but it referred only to the report that the ship had been torpedoed. However, he would take the matter up in his department.

DUMONT

No. 346

1877/424255

The State Secretary to the Embassies in Great Britain, France, Italy, Spain, Poland, the United States, and the Soviet Union

Draft Telegram

RM 468 BERLIN, June 21, 1937.

As DNB has probably reported there in the meantime, the Foreign Minister has had to postpone his planned visit to London. The reason for the postponement can also be gathered from DNB; that is, the situation resulting from the repeated Red Spanish attacks on German warships does not permit the Foreign Minister to absent himself from Berlin at the present time.[1]

MACKENSEN

---

[1] Unsigned marginal note: "At the direction of the Foreign Minister."

No. 347

3242/712254

The Embassy in Italy to the Foreign Ministry

Telegram

No. 166 of June 21   ROME (QUIRINAL), June 21, 1937—10 : 45 p.m.
Received June 22—2 : 30 a.m.

With reference to your telegram No. 188 of June 20 [1] and today's telephone conversation between von Hassell and von Mackensen.

The Chef de Cabinet requested me to come and see him this afternoon and told me the following:

Agreement was expressed on points 1 and 3.[2]

Re point 2: For reasons of principle, Italian support was not possible in the question of the surrender of submarines. An international commission could not be permitted to give demobilization orders against single units, since there was danger that on another occasion these orders might be applied to volunteer units, air forces, etc.[3] Since unilateral surrender of Red submarines was out of the question, the Italian Government requests that we do not insist on the surrender of submarines. Grandi and Attolico have received instructions in this sense.

SCHAUMBURG

---

[1] Not printed (3357/E009412). The telegram indicated that the German Government preferred the surrender of submarines by both sides.
[2] For the German proposals before the Non-Intervention Committee see telegram No. 343 of June 19 from London, document No. 341, p. 356.
[3] Marginal note in Neurath's handwriting: "Correct."

No. 348

424/217511–12

The Minister Counselor of Embassy in Great Britain to the Foreign Ministry

Airgram

No. 347 of June 22   LONDON, June 22, 1937.
Received June 23—9 : 00 a.m.
Pol. III 3221.

1. At the beginning of yesterday's session of the main subcommittee the chairman read the British Government's declaration. The following was expressed therein:

(a) The British Government's great disappointment at the success so far achieved by the non-intervention policy;

(b) The problem which needs the greatest attention at present is that of combing the volunteers out of Spain.

The British Government recognized the great difficulties involved in carrying this out and was aware that a considerable length of time would have to pass before this combing-out process, according to the experts' reports, could begin. In order to bridge this long period of time, the British Government offers the following: Aside from the general and complete combing-out of Spain in accordance with the experts' plan, the British Government should be empowered to take up negotiations with both parties to the end of having an equal number of volunteers, still to be determined, withdrawn from each side in Spain upon the British Government's guaranty of absolute impartiality.

The text is being forwarded in a written report.

The chairman urgently requested all representatives to express an opinion as soon as possible on the report of the experts as well as on the new proposal of the British Government which had just been read. All representatives agreed to transmit the new British proposal to their Governments. The Soviet representative declared that his Government was willing to accept the report of the experts as a basis for discussion but found fault even now with the insufficient control measures in it and the incorrect distribution of costs, and demanded that the Moroccans be included in the combing-out process. As to the new British proposal, he believed that the withdrawal of an equal number of volunteers from each side was not acceptable to his Government, and he demanded a withdrawal proportionate to the number of volunteers present on each side. The French and Czech representatives declared that they would accept the report of the experts as a basis for discussion, whereas the Belgian, Swedish, Portuguese, and Italian representatives still had no instructions on this point.

2. To the question how the control system could be given a more neutral and international character, the French representative suggested setting up a technical subcommittee of naval experts to work out practical proposals. In the course of the discussion he reverted to his familiar proposals to employ neutral observers as well as to treat the separation into zones less rigidly than before, but did not discuss them in detail. It was decided to establish this subcommittee, and each representative was invited to volunteer practical suggestions to this committee.

3. In the question of extending the agreement to non-European powers, it was resolved to commission the British Government to sound

out in a very general way the governments which seemed suitable without making any definite proposals.

4. Since very few of the representatives had received instructions concerning the last point on the agenda, the problem of ships sailing under the Spanish flag, this was postponed.

WOERMANN

No. 349

307/188388–89

The Ambassador in Great Britain to the Foreign Ministry

Telephone Message

LONDON, June 22, 1937—12:30 a.m.

In today's evening session all participants insisted on their previous standpoints. I explained the German standpoint once more, as agreed during today's telephone conversation with the Foreign Minister, insisting on an immediate naval demonstration and expressing agreement with the sharp warning to the Spanish parties, on condition that certain changes in text were made, as was also arranged with the Foreign Minister. As far as an international investigation of the case is concerned, I stated that we considered this useless, but I finally agreed to an investigation being carried on concurrently if an immediate naval demonstration was decided on.

The British Foreign Secretary and the French Ambassador declared that an investigation must absolutely precede any action. Eden in particular emphasized that he could not prevail upon his ministerial colleagues to agree to an action without a prior investigation, and he could not advocate such action himself, either. The French Ambassador stated that the proposed warning was an action in itself, which in his opinion would be much more effective than a naval demonstration.

As far as the further points for protecting the patrol ships are concerned, Eden defined his suggestions of the last session, after consulting his ministerial colleagues, to the effect that it could be agreed that submarines of the patrol powers in Spanish waters (including the western Mediterranean) should not proceed submerged, and that the Spanish parties should be informed that they must follow this procedure. If Spanish submarines should proceed submerged, the patrol powers would be justified in taking immediate military action against them.

Since no agreement could be reached after almost two hours of debate, the following communiqué was decided on:

"Meetings were held at the Foreign Office on June 19 and 21 between the Secretary of State for Foreign Affairs and the French,

German and Italian Ambassadors to consider the question of the incident in which the German cruiser *Leipzig* was involved on June 15 and June 18. At these meetings a number of proposals were considered for determining the most appropriate method of dealing with the situation.

"No definite agreement having up to the present been reached on the measures which should be adopted, it was decided that the four representatives should refer again to their Governments before their next meeting, which will take place tomorrow Tuesday." [1]

A further report will follow separately.

RIBBENTROP

---

[1] The quoted passage is in English in the original.

No. 350

1877/424259–60

The Ambassador in Great Britain to the Foreign Ministry

Telegram

VERY URGENT   LONDON, June 22, 1937—4 : 17 a.m.
No. 345 of June 22   Received June 22—6 : 00 a.m.

The following is by way of supplement to this evening's telephone message :

In a conversation after the close of the official session, Eden expressed his regret that the Foreign Minister's visit to London is not to take place at present.   I told him that considering the uncertain situation it could only be advantageous to postpone the visit, since after all it was intended to improve the atmosphere.

When I expressed regret that the seeming solidarity of the four powers failed at the first test, Eden said that it would be very much easier to agree to the German proposals if we could make some progress in the question of evacuating volunteers and that of placing neutral observers on patrol ships.   This afternoon the session of the Non-Intervention Committee had taken place, and there had not been one centimeter of progress in the evacuation question (a report on this will follow).   He could not make plausible to his ministerial colleagues, with whom he had conferred this evening, the necessity of a naval demonstration as a sign of the solidarity of the four powers, since there was no progress on the most important question of evacuation, where after all solidarity should first be demonstrated.

I answered Eden that in my opinion this question of evacuation had nothing whatsoever to do with the *Leipzig* case.

In the course of the conversations with Eden and other Ambassadors the idea was discussed of having a naval demonstration along the entire Spanish coast, e.g. from Valencia to Málaga, in order to make it easier from a domestic standpoint for the British and French Governments to obtain consent for the demonstration.   Since in my opinion such a demonstration would in any case appear to the outside world mainly as connected with the *Leipzig* incident, I indicated to him as my personal view that such a compromise might be made. Eden answered that a demonstration along the Red and the Franco coasts might give the question a different aspect.

It was suggested that further negotiations be carried on tomorrow on the following basis:

1. A naval demonstration, roughly from Valencia to Málaga;
2. A sharp warning, as agreed upon;
3. Approval of a concurrent investigation;
4. Measures for safeguarding our ships in the manner reported.

To judge from Eden's statement reported above, an agreement concerning a naval demonstration does not seem entirely hopeless. Because of the French position, which is evidently particularly difficult in this regard on account of Russia, agreement should not be considered a certainty, however. In case no agreement on these points can be reached tomorrow, the failure of the negotiations and the appearance of a new situation would have to be made public in the session and communicated to the press, in accordance with the decision of June 12.

I told Eden that I had only spoken privately and beyond my instructions and added that if agreement on this minimum of solidarity in the face of the serious *Leipzig* case could not be reached, cooperation of the four powers in the future was entirely illusory. The next conference will probably be tomorrow in the early afternoon. I request instructions.

RIBBENTROP

No. 351

3242/712275–76

Memorandum by the Foreign Minister

BERLIN, June 22, 1937.
e.o. Pol. III 3227.

In today's 9:30 a.m. conference with the Führer to consider the telephone communication from Ambassador von Ribbentrop of June 22, 12:30 a.m., and telegram No. 345 of June 22, the following instructions for Ambassador von Ribbentrop were drawn up:

1) The demand for the naval demonstration is to be maintained, but without consenting to its extension to the White coastal areas.

Grounds: It is absolutely certain that the attempt to torpedo the *Leipzig* was not made by White submarines. There is no reason, therefore, to extend the naval demonstration equally to White coastal areas also.

2) The demand for a stern warning, as agreed upon, is to be maintained.

These two actions are to be started immediately.

3) There are no objections to a concurrent investigation.

4) Negotiations on measures for safeguarding the ships are to continue in the sense reported.

5) The proposal to take foreign observers on board is to be refused. Instead of this a mixing of the patrol ships is to be proposed in such a way that British ships are interspersed between the German observation ships, etc.

6) A linking of the evacuation question with the *Leipzig* case is decidedly to be rejected.

7) The proposal for safeguarding the patrol ships by demanding that submarines of the patrol powers should not proceed submerged in Spanish waters and that the Spanish parties should be informed that they must conform to this procedure is pointless, since this would simply facilitate the activity of the pirate ships. The proposal is therefore to be rejected.

8) The surrender of the Red submarines may be dispensed with, in consideration of Italian objections.

v. N[EURATH]

No. 352

1877/424283–84

The Foreign Minister to the Führer and Chancellor

BERLIN, June 22, 1937.

According to a telephone message from Ambassador von Ribbentrop at 7:20 p.m., the Control Committee of the four powers in its session today rejected the German demand for an immediate naval demonstration as a proof of the solidarity of the four control powers, on the ground that an investigation of the circumstances surrounding the attempted torpedoings must precede any step against the Red Spanish party. I informed Herr von Ribbentrop by telephone that we had herewith recovered our freedom of action, and that the measures to be taken by us would be communicated to him tomorrow morning for transmittal to the four control powers.

The press has been informed to this effect.

I shall prepare by tomorrow morning the outline of the declaration to be issued by us concerning our withdrawal from the Control Committee.

I have communicated with the Italian Government to ascertain its attitude but up to now have been unable to obtain an answer.

BARON v. NEURATH

No. 353

3357/E009422–23

The Ambassador in Great Britain to the Foreign Ministry

Telegram

No. 348 of June 22   LONDON, June 22, 1937—10 : 43 p.m.
                                                        Received June 23—12 : 35 a.m.
                                                                    Pol. III 3242 a.

For the Führer and Chancellor and the Foreign Minister.

Today's four-power conference yielded no new points of view.   At the beginning of the session I stated that Germany, by way of cooperation, was prepared to drop the demand for surrender or internment of the Red submarine fleet and also would not raise any objection against a concurrent investigation.   Eden's suggestion that submarines should be permitted to sail in Spanish waters only if surfaced was rejected by us as ineffective, but the search for other ways of increasing the safety of the patrol ships should be continued.   However, the demand for an immediate naval demonstration off Valencia and for a warning had to be upheld.

Eden summarizes the differences of opinion as follows: There is lack of agreement on the following two points:

1. A naval demonstration without previous investigation.

2. A warning to one party only.

For the rest I refer to the communiqué agreed upon.

I for my part called attention once more to the exceptionally moderate German conditions in relation to the first incident and the bad impression which would be created in the world by a rejection on the part of this first four-power conference; but it was evident today from the very beginning that the British and French representatives came to the session with their course fixed.

At the end of the session Eden asked whether the other three participating powers considered the agreement of June 12 still binding and added that he believed the agreement was still valid unless the other participating powers informed him of a contrary viewpoint. The representatives of the other powers reserved their position on this point.   Our opinion is that according to the text the agreement of June 12 continues to be valid.   Please send instructions.

RIBBENTROP

No. 354

307/188344–45

The Foreign Minister to the Embassy in Great Britain

Telegram en Clair
(To be transmitted immediately by telephone)

No. 264   BERLIN, June 23, 1937.
                                                      Pol. III 3242.

With reference to your telegram No. 348.[1]

I request that you transmit to the Government there the following note:

"The Reich Government after learning of the attacks on the cruiser *Leipzig* on June 15 and 18 immediately informed the other powers participating in the naval patrol in Spanish waters that it was not prepared to expose its ships engaged in an international undertaking to further target practice on the part of Red Spain. It had reduced its requests for guaranties of the security of its ships to a minimum, namely, a naval demonstration on the part of the four control powers to be carried out at once, in order in this manner to give a clearly recognizable warning. Since the British and French Governments are not prepared to accede to this minimum request, the German Government to its regret feels itself compelled to state that there is lacking the sort of solidarity of the control powers which would be a prerequisite for an internationally conducted undertaking. The Reich Government has therefore finally decided to withdraw from the control system once and for all."

End of note.

Please present a copy of the preceding note to the chairman of the Non-Intervention Committee. I request that after presenting the note you return immediately to Berlin to report.

The answer to the question at the end of your telegram No. 348 is that, by the decision of the Reich Government to withdraw from the control system once and for all, the agreement of June 12 has become of no consequence to Germany.

NEURATH

---

[1] Document No. 353, *supra*.

No. 355

3242/712230

Memorandum by the Foreign Minister

RM 476   BERLIN, June 23, 1937—10 : 30 a.m.

On Eden's instructions the British Ambassador just called on me to voice the British Government's wish that we should not undertake any action of our own vis-à-vis the Valencia Government, for in the opinion of the British Government this would render more difficult a situation that was already very serious.

I reassured the Ambassador by referring to the instruction just being sent to Ambassador von Ribbentrop, according to which we intended merely to withdraw our naval forces from the control system once and for all, and for the very purpose of avoiding in so far as possible any further complication of the situation. The Ambassador then left, visibly relieved.

BARON V. NEURATH

No. 356

3242/712264

Memorandum by the Head of Political Division III

BERLIN, June 23, 1937.

Captain [*Kapitän*] Frisius of the War Ministry, Foreign Department, let me know by telephone for our information that our naval vessels were being withdrawn from the Mediterranean. For the time being there remains a force of one pocket battleship, one cruiser, four torpedo boats, and two U-boats in the Gulf of Cádiz. For the protection of our merchant shipping this force, with the exception of the two U-boats, will carry out cruises into the Mediterranean. In essentials, the situation will be the same as before the participation of the war vessels in the naval patrol.

DUMONT

No. 357

3242/712227–28

The British Ambassador to the Foreign Minister [1]

BERLIN, June 23 [, 1937]—3 : 00 p.m.

MY DEAR REICHS MINISTER: Mr. Eden has just rung me up on the telephone about the announcement which he is making in the House of Commons this afternoon. Roughly it is to the effect that the German Government is confining its action to withdrawing from the Naval Control and that it is taking this action with a view to avoiding the possibility of dangerous international complications.

Mr. Eden told me that there was some story from Paris that Germany intended to take independent action as well, such as a demonstration or something. I said "No," that you had told me quite definitely that German action would be confined to withdrawal and that he could make statement as he proposed. I trust I am right but if I am

---

[1] This letter, in handwriting on stationery of the British Embassy in Berlin, is in English.

wrong I should be very grateful if you would warn me. Mr. Eden is acting on my information and I do not want to let him or the German Government down.

Yours sincerely,

NEVILLE HENDERSON

No. 358

3242/712224

The Foreign Minister to the British Ambassador

BERLIN, June 23, 1937.

MY DEAR AMBASSADOR: In order to prevent any misunderstanding from arising with respect to our conversation this morning, such as I infer from your letter of 3 o'clock this afternoon, I should like to emphasize once more that the German Government regained complete freedom of action after Mr. Eden rejected its minimum demand and it then became evident that it was impossible to reach an agreement in the Control Committee. What measures the German Government will take to protect its naval forces now that the Control Committee has failed is exclusively its own concern. To begin with, as you know, we have conveyed to London that we are withdrawing from the control system once and for all.

I request that Mr. Eden be informed to this effect.

With highest consideration, I am

Sincerely yours,

BARON V. NEURATH

No. 359

307/188310

The State Secretary to the Embassy in Spain

Telegram

No. [237][1]

BERLIN, June 26, 1937.

In the London Non-Intervention Committee, as you probably know, the offer of the British Government to lend its good offices to both Spanish parties for the purpose of withdrawing volunteers will come up for decision in the near future. The proposal is that, before a general combing-out, the first step would be to withdraw from Spain an equal number of volunteers from both sides.

The debate in the committee will take place on Tuesday. I should be grateful for a telegraphic report before then as to what position you think Franco would probably take on the British offer.

MACKENSEN

---

[1] See telegram No. 315 of June 27, document No. 363, p. 375.

No. 360

424/217540–42

The Ambassador in Italy to the Foreign Ministry

Telegram

No. 170 of June 26   ROME, June 26, 1937—5 : 00 p.m.

Received June 26—7 : 30 p.m.

With reference to your telegram No. 193 of June 24[1] . . . (two groups garbled).

I have just discussed the whole complex of questions with Ciano:

I. *The question of volunteers:*

Ciano declared that the Duce, as the situation now stands, is against the withdrawal of the volunteers; this will only enter into question when Franco says that he can dispense with them. To my remark that the Duce had on occasion taken a less radical view, Ciano declared that more recent developments had been such that the withdrawal was out of the question. He asked whether the Führer perhaps had other ideas on the subject. I replied that I was convinced that the Führer, too, was not considering withdrawal, but that it was now solely a question of tactics. We wanted neither to be the scapegoat nor to be the ones to bring matters to a head in London. I assumed that the Italian Government thought likewise. Ciano agreed with this absolutely. We naturally had to distinguish between what we thought among ourselves and what sort of tactics we wanted to pursue. In respect to the former, the impossibility of a withdrawal was, as stated, to be maintained at present, particularly since after the withdrawal of volunteers began the other side would presumably demand the withdrawal of submarines and airplanes. While the recall of volunteers, who constitute one-tenth of the White troops, was still theoretically conceivable, the withdrawal of submarines and, above all, of planes, meant stripping Franco of these weapons completely. With regard to the volunteers, the following points were to be considered:

1. The standpoint was to be maintained that the Italian Government did not dispatch the volunteers but had indeed previously proposed in vain extending non-intervention to volunteers;

2. Consequently the volunteers' own wishes were primarily decisive both as to participation and as to withdrawal;

3. The sole authorities for releasing the volunteers were the White and Red Governments;

---

[1] Not printed (4906/E255219–21).

4. Above all, any discussion of withdrawal without the existence of effective, impartial supervision was pointless. When I referred to the idea of the impartial execution of Plymouth's proposal by the British, Ciano replied that the British could not qualify as impartial either. In summary, Ciano stated that the tactics must therefore amount to obstruction, and that Grandi had also been instructed to this effect. I replied that it was necessary, nevertheless, to consent to negotiations and once more stressed the scapegoat aspect. Ciano replied that it would in fact have been better not to negotiate in the matter as yet, but that negotiations were already in progress and would naturally have to be continued, but, as stated, in an obstructive manner. From this I inferred that perhaps the tactical standpoint was to be advanced that before effective supervision was guaranteed there was no practical possibility for withdrawal.

Therefore, from this standpoint also, German-Italian tactics on the control question were important.

II. *Control question:*

On this Ciano emphasized that it was neither acceptable to leave the patrol to England and France nor possible in practice to include small neutral naval vessels. On the other hand, we had to realize that if the German-Italian position was perhaps legally strong, it was nevertheless, in fact, highly unfavorable to us as well as to Franco, so that it approximated a sort of blockade exclusively against Franco. From this I deduced the necessity of bringing about as speedily as possible a practical understanding regarding German-Italian tactics and made statements in accordance with telegram No. 194.[2] Ciano agreed to the latter and thought that the possibility of letting Portugal appear as spokesman was worthy of consideration; for the rest, however, he still had no clear conception of what the Germans and Italians could do to eliminate the present unfavorable situation. I referred to Lord Plymouth's statement that the present control measures had not functioned, upon which we could perhaps base the demand that an entirely new system be set up in place of the present one, possibly through Portugal. Ciano, who grasped the significance of this, stated in conclusion that he would immediately get in touch with the Duce on this subject and inform me very soon as to what procedure the Italians had in mind. Above all, he stressed Mussolini's absolute determination to take joint action with us in the whole complex of questions.

HASSELL

---

[2] Not found.

No. 361

424/217543–44

The Ambassador in Italy to the Foreign Ministry

Telegram

No. 171 of June 26   ROME, June 26, 1937—11 : 05 p.m.
                                             Received June 27—2 : 40 a.m.

With reference to my telegram No. 170 of June 26.

Ciano asked me to call on him once more this evening in order to confirm, after conferring with the Head of the Government, the statements made to me this morning concerning the question of volunteers and the control system. As regards the control system in particular, Mussolini's opinion was as follows:

1. No decision should be made without the committee.

2. No solution was acceptable which in effect transferred all control measures to France and England and thus made possible a blockade of Franco. Should England and France actually bring about such a system, Mussolini would be for denouncing the non-intervention pact, a move which could be threatened even now if necessary.

3. On the other hand, Italy and Germany should declare that, since the present control system had not worked, they were willing to study with the other powers new and better methods which would avoid the present inadequacies and would permit Germany and Italy to cooperate once more. At least in the first stage, it was not the affair of Italy and Germany to make proposals in this direction.

Ciano added—in confidence, as he said—that it must be admitted that the present state of affairs, i.e. cooperation in the committee but not in the control system, was absurd; therefore it was desirable to obtain some more or less satisfactory changes in the present system, in order to be able to take part again.

With regard to the political situation, Ciano declared that no American move of any kind had been made in Rome; the British Ambassador had only complained about a very belligerent article by Farinacci [1] in the *Regime Fascista*, which Ciano had dismissed as a private statement; the French Chargé d'Affaires had reported the statements by the French Ambassador in Berlin advising moderation. In addition, however, Delbos had complained to Cerrutti concerning the publication of names of fallen legionnaires as violating the principle of non-intervention. Mussolini had been very indignant about this and had instructed Cerrutti today to reject these statements; the Italians honored their dead soldiers as they wished, and this was no concern of either France or Delbos. At my question Ciano added that Chautemps had more understanding for Italy than some others,

---

[1] Roberto Farinacci, editor of the *Regime Fascista*.

to be sure, but that this would not have any practical effect at the moment. Ciano remarked finally that Cerrutti was too much of a Francophile and was hardly the right man for the post any more.

HASSELL

No. 362

3242/712194–97

Memorandum by the Foreign Minister

June 27[, 1937].

REMARKS ON TELEGRAM 171 [1]

Re 1. Agree

Re 2. For us, too, the assumption of all controls by England and France is unacceptable. Neutral observers make no difference in this.

Re 3: The proposal to study a better control system can possibly be supported, but it is clear that we can participate only if an entirely new formula is found.

As concerns the question of withdrawing the volunteers, a decision on this must be left exclusively to the Red and White Governments.

In discussing the control question Woermann can, in my opinion, declare openly, on the proposal to have England and France take over, that we have no confidence in the impartiality of the two countries in view of the attitude displayed by them so far. This might perhaps change if they would decide in London to recognize Franco as a belligerent party.

If the question of denouncing the non-intervention pact should be broached to Woermann, he should not exclude the possibility of denunciation.

v. N[EURATH]

---

[1] Document No. 361, *supra*.

No. 363

307/188295

The Ambassador in Spain to the Foreign Ministry

Telegram

No. 315 of June 27   SALAMANCA, June 27, 1937—9 : 15 p.m.
Received June 27—11 : 00 p.m.

I have just spoken with Franco as directed in instruction No. 237 of June 26. He declared that the first attack on Madrid last fall would have succeeded and the war would have been won long since if the Reds already at that time had not had about 20,000 foreign volunteers at their disposal. At present, after deducting the large numbers killed and those who had left Spain because of war-weariness, he estimated the number of volunteers on the Red side at 40,000 to 45,000.

In principle he did not oppose a withdrawal of volunteers, but he had to make certain reservations. The first condition was that his Moroccan troops should in no case be included in the concept of foreign volunteers. In addition, absolutely effective measures would have to be instituted against deceptive Red maneuvers. For instance, it was to be expected that the volunteers removed by ship to France would be brought back to Red Spain across the border. Today volunteers were still coming to Red Spain unceasingly across the French border as well as by ship from Marseille; they were fewer in number than before, to be sure, since the heavy losses of the Red troops had had a deterrent effect.

Since he placed a low estimate on the combat value of the Italian divisions, after the experiences at Guadalajara, he would have no objections from the military standpoint to their removal, if they left all their weapons here. Franco concluded with the remark that he did not have the slightest confidence that the Reds would faithfully fulfill any sort of agreement, and he saw great difficulties in the way of practical execution of an equal withdrawal of volunteers from both parties.

FAUPEL

No. 364

3242/712204–05

The Foreign Minister to the British Ambassador

BERLIN, June 27, 1937.

MY DEAR AMBASSADOR: In reply to your letter of June 26,[1] I wish to inform you that the German representative in the Non-Intervention Committee has so far not received any final instructions from here concerning the manner in which the deficiencies of the naval patrol around Spain are to be eliminated. In any case we shall not be able to agree to any new arrangement tantamount to shifting the present equality of treatment of the coasts of White and Red Spain; therefore we shall be unable to accept the new proposal for a naval patrol which you have described.

The German Chargé d'Affaires in London has already given the President of the Non-Intervention Committee a note concerning the withdrawal of German personnel from the patrol service; it states

---

[1] Not printed (3242/712203).

that in withdrawing from the patrol system we consequently intend also to withdraw all Germans active in the patrol service.

I take this occasion to express, Mr. Ambassador, the renewed assurances of my highest consideration.

NEURATH

No. 365

424/217554–55

Memorandum by the Foreign Minister

RM 495   BERLIN, June 28, 1937.

The British Ambassador called on me today and asked me what position we would take tomorrow in the committee meeting in London, and in particular whether we would reject the taking over of the control measures by France and England. I answered that I had to inform him that this was the case. We could not agree to such a settlement, because we did not have faith that control by England and France, who in the past had always been on the side of the Valencia Government, would be carried out impartially. The Ambassador sought to refute this point of view with the remark that the British naval officers were certainly anti-Bolshevist. I answered that I had no doubt of that; on the other hand, I did not have the same impression of the attitude of the British Government, and after all the naval officers had to follow the instructions of their Government. The Ambassador then asked whether we knew of any other solution. I told him that after the unity of the four powers, which had been obtained with so much effort, had been destroyed by the—to me—incomprehensible attitude of the British Government on the *Leipzig* incident, it was not up to me to think up proposals as to what could be substituted for cooperation by the four powers. To the Ambassador's further remark that our negative attitude would ruin the good impression which our moderation in the *Leipzig* incident had made in London, I replied that I regretted that I could not change that. Moreover, I could only repeat that it was not our fault that matters had developed in that manner. I answered the Ambassador's question whether we would not perhaps accept neutral ships for the patrolling with the counterquestion whether he believed that any smaller countries could be found to take over this doubtful task. I could not imagine that Holland or Sweden or any other country would want to gamble with its ships.

In closing I told the Ambassador that Herr von Ribbentrop, who was en route to London, had exact instructions concerning our attitude toward the principal matters that would probably come up for discussion tomorrow.

BARON V. NEURATH

No. 366

424/217547–51

The Foreign Minister to the Embassy in Great Britain

BERLIN, June 28, 1937.
Pol. III 3334.

With reference to my telegram No. 267 of June 25.[1]

Concerning the question now in the foreground, as to how the control measures for Spain should be reorganized and at least brought to the state of effectiveness which they possessed at the beginning of June, there has been an extensive exchange of views during the last few days between here and Rome. The British and French Governments have also been in contact with us through various channels. Nothing is changed, however, in the basic instruction given you in the preceding telegram.

During discussions in the Non-Intervention Committee you will still have to proceed from the standpoint that we greatly regret the difficulties which have arisen due to the disruption of international solidarity, but that these difficulties are in no way our fault and therefore we make no proposals for a new adjustment; however, we do not wish the whole problem to become more acute.

More specifically, please take the following position in the committee:

(*a*) Control measures:

If, as is to be expected, the question is asked in the committee whether we are prepared to transfer the naval patrol to the British and French fleets alone or to them with their satellites, please put the counterquestion whether the members of the committee would be willing to give the naval patrol over entirely to Germany and Italy. For justifying our rejection of an Anglo-French naval patrol, you may state the following:

We could not recognize assumption of the naval patrol by the British and French fleets as an impartial solution, regardless of how they are distributed along the coast. Even if presumably neutral observers were taken aboard the ships, or if ships of neutral countries were interspersed, our attitude would not be changed. Since the experiences of recent date our trust in a neutral attitude of England and France is not sufficient to enable us to surrender all control over the Spanish Civil War to these two powers and thus to prejudice the situation.

---

[1] Not printed (307/188312–15). This telegraphic instruction directed the Embassy to notify the chairman of the Non-Intervention Committee that the German Government was withdrawing all German personnel in the service of the committee at the earliest possible moment, except employees in the London offices of the committee.

(In the British Parliament the question of recognizing Franco's Government as a belligerent has occasionally been discussed. Should the British Government follow this course, then our judgment of England's attitude would change for the better. No use should be made of this consideration in the committee, however.)

It is naturally out of the question that a decision concerning the reorganization of the control measures could be reached without the committee or outside it. If such a thing were suggested, the Italian representative would probably threaten to denounce the non-intervention pact. You are also empowered in such a case, following the Italian example, not to exclude the possibility of denunciation.

(b) In our opinion the moment for discussing the question of withdrawing volunteers has not yet arrived. So long as no effective neutral control measures are assured, the prerequisite for a recall of volunteers, however organized, does not exist either politically or technically. Moreover, please emphasize that the question of withdrawing volunteers mainly concerns the two combatant parties, and that therefore an opinion and proposals must first be obtained from both Spanish parties. Thus please limit yourself to the above points in discussions on the question of volunteers and reject a continuation of the debate at this stage.

I wish to remark confidentially that a certain disgust on Franco's part with regard to the Italian volunteers is evident in the latest reports from Salamanca. There are also other signs that Franco is interested in better contact with the British Government. Any observations of this sort on your part would be of interest here.

(c) From the whole situation pictured above, it follows that we are continuing to withdraw our control officers as ordered, although the British Ambassador has made representations here against this. The details of the withdrawal must be discussed further in London and if necessary settled after inquiry in Berlin.

(d) We intend to make our monthly contribution toward the control system on July 1 as usual. For later ones we reserve our decision.

(e) For the time being the orders to German commercial shipping to Spain to comply with the rules of the control system remain in effect. The Italians have agreed to this procedure until further notice, although with some hesitation.

It goes without saying that our general attitude should be brought into harmony with that of the Italian representative as may be indicated, and if need be also with that of the Portuguese representative. It is not our intention, however, to assume the leadership at any point in the debate in the Non-Intervention Committee but rather to leave this as far as practicable to the Italians or the Portuguese. It is possible that after certain changes in procedure the Italian representative will show an inclination to compromise with regard to reestablishing the conditions prevailing at the beginning of June. I refer in this matter to copies of reports from Rome, which we are sending you simultaneously with this instruction.

BARON V. NEURATH

No. 367

3242/712199–200

Memorandum by the Deputy Director of the Political Department

BERLIN, June 29, 1937.

I have just telephoned Herr Woermann, who conveyed to me the following regarding the result of today's session of the Non-Intervention Committee:

At the beginning of the session Lord Plymouth presented to the committee the British and French proposals, which aim at having the naval patrols carried out exclusively by Britain and France in the future. It was proposed that the distribution of the naval forces of the two powers should be such that the British fleet would patrol the entire Red coast and a small part of the White coast, whereas the main part of the White coast would be patrolled by France. The exact division of the White coast was still to be made in accordance with this scheme. The ships of both powers would take neutral observers on board. No proposals were made concerning the nationality of these observers. All powers represented on the subcommittee, with the exception of Germany, Italy, and Portugal, had accepted this proposal at once. The Italian Ambassador had advanced a number of serious objections to this proposal and had pointed to the shift in the balance of power effected thereby, but had stated that despite this he was willing to submit the proposal to his Government for a decision. Then Herr von Ribbentrop had taken the floor and had also expressed most serious objections which were in effect equivalent to a rejection, but he also, like Grandi, had promised to transmit the proposal to the German Government. In the course of his statements Herr von Ribbentrop had also put the counterquestion of how England and France would react if Germany and Italy should take over the patrol alone.

The next point which was discussed was the question of the withdrawal of volunteers. The Portuguese representative had pointed out that, as long as the question of the patrol was not decided, a treatment of the question of volunteers could not be considered. The German and Italian representatives had supported his statements. The question of volunteers was thereupon postponed until the next session on Friday.

When I asked Herr Woermann whether the Anglo-French proposal regarding the patrol contained anything new, Herr Woermann said that at the most one might consider as something new the heretofore unknown fact that the French fleet would patrol exclusively the White coast.

BISMARCK

No. 368

307/188253–59

Memorandum by the Ambassador in Great Britain [1]

LONDON, June 29, 1937.

I. Enclosed is a report [2] concerning today's session of the Non-Intervention Committee. It should be added that the session proceeded very quietly and no one showed any inclination to aggravate the situation.

II. I asked the Italian and Portuguese Ambassadors to call on me today in order to discuss the further procedure for Friday. After a detailed discussion of the situation I proposed to Grandi that he send Crolla, his Counselor of Embassy, to Rome tomorrow morning, and I would send Minister Woermann to Berlin at the same time in order to discuss our plan of action with the offices concerned there, such as the Foreign Ministry, the Navy, etc. At the same time it will probably be necessary to consult Franco on the matter, and this can be done only from Berlin; furthermore, it is necessary to coordinate the stands of Berlin and Rome for Friday, and this again can be done better from Berlin by telephone than from London, because of the danger of being overheard.

III. After a detailed discussion with Grandi and the Portuguese Ambassador I conceive of our procedure on Friday as follows:

(*a*) The Italian and I will state that for the reasons already presented in today's session we cannot agree to having England and France take over the patrol.

The Portuguese Ambassador just stated that his Government would in general probably follow the German-Italian course.

(*b*) As I already indicated in today's session, we shall state jointly with the Italians that control has failed on land and sea; at sea because of the two well-known shortcomings (the impossibility of stopping ships flying the Spanish flag and the flags of nations not participating in the Agreement); on land because of

---

[1] There is no heading on this document. Whether it was prepared by Ribbentrop for his own files or was transmitted to the Foreign Ministry cannot be determined.

[2] Not found.

the entirely inadequate patrol personnel.   As is known, the ships of
the four patrol powers have so far confined themselves merely to
checking whether ships of powers belonging to the committee carried
the patrol officer.

The committee should therefore consider whether the present inadequate control system can be replaced by a better system.   We could
make the following suggestions:

1. The 27 countries represented on the committee might grant
belligerent rights [3] to both Spanish parties.   This means that at sea
they would have the rights of a belligerent nation, that is, they could
stop and search ships and remove contraband.   Furthermore, this
would also permit establishing a blockade.   Naturally it is impossible to foresee from here exactly what effects, military and otherwise, might result.   But according to the discussions which we have
had here with the Italians and statements by Foreign Secretary
Eden, such a measure would seem to favor Franco.   Herr Woermann will clarify all aspects of the matter in Berlin.   Should the
granting of belligerent rights in the last analysis prove favorable
to Franco, this proposal could replace the naval patrol so far carried
out by the warships of the four powers.

2. We have discussed here whether the present control system
should not be retained for the present—that is, the requirement that
all ships of non-intervention powers put into certain control harbors
to take aboard observation officers, whose duty, as is known, consists
in inspecting the cargo aboard and supervising the unloading in
the Spanish port of destination.   This would have a certain advantage, since then the Spanish-French land patrol could also be
maintained.   For if the sea patrol is eliminated, the French will
then certainly demand that the land patrol likewise be eliminated.
Tonight it is not possible on the spur of the moment to judge adequately whether it is feasible to maintain this control system and
simultaneously to grant belligerent rights to the two Spanish
parties.   Herr Woermann will also study this question with the
competent offices in Berlin, especially the Navy.   Politically it
would be well if the control system could be maintained in this
form for the time being, since England and France would like to
do so for domestic reasons.   In practice this system is, of course,
ineffective, and after the granting of belligerent rights it would
probably soon break down in any case; this in turn would have the
advantage of saving considerable amounts of foreign exchange.
The troublesome question of providing warships, which in any
event had only a subordinate function from the standpoint of con-

---

[3] These two words appear in English in the text.

trol, and also the question of what powers should furnish these warships [would also] cease to exist.[4]

It is clear, of course, that if this proposal should prove to favor Franco, England and France would give their consent only very unwillingly. Even if this is the case, and nothing comes of this proposal in the end, then we at least have the advantage that we cannot be reproached for having put an end to the control system without having made any positive and constructive proposals.

3. The Non-Intervention Committee and the obligation of non-intervention would be maintained. We would even recommend as a further proposal that all nations which in any way come into question be immediately asked to participate in the Non-Intervention Committee and join in the obligation not to send volunteers to Spain.

4. We shall again raise the question of the gold belonging to the Bank of Spain.

5. We might perhaps consider making concessions in the question of the ban on the sale of merchant ships to the two Spanish parties.

IV. Withdrawal of volunteers.

There are two possibilities for procedure on Friday:

(*a*) We and the Italians might state (the Portuguese Ambassador accepted this idea today) that it would for the known reasons be useless and a waste of time to discuss the withdrawal of volunteers before the control question and the other questions connected therewith are settled; or

(*b*) We might accept with every reservation the present report of the committee as a basis for discussion, and authorize the British Government to give it to the two Spanish parties and obtain their stand on this matter.

I suggest proceeding as under (*a*), if we can make a sufficient number of positive proposals with reference to the alternative for the control system described above. Thus this depends mainly on whether it is in our interest to grant belligerent rights. If we cannot offer anything positive enough, I see no objection to proceeding as under (*b*), since we can then handle matters through Franco as we like, and even Valencia will make all sorts of reservations. We can then draw out the discussion of this question over as many months as we like, for in the end no withdrawal will ever take place, of course. On the other hand, we must see to it that in case the control system or the naval patrol should definitely be scrapped we could offer the British and French Governments something positive in order to pacify their opposition at home.

R[IBBENTROP]

---

[4] This sentence was garbled in the original.

No. 369

424/217570–71

The Ambassador in Great Britain to the Foreign Ministry

Telegram

No. 366 of June 30   LONDON, July 1, 1937—11 : 35 a.m.
                                              Received July 1—1 : 30 p.m.

For the Führer and Chancellor and the Foreign Minister.

Today I called on Eden.   After I had spoken with him of the general situation in the sense of the Führer's instructions, he asked me what was to be done about Spain.   He read me his instruction of today to Henderson, which he had discussed with the Prime Minister. According to this it is considered incomprehensible that patrol by the British and French fleets is not given complete confidence, particularly in view of their readiness to take neutral observers on board.   If, in spite of this, the German Government persisted in its negative attitude, he hoped that the non-intervention policy would be adhered to and that positive proposals would be made in accordance with it.

I left Eden in no doubt concerning the negative reply which was to be expected from Germany to the French proposal, and I stated once more that non-intervention had failed and that therefore one would perhaps have to pursue new methods.   In this connection the conversation turned to the newspaper reports and Eden's declaration in the House of Commons that if the non-intervention policy failed the two Spanish parties would in the end have to be accorded belligerent rights by England.   Eden thought that this solution would not yet be considered seriously, since the British Government urgently wished to adhere to the non-intervention policy.   In the further course of the conversation Eden indicated that in the interest of retaining the principle of non-intervention, perhaps a combination of non-intervention, recognition of rights as belligerent states, and withdrawal of volunteers could be considered.   Eden did not respond to my question as to how he pictured this combination in detail.

I received from the conversation the impression that the possibility of, and the prerequisites for, a *rapprochement* with Franco were being considered by the British Government.

I told Eden that there was no doubt that the Reich Government also wished to adhere as much as possible to the non-intervention principle, and that I expected Woermann back with instructions before the next session of the committee.

RIBBENTROP

No. 370

3242/712189-90

Memorandum by the Deputy Director of the Political Department

BERLIN, July 1, 1937.

Ambassador von Hassell telephoned me today at 1:30 a.m. and told me the following:

Count Ciano had discussed the situation in the Non-Intervention Committee with Mussolini. As a result it could be stated that the Italian Government is not opposed to the proposal for recognizing the two belligerent parties but considers it worthy of consideration and clarifying. This would result in the powers of the Non-Intervention Committee declaring their neutrality, but the neutrality concept would have to be supplemented appropriately by acceptance of the already existing agreements concerning non-intervention, including the ban on volunteers. As for the question of what goods should be declared contraband, they had not yet had time in Rome to go into this matter in detail and were leaving further consideration to the German and Italian representatives in London. In addition, it would be advisable that some system of supervision be maintained, not in the form of the naval patrol, but in the form of supervision by the Non-Intervention Committee. For example, one would have to consider leaving the control officers aboard the ships. At any rate the Italian Government, too, in pursuance of this proposal, was prepared to recognize the Valencia Government.

As for the question of volunteers, Grandi had been instructed that they did not wish to discuss it at the present time; they would have to get a clear picture of the supervision system first. Moreover, the entire problem of withdrawing the volunteers could no longer be brought back to its original status, since it had undergone the most varied changes in the course of the last few months.

In reply to my question Ambassador von Hassell confirmed to me that the Italian Government continued to reject the Anglo-French plan. Likewise, Italy's participation in the naval patrol without Germany was out of the question.

BISMARCK

No. 371

424/217592-93

Memorandum by the Foreign Minister

RM 507   BERLIN, July 1, 1937.

This morning the French Ambassador called on me in order urgently to request us once more to agree to the Anglo-French proposal for at least temporary exercise of control by the two countries named.   The Ambassador described the dangerous situation which would arise if, as a result of our refusal, the whole Non-Intervention Committee should break up.   I answered the Ambassador: First, I wished to repeat once more that the present situation was not our fault but exclusively that of the British and French Governments, for they had been unable to make up their minds to agree to our demands, which had been recognized even by Mr. Chamberlain as reasonable and moderate.   Moreover, I wished to explain to him the following concerning our attitude:

1. We refused to enter again into any control measures.

2. We rejected the Anglo-French proposal to take over sole control, even with neutral officers as observers.

3. We invited discussion on the recognition of both Spanish parties as belligerents with the rights implicit therein.

4. We proposed that a declaration of neutrality be made, at least by those powers represented on the Non–Intervention Committee.

5. We agreed to retention of the Non-Intervention Committee and of the obligations assumed by the members of the committee.

The French Ambassador then stated that he did not believe that his Government was prepared to recognize Franco, whereupon I told him that it would then have to take the blame for the consequences.   Moreover, the French Government's partiality, which led us to reject the Anglo-French proposal, would once more be very clearly shown by such a refusal.

Baron v. Neurath

No. 372

424/217594–95

Memorandum by the Foreign Minister

RM 508   Berlin, July 1, 1937.

The British Ambassador called on me this afternoon and made the same representations in the name of his Government as the French Ambassador had made this morning.   I outlined our standpoint to him once more and gave him the same explanation which the French Ambassador had already received concerning the instructions given to our representative in London.   Sir Nevile Henderson, who had previously expressed his personal opinion that recognition of Franco as a belligerent party was advisable, admitted this again today but expressed his fear that his Government was not ready for this.   I told him that he should urgently point out to his Government that our proposal contained not only the retention of the Non-Intervention

Committee but also the maintenance of all obligations undertaken there. If his Government would not recognize this concession on our part, then it was to blame for further developments. The Ambassador then pointed out the breach which had been created by the withdrawal of the German and Italian ships from the patrol. I told him that this breach had no significance whatsoever, for the present state of affairs was nowise different from that at the time of the so-called control. I had been informed just this morning by our representative on the Non-Intervention Committee that during the existence of the so-called control not a single case of violation of the obligations undertaken in the Non-Intervention Committee had been reported by the control officials. We as well as the Italians considered ourselves still bound by our promise given to the Non-Intervention Committee. But this, of course, could not last forever. We would then withdraw from the Non-Intervention Committee.

The Ambassador said finally that what I had proposed was not very much, to be sure, but it did allow the possibility of discussion, and the essential thing was that no new incident should occur anywhere. I informed him that if this was the case, as I hoped, England could only be grateful to us, since by our immediate withdrawal of our naval vessels the danger had at least been lessened.

BARON V. NEURATH

No. 373

307/188242–46

The Foreign Minister to the Embassy in Great Britain

[Pol. III 3423] [1] BERLIN, July 1, 1937.

The intention discussed by you and Ambassador Grandi to make a positive contribution during tomorrow's session of the Non-Intervention Committee is approved here. The idea which is at the bottom of the proposal, namely, to move the other Governments, primarily the British Government, to recognize the Franco government as a belligerent power, was discussed here in general terms some time ago with the British Ambassador and, as you know, was taken up in the international press as well as in the British House of Commons. It remains to be seen whether the British Government, and particularly the French Government, as well as the other Governments represented on the Non-Intervention Committee, will be willing to accept the idea of recognition of Franco as a belligerent power. Particularly the Russian Government will hardly feel any great inclination to do so.

---

[1] See document No. 379, p. 398.

Since, however, we are expected to make a positive contribution, such doubts will not be able to prevent us from developing before the committee a new plan which, proceeding from the basic idea of the recognition of Franco as a belligerent power by the 27 countries represented in London, can be discussed in detail and in any case can help us over the present difficulty.

It was not possible in the short time available to examine here all details of the plan discussed between you and Signor Grandi. In particular the answer of Ambassador Faupel, who was instructed to obtain Franco's opinion on the basic idea, has not yet been received. No military considerations which would make it impossible to present the plan have yet appeared. An exchange of views with the Italian Government has shown that it likewise agrees. Thus there are no fundamental objections. Nevertheless, it will be necessary that you and Ambassador Grandi only sketch the plan under discussion in broad outline before the committee and not let yourselves be committed to details. We are quite aware that recognition of Franco by the other countries represented in the Non-Intervention Committee implies that Germany and Italy accord the same character to the Red Spanish Government also. It does not, to be sure, expressly include a recognition of this Government in the actual sense under international law. However, the rights of a belligerent would accord the Red Spanish rulers certain possibilities, particularly at sea, which should be forestalled insofar as possible. On the basis of the above, please proceed tomorrow in the Non-Intervention Committee according to the following guiding principles:

1. The position stands that Germany will not participate again in the control measures as they were originally envisaged.

2. It is still out of the question to leave the naval patrol of Spain to the British and French fleets, even if neutral observers are taken aboard.

3. Recognition of the two Spanish parties as belligerents should be proposed as the basis for a new solution. Before this recognition, however, various questions would have to be discussed, among others the definition of goods to be considered contraband.

4. The non-intervention obligation of the powers represented in London, as well as the Non-Intervention Committee, should continue to exist.

5. It will be expedient to propose that at the same time as the two Spanish parties are recognized as belligerents the non-intervention powers, at least, make a neutrality declaration. It would be well to

supplement this with the existing agreements concerning non-intervention, including the obligation not to send any volunteers to Spain.

6. In order to restrict as much as possible the privileges arising for both belligerents from the rules of naval warfare, there should be maintained a system of control officers (including German control officers), who would, however, have a different function from hitherto. These new functions would mean that these control officers would be considered as a guaranty to the belligerent parties that the ships in question do not carry goods to Spain which the non-intervention powers have obligated themselves not to export to that country.

7. In order to define the above obligation more specifically for the belligerents, too, there would have to be drawn up and agreed upon with the belligerents a list of contraband which would be identical with the war materials that the non-intervention compact has already listed.

It might be well to make only such use of the above points in the discussion at tomorrow's session as seems necessary in the course of the debate.   It would be expedient not to go into points 6 and 7 at all, or only in very general terms.   At first the reaction which is called forth in the committee by the basic idea, that is, recognition of the Franco government as a belligerent power, should be observed in particular.

Before going into a discussion of the plan you are to bring up or of any proposals from other sources for reinstituting controls, you should, with the arguments at your disposal, put off the question of withdrawing volunteers, which is also scheduled for discussion during tomorrow's session.   You are empowered, however, to take part in a discussion of withdrawal and of the exchange of wounded by the two sides and to advocate the practical execution thereof by the International Red Cross.   These measures should not be put in the hands of other governments.

BARON VON NEURATH

[EDITORS' NOTE.   On July 2, 1937, Ambassador Ribbentrop presented in the chairman's subcommittee a statement on behalf of both the German and Italian Governments containing suggestions in reply to the Anglo-French proposals of June 29.   The German-Italian suggestions were (1) that belligerent rights be granted to the two parties in Spain, and (2) that the system of supervision, with the exception of the patrol system, be maintained.   For text of these suggestions see *Survey of International Affairs, 1937*, vol. II, pp. 325–326.]

No. 374

3360/E009628–29

The Ambassador in Italy to the Foreign Ministry

No. 2684   ROME, July 2, 1937.
                                                      zu Pol. III 3443.

POLITICAL REPORT

Subject: Italy's attitude in the control controversy.

In the course of the lively diplomatic activity of the last few days the question arises for the observer here whether the responsible Italian authorities are consciously working toward sharpening the conflict with England, or whether the desire to ease the situation is decisive. Although the impression gained from Attolico's statements, according to telegraphic instruction No. 197 of June 25,[1] points more toward the former supposition, Ciano's words, transmitted in my telegraphic report No. 171 of June 26—that the present state of affairs was absurd and one must believe that it was possible by new formulations to arrive at cooperation in the control measures—incline more to the latter view.

A similarly two-sided picture appears from the press. The enclosed provocative article by Farinacci in the *Regime Fascista* of June 25, which practically demands a preventive war, was disavowed by Ciano to the British Ambassador, to be sure, as is known from my report, and it was described to me personally as being much too extreme and inopportune for Mussolini. I doubt, however, whether this latter remark of Ciano's gives the whole picture. Mussolini himself recently published two articles in the *Popolo d'Italia* ("Il grido e la valanga", June 26, and "I volontari e Londra", July 1) which, although objectively sounding much more responsible than Farinacci's attack, nevertheless use very sharp language, also not free of abusive turns of phrase, against the Western powers and particularly England. The article "Italiani nuovi" in the *Popolo d'Italia* of June 29, not written by Mussolini himself but inspired by him, is also significant in the same sense. On the other hand there are quite a number of editorials in the *Giornale d'Italia* and particularly in northern Italian papers which, though they support our arguments in the control question uncompromisingly, still seem to aim at avoiding an unnecessary widening of the breach and at keeping the road open for a return to international cooperation in the Spanish question. The dispatch from Rome in the *Gazzetta del Popolo* of July 1 is enclosed as an example; in a hopeful and conciliatory manner it goes into the possibility of a "way out."

---

[1] Not printed (3358/E009453–54).

From the conversations I have held and from the whole picture in the press I get the impression that the feeling prevails here that they, together with the other great powers, are in a blind alley which they would do well to get out of, preferably without loss of prestige.

Final victory by Franco seems to be the essential thing; this is not being advanced by the current situation. It is considered the best procedure, however, on the basis of experience gained during the Abyssinian war, to confront the ambiguous and evidently wavering British attitude with a firm bearing which becomes at certain moments threateningly severe. Thus such wild articles as that of Farinacci represent a perhaps not unwholesome reemphasis of the tone chosen by Mussolini himself in the *Popolo d'Italia*. I do not believe that with all this they are consciously working toward a deterioration of the situation.

HASSELL

No. 375

424/217619–21

Memorandum by the Director of the Political Department

[July 4, 1937.] [1]

1. As a consequence of the latest development in the Spanish crisis a diplomatic alinement has formed against us, the causes of which will not be discussed here. Barring a reversal by England, this alinement must be regarded as fixed.

The situation at the moment is not an immediate threat to peace. Germany refuses to permit the Spanish crisis to lead to war. Nor is there at present any such inclination on the opposing side, although it would have an incomparably better point of departure both politically and militarily.

2. If we simply persisted in the position maintained thus far, the situation would become more acute. Developments could then no longer be controlled. Therefore our goal now should be rather the prevention of a general conflict than the unconditional and complete victory of the Franco party in the Spanish Civil War.

3. If the proposals made thus far for a solution of the crisis should prove finally to be unavailing—which is not yet definite—new solutions must be found.

The previous bases, namely the pretended isolation of Spain from foreign military help, gave White Spain sufficient prospects of success. If the isolation should cease altogether, open support of both sides would set in. Franco would then probably fare no better; above all,

---

[1] The date has been supplied from another copy of this memorandum (137/ 128139–41).

however, the extension of the conflict would then be almost unavoidable.

4. According to the principle accepted so far, the European powers kept a check on one another regarding the observance of their non-intervention pledge. There is in the air a new principle which is now often called "blockade," namely the barring of all deliveries of war matériel to Spain, perhaps on the basis of an expanded contraband list. This would no longer be non-intervention, but the opposite, namely a military strangulation of the two Spanish sides, coupled with extensive obstruction of their non-military imports.

(The open land boundaries would, however, still leave numerous gaps. Furthermore, a long time would elapse before the establishment of a new blockade, since non-European states would also have to be included, and great technical difficulties would have to be overcome before such a "blockade" was established.)

Even the German Navy might in the end participate again in establishing the "blockade"; in any case no obstacle should be placed in the way of the Italian Navy in this regard.

There could then, however, no longer be any opposition purely *on principle* to the withdrawal of the so-called volunteers.

A political advantage of the "blockade" idea would lie in the fact that England would doubtless be much more open to it than, for example, France and Russia.

5. Such a procedure would do violence to both sides. It would be a departure from our previous policy of unmistakable support for Franco. Whether Franco would actually suffer any disadvantage thereby in comparison with Red Spain would still have to be determined. The extinguishing of the Spanish conflagration would, however, be justified if its general spread could otherwise no longer be prevented.

The meaning of the "blockade" could, of course, only be to make the sides willing to negotiate, and then to rely on the strength of the principle of order embodied in France.

WEIZSÄCKER

No. 376

424/217622–28

The Ambassador in Great Britain to the Führer and Chancellor

A 3054   LONDON, July 4, 1937.

Subject: Report on the situation as it appears from here.

I. No serious complications for the general European situation are to be expected from the present tension in non-intervention policy.

England desires peace, as does France also; in spite of the sharp line followed at present, neither of them will push things to the limit. We can continue to count on this as an absolutely certain factor and can make our future decisions without being influenced or disturbed.

A real complication could arise from:

(*a*) A serious incident in Spanish waters, against which, however, precautions have been taken as far as possible by withdrawing our ships from the patrol; and

(*b*) The dispatch of large military contingents to Spain by Italy and Germany.

In a speech yesterday Eden mentioned England's anxiety over her position in the Mediterranean and her sea route to East Asia and stated that the integrity of Spanish territory was an important question for Britain; this also applies to France on account of her strategic connection with Africa.

The intervention of large, wholly German and Italian military units, which, after all, could not be brought there and be led to victory overnight, would therefore, in the present general political situation, involve the danger of serious complications. Additional arms and air aid to Franco from Italy and from us without the dispatch of *larger* contingents of volunteers would in my opinion not cause any serious complications.

II. The question is what goal we are to aim at in the coming week: the ending of all non-intervention (hence of the agreement and of the committee), or retention of the principle of non-intervention and the achievement of one of the possible compromise solutions favorable to Franco.

III. If it is considered at all in Berlin that the ending of non-intervention would be favorable to Franco, we would operate in such a way that the responsibility for the failure will be attributed as far as possible to England and France as a result of the rejection of our plan. From Eden's statement in the House of Commons it is to be assumed that England will then declare her neutrality and probably in the end grant belligerent rights to both Spanish parties anyway. Whether Franco will then be in a better position, only he himself can judge and decide. He would perhaps control the sea and be able to make it difficult to bring in supplies to the Bolshevists; on the other hand, France, and through France other nations as well, would probably deliver a great deal by land.

Since the ending of non-intervention would, however, make possible the influx of volunteers, especially from France, Russia, etc. (with the corresponding propaganda and support in those countries) and as a result would also necessitate starting a new influx of volunteers from

Italy, Germany, etc., the intensity of the Spanish war would probably increase considerably—a condition which in the long run would involve the possibility of complications of greater magnitude.

IV. Therefore it appears from here that for the time being it is in our interest to work toward maintaining the principle of non-intervention and finding a compromise acceptable to us. This will also prevent the open shipment of arms and volunteers, which lately has apparently not worked out to the disadvantage of Franco. However, the total situation cannot be surveyed to its full extent from here; nor, for that reason, can it be definitely decided whether the retention or the ending of non-intervention would favor Franco.

In the search for a compromise we should first bear in mind:

The unilateral Anglo-French naval patrol already rejected by us, and the rejection of the participation of German warships in the patrol, since on account of the danger of major incidents we do not wish to expose our ships singly in the future either.

We might be approached with the following ideas and compromise proposals:

(*a*) The non-intervention agreement—that is, the obligation not to send any arms or volunteers to Spain—will remain in force; on the other hand, all patrolling by sea and land is to be discontinued. The same situation as existed before March 12 would thus arise. This means that the hitherto illegal arms traffic to Spain will probably be carried on to a greater extent, because of the absence of control. Volunteers also will then probably reach Spain more easily.

(*b*) Non-intervention and control measures are to be maintained. The patrolling of Spanish waters would be taken over by an international flotilla of fishing boats. The navies of the powers could then remain in Spanish waters only in order to protect their interests. It would have to be determined whether participation by Germany and Italy in such a flotilla of fishing boats would be possible. Consideration could also be given to taking neutral observers on board the fishing vessels.

(*c*) The German-Italian plan will in some form be connected with the question of the withdrawal of volunteers. This thought has come up in various forms. It would be useless to speculate on this before the exact details of such a combination are known.

(*d*) Non-intervention will be maintained; however, the patrolling in Spain will no longer be done at sea and on the Portuguese or French side of the borders on land, but everywhere on the Spanish mainland. This idea was discussed yesterday by some newspapers. This would mean that for the sea frontiers the control officers would be located in the Spanish harbors. This type of control would have the disadvantage that such officers might possibly ascertain the presence of German and Italian formations. On the other hand, however, it would hardly be possible ever to obtain the consent of both sides in Spain to admit such officials. This has already been rejected once by both sides. Eventual acceptance of this idea for the sake of further dilatory negotiation should, if appropriate, be considered.

V. As regards the tactics to be followed in the coming non-intervention meeting, it seems to me that there are the following possibilities:

1. It is conceivable that the British and French will put to a vote their proposal for naval patrol by them alone. Presumably the overwhelming majority of the countries would vote for the acceptance of this proposal. Naturally the German-Italian proposal would then also have to be brought to a vote. Unanimous approval could not be obtained for either of the two proposals:

(*a*) If England and France should then make some sort of declaration that, even against the votes of Germany and Italy, they would presume now to undertake the naval patrol as a mandate from the great majority of the committee, the Italians and we would have to leave the Non-Intervention Committee immediately and withdraw from the non-intervention agreement. A sharp declaration to that effect would have to be issued simultaneously by us and the Italians. However, I consider such an action by the British and French as highly improbable.

(*b*) After rejection of both proposals the following would also be conceivable:

The British and French declare—since neither their proposal nor ours has been approved—that non-intervention has failed and that consequently they must reconsider their entire attitude toward nonintervention. The Italians and we would take the same position. We should likewise issue a sharp statement placing the blame for this crisis in non-intervention squarely on England and France. If England should immediately declare that she would no longer participate in non-intervention, it would be easier for us to assign them the blame.

2. The British will try in the next few days, covertly or through calling a new session of the subcommittee, to find a compromise solution. I regard this as probable. In this case we would work for a compromise acceptable to Italy, to us, and to Franco and reserve the definitive attitude of the Reich Government on any compromise proposal.

A further report may follow.

RIBBENTROP

No. 377

424/217636–37

The Ambassador in France to the Foreign Ministry

Telegram

No. 442 of July 5

Paris, July 5, 1937.
Received July 5—10 : 30 p.m.

My judgment of the present attitude of the French Foreign Ministry toward the control question, so far as such judgment is possible at all, considering the complexity of the problem and the difficulties of the French Government in handling it, is as follows:

At the moment when Germany's rejection of an Anglo-French patrol became known, the French Government was seriously considering the idea of abolishing all control measures, in particular those on the Red Spanish land frontier. The belief was that the possibility of thus being able, immediately and without hindrance, to supply Red Spain with arms on a large scale would mean a great, perhaps decisive, advantage for Red Spain. An additional factor was the feeling of being able for once to show the Italians, who were constantly reproaching the French for violating the principle of non-intervention, what effect large-scale French intervention in favor of Red Spain would have. Today, for the moment, the idea of abolishing the land patrol seems again to have receded somewhat. For one thing, the French Government does not seem entirely certain of the British Government's consent to this. As I hear, the view is held in Government circles here that England does not desire a victory for Red Spain; furthermore, it is alleged that very recently reports have been received here from Rome according to which Mussolini is prepared to discuss in London the withdrawal of volunteers. The French view seems to be that such discussions if proposed could not be refused. Of course, France could agree to a discussion only on condition that it was a question of a *supervised* withdrawal of volunteers. In this connection they seem to have in mind here the type of control previously suggested by the British (gradual withdrawal of the volunteers under neutral supervision), whereby Anglo-French agreement would at the same time be fully assured. Ultimately, according to opinion here, such supervised withdrawal of volunteers might perhaps even lead to the restoration of all control measures on the previous scale, but in a new form. The difficulties of such a procedure seem in no way to be underestimated here, especially since recognition of Franco as a belligerent power is still regarded as unacceptable both to France and to England. Still the belief here seems to be that in case the Italians bring up the withdrawal of volunteers for discussion in London, it must lead to new and certainly difficult negotiations.

WELCZECK

No. 378

424/217617–18

Memorandum by the Foreign Minister

RM 610   BERLIN, July 5, 1937.

The British Ambassador called on me this morning in order, as he said, to hear from me once more what our position was on the proposals under discussion in London. I told him that there had been no change in our position; for the rest, I wished to request that he report the following to his Government: It had come to my knowledge that the British Government had had instructions sent to its representatives in the countries participating in the Non-Intervention Committee that they should make earnest representation to obtain the support of these countries for the Anglo-French control plan. I did not doubt that under the pressure of these representations the majority of these countries would give their consent. If, however, the British and French Governments should, on the basis of the majority then obtained, claim the right to carry out their control plan, we would immediately withdraw from the Non-Intervention Committee and again assert our full freedom of action. I was telling him this in order not to receive later another reproach from the British that our decision had come as a surprise.

The Ambassador, who from the outset had not been in complete agreement with the attitude of his Government, attempted to obtain a promise that we would declare ourselves in agreement on the matter of discussing the withdrawal of volunteers. I told him that this discussion had, after all, taken place long since and that it would in my opinion be much more important finally to ask the two Spanish sides what their attitude was toward the withdrawal of volunteers. There was no object in further discussion until the position of those who were chiefly interested had been ascertained.

BARON V. NEURATH

No. 379

424/217656–57

The Foreign Minister to the Embassy in Great Britain

Draft Telegram

No. . . .   BERLIN, July 6, 1937.
                                                                Pol. III 3498.

With reference to your report of July 4, A 3054.

The dispatch of larger military contingents to Spain by Germany is out of the question. Nor has Franco thus far approached us or the

Italians with any such request. From Rome, also, there are no indications that the Italian Government is planning to send further military contingents to Spain.

On the basis of information available here, we too regard it as probable that the British Government will try to find a compromise solution; this is also indicated by the fact that the committee will not be convened until the end of this week. Since we hold that it is not our responsibility to come forward with new proposals after the German-Italian proposal has already been definitely rejected by England without further discussion, I request that you leave the initiative in any new proposals to the British Government. In case the British Government should submit a compromise solution to you secretly or in the subcommittee, I request that you limit yourself to receiving it and forwarding it to us together with your own opinion. This also corresponds to the view of the Führer and Chancellor, with whom I have just spoken on the telephone regarding the content of your report.

For your information I remark that the guiding principles transmitted to you in instruction Pol. III 3423 of July 1 [1] under points 1 to 7 are still authoritative for the German attitude. Accordingly, it is our aim to have the non-intervention obligation of the powers represented in London, as well as the Non-Intervention Committee, continue insofar as possible (point 4 of the above instruction).

In case no compromise proposal is submitted by the opposing side before the next session and, as a result, only the Anglo-French and the German-Italian proposals are up for debate, I request that you adopt the attitude you proposed under V, 1 (a) and (b) of your report A 3054. [2]

NEURATH

---

[1] Document No. 373, p. 387.
[2] Unsigned marginal note: "The Foreign Minister, to whom the stenographic draft was read, expressed approval."

No. 380

3406/E013833

The Ambassador in France to the Foreign Ministry

A 2677 PARIS, July 6, 1937.
Pol. III 1909.

As reported by telephone, Hauptamtsleiter Stabsleiter Stenger and Amtsleiter Leitgen [1] were received by Premier Chautemps on July 4, in the presence of Count Brinon, vice president of France-Allemagne. The interpreter was Herr Abetz of the Dienststelle Ribbentrop. The

---

[1] Adjutant to Rudolf Hess.

suggestion for the meeting came from the office of the Premier. The two Germans informed me of the invitation immediately and asked me to advise them whether they should accept; I recommended it very strongly. Herr Leitgen visited me shortly before his departure, informed me in broad outline of the substance of the conversation, and promised me that he would send a memorandum on the conversation to the Foreign Ministry; this has probably been done in the meanwhile. The renewed affirmation by Chautemps that to him ideological points of view would never constitute a reason for obstructing a *rapprochement* with another country seems to me worthy of note.

Since Herr Leitgen had not heard the last words addressed to Herr Abetz, I invited Count Brinon to call on me, and he repeated them as follows: "Please tell the gentlemen that we are letting ourselves be guided in Spain not by ideological motives but by vital interests. Spain is our neighbor and the Mediterranean is the life line to our African empire. I take it for granted that the authorities in Germany will understand this."

H. WELCZECK

No. 381

2938/569723–24

Note from the British Embassy [1]

No. 265   July 7, 1937.
(212/24/37)

YOUR EXCELLENCY: Under instructions from my Government, I have the honour to bring to your notice as a matter of urgency the question of the affairs of the Rio Tinto Company. The situation of the British mining companies in Nationalist Spain is causing His Majesty's Government the most serious preoccupation, and His Majesty's Government, being unwilling to allow the situation in regard to these companies to continue thus, are considering what steps can be taken to protect these important British interests. It is therefore hoped that the German Government will understand the attitude of His Majesty's Government and urge the German representatives now in negotiation with the representatives of the company in London to adopt a conciliatory attitude with a view to arriving at an early solution of the matter.

2. I would add, with reference to the Note of the Ministry for Foreign Affairs W II WE 2586 II of the 15th May last,[2] that, although negotiations are at present being carried on in London in regard to the sale of pyrites to Germany, it appears that the question of past

---

[1] This document is in English in the original.
[2] Not printed (2938/569713–18).

requisitions of the company's precipitate has not been mentioned. His Majesty's Government attach particular importance to this matter, and I trust therefore that either the delegation in London will be instructed to discuss it, or the competent German authorities will be willing to receive representatives of the company in Berlin, who, supported by my Commercial Counsellor, would be ready to enter into negotiations on the subject.

I avail myself of this opportunity to renew to Your Excellency the assurance of my highest consideration.

NEVILE HENDERSON

No. 382

1819/416252–53

The Ambassador in France to the Foreign Ministry

Telegram

SECRET   PARIS, July 7, 1937.
No. 451 of July 7

With reference to our No. 448.[1]

I hear from a reliable source that the Quai d'Orsay at the present time judges the negotiations between England and Franco rather optimistically. The subject of these is not only the question of northern Spanish ores. Rather it is believed that England thinks the time has come for strengthening her ties with Franco. England has always looked at the Spanish problem only from the British point of view, that is with a view to preserving strong British influence in Spain, regardless of the outcome of the Civil War. She expects that Spain will in any case be dependent on British financial and economic help after the Civil War.

At the Quai d'Orsay the moment is considered propitious for England to establish relations with Franco, since Franco is now more in need of help than ever before, while Italy and Germany, on the other hand, are not quite clear about their further attitude. As for Germany, they continue to assume in London and Paris that she is averse to greater intervention. Britain wants to take the ground out from under Italy's intervention policy, especially by influencing Franco in the volunteer question.

The situation in general is said to be judged more optimistically by the Quai d'Orsay.

WELCZECK

---

[1] Not printed (1819/416249).

No. 383

424/217669–71

Memorandum by the Foreign Minister

RM 621   BERLIN, July 7, 1937.

The British Ambassador called on me again today and asked me whether I still had no new proposals to make for the solution of the Spanish conflict. I told him that not only had I no proposals to make, but I also refused to give the matter any further thought after our last proposals, which had expressly been made as such and not as demands, had been rejected by the British Government without any reason being given and without even any attempt being made to start a discussion on this basis.

The Ambassador then asked again whether we would agree to the withdrawal of volunteers from Spain. That was the main point, to which his Government attached the greatest importance. I replied that in our last conversation I had already stated that the decision regarding the withdrawal of volunteers did not rest with us but with the Spanish belligerents. I could therefore only repeat that before there was any discussion of this question the Spanish parties would have to be heard regarding their attitude toward it and the conditions which they might lay down. The Ambassador wished to know further whether we would take measures to remove the German volunteers in case Franco agreed. I told him that if Franco no longer wanted any German volunteers, we would naturally do everything in order to bring the Germans back. For the rest, however, I wished to emphasize that the withdrawal of volunteers naturally would have to be on a basis of parity for the two sides.

The Ambassador then again brought up the question of the naval patrol. I emphatically rejected his inquiry as to whether we would not participate again after all, remarking that there was no object in now raising this question once more. He asked further whether we would agree to the extension of the British naval patrol in the Mediterranean if England recognized Franco as a belligerent. I told him that I would have to reject this also for the time being. Moreover, after the granting of belligerent rights to Franco and, as I assumed, also to the Red Government, it would be the responsibility of these two to exercise the control insofar as they were able to do so. When the powers had made declarations of neutrality, there would no longer be any occasion for carrying on the naval patrol.

When the Ambassador insisted on consent to the extension of the British naval patrol, I stated further that on this point no concession by us and, I assumed, by Italy could be expected.

Finally I suggested to the Ambassador that at the next session of the Non-Intervention Committee his Government ought really to ask the 23 other nations represented there whether they had any proposals to make. It seemed to me that owing to the brusque rejection of our proposal by Lord Plymouth this possibility had by no means yet been exhausted, and in my opinion the purpose of the Non-Intervention Committee was to discuss these questions.

The Ambassador promised to transmit my statements to his Government.

Baron v. Neurath

No. 384

424/217666-67

The State Secretary to the Embassy in Spain

Telegram

No. 251   Berlin, July 7, 1937.

Drafting Officer: Counselor of Legation Dumont.

Recently the assertion is becoming more and more pronounced in the British and French press that Franco is beginning to seek a *rapprochement* with Britain. He has recognized, it is said, that Germany and Italy cannot give him the desired help after all and that the military, naval, and economic power of the Anglo-French bloc is of greater importance for the future fate of Spain than the interested help of Italy and Germany. The papers refer in this connection to an article in the *Diario de Burgos*, according to which Franco has agreed to the withdrawal of the foreign volunteers. This would be in agreement with your telegraphic report No. 315 of June 27 to the effect that Franco in principle, i.e. on certain conditions, no longer opposes the withdrawal of volunteers.

The international press further stresses the favorable progress of the negotiations between England and Franco concerning the British mining interests (compare telegraphic instruction 249 of July 5[1]). Conversations about financial questions between Franco and the British Government are likewise said to have been concluded in the last few days.

Finally, information is available here that Franco has instructed his propaganda offices not to let through the censorship any further articles which are hostile to England. The director of the Portuguese radio system, who recently praised the British non-intervention policy in a radio talk which attracted much attention, is said to be a confidant of Franco.

---

[1] Not printed (2938/569720–21).

In the meantime your telegrams 329 [2] and 330 [3] have arrived here. Nevertheless, I request that you speak to Franco about the development described above and ask him to explain his aims. Please send a telegraphic report.

MACKENSEN

---

[2] Not printed (1819/416259).
[3] Not printed (424/217649–50).

No. 385

424/217675–76

The Ambassador in Italy to the Foreign Ministry

Telegram

No. 181 of July 7   ROME (QUIRINAL), July 7, 1937—11:25 p.m.

Received July 8—2:20 a.m.

With reference to your telegram 214.[1]

Today I spoke to Ciano in the sense of your telegrams No. 212 [2] and No. 214, whereupon Ciano stated most emphatically that all reports about a change in Mussolini's stand on the withdrawal of volunteers were absolutely false and part of a systematic press propaganda. An instruction to this effect had been sent to Attolico only recently. Thus Mussolini continued to reject discussion of the problem of volunteers now for the reason known to you, which was reported by telegram not long ago. The return of the volunteers came into question at all only if Franco desired it. Ciano gave a negative reply to my question whether there was indication of such a desire on the part of Franco or of any attempts by him to approach the British. He stated further that one did not need to worry about the French pressure for control to be abolished altogether and non-intervention to be abandoned, or about the realization of the proposal of the British and French that they alone take over the naval patrol. The first was no problem because France in fact was virtually incapable of action at the present time; for this reason he had also given the French to understand that in such an event Italy would dispatch a plane for every plane and a regiment for every battalion. Moreover, the view of the British was far more consistent and in any case was not for abandoning non-intervention. Insofar as a possible decision of the committee in line with the Anglo-French proposal was concerned, the Italian and German endeavors had been successful with just as many powers, so that an overwhelming majority was hardly conceivable. Aside from Portugal, Austria, Hungary, and Albania, which were for us, Yugoslavia would in any case not vote against us, and likewise Bulgaria,

---

[1] Not printed (3360/E009638–39).
[2] Not printed (5068/E292201–03).

Greece, and one or another of the Baltic states; Poland and Japan were good bets, especially if German influence was further brought to bear there.

Mussolini's absolutely firm stand resulted from his conviction that in the face of unwavering persistence the opposition would finally give in. The present moment was all the more unsuitable for weakening on our part as the situation in Spain was entirely favorable for Franco; a promising offensive against Santander with participation of Italian volunteer units was immediately impending, while, with Italian mediation, delegates of the Basques were negotiating the surrender of all Basque fighting forces; the Italian Government was using its influence with Franco in the direction of lenient conditions.

I replied that the real standpoint of the Italian Government was clear to me, but that it was necessary to adopt appropriate tactics in the committee on Friday. Ciano thereupon read me an instruction being sent today to Grandi; it corresponds to the substance of my telegram and gives him the tactical instruction not to enter into any discussion of the volunteer question and in general to gain time until events in Spain improve our position still further; on Friday he was to try through skillful maneuvers to prevent any unfavorable decisions.

HASSELL

Addition by the Code Room: Ambassador von Hassell requested by telephone that the second half of the paragraph beginning with "Mussolini's absolutely firm stand," that is, the passage "a promising offensive" to "lenient conditions," be treated as strictly secret.

No. 386

47/32197–99

The Ambassador in Spain to the Foreign Ministry

CONFIDENTIAL SALAMANCA, July 7, 1937.
Pol. I 3817.

Subject: General Sander's attitude toward Hisma.

During the last six months I have had to observe again and again that General Sander has a definitely hostile attitude toward Hisma. This fact would not in itself be important if General Sander would keep his views about Hisma to himself. This he has not done, but on numerous occasions has made derogatory remarks about Hisma.

During the first months of this year, therefore, I pointed out to General Sander several times in conversations that it was the director of Hisma, Herr Bernhardt, who had called the attention of the German Government to the possibilities of intervening against world Bolshevism in Spain; that it was Hisma, furthermore, which had arranged for obtaining considerable amounts of raw material in Spain for Germany, thus covering part of the debts which Spain owed us; and, finally, that the position of Hisma was decisive for the outcome of the negotiations, even then in preparation, the purpose of which was to conclude several German-Spanish economic agreements, by which many raw materials indispensable to us were to be assured us in the future.

I called General Sander's attention especially to the fact that in the interest of these economic agreements the prestige of Hisma ought not by any means to be damaged. Nevertheless General Sander did not stop his derogatory remarks about Hisma, and these gradually spread even among the Spaniards.

On June 23 the First General Staff Officer of General Kindelan (Commander in Chief of the Spanish Air Forces), Comandante Arranz, asked me if he might discuss a few matters frankly with me. He told me that General Sander frequently made very pessimistic statements concerning the progress of the war and derogatory remarks concerning Spanish conditions without considering that Spanish officers who spoke German, or at least understood it, were frequently present. Thus Sander had also expressed himself in a very derogatory manner about Hisma. He, Arranz, knew the importance of Hisma for German-Spanish economic relations very well; he knew that Hisma was not a profit-making enterprise and that such attacks on Hisma were calculated to damage German-Spanish cooperation, especially in the economic field.

The fears of Comandante Arranz have been fully substantiated. The difficulties which our economic mission has encountered in Burgos during the past weeks can be attributed to the hostile attitude of certain Spanish circles toward Hisma; this attitude is becoming especially apparent lately and can be traced not only to the intrigues of German and Spanish businessmen representing private interests but also to numerous careless and completely unfounded statements by General Sander.

Since my efforts to influence General Sander in this matter have been unsuccessful, I feel obliged to report the affair with the request that General Sander be required to exercise the necessary self-discipline in his statements about Hisma and to direct any complaints which he feels entitled to make against Hisma to the proper German authority, namely, General Göring.

FAUPEL

No. 387

1819/416270

The Deputy Director of the Political Department to the Embassy in Spain

Telegram

BERLIN, July 8, 1937.
Pol. III 3540.

Ambassador von Ribbentrop received today the following instruction for tomorrow's session:

"In the tactics that you are to follow please bear in mind that we want above all to gain time, and we wish to make no proposals ourselves which it is the business of Franco or the Non-Intervention Committee to make.   This also applies to the last paragraph of telegraphic report No. 334 [1] from Salamanca, and therefore I request that, if the Portuguese representative makes the statements mentioned therein, you refrain from taking any stand on them at tomorrow's session."

End of instruction to London.

BISMARCK

---

[1] Not printed (5068/E292206–07).

No. 388

424/217696

Memorandum by an Official of the State Secretary's Secretariat

BERLIN, July 9, 1937.

Prince Bismarck reports that he informed the Foreign Minister by telephone of his telephone conversation with Herr Woermann about the outcome of today's session of the Non-Intervention Committee.

The Foreign Minister replied that if the British made new proposals, this was only to be welcomed.   We should, however—and this was also the Führer's opinion—remain entirely noncommittal for the time being.   Especially if the British Ambassador took new steps at the Foreign Ministry tomorrow or the day after, he was to be told that, before further action, the return of the Foreign Minister, who would not arrive in Berlin before Monday, would have to be awaited.

SIEGFRIED

No. 389

424/217687–89

The Ambassador in Spain to the Foreign Ministry

Telegram

VERY URGENT   SALAMANCA, July 9, 1937—7 : 37 a.m.
No. 336 of July 8   Received July 9—3 : 00 p.m.

With reference to your radiogram 251 of July 7.[1]

I had a lengthy discussion with Chef de Cabinet Sangroniz in the presence of Foreign Secretary Muguiro. I informed Sangroniz of the doubts of the German Government and used the opportunity also to call attention to the somewhat peculiar and undesirable delay in signing the economic agreement long since worked out by the two delegations. Sangroniz replied that Spain unfortunately did not have at her disposal agencies which worked with such mathematical precision as the German agencies. The as yet completely inadequate organization of the agencies here made procedure extremely slow in spite of the best intentions. This was the reason for the delay. This part of Sangroniz's statement is not quite correct; intrigues against Hisma play an important part. Sangroniz told me that the signing of the agreement would still take place this week in accordance with Franco's latest promise.

Sangroniz then assured me on his word of honor that Spain was not thinking of changing her policy toward Germany. Announcements in the French and British press were a systematic attempt to drive a wedge between Germany and the Franco government.

Chilton had asked Sangroniz personally a few days ago for permission to send a British consul to Bilbao because of special British interests there. Sangroniz had answered that the Nationalist Government would grant an exequatur for a British consul only after being recognized by England as a belligerent power. Sangroniz continued that the Spanish Chargé d'Affaires had of late addressed very sharp notes to England. (This refers to the note concerning the securities removed from Bilbao—compare my report of June 27, Sa. 3–2395 [2]—as well as to the note transmitted by telegram 330 of July 6,[3] which has since been published. England had given the Franco government to understand semiofficially through Portugal that she was ready to recognize Franco as a belligerent power. In order not to ruin this possibility the Spanish press had been instructed to moderate its previous very sharp tone toward England until further notice.

---

[1] Document No. 384, p. 402.
[2] Not found.
[3] Not printed (424/217649-50).

As for Franco's consent to the withdrawal of volunteers, it was only a hypothetical readiness. Franco was laying down so many conditions on this point that in practice the measure would not be carried out.

With reference to the somewhat peculiar procedure of transmitting the Spanish note by my telegram 334 of July 7,[4] Sangroniz told me in answer to my question that Franco's signature to this note had been forgotten. Since Portugal had to have a quick reply, which Franco did not wish to give without Germany's consent, they had chosen the method via the German Embassy used tonight as the quickest one. I ascertained that the Italian Chargé d'Affaires received an identical note with the request for transmittal to Rome.

FAUPEL

[4] Not printed (5068/E292206–07).

No. 390

47/32155–63

The Ambassador in Spain to the Foreign Ministry

SECRET   SALAMANCA, July 9, 1937.
Sa. 3–2487   Pol. I 3562 g.
Subject: The military situation and the duration of the war.[1]

The attack on Bilbao by Franco's troops began in the last days of March; the capture of the city took place on June 19. The operation thus took 11 weeks, in the course of which an air-line distance of approximately 40 kilometers was covered—from the initial position of the attacking troops to Bilbao. Although the mountain terrain to be crossed along the Biscay coast offers certain difficulties, it would unquestionably have been possible with the right operational leadership, but especially with troops better trained and better equipped for the attack, to carry out the operation in much shorter time in view of the great superiority of the attacking forces in artillery and planes. Through a timely advance via Orduña-Amurrio the retreat of the Red troops fighting east of Bilbao could have been cut off and thus a considerable part of the enemy forces on the northern front could have been annihilated. As a result of the exceptional slowness of the operations the Reds were able to throw up numerous fortifications and finally to escape encirclement from the south in time. Thus an altogether possible Cannae became an "ordinary victory." In spite of all mistakes in command the total number of prisoners taken

[1] A file note dated July 13, 1937 (47/32173), from Pol. I to Dumont of Political Division III states that on the instruction of the Foreign Minister this report was submitted to the Führer and Chancellor on that date.

so far in the fighting around Bilbao amounted to 14,000, according to the figures published in the Army reports.

While many, in part senseless, shootings occurred following the entry of the Spanish troops into Málaga last February, General Franco, evidently having learned from the experiences there, had this time forbidden large troop detachments from entering and remaining in Bilbao, and thus avoided possible excesses.

The capture of Bilbao signifies not only a military and a great moral victory but also possession of one of the most important harbors of Spain, and, above all, of the iron ore mines, which are extremely valuable for the manufacture of war matériel and ammunition, their importance being readily apparent from the fact that, according to a report received by the Embassy 2 months ago, England lately received 100,000 tons of iron ore per month from Bilbao, in other words 20 percent of her total import.

The importance attributed by the enemy to the fall of Bilbao is indicated among other things by an article in the *Solidaridad Obrera*, an Anarchist paper published in Barcelona, which appeared the day of the capture of Bilbao but had become known before this in the rest of Red Spain.   This article states as follows:

"In May our military situation was favorable.   Expressed in figures, one can say that our chances for victory were 80 percent to the enemy's 20.   In the middle of June our prospects grew worse, and if Bilbao should fall the ratio would be reversed.   Franco would then have an 80-percent chance for victory to our 20."

After the fall of Bilbao the press of Nationalist Spain published statistical comparisons of the area occupied by Franco and that occupied by the Reds, in which it was pointed out, among other things, that of a total of 50 provincial Spanish capitals, 34 are now in Franco's hands.

The disproportionately long duration of the operations against Bilbao is due in part to the differences of opinion between Franco and the Italian General Doria.   The four Italian divisions involved in the defeat of Guadalajara of March 18 had been merged into only two divisions after the elimination of numerous unsuitable officers and men and were again ready for action at the end of May, following 2 months of rest and training.   Franco wanted to use them for an easier task first in order to condition them for battle.   Instead of quietly accepting this and, assuming that his troops actually possessed the fighting spirit and quality he claimed, overthrowing the enemy before him and then advancing as far as possible, General Doria refused to comply with Franco's instructions and demanded that his army corps be used only for a decisive action which promised great success.

Franco, on the other hand, rightly took the stand that another military reverse for the Italians, who were also responsible for the temporary set-back at Bermeo,[2] was intolerable for political reasons and that therefore they could be assigned a decisive attack only after they had proved their ability through easier tasks.   Since it was not possible to reach an agreement, the bulk of the Italian troops remained inactive in reserve during the entire fighting around Bilbao. Only the Italian artillery and fliers, especially the generally acclaimed fighter pilots, successfully took part in the fighting.   It is clear that this conduct has not increased the prestige of the Italians nor improved their relations with Franco, who in talking to me a few weeks ago termed the entire role of the Italian divisions in Spain a tragedy.

The Italians are trying first of all to make up as much as possible for their loss of military prestige by propaganda carried on through the newspapers, films, etc., with the expenditure of extraordinary sums of money.   It is said that the Italian press and propaganda director here, Danzi, has 240,000 pesetas at his disposal for this purpose each month—according to other accounts even 500,000 pesetas. The result is that the heroic deeds of the "Legionarios"—as the Italian troop units here call themselves—are constantly being praised in the press and in other ways.   For some time they have also been mentioned with praise whenever possible in the official Army reports, evidently as the result of influence exerted by the Italian Embassy. On the other hand, Franco, General Kindelan, and all other persons familiar with the circumstances fully realize that the taking of Bilbao was accomplished to a great extent by the German fliers and by the German antiaircraft batteries committed in the ground fighting, and they give full recognition to this.

It is a noteworthy fact that with regard to the direction of operations the Generalissimo undoubtedly feels relieved by the death of General Mola.   He told me recently: "Mola was a stubborn fellow, and when I gave him directives which differed from his own proposals he often asked me: 'Don't you trust my leadership any more?' "

Franco had planned the continuation of the operations in such a way that part of the troops so far committed against Bilbao were now to advance parallel to the coast on Santander, while the Italian army corps under General Doria was simultaneously to be committed against Santander in a direction from south to north along and on both sides of the highway from Burgos, flanked by one Spanish column advancing on its right and one on its left.   (Compare the enclosed map with explanations.[3])   Franco hoped to conclude this operation as well as

---

[2] Footnote in the original: "The so-called *Flechas Negras* brigade had been committed at Bermeo.   It consists of Italian officers, non-commissioned officers, and specialists, and Spanish troops trained and commanded by Italians."
[3] Not found.

the subsequent attack on Asturias in the months of July and August and thus mop up the entire northern front in the course of the summer.

The necessary regrouping of the troops was done with the greatest slowness. The beginning of the attack was postponed again and again until a few days ago the Reds succeeded unexpectedly in seizing the initiative by an advance west of Madrid, which was not without danger, and in making it impossible for the time being to carry out the offensive started by Franco against Santander.

The advance west of Madrid and other local attacks by the Reds prove that the hope for their early moral collapse, already voiced on occasion, was premature. Even if Franco succeeds in quickly halting the attack west of Madrid, which is probably directed by the Red General Miaja, and to resume the offensive against Santander, the enemy there nevertheless has at least gained time to bring up new equipment and ammunition, to improve the training of his troops, and to build fortifications. Therefore even if the further course of Franco's operations is favorable, the defeat of the enemy forces around Santander and in Asturias can hardly be expected before fall. Thus the prospects for a victorious conclusion of the war before the end of the year become considerably less than heretofore.

For months the conduct and duration of the war in Spain have been less an operational problem than one of organization and training. There are many points where Franco can attack with prospects of success. The first thing for him to do after overcoming the present crisis will be to continue the operation prepared against Santander. Resumption of the earlier attack against Madrid, carried on for months, should absolutely be avoided. The quality of the attacking troops, however, is decisive under all circumstances.

Franco needs a number of assault divisions especially trained for the purpose; with them an attack such as the one on Bilbao, for example, would probably have lasted not 11 but perhaps only 3 weeks. The possibility of forceful blows in quick succession can be created only through organizing such assault divisions.

The Spaniard as such is a good soldier. What Franco's troops lack is training, especially assault training, although this is probably even more true of those of his enemies. With their present corps of officers and non-commissioned officers the Spaniards are not in a position to lead and successfully conclude attacks independently and without foreign aid. The experiences with the two brigades of *Flechas Negras* and *Flechas Azules* have proved that the Italians likewise are not capable of doing this. Both brigades were organized 6 months ago with Italian officers, non-commissioned officers, and specialists (20 percent) and with Spanish men (80 percent) and were trained and commanded by the Italians. They have accomplished extremely little, so that Franco evaluates their fighting quality as far inferior to that of his purely Spanish units.

We Germans can say without any presumption that our combat training and especially our assault training is better than that of any other army. But even our best officers and non-commissioned officers are worthless here as instructors if they do not speak the language of the country and consequently cannot make themselves understood to their Spanish students. Experience has shown that, if he works very hard and has considerable linguistic talent, it takes an instructor newly arrived in a Spanish-speaking country approximately 6 months before he can perform useful work.

On the basis of these considerations I had requested and received consent as early as last December to utilize officers proved in South America, as well as the 50 to 60 so-called Spanish refugees sought out by the Auslandsorganisation of the NSDAP. These instructors proved excellent, first with the Falange and now with the training courses for the officers and non-commissioned officers of the Army, and are at the present time the backbone of combat training here. Nevertheless, because of a number of wrong measures, the results in the sense of creating assault divisions are entirely inadequate. The number of such instructors familiar with the language is also too small. It would pay to discuss in greater detail the measures for eliminating all these faults only if there is a possibility of carrying them out.

If no assault divisions are organized, victory and defeat are left to chance; then the end of the war cannot be foreseen. A quick final victory could then probably be achieved only through the moral collapse of the Reds, which at the present time we have no reason to expect and which can under no circumstances be a factor in making our decisions.

FAUPEL

No. 391

2938/569743–44

Memorandum by an Official of the Economic Policy Department

BERLIN, July 10, 1937.
zu W II WE 4785.

On the occasion of a conference concerning the Spanish iron mines in the Basque country, Herr Bethke of the Rowak firm gave the following information:

He had inspected Bilbao personally. The mines, blast furnaces, and rolling mills in the vicinity of Bilbao were undamaged and could start work at once. The production of the iron mines would be hampered by the fact that part of the workers had left with the Reds and another part had been killed or wounded. However, it could be assumed that within a short time the output would amount to about half of the former production. There were stocks of 300,000 tons of iron ore piled up.

About 60 percent of the Basque iron mines had been in Spanish possession and 40 percent in British (also some in French and Belgian possession), and in this way the mines had been either purely Spanish or purely foreign-owned. Of the exports, about half had formerly been sent to Germany and the other half to England, except for a fraction which went to French and Belgian smelting works. Recently the total output had been sent to England; the Basque Government had obliged the mines to do this. Now the former treaties, according to which Germany participated in the exports, would be put in force again. It was further intended that there should be sent to Germany what had been delivered to England instead of to Germany in recent months. In the future, of course, the Spanish smelting works should continue to receive the iron ore necessary for their operation. It was hoped, however, that all other ore would be sent to Germany for the foreseeable future, although it was not the intention to disregard the British in the long run. The British were particularly interested in receiving the Basque iron ores, because these were so-called well-tempered ores [*sogenannte gutmütige Erze*], and the British blast furnaces needed about 50 percent of such ores in order to operate smoothly. Germany was in a position to smelt up to 100 percent of the much harder Swedish and other iron ores in her blast furnaces, which was impossible for the British. Hence England's particular interest in the Basque iron ores.

The negotiations recently begun with the mine owners had started out favorably; in particular, the Basque owners had shown themselves very willing to make deliveries to Germany.

KREUTZWALD

No. 392

3205/697636

Protocol Signed at Burgos on July 12, 1937 [1]

SECRET

The German Government and the Spanish Nationalist Government agree in the view that under the circumstances obtaining at present it is advisable to postpone until a later, more suitable time a comprehensive settlement of the economic relations between their countries.

If the two Governments accordingly refrain from making detailed agreements in this field at present, it is nevertheless their intention to

---

[1] The same signatories signed on the same day at Burgos an agreement supplementary to the German-Spanish commercial treaty of May 7, 1926, providing for unrestricted most-favored-nation treatment. This supplementary agreement appears in the *Reichsgesetzblatt*, 1937, vol. II, p. 521.

place economic cooperation between their countries on a firm basis now and also for the future. From this standpoint, the Spanish Nationalist Government declares that it is prepared to conclude with Germany its first general trade agreement with any country. Accordingly, if it intends to enter upon international economic negotiations, it will inform the German Government in good time, in order to give the German Government the possibility of previously concluding an economic treaty.

If for special reasons the Spanish Nationalist Government should feel impelled to take up comprehensive economic negotiations with a third country before doing so with Germany, it will inform the German Government concerning such negotiations, insofar as they could be of interest to Germany, in order to give it the possibility of expressing its wishes in time. The carrying through of such negotiations shall not be affected thereby.

Without prejudice to the agreement reached in this protocol, the Spanish Nationalist Government reserves the right to accord Italy the same treatment which is here promised to Germany.

Done in duplicate in the German and Spanish languages at Burgos on July 12, 1937.

For the German Government:

FAUPEL
WUCHER

For the Spanish Nationalist Government:

FRANCISCO GÓMEZ JORDANA
J. BAU

No. 393

307/188205–10

The Minister Counselor of Embassy in Great Britain to the Foreign Ministry [1]

[July 14, 1937.]

The text of the proposals which have just been received is transmitted herewith. The Ambassador's comments will follow in the course of the afternoon.[2]

NON-INTERVENTION IN SPAIN

Statement by United Kingdom's Government

At the last meeting of the Non-Intervention Committee held on the 9th July, His Majesty's Government in the United Kingdom were entrusted by their colleagues on the commission with the task of drawing up proposals which should aim at closing the present gap in the control scheme and enable the policy of non-intervention to be con-

[1] There is no indication whether this undated communication is a telegram or a dispatch.

[2] The remainder of this document is in English in the original. The text as received in the Foreign Ministry differs somewhat from that printed in the British White Paper, Cmd. 5521.

tinued. This task has been no easy one. For any proposal which can be put forward with any hope of success must not only harmonize the widely divergent views which have been expressed but must also give promise of an effective system of non-intervention.

His Majesty's Government have, however, bent their best endeavours to their task, and have evolved a scheme which they herewith submit to other Governments represented on the Committee in the hope that it may lead to an agreed solution of the present difficulties. In submitting it, they will however make one observation. It is admittedly a compromise between varying points of view; it can only be successful if it is accepted by the Governments concerned in a spirit of compromise. All the Nations represented on the Committee have repeatedly expressed the view that they wish non-intervention in the Spanish conflict to continue. They have now an opportunity to give to that wish practical effect. Unless a greater spirit of international cooperation is evident than has been achieved in the past, this scheme will fail and the nations of Europe will be faced with a new and infinitely more dangerous situation. His Majesty's Government in the United Kingdom therefore urge other nations represented on the Non-Intervention Committee to give to these proposals their immediate consideration, and in the event of their being accepted to devote a real spirit of international collaboration to their practical application.

Outline of Proposals

A. Reconstruction of the system of supervision.

1. Supervision of traffic entering Spain by sea.

(*a*) The system of placing observers on ships visiting Spanish ports to be continued.

(*b*) The naval-control system to be discontinued and replaced by the establishment, with the consent of both parties, of international officers in Spanish ports under proper safeguard. These officers would perform the functions hitherto carried out by the naval control, i.e. ascertaining that the requirements of the scheme as regard carrying observers on board are complied with.

2. Supervision of traffic entering Spain by land.

The system of supervision on the land frontiers to be restored at once.

B. Further measures for meeting the present situation and for filling certain gaps in the supervision system.

3. With a view to the more effective application of the policy of non-intervention all Governments parties to the Non-Intervention Agreement, to recognize the two parties in Spain as possessing a status which justifies them in exercising belligerent rights at sea, in accordance with the rules governing such exercise but subject to the following special conditions:

(*a*) That the contraband list adopted by the belligerent shall be identical with the list of prohibited goods adopted by the Non-Intervention Committee. In other words, the Powers will recognize limited contraband lists only. This, however, will not preclude them from adding certain goods to those regarded as contraband under the Non-Intervention Agreement. Such addition will be subject of negotiation between the Committee as a whole and the two belligerents.

(*b*) That as a corollary to (*a*) the two parties will agree in the exercise of belligerent's rights at sea, to allow the unmolested passage of ships carrying observers and flying the flag of the Non-Intervention Committee. This, however, will not apply where the ship is engaged in a neutral [*unneutral*] service (such as the carrying of troops or the transmission of intelligence) or breach of the blockade which has been duly notified and is effectedly maintained.

(*c*) That since international shipping between countries other than Spain is obliged in certain areas to pass near the Spanish coast, no steps shall be taken by either party to impede or interfere with the passage of neutral ships not engaged in traffic with Spain.

(*d*) A Government which is a party to the Non-Intervention Agreement will be entitled to protect ships flying its flag against the exercise of belligerents rights in cases where the conditions laid down in (*a*), (*b*), or (*c*) are not being complied with.

4. In order to preclude the carrying of arms on ships which are entitled to have observers on board, the Non-Intervention Agreement to be extended so as to prohibit the carrying to Spain, from any port, by ships entitled to fly the flag of any of the parties to the agreement, of goods on the prohibited list.

5. The Committee to inform non-member powers of their intention to recognize the belligerent status of the two parties on the above terms and to invite their cooperation with a view to making the policy of non-intervention more effective. Any Governments which are prepared to become party to the Non-Intervention Agreement and to recognize the belligerent status of the two parties on the above terms to be invited to avail themselves, for ships flying their flag, of the facilities for taking on board observers at the established "control" ports.

6. The Committee to consider further the question of the employment by the two parties of foreign aircraft which enter Spain under their own power, and to examine in particular the possibility of requesting the two parties to accept foreign observers in specified aerodromes in Spain.

C. Withdrawal of foreign nationals.

7. (*a*) The Committee to pass a unanimous resolution in favour of the withdrawal from Spain of all persons whose evacuation is recommended in the report of the technical sub-Committee (N.J.S. (36) 525).

(*b*) A commission to be sent out to either party in Spain to make arrangements for and to supervise the withdrawal of the persons in question as soon as possible.

(*c*) All Governments to undertake to collaborate in such practical measures as may be found necessary for effecting these withdrawals.

D. Execution of above program.

8. His Majesty's Government propose that the above program should be carried out in the following stages:

I. Establishment of officers in Spanish ports, and withdrawal of naval patrol, as soon as possible;

II. Establishment of commissions to make arrangements for and supervise the withdrawal of foreign nationals, and extension of the Non-Intervention Agreement as proposed in § 5, to follow I as quickly as possible;

III. Recognition of belligerent rights to become effective when the Non-Intervention Committee place on record their opinion that the arrangements for the withdrawal of foreign nationals are working satisfactorily and that this withdrawal has in fact made substantial progress.

E. Immediate action by His Majesty's Government to be authorized by the Committee.

9. His Majesty's Government to be authorized by the Committee to enter immediately into discussions with the two parties in Spain on the following points:

(1) The establishment of officers in Spanish ports (§ 1 (*b*) above).

(2) Withdrawal of foreign volunteers (§ 7 above) including the establishment of the commissions in Spain.

(3) The conditions on which belligerent rights are to be granted (§ 3 above).

WOERMANN

No. 394

3205/697638

Protocol Signed at Burgos on July 15, 1937

SECRET

Although the German and the Spanish Nationalist Governments are refraining for the time being from concluding new agreements for the regulation of the German-Spanish exchange of goods and payments, they still desire to affirm in a general and binding form their mutual endeavor to advance commerce between their countries in a manner which will result in the greatest possible expansion. In particular, the two Governments declare that it is their earnest desire to assist one another to the greatest possible extent in the delivery of such raw materials, foods, and semifinished and finished goods as are of particular interest to the recipient country. Likewise, each Government will take into account the export interests of the other country, insofar as possible. Both Governments will accordingly contribute to the greatest possible extent toward facilitating the execution of private contracts in German-Spanish trade.

Done in duplicate in the German and Spanish languages at Burgos on July 15, 1937.

For the German Government:	For the Spanish Nationalist Government:
FAUPEL	FRANCISCO GÓMEZ JORDANA
WUCHER	J. BAU

No. 395

428/218216–18

The Ambassador in Great Britain to the Foreign Ministry

Telegram

VERY URGENT   LONDON, July 15, 1937—12:11 a.m.
No. 399 of July 14   Received July 15—3:00 a.m.

With reference to my 398 of July 14.[1]

For the Führer and Chancellor and the Foreign Minister.

The British proposal contains a combination of all the ideas discussed so far and gives extensive recognition to the German-Italian proposal in particular. The plan itself, which is contained in points 1 to 7, appears suitable as a basis for discussion. In any case we must follow such tactics that a possible failure of the negotiations would be attributed not to us but to other powers.

With regard to particular points, the following should be noted:

Re 1 (*b*). The proposal to permit surveillance of Spanish harbors was long ago accepted unanimously by the Non-Intervention Committee and came to nought only because of rejection by the Spanish parties. The proposal then made even gave the observers in Spain considerably greater power, since they could inspect the entire harbor area, whereas the present proposal is linked to the provision for retaining observation officers on board and the observers in Spanish harbors will therefore have to confine themselves to ascertaining whether ships have observers on board. A considerably smaller staff would suffice for this task.

The strong objection to this proposal, that these commissions would be able to get an insight into conditions in Spain, might be countered by narrowly limiting their duties.

A rejection in the present situation would probably be possible only if we could make other equally effective proposals.

Re 2. At the proper moment a strengthening of the land control measures would have to be requested.

We might furthermore inform the committee that the German observation officers would cancel their notice of withdrawal after agreement was reached on the plan as a whole and the land control measures were reestablished.

Re 3. The question as to why belligerent rights are to be given at sea only should be discussed.

In addition, the German-Italian proposal linked the granting of belligerent rights with declarations of neutrality by the non-intervention states. Since this proposal is politically effective, it might be adopted by us.

---

[1] Not printed (428/218215).

The details under (*a*) to (*d*) appear to be acceptable and in the main correspond to our suggestions.

Re 4. The proposal to forbid ships of the non-intervention states to carry contraband was made by England some time ago and accepted by us in principle.

Re 5. Extension to non-European nations is in accordance with the German suggestion. As is known, the British Government has already undertaken to sound out other countries, but no results on this have been reported yet. From our point of view it would be desirable if, for example, the South American countries, which are quite overwhelmingly on Franco's side, would join the committee directly. Could soundings in this matter also be made from there?

From the conversation with the Italian and Portuguese Ambassadors it appeared that they are also in favor of this proposal. Attolico's statements to the contrary are evidently based on a misunderstanding.

Re 6. The reexamination of the question of air control measures is formulated very vaguely and might be blocked by the opposition of the Spanish parties. Please send telegraphic instructions on the view there.

Re 7. We might propose that No. 7 be replaced by a different version which would confine itself to taking the report of the experts as a basis for further action and submitting it to the Spanish parties for their opinion. The commission mentioned in paragraph (*b*) has more extensive powers in the British proposal than in the report of the experts. In any case its full powers would have to be clarified in detail.

Re 8. The proposal regarding the sequence of the individual measures reveals that the British Government considers the reestablishment of the control system around Spain as the first stage and the withdrawal of the volunteers and the granting of belligerent rights as the second stage. This seems to me acceptable. However, the latter two questions are to be linked in a manner which, as already reported in the previous telegram, is unacceptable to us. We could make the counterproposal that belligerent rights will be granted as soon as agreement on a new control system has been reached in the committee and the Spanish parties have approved the principle of withdrawing volunteers. The prospects for such a proposal are, however, uncertain at the present time. Some sort of a link between the two questions seems unavoidable. It may be assumed that the actual carrying out of the two measures will thereby be delayed for a long time in any event.

Re 9. The Italians and the Portuguese have strong objections to granting England somewhat the role of an arbitrator by making her mediator in all important questions vis-à-vis both the Spanish parties.

These objections might be met by a different formulation, but the initiative on this should be left with the Italians and the Portuguese. Above all, it is important that England does not enter into binding agreements with the Spanish parties, for example, on the withdrawal of volunteers, by which the other committee members would later be bound.

RIBBENTROP

No. 396

428/218219–20

The Foreign Minister to the Embassy in London [1]

Telegram

No. 302

BERLIN, July 15, 1937.
Pol. III 3691.

With reference to your telegrams 398 [2] and 399.[3]

I am agreed that in tomorrow's session of the Non-Intervention Committee you term the British proposal a "basis for discussion." I also agree to your proposed tactics in tomorrow's session. Since detailed examination of the British proposals has not yet been completed, and further, since reactions from Rome and Salamanca have not yet come in, it would be desirable if tomorrow's decision was confined to matters of procedure and our attitude on all details reserved.

In principle, care should be taken to make it impossible for the opposing parties to be treated merely as the object of an action by the European powers; this applies particularly to the withdrawal of volunteers. We have reason to believe that the Italians wish to adopt an intransigent attitude on the question of volunteers. But blame for a possible failure must on no account fall on the German-Italian side. Therefore, perhaps in the first stage of the discussion your possible objections regarding item D paragraph 8 under III might take the form of the question: Does recognition of belligerent rights, *after* the envisaged confirmation that the withdrawal of volunteers was functioning, imply the grant of belligerent rights *in addition to* those mentioned above in the British compromise proposal (3)? In any case, the impression must not take root that from the outset we accept the idea that granting of belligerent rights at sea should depend on prior implementation of the actual evacuation.

NEURATH

---

[1] Copies of this telegram were sent to Rome as No. 230 and to Salamanca as No. 265.

[2] Not printed (428/218215).

[3] Document No. 395, *supra.*

[EDITORS' NOTE. Neurath's instructions were carried out, and at the session of July 16 the Axis Powers agreed to accept the British proposal as a basis of discussion while details could be discussed in a subcommittee. The French Ambassador, however, indicated that he was without instructions and proposed an adjournment. On July 19 Ribbentrop was instructed that, despite the fact that Franco rejected the British proposal out of hand, he should continue discussions in committee. At the meeting on July 20, however, Grandi brought matters to a deadlock by introducing unacceptable questions of procedure. Grandi was, however, provided with new instructions which would in fact allow the British plan to be defeated as much by Russian and French opposition as by that of the Axis Powers.]

No. 397

3205/697642, 697644

Protocol Signed at Burgos on July 16, 1937

SECRET

I.

The German Government and the Spanish Nationalist Government agree that under the present circumstances it is not feasible to reach definitive agreements concerning the manner of settling obligations for payment which have arisen as a result of the special deliveries made by Germany to the Spanish Nationalist Government.

However, it is fixed in advance that these obligations are payable exclusively in German reichsmarks. The Spanish Nationalist Government declares itself prepared in principle to pay 4 percent interest annually on the balance of the debt; the German Government agrees, however, to discuss the question of interest thoroughly once more at the final settlement of the obligations.

II.

In order to give the German Government a certain assurance with regard to the liquidation of the obligations mentioned under I, the Spanish Nationalist Government will arrange that goods, especially raw materials, which the German Government desires to obtain from Spanish sovereign territory, including the Spanish protectorate in Morocco, are delivered to Germany according to periodic agreements between the two Governments and charged against the German claims in question, and furthermore, that payments in discharge of these claims, which will be agreed upon periodically between the two Governments, will be made available to the German Government for application to economic purposes in the above-named areas.

III.

Considering the circumstance that Germany and Spain are in the fortunate position of being able to complement one another economically, the German Government and the Spanish Nationalist Government consider that it is in both their interests to support one another mutually in advancing production, thus contributing to increasing the well-being of their countries.

The German Government declares its willingness to cooperate in the economic reconstruction of Spain, particularly in opening up and utilizing the mineral resources and other raw materials in Spanish sovereign territory, including the Spanish protectorate in Morocco. Accordingly it proposes to provide both expert personnel and necessary technical equipment, insofar as the Spanish Nationalist Government desires this.

The Spanish Nationalist Government will facilitate as far as possible the establishment of Spanish companies for the opening up and economic utilization of mineral resources and other raw materials and for other economic purposes serving the general welfare, under participation of German citizens or German firms, as compatible with the general stipulations of Spanish law.

Done in duplicate in the German and Spanish languages at Burgos on July 16, 1937.

For the German Government:

FAUPEL
WUCHER

For the Spanish Nationalist Government:

FRANCISCO GÓMEZ JORDANA
J. BAU

CHAPTER IV

THE POWERS AND NON-INTERVENTION
JULY 19–NOVEMBER 1, 1937

No. 398

428/218256

The State Secretary to the Embassy in Great Britain

Telegram

No. 309   BERLIN, July 19, 1937.
                                                         Pol. III 3744.

With reference to your No. 413.[1]

I assume that your questions have in the main already been answered by today's air-mail instruction.[2] Fundamentally there exists here a strong interest in strict control on land and little interest in the naval patrol. Under certain circumstances, the military would prefer a delay in reinstituting general control measures and a continuation of the present state of affairs rather than strict naval patrol without strict control on land at the same time.

I am in accord with the tactical procedure which you proposed in the above-mentioned telegraphic report.

MACKENSEN

---

[1] Not printed (428/218249–50).
[2] Not printed (3361/E009678–85). Ribbentrop had inquired in telegram No. 413 of July 18 whether he might discuss control measures in Spanish harbors separately from the questions of volunteers and belligerent rights. The air-mail instruction informed him that he might proceed tactically as he thought best; Franco's opposition would in any case defeat any measures designed to cut off his supplies by the sea route. The important consideration was that Germany should not be blamed for failure of the British plan.

No. 399

428/218272–73

Memorandum by the State Secretary

BERLIN, July 20, 1937.

Ambassador Faupel, in the last part of a 1½-hour conversation which I had with him yesterday, introduced the subject of the untenable situation which had arisen between him and General Sander. He explained it in detail and asked whether I could give a cue as to

423

what he might do to find a solution for this situation. He emphasized that as early as several months ago he had submitted the matter to the Führer in person but that the latter, after consultation with Field Marshal von Blomberg, had refused to interfere in a question of military personnel. In the meantime the situation had become worse from week to week, although he, Faupel, had been keeping entirely out of military questions for about 2½ months, which until then he had not been able to do, considering the personality of General Franco and his habit of speaking with him about military questions, too. My advice for a frank discussion between him and General Sander was also too late, for he had made such an attempt just a few weeks ago, with the negative result that during a motor trip to Bilbao he had called at the Victoria, General Sander's hotel, but to his inquiry, transmitted by an officer, as to whether he might shake hands with the General, he had received the answer that the General was sorry but he was not feeling well and was lying down. He could not expose himself to such an affront a second time. The worst thing in the whole controversy was that it had become public, in Spain, too, mainly through the indiscreet conduct of General Sander, and had become a general topic of conversation. This state of affairs could not continue.

I told the Ambassador that in my opinion a solution could be reached only by a renewed report of the whole affair to the Führer and Chancellor. I was willing to speak in this sense to the Foreign Minister, and I could imagine that during the Führer's pending stay in Bayreuth an opportunity might arise for the Ambassador to make such a report.

In following up this idea it should be remembered that on the one hand, as I heard in strict confidence, General Franco is supposed to have applied to Berlin by way of General Sander to have Ambassador Faupel, who is no longer acceptable to him in any way, replaced by some other person, and on the other hand, and independently of this, the War Ministry is said to be thinking of replacing General Sander by another commander, mainly because of Admiral Canaris' report on his latest impressions in Spain. State Secretary Milch is said to have been won over to this idea already and to be willing to make General Kesselring [1] available as a replacement.

In this situation it might be well to consult with the War Minister before making further decisions.

According to official information from the War Ministry, Field Marshal von Blomberg will be in Bayreuth from 1:30 p.m. on July 23 until 8 a.m. on July 25.

v. MACKENSEN

---

[1] General Albert Kesselring of the German Air Force.

No. 400

428/218291–92

The Ambassador in France to the Foreign Ministry

Telegram

URGENT   PARIS, July 22, 1937.
No. 478 of July 21   Received July 22—11 : 55 a.m.

Information from a political source gives the following picture of the official view here on the Spanish question:

1. The prospects for the resumption of control measures are viewed very unfavorably.

2. An effort by Italy and Germany, who are playing for time, to try to impede and prolong the negotiations with counterproposals is counted on.

3. Both countries estimate Franco's situation too favorably. In reality the Reds are stronger. But the end of the Civil War is more remote than ever, particularly since both sides will certainly use the present intermediate stage to strengthen themselves.

4. The intermediate stage signifies a state of tension which, from the standpoint of foreign policy, cannot be borne much longer. Among the French people, too, the feeling is growing that the present uncertainty is intolerable in the long run.

5. Accordingly the Government's disinclination to make concessions and its desire to take a firm stand are increasing.

This possibility is present because:

(*a*) The opening of the land frontier with northern Spain to the transport of weapons and munitions would open the eyes of the Italians and would certainly shift the situation in favor of the Reds.

(*b*) The psychological relations between France and Germany as well as Italy are in the process of changing. As a result of the long-continued tension and under the influence of the recent parade of army and air power, the French people are beginning to get used to the conviction of their own strength, so that they no longer need to accept further "provocations." This mood affects the attitude of Delbos and of Blum, who is particularly under the influence of the decisions of the Socialist Congress and who has already brought up for discussion in the Council of Ministers the necessity of more stringent measures. Mussolini can be kept within bounds only by firmness.

6. A necessity for firmness will appear if the question of an Italian artillery base between Gibraltar and Algeciras should become acute. The French Government is resolved to take a determined and stern stand in this matter. It can do this all the more readily since, as the

Morocco incident at the beginning of this year has shown, the whole French people is united behind it in this question and realizes that French national interests of the first order are involved. On this point in particular it can also count on the unreserved support of the British Government, whose own interests are likewise engaged.

WELCZECK

No. 401

2938/569735–40

The Foreign Ministry to the Embassies in Spain and Great Britain and to the Economics Ministry

BERLIN, July 22, 1937.
W II WE 4637/IV.

With reference to the instruction (letter) of May 15, 1937, W II WE 2586.[1]

The British Embassy reverted to the Rio Tinto affair in the note of July 7,[2] a copy of which is enclosed. For your information, the following supplementary facts are communicated:

Before the note was answered, the Commercial Secretary of the British Embassy telephoned on July 12 and, referring to the note, stated that Messrs. Buchanan and Robbins of the Rio Tinto Company in London had arrived in Berlin. He requested that they be received at the Foreign Ministry in order to present their standpoint and that he might take part in the conference. He was told that we were willing to receive them but was informed at the same time that we were rather surprised that after the negative stand taken in our note of May 15, 1937, W II WE 2586, the British Embassy renewed its support for a claim, which we considered unjustified, in the question of the confiscated copper precipitate.

The conference took place on July 13. At first, the Englishmen did not mention the question of indemnification for the confiscated copper precipitate at all, and they did so later only incidentally in the course of their further statements. The German standpoint was most definitely reaffirmed, to the effect that neither the German Government nor any private German firm could be made responsible for the confiscation undertaken by the Spanish Government.

The aim of the statements made by the Englishmen was to gain a basis on which the heretofore satisfactory relationship of the Rio Tinto Company with the German purchasers of its copper ores, etc.,

---

[1] Not printed (2938/569713–18). Reference is to the note handed to the British Embassy on that date.

[2] Document 381, p. 399.

from Spain (and other parts of the world: Southern Rhodesia) could be established for an indefinite period.

They pointed out that a 2-year contract on German purchases of pyrites from the Spanish mines of the Rio Tinto Company recently had been negotiated and set down in draft form in London with the Duisburger Kupferhütte (Dr. Rudolf Kissel and Dr. von Bodelschwingk), who represented all German buyers interested in obtaining pyrites, but that its final conclusion still depended upon regulation of the price question. In a letter accompanying the draft of the contract it was already arranged that the Rio Tinto Company agreed to permit Germany, as an exception, to make part payment in pesetas (whereas all of its other contracts provided for payment in pounds sterling in London). The company had to insist, however, that

1. the confiscation of its products by the Spanish Nationalist Government cease; and

2. that further deliveries to Germany be paid for partly in pounds sterling or in refined copper.

The British representatives stated with regard to point 1 that in spite of the state of war in which the country finds itself they consider confiscation by the Spanish authorities unjustified, since in the first place the Rio Tinto Company is a British firm (not a Spanish firm) and its products are British property on the basis of the treaty concerning concessions for Spanish mines, and because, in the second place, even in case of war, confiscation may be carried out only for purposes of warfare but not in order to gain possession of properties for trading with third countries. They took the view that General Franco would be willing to forego confiscation if it were made clear to him by a joint action of the British and German parties interested that he would fare better by regulating the production and sale of pyrites through commercial channels.

With regard to the question of price, they believed that the German Government would be able to induce the German purchasers to accede to the desires and proposals of the Rio Tinto Company.

In spite of lively discussion of the various proposals, we mainly confined ourselves to taking note of their desires and suggestions. For the rest the conversation was spirited but friendly, and the Englishmen were assured, in response to their evident desire to come to a long-term agreement, that we wished to work in this direction, even though no promises could be made.

The Englishmen understood this but hoped that during their stay in Berlin it would be possible for them to receive a definite answer concerning the German stand on their suggestion. They were particularly interested in locating not only the proper Government authorities but also an authoritative representation of the German copper interests with whom they could continue the negotiations. They were promised that efforts would be made in this direction.

The representative of the British Embassy acted merely as an observer during the whole negotiation.

After the conference which Messrs. Buchanan and Robbins of the Rio Tinto Company had here, they made an appointment with the Rowak firm on their own initiative, without being introduced by the Foreign Ministry; they were received there on July 14. They had let us know that they had to return to London the same evening but would be available during the next week in case they were informed that Germany desired the continuation of the negotiations on their suggestions.

Concerning the content of their conversation with the Rowak firm, where they were accompanied by Herr Fellner of the Metallgesellschaft, Rowak reported that the conference had been very friendly and that the Englishmen's desire had been summarized to the effect that they wished to induce the Spanish Nationalist Government to unblock 37,000 pounds sterling per month. They had been told that Rowak could only transmit this desire to its Spanish friends but that Rowak hoped that these friends would have sufficient opportunity to support their desire with the Spanish Government.

Rowak also reported that there had been only a short discussion of the question of indemnification for the confiscated copper precipitate but that the Englishmen would apparently drop this claim if a satisfactory solution of the whole question was reached.

The Commercial Attaché of the British Embassy was invited here for the final reply to the British Ambassador's note of July 7, 1937. He was first informed of the course of the conversation between the British representatives and Rowak, of which he had not yet learned, and then he was told the following:

The Foreign Ministry had been glad to contribute to a settlement of the controversial questions, and had therefore complied with the desire of the Embassy to receive Messrs. Buchanan and Robbins. We were therefore very happy to see that these gentlemen had already on their own initiative found their way to Rowak, since we, too, could only have named Rowak as the proper German agency to which the Rio Tinto Company should turn for further discussion of the matter. In any case we had to adhere to the position expressed in our *note verbale* of May 15, 1937, W II WE 2586, that we reject any claim by the Rio Tinto Company resulting from the confiscation of the copper precipitate, insofar as it is made against the German Government or a German firm, and that we are still of the opinion that the affair can be further dealt with only through purely commercial channels and by the firms concerned.

The British Commercial Attaché took note of this answer. He will report it to the Foreign Office in London; he added only that the British Embassy had to adhere to its stand on the legal aspect of the situation, just as did the Foreign Ministry, but that he hoped that the further course of the negotiations had now been put on the right path.

By direction:
K[REUTZWALD] (?)

No. 402

428/218308

Minute by the Director of the Political Department

BERLIN, July 24, 1937.

The report in the *Völkischer Beobachter* of July 22 concerning the dispatch of troop contingents of the French Foreign Legion to the Red Spanish front is based on the interrogation of an alleged deserter from the Foreign Legion. The report in the *Völkischer Beobachter* was, however, given a somewhat positive turn in comparison with the interrogation of the legionnaire. In transmitting the interrogation to the Propaganda Ministry the Gestapo remarked as follows:

"It has not yet been possible to check the veracity of the information. I therefore pass it on with reservations and consider that a certain caution is advisable in any use made thereof."

Aside from the fact that the French Ambassador expressly asked that the matter be brought to the Führer's attention,[1] since faith in the authority of the Führer is at stake, this is in my opinion another instance which shows that a press policy in international matters without the participation of the Foreign Ministry must have unfavorable results.

Since the French *démarche* was published today in the French press with detailed comment, it did not seem advisable to preserve complete silence on the matter in the German press. Therefore the corresponding Havas report was given to DNB today with the enclosed addendum.[2]

Herewith submitted to the Foreign Minister.

WEIZSÄCKER

---

[1] Weizsäcker memorandum of July 23, not printed (428/218304–07).
[2] Not printed (428/218309).

No. 403

307/188156

The Director of the Political Department to the Embassy in Great Britain[1]

Telegram

No. . . .   BERLIN, July 24, 1937.
                                                          Pol. III . . .

For your information.

The following strictly confidential report from a reliable source, although not officially from the Italian Government, may serve to explain the instruction to Grandi concerning treatment of the question of withdrawing volunteers:

The report states that the Italian Government is ready to agree to the withdrawal of volunteers as soon as Franco gives the cue to do so. The Italian Government, however, does not wish to assume the odium vis-à-vis Franco and world opinion of having itself urged the withdrawal of the volunteers.

                                                          WEIZSÄCKER

---

[1] The same text was sent for information to the Embassies at Rome and Salamanca.

No. 404

4446/E086578

The Ambassador in Italy to the Foreign Ministry

Telegram

No. 120 of July 29   ROME, July 29, 1937—9 : 20 p.m.
                                       Received July 29—11 : 25 p.m.
                                                          Pol. III 3924.

Ciano stated today that we could be satisfied with the progress of the deliberations of the London committee. The type of Olympic contest in progress there at present, in which now one, now another Ambassador claimed victory, was not injurious to our interests. We could calmly await the further course of events. In Spain itself the military situation was not unfavorable, but unfortunately nothing decisive was happening; rather, the situation was similar to that of two boxers who, somewhat tired after a long fight, continued to exchange blows mechanically. A well-organized and also numerically strong army group of Italian volunteers had been ready for action for some time but was not being used. On the whole Ciano's mood inclined again toward resignation.

                                                          HASSELL

No. 405

4446/E086578/1

The Head of Political Division III to Secretary of Legation Brücklmeier of the Embassy in Great Britain

BERLIN, July 31, 1937.
Pol. III 3924.

DEAR HERR BRÜCKLMEIER: Enclosed I am sending you a copy of a telegram from Rome for your information.[1]

As you may know, the Italian volunteers have been standing at ease for weeks and cannot be persuaded to launch even the smallest attack. Consequently the Bilbao offensive required considerably more time than Franco's General Staff had assumed it would and the offensive at Santander has made no progress at all. The feeling of the Spaniards toward the Italians is said to be anything but a happy one.

With best regards and Heil Hitler!

As ever,
DUMONT

---

[1] Document No. 404, *supra*.

No. 406

4078/E068923

The Chargé d'Affaires in Spain to the Foreign Ministry

Telegram

No. 385 of August 3   SALAMANCA, August 3, 1937—time not indicated.
Received August 3—11:40 p.m.
Pol. III 4004.

Sangroniz, Chief of the Diplomatic Cabinet, just told me that the Vatican has requested that the present unofficial Spanish Nationalist representation at the Vatican be changed into an official mission, which could be taken as recognition of the Franco Government by the Vatican.

Sangroniz further told me that British Ambassador Chilton assured him Britain would recognize the Franco Government as a belligerent power in any case.

HEBERLEIN

No. 407

47/32282–84

The Director of the Political Department to the Embassy in Italy

Telegram

No. 252   BERLIN, August 4, 1937.

Pol. I 4305 g.

Drafting Officer: Counselor of Legation Dumont.

According to a wire from the Embassy at Salamanca, the Franco Government sent an urgent telegram to the Spanish Ambassador in Rome on August 3, from which I transmit the following passages:

"All reports of the last few days agree in announcing strong Russian aid for the Reds consisting of 100 heavy, 500 medium, and 2,000 light tanks; 3,000 motorized machine guns; 300 planes, and tens of thousands of machine guns, all of them with Red maintenance personnel and command units.

"The report seems exaggerated, since the numbers appear to exceed the capacity of one nation to provide assistance.

"In case the report is confirmed, however, urgent action is necessary to stop the transports as they pass through the straits south of Italy and to block the route to Spain.   This can be done by providing Spain with the necessary number of ships or through intervention by the Italian fleet itself.   A number of destroyers operating along the Italian coast and harbors can prevent any Russian assistance via the Mediterranean, either openly under the Italian flag or with a Spanish officer and several men on board, and a hoisting of the Spanish Nationalist flag during the capture.

"I am sending a delegate to Rome at once to negotiate this important matter.   In the meantime, in order to prevent the arrival of ships already en route, ask the Italian Government to observe and report the position and route of Russian and Spanish ships which leave Odessa.   The ships must be observed and followed by Italian destroyers and their positions reported to our fleet.

"Please transmit the above information and request to the Duce or Count Ciano with the utmost urgency, at the same time assuring them of the Generalissimo's unshakable friendship and gratitude to the Italian nation."

End of the Spanish telegram.

Nothing is known here concerning increased arms transports by Russia.   Franco's demand for intervention by the Italian fleet sounds very strange.   Please send a telegraphic report later concerning the reception of the Spanish *démarche* by the Italian Government.

WEIZSÄCKER

No. 408

428/218383

The Ambassador in Italy to the Foreign Ministry

Telegram

No. 206 of August 5   ROME (QUIRINAL), August 5, 1937—9 : 00 p.m.

Received August 6—12 : 10 a.m.

With reference to your No. 252.[1]

As Ciano informed me, Nicolás Franco arrived here this morning to follow up on [Franco's] message, had a conversation with Ciano, and will speak with Mussolini and Ciano this evening; in addition, there will be a conference today between the deputy chief of the Spanish Admiralty Staff, who is accompanying Franco, and the Italian Admiralty Staff. With regard to the subject matter, Ciano declared that, although the estimates regarding Russian transports might be somewhat exaggerated, the Duce was in principle still inclined to do everything he could to put a stop to them—not with surface vessels, to be sure, but only with submarines, in Sicilian waters; in case the submarines had to surface, they would display the Spanish flag. The question whether it would be feasible to turn two or three older warships over to Spain, if necessary changing the silhouette, was still being considered. He would keep us informed regarding the outcome of further consultations and deliberations.

HASSELL

---

[1] Document No. 407, *supra*.

No. 409

47/32290

The Director of the Political Department to the Embassy in Italy

Telegram

SECRET   BERLIN, August 13—4 : 40 p.m.
No. 261   zu Pol. I 4308 g.

Drafting Officer: Counselor of Legation Haidlen.

With reference to your telegram No. 206 of August 5.

The Embassy at Salamanca telegraphed as follows on August 11:

Chief of the Diplomatic Cabinet Sangroniz just informed me that Mussolini had declared that he was prepared to carry out the measures requested by Franco for preventing the transit of Russian war matériel through the straits south of Italy. Whether this action will be undertaken under the Italian or the Spanish flag was still uncertain.

WEIZSÄCKER

No. 410

47/32273

The Chargé d'Affaires in Italy to the Foreign Ministry

Telegram

No. 216 of August 16   ROME, August 16, 1937—3 : 25 p.m.
                                        Received August 16—7 : 20 p.m.
                                        Pol. I 4283 g.

Ciano, who received me today in regard to another matter, asked me to inform [Berlin] very confidentially that he had good news concerning the operation in progress near Santander, which was expected to be captured sooner than had been foreseen. Further, the Italian "blockade" of the Spanish coast was functioning excellently; in the last few days seven transport vessels had been sunk, and he assumed that shipments would soon cease. Ciano was obviously very well satisfied and optimistically inclined.

In regard to the Far Eastern conflict, Ciano was of the opinion that this was a favorable development insofar as Russia and England would thereby be diverted from Spain. It was for this reason that the present moment had been chosen for the operation at Santander. As far as England and Italy were concerned, there was nothing to be added to his last communications to Ambassador Hassell. The most important thing now was to clear up the Spanish question, which had been dragging on much too long; settlement of other questions would become considerably easier after that.

PLESSEN

No. 411

1819/416299–302

The Ambassador in Spain to the Foreign Ministry

Sa. 3–3174   SALAMANCA, August 21, 1937.
                                        Pol. III 4255.

Subject: Report on my farewell visit to General Franco.[1]

On August 20, I took leave of General Franco in Burgos. He said to me first that the news of my departure was most unwelcome to

---

[1] In a memorandum of Aug. 19 for the Director of the Personnel Department (54/36045) State Secretary Mackensen had noted that "during his visit today General Keitel inquired about the status of the Faupel affair. He assumed that the Führer and Chancellor had ordered the recall of Ambassador Faupel as well as of General Sperrle. The latter, however, in order not to arouse any unnecessary attention, was not to be recalled until a certain imminent change in the military situation had occurred. The General desired to know when Ambassador Faupel's recall could be expected. I informed him regarding the status of the matter." Ambassador Faupel was recalled. On Aug. 27 Eberhard von Stohrer was appointed Ambassador to the Franco Government and assumed his post at Salamanca on Sept. 19. Stohrer had previously been named Ambassador to Spain on July 16, 1936, but had not proceeded to his post at that time because of the outbreak of the Civil War.

him, and then he proceeded to expound to me once more in detail his view of the international situation.

He began with Portugal, where the recognition had come very late that the regulated police state there required an ideological and party foundation. In the last year, to be sure, considerable success had been achieved in this field; nevertheless, the Portuguese Government had informed him recently that there was a strong Communist movement afoot in one of the border provinces west of Badajoz, and it had inquired of him whether he was in a position to close the frontier by military force. Franco had, he informed me, not only promised to do this but also declared his willingness to cooperate with the Portuguese authorities in every way in suppressing this Communist movement.

Franco continued that, if Spain should once go Red as a result of the victory of his opponents, the Government in Lisbon would find it impossible to remain in power; Portugal would then be inundated within a week by the wave of Communism.

Passing on to France, he again spoke of his agent with Laval, whom he had mentioned to me a number of times before. Laval was well aware that the elections scheduled for October 10 (Franco called them *elecciones cantonales*) would be a test of strength for the Popular Front. Lebrun was undecided as to what was to be done and was considering the idea of making Daladier premier. Franco went on to say that the agent to whom he owed this information had also recently spoken to Pétain and asked him what he for his part intended to do. Pétain had answered that he would place himself at the disposal of whatever political figure he believed would be in a position to save France.

I repeat this part of the Generalissimo's remarks dealing with the political situation in France with special reservations.

The French Army, Franco went on to say, would decline in morale from year to year, if only because the young people in the schools were increasingly being subjected to Communist teachings.

According to what Franco told me, he had learned recently from an agent that the French General Staff in Toulouse had prepared a plan of attack on Aragón for the Reds. A copy of this plan would be given to Franco in a few days.

Regarding England, the Generalissimo said that he was constantly trying through the Duke of Alba and other Spaniards at present in London to point out to British circles that a *rapprochement* of England with Germany and Italy was indicated; France was no suitable ally for England in the long run.

It is obvious that Franco would welcome a *rapprochement* between England and Germany. Our oft-repeated inquiries regarding possible loan negotiations with England, the export of ore from Bilbao, etc., have shown the Generalissimo with what interest we follow and watch over his relations and negotiations with England. The longer the war lasts, the more Spain is bled white financially and all the more important it is for Franco to find an understanding and cooperative attitude in Germany on the question of a British loan.

Franco considers the deliveries of Russian war matériel to the Reds, which were recently resumed on a large scale, a very serious matter. To be sure, the first reports regarding the transports by sea now under way had been exaggerated; nevertheless, because of their volume, these deliveries constituted a very great danger.

Russia was in his opinion scarcely in a position at the present time to carry on a foreign war, since her army was badly shaken by the shooting of a large number of the leaders. The Soviet Government was exerting itself all the more to stir up unrest in foreign countries. Russia did not need to fear being attacked in Europe; therefore, she could without danger supply Red Spain with considerable armament, for which she was getting a good price in gold or in art objects and other articles of value.

Franco told me that stopping arms deliveries through the Mediterranean and preventing unloading in Red harbors were the most effective ways to shorten the war for the nations interested in bringing it to an end.

When Franco referred to the present decreased strength and striking power of the French as well as the Russian Army, it appeared to me that he wished to intimate that Germany could support him more effectively than heretofore without incurring any risk herself, in order that he could soon conclude the war.

Finally, Franco, in an almost conspicuous manner, called attention to the importance of the Canary Islands, which were of the greatest value as a naval and air base for Spain herself as well as for all powers who were her friends or allies. Harbor defense installations, as he explained, could be easily erected there.

FAUPEL

[EDITORS' NOTE. Meantime, debate had been continuing in the Non-Intervention Committee on the British proposals, and on August 27, 1937, there was presented a report prepared by the chairman and secretary of the Non-Intervention Committee, Vice Admiral van Dulm and Francis Hemming, on means for restoring and improving the naval patrol along the Spanish coasts. Its conclusion was that the naval patrol system had been extensively evaded and that it had not produced results justifying its costs. It recommended instead a system of observers in Spanish ports.]

No. 412

3361/E009718–19

The Chargé d'Affaires in Great Britain to the Foreign Ministry

Telegram

No. 517 of September 2   LONDON, September 2, 1937—9 : 10 p.m.
Received September 2—11 : 30 p.m.
Pol. III 4328.

With reference to my telegraphic report No. 515 of September 1.[1]

I have learned from the French Embassy that no step is intended in the Non-Intervention Committee at the present time because of the situation which, in French opinion, was brought about by the Italian attitude.

According to a confidential communication from the French Embassy, the Quai d'Orsay would actually have been inclined to renew the expired French law dealing with the ban on foreigners. In Government circles, however, they considered rejection of such a law probable in view of the sentiment in the country and consequently were refraining, for the time being, from renewing it. Administratively the ban on volunteers is maintained, but no penalties can be imposed.

France expressly assumed no international obligation to impose penalties. But the agreement concerning the ban on volunteers was made at the time with the understanding that all countries would adopt essentially similar regulations, including penalties, as provided in paragraph . . . (group garbled; the figure received was "52") of the report of the experts, document No. 259 of January 6,[2] and as accepted by the French Government (document No. 303 [2]). Moreover, in the German memorandum of January 25 (Pol. III 416) [3] the statement was made that an agreement regarding the content of the measures to be taken was prerequisite to the German acceptance of a ban on volunteers.

I suggest studying, in consultation with Rome, whether in view of the French attitude a change should be made in the German law of February 18 (provision for the imposition of penalties). I have gained the impression here that the previous announcement of such intention to the French Government would perhaps strengthen the

---

[1] Not printed (428/218424–25).
[2] Of the Non-Intervention Committee.
[3] Not printed (5067/E292194–97).

stand of the Quai d'Orsay on the matter of proclaiming a new French law.[4]

WOERMANN

---

[4] A handwritten note initialed by Dumont reads as follows: "The French law of January 21, 1937, concerning the ban on volunteers, published in the *Journal Officiel* on January 22, 1937, stipulates in article 1, section 2, paragraph 2 that the provisions of the ban are to go into effect for a period of 6 months on the date set by international agreement. The ban on volunteers went into effect internationally (i. e. for the non-intervention powers) on February 21, 1937; thus the French law expired on August 20, 1937."

Below this there is a typed note reading as follows: "I discussed the matter with Herr Woermann over the telephone before the October 16 session of the Non-Intervention Committee. Herr Woermann shares my opinion that this is undoubtedly a loophole. He is, however, of the opinion that it is not necessary for us to do anything because, as he had heard, the question would be brought up by someone else during the session of October 16. I reported the matter to the Director of the Political Department. To be resubmitted on October 20. Berlin, October 16, 1937."

A further note in Dumont's handwriting reads as follows: "Utilized in airgram of October 18 to London."

[EDITORS' NOTE. In apparent connection with the Spanish Civil War, widespread attacks upon merchant vessels in the Mediterranean Sea during the summer of 1937 by submarines of undeclared nationality culminated in an attempt to torpedo the British destroyer *Havock* while engaged on patrol north of Alicante, Spain, during the night of August 31–September 1, 1937. This was reported to have been the eighteenth attempt in a month to sink neutral ships without warning and without regard to whether they were bound to a Spanish port or whether they were carrying observers of the Non-Intervention Committee on board.

At a special cabinet meeting on September 2, the British Government decided to reinforce its naval strength in the western Mediterranean. It also accepted a French proposal for calling a conference of Mediterranean powers and others concerned to deal with the situation.]

No. 413

3368/E010487–88

The Chargé d'Affaires in Great Britain to the Foreign Ministry

Telegram

No. 521 of September 3   LONDON, September 3, 1937—10:39 p.m.
Received September 3 [4?]—1:05 a.m.
Pol. III 4354.

I called on Eden today and asked him for information regarding the projected conference of Mediterranean powers. Eden confirmed the fact that, contrary to the evasive statement of the French Embassy, the initiative had been taken by France. There was agreement between the two powers that England, France, Italy, Yugoslavia, Greece, Turkey, and probably also Albania and Egypt should participate. The newspaper report that the exclusion of Italy was intended was completely false. In addition, the French wanted to invite the Red Spanish Government. England was against this, however, if only because it would be difficult to invite only one of the Spanish Governments.

I asked Eden on what basis the powers had been selected. Eden replied to this that it was desired to limit the conference to the powers bordering on the Mediterranean. In reply to my repeated question why these particular powers had been selected, Eden answered that the reason was certainly not to exclude Germany. He desired to have a conference on practical measures and no political discussion of the past. This would presumably not be possible if, for example, the Soviet Union and Red Spain were represented. At a later stage, however, it was intended to inform all interested parties of the outcome of the deliberations. These nations were then presumably to be given the chance to join. Thus, Holland had already indicated her interest. I stated that I was not informed regarding my Government's stand. As object of the discussions Eden designated measures in the Mediterranean Sea which would make a recurrence of incidents impossible or less likely. He had no definite ideas on the subject as yet. For example, they might consider an agreement not to use submarines in the Mediterranean, and concerted action of the fleets involved.

The conference is to take place outside the League of Nations in Geneva, or, if the Italians object to this, in a neighboring town.

Eden expressed himself cautiously regarding the perpetrators of the attacks on the two British warships. First he stated that he had expressed to the Admiralty the opinion that there was no other possibility than that the British warships had been mistaken for Spanish ships. In the further course of the conversation, however, he dropped the remark that there were several countries which assumed too great risks. Eden went on to say that he considered the situation very serious and that public opinion in England was exceptionally alarmed.

From the conversation I obtained the impression that under certain circumstances Eden might yield to French insistence on the participation of Red Spain.[1]

WOERMANN

---

[1] Marginal note in Neurath's handwriting: "In the event the conference takes place, we must reserve the maintenance of all our rights."

[EDITORS' NOTE. On September 6 the British and French Governments jointly issued invitations to Germany, Italy, the Union of Soviet Socialist Republics, Albania, Yugoslavia, Greece, Turkey, Egypt, Bulgaria, and Rumania to send their representatives to a conference at Nyon, Switzerland, beginning on September 10.]

No. 414

3368/E010494

Memorandum by the Director of the Personnel Department

BERLIN, September 6, 1937.
e.o. Pol. III 4383.

This afternoon the First Secretary of the British Embassy handed me the English text of the invitation to the Mediterranean conference.

He stated by way of explanation that his Government wished to discuss the situation in the Mediterranean only insofar as it concerned the uncertainty which was caused by the attacks of submarines and planes of unknown nationality. All other questions came within the competence of the Non-Intervention Committee and were not to be drawn into the discussions of the conference. Regarding the place of the conference, for which Nyon had been proposed, nothing had been decided; Lausanne or Montreux also were possibilities. The countries bordering on the Black Sea, thus also Soviet Russia, had been invited, because the Black Sea was directly connected with the Mediterranean and so to speak formed a part of it. Mr. Kirkpatrick also confirmed to me that no program for the negotiations had yet been worked out.

Respectfully submitted herewith to the Foreign Minister through the State Secretary.

PRÜFER

No. 415

3368/E010490

Memorandum by the Director of the Personnel Department

BERLIN, September 6, 1937.
e.o. Pol. III 4396.

The Italian Chargé d'Affaires, Count Magistrati, called on me today (at 6:30) and informed me that his Government had received a note from the Soviet Government today at about 5 o'clock in which Italy was held responsible for the torpedoing of a Soviet ship near the Greek coast and in which, first, compensation and, secondly, punishment of the guilty parties were demanded.

The Italian Government had immediately replied to the note and declared that this was a completely arbitrary judgment and that Italy disclaimed all responsibility and disputed the right of the Soviet Government to render a unilateral judgment in the case.

The invitation [to the Mediterranean conference] was to be delivered in Rome at 7 o'clock by the French and British Embassies. A new situation as regards this invitation had arisen as a result of the Russian step. The Italian reply would now be somewhat to the effect that, in view of the Russian note, they would now have to study the invitation, which originally had not been looked upon unfavorably, and ask with whom they would be sitting down at the conference table.

I informed Count Magistrati that Soviet Russia was among those invited. This fact, he thought, would probably make participation on the part of Italy impossible.

Respectfully submitted to the Foreign Minister through the State Secretary.

PRÜFER

No. 416

3368/010489

Memorandum by an Official of Political Division I

URGENT   BERLIN, September 6, 1937.
                                                   e.o. Pol. III 4381.

In a staff meeting of the Foreign Department [*Abteilung Ausland*] of the War Ministry it was decided that action on the Mediterranean conference was primarily a matter of foreign policy and should therefore be left essentially to the Foreign Ministry. The technical questions mainly concern matters affecting the Navy, so that the latter should take care of preparations for the conference.

At the Supreme Command of the Navy I was subsequently told that the following persons were being considered for a delegation that might be sent to Nyon:

1. Rear Admiral Guse
2. Lieutenant Commander Wagner
3. Ministerial Counselor Dr. Eckardt

It was stated in this connection that it would be desirable, in the Navy's opinion, to send a German delegation to the conference.

Herewith respectfully submitted to Counselor of Legation von Kamphoevener.[1]

VON DER HEYDEN-RYNSCH

---

[1] Head of Political Division I.

No. 417

3368/E010499–500

Memorandum to the British and French Embassies

BERLIN, September 9, 1937.
Pol. III 4418.

The German Government has the honor to give the following reply to the proposal of the French and British Governments, conveyed to it on September 6, to call a meeting of the interested powers on September 10 in consequence of the difficulties which have recently arisen in the Mediterranean:

The German Government naturally welcomes every attempt calculated to put an end to the insecurity in the Mediterranean caused by the Civil War in Spain, and would be happy if a way were found to bring about an understanding among the interested powers concerning the joint measures to be taken to that end.   It cannot refrain, however, from recalling that when a few months ago it took the initiative of making a similar proposal it met with an attitude on the part of the French and British Governments which gave it little encouragement to put its faith in new collective agreements in this field.   Although at that time, following the attack on the German pocket battleship *Deutschland*,[1] which entailed such grave consequences, a binding agreement was reached regarding the handling of such cases, the French and British Governments could not see their way, following the immediately subsequent torpedo attack on the German cruiser *Leipzig*,[2] to exhibiting even a minimum of solidarity vis-à-vis the German Government.

Added to this is the fact that, as the German Government has learned, the Government of the Union of Socialist Soviet Republics has deemed it appropriate in recent days in connection with certain incidents in the Mediterranean to level unproved accusations against the Italian Government and link them with far-reaching demands. The German Government concurs with the Italian Government that the latter cannot be expected to take part in a special conference of the sort planned as long as the incident caused by the note of the Government of the Union of Socialist Soviet Republics has not found a satisfactory resolution.

These complicating circumstances notwithstanding, however, the German Government, desirous to give new proofs of its good will, does not wish to cause any delay in the attempt to ease the situation through joint consultation.   It proposes therefore, in accord with the Italian Government, that instead of calling a special conference the London Non-Intervention Committee be authorized to handle the mat-

---

[1] See documents Nos. 267–277, pp. 296–305.
[2] See documents Nos. 339–346, pp. 354–361.

ter, since its sphere of action is very closely related to the issues in question, and since its organization affords the possibility, if all sides show good will, of reaching a prompt settlement. Deliberation in the London committee would also offer the advantage that other interested governments besides those enumerated in the Anglo-French proposal could participate.

No. 418

47/32334

The Foreign Minister to the Embassy in Italy

Telegram

IMMEDIATE   NUREMBERG, September 12, 1937.
STRICTLY SECRET
No. 294

For the Chargé d'Affaires. To be deciphered personally.

Please inform Ciano personally that it appears from a statement made to me by the British Ambassador here that the British have intercepted and deciphered radio messages of Italian submarines operating in the Mediterranean.[1]

NEURATH

---

[1] As appears from marginal notes, the message was sent first to Berlin and dispatched from the Foreign Ministry there as telegram No. 294 of Sept. 13, 12:40 p.m.

[EDITORS' NOTE. An agreement between the representatives of the governments represented at Nyon was reached on September 11, 1937, and the agreement was signed September 14. A summary of the provisions, issued on September 11, may be found in *Survey of International Affairs, 1937*, vol. II, pp. 347–348, and the text was published in the British White Paper, Cmd. 5568 of 1937. A supplementary agreement dealing with attacks by airplanes was signed September 17. Its text was published in the British White Paper, Cmd. 5569 of 1937.]

No. 419

3368/E010531

The Chargé d'Affaires in Spain to the Foreign Ministry

Sa. 3 Ia–3471   SALAMANCA, September 16, 1937.
                                             Pol. III 4524.

Subject: The Nyon agreements.

In the course of a conversation which I had with him yesterday the Italian Ambassador here, Count Viola di Campalto, expressed con-

siderable concern about the probable effects of the Nyon agreements,
which he termed entirely one-sided discrimination in favor of Red
Spain.   The measures for putting a stop to Russian deliveries of war
matériel, which so far had proved exceptionally effective, would in
the future be made extremely difficult if not impossible by the carrying
out of the surveillance decided upon at Nyon.   In view of the increase
in arms on the Red side to be expected as the result of this, the only
remedy would be to increase correspondingly Italian and German
support of Franco in order to prevent the victory of the Spanish
Nationalist cause from being jeopardized.   He hoped that Mussolini's
visit to Germany would also be significant for German-Italian cooperation in this respect.[1]

HEBERLEIN

---

[1] Mussolini's visit to Germany took place Sept. 25–29, 1937.   See vol. I, documents Nos. 1–3, pp. 1–8.

No. 420

3368/E010532

Memorandum by the Director of the Political Department

BERLIN, September 18, 1937.

Pol. III 4540 a.

The Spanish Ambassador asked me today about our stand on the
Nyon arrangement.
I told the Ambassador that we were still occupied in studying the
various points of the Nyon arrangement which concerned us in particular.   We would hardly be interested in having German warships
participate in patrolling the Mediterranean.   Naturally we would let
the Italians take the lead in regard to the further treatment generally
to be accorded the Nyon decisions.

WEIZSÄCKER

No. 421

3368/E010535–36

The Consul at Geneva to the Foreign Ministry

Telegram

URGENT   GENEVA, September 23, 1937—7 : 58 p.m.
No. 90 of September 23   Received September 23—9 : 45 p.m.
Pol. III 4613.

The sensational reports of Geneva and Paris newspapers concerning
alleged negotiations in high policy between Delbos and the Italian
delegate in Geneva [1] do not conform to the facts and are merely the

---

[1] Signor Bova-Scoppa.   On these conferences see also vol. I, document No. 3,
pp. 7–8.

first attempt of Popular Front circles to disturb the atmosphere for Mussolini's visit to Germany. The only element of truth is that Bova-Scoppa received instructions from Rome to counteract once more the rumors concerning Italy's alleged territorial aspirations in Spain spread by the French in Geneva on the occasion of the present Mediterranean negotiations in Paris. The Italian delegate therefore called on Delbos yesterday morning and told him that, contrary to the rumors again being circulated concerning Italy's alleged territorial aspirations in Spain, the Duce's well-known statements retained their full validity. Delbos then asked Minister Bova-Scoppa to call on him once more yesterday afternoon and asked him whether "under the given circumstances the Italian renunciation of territorial acquisitions in Spain might not be made still more specific." Bova replied that the Duce's statements did not need any supplementation since they were entirely clear and were valid for the future too. Bova declared that all other accounts of his conversations with Delbos were malicious inventions intended to interfere with Mussolini's visit to Germany and with the growing relaxation of tension in the Mediterranean. I was informed today by an authoritative Turkish source that in the negotiations with the naval experts in Paris it was intended to establish three patrol zones in the Mediterranean and thus to give the Italians full equality of rights. Presumably the French zone would comprise the western, the Italian the central, and the British the eastern Mediterranean. The Turkish delegate asserted that the Balkan Entente, under Turkish leadership, was advocating full equality of rights for Italy in the Mediterranean conference and termed the Paris negotiations, though outwardly of a purely technical character, a marked political victory for Italy, to which great importance would have to be ascribed in the political situation as a whole in case an accord was reached in Paris.

KRAUEL

No. 422

3368/E010544–48

The Chargé d'Affaires in France to the Foreign Ministry

A 3606   PARIS, September 25, 1937.
                                           Pol. III 4707.

Subject: French-Italian policy; Nyon conference.

French policy regards Italy from two standpoints. France considers Italy an impetuous neighbor and frequently, because of her large population and her aggressive leadership, a troublesome one for French possessions in the Mediterranean and North Africa. However, she also sees in Italy a factor in world politics, whose political and military weight she wishes to have on her side in any European conflict. As long as French policy assumes Germany to be the main enemy in Europe, France will try to prevent close German-Italian cooperation, or, if such should nevertheless come about, to disrupt it. In order not to forfeit a future alliance which might become necessary, France has always carefully handled friction arising from proximity with Italy and has always avoided taking an open stand against Italy. In the Abyssinian question, in spite of her commitments to the League of Nations, she took an attitude of mediation, one which helped the Italians as far as possible. In 1935 Laval was able to side-step the British proposal for joint political and military action directed against Italy in the Mediterranean. During the Anglo-Italian tension France avoided everything that might aggravate the differences. In the Spanish question even the Popular Front Government refrained from making any open and direct attack on Italy, although there is a lively ideological opposition to Fascist Italy in Popular Front circles and although French interests seemed greatly endangered. In safeguarding French interests France has always considered Italian sensibilities. Thus she took account of Italy's dislike for the League of Nations by establishing the Non-Intervention Committee outside Geneva, and before the Nyon conference also moved away from the aggressive Soviet attitude toward Italy.

In spite of all care and consideration, French policy could not prevent French-Italian relations from becoming more and more tense in the Mediterranean area common to both countries as well as in general European politics. Italy did not agree to settling the Spanish question in the manner advocated by Britain and France. The growing Italian influence in Spain touches immediate and vital French interests (Spanish Morocco, communication between France and her North African colonies). For a while the Anglo-Italian tension seemed headed toward settlement without French mediation. But what alarms France above all is cooperation between Rome and Berlin. All attempts to make Italy understand that she was separated from Germany by insuperable differences of interest in central Europe remained unsuccessful. The fear that Germany and Italy might even agree on central Europe increased. And France was and still is too much hindered in her political freedom of movement by the war in Spain to participate with full attention in central Europe. Sooner or later a way out had to be found. The idea suggested itself to try, in accordance with the tactics followed so far, to divorce the geopolitical problem of proximity in the Mediterranean, in which Spain can also be included, from the general political problem, thus settling the one group of questions in order to obtain a free hand for the other. The question was, however, how this could be done without offending Italian prestige, provoking Italy, and thus pushing her even closer to Germany.

In this situation the sinking of several freighters in the Mediterranean by unidentified submarines was not unwelcome. By attributing general significance to these isolated incidents they cleverly created a basis for appearing as the representative and champion of injured international law, strengthening their own power in the Mediterranean as they wished and putting Italy in a position in which participation or refusal alike would result equally in limiting her previous freedom of action. The very fact that the question was represented as a general problem was intended to make it more difficult for Italy to refuse her participation. How could Italy oppose a discussion concerning suppression of the "pirate pest"? How could she complain about the calling of a conference in which she had been invited to participate on an equal basis and to which, out of consideration for Italy, the *Temps* emphasized, Germany had also been invited although she was not a Mediterranean power?

If the invitation was accepted, Italy was thereby involved in a discussion which she had previously tried to evade. The initial rejection of the invitation was probably not unwelcome here, for that meant the agreement could quickly be concluded along Anglo-French lines and Italy could be confronted with an accomplished fact. This, to be sure, first created a critical situation for a few days. If Italy had flatly refused to accede to the agreement, events of great consequence might have resulted. Of course, Anglo-French policy would have been in a position to provoke or avoid incidents as needed, to make light of them or to magnify them, but it would not have been master of everything happening in the Mediterranean. From conversations here I have gained the impression that this risk was taken deliberately. Italy's accession in principle has eliminated this danger for the time being.

The Nyon results are evaluated more or less as follows from the French point of view:

The military potential of France and England in the Mediterranean has been strengthened to such a degree that French interests seem assured even from a military point of view. Political and military cooperation with Britain in the Mediterranean, which Laval had avoided, has now become a fact. All states bordering on the Mediterranean have at the very least been neutralized in relation to Italy in case of a conflict. These results were achieved without France having to take an open position against Italy and without the strengthening of the power potential appearing as an anti-Italian demonstration; for Italy was explicitly invited beforehand to work out the agreement and later to accede to it.

France thereby hopes to have confirmed the confidence of the small states in French strength and to have brought Italy to realize that she cannot expect any decisive support from Germany in the Mediterranean.

The most important gain, however, is considered to be the fact that Italy, following her accession at Nyon, is for the first time in a long while again negotiating directly with France. The Delbos - Bova-Scoppa conversations were accordingly exaggerated and represented as a sensational event. They hope to be able to expand the discussions into three-power talks among Italy, England, and France, to clarify in this manner other pending questions also, especially the Spanish problem, and to exclude both Germany and the Soviet Union from the discussion for the time being.

The further tactics vis-à-vis Italy cannot yet be discerned with certainty. The lifting of the patrol around Spain does not yet give a definite clue. It is evident, however, that French as well as British policy vis-à-vis Italy seems to be getting sharper lately, not in tone, to be sure, but in effect. This probably involves no move equivalent to an ultimatum, however, but an attempt at the same time to win over Italy through concessions, if possible. How far these concessions are to go is not evident at the present time. Probably it is not seriously believed in France either that recognition of the Italian Empire and even granting of belligerent rights to Franco could bring about a change in the current Italian policy in Spain. The question therefore arises whether another offer, perhaps of an economic nature, might not be in preparation by France and England. This is probably what Pertinax[1] is alluding to when he emphasizes again and again lately that Britain and France would not be niggardly in clearing up old difficulties, if they could be convinced of Italy's desire for peace.

That the Anglo-French invitation to three-power talks was issued precisely on the day of Mussolini's departure for Berlin was surely no accident. Also the somewhat nervous activity of French policy during the past weeks and the all too obvious reference to alleged improvement in the French-Italian atmosphere betray the intention, openly admitted by a part of the press, to dissuade Mussolini from further *rapprochement* with Germany and to create doubts in Germany concerning the reliability of Italian friendship. In my opinion, however, one underestimates the significance of the events if one regards them merely as maneuvers calculated to interfere with Mussolini's visit. Rather, the developments of the recent past suggest the question whether French Mediterranean policy and, together with it, British policy may not be about to enter a new phase.

FORSTER

---

[1] André Géraud, writer on foreign affairs for the *Echo de Paris*.

No. 423
3374/E010958–59

The Chargé d'Affaires in Great Britain to the Foreign Ministry

Telegram

No. 566 of September 28   LONDON, September 28, 1937—9 : 12 p.m.
                               Received September 28—11 : 10 p.m.

With reference to our No. 564 of September 27.[1]

In the Foreign Office I have heard the following about alleged British-French-Italian discussions regarding the Spanish question: The British and French Governments have not yet approached the Italian Government. Discussions with France on this have not been concluded. The intention to approach Italy actually is held. The discussions, however, are to take place not in the form of a three-power conference, but through the usual diplomatic channels. The purpose is to determine the real intentions of the Italians in regard to the Spanish question, particularly in the matter of volunteers, and to try to come to an agreement. I said that my personal impression from the newspaper accounts was that it was desired to set up a Stresa front in regard to the Spanish question. In reply it was stated in the Foreign Office that the reason for the contemplated procedure was that a question was involved which concerned mainly Italy. The Non-Intervention Committee had not proved to be a suitable place for the discussion of delicate questions, since all matters were made public there.[2]

WOERMANN

---

[1] Not printed (3368/E010542).
[2] Marginal note in Neurath's handwriting: "Mussolini and Ciano told me today that they had rejected the plan of Paris and London to arrange a conference to discuss the question of volunteers. The inquiry had been made only unofficially so far."

No. 424
3374/E010962–63

The Chargé d'Affaires in Great Britain to the Foreign Ministry

Telegram

No. 568 of September 29   LONDON, September 29, 1937—3 : 53 p.m.
                               Received September 29—5 : 35 p.m.
                               Pol. III 4679.

With reference to our telegraphic report No. 566 of September 28.

I have heard from a well-informed source that Chamberlain takes a lively interest in the contemplated Anglo-French step in Rome in regard to the Spanish question and that he fully approves of the policy initiated. From this source the impression gained here from other sources has been confirmed, that the intended step is not a usual routine diplomatic performance, but that England and France want to compel Italy to reach a decision upon which they will make their own future non-intervention policy depend.

Yesterday in the Foreign Office the Italian Counselor of Embassy, without specific instructions to that effect, urged that they exchange views with Rome before sending such a note. He took the position that a note sent to Rome without diplomatic preparation would necessarily result in failure. During the intended Anglo-Italian discussions, which were to take place soon after Lord Perth's return, there would be sufficient opportunity to discuss Spain also. The Counselor of Embassy had no definite impression as to what "the reaction was to his suggestions."

WOERMANN

No. 425

3374/E010964

The Foreign Minister to the Embassy in Great Britain

Telegram

No. 382 BERLIN, September 30, 1937.
zu Pol. III 4679 I.

With reference to your No. 568 of September 29.

For the Chargé d'Affaires.

In case you should be asked for your opinion regarding the contemplated step, please for your part take the position that diplomatic preparation in Rome would be advisable before sending the note to the Italian Government, in order to prevent unfavorable repercussions.

NEURATH

No. 426

3206/697733

The Ambassador in Great Britain to the Foreign Ministry

LONDON, October 2, 1937.
Pol. III 4736.

Subject: Spanish Non-Intervention Committee. Negative Soviet Russian note on the Dulm-Hemming report.

In the statement of the Soviet Union on the Dulm-Hemming report,[1] to which a special significance attaches, the Soviet Union takes the

---

[1] See Editors' Note, p. 436.

stand that the ending of the naval patrol renders the remainder of the naval surveillance meaningless. Without naval surveillance, control measures on land are impossible. At the same time, however, the Soviet Union makes the continuance of the non-intervention policy dependent upon the maintenance of effective control. It is therefore not excluded that in the end, upon Russian initiative, the policy of non-intervention cannot be continued. The positive stand which Germany intends taking on the report is calculated to fix the blame for a possible collapse of non-intervention clearly upon the Soviet Union.

By direction:
WOERMANN

[EDITORS' NOTE. On October 2 a joint Anglo-French note was presented in Rome which invited the Italian Government to examine with Great Britain and France "in a spirit of perfect frankness the situation arising from the prolongation of the Spanish conflict." It referred to the difficulties which had been encountered in the question of the withdrawal of volunteers and expressed the opinion that an agreement between these three powers would be necessary to overcome these obstacles.]

No. 427

3374/E010992

Memorandum by the Head of Political Division III

BERLIN, October 4, 1937.
zu Pol. III 4762.

In a conversation with the French Ambassador, whom I met at a reception Saturday evening, I brought up the subject of the Anglo-French note on the Spanish question which had been delivered to the Italian Government. M. François-Poncet stated emphatically that this was a case of an *Italian* initiative. In reply to my question as to the basis of his statement, he expressed himself as follows: The conversations that Delbos and Bova-Scoppa had had in Geneva were based by no means on a French but rather on an Italian initiative. After Italy had of her own volition desired an agreement of a technical nature with Paris and London on the Spanish question, it had seemed to the Governments in Paris and London to follow that this conversation among the three of them should also be extended to the political side of the matter. To my question as to whether he expected any results from the Anglo-French note, M. François-Poncet replied in the negative, stating that he thought the situation was more likely to deteriorate.

Submitted herewith to Ministerialdirektor Baron von Weizsäcker.

D[UMONT]

Note by the State Secretary: The Frenchman recently told me exactly the same thing. I replied that we were of a different opinion with respect to the Bova-Scoppa - Delbos conversation.

M[ACKENSEN] Oct. 5.

No. 428

428/218467–68

Memorandum by the State Secretary

BERLIN, October 4, 1937.

The Italian Ambassador called on me today to give an oral commentary on the Anglo-French note addressed to the Italian Government, which he had sent me earlier in the day. Thus far the Italian Government had confined itself, as we already knew, to the reply delivered orally to the two Chargés d'Affaires by Ciano, that Mussolini had left Rome and therefore could not decide at once. Attolico sees in this a clear proof of his Government's desire to treat the whole matter in a rather dilatory way.

As far as the text of the actual reply is concerned, it was the intention in Rome, the Ambassador stated further, to base it on two points:

1. The question broached in the note came under the exclusive jurisdiction of the Non-Intervention Committee.

2. Any discussion of the matter without Germany's participation was out of the question.

Attolico asked me to inform the Foreign Minister of the above and added that his Government would, moreover, be grateful for any "suggestion" with respect to the content of the reply. I told him that I would transmit his message at once to the Foreign Minister, from whom I could expect to receive a decision tomorrow. If I might make a personal comment on the matter, I had really expected that the Italians would emphasize a different point of view in their reply, namely, the one *we* had always primarily stressed: the decision on the question of the withdrawal of volunteers lay primarily with Franco and Valencia. Not until we had received the statement of their opinion was there any object in discussing it in other circles. Attolico said that this idea was very worthy of consideration and thought that the reply now contemplated by Ciano was attributable to the fact that he had wanted to word it as much as possible like that first reaction to the step taken by the British and French in Rome immediately after Mussolini's departure. As we knew, Ciano immediately had sent from the train a telegram of curt refusal with similar content.

MACKENSEN

No. 429

3374/E010996–97

Memorandum by an Official of the Foreign Minister's Secretariat

BERLIN, October 5, 1937.
zu Pol. III 4785.

The Foreign Minister has sent the following communication through Amtsrat Köppen:

For the time being the Foreign Minister has no further proposals to make with regard to the Italian reply. In his personal opinion, the main emphasis should be placed on affirming once more that the question of the volunteers can be taken up only after the attitude of General Franco and the Valencia Government has become known.[1]

MARCHTALER

---

[1] Marginal note: "I informed the Italian Ambassador of the above by telephone this evening, and he will report to Rome accordingly this very evening. M[ackensen], Oct. 5."

No. 430

3374/E010995

The Foreign Ministry to the Embassies in Great Britain, Italy, and Spain

BERLIN, September [1] [*October*] 5, 1937.
Pol. III 4772.

For information.

The French Ambassador stated in a conversation with the State Secretary that the Italians had not proceeded logically in the matter of the three-power conference. If they now made difficulties, that was in contradiction to what Bova-Scoppa had said earlier in Geneva. The idea of such a conference had really originated with him. It was also false if the Italians now represented the conference idea as an attempt to undermine the solidarity of the Rome-Berlin Axis.

The State Secretary replied to the French Ambassador that this interpretation did not seem to him personally to be so very far-fetched, but it was an attempt which was condemned to failure from the outset. Moreover, we regarded the development of this question with complete calm, in view of the impressions received in the conversations just ended, which had left the fullest confidence on both sides that neither of us if involved in discussions with third parties would forget the interests of the other.

By direction:
DUMONT

---

[1] Evidently a typist's error. The document was initialed by Dumont and dispatched on Oct. 5.

No. 431

3374/E011000

The Chargé d'Affaires in Great Britain to the Foreign Ministry

Telegram

URGENT
No. 582 of October 7

LONDON, October 7, 1937—9 : 36 p.m.
Received October 8—1 : 00 a.m.
Pol. III 4795.

With reference to your telegram 388 of October 7.[1]

The French are today circulating the following version of the Spanish question:

France had indications from Rome to the effect that the Italian Government would reply with a counterproposal for conversations to include Germany or referral to the Non-Intervention Committee. France regarded such a reply as a rejection of the Anglo-French note.

Corbin yesterday had proposed to the British Government answering with measures in ascending series, the first to be the opening of the French border.

According to the same source, Eden is said to have agreed in principle after consulting Chamberlain.

In the Foreign Office journalists were refused information as to the conditions under which a reply would be considered unsatisfactory and the measures which might then be taken. On the other hand, it was confirmed that accord had been reached between England and France regarding the reaction to an unsatisfactory reply from Rome.

Finally, I hear from a reliable source that after another Anglo-French step is taken in Rome today, a last appeal is to consist of the speech which Chamberlain is making at the Conservative Party Congress at Scarborough Friday evening.[2]

WOERMANN

---

[1] This telegram transmitted a report from Ambassador Hassell in Rome stating that the Italian reply to the Anglo-French note would be negative and would allege the grounds already discussed between State Secretary Mackensen and Ambassador Attolico on Oct. 4. See document No. 428, p. 452.
[2] Oct. 8, 1937.

No. 432

428/218472

The Chargé d'Affaires in Great Britain to the Foreign Ministry

[Telegram]

No. 581 of October 7   LONDON, October 7, 1937.

Pol. III 4808.

With reference to telegraphic instruction No. 385 of October 4.[1]

The competent official in the Foreign Office gave the following strictly confidential information regarding the establishment in England of Spanish Nationalist consulates of a semiofficial character:

General Franco had made such a request of the British Government as early as the beginning of September. The British Government had recently replied to this via Hendaye and had given its consent in principle to the dispatching of agents of a semiofficial character who were to enjoy neither the title of consul nor diplomatic privileges but should in effect possess the duties and rights of a consul. Final consent was made conditional, however, upon a satisfactory solution of certain questions. Inquiry revealed that among them were presumably the following:

Release of certain British ships, unhampered activity of the British consuls in Nationalist Spain, and solution of some economic questions.

Franco had further been promised that a British commercial agent would be sent to Salamanca.

WOERMANN

---

[1] Not printed (428/218464).

No. 433

435/220516

Memorandum by the State Secretary

BERLIN, October 8, 1937.

I telephoned the Italian Ambassador today to inform him that we agreed to the text of the Italian reply to the French and British as drafted.[1]

Signor Attolico thanked me for the information and then asked whether we were also prepared, in case the note met with a favorable reception—which was hardly to be expected—to participate in future developments in accordance with paragraph 6.[2] I told the Ambassador that I personally entertained no doubts on this score, particularly

---

[1] In the files is a German translation of the proposed Italian reply (3374/E011009–12).

[2] Paragraph 6 of the draft referred to in the preceding footnote read: "The Fascist Government in conclusion states that it will in no case take part in conversations, meetings, or conferences to which the German Government is not also formally invited and in which that Government does not also take part."

since it then lay more or less within our power, too, to determine the course of developments. I would, however, consult my colleagues here in the Ministry and then call him again.

MACKENSEN

No. 434

435/220521

The Ambassador in Italy to the Foreign Ministry

Telegram

No. 273 of October 8   ROME (QUIRINAL), October 8, 1937—9 : 25 p.m.
Received October 9—12 : 05 a.m.

In a discussion of the Italian reply, which has been communicated to Berlin, Ciano told me today that it would now become evident whether Britain and France were bluffing and in reality desired an agreement, or whether France was actually striving to end non-intervention. The situation was certainly not rosy and was not improved by the American attacks. Nevertheless, he was inclined to believe that England and America, in any case, basically did not desire a conflict. On the French side, to be sure, an increasing sharpness in tone had become noticeable of late, while the British always indicated a desire for an amicable settlement. Of course, the Anglo-Italian conversations were again adjourned for the present after the British Ambassador had delivered a friendly memorandum in which the suggestion was made first to await the clarification of the present situation, which was especially complicated by the Spanish question. I informed Ciano of the contents of your telegraphic instruction No. 315 of October 7,[1] which he found very interesting since it was entirely new to him. He promised to make inquiries and to inform me of the results.

In order not to aggravate the situation, Ciano declared that now, after the departure of the latest reinforcements, no more volunteers would be sent and the Nationalist submarines would be held back; the torpedo attack on the *Basilisk* must have been done by the Reds.

Bastico, the leader of the Italian volunteers in Spain, who had proved his mettle but was hard to get along with, was being replaced by Berti, his former deputy, because of conflict with Franco.

HASSELL

---

[1] Not printed (5066/E292186–87).

No. 435

4445/E086245

Spanish Decree of October 9, 1937, on Mining Concessions [1]

Article I. Until provision is made to the contrary, all acts disposing of mining property, or the purchase, sale, or transfer of shares in mining companies or leases, shall be suspended.

Article II. All titles to mining property, leases, exchanges, sales, or purchase of material, or of properties used in the exploitation of mines or the immediate processing of their products, obtained since July 18, 1936, are declared to be null and void.

Article III. Any arrangements contrary to this decree are dissolved.

Issued at Burgos on the 9th of October, 1937, Second Year of Triumph.

FRANCISCO FRANCO

---

[1] Translated from the Spanish official text published Oct. 12, 1937, a copy of which was found in the files of the German Embassy in Spain.

No. 436

435/220529

The Chargé d'Affaires in Great Britain to the Foreign Ministry

Telegram

No. 593 of October 13   LONDON, October 13, 1937—7 : 55 p.m.
                                       Received October 13—11 : 00 p.m.

I hear from the Foreign Office that the newspaper reports that England and France are agreeable to having the question of volunteers brought before the Non-Intervention Committee are correct. No date has yet been set, but an early meeting is expected, perhaps even Friday of this week or Monday of next week. I shall report further on Thursday.

In my opinion, an unprepared discussion in the Non-Intervention Committee is dangerous. A certain amount of diplomatic preparation would be much more advisable. Leadership in the committee should probably be left to the Italian Embassy.

Please send instructions in general terms for all eventualities, also as to whether the question of volunteers is to be linked by us to the old counterdemands, particularly to the question of belligerent rights. Previous discussion with the British Government would be urgently desirable in this case especially.

The Italian Embassy here likewise lacks detailed information regarding its Government's intentions.

WOERMANN

No. 437

435/220527–28

The Ambassador in France to the Foreign Ministry

Telegram

No. 602 of October 13   PARIS, October 13, 1937.
                                        Received October 14—1 : 00 a.m.

For France the Spanish problem divides itself more and more distinctly into two groups of questions. One concerns the Spanish Civil War directly, that is, the struggle between White and Red. Here French policy is as uncertain as ever because there are conflicting sympathies and because the view of the French Government differs from that of the British Government: The former is against a White victory, the latter increasingly against a Red victory.

The second group of questions concerns the preservation of Spain's territorial integrity, that is, preventing Italy from establishing herself in the Balearics, on the mainland, or in Spanish Morocco. In the opinion of the French Government, vital interests in connection with the transport of troops from North Africa and the French position in the Mediterranean are involved. In this, public opinion was solidly behind the Government and the British interests were in agreement with the French. France cannot yield here; in fact, the French attitude is becoming more and more firm. Nevertheless, French tactics even on the last question have thus far been cautious. The French Government made constant efforts to avoid provoking the Italian Government and to gain by negotiation the objective of protecting Spain's territorial integrity. Recently there have appeared indications that the French Government had reached the point where it considered its previous tactics ineffective and considered it necessary to use much sharper language (proposal of the three-power conference on Spain, statements on the opening of the French frontier with Red Spain). Although these indications have taken very definite shape, the probability of an imminent change in French tactics was already viewed with skepticism in report A 3602 of September 28.[1] This judgment seems to be confirmed today. Although the last Italian reply was regarded here as a flat refusal and subjected to very unfriendly criticism, the impression prevails today that this time no recourse will be taken to the measures threatened in case of a negative Italian stand or to the language of an ultimatum. Comments in the press would indicate, rather, that the French Government will for the present postpone the formal opening of the Red Spanish border and, together with the British, once more accede in some form or other to the Italian proposal for negotiations. For the last point the con-

----

[1] Not printed (3374/E010978–80).

sideration mentioned at the outset may be decisive, namely, that the opening of the border could today lead not only to internal political difficulties but also to difficulties with England. In addition, it is believed that the opening of the border would now no longer have so strong and, in any case, so immediate an effect as had previously been assumed or asserted.

In some newspapers there is also talk today of an Anglo-French occupation of Minorca or of an Anglo-French naval demonstration off Minorca. I consider the first entirely incredible at present; but it is not to be entirely excluded that several French and British ships which are in the western Mediterranean in accordance with the Nyon agreement might assemble off Minorca as a warning to Italy against the occupation allegedly intended by her. The French might be inclined to push this measure, which would be in line with their guiding principle of safeguarding Spain's territorial integrity, because they believed that they could carry it out without attracting too much attention.

WELCZECK

No. 438

3362/E009769–71

The State Secretary to the Embassy in Great Britain

Telegram

No. 398

BERLIN, October 14, 1937.
Pol. III 4892, Ang. II.

With reference to your telegram 593 of October 13 and our telegram No. 397 of today.[1]

In discussing the subject of volunteers in the Non-Intervention Committee, please, as you yourself suggested, let the Italian Embassy take the lead. Naturally you will have to give support.

You can take the position that the rejection of the three-power conference on the question of volunteers, proposed in Rome by London and Paris, was, among other things, due to the fact that the Italians at the present stage of the Spanish conflict wished to avoid an intimate conversation on the question of supporting Franco. Likewise, no value is attached to further general debate on the recall of volunteers nor to a repetition of the futile discussions in the committee. The tactical objective of exposing Russian obstructionism was adequately realized in the committee this past summer.

Without expressly dropping our former counterdemands, we therefore raise no objections but now advocate asking the Spanish parties how they stand on the withdrawal of volunteers (see telegraphic

---

[1] Latter not printed (435/220530).

instruction 326 of August 4 [2]).   Valencia's alleged promises to deport
the volunteers, not yet officially known to us, are naturally not to be
considered sufficient.   They should, rather, be made much more specific.   It remains to be clarified by what criteria the selection of volunteers to be deported would be made, what countries would be ready
to receive them—particularly those who had meanwhile become naturalized in Red Spain—and what security would be given for their
effective deportation and against their return to Spanish territory.
We shall, if the occasion arises, try to exert the necessary influence
toward a suitable reply from the Franco Government.

Should the idea of first experimentally deporting a small number
of volunteers be brought up again, no objections in principle should
be raised against it, but on this point also the Spanish parties should
be allowed the first word.

Rome has been informed from here.

MACKENSEN

---

[2] Not printed (428/218365–66).

No. 439

435/220535

*The Minister Counselor of Embassy in Great Britain to the Foreign
Ministry*

Telegram

URGENT   LONDON, October 15, 1937—3 : 11 p.m.
No. 597 of October 15   Received October 15—5 : 35 p.m.

I had a conversation with Grandi, who received the following
communication from Eden regarding British intentions at the Saturday session:

1. Acceptance of the British plan of July 9 as a basis of negotiations (see document 599 [1]).

2. Immediate, symbolic withdrawal of a part of the volunteers;
Eden suggested a ratio of 3 : 2 in favor of the Reds, without committing himself to this.   Grandi thereupon replied that in that case it
would be necessary to ascertain the number of volunteers on both
sides.

3. Support of the committee's resolutions vis-à-vis the belligerent
parties.

4. A renewed solemn pledge not to send any volunteers or matériel
to Spain.   The word "volunteer" is in this connection to be construed
in the broadest sense.

In speaking to Grandi, Eden once again termed the British proposal
a last attempt.   Grandi did not enter into a detailed discussion for

---

[1] Of the Non-Intervention Committee.

want of instructions. He intimated to Eden an acceptance in principle but made any settlement of course contingent upon unanimity for the resolutions in the committee, in order, in this way, to be able to pin the responsibility on the Soviet Union in case the latter persisted in her negative attitude.

Today, too, Grandi had no instructions from his Government. I informed him of the content and purport of telegraphic instruction 398.[2] Grandi agreed with the inclination to take a positive line and will inform his Government accordingly. He will probably receive the British proposals only in order to report them.

WOERMANN

_____

[2] Document No. 438, p. 459.

No. 440

2946/576037–39

The Foreign Ministry to the Embassy in Spain

BERLIN, October 16, 1937.
W II WE 6664.

With reference to the Anglo-Spanish economic negotiations.

According to the pouch reports from the Embassy on September 27, Sa. 3 I c–3569,[1] and on September 30, Sa. 10 B–3693,[2] as well as telegraphic report No. 495 of October 11,[3] Spain intends to enter into negotiations with the British agent to be sent to Spain concerning arrangement of an economic *modus vivendi.* In so doing she had no thought of "prejudicing her future trade relations in any way by an economic agreement with England."

Despite this limited subject matter, the Anglo-Spanish negotiations require our attention.

Even if we may assume that General Franco does not intend to satisfy England's wishes to the detriment of Germany's interests, nevertheless any negotiations by Spain with a third country are potentially dangerous to the position of preeminence which we have won in Spain in the economic field. This is especially true with relation to England; for German and British interests, as is well known, confront one another on Spanish soil, particularly in the case of iron ores, which are especially important for Germany, and also in the case of copper and pyrites, so that it requires a special effort to maintain as long and as fully as possible the preeminence we have won with regard to these raw materials.

That England cannot permanently be kept from the Spanish market as in the past is a fact with which we have to reckon. England's old

_____

[1] Not printed (3359/E009550–51).
[2] Not found.
[3] Not printed (3359/E009557).

relations with the Spanish mines and the Generalissimo's desire, based on political and economic considerations, to come to an understanding with England place certain limits on our chances of reserving Spanish raw materials to ourselves permanently.   Moreover, we also have an interest in not having the competition between us and England in the Spanish market lead to unnecessary tension.   It is therefore a question of finding a settlement while preserving our advantage to the greatest possible extent.

In order to be able to do this successfully we must first be informed in time and as fully as possible as to the subject matter of the negotiations.

In view of the good relations with Spain, it is to be assumed that General Franco will readily accede to such a request; in case of need, however, we could also invoke the promises of the Franco Government. The restrictions on her freedom of movement in concluding economic agreements with third countries, which Spain accepted in the protocol of December 31, 1936,[4] and later in the secret protocol of July 12, 1937 (consultative pact),[5] were demanded and put through by us in no small measure in order to safeguard the supplies of the above-mentioned raw materials.   To be sure, the protocol of July 12 states that "comprehensive economic negotiations" should be held with Germany before any other country and that, in case *such* negotiations had to be concluded with a third country sooner than with Germany, she should be given the opportunity to make her wishes known in time. With this wording, the objection could be raised that the consultative pact was not applicable to the Spanish-British negotiations, because "comprehensive" economic negotiations were not intended.   Nevertheless the consultative pact is applicable if we consider its intent. It was concluded with the express intention of "placing economic cooperation on a firm basis for the future, too."   The purpose of the agreement would be defeated, however, if, by special adjustments in the separate fields important to us, we, as a purchasing country, were forced step by step out of the market.   What matters in the case of a *modus vivendi*, therefore, is its substance rather than its scope.   Even the granting of rights with a time limit would not be without danger, since possession once conceded is difficult to nullify and therefore prejudicial in its effect.

Please keep us informed of the course of the Anglo-Spanish negotiations and intervene to protect German purchasing interests, even without special instructions, in case they seem directly menaced.

By direction:
BENZLER

---

[4] Document No. 180, p. 199.
[5] Document No. 392, p. 413.

No. 441

3362/E009780–84

The Chargé d'Affaires in Great Britain to the Foreign Ministry

Airgram

No. 604 of October 17   LONDON, October 17, 1937.

Received October 17—11 : 00 p.m.

Procedure for Tuesday's session of the Non-Intervention Committee could not yet be discussed with Grandi because of the week end. The following points of view should be considered in determining our attitude:

1. In the question of volunteers a French proposal provides for three stages:

(*a*) Withdrawal of a certain number of volunteers (so-called symbolic withdrawal). The French proposal does not provide for any concession in return.

(*b*) The beginning of complete withdrawal. As soon as a commission has determined that withdrawal "is proceeding on an adequate scale," the Spanish parties are to be accorded limited belligerent rights.

(*c*) Complete withdrawal of all volunteers. It is not clear from the French proposal at what stage control measures are to be restored in accordance with the van Dulm - Hemming report. It appears from paragraph 5 of the proposal that this would take place as soon as possible. No direct connection is made with other points, particularly the question of volunteers.

2. We should in any case lay value on having control measures instituted at the very moment when the first contingent of volunteers is withdrawn. Control measures would therefore have to be resumed, at the latest, at the moment of the first "symbolic" withdrawal.

3. Perhaps we need not make a symbolic withdrawal contingent upon the *prior* granting of belligerent rights. The statements made by Grandi and Ambassador von Ribbentrop leave the door open here also.

4. There would probably be no risk involved in deciding immediately, as early as at Tuesday's session, without a promise of a concession in return, to approach the Spanish parties on the subject of a symbolic withdrawal, in accordance with the supplementary Italian proposal. There are two approaches, and these can also be combined. Either we can leave it entirely to Franco first to state his conditions for a symbolic withdrawal, and effect our wishes in this way, or we can make our desires known, at least partially, as early as at Tuesday's session. Even for a symbolic withdrawal, a number of additional agreements naturally will be needed.

(*a*) The conflict will surely revolve around the questions of the proportionate shares and the size of the first contingent. Probably none of the governments is in a position to furnish conclusive material regarding the number of volunteers on both sides. If only for this reason, we would adhere to the demand for withdrawal of an equal number on both sides, at least for the first symbolic withdrawal.

(*b*) As far as the number is concerned, newspaper reports speak of 3,000 or 5,000 men on each side. This number seems too high for a symbolic withdrawal. Perhaps, to name some sort of figure, we could suggest 500 on each side. What is the highest figure which could be conceded?

(*c*) We would also have to discuss the manner of the first withdrawal, which might be easier than agreements on further withdrawals. Plymouth has already suggested sending one ship to each of the parties with a certain number of officer-observers aboard, who could be charged with supervising the withdrawal on the spot. There would probably be no difficulties on this point.

5. Discussion of further withdrawals would thus, according to this plan, be undertaken only when the answer of the two parties regarding the symbolic withdrawal had been received. It is not necessary, therefore, to start considering this matter today.

6. The French desire for a new pledge not to send any volunteers or aviation matériel is probably acceptable. Have we any interest in bringing up the question as to why the French proposal refers to aviation matériel but not to other arms and munitions?

In summary, our proposal would therefore look somewhat as follows:

(*a*) Deliberations on the establishment of the control measures will start on Monday and will be expedited so that control measures will go into effect, at the latest, when the first contingent of volunteers leaves.

(*b*) At the Tuesday session the pledge to send no volunteers or air matériel, provided for in paragraph 4 of the French proposal, will be renewed.

(*c*) Otherwise we shall, in the matter of a symbolic withdrawal, advance only our wishes as regards the number involved and the manner of execution. It could perhaps be left to the Embassy to decide, as the course of the negotiations may indicate, whether and to what extent these desires should be made known through Franco or in part here, too.

(*d*) Naturally the demand for belligerent rights remains. This would have to be explicitly stated at Tuesday's session. This could best be done by making a German or Italian proposal to the effect that, in contrast to the French plan, belligerent rights be granted at the moment when a symbolic withdrawal takes place.

8. These proposals take into account the fact that it must be regarded as very dubious whether Franco really desires the withdrawal of volunteers. It cannot be ascertained here whether he, for his part, agrees to the proposal of a symbolic withdrawal or intends to make it contingent upon conditions that would be unacceptable to the other side.

9. It can probably be assumed from the attitude of the Soviet Ambassador at the Saturday session and the Russian reply to the van Dulm - Hemming plan that the Russians are continuing their obstructionist tactics. We could therefore probably play our hand so that the French plan would also fail because of the Soviet Russian attitude. Our prior performance of symbolic withdrawal is of no great moment here, since there are probably a great number of wounded and sick on Franco's side, too, and in practice the withdrawal could begin with them.

Another possibility would be to take up the Portuguese suggestion to reach agreement of all the powers without the Soviet Union. This would naturally be politically advantageous, since it would lead to a clear isolation of the Soviet Union. It would require that, even after the symbolic withdrawal, we continue to collaborate to a certain extent on the French plan. Agreement of the powers without Russia would be conceivable only if there were certain assurance that in that case unilateral Soviet Russian support via the sea could in the main be suppressed. This cannot be judged from here.

We are of the opinion here that the better course would be to leave the Soviet Union in the game as a troublemaker, since we would then more readily find an alibi in difficult situations, and, if the particular circumstances render it desirable, we could more easily pursue dilatory tactics than in the case of the second possibility.

WOERMANN

No. 442

3362/E009785–89

The Foreign Minister to the Embassy in Great Britain

Airgram

TODAY
By air mail

BERLIN, October 18, 1937.
zu Pol. III 4937.

With reference to your No. 604 of October 17.

At the coming negotiations of the Non-Intervention Committee please continue to allow the Italian representative to take the lead, since Italian interests predominate in accordance with Italy's greater commitments. By following the Italians and supporting them with your arguments, you will adequately document the German-Italian united front.

Here, too, it seems entirely desirable that first of all a symbolic step be taken by withdrawal from Spain of a limited contingent of volunteers. Such a procedure would serve to relieve the general tension and would not interfere with our Spanish policy. The symbolic gesture contemplated will then also provide sufficient practical experience for the plan of a general withdrawal of the volunteers.

I wish to comment in detail as follows regarding airgram 604:

Re 1(*a*) to (*c*) : No comment.

Re 2 : Agreed, but we realize that the control measures contemplated can hardly be organized on a really effective basis anyway.

Re 3 : Agreed.

Re 4 (*a*) : Agreed. The demand for the withdrawal of an equal number of volunteers on each side as the first symbolic step will not be difficult to justify, if necessary, with the argument that a preliminary investigation to establish a ratio corresponding to the actual number of volunteers on each side would be very time-consuming and would therefore unduly delay the symbolical step desired by all.

Re 4 (*b*) and (*c*) : With regard to the number to be withdrawn under the symbolic action, we do not need to be ungenerous. Please agree to a figure of, say, 3,000 men, who could be quartered on a medium-sized transport steamer for a short time.

Should the question of the nationality of the volunteers scheduled for withdrawal come up in the committee, please refrain from entering into a discussion on this, but try to arrange for the choice to be left to the Spanish combatants.

It would also be undesirable at this time to go further into the question in the London committee as to where the volunteers scheduled for removal are to be sent. This first symbolic gesture involves only an experiment. If withdrawal of volunteers on a large scale comes up for discussion later, the questions touched on here will naturally have to be taken up more thoroughly and will play a decisive role.

Re 5 : Agreed.

Re 6 : There is no objection here to a renewal of the pledges made by the non-intervention powers in the non-intervention agreement. The only condition for this is that all these powers renew their non-intervention pledges in like manner and that all previous pledges be included. This renewal would therefore apply not only to the volunteers and air matériel, but also to all other war matériel.

It is left to your discretion to bring up for discussion in this connection the question as to whether the law is still in effect in France forbidding volunteers to cross over into Spain.

Re 7 (*a*) : Agreed.

Re 7 (*b*) : See remarks on point No. 6.

Re 7 (*c*) : Agreed. Please continue the reservation with regard to consent of the Spanish combatants, but bear in mind what was said on point No. 4, as well as my introductory comments, to the effect that we have a decided interest in bringing about the symbolic gesture.

Re 7 (*d*) : With regard to granting of belligerent rights, we agree with your previous remarks in the committee. Please treat this question in such a way, however, that it does not make impossible the execution of the first symbolic gesture of the withdrawal of volunteers. I therefore suggest your saying something to the effect that, as soon as that first gesture is carried out, the problem of recognition of the rights of belligerents must be given priority.

Re 8: Another communication will follow regarding Franco's attitude on the question of the withdrawal of volunteers and regarding the problem of the recognition of belligerents, as soon as we have further information on these points.

Re 9: We agree to the concluding paragraph.

The Italian Ambassador was informed orally today regarding the contents of the above instruction.[1]

NEURATH

---

[1] Marginal note in Weizsäcker's handwriting: "The War Ministry (Lieutenant Colonel Scheller) agrees with the basic principles of the instruction."

No. 443

3362/E009790

The State Secretary to the Embassy in Great Britain

Telegram

URGENT   BERLIN, October 18, 1937.
No. 400   zu Pol. III 4937.

With reference to your No. 604 of October 17 and to our airgram of today.[1]

On point No. 8: By direction of his Government, the Spanish Ambassador communicated today, leaving a memorandum to that effect, that Franco regarded the granting of *limited* belligerent rights as not in his interest, since the advantages arising from limited rights would be less than the disadvantages. Please take this into account in future debates in the Non-Intervention Committee.

With reference to the withdrawal of the volunteers, the Spanish Ambassador emphasized that under no circumstances were Moroccan troops to be included in the concept of volunteers.

MACKENSEN

---

[1] Document No. 442, *supra.*

No. 444

435/220562

The Ambassador in Italy to the Foreign Ministry

Telegram

SECRET   ROME, October 19, 1937—8 : 35 p.m.

No. 292 of October 19   Received October 19—11 : 05 p.m.

For the Foreign Minister.

Mussolini told me today that he had received a telegram from Franco this morning asking for the dispatch of one more division with which to accomplish the final liquidation of the Asturian front. Mussolini expressed his pained astonishment; he said the Spaniards were very good soldiers but had no idea of modern warfare and were making exceedingly slow progress in Asturias. He had instructed the War Ministry to dispatch a division and to do this as soon as possible, naturally, in view of the political situation. He said in reply to my question that the militia involved had been organized into units for the purpose and was adequately trained and ready for action; he apparently wished to stress the difference between this and the militia originally sent.

HASSELL

No. 445

435/220565–67

The Chargé d'Affaires in Great Britain to the Foreign Ministry

Telegram

No. 606 of October 19   LONDON, October 19, 1937—11 : 59 p.m.

Received October 20—3 : 00 a.m.

I. Eden presided at today's session because Plymouth was prevented by other duties from doing so.

Eden opened the session with a request to the individual representatives to state their position on the five points of the French proposal.

Grandi read a statement to the effect that the British plan of July 1937,[1] rather than the French proposals, should be the basis of the negotiations. Thereupon the Portuguese Ambassador made a lengthy statement, at the close of which he declared that Portugal was willing to permit border supervision once more if France did the same. I stated that I supported the Italian proposal to make the British plan the basis of negotiations, and suggested discussing the French proposals in conjunction with individual points in the British plan. I

---

[1] Document No. 393, p. 414.

stated that I would then go into details of the French proposal during the subsequent discussion.   I also said that the committee must be informed as to the real status of the French volunteer law, which had lapsed in the summer and had not been renewed.

The Belgian, Czech, and Swedish representatives gave the French proposals their approval.

The Soviet Ambassador stated once again that his Government regarded the policy of non-intervention as a failure and rejected responsibility for its continuation.   If the other governments were of the opinion that this policy could be continued, the Soviet Government did not wish to interpose any difficulties for them.   With regard to the French proposals he stated, among other things, that the Soviet Union could not consent to a discussion of the question of belligerent rights until the last volunteer had left Spain.

Eden stated emphatically that, in accordance with the communiqué of the last session, only the French proposals were up for discussion. He tried to obtain alternately from Grandi and from me more positive statements on the details of the French proposal.   In conformity with the tactics adopted by Grandi, I had to reply to this that first of all agreement had to be reached on the question of procedure.   Like Grandi, I stated, however, that in the German reply to the British plan essential points of the French proposal had already been answered.   I added that the German Government likewise agreed to a partial withdrawal by the methods proposed by Grandi at the last session.

After further discussion Eden stated that an agreement had not been reached, and he recessed the session.   It was not possible to reach an agreement in private conversations during the recess either. Grandi, in particular, was not inclined to depart from his position. It was thereupon decided to adjourn the session to Wednesday at 3 : 30 p.m.   Eden again spoke of the grave situation and addressed an appeal to the members of the committee to revert to the French proposals.

II. Grandi had informed me this morning of his intention to bring forward the British plan.   In the text that he read to me, however, he nevertheless had some positive replies to the French proposals. At the meeting, the reading of his statement concerning the return to the British plan met with an extraordinary coolness which made it seem to Grandi inadvisable to go into further detail.   I was not able to ascertain with certainty whether Grandi was acting on instructions.   I had informed him precisely of our instructions to be conciliatory.   In view of Grandi's attitude, however, I was not able to make any use of these at the session.   Grandi's view is that there is no reason to drop the British plan, which had been accepted by everyone with the exception of the Soviet Union, and now to give undue prominence to the question of volunteers.

In my opinion Grandi's procedure at the session was tactically somewhat unfortunate. Since he spoke before the Soviet Ambassador did, there was no further opportunity to take advantage of the negative Soviet attitude.

III. Grandi was not entirely disinclined to yield on the question of procedure, but wished under no circumstances to do so at today's session. No way out for tomorrow's session has appeared as yet, even in private conversations. As a possible way out, it was suggested that neither the British plan nor the French proposals be discussed, but rather the single problems as such. As the situation stands, there will be no course left at tomorrow's session but to continue to follow cautiously the Italian procedure. It would be very desirable to use our influence in Rome so that Grandi will receive new instructions by tomorrow noon.

WOERMANN

No. 446

3206/697740

The Chargé d'Affaires in Great Britain to the Foreign Ministry

STRICTLY CONFIDENTIAL   LONDON, October 19, 1937.
A 4526   Pol. III 5057.

Subject: Alliance agreements between Italy and Nationalist Spain.

As a member of the Embassy has heard from a member of the British Foreign Service with whom he is on friendly terms, the Foreign Office believes less in future territorial concessions by Franco to Italy than in already existing alliance agreements between Italy and Nationalist Spain, which at the same time give Italy certain rights in the form of leases of land for the construction of naval bases in Spanish Mediterranean ports, on the Canary Islands, and in Majorca. The Italians would thus obtain a legal position on Spanish territory such as the British, for instance, have in Egypt. The Foreign Office believes it has reliable information to the effect that such arrangements have been made and they wonder what the Italians intend by this policy, which will endanger the British shipping routes to South America, South Africa, and India. The official in question, who can be considered especially well informed because of his official position, perceives therein the continuation of an anti-British policy of expansion on the part of Italy, which started with the campaign in Abyssinia.

WOERMANN

No. 447

435/220575–76

The Ambassador in Spain to the Foreign Ministry

Telegram

VERY URGENT   SALAMANCA, October 20, 1937—12 : 30 a.m.
No. 506 of October 19   Received October 20—2 : 00 a.m.

The Government here has just delivered a note of today's date, setting forth the attitude of the Nationalist Government on the nonintervention deliberations. The chief points in the note are as follows: The Nationalist Government, in the interest of preserving peace, is prepared in an extreme case to make the sacrifice of having volunteers withdrawn. The withdrawal must take place in good faith on both sides and under the following conditions:

1. The withdrawal is to be only partial and confined to infantry without their equipment, excluding artillery, tanks, technical troops, and especially the air force.

2. The withdrawal must take place simultaneously and on the same scale on both sides.

3. Execution is to be guaranteed by complete closing of the land and sea frontiers under neutral supervision—by Germany and Italy on the Red side and England and France on the Nationalist side.

4. The volunteers are not to be determined by their mother tongue, but by their original nationality, Moroccans and members of the Foreign Legion, in any case, to be excluded.

5. The removal is to take place only by sea, from small ports, and under convoy.

6. Ports of disembarkation are to be so chosen that return of the volunteers to Spain is impossible.

7. The removal is to be on a small scale at first, possibly a thousand men on either side.

8. The *quid pro quo* is to be full recognition as a belligerent power.

I am sending the text of the note with translation by plane tomorrow. The note is the reply which the Nationalist Government has given the Italian Embassy to its inquiry on the question of volunteers that had been addressed to the Spanish Government at the direction of the Italian Government.

STOHRER

No. 448

47/32380–81

Minute by the Director of the Political Department

BERLIN, October 20, 1937.
Pol. I 5539 g.

The Italian Ambassador informed me in confidence today that an Italian division had been ordered transferred from the Aragón front to Asturias and that the shift was made at Franco's express desire.

Attolico knew nothing about the intention, reported by Herr von Hassell, of dispatching another division to Spain.

WEIZSÄCKER

No. 449

435/220582

Memorandum by the Foreign Minister

RM 819   BERLIN, October 20, 1937.

I approached Ambassador Attolico again this afternoon regarding Grandi's attitude in yesterday's session of the Non-Intervention Committee and explained to him that it would have seemed correct to us if Signor Grandi had been conciliatory in the matter of the "symbolic act," since it would then have been easier for us to remain unyielding on the essential points. To take a fixed position on a question of procedure was, in my opinion, not to our purpose. We could very well leave it to the Bolshevists by their opposition to sabotage a serious treatment of the question of the withdrawal of volunteers.

The Ambassador told me that he had telephoned to Rome this morning immediately after the conversation with Herr von Weizsäcker and had again reported our view.

BARON V. NEURATH

No. 450

435/220589–91

The Chargé d'Affaires in Great Britain to the Foreign Ministry

Telegram

URGENT   LONDON, October 21, 1937—12 : 22 a.m.
No. 610 of October 20   Received October 21—3 : 30 a.m.

I. At noon today Grandi received instructions by telephone from Ciano, which, in the main, follow our line. He revealed them at the beginning of today's session, over which Eden again presided. He took up the questions of control measures and neutrality, including belligerent rights and volunteers, and declared:

1. The readiness of the Italian Government to agree to the immediate dispatch of a commission to Spain. This commission is also to determine the number of volunteers in Spain. The investigations of this commission are to serve as the basis for deciding how and in what ratio the volunteers are to be withdrawn. On the basis of the commission's report, the committee is also to decide how and in what manner belligerent rights are to be granted.

2. Readiness to consent to an immediate partial withdrawal of volunteers in like number on both sides and to approach both Spanish parties on this score.

Grandi linked these points to the corresponding sections of the British plan in order thus to adhere to his proposal of yesterday.

I stated that my instructions were along the same lines. Germany acceded to the proposal to approach the Spanish parties with regard to a partial withdrawal of like numbers and to dispatch to Spain a commission such as Grandi proposed in connection with the British plan. I also stressed the need of further progress on the question of belligerent rights and restoration and strengthening of control measures. I mentioned in this connection that the first partial withdrawal was not being made contingent upon the granting of belligerent rights.

Eden and Corbin welcomed our cooperative attitude.

The Portuguese Ambassador [1] thereupon proposed immediately incorporating the results in resolutions.

During a recess the committee secretary drafted a resolution which failed to meet the viewpoints of any of the principal powers concerned. Another draft of a resolution submitted by Corbin was also rejected by Grandi and me, particularly since it made no mention at all of belligerent rights. In the case of the third draft, prepared by Eden, it was also impossible to achieve unity. I therefore proposed dispensing with the resolution altogether today and deferring it to the next session. This proposal was finally accepted. The only resolution that was adopted was to authorize the chairman of the committee to make the necessary preliminary preparations for dispatching the commission to Spain and to report on this to the committee.

II. The progress made today will make it possible at the next session to adopt resolutions regarding the dispatching of the commission to Spain and the step to be taken with the Spanish parties concerning the first partial withdrawal. The solemn pledge in the French proposal not to send any volunteers or war matériel will likewise be brought up for a vote.

I shall press for acceptance by all participating powers through the full committee; I shall also be concerned to see to it that the question

---

[1] Armindo Monteiro.

of belligerent rights and control measures receives proper emphasis in the resolution.

The rather confused debate concerning a draft resolution showed that, despite agreement on points of principle, it will be quite difficult to find a text satisfactory to all parties.

Besides this, the attitude of the Soviet Union remains doubtful. Maisky evidently intended making a statement today but was dissuaded from this by Eden outside the meeting.

WOERMANN

No. 451

435/220594

The Foreign Minister to the Embassy in Great Britain

Telegram

No. 404   BERLIN, October 21, 1937.
                                            Pol. III.

With reference to your 610 and 611 of October 20 and 21.[1]

For the Chargé d'Affaires.

1. At tomorrow's session please insist absolutely on having all resolutions accepted unanimously, that is, also by the Russians. Should the British try, in case of a Russian refusal, to carry out anyway the concessions made by the Italians and us, please oppose such an attempt on the ground that we see no reason to absolve the Russians from co-responsibility in the contemplated measures and that Russian non-participation would mean that the withdrawal of volunteers could not be carried out on the Red side.

2. On the granting of belligerent rights to Franco, please insist only up to the point that Russian opposition to this is thereby increased.

3. A renewed solemn assurance not to send war matériel, etc., could perhaps be avoided by a reference to declarations previously made.

NEURATH

---

[1] Latter not printed (435/220592-93).

No. 452

435/220607-09

The Chargé d'Affaires in Great Britain to the Foreign Ministry

Telegram

No. 619 of October 22   LONDON, October 22, 1937—11 : 15 p.m.
                                     Received October 23—2 : 45 a.m.

I. The British draft of a resolution [1] was on the agenda at today's session. Grandi had also prepared a draft in collaboration with us

---

[1] Transmitted to Berlin in report No. A 4539 of Oct. 23 (5068/E292213-20/1).

and the Portuguese. He stated that before entering the discussion he would have to clarify thoroughly the question as to whether all powers were unconditionally for the British plan,[2] in which connection he referred again to the principle of unanimity.

Maisky repeated his statement that the Soviet Government refused to accept responsibility for continuation of the non-intervention policy but raised no objection to its continuation by the other powers. He then went into the details of the draft. He stated, first, that the Soviet Union had no objections to sending the commission to Spain; second, that the question of belligerent rights should be examined only when the last volunteer had left Spain; and, third, that he had no objection to a symbolic withdrawal but that this must take place on a proportional basis.

Eden thereupon asked Maisky what his statement meant. Did Russia desire to let the other powers work alone on the plan submitted, without disturbance on her part, or did Russia herself wish to collaborate? Maisky then stated that Russia did not wish to assume any political responsibility but wished, as a member of the committee, to take part in the deliberations and resolutions on all questions, in which connection he likewise referred to the principle of unanimity. Eden obtained from Maisky the promise that he would once more report to his Government on these questions before the next session. An immediate collapse at today's session was thereby avoided. Grandi and I stressed the importance of the Russian statement but did not consider it desirable to let the session break up on this issue today, since we can wait for the final reply of the Russian Government.

We then proceeded to discuss the British and Italian drafts, from which a joint draft was produced. The draft contains all the familiar points, including control measures and belligerent rights.

1. On the question of a symbolic withdrawal, all the powers with the exception of France and the Soviet Union were in favor of withdrawing equal numbers. A tentative figure of 1,000 men was decided upon. Eden was not disinclined to let the matter of the symbolic withdrawal drop completely because of the difficulty that arose.

2. Further differences of opinion arose over whether the commission being sent to Spain should itself decide the final number of volunteers or whether the decision should rest with the committee. Italy, Portugal, and we came out for the second alternative, while all the other powers were in favor of the first.

3. Difficulties also arose over the date when control measures were to be restored on land and sea. There is agreement that the control measures must be reinstituted before the symbolic withdrawal.

[2] The reference is to the British proposals of July 14. See document No. 393, p. 414.

Grandi proposed immediately restoring control measures on land in their former magnitude and at a later stage strengthening control measures on land and sea in accordance with the van Dulm - Hemming report.

4. Finally, no unity could be achieved on Grandi's proposal for express commitment on the nine points of the British plan.

II. In the course of the discussion, Maisky asserted that there were 15,000 Germans and over 85,000 Italians on the White side and only 10,000 to 12,000 volunteers on the Red side. Grandi and I rejected these assertions without going into detail.

III. In the Russian question the tendency became apparent, on the part of the British and French, to keep Russia in the committee with full responsibility for the non-intervention policy but to accept the fact of her being the only power not granting belligerent rights.

IV. The next session is to convene on Monday afternoon at 4 o'clock. Please send me instructions by Monday morning on the draft of the resolution. A statement of opinion on it is being sent today together with the draft.

WOERMANN

No. 453

3362/E009834–35

The Chargé d'Affaires in Great Britain to the Foreign Ministry

Telegram

URGENT
No. 621 of October 23

LONDON, October 23, 1937—8: 33 p.m.
Received October 23—11: 30 p.m.
Pol. III 5065.

With reference to our report of October 23, A 4539.[1]

I discussed the draft of the resolution with Grandi and the Portuguese Ambassador today with the following result:

I. Russian question: Grandi had the same instructions as those in telegram No. 404.[2] The situation anticipated in them had not arisen at the last session. We were in agreement that the moment for pinning down the Russians should be made dependent on the course of the session. Grandi intends at a given point, perhaps during the discussion of the preamble (general note on the last page of the draft resolution) to ask the British and French how they stand on the Russian problem. If the British and French, as reported in telegraphic report 619,[3] section III, do commit the Russians to the policy of non-intervention but want to release them from granting belligerent rights, we intend to state that that has created a new situation which

---

[1] Not printed (5068/E292213–20/1).
[2] Document No. 451, p. 474.
[3] Document No. 452, *supra*.

makes it necessary to obtain new instructions. Actually the question does not amount to much, provided that all other powers grant belligerent rights. It is to be noted on this point that all the traffic between the Soviet Union and Spain is carried on by ships that, legitimately or otherwise, fly non-Russian flags.

II. On the question of belligerent rights (telegraphic instruction 404, point 2) Grandi also has the same instructions. The expectation entertained there (increase of Russian opposition) is already fulfilled. We have thus far acted on the assumption that Franco was interested in the granting of belligerent rights and that for tactical reasons also we had to keep the issue going.[4] The reasons for the instruction are not known to Grandi either. I would be grateful for information.

III. On the details of the draft resolution:

Re 1 (*b*). Yielding on the question of an equal number of volunteers for a symbolic withdrawal is out of the question. Would there be any objections if a symbolic withdrawal did not take place?[5] We would put the blame on others and make them responsible for it.

Re 1 (*c*). The dispute as to whether the final decision on the number of volunteers is made by the commissions or the committee could, if the other side does not yield, be postponed by our saying that this depended on the composition, duties, and working methods of the commissions. A decision could not be reached until these points had been resolved.[6] Tactically it would hardly be correct to let the collapse of the negotiations result from German-Italian opposition on this point instead of from the Russian question. We intend to work out proposals for the composition of the commissions, etc., which will make an independent decision difficult for them. Besides, Franco can make collaboration on withdrawal contingent upon the correct decision of the commissions.

Re 3. The present formula for the entry into force of the control measures is satisfactory. It means that control measures on land and sea shall enter into force before the symbolic withdrawal and that at this time the strengthening of the naval patrol must only be decided on but not carried out.

IV. We agreed that the treatment of the Friday session in the British press is entirely biased, since it attempts to ascribe to the Italians greater responsibility than to the Russians. We intend to bring up the matter jointly at the beginning of the next session.

V. The next session was postponed to 4 p.m. Tuesday at German and Italian request.

WOERMANN

---

[4] Marginal note in Neurath's handwriting: "Meanwhile Franco again desires belligerent rights."

[5] Marginal note in Neurath's handwriting: "No."

[6] Marginal note in Neurath's handwriting: "Yes."

No. 454

2946/576040-43

The Ambassador in Spain to the Foreign Ministry

Sa. 10 d–4048   SALAMANCA, October 24, 1937.

Subject: Anglo-Spanish commercial relations.

With reference to my telegram No. 511 of October 22 [1] and to your instructions W II WE 6405 of October 2 [2] and W II WE 6664 of October 16. [3]

On the basis of the above-mentioned instructions, I took the opportunity once more to discuss with Secretary General Nicolás Franco the current Anglo-Spanish negotiations, which, as you know, are to arrange for the exchange of semiofficial missions between Nationalist Spain and Great Britain.

Don Nicolás repeated to me that England had neither demanded nor obtained economic advantages of any kind at these discussions. When I interjected that the British press had been informed by a competent British source that the British Government had also demanded the solution of some economic questions, for example, the release of some British ships (your telegram No. 366 of October 9 [4]), the Generalissimo's brother replied that this assertion was incorrect; on the Spanish side, to be sure, the question of Spanish Nationalist shipping had been tied up with the consular question. At present, ships flying the flag of Nationalist Spain could not enter British ports; the Spanish Government had therefore demanded the freedom of Spanish Nationalist ships in British waters as the natural corollary of an agreement regarding exchange of semiofficial missions.

Following this explanation, Don Nicolás told me that at present there existed only three agreements of a commercial nature between Nationalist Spain and England:

1. A clearing agreement concerning Spanish shipments of sherry, tomatoes, and oranges in return for British goods. This agreement had been in force for months. During those negotiations Spain had rejected the British desire that the clearing debt arising out of former agreements with the whole of Spain be recognized even now but had stated that Nationalist Spain was not thinking of going into bankruptcy after the victory; on the contrary, she intended to liquidate the old debts, provided she was granted a suitable moratorium. Spain

---

[1] Not printed (3359/E009560).
[2] Not found.
[3] Document No. 440, p. 461.
[4] Not printed (5066/E292188–89).

would fulfill these obligations the more readily if the governments of the creditor nations confiscated the gold shipped out of Spain by the Reds contrary to the provisions of constitutional law. Since England did not, however, desire to incorporate this latter remark in the agreement, she finally waived the above-mentioned qualified promise of later recognition of the old clearing debt.

2. An agreement concluded by the Junta Técnica [5] in Burgos regarding payment for ores shipped from the Rio Tinto mines to England. England paid for these ores in pounds, and the Spanish Government in each case transferred the amount to the Rio Tinto Company in pesetas at the official rate of exchange. The company then established that it had commitments abroad (e.g. orders for machinery) and therefore needed a certain amount in foreign exchange. The Junta had therefore agreed to place at the company's disposal 10,000 pounds sterling a month out of the payments coming from England. The agreement could be terminated at any time.

3. An agreement concerning ores from the Bilbao area. The British Government had informed the Spanish Government that it attached the greatest importance to receiving regularly a definite quantity of certain ores—which could only be procured from Bilbao—in order that the British factories processing these ores would not have to suspend operations. (Don Nicolás was unable to give precise information as to what ores were involved). The Spanish Government had promised to do its best to meet this wish, which did not conflict with German interests, but had rejected the demand of the British that they be allowed to pay for these ores in pesetas. This agreement, too, could be terminated at any time. Perhaps the report from London communicated in instruction W II WE 6405 of October 2,[6] refers to this agreement.

We thus have the statements of Nicolás Franco, Chef de Cabinet Sangroniz, and the proper director of the Junta, all of which are to the effect that commercial questions are not to be settled in the "consular agreement" between Nationalist Spain and England which is apparently about to be concluded. Moreover, the Generalissimo told me himself (cf. report of Sept. 30, No. Sa. 10 B–3693 [6]) that German interests "would be given full consideration in the later development of Spanish commercial relations."

The matter will be kept in mind. If further interest in the above-mentioned agreements exists there, I shall try to obtain more details.

v. STOHRER

---

[5] Council of State of the Nationalist provisional government, headed by General Count Gómez Jordana. See also document No. 455, *infra.*

[6] Not found.

No. 455

435/220636–43

Memorandum by the Ambassador in Spain

STRICTLY CONFIDENTIAL   **October 25, 1937.**

SUMMARY OF PRELIMINARY IMPRESSIONS OF THE SITUATION IN SPAIN

I. *Military situation*

In the view of military experts the military situation is very favorable for Nationalist Spain. But the war has not yet been won!

There is great confidence on the Nationalist side; but reverses for Franco could occur at any time and worsen the situation again, and even have serious consequences, since 40 percent of the population in the liberated region is still considered as politically unreliable.

Among the Reds, morale is low; their aggressiveness is gone. Nevertheless, another strong attack under international leadership is considered possible. In spite of the victorious conclusion of the Asturian campaign, the collapse of the Reds is not to be expected before a new and successful Nationalist offensive.

This offensive is planned for the vicinity of Saragossa, in order to intensify the war weariness of Catalonia. Whether the offensive can still be carried out successfully before winter is doubtful. Therefore continuation of the war until at least spring is to be counted on. The winter will perhaps be used for mopping-up operations and straightening out the front in the south.

A delayed decision can easily be borne by Franco militarily, politically, and economically. Only in foreign policy is prolongation of the war hazardous.

II. *Economic situation*

Economic life in Nationalist Spain is almost normal; the currency is stable and in no danger; the prices of simple foods, which are available in abundance, have risen very little for the masses. The stocks will even suffice later to supply the areas still held by the Reds at present. Almost all other daily necessities, especially coal or motor fuel, are available in sufficient quantity. The distribution of food is encountering no difficulties; transportation is adequate.

In Red Spain, on the other hand, there is a severe shortage of food, a scarcity of coal, etc., as a result of internal confusion, poor organization, and the scarcity of foreign exchange.

III. *Organization and seat of the Nationalist Government*

There is a strong, presumably intentional decentralization in the provisional administration. Despite advantages to be expected in foreign policy, Franco has refrained up to now from forming an actual government (ministries), in view of personnel and party difficulties. Governmental affairs are therefore still performed in Burgos by the so-called Junta Técnica, which works slowly and not always reliably as a result of a small staff. Franco's headquarters are also in Burgos at present; transfer to Tudela is envisaged.

Secretary General Nicolás Franco resides in Salamanca but is often at headquarters with his brother, in San Sebastián, or at the Junta Técnica in Burgos. Part of the "Diplomatic Cabinet," the so-called "Secretariat for Foreign Affairs," and the Spanish press department also are located in Salamanca. The chief of the "Cabinet," Sangroniz (who besides matters of protocol takes care of all the more important political matters as a sort of foreign minister), is rarely to be found in Salamanca any more; he has moved with the greater part of his staff to San Sebastián, where he maintains contacts with Burgos and with the diplomatic missions accredited to Red Spain and located in St. Jean de Luz and Biarritz. The chief of the afore-mentioned "Secretariat," on the other hand, is usually in Salamanca but handles only routine and less important matters.

This decentralization is very burdensome to the Embassy since the more important political affairs are handled at headquarters, in Burgos, in San Sebastián, but hardly ever in Salamanca any more. This continually requires trips by the Ambassador and the personnel of the Embassy.

Now that the Asturian campaign has been concluded, the transfer of at least part of the German Embassy to San Sebastián will be necessary. The Italian Ambassador has the same intention. In case of a winter campaign in the south, Seville is also possible as headquarters and provisional seat of government.

IV. *Internal political situation in Nationalist Spain*

The mood is good and hopeful. Behind the front there is hardly anything to be noticed of the war. Those parts of the population which are against the military control of Franco are silent as long as the military situation is favorable; after the victory they can very easily be converted to the new regime. For how long depends on the social reforms!

Within the "Party of Unity" built by Franco, the "Falange Tradicionalista y de las JONS," there are several sharply defined tendencies:

1. The old fighters and adherents of the original Falange (*Camisas viejas*), founded by José Antonio Primo de Rivera, who are urging thorough social reforms;

2. The very pro-Vatican and reactionary Requetés, which developed out of former Carlist units;

3. The adherents of the Acción Española, a small party consisting of highly placed intellectuals of a conservative and monarchistic trend;

4. The Acción Popular, representatives of political Catholicism (Center!);

5. The "Tradicionalistas," a small group of pure monarchists.

The "Party of Unity" exists therefore only on paper. After the victory these divergences may, under certain circumstances, be intensified.

Franco cleverly keeps himself above these parties. Around him there are at present strong forces at work to give Catholicism its dominant position in Spain again. The Vatican has lately put itself entirely on the Nationalist side. The prospects for the establishment of a Spanish National Church independent of Rome are not very great. There are, moreover, increased efforts, supported by Italy (and England), to reestablish the monarchy. The Spanish people are sharply divided on this latter point. Restoration must nevertheless be reckoned with.

On the other hand, there is a prospect that certain social reforms will be carried out to eliminate the previous domination of the nobility, capital, and landownership, and improve the situation of the working classes.

V. *The position and condition of the German element in Spain*

(*a*) General and political.

Germany stands ace-high in Spain at present. German aid is gratefully acknowledged. The splendid achievements and the personal bearing of the members of our Air Force and other German volunteers have won us general respect. The restraint in our propaganda in comparison to Italian forwardness is reckoned greatly to our credit. After the war, however, we should not rate gratitude for wartime help too highly in our calculations.

Efforts to win friends for Germany are bringing excellent results. The relations of the Propaganda Ministry's local press and propaganda office (Consul General Köhn, director) with the Spanish Nationalist Government's central press and propaganda office are first-rate and intimate (as Franco himself confirmed to me). On request the Falange receives from the German press office a wealth of material on German conditions and the organization, etc., of the NSDAP. There is no importunate propaganda or "intervention in the internal affairs" of Spain. Any objection of this type formerly made can at most refer to the beginnings of the Falange (the Hedilla affair). The factual German publicity is far superior to and more successful than the Italian. The independence of the above-mentioned local office of the Propaganda Ministry from the Embassy has hitherto been unobjectionable.

At present the soil of Nationalist Spain is very favorable for cultural propaganda. German schools are enjoying a strong influx from the Spanish element. Conflicts of jurisdiction and other dissensions within Spanish agencies, however, militate against the conclusion of a cultural agreement.

(*b*) Economic position of the German element.

There have been very great property losses for the German element in Spain as a result of the Civil War! The losses are especially large because the Germans were advised by official German sources to leave Spain immediately in order to save their lives and because Germany's stand in favor of Franco caused the Red mobs to rage particularly against German property. The losses of Germans in Spain cannot therefore be equated with the losses of Germans in other wars (China); the German Government has greater moral responsibility with respect to the Germans in Spain.

The rebuilding of the German element in Spain (12 to 15 thousand before the Civil War [of whom] 9 to 10 thousand have fled) must therefore be vigorously promoted; the will to rebuild among numerous Germans who have already returned is present to a most gratifying extent. Cooperation between official German agencies and the Party organization has been smooth almost everywhere. It is to be hoped that a beginning can soon be made in the granting of reconstruction credits (600,000 **RM** are available, negotiations regarding clearing with Spain are pending). The problem of indemnification by the Spanish Government for damages suffered by Germans is being treated and furthered separately. The Spanish Chief of State recently assented in general terms (strictly confidential!). German damages filed (but in part filed as a precaution, that is, with actual destruction of the property not confirmed): approximately 90,000,000 **RM**; debts outstanding for delivery of goods to Spain: 70,000,000 **RM**. This last will probably be paid later to a great extent. The final total loss will probably not exceed 70 to 80 millions.

The Embassy is ably supported by the Landesgruppe and the Ortsgruppen of the NSDAP in its work of organizing and aiding the German element.

(*c*) German economic policy.

This policy is determined by the state of war, wartime deliveries to Spain, and our needs (Four Year Plan). The clearing office is the Treuhandgesellschaft Hisma (Herr Bernhardt, director), through which practically the whole present traffic in goods goes or is controlled. Hisma deserves the greatest credit with regard to the initiation of German-Spanish trade after the beginning of the Civil War, the rapidly growing German exports to Spain (which are *far* greater, for example, than Italian exports), and the importation of important raw materials to Germany (within the framework of the Four Year Plan). (Franco himself mentioned to me the valuable services of Hisma.)

On the other hand the constantly increasing scope of the transactions instituted and controlled by Hisma constitutes a certain hindrance to free trade and in specific cases also makes the efforts at reconstruction by the Germans in Spain more difficult. Thus in these circles there are ill will and complaints against Hisma which are in part demonstrably incorrect. On the Spanish side, too (the export trade, the Junta Técnica, the Spanish colony in Germany), there is a growing opposition which has hitherto been kept harmless by Franco. Consideration is at present being given by the Embassy and Hisma as to how the true aims and purposes of Hisma can be clarified for these German and Spanish circles and thus a calming influence exercised.

How far the requirements of raw materials and the promotion of our exports compel us to accept possibly increased opposition of this type cannot be determined here; but we surely ought not to fail to take into consideration both the interest of the Germans with a will for reconstruction and the feelings of Spanish economic circles, some of which threaten to turn to trade with other countries.

The aim of our policy in Spain must be, after the attainment of a peace which excludes all Red influences in Spain, to create an atmosphere in Spain which, in its effect on political and economic relations between the two countries, will justify the great sacrifice of life and property and especially the diplomatic risks which we have undertaken for Spain.

Whether this is successful will depend principally on the correct judgment and consideration of Spanish mentality and on our economic policy.

VON STOHRER

No. 456

3362/E009836–37

The Foreign Minister to the Embassy in Great Britain

Airgram

Via tonight's plane   BERLIN, October 25, 1937.
                                                            Pol. III 5065.

With reference to your report A 4539 of October 23 [1] and telegram 621 of the same day.

We are not interested in having the non-intervention policy as carried on in the London committee fail in the near future. We are not at present seeking a test of how Britain and especially France would

---

[1] Not printed (5068/E292213–20/1).

act in case of the failure of this policy. On the contrary, a further gain of time will probably favor Franco's military fortunes and create a new situation which would also be advantageous for us in the Non-Intervention Committee.

From this point of view it would be very regrettable if the plan for a symbolic gesture of withdrawal of volunteers, having been brought up and having reached a rather advanced stage, should be dropped. I therefore ask you, together with Grandi, to attempt to bring this plan further into the foreground again and, if at all possible, cause it to be carried out. For this purpose you may, in case of Russian obstruction, depart from the demand for unanimity in this one case. Should the plan nevertheless be in danger of being wrecked— by France's resistance to the withdrawal of equal numbers of volunteers from both sides, for example—I leave it to your discretion to consult Berlin again.

In order not to upset the above plan, however, it will also be necessary, insofar as possible, to defer questions with regard to which dissension will be unavoidable in the committee. This would entail Grandi's refraining from pressing for the adoption of his draft preamble (concluding sentence of the draft resolution of October 22), which is obviously unacceptable to the Russians. A further objection to this preamble, from our point of view, is the fact that in the British plan of July 14, on which Grandi bases his draft, the time of granting belligerent rights to Franco is unfavorably formulated. The same is also true, by the way, of the draft resolution of October 22, No. 1 (d). Grandi, as we hear through Attolico, has meanwhile received the instruction—which I also extend to you—to advocate that belligerent rights be granted the two parties in Spain when the symbolic gesture has been carried out and a plan is fixed for the total withdrawal of the volunteers. Finally, as you will have seen from Ambassador von Stohrer's report,[2] which has meanwhile been sent to you, Franco himself—in this he goes beyond the British plan—attaches great value to the granting of *unlimited* belligerent rights. All this speaks against forcing through the British plan as a whole at this time.

With regard to the duties and competence of the commissions to be sent to Spain, I agree with your intention explained in telegram No. 621, but the commission should be allowed no final decisions or executive authority. As regards both the number of volunteers to be withdrawn and the manner of their withdrawal, the London committee must retain the last word. The commissions should have power exclusively to investigate and to report.

---

[2] On Oct. 22, Stohrer reported (telegram 509 of Oct. 22, 435/220600) that Franco had found that lack of belligerent rights in naval warfare had held up the campaign on the northern front. He foresaw similar difficulties in regard to the final offensive against Catalonia and Valencia.

We also consider satisfactory the formula for the resumption of the land and sea patrol as proposed under No. 3 in the draft resolution. In this connection, however, please take up again the idea of an air patrol in accordance with the van Dulm-Hemming report.

Attolico, who informed us of the instruction to Grandi, has been informed regarding the essential content of the present instruction.[3]

NEURATH

---

[3] Marginal note in Weizsäcker's handwriting: "Attolico visited me early today of his own accord."

No. 457

435/220623-25

The Minister Counselor of Embassy in Great Britain to the Foreign Ministry

Telegram

VERY URGENT   LONDON, October 26, 1937—12 : 06 a.m.
No. 623 of October 25   Received October 26—3 : 40 a.m.

I. Eden asked me to call on him this evening, after he had previously spoken for an hour and a half with Grandi and, during the course of the day, with other ambassadors too.

Eden said he believed, on the basis of conversations during the last few days, that he had to assume that the Soviet Union wanted to hold entirely aloof from non-intervention. I referred him to the report in the evening papers, according to which the Russians had suspended their membership payments for political reasons and were waiting only for an appropriate moment to announce it. Eden pretended that he was ("not" apparently missing) informed, although, as we know through confidential reports from a reliable source, he has been concerned with this matter for 2 weeks.

Eden went on to say that the British view was that they should let Russia withdraw quietly. He thought he could assume that this was also the French conception. He asked about the German view of the matter. I answered that I had absolutely strict instructions. Germany had adhered to the non-intervention agreements on the condition that all the European powers concerned assume the same commitments. From the practical point of view, too, it was completely impossible that the Soviet Union retain freedom to intervene. Moreover, its cooperation was necessary in the question of volunteers, for example.

Eden answered that from the general political point of view Germany could only be pleased if Europe reached agreement without the Soviet Union. The question of volunteers could solve itself, in that the Russian volunteers would in that case be forced out of Spain. I repeated reasons which made such a proposal unacceptable.

Eden then said that at the beginning of tomorrow morning's session the status of the Russian question would have to be clearly determined, with which I agreed. But, he continued, things could not be left in such a state of collapse. We would have to look for ways and means to maintain non-intervention in spite of that. All participating powers would have to join in efforts to this effect. I asked Eden whether he had any ideas on this point, to which he answered that his idea was precisely that of leaving the Russians entirely out. In case this was not possible, he had no suggestions either at the moment but he would continue to think about it.

Eden then said quite frankly that the main problem was after all not the details of the resolution but the fact that the Italians had established themselves in the Balearic Islands. Perhaps we could do something for public opinion by sending a commission to the Balearic Islands to determine the actual situation there. I asked Eden whether he really believed that any volunteers who might at the moment be on the Balearic Islands wanted to remain there permanently. Eden replied he had formal assurances from Italy on that score which the British Government had accepted. For that very reason such an international commission would be a good thing. I remarked that I could take no stand on that idea. If such an idea appeared acceptable at all to the participating governments, on which subject I had no opinion, at any rate the idea of a unilateral dispatching of a commission was unacceptable from the very beginning.

In the course of the conversation Eden also mentioned the difficulties which had arisen regarding the question whether the number of volunteers was to be determined by the commissions on the spot or by the Non-Intervention Committee. Here I advocated our point of view anew but referred to the fact that differences of opinion had become unimportant in view of the Russian attitude.

I was unable to see Grandi between his conversation with Eden and mine. An appointment with the Portuguese Ambassador and Grandi for this evening had to be given up on account of the late hour and will not take place until tomorrow.

Eden's idea of the further course of events was that if an impasse should occur tomorrow as a result of the Russian attitude the matter would be referred to the full committee, whereby 48 hours would be gained which could be used for diplomatic discussions.

I just had a short conversation with the Counselor of the Italian Embassy. We agreed that we must now put the whole emphasis on Russia's attitude and reject any discussion of details of the draft resolution.

II. Correction to telegram No. 609.[1] The Italians have received our instruction No. 404 [2] not as their own directive but only for their

---

[1] Not printed (435/220583–87).
[2] Document No. 451, p. 474.

information. But, in accordance with the general line, Grandi will not place himself in conflict with it.

WOERMANN

No. 458

1819/416321–22

The Foreign Minister to the Embassy in France

BERLIN, October 26, 1937.
Pol. III 5035.

With reference to cipher letter Pol. III 4328 of September 4, 1937.[1]

The French law of January 21, 1937, concerning the ban on the departure of volunteers for Spain provides in article 1, section 2, paragraph 2, that the provisions of the ban shall become effective on the date set by international agreement *for a period of six months*. The ban on volunteers went into effect for all non-intervention powers on February 21, 1937, in accordance with an agreement of the governments participating in the non-intervention agreement. The French law therefore expired on August 20, 1937.

Our Chargé d'Affaires in London has learned confidentially at the French Embassy there that they were inclined in Government circles in France to renew the law but avoided doing so because they feared rejection of the law in view of the mood of the country. The ban on volunteers had meanwhile been maintained by administrative measures.

In the meeting of the main subcommittee on October 19 our Chargé d'Affaires in London brought up the question of the status of the French ban on volunteers. M. Corbin urged Herr Woermann outside the meeting not to press this question; the law could not be revived until the Chamber of Deputies met again. Meanwhile the very same effect as the law had was accomplished by administrative measures. The adoption of the law would in any case be made more difficult if it were demanded under outside pressure.

We do not intend to force the issue, but clarification appears indispensable, all the more so since a renewed commitment to send no volunteers and no matériel to Spain is provided in paragraph 2 of the well-known draft resolution of October 22 (cf. dispatch Pol. III 5084 of October 25 [2]). Such an assurance could only be given on the assumption that the legislation of all non-intervention states will be brought into harmony with it, that is, that the French Government will make the necessary legal arrangements as soon as the Chamber meets.

---

[1] Not printed (5068/E292209–11).
[2] Not printed (5068/E292213–20/1). It transmitted for information report No. A 4539 of Oct. 23 from Selzam, of the London Embassy.

Please call the attention of the Government there to the significance of the matter in a manner deemed suitable.

By direction:
WEIZSÄCKER

No. 459

435/220631–32

The Ambassador in Great Britain to the Foreign Ministry

Telegram

URGENT   LONDON, October 27, 1937—10 : 14 p.m.
No. 628 of October 27   Received October 28—1 : 00 a.m.

I. Grandi's insistence on the British plan [1] was due to two considerations: In the first place, the whole intermediate stage, with the desire for three-power conversations, was thereby eliminated. The Italo-German thesis that the matter belonged in the Non-Intervention Committee was proved correct as against the Anglo-French view. Secondly, in this manner we succeeded in obtaining a unanimous decision against the Soviet Union.

We now have the following possibilities:

1. We could state that the whole plan has collapsed because of failure to agree. We would thereby be giving the opposition freedom of action and could claim it ourselves.

2. The second possibility would be that Russia withdraws from nonintervention. In this case other participating powers would have to guarantee that they would oppose Russian attempts at non-intervention [*sic*] and would not support Russia in case of a conflict arising from the exercise of belligerent rights by Franco.

3. The third possibility would be to concede that Russia remains a non-intervention power but that the question of belligerent rights is to be handled only by the remaining powers. In this case, too, guaranties against the possibilities of a conflict between Franco and the Soviet Union would have to be demanded. In addition, we could attempt to correct the disadvantageous association of belligerent rights with the withdrawal of volunteers in the draft resolution.

A decision on these possibilities need not be made during Friday's meeting. I agree with Grandi that the best tactics for this session would be for the draft resolution to be brought to a vote and later

---

[1] At the subcommittee meeting of Oct. 22 the Italian and German delegates had stated that their acceptance of the British plan of July 14 would have to be dependent upon its acceptance by all members of the Non-Intervention Committee. On Oct. 25 Neurath sent instructions to London permitting a slight modification of this attitude (document No. 456). At the session on the next day, the Soviet delegate, Ambassador Maisky, intimated that his Government might be prepared to examine the question of belligerent rights when "the bulk of the volunteers had been withdrawn." It was thereupon agreed that delegates should submit the British plan as a whole for consideration by their respective Governments.

brought before the full committee, in which connection it would have to be established that agreement could not be attained. On Friday we could put before the British and the French the question of what conclusions they were ready to draw from this situation. In case an answer is given at that session we could state the necessity of reporting to our Governments. As delaying tactics in this procedure we could permit further discussion regarding the practical execution of the resolution, could push particularly the question of control and of belligerent rights in the subcommittee, and could collaborate in working out the composition of the commissions and instructions for them. But we have to bring out quite clearly that any action on the basis of these decisions, especially any approach to the Spanish parties and dispatch of commissions, is out of the question until the Russian situation is clarified. Grandi also favors this procedure and will recommend it to the Italian Government.

II. It is not entirely impossible that the Soviet Union will make further concessions. In that case we would insist that the draft resolution was to be accepted as such and a halfway concession by the Soviet Union was to be rejected.

III. Our acceptance of the British plan became inevitable as a result of the tempo proposed by the Italians. I consider acceptance as not dangerous, however, since we have a whole series of possibilities for playing for time as long as desired. We can also attempt to have the provisions of the draft resolution improved when Franco's wishes are stated.

RIBBENTROP

No. 460

3362/E009852-54

The Foreign Minister to the Embassy in Great Britain

Telegram

URGENT BERLIN, October 28, 1937.
Today (this morning if possible) zu Pol. III 5123, 5126.
No. 419

With reference to your telegrams 626 [1] and 628 of October 27.

Since we must continue our effort to gain time for Franco, I judge the possibilities listed under I in your telegram 628 as follows:

Re I (1): Stating that the whole plan has collapsed is at present absolutely not desired.

The possibility mentioned under I (2) must also be eliminated, as we cannot now release Russia from her non-intervention obligations while we ourselves remain committed.

---

[1] Not printed (435/220628-30).

Under existing circumstances, therefore, the possibility described under I (3) is probably the one most to be recommended. What rights and duties Russia would retain if the question of belligerent rights were treated among the non-intervention powers with the exception of Russia is not quite clear here, however, and would have to be worked out in the discussions in the committee. Even though, as you mentioned in an earlier report, there is not much of practical value in this question, we nevertheless have no reason to release the Russians from an engagement that is particularly onerous for them and on the other hand to give them a chance to disturb the other decisions of the committee and the execution thereof by all sorts of maneuvers. From our point of view it would suffice if the Russians were to remain bound to all the original non-intervention commitments and later provisions for their execution. Clarification of this point in the committee seems necessary to me.

I further agree with you that, if the Russians do not grant Franco belligerent rights, guaranties against the possibility of a conflict between Franco and the Soviet Union would have to be provided.

As for the details of the resolution, it would be desirable if, with respect to the powers of the two commissions to be sent to Spain, the complete and continuing dependence of the commissions on the Non-Intervention Committee were worked out more clearly than heretofore. The provision according to which the committee retains the power to fix the date for the evacuation of volunteers is valuable, it is true, but in my opinion hardly sufficient.

The concession desired by us in the matter of the powers of the commissions can perhaps be obtained in return for exempting the Russians from the granting of belligerent rights to Franco.

I agree to your statements under II in telegram 628.

NEURATH

No. 461

435/220656–59

The Ambassador in Great Britain to the Foreign Ministry

Airgram

VERY URGENT   LONDON, October 30, 1937.
No. 638 of October 30   Pol. III 5186.

I. In a conversation which I had today with the Italian Ambassador we considered the situation as it developed in the last session of the main subcommittee.[1] We agreed to submit the following to our Governments.

---

[1] On Oct. 29 Maisky stated the refusal of the Soviet Government to accept the British plan and French suggestions but offered to accept some portions of the draft resolution of Oct. 22.

We have two possibilities. Either we block further discussions until the situation arising from the attitude of the Soviet Union is clarified, or else we accept with some changes Plymouth's proposal according to which he would be empowered to present the draft resolution in its entirety to the Spanish parties immediately while the work in the subcommittees would continue.

II. We agreed that in deciding in favor of the first possibility it would be preferable not to enter into discussions in the subcommittee next Tuesday, since we would have to adopt a negative attitude there which would be exploited by a certain section of the press. We are of the opinion that it would be better in that case not to take part in the meeting and to write a letter of the following content to the chairman on Monday:

(*a*) We confirm our complete and unreserved acceptance of the draft resolution.

(*b*) We confirm that our acceptance has been made on the condition that all other participating governments accept the draft resolution.

(*c*) We state that, in view of the refusal of the Soviet Government to recognize several essential points in the draft resolution, it would be practically useless to continue the discussions for putting the resolution into effect, so long as the questions arising from the attitude of the Soviet Union are not clarified.

(*d*) We propose that an immediate exchange of views through diplomatic channels take place among the governments mainly interested, in order to put the resolution into effect as quickly as possible, or else that some other quick solution to the present difficulties be found.

We agreed that, if this course was adopted, we would have to be prepared to withstand the pressure of the French and British Governments which would surely be forthcoming.

We further agreed that such an attitude would at the moment bring with it no serious risk of international complications.

III. If the second alternative is chosen (acceptance of Plymouth's proposal with some changes), we agreed that it would be advisable to issue the following explanation at the session Tuesday regarding the attitude of our Governments:

(*a*) In his approach to the Spanish parties the chairman must make clear to them that the resolution has not been accepted in all parts by the Soviet Government.

(*b*) It must also be clearly established that, aside from the approach to the Spanish parties, execution of the resolution cannot take place until all participating governments have actually accepted it in entirety, or until some measures have been agreed upon to fill the gaps which have arisen as a result of the present attitude of the Soviet Union.

(c) It would further have to be brought out that the dispatching of the two commissions to Spain actually represents a step in the execution and therefore cannot take place until a satisfactory solution of the questions mentioned in (b) has been arranged.

(d) Finally, in this case too, a diplomatic exchange of views should be entered upon in the interest of a rapid solution of the Russian difficulties.

We would of course attempt to have these proposals approved by the full committee. If this cannot be attained, we would have to insist that points (a) to (c) be entered not only in the minutes of the meeting but also in the documents to be communicated to the Spanish parties.

Grandi and I agree in the view that, if the second course is followed, it will depend on Franco's diplomatic skill to give the proper answers and that this second possibility does not necessarily mean increasing the tempo as compared with the first possibility.

Grandi will send his Government a telegram identical with the present one.

The procedure provided in No. II assumes that the Italian Ambassador and I will receive instructions by Monday afternoon at the latest. Since Tuesday's session is to begin at 11 a.m. it would be too late if the note was sent Tuesday morning.

RIBBENTROP

No. 462

3362/E009860-62

The Foreign Minister to the Embassy in Great Britain

Telegram

URGENT　　　　　　　　　　　　　　　BERLIN, November 1, 1937—4 : 30 p.m.
No. 428　　　　　　　　　　　　　　　　　　　　　zu Pol. III 5186 I.

With reference to your telegram 638.[1]

The idea of inducing the leaders of the committee really to clarify the Russian attitude by ostentatiously absenting yourself from the next session may appear enticing as a means of pressure on them. But please drop that alternative. I fear that through such a staged withdrawal, so to speak, we will permit the misconception to arise that it is not the Russians but we who are being isolated—an impression that must by all means be avoided.

---

[1] Document No. 461, *supra.*

For the same reason, in order to forestall this, please give up the idea that we could effectively further our aims in London by stopping our contributions.

What still really matters is to work out in the committee, in the sense of my telegram No. 419 of October 28, what rights and duties the Russians would retain if they were exempted from granting belligerent rights to Franco. As has already been attempted various times by Grandi (cf. your telegram 635 [2]), that would have to be defined in the committee discussions in all its details, for we cannot, as I have already said, release the Russians from a commitment which is especially onerous to them and on the other hand leave them every possibility for maneuvers to disturb the committee.

If in the course of these discussions it should result that (cf. your telegram 640 III [3]) the Russians were expressly declared to have lost the protection of the provisions of the Nyon agreement, that would indirectly mean at least a moral victory, which we should welcome.

To approach the two combatants before a thorough clarification of the Russian question can have no practical results. It can be foreseen that Franco's Government would only hand the question of the rights and duties of the Russians back to the committee. The committee therefore cannot avoid the foregoing task of clarification if, as is desired, it wants to advance materially.

It may be that the task thus set for the committee will take some time. This delay, however, is unavoidable and is exclusively the fault of the Russians. Moreover, we will not object if, parallel to the discussions in the committee, there is an attempt to obtain clarification of the Russian attitude through diplomatic channels (cf. your telegram 640).

In addition we have no objection to continuing the discussions meanwhile as to the detailed composition of the two commissions to be sent to Spain and as to how they are to carry out their functions. On the other hand, any discussion of future measures to be taken in case the resolution fails, mentioned in your telegram No. 636 (b),[4] should be dropped. This can be discussed only when the resolution has actually failed.[5]

NEURATH

---

[2] Not printed (435/220649).
[3] Not printed (435/220664–65).
[4] Not printed (435/220651–52).
[5] Marginal note in Weizsäcker's handwriting: "Attolico has been informed in broad outline. He will obtain Rome's answer as soon as possible."

[EDITORS' NOTE. On November 2, 1937, the chairman's subcommittee of the Non-Intervention Committee agreed, with the exception of the Russian representative, upon the text of two resolutions for submission to the full Non-Intervention Committee. The resolutions were adopted on November 4 by the Non-Intervention Committee. These resolutions were somewhat similar to the British proposals of July 14, 1937. The subcommittee's plan may be found in the London *Times* of October 30, 1937. For a German analysis of the plan see the circular instruction of November 9, 1937, printed as document No. 466, p. 504.]

CHAPTER V

GERMAN ECONOMIC PRESSURE ON FRANCO
NOVEMBER 4, 1937–MARCH 10, 1938

No. 463

2946/576069–71

Memorandum of the German Embassy in Spain [1]

CONFIDENTIAL   BURGOS, November 4, 1937.
Ps/Z

REPORT OF PARTY COMRADE PASCH ON THE MONTANA PROJECT

On October 20, 1937, Herr Klingenberg and I first took the memorandum of the same date to Bau and let him read this report. He stated that in principle he approved of our ideas, except that the "*igualdad absoluta*" that we had stressed was out of the question, since this was incompatible with the "*leyes existentes*," which permitted only 25 percent to 30 percent foreign participation. I informed Bau that I could under no circumstances visualize any other condition than that

---

[1] This and the following memorandum from the files of the German Embassy in Spain refer to efforts of German businessmen active in Spain to secure control of Spanish mining companies in order to guarantee to Germany a steady supply of Spanish mineral raw materials. These efforts formed a part of the activities of the Hisma Company. The Montana project was the name applied to the Hisma activities in this field, which included efforts to bring about German control of five mining companies operating in Spain. They suffered a set-back when the Nationalist regime in Spain issued the decree of Oct. 9, 1937, annulling mining concessions and other arrangements for securing control of mining concerns obtained since the beginning of the Civil War (document No. 435, p. 457).

Wilhelm Pasch, whose report is given in this document, was an employee of Hisma engaged in securing mining concessions and in purchasing shares in mining companies.

Johannes Bernhardt, whose report appears as document No. 464, *infra*, was the head of the Hisma Company.

Another memorandum of Nov. 4 in the files of the German Embassy in Spain (2946/576066–68, not printed) indicated that officials of Hisma had protested on Oct. 12, 1937, to General Jordana and General Franco against the decree of Oct. 9, 1937, insofar as it adversely affected Hisma's efforts to secure extensive German participation in the Spanish mining industry. Somewhat indefinite assurances were given to the effect that the decree was not directed against German interests. Jordana requested that the views of Hisma be put in writing. This was done, and a memorandum drafted by Pasch was presented to Jordana on Oct. 20, 1937. The text of this memorandum has not been found. Its contents are indicated by the following document which discusses Jordana's views regarding it.

of "*igualdad absoluta*," since really profitable cooperation was only possible with equality of interests. Thus I purposely left open the definition of "*igualdad de derechos*," not applying it exclusively to capital, for instance, but purposely leaving freedom in the interpretation of how equality would take its final form.

Bau used this opportunity to recommend warmly a lawyer friend of his from Valencia, now in Burgos, to assist in working out the statutes of a company. He also remarked that the man mentioned would be particularly suitable as attorney for the board of the new company. His suggestion was gratefully acknowledged but was not discussed further. Subsequently the report of October 20, 1937, was presented to Jordana in the presence of Klingenberg. Jordana stated that he was expecting a visitor immediately and would study the note later. Therefore he could make no comment. And General Dávila was, in fact, announced after us, so that an immediate statement was impossible for him. After leaving Jordana's room we again met Sierra Pomares, who had been present during our discussion with Bau and who in the meantime had continued to discuss our note alone with Bau. Sierra Pomares indicated that in Bau's opinion it would probably be possible to find a way to provide absolute equality in practice. Since Jordana had asked for several days' time to study our note, Klingenberg and I did not go to him until October 26, 1937, and then asked him for his basic attitude on our note. The result of this conference is set down in the following minute for Party Comrade Bernhardt:

"After we had recently given General Jordana the basic program for cooperation in mining matters in the form of a short memorandum, and he had asked for time to study it, Herr W. Pasch and Herr Klingenberg visited him again this morning in order to make some progress in the matter.

"Jordana told us that he had read the memorandum but that it did not go beyond general basic principles and that it would be necessary for us to present concrete data, etc., etc. We replied that, after all, the memorandum did contain the basic ideas and that we expected first to obtain the Government's full approval of this basis in order then to continue the work as fast as possible in a concrete manner.

"General Jordana answered us quite evasively. He said that the matter was of great importance and should be handled with great care. He was of the opinion that the Government in its present form perhaps did not even have the power to decide a matter of such scope and of possible great consequences. For this reason he considered it best to put the matter off and gave it as his opinion also that even the Generalissimo would not take it upon himself to reach a quick decision in a matter of such importance as this. Besides, the memorandum contained the expression 'equality of rights,' and he must point out that the Government had to keep strictly to the Spanish laws. He also indicated that the treaties between Germany and Spain were surely to be understood as meaning that Spanish laws would always be observed.

"We repeated that in this case, however, a very special, new type of close cooperation would be involved, and that it was tremendously important not to lose any time and not to interrupt the preparatory work which had been done. General Jordana answered that setting the time was, after all, a matter for the Spaniards to decide. With regard to the decree, Jordana said that he had, to be sure, told Herr Bernhardt that it was not directed against Germany, but the decree existed, and of course it applied to us exactly as to anyone else; the law as such knew no exceptions.

"For us the clear result of the conference is the realization that in this manner we are not making one step of progress and are only losing valuable time. The matter can be speeded up only through intervention at the highest level."

After this statement of Jordana we considered it expedient to speak to Bau about this matter once more, and it was clear to us that a clarification could be brought about only through discussion with State Secretary Nicolás Franco or the Generalissimo.

On October 29, 1937, I learned through Amann in Bilbao and through Enrique Ocharan that, during Jordana's last stay in Bilbao, Merello of Altos Hornos, in particular, had been working for a ban on the acquisition of mines by foreigners, and, according to the information obtained by Amann and Ocharan, Merello had had especially the Germans in mind. Jordana promised the Fuerzas Vivas of Bilbao that he would study such a prohibition. The facts show that Jordana needed only a short time to carry this suggestion over into the well-known decree.

In Burgos on the evening of November 1 I met Fr. Lipperheide, who told me confidentially that, according to a statement made to him by Taberna, the decree had been worked out by Bastos, Juan Zabala (Chief of Mines of Vizcaya), and Taberna, and Taberna had mentioned that the decree was directed particularly against us, since they were well informed concerning my activities. Lipperheide is himself exploiting a mine near Bilbao, and he asked Taberna to what extent he would be affected by this decree. Since Lipperheide is working the mine under the name of his Spanish company, in which his share is allegedly about one-third, Taberna told him that upon presenting a petition he would surely be given permission for further exploitation.

On the same evening we drove to Salamanca and gave Party Comrade Bernhardt this important information. After detailed discussion we agreed once more that this untenable situation must be brought to an end as soon as possible by appealing to the Generalissimo.

No. 464

2946/576072–76

Memorandum of the German Embassy in Spain

CONFIDENTIAL   BURGOS, November 4, 1937.
B/Z

REPORT BY PARTY COMRADE BERNHARDT ON THE MONTANA PROJECT

After my trip to Lisbon (a report on the Portuguese economic situation is being sent separately) I went to Seville, where Sierra Pomares had already arrived on October 22. In the main conferences concerning bookkeeping, auditing of books, and internal liquidation of October 25, 29, and 30, the following was revealed:

Sierra Pomares was instructed to give Burgos a clear picture of our activities up to the present time. Evidently he was reproached for not being sufficiently well oriented. The former Spanish personnel were absolutely inadequate, so that Zschiesche [1] quite correctly took a negative attitude toward them. This attitude was evidently misunderstood by the suspicious-minded Spaniards, who evidently thought in their hearts that we had something to hide.

Any help from Sierra Pomares in our Montana project presupposes that he is fully oriented concerning the status of the whole Hisma organization. We must supply him with the material ourselves, since he himself is not capable of making an investigation.

The balance as of October 31, 1937, is now being drawn up, without any reservations, so that we can give a full report concerning our trustee activities. There must be no holding back of any kind, not for bookkeeping reasons or because of irritation, either, since this would be falsely interpreted. In a detailed discussion with Sierra Pomares I explained to him the basic ideas of our long-term investments, repeatedly describing clearly the necessity not only of a military and political alliance but also of an economic one. Sierra is now more than ever convinced of our aims. If we now fill in the gaps in his knowledge with regard to the accounting, we will strengthen his position with his superiors and will have a valuable collaborator in him.

On the suggestion of Sierra Pomares it was decided to take up the Montana project first with Nicolás Franco, then with Jordana, not again with Bau, and finally with the Generalissimo. Sierra's activity ends with Jordana's intervention.

On November 3, 1937, Sierra Pomares and I called on Nicolás Franco. The conference lasted 2 hours in all. In a surprisingly clear manner Nicolás confirmed the following:

1. The decree by no means referred mainly to the Red zone but applied to us.

---

[1] German employee of Hisma.

2. The Montana affair could not be settled by the Generalissimo alone, since he could not bear the responsibility for the mortgaging of Spanish property.

3. The early formation of a [permanent] government was necessary for the handling of our request.

4. The Government did not desire our independent handling of the mine affair as heretofore.

5. The Montana affair had called into the arena contending elements from all camps in Spain.

After detailed discussion of the political and economic aims and the expediency of the alliance between Spain and Germany, we proceeded to the formulation of the main questions. The following questions arose for us:

1. Should we report to Germany the fact of the nullification and the resulting cessation of the economic and technical preparatory work?

2. Should we interrupt the work of exploitation and extraction already begun, as the law actually decrees, and thus also dismiss all workers?

Nicolás answered as follows:

Re 1. We should do nothing, since the fundamental study would take place immediately after formation of a government. The government would be formed in the immediate future.

Re 2. On this point he stated that we must stop work, since the law had to be complied with.

We objected that to stop work would of necessity be not only anti-social but also injurious to an unpredictable extent, when the public became aware of the brusque interruption of the work already begun by the organization. Moreover, we had to report such a decision of the Spanish Government to Germany anyway; for it was just as important in its effect as any decision on the whole project.

Nicolás understood this, and it was decided that with reference to point 2 (cessation of work) we would make an application at once to the Junta in Burgos asking that the work in the mines which had already begun operation might be continued. The decision on the matter would have to be made at once.

It was agreed with reference to point 1 that a suitable request would be submitted at this time, but we realize that a decision cannot be expected until after formation of the government.

After the conference we agreed to talk over the texts of the documents to be submitted in cooperation with Sierra Pomares. Sierra was to speak with Jordana first, in order to prepare the ground. The main conference is to take place in the presence of Sierra Pomares, Pasch, and Bernhardt, whereas the discussion with the Generalissimo is to be carried on by Party Comrade Bernhardt, if possible including Pasch.

General impression of the present situation:

It is clear to us that the Montana project constitutes the whole aim and purpose of our assistance in Spain in the economic field; for all our acquisition of raw materials by purchase signifies nothing permanent, as is known to all purchasing firms, but is only a hand-to-mouth existence as regards raw materials.

The objective of our economic interest in Spain must be the deep penetration into the main sources of Spanish wealth, namely, agriculture and mining. Whereas the products of agriculture fall to the share of the German Reich more or less without effort, since the Spaniards are forced to find a market, the mining problem is of tremendous importance in every respect.

Reduced to a clear formula, it may be said that the success or failure of our efforts in Spanish mining will determine whether our assistance to Spain was successful or misplaced. Clearly recognizing that the Montana problem is the real objective of our economic effort, we must resolve this problem with all the means available. It must be stated here that these means must be found and applied in all fields and that we must, therefore, exert diplomatic, military, and cultural influence in order to attain this single objective of establishing ourselves economically.

Since this problem brings all forces to the fore, forces both pro and con (the old capitalism, Freemasonry, the British, the French, the Vatican, envy, lack of understanding, mistrust, ignorance, laziness, etc.), it is necessary to recognize all the aspects which the task really presents.

We must proceed step by step, since only in this way can we gain followers for our fine ideas. We will be able to show successes in the continuation of our present extraction operations which will be convincing. And, for one thing, we will be recognized by this as a partner who will be eligible under the exceptions which are envisaged for the decree.

The solution of the whole problem as it stands now will have to be forced if it cannot be attained by reasonable means. We must be clear from the very beginning concerning this necessity. It will be our task, however, not to exercise this pressure until persuasion, conviction, and actual successes have failed to attain the end desired.

The whole action must be managed from the start in such a way that the step-by-step procedure is left to a certain extent to private initiative but that in the solution of the entire problem the official German authorities, Four Year Plan, etc., are brought in. Consequently the presentation of the application with regard to the founding of Montana and the list of the acquired mining rights should be placed under the sponsorship of the German Reich by having the Embassy transmit the documents.

In the negotiations we should not only emphasize again and again the real effectiveness of our efforts in the interests of the two nations but also point out in particular that Germany could not tolerate and would not understand a denial by the Spaniards of rights already acquired. Germany would doubtless draw the logical consequences from this deep disappointment and would exercise reserve in all economic matters. German capital, German technology and science will then be utilized in other countries which have more understanding for our honest intentions and present needs.

We are quite aware that all means must be utilized in the treatment of this central problem. We may, therefore, have to take steps to inform the second ally in the Spanish question, Italy, concerning this conduct and manner of procedure, in order to utilize these additional forces for attaining our objectives.

The resistance which the Spaniards have demonstrated forces us more than ever to insist under all circumstances that the rights of the two parties are absolutely equal. Thus we shall insist more on this equality of rights then we previously expected. This equality of rights does not need to be expressed directly in the relative amount of capital invested, but in its final effects it must be so clearly formulated that an arbitrary shifting of the equality of legal status in favor of the Spaniards is impossible. Thus we shall under no circumstances tolerate the frauds, impositions, exploitation, and such similar maneuvers which were formerly so frequent.

After having saved the Spanish people from destruction and prepared the way for their recovery, we must insist on written pledges of the acquired rights on a long-term basis.

MONTANA PROJECT (SUPPLEMENT)

BURGOS, November 4, 1937.

Putting the Montana into operation could take a considerable length of time for the most varied reasons of a political, material, and legal nature. Since, however, the mining of ores is a most urgent necessity for Germany, the objections which justify a delay must be countered. We must be clear about the fact and must make it evident to the leading figures in Nationalist Spain that Germany is engaged in an economic war and thus is also at war. Just as Germany immediately sent her help to her Spanish partner, who finds herself in a real war, Germany has a claim to immediate deliveries by Spain for her own economic war.

In order to prevent the formal legal difficulties, which are undoubtedly justified in many points, from taking effect, the principle which was dominant in Germany's assistance to Spain should be utilized here, too. There should be established, therefore, a sort of

Montana-Hisma.

Under the name of "Araelsa & Pasch," for instance, this would be administered in a trustee capacity, exactly as the original Hisma was at the time, and would work just as actively. Then the final change-over of this enterprise designed for economic warfare into a peace-time enterprise could be undertaken at leisure and according to the situation.

The argument of now repeating the establishment of the original Hisma for the benefit of the economic war in Germany might meet with understanding.

[EDITORS' NOTE. For Hitler's views of the political implications and importance of the Spanish Civil War as expressed at his conference held in the Reich Chancellery with Blomberg, Fritsch, Raeder, Göring, and Neurath on November 5, 1937, the so-called Hossbach Conference, see volume I, document No. 19, pp. 36–37.]

No. 465

1819/416356–57

The State Secretary to the Embassy in Spain

Telegram

No. 409 BERLIN, November 8, 1937—7:45 p.m.
e.o. Pol. III 5317.

With reference to our instruction No. 406 of November 6 [1] and No. 408 of November 7.[2]

After communicating in detail with the Italian Ambassador, please call on Franco and explain to him our view regarding the reply to the draft resolution as follows:

As already stated in telegram No. 406, we consider it desirable to let Barcelona reply first.

In our view, too, the content of Franco's reply should be basically favorable and limited to principles without going into detail. We agree with the proposals of our London Embassy (cf. telegram No. 408 of November 7 [2]) made in agreement with the Italian and Portuguese representatives.

As regards the London proposal to demand immediate granting of belligerent rights, we believe that we are right in assuming that this will not be demanded in the form of a categorical condition but that the intention is to work it into a considered counterproposal which will be joined to the request for clarification of other general ques-

---

[1] Not printed (435/220718).
[2] Not printed (435/220722).

tions connected with the resolution. The questions transmitted in telegram No. 408, V 1 to 5 appear to us also to suit the purpose.

The War Ministry is anxious that at the proper time the following viewpoints should be considered:

1. A real strengthening of the land control;

2. A possible counterproposal to withdraw 5,000 men from each side at first as a trial;

3. The Red and White volunteers evacuated must be sent back to their native lands;

4. The task of the commissions set up cannot consist of their traveling around in the country on their own initiative; they must rather be bound by definite instructions.

It probably goes without saying that Franco will bear in mind the purely general character of his answer at present and will not bring forward at this time the demand contained in the *note verbale* transmitted in the report of October 19, Sa. 3 I a 3940/37,[3] that the withdrawal of the volunteers should be restricted to infantry forces. Likewise, the demand that the patrol on the Red side should be undertaken by Italians and Germans would appear unacceptable to the other side and therefore not suitable as a proposal at the present stage.

The view of the German Government in this sense was brought to the attention of the Spanish Ambassador this morning.

MACKENSEN

---

[3] Not printed (435/220568–77).

No. 466

1819/416359–63

The Foreign Ministry to Various German Diplomatic Missions [1] and the Consulate at Geneva

BERLIN, November 9, 1937.
Pol. III 5330.

The Non-Intervention Committee in London decided in the plenary session of October [*November*] 4, 1937, to submit to the two Spanish parties the questions under discussion (withdrawal of volunteers, granting of belligerent rights, and reinstitution of control measures) and for the time being to leave to them the decision on these three basic questions.

The resolutions appended hereto which were accepted by the committee are in substance similar to those in the British plan of July 14, 1937, which also emphasized these three points: reinstitution of a patrol system, withdrawal of foreign volunteers, and conditions for granting belligerent rights.

---

[1] List of addressees not printed.

As is known, the negotiations on the British proposals failed last summer because of the obstruction by the Soviet Government, which refused to accord belligerent rights to the parties—meaning Franco. The negotiations which were resumed on October 16, 1937, also suffered under the continued attempts at disruption by the Soviet representative, who again tried to extract an essential part of the whole plan by means of his opposition to the idea of granting belligerent rights.

This time the Russian went even further in his obstruction. He stated that his Government regarded the non-intervention policy as having failed and refused responsibility for the continuance of this policy. He did not, however, carry out the logical conclusion of this declaration. Rather, he participated further in the discussions of the committee and he also agreed to the draft of the resolutions, except for those parts which referred to the question of belligerent rights. He refrained from voting on those.

The Soviet attitude was also contradictory in another essential point. The Soviet representative agreed without reservation to the paragraph concerning the reinstitution of land and sea patrol measures, disregarding a note of the Soviet Government he had given the chairman of the committee a few days earlier which represented the control measures in the form contemplated as useless and only causing unnecessary expense. The Soviet Government remained consistent on only one point; it refuses to continue to pay the contributions to which it obligated itself along with the other non-intervention powers.

Considering this attitude of the Soviet Government, there existed the following possibilities for our further procedure: to state that because of lack of unity on the main points the whole plan was a failure; or to continue the non-intervention policy without Russia; or, finally, to consider Russia as still belonging to the circle of the non-intervention powers but to free her from the obligation of granting belligerent rights.

Considering the German Government's basic commitment to the non-intervention policy, the first possibility had to be eliminated. Proceeding from the same principle of avoiding anything which might upset the non-intervention policy, the second possibility was also out of the question, for a state of affairs which left the Russians the freedom to attempt intervention would have involved the danger of serious international complications. Thus only the third possibility remained: to continue to regard Russia as a non-intervention power but to handle the question of belligerent rights only among the other powers. The Italian Government followed the same line, and we remained in close contact with the Italians during the whole course of the negotiations, taking care to harmonize our respective attitudes. Therefore, without regard for the attitude of the Soviet Government, we gave our approval to the draft resolution.

We would have considered it desirable, to be sure, to have defined in the committee, before the queries were sent to the combatants, the rights and duties which the Russians would retain in case of acceptance of the plan by the two parties. For it is contradictory on the one hand to free the Russians from a commitment which is onerous to them and on the other hand to leave them every opportunity for disruptive maneuvers in the committee. In any case it can be expected that the Franco Government will ask the committee in the near future for a full definition of the rights and duties of the Russians. We, however, did not insist on a previous clarification of the Russian position in order not to delay the transmittal of the decision to the two parties and in order to make a contribution toward overcoming the difficult situation.

In any case the resolution provides, at our request and that of the Italians, which the Governments of Portugal, Austria, Hungary, and Albania have also joined, that measures will be taken to fill the gap caused by Soviet Russia's breaking away in the question of belligerent rights. Obtaining a clarification of the Russian attitude by diplomatic means at the same time as the discussions in the committee is also being considered.

In order to give proof of its readiness to achieve practical results as soon as possible along the lines now indicated, the German Government agreed from the very beginning to the symbolic gesture originally contemplated, that is, to withdraw a certain number of volunteers at once from both sides. Unfortunately the committee dropped this idea, since it developed that the Soviet Russians as well as the French did not want an *equal* number of volunteers withdrawn from both sides but a number corresponding to the relative strength of the two parties. Changed in this manner, the proposal would have required extensive investigations on both sides and would therefore have made the meaning of the symbolic gesture illusory.

Until the arrival of the replies of the two parties, the committee is to continue discussion of the composition and powers of the commissions to be sent to Spain in connection with the withdrawal of volunteers.

I suggest that on occasion the points of view discussed here be utilized. A further instruction may follow.

By direction:
BISMARCK

No. 467

435/220749

The Chargé d'Affaires in Spain to the Foreign Ministry

Telegram

SALAMANCA, November 13, 1937—12 : 30 a.m.
No. 559 of November 12 Received November 13—2 : 10 a.m.

With reference to your telegraphic instruction No. 409 [1] and our telegraphic report No. 556.[2]

Franco, who received the Italian Ambassador and me today in the presence of Chef de Cabinet Sangroniz, stated that he was generally in agreement with our proposals, to which the Italian Ambassador added his support, and confirmed particularly his intention to give an affirmative answer in principle. He wishes to let Barcelona make the first move but believes that he cannot indefinitely delay his answer, which is due by November 17, if the Red Government follows the same tactics. Franco also considers it desirable to fix the mandate of the commissions exactly but does not wish to submit objections in the present stage regarding the freedom of movement of the commissions in Nationalist territory in order not to arouse mistrust. Franco does not seem to accord great importance to the Soviet Union's not granting belligerent rights, since he believes that he, for his part, will then have a free hand with regard to Soviet intervention.

At my request Franco promised to inform the German and the Italian Governments of the text of his answer before dispatching it.

HEBERLEIN

[1] Document No. 465, p. 503.
[2] Not printed (435/220736).

No. 468

3372/E010766

The Ambassador in Spain to the Foreign Ministry

Telegram

No. 566 of November 17 November 17, 1937.

With reference to your telegraphic instruction No. 379 of October 19, 1937,[1] and our telegram No. 563 of November 15.[2]

Franco told me yesterday, with regard to the draft of the reply to the Non-Intervention Committee which he is now considering, that he has become somewhat doubtful as to whether the granting of belligerent rights would not now bring him more disadvantages than advantages. If all countries except Russia should grant him belligerent rights, he was uncertain as to whether he might not also have

[1] Not printed (435/220563).
[2] Not printed (435/220759).

to follow the rules of naval warfare with reference to Russia; also, the capture of contraband ships by airplanes was hardly practicable under the rules of warfare. In spite of this, however, for reasons of principle and in the interest of a blockade of the Spanish east coast he would demand the granting of belligerent rights in his reply.

STOHRER

No. 469

435/220767

The Ambassador in Spain to the Foreign Ministry

Telegram

No. 568 of November 17   SALAMANCA, November 17, 1937—10 : 00 p.m.
Received November 18—1 : 50 a.m.

With reference to my report of October 18, Sa. 10 g 3933,[1] and your instruction of October 22, II WE 6815.[1]

I spoke with Franco again yesterday concerning the new mine decree and the concern which it had recently caused with regard to mining rights acquired and to be acquired by Hisma. The Generalissimo stated once more that the decree had been issued because of the danger that the Red Government might sell out everything, and that German interests would be protected.

I stressed repeatedly and emphatically that the delivery of ores from Spain was of the greatest importance for us at present and in the future and absolutely must be guaranteed.

At the same time I asked for a study as to whether further amounts of grain could not be released for us, and Franco promised this likewise.

Please inform Director Bernhardt of the above; he is now in Berlin for a few days by order of General Göring.

STOHRER

---

[1] Not found.

No. 470

2938/569762–65

Memorandum by the State Secretary

BERLIN, November 25, 1937.

After being announced by State Secretary Körner, Herr von Jagwitz called on me today to ask our view of Colonel General Göring's instruction to him concerning clarification of General Franco's stand on the question of Germany's economic position vis-à-vis Spain. On the basis of certain reports which Colonel General Göring considered entirely reliable, but which Herr von Jagwitz evidently considered somewhat questionable, the former had the definite impression that of late General Franco was increasingly granting rights to the British, the effects of which could seriously threaten our economic position in Spain. The Colonel General took the view that his unusually great personal assistance to General Franco gave him the right to make very definite demands with regard to the safeguarding of the German "war booty" (the Colonel General's literal expression). Herr von Jagwitz was therefore supposed to go to Salamanca at once and "hold a pistol to General Franco's breast." Herr von Jagwitz remarked about this order that at the present moment such an approach in terms of an ultimatum did not seem to him to be in our interest. Certain things, no doubt, were under way between Franco and England which we regarded as suspicious, if only for the reason that Franco did not put his cards on the table in these matters, but it should not be overlooked that Franco quite naturally had to take British commercial interests in Spain into account. What we had received thus far from Spain on the basis of the current contracts was, after all, a very considerable amount; about 90 millions was involved, almost exclusively in vital raw materials, whereas formerly the main part of our commercial transactions in Spain had been taken up with the non-essential import of oranges to the sum of over 40 million marks. One should also consider whether a threat made to the General that we would reduce our present military support or perhaps even stop it altogether would still have the same effect at the present military stage, which is favorable for Franco, as it would have had about 3 months ago. If the threat were not effective with Franco and he accepted the consequences, then we would have completely lost our commercial connections with Spain. For these reasons it appeared to him, Jagwitz, more expedient not to proceed in this vigorous way for the time being but rather to have our Ambassador visit General Franco at once and, referring to a certain anxiety which had arisen here with regard to the security of our economic claims and rights in Spain, to inform Franco that he had been called to Berlin to make an immediate report concerning these matters and therefore must receive very clear explanations from the General in this regard before starting his trip. If Franco should answer evasively or should even refuse, further steps could be discussed when the Ambassador makes his personal report here. There would still then be time to send him, Jagwitz, to Salamanca as a special envoy with appropriate instructions in the nature of an ultimatum. He, Jagwitz, had explained these ideas to State Secretary Körner and had been authorized by him to get our opinion. I told Herr von Jagwitz that in my opinion the middle course suggested by him, which provided that first the person appointed for such tasks, that is, our Ambassador, should bring his influence to bear on Franco, would be proper in this situation. If General Franco should evade an explanation which provides us with the necessary assurances, particularly with regard to our mines, which are said to be particularly endangered, then there would still be time enough to proceed in the manner ordered by Colonel General Göring. Herr von Jagwitz intended to report in this sense to State Secretary Körner, who would then on his part get in touch with Colonel General Göring. He asked me also to transmit my opinion directly to Herr Körner, which I promised to do.

Herr von Jagwitz introduced Herr Bernhardt to me at the close of the conference and in his presence recapitulated briefly the contents of our conversation. Herr Bernhardt is also of the opinion that a move should first be made through Herr von Stohrer. Herr Bernhardt in addition made the request, energetically supported by Herr von Jagwitz, that I regularize his passport status, which is somewhat involved on account of its manner of origin (he is still traveling on a false passport), and that I see that his traveling papers are made out in such a manner that he would be enabled without difficulty to take along secret and important documents through France. They considered a diplomatic passport most suitable for this purpose. I told them that a diplomatic passport was out of the question under the present regulations but that I would be glad to take up the matter; for the rest, as far as carrying secret documents was concerned, I could say even now as my personal opinion that the surest solution seemed to me that of periodically designating Herr Bernhardt as a courier with the necessary papers. If we were to make out a different passport for Herr Bernhardt than the usual police passport, then provision should first be made to have Colonel General Göring, representing the Four Year Plan, inform us what official title Herr Bernhardt should be given in the passport.

For the rest, both men stressed that they were greatly concerned to state emphatically that their relationship with Ambassador von Stohrer was excellent and that their recent remark (which they have in the meantime explained to Herr Clodius) had nothing in the remotest to do with a complaint.[1]

Mackensen

---

[1] Unsigned marginal note: "To the Acting Director of W. with a request for an early conference (Herr Bernhardt's present passport is supposedly in Herr Ripken's possession at the moment)."

No. 471

136/73542

Memorandum by the Deputy Director of the Economic Policy Department

BERLIN, November 27, 1937.

Herr von Jagwitz telephoned at noon today and informed me that the procedure proposed in the conference he had with State Secretary von Mackensen on November 25 with reference to safeguarding our economic rights in Spain had been approved by State Secretary Körner. Herr von Jagwitz requested that Herr von Stohrer now be instructed to this effect as soon as possible. He emphasized again that in the main it was a question, first, of securing our mining concessions after the proclamation of the new Spanish mining law and, second, of preventing Anglo-Spanish agreements detrimental to us.

In discussing the question whether it was advisable to summon Herr von Stohrer to Berlin after he had made his *démarche*, I told Herr von Jagwitz that I did not consider that wise since, after his first *démarche*, Herr von Stohrer had to be available for further discussions in Salamanca. Herr von Jagwitz agreed.

CLODIUS

No. 472

2946/576078–79

The Foreign Ministry to the Embassy in Spain

W II WE 7512 BERLIN, November 27, 1937.

Subject: German mining rights in Spain.

With reference to your telegraphic report No. 568 of November 17.

A long conversation was held with Herr Bernhardt in the Foreign Ministry on November 24 regarding the possible effects of the Spanish law of November [*October*] 9 on the mining rights acquired by Hisma. The anxiety of Hisma and the foreign-trade group under Minister President Colonel General Göring, Commissioner for the Four Year Plan, is not altogether dissipated by the statements of Generalissimo Franco that German interests would be safeguarded. In order to give Franco's assurances a more definite content, I therefore request that the enclosed list [1] of mining rights acquired by Hisma be handed to General Franco and that a binding pledge be obtained from him to the effect that the rights of Hisma specified in the list receive the protection of the Spanish Government.

---

[1] Not printed (2946/576081–84).

By way of precaution I wish to remark that the list contains only the present mining rights of Hisma. It is not known here whether an expansion of mining interests beyond the rights specified in the list is contemplated. Therefore, in order not to restrict Hisma's freedom of action, the list should not be represented as setting limits to Hisma's plans.

Only one copy of the list is available here. Because of lack of time, copies could not be made. I therefore request that three copies be sent to the Foreign Ministry.

Please report as soon as possible on the outcome of your approach to General Franco.

By direction:
SABATH

No. 473

322/193713–20

The Ambassador in Spain to the Foreign Ministry

IN PART CONFIDENTIAL   SALAMANCA, November 27, 1937.
No. 4721   W II WE 7682.

Subject: German-Spanish commercial relations.

With the *de facto* recognition of the Franco Government by England [1] a new phase in the relations of Nationalist Spain with the rest of the world has begun. Japan is about to follow the example of Germany, Italy, Albania, and several small South and Central American countries in recognizing the Franco Government *de jure;* Austria, Hungary, Switzerland, and Holland have taken up semiofficial relations with Nationalist Spain, and other states such as Yugoslavia, Poland, and recently Belgium, too, show that they are likewise anxious to regularize their relations with the new Spain.

This race finds its explanation, not in any sudden necessity for the various governments to protect and serve their citizens in Nationalist Spain or to safeguard other general interests, but—exactly as with England—in the well-considered effort to conclude advantageous trade agreements under favorable conditions before the final victory of the Nationalist movement and to secure their future commercial relations with Spain.

Under these circumstances it might be useful to examine the present status of German commercial relations with Spain and their prospects for the future.

---

[1] On Nov. 16 Sir Robert Hodgson was appointed British agent in Nationalist Spain. On Nov. 22 the Nationalists replied by accrediting the Duke of Alba as their agent in London. On Dec. 1 Japan recognized the Nationalist administration *de jure.*

Since the beginning of the Spanish Civil War, that is, for more than a year, almost all commercial intercourse between Germany and Spain has been conducted through Hisma, the commercial company established *ad hoc*, whose contractor in Germany is Rowak. The undeniable success of these establishments and their work is based, first, on the selection of the goods exchanged between Germany and Spain— that is, the goods which are vital for Germany and Spain at the present time—and, second, on the balancing or settling insured by this organization for all deliveries made to Spain from Germany, in particular war deliveries, by means of the goods passing via Hisma to Germany. A great advantage of the monopoly-like position of Hisma is, for the moment, that unrestricted private arrangements are avoided, since German goods are imported into Spain in practically no other way, and consequently—as Spain does not pay in foreign exchange— an increase in Spain's debt to us is avoided. Moreover, as a trust company, Hisma can divert sums of pesetas, which it obtains from the Spanish Government in payment of debts, to investments in the interest of our supply of raw materials (Four Year Plan and the future).

With the numerous foreign competitors, especially England, which are now expected to appear in the Spanish market, it is a question, however, whether we must not take still further precautions in order to insure the sale of German goods for the future.

Recently there have been numerous—sometimes very violent—complaints from German firms, from Spanish firms which seek to maintain trade with Germany, and from individual merchants on account of the refusal to issue import permits for German goods which would find a good market in Spain (see the annex,[2] for example). Often Hisma is unjustly blamed—perhaps not entirely without the assistance of the responsible Spanish authorities—for the rejection of such applications; in general, a stiffening toward our requirements and wishes can be noted of late on the part of these not very objective authorities. In most cases the reason for not granting an import license is rather to be sought in the fact that we have to demand payment in foreign exchange for the imports to Spain that do not go through Hisma. There are reports here of the refusal of applications for importing German goods when at the same time the interested party was informed that he could obtain an import license for the same goods from England, etc., since the country in question either gave credit or was satisfied with full or partial payment for the goods in pesetas or some other kind of compensation. It seems that here and there England, in placing orders for Spanish goods for which she pays in foreign exchange, even makes the purchase of some British goods a condition and so assures herself of further sales. The agitation of

---

[2] Not printed (322/193721).

the German businessmen and their uneasiness with regard to the future are therefore understandable.

At various times I have already been able to report more or less confirmed rumors according to which the British are also negotiating with Spanish agencies regarding a grant of credit.

As appears further from two reports by the New York correspondent in the *Nachrichten für den Aussenhandel* of November 6 and 18, a representative of the Spanish Nationalist Government is said to be negotiating with North American business groups for a resumption of reciprocal trade relations. The Americans are said to have become convinced that it is necessary to invest American capital in Nationalist Spain in order not to fall behind other countries.

I also hear that just in the last few days a trade agreement has been concluded between Nationalist Spain and Switzerland in which Switzerland apparently promises 30 percent in foreign exchange in payment for Spanish goods, and demands the purchase of Swiss goods only for the remainder. I shall send a further report on this agreement.

It is especially noteworthy that French business also is already stirring; thus in a telegram to Paris the French Chamber of Commerce in San Sebastián urgently requested the establishment of commercial relations with Nationalist Spain.

The other countries will follow the example of the foregoing and try to insure for themselves as large a share as possible in the future Spanish market.

Accordingly it would hardly be saying too much to state that today we are standing at the crossroads. One road—hitherto followed with success—may lead to at least a partial loss of the Spanish market if, in view of the great increase in our credit balance as a result of the war deliveries, we believe that we must limit or even halt completely our other exports to Spain. The choice of the other road—further capital export through a grant of credit or acceptance of payment in pesetas—which has become virtually impossible as the result of our foreign-exchange position, would hardly meet with fewer objections than the former.

According to what the Italian Ambassador tells me, the Italians have the same difficulties. After apparently considerable reductions or cancellations, the "war debt" which the Spaniards owe Italy amounts—as Count Viola tells me—to 3 billion lire. The payments in goods promised by Spain seem already to have resulted in a very serious curtailment of Italian exports to Spain.

It is certain—always presupposing, naturally, that in the not too distant future the Civil War will end in favor of Franco—that Nationalist Spain will have a very great shortage of goods. In order to reconstruct the devastated areas and her entire economy, she will have to draw on foreign help and consequently foreign capital in every form, since after the conclusion of peace she will not be in a position to pay in full for the very considerable imports of foreign goods needed either with the proceeds of the Spanish goods available for export or in any other way.

According to the fundamental principles of the new Nationalist regime, it will presumably be less eager to obtain large cash credits than credits in goods, especially in the form of short-term emergency credits.

Can we, or even must we, meet the expected—or, rather, already present—credit requirements of Spain in order, in addition to obtaining payment for our war deliveries by deliveries of goods (especially raw materials), to retain for ourselves the Spanish market? From various sides the question is answered in the affirmative, and it is pointed out that if we refuse business which does not bring in any foreign exchange we shall do no business at all and shall possibly be ousted permanently from the market—for the future, too, when the shortage of foreign currency may have become less acute; whereas, if we forego payment in foreign exchange—either by granting credit or by accepting pesetas—we could promote our exports, assure work for the German worker, and retain the market for ourselves, perhaps even expand it.

One party, who requested not to be named, sent me the annexed draft [3] of a plan along these lines which contains certain proposals for settlement, although only in broad outline.

I do not agree altogether with the view advocated in the memorandum; in my opinion too little account is taken of the factor of the growing indebtedness, which would be especially serious in the event of a later devaluation of the peseta; it also seems to me necessary to give greater latitude to private initiative and hence also introduce more private risk. Moreover, I am not in a position to judge whether such a plan is at all practicable without encroaching on the useful work of Hisma for the Four Year Plan. In any case it would be necessary to include a guaranty for the transactions of Hisma. Nevertheless I felt that I should submit this plan, since the same or similar lines of reasoning have been expounded to me repeatedly.

In any case, however, it would seem, now that the Civil War appears to be drawing to an end, that the moment has come for immediately giving thorough study to the problem of securing German trade with

---

[3] Not printed (322/193722–25). It consisted of a proposal for extension of credit to Spain.

Spain in the future, considering all possibilities whereby, after the end of the Spanish Civil War, we might retain the Spanish raw-materials market and at the same time assure the sale of German products in Spain. It should also not be overlooked, with regard to the former, that a considerable decrease in Spain's ability to export will set in with respect to a number of raw materials (especially wool) when the needs of the part of Spain which is still Red make themselves felt and the industries located there become purchasers once more.

I should appreciate being informed as soon as possible concerning the view held there on these questions.

I intended to inform Herr Bernhardt, the head of Hisma, of this report before dispatching it; since he is now in Germany, I shall send him a carbon copy of the report upon his return and request an opinion on the basis of his experience and his knowledge of economic conditions here.

v. STOHRER

No. 474

322/193726–29

Memorandum by the Director of the Economic Policy Department

BERLIN, November 30, 1937.

As Herr von Jagwitz had conveyed previously, Minister President Colonel General Göring intends to appoint Herr Bernhardt as his special representative for economic questions in Nationalist Spain. Since the Minister President feels it important that this appointment be made only after previous concurrence of the Foreign Ministry, he instructed Herr von Jagwitz to agree with us beforehand about the text of the communication by which the Foreign Ministry would be informed of the appointment. Herr von Jagwitz has delivered the attached draft, of which the first three paragraphs have already been discussed with us. I propose that Herr von Jagwitz be informed that we are in agreement with regard to these three paragraphs but that we would like to request that the notification to the Spanish Government of the appointment of Herr Bernhardt, as proposed in the fourth paragraph, be omitted, at least for the time being. The task assigned to Herr Bernhardt does not require that he carry on negotiations with the Spanish Government except in matters which involve Hisma. Apart from the fact that such negotiations would be undesirable from the point of view of the position of the Embassy, it would be decidedly objectionable on political grounds were Herr Bernhardt to approach the Spanish Government on such a mission just at the moment when

Herr von Stohrer has been directed to carry on the negotiations with General Franco for the protection of German economic interests in Spain.

Herewith submitted to the State Secretary with the request that I be authorized to communicate with Herr von Jagwitz in the sense proposed.

WIEHL

[Enclosure]

DRAFT

BERLIN, November 27, 1937.

Minister President Colonel General Göring, Commissioner for the Four Year Plan, has appointed Herr Johannes G. F. Bernhardt, head of Hisma Ltd., as his special representative for economic questions in Nationalist Spain. In continuing his previous activity as head of Hisma, Herr Bernhardt will have the duty of seeing to it that the raw materials and vital foodstuffs necessary for the execution of the Four Year Plan shall, insofar as Spain figures as a source of these products, be secured for the German economy on the largest scale possible. Beyond this, he has been instructed to devote his attention to all questions which concern future reciprocal economic relations between Germany and Spain, in order to see that Germany's economic position in Spain at this time, and especially after the restoration of normal conditions in Spain, is expanded and rendered secure.

Herr Bernhardt has been instructed further to observe the economic efforts of other countries insofar as they affect relations between Germany and Spain, and especially to report in case they might seriously curtail our economic position in Spain.

Since the task assigned to Herr Bernhardt partly coincides with the duties of the German Embassy in Spain, Herr Bernhardt has been instructed to maintain the closest contact with the Embassy in the performance of his task and to send his pertinent reports through the Embassy. In order to insure as close cooperation as possible between Herr Bernhardt and the Embassy, I request that the latter be informed of the task assigned to Herr Bernhardt and that the Ambassador be asked in reporting on economic questions of a fundamental nature to get in touch with Herr Bernhardt beforehand insofar as possible and, in the event of a difference of opinion, to report at the same time the divergent view of Herr Bernhardt.

I request further that the Embassy in Salamanca be asked to inform the Spanish Nationalist Government in a suitable manner of the mission assigned to Herr Bernhardt.

By direction:

No. 475

435/220791–92

The Foreign Minister to the Embassy in Spain

Telegram

SECRET   BERLIN, November 30, 1937.
No. 433   W II WE 7557.

For the Ambassador personally.

With reference to our telegraphic instruction 431 of November 27 [1] and written instruction W II 6664 of October 16.[2]

1. Nicolás Franco's statement on agreements between Spain and England is, according to reports from a reliable source, either incomplete or outdated by further developments withheld from us by the Spaniards. We have reliable information that Franco is supposed to have offered England very considerable concessions, which, though they are not known to us in detail, represent a serious threat to our interests. I therefore request that the Generalissimo be asked personally for an explanation and that it be made quite clear to him that, apart from all priorities granted us by treaty and simply on the basis of our exceedingly effective moral, financial, and military support of Franco in the critical moments of his rebellion, we insist absolutely on our well-founded demand that our vital economic interests are not sacrificed to the interests of third parties but are satisfied in full. In particular, we must insist that the major part of the ore and iron production of the Bilbao and Asturias mines is reserved for us and that, in addition, we are given an unlimited concession for the purchase of scrap. To be sure, we recognize the necessity, as already stated in the instruction of October 16, of letting England also have a share in the trade with Spain. But we will by no means put up with a favoring of England which displaces us from our economic position, especially in the purchase of raw materials. If General Franco should reply evasively or indeed confirm the correctness of our information, at the same time refusing to give satisfactory explanations as to how he will give our justified interests their due, please inform him plainly that in this case we on our part shall also unfortunately be forced to reexamine our attitude toward the Spanish Nationalist Government on various questions in view of this new situation.

2. As a test of the extent to which Franco is willing to consider German interests, please demand recognition of the list of German mining rights transmitted with the instruction of November 27.[3]

---

[1] Not printed (2946/576080).
[2] Document No. 440, p. 461.
[3] See document No. 472, p. 511.

3. Since Franco's negotiations with England are probably still in progress and a speedy decision may be necessary, please make the *démarche* with the Generalissimo immediately and report by wire.

NEURATH

No. 476

1819/416386–88

The Ambassador in Spain to the Foreign Ministry

SECRET
SS 8

SAN SEBASTIÁN, December 3, 1937.
Pol. III 5694.

Subject: Armistice negotiations between White and Red Spain.

According to all I have been told by old and well-informed Spanish friends here, non-binding conferences on ending the Civil War have actually taken place recently between White and Red Spain. Evidently the Red Spanish Ambassadors in Paris and London, especially, have used their influence toward stopping the war. This exchange of ideas, however, never reached the stage of actual negotiations, since the military leaders on the Red side violently opposed the idea of a negotiated peace from the very beginning on the ground that Franco has said that he would bring the Red Spanish officers before a military court without mercy. On the other hand Franco's demand for an unconditional surrender, which is understandable in view of the present war situation, deprived the conferences of any prospect of success from the very outset.

Under these circumstances foreign intervention for the purpose of ending the war, which the Reds had definitely expected lately, was also made impossible. On the Red side companys, in particular, had hoped to bring about a "Federación Española," that is, a partitioning of Spain into two parts, whereby the Reds would have been prepared to cede Madrid and all of Andalusia to Franco. In order to bring about this solution, the Reds were thinking of a radical change in government, about which in fact the entire foreign press had been writing for the past weeks. It was planned to call upon moderate men like Miguel Maura, Sánchez Ramón, Portela, and Madariaga and to give the presidency to the well-known scholar Altamira [1] because of his international reputation. This government was to negotiate with Franco. Emigration was to be facilitated for the Republican and Socialist leaders of the Red party, and in the "Federación Ibérica" or "Española" then formed each side was to choose the regime which appealed to it the most.

---

[1] Rafael Altamira y Crevea, Spanish jurist and historian, professor of history, University of Madrid, 1914–36; judge, Permanent Court of International Justice, The Hague, 1922–46; professor, National University of Mexico, 1946–.

This whole plan failed because of the aforementioned attitude of the Red military leaders and Franco's decisive refusal to negotiate—which, as was reported by telegram, he recently expressed so energetically in public, probably just because of the plans mentioned.

It is probable that this unofficial and indirect communication between Red and White is the reason for the delay in the offensive planned by Franco, even though he withheld this from his German and Italian military advisers. This is the only way to explain the fact that in the face of approaching winter valuable time was permitted to elapse without an attempt to force the enemy to surrender to one more powerful assault. According to my information, however, still other considerations have induced Franco to hesitate and permit the Reds to hope that a negotiated peace would be possible without further fighting. Both sides told themselves that a big new offensive, which, as is known, was to be directed against rich Catalonia, would destroy so much national wealth and would render 100,000 to 150,000 Spanish men incapable of fighting and perhaps of working, so that through these losses the future credit and the economic reconstruction of Spain would suffer decisively. In line with this reasoning, another argument used against a big, costly offensive was that on the Red side thousands of Spaniards who in their hearts were for Franco would be forced to die for the false Red "ideal."

As I have also learned from a source which repeatedly proved reliable as early as during the World War,[2] there now remains, following the rejection of these feelers put out by the Reds, only one contact between the Whites and the Reds, which is maintained with the commander of Irún by a certain Angel Baza, a secretary of Indalecio Prieto. Even in very recent days Baza has flown several times from Barcelona to Biarritz; from there he gets in touch with the above-mentioned authority in Irún through an intermediary. During one of his last visits to Biarritz he stated that considerable improvement had been achieved lately on the Red side with regard to the reestablishment of discipline in the army and order in the rear echelons, as well as with regard to the supplies of ammunition and weapons. For this reason the Red Spanish Government had considered it safe to invite several British M.P.'s to visit Barcelona and Valencia. The Red Spanish Government hoped to be able to alter British expectations of an early Franco victory by means of the favorable impression which the British parliamentarians would gain.

According to today's press reports the leader of the British opposition, Mr. Attlee, is in fact already en route to Barcelona.

VON STOHRER

---

[2] Stohrer had served in the German Embassy in Spain during World War I.

No. 477

1819/416390

The Ambassador in Spain to the Foreign Ministry

SECRET   SAN SEBASTIÁN, December 3, 1937.
SS 9

Subject: Spain and Italian aid.

According to information consistently given to me on my travels in northern and southern Spain and especially here in the present political milieu of San Sebastián, there is increasing annoyance over the attitude of the Italians and the conduct of Italian officers and troops, not only in the military and political circles of Nationalist Spain but also quite generally among the Spanish people. It can even be said that in circles at Franco's headquarters they have pretty much had their fill of the entire Italian military aid. The extravagant glorification of Italian deeds of arms, the presumptuousness of Italian military authorities, the conduct of the troops at the front and especially in the rear echelons, the smuggling of Italian goods promoted by the Italian military, which appears now and again, and other encroachments are causing an increasing dislike for the Italians.

With regard to Italian military assistance in the impending operations, I know from eyewitnesses that a violent scene occurred between Franco on one hand and the Italian Ambassador and the former Italian commander in chief, General Bastiani, on the other. Franco has also occasionally spoken disparagingly to the commander in chief of the Condor Legion about Italian military aid and at various other times has complained about the failure of military operations because of conflicts in the Italian military command over matters of vanity and prestige. I hear that on account of the comparatively poor military quality of the Italian units Franco intends to flank the Italians with the excellent Spanish Navarra brigades in the next offensive.

Moreover, General Franco told me a few days ago that, in view of the latest decisions of the Non-Intervention Committee in London, 3,000 Italian troops, which, to be sure, consist partly of sick and unreliable elements, have already been withdrawn and prepared for immediate shipment home.

Now as in the past the steady and unostentatious soldierly conduct and the reserve of the German volunteers are widely praised and contrasted with the conduct of the Italians. I am by no means basing this statement on the praise expressed every day to me or other members of the Embassy but on the report of appraisals spoken outside the range of German hearing.

VON STOHRER

No. 478

136/73546

The State Secretary to the State Secretary in the Office of the Commissioner for the Four Year Plan

BERLIN, December 3, 1937.

DEAR HERR KÖRNER: In confirmation of my telephone call I convey to you the following text of the telegraphic report just received from Herr von Stohrer:[1]

"The instruction has just been carried out in Burgos.

"Franco stated most emphatically that all reports of concessions granted to or intended for England, or possibly demanded by England, were pure fabrications.

"Further particulars on the conversation will follow tomorrow by the usual radio channel.

STOHRER"

The detailed report in prospect will be sent to you by the quickest means as soon as it arrives.

Heil Hitler!

Faithfully yours,

v. MACKENSEN

---

[1] This was Stohrer's telegram No. 1 of Dec. 2, sent from San Sebastián at 1:30 a.m. on Dec. 3 (136/73547).

No. 479

2946/576087–89

The State Secretary to the Ambassador in Spain

BERLIN, December 3, 1937.

DEAR HERR VON STOHRER: Although in today's telegram [1] we have meanwhile received your answer to our telegraphic instruction of November 30,[2] I should like anyway to explain to you in a few words how our instruction originated; unfortunately I have not found time to do this during the last few days. I probably do not need to stress that the content of this letter is meant exclusively for your personal information.

State Secretary Körner recently informed me on instructions of Colonel General Göring during one of my visits to Carinhall that the Colonel General had been convinced on the basis of information in his possession, which he considered completely authentic, that General Franco had entered into discussions with the British, in the course of which concessions of such a nature as to cause most serious injury

---

[1] See document No. 478, *supra.*
[2] Document No. 475, p. 518.

to our interests in Spain had already been made and would still be made to the British. He was by no means disposed to put up with such conduct on the part of the Generalissimo, whom he had aided in the most difficult times with the full weight of his personal prestige and whom he had continued to support to the utmost extent possible. His responsibility to the German people obligated him to see to it that now the Spaniards also did what was humanly possible to satisfy German interests (mines, raw materials, etc.). He had no idea of accepting in silence the situation as it appeared to him today and had consequently decided to send Herr von Jagwitz to Spain immediately in order to "hold a pistol to the Generalissimo's breast." Herr von Jagwitz was to leave no doubt that he, the Colonel General, was resolved to take the most stringent measures if the Generalissimo did not guarantee our rights and interests in an absolutely clear form.

A few days later Herr von Jagwitz made an appointment with me through State Secretary Körner in order to discuss the whole situation. He made it clear that he himself thought the Colonel General went somewhat beyond what was called for at the moment and indicated that the Colonel General had not permitted him to look at the documents on the basis of which he had thought it necessary to conclude that the Spaniards were engaged in machinations injurious to us. I got the impression that Herr von Jagwitz himself did not regard the situation as so serious. In the course of the conversation he himself made the suggestion that before the mission assigned to him was carried out an intermediate stage should be inserted and General Franco should first be approached once more through our diplomatic representative. I was convinced by his reasoning, and on the basis of our conversation I proposed to State Secretary Körner that the Colonel General be advised to follow the procedure which was formulated in our telegram to you. State Secretary Körner informed the Colonel General to this effect and received his full approval for our proposal. Naturally the path is open for a return to the original ideas, if Franco does not give the assurances which the Colonel General considers necessary, and which cannot consist only in promises. A denial of the rumors regarding his transactions with the British is naturally not sufficient for this; rather we must receive something quite tangible. For the time being we are waiting for the radio report which you announced for tomorrow. I regard it as desirable, however, to orient you as to what led up to our telegraphic instruction of November 30.

With cordial greetings and Heil Hitler!

As ever,

MACKENSEN

No. 480

2938/569781–82

The Ambassador in Spain to the Foreign Ministry

Telegram

No. 601 of December 4   SALAMANCA, December 4, 1947—10 : 00 p.m.
Received December 5—1 : 10 a.m.
zu W II 7711.

With reference to your telegram 433 of November 30 and my telegram 1 of December 2 from San Sebastián.[1]

Franco showed great surprise—and he seemed to me entirely sincere—at the reports of supposed concessions made by Spain and England, or promised to or demanded by England. Repeatedly and very decisively he replied to all my counterquestions as to whether England might after all have been given some commitment of an economic nature lately, or whether perhaps concessions had been made to private British firms, etc., that this was not the case. He said that he was in fact surprised that England—as he had told me once before a short while ago—"paid so little attention to Spain" in economic matters.

Nevertheless, pointing out that I was speaking by official order, I once more stressed to Franco the stand emphatically expressed during my last conversation with him (my telegram No. 568 of November 17) concerning the importance of the Spanish raw materials market for Germany and made extensive use of the arguments supplied me in telegram No. 433.

With regard to mining rights, Franco, in receiving the list of concessions acquired by Hisma, promised immediate and friendly consideration as to how our demands could be assured under the new law. I shall press for speed.

He stated, on the other hand, that scrap metal had been exported at best only occasionally, and that the Spanish armament industry was in urgent need of scrap at the present time, so that they had even introduced scrap collection days. After this conversation Franco is no longer in any doubt as to the great extent of our interest in Spanish exports of raw materials, especially ores, and our determination to advance it energetically.

In spite of the above-mentioned denials by Franco, I still intend to discuss the matter seriously with the Chef de Cabinet too, if only as a matter of precaution for the future in view of the early arrival of a semiofficial British delegation. For this reason it would be very

---

[1] See document No. 478, p. 522.

useful for me to know what the objectionable concessions are that are supposed to have been promised England according to the information available to you.

STOHRER

No. 481

1819/416385

The Ambassador in Spain to the Foreign Ministry

SS 44   SAN SEBASTIÁN, December 10, 1937.

Pol. III 5819.

With reference to my report No. SS 10 of December 4.[1]

Subject: Red Spanish feelers for ending the Civil War through negotiations.

I have learned, in addition to the information sent in my previous report, that the first unsuccessful exchange of views on a possible end of the Spanish Civil War through negotiations took place between representatives of the Red Spanish Embassies in Paris and London and some Franco agents in Belgium.

The contact has not been broken off entirely even now. In addition to Indalecio Prieto's secretary, Angel Baza, mentioned in the previous report, another Red Spanish agent, Heliodoro de la Torre, the former "Minister of Justice" of the Red Basque "Government," who travels back and forth between Bayonne and Barcelona, is making efforts at present to pursue the matter further in communication with the Spanish Nationalist commander or Irún.

STOHRER

---

[1] Not printed (5150/E303649–53).

No. 482

2946/576092–94

The Foreign Ministry to the Embassy in Spain

W II W E 7799   BERLIN, December 13, 1937.

Drafting Officer: Counselor of Legation Sabath.

Subject: Mining rights.

According to telegraphic report No. 601 of December 4 General Franco promised to give immediate and friendly consideration to the list of Hisma's mining rights given to him for recognition. When the representations were repeated to the Chef de Cabinet on December 8 (telegraphic report No. 608 [1]) no commitment beyond this was made.

---

[1] Not printed (136/73551).

The statements of Franco and his Chef de Cabinet are unsatisfactory. Even if no immediate commitment could have been given, their statements should still have had a more positive character. General Franco knows the German raw materials situation very well and consequently the importance of German participation in Spanish mines. This has repeatedly been the subject of conversations and negotiations. Finally, so much time has elapsed since the list was presented on December 4 that any necessary examination, the urgency of which was obvious, could have been concluded long ago.

The mining decree of October 9 does not limit the decision of the Spanish Government. Rather it extends its freedom of action. Furthermore, recognition of the mining rights would have been the most convincing confirmation of Franco's assurance that the decree is not directed against Germany. Since he was aware of the concern which the decree caused us, if he had the attitude toward Germany which we expect of him he should even have welcomed being given an opportunity to reestablish, by means of a generous action, the clear and unequivocal situation which existed formerly.

We have always preferred to speak with Franco on a basis of complete mutual trust and to consider the similarity of interests of the two countries and the ability of their economies to supplement one another as the decisive factor. We have therefore been reluctant to appeal to contractual obligations which were merely the expression of this basic attitude. Should Franco's delaying attitude remain in evidence, however, in the case of recognition of the claim to mining rights, in other words in a question which is of overwhelming importance for the German economy, please insist with utmost emphasis on adherence to the obligations entered into in the secret protocol of July 16. Franco is well aware of the full scope of this agreement. He participated personally in formulating article III of this protocol, which applies in this case.

If the Spanish Nationalist Government is supposed to facilitate the organization of Spanish companies for developing and exploiting mineral resources, with the participation of German firms as far as possible, then it is thereby obligated to engage in activity which can be limited at best only by Spain's own vital needs. That is much more than mere "friendly consideration."

Please demand once more most emphatically, making use of the above arguments, recognition of Hisma's mining claims, and report by telegram.

By direction:
WIEHL

No. 483

136/73556

Memorandum by the State Secretary (Excerpt)

December 16, 1937.

The Italian Ambassador called on me this evening to discuss several separate questions:

1 . . . . (¹)
2 . . . . (¹)
3 . . . . (¹)

4. From Rome reports, the Ambassador gathered that they were somewhat concerned there with regard to the activity of the Duke of Alba in London and Quiñones de León in Paris. Especially were they watching with some skepticism the *British* activities in Nationalist Spain. Signor Attolico wished to know whether we shared this feeling. I told him that we, too, were watching this activity very closely and had just recently requested our Ambassador to express his opinion on the status of Anglo-Spanish relations, giving special consideration to what success, if any, British activities may already have had in the economic field. The Ambassador's statement was not yet available. Signor Attolico requested that as soon as it arrived I tell him whatever it contained that might interest the Italians. He also asked that Herr von Stohrer be requested to maintain close contact with his Italian colleague in these questions.

---

¹ Omissions indicated in the original.

No. 484

2946/576101–04

Memorandum by the Ambassador in Spain

SALAMANCA, December 16, 1937.

On December 14 I again visited Chef de Cabinet Sangroniz in San Sebastián to present to him once more in the most urgent manner the necessity of an early affirmative reply with regard to our mining rights. Señor Sangroniz promised to discuss the matter in this sense with the Junta and, if possible, with the Generalissimo when he was in Burgos on the following day and to push it as much as possible. He also promised to inform me of the outcome in Salamanca on December 16. During this conversation I pointed out to Señor Sangroniz that we must definitely have at least a tentative affirmative answer at once.

When I called on Señor Sangroniz here in Salamanca today, he reported to me that he had spoken with the members of the Junta and had urged them to settle the matter as soon as possible, and that he had also spoken about it with the Generalissimo, who likewise showed the greatest interest. To my question as to when this answer could be expected, Señor Sangroniz replied that he did not know, since this decision depended on the technical agencies of the Junta. At my insistence he stated as his personal opinion that this question was of the greatest importance for Spain and therefore could not be disposed of in a hurry. After all, the matter involved access to Spanish mineral resources, and therefore very considerable values were at stake. It should not be forgotten that the Spanish Government was a provisional government which could not proceed precipitately in such matters. Great responsibility rested with the Generalissimo, too, in this respect. Upon my remark that 10 days, after all, gave sufficient time for studying the matter, Señor Sangroniz protested—always emphasizing that he was not competent in this question—that 73 mine concessions represented an equal number of different rights, which had to be examined one by one. When I then referred to the protocol of July 16 of this year in which Spain had expressly agreed to our participation in the economic reconstruction of Spain, especially in the development and exploitation of mineral resources, and had consented to the organization of Spanish companies for such development with German citizens or German firms participating, Señor Sangroniz emphasized that he knew this very well since he had taken part in the discussions at the time, but that it was expressly stated in the provisions of the protocol in question that such enterprises, etc., "had to be compatible with the general stipulations of Spanish law." Consequently it had to be examined in each individual case whether the legal provisions had been observed in the acquisition of the various concessions, especially with regard to the percentage of ownership.

In addition, I also spoke once more to Nicolás Franco yesterday about the importance of Spanish mineral deliveries to Germany and about the Montana affair and also explained to him in an unmistakable manner the importance of this question for us and for the future of German-Spanish economic relations. Nicolás Franco, who had had an exhaustive conversation on the matter with Herr Bernhardt about 4 weeks ago (see Herr Bernhardt's memorandum on this subject), repeated to me what he had said then. He, like Sangroniz, emphasized that an examination of the separate concessions was absolutely necessary, and for the first time he brought up the argument that it was "well known" that the Spanish mining laws permitted only 25 percent foreign ownership in mining companies. Naturally I pointed out to Don Nicolás that perhaps it might be possible to change these laws as applied to Germany in view of our good relations and the help which we had rendered the Nationalist movement, whereupon Nicolás Franco answered neither yes nor no but stated only that a solution would have to be found somehow, of course, so that we could obtain the ores necessary to us. He expressed the opinion that even with only 25 percent ownership Germany could obtain through contracts with the mining companies—subject to guaranties for Spanish interests—by far the greater part of the ores produced in the mines. These questions had to be examined closely. He, too, emphasized once more that the present Spanish Government was a provisional government, which was in need of a number of mining experts who were still in Red Spain, and that therefore for this reason, too, it was unable to make such decisions so easily and quickly.

STOHRER

No. 485

3362/E009976

The Director of the Political Department to the Embassy in Italy

Telegram

No. 400 of December 18   BERLIN, December 18, 1937.
e.o. Pol. III 5850.

Drafting Officer: Counselor of Legation Dr. Dumont.

With reference to our telegraphic instruction 396.[1]

Despite Plymouth's statements on the percentage of volunteers to be withdrawn as a condition for granting belligerent rights, there is no inclination here at present to go beyond Franco's proposal. Provided Franco agreed, we would be prepared to offer to withdraw 5,000 immediately, and we consider it advisable to direct the discussion first to the preliminary questions, the clarification of which Franco requested in his note of reply to the resolution of November 4.[2]

Please ascertain and report by wire the position of the Government there.[3]

WEIZSÄCKER

---

[1] Not printed (5152/E303661–63).
[2] Marginal note in Dumont's handwriting: "The telegram is based on information from the Foreign Department of the War Ministry."
[3] Not printed (5152/E303665–66).

No. 486

2946/576116–17

The Ambassador in Spain to the Foreign Ministry

Telegram

No. 632 of December 18   SALAMANCA, December 18, 1937.

Our renewed and very emphatic representations with the Junta in Burgos, as well as with Secretary General Nicolás Franco and Chef de Cabinet Sangroniz in Salamanca, have in every case demonstrated complete willingness to cooperate with us in the question of German participation in the Spanish mining industry. Nevertheless, it has thus far been impossible to obtain any binding commitment in the sense of our demands regarding the 73 mining rights claimed by us. The Spaniards assert that it has not yet been possible to complete the absolutely necessary examination of the legal situation.

In spite of all references to the necessity of a speedy settlement of this question it will not be possible to prevail upon the Spanish Nationalist Government to take a different stand for the time being unless we can resort to other measures, perhaps of the kind indicated in telegraphic instruction No. 433 of November 30. We recommend, however, that special pressure not be applied at the present time. More will be reported orally on the occasion of my impending visit to Berlin.

The planned joint *démarche* with the Generalissimo has not been possible so far and will presumably not be possible in the near future, since Franco is very busy at the front because of the military situation and cannot be reached. Should a conference still be possible prior to our departure, we shall try to obtain from Franco a more concrete promise with regard to our participation in the development of Spanish mineral resources and the launching of this enterprise.

BERNHARDT
STOHRER

No. 487

3370/E010604–06

The Ambassador in Spain to the Foreign Ministry

CONFIDENTIAL   SAN SEBASTIÁN, December 19, 1937.

From the Spanish point of view today's luncheon had the purpose of pointing out to the German Ambassador in a confidential manner a danger which—in their opinion—must automatically work to the disadvantage of the future trade relations of Germany and Spain if the present monopolistic situation in commercial relations between the two countries is maintained.

The following disadvantages in the present system were pointed out:

1. a throttling of the normal development of the Spanish economy with reference to Germany.

2. a gradual increase in the resentment of Spanish economic and banking circles against Hisma, which is making their independent development more difficult and which consequently

3. increases the probability of stronger ties with England, whereby

4. the possibilities for Germany would be limited considerably even in the near future.

It was mentioned repeatedly that they were now at a "turning point," which in my opinion was meant to imply that Germany must either decide to relax the present arrangements or to reconcile herself to having the Spanish economic interests orient themselves toward other countries, especially England and America, thus obtaining the possibility once more of drawing profits themselves from their activity.

In this connection it was termed desirable to find a combination which would result in cooperation of Spanish, German, and British economic interests in the Spanish market. This cooperation, for example, would apply especially to the ore industry.

With regard to the German wishes for insuring Spanish ore deliveries, it was termed necessary to organize German-Spanish companies which would be formed for every type of ore in order to develop the Spanish resources in iron, copper, pyrites, manganese ore, etc., and would be grouped together under one parent company on the order of Hisma. It was hinted that the ores were to be paid for in foreign exchange, which the German economy could obtain through cooperation with the British.

In this connection the Spaniards also discussed the definite possibility that we might by means of negotiations secure for ourselves rights going beyond the present property law limiting foreigners to 25 percent ownership.

The activity of Hisma was recognized as useful and worthy of gratitude, since it had effectively closed a big gap in the Spanish economy created by the Civil War. So far the activity of Hisma had been in the interest of both the German and the Spanish Governments and economies. It had helped to free the Spanish economy from the shortages created by the abnormal conditions. With the internal situation in Spain growing increasingly normal, however, Spainsh forces were becoming free which even now could take over a part of Hisma's activity and which from the standpoint of Spanish interests must do so. At the present time, however, these forces found themselves excluded from any participation in German-Spanish trade through the virtual economic monopoly exercised by Hisma. If these forces were not permitted to engage in trade in competition or together with Hisma, then they were forced to seek other channels of activity and enterprise in the interest of Spain. But such a change would presumably result in halting, or at least in decreasing, German-Spanish trade.

Upon inquiry it was stated that in Spanish opinion the time for reorganizing the economic system, at present geared to abnormal conditions, had not yet come. But a turning point was in the offing, and therefore preparations should be made even now for the future organization of German-Spanish economic relations. It was pointed out with special emphasis that the conditions for a German-Spanish economic agreement were more favorable at the present time than ever before and that Germany should utilize this propitious moment, which presumably could not return later.

There was lively interest on the part of the Spanish banking and trade groups in the preparation of this possible broad-based relationship for the future. The banking groups concerned were especially willing to participate in and be incorporated into Hisma in its future form.

It was suggested that the ideas outlined above be made the topic of a discussion among German bankers and businessmen and leading personalities of Hisma.

On the German side it was termed natural that Spain should take under her own responsible direction the commercial apparatus necessary for German-Spanish trade, insofar as her share was concerned. Germany was thinking of economic cooperation on a basis of parity.

RIPKEN [1]
STOHRER

---

[1] Dr. Georg Ripken was at this time Secretary of Legation in the Economic Policy Department. He was sent to Spain in July and November 1937 in order to assist the German Embassy in difficult economic negotiations with the Spaniards.

No. 488

2128/463777

The Ambassador in Spain to the Foreign Ministry

STRICTLY CONFIDENTIAL   SALAMANCA, December 19, 1937.
No. 4609

With reference to your instruction of November 15, Pol. III 5375.[1]

Here, too, one hears much about the—for us—none too gratifying

---

[1] Not printed (3359/E009581–82).

activity of the Spanish Nationalist representative in London, the Duke of Alba. Not only did he make a statement to the press when he assumed the post in which he praised England extravagantly as Spain's best customer and gave the assurance that the resumption of commercial relations between England and Nationalist Spain was heartily welcomed; in a new interview given to the *Daily Telegraph* a few days ago—against which, if correctly reported by the *Temps* of December 9, not much objection can be made—he also stated quite unnecessarily, that 6,000 German "technicians" were active in Spain.

Alba, I am told, is trying through his connections here in Spain, which include chiefly Merry del Val, formerly Spanish Ambassador in London for many years, to work for England and to create sentiment against German and Italian influence in Spain.

Unfortunately, almost the same must be said about the Spanish Nationalist representative in Paris, Quiñones de León, the former Ambassador and confidant of King Alfonso.

Both men, it is said, are working hard against the influence of the Falange in Spain and for the restoration of a moderate regime of liberalistic tendencies and for a constitutional monarchy.

VON STOHRER

No. 489

309/189279

The Ambassador in Italy to the Foreign Ministry

Airgram

No. 365 of December 20   ROME, December 20, 1937.
Received December 22—6 : 15 p.m.

Ciano expressed little satisfaction today with the situation in Spain : Franco was a good soldier but no great military leader with broad vision; he had missed the most opportune moments, had given the Reds the opportunity to rally again, and would evidently postpone the offensive this time, too. If the war should continue to drag on like this, the question of volunteers would become seriously acute after all. There were 40,000 Italians in Spain, some of whom had been there for 16 months; 2,000 of them were living in tents. They were fighting for a cause which could not be close to the heart of the ordinary man, a cause which he could hardly understand. It was hardly justifiable to leave them there for months during the winter when the determination to force a decision was lacking. Therefore Franco had been informed that a partial withdrawal of volunteers would have to be considered if the situation developed in this manner.

HASSELL

No. 490

322/193699–706

Memorandum by the Ambassador in Spain [1]

SAN SEBASTIÁN, December 21, 1937.

After the return of Herr Bernhardt from Berlin there was a detailed discussion on December 18 in the Embassy at Salamanca on the background and development of the Montana affair. Besides Herr Bernhardt the following participated: Secretary of Legation Dr. Ripken, who was sent from Berlin and arrived with Herr Bernhardt, Counselor of Embassy Heberlein, and I, as well as Herr Pasch and Herr Brinkmann of Hisma during almost the entire conference.

I stated that actually the Montana affair had first come to the attention of the Embassy through the well-known decree of October 9 (which prohibits the cession of mining rights, etc.). To be sure, we had heard of the founding of Montana by Hisma, and Herr Bernhardt had incidentally told Herr Heberlein and me that he was instructed to obtain mining rights, etc., in Spain in order to secure the raw materials needed by us in Germany. The Embassy had not sent a report on the decree to Berlin at once, but I had had a conference with Herr Bernhardt, which took place about two days after the publication of the law, after Herr Bernhardt had already discussed it with Franco and the members of the Junta. Herr Bernhardt had told me at that time that all, including the Generalissimo, had informed him that the law had become necessary to prevent the selling out of Spain by the Reds, but that our rights would not be affected. I sent a report to this effect to Berlin. In this conversation, however, I requested Herr Bernhardt to see to it that his rights were somehow made legally invulnerable, since a law was a law and according to its text the law of October 9 doubtless referred to German rights too. Herr Bernhardt told me that he was also of this opinion and intended to safeguard himself. He also requested me, on my next visit to Burgos, to ask the Generalissimo and the members of the Junta once more how the law was to be understood. This was done. Señor Bau, the Generalissimo, Nicolás Franco, and Sangroniz all told me the same thing as the Generalissimo had told Herr Bernhardt in the presence of General Jordana and Señor Bau. The keynote of all the answers was: German rights will be protected somehow as a matter of course.

With these impressions I went to Berlin at the end of October to make a report. On November 13 I returned and had a long conversation on the same day with Herr Bernhardt, who had to return to Berlin that evening on instructions from there.

[1] Notation in Stohrer's handwriting at the top of the page: "Strictly confidential! To Herr Ministerialdirektor Wiehl, for the present for his strictly personal information."

In this conversation Herr Bernhardt said to me: "Let's not let them pull the wool over our eyes; the mining decree of October 9 is aimed at us! A few days ago I spoke with Nicolás Franco, who told me in so many words." Herr Bernhardt then handed me three memoranda,[2] which described the actual situation as he had explained it. I was very much astonished and promised, at the request of Herr Bernhardt, to speak to the Generalissimo about the matter again on my next visit. In addition, I promised to continue making representations to the other competent authorities as well in favor of recognition for our mining rights.

I spoke to the Generalissimo on November 16; he repeated the statement which had been made to Herr Bernhardt with regard to the decree. I sent a telegram to this effect to Berlin and requested that Herr Bernhardt be informed there.

I then described the outcome of my very serious *démarche* with the Generalissimo on December 2,[3] which I undertook on instructions from Berlin (telegram No. 433 of November 30 from the Foreign Ministry). The outcome was well known.

All my further *démarches* as well had shown that the alleged concessions to England, which were the occasion for our sharp protest and our demand for the immediate recognition of the 73 mining rights hitherto acquired by Hisma, were non-existent.

(A memorandum in the files [4] gives information on additional *démarches* to the same effect which I repeatedly undertook with Señores Nicolás Franco and Sangroniz.)

In the conference on the Montana affair at the Embassy on December 18 I reported the result of my repeated *démarches* with Nicolás Franco and Sangroniz during the last few days, and Herr Bernhardt gave his impressions of his conversations with Jordana and Bau on the preceding day in Burgos.[5] The statements of Señores Nicolás Franco and Sangroniz to me are recorded in the aforesaid memorandum. Herr Bernhardt expressed satisfaction over his conversations in Burgos; he thought he had ascertained the honest desire to cooperate with us in the field of mining. But he, too, did not obtain any positive assurance that the 73 mining rights enumerated in the well-known Hisma list would be recognized. While Herr Bernhardt was now of the opinion that especially Señores Jordana and Bau were so favorably disposed that they should be decorated, he thought that the obstacles in the way of recognition of the Montana rights were to be attributed to intrigues originating with Nicolás Franco, Sangroniz, and Ambassador Magaz. I stated that Señor Bau had also made sat-

---

[2] See documents Nos. 463 and 464, pp. 496 and 499, and footnote 1, p. 496.
[3] See document No. 478, p. 522.
[4] Document No. 484, p. 527.
[5] See document No. 486, p. 530.

isfactory statements to me formerly regarding cooperation with Germany but that Herr Bernhardt had formerly regarded him with the greatest distrust.

Then Herr Pasch and Herr Bernhardt told how the agencies in Vizcaya (banks and mining companies), from which the initiative for the issuance of the decree of October 9 evidently came, had recently informed the Hisma people that they still desired to cooperate with us.

Herr Bernhardt stated further that we should under no circumstances permit the Spaniards to make such difficulties for us in the Montana affair and refuse to recognize immediately the 73 rights in question. Herr Bernhardt, supported by Herr Pasch, stated that the La Cierva mining law of the year 1921, which was in their files and which had established a limitation on the rights of foreigners in the field of mining, formed the basis for our acquisition of mining rights. This law, however, had been violated at various times in the interest of England. Thus with regard to the Tharsis Company (Huelva province) and mining rights in Guipúzcoa the British had been permitted in the following years to acquire 100 percent rights. In view of the help that we had given to the Spanish Nationalist movement, it would be outrageous if the Spaniards did not grant us at least the same rights, especially since by the agreement of July 12 of this year we had acquired unlimited most-favored-nation treatment.

Here Herr Ripken and I interposed that in the latest discussions the Spaniards had made constant references to a law of 1925 or 1926 (the period of Primo de Rivera), in which the property rights of foreigners with regard to mines and mining rights had been limited to 25 percent. It was therefore important to determine whether *after* this period there had been a deviation from the principle laid down in the law or decree. The gentlemen had no information on this point. Herr Pasch at first denied the existence of a law or decree dating from the aforesaid two years. Herr Ripken stated, however, that the Spaniards had already made reference to this law in the negotiations for a commercial treaty last July. To be sure, this law or decree had never been seen. The Spaniards had stated that in the small inland cities of Salamanca and Burgos these decrees were unobtainable. Herr Ripken also said that even during these negotiations in July General Jordana had insisted, in deference to this law, that it should be expressly stated in article 3 of the secret protocol of July 16, 1937, that in the founding of mining companies and in the exploitation of Spanish mineral resources by Germany "the general stipulations of Spanish law" had to be observed. After some discussion back and forth, Herr Ripken said, Ambassador Faupel and the delegation had agreed to this restriction and had not insisted on seeing the law or decree. Under these circumstances the Spaniards were consequently right when they then insisted that the mining rights acquired by Hisma be in harmony with "the existing Spanish laws."

The Hisma representatives stated that this was quite true. Up to now, however, they had not known of any mining law or decree of 1925 or 1926, so that actually it could not be ascertained whether the legal basis for our demand exists.

Herr Pasch or Herr Brinkmann suggested here that the law or decree constantly cited by the Spaniards was perhaps the general Law for the Protection of National Property, which dated from about that period and which was said to provide for a limitation of 25 percent on foreign ownership in concerns of national importance. However, the Hisma representatives did not know anything further about this, either. I asked them to see to it that they procured the necessary legal documents as soon as possible from their files or, in case the documents could not be found there, from the Junta.

When Herr Ripken asked what share of the mines in question the Montana had acquired, Herr Pasch answered that a number of the rights contained in the list were only "concessions" (which, however, included the right of full exploitation and acquisition) but that others involved ownership to the extent of about 40 percent to 100 percent.

Herr Bernhardt remarked in this connection that in his opinion the present legal regulations should not be or remain the basis of our rights but that we simply had to prevail with our more far-reaching claims.

I agreed and, turning to the practical side of the question, stated that in view of the opposition hitherto shown by the Spaniards there were only two ways open to us to achieve this: 1. By initiating negotiations with the Spaniards immediately in order to induce them to recognize the Montana rights and, if necessary, amend in our favor the decree of October 9 or other legal regulations. 2. By enforcing our demand through vigorous pressure methods such as already suggested by telegram No. 433 of November 30 from the Foreign Ministry.

Herr Bernhardt was of the same opinion; it was agreed that the latter procedure was not indicated as yet and also that it could only be adopted after previous approval from Berlin. A telegram (No. 632 of December 18) in the above sense was then sent to Berlin with unanimous approval. It was also decided that on that same evening Herr Bernhardt and I should make a joint visit to Nicolás Franco in order to try, as Herr Bernhardt wished, to find out the real reason for the Spanish opposition. This conference could not take place, because Don Nicolás was in Valladolid.

In addition, my proposal was adopted that, in spite of the strong claim on the Generalissimo's time made by the present events at the front, an attempt should be made to obtain a joint audience for Herr Bernhardt and me before Christmas in order to try as far as possible to influence and commit Franco in line with our wishes.

This conversation actually took place in Burgos on Monday, December 20. For particulars regarding it see the following memorandum.[6]

RIPKEN
STOHRER

[6] Document No. 491.

No. 491

322/193694-98

Memorandum by the Ambassador in Spain[1]

[Undated]

On December 20 Generalissimo Franco received Herr Bernhardt and me in Burgos at my special request that we be granted this audience before Christmas despite the General's intense preoccupation with events at the front.

I took the opportunity to tell the Generalissimo first of all that I was going to Germany shortly. I said that the main reason for seeing him, however, was my desire to introduce Herr Bernhardt, at his request, as the official representative of the Four Year Plan, and to state that this appointment and our appearing together were meant to show that Hisma and the Reich representation were of one mind.

Referring to my previous repeated *démarches* in the Montana affair, I then stated once more with emphasis that the guaranty of ore imports from Spain was a vital question for us and that in view of our special relations with Spain we felt we had the right to count on full support from the Nationalist Government in this question.

I then asked the Generalissimo to permit Bernhardt, who had just returned from Berlin and had obtained the latest instructions of Colonel General Göring there, to present this question in detail.

Herr Bernhardt did this exhaustively. He emphasized once more the necessity of securing Spanish ores for ourselves, not only by delivery contracts but also by participation in the exploitation of Spain's mineral resources; but he also emphasized that in this procedure, which had indeed been granted us by treaty, we naturally had in mind collaboration with Spain and not independent exploitation. For this reason, Herr Bernhardt explained, we had to request urgently that the 73 mining rights acquired by Hisma or Montana

[1] Notation in Stohrer's handwriting at the top of the page "Strictly confidential! To Herr Ministerialdirektor Wiehl, for the present for his strictly personal orientation."

be approved by Spain. The matter had already been protracted for such a long time that they had become uneasy in Berlin. Therefore he requested, as I had repeatedly done already, that the matter now be decided quickly in our favor.

The Generalissimo, who had greeted me very cordially, but then had been visibly cool and aloof during the conversation, now spoke for the first time, saying to begin with that he knew our position exactly and that he naturally stood by his statement that our interests in the mineral exports from Spain would be safeguarded. However, it would not do to hurry this matter unduly; it was a question of 73 different rights which had to be investigated, and this required time. Nevertheless, in response to my *démarches* he had again summoned General Jordana and instructed him to expedite the investigation "on which the Ambassador had insisted so strongly." This had been done, and the investigation was already far advanced. In many things, however, General Jordana still needed information, which Herr Bernhardt would have to give him. The data given by Hisma in the list were insufficient. Alongside a whole series of rights the only explanation given was the word *contrato* (contract, agreement), which meant nothing. Herr Bernhardt promised to go to General Jordana that very afternoon and supply him with the information.

In reply to these last statements of Franco, Herr Bernhardt said that *contrato* sometimes referred to the acquisition of ownership and sometimes to leases and similar contracts.

The Generalissimo objected further that he was bound by the Spanish laws. These provided for a limitation of foreign ownership of mines, etc. There was, as far as he recalled, a law or decree of 1932 or 1933 which limited foreign ownership to 25 percent. Herr Bernhardt interposed here that it was in large part only a question of concessions (*denuncia*), which were not equivalent to property rights. To this the Generalissimo replied that it was precisely the concessions which had also been affected by the law or decree. (I took this remark of the Generalissimo to mean that the law of 1932 or 1933 cited by him, which has never been mentioned before and which is also unknown to Hisma, prohibits the acquisition by foreigners of concessionary rights. Herr Bernhardt, however, said that in his opinion the Generalissimo meant to refer to the new decree of October 9. It is quite possible that Herr Bernhardt is right. It is necessary first of all to clarify the judicial and legal situation.) In the further course of the conversation, which lasted almost three-quarters of an hour, Herr Bernhardt pressed for an explanation of what he called a certain change that seemed to him and also to certain authorities in Berlin to have occurred in the attitude of the Spanish Government toward Hisma and himself, as was evident in the handling of the

Montana affair. The Generalissimo evaded this question at first but then said finally in approximately the following words: "Well, yes. It did indeed surprise (or annoy) me (*me ha extrañado*) that Hisma, which I entrusted with the task of regulating trade and payments, is now secretly (*clandestinamente*) trying to acquire and is acquiring mining rights as well."

Herr Bernhardt immediately replied that this task had been assigned to Hisma from the outset. This had been clearly stated in the negotiations of last July, when, as the protocol of July 16 showed, the formation of companies for the exploitation of Spanish mineral resources with the cooperation of German citizens and firms had been anticipated. Franco replied: "I was not aware of that. Therefore I was surprised that it happened." When Herr Bernhardt expressed his regret at this misunderstanding, the Generalissimo, who had become somewhat more affable in the course of the conversation, smiled and said in a conciliatory tone: "Well, when you're surprised, you're just surprised."

Under these circumstances it was clear that no progress could be made this way in the matter itself. Herr Bernhardt therefore proposed, with my support, that negotiations on the whole matter should be conducted as soon as possible. To this the Generalissimo agreed, and it was decided, subject to the approval of Berlin, that immediately after Christmas a mixed commission would be convened, which was to consist of members of the Junta, members of Hisma, and a representative of the Embassy. This commission was to make an expert study of the legal situation and try to come to a conclusion. Herr Bernhardt and I then sent a telegram to this effect to Berlin.

STOHRER

No. 492

294   )–30

Memorandum of the Embassy in Spain

SAN SEBASTIÁN, December 22, 1937.

After the conferences with Herr Bernhardt and Herr Ripken on December 18 (Salamanca) and December 20 (Burgos, Generalissimo) the following may be stated with reference to the Montana affair:

1. The Spanish by no means deny in principle our right to acquire ownership of mines, etc., in the sense of our agreement of July 16. They only demand that this acquisition—in strict correspondence with article III of the agreement of July 16—be kept within the framework of the existing Spanish laws.

2. The Spaniards—see the memorandum of the conference with the Generalissimo on December 20—are unpleasantly surprised that Hisma

is engaged in buying up mining rights and forming mining companies without having previously consulted the Spanish Government on this matter. (Herr Ripken did not recall that anything was said in the negotiations of last July about Hisma's taking over this task as well.)

3. The preparations for these purchases of mining rights by Hisma were technically faulty. Conformity with existing treaty and legal provisions was not achieved. Moreover, the Spaniards (Generalissimo, December 20) complain that the list of 73 mining rights submitted by me for immediate acceptance by instruction of the Foreign Ministry contains insufficient data regarding the nature of the rights acquired, so that an examination is not possible as matters now stand.

No. 493

2946/576131–33

Memorandum by an Official of the Economic Policy Department[1]

1. German-Spanish imports and exports are dependent, on both the German and the Spanish sides, on specific permits.

2. Within the framework of these controls it is possible at present, and in fact has been possible since November 1936, to trade only through the firms of Rowak in Berlin and Hisma in Seville.

3. The task assigned to these two firms consists in:

(*a*) Providing a channel for so-called normal, that is, peacetime, trade and serving as a clearing house for it;

(*b*) Providing Germany with the raw materials and vital foodstuffs necessary for her economy, especially for the Four Year Plan;

(*c*) Providing payment for special deliveries of war matériel which cannot be paid for in foreign exchange.

Re(*c*) Included here is the task of financing current war deliveries which cannot be charged to the large-scale credit which has been set up for other deliveries of the same kind, and providing for a small amortization of the large-scale credit even at this time.

4. German-Spanish trade is basically restricted by the value of the Spanish products exported to Germany, that is, the monthly average of German goods exported to Spain cannot exceed the value of Spanish exports to Germany. In recent months (September, October, November) the monthly average of Spanish exports to Germany amounted to approximately 10 million RM. The German outlay for Spain is divided as follows:

(1) Amortization of the large-scale credit, for the time being, is taking place in the amount of 350,000 RM per month;

---

[1] This memorandum is from the files of the German Embassy in Spain and bears the notation: "Herr Ripken's memorandum, Dec. 22, 1937."

(2) Financing of current deliveries of war matériel, at present in the amount of 4 million RM per month;

(3) Financing of deliveries under so-called free trade; at present 5.5 million RM are available per month for this purpose.

5. The trade through Hisma-Rowak by no means excludes so-called free trade. Within the range of the funds for carrying on free trade that are made available from time to time through Spanish exports to Germany, the representatives of the so-called free trade can carry out orders for the delivery of German goods that have been obtained in free negotiation of contracts between Spanish purchasers and German suppliers. A further requirement, of course, is the authorization of the Spanish control agency for the importation of the German articles in question.

6. The German Government agencies are fully aware that carrying on German-Spanish trade exclusively through the Hisma-Rowak firms almost completely eliminates the Spanish and German private trade apparatus. It was necessary to make this arrangement, however, because in view of the needs of the Four Year Plan it did not seem possible in any other way to insure that all the raw materials and foodstuffs available in Spain that were necessary for the German economy would be obtained.

With the approval of the Spanish Nationalist Government it was decided last June by all the appropriate German Government agencies that this system of trade should be adhered to as long as the abnormal war conditions in Spain continue (constant need of war matériel, lack of a proper administration). A study of the situation has shown that there is still no reason for revising the decision now in force.

7. Within the range of the possibilities open to free trade, the Hisma and Rowak firms exercise control over the transactions reported for clearing and execution to the extent that they carry out the deliveries of those German goods in particular that the German economy has a permanent interest in exporting to Spain. Transactions of other kinds, and also those requiring disproportionately large funds, are carried out only if funds are left over from the trade in the so-called goods of the first order.

At present Hisma still has to balance advances which had to be made for financing war matériel. By financing of this kind, postponements may result with regard to the amounts to be made available each month for free trade.

8. The German Government has no thought as yet of amortizing the afore-mentioned large-scale credit at the expense of the normal course of free exchange of goods. The exchange of goods in 1935 is regarded as "normal."

No. 494

309/189277-78

Memorandum by the State Secretary

BERLIN, December 29, 1937.

Count Magistrati told me during his visit today that the Duce had recently had a big conference in Rome on the question of Italian participation in the Spanish Civil War. In addition to high Italian military personnel, the general commanding the Italian legions in Spain had also been included. The outcome of this conference had been:

1. The clear decision by the Duce that the Italian legionnaires should remain with Franco for the time being;

2. The recognition that Franco's attitude as observed by the Italians, that the decisive victory should no longer be sought in the military field but through the gradual combined effect of political factors, in no wise corresponded to Italian interests. A final decision such as Franco seemed to visualize might not come for months, even years. The Italians, however, were not inclined to invest money and gold *ad infinitum* in the Spanish undertaking. Therefore it had to be made clear to Franco that he would have to return to the idea of seeking the final decision by force of arms.

3. This was possible, however, only if a "unity of command" was finally achieved in Spain, the lack of which had made itself felt from the outset—not least of all in the fighting in the north—in a way that was profoundly disturbing.

The general commanding the Italian troops in Spain had been sent back to Spain by Mussolini with the instruction that he should make plain to General Franco with the proper emphasis the great sacrifice on the part of Italy that was involved in the Duce's decision to leave his legions at the further disposition of Franco, but that he should also explain to him with the same emphasis that he now had to seek a military decision with all available means, and that this required a unified high command over the Spanish, Italian, and German troops.

In reply to my question as to whether the General was to transmit the last demand to the Generalissimo at once or was to wait until our position was known, Count Magistrati replied that his instruction contained nothing on this point; he could therefore assume that this subject was also to be taken up immediately with General Franco.

I promised Count Magistrati that I would find out our position on the question of a unified high command and then notify him. We could not announce our position until we had consulted with our responsible military authorities. Although for many reasons, and especially on the basis of many experiences made in the course of the war, a unified command was undoubtedly desirable, still it should be remembered that such a command would also burden us with a certain responsibility for the course of the operation which in the past we had avoided assuming.

Count Magistrati requested a reply as soon as possible.

MACKENSEN

No. 495

586/242957–58

Memorandum by the Director of the Political Department

CONFIDENTIAL   BERLIN, January 2, 1938.

On the basis of prior conferences with General Keitel I gave Count Magistrati the following reply today to his communication of December 29 [1] to the State Secretary regarding the settlement of certain military questions in Spain:

Re 1: I took cognizance of the Duce's decision to the effect that the Italian legionnaires were to remain at the disposition of Franco for the time being. There had not been any similar problem here.

Re 2: We noted with interest and agreed with the view that the war had to be brought to a speedy and victorious conclusion by force of arms.

Count Magistrati added that it would be made clear to Franco that the Italians did not want to let themselves be expended in trench warfare or on service in rear echelons. Mussolini wished to see them committed in direct and active fighting.[2]

Re 3: I told Magistrati that in our opinion there was already a unified high command in the person of General Franco, whose place, after all, could not be taken by anyone else. The top German commander had been instructed from the outset to maintain close contact with the top Italian commander and together with him to submit his recommendations to the Generalissimo. The latter would then make the final decision in each case. As far as was known here, the relations between the top German and Italian commanders were close and friendly. We had no information to the effect that this procedure had not worked thus far.

Count Magistrati did not contradict this statement as such but said that the fault had lain in the proper execution of General Franco's orders, especially by his own Spanish generals. It was the opinion in Rome that in order to remedy this General Franco should have a general staff including Italians and Germans too, so that a stronger

---

[1] Document No. 494, *supra*.
[2] Marginal note in Neurath's handwriting: "But not his troops."

influence might thus be exerted on the Spanish subordinate commanders. I replied to Magistrati that one might thereby also obtain the opposite of the desired effect. The weight of the direct influence of the top German and Italian commanders on General Franco might be lessened under certain circumstances by the establishment of a general staff, which could constitute a wall of partition [separating them from Franco]. Moreover, by this procedure we would assume certain responsibilities for the Spanish war which were difficult to support.

Magistrati did not shut his mind against this objection and added for his part that the Spaniards had their own peculiar mentality; they were rather sensitive and would perhaps not look with favor on the establishment of a general staff at the present stage, shortly before the final victory.

Magistrati will now consult with Rome again, and he also mentioned that in order to achieve a unified German-Italian position an Italian officer might be summoned from Rome.

Further communications from the Italians will now have to be awaited.

WEIZSÄCKER

No. 496

322/193688–90

Minute by the Director of the Economic Policy Department

BERLIN, January 5, 1938.

CONFERENCE ON SPAIN IN THE FOREIGN MINISTRY ON DECEMBER 29, 1937
Present: Major van Jagwitz (Ret.); Ambassador von Stohrer; Ministerialdirektor Wiehl; (Herr Bethke and Secretary of Legation Ripken during part of the conference).

The conference had the following results:

I. *Mining Rights*

The negotiations already under way between the Embassy and the Spanish Nationalist Government to clarify the mining rights acquired by Hisma are to be continued at an accelerated pace with a view to effecting an affirmative declaration by the Generalissimo at the earliest possible date. The Spanish legal situation with regard to these mining rights is not clear and needs to be investigated at once. Hisma will give the necessary explanations concerning the actual nature of the rights which it has acquired. Whatever the results of the investigation of the factual and the legal situation may be, it is agreed that we must strive with all possible energy and speed toward recognition by the Generalissimo, if possible without reservation, of the present actual substance of Hisma's rights; it is also agreed that we cannot be content with a limitation of these rights to the 25 percent provided for by Spanish law, for instance; and that treatment of Hisma's rights by the Spaniards on a purely formal legal basis would not do justice to the moral claims which Germany has won by her extensive support of the Spanish Nationalist Government.

The Embassy will continue to work toward realization of these claims with all diplomatic means available. Resort to an ultimatum, however, as indicated in the Foreign Ministry's telegram No. 433 of November 30, 1937, is not to be taken with respect to the Generalissimo unless it becomes evident that the desired result cannot be reached without this. In this case the decision of a higher authority should again be obtained before taking this step.

The contradictions between Franco's statements to the Ambassador and the reports received by the Colonel General [Göring] need to be clarified. The Embassy can only attempt such clarification if the Ambassador is given more exact information about the content of the reports. Herr von Jagwitz agrees to inform the Colonel General to this effect.

II. *Organization of German-Spanish Economic Relations*

Herr von Stohrer stated that in German-Spanish economic relations, too, everything, of course, had to be done to assist in the execution of the Four Year Plan. He had to be careful, however, that an atmosphere did not develop in Spain which, after the end of the Civil War and thus after the end of Spanish dependence on German help, would make it impossible for Germany to realize what she expected from her great assistance to Nationalist Spain. The alarm signal which he had wanted to raise in his report of November 27, 1937,[1] was meant to indicate that the atmosphere in Spain was threatening to grow unfavorable to German economic aspirations.[2] Lately German and Spanish commercial interests were to an increasing degree presenting their claims for participation in German-Spanish trade, from which they allegedly felt themselves excluded up to now.

Herr von Jagwitz emphasized that the coordination of German-Spanish trade under the organization of Rowak-Hisma had proved satisfactory beyond all expectation, and that it had been possible to obtain a much greater amount of the most important raw materials from Spain and to do more for safeguarding our claims on Spain than would have been possible without this organization.

---

[1] Document 473, p. 512.
[2] The sentence was corrected; it originally read: "He had wished to suggest in his report of November 27, 1937, that there were certain indications in Spain of an imminent deterioration of the atmosphere in this direction."

Herr Wiehl stated that under these circumstances it would be inexpedient to permit a change to be made in the present state of affairs, which offered Germany great advantages in Spain in comparison with competing countries. However, both the Embassy in Spain and the responsible authorities here should continue to observe closely the indications reported by the Embassy, so that we could accommodate ourselves promptly to further developments in the situation, as soon as new decisions were required.[3]

Everyone concurred in these statements.

Herr von Jagwitz promised that the plan, already made, to give greater consideration than in the past to Spanish economic circles would be carried out insofar as possible.

W[IEHL]

---

[3] Another version of this sentence written by hand in the margin reads: "However, the indications of further developments reported by the Embassy would have to be observed closely both by the interested authorities here and by the Embassy, which would continue to report on them, so that we could make new decisions promptly as soon as they were required."

No. 497

1557/377675-76

Memorandum by the State Secretary

SECRET   BERLIN, January 5, 1938.
                                                              Pol. I 59 g.

Today Count Magistrati reverted once more to the information he gave me recently concerning Mussolini's conversations with the Commander in Chief of the Italian troops in Spain and other high Italian military personages. He was now in a position to be more specific concerning the contents of the instruction which Mussolini gave to the Italian Commander in Chief to be passed on to General Franco. According to the instruction the General was to inform Generalissimo Franco of the following:

1. The Fascist Government was resolved to declare its solidarity with Franco's cause until its final victory.

2. Accordingly, it made available to the Generalissimo its volunteer forces as in the past, naturally insofar as he wished to make use of them.

3. It was necessary that these troops be employed in accordance with their quality; this meant that the two Italian divisions should not be used in a battle of attrition, but rather in engagements in which decisive results could be expected.

4. It was urgently necessary to accelerate the pace of operations and not to believe, for instance, that victory had already been attained

because a certain amount of diplomatic recognition had been given. Likewise, it would be wrong to count on the collapse of the Reds' supply lines, which had even survived the serious crisis of the revolt in Barcelona. A final collapse of the Reds' supply lines was, in the opinion of the Duce, only conceivable after a full military success.[1]

5. General Franco should not indulge in any illusions concerning the attitude of the British and the French. There would never be any change in their hostile attitude toward the Spanish Nationalist cause.

6. It was necessary to form a really *single* command with German and Italian participation. On this point Count Magistrati had me confirm once more what Herr von Weizsäcker had told him some days ago concerning the attitude of our military on the question of a unified command in Spain. He repeated correctly the substance of what had been communicated to him at the time, saying that he had also reported to Rome to this effect.

MACKENSEN

---

[1] Marginal note: "My opinion, too. Schw[endemann]."

No. 498

1557/377689

Memorandum by the State Secretary

BERLIN, January 10, 1938.
Pol. I 139 g.

As General Keitel informed me during his visit today, Count Magistrati called on Field Marshal von Blomberg in person a few days ago in order to communicate to him—evidently following closely the statements he made to me recently on the subject—the message which General Berti was supposed to transmit to General Franco in Mussolini's name. In his remarks Count Magistrati placed in the foreground the question of a unified top command. General Keitel stressed that in his answer the War Minister had stated almost exactly what Herr von Weizsäcker had already told Count Magistrati here. The War Ministry considered the affair thus finally decided in the negative and did not expect that this opinion would be changed by General Volkmann's report, which Herr von Stohrer had announced in a telegram.

MACKENSEN

No. 499

2946/576148–50

Memorandum of the Embassy in Spain

SALAMANCA, January 10, 1938.

CONFERENCE ON THE MONTANA PROJECT, JANUARY 10, 1938

Present: The Ambassador; Herr Enge;[1] Secretary of Legation Stille;[1] Herr Bernhardt; Herr Brinkmann; Herr Zepp of Hisma.

The Ambassador emphasized once more that the matter had by all means to be accelerated. Herr Bernhardt replied that it was for this reason that Herr Pasch had already returned to Burgos this morning in order to continue the conferences on technical questions there with the experts entrusted by the Junta Técnica with the handling of the Montana affair. This further technical preparation was being carried out on one hand by conferences in Burgos with the two experts, Señor Marín and Señor Guistózaga, and on the other hand by tours of inspection and collection of data at the various mines and fields by one or another of the experts. The legal questions were being dealt with further by lawyers in Bilbao and southern Spain.

Herr Bernhardt then presented the memorandum which had been drawn up as a result of yesterday's conferences at Hisma. The Ambassador asked why the memorandum had not been drawn up by Hisma 4 weeks ago; Herr Bernhardt replied that he had not known that the Junta Técnica was so uninformed concerning the legal situation as it had proved to be in the conference with Jordana on January 7. Jordana should have stated in detail in that conference what the reasons were which stood in the way of recognition of the mining rights. Although it was really, now as before, the Junta Técnica which had to show reasons against the recognition of the rights, in the interest of speed the laws were now being studied and submitted for discussion by the Germans. Hisma had known from the start that in acquiring the mining rights it had kept within the bounds of the law, and it had been a great surprise [*eine grosse sorpresa*] for Hisma that it was now being said that this acquisition was illegal.

It was agreed that all material suitable for answering any objections which the Spaniards might still raise would be examined and assembled at once. For this purpose Herr Pasch, in cooperation with his lawyers, was to continue to clarify the technical questions in conferences with Marín, whereas the Embassy will continue to occupy itself with the legal questions. In particular, the treaties with Japan, Portugal, and France are to be utilized and examined to see whether

---

[1] Member of the staff of the German Embassy in Spain.

they provide us with an argument for additional legal backing of our claims.

Herr Bernhardt answered in the negative the Ambassador's question whether Herr Bernhardt knew any other means of expediting the matter. In his opinion we must now allow about a week's time for the experts to study the technical questions and for the Junta to study our memorandum. Everyone agreed that too great pressure would not be in our interest, since work begun at various mines before the decree of October 9, 1937, was, after all, being continued on full scale with the tacit consent of the Spaniards.

STILLE

No. 500

3363/E010011–13

The Chargé d'Affaires in Great Britain to the Foreign Ministry

A 139   LONDON, January 13, 1938.
                                            Pol. III 116.

With reference to our airgram No. 9 of January 11.[1]

Subject: Spanish Non-Intervention Committee; an early decision is necessary on the question of "substantial withdrawal".[2]

The question of the so-called "substantial withdrawal" is now reaching an acute stage. As reported, it was decided in the session of the Non-Intervention Committee on January 11 that the matter should next be discussed in informal conferences between Lord Plymouth and individual representatives in the Committee.

In a private conference with Lord Plymouth before the last session I said that the German Government took the position that in this question Franco's proposal should be followed, that is, belligerent rights should be granted after 3,000 men had been withdrawn equally from each side (it is not entirely clear here whether Franco's last demand was for 3,000 or 5,000 men).

It is now quite certain that we have no prospect whatsoever of putting through this proposal, and there arises the question of what tactics we should use henceforth. I have already indicated in the conversation with Lord Plymouth that one might perhaps leave the point open until the reply of the Spanish parties to the proposals submitted to them had been received. Lord Plymouth, however, was completely opposed to this suggestion and it is certain that it will not meet with any favor from the other delegates either, especially the French.

---

[1] Not printed (586/242972–74).
[2] This phrase is in English in the original.

In the session of January 11 Lord Plymouth tried to make substantial progress in the question. The Italians and we, however, did not agree to any substantive discussion in the session. The reason for this was partly the fact that we still have no final instructions on this point and partly the tactical consideration that it was not advisable to take this point up prematurely when in other points, especially in the question of controls, the main difficulties are on the side of the Soviet Union.

The proposal now officially made by Lord Plymouth that belligerent rights are to be granted after 75 percent of the volunteers have been withdrawn is not, as was quite clear from my conversation with Lord Plymouth, the last word of the British. It is rather a tentative figure mentioned only for the purpose of starting the discussion. It seems to me that the British are aiming at the figure of 50 percent but would even be satisfied with a still smaller percentage if general agreement could be achieved on it.

It is remarkable that the French Ambassador so far has taken no position whatever on the matter, although he obviously already has instructions in his pocket. I would assume, however, that the British and the French will proceed jointly in the matter and that the French as well intend to settle on about 50 percent or somewhat higher.

A further report will follow.

WOERMANN

No. 501

1557/377713–16

The Ambassador in Spain to the Foreign Ministry

SECRET   SALAMANCA, January 13, 1938.
No. 307   Pol. I 167 g (III).

With reference to my telegram of January 11, No. 10,[1] and personal letter of January 8 to Ministerialdirektor Baron von Weizsäcker.[2]

Subject: The battle of Teruel and its significance.

The calm prevailing on all fronts since the end of the Asturian campaign was suddenly broken about the middle of December by a surprise attack on Teruel by the Reds. The attack on this city took place at the moment when Generalissimo Franco, after hesitating for a long time and letting more than 7 weeks pass since the capture of Gijón, was preparing to launch a decisive blow against Madrid.

Whereas in the closing days of the year it seemed as if the White Spanish troops brought up in all haste from assembly areas near

---

[1] Not printed (586/242969).
[2] Not found.

Guadalajara would succeed not only in stopping the Red penetration but also in freeing the city and its vicinity once more from the enemy, it developed after preliminary successes of the White counteroffensive that the Reds, contrary to expectation, were strong enough to stand their ground, to get all of Teruel into their hands a few days ago, and in addition to carry on further attacks against the Spanish front west and north of the city. At the moment the battle of Teruel is still in progress.

The main result of the battles around Teruel is the realization that in recent months the Reds have been able, with the help and direction of foreign organizers and officers, to inject an impressive degree of new fighting strength into their troops and thus to seize the initiative.

I was able to point out as early as the end of November and the beginning of December that, according to all reports available here, not only the discipline in the Red Spanish Army but also the arms, supplies, and provisions of the Red front had improved, whereas the political and economic situation in the Red zone was still growing worse at that time. It must now be stated, however, that reports agree that a certain turn for the better has come about in the latter respect, too. As I hear from the most varied sources, somewhat more order and discipline prevail of late among the Reds, even in the rear areas. The police have improved; common crimes are punished on the spot or prosecuted by orderly court proceedings. Even the supply of food seems to have improved somewhat, which is attributed in part to the considerable amount of foreign currency acquired by the Red Government through the export of oranges now under way. Moreover, the war industry located in the Red area—generally of no great importance, however—seems to have been restored to operation lately. Indalecio Prieto is given the main credit in Red Spain for the undoubtedly improved situation; he was untiringly active at the front and in the rear areas, and it is asserted that he also had a hand in the sudden large-scale attack on Teruel, which supposedly was prepared and launched within 5 days. If one adds to this the fact that the present Red leaders have been able to eliminate the Anarchists and other extreme elements and thus to bring about a certain order in the heretofore chaotic state of affairs, then, speaking quite generally, it must be recognized that there has been an unmistakable improvement in conditions on the Red side.

However, there is surely no question, as yet, of any lasting and decisive significance in this change. Although the capture of Teruel now gives a strong stimulus to the morale of the Reds, which had sunk to a very low point after the collapse of the northern front, nevertheless a new military success by Franco would no doubt severely shake the internal structure of the Red zone once more. Whether it is possible, however, for the Spanish Nationalist leaders to make such a successful thrust in the foreseeable future is more than doubtful in the opinion of non-Spanish military experts. At the present time we have reached a stage in which forces are equally balanced—as has been the case several times during the Spanish Civil War.

In this new situation the question arises whether and how Franco can succeed in regaining such superiority over the Red opponent as will give promise of success. Considering the support which the Red side is still receiving from outside—evidently even to an increasing extent, to judge from the victory at Teruel—this would probably be very difficult, if not impossible, for him to do unaided.

Thus the German and Italian Governments are again confronted with the question whether they will and can make renewed and probably quite considerable sacrifices for Franco in order to insure his victory over the Spanish Bolshevists and to prevent his being forced into a negotiated peace, which at most would mean a "pink" (neither White nor Red) solution to the Spanish problem. The German and Italian military unconditionally recommend this assistance. With regard to the proposals drawn up by the Italian Commander in Chief of the Italian volunteer units in Spain and the German military view on these proposals, I should like to refer to General Veith's reports.

If we proceed on the assumption that Franco, considering his strong economic position, is not hoping for the conclusion of the war as a result of internal and economic disintegration of the Reds—which would first have to be determined—but rather that he is resolved to continue the war in a more active manner than in the last few months, then it also seems to me insufficient to try to give Franco military superiority over his enemies again only by means of deliveries of matériel. We—that is, Germany and Italy—will rather have to put at his disposal at least a much greater number of technical personnel and officers with general staff training. The absolute prerequisite for this would be, however, that in the future our military would be assured of a much greater—even decisive—influence on the conduct of the war and the execution of the orders issued by the Army high command; of course, the present "unified supreme command" must remain under Franco.

Considering the well-known Spanish mentality, this last point particularly will offer great difficulty and will require cautious but very firm treatment.

Since, moreover, quite apart from international considerations, time is working against Franco militarily, the proverb is appropriate here, too, that "he who gives quickly gives doubly."

STOHRER

No. 502

4446/E086609–15

Memorandum by the Head of Political Division IIIa [1]

BERLIN, January 15, 1938.
zu Pol. III.

From the available reports about events in Teruel it appears that the favorable military situation which arose for Nationalist Spain after the mopping up of the Spanish northern front has deteriorated considerably. It is termed serious although not dangerous. As yet none of the observers goes so far as to believe that Franco's final victory is jeopardized. However, it seems certain that no offensive by Franco for the purpose of deciding the war can be expected before spring and that there is even danger that Franco might by spring have used up the reserves which became available for an offensive through the mopping up of the northern front and might no longer be capable of an offensive that would decide the war.

The political consequences of this situation are considerable. While before the events in Teruel the end of the Spanish Civil War seemed to be in sight, today the end of the war seems once again to have moved into the far distant future. While the prospects for a Red victory were hitherto generally considered very poor, the Leftist circles in many countries (compare, for example, the British and French press) have found new hope for a Red victory. If the war continues to drag on indefinitely, our position in the Non-Intervention Committee in London will not become easier. In the final analysis, although England is very much occupied for the time being with problems in the Far East and France has enough troubles of her own, it cannot be foreseen how our present comparatively favorable situation with reference to the Spanish war will develop if the latter drags on for many more months, or even into the next year, quite aside from the disturbances which our help to Nationalist Spain will cause in our military and economic armament program.

This situation forces us to study the question what can be done to insure once more Franco's military superiority and bring about a victorious conclusion of the war as quickly as possible.

A prerequisite for posing this question is the recognition that neither a Red victory nor a *partie remise* can be considered. As for the latter possibility, it is well known that from the beginning of the Spanish Civil War England and France have considered it the desirable solution, since both countries, for obvious reasons, cannot desire the

---

[1] Political Division IIIa was in charge of German relations with Spain and Portugal.

establishment of a Spain which is authoritarian and militarily strong, and which inclines politically toward Italy and Germany. An understanding between Red and White, perhaps in such a form that an armistice would be concluded first and a decision about the new form of government made later by a referendum—which is what they have in mind in England—would give the Red party by ballot the victory which it is unable to achieve on the battlefield; the reason for this would be that the present Red part of Spain has been under the skillful Red propaganda for so long that a Red majority would certainly be assured there, while in the White area the Red propaganda would likewise find sufficient openings, especially when the high tension of the war period ceased and the misery of the postwar period made itself felt so much the more.

A compromise between the fighting parties appears impossible, above all for ideological reasons, but also because too much unjustly shed blood has flowed between the two, and finally because the political organization of the authoritarian state has already progressed very far in Nationalist Spain, while the democratic parliamentarian façade still stands in Red Spain and has of late even been strengthened again as against the Anarchists and Communists. It is impossible to see how two so fundamentally different forms of government could be combined.

As matters stand, only a radical victory of one of the two parties appears thinkable, with the consequence that the leader stratum of the losing side will be literally eliminated far down to the leaders of middle and lower rank, either by flight abroad or by execution after more or less summary proceedings. At any rate that is what has happened in the areas so far conquered by Franco. It is actually a life-and-death struggle between the two Spains: nationalist, traditional, agrarian, monarchist, Catholic-clerical Spain, which is now also strongly oriented toward a social program and syndicalism through the influence of the Falange; and the Spain of the Liberals, Socialists, Communists, Anarchists, Freethinkers, and Freemasons, which in some way stems from the French Revolution of 1789. In case of a Franco victory the result will be a Spain which renews the centralized, nationalist, and Catholic tradition with a strong social tendency.

Even if the war lasts a long time, the greater power of resistance may well be on Franco's side, principally because he controls the areas with agricultural surpluses, whereas there is in the Red areas a shortage of grain, meat, and fish, which has for a long time made the urban population feel the pressure of hunger; then, too, because the population which is the most valuable from a military point of view (Navarre, Galicia, Castile) is on his side, and because so far he has been given assistance from abroad which, while not the greater materially, to be sure, has been more effective from the military standpoint, mainly because of the commitment of complete units.

The only question involved here is how long it should and may take until the war is brought to a victorious conclusion. One of the handicaps on the way to this goal is, according to my experience in Spain, the frequently exaggerated optimism in the Nationalist headquarters, whose officers take great pride in their General Staff training, and the inadequate mobilization of the manpower resources of the country as the result of insufficient insight into the extent of the difficulties still to be mastered.

According to the latest compilation of Special Staff W [*Sonderstab W*], Franco has the following forces at his disposal:

At the front	470, 000 men
Reserves in the interior	
(*a*) Ready for action	40, 000 men
(*b*) Incompletely equipped reserves and replacements	35, 000 men
In process of organization	12, 000 men
Security troops in the interior	25, 000 men
	582, 000 men

These figures are approximate, since the exact strength is probably not known even in Franco's headquarters itself, in view of the faulty Spanish organization.

According to the latest compilation of Special Staff W, the Red Forces are composed as follows:

At the front and front reserves	342, 000 men
Reserves	
(*a*) Ready for action	75, 000 men
(*b*) In process of organization, at least . .	45, 000 men
Security troops in the interior, at least . . .	30, 000 men
	492, 000 men

Thus Franco has approximately 90,000 more men at his disposal than the Reds, but it should be kept in mind that among his troops there are probably at least 50,000 to 60,000 Moroccans. In comparing the above figures it is especially noticeable that the Red reserves in the interior and the reserves in process of organization are considerably stronger than Franco's; that is, the Reds are recruiting more, which is evident also from other reports.

This is primarily where the efforts to assure Franco's military superiority, now as well as in the future, and to increase it, must begin; Franco should be induced to recruit more men in order to make up for the losses at Teruel as well as for further losses which will occur in other Red offensives to be expected in the near future, so that in the spring he will have ready the reserves necessary for an offensive that will decide the war.

This is altogether possible. Franco's area probably has approximately 11 million to 13 million inhabitants; if one reckons on a loss of 100,000 men killed or no longer fit for the front, then Franco has so far mobilized 700,000 men in his area, including the Moroccans. Compared to the military efforts of Germany in the World War, for example, this is a very modest figure (not one-third of Germany's effort with regard to personnel). All the cities of Nationalist Spain are full of young men who have not yet been drafted. In my opinion Franco could without trouble call a quarter of a million men to the barracks. Difficulties would probably arise only in quartering, arming, and training the men. Quarters could surely be improvised, since there are many partly or completely empty monasteries, noblemen's palaces, etc., in Nationalist Spain. As regards arms, German and Italian help would probably be necessary, as it would for training.

As far as the deliveries of further materials to Franco are concerned, it should be kept in mind as a general principle that it is cheaper to double deliveries for half a year than to deliver only half as much for twelve months, quite aside from the other disadvantages of doubling the length of the war.

Thus it follows that our efforts to hasten the victorious conclusion of the Spanish Civil War, necessitated by weighty political reasons, should not be aimed at greater influence in the Supreme Command of the Nationalist forces, as was recently demanded again by the Italians, but at a greater mobilization of the war potential of Nationalist Spain in manpower, to be carried out with our help and Italy's. This appears altogether possible and alone worthy of the Nationalist Government and the Spanish people.

Submitted to the State Secretary, the Director of the Political Department, and the Deputy Director of the Political Department.

SCHWENDEMANN

No. 503

586/243017–19

The Ambassador in Spain to the State Secretary

SECRET SALAMANCA, January 15, 1938.[1]

DEAR HERR VON MACKENSEN: Yesterday I reported officially (No. 307 of January 13) about Teruel and stated that according to the judgment of German and Italian military men Franco could win the

---

[1] The initials of the State Secretary indicate that this letter was in his hands on Jan. 18 and was also shown to the Foreign Minister on that date.

war militarily only through increased military aid. That may perhaps be somewhat pessimistic; but my judgment is, of course, not authoritative in such a purely military question.

What will the situation be, however, if for one reason or another we have to or wish to refrain from making further, conceivably very large, sacrifices for Franco? What, in particular, would happen if from now on we advocated an early withdrawal of all volunteers active at the front with the Whites and the Reds and if it proved possible to carry out this withdrawal speedily and with some degree of impartiality? Which side would then have the better prospect of success? That is, of course, a military question; nevertheless, I believe that the Whites, whose discipline and morale are undoubtedly better than the Reds', in spite of the prestige victory of the Reds at Teruel, and whose far more favorable economic situation permits continuing the war for a long time, would then have the better chances.

This is, of course, not certain, but a military victory, in the opinion of the military, is not certain unless Germany and Italy are prepared to make much greater sacrifices *and if* no international complications occur. Even then, Franco could lose the war or be obliged to conclude a "pink" peace.

I admit that in case of such a sharp change in the political course there is danger that we shall displease Spain very much and that we shall be in a difficult position as to the protection of our economic interests in Spain and generally as to the development of our future relations with Spain. Since, however—as you know—I have no very great illusions on this score as it is, I would not attach too much importance to the latter danger.

The above statements merely reflect thoughts which have occurred to me during the last few days but which I purposely have not discussed with the responsible military authorities because I do not know what opinion is held in Berlin about the Italian and German military proposals. However, without committing myself, I at least wanted to put these ideas on paper.

Nothing new occurred on the Teruel front during the last two days.

With cordial greetings and Heil Hitler!

As ever,

STOHRER

P.S.: Admiral Canaris called on me just now; he had been at the front with Franco and had far more favorable impressions than Berti and Veith. Franco expressed complete confidence but also admitted to the Admiral that he could not undertake any large offensive for several months.

At the request of Admiral Canaris I am telegraphing [2] today that in his opinion it would be useful, before making any far-reaching decisions, to await the report which he will submit upon his arrival in Berlin on January 22. On January 20 Admiral Canaris will arrive in Rome, where he is to see Count Ciano.

St[OHRER]

[2] Not printed (3363/E010407).

No. 504

3176/683036–39

Minute by an Official of the Economic Policy Department

BERLIN, January 17, 1938.
W II WE 140.

CONFERENCE IN THE MINISTRY FOR FOOD AND AGRICULTURE ON JANUARY 14, 1938, ON LAND ACQUISITION IN SPAIN [1]

In continuation of the conference of December 3, 1937.

Participants:

From the Food Ministry:	Ministerialdirektor Walter
	Ministerialdirektor Riecke, State Minister (Ret.)
	Ministerialrat Ebner
	Ministerialrat Weber
From the Finance Ministry:	Ministerialrat von Knorre
From Rowak:	Herr Bethke
	Herr Wahle

Herr Walter reported that Minister Darré and State Secretary Backe agreed with the plans in principle. They considered it useful for Germany to engage in agricultural activity in Spain, partly in view of the expected colonies, since there were in Spain and the Canary Islands possibilities of training for work in the colonies.

Herr Walter brought up for discussion the following questions:

1. Whether the plans might not be ruined by a Spanish agrarian reform;

2. Whether increasing monopolization might not also hinder export;

3. How far management would be conducted;

4. How the purchase was to be financed.

The Reich could not appear officially as the owner. Its financial participation, however, seemed necessary, since industry could not make sufficient means available.

Herr Bethke explained that there was no thought of buying big estates, because there was a plan to subdivide the large estates. Only

[1] For further material on this subject see document No. 809, p. 919.

farms of 3,000 to 4,000 hectares could be considered. He pictured these farms as model enterprises, the purpose of which was gradually to increase Spain's total production. (How the Guadalquivir project, however, which comprises an estate of approximately 20,000 hectares, is to be reconciled with this remained unexplained.)

The question of financing might perhaps be solved through a plan whereby Franco would repay his debts to us by transfers of land.

After an exhaustive discussion, the opinion of the Food and Finance Ministries, and partly also of Rowak, was revealed to be as follows:

1. If it is decided to purchase land in Spain for agricultural exploitation, this should be done only after the Spanish Government has been informed of it and has given its consent;

2. The land can be purchased only by a Spanish company with predominant German influence;

3. Seen from the standpoint of Germany's food situation, the project does not offer any immediate advantages. If any success is to be expected at all, it can come only after from ten to twenty years. It cannot be assumed that the Franco Government will permit us to export agricultural products independently of the needs and the laws of its own country. The sizable capital which would have to be raised can be invested in Germany with greater immediate results in production.

Herr Riecke thought therefore that the result could probably also be achieved through advisory agricultural commissions. Perhaps it might be advantageous if, first of all, representatives of the German Food Ministry communicated with the Spanish Ministry of Agriculture in order to inform themselves of Spain's wishes. At such a conference it might happen that the suggestion of Rowak would be realized in that the Spaniards would express on their own initiative a desire for the establishment of model farms.

The Food Ministry declared at the end of the discussion that the question was to be judged exclusively from the political standpoint. It would make its good offices available in case the Foreign Ministry desired the purchase of land. But on the basis of food policy the Food Ministry could undertake nothing.

I thereupon made the following statement:

The discussion had brought about a complete change in the situation. While earlier the Foreign Ministry was only to state whether or not the purchase of land in Spain was politically objectionable, it was now supposed to state whether it was politically desirable. The responsibility had thus been placed upon the Foreign Ministry.

During the first stage of the discussions the stand of the Foreign Ministry had been very simple. If the Food Ministry had expected an easing of Germany's food situation from a purchase of land, the

Foreign Ministry could have given its support. No objections would have been raised.

I did not wish to take any definitive stand yet on the present question, since I first wished to present the matter in the Foreign Ministry. I could not imagine, however, that the Foreign Ministry would appear as the driving force. I could not yet see any *political* reasons which made it appear advantageous to engage in agriculture in Spain on a large scale through companies under German influence.

SABATH

No. 505

309/189261–62

The Director of the Political Department to the Embassy in Italy [1]

Telegram

No. 16
BERLIN, January 18, 1938.
zu Pol. III 114 Ang. 2.

The London Embassy reports that it will become necessary in the very near future to take a stand in the Non-Intervention Committee on the question as to when belligerent rights are to be granted and what connection is to be made between this question and the question of withdrawing the volunteers. The further procedure was the subject of a discussion with the Italian and Portuguese Embassies. As a result of this conference the London Embassy mentions the following proposal as the most acceptable for our further conduct:

"We shall declare in the London conferences that we continue to consider Franco's proposal the correct one, namely, that prior to the granting of the belligerent rights a certain number of volunteers be withdrawn—the same number from each of the warring parties; we could also throw into the discussion the idea of recognizing Franco and further declare that, as an experiment, we were also ready to enter into discussions of proportionate figures. In this connection we would mention as our figure 20 percent and would in any case insist on it as long as the Soviet Russians do not improve their offer of from 80 to 85 percent. At the same time final compromise on this point could be made dependent on the settlement of other questions, the choice of which would best be left to the Embassy in consultation with the Italians. This procedure appears to us the most acceptable. Naturally we should have to decide rather definitely to what percentage we would finally want to come. No decision on this point is necessary today, however. As matters stand, an agreement on 50 percent seems possible, perhaps even on 40 percent. We were unanimously of the opinion that, once a percentile solution is adopted, it is relatively unimportant whether 10 or 20 percent more or less is conceded.

---

[1] The same message was sent for information to the Legation in Portugal as No. 6 and to the Embassy in Spain as No. 17. To the message to Lisbon was added the instruction "Please inform the Government there."

"During the last few days Plymouth has repeatedly urged all participants to begin the informal conferences decided upon on Tuesday as quickly as possible."

End of telegraphic report from London.

I informed the Italian Ambassador of this proposal today and told him that we approved of it. He declared himself in agreement, on the condition that an effort should be made to gain as much time as possible and that no intimation of a possible compromise on the figure of approximately 50 or 40 percent should be given for the time being. We were further of the opinion that in case a stalemate was reached in London one might revert to a suggestion made by Lord Plymouth to the Italian Chargé d'Affaires to the effect that Franco be given more of a voice in the matter and that the commission to be sent to White Spanish territory be instructed to negotiate with him about the percentages.

WEIZSÄCKER

No. 506

3374/E011036–41

The Chargé d'Affaires in Great Britain to the Foreign Ministry

CONFIDENTIAL   LONDON, January 20, 1938.
A 351   Pol. III 198.
Subject: The political situation in the Non-Intervention Committee
    at the turn of the year.
        I. The grouping of powers
        II. The tactical situation
        III. Prospects for the future

I. The group formed by Germany, Italy, and Portugal presents a more united front in the Non-Intervention Committee than ever before. Cooperation and support are given without friction. Count Grandi, who, as is known in Berlin, during certain phases last year made surprise moves about which he had not informed us in advance or had not fully informed us, has now abandoned such tactics. If Portugal is perhaps thinking more than before, in her entire policy, of British friendship, cooperation with our group in the committee does not suffer thereby. The community of interest leads of itself to joint action.

In accordance with the instruction given at the very beginning we have frequently, though not always, given the lead in the committee to the Italian representative, especially in questions in which Italian interest predominates. Count Grandi told me once in the fall without any apparent reason that we should not only support one another in the committee but also make it evident that we pursued a joint policy. Perhaps this was intended as a slight criticism. In general we agree beforehand who will speak first on the various questions. I believe that this continues to be only an expression of the division of interests if, at least at "big" sessions and on certain questions, especially, for example, on the withdrawal of volunteers, the first word is left to the Italians.

At the last session of the full committee our group for the first time had the full support of Austria, Hungary, and Albania. Whether other powers will now join this group cannot yet be foretold.

This closely knit group is not confronted by any other similarly united group. The British, French, and Soviet Russians continue to follow an essentially similar policy in many questions, especially in some of the most important ones. Thus all three are pressing for the withdrawal of volunteers. In other questions, however, their attitude is not so uniform. It must be recognized that, by the mere fact that Britain appoints the chairman and the very capable secretary, she has in general assumed the leadership and that in so doing she tends to take an impartial attitude. Unfortunately, at certain moments, especially at the time of the *Deutschland* and *Leipzig* incidents, the British adopted a different attitude. On the other hand the British plan of July was a fair attempt at mediation between the different views, in which England gave full support especially to the German-Italian demand for granting belligerent rights and furthered it in opposition to the wishes of France.

The French Ambassador in general keeps very much in the background on days when big issues are being contested, but he is generally the one who always tries to speed up the tempo. At any rate Red Spain has in France a much better helper than in England.

The Soviet Union has isolated itself to an increasing extent through unskillful tactical procedure. Finally, in the decisive sessions, Ambassador Maisky has repeatedly retreated, which has not exactly increased his prestige. In the summer the Soviet Union involuntarily did us a good turn by its conduct, so that the big split before the summer recess was charged mainly to the account of the Soviet Union even by British public opinion. Still more than the Ambassador, the Jewish Counselor of Embassy Kagan frequently aroused the impatience even of the British by his long and captious speeches.

Aside from the above-mentioned group of Austria, Hungary, and Albania, the smaller powers have shown an increasing tendency to treat the affairs of the Non-Intervention Committee as those of the Great Powers and to keep out of them as much as possible. In this connection the powers of the Little Entente and the Balkan Entente this summer for the first time agreed upon a joint procedure and also harmonized their conduct completely with that of the powers of the Oslo group. The former Swedish representative on the committee,

Baron Palmstierna, who has now retired, was generally the only exception to this. Until well into the summer Palmstierna had the tendency to go along with the Soviet Ambassador through thick and thin. Recently he no longer has involved himself in this manner, perhaps at a hint from Stockholm as the result of our complaints.

The Belgian Ambassador, on the contrary, frequently opposed the Soviet Ambassador in the early days of the committee, whereas he no longer does this now.

II. In accordance with the state of affairs we have had to follow essentially dilatory tactics in the committee throughout the entire past year. The question of withdrawing the volunteers has now been on the agenda for a whole year. It would, of course, have been relatively easy to reach a settlement, if this had been in the interest of all. It proved to be a good move on our part to throw the question of belligerent rights into the discussion. It was possible mainly through this to draw out the discussions again and again without our really getting into an awkward situation publicly. In this connection Soviet Russia involuntarily did us the services already mentioned above.

The entire negotiation in the committee has something unreal about it, since all participants see through the game of the other side but only seldom express this openly. The fact that questions concerning which no one knows whether they will ever become actual are discussed with great seriousness in all details also contributes toward making the whole thing often appear more of a game than a reality. The non-intervention policy is so unstable and is such an artificial creation that everyone fears to cause its collapse by a clear "no" and then have to bear the responsibility. Therefore unpleasant proposals are talked to death instead of rejected. We must, of course, take care to direct our tactics in such a way that we will not appear as saboteurs.

In general, politics has been taken out of the committee to a great extent during the past few months. This has had the result that the interest of the British public has decreased greatly. The time is past when photographers would stand outside the door before each session and when the press carried columns of reports, some true and some false, about the sessions. It can return at any time, of course. Apparently the main point of contention, namely, the question whether the volunteers are to be withdrawn or not, is no longer considered a vital question even in England. Here the main problem of the Spanish conflict is still considered to be whether Italy will establish herself permanently in Majorca or even on the Spanish mainland. The question of withdrawing the volunteers is in the main considered from this point of view and is regarded as a means of achieving the objective of Italian evacuation from Spain.

III. I reported some time ago that according to the normal course of committee procedure and without the introduction of special delaying maneuvers it cannot be expected that the withdrawal of volunteers will begin before May. Even today May can be regarded as the very earliest date to be considered, and it is altogether possible even to bring about a somewhat longer delay without special artificial means. At any rate Lord Plymouth and the secretary of the committee, Hemming, also stated in one of the last sessions that 2½ to 3 months will elapse between the moment when the commissions arrive in Spain and the real withdrawal. During the next week a provisional reply will presumably be sent out to the two Spanish parties, and it is possible that a formula will be found by approximately the middle of February for all questions remaining open. After the committee has taken almost 2 months to reply to the Spanish parties, Franco has, of course, the power to cause even further postponement, if this is desired, by delaying his reply and above all by asking additional questions. In the course of this summer, however, the time will come when the game played with petty means will have been exhausted. In my opinion, thought should be given even now to what should be done at that time if the withdrawal of volunteers is to be prevented further. It is not entirely excluded that the Soviet Union will offer us the chance that the entire negotiations will break down because of her. This applies especially to the general reservation which the Soviet Union has made in regard to the question of resuming control measures. I rather believe, however, that the Soviet representative here will again, as in earlier cases, change his attitude at the last moment. Of course, other strong possibilities remain for Franco himself. Finally, in case there is danger that we might otherwise get into an untenable situation, we shall probably have to consider whether we should not at a given time frankly tell the British and perhaps the French as well, outside the committee, that the withdrawal of volunteers is not possible at the moment, perhaps because of the fighting then in progress or some similar reason.

WOERMANN

No. 507

2938/569797–98

The Ambassador in Spain to the Foreign Ministry

SECRET   SALAMANCA, January 21, 1938.
No. 433   W II WE 508.

Subject: Ore shipments from Nationalist Spain and Spanish Morocco to Germany.

Director Johannes Bernhardt of Hisma Ltd., Seville, has transmitted to the Embassy a report, a copy of which is enclosed and which gives a picture of the quantities of ore shipped to Germany during the past year from Spanish Morocco and Nationalist Spain.

Herr Bernhardt has already forwarded these figures, which are *not meant for publication*, directly to the office of Minister President Colonel General Göring, Division of the Four Year Plan, Foreign Trade Group, in Berlin.

I shall later send further information about the total figures promised by Hisma on Spanish exports to Germany for the year 1937.

STOHRER

[Annex]

For your information we wish to report to you that ore exports were as follows during the month of December:

Iron ores: Bilbao shipments, approximately..	90,000 tons
Morocco shipments, approximately.	100,000 tons
Other shipments, approximately...	15,000 tons
Total....................	205,000 tons
Shipments of pyrites, approximately.........	55,000 tons
Shipments of ores such as tungsten, copper, and bronze, approximately................	152 tons

Thus during the month of December we achieved a record of approximately 260,000 tons.

The figures for the year 1937 are also now available. We shipped a total of 2,584,000 tons of ores, including:

Iron ores..............................	1,620,000 tons
Pyrites................................	956,000 tons
Miscellaneous ores, approximately.........	7,000 tons

The figures speak for themselves. We request therefore that contrary reports of a biased nature or coming from a less careful source be rejected.

At the same time we ask that we be informed of the agencies which so far have repeatedly given misleading figures, so that we can set the matter right.

The total figures for all exports from Spain to Germany are also already available; I shall send them to the Embassy shortly.

Heil Hitler!

BERNHARDT

No. 508

2946/576154–57

Memorandum of the Embassy in Spain

January 28, 1938.
PROTOCOL OF THE MEETING FOR CONSIDERATION OF THE MONTANA
PROJECT, BURGOS, JANUARY 25, 1938

Present: General Jordana, Ambassador von Stohrer, Secretary of Legation Stille.

After the Ambassador's introductory remark that he had come to Burgos in order to speak once more with General Jordana about the Montana project, on which, to his regret, no progress had been made during the last two weeks, and in order, as he hoped, to receive orally from General Jordana a few more detailed explanations, the latter replied that as a result of the great number of mining rights—namely 73—acquired by Germany, the examination was taking some time. After all, the protocol of July 16, 1937, stipulated expressly that utilization of Spanish mineral resources by or for Germany should be carried on only as compatible with the general stipulations of Spanish law. Therefore an extensive legal examination was necessary.

The Ambassador replied that this examination was certainly taking a long time. In his opinion the German-Spanish cooperation which was envisaged in the protocol of July 16, 1937—and which Jordana also desired—could become a reality only if a number of mining rights were already available as a basis for this cooperation, which was to be put into effect in the form of a Spanish company. For this reason Hisma had acquired these rights, but had always intended to utilize them only in the form of friendly cooperation.

General Jordana thereupon stated that unfortunately there was no clear legal text by which the question whether Hisma was permitted to acquire the mining rights could be answered clearly and simply. A number of laws, royal ordinances, and decrees had to be considered which were not closely coordinated in their details and consequently raised difficult questions of interpretation. To answer these, a very extensive examination was necessary, which unfortunately was made very difficult by the lack of suitable officials and especially by the lack of any precedents.

The Ambassador then asked that he be given a definite date on which a Spanish reply to our memorandum,[1] which was given Señor Jordana on January 12, could be expected. He well understood the difficulties but nevertheless had to attach importance to being given a definite date. At any rate he had to insist on being able to give

---

[1] Not found.

his Government a certain date by which the Spaniards would have their answer ready. When General Jordana would not commit himself to any date in spite of these strong representations, the Ambassador stated further that they were concerned, even alarmed, in Germany over the development of the Montana project. In view of the great importance which was attached in Berlin, especially by the Commissioner for the Four Year Plan, Colonel General Göring, to the question of obtaining Spanish minerals, it was quite possible that in case of further delays and excuses by the Spaniards a sudden change of sentiment might occur in Berlin. He would like to avoid this but saw the danger increasing unless a decisive step was taken soon in the sense of fulfilling our wishes.

In this part of the conversation, in which he also referred to the German sacrifices made for Spain, the Ambassador went as far as he could within the limits of a friendly treatment of the matter in accordance with Berlin instructions.

General Jordana thereupon replied that in his opinion the mining rights had only a relative value for us, since the mines in question first had to be developed and consequently had only a very small output at the present moment. Furthermore, one did not know at all how the situation would be in a month. Of course the Nationalist Government was prepared to cooperate, but this cooperation could become effective only if German participation was limited or less extensive.

The Ambassador thereupon asked at once that this opinion be given to him in writing so that he could send it on to Berlin. For the rest, he was of the opinion that, in order to simplify and advance the negotiations, those points about which there was agreement between Germany and Spain should be put into writing and taken out of the negotiations.

General Jordana replied that he was not authorized to give such confirmation, since everything first had to be approved by the Generalissimo. Because of the lack of a government the Generalissimo alone embodied governmental authority in Spain and consequently nothing could be done without his consent. The results of the studies made by the experts of the Junta Técnica, which were far advanced and which lacked only a few more data for their completion, likewise had to be submitted to the Generalissimo.

In order to make some progress the Ambassador then suggested that he send General Jordana a letter the next day asking him for confirmation that the further handling of the Montana project would be on the basis of the protocol of July 16, 1937, and thus in the sense of the German-Spanish cooperation expressed in this protocol, which had to be pursued further in the interest of both countries according to the opinion also expressed by General Jordana. If such a confirmation were sent on to the German Government in Berlin, it would at least see the Spanish Government's good intentions for honest cooperation.

General Jordana agreed to make such a statement in the form of a personal letter to the Ambassador but remarked that, even in the case of such a personal letter, he would first have to submit it to the Generalissimo.

At the end of the conversation General Jordana stressed once more that he had to abide strictly by the Spanish laws. The mentality of the Spanish people was such that it tended, following a change in government or in government parties, to call the members of the former government to account for its actions. Thus he himself, because of his actions under the dictatorship of Primo de Rivera, had later been condemned by the Republic, first to death and then to life imprisonment, and had spent 2 years in prison! Therefore he had to attach great importance to abiding most strictly by the Spanish laws since, after all, one could never know what might happen.

STILLE

Note: Following my return to Salamanca, Herr Brinkmann of Hisma told me that on the same day on which the Ambassador and I were with General Jordana the Spanish experts, especially the lawyers, had held a conference in the Junta Técnica, which lasted for more than three hours and was exclusively devoted to the Montana project. He, Herr Brinkmann, had the impression that the examination was now actually being speeded up by the Spaniards because of our oft-repeated insistence.

STILLE

No. 509

2946/576160–63

Memorandum of the Embassy in Spain

SALAMANCA, January 26, 1938.

Subject: Montana project.

With reference to the memorandum [1] of a thorough discussion with Señor Sangroniz on January 26, in which the Montana project is listed as point 1.

I informed Señor Sangroniz that my conversation with General Jordana in Burgos yesterday had not left very favorable impressions with me. We simply were not making any progress in the Montana affair, with which he, Sangroniz, was familiar. The matter had now been pending for 2 months. Early consideration was always prom-

---

[1] Not found.

ised, but we still had no reply. I did not need to explain to him once more the importance of this affair for us. But I did want to tell him very frankly that this treatment seemed to us improper and incorrect in view of the sacrifices made by us so far and still being made daily for the Spanish Nationalist state and the movement. After all no really large sum was involved: approximately one and a half million RM. In view of our services to Spain they could well make a gesture and, with a stroke of the pen, settle the Montana affair— in which the German Government and especially Colonel General Göring were so very much interested—in our favor.

Señor Sangroniz explained, however, as he had done earlier, that the matter was important from the point of view of principle and that the present provisional Spanish Government had to be exceptionally careful with regard to its disposition of the Spanish patrimony. He had again spoken with Jordana recently and believed that the matter would be settled in our favor. But first it would have to be determined whether the acquisitions were actually in accordance with Spanish law. Then one could proceed further.

I repeated once more that this manner of handling the affair did not appear right to me. I again pointed to the sacrifices which we were making for Spain and to the fact that after all we could also make some demands. Thereupon Señor Sangroniz asked that he be permitted to speak to me about this matter quite frankly, in a friendly manner and without witnesses. I expressed my agreement, where-upon Señor Sangroniz stated the following:

"I want to tell you very frankly that it was not correct to arrange the matter as Germany wanted to do. To begin with, it was a psychological error to alarm and in a sense to mobilize the interested parties and the entire Spanish administration [*administración española*] through the numerous purchases of mining rights. This aroused opposition which would not have appeared if Germany had stated that she wanted to organize a company at the present time; if Germany had purchased only a few mining rights to begin with and had discussed with Spain how the matter might now be continued and expanded in the sense of friendly collaboration [*colaboración*]. Instead of choosing this course, Germany bought up mines and mining rights to an incredible extent. (Señor Sangroniz used a still stronger expression with the request that this might not be held against him.) This, of course, aroused opposition everywhere, and through this sensation and this opposition the Spanish Government was forced to settle the matter fundamentally on the basis of Spanish law. If matters had been handled differently, the affair would have become less of a sensation and could have been settled more secretly."

I replied to Señor Sangroniz that we acted as we did because in the agreements of July 1937 we had, after all, obtained the Spaniards' consent to collaboration in the exploitation of Spanish mineral resources. From the very beginning we had never thought of keeping and exploiting all these rights 100 percent for ourselves—and Herr Bernhardt had always stressed this—but we had always thought of collaboration [*colaboración*] with Spain and had made plans for it. I could not suppose that the Spanish Government might perhaps for some reason or other not wish to keep the promises given us in July. But time and again it was visibly delaying the decision in this matter, which was so close to our hearts. From General Jordana's statements and his own statement it appeared that it was intended to leave any definite decision to the real government which was supposedly now being formed. I was urging Señor Sangroniz once more to use all his influence with the Junta Técnica for an early positive reply in this matter.

No. 510

2946/576158–59

The Ambassador in Spain to the President of the Junta Técnica [1]

SALAMANCA, January 26, 1938.
zu 10 g Mont.

MY DEAR GENERAL AND DISTINGUISHED FRIEND: [2] During our conversation in Burgos yesterday I had the honor to bring to the fore once more the great importance which the responsible authorities in Germany, especially the Commissioner for the Four Year Plan, Colonel General Göring, attach to as speedy a clarification as possible of the questions raised by the acquisition of the mining rights. I further stated that these authorities consequently are looking forward with great impatience to a speedy reply to the memorandum handed you on January 12 by Herr Bernhardt. You, on the other hand, pointed out that the absence of any archives, the lack of trained officials, and especially the nature of the governmental authority, at present only provisionally embodied in the person of His Excellency the Generalissimo, greatly complicate a thorough treatment of the legal questions which, in the opinion of the Spanish governmental authorities, were raised through Hisma's acquisition of the mining rights. Although I can understand that in view of the special circumstances these difficulties are an obstacle to the handling of the legal questions, nevertheless, as I pointed out in our conversation yesterday, I am of the opinion that by not making purely judicial arguments and considerations the sole basis for all decisions to be reached, it is possible to comply with the wish for speed expressed by Germany.

---

[1] The copy used is a draft in German. The letter was transmitted to General Jordana in the Spanish translation; the latter text is 5149/E303624–32.
[2] In Spanish in the original.

In order to give a contractual basis to the good understanding fortunately existing between Germany and Spain in the economic field, the various protocols were signed last July; they envisage honest cooperation between Germany and Spain, especially for the purpose of opening up and utilizing Spanish mineral resources and other raw materials. I believe that it would be desirable for the further fruitful development of this cooperation, and would be welcomed by the German Government as an indication of the Spanish Government's frequently demonstrated desire for honest collaboration, if at present you would give me for transmittal to my Government at least the confirmation that in your opinion, too, the further handling of the Montana project should be on the basis of the protocol of last July, in the drafting of which you had an essential part, and that consequently you, too, my dear General, will continue to work for the realization of the common desire of the Spanish and German Governments for friendly collaboration [*amistosa colaboración*] expressed in the protocol.

I take this opportunity, etc.   VON STOHRER

No. 511

3374/E011042–43

The Foreign Ministry to the Embassy in Great Britain [1]

CONFIDENTIAL   BERLIN, January 28, 1938.
                                               zu Pol. III 198 Ang. II.

Drafting Officer: Counselor of Legation Schwendemann.

With reference to your report A 351 of January 20.

All reports on the military situation in the Spanish Civil War indicate that the expectation which prevailed rather generally before the events at Teruel, that within a few months Franco would succeed by means of a large-scale offensive in bringing the war to a victorious close, was unjustified; that, on the contrary, the end of the Spanish Civil War is not yet in sight. This cannot fail to affect our attitude in the Non-Intervention Committee. Since our political aim in Spain remains the same, namely, to prevent a Red victory with all its attendant political and economic consequences for us, a change in our attitude toward Franco is out of the question. The setting of any definite time for the withdrawal of the volunteers, therefore, cannot be considered at present. From this it is evident that the time element

---

[1] It is not clear whether this instruction, which was prepared for Weizsäcker's signature but was not signed by him, was actually sent. Although Schwendemann initialed it on Jan. 29, the word "Cessat" was written on the margin by him on Mar. 8.

involved in solving the problem of the withdrawal of the volunteers, as contemplated in section III of the above-mentioned report, is not in our interest. Therefore please make it your primary aim in the negotiations in the Non-Intervention Committee and its subcommittees to gain as much time as possible and to defer as long as possible the time when we might have to commit ourselves to a fundamental decision on the further development of the non-intervention policy.

By direction:
(v. WEIZSÄCKER)
SCH[WENDEMANN]
Jan. 29.

No. 512

309/189218–19

The Chargé d'Affaires in Great Britain to the Director of the Political Department

CONFIDENTIAL   LONDON, January 28, 1938.

DEAR HERR VON WEIZSÄCKER: About a week ago I made a comprehensive report [1] on the situation in the Non-Intervention Committee. In the short interim I have arrived at a more pessimistic opinion.

Several times now the British Leftist press has carried reports that new Italian troop shipments to Spain are impending; we have also reported about this (report A 448 of January 27 [2]). From Germany likewise rumors have reached me according to which the Italians are planning something of the sort and had requested similar action by us, unsuccessfully, to be sure, insofar as manpower is concerned. I do not know with full certainty whether this is correct. At any rate it appears to me that there is no intention whatever of withdrawing the volunteers before victory.

On the other hand the difficulties in the committee have increased. I do not exactly consider it a danger signal, but it is indicative that Lord Plymouth did not even dare to call another session this week although the French Ambassador is trying hard to speed up matters.

As is indicated in our current reports, we must act very cautiously in this situation so that we will not be maneuvered into an unfavorable position—for which the prospects have now increased.

The worst point in our procedure is our opposition in the control question. In the last session of the technical subcommittee the British made a new compromise proposal,[3] as you will see from our report.

---

[1] Document No. 506, p. 562.
[2] Not found.
[3] This proposal concerned the powers of the observer officers in Spanish ports. It was reported by Woermann in airgram No. 34 of Jan. 25 (586/242999–243002).

I consider it very desirable that we should now accept this proposal.[4] If, on the other hand, there are really cogent reasons for rejection, I should be very grateful if we were informed thereof frankly and confidentially. Perhaps there is a certain connection with the events mentioned in the second paragraph of this letter. But even supposing that something is again pending, I should nevertheless plead for acceptance of the present British compromise proposal. The Italian Embassy has, to be sure, supported us as always in the technical subcommittee, even in our attitude on the control question, but it also shares our opinion that we should accept the compromise proposal and it is in a position to do so on the basis of its instructions. We have already reported a number of times that the Russians will be driven into isolation on the control question if an agreement is reached among the other powers on the point now at issue. I therefore request once more that we be given a positive instruction in this direction as soon as possible.[5]

I shall have a joint conference this afternoon with the Portuguese Ambassador and Grandi, and I do not know whether it will change the picture in any way. If necessary I would telegraph the results of this conference.

With cordial greetings and Heil Hitler!

As ever,
WOERMANN

---

[4] Marginal note in Weizsäcker's handwriting: "So do I."
[5] Marginal notes: "Are we in accord with the military to the extent that we can inform Woermann of our agreement by telegram? W[eizsäcker] Jan. 29." "The requested instruction has been issued in the meantime. Schw[endemann] Feb. 2."

No. 513

3363/E010030-31

Minute by the Head of Political Division IIIa

BERLIN, January 28, 1938.
zu Pol. III 244 Ang. I.

I discussed with Captains [*Kapitänen*] Frisius and Heinichen of the Foreign Department [*Abt. Ausland*] of the War Ministry today the question of our stand on the new British compromise proposal, as communicated to us in the airgram from the London Embassy.[1] They emphasized that the War Ministry had always been opposed in principle to any strengthening of the naval patrol, because the sea route was the only one by which Franco could receive reinforcements. I explained that the limited powers of the naval patrol officers as provided in the new British compromise proposal could not interfere with these supplies for Franco, since they arrived on ships flying the flags of

---

[1] No. 34 of Jan. 25. Not printed (586/242999-243002).

countries other than those represented in the Non-Intervention Committee. If these supervising officers had only the right to go ashore in order to check whether other ships of the non-intervention countries lying in port had patrol officers on board, then access to parts of the harbor in which a ship under the flag of a non-intervention country might be lying could always be denied them. Both officers, however, adhered to their opinions and expressed the fear that the other side would undoubtedly try in London to extend more and more the right of supervision of the new patrol agents in the Spanish ports. I replied that this would simply have to be prevented. The officers finally said that they did not wish to oppose an instruction to the Embassy accepting the British compromise proposal but would not assume responsibility for it.

Thus the instruction in the sense of the Embassy's proposal can now be sent to London, and it is enclosed herewith.[2]

Respectfully submitted to the Director of the Political Department.

SCHW[ENDEMANN]

[2] For the instruction as sent, see the following document.

No. 514

586/243008

The Director of the Political Department to the Embassy in Great Britain

Telegram

No. 23   BERLIN, January 29, 1938.
                                                         zu Pol. III 244/Ang. II.

With reference to your airgram No. 34 of January 25.[1]

There are no objections here to accepting the new British compromise proposal, provided that the strengthening of the naval patrol is limited exclusively to giving observation officers authority to go ashore only for the purpose of ascertaining whether other ships lying in port that belong to treaty powers have observation officers aboard and, if not, to assume their function in their stead.

WEIZSÄCKER

[1] Not printed (586/242999–243002).

No. 515

586/243020–23

The Ambassador in Spain to the State Secretary

SALAMANCA, February 1, 1938.

DEAR HERR VON MACKENSEN: I have not called on the Generalissimo since meeting him on January 6, as I did not know and do not know even now what position Berlin contemplates taking on the new situation created by Teruel and the wishes expressed by the military, and I therefore wished to avoid any embarrassing questions.

My Italian colleague, with whom I work very well, was heretofore in the same situation, and for that reason he did not visit Franco either. A few days ago, however, he received, at least through private channels, news about the attitude taken by Mussolini, and now—as I reported by wire on January 31—the Italian Commander in Chief, General Berti, has received specific instructions from Rome which, in the presence of Count Viola,[1] he reported to the Generalissimo at Burgos on January 29.

As my Italian colleague tells me, Mussolini was very much annoyed with Franco and his manner of conducting the war; he had nevertheless promised him his help once more, but for a limited time only. He does not wish to go along with him for more than 4 to 6 months longer, however. Franco should proceed somewhat more energetically. For this purpose, however, he could have renewed support from the Italians in matériel and perhaps also in troops. To be sure, General Berti gave Franco plainly to understand, a stricter organization of the army command and a better coordination of the individual units must be assured. At the same time Berti also made it plain that Franco must lend a more willing ear than heretofore to the advice of the Italian military.

Franco replied to these statements, as always, in a calm and friendly tone, stating that in his opinion the war situation was very good; the enemy was throwing more and more of its reserves into the witches' caldron of Teruel (from other reports, however, they are still supposed to have a few more divisions in reserve) ; in a few days he would launch a sizable operation near Teruel once more in order to organize his front there better, and possibly even occupy the city again. Then—Franco told General Veith and Admiral Canaris the same thing—he would first undertake occasional small operations in order to shake the enemy's confidence and to train his own men. Then in the spring the big drive would take place. In order to carry this out he was now strengthening his present front considerably, so that he would have to use only very few troops to man it and would be able to concentrate all his forces for this drive. Moreover, he had now drafted an additional 40,000 new recruits. He did not need much more equipment, at the most antitank guns, heavy infantry equipment, and so forth. Franco supposedly said nothing about troops.

General Berti and the Italian Ambassador still have the impression that Franco shrinks from a decisive blow, the failure of which could mean for him the loss of the war, or at least the impossibility of a

---

[1] The Italian Ambassador to the Nationalist Government.

victory; and for this reason he still prefers the simpler operation against Madrid—which, from the military standpoint, is not regarded as absolutely certain to end the war—rather than the plan of a drive in Aragón.

There is no doubt—and this view is shared by both our military and the Italian—that the situation at Teruel has recently shifted somewhat in favor of Franco again. This does not alter the fact, however, that a balance of forces now exists.

I should be very grateful to be informed of the attitude taken in Berlin—at least in principle—toward General Veith's wishes and proposals, and what influence, if any, Berlin intends to exert on further developments in Spain.

Should we desire to make available more matériel and possibly personnel, also—other than through purely commercial channels— I should advise *immediately* formulating counterdemands with respect to the conduct of the war, etc., in a suitable way, for otherwise in half a year we will be in exactly the same position as now. [It would help greatly] if we could obtain belligerent rights for Franco; the food question (see report No. 242 g of January 31,[2] being sent today) has become vital for the Reds. I believe that in return for these belligerent rights Franco could well dispense with almost all foreign ground troops (see my private letter of January 15) ; a successful blockade would compensate for their loss.

With cordial greeting and Heil Hitler,

Ever faithfully yours,
STOHRER

---

[2] Not printed (1557/377775–80).

No. 516

586/243024–24/1

The Director of the Political Department to the Ambassador in Spain

CONFIDENTIAL   BERLIN, February 2, 1938.

DEAR STOHRER: According to your many letters of recent date and the oral accounts of C.[1] and of your Counselor of Embassy Heberlein, you have surely been waiting for some time for a statement as to whether our Spanish policy has been reexamined, and with what result.

I am writing you today only to tell you that we have not allowed the subject to rest. On the contrary, we are very much occupied with it; we have not yet come to the conclusion, however, that there must be an immediate change. If the military revival on the Franco side, which seems at present to be impending, should last, everything would take a turn for the better again, politically, too. But if, as is to be

---

[1] Admiral Canaris, who had returned from Spain on Jan. 22.

feared, only partial successes and smaller demonstrations of activity are involved, then we shall have to consider something such as you reported to us yesterday with regard to the Italians. In any case, we should like to have available the considered judgment of our own military on the present situation, which we do not yet have. Moreover, if we want to make more of an impression on Franco than the Italians succeeded in doing, it will be necessary to discuss with you personally the means of doing so. This has not yet been suggested to the Foreign Minister, since it is not urgent.

As I said, I only wish to assure you that your various communications and suggestions have not gone unheeded here.

Cordial greetings and Heil Hitler,

Yours,

WEIZSÄCKER

No. 517

309/189215–16

The Chargé d'Affaires in Great Britain to the Foreign Ministry

Telegram

No. 53 of February 2   LONDON, February 2, 1938—9 : 08 p.m.
Received February 3—12 : 30 a.m.

In connection with the *Endymion* incident [1] Eden summoned the Italian and French Ambassadors today as the representatives of the two powers which, together with Great Britain, provide patrol service in the . . . (group missing) on the basis of the Nyon-Paris agreement.

Grandi informed me as follows regarding this: The conversation had lasted only 10 minutes. Eden had read and handed both Ambassadors a statement. It was to the effect that the attack on the British ship was a clear-cut violation of the rules of international law. It had not been possible thus far, however, to identify and seize the attacking ship. The British Government considered it urgently necessary to take strict measures against a revival of this piracy. For this purpose more drastic measures were needed than were provided for in the Nyon agreement. The British Government therefore reserved the right ("they . . . propose to reserve . . . the right" [2]) from now on to destroy every submerged submarine encountered in the part of the western Mediterranean reserved for the British patrol ships. The British Government had decided to notify the French and Italian Governments of this

---

[1] The British vessel *Endymion* had been torpedoed and sunk by a submarine off Cartagena on Feb. 1 with loss of 10 lives. The observation officer on board was killed.

[2] In English in the original.

action. The two Spanish parties would be notified of the measures.

Grandi thereupon asked Eden how the words "they propose to reserve" were to be interpreted—whether this was a proposal or an announcement. Eden, according to Grandi, gave no very clear-cut answer, but it was plain that an announcement was meant. Eden also requested the two Ambassadors to inquire of their Governments whether they wished to take like measures in their zones.

There was no talk of calling a conference of all the signatory powers of Nyon. I also wish to point out that the measures which the British Government now intends to take were already discussed at Nyon, but rejected. The measures contemplated have not yet been published.

WOERMANN

No. 518

309/189209–10

The Director of the Political Department to the Embassy in Great Britain

Telegram

No. 31
BERLIN, February 4, 1938.
Pol. III 357.

With reference to your telegram No. 55 of February 2.[1]

The Italian Ambassador informed us today of the contents of the instruction to Grandi, which either will be or has already been sent, regarding the line he is to take on the question of the percentage of volunteers to be withdrawn and the time for granting belligerent rights. According to this, Grandi is instructed not to go beyond an offer of 20 percent, at first. Should it not be possible to reach an agreement on this basis, he is to propose again that the commissions to be sent to Spain be authorized to negotiate the date for the granting of belligerent rights. In this connection, he is to avail himself of the argument that it is of no use at the present time to engage in long debates on the percentage in London, before it is clear what position the Spanish parties will take on this question. Should this proposal be rejected by Plymouth again, as in the past, Grandi is empowered to give his consent to a 30 percent withdrawal of volunteers, but this offer is as far as the Italian Government will go.

On the basis of this new Italian attitude, please do not go beyond an offer of 30 percent either, for the present, in the interest of a common German-Italian procedure. Should negotiations fail to produce an agreement on this basis, a renewed discussion with the Italian Government on further procedure will be necessary.

WEIZSÄCKER

---

[1] Not printed (586/243031).

No. 519

3374/E011047–48

The Chargé d'Affaires in Great Britain to the Foreign Ministry

A 588   LONDON, February 4, 1938.
                                                            Pol. III 369.

Subject: Rumors of the dispatch of German and Italian reinforcements to Spain.   Grandi's statements on the number of volunteers in Spain.

In the last few weeks the Leftist press here has repeatedly published reports of the alleged dispatch of more Italian troops to Spain, in which connection the figure of 50,000 was mentioned in some cases as the strength of the reinforcements (cf. reports A 393 of January 26 [1] and A 448 of January 27 [1]).

In the Commons' session of February 2 there was a question on this matter, to which Eden replied that the British Government was not in possession of such reports (Hansard of February 2, vol. 331, No. 45, column 215). On February 3 even the Manchester *Guardian* confirmed the fact that there was no proof on hand that Italian troops were being made ready, in this manner, and attributed the earlier incorrect reports to the fact that the Italian troop reinforcements had been assembled for Libya. The *Daily Express*, too, in its edition of February 4, publishes a report to the effect that the Italian Supreme Defense Council, with Mussolini presiding, had decided to make radical changes in its policy with respect to military assistance for Franco. At present, therefore, no further reinforcements of any kind were being sent to Franco. In this decision Mussolini had been influenced in the first place by his desire not to render the Anglo-Italian conversations impossible because of the Mediterranean question, and also by the conviction that today there was no longer any danger of a Soviet administration in Spain if the Government won the war.

On the other hand the Manchester *Guardian* of February 4 now publishes a report from Geneva to the effect that the German Government was dispatching to Spain 2,000 technicians, who were leaving Berlin in detachments of 120 men at 2- to 3-day intervals and proceeding by way of Italy to Franco.

The Italian Ambassador told me in the course of the conversation that the maximum number of Italian volunteers had been 60,000 to 70,000 men in March 1937. The numbers had now been reduced to some 30,000 men. When he had asked in Rome why they had not let him exploit this fact as a favorable bargaining point, he had been

---

[1] Not found.

informed that Rome wished to decide independently, without being influenced in any way, whether or not its own volunteers were to remain in Spain.

I enclose the two articles from the Manchester *Guardian* of February 3 and 4, as well as the one from the *Daily Express* of February 4.[2]

WOERMANN

[2] Not reprinted.

No. 520

586/243043

Minute by the Head of Political Division IIIa

URGENT   BERLIN, February 7, 1938.

Pol. III 398.

Captain [*Kapitän*] Frisius of the Foreign Department of the War Ministry told me, when I asked him what consequences the new Anglo-French measures[1] in the Mediterranean on the basis of the Nyon agreement had for us, that these measures entailed no consequences of any kind for us. Our submarines in Spanish waters had the strictest orders to stay only in the Atlantic. Their duty was solely to protect our transports. Submarines had been used for this task only because we needed our few other warships for training purposes, whereas we were relatively well supplied with submarines.

Respectfully submitted to the State Secretary, the Director of the Political Department, and the Deputy Director of the Political Department.

SCHWENDEMANN

[1] Following a renewal of submarine attacks in the Mediterranean, culminating in the sinking of the *Endymion* on Feb. 1, the British, French, and Italian Governments agreed to instruct their naval vessels to the effect that submerged submarines in the areas under patrol should be regarded as contemplating an attack on merchant shipping and were to be attacked accordingly.

No. 521

1557/377797

The Ambassador in Spain to the Foreign Ministry

STRICTLY CONFIDENTIAL   SALAMANCA, FEBRUARY 7, 1938.

No. 244 g   Pol. I 385 g III.

With reference to my telegram No. 44 of January 31.[1]

The Italian Ambassador has informed me in strict confidence that Mussolini had abruptly given General Berti, who was in Italy on private business for two days last week, a letter for Franco, in which the latter was asked in friendly but firm language to take more energetic action.

[1] Not printed (1557/377754).

In view of the present successful Nationalist offensive near Teruel, Berti, by agreement with the Ambassador, did not deliver the letter.[2]

STOHRER

---

[2] In report No. 259 g of Feb. 17, 1938 (1557/377841) Ambassador Stohrer reported that he had been informed that General Berti sent Mussolini's letter to General Franco a few days later after all.

No. 522

586/243040–41

The State Secretary to the Embassy in Great Britain[1]

Telegram

No. 34   BERLIN, FEBRUARY 8, 1938.
                                                      Pol. III 378 Ang. I.

With reference to your No. 63.[2]

In response to the announcement concerning British measures against submerged submarines in the British Mediterranean zone, please read the following statement of the Reich Government verbatim to the Government there and leave a written copy upon request:

The German Government has taken cognizance of the announcement concerning British measures against submerged submarines in the Mediterranean zone patrolled by the British fleet in accordance with the Nyon agreement. It feels impelled to register a legal reservation with reference to the action decided upon by the British Government. The German Government takes the stand that a unilateral measure of this kind in the open sea has no binding legal force for those powers whose consent was not secured in advance. But, since German naval forces are not affected *de facto* by this measure, the German Government does not (at present)[3] intend to take any action in consequence of this legal reservation.

MACKENSEN

---

[1] The text of this telegram was communicated for information to the Embassy in Italy as No. 32 and to the Embassy in France as No. 41.
[2] Of Feb. 5, 1938; not printed (586/243039).
[3] Marginal note: "The Director of the Political Department approved by telephone, adding the words in parentheses. v. M[ackensen]."

No. 523

309/189190–93

The Chargé d'Affaires in Great Britain to the Foreign Ministry

Airgram

No. 69 of February 9   LONDON, FEBRUARY 9, 1938.
                                                      Received February 9.

From the discussions which he had with Eden last Friday and Saturday, Grandi gained the impression that he had won Eden personally over to his old idea of leaving to the commissions the task of fixing the date for withdrawal of volunteers. Grandi told me that he was, to be sure, skeptical as to whether Eden would gain acceptance of this, his personal view, among the experts in the Foreign Office.

Lord Plymouth received the representatives of Italy, France, the Soviet Union, Portugal, and Germany yesterday and today and once more explained to them the British view on this question. In view of the conversation between Grandi and Eden, I arranged that my visit took place only after Grandi had already called on Plymouth.

Plymouth presented the matter to me essentially as he had to the Italian Ambassador and the Portuguese Chargé d'Affaires. According to his statements the British Government submits the following four proposals for consideration:

1) The Italian-German proposal for leaving the dates to the decision of the commissions. Plymouth told me that he considered it almost hopeless to obtain unanimous acceptance of this proposal. Nor did he consider it expedient. But he was submitting it for discussion nevertheless.

2) Variants of proposal 1 to the effect that commissions are to be sent to Spain to verify the number of volunteers there, and perhaps also to get in touch with the parties concerning the date of withdrawal; then they are to come to London and here submit to the committee a joint proposal for the withdrawal. Plymouth does not hold out much hope that this proposal will pass, either. In his opinion this proposal had the advantage, over against proposal 1, that the decision would be rendered by the appropriate and responsible agency, namely, the Non-Intervention Committee. In reality, however, the proposal merely meant postponing the decision to a later date, when expenses would have been incurred and it might be more difficult politically to arrive at an agreement than it would be today.

3) The idea of a proportionate withdrawal is replaced by the introduction of the time factor. It is assumed that 50 days are required for sending the volunteers on their way from the moment they are withdrawn from the camps. Belligerent rights are to be accorded on a specified day, perhaps the fifteenth, the twentieth, or the twenty-fifth day, with the understanding that the granting of the rights will be postponed if the withdrawal has not proceeded according to plan up to that date. I told Plymouth that this seemed to me merely another way of expressing proportionate withdrawal, and he agreed with me.

4) Not a definite proposal but merely a suggestion: The committee is to fix in advance a definite number, for instance 20,000 men, as a standard for "substantial progress." [1] This number is to represent the number of volunteers to be withdrawn from the side having

---

[1] This phase is in English in the original.

the smaller number according to the findings of the commissions. The other side is to withdraw a proportionately larger number, using as a criterion the figures established by the commissions. The following is an example: If the commissions find that there are 60,000 volunteers on the White side and 40,000 on the Red side, then, for instance, 20,000 volunteers are to be withdrawn from the Red side and 30,000 from the White side before belligerent rights are granted. Plymouth offered to have this proposal first submitted unofficially through the British Government to the two Spanish parties, while at the same time the proposal should be supported in Salamanca and Barcelona by friendly powers.

I told Plymouth that I continued to be in favor of proposal 1 but perhaps considered proposal 2 even better. The German Government, like the Italian, considered it inadvisable to submit to Franco proposals which, one could assume from the beginning, he must reject. But I was ready to submit the four proposals to my Government for a decision. In this connection I assumed, of course, that, simultaneously with the acceptance of any such proposal, Soviet Russian resistance in the control question would be abandoned and France would be ready for a sensible settlement of the question concerning the date for resuming control measures at the land borders.

Plymouth will not set the date for a new session until the matter is further advanced. He urged me to call on him again as soon as possible and to inform him of my Government's stand.

My views will be sent tomorrow after discussion with the Italian Embassy.

WOERMANN

No. 524

309/189188–89

The Chargé d'Affaires in Great Britain to the Foreign Ministry

Telegram

No. 72 of February 10   LONDON, February 10, 1938—11:31 p.m.
                                          Received February 11—3:15 a.m.

With reference to my airgram No. 69 of February 9.

I have discussed with the Italian Embassy the four proposals submitted by Plymouth, with the following result:

Proposal 1:

The Italians continue to cling to proposal 1 but realize that it can hardly be carried out. For tactical reasons they intend to bring it up once more, and I promised my support.

Proposal 2:

I consider proposal 2 particularly favorable because it makes it possible to gain the most time. The Italians incline—not too willingly—toward this view but consider it necessary that a guaranty be inserted to the effect that the proposal to be submitted to the committee by the commissions should not from the outset be regarded as binding.

I agreed with this view.

Proposal 3:

We are agreed that proposal 3 is essentially another version of the old British proposal to choose a proportional basis.

But this proposal has the disadvantage that by insertion of the time factor Franco would be put under pressure to expedite the withdrawal as much as possible. Nevertheless, proposal 3 does not fall outside the scope of our previous instructions, provided the fifteenth or twentieth day could be agreed upon.

Proposal 4:

We were agreed that this was an interesting proposal which was worth studying and that it probably had the greatest chance of being generally accepted. However, it operates in Franco's favor only if it is established that the number of volunteers on both sides is approximately equal or that Franco has fewer volunteers. This is shown by the following example: Assuming that Maisky was right in his assertion that there were only 15,000 volunteers on the Red side and 60,000 on the White side, then, if 10,000 were accepted as the basic number, belligerent rights would be granted if 10,000 men were withdrawn from the Red side and 40,000 from Franco's side. Since the Russians have insisted with great stubbornness vis-à-vis Plymouth that there are only 15,000 men on the Red side, they could not accept for a basic number a figure much higher than 10,000 to 12,000. If it should subsequently transpire that there are about 30,000 men on each side, belligerent rights would have to be granted after 10,000 to 12,000 men had been withdrawn from each side.

It appears that the British are now aiming at proposal 4.

I request telegraphic instructions as soon as possible, following an understanding with Rome. I should be particularly grateful if it were possible to send the German and Italian Embassies substantially the same instructions, which might also state that we are being granted freedom of action to a certain extent.

WOERMANN

No. 525

309/189187

The Chargé d'Affaires in Great Britain to the Foreign Ministry

Telegram

No. 73 of February 10   LONDON, February 10, 1938—11:31 p.m.
                               Received February 11—3:30 a.m.

With reference to my telegram No. 72 of the 10th.

Eden asked Grandi to call on him today, mainly to discuss with him once more the situation in the Non-Intervention Committee. Grandi told me that Eden concentrated exclusively on the fourth proposal. However, he has already modified it so that the fixed number of volunteers which is to be set down as . . .[1] for a "substantial withdrawal"[2] is reduced to between 15,000 and 12,000. For instance, if there are 60,000 men on one side and 40,000 on the other, then the latter is to evacuate 15,000 (or 12,000), and the other party 22,500 (or 18,000). In the course of the conversation Grandi rejected the third proposal (insertion of the time factor) as too complicated. He is not opposed to proposal 4 in principle. He once again stated his readiness to transmit it to Rome in its new form, but in his conversation with Eden termed the new figure still too high and mentioned the figure of 9,000 in its stead, without thereby committing himself to the proposal itself.

In his report to Rome he called the new British proposal "interesting," but apparently refrained from any direct recommendation.

WOERMANN

---

[1] The word not translated is *Kriegsbereitschaft*, apparently a mistake in transmission.
[2] These words appear in English in the original.

No. 526

2946/576166–69

The Ambassador in Spain to the Foreign Ministry

No. 840   SALAMANCA, February 10, 1938.

With reference to my report No. 346 of January 20.[1]

Subject: Hisma mines.

Since the above-mentioned telegraphic report, I have let no opportunity go by without trying to push and expedite the settlement of the Montana affair through the proper Spanish authorities. Herr Bernhardt has done the same. Both he and I, after our joint talk (on January 6) with the chief of the Junta Técnica, General Jordana, again called on the General to point out to him the need for a speedy

---

[1] Not found.

conclusion of the investigation of the question required by the Spaniards. At various times I likewise discussed this matter very seriously with Chef de Cabinet Sangroniz, who thereupon—as I ascertained—again brought it to the Generalissimo's attention.

During my last visit to General Jordana, which took place before the recent formation of a government—in which the General was appointed Vice President and Foreign Minister—he could only say, in reply to my definite inquiry as to when our memorandum would be answered, that he hoped the investigation would be completed soon. With regard to this I may say that, as Hisma has also ascertained, the investigation of the Montana project is actually being carried on energetically. However, in order to impress upon the General that we could not declare ourselves in agreement with this dilatory treatment and that we would have to receive at least a provisional statement on the fundamental view of the Spanish Government in the Montana affair, I asked the General orally and—at his request and in agreement with Herr Bernhardt—in writing the next day,[2] what the attitude of the Spanish Government was on our view that any further action in the Montana affair had to be taken on the basis of the protocols of July 1937 and thus in the spirit of the German-Spanish cooperation expressed therein. In reply to this inquiry the new Foreign Minister's letter, enclosed in Spanish with a German translation,[3] has just reached me; in it he explains the delays by the administrative reorganization now taking place, promises more detailed information within a short time, and states as follows with regard to my above-mentioned question:

"I should like to state in advance, however, for the information of your Government, that Nationalist Spain is at all times endeavoring to insure friendly and close collaboration with Germany in the economic field, in accordance with the agreements concluded between the two countries in July 1937 to which you referred."

Even if this answer does not seem to say much, it will, as I had hoped, give us a point of advantage at least with respect to the difficulties created by the mine decree of October 9, for "economic collaboration in accordance with the German-Spanish agreements concluded in July 1937," to which the General now again commits himself, would not be possible if the above-mentioned decree were carried out. On the legal side of the matter, to be sure, the letter, as was to be expected, adds nothing new.

I have heard confidentially that this exchange of correspondence was taken up with the Generalissimo and that Jordana's reply received his approval.

---

[2] See document No. 510, p. 571.
[3] The English translation appearing as the enclosure has been made from the German translation in the files.

In agreement with Herr Bernhardt, I am of the opinion that it would be pointless at present, that is, during the administrative confusion caused by the formation of a government, to insist more strongly on the matter.

VON STOHRER

[Enclosure]

The Minister for Foreign Affairs of the Spanish Nationalist Government to the German Ambassador

BURGOS, February 7, 1938.
IId Year of Triumph.

MY DEAR AMBASSADOR AND FRIEND: I have the honor to acknowledge receipt of your friendly letter of January 26, in which you indicate your interest in an early reply to the memorandum which was handed to me by Herr Bernhardt in reference to the acquisition of certain mining rights.

You will not be surprised, Mr. Ambassador, that the changes involved in the administrative reorganization of Nationalist Spain attendant upon the formation of a new government delay the prosecution of all matters accordingly. I shall nevertheless continue to make an effort to have the matter in question, which is of special interest to you, settled as soon as possible.

I should like to state in advance, however, for the information of your Government, that Nationalist Spain is at all times endeavoring to insure friendly and close collaboration with Germany in the economic field, in accordance with the agreements concluded between the two countries in July 1937 to which you referred.

Hoping to be able to send you further information within the near future, I take this occasion to express to you my highest consideration.

JORDANA

No. 527

586/243057–58

Memorandum by the Director of the Political Department

BERLIN, February 11, 1938.

Referring to an earlier conversation concerning joint action in the Non-Intervention Committee, I spoke to the Italian Ambassador today about Italian policy in Spain. I told the Ambassador that we had been informed that General Berti and Italian Ambassador Viola had visited Franco to urge a more energetic conduct of the war.

But Franco, it seems, had merely paid them a few compliments without volunteering any information concerning his strategic plans.

Attolico replied that the two men had a letter from Mussolini to deliver to Franco in order to put life into Franco's decisions (actually, according to Herr von Stohrer's report,[1] this letter was not delivered to Franco).

I then told Attolico that whereas a stubborn fight was being waged in London concerning percentages of volunteers to be withdrawn, according to our information the number of Italian volunteers, which previously amounted to 50,000 or more, had already been reduced to 30,000.

In general Attolico sought to explain this reduction by natural losses and repeated the statement he had made previously, namely, that Mussolini had, to be sure, ordered a gradual reduction in the number of volunteers but had stopped it again after the defeat at Teruel.

In reply to my concrete question as to what policy Italy was now really intending to pursue in Spain in view of Franco's somewhat confused conduct of the war, nothing definite was said. Attolico merely thought that Franco would have to hasten the day of victory or other ways would have to be found for removing the Spanish problem from the field of European tension. For, in the long run, it did disturb general political affairs in Europe too much.

I suggested to Attolico that the next time he called at the Foreign Ministry he might be more explicit about the constructive ideas entertained in Rome concerning the Spanish problem.

WEIZSÄCKER

---

[1] Document No. 521, p. 581.

No. 528

1557/377806

The Ambassador in Spain to the Foreign Ministry

Telegram

SALAMANCA, February 14, 1938—time not indicated.
Received February 15—12:50 a.m.
No. 76 of February 14   Pol. I 410 g (III).

With reference to my telegram No. 44 of January 31.[1]

The Italian Ambassador informed me that Franco has now communicated in writing his rather extensive wishes with respect to more war matériel.

The Italian Ambassador still lacks instructions on the whole question of Italy's further attitude. The entire matter has thus far been handled only by the military authorities.

STOHRER

---

[1] Not printed (1557/377754).

No. 529

309/189096–113

Memorandum by the Ambassador in Spain[1]

SECRET   February 1938.

STATUS OF OUR DE FACTO AND DE JURE RELATIONS WITH
NATIONALIST SPAIN

I

The former are characterized by the support which we make available to the Spanish Nationalist movement under General Franco.

Our *de jure* relations with Nationalist Spain, on the other hand, are incorporated in a number of agreements which for the most part, however, deal with matters of principle and have brought us relatively few positive rights.   These agreements and protocols are as follows:

1. The secret protocol of March 20, 1937,[2] by which the political and economic principles for the relations between the two countries are established.

2. The so-called second supplementary agreement of July 12, 1937,[3] to the German-Spanish commercial agreement of May 7, 1926, whereby Germany is accorded unconditional and unrestricted most-favored-nation treatment with respect to customs and charges in Spain as well as in shipping matters.

3. The secret protocol (consultative agreement) of the same date,[4] whereby a comprehensive settlement of the economic relations between the two countries is deferred until later, but provision is made that Germany is not to suffer disadvantage from commercial agreements concluded earlier by Spain with third countries.

4. The secret protocol of July 15, 1937, regarding deliveries of raw materials,[5] by which both Governments state their intention to promote commerce between their countries as much as possible, to extend to each other all possible support in the exchange of those raw materials, etc., which are especially important for the other party, and to consider each other's export interests.

5. The secret protocol of July 16, 1937, on liquidation of credits and German participation in commercial enterprises in Spain,[6] whereby certain fundamental principles are established for the payment of the liabilities incurred as a result of special deliveries to Spain; it further

---

[1] This memorandum was later mentioned by Stohrer as dating from the middle of February.   The copy used here bears Weizsäcker's name in his own handwriting.   For an extended commentary on it by Schwendemann see document No. 544, p. 615.

[2] Document No. 234, p. 256.

[3] See *Reichsgesetzblatt*, 1937, vol. II, p. 521.

[4] Document No. 392, p. 413.

[5] Document No. 394, p. 417.

[6] Document No. 397, p. 421.

provides that instead of cash payments in settlement of claims originating from the special deliveries raw materials of special interest to Germany will be supplied to Germany and, further, that in settlement of these claims, amounts to be agreed upon from time to time by the two Governments can be placed at Germany's disposal for investment in Spain. Finally, it is stated in this protocol that the two countries are to help each other in increasing production, that Germany declares herself ready to cooperate in the economic reconstruction of Spain and in the development and utilization of mineral resources, etc., and that for this latter purpose the Spanish Government will facilitate as much as possible the founding of Spanish companies for the development of mineral resources, etc., with German nationals or firms participating as compatible with the general stipulations of Spanish law.

A closer inspection of the contents of these agreements or protocols shows that in a political respect, in return for our support of the Nationalist movement, we have thus far not acquired any positive compensation from Spain. Aside from the promise (protocol of March 20, 1937) that both Governments wish to consult constantly on measures to be taken against Communism and in general wish to keep each other informed on questions of international policy affecting their joint interests, nothing really tangible is to be found except for the provisions in numbers three and four of the same protocol, whereby each country promises to maintain benevolent neutrality in case of an attack on the other.

In the important question of indemnifying the German residents of Spain for losses sustained by them in the Spanish Civil War, we have likewise been able to obtain no assurances in the form of an agreement. There is on this point only an oral promise by General Franco, in which, however, nothing is said regarding the extent and the methods of indemnification (see reports No. 161 g of October 24, 1937,[7] and No. 161 g II of November 17, 1937 [8]).

Economically, on the other hand, we have acquired certain positive rights through the above-mentioned protocols. For the time being, however, there is in the protocol of March 20, 1937, only the general promise that the two countries will extend their economic relations as much as possible and cooperate economically in every respect.

The above-mentioned provisions of the supplemental agreement to the commercial treaty of July 12, 1937, merely state that in place of the general most-favored-nation treatment in respect to charges and customs as well as in shipping, Germany is now accorded unconditional and unrestricted most-favored-nation treatment in these matters.

---

[7] Not printed (47/32476–79).
[8] Not printed (47/32480).

The further protocol of July 12 gives us no guaranty, either, of actually being able to be the first country to undertake a general treaty regulation of economic relations with the Spanish Nationalist Government. Spain promises, however, that in case she intends to enter into detailed economic negotiations with a third country, she will give us a chance to conclude such an agreement first, or at least will inform us in order to make it possible for us to explain our wishes in this connection in good time. Spain reserves the right, moreover, to accord Italy the same treatment.

The protocol of July 15, like the protocol of March 20, confirms the endeavor of both countries to extend commerce between them as much as possible and to give each other support with respect to those goods which the other particularly needs.

It is only the protocol of July 16 that, quite apart from certain valuable provisions regarding the payment of the special Spanish obligations, contains positive assurances for us. These are as follows:

1. We can demand, following agreements concluded in each instance, that goods, especially raw materials, which we desire to obtain from Spain and Spanish Morocco be delivered to us and charged against the German claims in question.

2. Furthermore, following agreements concluded between the two Governments in each instance, sums which are to be used to liquidate these same Spanish debts and are charged against the German claims can be placed at the disposal of the German Government for economic purposes in Spain (investments).

3. The Spanish Nationalist Government obligates itself to facilitate as much as possible the establishment of Spanish companies for the development and economic utilization of mineral resources, etc., with German nationals or German firms participating.

(This latter promise is in return for the German Government's readiness, likewise expressed in article 3, second paragraph of said protocol, to assist in the economic reconstruction of Spain and the development of mineral resources and to make experts and technical equipment available for this purpose.)

The protocols stress time and again that the provisions contained therein are only tentative agreements. In section 6 of the protocol of March 20, 1937, it is explicitly stated that the two Governments "at the proper time will regulate their political, economic, and cultural relations in detail by special agreements in accordance with the principles laid down above." On the basis of this clause we can therefore ask the Spanish Nationalist Government at any time to enter into new negotiations for regulating our political, economic, or cultural relations.

II

If, in the light of the above, we consider from the standpoint of our German interests and their future development the actual relations existing between the German and the Spanish Governments on the one hand and the legal relations established by the agreements thus far concluded on the other, we necessarily reach the conclusion that, in return for the great sacrifices we have made for the Spanish Nationalist movement, we have thus far received only very meager equivalents and few assurances for the future.

Even if it is clear to us that our political aim not to let Spain fall into the toils of Bolshevism justifies great sacrifices, there can nevertheless be no doubt that we have sufficient reason—above all, if the war lasts a long time and German assistance continues accordingly—to demand more and to obtain guaranties for ourselves which will to a certain extent justify the sacrifices made for Spain in life and property, and the foreign-policy risk. We shall, in this connection, have to think not only of a victorious ending of the war for Franco but also of a compromise peace. Whether or not we are still in a position today to make suitable demands with some chance of success after having thus far "given without taking," is, to be sure, open to question. Nevertheless, it is worth investigating what demands we could profitably make of Spain, if the occasion arose.

As far as political aims are concerned, to begin with, we have from the very start and in repeated public statements denied having any territorial demands of any kind on Spain or her colonies. This must remain unchanged even today, especially since it would mean completely misunderstanding the Spanish mentality if we assumed that Nationalist Spain would ever be prepared to yield to any country at all even so much as a foot of national soil.

On the other hand, we might perhaps give thought to a development of the clause regarding benevolent neutrality contained in articles 3 and 4 of the protocol of March 20, 1937. This might consist in a more extensive promise on the part of Spain to prevent the transit of troops of a third power and their supply and, in case of a conflict, to provide the other country [that is, Germany] with supplies of any kind that it might need and to concede it any assistance in the utilization of harbors, airlines, etc., as laid down in an undated protocol available here, which was apparently concluded between the Italian Government and the Spanish Nationalist Government in the spring or summer of 1937. (See enclosure.[9])

We could also try to exert more influence on the later training, development, and equipment of the Spanish Army through an agreement regarding exchange of officers, the dispatching of a military mission

[9] Not printed (309/189114–16).

to Spain, etc., in order by these means to set up in the future a counter-weight to France.

Following up on number 1 of the protocol of March 20, 1937, we could try to win the Spaniards over to joining the anti-Comintern pact. To be sure, a French newspaper has asserted that Franco told a French journalist that he was not thinking of joining any "international pact." However, numerous statements allegedly made by Franco and circulated by the French and British press were denied at the time by the Nationalist Spanish Government.

We could also consider a promise by the Spaniards to support Germany's colonial demands and our interests in the Tangier Zone.

It would also be very valuable to us if we could obtain in written form the promise given thus far only orally that Spain would make restitution for the damages sustained by Germans in Spain. I believe, however, that we could at best obtain this by relaxing our demands for special deliveries.

With respect to further Spanish-German collaboration and facilitating reconstruction of the German community here, we could also demand of the Franco Government certain guaranties concerning the freedom of our countrymen in Spain to sojourn, settle, and work there.

In the economic field it might perhaps be worth while to give thought to advantages for German merchant shipping and civil aviation and to assuring our influence upon Spain's currency policy. Thought might also be given to expansion of our supply of raw materials from Spain and to a more extensive guaranty—one less hampered by restrictive clauses—of the acquisition of mining rights and other participation in Spanish enterprises.

In the cultural field, a cultural treaty, as already provided for in the protocol of March 20, 1937, which should include particularly the introduction of the German language in certain Spanish institutions of learning, would be valuable to us.

Finally, there might be mentioned the usefulness of a police agreement for which preparations could be made by the delegation of German police officials at present with the Spanish Ministry for Public Safety.

III

Now how could we hope to obtain some of the above-mentioned or other conceivable desires and demands?

Part of the above concessions of value to us we could presumably obtain by the usual method of negotiation, without it being necessary for us to make significant new commitments or to exert stronger pressure.

Presumably—soundings might be worth while—we could obtain the following demands in this manner, though not all at once:

1. Expansion of the benevolent neutrality clauses (articles 3 and 4 of the protocol of March 20, 1937).

2. Greater influence upon the training, development, etc., of the Spanish Army through an agreement regarding exchange of officers, etc.

3. Accession of Spain to the anti-Comintern pact.

4. Support by Spain of our colonial claims and interests in the Tangier Zone.

5. Guaranties of freedom of sojourn, settlement, and work of German nationals in Spain (at present negotiations are in progress concerning preferential treatment of the Reich Germans in the issuing of work permits prescribed for all foreigners active in Spain).

6. Privileges for German merchant shipping and the like.

7. Conclusion of a cultural treaty.

8. A police agreement.

Other economic demands—particularly more extensive ones which are, however, of prime importance to us—will be more difficult to obtain. Negotiations of this kind (the Montana affair) have shown that in this respect there is strong opposition to overcome, which results, first, from the anxious efforts of the Spaniards to act within the narrow limits of the agreements concluded between us and them and in accordance with general Spanish law, and then from the highly developed and strongly emphasized sense of responsibility on the part of a government which dominates only a portion of Spain, is therefore only a provisional one, and wishes to avoid alienating or encumbering Spanish "national property."

Since the well-known Montana affair is not yet settled, it cannot be stated with certainty what progress, if any, we will make with the investment policy we have adopted in Spain and the safeguarding of our raw material supply contemplated thereby.

In view of the vital significance of this question for Germany it is indeed appropriate to consider whether, if we make no headway through negotiation—which is always very difficult with Spain—we might not possibly employ other means of pressure, stemming from German military support, which is indispensable to Spain at present.

To clarify this question as well as the general question, discussed above, of bargaining with Spain for certain privileges, the present moment seems entirely opportune, since for the first time we are dealing with a regular government as a treaty partner and opposite number. Even if this government is not yet a government for the whole of Spain, it can nevertheless conclude treaties and make commitments with considerable prospect of future and lasting recognition.

I consider it entirely possible that through energetic pressure of the kind indicated—particularly at a time of military uncertainty or even crisis—we can achieve one or another of the demands which are not obtainable through negotiation.

However, leaving aside military demands, which are outside the scope of these discussions altogether and which can probably be made as the occasion arises, after careful deliberation I would urgently advise against this course.   In the first place, it is by no means certain that the result of such pressure in the nature of an ultimatum will offset the disadvantages that may be expected with certainty with regard to the political atmosphere.   Thus a success might be only a momentary success; Spain—once she no longer needed our help— would know how to shake off the obligations she assumed, indeed, beyond this, even to make difficulties for us with respect to the promises she voluntarily made in the protocols of July 1937 and possible additional agreements.   It must also not be forgotten that war debts constitute a very uncertain factor.

Over and above this, however, there is another argument against taking a course other than that of amicable negotiations, namely, the possibility of a negotiated peace, which is not to be lightly dismissed just now in view of the present development of the Spanish problem as a whole.   In that case, Franco, on whom we have "put our money" for lack of other possibilities, would hardly remain at the head of the government of all Spain and that government would certainly annul all concessions made by methods which were not absolutely legal.   For this reason we shall have to be very cautious in general.

IV

The view taken above follows, moreover, from the instructions issued by the highest quarters to avoid any interference in the internal affairs of Spain.   In view of the above-mentioned balance between our assistance to Spain and the advantages that we have received in return, which clearly is unfavorable to us and in which we shall not easily make a decided improvement if we stick to negotiations, it may be justified to question whether or not we should revise this attitude of ours toward Spain.

If we reject pressure in the nature of an ultimatum for the reasons stated above, we could, on the other hand, give thought to creating conditions that could bring us equivalents on a larger scale for the sacrifices we have made for Spain—by exerting influence upon the development of Spanish internal politics.

We have thus far confined ourselves to indicating our particular sympathies for that movement in the Falange which is called the "original Falange," the "revolutionary Falange," or the *Camisas viejas*," which is closest to us ideologically and whose aims, in our opinion, also offer Spain the best guaranty for the successful establishment of a new and strong national state which could be useful to us. We have, therefore, readily placed our experience at the disposal of the Falange, have shown our Party organizations, social institutions, etc., in Germany to picked representatives of the Falange, and have advised them upon request. We have thereby considerably lightened their task here, but we have naturally not been able to strengthen them to the extent that the victory of this element is assured.

As such it would be entirely possible to increase our support of the original Falange in the sense of fighting the reactionary forces. The Spanish mentality—one must always bear in mind that there is hardly a people in the world so difficult to handle as the Spanish—would impose very narrow limits on the scope of this influence, and if we disregarded these we would only achieve the opposite.

Quite apart from this consideration, however, it is very questionable whether we would succeed with our efforts and bring victory to the original Falange. It is, indeed, to be expected that the young people now at the front tend largely to be followers of the original Falange and will have an important voice in affairs after the war. The differences within the Falange, as a whole, are very great nevertheless. The Rightist (reactionary, Carlist, monarchistic) Requetés have many supporters; in some parts of the country, as in northern Spain, they possess not only influence but dominance. Their numbers are even increasing in some places in view of the growing influence of the Catholic Church. Nor is the original Falange completely antimonarchist, and the question of restoration (after a victorious ending of the war) will depend primarily on the attitude of Franco, who has not committed himself on this question.

Since it is evidently at present in Franco's interest and is his aim not to let any portion of the Falange become too strong—a game that the "Falangist" Serrano Suñer (Minister of the Interior, press chief, and brother-in-law of Franco) has thus far played superbly—we should soon find ourselves confronted with the official opposition of the Spanish Government, which would reject any "interference in Spanish domestic affairs."

Even if we ought not to be too fearful in this matter of "interference in the internal affairs of a country" if interference is profitable, it is nevertheless better to dispense with it if one is not absolutely sure of success. And in this case success is even quite improbable.

If, therefore, in view of the political situation and the mentality of the Spaniards, I expressed myself above as opposed to action amounting to an ultimatum for obtaining economic privileges or concessions, for the same reasons I must advise against a change in the policy of non-intervention in Spanish internal affairs, which has been pursued thus far in accordance with instructions. In fact, in view of the consolidation of Spanish affairs which has now resulted from the formation of a government, I should like to advise exercising the greatest caution, especially with respect to our relations with the individual parties, avoiding any official favoritism being shown one or the other group, and not coming into conflict with the Franco Government's aim regarding domestic policy just mentioned. Otherwise it is to be feared that our propaganda work in the press, which has thus far been successful, will be made more difficult by the governmental and Party press control, now united in one hand, that of Minister of Interior Suñer, and that the atmosphere which has thus far been favorable will change for the worse.

V

Since we have from the beginning of the Spanish Civil War quite deliberately refrained from making counterdemands for our services on a *quid pro quo* basis, the moment no longer seems opportune for replacing this policy by an ultimatum-like procedure (here, too, I stress the fact that I have omitted military questions from this whole discussion). We shall therefore have to try, through negotiation, to give more substance to our relations with Spain, constantly stressing that we are only concerned with friendly collaboration.

For this purpose I propose that we make up our minds which of the eight questions mentioned above (page 10)[10] seem most important to us and should be settled soon by treaty and that we then sound out the Spaniards to ascertain what extent they seem inclined to negotiate these matters. As soon as we know what position the Spanish Government is taking in the Montana affair, we can also include in these deliberations the question of guaranteeing for the future our supply of raw materials. For the rest, the above-mentioned eight subjects are probably not the only ones with respect to which an improvement and fixing by treaty may seem desirable for us. This is the proper moment for approaching the Spaniards with requests for negotiation, in view of the recent formation of a regular government.

Thus, although I believe that by continuing our previous policy of bringing friendly influence to bear and of non-intervention in Spanish internal affairs we can nevertheless achieve an improvement in

---

[10] See p. 595.

our legal situation with regard to Spain and thus at least obtain some equivalents for all the sacrifices we have made her, I nevertheless warn against too great optimism, as I did even before assuming my post at Salamanca.

One must not count on political gratitude; coercive measures will prove only momentarily successful with the Spaniards, and after the war the country's situation even at best will not be such that there is much left for its allies.

STOHRER

No. 530

586/243064

The Chargé d'Affaires in Italy to the Foreign Ministry

Telegram

No. 34 of February 17   ROME, February 17, 1938—1 : 25 p.m.
                              Received February 17—3 : 45 p.m.
                              zu Pol. III 462.

Also for the Supreme Command of the Navy.

Last night, in accordance with instructions, the Naval Attaché delivered the letter containing the notification of legal reservations concerning the combating of submarines in the Mediterranean. The Chief of Staff took cognizance thereof and expressed his appreciation of the step. At the same time he stated :

1. Italy had to go along in order not to come under suspicion.

2. He thought he could state confidentially that no damage would be done in the Italian zone as the matter was very delicate.

3. Compared with the British and French submarine-attack zones, the Italian zone was particularly small; it did not touch any territorial waters [1] and, furthermore, was probably seldom entered by submarines.

4. There was no danger for German submarines in the Italian zone because their locations were known to the Italians, but, if German submarines touched the Italian zone, instructions would naturally be issued not to take any action against them.

LANGE [2]
PLESSEN

---

[1] A marginal note in Mackensen's handwriting queries this clause as follows : "Is that of any significance? It is precisely a question of the open sea !"
A handwritten reply reads : "Yes. The Italian reply is not very intelligent. W[eizsäcker] /19."

[2] Captain Lange, Naval Attaché of the German Embassy in Italy.

No. 531

4446/E086628–30

The Ambassador in Spain to the Foreign Ministry

STRICTLY CONFIDENTIAL   SALAMANCA, February 17, 1938.
No. 256 g   Pol. III 572.

With reference to my reports No. SS 8 of December 3, 1937, No. SS 44 of December 10, 1937, and No. 242 g of January 31, 1938.[1]

Subject: Efforts to end the Spanish Civil War by negotiation.

With reference to the attempts last November, which I reported, to effect a settlement of the Spanish Civil War through negotiation, I have received supplementary reports from a reliable source from which it appears that England was already then seriously concerned with the question of a negotiated peace.   The Red Spanish Government, that is, Companys and Prieto, stated at the time in reply to a feeler put forward by England that a military victory was unlikely for either party and that one must therefore avoid further sacrifices and try to achieve a negotiated peace.   Since no cooperation of any kind was to be expected from Franco then, however, in view of his favorable military situation, the idea of intervention by England was again postponed in December.   The Red Spanish side, nevertheless, is said to be occupied more and more with the thought of effecting a negotiated peace.   Thus in the ensuing period, also, the rulers on the Red side did not entirely abandon the idea of a Spanish *federación*, while on the other side the plan for the establishment of a constitutional monarchy under the Crown Prince Don Juan was also discussed.   The British, in view of the difficulties of making a federation palatable to Nationalist Spain and a monarchy to Red Spain, are said to have proposed the idea of effecting an interim solution under a group of politicians who were committed neither to the Whites nor to the Reds, and who would be given the protection of the Army, after which a plebiscite could decide on the future regime.   The Spanish politicians living in France (mentioned in my report No. 242 g of January 31, 1938) got in touch with British officials in this sense; the former Spanish Ambassador to Washington and Paris, Salvador de Madariaga, who has become known particularly as Spain's delegate to the League of Nations, played an especially prominent part.   He is considered a politician of moderate tendencies and a decided foe of the Communists.

The initial successes of the reorganized Red Army at Teruel revived the hope in Red Spanish circles, as well as in circles of the above-mentioned Spanish émigrés and in London, that mediation held promise

---

[1] Not printed (1557/377775–80).

of success. This hope was destroyed once more by Franco's successes at the end of last year and the beginning of this month, since it is assumed—and rightly—that Franco today is still not thinking of negotiating. But none of the interested parties mentioned seems to have given up these attempts. The Reds hope to break down Nationalist Spain from within by means of the extremely strong propaganda behind the Nationalist front and abroad, which I have reported at various times, and thus to make it more amenable to the idea of a compromise peace.

Without being able to vouch for the correctness of the information, which reached me from a reliable source, I should like to mention another statement emanating from the intimate circle of acquaintances of the Red Ambassadors at Paris and London, Osorio Gallardo and Azcarate, according to which new hopes of ending the Spanish Civil War are being created by the *rapprochement* now taking place between England on the one hand and Germany and Italy on the other. England—it is said—would try to make clear to Franco's two allies that their diplomatic goal had been attained, since the end of the war would by no means result in a victory of Communism. Through these negotiations it would perhaps be possible to obtain political advantages for Germany and Italy that might cause both powers to lose interest in the Spanish affair and thus provide the opportunity for a negotiated peace.

STOHRER

No. 532

2946/576182–83

The Ambassador in Spain to the Foreign Ministry

No. 1159   SALAMANCA, February 17, 1938.
Subject: Hisma mines (Montana).

With reference to my report No. 840 of February 10.

During my first call on the new Minister for Commerce and Industry I spoke primarily about the Montana affair. Señor Suances, who had just taken over his Ministry and was still moving into the new office building at Burgos, told me that as yet he had not been able to look into the documents in the matter; on the other hand, General Jordana, the former director of the Junta Técnica and present Minister for Foreign Affairs, had informed him in detail concerning the question and our interest in it.

After I had once more described to the Minister in full detail the great importance of this matter for Germany and asked him to speed the settlement as much as possible, the Minister stated approximately the following, stressing that these were, of course, merely his own tentative impressions and that a definitive stand could only be taken jointly with General Jordana, who was responsible for foreign affairs:

"I am of the opinion that we must proceed with utmost caution in this matter in the interest both of Spain and of Germany. Everything possible must be done to prevent the occurrence of circumstances similar to those in the case of the Rio Tinto Company. In a combination of circumstances favorable to her, England took these mines from us at the time. Even now this incident has not been forgotten by the Spanish people. The Rio Tinto is still 'a thorn in Spain's side.' Concerning the Montana project and the cooperation between our two countries in the mining field generally, as laid down by the protocols of July of last year, care must be exercised lest Spain—and I mean also all of Spain later—and the outside world become alarmed. The *colaboración* provided for in the protocols must therefore be so formulated that certain percentages of the individual mines belong to Spain or Germany. Since we are familiar with your great interest in the delivery of minerals from Spain, I consider it altogether possible to secure for Germany by contract a larger percentage as regards the division of the yield, regardless of the percentage of Germany's share in ownership."

Since in these statements the Minister based everything on the example of "approximately 60 percent Spanish-owned and 40 percent German-owned," I interjected that, after all, this ratio should also be reversed now and then and one mine or another even belong to us entirely, whereupon the Minister replied:

"In my opinion a reversed ratio in regard to share in ownership can be considered. But, at any rate, it must always be a matter of *colaboración*. As far as organization of the German-Spanish company is concerned, I am at the present time against combining in one company as many mining rights as apparently have already been acquired by you. Precisely for the reasons given, I consider it more expedient to set up a number of small companies, perhaps of a local character, with these rights. The whole matter has already attracted a certain amount of attention because of the extensive mine purchases—something that must be avoided in the future."

My general impression from the conversation, which—as the Minister also mentioned expressly—represented nothing but a tentative expression of opinion on his part, is that Señor Suances will with utmost readiness agree to our efforts at participation in the exploitation of Spanish mineral resources but that he will at the same time insist on the idea of *colaboración*, that is, on Spain's participating in the companies—probably to a considerable extent—in accordance with the July protocols and in the sense of the written communication which I recently received from General Jordana (see the report referred to above).

v. Stohrer

No. 533

586/243068

The Chargé d'Affaires in Great Britain to the Foreign Ministry

Telegram

URGENT LONDON, February 21, 1938—11:40 a.m.
No. 104 of February 21 Received February 21—2:30 p.m.

Grandi intends to take immediate advantage of the situation created by Eden's resignation,[1] and to that end, as he just informed me, he made an appointment with Chamberlain even before today's session of Parliament. For this purpose he obtained authorization from Ciano by telephone to accept proposal 4 in the question of the Spanish volunteers.

WOERMANN

---

[1] Eden resigned as Foreign Secretary on Feb. 20, 1938, as a result of disagreement with the Prime Minister over the handling of relations with Italy.

No. 534

309/189166–68

Memorandum by the Foreign Minister

RM 110 BERLIN, February 21, 1938.

The Spanish Ambassador called on me at noon today and handed me the enclosed *aide-mémoire* in the Spanish language.

He expressed the hope that Germany would continue her policy of giving support to the Nationalist Spanish Government as heretofore.

Referring to yesterday's speech by the Führer,[1] I assured him that there had been no change in our policy and that we continued to hope for a victory of the Nationalist Government and expulsion of the Bolshevist Government.

v. RIBBENTROP

[Enclosure] [2]

BERLIN, February 21, 1938/II.

The Spanish Nationalist Government is interested in pointing out the maneuver on the part of certain powers, consisting in an attempt to represent the Spanish and Italian standpoints on the recognition

---

[1] In Hitler's speech before the Reichstag on Feb. 20 he had referred to German policy toward Spain. He had stated that Germany had no territorial interests connected with the Civil War. He said that "the German Government would see in the bolshevizing of Spain not only an element detrimental to the peace of Europe but also one disturbing to the balance of power on the Continent."
[2] The copy in the files is a translation into German from the Spanish original.

of belligerent rights and the withdrawal of volunteers as being out of harmony with one another. This recognition, in the opinion of the Nationalist Government, must not depend on the withdrawal of foreign volunteers. This viewpoint is the same as that held by the Italian Government.

The Nationalist Government, in agreement with the directives that the Imperial and Royal Government of Italy has given its representative on the Non-Intervention Committee, has again expressed its opinion that a full guaranty was necessary against the return to the Red Army, such as is happening at present despite the guaranties given, of volunteers coming from the Red zone and withdrawn through the Non-Intervention Committee. The Spanish Nationalist Government also believes that in the event of a withdrawal of the volunteers it would be desirable that this be done in equal numbers for each of the two parties, since proportionate withdrawal is impossible and would entail serious disadvantages to Nationalist Spain. This is true if only because the form of organization of the international Red brigades and their command authority make it very easy to conceal volunteers, while the case would be entirely different for Nationalist Spain, where it would be impossible to conceal such elements. The three systems proposed by the Non-Intervention Committee do not permit exact definition of the obligations assumed. The Nationalist Government therefore believes that, in case the number of volunteers to be withdrawn should be fixed, it would be preferable to have this figure set directly by the Non-Intervention Committee and to have the agreement arrived at there submitted to the Nationalist Government for approval before putting it into effect.

In all the points mentioned above, the opinion of the Nationalist Government coincides fully with the directives of the Italian Government.

No. 535

309/189160–62

The Chargé d'Affaires in Great Britain to the Foreign Ministry

Telegram

No. 112 of February 24   LONDON, February 24, 1938—8 : 28 p.m.
                            Received February 25—12 : 45 p.m.

With reference to your telegram 44.[1]

In his conversation with Chamberlain on Monday Grandi had, as reported, accepted in summary form the British proposal 4 in the question of the withdrawal of volunteers and of belligerent rights (cf. telegraphic report 104 of February 21). Grandi then had a discussion with Plymouth yesterday. Plymouth asked Grandi, among other

---

[1] Of Feb. 19; not printed (586/243053–54).

things, what number he considered acceptable for proposal 4. Grandi's reply, he told me, was that he had at one time agreed with Eden on 10,000 men as a basic number and had submitted this figure to his Government (on the other hand, see the account of the latter conversation in telegraphic report 11 of February 10 [2]). Like the Portuguese Chargé d'Affaires, who also called on Plymouth yesterday, Grandi expressed the wish that control be reestablished on the land frontier upon the arrival of the commissions in Spain.

About his conversation with Chamberlain, Grandi told me further that Chamberlain had inquired as to the attitude of the German Government, whereupon he (Grandi) had replied that in this question as in all other corresponding questions there was, of course, agreement between Berlin and Rome.

Today I had a talk with Plymouth, who, among other things, told me of the conversation with Grandi but added that he was not clear about the question of the basic number. He did not have the impression that any previous agreement had been reached on a definite number. Here, then, was a certain difficulty, but he did not regard it as very considerable.

Under the given circumstances I told Plymouth that I wished to speak quite frankly with him. My instructions,[3] which had been drawn up before the conversation between Grandi and Chamberlain, had been to make another attempt first with proposals 1 and 2. From his account I saw that any long discussion of proposals 1 and 2 was now out of the question. I could therefore inform him of my Government's acceptance of proposal 4. I likewise assumed that control on the land frontier would go into effect again simultaneously with the arrival of the commissions and that, in general, agreement would be reached on the other questions that were pending. Plymouth concurred in the view that any agreement on an individual point depended on agreement with regard to the total plan and then asked me about the basic figure. I told him that I wished to reply "undiplomatically" and confidentially. I had not been given any fixed basic number by my Government but was to arrive at one by negotiation. However, I was not authorized to accept any figure definitively but first had to report. Hence there was no purpose in discussing any higher figure, since that would then not be accepted anyway; I likewise regarded the figure of 10,000 as a suitable basis.

Plymouth then expressed the hope that no difficulties would arise in the question of financial contributions. I replied that my Government was prepared to continue paying the current contributions

---

[2] The telegram number appears to be in error; presumably the reference is to No. 73 of Feb. 10, document No. 525, p. 586.

[3] Contained in telegram 44, which was sent on Feb. 19 before Eden resigned. Meantime, Grandi had been authorized to accept British proposal 4.

for the old system of supervision, but that I had not yet received any instructions in regard to the new payments for the withdrawal of volunteers. I should appreciate instruction in this matter.

From his conversation yesterday with the French Ambassador, Plymouth had the impression that France would likewise accept proposal 4; but he was doubtful about the attitude that the French would take on the question of the reestablishment of land control. In this question the resolution of November 4 was counter to our demand. In France, moreover, the question was strongly overlaid with internal politics.

Plymouth will speak with the Soviet Ambassador today or tomorrow.

The next meeting of the main subcommittee will not be called until the discussions have made further progress—the middle of next week at the earliest.

WOERMANN

No. 536

309/189147-48

Minute by the Director of the Political Department

BERLIN, February 26, 1938.

The Spanish Ambassador wished to see me urgently today to obtain a clear picture of the proceedings in the London Non-Intervention Committee. I first explained to the Ambassador the various proposals concerning the withdrawal of volunteers which had been under discussion in London up to the beginning of this week. I then told him that we, together with the Italians, had insisted on either proposal 1 or proposal 2. In the course of the Anglo-Italian discussions of a general political nature, the Italian Government had then approved proposal No. 4, with the result that we too had to support this proposal. As a result of these events two viewpoints expressed in the *aide-mémoire* which the Ambassador had handed to the Foreign Minister on the 21st were superseded. In this *aide-mémoire* Spain had assumed that the Italian Government would not agree to the proportionate withdrawal of volunteers but would insist instead on the withdrawal of an equal number of volunteers from both parties. Likewise, proposal 4, in contrast with the Spanish *aide-mémoire*, makes the withdrawal of a certain number of volunteers a condition for the granting of belligerent rights to the combatants.

The Ambassador understood the circumstances which had led to the new Italian stand and then the new German stand in the Non-Intervention Committee. But he did not conceal a certain uneasiness concerning the possibility that the problem of withdrawing the volunteers might now enter a new and perhaps more accelerated phase. He intimated that Spain would without regret permit a considerable number of Italian infantrymen to go home but expressed the hope that the Condor Legion and the Italian specialists could be retained to the end of the war.

I reminded the Ambassador that the Foreign Minister had recently assured him of our full sympathy and good intentions for further diplomatic and material assistance within our ability. I further told him that even now a number of differences would have to be removed before achieving complete unanimity in the Non-Intervention Committee (the closing of the French border, Russia's consent to the granting of belligerent rights, and the like) and that finally the combatants themselves would of course have to be heard before international commissions of inquiry were sent to their country. Therefore one might well assume that these commissions would not arrive before the spring flowers. Nevertheless, embarrassing situations would arise for the foreign volunteers once the commissions arrived on the spot, and I did not at the moment see any real way out. One must therefore face the possible development indicated here with greater seriousness than had been necessary in the course of the last 12 months' empty bickering in London.

I carried the conversation this far in order to prepare the ground somewhat for Herr Stohrer's next conversation with Franco (cf. telegraphic instruction No. 59 [1]). It will be necessary to follow up this telegraphic instruction to Salamanca with a short information telegram concerning the preceding conversation and also to inform London and Rome accordingly.

WEIZSÄCKER

[1] Document No. 539, p. 610.

No. 537

309/189155–56

Memorandum by the Director of the Political Department

BERLIN, February 28, 1938.

During his visit today the Counselor of the Italian Embassy also touched on the subject of Spain. He referred to his (or Attolico's) earlier communication [1] to the effect that General Berti had a letter to deliver to Generalissimo Franco in which Franco is urged to decide on and communicate his strategic intentions. Count Magistrati read me the letter, which informs Franco in a friendly but rather pointed way that he could keep the Italian legionnaires if he would gird himself for a great military blow. Should Franco

[1] See document No. 527, p. 588.

desire to make an end by other means than military blows, however, then it was useless to keep the Italian legionnaires in Spain any longer.

Magistrati continued that he did not know whether this letter had been answered. It appeared to him, however, as if Franco had not expressed himself. For several days, consequently, the Italian legionnaires had been ordered to stand inactive until Franco had made a decision. The Italian air forces on the Balearic Islands had been ordered to exercise the same restraint.

I took the occasion to inform the Counselor of the Italian Embassy of the conversation that I had last Saturday with the Spanish Ambassador (cf. minute of February 26). I added that Herr von Stohrer would probably receive an instruction in the next few days which would likewise be to the effect that he induce the Generalissimo to make a decision regarding his future conduct of the war.

Magistrati and I found that our attempts to influence Franco were thus running quite parallel.

In conclusion I reminded Count Magistrati that I had already suggested to Ambassador Attolico some time ago that he inform us of the constructive ideas of his Government with respect to Spanish policy.

WEISZSÄCKER

No. 538

3363/E010074–77

Memorandum by the Head of Political Division IIIa

BERLIN, February 28, 1938.
Pol. III 613.

Since we and the Italians have agreed with the British to accept the fourth of the four proposals on the removal of volunteers, this matter has again made a little progress. This gives rise to the following considerations:

1. The situation on the Red and White sides with regard to the volunteers is quite different. On the White side, aside from complete German and Italian units, there are no appreciable numbers of volunteers. On the Red side, aside from the fliers, other officers, and specialists sent by Russia and other governments, there are many thousands from all countries, who mainly make up the international brigades. These people are not under any foreign command but only under the Red Spanish military authorities. Most of them probably have Red Spanish passports and are thus formally not foreigners. The fact that the Russian Ambassador in London has committed himself to a figure of 15,000 volunteers on the Red side while the actual number must be considerably greater permits the conclusion that the

Reds already realize which men, and how many, they can give up if necessary, without jeopardizing their own fighting strength. Locating the others would probably be very difficult, in view of the unlimited possibilities for concealing them and since they hold Red Spanish passports.

A combing-out of the volunteers according to the methods contemplated by the London committee would therefore work out one-sidedly to the disadvantage of the Whites.

2. Naturally it is out of the question either for the Italians or for us to permit the volunteers on the White side to be combed out by the methods of the Non-Intervention Committee. These methods provide for disarmament, delivery into a camp, and shipment home, at all times under strict supervision.

The withdrawal of the volunteers on the White side would therefore have to take place without any collaboration on the part of agencies of the Non-Intervention Committee. That would make the control and verification of the withdrawal by the committee and its recognition of the withdrawal illusory and thus throw open the door for reproaches by the other side that we had not adhered to the procedure for withdrawal which we ourselves had accepted in the Non-Intervention Committee.

3. In one of the last telegrams from London—Pol. III 613 [1]—an instruction is requested with regard to our financial contribution for the withdrawal of the volunteers. It follows from the above that the withdrawal of the German and Italian volunteers can take place only outside of the collaboration of the London committee and its agencies, and naturally at our expense or that of Italy.

The costs of withdrawal are estimated by the London committee as one and a half million pounds, of which one-fifth, or 300,000 pounds, would be our share. Herr Sabath has been sent in order to determine to what degree our contribution can be covered by deliveries in kind. This can, of course, be done only to a partial extent.

Consideration of the further development of the question of the cost of withdrawing the volunteers leads to difficulties. It follows from the foregoing that the erection of camps for volunteers in White Spain who are to be withdrawn, as well as any sort of large expenses for the withdrawal on the White side, will not materialize for the London committee. The committee in London, however, in its zeal for carrying out its utopian tasks, will want to make practical preparation for the installation of camps on both the Red *and* the White sides. It will therefore approach us with regard to making the deliveries in kind and paying advances on the sum of 300,000 pounds which theoretically falls to us.

[1] Document No. 535, p. 604.

Thus we would practically be paying twice, once for the withdrawal of our people by ourselves and then for the withdrawal of the volunteers from Red Spain.

4. If it came to an agreement for actual withdrawal of volunteers, we would have to show our colors eventually by stating to the committee that the German volunteers had already been withdrawn or would be withdrawn by a certain time, which would amount to an admission that they were contingents sent by the Government, that is, a proof of our intervention. Such a statement could not be made, however, before the withdrawal of the volunteers on the Red side was certain. But this is supposed to be done by the very procedure worked out by the Non-Intervention Committee (dispatching of a control commission). According to the above, however, this procedure is applicable only to the Red side. The condition for an actual withdrawal of volunteers on the White side is therefore only to be created if the method of combing out, which can by no means be used with the Whites, is employed on the side of the Reds. It is not clear how the Reds can be persuaded to accept this.

Submitted to the Director and the Deputy Director of the Political Department.

SCHWENDEMANN

No. 539

309/189151–54

The State Secretary to the Embassy in Spain

Telegram

No. 59 BERLIN, February 28, 1938.

zu Pol. III 610.

Our future policy in Spain will possibly be strongly influenced by the course of the Anglo-Italian negotiations for a general settlement of the questions at issue between the two countries. Should an understanding be reached on a gradual withdrawal of the Italian volunteers from Spain, we would also have to adapt ourselves to this procedure.

The War Ministry is convinced that a decisive military success is impossible for Franco without German and Italian volunteers, particularly fliers, but that, on the other hand, Franco will no longer need German and Italian volunteers once he has succeeded in breaking through. Since a withdrawal of all the Italian volunteers could be expected only after several months, at the earliest, even in case of rapid progress in the Anglo-Italian negotiations, Franco can in all likelihood still count on the cooperation of German and Italian volunteers for the next few months. A longer stay, however, as already stated, is uncertain.

There are doubts here whether Franco realizes this situation and whether he is not taking too optimistic a view with regard to the duration of Italian and thus also of German armed assistance (cf. your report No. 1006 of February 19 [1]) and is not basing his decisions regarding the further conduct of the war on this view. This would entail the danger that he would not yet have forced a decision on the war by the time the Italian and German volunteers are withdrawn on the basis of political decisions which go beyond the Spanish question.

The above considerations, it is true, only define the possibilities which stand out and which can be viewed in their entirety only after better knowledge of the present aims of Italian policy with respect to England, as well as after the further progress of the Anglo-Italian negotiations. Franco, however, should take them into account even now in his conduct of the war.

Therefore please take the opportunity soon to give Franco to understand in any way you see fit that our military assistance in the form of personnel does not depend on our good will alone but also on developments in the London Non-Intervention Committee. At the same time please ascertain Franco's further military plans and impress upon him the need for a speedy, decisive military blow.

For your own information I add the following:

The Spaniards can continue to be assured of all our good will as well as our diplomatic and material aid within the limits possible, as Foreign Minister von Ribbentrop also stated to the Spanish Ambassador here on the occasion of his first official visit. But they should not entertain too great illusions beyond the limits of this aid and should not be misled, by confidence in our continued armed assistance, into regarding the heretofore rather one-sided performance in the relations between Germany and Nationalist Spain as a permanent condition. There exists between us, to be sure, the secret agreement of March 20, 1937, which gives us certain advantages. Besides, Spain has made a modest return by deliveries of raw materials to us. However, as a result of general political developments between Berlin and Rome, on the one hand, and Paris and London, on the other, it may become necessary in the near future to draw up a political interim balance with Franco and in a frank manner discuss anew the future of German-Spanish relations. In such a conversation with Franco, which would have to extend to the economic and cultural fields as well as the political field, it would seem to us desirable to proceed from the standpoint that the agreement of March 20, 1937, still provides the proper basis for future German-Spanish relations, as in the

---

[1] Not printed (3363/E010060–64).

past. We could have Franco confirm this to us and could introduce any desirable additions or elucidations.

Please give me your own reaction to this first, however; I should like to make use of it during the contemplated clarification with the Italian Government of our joint Spanish policy.[2]

MACKENSEN

[2] Unsigned marginal notes: "The Italian Ambassador was last asked on February 11 to express himself more clearly on the constructive ideas held in Rome with respect to the Spanish question. This subject should probably be discussed once more very plainly with the Italian Ambassador." "Refer back to the [Spanish] desk for transmission of this telegram to Rome and London, as well as to the War Ministry."

No. 540

F3/0223–25

Memorandum by the Head of the Political Division IIIa

TOP SECRET

BERLIN, March 2, 1938.
zu Pol. I 139 g Rs.

After Germany had supported the Spanish Nationalist Government since August 1936, given it recognition on November 17, 1936, and entered into official diplomatic relations with it, it was logical to formulate in an agreement the particular political relation between Germany and Nationalist Spain which had resulted from this development. The final impulse to do so was provided by the fact that Mussolini concluded a very extensive secret agreement with Franco which only came to our attention later.

On March 20, 1937, a secret protocol was concluded with Nationalist Spain, providing in point 1 for continuous consultation to keep Communism in check, in point 2 for continual contact with regard to joint interests in questions of international policy, in point 3 for non-participation in agreements with third powers directed against one of the two countries, in point 4 for exclusion of all support of a third state in case of an attack, in point 5 for promoting of economic relations, and in point 6 for the conclusion of treaties in the future with regard to the political, economic, and cultural relations between the two countries.

The purpose expressed in point 6 has already been partly realized with respect to economic relations (point 5 of the protocol) by the July agreements of 1937. In July 1937 the following agreements were entered into:

1. The second supplementary agreement to the German-Spanish trade agreement of May 7, 1926, providing for an absolute and unrestricted most-favored-nation position for German exports to Spain which is also extended to shipping.

2. The secret protocol of July 12, in which the Spanish Nationalist Government states its readiness to conclude with Germany its first general economic treaty.

3. The secret protocol of July 15, establishing the principle of promoting commerce between the two countries as much as possible and stating the readiness of both Governments to support one another to the greatest possible extent in the deliveries of those raw materials, foods, and half-finished and finished goods which are of particular interest to the purchaser country.

4. The secret protocol of July 16 regarding the settlement of debts that originated from German deliveries of arms to the Spanish Nationalist Government.

The July agreements are similar in nature to the protocol of March 20, 1937, insofar as they establish, particularly in the three secret protocols, principles and guide lines which are subsequently to be given concrete form by further agreements.

The main object of our future Spanish policy will have to be to give increasingly concrete form to the principles and aims expressed in past agreements between Germany and Nationalist Spain.

The past agreements with Nationalist Spain were concluded on the assumption of a victorious end of the Civil War in favor of Franco. The same prerequisite holds good for future agreements made in the spirit of the present ones.

The texts of the protocol of March 20, 1937, and of the July agreements are enclosed.

Submitted to the Foreign Minister through the Director and the Deputy Director of the Political Department and the State Secretary.[1]

SCHWENDEMANN

[1] Marginal notation in Weizsäcker's handwriting: "The Italians are acquainted with the contents of the agreement of March 20, 1937."

No. 541

309/189131–32

The Ambassador in Spain to the Foreign Ministry

Telegram

No. 110 of March 4   SALAMANCA, March 4, 1938—9 : 30 p.m.
                                           Received March 5—12 : 35 a.m.

With reference to your telegram No. 59 of February 28, and No. 61 [1] and No. 63 [2] of March 1.

The instruction contained in the first-named telegram has been carried out.

[1] Not printed (586/243082–83).
[2] Not printed (586/243084–85).

Franco replied by giving a detailed description of the military situation, his plans, and his objectives:

"Unfortunately the regrouping after the ending of the military campaign in the north took more time than was expected.   The sole reason was the fact, which had remained hidden from the outside world, that there continued to be guerrilla warfare, particularly in Asturias, which had not ended until just recently.   After the capture of Gijón there were still 18,000 armed men scattered throughout the country; quite recently probably the last ones—2,000 men with 18 machine guns and 1,500 rifles—were captured.   Thus the enemy was able to seize the initiative and, because of the failure of the local commander at Teruel, to obtain initial successes there which prevented execution of the December offensive against Madrid.   I also explained this a short while ago in a letter to Mussolini (cf. your telegram No. 63).   The military situation at the present time is very satisfactory once more.   The Reds have suffered very severe losses at Teruel.   Their reserves have been depleted and their morale shattered."

Franco then sketched his next military objectives, which I reported in cipher letter No. 274 g of March 3 [3] and which I am not repeating here for reasons of security.

Contrary to the concluding sentence of the cipher letter, Franco declared that he had in mind the more far-reaching objectives mentioned there, after all; he was convinced that the projected offensives, which should be carried out without any interruption, as it were, would be successful and bring the war to an end.

Franco went on to describe the economic situation in the Nationalist zone as excellent but that in the Red zone as desperate.   Particularly recently (see report 255 g of February 17 [4]) a serious deterioration had set in there again.

Whereas a few days ago Franco had expressed to the Italian Ambassador serious misgivings regarding the withdrawal of volunteers, particularly on account of the psychological effect to be expected, he did not do so to me; rather he stated with great assurance that he hoped to bring the war to an end militarily, without having the question of the withdrawal of volunteers enter an acute stage.

I have informed the Italian Ambassador of this discussion.

I have refrained from touching upon the questions mentioned in the next to the last paragraph of your telegram No. 59 in consideration of the wording of the last paragraph of said telegram.

STOHRER

---

[3] Not printed (1568/379476).   In this report Stohrer states that Italian legionnaires were being held ready for action in extensive operations which were planned south of the Ebro.   If this offensive succeeded, further operations on the north bank were envisaged.   There was no intention as yet to drive to the Mediterranean.   The Ebro offensive opened on Mar. 9.

[4] Not printed (5148/E303618–20).

No. 542

586/243099

The Ambassador in Spain to the Foreign Ministry

Telegram

No. 111 of March 4   SALAMANCA, March 4, 1938—9 : 30 p.m.
Received March 5—12 : 35 a.m.

With reference to my telegram No. 100 of March 1.[1]

The Generalissimo told me that, since the end of December, 14,500 prisoners have been taken at Teruel but there were only a very few foreigners among them; he asked that this latter fact be treated as strictly confidential.

STOHRER

---

[1] Not printed (4446/E086637).

No. 543

1547/376099

The Ambassador in Spain to the Foreign Ministry

No. 119 of March 9   SALAMANCA, March 9, 1938.
Pol. III 753.

With reference to my telegram No. 110 of March 4.

The Italian Ambassador told me that Mussolini replied in a very amiable manner to the very detailed letter of Franco, with which you are familiar, regarding the war situation and expressed the hope that the Italian volunteers would still render useful service to Franco before their final withdrawal, which was after all absolutely necessary.

Yesterday the Italian Ambassador gave the reply to the Generalissimo, who is said to have been very well satisfied with Mussolini's letter.

STOHRER

No. 544

309/189122–28

Memorandum by the Head of Political Division IIIa

BERLIN, March 10, 1938.
zu Pol. I g 649 g III.

With regard to Ambassador von Stohrer's memorandum[1] on the status of our actual and legal relations with Nationalist Spain the following is noted:

---

[1] Document No. 529, p. 590.

A. General

1. The statements made regarding the disparity between our services to Nationalist Spain and the advantages which we have been assured by treaty are correct.

2. The same is true with regard to the statement that there is no prospect of improving this situation in the long run by means of pressure in the nature of an ultimatum or by interference in the internal politics of Nationalist Spain.

3. It is no less true that we must strive for an improvement in our position and that the proper time for this is after the formation of a regular government, in view of the fact that Franco still needs us.

4. The possibility of a compromise peace between the Reds and the Whites, described as quite probable, with the resultant loss by Franco of his present dominant position, appears very doubtful. In spite of the undeniable efforts in the Red and the White camps and by the émigrés toward a compromise—efforts which are encouraged by England, in particular—it seems to me that no compromise is possible. There is complete incompatibility between the authoritarian pattern of the state in Nationalist Spain, which is now essentially complete, and the form of the Red Spanish Republic, of which the façade at least is parliamentary and democratic. It therefore appears proper for us to base considerations of our future policy in Spain fundamentally on the assumption that Spain will be an authoritarian state with a strongly developed social policy. This state, both on account of the regime and because of the fact that such a strong Spain is in the interest neither of England nor of France, will be forced to incline toward the Rome-Berlin Axis.

5. The result of this is, on the one hand, our interest in the military victory of Franco and, on the other, the necessity of formulating the treaties guaranteeing our future interests in Spain in such a way that they will be compatible with the ideology and the attitude of the authoritarian-social state. A further consequence of this is that in our search for possibilities of guaranteeing our interests we must be guided by the question as to what the fields are in which an actual community of interests between the two countries exists or can be created, or at least can be made to appear plausible.

6. The following are to be considered as common interests of this kind:

(a) A common type of regime and consequently a mutual interest in taking up similar battle positions against fundamental opponents of the regime and in using similar methods to combat them. This would give Spain an interest in joining the anti-Comintern pact and a police agreement, and in borrowing extensively from our social and political methods; it would also give rise to an interest in cooperation in the field of the press and propaganda in international discussions regarding the regime; and this would again give rise to the possibility of a press and radio agreement with us in line with the statements contained in the Führer's latest Reichstag speech on combating press agitation.[2] (This point was not mentioned in Herr von Stohrer's memorandum.)

(b) Since an authoritarian state by its very nature must be strong both within and without, and since a strong Spain is a great advantage to us for reasons of high policy, it is consequently in the common interest of Germany and Nationalist Spain that the latter be militarily and economically strong. This gives rise to a common interest in building up a strong system of armaments, i. e. cooperating with regard to the armaments industry, the training of the army, officer training, etc., and, furthermore, a common interest in the exploitation of Spanish mineral resources. The question of the part we are to play here is principally a question of defining the extent of our participation and that of Nationalist Spain.

(c) If the relationship and the community of interests between the two countries are envisaged as under (a) and (b), then there logically arises a common interest in strengthening cultural exchange and in assuring a feeling of community of interest among wide sectors of the people by cultural-political measures. This will result in a desire to conclude a cultural agreement to serve these purposes.

(d) The activity of numerous Germans in Spanish economic life before the Civil War was in the interest of Spain as well as that of Germany. In an orientation of the two countries as outlined in this memorandum such activity would be all the more in their mutual interest, and therefore there would be a common interest in reestablishing Germany's economic position in Spain and consequently in giving compensation to the refugees from Spain.

B. The following is noted regarding the questions listed on page 10 of Herr von Stohrer's memorandum[3] in which he envisages an immediate possibility of negotiating with the Nationalist Spanish Government:

From the ideology of the Spanish Nationalist movement as well as from the Spanish character it is apparent that any subordination to the will of one or more allies, particularly if it is forced, would meet

---

[2] In his speech before the Reichstag on Feb. 20, Hitler had said that little result could be expected from conferences and conversations of statesmen because false interpretations were placed upon such meetings in the foreign press. He advocated an international agreement "to prevent the circulation of those newspapers which do more harm to the promotion of friendly relations between nations than any poison or incendiary bombs."

[3] See p. 595.

with the strongest internal resistance. Consequently, in the course of the projected negotiations we ought to emphasize the idea not of a claim or a counterclaim in return for our services but of the logical development of the community of interests which arose during the Civil War and which is based on geopolitical and historical factors. We should approach the Spaniards in the sense of what was stated under 6(a)–(d) with the request and the desire to talk over the whole complex of our relations and to ascertain our common points of interest in open discussion, in order to proceed to agreements on individual points as soon as the discussion has brought about the necessary clarification.

If this method is approved, it follows that it is not possible at the present time to draw up a schedule of questions concerning which we could come to a settlement with Nationalist Spain, since such a schedule could only grow out of the discussion with the Spaniards. We could, however, very well draw up a schedule of questions according to their importance or urgency for us, in the light of which—naturally without letting this be known to the Spaniards—we could direct the negotiations. This schedule might, however, differ greatly in many respects from that which would probably result from the discussion with the Spaniards. The agreements which it ought to be possible to reach most quickly are those on a cultural treaty, a police agreement, and perhaps a press and propaganda convention, because the ideological argument can be used here and the ideal community of interests is not disturbed by any clash of economic interests.

It might be more difficult to induce the Nationalist Spanish Government to commit itself by treaty agreement with regard to its international policy, since it has time and again shown the desire not to commit itself in advance in this respect. It is consequently doubtful whether Spain's adherence to the anti-Comintern pact can be obtained or whether the extension of the clause regarding benevolent neutrality (articles 3 and 4 of the protocol of March 20, 1937) can be achieved at this time, but this does not mean that attempts in this direction cannot be undertaken even now.

The safeguarding of our German element in Spain by guaranteeing freedom of residence, settlement, and work for German nationals in Spain, as well as the assurance of indemnification, is particularly important for us. Although it is largely an economic question, nevertheless moral and ideological arguments can be used here to a considerable extent. In spite of objections against this which could be raised, this should be done immediately, so that after the war is over—surprises are not at all impossible in this regard—the necessary bases exist for the reestablishment of the German element in Spain.

With regard to the other economic questions (conclusion of an extensive commercial treaty, exploitation of natural resources, payment for our deliveries, assurance of Spanish raw materials, shipping questions, etc.) there arises the fundamental question as to the form of our future economic activity in Spain, which will not be discussed here for the present. From a knowledge of the Spanish national character and the ideology of the Spanish Nationalist Movement, the fundamental observation may be made that Nationalist Spain will resist any attempt at excessive foreign control, monopoly, or any sort of subordination, as soon as she has freed herself from the emergency in which she needs direct assistance. In further negotiations on economic questions, this should be taken into consideration even now. It is very apparent from Herr von Stohrer's last report [4] regarding his conversations with Spanish Minister of Economics Suances that in the Montana affair the Spaniards are not disposed to grant us participation in the exploitation of the Spanish mineral resources in the form of majority participation on our part. It is illogical for us on the one hand to adopt the ideology of a reawakened, newly strengthened Spain, a Spain *una, grande e* [*sic*] *libre*, and to support this with our blood and money, and then in the economic sphere to make use of methods of majority control and monopoly in our dealings with this country.

As far as the military cooperation of the two countries in the future is concerned, it is questionable whether agreements are necessary or possible at present. The War Ministry should be consulted on this point.

Herewith submitted to the Deputy Director and the Director of the Political Department.[5]

SCHWENDEMANN

---

[4] See document No. 532, p. 601.
[5] On Mar. 31, 1938, Stohrer wrote a personal letter to Weizsäcker suggesting, with reference to the new Spanish mining law, that it was time to prepare a really generous financial settlement with Spain to be negotiated immediately after the end of the war. In this, Germany should not let herself be anticipated by the Italians.

CHAPTER VI

CONTINUED AID TO FRANCO AND NEGOTIATIONS FOR A TREATY MARCH 16–DECEMBER 19, 1938

No. 545

3374/E011070

Memorandum by the State Secretary

BERLIN, March 16, 1938.
Pol. III 981.

The Spanish Ambassador, who called on me today with regard to another matter, spoke with lively concern of certain reports according to which Léon Blum and Paul-Boncour[1] were considering initiating active French intervention in favor of Red Spain. His information was not yet absolutely certain, but still enough was known to necessitate serious consideration of what was to be done in the situation which would thereby be created. It would really be ironical, to be sure, if Léon Blum, whom he might well term the father of non-intervention, should now decide to take such a step. The Ambassador asked me what Germany's attitude would be if France should initiate such active intervention. I answered that we had not considered this question up to now; it was certain, however, that in this case an entirely new situation would have to be faced. Moreover, the Foreign Minister was expected to return to Berlin this afternoon, and then there would be an opportunity to ask his opinion.

At his request I promised the Ambassador to inform him in case there should be a clarification of our attitude on this question.

MACKENSEN

---

[1] Joseph Paul-Boncour, Foreign Minister in the Blum Cabinet, Mar. 13–Apr. 10, 1938.

No. 546

586/243105

The Ambassador in France to the Foreign Ministry

Telegram

No. 148 of March 17   PARIS, March 17, 1938.
                                              Received March 17—6:15 p.m.

For the Foreign Ministry, the War Ministry, the General Staff, and the Supreme Command of the Navy.

According to a number of reports to the same effect, the Supreme Council for National Defense in its session of March 15 took up particularly the situation in Spain in addition to the Czechoslovak question.[1] The French Mediterranean squadron is then reported to have received orders to be prepared for action. The press reports that four units have left for Barcelona to protect French nationals; other units have left to be stationed in Port Vendres. The Army is preparing certain safety measures in the Sixteenth, Seventeenth, and Eighteenth Districts. It also appears that reinforcements from the interior of France are being brought in for these districts, which are short of troops, without affecting the condition in the eastern frontier zone which I have reported. As far as air defenses go, the southern regions (Bordeaux, Toulouse, and Toulon) have been put on the alert.

With the Army it appears for the moment to be a matter of protecting the Pyrenees boundary, which seems to be in greater danger because of events in Spain, while, for the Navy and the Air Force, action to safeguard the French communications in the western Mediterranean does not appear to be out of the question.

                                                         KÜHLENTHAL
                                                         WELCZECK

---

[1] See also vol. II, document No. 87, p. 170.

No. 547

F14/008

Memorandum for the Führer by the Foreign Minister

RM 169   BERLIN, March 17, 1938.

The Italian Counselor of Embassy, Count Magistrati, who called on me today in regard to another matter,[1] gave me the following information:

According to reports available to the Italian Government, the military situation has greatly improved in favor of Franco. There were also reports, however, to the effect that the French Government was

---

[1] For other matters discussed at this interview see vol. I, documents Nos. 396 and 728, pp. 610 and 1059–1060.

considering intervention with troops and matériel in favor of Barcelona. The Italian Government was determined in that event to answer with like measures and on a large scale.

RIBBENTROP

No. 548

309/189091–92

Memorandum by the Foreign Minister

RM 200   BERLIN, March 21, 1938.

The Italian Counselor of Embassy, Count Magistrati, called on me today at 1 p.m. to give me the following information:

The British Ambassador, the Earl of Perth, had transmitted an *aide-mémoire* by direction of his Government. It was stated therein that the reports regarding the bombing attacks on Barcelona by General Franco's Italian airplanes had created a sensation in England. In view of British public opinion it would be difficult in case of repetition of such attacks to bring the negotiations with Italy to a successful conclusion. The British Government requested the Italian Government to exert its influence on General Franco to the end that such bombing attacks would be discontinued in the future.

The Earl of Perth had added that a delicate situation would arise for Chamberlain in case the bombing attacks did not cease. England was still trying to keep France, which was already nervous because of the *Anschluss*, from interfering in Spain.

Count Ciano had replied that Barcelona could not be considered an open city. The city was fortified and was the seat of the Red Government. However, Italy would exert her influence in the desired manner. The initiative for the bombing attacks originated not with Italy but with Franco. Moreover, the Italian forces now amounted to only 60 percent of their former maximum strength.

Count Ciano had added that, in case of an attack in Spain, Italy would retaliate with like measures. This could lead to consequences the importance of which could not be foreseen at present.

I answered Count Magistrati that in my opinion the French Government was not committed to intervention, in particular not without England's approval. I could not imagine, however, that the British Government was bent on a policy of adventure.

RIBBENTROP

No. 549

F19/151–53

The Supreme Command of the Wehrmacht to the Foreign Ministry

No. 223/338 geh. Kdos. Ausl. Ib   BERLIN, March 22, 1938.

Attention: Ministerialdirektor Baron von Weizsäcker.

The Supreme Command of the Wehrmacht takes the following stand on two questions connected with events in Spain, which were brought up for discussion here by the Foreign Ministry:

I. Is military intervention on the part of France to be expected?

France would like to see Red Spain avoid a rapid and complete collapse under the blows of the Spanish Nationalist armed forces. Such a collapse would also have the effect of doing still further harm to France's prestige, which has greatly declined of late; of making Franco the unopposed sole master of all Spain; and possibly of maintaining or even strengthening the German-Italian influence south of the Pyrenees.

Military intervention, i.e. the employment of French forces south of the Pyrenees, might be able to prevent this Red collapse. In any case, however, it would entail the possibility that the localized Spanish Civil War might develop into a European war. For France knows that south of the Pyrenees she would encounter not only the whole of the Spanish Nationalist armed forces but also Italian and German troops, behind which stand the armed forces of both of these great military powers. A very considerable number of French troops would therefore have to be used. But this would result in a weakening of the eastern frontier facing the allied German-Italian armed forces. Whether France is able and sufficiently strong to assume this dangerous risk, especially in regard to a matter which has already been decided militarily, may be doubted. For in order to do this she would probably be unable to forego the active cooperation of England. It is not likely that she could obtain this. Moreover, the lack of internal unity and the weak position of the present French Government make it appear improbable that so serious a decision can be made and executed.

If French military intervention in the Spanish conflict thus appears improbable at the present time, there is all the more possibility of intervention of a political nature. The military measures taken by France, as, for instance, outlined in telegram No. 156 of March 19 from the Embassy in Paris,[1] would also serve this purpose. They could also be explained, moreover, by pure military necessity, namely, in order sufficiently to safeguard the French-Spanish border in the

---

[1] Not printed (586/243109).

face of the possibility that Red Spanish troops or other undesirable elements might cross over or that the war might be carried up to or even beyond the border.

II. Are there any military objections to the establishment of a neutral zone approximately 50 kilometers wide on Spanish soil along the French-Spanish border?

The alleged desire of France to establish such a zone may be explained by her wish to keep the Nationalist troops, and more especially the German and Italian troops, away from her borders.

If, as is assumed here, we continue to maintain, as heretofore, the fiction that no German troops are committed in Spain, we are not immediately concerned in this question.

It is not known here what attitude the Italians will asume on this matter.

Franco's opinion is decisive in this matter. In the opinion of the Supreme Command of the Wehrmacht he would scarcely approve any such proposal. For, if this idea should materialize, it would give the Red Spaniards a safe zone of refuge on Catalonian soil and deprive Franco of the possibility of mopping up all Spain.

The Chief of the Supreme Command of the Wehrmacht,
KEITEL

Re II. This does not quite apply to the question which was asked. According to oral information there is no objection (e.g. on the part of Admiral Canaris, who will see Franco next week) to proposing a regulation according to which bands of *volunteers* on the White side may not be brought closer than 50 kilometers to the French boundary.

Signed March 22, 1938.

No. 550

1568/379558–61

The Ambassador in Spain to the Foreign Ministry

SECRET   SALAMANCA, March 23, 1938.
No. 291 g   Pol. I 767 g III.

Subject: The effects of the recent air attacks on Barcelona.

With reference to my telegram No. 149 of March 20.[1]

I hear from Barcelona that the results of the recent air raids on Barcelona carried out by Italian bombers were nothing less than terrible. Almost all parts of the city were affected. There was no evidence of any attempt to hit military objectives in Barcelona. Hundreds of houses and whole streets are said to have been destroyed by the bombs, which were evidently of a particularly destructive type. So far 1,000 dead have been counted; it is assumed, however, that

---

[1] Not printed (3366/E010413).

many more dead will be found beneath the ruins. The number of wounded is estimated at over 3,000. One bomb is said to have killed a whole group of women waiting in line to get their milk rations, while another one struck a subway entrance and tore to pieces the people who had sought refuge there.

The Red Government is using the general indignation aroused by these air attacks to encourage the resistance and endurance of the population, who had been thrown into consternation by Franco's military successes in Aragón. As a sign that these bombing attacks did not result in an effective demoralization of the population of Barcelona, it has been pointed out that many of the wounded, while being carried on stretchers to first-aid stations and hospitals, exhorted the public with clenched fists and exclamations of hatred to carry on further resistance.

According to what I hear, the Red leaders in France are making good use of the heavy losses suffered by the civilian population in Barcelona. In southern France (e. g. Biarritz) posters even are said to have been put up which contain very sharp attacks on Fascism, National Socialism, and the Führer himself, with the plain intent of alarming the French people and supporting the efforts being made by the Reds in France to obtain reinforcements in matériel and personnel there. Among the international journalists who have seen the results of the air raids in Barcelona there is the greatest indignation, which is apparent in the reports they have sent their papers. In these circles it is said to be the conviction that the indiscriminate dumping of bombs on the city of Barcelona was principally a matter of experimenting with new bombs.

I fear that in a civil war like that in Spain destructive air raids in cases where military objectives are not clearly recognizable do not have the intended psychological effect but rather entail considerable danger for the future. I am convinced that both in Spain and in other countries they will stir up hatred against us and Italy after the war, in the worst possible manner, by pointing out that Spanish airplanes had naturally not subjected their own cities to such devastating bombardments but that it had been done by their Italian and German allies.

For this reason, even at the time of the first severe air raids on the inner city of Barcelona by Italian aviators 2 months ago, raids which led to the bombing of cities in the rear areas of Nationalist Spain and which were first blamed on German planes, I spoke with the Italian Ambassador and responsible Spanish authorities and expressed the above-mentioned apprehensions. I met with a very sympathetic reception. Particularly Count Viola was entirely of the same opinion, which—as he told me later—he also expressed to the

Italian Commander in Chief and to Rome.   General Veith also shared my apprehensions.

Since consideration has subsequently been shown by the Spaniards with regard to bombing cities in the Red rear areas, I do not know whether the recent destructive air attacks on Barcelona are to be attributed to the initiative of the Italians themselves, or whether a new instruction has been issued by the Spanish High Command.

STOHRER

I have just learned from the deputy of the Naval Attaché, who is absent just now, that according to information from the Deputy Chief of the General Staff of the Spanish Nationalist Navy, Generalissimo Franco has given orders that the city of Barcelona is not to be bombed any more.   The instructions also apply to harbors in which there might be neutral ships.   The reason for the second part of this command is said to be the fact that a few days ago a British ship [2] was sunk by a direct hit in the harbor of Tarragona, causing the death of an official of the Non-Intervention Committee and several British seamen, and wounding a number of persons.

STOHRER

---

[2] The *Stanwell*, bombed and set on fire during a raid on Tarragona on Mar. 15.

No. 551

1568/379578

The Ambassador in Spain to the Foreign Ministry

VERY SECRET   SALAMANCA, March 24, 1938.
No. 300 g   Pol. I 776 g.

With reference to my report No. 291 g of March 23.
General Veith just wired me the following:

"The liaison officer with the Generalissimo informs me that Mussolini, 'to the great indignation' of Franco, personally ordered the March 18 bombing of Barcelona.   The Condor Legion is not implicated, since I have forbidden the bombing of open cities without military objectives.   The Generalissimo told me on March 23 that bombs had been dropped on the residential section of the city, which was four kilometers from the industrial part.   He considered this a blunder.   The bombing had now strengthened morale and had united diverging interests.   Moreover, the population was partly Nationalist.   England and France had sent notes of protest; the French note would not be answered, while the British note would be answered by making reference to the military installations in Barcelona.   I have been told by the liaison officer that Franco requested Mussolini through the Ambassador in Rome to refrain from issuing direct orders to plane units at Majorca."

The above is the shortened text of the telegram.

STOHRER

No. 552

586/243127–28

Memorandum by the Deputy Director of the Political Department

BERLIN, March 25, 1938.

At my request Count Magistrati called on me today, and I told him that we considered it advisable, in conjunction with the Italian Government, to advise General Franco that in case of further military advances in the neighborhood of the French-Spanish border he should not commit the German and Italian volunteers fighting in the Spanish Nationalist Army any closer than 50 kilometers from the French-Spanish border.

This referred principally to the volunteers in the land forces; we would recommend to General Franco, however, that he not commit the German and Italian airplanes within the 50-kilometer zone, either. In the opinion of the Supreme Command of the Wehrmacht there was no objection from a military standpoint to such a regulation. Count Magistrati, to whom I showed the French Foreign Minister's statements before the Foreign Affairs Committee Wednesday, according to which France would never tolerate "a permanent or even a temporary stationing of non-Spanish military forces in the vicinity of French territory," found this proposal entirely satisfactory, and he promised to transmit it to Rome immediately with his recommendation. As soon as a reply was received he would notify me. We agreed that it would be best to discuss at a later stage the question whether such a regulation should be published by Franco.

BISMARCK

No. 553

1568/379579

The Ambassador in Spain to the Foreign Ministry

STRICTLY CONFIDENTIAL   SALAMANCA, March 26, 1938.

No. 1717   Pol. I 785 g III.

Subject: The recent air raids on Barcelona.

With reference to my report No. 300 g of March 24.

The Italian Ambassador just informed me that in his absence the Vatican Chargé d'Affaires had requested the Counselor of Embassy to see that the Italian Embassy uses its influence in order to prevent air raids on open cities in the future. Monsignor Antoniutti had also informed the Italian Embassy at the same time that he had made a similar *démarche* with Franco in the name of the Vatican.

The Italian Ambassador added that he is of the opinion that such bombings are, to say the least, exceedingly unwise politically, as he had also frankly stated in Rome following our previous discussion.

STOHRER

No. 554

586/243137

The Director of the Political Department to the Embassy in Spain

Telegram

No. 112   BERLIN, March 30, 1938.

General Volkmann received instructions from the War Ministry to urge Franco to continue the military operations until all of Catalonia is conquered and not to call a halt there in order to go over to the offensive at other fronts, for example at Madrid. We share the opinion of the War Ministry. I leave it to your discretion, therefore, on a suitable occasion and in a manner which seems advisable, to make similar representations to Franco.

WEIZSÄCKER

After dispatch:

To Pol. III, with the request that Captain [*Kapitän*] Frisius be informed of the contents of the telegram.

No. 555

309/189079

Memorandum by the Director of the Political Department

BERLIN, March 31, 1938.

The Italian Chargé d'Affaires declared today in the name of his Government that he agreed with the plan to request General Franco not to permit the volunteers in his ranks (including the Air Force) to approach closer than 50 kilometers to the French border during future military operations; this would prevent incidents from occurring there.

WEIZSÄCKER

No. 556

309/189077–78

The Chargé d'Affaires in Great Britain to the Foreign Ministry

Telegram

No. 186 of March 31   LONDON, March 31, 1938—11 : 15 p.m.

Received April 1—2 : 50 a.m.

With reference to our telegram No. 180 of March 29.[1]

I. In today's session of the main subcommittee of the Non-Intervention Committee, Plymouth first gave a survey of the progress of its discussions. I should like to stress the following points:

1. Plymouth stated that the French, German, Italian, Portuguese, and Soviet Governments had accepted in principle the British formula for the withdrawal of volunteers. The French, Italian, Portuguese, and British Governments had accepted 10,000 as a basic figure. The German Government had accepted this figure as a basis for discussion, but the Soviet Government had rejected it as too low.

At the beginning of the discussion I likewise accepted 10,000 as a basic figure. The Soviet Ambassador said that he would have to ask his Government for its stand.

2. Regarding the reestablishment of supervision on land, Plymouth submitted a new British compromise proposal. According to this, supervision on land would be reinstituted as soon as word was received from the two commissions that they were ready to begin the count. Supervision would be automatically discontinued in case withdrawal had not begun by the fifty-sixth day after the plenary session of the committee had finally accepted the resolution.

All the representatives stated that they would present this proposal to their Governments. The French Ambassador declared that the British proposal, on which he reserved his comment, represented a divergence from the resolution of November 4, 1937.[2] His Government would have to request reinforcement of the naval patrols. It desired that the observers at the various harbors also be given the right to enter other harbors and that there be an observer at all Spanish harbors in which war matériel could be unloaded.

3. With regard to the memorandum of the Secretary General of the non-intervention secretariat (36731), Plymouth declared that the proposed elimination of categories was not completely satisfactory. The British Government would take the recommendation of the Secretary General into sympathetic consideration.

Grandi and the Portuguese Ambassador accepted Hemming's recommendations. The Soviet Ambassador declared that his Government

---

[1] Not printed (586/243134).
[2] See Editors' Note, p. 494.

attached very great importance to withdrawal according to categories. I reserved the German stand on this matter.

II. I have no objections to acceptance of the British compromise proposal under section 2.

The French proposal would probably come to nought, if only because of the Spanish parties. Please consult with Rome as to whether it could be accepted with this expectation. The exact text will follow later.

III. The time for the next meeting has not yet been fixed.

IV. The meeting was obviously called by Plymouth principally in order to demonstrate to British public opinion that the work of the Non-Intervention Committee is progressing. Probably no one believes any longer that a withdrawal of the volunteers can actually be carried out by the methods of the present plan. Plymouth hinted cautiously that he had his doubts regarding the whole plan, by dropping the casual remark that he was aware that the latest events in Spain had clearly put the work of the committee in a somewhat different light.

WOERMANN

No. 557

309/189068-69

The Ambassador in Spain to the Foreign Ministry

Telegram

No. 188 of April 5   SALAMANCA, April 5, 1938—1:50 a.m.

Received April 5—2:55 p.m.

For the State Secretary and the Chief of the Supreme Command of the Wehrmacht.

During yesterday's discussion Franco brought up in a cautious manner the question of a possible withdrawal of the Condor Legion, after both Torres and Foreign Minister Jordana had broached the subject in previous conversations. Assuming a favorable military development which made a rapid conclusion of the operations seem likely, Franco stated that the negotiations in the Non-Intervention Committee as well as a regard for French and British sensibilities suggested a withdrawal of the foreign volunteers. If the military situation continued to develop favorably, the time might also come soon for a withdrawal of the Condor Legion. General Kindelan already had about 50 Spanish pilots at his disposal who could take over the German planes; he had in mind a kind of transition arrangement (instruction by German personnel). Franco requested that I ask General Veith to make further arrangements with Kindelan. He was also considering something similar with regard to the Italians, but he did not define these plans. Considering the political importance of the whole question, I asked Franco in the course of a short second conference not to inform Veith for the present since I wished to report the matter to Ambassador Stohrer. Franco agreed to this proposal.

In a lengthy discourse Franco also informed me of his conception of future peacetime military cooperation. He expressed a desire merely to have several German naval officers placed at the disposal of the Navy for training purposes, as inconspicuously as possible. Regarding the training of the Army and the Air Force, Franco emphasized repeatedly that the Spanish planned to carry this out themselves and merely needed a few specialists. In general, he stressed throughout that he intended to apply the same principles to the Italians. It was noteworthy that this time Franco praised the Italians very strongly. The total impression was that Franco is evidently trying to secure a free hand for himself. I shall report details on my return.

The Ambassador is acquainted with the above telegram.

CANARIS
STOHRER

No. 558

F19/169

Memorandum for the Führer by the Foreign Minister

[Undated]

Enclosed:

1. The translation of the Italian-Spanish secret protocol which was signed in the beginning of 1937 and of which the Italians did not inform us until after it had been signed; [1]

2. The German-Spanish secret protocol which was subsequently signed on March 20, 1937; [2]

3. A telegram from Admiral Canaris which arrived yesterday,[3] according to which Franco, referring to French and British sensibilities, broached the question of the withdrawal of German and Italian volunteers.

I consider that the time has now come for us to clarify with Franco our future political relations with Spain. For that purpose a treaty could be considered along the basic lines of our secret protocol and somewhat like the draft enclosed as annex 4. A treaty of this type would, without involving the obligations of a military alliance, bind Franco closely to the Berlin-Rome Axis and assure us that Spain

---

[1] See document No. 137, p. 147.
[2] Document No. 234, p. 256.
[3] Document No. 557, *supra*.

would not be used by France and England as an area for military operations or transit of troops. I have instructed Ambassador von Stohrer to sound Franco first in a general way, without giving him the draft, in order to ascertain whether he is prepared to enter into negotiations for a treaty of this kind. I have also requested Stohrer to inform his Italian colleague in broad outline of our intentions.

RIBBENTROP

F19/177–178
F3/0215–0217

[Enclosure]

DRAFT OF A GERMAN-SPANISH TREATY OF FRIENDSHIP [4]

VERY SECRET

The German Chancellor and the Chief of the Spanish Nationalist Government,

realizing that the German Government and the Spanish Nationalist Government, because of important common interests, affinity of political views, and the feeling of cordial good will which has always existed between their peoples, have the mission to collaborate closely,

filled with deep satisfaction over the fact that their friendly association has thus far proved so successful,

convinced that the progressive development of their relations will serve the welfare of both peoples in the future also and will be a certain factor in the preservation of the highest cultural values as well as in the maintenance of peace,

are agreed in their desire to affirm their common purposes by a solemn treaty based on the principles of equality of rights and independence of both parties. For this purpose they have appointed as their plenipotentiaries:

The German Chancellor:

. . . .

The Chief of the Spanish Nationalist Government:

. . . .

who, having communicated to each other their full powers, found to be in good and due form, have agreed upon the following provisions:

Article 1

The High Contracting Parties will constantly maintain contact with each other in order to inform each other concerning questions of international policy affecting their common interests.

---

[4] As appears from a minute by Weizsäcker dated Apr. 2 (136/73612) the draft was prepared for submission by the Foreign Minister to the Führer.

Should their common interests be jeopardized by international events of any kind, they will enter into consultations without delay regarding the measures to be taken to safeguard these interests.

Article 2

The High Contracting Parties are both aware of the dangers facing their countries through the aspirations of the Communist International and will consult constantly as to measures that seem appropriate for combating these dangers.

Article 3

In the event that the security or other vital interests of one of the High Contracting Parties should be externally threatened, the other High Contracting Party will grant the threatened Party its political and diplomatic support in order to contribute to the best of its ability toward eliminating this threat.

Article 4

In view of the close friendship in which Germany as well as Spain is bound with Italy, both the High Contracting Parties will be mindful in the execution of the agreements made in articles 1 to 3 above of assuring also the collaboration of the Royal Italian Government in each instance.

Article 5

Neither of the High Contracting Parties will enter into treaties or other agreements of any kind with third powers which are aimed directly or indirectly against the other High Contracting Party.

The High Contracting Parties agree to inform each other regarding treaties and agreements affecting their common interests which they have previously concluded or will in the future conclude with third countries.

Article 6

In case one of the High Contracting Parties should become involved in warlike entanglements with a third power, the other High Contracting Party will avoid anything in the political, military, and economic fields that might be disadvantageous to its treaty partner or of advantage to its opponent.

Article 7

The High Contracting Parties will in special agreements arrange for measures which are calculated to promote the fostering of comradely relations and the exchange of practical military experience between their armed forces.

Article 8

The High Contracting Parties are agreed in their desire to intensify the economic relations between their countries as much as possible. They reaffirm their purpose that Germany and Spain shall henceforth cooperate with and supplement each other in economic matters in every way. The implementation of these principles shall be reserved for special agreements.

Article 9

The present treaty shall be ratified and the instruments of ratification shall be exchanged at . . . as soon as possible.

The present treaty shall enter into force on the date of the exchange of instruments of ratification and from then on shall remain in full force for a period of 5 years. If within 1 year before the expiration of the aforesaid period neither High Contracting Party notifies the other of its intention to terminate the treaty, it shall remain in force for 5 more years and in a like manner continue in the following periods of time.

In witness whereof the plenipotentiaries have signed this treaty.

Done in duplicate in the German and Spanish languages . . . .

No. 559

F19/162–65

Memorandum by an Official of the Foreign Minister's Secretariat

SALZBURG, April 6, 1938—evening.

Memorandum for the Foreign Minister!

I have given the Führer the memoranda in accordance with instructions and added what I was to say orally.

The Führer took a very long time to read the memorandum through attentively; first, he put a question mark on page 3, article 3, in the middle of line 4 next to the word "political." [1] Further, in article 4, line 2, he changed "is" to "are" and declared finally that he considered articles 5 and 6 useful. At article 7, opposite "exchange of comradely relations and practical military experience," he placed another question mark.

The Führer declared that he considered a commercial treaty better than this project, which actually was of little value (with emphasis on "actually"!).

He declared further that it would not be bad at all if we could withdraw our troops and, above all, our air forces. Naturally, there

---

[1] See document No. 558, *supra*, and document No. 773, p. 885.

would first have to be an understanding with the Italians. After all, a considerable part of our air strength was in Spain, whereas it was very much needed and would be of extremely great value for rebuilding the air force in Austria. Since in his opinion, too, the war was drawing to an end, our soldiers could not learn anything more in any case. In the territory of former Austria, however, the troops, and particularly the air force, could be utilized to very good advantage for rebuilding our forces. In the final analysis the troops had to be withdrawn from Spain some time or other. We had already tried to do so several times.

I had called the Führer's attention to the Foreign Minister's view of the value of the Canaris telegram. He is of the opinion, however, that the Italians should be informed immediately of the fact that Franco, in view of French-British sensibilities, has expressed a wish for the withdrawal of volunteers, and also of the fact that Franco believes that the war is now drawing to an end. The Italians should be told that we would naturally be grateful if we could make use of this offer, and they should be asked what their opinion is in this matter.

The Führer requests the Foreign Minister to have this done immediately but to delay the question regarding the treaty until his return on Sunday.

Spitzy

Note: I am returning herewith the memorandum regarding the conversation with Henlein,[2] which the Führer read day before yesterday and noted without comment.

Sp[itzy] Apr. 6.

---

[2] A memorandum of an interview between Henlein and the Führer on Mar. 28, 1938, is printed in vol. II as document No. 107, p. 197, and minutes of a conference with Henlein at the Foreign Ministry on Mar. 29 appear in the same volume as document No. 109, pp. 204–205.

No. 560

136/73613–15

The Foreign Minister to the Embassy in Spain

Draft Telegram [1]

VERY SECRET   BERLIN, April 6, 1938.

No. . . .   zu Pol. I 649 g III.

We consider that the time has now come to clarify with Franco our future political relationship with Spain. We have in mind the negotiation of a treaty to be made public, keeping within the framework of our secret protocol of March 20, 1937, and merely putting its funda-

---

[1] This telegram is endorsed "Cessat" and apparently was not sent.

mental ideas in concrete form. A draft for such a treaty will be sent by the next courier.

Please approach Franco as soon as possible, even before the arrival of the draft treaty if an opportunity should arise, and sound him out in an appropriate manner in order to determine whether he is now prepared to enter into negotiations with us on such a treaty.

I suggest that you open the discussion in somewhat the following manner: In view of Franco's impending final victory, German-Spanish relations are now entering a new phase. Franco's recent statements to Canaris, mentioned in your last telegraphic report, No. 188 of April 5, also obviously proceeded from this point of view. Consequently, we considered it advisable to clarify our future relations now in the interest of both parties and to realize the fundamental ideas of the secret protocol in a political treaty. Naturally we had in mind only agreements which preserved the principle of complete equality and independence of both parties, and which resulted only in close political cooperation and not in a military alliance. We believed that we could take it for granted that such a treaty was also in accordance with Franco's wishes, since it constituted the natural culmination of our cooperation up to the present. It served the Spanish interest, since it permitted the Spanish Government close association with the Berlin-Rome Axis without compromising it with regard to third powers.

Our draft should not be submitted at this stage.

If you are unable to reach Franco in the near future, it would be advisable to discuss the matter first with the Foreign Minister.

At the same time please give your Italian colleague a general picture of our intentions.

If the execution of the above-mentioned mission should necessitate a short postponement of your trip, which was approved in a personal letter of April 4,[2] this would have to be accepted.

v. Ribbentrop

---

[2] Not found.

No. 561

2946/576207–09

The Director of Hisma to the Ambassador in Spain

SALAMANCA, April 6, 1938.

MY DEAR AMBASSADOR: I enclose the comments on the mining law which you desired for your conference with Minister Suances.[1]
I am leaving for Germany but shall definitely be back this month.
Heil Hitler!

As ever,
J. BERNHARDT

[Enclosure]

MEMORANDUM

SALAMANCA, April 6, 1938.

Subject: For the discussion with Minister Suances.

1. A restriction on the participation of foreign capital in Spanish mining companies or other enterprises is unjust and, above all, unwise. Such a law will keep foreign capital away and hamper the reconstruction of Spain.

Such a law would bear the mark of the provisional and would have to be changed within a few months.

2. The state has means at hand to supervise and control this foreign capital.

3. The state can superintend the output of these companies and secure the proceeds thereof mainly for itself.

4. It would be politically unwise to include the desired restrictions especially in a mining law. Any mining law will particularly arouse the attention of international capital, etc. Precisely the Generalissimo's realization that England "is a great power which can be reduced in strength only over a number of years" should prevent him from

---

[1] In the 4 weeks following Stohrer's conversation with Suances on Feb. 17 (see document No. 532, p. 601) little change took place regarding the German claims for mining concessions. On Mar. 19, however, General Franco ordered the Council of Ministers to decide the question one way or the other. The result was a decision to draft in place of the law of Oct. 9, 1937, a general decree applicable to all foreign powers, which would nevertheless leave the door open for privileges to be granted to the Axis Powers. The new decree, however, specifically reserved to the Spanish Government the right of granting or refusing changes of ownership in Spanish mines. On Mar. 30 Stohrer informed both Suances and Foreign Minister Jordana of his dissatisfaction with the terms of the new draft law and requested an interview with General Franco. This course of events was described by Stohrer in his report No. A 1886 of Mar. 31, 1938 (5149/E303633–40). His interview with Franco took place on Apr. 6 (see document No. 566, p. 641). The document printed as the enclosure to No. 561 is a brief prepared by Bernhardt for use in following up this conversation by further negotiations with Suances.

passing a mining law greatly limiting the participation of capital. It would be much more advisable:

5. To issue a generally applicable mining law in which the state reserves the right to grant concessions in individual cases and in which the products of the mines, in case of emergency or war, are reserved for the needs of the nation, and the like.

6. The greatest value, however, should be attached to the *finance law*, which would be intelligible even to the British since everyone knows the severe damage which has been wrought in Spain. Furthermore, a nationalization of the invested capital is in the interest of the Spanish state and at the same time in our own interest. It is, however, indirectly contrary to the special rights which the British and the French have been accorded in the past.

J. BERNHARDT

No. 562

586/243149

The Ambassador in Spain to the Foreign Ministry

Telegram

No. 190 of April 6   SALAMANCA, April 7, 1938—12 : 59 a.m.
Received April 7—2 : 20 a.m.

With reference to my telegram No. 187 of April 5.[1]

The instructions contained in telegraphic instructions 112 [2] and 115 [3] were carried out with the Generalissimo today, taking 118 [4] into account.

Franco is determined to continue the offensive until the collapse of the enemy. On account of difficulties in terrain, however, the Mediterranean will not be reached for several days. Victory is certain; further desperate resistance by the Reds is quite possible, and he has included this in his calculations.

In spite of the reassuring reports which he has received recently from Paris, he agrees entirely with the opinion of the Germans and the Italians that the French interventionists should be deprived of any pretext; he is therefore willing, in accordance with our proposal, not to use foreign volunteer troops near the French border and, insofar as possible, also to follow our suggestion not to use German and Italian aircraft there either.

He would consider what would be the best possible method of making this concession known in France; perhaps he could do it best by way of England.

---

[1] Not printed (586/243145).
[2] Document No. 554, p. 628.
[3] Not printed (2129/463809).
[4] Not printed (2129/463809–10).

The Italian Ambassador made a similar *démarche* with Franco today and met with the same compliance.

STOHRER

No. 563

586/243150-51

The State Secretary to the Embassy in Great Britain

Telegram

No. 114   BERLIN, April 7, 1938.
                                          zu Pol. III 1088 Ang. I, Pol. III 1059.

Drafting Officer: Counselor of Legation Schwendemann.

With reference to your telegraphic report No. 186 of March 31 and written report No. A 1589 of April 1.[1]

Since the development of the military situation in Spain permits the expectation of a speedy final victory by Franco and since the entry into force of the British plan regarding the combing-out of volunteers need therefore no longer be reckoned with, we can permit our stand on special questions to be dictated purely by considerations of tactical policy. In doing so we should naturally stay within the general framework of our previous position. I therefore request that you take the following stand on the questions mentioned in previous reports:

1. We agree either to withdrawal according to categories or to a general withdrawal, whichever the majority of the committee may prefer.

2. No objection to acceptance of the British compromise proposal on the resumption of land control.

3. With regard to the strengthening of naval patrols, please maintain the previous standpoint that this is not desirable.

4. Since the Reich Foreign Exchange Control Agency has now granted permission for the transfer of 426,000 RM, amounting to approximately 35,000 pounds sterling, we can now pay our outstanding current obligations.

A definitive instruction will follow. You may in the meantime state that we are in principle prepared to make payment. Please get in touch with the Italian Embassy in advance, however, in order to arrange a common method of procedure.

Please wait until Woermann's return before carrying out the above instruction.

WEIZSÄCKER

---

[1] Not printed (5152/E303669-74).

No. 564

1568/379607

Memorandum by the State Secretary

BERLIN, April 8, 1938.
Pol. I 889 g.

This morning I gave the Italian Chargé d'Affaires the following information:

General Franco had let us know through military—not diplomatic—channels that he would now like to suggest the withdrawal of volunteers from Spain. The war was drawing to a close. I added that the subject of the withdrawal of volunteers had already been up for discussion and the concrete suggestion Franco had just made to us was welcome. We could make good use at the present time of the withdrawal from Spain in building up our Air Force at home. We had not yet discussed the subject in detail with Franco, however, nor had we made any decisions or issued any orders on our own, but we were interested in finding out from the Italians as soon as possible what their basic stand was with regard to Franco's suggestion.

Count Magistrati promised to try to get at least a provisional reply from Rome as soon as possible.

WEIZSÄCKER

No. 565

136/73617

Memorandum by the State Secretary

BERLIN, April 8, 1938.

Former Ambassador Faupel visited me today in order to give the Foreign Ministry some advice regarding our future policy in Spain. As far as cultural relations are concerned, the enclosed French-Spanish propaganda newspaper which is now appearing is of importance.

With regard to our political contacts in Spain, Herr Faupel thought we should work with the Falange and cultivate good relations with this group just as Herr Bernhardt and he, Faupel, had done in the past.

I merely listened to Herr Faupel. My own personal opinion is that we shall not get very far with Franco by working with the Falange as long as it is anticlerical, since Franco really appears to be trying to effect a synthesis between a social and a clerical course.

To Pol. III through the Deputy Director of the Political Department.

WEIZSÄCKER

No. 566

136/73616

The Ambassador in Spain to the Foreign Ministry

Airgram

No. 195 of April 8   SALAMANCA, April 8, 1938—time not indicated.

Received April 8—11:30 p.m.

With reference to my report No. 1886 of March 31.[1]

The day before yesterday Franco made some very reassuring statements to me regarding the projected new Spanish mining law. The Finance Minister, who is also interested in the matter, did likewise. I received the impression that there will be no percentile restriction of foreign participation.

STOHRER

---

[1] Not printed (5149/E303633–40).

No. 567

586/243154

The Ambassador in Spain to the Foreign Ministry

Telegram

No. 196 of April 8   SALAMANCA, April 8, 1938.

Received April 8—11:30 p.m.

With reference to your telegraphic instruction No. 123 of April 7[1] and to my telegraphic reports Nos. 190[2] and 191[3] of April 6 and April 7.

Franco has not yet mentioned to me the questions of further employment of the Condor Legion and future peacetime military cooperation, which I also have purposely not brought up.

The ideas concerning withdrawal of the Condor Legion which Franco expounded to Admiral Canaris seem to proceed from the assumption that our matériel, particularly the planes, will remain in Spain. To judge from a chance remark by General Veith the military has no objection to this. The arrangement proposed by Franco, which, however, depends upon how the military situation develops, is therefore probably expedient.[4]

Franco evidently intends to make the same arrangement with the Italians. According to press statements, however, the demand not only for withdrawal of the Italian volunteers but also for removal

---

[1] Not printed (586/243152).
[2] Document No. 652, p. 638.
[3] Not found.
[4] Marginal note: "RM: The connection with the political balance sheet of our commitments in Spain is not mentioned in this telegram. W[eizsäcker]. [April] 9."

of the Italian matériel is said to have been made in the Anglo-Italian negotiations.

Franco's plans for later military cooperation, on the basis of the statements he made to Admiral Canaris, are unsatisfactory; however, in Canaris' opinion they do not exclude the training of a number of Spanish officers in Germany.

STOHRER

No. 568

136/73618

The State Secretary to the Embassy in Spain

TOP SECRET   BERLIN, April 8, 1938.
By courier on April 9   zu Pol. I 225 g Rs. Ang. II..

For the Ambassador personally.

I am sending you, enclosed, a Foreign Ministry draft, still known only within the Ministry, of a political treaty between Germany and Nationalist Spain.[1] For your personal information I wish to remark that it has not yet been definitely decided whether you are to be asked to negotiate with General Franco on a treaty based on the draft, since the Führer has reserved for himself the last word as to whether such a method of procedure should be followed at all. Therefore please keep the draft strictly confidential until you have received further telegraphic instructions.

WEIZSÄCKER

---

[1] Document No. 558, enclosure, p. 632.

No. 569

136/73620–22

The Ambassador in Spain to the State Secretary

VERY SECRET   SALAMANCA, April 11, 1938.

DEAR WEIZSÄCKER: Thank you very much for your letter of April 7,[1] which just arrived, together with the provisional instruction of April 8 (Pol. I 225 g Rs).

While awaiting the promised supplementary telegraphic instruction, I should like as a precautionary measure to call attention to two points:

---

[1] Not found.

1. F[ranco] will presumably inquire whether we already have definite proposals to make with regard to articles 7 and 8, and when we wish to negotiate on them.

2. In the provisional instruction nothing is said regarding the regulation of cultural-political relations.

I should be grateful if this could be taken up in the promised telegraphic instruction.

Also, upon the arrival of the final instruction there will hardly be any objection to my giving F[ranco] the draft; or should he be sounded first with regard to his basic inclination? In the latter case, please send further instructions.

In my opinion we should attempt to negotiate as soon as possible on the matters relating to articles 7 and 8 as well as on the question of cultural relations.

The moment the war ends the "general settlement" which I mentioned in my personal letter of March 31 [2] will also become acute. The more I think about it, the more it appears to me that a gesture of this kind could be useful.

Well, I hope to be able to discuss this question with you very soon, too.

In great haste, just before the courier mail is collected.

Cordial greetings and Heil Hitler.

As ever,
STOHRER

---

[2] Not found.

No. 570

1568/379608

The Deputy Director of the Political Department to the Embassy in Spain

Telegram

BERLIN, April 11, 1938.
e.o. Pol. I 894 g.

For the Ambassador personally.

The Italian Chargé d'Affaires informed me that the Italian Government had not yet received a proposal similar to the one Admiral Canaris transmitted to us with respect to the withdrawal of volunteers in Spain. As soon as it receives a similar hint from Franco it will immediately get in touch with the German Government.

BISMARCK

No. 571

F19/157

The Ambassador in Spain to the Foreign Ministry

Telegram

No. 203 of April 12   SALAMANCA, April 12, 1938—11: 30 p.m.
Received April 13—12: 45 a.m.

With reference to your telegram No. 130 of April 11 and to my telegraphic reports Nos. 196 and 198 [1] of April 8.

Please wire instructions if it is desired that I discuss the recall of volunteers at my meeting with Franco within the next few days; as I reported, I have thus far intentionally avoided doing so.

STOHRER

---

[1] Latter not printed (586/243155).

No. 572

3374/E011100

Memorandum by the State Secretary

BERLIN, April 14, 1938.
e.o. Pol. III 1251.

In the course of a conversation with me, the Spanish Ambassador today again expressed his anxiety over French military intervention on behalf of Red Spain. I told the Ambassador that I could not quite conceive of France yielding to pressure from Red Spain without British approval, but that the latter, in my opinion, was not obtainable at the present time.

WEIZSÄCKER

No. 573

1568/379634–37

Memorandum by the Ambassador to Spain

STRICTLY CONFIDENTIAL   BERLIN, April 22, 1938.
Pol. I 1080 g III.

I have just received from a reliable source the following information with regard to Spain:

1. Contact has been established between Paris and Burgos regarding the appointment of a French diplomatic agent in Nationalist Spain (after the example of England). A hint in London to the French Government that France should assure herself a share in Spain's reconstruction after the war supposedly was a contributing factor in this.

2. The dejection bordering on panic which was reported to exist in the Red Spanish zone has changed to a more optimistic view of

the military situation since about April 10 for the following reasons: first of all, the really tremendous deliveries of military supplies which Barcelona has recently received (planes, tanks, machine guns, bombs, etc., of not only Russian origin), and secondly Russia's promise to make the greatest effort with respect to further deliveries if Red Spain should continue to hold out. Stubborn resistance may therefore be expected now, particularly in Catalonia.

3. The Reds are supposed to have at the Catalonian front 40 battalions consisting of foreign volunteers (?).

4. Red Spain further expects extensive help from France (but not direct intervention), because France is convinced that a strong Nationalist Spanish Army under German leadership would constitute a serious threat to the Pyrenees border. The Red Spanish press, the radio, and the Red Spanish agents in France are directing the attention of the French public to this danger in every way possible.

Unconfirmed reports claim that the French have assembled heavy artillery at certain Pyrenees passes.

5. In a letter written by the Spanish Nationalist diplomat, Silio, who is employed in the Spanish Nationalist Mission in Paris, a statement is made to somewhat the following effect:

"In political circles in Paris it is quite generally assumed that Franco's victory is unavoidable. It is feared that an army that has such achievements to its credit as the Spanish Nationalist Army now has, when cooperating with Germany, constitutes at every moment a most serious danger to France. France is no longer at all interested in the fate of the Reds; she is thinking only of this danger for the future. For this reason the French are trying with all the means at their command to interfere with a Franco victory and to defer it. They are making all kinds of plots and maneuvers and are helping the Reds at every turn in order to injure the cause of Nationalist Spain as much as possible even at the last moment. The French have the full support of the London Government in this policy."

6. Particularly strong propaganda against Germany is being carried on by the "Basque Government" in Barcelona at the present time. It is claimed, among other things, that the Basques captured by Franco during the fighting on the northern front must perform what is virtually slave labor in the mines there in order to meet the German demands with respect to ore deliveries. The Basque propagandists have also compiled abundant material on alleged atrocities in Nationalist Spain, on arbitrary acts of destruction by German fliers, etc., and have given some of it to Mr. Churchill, who was in Paris a short time ago. (A detailed report on this Basque propaganda activity against Germany will follow.)

7. As I have already reported on various occasions, Mr. Brewer,[1] the American Ambassador accredited to Red Spain and residing in

---

[1] The American Ambassador to Spain was Claude Bowers.

St. Jean de Luz (whose grandfather was German!), continues to distinguish himself with his sympathy for the Reds. His reports are said to contain all the propaganda reports regarding conditions in Nationalist Spain and to be responsible for the reports in the American press, some of which are often hair-raising. Various diplomatic representatives of South American republics represented at St. Jean de Luz—who report quite differently—attribute to these reports the growing pressure of the United States on these republics, whereby the United States hopes to achieve the non-recognition of Franco by the South American governments.

It is stated with certainty that the automatic weapons which Red Spaniards have received in recent weeks via Bordeaux come not only from Mexico but also from the United States and that the volume of shipments from there continues to grow considerably.

STOHRER

No. 574

3359/E009612

The Chargé d'Affaires in Great Britain to the Foreign Ministry

A 1901   LONDON, April 25, 1938.
                                          Pol. III 1353.

Subject: Sir George Mounsey [1] on the Spanish question.

During my farewell visit today,[2] Sir George Mounsey made the following statements, which were evidently not improvised: It seemed to him very desirable that the losing party in Spain should receive moderate treatment. I asked him whether he was informed of any negotiations in this respect or whether the British Government wanted to do something about it. Mounsey answered both questions in the negative: It was a thankless task to give advice unasked. However, he was the more insistent on the matter itself and also pointed out how desirable it was for a permanent pacification of Spain that Catalonia, in keeping with tradition, should receive a certain kind of autonomy within Spain. He mentioned in this connection that the Duke of Alba had informed him that the Basque provinces had retained their former autonomous position since they had accepted the terms of surrender, which was entirely new to him, Mounsey. It was apparently the purpose of this talk to suggest to us that we speak with Franco on these questions.

---

[1] Assistant Under Secretary of State in the British Foreign Office.
[2] Woermann was leaving the London Embassy on appointment to the position of Director of the Political Department in the Foreign Ministry.

It seems apparent from the conversation that the British have reconciled themselves entirely to a Franco victory.

WOERMANN

No. 575

586/243168

The Ambassador in Spain to the Foreign Ministry

Telegram

No. 218 of April 27   SALAMANCA, April 27, 1938—9 : 30 p.m.

Received April 27—10 : 50 p.m.

Since it will be a few days before I can see Franco, I spoke to Foreign Minister Jordana today about the question of the time and the methods of withdrawing the Condor Legion, which he as well as the Generalissimo had discussed with Admiral Canaris. Jordana replied that, according to a very recent statement by Franco, the latter did hope to be able to count on our volunteers being permitted to stay until final victory was assured, but that he did not wish to anticipate the Generalissimo with this confidential information.

To his knowledge, the corresponding question had not yet been discussed with the Italians.

STOHRER

No. 576

309/189063

The Ambassador in Spain to the Foreign Ministry

Telegram

No. 219 of April 29   SALAMANCA, April 30, 1938—12 noon.

Received April 30—1 : 25 p.m.

With reference to my telegraphic report 203 of April 12 and to your telegraphic instruction 130 of April 11.

According to the Italian Ambassador, Franco has not spoken of the withdrawal of Italian volunteers in the last 2 weeks. Quite the contrary—about a week ago, in discussing the retirement to a rest area of the Italian units which are at present very exhausted, Franco gave my Italian colleague to understand that he intended to make further use of Italian ground troops also and by no means desired the withdrawal of the volunteers before victory was finally assured or pressure was exerted through the Non-Intervention Committee.

STOHRER

No. 577

586/243171–75

Memorandum by an Official of the Economic Policy Department

SECRET   BERLIN, April 30, 1938.

W 354 g

Subject: Settlement of our military expenditures in Spain.

I. The Führer has reserved to himself the decision on

(*a*) whether the military equipment used in Spain should be left there when the volunteers are withdrawn,

(*b*) the amount of the financial claims that should be made on the Spanish Government.

The intention, it is stated, is to coordinate our step with that of Italy and to discuss it in Rome.

In addition to its military and political significance, the question also has economic significance.

II. It had originally been intended to have Spain pay for all expenditures on a cash basis. This could not be done because German assistance went beyond the capacity of Spain to pay at once in foreign exchange and raw materials. Only a relatively insignificant portion has been paid for.

The deliveries by industry (approximately 58 million RM) have been paid for in full. They may, therefore, be disregarded.

The expenditures of the *Wehrmacht* amounted to 338 million RM on March 31, 1938. The Wehrmacht account is as follows:

135 million RM (including 1 million RM for personnel expenses incurred in Germany. The Spanish Government is currently paying the other personnel expenses). A bill for this amount has been submitted to the Spanish Government. It has acknowledged this and thus far paid 45 million RM (19 million RM thereof in foreign exchange).

203 million RM (including 52 million RM for personnel expenses). No bill has as yet been submitted for this amount, and no payment has as yet been made.

The charges for goods correspond to the value of the material at the time of shipment.

The different treatment of the two groups is explained by the fact that it was originally intended to charge Franco only for the equipment that was *turned over* to him and to defer a decision on the settlement for the equipment that remained in the hands of the German volunteer formations. This clear-cut line of differentiation could not, it is true, be adhered to entirely, but in a general way a distinction can still be made between the groups.

Of the 338 million RM, therefore, $338-45=293$ million RM are not yet paid. This amount includes 53 million RM for personnel expenses, so that 240 million RM expended for equipment still remains unpaid.

The Wehrmacht is no longer interested financially. The Finance Ministry has assumed the budgetary liability.

III. The following possibilities are open to us:

(1) The Spanish Government will be charged for all expenditures for materials and personnel.

(2) No charge will be made for supplies that went to the German volunteer units. This would mean that the sum of approximately 203 million RM would be canceled.

(3) In case the matériel is left with Franco—which the Wehrmacht is inclined to do because of the considerable depreciation in the equipment—compensation will be asked.

What this amount will be we cannot yet tell.

A large portion of this equipment is no longer recoverable (ammunition, airplanes). The remainder is worth much less than at the time of its valuation in the accounting.

This undetermined remainder which enters into consideration for a transfer can be charged as follows:

(*a*) either at its value when new, or

(*b*) at a value allowing for depreciation.

Tentative appraisal:

$$203 - 52 = 151 \text{ million } \mathbf{RM}$$
$$50\% \text{ depreciation} = 75 \text{ million } \mathbf{RM}$$
$$\text{Depreciated value} = \text{about } 40 \text{ million } \mathbf{RM}$$

IV. In deciding whether and how far we should accommodate Franco, our hands are to a certain extent tied.

Our assistance to Spain is to be compensated by deliveries of raw materials otherwise requiring foreign exchange, and by investments (secret protocol of July 16, 1937).

The compulsion to deliver raw materials decreases with the lessening of the pressure of the financial obligations.

Hisma has acquired mining rights; negotiations as to their recognition are still pending, but indications are that the outcome will be satisfactory. Franco is to make available the peseta amounts for their acquisition. He has thus far given pesetas in an amount equivalent to some 10 to 12 million RM. Hisma is claiming some 100 million RM.

The actual amounts paid, accordingly, are:

$$45 \text{ million } \mathbf{RM}$$
$$12 \text{ million } \mathbf{RM}$$
$$\overline{57 \text{ million } \mathbf{RM}}$$

If we add approximately 90 million RM more for Hisma, the result is an amount of 147 million RM.

In a settlement in accordance with **III** 3 (*b*), we should accordingly already have reached the limit below which we could make no concessions (135 plus 40 equals 175 million RM).

V. Conclusions

Our position with regard to Spain is not to be simply assimilated to that of Italy in the matter of claims for military assistance. A different treatment may therefore be justified.

(1) Italy's expenditures are greater than ours. The greater the claim, the greater is the uncertainty of recovery. Above a certain amount, cancellation is no longer a sacrifice for the creditor but only a recognition of inability to pay.

(2) In contrast to Italy, we have already disposed of a considerable portion of the claims on Spain.

We need some 100 million RM for investments and at least 100 million RM [1] as a means of enforcing *additional* deliveries of raw materials, especially of ores. A lessening of the financial pressure might endanger our supremacy in the economic field. England and France would be the gainers.

Purely from the standpoint of economic policy, payment of all expenditures should be required. In the question of interest (in the secret protocol of July 16, 1937, 4 percent is tentatively promised) we could show a cooperative attitude. Should a reduction of the capital debt be desirable for political or economic reasons (concessions in other fields), the following solution would be conceivable in the case of the deliveries by the Wehrmacht in the amount of 338 million RM as of March 31, 1938:

Germany's interest in the amount of the debt:

        100 million RM investments (10 to 12 million RM already
             made available by Franco in pesetas)
        100 million RM additional imports (by comparison: in 1937
             ores were imported for a total amount of 25 million RM)
         45 million RM already paid

approx. 250 million RM minimum interest.

Accordingly, Germany claims:

        135 million RM recognized indebtedness (first group)
         75 million RM equipment used up, replacement value (the
             203 million RM of the second group less 52 million RM
             personnel expenses, the remainder divided by two)
         40 million RM for the equipment to be left behind, with al-
             lowance for depreciation

        250 million RM

[1] Footnote in the original: "Not yet agreed with the Four Year Plan."

We would then relinquish our claim to 52 million RM for personnel expenses in Germany and 35 million RM constituting the difference between the value of new material and the depreciated value of the equipment transferred. (In round figures, 250 plus 52 plus 35 equals 337 million RM.) Spain's foreign debt to us would be only 100 million RM.

SABATH

No. 578

1568/379624

The Ambassador in Spain to the Foreign Ministry

Telegram

No. 222 of April 30   SALAMANCA, April 30, 1938—11:30 p.m.
Received May 1—1:30 a.m.
Pol. I 1045 III.

General impression concerning the present military situation:
The Spanish Nationalist advance has been halted on all fronts. This is explained by certain regroupings but above all by unfavorable weather and surprisingly increased resistance from the Reds; the latter, in turn, is to be explained by extensive deliveries of war matériel of all kinds from abroad, particularly antiaircraft guns, artillery, tanks, and ammunition. Spanish Nationalist losses have increased in the last few weeks.

STOHRER

No. 579

1568/379638–40

The Ambassador in Spain to the Foreign Ministry

SECRET   SALAMANCA, April 30, 1938.
No. 344 g   Pol. I 1089 g III.

I am enclosing a translation of a letter of April 18 from Generalissimo Franco to Italian General Berti, which General Veith placed at my disposal. The contents refer to a controversy regarding the retirement of battle-weary Italian units (see also my telegraphic report No. 219 of April 29 [1]).

Under No. 5 mention is made of the fact that the Duce has expressed the wish that the Italian troops of volunteers should "not be used north of the Ebro." Thus Mussolini went considerably farther than our recommendation not to use foreign volunteers within 10 kilometers of the French border.

STOHRER

---

[1] Document No. 576, p. 647.

[Enclosure]

Translation of Franco's Letter to General Berti

TERMINUS, April 18, 1938.

To His Excellency General Berti,
     Commander of the CTV,[1] Alcañiz.

In reply to your letter No. 753 of April 16 which has come to my attention, I wish to tell you the following:

1. I understood the Duce's directives with regard to the employment of your troops to mean that they were to be employed in a manner conducive to as speedy an ending of the war as possible.

2. Since the war is not yet at an end the inactivity of the volunteer troops would practically mean giving the enemy a whole corps and would force me to pull out another Spanish corps to man this line, and this at a time when I need the troops for operations.

I therefore cannot accept your proposal not to man the Ebro line, a line which because of the river is simply a patrol line.

3. The Ebro line which was assigned to you in accordance with order No. 10 of the Northern Army can be supplied from Morella by paths which are to be cut in the mountain spurs parallel to the Ebro and connected with the roads already there.

4. I consider one division adequate for the manning of the line, with one brigade in a second line.

The other volunteer division could be held in reserve and could rest. In this manner a change could be made every week.

5. The desire evidenced by the Duce not to use the volunteer units north of the Ebro unless absolutely necessary obliges me to leave them in a quiet sector, in which connection, however, a mission can be accomplished which will permit them at the same time to recuperate from the losses and exertion that they underwent in this brilliant campaign [*Etappe*].

6. The need for speeding up pursuit of the enemy and not to interrupt it for a minute explains why I am unable to release your corps from service entirely.

7. The stay at this front, I believe, will be very short. The course of operations will shortly eliminate this front and thereby place the CTV in general reserve.

8. The efforts made by the enemy with regard to organizing new units make us look ahead and prevent us from reducing the number of our troops.

9. Since new Spanish units are at present being trained and in view of the great losses sustained by the volunteer units, we could reduce the two divisions to one, form another with Spanish personnel, and

---

[1] Comando Troupe Volontarie.

equip the latter with matériel from the disbanded division. This could be done about the end of this month.

FRANCO

No. 580

4446/E086664

The Ambassador in Spain to the Foreign Ministry

Telegram

No. 2 of May 4 SAN SEBASTIÁN, May 4, 1938—2 : 30 p.m.
Received May 4—4 : 15 p.m.
Pol. III 1426.

The Foreign Minister confirmed to me that lately the amount of war matériel reaching Red Spain via France was really tremendous and was the only thing that made further resistance by the Reds possible; he hoped that the French Ministers had been prevailed upon in London [1] to limit deliveries of war matériel across the French frontier.

French diplomatic circles in St. Jean de Luz say that this was the case but that the French Government had to proceed carefully, one step at a time, because of the threat of a general strike.

STOHRER

---

[1] On Apr. 28–29 Daladier and Bonnet had consultations with Halifax and Chamberlain in London. For reports on this meeting, see vol. I, document No. 757, pp. 1103–1104, and vol. II, document No. 139, pp. 246–247.

No. 581

586/243182

The Ambassador in Spain to the Foreign Ministry

Telegram

VERY URGENT SAN SEBASTIÁN, May 4, 1938—9 : 30 p.m.
No. 4 of May 4 Received May 5—1 : 00 a.m.

Please transmit the following to Rome at once: [1]

"On the question of the withdrawal of the Condor Legion, Franco stated, in complete accordance with the statement of his Foreign Minister reported earlier, that he requested retention of the German volunteers for the present; it was to be expected that the Reds would continue to offer tough resistance; this would finally change into local fighting. With the beginning of 'guerrilla warfare' (not just when it was possible to speak of the beginning of police action) the time would have come when he could, without damage to his cause, dispense with the German volunteers. His statement to Admiral Canaris [2] had been prompted by the consideration that, in case of

---

[1] Because of the visit of the Führer, the Foreign Minister, and the State Secretary to Rome. See vol. I, document No. 761, pp. 1108–09.
[2] See document No. 557, p. 630.

political expediency (London committee) or political complications, we and Italy had to have a chance to reduce our Spanish operations without too great damage to the Spanish cause. He had therefore seen to it that, later on, Spanish investment capital could take over German equipment, although, as Franco repeatedly stressed, it would not be possible for them even approximately to replace the excellent German pilots."

(The change in the military situation, which is, however, favorable, thus has caused Franco to alter his view since the time he had made his statements to Canaris.) To the Italians, Franco stated that he entertained the same view; because of recent great Italian losses and the removal of the exhausted troops, to be sure, a single division was now being formed out of the two Italian divisions comprising 25 battalions, which meant a reduction of the Italian ground troops by about one-third.

Franco promised to inform us in due time and quite frankly when he believed that, from his standpoint, withdrawal of the Condor Legion could begin.

STOHRER

No. 582

136/73624

The Ambassador in Spain to the Foreign Ministry

Telegram

VERY URGENT   SAN SEBASTIÁN, May 4, 1938—11 : 30 p.m.
No. 6 of May 4   Received May 5—2 : 00 a.m.

Please transmit the following to Rome at once :

"In a long talk today I explained to Franco, as instructed, our stand as to the nature of future German-Spanish relations and informed him of our intention to conclude an agreement with Spain accordingly. Referring to the provisions of the German-Spanish secret protocol of March 20, 1937, and handing him a short memorandum, I discussed with Franco in detail various points in the new agreement which we contemplate.

"Franco agreed entirely. He authorized me to negotiate with the Foreign Minister on the basis desired by us and, above all, to initiate immediately discussions regarding a cultural agreement. I informed the Foreign Minister of the result of the conversation at once. Further details will follow by letter."

Please instruct me whether or not to enter into negotiations and whether to communicate the substance of article 4 of our draft agreement (consultation with Italy).[1] I also request instructions as to the extent to which I may inform the Italian Chargé d'Affaires.

Very secret: To the question that I asked only casually, in accordance with instructions, whether the accession of Spain to the Anti-

---

[1] See document No. 558, enclosure, p. 633.

Comintern Pact was not desirable, Franco stated that in practice he was really pursuing a very vigorous anti-Comintern policy already; accession to the pact was probably impractical while the war lasted, since otherwise a strong reaction was to be expected from England, who—he knew for a fact—had by threats prevented Portugal and Greece from adhering to the Anti-Comintern Pact. After the war, however, he would consider accession.

The total impression was very favorable. The atmosphere was one of mutual confidence and friendship.

STOHRER

No. 583

136/73628

The State Secretary to the Foreign Ministry

Telegram

No. 5 of May 7   ROME, May 7, 1938—8 : 00 p.m.
Received May 7—11 : 40 p.m.

With reference to your telegram No. 151 of May 5.[1]

Please authorize Ambassador von Stohrer to commence negotiations now. The article in our draft treaty with regard to consultation with Italy may likewise be brought up and the Spanish reaction to it ascertained. Regarding the basic outline of the intended German agreement with Spain, the Foreign Minister has informed Ciano here orally. Stohrer may inform the Italian Chargé d'Affaires in the same measure without, however, giving him the draft agreement or telling him all the details.

WEIZSÄCKER

---

[1] Transmitting the contents of telegram No. 6 of May 4 from San Sebastián, document No. 582, *supra*.

No. 584

586/243191

Memorandum by the State Secretary

BERLIN, May 12, 1938.

The Spanish Ambassador spoke to me with some anxiety today regarding the rumor that Germany was considering withdrawing her volunteers from Spain.

I told the Ambassador that we had not been considering such a move of our own accord. In view of the rapid progress of the Spanish offensive a few weeks ago, however, Generalissimo Franco had dropped a hint to Admiral Canaris regarding the withdrawal of our volunteers. Naturally we were not thinking of leaving the volunteers in Spain any longer than they were urgently needed there. Since the Franco-

Canaris conversation, Herr von Stohrer had heard from Franco himself that the latter was still absolutely counting on the volunteers until the conclusion of the actual military action and its transition into a police action. Franco had told Stohrer that he would inform him frankly at the proper time regarding his view as to the opportuneness of our withdrawing from Spain.

Señor Magaz showed his satisfaction with the information I had given him.

WEIZSÄCKER

No. 585

3374/E011128–29

The Ambassador in the United States to the Foreign Ministry

No. 853   WASHINGTON, D.C., May 16, 1938.
                                                 Pol. III 1650.
With reference to previous reports.

Subject: Lifting of the arms embargo against both parties in the Spanish Civil War.

Within the scope of the most recent move to lift the arms embargo against the Red Spanish Government, the enclosed bill [1] for lifting the embargo and amending the neutrality act was introduced by Senator Nye [2] on May 3. Senator Pittman, the Chairman of the Foreign Relations Committee of the Senate,[3] before submitting it for open debate, sent the bill to Secretary of State Hull with a request for his opinion. The Secretary of State waited until the President's return before giving his opinion and has now made it known in the form of a letter of reply to Senator Pittman. The reply is a flat *no* to Nye and his supporters with respect to the lifting of the embargo. As to the amending of the neutrality act, which is considered inevitable by ever-growing sectors of the American public, Mr. Hull simply said in his reply that the question was too serious to be discussed profitably in the closing weeks of this session of the Congress. I am also enclosing the text of the letter.[4]

At the recommendation of Hull, the Senate Foreign Relations Committee with unusual speed (17 votes to 1) postponed consideration of the Nye resolution for an indefinite time. The fate of the resolution is thereby sealed.

This development shows that the Administration is still not inclined to take a step which, as it was planned, would have benefited only the Red Spanish Government—though perhaps only in the

---

[1] Not reprinted.
[2] Senator Gerald Nye, Republican, of North Dakota.
[3] Senator Key Pittman, Democrat, of Nevada.
[4] For text of this letter see *Peace and War: United States Foreign Policy, 1931–1941* (United States Government Printing Office, Washington, 1943), pp. 419–420.

form of moral support. Decisive for the attitude of the Administration on this question is the British attitude; strong internal political factors to which I have repeatedly referred in my reports on this matter also play a considerable role.

DIECKHOFF

No. 586

3206/697774–85

The Ambassador in Spain to the Foreign Ministry

STRICTLY CONFIDENTIAL   SAN SEBASTIÁN, May 19, 1938.
No. 367 g   Pol. III 1691.
Subject: The political situation in Nationalist Spain.

When military reverses occur internal political differences come to the fore.

Every time a military reverse or even a stalemate occurs in the military operations of Nationalist Spain, the same phenomenon appears again and again; the optimistic appraisal of the situation and the confidence in victory change to the opposite, giving way to deep disappointment, great mental depression and dissatisfaction, and allowing the internal political differences to come more strongly to the fore.

This phenomenon is now also appearing in the course of the present slowdown in the military operations.

This has been experienced once more since the brilliant advance of Franco's troops to the Mediterranean has more or less come to a halt and the collapse of the Reds, which many had been expecting, has not occurred.

Unity and solidarity are still lacking in Nationalist Spain. 40 percent of the population are still politically unreliable. The consequences thereof: Regime not endangered, however.

Such phenomena clearly show that Nationalist Spain still lacks unity and solidarity in many respects. As early as my memorandum of October 1937 concerning my first impressions in Spain,[1] I called attention to the fact that persons who know the situation well estimate the number of politically unreliable people in White Spain at about 40 percent. This fact is emphasized by a number of assassinations, on some of which I have made separate brief reports; attempts to destroy bridges; accidents in powder magazines; acts of incendiarism; and the guerrilla fighting still in evidence in southern Spain (Cáceres) but especially in Asturias. Severe reprisals—which naturally produce counteraction, however—have prevented these events

---

[1] Document No. 455, p. 480.

from assuming dimensions which could be dangerous to the security of the regime and have succeeded in preventing the strong and constantly growing propaganda of the Red Spanish rulers and particularly of the Basques, mentioned at various times in my reports, from having any substantial success in Nationalist territory.

Lack of unity often exists even among the elements well disposed toward the regime.   Spanish individualism.

On the other hand, however, the length of the war and the fading of hope for peace in the near future due to the slowdown in war operations have again brought to the fore controversies among the elements who are unquestionably well disposed toward the regime.   The Unity Party created by the Generalissimo is today still far from having a uniform direction and uniform aims.   Moreover, the strongly individualistic character of the Spaniard tends very particularly toward criticism which is often very outspoken, toward particularism and advocacy of the view that only he, or he and some of his friends or, at the most, his particular party comrades, are right in political affairs. The result is that, although the war and the needs of the hour require unity in political action, one can hear quite different opinions on this or that problem even in military and governmental circles.

Generals in politics: The strongly critical speech of General Yagüe. Franco's reaction to this "lack of discipline."

The speech which General Yagüe, noted and able leader of the Moroccan Corps, made in Burgos on April 19 at the celebration of the anniversary of the establishment of the Unity Party threw an interesting light on these conditions.   In his speech, excellent in itself, which only a few newspapers were able to publish (apparently in a milder form), the General expressed his ideas concerning the comprehensive social reforms which he considered necessary, the need for an honest and incorruptible administration of justice, patriotism which is always ready for sacrifices, Christian charity and Spanish chivalry, with a frankness and a critical attitude which were at the very least inconvenient for the present Government.   In particular, it was felt that the parts of his speech in which he gave free recognition to the bravery of the Red Spanish opponents, defended the political prisoners—both the Reds and the "Blues" (Falangists), who were arrested because of too much political zeal—and severely attacked the partiality of the administration of justice, went beyond his authority and represented a lack of discipline; the answer was his recall from his command, at least temporarily.   Although the rumors that General Yagüe has been arrested have proved to be untrue, it does seem to be the case that he was ordered to remain at the disposal of the Generalissimo in Burgos or in the vicinity of the city until further notice. It cannot be ascertained at the moment whether this incident will be followed by a court martial.

Differences between Franco on the one hand and Yagüe and Queipo de Llano on the other are not serious for the time being but are noteworthy as a symptom.

If the antagonism between Franco and the "Falange's General," Yagüe, which was brought out once before in the past, has thus entered an acute stage, it is not surprising that there is again talk of disagreements between the Generalissimo and the "social General," Queipo de Llano, in Seville. I consider the Yagüe incident and the fundamental differences between Franco and Queipo de Llano, which undoubtedly exist, as by no means serious at the present time; these events, however, do show that the spirit from which the typically Spanish *pronunciamientos* originate has not yet been destroyed, and that in this respect surprises are not impossible if the fortunes of war should prove capricious or if after the war internal political and social antagonisms should clash.

Franco has wisely understood how to straighten out differences within the Unity Party and to preserve his authority. In view of conflicting opinions concerning Franco's position with regard to Falange, Requetés, Monarchy, and Church, it is difficult to evaluate Franco's actual commitments and aims.

Moreover, Franco has undoubtedly succeeded in preserving his authority up to this time. As I brought out in my memorandum on "The *de facto* and *de jure* relations between Germany and Nationalist Spain" in February,[2] he has very cleverly succeeded, with the advice of his brother-in-law, Minister of the Interior Serrano Suñer, in not making enemies of any of the parties represented in the Unity Party which were previously independent and hostile to one another—particularly the old (original) Falange and the Requetés—but, on the other hand, also in not favoring any one which might thus grow too strong. When shortly after the formation of the Government (report No. 257 g of February 17, 1938 [3]) the dissatisfaction of the original Falange concerning appointments in certain ministries—particularly the Foreign Ministry—became very evident, the matter was immediately settled in compromise form by Franco or Serrano Suñer, by having important positions in the latter's Ministry, particularly in the press and propaganda departments, occupied by very aggressive Falangists—who, to be sure, are also intimate friends of Serrano Suñer. There are other examples of thoughtful arrangements of a

[2] Document No. 529, p. 590.
[3] Not printed (4446/E086631–32).

similar nature. It is therefore comprehensible that, depending on
the party allegiance of the person concerned, one is just as apt to
hear the opinion in Spain that "Franco is entirely a creature of the
Falange," as that "Franco has sold himself completely to the reaction," or "Franco is a pure monarchist," or "he is completely under
the influence of the Church." Under these circumstances it is not
easy to form an unbiased opinion as to the actual strength of the commitments of Franco and his Government with these forces.

*It is certain, however, that the influence of the Church has increased
immensely in the last few months. Proof: Readmission of the
Jesuit Order . . . which is welcomed by public opinion . . .
but disapproved by the Falange.*

Probably only one thing is certain as matters now stand, and that
is that under the present regime the influence of the Catholic Church
in Nationalist Spain has greatly increased in the last few months. A
proof of this that is publicly evident is the release of the decree,
mentioned in report No. 2544 of May 5, 1938,[4] according to which
the Society of Jesus is again permitted in Spain, its former rights
have been restored, and it is given a position, through recognition of
the Society as a legal entity, which it did not possess even under the
monarchy. The newspapers report that the responsible Minister of
Justice, Conde de Rodezno, who is from the ranks of the Requetés,
received countless congratulations from all parts of the country because of this decree, on the significance of which I reserve a further
report; the press controlled by Minister of the Interior Serrano
Suñer, who is well known as an ardently religious man, commented
throughout in the same way. But it is none the less certain that the
readmission of the Jesuits in Spain meets with great disapproval in
the ranks of the Falange.

Prospects for forming a separate State Church have diminished.

Apart from this sharp change in the Church policy of Nationalist
Spain, to which the Vatican has replied by dispatching a nuncio,
there is such a plethora of lesser observations and phenomena that
one is forced to draw the conclusion that a victory of the Catholic
Church and its influence is assured, and that the reactionary forces
in Spain have thus been strengthened. This is not to say, however,
that the strong demand of the original Falange, that Spain should
create a Catholic State Church of her own, has become entirely un-
realizable; but the prospects for attaining this end have without doubt
greatly diminished because of the development described above.

---

[4] Not printed (5157/E303713).

Church influence in the entourage of Franco.

It is certain that the Vatican is attempting to exert a strong influence on Franco's entourage, and thus on the Generalissimo himself, and this is strongly underscored by the above-mentioned restoration of the rights of the Jesuit Order. The Spanish Dominicans—Padre Menéndez Reigada, who belongs to this order, is one of the Generalissimo's advisers—and other churchmen, among others the Apostolic Administrator of the Basque diocese, Monsignor Luzurika (who, by the way, is considered an enemy of the Jews and the Freemasons), have access to the very pious family of the Generalissimo and have the possibility of exerting a strong influence there. The religious atmosphere of Franco's house is clearly characterized by the recent solemn initiation of the young daughter of the Generalissimo into a Catholic youth organization of the Falange.

Franco is nevertheless an honest supporter of the basic principles of the Falange. He must take account of other tendencies, however.

As regards Franco's attitude toward the Falange, after taking due account of the many contradictory reports which come to me I nevertheless adhere to the opinion which I have expressed in the past: that Franco is entirely serious in recognizing and defending the basic principles of the Falangist program but that in consideration of the very strong position in certain parts of Spain of the Requetés and of conservative and monarchist organizations close to them, as well as of the wishes of the Church, he considers it advisable to proceed slowly with regard to the extent and tempo of the reforms. When occasional statements by Franco, as in his speech on the anniversary of the founding of the Unity Party on April 19, 1938 (report No. 2268 of April 21[5]), or the measures taken against Yagüe, are interpreted as indicating that he meant to renounce the original Falange, in my opinion this is going much too far.

At the moment one cannot speak of either victory of reaction or victory of the Falange.

Thus there can be just as little question of a victory by the reaction at the present time as of the opposite extreme, that is, that the original Falange has won out—although one might incline to this supposition after superficial observation, considering the work which it is performing with confidence and enthusiasm, the greater prominence of the Falange organizations, and the speeches of their leaders.

---

[5] Not printed (5159/E303735-37).

The success of a pacification of the country will depend on whether sufficient reforms are carried through.

The most important question for further developments in Spain after the war is probably the following: Will it be possible, in spite of the very considerable obstructing forces, as described above, to carry through social reforms in Spain to such a degree that, as a result of obvious improvement of the situation of the working classes, the unreliable elements who are inimical to or at least distrustful of the new Spain—certainly much more than 40 percent of the total population after conquest of the remaining Red territory—can be won for the new state?

Possibilities of conflict on this question after the war. There is danger that the Falange will become more radical, since the social aims of the Red Spaniards resemble the aims of the Falange.

Since the Falange, that is, the original Falange, constantly emphasizes its resolve to carry through these reforms, this provides a greater possibility of conflict in the period after the end of the war. There is some cause for alarm in the fact that the social program of the Falange is essentially not at all far removed from the demands which THE MORE MODERATE circles in Red Spain have advanced (cf. report No. 242 g of January 31, 1938,[6] for Prieto's efforts, based on this fact, to lure the Falange away from Franco). A Falangist who has an official position with the Government and incidentally comes from a very conservative family once told me that he had many more points of contact with the Reds in the other zone than with the clerical and reactionary circles here. In case the reaction should become greater after the war, therefore, it is not impossible that the Falange might become increasingly radical; this would greatly endanger Franco and possibly push him toward the path of military dictatorship. The Caudillo will thus have need of great skill in order to reconcile these opposing factors to some extent after the victorious conclusion of the war.

The question of a restoration of the monarchy. Summoning of the Infante Juan possible. Franco's role in this question.

As regards the question of the monarchy, the Spanish people continue to be very divided, as in the past. Persons who are acquainted with conditions—as I have previously reported—believe that a plebiscite at this time would show a majority against the monarchy.

---

[6] Not printed (1557/377775–80).

Considering the strong forces which are for a monarchy, however, namely, the Church, the Requetés, the other monarchist organizations in Spain, and the objectives of foreign countries (Italy, England), it can be considered certain that after the end of the war the monarchists will gain many adherents. I therefore believe it very possible that there might be a restoration, with the third son of former King Alfonso XIII, the Infante Don Juan, summoned to the Spanish throne. If, as is to be hoped, Franco emerges from the war with greater strength, and if he succeeds in mastering the initial domestic political difficulties referred to above, which he will certainly not be spared, he will have it in his power to decide this question. It is generally considered true that Franco is very seriously considering a restoration of the monarchy. The statements he made to me on the question of the monarchy, which I reported at the time (see report No. 142 g of September 30, 1937 [7]), at least do not contradict this view.

The conclusions which we should draw from the present situation: 1. Continued adherence to non-intervention in Spanish domestic affairs. 2. Discretion in our ideologically justified inclination toward the Falange. 3. Maintenance of contact with other parties, also. A return for the sacrifices we have made for Spain?

If the above description of the present situation and probable future developments is accurate, it naturally follows that it is advisable for us to adhere strictly to the same policy of non-intervention in Spanish domestic affairs which we have followed in Spain in the past. At the end of the war the German interests in Spain will best be served if we do not emphasize politically our ideologically justified inclination toward the original Falange and its demands to such an extent that this attitude brings us into opposition with the other forces in question—as interested parties are already attempting to do—and prevents us from keeping in contact with them, also. Only in this way shall we be able to possess a sufficient foothold in Spain under any one of the possible final solutions in order to secure for the future some return, even if not in full, for the sacrifices which we have made for Spain. Perhaps we should already insure this return by means of negotiations with Spain.[8]

v. STOHRER

---

[7] Not printed (3206/697735–37).

[8] The italic subheadings in this and several subsequent reports from San Sebastián appear in the margin of the original documents as summaries supplied by Stohrer.

No. 587

136/73629–33

The Ambassador in Spain to the Foreign Ministry

SECRET   SAN SEBASTIÁN, May 19, 1938.
No. 369 g   Pol. I 396 g Rs.

Subject: Negotiations regarding conclusion of a German-Spanish agreement.

With reference to our report No. 2571 of May 13, 1938.[1]

The Foreign Minister, General Jordana, asked me to call on him today in order to tell me that the Generalissimo and he, after thorough discussion of the draft of a German-Spanish agreement which we had delivered, considered it necessary to make two objections, which—he wished it understood at once—were not of a substantive but only of a formal nature. Against the content itself—subject to a review, probably in the main only of an editorial nature—there were no objections, particularly since the draft agreement contained nothing substantially different from the protocol of March 20, 1937.

First of all, the Generalissimo and he were of the opinion that the agreement—like the earlier protocol—should remain secret; if, however, the form proposed by us of a regular treaty between states were chosen, it was inevitable that a rather large number of people should learn of it and that at least the fact that a treaty was concluded between Germany and Spain would then become generally known. It was then inevitable that false and exaggerated rumors regarding the content and purport of this agreement should be circulated, which, in his opinion, would necessarily be undesirable for both contracting parties at present.

The second objection, the Foreign Minister stated, referred to the time for the conclusion of the agreement. He could tell me in strict confidence that the Spanish Government had the impression that England was on the point of considering a more positive *rapprochement* with Nationalist Spain. The British Government had given the Duke of Alba to understand that it was endeavoring to have the French border closed to shipments of war matériel to the Reds. It had even urged that the Spanish Nationalist Government use its influence with Mussolini to get him to take a stiffer attitude toward France and that it suggest to him that he for his part demand in Paris the closing of the French border. The part of Mussolini's speech at

---

[1] Not found.

Genoa referring to French-Italian relations,[2] as well as the report broadcast over the radio tonight that Mussolini had stated that he did not wish to continue the French-Italian conversations so long as deliveries of matériel to the Reds across the French border continued, seemed to him to be a result of this step. He was very grateful, moreover, that, according to newspaper reports, the German Government also, through its Ambassador in London, had made similar representations. Therefore the present time was perhaps a very important turning point in the Spanish Civil War, for an actual closing of the French border meant that the Reds would soon have to lay down their arms. To undertake anything at all precisely at this difficult moment that might be disquieting to one of the powers concerned, particularly England, seemed to the Generalissimo and him dangerous. Through rumors, however inaccurate, regarding alleged German-Spanish agreements, the atmosphere, which was at present very promising, might be irreparably troubled. A few weeks ago he would still have had no objection to the conclusion of the agreement proposed by us— though perhaps not in the form of a regular treaty—and it was possible that the objections raised would soon be pointless again, but just now they seemed to him very worthy of consideration.

The Foreign Minister stated further that these objections, frankly expressed to me, were by no means to be taken as a rejection of the official treaty proposed by us. Such a thing, in view of the mutual trust that characterized German-Spanish relations—for which the Spanish were very grateful—was out of the question. He was asking me, rather, to submit to my Government for its opinion the views which he expressed. Since we, too, were surely interested in an early end of the Spanish Civil War, he thought that we would have understanding for Spain's present situation, which had just been explained to me in complete confidence. He requested me urgently, however— Jordana repeated this several times—so to word my report about our conversation as to avoid under all circumstances giving the impression that possibly the Spanish Government had suddenly changed its mind and had objections to make to the conclusion of the agreement contemplated by us as such. This was by no means the case as was evident from the very fact that Spain of course adhered fully to the

---

[2] In his speech at Genoa on May 14, 1938, Mussolini had stated that he did not know whether French-Italian negotiations which were in progress would reach a conclusion since in the Spanish war the two countries were on opposite sides of the barricades. For extracts from Mussolini's Genoa speech see *Documents on International Affairs, 1938*, vol. I, pp. 239–241, and for the report by the German Ambassador in Italy on the speech, see vol. I of this series, document No. 764, pp. 1112–1114.

protocol of March 20, 1937, and that the new agreement by no means contained anything essentially new.

I tried to overcome Jordana's objections with regard to the impossibility of keeping the conclusion of this agreement secret by explaining to him that, according to his own statements, only he and the Political Chief of the Ministry, aside from the Generalissimo, at present knew anything of this intention, and that on our side, too, only very few officials knew of it. To this he replied that in Spain an official agreement had to be submitted for decision to the Council of Ministers under any circumstances and, according to the new decrees regarding the competency of the Falange, also to Party officials. It was therefore practically impossible to guarantee absolute secrecy.

In order to discover whether the question of maintaining secrecy as to the agreement, which Jordana repeatedly stressed, was really at the bottom of the reasons now given against concluding the agreement and also of the change in the attitude of the Generalissimo and the Foreign Minister—emphasizing that I naturally spoke quite unofficially—I raised the question whether, under these circumstances, the agreement proposed by us could not perhaps again be concluded in the form of a secret "protocol." General Jordana eagerly assented to the idea and declared that this would surely facilitate the matter very much.

I do not have the impression that either Franco or Jordana has suddenly conceived any substantive objections to the agreement proposed by us or to parts of it, but that they fear, for the reasons alleged by Jordana and perhaps also for other reasons at present not easily discernible, that by the conclusion of an agreement with us which would necessarily become known they would disturb their present political circles. Perhaps, in view of Mussolini's strong support of Nationalist Spain, consideration for Italy plays a part. An argument in favor of this assumption is the interest shown by the Foreign Minister at the last conference (mentioned in the previous report) with respect to the question of informing Italy.

Should we not wish to adhere unconditionally to the form of agreement proposed by us, we might perhaps again try to conclude the agreement in the form of a secret "protocol" or have the new or redrafted points signed by means of a secret "supplementary protocol."

Please send me instructions—by telegram if possible—as to my future attitude.

STOHRER

No. 588

136/73635

The Ambassador in Spain to the Foreign Ministry

Telegram

URGENT SAN SEBASTIÁN, May 31, 1938—2 : 15 p.m.
No. 40 of May 31 Received May 31—3 : 45 p.m.

With reference to our No. 30 of May 25 [1] and to telegraphic instruction No. 182 of May 30.[2]

The Foreign Minister has replied to my personal letter (report No. 2749 of May 27 [3]) that my views were being taken into account in the formulation of the law, but that an announcement of the contents could not be made until after the text had been decided on and approved by the Generalissimo. The Minister of Commerce informs me that it will take another two or three days to complete the law and that Jordana will then inform me of its contents.

So far Hisma has also been unable to find out more about the contents, other than that, as already reported, there will probably be a limitation of foreign participation to 25 percent, although with exceptions.

I have requested an immediate audience with the Generalissimo in order to make the authorized *démarche* and have told the Foreign Minister that I expect that until that time no final decisions will be made.

The *démarche* with the Spanish Ambassador in Berlin must be made at once in order still to exert an influence on the final text of the law.

STOHRER

[1] Not printed (2946/576227).
[2] Not printed (2946/576228).
[3] Not printed (5149/E303641–44).

No. 589

3204/697617

The Ambassador in Spain to the Foreign Ministry

Telegram

URGENT SAN SEBASTIÁN, May 31, 1938.
No. 41 of May 31 Received May 31—9 : 30 p.m.

With reference to my reports Nos. 369 g of December 22 [*May 19*] [1] and 380 g of May 27 [2] and in connection with our telegram No. 40 of today.

I might wish to use the opportunity of the impending discussion of the Montana project with the Generalissimo in order to ask Franco

[1] Document No. 587, p. 664.
[2] Not found.

about the changed attitude of the Spanish Government in the question of concluding a political treaty. Please wire instructions as soon as possible as to whether we could agree to concluding a secret protocol or a supplementary protocol instead of a solemn treaty.

STOHRER

No. 590

136/73634

The Foreign Minister to the Embassy in Spain

[Telegram]

SECRET   BERLIN, May 31, 1938.
No. 183   Pol. I 396 g Rs.

For the Ambassador personally.

With reference to your report No. 369 g of May 19.

Since the Spanish Nationalist Government objects to the draft agreement at the present time, we do not want to give the impression that we had greater interest in concluding it than the Spaniards. Our objective in offering the agreement would not be attained if the agreement were concluded and kept permanently secret, nor if a secret protocol were concluded which was not sufficiently different from the protocol of March 20, 1937, to justify the signing of a new document. Therefore please do not force matters but continue to pursue the idea of concluding the agreement at an opportune time.

RIBBENTROP

No. 591

322/193662–65

Memorandum [1]

BERLIN, June 1, 1938.

1) The secret protocol of July 12,[2] 1937, provides:

"The Spanish Nationalist Government will facilitate as far as possible the establishment of Spanish companies for the opening up and economic utilization of mineral resources and other raw materials and for other economic purposes serving the general welfare, under participation of German citizens or German firms as compatible with the general stipulations of Spanish law."

---

[1] This memorandum, which was initialed by Kreutzwald and Wiehl, provided an outline of the arguments used by Weizsäcker in a talk with the Spanish Ambassador on June 1 (136/73637), when he also handed the Ambassador the aide-mémoire printed here as an enclosure. On June 9 he again saw the Ambassador, who said that the British interest in the Rio Tinto mines would also be limited by Franco's government and hinted that this action might be turned to Germany's benefit. Weizsäcker noted that the Ambassador's statement was otherwise not very satisfactory (136/73640).

[2] The passage quoted is from the secret protocol of July 16, 1937.

2) Hisma (Montana in Bilbao) claims about 80 mining concessions in Spanish Nationalist territory, for the acquisition of which it used peseta funds amounting to about 10 million RM which it obtained for special services. In all, about 100 million RM are said to have been invested.

3) On October 9, 1937, a decree was issued which, among other things, declares all mining rights acquired after July 18, 1936, to be null and void.[3]

4) We made repeated representations against the application of this decree to Montana, and these led to assurances by General Franco and other persons in authority that the interests of Hisma were to be safeguarded.

5) Regarding the legality of the acquisition of the mining concessions the Embassy in January submitted a memorandum to the Spanish Government.[4]

6) From a conversation of Ambassador von Stohrer with the Spanish Minister of Commerce last February[5] it appeared that the Spaniards are hesitant to permit foreign companies a 100 percent interest in companies engaged in mining. The Spaniards would like to permit only an interest of less than 50 percent. Hisma believed nevertheless that it could obtain a 100 percent ownership in some mines.

7) Last March the Minister of Commerce was instructed to draft a new mining law to replace the decree of October 9, 1937. In this connection, too, reassuring promises were made by General Franco and the Minister of Finance.

8) According to a recent report Hisma does not insist on a 100 percent interest, because it recognizes the right of the state to dispose of mineral resources. The 100 percent interest of the British in Rio Tinto has always been very annoying to the Spaniards. If the 100 percent interest of the British in Rio Tinto should be recognized, however, Hisma likewise would want 100 percent interest in certain mining rights. Hisma would also like the new mining law to fix no definite quotas for foreign ownership.

[Enclosure]

AIDE-MÉMOIRE

BERLIN, June 1, 1938.

On October 9, 1937, the Spanish Government issued a mining decree, which, among other things, declared that all mining rights acquired since July 18, 1936, were null and void. The decree aroused the fear

---

[3] Document No. 435, p. 457.
[4] See documents Nos. 508 and 510, pp. 567 and 571.
[5] See document No. 532, p. 601.

that it might prejudice the rights acquired by Hisma (Montana) and not conform to the provisions of the German-Spanish secret protocol of July 12 [*16*], 1937. These misgivings were later confirmed by the regulations in the Spanish Finance Minister's decree of April 29. The German fears were repeatedly communicated to the Spanish Government—among others, to His Excellency, the Chief of State, Generalissimo Franco, by the German Ambassador personally. Franco promised that the rights acquired by Hisma (Montana) would be examined and that German interests would be fully taken into account in the contemplated new mining law. The new law is to be completed soon. Though it fully understands the national interests of Spain that must be protected in the new mining law, the German Government, which desires economic cooperation in the interest of both parties, hopes that the new law will recognize the great importance of German-Spanish cooperation and will give the rightful German interests full consideration.

No. 592

586/243220–22

Memorandum by an Official of Political Division I

BERLIN, June 2, 1938.

General Keitel asked me to call on him today so that he could make the following statement for transmittal to the State Secretary:

He had recently reported to the Führer and Chancellor that from the military point of view the situation of the Condor Legion in Spain required a decision. Either we should decide to leave it there longer, in which case we should give it replacements for the constant loss of matériel; or, if we did not intend to do this, we should consider an early withdrawal of the Condor Legion from the battlefront, because it could not be expected to continue fighting with inadequate matériel (wear on airplanes, wearing out of gun barrels). The Führer agreed that from the military point of view a decision should be made and stated that he was prepared to make a decision. It was necessary, however, to find out what the intentions of the Italians were in this matter. General Keitel might get in touch with Foreign Minister von Ribbentrop in this matter.

General Keitel explained on this occasion that the military were not entirely clear about the intentions of the Italians. According to the reports available there were between 20,000 and 25,000 infantry and artillery troops in Spain. In addition there were about 7,000 flight personnel and ground personnel, so that one might reckon approximately 30,000 men. According to a recent report of Colonel von

Rintelen, the Military Attaché in Rome, numerous return transports from Spain were lately to be noted, while there were no corresponding embarkations to Spain.

On June 1 General Keitel discussed with the Foreign Minister the question of leaving the Condor Legion in Spain.

General Keitel remarked further that he was very worried about the fate of the German airplane crews which had been in Red captivity for many weeks, and that he had therefore requested the Foreign Minister to take vigorous action once more for success of the exchange negotiations. The Foreign Minister had promised to do this.[1]

$\cdot$ $\cdot$ $\cdot$ $\cdot$ $\cdot$ $\cdot$ $\cdot$ $\cdot$

HEYDEN-RYNSCH

---

[1] The remaining paragraph of this document is concerned with the question of the return of German military advisers from China. See vol. I, ch. IV.

No. 593

586/243214–19

Memorandum by the State Secretary

BERLIN, June 4, 1938.

The enclosed description of the military situation in Spain is submitted to the Foreign Minister for his attention.

According to this account by an expert we probably must expect a continuation of the Spanish Civil War into the winter. Franco, as is well known, had requested that our volunteers be left with him till the conclusion of the military action and be withdrawn only when police action began. Obviously this time is still remote. Both our volunteers and the Italian fliers and technicians are still very important to Franco militarily; at most the Italian infantry might be regarded as superfluous.

Under these circumstances the withdrawal of our own and the Italian volunteers at the present time would be interpreted by Franco and also by the world outside as a political retreat and would give an undue lift to the cause of the Reds. I should therefore like to recommend that for the time being the German-Italian military effort in Spain be maintained at approximately the level of the present nominal figure, with replacements for gaps—in matériel, too—which have arisen. An agreement to that effect should be made with the Italians. With the cooperation of Franco, the non-intervention policy should be conducted in such a way that for the time being there will be no withdrawal.

WEIZSÄCKER

[Enclosure]

ABSTRACT OF THE REPORT BY COLONEL JÄNICKE OF THE GENERAL STAFF,
SPECIAL STAFF W, ON THE MILITARY SITUATION IN SPAIN, GIVEN
ON JUNE 3, 1938, BEFORE THE STATE SECRETARY

BERLIN, June 3, 1938.

1) The military situation on the southern front. After Franco's
troops had succeeded in breaking through to the sea, their first need
was to obtain a more favorable position in view of the poor rear communications of their lines facing Valencia. The extremely difficult
fighting in the impassable mountain terrain had been hampered still
further by a very long period of bad weather. Still it was to be
noted that Franco, with about three corps against six Red Spanish
corps, which, furthermore, occupied well-consolidated positions, was
now advancing several kilometers a day, so that continued progress
of the attack was to be expected. The Reds had concentrated all
available reserves of troops and munitions in this sector of the front.
A lack of matériel was already making itself noticeable, as not enough
supplies were being brought in from Catalonia. The next goal of
the White attack would be to reach Sagunto along the main highway
leading southward from Teruel. Then, according to the reports so
far available, the plan was to turn westward and, with a simultaneous
thrust from Toledo, cut off Madrid completely. It was further intended to close the great Ciudad Real arc by a corresponding operation from Toledo and Córdoba and thereby obtain possession of the
valuable mining regions, especially Almadén. In this connection
reference was made to the passivity of General Queipo de Llano's
group, which was dictated by internal political considerations.

Colonel Jänicke expressed the opinion that the planned operations would in the course of time undoubtedly lead to victory but
that, unless a so-called Abyssinian miracle should occur, a long duration would still have to be expected.

2) With regard to the situation on the eastern front it could be
said that, with sufficient forces and bridgeheads on the Ebro and
Rio Segre sector, the Whites had obtained a good jumping-off position. After the initial feeling of panic the Reds had recovered and
reorganized under the leadership of the French Communist Deputy,
Marty, and had strongly fortified the Catalonian sector. Every
arms smuggler in the world was now bringing arms and munitions
of every conceivable type into Catalonia. In the recent attacks of
the Reds on the bridgeheads of the Whites it had been shown that
the Reds had at their disposal an unusually large amount of matériel and numerically strong bodies of troops as well, but probably
because of lack of officers and insufficient training the fighting qual-

ity of the troops was no longer being maintained at the desired level and was obviously beginning to deteriorate. At any rate the Reds had suffered very bloody losses in the attacks on the eastern front without having obtained any noteworthy successes.

Colonel Jänicke expressed the opinion that Franco probably hesitated to tackle the problem of Catalonia militarily and probably intended to undertake a complete mopping-up in the south before being able to attack here with his combined forces.

3) Regarding the employment of the Condor Legion, Colonel Jänicke expressed the view that its military value for Franco was still extremely great—greater proportionately than its numerical ratio to the entire air force at his disposal. Colonel Jänicke emphasized that from the military point of view the Condor Legion was already in such a position that the only choice was either a fresh supply of matériel or an early withdrawal, and he gave figures for the deficiency in the fighting strength of the Legion, which has about 150 front-line planes. In conclusion Colonel Jänicke expressed the opinion that from the military point of view a withdrawal of the Condor Legion was not advisable, stating in this connection that possibly a few fighting planes in Spain might be of more value to us than the availability of numerous planes on the western front.

4) The employment of the Italians at present was as follows: The *Flechas Negras* division (80 percent Spaniards, 20 percent Italians) was at present in the southern Ebro sector. The nucleus of the Italian infantry, namely about two divisions, was in the general headquarters reserve in the vicinity of Logroño. The Italian fliers were at present employed at the front. Here Colonel Jänicke mentioned that, though there was a great deal of aircraft matériel on the Red side, the flying personnel was so poor that it was possible to shoot down planes one after the other. In this connection he reported that in the recent attack by nine Martin bombers on the Condor Legion's airfield, five of them were shot down by the fighters that went up and one was destroyed by antiaircraft fire.

5) With regard to the value of the Red fleet, Colonel Jänicke's appraisal was that it did possess considerably more tonnage than that of the Whites but that as a result of the murder of almost all officers at the beginning of the revolution an effective employment had not yet materialized and was probably not to be expected either. On the other hand, the White fleet was sparing itself because since the sinking of the *Baleares* [1] it had become doubly cautious.

6) The general impression given by Colonel Jänicke's statements is that Franco probably has a military superiority which can now

---

[1] The cruiser *Baleares*, which had fallen into the hands of the Nationalists at the beginning of the war, was sunk by Government forces in a naval action on Mar. 6, 1938.

hardly be shaken. Nor should it be doubted that Franco will gradually attain his objective of conquering the parts of southern and
central Spain which he does not yet have and then turn with his
combined forces on Catalonia. At the present time there is no way
of telling when these objectives will be attained, but, unless unforeseen circumstances arise, a rather long duration of military operations must be expected.

No. 594

3366/E010429

The British Ambassador to the State Secretary [1]

BERLIN, 4th June, 1938.

MY DEAR STATE SECRETARY: The recent indiscriminate bombing of
towns and villages by Spanish Nationalist forces has greatly exercised public opinion in England. His Majesty's Government have
once more addressed a strong protest to the Government of General
Franco. They have asked the French Government and the Vatican
to make similar protests and they have asked the Italian Government
to exercise their influence with General Franco with a view to putting
a stop to these barbarous methods of warfare which are likely in their
turn to evoke reprisals on the part of the other side.

I have been instructed by my Government to approach the German
Government and ascertain whether they would consider similarly
using their influence with General Franco.

Yours sincerely,
NEVILE HENDERSON

---

[1] This document is in English in the original. For Weizsäcker's reply, see
document No. 605, p. 690.

No. 595

136/73638–39

The Ambassador in Spain to the Foreign Ministry

Telegram

No. 52 of June 5   SAN SEBASTIÁN, June 5, 1938—12 midnight.
Received June 6—3 : 00 a.m.

With reference to our telegram No. 40 of May 31.

The Generalissimo informed me through the Foreign Minister, with
whom I had a long conversation in Burgos today, that the demand
which I had repeatedly expressed to him, to the Foreign Minister,
and to the Minister of Commerce that our interests should be considered in the drawing up of the new mining law had been taken
into account and that as a result of my last strong representations
new amendments intended for us, which went to the absolute limit
of what the Spanish Government could accept, had been made in

the final form of the text of the law. The Generalissimo had feared that, if he himself received me during these last few days of the final revision of the law, the impression might have arisen that these changes were made in response to German pressure.

According to the statement of the Foreign Minister, the changes made in the last few days are:

1) Legalization of 40 percent instead of 25 percent foreign capital interest;

2) Greater possibility for the Spanish Government to make exceptions in our favor.

The Foreign Minister declared further that the law had already been signed by the Chief of State and that changes were therefore no longer possible. As a courtesy to the German Government, however, he would request of the Generalissimo that the law should not be published for a few days so that Berlin might be informed in advance. I replied to the Minister that this unfortunately was only a formal gesture and that without knowing and examining the law thoroughly I could not judge from his statements whether it met our just expectations.

Since the Foreign Minister had only the copy signed by Franco, he promised to send me another copy of the law immediately.

As soon as this is received a copy and a translation will be delivered by a civilian pilot as a special courier and the dispatch will be announced by wire.

Bernhardt, who is fully informed, will also receive a copy of the law under the obligation of strictest secrecy demanded by the Minister. A supplementary written report follows.

STOHRER

No. 596

2946/576244–56

Memorandum by the Ambassador in Spain

SAN SEBASTIÁN, June 6, 1938.

After I had had several calls put through to Burgos during the last few days in order to ask time and again when the Generalissimo could receive me in the important Montana matter, the Foreign Minister suddenly notified me that he himself would like to talk to me. This message was given to me on Saturday afternoon after I had already left the Embassy. This suited me very well, for I had no reason to tell the Foreign Minister what, according to my instructions, I was to discuss with the Generalissimo.

When I returned to the Embassy on Saturday evening, the local representative of the Foreign Ministry, Minister Espinos, called on me to tell me that the law had just been signed, according to a statement which General Jordana made by telephone, but that Jordana wished to show it to me before the impending publication. I told Señor Espinos very sharply that this was by no means the information which I had expected. I had requested an audience with the Generalissimo in the name of my Government and had expressed the expectation that until that time nothing definite would be done; I was extremely surprised that these two requests which the German Ambassador had made at his Government's order had not been fulfilled; I had no reason whatever to call on General Jordana; my instructions stipulated that I speak to the Generalissimo; now that the law had been signed I could do nothing but inform my Government accordingly; furthermore, I personally had to ask myself whether I was perhaps no longer *persona grata* with the Generalissimo. I would also ask this question in Burgos and would at once draw the necessary conclusions from an affirmative reply. Señor Espinos rejected this assumption most decidedly and said that during the last few days the Generalissimo had been busy "como un loco" (not a very nice expression, which he repeated a number of times). Thereupon I told him that I by no means demanded that the Generalissimo receive me at a certain hour or on a certain day, and that I also did not mind if the matter remained *in suspenso* until he had more time. I assumed at any rate that under the given extraordinary circumstances the Spanish Chief of State could find half an hour for the German Ambassador at some time or other.

When Señor Espinos asked me what he should do now, I told him that he should transmit everything I had said to the Foreign Minister word for word.

Two hours later Jordana himself called me from Burgos and told me the following:

He absolutely had to see me in person. He would be at my disposal all day tomorrow, Whitsunday, at any hour. I replied that I had the order and the wish to see the Generalissimo and to transmit my instructions to him. As happy as I was at all times to speak to him— Jordana—I still could not consider my instructions carried out by such a meeting; if I were received by Franco shortly before or after, I should be very happy to inform him, the Foreign Minister, also. Otherwise, a meeting in this matter would be of no value.

Jordana replied that he had to give me an explanation, which he could not do by telephone, as to why I had not received an affirmative answer in the 5 days during which I had been requesting the audience. He also had to give me "other" urgent information from the Generalissimo.

Under these circumstances I could, of course, do nothing but agree that I would call on him the next day, and the Foreign Minister left the choice of the time entirely up to me. During the conversation I stressed, however, that my instructions were not carried out by this meeting.

On Whitsunday at 1 o'clock I called on Jordana. A serious conversation lasting an hour and a half ensued, during which I purposely permitted the General to make his statements first.

Jordana explained first that the Nationalist Government had decided right after the beginning of the Nationalist movement to settle the mine question which was so important for Spain. The absence of laws, and especially excessive sales of mineral resources by the Reds in their zone, had been the cause for publishing several decrees— especially the decree of October 9, 1937, which, however, had created conditions that were untenable in the long run. Now, at last, the moment had come to settle this matter by law. In consideration of the great importance which we attributed to participating in the exploitation of Spanish mineral resources and which we had emphasized again and again, the Government had taken our wishes into account. The law originally submitted by the Minister of Commerce had been amended in our favor by the Council of Ministers. As the result of my constantly increasing insistence during the last 2 weeks and my representations vis-à-vis the Generalissimo, the Foreign Minister, and the Minister of Commerce, the Council of Ministers had incorporated into the law additional improvements in our favor during the last few days. In view of the promises given us, he—Jordana— and the Generalissimo had become very much the champions of our stand in the face of dissenting opinions. It was remarkable what had been achieved thereby, and he hoped that we were satisfied with it.

Following some eulogies concerning my energetic action, which was fully understandable from the standpoint of the German Government, he stated that two more improvements of considerable import had now been incorporated as compared with the first draft of the law approved by the Council of Ministers: The foreign share in mining rights had been increased from 25 percent to 40 percent, and the possibility had been expanded for the Spanish Government to make exceptions even beyond this in special cases. In the opinion of the Generalissimo and the entire Government, however, the absolute maximum had herewith been achieved for which the Spanish Government, in consideration of other countries and of its full responsibility regarding Spanish national property, could be responsible. For this reason the Generalissimo had already signed the law yesterday. In order, however, to satisfy at least to some extent my demand not to learn about the law first from the newspapers, he was herewith submitting the law and asking me to transmit its contents to my Government. It would then be published at once.

In reply to the General's long explanations I answered very seriously that I had made two requests at the instruction of my Government:

1. That I might speak to the Generalissimo in this question, which was vital for Germany;

2. That nothing definite be done until that time.

Unfortunately I had to note that both requests, made not only by the German Ambassador but also by the German Government, had remained unfulfilled. I was being kept from the Generalissimo, and definite decisions had been made. I regretted that I had to consider the whole handling of this matter, concerning which we had spoken sufficiently for months, practically as an unfriendly act toward Germany. I first requested to be told why the Generalissimo did not receive me. If I was perhaps no longer *persona grata* with him, I would draw the necessary conclusion at once and ask for my recall.

General Jordana assured me in every possible way that this assumption was completely erroneous; the Generalissimo and he himself esteemed me highly, and he urged me not to entertain such thoughts. On the contrary, he had the Generalissimo's order to give me the reason, which could not be trusted to the telephone, why, after due deliberation, he had not wished to receive me in the last few days. I knew how enemy propaganda constantly stressed that Spain was dominated by Germany and that she was subjected to and acted under German pressure and perhaps occasionally under Italian pressure, too. Following my representations he and the Generalissimo had been convinced that we had to be given even greater consideration. For this reason the law had been discussed once more by the Council of Ministers. If Franco had received me during those days, enemy propaganda would have claimed generally and to an increasing extent that the Spanish Government acted under pressure from the German Ambassador. That had to be avoided under all circumstances.

I thereupon told General Jordana that this explanation was hardly plausible. The newspapers never reported when an ambassador called on the Generalissimo. Therefore, public opinion would remain in the dark.

Jordana replied that the audience would have become known in Government circles, at any rate, and would have been interpreted accordingly; this interpretation might easily have reached broader circles.

I also stated that I was extremely surprised that the law had already been signed in spite of my request; Jordana explained this by the fact that after due consideration, as he had already told me, the absolute maximum for which the Chief of State and the Government could assume responsibility had been achieved in this version. I stated that I was not satisfied, however, and said that it was very distressing for me to see that so little friendly understanding was shown by the

Spanish Government in a matter which we had termed vital. He—Jordana—had told me in his letter of May 29, 1938,[1] that it was not "customary" for the Spanish Government to make a law known before it had been definitely accepted, signed, and published—a statement which had deeply offended me personally. I could not help pointing out to him in a friendly but very serious way that it was also probably not "customary" for one government to put at the disposal of another several thousand soldiers and large quantities of war matériel and to permit the soldiers to be killed and the matériel to be destroyed. I even had to remind him that under the monarchy and also under the republic (perhaps with the exception of Primo de Rivera's dictatorship) all laws had been submitted openly in parliament, so that a foreign power could have taken cognizance of the content and raised objections. The German-Spanish relationship seemed to me to require an entirely different handling of such matters.

In reply to these reproaches, made in the most serious manner, Jordana said somewhat meekly that it was, after all, not possible for a sovereign state first to ask the permission, as it were, "of all friendly governments" in order to publish a law. I replied very firmly that Spain, to my knowledge, unfortunately had very few "friendly governments," two at the most, which had drawn actual consequences from this friendship in Spain's interest, and that the present case by no means involved some insignificant law but the settlement of a matter which affected us very closely.

I finally asked Jordana the direct question what he thought would happen if I were to report the actual facts to Berlin without any embellishment; namely, that I had been refused an audience with the Generalissimo and that definite decisions had been made before hearing the German Government. I could not anticipate either the judgment or the decisions of my Government, but I personally had to say that I would then have to consider the situation as very serious; he should place himself in my position and tell me what he—Jordana—would report to his Government in such a case. Visibly impressed, Jordana replied that I could do very great harm by such a report and that he urged me as a friend not to present the matter so crassly. When I asked how I should proceed with regard to my Government, he told me the following, which I took down in order to commit him. After some hesitation he expressed himself approximately as follows:

Because of the Generalissimo's exceptional burden of business and because of his opinion that in view of the delicacy of the question the impression might be created and spread in a distorted version that the Spanish Government had acted under pressure from the

---

[1] Not printed (4445/E086250–53).

German Ambassador, I was not able to discuss my instructions with the Generalissimo himself, but with the Foreign Minister, who has the Generalissimo's full confidence and is in constant contact with him in the matter.   At any rate, according to the Foreign Minister's express statement, I was able by my emphatic representations in the last few days to get the law, as it had first been accepted by the Government, changed in our favor so that the foreign share in mining rights was increased from 25 percent to 40 percent and so that the Spanish Government reserved the possibility "of increasing this percentage in cases in which the mines are not being exploited properly or mines in which the Spanish Government does not have an official interest."   In this connection, moreover, the Minister also emphasized that these far-reaching concessions had been made only for Germany, since they felt much the greatest gratitude toward this country.

At this point I purposely adopted a somewhat more conciliatory tone and told the Minister that I in no way considered myself a letter carrier who only passes something on or a phonograph record which reproduces word for word; quite to the contrary, as an old friend of Spain I considered it my duty, which he (Jordana) also shared, not to poison the relations between our two countries but rather to strengthen them.   I was therefore willing to report to my Government in the sense suggested by him.   Of course, since I still was not familiar with the law, I could not foretell what the reaction would be.   At the very least, however, my Government would be greatly surprised not to receive the law until just before its publication and only after it had been signed by the Chief of State.   In order not to permit this impression to become too strong I asked him to give me the law for transmission to Berlin by courier and to permit about a week to pass before its publication.   This was, Heaven knows, only a small contribution on his part as compared to my attitude, which had been conciliatory almost to the point of irresponsibility.

Jordana promised to ask the Generalissimo and to give me a reply in the evening.

After my return to San Sebastián Jordana did call me at once and said with a note of regret that he had unfortunately only been able to get the law held back until June 8.   On that day it would be given to the press.   I replied that I considered this concession extremely small and regretted that fact deeply.   Thereupon Jordana again poured forth all sorts of assurances.

I purposely conducted the entire conversation with the Foreign Minister very seriously and emphatically, since the whole question of the mining law appeared to me a sort of touchstone of the new Spanish Government's attitude toward us.   The result is by no means pleasing or gratifying, even though the new law—which was actually delivered to me in San Sebastián during the night—seems acceptable to our interests.

Another memorandum will follow concerning the peculiar efforts to keep me from the Generalissimo as well as on the evaluation of the law itself.[2]

St[OHRER]

[2] See document No. 603, p. 687.

No. 597

586/243235–37

Memorandum by the Foreign Minister

RM 231 BERLIN, June 8, 1938.

1. The Italian Ambassador called on me today at my request. I told him that the Führer had congratulated the Swiss Minister today on the Geneva resolution concerning the neutrality policy of Switzerland [1] and had stated to him that Germany saw and acknowledged in Swiss neutrality an important factor in guaranteeing peace. I now intended, in line with my conversation on this subject with Ciano in Rome, to confirm to the Swiss Government our respect for its neutrality and acknowledge receipt of the declaration of May 20, 1938. I should be pleased to decide upon the tenor and the timing in agreement with Italy and asked him to get in touch with Ministerialdirektor Gaus for further details.

Attolico replied that this procedure was in accordance with the wishes of his Government.

2. I informed Attolico that about 2 months ago Franco had given us to understand unofficially that the time would soon come for the withdrawal of further volunteers. I asked Attolico whether Franco had made any similar statement to Italy.

Attolico replied that occasionally Franco had expressed such ideas, probably for reasons of domestic politics. In reality, however, he could dispense neither with us nor with the Italians. Attolico will inquire in Rome on occasion whether they had given this question any thought there.

From the rest of the conversation with Attolico it was clearly evident that Mussolini had no intention of withdrawing the Italian troops, which still amount to about 30,000 men; however, the Italian generals in Spain would like very much to get out of Spain. I told Attolico that we had not yet given any consideration whatever to a possible withdrawal of our troops; however, we could not force ourselves on Spain.

[1] On May 14, 1938, the Council of the League of Nations declared that complete neutrality on the part of Switzerland was compatible with membership in the League and took note that Switzerland would no longer participate in any sanctions. This position was communicated by the Swiss Government to the German Government. For German documents on this subject see vol. V of this series.

Subject to further communications from the Italians, it seems to me that under these circumstances a liquidation of our part in the Spanish war is out of the question for the time being. It can therefore only be a question of determining whether a partial, tacit reduction of our forces is possible. This should be clarified in a conference with the War Ministry, to which the commander of the German forces in Spain should also be summoned.[2]

3. Attolico asked me whether I had heard anything about the idea of an international commission to verify bombings on Spanish territory.

I replied that so far no one had approached us. He himself did not know anything about such steps in Rome either but indicated that such a step was expected there in the next few days. He stated with reference to this that in the idea of sending commissions he saw the danger that an attempt would be made by England, America, France, etc., to carry on propaganda against Germany and Italy. I told Attolico that we had received a letter from the British Ambassador[3] in which he inquires whether we would be prepared to use our influence with Franco to stop the bombings. A reply was still being drafted. It was possible that the British Ambassador would broach this question tomorrow. I mentioned that we on our part would call attention to the Red atrocities as well as their repeated bombings of open cities in White Spain and would declare further that we could not agree to participation by Germany in such one-sided observations by commissions which went only to Red Spanish territory.

Attolico replied that his Government, too, would surely take the same position.

RIBBENTROP

---

[2] Marginal note: "Taken care of. See separate memorandum. W[eizsäcker]."
[3] Document No. 594, p. 674.

No. 598

309/189031–32

Memorandum by the State Secretary

BERLIN, June 9, 1938.

I asked the Spanish Ambassador, who came to see me today on his own initiative, what he had to say about the British measures against the bombings by Franco's troops. I also intimated to the Ambassador that the British were suggesting that we talk the Generalissimo out of bombing Spanish cities in the future.

Señor Magaz thought this British demand ambiguous, for one could read in French newspapers that it was really not Franco himself but the Italian and German volunteer air forces alone which were dropping bombs on Red Spanish cities. Señor Magaz continued that actually it was always difficult to wrest permission from Generalissimo Franco for bombing Red Spanish cities. He realized that 50 percent of the population there were for him in their hearts; besides, such air raids also always hit relatives of his own followers.

The Ambassador did not go so far as to suggest to me that we might actually exert our influence toward reducing these air raids. Perhaps his remark deserves study nevertheless.

As an argument against the British demands, the Ambassador then stated that cities like Seville, Salamanca, Valladolid, and Saragossa had likewise suffered from Red air attacks. If similar attacks were not being repeated at the present time, this was due only to the inferiority of the Red air forces. If humane warfare were to be discussed, it should be mentioned that the Red Spanish leaders had the shooting of approximately half a million people on their conscience. As far as the bombing of harbor cities was concerned, however, everyone knew that enemy war matériel was imported there. The British Government could therefore do nothing better to prevent the air attacks than putting an effective stop to these imports.

WEIZSÄCKER

No. 599

309/189035

The Ambassador in Italy to the Foreign Ministry

Telegram

SECRET   ROME, June 9, 1938—11 : 30 p.m.
No. 152 of June 9   Received June 10—4 : 15 a.m.

With reference to your telegram No. 204 of June 8.[1]

Ciano replied to me that in their last conversation on June 3 Lord Perth, although he had not brought up the subject since, had already suggested very gently, recalling the gratifying and successful Italian influence on Franco in the past, that influence be brought to bear on Franco again in the question of aerial bombing. Ciano had told him in reply that this was quite a good deal to ask as long as France did not change her attitude. He would inform the Duce of the British suggestion. "Actually," Ciano added, "we have of course done nothing and have no intention of doing anything either." Very confidentially he wished to tell me that some shipments were at this very moment again going to Franco—"little groups of two to three hundred men" [2]—especially pilots and technicians.

Finally Ciano told me, likewise very confidentially, that according to a radio message from a French ship, intercepted by the Italians, all

---

[1] Not printed (4446/E086669).
[2] The quoted expression is in French in the original.

Barcelona was like a flaming inferno and gasoline explosions had started fires which threatened to destroy the greater part of the city.

MACKENSEN

No. 600

309/189033

The Ambassador in Great Britain to the State Secretary (Excerpt)[1]

June 9, 1938.

.   .   .   .

I should like to forward to you today by private letter a request which Lord Halifax addressed to me yesterday. He brought up the question of aerial bombing by Franco's troops in Spain and very cautiously and discreetly made the following statement: Since German volunteers too were fighting in Spain and it was possible that they were pilots and took part in aerial bombing, he wished to point out to me that the aerial bombings were causing increased concern in British public opinion and that it would be of great value to the British Government if it were possible to eliminate the bombing of British ships and non-military areas. He knew that this was a very delicate matter and he wished *at all events* to avoid creating any ill feeling in Germany, and therefore he made the communication to me orally and confidentially and requested me to forward it in the appropriate manner.

Lord Halifax's cautious manner of handling this question is also the reason why I am choosing the method of a private letter to you, with the request that you inform me what action, if any, it may have been possible to take in this question.

.   .   .   .

DIRKSEN

---

[1] The document in the files consists of this excerpt only. It was circulated to the Foreign Minister, the Under State Secretary, and the Director of the Legal Department.

No. 601

586/243248–49

Memorandum by the Foreign Minister

RM 232   BERLIN, June 10, 1938.

The British Ambassador called on me today to discuss several questions. Sir Nevile [Henderson] first spoke of the air raids in Spain and then reverted to his letter to the State Secretary.[1] He asked whether we were willing to do something in this matter with

---

[1] Document No. 594, p. 674.

Franco. I told the Ambassador that his letter had seemed somewhat peculiar to me. It was strange that, every time something happened that the Reds disliked, some special measure followed in their favor. If British ships entered Red harbors today, they had to realize that they were going into the midst of a combat area and had to do so on their own responsibility. Moreover, ships which were in Red harbors probably carried war matériel, so that attacks by the Spanish Nationalists on all ships, regardless of nationality, were understandable. Moreover, this matter could not be handled unilaterally. The Spanish Reds were likewise bombing open cities in White Spain, and, if one wished to talk of humanizing the Spanish Civil War, then it was also necessary to call attention above all to the constant atrocities and executions by the Reds. According to the latest reports, Franco found White Spanish hostages executed in every conquered village. The total number of persons murdered was by now estimated at half a million. This was cold, stark cruelty, while the air raids by the White Spaniards, regrettable as they were, were merely a consequence of the war risk. Finally, the question of air raids was the concern of General Franco, to whom, moreover, we could give no advice regarding his conduct of the war. Sir Nevile would also be sent a written reply to his letter.[2]

The British Ambassador told me that he had thought we would not particularly welcome his letter. He had raised the question merely because he had orders from his Government to do so and a similar invitation had been sent to all governments, thus also to the German Government.

RIBBENTROP

---

[2] For the reply, see document No. 605, p. 690.

No. 602

309/189029–30

The Ambassador in Great Britain to the Foreign Ministry

Telegram

No. 276 of June 10   LONDON, June 10, 1938—10 : 10 p.m.
                                      Received June 11—1 : 45 a.m.

With reference to telegraphic instruction No. 185.[1]

I. Today's session of the main subcommittee was postponed; no new date has as yet been set. Plymouth asked me to call on him, however, in order to tell me the British compromise proposal concerning the question of strengthening the naval patrol. It provides for the appointment of a permanent observer in each of a limited number of

---

[1] Not printed (5158/E303725–27).

important harbors in Franco's area and in an equal number in the
Red area. The text will follow *en clair*.[2]

II. I had a long conversation with Grandi, whom I informed
of the contents of the above telegraphic instruction.

1. He is of the opinion that the blame for non-unanimous acceptance of the combing-out plan must be fixed indisputably on Russia
and that it is therefore advisable to accept the British proposal.
This would at least force the Russians into the position of having
to accept or reject the plan in its entirety. Grandi believes that
no risk is incurred by accepting Plymouth's proposal, since Franco
can reject the plan, and Barcelona will probably do so. Italian opposition to a strengthening of the naval patrol had been based so
far mainly on tactical considerations which were lacking at the
present time.

2. With reference to assuming a quarter of the cost of the combing-out process in case of Russian non-participation, his Government was inclined to agree, on condition that guaranties are granted
for effectively carrying out the process, the formulation of this
guaranty being left to the British for the present.

3. Grandi added that the Italian Government was interested in
strengthening Chamberlain's position in order to prevent Eden
from returning or the post of Foreign Minister from being filled
by a person with a similar attitude; this might be feared in case
Chamberlain's policy was not sufficiently successful. For reasons
of internal policy it was important for him to be able to show an
early success. This might include the acceptance of the combing-
out plan and the implementation of the Anglo-Italian agreement.

---

[2] It was sent as telegram No. 280 of June 11 (586/243253–54). The text (in
English) is as follows:

"The International Committee recognize the importance of ensuring that no
ship having the right to fly the flag of any of the participating countries, which
has failed to embark an Observing Officer in accordance with the scheme, enters
a Spanish port engaged in foreign trade, where technical facilities for the
unloading of war material exists, without being detected and the fact reported
to the International Committee.

"In order, therefore, to ensure that this object is fully secured, it will be the
duty of the Board to take all measures, within the framework of the present plan,
which they may consider appropriate and in particular to make arrangements to
ensure the constant presence of Observing Officers in all Spanish ports engaged
in foreign trade, where such facilities exist.

"In the six or ten principal Spanish ports where these facilities exist—which
would be equally divided between the two sides in Spain—the Board will station
permanent Observing Officers.

"The Board will draw up and communicate to the members of the Committee
daily lists showing the movements (entry, departure, stay) in each Spanish port
of non-Spanish merchant ships.

"Further the International Committee agree that, as soon as possible after
the expiry of a period of thirty days from the date on which the provisions of
the present Pact are brought into operation, the Bureau of the Board shall submit
a report on the working of the Observation Scheme as a whole, as now strengthened, with special reference to the objects of the Committee set out above."

The Italian Government was therefore basically inclined to co-operate with the British in the Non-Intervention Committee.

III. In view of Grandi's stand, please supply me with new instructions, also with reference to the British compromise proposal, since the united front with the Italians would be jeopardized by carrying out the previous instructions.

DIRKSEN

No. 603

2946/576260-64

The Ambassador in Spain to the Foreign Ministry

No. 2998   SAN SEBASTIÁN, June 10, 1938.

With reference to our telegram No. 52 of June 5.

Subject: The Montana affair and the mining law.

I could not help feeling in recent weeks that the promises given me in the Montana affair and the mining law matter by the Generalissimo and the ministers were considered onerous by the Spanish Government and that they were looking for a way to avoid my repeated inquiries and to confront us with a *fait accompli* by issuing the law, a method which, moreover, was not unpopular under other regimes in Spain either. Therefore, as is known in detail from my reports, I tried to keep this intention from being carried out, in the case of the Generalissimo by means of a private letter to his adjutant and through a request for an audience, and in the case of the Foreign Minister, the Minister of Commerce, and the Finance Minister by means of repeated urging and more and more emphatic representations. This was the more necessary since—quite contrary to the usual Spanish practice—in this case neither Hisma nor I succeeded in finding out anything specific about the contents of the proposed new law.

The especially non-committal and evasive information which I received from the Foreign Minister and the Minister of Commerce after the first discussion of the law by the Council of Ministers finally prompted me to request approval in Berlin for an emphatic *démarche* to be made by me with the Generalissimo. As a result of the authorization which was granted me with all conceivable speed and the audience which I consequently requested at once with the Generalissimo, the situation was saved at the last moment. With the Generalissimo presiding, the Council of Ministers discussed the law two more times and incorporated the important changes reported by wire, which probably make the law acceptable for us. To be sure, the Generalissimo did not receive me himself for the reason already reported by telegram, in order not to have to admit German pressure in this matter, but he finally acted after all as though I had personally reminded him of the promise given me earlier and had spoken to him once more about the matter.

In the opinion of Director Bernhardt of Hisma, the law fully offers us the possibility of participating in the exploitation of Spain's mineral resources in the manner desired by us, especially considering that foreign participation in mines was finally set as high as 40 percent and that the possibility exists for the Spanish Government to make still more far-reaching exceptions.

It may not be without interest to record how General Jordana formulated these exceptions to me during the conversation of an hour and a half which I had with him on Whitsunday before I was familiar with the law itself.[1]   He said that foreign participation higher than 40 percent, a participation which could go as high as 90 percent and perhaps even 100 percent, could be permitted in such cases "in which mines were involved which were not being exploited or mines in which the Spanish Government had no special interest."   To be sure, the text of the corresponding passage in the law reads somewhat differently, namely:

"In special cases in which Spanish capital is not raised in the ratio provided in the previous section for the exploitation of mining concessions by interested nationals, the Minister of Industry and Commerce may, on the basis of a decision of the Council of Ministers, permit lowering the percentage mentioned (60 percent) to the extent and under the conditions which may appear expedient in each case."

Undoubtedly, however, the great limitation of the rights of foreigners with regard to the leading positions in the mining concerns is inconvenient.   The pertinent provisions of article 4 conform to Cierva's law of 1925 for the protection of industry.

But just as it will, of course, not be difficult for us to secure through dummies the 11 percent lacking for a majority of the shares whenever we have a special interest in a mine and the Government should not be inclined to make the exception provided for, so, too, it will be entirely possible for us, with reference to the choice of personnel, to insure German influence upon the commercial and particularly the technical direction.

For the rest, Herr Bernhardt has taken it upon himself to have his specialists undertake a thorough study of the new law.

In the final analysis we have thus probably achieved substantially what we had to achieve from the standpoint of our interests and what we could demand in consideration of the claims of other countries, which, of course, are based on the same law, and Spain's understandable desire to safeguard her own interests.   This opinion is shared also by Herr Pasch, Hisma's representative in mining matters.

[1] See document No. 596, p. 675.

As soon as the result of the study of the law by Hisma's specialists and the appropriate agencies in Berlin is available, I shall take the liberty of suggesting proposals with reference to our further procedure in the matter in order to make the actual execution and application of the law as favorable as possible for us. The Spanish Government has retained the greatest possible degree of freedom for this through the wording of the law, so that it has every opportunity to encourage or limit foreign participation in the exploitation of Spanish mineral resources.

Whether we receive what we are asking will consequently depend on the practical application of the law, that is, on the good will of the Spaniards. I should therefore like to reserve my opinion on the formal treatment of the whole matter by the Spaniards, in which, to be sure, a number of things may be criticized, until it becomes possible to gain a general view of the practical effects of the new legislation.

v. Stohrer

No. 604

309/189024–26

Minute by the Head of Political Division IIIa

Berlin, June 11, 1938.
e.o. Pol. I 1348 g (III).

In a conference which took place yesterday in the State Secretary's office General Volkmann expressed his opinion on the following questions:

1) The present fighting power of the Condor Legion in relation to its authorized effectives: The Legion had not received any supplies of matériel (aircraft and artillery) since the beginning of March. The 88-mm. antiaircraft artillery (20 guns) had been completely worn out by firing and ought to be reconditioned. On account of the inaccurate firing resulting from the condition of the guns hardly any more planes were being shot down. The combat power of the combat planes had been reduced by one-half (16 out of 30 fighter planes were usable). In view of the enemy's superior numbers, often three to four times as great, the number of pursuit planes was no longer adequate to protect the bombers, while the low-level planes [*Tiefflieger*] could no longer be sent into action because of their poor condition, which recently had resulted in very high losses.

2) In reply to the question whether the Condor Legion could be reduced in size to the point where it would be able to get along with the present matériel, General Volkmann stated that this was impossible. The Legion had from the outset been made up in such a way that collectively it represented an effective unit which could not

be reduced without lessening the value of the unit as a whole. It should further be considered that the Legion had won high military recognition because its operations had always been carried out according to plan. This prestige would be jeopardized if its efficiency were reduced. Moreover, it should be borne in mind that, from the time the matériel was sent from Germany till it was ready to be used at the front in Spain, 4 to 6 weeks would elapse. This made the need for the supplies particularly urgent.

3) General Volkmann came to the conclusion that only two possibilities were open: either to restore the Legion to its original effectiveness by supplying matériel and maintaining it at this level by continued supplies, or to withdraw it. When asked what the military effect of a possible withdrawal would be, General Volkmann emphasized that the morale of the Reds would thereby receive a very strong lift. As a result of the enormous deliveries of matériel from Russia and France in the last few months the situation of the Reds had been greatly consolidated and the ratio of air strength in particular had been changed in their favor. Departure of the German fliers, and possibly the Italian as well, would be serious from a military point of view. As for the possibility of the Spaniards taking over the German matériel if the Condor Legion withdrew, it should be pointed out that, without the competent and thorough German maintenance, the planes would be worn out much faster still, and that if the already greatly reduced effectiveness of our planes was to be maintained after they were turned over to the Spaniards, the problem of replacements would still be present, since Nationalist Spain did not have any production of her own.

Herewith submitted to the Foreign Minister.

SCHWENDEMANN

No. 605

3366/E010432–33

The State Secretary to the British Ambassador

Draft[1]

TODAY

BERLIN, June 11, 1938.
zu Pol. III 1881.

DEAR SIR NEVILE: In answering your letter of June 4 I have the honor to reply to you that the German Government from the outbreak

---

[1] This copy was prepared for Weizsäcker's signature and was initialed by him and by Ribbentrop. It appears to be the final draft. In a letter of the same day to the Ambassador in Great Britain (3366/E010434) written in reply to Dirksen's letter of June 9, of which an excerpt is printed as document No. 600, p. 684, Weizsäcker included a copy of his reply to Henderson and wrote: ". . . Originally we intended making the language of this reply somewhat more forceful. That we could not, in fact, comply with the British suggestion is natural, of course. . . ."

of the Spanish Civil War has welcomed and willingly supported every attempt at general humanization of the conduct of the war which applied equally to both parties and is prepared to continue to do so. In accordance with the principle of equal treatment in this connection the German Government could not undertake an approach to General Franco, which by its very nature would represent a one-sided interference with his conduct of the war, especially as according to all reports available to us the methods of conducting the war being followed by the Spanish Reds and their behavior toward the civilian population are lacking in any consideration for the principles of humanity.

The German Government, moreover—and this is important in this connection—has no information that bombing attacks by Nationalist fliers have had other than military objectives.

Sincerely yours,
WEIZSÄCKER

No. 606

309/189020

Memorandum by the State Secretary

BERLIN, June 11, 1938.

I reported to the Foreign Minister today that, in the opinion of the leading military authorities, no reduction in the combat strength of the Condor Legion can be considered. And since a complete withdrawal also would be inadvisable at the present time for political and military considerations and would, moreover, not be in agreement with the Italian view, the Foreign Minister will suggest to the Führer replenishing the equipment of the Legion to the extent necessary for maintaining its fighting strength.

The Italian Ambassador has been informed by me in the above sense at the direction of the Foreign Minister.

The Foreign Minister also wants the War Ministry to receive the same message. Another conference with General Keitel was no longer possible because of the latter's absence but was no longer necessary, either, because of the concurrence of opinions.

WEIZSÄCKER

No. 607

309/189016–17

Memorandum by the Under State Secretary

BERLIN, June 13, 1938.

Count Magistrati called on me today in order to discuss current non-intervention matters. On this occasion I mentioned that Count Grandi had stated to our Ambassador that it was essential for Chamberlain to achieve an early success. This included the acceptance of the combing-out plan and the implementation of the Anglo-Italian agreement.[1] I asked him the meaning of this statement. Was it to be concluded from this that Italy was now really thinking of a withdrawal of volunteers? Count Magistrati, who evidently agrees with Grandi on this point, replied as follows:

It did indeed appear necessary for the implementation of the Anglo-Italian agreement of April 16, 1938, that Italy engage in no policy in the committee that would lead to conflict with England. England had in a very vague manner made the implementation of the agreement of April 16 dependent on a settlement of the Spanish question. No exact definition of what "settlement of the Spanish question"[2] meant had been given, however. In any case there could be no talk of such a settlement if Italy and England disagreed in the committee. The time might come, however, when England declared herself satisfied in this respect without the actual withdrawal of the volunteers having been carried out.

In reply to my question to this effect, Count Magistrati confirmed to me that nothing concrete would of course be done in the question of withdrawal without reaching a previous agreement with us, and that there would be no change in German-Italian cooperation in the committee. Count Magistrati was convinced that there was no thought of an actual withdrawal at the present time.

WOERMANN [3]

---

[1] The text of the Anglo-Italian agreement of Apr. 16, 1938, and accompanying documents are printed in the British White Paper, Cmd. 5726; also in *Documents on International Affairs, 1938*, vol. II, pp. 141–156. A detailed analysis of the agreement, prepared in the German Foreign Ministry on Apr. 27, 1938, is printed in vol. I of this series as document No. 755, p. 1097.

[2] This phrase is in English in the original.

[3] After his return from the Embassy in London, Woermann became Director of the Political Department with the personal title of Under State Secretary.

No. 608

3367/E010480–82

Memorandum by an Official of the Economic Policy Department

June 13, 1938.
e.o. W II 3172.

Director Kissel of the Duisburger Kupferhütte called on me today and stated the following:

As we knew, the Duisburger Kupferhütte had for many years obtained large amounts of pyrites from Spain. These transactions were formerly on a shilling basis with optional payment in pesetas. Furthermore, at one time 200,000 tons of pyrites had been obtained for 10,000 tons of nitrogen. The Kupferhütte's consumption of

Spanish pyrites amounted to 500,000 to 600,000 tons per year. Imports had now been increased to 1,200,000 tons in order to provide stock piles.

After the outbreak of the Civil War there had arisen the well-known difficulties in obtaining pyrites from Spain because the British companies, Rio Tinto and Tarsis, owned the pyrites mines in Spain. In June 1937, as was also known, new delivery contracts had been concluded with the British. The contracts had not been signed but nevertheless had been carried out.

The British had desired in particular that the production of their pyrites mines in Spain should no longer be confiscated and that a certain percentage of the proceeds of the sale of the pyrites should be transferred to them in London in pounds.

The British had also actually received a certain remittance in pounds from the Spanish Government.

Now the British were suddenly demanding a price increase of 25 percent. The reason for this price increase was that the British had to pay a higher rate of exchange for the pounds transferred to them by the Spanish Government than they were credited with for the pounds which they received in payment for the pyrites. The difference amounted to 10 pesetas per pound. The British admit freely that they wanted to make good the loss involved in changing pesetas to pounds by raising the price of pyrites.

With regard to the British demand it could be said that it was unjustified because: (a) Germany had nothing to do with this conversion and it was not in the same category as pyrites deliveries; (b) Germany purchased only part of the production of pyrites; and (c) the British companies claimed and required pounds for only part of the proceeds of the sales.

The Duisburger Kupferhütte was, however, confronted with the unpleasant fact that no contract existed concerning deliveries of pyrites on the basis of which it could demand further delivery at the prices fixed, and it could therefore not flatly refuse an increase in price if the pyrites deliveries could not be obtained in any other way. He therefore asked us to consider whether the Spaniards could not be told that a measure directed by the Spaniards against England would be injurious to Germany and that it was therefore requested that this measure be set aside. Moreover, the measure was unjustifiable, since it was incomprehensible why the Spaniards should ask the British for a higher rate of exchange for the pounds sent to London than they credit the British companies with in the proceeds from their sales.

I objected that the British were probably interested in hitching Germany to their wagon and thus with her help making an end to a measure which was inconvenient for them. Director Kiss[e]l admitted this but on the other hand pointed out that the Spaniards had asked Germany (Herr Bernhardt) to conclude a contract with the British companies in order to avoid confiscation. This had been done in accordance with Spanish desires and justified Germany in now asking Spain not to permit Germany, after having complied with the Spanish desire, to be the one injured by the agreement. I replied that, if the Spaniards had expressed this wish to Herr Bernhardt, it would be most efficacious if Herr Bernhardt would speak with the Spaniards again, if necessary. It would be well to hear Herr Bernhardt's opinion. Herr Kiss[e]l answered that he had already had the intention of calling on Herr Bethke. He would do so now and report on the result of his conversation with Herr Bethke.

KREUTZWALD

No. 609

309/189011–12

Memorandum by the Head of Political Division IIIa

BERLIN, June 16, 1938.
e.o. Pol. III 1914.

Drafting Officer: Counselor of Legation Dr. Schwendemann.

Captain [*Kapitän*] Frisius informed me today that the stand of the Supreme Command of the Wehrmacht with reference to the strengthening of the naval patrol was as follows:

Carrying out the planned reinforcement of the naval patrol would jeopardize the supplies for the Condor Legion. As long as this supply was needed there could therefore be no question of the institution of the reinforced naval patrol. But since the reinforced naval patrol was to be instituted only within the framework of the British plan and it was agreed that the German volunteers had to be withdrawn before this plan was instituted because there could be no question of their withdrawal on the basis of the combing-out plan, the Supreme Command of the Wehrmacht had no objection to the acceptance of the reinforced naval patrol in the London Non-Intervention Committee as a tactical diplomatic measure.

I pointed out to Captain Frisius that even after acceptance of the British plan in London, which was, of course, not assured in the near future because of Russian opposition, the Spanish parties would first have to be asked. By asking questions and similar means Franco had the power to delay the implementation of the British plan and thus of the reinforced naval patrol as long as he needed the foreign volunteers. According to our latest information the Italians continued to take the stand that the war must at all events end in a victory for Franco; they were continuing to supply matériel but nevertheless were cooperating with the British in the Non-Intervention Committee.

Captain Frisius then confirmed that the Supreme Command of the Wehrmacht had no objection to our agreeing to the reinforced naval patrol in the London committee as a tactical measure.

Herewith submitted to the Under State Secretary.

No. 610

586/243261

The Under State Secretary to the Embassy in Spain

Telegram

VERY SECRET   BERLIN, June 16, 1938.
No. 202 of June 16   e.o. Pol. I 456 g Rs. Ang. I.

Drafting Officer: Counselor of Legation Dr. Schwendemann.

For the Ambassador personally.

The question of additional supplies for the C[ondor] Legion has been thoroughly examined here. In the face of practically the only expedient alternatives—whether the fighting strength of the Legion, which has been reduced considerably in recent months by wear and tear on the equipment and by losses, was to be restored to its authorized strength, or whether the Legion was to be withdrawn—the decision was made in favor of restoration of its full combat strength, in view of the weighty political reasons which speak for the Legion's remaining longer. The decision obligates us to deliver replacements which mean a considerable sacrifice for us. Please point this out to the Foreign Minister and, when the opportunity arises, to Franco, too.

WOERMANN

No. 611

586/243255

The Under State Secretary to the Embassy in Great Britain

Telegram

No. 196   BERLIN, June 17, 1938.
                                        zu Pol. III 1853–1856 Ang. I.

With reference to your telegraphic reports No. 276 of June 10 and No. 280 of June 11.[1]

We are prepared to accept the British compromise proposal but not to take over the payments refused by Russia.

---

[1] See document No. 602, p. 685.

For your confidential information:
Approval of the British compromise proposal is possible since the reinforcement of the naval patrol will be carried out only when the British plan is implemented, and the implementation of the plan presupposes the previous withdrawal of German and Italian volunteers.

WOERMANN

No. 612

586/243262

The Ambassador in Spain to the Foreign Ministry

Telegram

VERY SECRET   SAN SEBASTIÁN, June 18, 1938—8:30 p.m.
No. 81 of June 18   Received June 18—9:50 p.m.

With reference to your telegram No. 202 of June 16.

I would be grateful for information as to whether the measure in question is being carried out at Franco's request or suggestion or on our own German initiative, since the form of the *démarche* which I have been ordered to make depends on this and perhaps also the question of whether we could demand a return for this new sacrifice.

STOHRER

No. 613

309/189007

The State Secretary to the Embassy in Spain

Telegram

VERY SECRET   BERLIN, June 20, 1938.
[No. 210 of June 20] [1]

With reference to your telegram No. 81.[2]

After Franco told you on May 4 [3] of his wish that the volunteers be left until further notice, the question was studied here once more by the Wehrmacht in agreement with the Foreign Ministry and General Veith. The conclusion was that it is not possible to leave the Legion in its present condition because of the loss of matériel and personnel. Consequently only complete withdrawal or replacement could be considered. In compliance with Franco's wish of May 4 the decision was in favor of replacement. It is not intended to make this dependent on a return service. On the other hand, it would be considered expedient here, too, if, when you inform him of the replacements, you would at the same time bring up once again our other wishes. A de-

---

[1] The telegram number has been supplied from the copy in the Embassy file (2948/576476).
[2] Document No. 612, *supra.*
[3] See document No. 581, p. 653.

tailed written instruction will follow concerning the indemnification demands.

WEIZSÄCKER

No. 614

586/243267–68

Minute by the Head of Political Division IIIa

BERLIN, June 20, 1938.
zu Pol. I 1382 g.

According to information from Colonel Jänicke (of Special Staff W of the Air Ministry), General Orgaz, by order of Franco, made the following three requests of General von Brauchitsch a few days ago:

1. Access to the training regulations of the German Army.

2. Transfer of training officers for the formation of a training unit in Spain, which would be drilled according to the German training regulations.

3. The Spanish war industry should be developed in close connection with the German industry. The Spanish Nationalist Government wished to enter into conferences on this subject.

The requests expressed by General Orgaz signify something essentially new in comparison with the statements which General Franco made to Admiral Canaris in the well-known conference of April 4,[1] according to which the Spanish Nationalist Army wished to carry out its training independently.

Lieutenant Colonel von Thoma, who, under Orgaz, directs the training courses in Spain given by German training officers, told me that 25,000 officers and officer-candidates had already completed these courses, that because of the combat training received in these courses the losses of the Spanish Nationalists had been reduced by one-half, and that just a short time ago Franco had acknowledged the German training activity in a special letter of thanks. Herr von Thoma also told me that General Orgaz himself was deeply convinced of the superiority of the German training, that he wished and hoped to be able to direct the development of the Spanish Army himself as War Minister, but that there was a great deal of opposition to him among the Spanish generals, who feared Orgaz's energy. Unfortunately there were in the Spanish officer corps, especially from staff officers on up, opinions which were not favorable to the development and training of the Army according to the German pattern. The young officers, however, who had gone through the German school, were entirely won over to our methods, and there was lively competition for participation in the German courses. Also, it had already

---

[1] See document No. 557, p. 630.

been possible to push back the Italians considerably; they had been favored at first where aviation and artillery training was concerned, while infantry training was in our hands. Herr von Thoma was quite optimistic with regard to the possibility of getting the training of all branches of the service in our hands.

Herewith submitted to the Under State Secretary and the State Secretary.

SCHWENDEMANN

No. 615

3206/697795-96

The Ambassador in the Soviet Union to the Foreign Ministry

No. A 897   Moscow, June 20, 1938.
                                                            Pol. III 1975.

POLITICAL REPORT

Subject: The Soviet Union and the Civil War in Spain.

Until recently the local newspapers attempted to make the military situation and Red Spain's chances of victory look as favorable as possible on the basis of Red Spanish Army reports. The advance of the Spanish Nationalist troops was, as a rule, admitted only between the lines and was presented as insignificant. On June 17, however, *Izvestiya*, the official Government organ, published an article by its well-known special correspondent, Ilya Ehrenburg, which bluntly admits the seriousness of the situation for the Valencia Government. Ehrenburg has occupied himself for years with the Spanish problem and consequently is considered an authority here in this field. The article was transmitted to Moscow by telegram on June 16 and was written with the occupation of Castellón fresh in his mind. He depicts the life and morale of the population behind the Red Spanish front in very somber colors. His statements about the spirit and discipline of the Red Spanish troops do not sound very encouraging.

Ehrenburg's statements about the Falangists appear to me worthy of note: "The dispatch of further Italian reinforcements to Spain would really enrage the Falangists, who are already indignant about the preponderance of foreigners as it is." At another point Ehrenburg calls the Falangists "the Spanish patriots on the other side of the trenches" and intimates that their attitude could become significant for the further political development in Spain. In this connection it is worth emphasizing that the Soviet press during recent weeks repeatedly carried reports about insubordination on the part of the Falangists and explained these rebellions against Franco above all by the increasing hatred for foreigners. From these press statements one gets the impression that the Soviets believe an understanding between the Falangists and parts of the Red Spanish side is possible. This is confirmed to a certain extent by Litvinov's statements to the French Counselor of Embassy here, Payart, who recently returned to Moscow after being assigned to Valencia for over a year. Litvinov supposedly said that the Soviet Government would be prepared to withdraw from Spain under the proviso, "L'Espagne pour les Espagnols." Litvinov intimated thereby that such an understanding between the two Spanish combatants was an acceptable compromise, since it would permit the Soviet Union to liquidate its Spanish adventure.

COUNT VON DER SCHULENBURG

No. 616

586/243292–93

Memorandum by the State Secretary

BERLIN, June 23, 1938.

I informed the Italian Ambassador today that Herr von Mackensen will probably be in Rome today or tomorrow in order to discuss Italian intentions in Spain. Developments in the Non-Intervention Committee would shortly confront Franco with the question whether he should accept the British plan and thus permit the withdrawal of the Italian and German volunteers. For us it was therefore a matter whether we had any advice to give Franco concerning the treatment of the British plan and, if so, of what nature.

To begin with, Attolico stated that Franco was certainly justified in also demanding a withdrawal from Red Spain of foreign elements which were not of a purely military nature, such as foreign agitators, organizers, etc. I added for my part that Franco could also demand with good reason that the French - Red Spanish border should be hermetically sealed, so that the persons withdrawn from the Red Spanish side would not return to their field of activity. Advice to Generalissimo Franco on his treatment of the British plan, however, should in my opinion also be based on knowledge of German-Italian objectives and intentions. Since the Italian commitments were larger than the German commitments it would be useful for us to know Italy's plans. To our knowledge, Count Grandi's attitude in the Non-Intervention Committee was greatly influenced by the desire to safeguard the Anglo-Italian agreement.

Attolico understood my question very well. He stated that Mussolini had really wished for a long time to withdraw the volunteers from Spain. He had just not been able to leave Franco in the lurch in the hour of need. The Italian generals were pressing urgently for the withdrawal of the volunteers. But Franco's attitude had time and again been somewhat ambiguous. If the return of the Italian volunteers had hitherto been postponed, still a situation was very well to be imagined—for instance, as a result of a slackening in the transport of war matériel from France—in which the Italian and German commitments in Spain could cease without injuring Franco too greatly.

Attolico was of the opinion, however, that Franco should first be sounded out on his opinion as to how the war should be continued and how the British plan should be treated. Then it should be deliberated whether we ourselves wished to consider the possibility of withdrawing our volunteers, and finally whether and how our view should be made clear to Franco.

It was noteworthy during the whole conversation that Attolico was obviously trying to say nothing which could obstruct the reduction and withdrawal of the Italians from Spain. Very little was to be noted of his otherwise customary attacks on the British Government or of consideration for Franco or the future fate of Spain.

WEIZSÄCKER

No. 617

2134/467183–85

Memorandum by the State Secretary

BERLIN, June 28, 1938.

The Spanish Ambassador paid me an urgent visit today in order to discuss the bombing of British ships. He said that Chamberlain was in a difficult situation and evidently needed support if Eden was not to come to the fore again. Renewed bombing of British ships in Valencia [1] had made the situation still more difficult. Chamberlain intended to inform the Commons, perhaps even today, that Mussolini was prepared to urge Franco to spare British ships (or had Mussolini done this already?). Now the rumor was circulating—in non-Spanish foreign countries, the Ambassador said—that the British ships had been bombed by German planes on instructions from Berlin. Señor Magaz asked what could be done to combat these rumors and how Chamberlain could be given support.

When I for my part asked him the question what the Spanish Government could suggest, Magaz replied that he had no instructions and could give no advice whatsoever. When I insisted, Magaz said per-

---

[1] On June 22 two British ships were damaged at Valencia by air attack, and on June 27 one was sunk at Alicante and another at Valencia.

haps the German Government could deny that German planes had dropped bombs on British ships on orders from Berlin. Perhaps also an announcement in London could be considered to the effect that the German Government had advised Franco to refrain from bombing British ships.

I replied as follows to these ideas of the Spanish Ambassador (which are somewhat peculiar from two points of view) :

1. Rumors—which also seemed to be circulating in Spain—had likewise come to my ears, to the effect that the bomb attacks in Red Spanish harbors were the result of willful action on the part of planes manned by German volunteers. In two directions, the Spanish and the British, these rumors had to be taken seriously. Particularly in Spain herself such talk must necessarily confront our volunteers with the serious question why they were not protected and supported in their unselfish activity on behalf of Nationalist Spain. It would not surprise me, considering such talk, if the volunteers wished to return home. Nothing would appear to me more effective and more natural than that Generalissimo Franco himself should declare unambiguously and publicly that no one but he was directing the military operations in Spain and that the whole responsibility for it all rested upon his shoulders; rumors to any other effect were ridiculous.

2. As for the other suggestion, I told Magaz I did not wish to answer without time for consideration. On first thought I could imagine a *démarche* undertaken by Herr von Stohrer with General Franco in the form of a question as to whether it would be possible to find ways and means of avoiding the bombing of British ships, with its unfortunate consequences. Then one could indicate in London that, although we had absolutely nothing to do with the matter and were avoiding unilateral intervention in the Spanish Civil War, we had consulted with our friends in Nationalist Spain as to how the calamity of the bombing of British ships was to be dealt with.

The Spanish Ambassador will not report to his Government today but will call on me again tomorrow—Wednesday—at noon.

Ambassador Attolico, with whom I spoke afterward on the telephone in another matter, allegedly knew nothing about the above-mentioned telegram of Mussolini, but will make inquiries in Rome.

It is reported by a military source that Franco has forbidden the bombing of Red Spanish harbors for the next 4 days.

There is no report at hand from Ambassador von Dirksen in this matter. In any case we shall have to proceed in a suitable manner in London to combat the rumors mentioned by Magaz.

WEIZSÄCKER

No. 618

586/243312-13

Memorandum from the Spanish Embassy [1]

No. 116   BERLIN, June 28, 1938.
IId Year of Triumph.
Pol. III 2080.

During the last bombing of the harbors of Valencia and Alicante, two more British steamers were hit, which made the situation previously created still more difficult. The head of the British Government, Chamberlain, had the intention, in order to pacify the Opposition, of communicating to the Commons a telegram from Mussolini in which the latter offers his services to negotiate with General Franco in order to stop the attacks on British ships.

The last bombing deeply impressed the head of the British Government, since he considers that public opinion in his country was deceived, and he fears the consequences. Since they are acquainted in London with Mussolini's desire to come to an understanding with England and with General Franco's inclination to accommodate England, it seems that the last attacks are considered as having been carried out by Germans—and on the basis of instructions from Berlin—which gives cause for alarm for the future.

The Spanish Embassy hastens to state that it is not a question of planned attacks on British ships but of attacks on the harbors in which the above-mentioned ships are located, together with those of other nations, and that it would be the best solution if the above-mentioned ships would give up traffic in war matériel. The Nationalist Government is prepared to designate a neutral harbor, and it renewed its offer in another communication transmitted yesterday.

---

[1] The copy used is not the Spanish original but a German translation.

No. 619

586/243319-20

Memorandum by the State Secretary

BERLIN, June 29, 1938.

Attolico, after consulting with Rome, answered as follows the question which I asked him yesterday by telephone as to what he knew concerning the alleged telegram sent by Mussolini to Chamberlain on the subject of the bombing of British ships in Red Spanish harbors: Señor Magaz's information was false; the contrary was correct. No telegram from Mussolini to Chamberlain existed; on the other hand the following was true: Franco, for his part, had told the Italian Government:

1. He had forbidden the Spanish Nationalist Air Force to attack British ships which were under way.

2. He had ordered that British ships in Red Spanish harbors should also be spared, insofar as possible.

3. He had offered to have the harbor of Almería reserved as a sort of neutral unloading port for legitimate imports, that is, food on British ships.

The Italian Government had discussed these statements of Franco in London and had stated that in the opinion of the Italians Franco had thus done all that was possible to protect British interests.

Although Attolico wished emphatically to deny the Spanish version, a conversation on the subject between Rome and London did take place after all, of which we have now learned by roundabout means and which is more or less embarrassing to us, since we had refused in London to interfere in the bombing affair and had informed the Italian Government to that effect.

WEIZSÄCKER

No. 620

586/243317–18

Memorandum by the State Secretary

BERLIN, June 29, 1938.

During his call, which had been arranged for today, the Spanish Ambassador mentioned that the reference in his memorandum of yesterday had been to a personal telegram from Mussolini to Chamberlain. But since Attolico denied that there was such a telegram, he did not wish to insist on the point but would assume a misunderstanding on the part of the Duke of Alba in London.

I then told the Ambassador the following:

1. The Foreign Minister wished to refrain from any conversation in London as discussed by Magaz and me yesterday. In the bombing affair we had taken the clear position vis-à-vis the British that we refused to undertake unilateral intervention or to give advice in the Spanish Civil War. Also, a German offer in London to try to restrain Franco might be interpreted as a sign of lack of German-Spanish solidarity and loyalty.

Magaz, it is true, said his Government could refrain from bombing raids more easily on the advice of its friends than under the pressure of its foes. But he showed understanding and then let this subject drop.

2. I informed the Ambassador that, as I had already told him yesterday, the rumor we discussed concerning German willfulness and abuses in dropping bombs on Red Spanish harbors was very disturbing to us. We had no interest in upsetting our relations with England by such air raids. In particular, however, we did not wish to allow our fliers, in carrying out the commands of Franco and his generals, to get the reputation of destroying life and property on Spanish soil against the real wish of the Spanish Government, and this in thanks for the fact that our fliers in Spain were giving their all for the fight against Bolshevist Red Spain. If such rumors were not silenced in Spain—and unfortunately, contrary to the information from Magaz, I had reports that they actually were circulating there—this would without doubt exert a direct influence on the activity of the Condor Legion, to which, as was known, we had just recently sent fresh supplies.

I added that the Ambassador should not underestimate the significance of my remark. Herr von Stohrer would receive instructions from us to speak very clearly with the Generalissimo.

WEIZSÄCKER

No. 621

1568/379696–97

Memorandum by an Official of Political Division I

BERLIN, June 29, 1938.
Pol. I M 2276 g.

The following took part in the conference called by Prince Bismarck: Colonel Jänicke, Lieutenant Commander Heinichen, Counselor of Legation Schwendemann, and Counselor of Legation Baron von der Heyden-Rynsch.

Colonel Jänicke expressed himself as follows concerning the bombing attacks on British ships in Spanish harbors during the last few days:

The bombing of Red Spanish harbors took place on the basis of general orders from General Franco. The responsible military leaders of the plane units discussed the details. The special order of May 17 is appended to today's situation report.

However, only Italian and German planes could be used for the bombardment, as they were the only ones which were fast enough and had a large enough radius of action. As far as land planes were concerned, the attacks were made from high altitudes of 4,000 or 5,000 meters, and the bombs were dropped in sticks; it was not possible for the fliers to see exactly what kind of steamers were involved. The seaplanes from Palma usually flew at night, because they were too slow. Their attacks were made at night, and they descended from high altitudes, throttling down their engines for the sake of conceal-ment, so that the attacks actually were made at an altitude of from 60 to 70 meters.

Colonel Jänicke stated that the order had now been given not to undertake any attacks for the next 4 days.

In summary it can be said that during the attacks it is impossible to determine the nationality of a steamer. The harbor installations were simply under attack and also the ships located there, no matter whether they carried war matériel or food cargoes.

Colonel Jänicke also said that the bombing of two British steamers the day before yesterday had been carried out by the Italians, as was also the bombing of five more ships yesterday afternoon.

Colonel Jänicke emphasized, moreover, that neither the Condor Legion nor the seaplane squadron had made any bombing attacks whatsoever against Barcelona.

Herewith respectfully submitted to Prince Bismarck as directed.

V. D. HEYDEN-RYNSCH

No. 622

F6/0271-73

Memorandum by the Foreign Minister

RM 242   BERLIN, June 30, 1938.

The Italian Ambassador, who had made an appointment with me, called on me today at 5 p.m.

I first informed him of the Spanish Ambassador's step, which had left a strange impression upon us. The German Government had rejected in writing the request of the British Government that we induce the Spanish Nationalist Government to cease making air attacks, on the grounds that we did not wish to interfere in the internal conduct of the war, and we also rejected unilateral intervention. The Italian Government had been informed at the time that this was our view. I said I should appreciate information as to whether the Italian Ambassador in London, Count Grandi, might have taken a different position.

The Italian Ambassador replied that he did not think Grandi had taken such a step. As far as he knew, the Italian Government, in reply to the initiative of the British Ambassador, the Earl of Perth,[1] had merely pointed to the declaration made in the meantime by General Franco.

I told the Italian Ambassador that in my opinion the impression had meanwhile arisen that mainly German fliers had participated in the bombing attacks. Ambassador Attolico replied that the whole

---

[1] Ciano, *L'Europa verso la catastrofe*, pp. 339–341.

world knew very well that those involved in the bombing attacks on the harbor cities, especially Barcelona, had been Italian fliers. I referred the Italian Ambassador to the editorial by Gayda which appeared a few days ago in the *Giornale d'Italia*, in which the latter had spoken of an "unobtrusive Italian influence on Franco for moderation." Since on the Spanish Nationalist side only German and Italian fliers could be meant, it seemed unfortunate to me if by such statements the impression should be created in England that Signor Gayda wished to exert a moderating influence on the German fliers.

Ambassador Attolico said that he had in the meantime received a reply from Rome to the question which had been asked by the State Secretary in his recent conference and would give it to the State Secretary tomorrow.

I then asked the Italian Ambassador how he conceived of the implementation of the British plan with regard to the combing-out of the volunteers in Spain.

The Italian Ambassador replied that, after the proposal had been accepted in the committee, it was necessary first of all to approach the two Spanish parties. As soon as the plan was submitted to General Franco, it would be well for the German and Italian Governments to consult in order to advise Franco on the further handling of the plan.

I approved of this suggestion.

Finally the Italian Ambassador also spoke to me about the Confédération Internationale des Étudiants, which was predominantly under the influence of radical Leftists and Communists. The Confédération was consequently strongly anti-Italian in orientation. He had now heard that the German student organization belonged to the Confédération. He would appreciate it if I would have a report made on this question at some time.

RIBBENTROP

No. 623

586/243323-25

The State Secretary to the Embassy in Spain

Telegram

No. 224   BERLIN, June 30, 1938.
                                            zu Pol. I 510 g Rs. Ang. I.

Drafting Officer: Dr. Schwendemann.

Yesterday the Spanish Ambassador here handed me a memorandum [1] which first points out that the situation already created by air

---

[1] Document No. 618, p. 702.

raids was aggravated by the sinking of two more British steamships. The memorandum then refers to the telegram which Mussolini allegedly sent Chamberlain, in which Mussolini offers to negotiate with Franco regarding attacks on British ships. The memorandum says further that in England the latest bombing attacks on British ships in Red Spanish harbors were charged to German fliers acting on orders from Berlin since it was known that Mussolini wished to come to an understanding with England and that Franco was inclined to accommodate England. The Ambassador is not making any proposals of his own accord, but he suggested upon inquiry that we might have an oral statement made in London to the effect that we would advise Franco to cease air attacks on harbors.

By direction of the Foreign Minister I told the Spanish Ambassador yesterday in reply to his *démarche* that we preferred not to take any steps in London. In the question of air raids we had taken the clear position vis-à-vis the British that we refused to undertake unilateral intervention or to give advice in the Spanish Civil War. Also, a German offer in London to exert a modifying influence on Franco might be interpreted as an indication of a lack of German-Spanish solidarity. Furthermore, I repeated to the Ambassador that the rumor cited in his memorandum, the rumor of German willfulness in regard to the bombing of Red Spanish harbors by Germans, really astounded us very much. We had no interest in disturbing our relations with England by such air raids; in particular, however, we did not want our fliers, in executing Franco's orders, to get the reputation of being destroyers of life and property on Spanish soil against the will of the Spanish Government. Unless such statements in Spain ceased—and unfortunately we had reports, contrary to the information which he had given us, that they were actually circulating there— this would undoubtedly have an immediate effect on the activity of the Condor Legion. I added that the Ambassador should not underestimate the importance of my remark. You would receive instructions from us to speak plainly to the Generalissimo.

Please call on Franco himself now and, making use of the foregoing, point out to him very clearly that our fliers, who are working unselfishly for Nationalist Spain, might under any circumstances expect from Franco and all responsible Spanish authorities to be protected from having the odium of the bombings shifted directly or indirectly to them. Moreover, according to reports available in Berlin, the bombing of British ships during the last few days has been done in the main by Italians.

On the basis of today's conference with the Supreme Command of the Wehrmacht, the latter will immediately inform the Condor Legion. There is no doubt that the aerial warfare of the German volunteers is kept strictly within the scope of the orders issued by Franco.[2]

WEIZSÄCKER

---

[2] The interviews of June 28–30 with the Spanish and Italian Ambassadors and the instructions to the German Ambassador in Spain given in this document were summed up in informatory instructions signed by Prince Bismarck to the Ambassadors in Great Britain and Italy. These instructions (2129/463839–44) concluded as follows:
"Actually the bombing of Red Spanish harbors was carried out by German and Italian planes by orders from Spanish headquarters. The purpose is to cut off the food and war matériel imports of the Reds and thus effect the collapse of the Red front. There were no instructions of any kind from Berlin with regard to the employment of the Condor Legion. The Condor Legion will now be formally instructed in any case during its future operations to keep strictly within the framework of the orders given by Franco and his agencies and to refrain from any war activity beyond the scope of these orders."

No. 624

586/243334

The Ambassador in Spain to the Foreign Ministry

Telegram

SECRET   SAN SEBASTIÁN, June 30, 1938—8 : 30 p.m.

No. 96 of June 30   Received June 30—11 : 00 p.m.

General Veith states that General Kindelan proposed to him, with Franco's approval, that Spanish crews and mechanics take over several complete multiple-engined squadrons of the Condor Legion. General Veith telegraphed this proposal to Berlin but asked that in case it was accepted the Spaniards in question be placed under German command. Kindelan seems to have made the same proposal to the Italians; the Italian Ambassador, however, has not yet been informed of this.

STOHRER

No. 625

632/252367–68

Memorandum by the State Secretary

BERLIN, July 1, 1938.

Today the Italian Ambassador, after some conversation on other subjects, brought up the recent *démarche* of Spanish Ambassador Magaz, in which, as is known, the Italian attitude toward England in the Spanish conflict was put in a somewhat strange light.

At the request of Attolico I described to him the communications of Señor Magaz and told him that Magaz's statements, which Attolico wished to represent as somewhat senile, were made on instructions from the Spanish Government. For the rest, in discussing this matter I kept to the statements made by the Foreign Minister to Attolico on June 30 (RM 242).

Attolico did not make any very determined attempts to explain or defend the Italian procedure.

I then turned to future developments in Spain. Without informing the Ambassador that the Spanish had already made proposals to us for replacing one-third of the Condor Legion with Spanish fliers, I mentioned that presumably Franco would soon have to express himself with regard to the so-called British plan. We, that is Italy and Germany, would then have to know what advice, if any, we should give Spain with regard to her attitude toward the British plan. The German Government did not yet have any definite view in this matter. With Attolico's permission I would outline to him briefly my purely personal and unofficial thoughts on the subject: We had no interest in getting into conflict with England or with anyone else on account of the activity of our volunteer fliers in Spain. Our operations there had been self-sacrificing and disinterested. Since Italy had now been working insistently for acceptance of the British plan and Franco was perhaps inclined to accept the plan, I did not see why Germany should deter Franco from having it carried out. However, the procedure which was provided for in the British plan would put the volunteers in Spain in the awkward position of being inspected, counted, made ready for departure, and sent home by an international commission. If I were a German officer in Spain I would certainly say "No, thanks!" to this procedure. From this point of view, therefore, my opinion would be—subject, as I had said, to the official view of the German Government—that, in case the British plan is accepted, our volunteers there should be shipped home posthaste. Attolico might turn these things over in his mind; in the meantime I would see to it that we, for our part, also examined and clarified this question further.

WEIZSÄCKER

No. 626

1568/379726–30

The Ambassador in Spain to the Foreign Ministry

SECRET   SAN SEBASTIÁN, July 1, 1938.
No. 432 g   Pol. I 1562 g.

With reference to my reports No. 412 g of June 19 [1] and No. 404 g of June 16,[2] and telegram No. 94 of June 30.[3]

Subject: Internal political situation in Nationalist Spain and the question of ending the Civil War.

Rumors of intervention in the Spanish Civil War by the powers.

There have been categorical statements by Franco that he will fight on until complete capitulation by the Reds. There have been state-

---

[1] Not printed (3366/E010436–46).
[2] Not printed (1568/379710–13).
[3] Not printed (5159/E303739).

ments by Chamberlain in the House of Commons that, although the British Government is indeed prepared to undertake intervention in the Spanish Civil War, it sees at present no prospects of success for such a step. Nevertheless, the opinions being voiced—especially abroad—to the effect that there will soon be an intervention by the powers in the Spanish Civil War leading to an armistice and to a compromise peace in the near future refuse to be silenced.

Reds hardly believe any longer in military victory over Franco but hope for international events that will better the position of the Republic.

As I have reported at various times, the Red authorities, in spite of all the confident statements circulated by them in the Red zone, hardly expect seriously any longer that they will be able to achieve a military victory over Franco; the Reds still hope, however, for international events which might improve their position—especially a change in British policy in the fall, the outbreak of a European war, or intervention by the powers for eliminating the Spanish danger spot. With regard to the last-mentioned, Barcelona now seems to be very active again, especially in Paris, through the Spanish politicians living there whom I have mentioned at various times in my reports.

Reds would reconcile themselves to a Franco victory if "the independence of Spain and the lives and property of Spaniards" were guaranteed. Red propaganda thus directed against German-Italian influence and the authority of Franco.

The Reds have recently been saying that they might be reconciled to a victory by Franco and his military but that a regime must be demanded which in addition to the independence of Spain (naturally from Germany and Italy!), guarantees the lives and property of the Spaniards. The terror practiced at present in the Nationalist zone by Police Minister Martínez Anido and the totalitarian leadership of the state are, however, unacceptable. The purpose of this propaganda, which is closely connected with the reported campaign against German and Italian influence in Nationalist Spain, is very clear: it tries to undermine Franco's authority and to represent his governmental methods as an obstacle to the conclusion of peace.

In view of the slow progress of the war and the unrest in the Nationalist zone this propaganda not entirely harmless. Voices even in Nationalist Spain allegedly favoring an end of the war.

In view of the present military situation, which again shows a certain equilibrium of forces, and the dissatisfaction and unrest which are consequently appearing again to an increasing extent in the Nationalist zone, this propaganda is not entirely without danger. This is especially true also because in circles of the original Falange, already greatly angered by the church policy of Franco and Suñer, the opinion is being expressed more and more that the regime of General Martínez Anido is unbearable and that it is desirable to bring about a change in these methods, regarded by wide circles in Nationalist Spain as unendurable in the long run. In this connection it is not without interest that the Falange recently demanded of Franco that the Ministry of Public Safety be given over to it and that a Ministry of Public Health be created for Martínez Anido. From a generally well-informed source I hear that even in high military circles of Nationalist Spain strong objections have also been raised occasionally against a further prolongation of the war, which is making slow progress and causing loss of Spanish lives and property, and the hope has been expressed that a formula may be found for ending hostilities.

Possibility of a peace by agreement? International prerequisites for it.

Under these circumstances the possibility of a negotiated peace such as appeared on the horizon at the time of the Teruel crisis (cf. report No. 242 g of January 31, 1938 [4]) is again perhaps not entirely to be discounted, in spite of all of Franco's rejections in the past. Given further deterioration of the internal political situation, as characterized by the reported arrests within the original Falange, the prerequisite might well be created for the success of international intervention, which might fulfill both the desire to see the war in Spain end soon, which is being expressed with increasing force in England, and the Italian (and British) desire to have the Anglo-Italian agreement enter into force.

Possible consequences of a long war.

On the other hand, if the war continues for some time and if Franco persists further in his demand for complete capitulation by the enemy, it is not entirely impossible either—in the event that he does not win great new victories soon again—that new developments will push Franco aside and so aggravate the internal political conflicts that serious new convulsions might result.

STOHRER

---

[4] Not printed (1557/377775–80).

No. 627

586/243335

The State Secretary to the Embassy in Spain

Telegram

No. 228   BERLIN, July 2, 1938.
                                           Pol. I 514 g Rs. I.

With reference to your telegram No. 96.[1]
General Veith will receive instructions today to state his agreement
with Kindelan's proposal, under the condition which he set of subordi-
nating the Spaniards to German command.[2]

WEIZSÄCKER

---

[1] Document No. 624, p. 708.
[2] Unsigned marginal note: "Both Field Marshal Göring and General Keitel
agree. The instruction to this effect was sent at once."

No. 628

3366/E010449–50

Minute by the Head of Political Division IIIa

BERLIN, July 5, 1938.
e.o. Pol. III 2798.

The Assistant Military Attaché at San Sebastián and liaison officer
at Franco's headquarters, Captain Wilhelmi, who has lived in Spain
for many years and who may be said to know Franco more intimately
than any other German because he has lived at headquarters for a
long time and also interprets for Franco, has told me some very
interesting things, the most important of which I list below:
Wilhelmi has a high regard for Franco as a personality. He
praised his great intelligence, skill, and energy. Franco actually
did everything at headquarters himself. In internal policy he had
maneuvered very skillfully and had been able to hold together and
balance off the divergent tendencies.
With reference to the position of the Catholic Church, Wilhelmi
said that it was unusually strong and that in the future Spain might
be expected to be much more Catholic than formerly. Any idea that
there might be some change in this regard, that the Falange was
pursuing anticlerical objectives, or that some change could be brought
about by propaganda from our side, was completely mistaken. Moreover, the clergy, especially in the northern provinces, had strongly
advocated neutrality toward Germany during the World War.
There was a very unfriendly feeling toward Hisma at headquarters.
Wilhelmi spoke very highly of the Spanish soldier. He praised the
bravery of the Spanish troops and their disregard for death and

was of the opinion that with good training and good commanders the fighting quality of the Spanish infantry could be called first-class. The fact that the Reds were Spaniards, too, explained the great severity of the fighting and the slowness of Franco's military victory. The piety of the Spaniard played an important part in his disregard for death; also the centuries-old Arabic influence and the character of the Iberian race, such as we knew it from the history of Numantia.

The prestige of the Condor Legion and of the German Army as a whole was very great, extending to the broadest sectors of the population.

Herewith submitted to the Deputy Director of the Political Department and the State Secretary.

SCHWENDEMANN

No. 629

632/252390

The Ambassador in Great Britain to the Foreign Ministry

Airgram

No. 324 of July 5 LONDON, July 5, 1938.

Received July 6—2:45 p.m.

Grandi informed me today that the Italian Government had advised Franco to stop bombing British ships in Red Spanish harbors. This had been done mainly to strengthen Chamberlain's position. When the British suggested exerting influence along these lines, the formalistic stand had been taken that the Italian Government was not in a position to exert such influence on Franco.

DIRKSEN

No. 630

1819/416418–21

Memorandum by the Ambassador in the Soviet Union

No. A 965 Moscow, July 5, 1938.

THE ATTITUDE OF THE SOVIET UNION IN THE SPANISH CIVIL WAR

The Ambassadors of Britain and France have of late repeatedly approached People's Commissar Litvinov in order to induce the Soviet Government to adopt a more conciliatory attitude in the Non-Intervention Committee and to accept the latest British proposals.

Twice the British Ambassador, Lord Chilston, has discussed with Litvinov the question of the Soviet Union's participation in defraying the expenses occasioned by the withdrawal of foreign volunteers from Spain. At first Litvinov rejected any Soviet participation on the ground that the Soviet Union could not be expected to pay for removing Germans and Italians. He at first did not want to concede Lord Chilston's objection that Soviet volunteers, too, were in Spain. Finally Lord Chilston proposed to Litvinov that the Soviet Union obligate itself to assume the costs arising in case Soviet volunteers were found to be in Spain and had to be removed. Litvinov agreed to this proposal.

The French Ambassador, Coulondre, called on Litvinov repeatedly, especially before the session of the Non-Intervention Committee on June 21, in order to induce the Soviet Government to give in. Litvinov personally, so M. Coulondre told me, had shown himself entirely ready to comply with the French wishes, but he had encountered opposition in the Politburo to his proposals in this sense. Finally, however, Litvinov had been able to prevail with his view in the Politburo.

Concerning the attitude of Litvinov as well as of the Politburo on the Spanish Civil War and the differences of opinion existing between the two, Coulondre gave the following account—probably on the basis of the impressions gained from his talks with Litvinov:

At the beginning of the Spanish Civil War Stalin and the Politburo had kept aloof. Only upon the urging of the foreign Communist parties, especially the French Communists, had the Kremlin considered itself obliged to support Red Spain to an increasing extent, chiefly for fear of a defection of the foreign Communists. After Stalin and the Politburo had decided upon intervention—even though perhaps against their wishes—they wanted to see their intervention crowned with success. It was understandable that, if only for reasons of prestige, they did not wish to see a defeat of the Reds. While the Politburo was guided more by considerations of ideology and sentiment in its evaluation of the Spanish Civil War, Litvinov's attitude was politically realistic and took into account the interests of the Soviet Union as a Great Power. From the standpoint of Soviet policy, Litvinov considered it best to withdraw from the Spanish venture without overly great losses. Under certain conditions, above all under the condition "L'Espagne pour les Espagnols," Litvinov apparently was ready to accept an agreement between the two Spanish combatants.

M. Coulondre seemed to be of the opinion that Litvinov would have further success in gaining acceptance in the Politburo for his realistic views.

M. Coulondre's judgment is confirmed to some extent by Litvinov's statements concerning the Spanish question in his well-known speech of June 23 [1] on foreign policy. Litvinov stated that vital interests of

---

[1] For extracts from Litvinov's speech of June 23, 1938, see *Documents on International Affairs, 1938*, vol. I, pp. 315–323.

England and France were being threatened in Spain by Germany and Italy. It therefore had to be expected of England and France that they would defend their threatened positions in Spain against Germany and Italy. The Soviet Government had accorded the Spanish Government only the "modest" help which the League of Nations had recommended.

Litvinov's remarks concerning the activity of the Non-Intervention Committee are also meant to leave the impression that no power interests are at stake in Spain for the Soviet Government, in contrast to England and France. From the manner in which Litvinov depicts the Spanish problem *sine ira et studio* as a question which does not affect the Soviet Government directly, it may be concluded that the Soviet Government believes a victory of the Red Spaniards rather improbable and therefore considers it better to prepare the public for such an outcome and for a disentanglement of the Soviet Union.

COUNT VON DER SCHULENBURG

No. 631

2129/463857

The State Secretary to the Embassy in Italy

Telegram

STRICTLY SECRET [BERLIN, July 6, 1938.]

No. 236 of July 6

To be deciphered by Chief of Mission personally.

With the British plan (accepted?)[1] in the Non-Intervention Committee, there comes up again the question previously raised in telegraphic instruction 224 of June 21[2] as to what attitude Italy and Franco will take with regard to acceptance of the plan by the Spanish parties.

Please inform the Italian Government that we do not intend to give Franco any unsolicited advice about his attitude. If, however, he should ask us for it, we would in any case not advise him against accepting the British plan. To be sure, we would add that the withdrawal of German volunteers within the framework of the combing-out measures provided for in the British plan is out of the question. We would then have to evacuate them from Spain in good time beforehand. We would make the same statement to Franco if he should accept the British plan without consulting us.

I request a telegraphic report concerning the intentions of the Italian Government with reference to the withdrawal of volunteers

---

[1] On July 5. The text of the plan is printed in the British White Paper, Cmd. 5793. It may also be found in N. J. Padelford, *International Law and Diplomacy in the Spanish Civil Strife* (New York, 1939), pp. 523–589.

[2] Not printed (586/243273).

under the new circumstances now existing, as well as with reference to advice to Franco in the question of accepting or rejecting the British plan.

WEIZSÄCKER

No. 632

2948/576481–84

The Ambassador in Spain to the Foreign Ministry

SECRET   SAN SEBASTIÁN, July 6, 1938.

No. 435 g

With reference to your telegraphic instructions No. 202 of June 16 and No. 210 of June 20.

Subject: Rebuilding the Condor Legion, and our mining interests in Spain.

Yesterday I carried out with Generalissimo Franco and Foreign Minister Jordana the instructions in the above-mentioned telegrams and called the attention of both to the fact that by bringing the Condor Legion up to strength and by restoring its full fighting power we were about to make a new sacrifice for Nationalist Spain, and that this time, too, we had refrained from asking for any sort of compensation for this contribution to Franco's prosecution of the war.

In accordance with my instructions I further stated that it would be understandable that in view of this new delivery of war matériel to Spain we had a justified interest in a friendly and cooperative attitude on Spain's part to insure our ore supply, since it would be recognized that Germany was a country relatively poor in raw materials.

I called the Generalissimo's attention in this respect to my constant emphatic representations in the matter of the Montana, which were well known to him, and told him we had regretted that the new mining law just published (on June 8) had been drafted without any confidential exchange of views with me or my Government; neither the Foreign Minister nor the responsible Minister of Commerce had replied to my repeated questions with any clear information concerning the intended content of the law and the consideration given in the law to our interests, so that we had been confronted by a *fait accompli* in spite of the communication of the content of the law to me shortly before its publication. The law had now been issued, and for us it would now depend on how the Spanish Government applied it. General Jordana had told me with reference to the law that "it left the door open for safeguarding our special interests." This appeared to me actually to be the case, but I hoped that this at most half-open door would not in the practical application be closed still further but would be opened more widely for us.

I told the Generalissimo that I was not yet fully informed about my Government's reaction to the law. (This line was indicated since I have expressed doubts about the instructions contained in telegram No. 203 of June 17 [1] and still do not know whether, in view of my doubts, it is planned to refrain from carrying out the original intention and first await—as I suggested—the practical application of the law.) However, I asked the Generalissimo even now to use his influence so that the most extensive use would be made of the "half-open" door for the Montana's interests—pursuant to the assurances which he had repeatedly given me. Franco assured me of this. In addition, he interrupted the above statements of mine several times in order to make remarks of his own. Thus he gave particular emphasis to the reason for keeping the draft of the law secret (to which I had objected) : This should by no means be regarded as directed against us or as lack of confidence; it was occasioned solely by the unbridled enemy propaganda I myself had previously described in detail, which was asserting more and more emphatically that the Spanish Government was dominated by Germany and Italy. If the draft had been made known to me by one of the responsible Ministers, the "undercover Reds," who unfortunately were also in the Ministries, would have passed this information on and have used it as propaganda against him, the Spanish Chief of State, and his Government and thereby would have rendered more difficult adopting the final version, which, after all, took our interests into account; enemy propaganda would have stated that the law was submitted to the German Government for approval and the attention of the entire world would thus have been called to the law and its alleged pro-German nature; this would not have been in the interest of either Spain or Germany. It was for this reason too that he had sent me his regrets and had preferred not to see me during these critical days.

I took a similar position vis-à-vis the Foreign Minister, General Jordana, referring in the matter of the Spanish Government's formal procedure in drafting the law, against which procedure I had objected, to the very serious conversation I had had with him on the same question on Whitsunday.[2] The Minister, too, promised me to use all his influence in the Council of Ministers for a loyal application of the law as regards the interests of the Montana Company.

Herr Bernhardt, the director of the Hisma Company, has been informed by me of these conversations with Franco and Jordana.

VON STOHRER

---

[1] Not printed (2946/576266).
[2] See document No. 596, p. 675.

No. 633

632/252397–98

The Ambassador in Italy to the Foreign Ministry

Telegram

STRICTLY SECRET   ROME, July 7, 1938—2 : 50 p.m.
No. 183 of July 7   Received July 7—5 : 20 p.m.

With reference to your telegram No. 236 of the 6th.

For the State Secretary.

I called on Ciano this morning and, pursuant to our last conversations on the subject, gave him the information as ordered and asked him to express himself as to the Italian Government's intentions concerning withdrawal of the volunteers and advice to Franco. Emphasizing that Italy would not do anything in either direction without consulting us, he replied that even today the attitude of the Italian Government on the question of volunteers was not yet settled. The British plan had undergone changes until very recently, and these had induced him to instruct the appropriate offices in his Ministry to make a careful study, which had not yet been concluded. Only then could he form an idea as to whether Franco should be induced to raise objections in the matter. He added that he hardly believed that objections of a serious nature would prove necessary, but he did not seem entirely in agreement with Grandi's conduct in the latest stages. As *modus procedendi* it appeared best to him to await the results of the examination to which we also would probably subject the details of the British plan and then to enter into an exchange of ideas concerning further coordinated procedure. He would ask me to call on him at a given time. Upon my remark that speed was probably required since Franco might reply any day, Ciano answered that in his opinion Franco would in no case reply without previous consultation; he was ready, however, to instruct the Italian Ambassador to keep a very watchful eye on developments in the matter of the reply. He indicated in this connection that the Government here was not interested in any special speeding up, since military operations on a large scale were impending during the next few days, operations in which the Italian volunteers were participating insofar as they were at all available.

MACKENSEN

No. 634

2946/576282

Memorandum by an Official of the Economic Policy Department

SECRET   BERLIN, July 9, 1938.

W II 3667 I

Herr Bernhardt gave us explanations in line with the enclosure to the letter of July 5 from the Economics Ministry.[1] He explained more fully how he envisages insuring predominant German influence in the Spanish mining companies in respect of capital investment. According to the mining law, German capital can participate only to the extent of 40 percent at the most. In order to prevent the remaining 60 percent from getting into the hands of *one* Spanish party, thus making the predominant influence of German capital impossible, Herr Bernhardt proposed the following to the Spanish Minister of Commerce, Suances:[2]

It was impracticable to have only *one* financial partner beside Hisma-Montana by including the big Spanish banks. The big Spanish banks do not represent any reliable capital. It would be more important for the Spanish state for Montana to grant it the right of repurchase in order to give the Spanish state the opportunity later to acquire the mine holdings of Montana. It was also necessary to have private Spanish interests participate in Montana, which would require a public sale of shares. Private participation was needed in order not to isolate Montana from the public. Interest should rather be aroused in Spanish middle-class circles for the efforts of Montana.

According to Herr Bernhardt these statements appeared plausible to Señor Suances. Herr Bernhardt therefore hopes that approximately 20 percent of the capital of the mining companies can be offered for public subscription and that in this manner Spanish agents of Hisma can acquire a sufficient portion of the shares to assure Montana a reliable majority.

KREUTZWALD

---

[1] Not printed (2946/576283–84).
[2] The conference between Bernhardt and Suances took place on June 21, 1938.

No. 635

632/252418

Memorandum by the Under State Secretary

BERLIN, July 13, 1938.

The Spanish Ambassador called on me today and, leaving the enclosed memorandum [1] together with a translation, requested an opinion and advice from the German Government concerning the plan accepted by the Non-Intervention Committee.

I told the Ambassador that we had visualized exactly the opposite procedure. An instruction was on its way to our Ambassador in San Sebastián directing him to make inquiries about the position of the Spanish Nationalist Government on the plan. The Ambassador said that a suggested though by no means final standpoint was already contained in the memorandum, especially in the reference to the dangers of international control in Spain.

I finally arranged with the Ambassador to give him definite information as to whether we would wish to adhere to the course we had set out upon or to follow his suggestion.

Since it was agreed with the Italian Government that we will proceed in the manner proposed by us, and it is to be assumed that the Spanish Nationalist Government has made a corresponding *démarche* in Rome, it will be advisable first to get in touch with the Italian Government once more. We would propose to them that the matter be permitted to rest with the inquiry in Burgos and that we should not take any position for the time being.

WOERMANN

---

[1] Not printed (632/252419).

No. 636

632/252424-25

The Ambassador in Spain to the Foreign Ministry

Telegram

No. 136 of July 13   SAN SEBASTIÁN, JULY 13, 1938.
                                  Received July 14—1:50 a.m.

With reference to your telegraphic instruction No. 240 [1] of July 6 and my telegram No. 16 of July 7.[2]

---

[1] The reference is to telegram No. 236 of July 6 to Rome, document No. 631, p. 715, which was presumably transmitted to the Embassy in Spain for information as telegram No. 240.
[2] Not printed (2129/463872).

The Foreign Minister first summoned the Italian Ambassador and me separately to inquire how our Governments felt about the British plan for withdrawal of volunteers from Spain which has now been received here and was acknowledged by the Spanish Government yesterday. According to his examination, which so far had been only superficial, the plan contained a number of provisions which were awkward and very difficult to reconcile with Spanish Nationalist sovereignty, but he did not name them in detail. The Minister merely thought that the international commissions would have an easy task here in view of the presence of entire German and Italian units, while determination of the number of foreign combatants dispersed on the Red side would be difficult and inexact. When the Minister asked whether I already knew my Government's stand, I replied that I was still without instructions, since the lengthy text of the plan had probably arrived in Berlin only a few days ago; I was convinced, however, that the German Government would examine the plan with interest in consultation with the Italian Government.

In reply to Jordana's question I stated quite non-committally that I had no cause to believe we would advise Franco to accept or reject the plan; this seemed to satisfy the Minister, who evidently wants advice but not concrete proposals.

Jordana asked me to request my Government to inform him of its stand on the plan; he made a similar request of the Italian Ambassador. In reply to my question whether he wished information concerning specific points, the Minister stated that he was chiefly interested in a statement of the general attitude of the German Government so that he could make a preliminary report to the Generalissimo about the situation created by the plan.

Referring to his remarks about the ease with which the number of volunteers fighting in Nationalist Spain could be determined, I said, in the sense of the request in the telegraphic instruction, but merely in the form of a spontaneous statement, that it would probably be difficult to expose the Condor Legion to the combing-out measures of the international commissions, which Jordana fully conceded.

Finally, the Minister thought that an attempt should, of course, be made to gain time through further inquiries, without, however, creating the impression that Nationalist Spain wished to sabotage the plan; it was also necessary to see how the Reds reacted.

The Italian Ambassador also stated that he was still without information; he promised Jordana to inquire in Rome.

STOHRER

No. 637

2129/463886–89

The Ambassador in Great Britain to the Foreign Ministry

TOP SECRET   LONDON, July 14, 1938.
A 3059   Pol. I 599 g Rs.

With reference to our report of July 6, 1938, A 2936.[1]

Subject: The Spanish question after acceptance of the combing-out plan by the Non-Intervention Committee.

The agreement reached in the Non-Intervention Committee on the combing-out plan is considered by the great majority of the public a success for Chamberlain, as is evident from numerous press utterances (cf. the previous report cited above). This event will certainly contribute to easing the position of the Government in the House of Commons until Parliament recesses, provided, of course, that no further opportunities for attack are offered the Opposition by any new bombing of British ships in Red Spanish harbors and waters.

The course of British domestic politics is lately being determined more and more by international developments, whereas internal questions of an economic and social nature and other domestic questions are losing in importance. Since Eden's departure from the Cabinet, however, the new course has not been able to show any really telling successes in foreign policy, which has made the position of the Prime Minister more difficult from month to month. Thus he has good reason to feel satisfied with the partial success recently achieved by his foreign policy.

Chamberlain doubtless knows, however, that the agreement reached in the Non-Intervention Committee signifies nothing more than the completion of one phase. Thus it can relieve him only in one sector and that only for a limited time. The settlement of the Spanish question as a whole, and therewith also the implementation of the Anglo-Italian agreement, has, in the opinion of the Opposition in any case, not yet entered the realm of probability. The Opposition will continue to make use of the Spanish problem. I should like to call attention to the questions in the House of Commons in the last few days and especially Eden's speech of July 7, in which he sharply condemned the Prime Minister's present policy. His moralizing statements indicate what direction British foreign policy might take in case of his return (cf. report of July 11, A 2970).[2] Chamberlain will therefore have to continue to reckon with the Opposition to a

---

[1] Not printed (3364/E010137–39). It reported the acceptance of the British plan by the Non-Intervention Committee on July 5.
[2] Not printed (5155/E303695–98).

greater or lesser degree until he can show a consolidated success, in other words, until the withdrawal of the volunteers has become a fact. In this regard the Government is evincing great optimism. The authorities hope that the plan will be accepted before 6 weeks have passed. If the combing-out really proceeds as planned, the conditions for the implementation of the Anglo-Italian agreement might possibly be created even before Parliament convenes in the fall.

I had a discussion a few days ago with Count Grandi, who has since gone on leave, and with the Portuguese Ambassador concerning the advice possibly to be given the Franco Government regarding its attitude toward the combing-out plan. Both of my colleagues were of the opinion that Franco could afford at the present time to await the answer of the Spanish Reds. This hesitation could simply be justified by the fact that he was the first one to take a stand on the resolution of November 4, 1937, and now it was the turn of the Red Spanish Government to speak first. It could be useful, however, if, in the light of the provisional answer of the Spanish Reds, Franco would not delay too long with a similar answer to indicate his good will.

My Portuguese colleague, Grandi, and I also agreed that Franco must try in any case to put the blame for a possible rejection of the plan unmistakably at the door of the Spanish Reds. British public opinion will make not only the appropriate Spanish party but also the powers friendly to it responsible for a failure of the combing-out. Thus it is to a certain extent also in our own interest to have the blame for any such failure and Chamberlain's consequent lack of success placed on Red Spain and the Soviet rulers who stand behind it, and not on Franco. The Spanish Chief of State should therefore, in the opinion of my Italian colleague, avoid everything that could give the impression of lack of good will. For this reason he should voice no petty reservations in case it should be necessary to postpone the final decision. Grandi has called the attention of his Government to three points which Franco could advance: first, the final clarification of his status, which the resolution does not go into; second, the promise of awarding belligerent rights even in the case of a withdrawal of the volunteers on his side before the start of the combing-out process; and third, the maintenance of the land control beyond the time anticipated if the Spanish Reds maliciously thwart the scheduled withdrawal.

The acceptance and execution of the plan will bring with it the implementation of the Anglo-Italian agreement. The Opposition, however, would suffer a heavy blow and, in particular, an end would be put for a long time to come to the efforts directed toward the return of Eden and his followers. Chamberlain would therewith have created for himself a platform in England from which he could pursue his realistic policy without being hampered by resistance in his own camp. A failure of the plan, however, and a consequent probable further delay in the implementation of the Anglo-Italian agreement might result in a serious crisis for Chamberlain's Cabinet. Since all parties reckon with the probability of new elections as early as the fall of 1939, although according to law they do not have to be called until 1940, campaign preparations will start in the coming winter. The domestic conflict will therefore become sharper in late fall, and this can only contribute to aggravating such a crisis.

In this connection the following information, which I received just recently from a reliable source, is not without interest. Sir Robert Vansittart [3] is said to have resumed sharp opposition to the Prime Minister's Spanish policy some time ago. Chamberlain has supposedly now resolved to remove Vansittart sooner or later also from his present position in the Foreign Office. This would confirm that Chamberlain wishes to keep to the course which he has taken. Even if Vansittart should not be removed in the near future, successes of Chamberlain's policy would make his position more and more untenable, while failures of the Prime Minister would strengthen Vansittart's position in the same proportion as the influence of the Eden circle increased in such a case.

In the question of the bombing of British ships, on which point, as will be recalled, the Opposition has been attacking the Government particularly of late, no basically new development can be noted. Sir Robert Hodgson, the British agent in Burgos, has been in London for some days in order to report. General Franco's answer on the bombing question, which he brought with him, is still being studied. In its present form it is considered unsatisfactory. It is evident from the conduct of the Prime Minister, however, that the Government will continue to treat this question with caution. In his statement in the House of Commons yesterday Chamberlain made a distinction between attacks on British ships in Spanish harbors and on ships outside the harbor waters, which amounts actually to a partial recognition of belligerent rights. The proposal for instituting a "protected harbor" [4] can be considered rejected. In the future the attitude of the British Government in this question will depend greatly on General Franco's stand on the combing-out plan.

Chamberlain also stated that Hodgson would remain in London for the present. This has given rise to the conjecture that if Franco should reject the plan Hodgson would not return to his post. Furthermore, Hodgson is said to have given his Government impressive mate-

---

[3] On Jan. 1, 1938, Sir Robert Vansittart had been transferred from his post as Permanent Under Secretary of State at the Foreign Office to a specially created post of Chief Diplomatic Adviser.

[4] See documents Nos. 618 and 619, p. 702.

rial concerning the occupation by Germans of key economic and military positions in White Spain.

In everything connected with the Spanish question the basic difference between Chamberlain's opinions and those of his opponents, whether among the Opposition or in his own camp, is clearly revealed. On the one hand there is the Prime Minister, who does not close his eyes to the actual facts; on the other, Eden and the Churchill group, who are bound by a rigid "moral principle" and are willing to go to extremes for the sake of this principle. It does not need to be particularly emphasized that the official Opposition parties consider the Spanish question an especially suitable platform from which they not only can cause difficulty for the Government as such, but, in addition, can attack Germany and Italy.

VON DIRKSEN

No. 638

632/252429

The Ambassador in Spain to the Foreign Ministry

Telegram

No. 140 of July 14 SAN SEBASTIÁN, July 15, 1938—2 : 20 p.m.
Received July 15—4 : 10 p.m.

Since telegraphic instruction No. 251 of July 13 [1] did not arrive until after my conference in the Foreign Ministry (telegraphic report No. 136 of July 13), I immediately called on the Minister again, who in the meantime had continued his study of the London plan. On being pressed he stated somewhat more concretely than yesterday that a way must be sought, on the one hand, to strengthen Chamberlain's position by accepting the plan in principle but, on the other hand, by means of skillful questions, reservations, and counterproposals, to win as much time as possible in order to prosecute the war in the meantime; according to a recent statement by Franco the support of the Condor Legion could not be dispensed with for the present.

Moreover, the Minister repeated urgently his request for advice from Berlin, pointing out that a Spanish position on the London plan was possible only in agreement with the two friendly Governments.

Franco was at the front on account of the new offensive and therefore had not been informed by the Minister of the contents and effects of the London plan. However, the highest military and naval authorities had received . . . (group missing) for the opinion of their departments.

In this connection the Minister mentioned several provisions of the London plan which were hardly acceptable, such as the stationing of

---

[1] Not printed (5153/E303682).

officers of the commission aboard warships, with the possibility of communication in code; also certain clauses referring to airfields and harbors, and the consequent impediment to imports from abroad.

Both conversations with the Foreign Minister revealed the great perplexity of the Spanish Government and pronounced anxiety, also expressed to me by the Minister of the Interior, concerning the danger to Chamberlain's position, this latter due also to the alleged cooling of Anglo-Italian relations.

Telegraphic instruction No. 252 of July 13,[2] according to which we wish to give the Spanish Government precedence in expressing a stand on the plan, did not arrive until after my return from Burgos. Another telegraphic report will follow immediately after further consultation with the Italian Ambassador.

STOHRER

---

[2] Not printed (309/188996).

No. 639

309/188968

The Ambassador in Italy to the Foreign Ministry

Telegram

URGENT   ROME (QUIRINAL), July 16, 1938—9 : 50 p.m.
No. 190 of July 16   Received July 16—12 : 00 p.m.

With reference to your No. 243 [1] and my No. 189.[2]

The Political Director summoned Plessen today and, asking him to transmit this information to Berlin at once, told him that directly after yesterday's conversation a report of July 12 from the Italian Ambassador at San Sebastián had arrived, to the effect that the Spaniards insist that the Italian and German Governments inform them of their stand on the London plan. The Italian Embassy had reported that the Spanish Nationalist Government found it difficult to form a correct opinion on the text of the London documents; it was very eager to have the Italian and German opinions and also advice.

The Political Director also stated that under these circumstances the Italian Government was of the opinion that it was very desirable politically to advise Franco to inform the London committee at once that he accepted the London plan in principle. Franco could say in his note addressed to the committee that he was studying the plan carefully and that his comment on the separate points of the plan would follow. Later (and this was not at all urgent) Franco should direct a second note to the committee, containing detailed comments

---

[1] Not printed (2129/463862–63).
[2] Not printed (309/188973).

and possibly questions. For preparing this second note Franco could utilize material which the Italian Foreign Ministry had sent to the Italian Embassy in Berlin during the last few days, as well as further comments which were now being prepared by the Foreign Ministry and would shortly be transmitted to the German Government, so that in case of agreement they could be sent on to Franco. The London plan offers every opportunity for objections and questions. Attolico is being informed.

The Foreign Ministry requests an answer as soon as possible and hopes for agreement.

MACKENSEN

No. 640

309/188959

The Ambassador in Spain to the Foreign Ministry

Telegram

SAN SEBASTIÁN, July 19, 1938—time not indicated.

No. 148 of July 19   Received July 20—12 : 25 a.m.

With reference to your telegram No. 262 of July 16.[1]

The Italian Ambassador gave me the comments of the Italian Foreign Ministry on the London plan mentioned in telegraphic instruction No. 261 of July 16.[2] In brief summary they are as follows:

1. Franco's answer has great importance for the future treatment of the problem of volunteers.

2. Franco should formally uphold the standpoint of his answer of November 18, 1937, that is, acceptance in principle, with reservations and counterproposals.

3. There is no hurry about the answer; Lord Plymouth supposedly does not expect an answer for from 4 to 6 weeks.

4. It would be useful to know Barcelona's answer beforehand.

5. The resolution of July 5 does not answer all of Franco's wishes and counterquestions of November 18, 1937, in particular with regard to the status of the Burgos Government under international law.

6. The combing-out procedure gives rise to numerous objections, particularly with regard to respecting territorial sovereignty.

7. Further objections are possible with regard to guaranties for identifying and removing Red volunteers.

8. The plan contains no formula which assures in a tangible way recognition of belligerent rights.

STOHRER

---

[1] Not printed (309/188969).
[2] Not printed (632/252431).

No. 641

168/132658–60

The State Secretary to the Embassy in Spain

Telegram

No. 269   BERLIN, July 21, 1938.

zu Pol. I 590, 597, 598, 599 g Rs. Ang. II und Pol. III 2405.

With reference to your telegraphic reports 140,[1] 142,[2] and 148.[3]

In agreement with the Italian Government I request that you inform the Spanish Government somewhat as follows in answer to its repeated inquiries:

1. We would consider it expedient for Franco to give a provisional answer to London as soon as possible, accepting the plan in principle and reserving comment on the separate points.

2. For the rest we agree with the eight points mentioned in your telegraphic report No. 148, which were also given us by the Italian Ambassador here and which can serve as a basis for advice to the Spanish Nationalist Government. In particular, we see no objection to having Franco, if he wishes, await the answer of the Spanish Reds, especially since in November he was the first to state his stand on the resolution.

3. Points 5 to 8 of telegram No. 148 should be utilized for the definitive reply. It would be extremely undesirable, however, if the reservations in the answer were so formulated that public opinion, above all in England, would blame Franco for a possible failure, especially since then part of the responsibility would be put on the friendly powers.

In supplement to points 5 to 8 the following viewpoints could be considered:

(*a*) A promise to grant belligerent rights even in case the volunteers on Franco's side are withdrawn before the combing-out process.

(*b*) Franco's desire to know the general instructions of the commission, which are not yet complete, before finally agreeing to the plan, with the possibility of expressing an opinion on them.

In making the *démarche* please proceed in agreement with the Italian Ambassador; in so doing please state once more that we do not wish to anticipate Franco's decisions by these suggestions.

In making the *démarche* please also point out that a withdrawal of the German volunteers naturally could not be made in the manner provided by the combing-out plan, so that they would have to be removed at a given moment well in advance.[4]

WEIZSÄCKER

---

[1] Document No. 638, p. 725.
[2] Not printed (309/188970).
[3] Document No. 640, *supra*.
[4] The text of this telegram was communicated to the German Embassy in Italy as No. 251 after agreement had been reached with the Italian Ambassador in Berlin.

No. 642

2946/576293

The Deputy Director of the Economic Policy Department to the Embassy in Spain

Telegram

STRICTLY SECRET

No. 290 of August 2

BERLIN, August 2, 1938.

Received August 3—9 : 00 a.m.

For the Chief of Mission only, or deputy.

To be deciphered personally.

With reference to your No. 179.[1]

The Embassy is empowered to undertake negotiations with the Spanish Government concerning the utilization of funds derived from war deliveries for financing investments. The matter has been discussed here with the Ambassador. If, because of the possible necessity of keeping within the well-known 60-day limit or for any other reasons, there is danger in delay, please start the negotiations at once without awaiting the arrival of the Ambassador and demand of the Spanish Government that it make available for investments at this time the peseta equivalent of 10 million RM.

Further telegraphic instructions will probably follow tomorrow with regard to full powers for Bernhardt to utilize the money paid out for Montana.

CLODIUS

---

[1] Not printed (2946/576291–92). In this telegram of Aug. 1 the German Chargé d'Affaires, Heberlein, had requested authority to proceed with negotiations with the Spanish Government on the Montana project.

No. 643

2946/576295

The Ambassador in Spain to the Foreign Ministry

Telegram

STRICTLY SECRET

No. 185 of August 4

SAN SEBASTIÁN, August 4, 1938.

With reference to your telegram No. 290 of August 2.

Since the question has not been entirely clarified here as to whether there is danger in delay as far as keeping within the time limit is concerned, to be on the safe side my representative yesterday personally requested of Foreign Minister Jordana that the Nationalist Government agree to the utilization of 15 million RM at this time for investment in mining companies. The sum of 15 million RM was mentioned as a precaution, since according to Hisma about 50 million pesetas are required. Jordana promised sympathetic and prompt consideration.

STOHRER

No. 644

1606/385658-59

The Under State Secretary to the Embassy in Spain

Telegram

No. 306   BERLIN, August 11, 1938—9 : 05 p.m.

zu Pol. I 1811 g.

With reference to our telegram No. 303 of August 10.[1]

The joint examination with the Italian Government of the Spanish Nationalist draft note [2] has been completed.   In conformity with the Italian Ambassador and after arranging an agreed line with him, please give the Government there the following answer:

We had indeed considered that a somewhat more accommodating note, also as regards contents, was possible, but we did not wish to raise any objections to the Spanish draft.   On the whole, however, it seemed to us that the offers, which were in fact quite strongly positive, tended to be lost sight of somewhat too much in the long note.   Perhaps a stylistic revision of the note as a whole might give it a somewhat more positive turn without changing the actual contents.   We merely wanted to bring up for consideration whether the part about the granting of belligerent rights, the arguments for which we considered very strong and effective, might not be placed before the part about the withdrawal of volunteers.

We believed that we should advise against sending a short preliminary note, since it was now too late for this.

The Spanish Ambassador here will be informed.

WOERMANN

---

[1] Not printed (5153/E303680).
[2] Not printed (1606/385680-92).

No. 645

1606/385659-60

The Under State Secretary to the Embassy in Great Britain

Telegram

No. 260   BERLIN, August 11, 1938—9 : 05 p.m.

For your information.

The Spanish Nationalist Government has sent us the draft of a note in answer to the British plan, to which we, in accord with the Italian Government, have made no objections.   The whole direction of the draft is decidedly negative.   The Spanish Nationalist Government demands immediate granting of belligerent rights and agrees to the withdrawal of volunteers only as an autonomous measure after the granting of belligerent rights.   It suggests the number of 10,000 on each side.   The note also contains a number of additional proposals, in particular the evacuation of two harbors in the Red Spanish zone.

It is probable that when the note reaches the Non-Intervention Committee it will be discussed and will immediately lead to considerable difficulties.

Further instructions and a copy of the draft note in its present form will follow.

Since the German and Italian answers are not being transmitted to Franco until August 12, the Spanish note, which will possibly still undergo slight revision, will certainly not arrive there before the beginning of next week.

WOERMANN

No. 646

1606/385660–61

The Under State Secretary to the Embassy in Italy

Telegram

No. 263   BERLIN, August 11, 1938—9 : 05 p.m.

Agreement has been reached with the Italian Embassy here to the effect that we agree essentially with the Spanish draft note sent here and to Rome.

The Embassy at San Sebastián has been instructed to relay this information in closest cooperation with the Italian Embassy.   The Spanish Ambassador here is being informed.

WOERMANN

No. 647

2946/576298–300

Memorandum by the Ambassador in Spain

SAN SEBASTIÁN, August 11, 1938.

Today Herr Bernhardt, who just returned from Portugal, told me that in the meantime the Montana project had been greatly advanced in Bilbao.   All concessions had been reported in the meantime and the founding of the five companies had been started.   He—Bernhardt—conceived the further course of events as follows:

Since the companies had now been established with 40 percent German capital, in accordance with the new mining law, exceptions should be demanded on the basis of this new law for the mines in which a higher percentage of ownership seemed useful to us.   In reply to my inquiry Herr Bernhardt said that, of the five companies to be established, higher percentages were desirable for four.   If the Spanish Government should object to this in the case of any of the mines, an exception could be made in a special protocol, but the Spaniards should be made to approach us in the matter. He wished to consider acquiring the majority by means of dummies only if we were not able to make sufficient headway with these demands for exceptions.

I declared myself fully in agreement with this course, particularly as regards refraining from an evasion of the law by means of dummies—an opinion which I had already expressed earlier—in order to see how the Spanish Government actually interprets the spirit of the law.

Herr Bernhardt answered a further question by saying that he had found general understanding for these plans in the Ministry of Commerce in Bilbao; the mining engineers, who had investigated the whole affair, were entirely on his side; Minister Suances was also in accord with the procedure. Suances had also taken up the idea that the entire capital might be advanced by Hisma at first, and then the 60 percent or less might be bought back, so to speak, by the Spanish Government. Only the director of the mining department, an elderly man with old-fashioned ideas, proved somewhat difficult in the whole affair.

Herr Bernhardt then presented his ideas as to the further treatment of the matter, suggesting that he give me the necessary data and that I then apply for the desired exceptions through official channels by way of the Foreign Minister, General Jordana. I agreed in principle but suggested that Herr Bernhardt first formally obtain the agreement of the Minister of Commerce, which had already been given him in a general way, by presenting the petition that had been prepared (by means of which the exceptions are requested). I explained that in this way the influence of the Foreign Minister, who was not unconditionally won over to our view, would be pushed somewhat into the background; for I feared that the Foreign Minister might pass my note on to Suances with the remark that these demands were, after all, too much of a good thing, and he would thus exercise an undesirable influence on Suances, who was already won over. If, however, I could tell the Foreign Minister at once on giving him the note that Suances was willing to agree to this request made of the Foreign Ministry, we would take the wind out of Jordana's sails. Herr Bernhardt declared himself quite in agreement; therefore, he will first submit the matter to Suances for his provisional approval; later it is to be dealt with through diplomatic channels and submitted to the Council of Ministers according to the law.

STOHRER

No. 648

1606/385748

The Ambassador in Spain to the Foreign Ministry

SECRET   SAN SEBASTIÁN, August 11, 1938.
No. 474 g   Pol. I 1925 g III.

Subject: The Italian volunteers on the Spanish Nationalist side.

A person who frequents Generalissimo Franco's headquarters and is therefore always very well informed regarding matters there has given me the following figures as of July 1, 1938, on Italian volunteers who would be considered for withdrawal:

Air Force:	Officers	339
	Enlisted men	1, 830
	Additional number of officers and men on the islands (Palma de Mallorca) . .	519
Army:	Officers	2, 528
	Enlisted men	34, 859
		40, 075

To this is to be added a total of 8,000 volunteers (300 of them officers) who have arrived in Spain as replacements since July 1.

STOHRER

No. 649

168/132621–22

Memorandum by the Under State Secretary

BERLIN, August 12, 1938.

Yesterday I arrived at an understanding with Count Magistrati, who had appropriate instructions from his Government, regarding the reply we wish to give the Spanish Nationalist Government concerning its draft note on the British plan.

The reply is to be to the effect that we considered it too late to send a short preliminary note now, but that we were in favor of sending the principal note. We had indeed had in mind a somewhat more conciliatory statement but would raise no objection to sending this one. As a detail, perhaps the last part of the note, containing the concessions, could be phrased in somewhat more friendly terms, since the note gives a decidedly negative impression. Furthermore, in deference to Italian wishes, it is recommended that the part regarding belligerent rights be placed ahead of the part dealing with the withdrawal of volunteers.

In an earlier discussion Ambassador Attolico and I had brought up the question whether we ought to advise Franco to strike out the last paragraph of the note, which repeats the solemn declaration that Nationalist Spain would not permit the slightest lien to be placed on her territory or economy either now or later. Count Magistrati told me that the Italian Government had come to the conclusion that such advice from us might be incorrectly interpreted and had better be omitted. I told him that we would therefore refrain from making such a suggestion, which actually would entail the possibility of a Spanish refusal.

I informed the Spanish Ambassador accordingly today.

Furthermore, the Embassy at San Sebastián has received instructions in line with this memorandum.

At the request of Department W [1] the Embassy in San Sebastián has been asked to make clear in a mild form that the reference to a lien on Spanish economy could not, of course, entail any prejudice to the current German-Spanish economic negotiations.

WOERMANN

---

[1] The Economic Policy Department.

No. 650

1606/385721–22

The Under State Secretary to the Embassy in Spain

Telegram

VERY URGENT   BERLIN, August 12, 1938—8:15 p.m.
No. 308   Pol. I 1875 g.

With reference to our telegram No. 306 of August 11.

The last paragraph of the Spanish draft note, which I assume you have or can procure, contains the statement that Nationalist Spain will not permit the slightest lien to be placed on its territory or economy either now or later. In conversation with the Government there please make it clear, but in a mild form, that it cannot be the sense of this paragraph to prejudice the goals of the economic negotiations between Germany and Nationalist Spain.

For your information:

We would have preferred deletion of the entire last paragraph, which has no direct connection with the British plan. But the Italians did not wish to approach the Nationalist Government with such a request.

We have not informed the Italian Government of these instructions to you, since conditions are not exactly the same in the economic field, but we have no objection to your informing the Italian Ambassador there.

WOERMANN

No. 651

1606/385731

The Ambassador in Spain to the Foreign Ministry

Telegram

STRICTLY SECRET   SAN SEBASTIÁN, August 14, 1938—9 : 15 p.m.
No. 206 of August 14   Received August 14—11 : 30 p.m.

Bernhardt, director of Hisma, states that the Spanish Nationalist Army urgently requires 88-mm. ammunition, since its supplies are entirely exhausted. The lack of this ammunition constitutes an acute military danger at the Ebro front. Shipment of BMW airplane engines is almost as urgent. It is to be feared that because of the urgency of war deliveries the Spanish Government will prohibit all free imports from Germany. Bernhardt has telegraphed to Berlin to request immediate intervention with Field Marshal Göring so that the promised additional credit of 25 million RM may be made available and especially so that 88-mm. ammunition may be delivered as quickly as possible.

At Bernhardt's request, I ask support for his efforts there insofar as possible.

By direction:
HEBERLEIN

No. 652

136/73641

The Ambassador in Spain to the Foreign Ministry

Telegram

No. 220 of August 20   SAN SEBASTIÁN, August 20, 1938.
          Received August 20—9 : 45 p.m.

With reference to your telegram No. 308 of August 12.

The instruction was carried out today in the course of an exhaustive conversation with the Foreign Minister. The Foreign Minister answered that in the reply to the Non-Intervention Committee the statement regarding rejection of any lien whatever on Spanish territory and economy had been included merely for the purpose of taking the wind out of the sails of Red propaganda, which had recently been maintaining that Spanish liberty and independence were the sole aim of the war; the Minister expressly assured me that the desired close economic cooperation between the two countries would not be prejudiced by this wording.

STOHRER

No. 653

632/252505

Memorandum by the Under State Secretary

BERLIN, August 22, 1938.

The Spanish Ambassador called on me today and gave me a copy of Franco's reply,[1] which I have handed on for circulation.

The Ambassador again requested Germany's support through diplomatic channels and in the press in view of the great difficulties encountered by the note in London. I told the Ambassador that we had already given the necessary instructions. As regards the press, we would not only support Franco in Germany in the situation caused by the note but also make an attempt to secure a favorable echo in foreign countries through agencies, etc.

In regard to diplomatic support I told the Ambassador again that our representative on the Non-Intervention Committee would, of course, receive instructions to give full support to the Spanish Nationalist viewpoint, but that in view of the nature of the Non-Intervention Committee's work we could not go so far as to identify ourselves with every point of Franco's note in the further course of the negotiations. I promised the Ambassador, however, that he would be consulted periodically on important points.

WOERMANN

---

[1] On Aug. 16 the Nationalist reply was handed to Sir Robert Hodgson at Burgos. In view of its negative character Lord Plymouth decided not to summon a meeting of the Non-Intervention Committee to discuss it. The text of Franco's reply may be found in Padelford, *op. cit.*, pp. 596–601.

No. 654

632/252506

The Ambassador in Spain to the Foreign Ministry

Telegram

VERY SECRET   SAN SEBASTIÁN, August 22, 1938—8 : 30 p.m.
No. 223 of August 22   Received August 22—11 : 15 p.m.

At Mussolini's instructions, the Italian General Berti has told Franco in the presence of the Italian Ambassador that he must exert the greatest efforts to bring the war to an early end. Italy could no longer participate indefinitely but was prepared, if desired, to send several new divisions, matériel, etc.—on condition, however, that she be permitted to exert a strong influence in the command.

Franco, who was full of confidence as always, neither accepted nor rejected this but asked for new matériel.

The Italian Ambassador told me personally and in strictest confidence that Italy's *démarche* was probably something of a bluff to induce Franco to take energetic action; for reasons of domestic policy alone, Franco could not relinquish command to the Italians even in part.

From a remark by Franco the Italian Ambassador infers that the former appears resigned to the sending of Hemming, the Secretary of the Non-Intervention Committee.[1]

STOHRER

----

[1] It had been proposed that Hemming should go to Spain to confer with General Franco in an endeavor to remove his objections to the plan of the Non-Intervention Committee.

No. 655

2946/576307–10

The Director of Hisma to the Ambassador in Spain

SECRET   SALAMANCA, August 27, 1938.

Subject: The question of the mines.

Enclosed we respectfully transmit for your information Herr Pasch's memorandum regarding the conversation of our [1] Herr Bernhardt with Under Secretary Fernández Cuevas.[2]

Heil Hitler!

J. BERNHARDT [3]

[Enclosure]

BILBAO, August 27, 1938.

Subject: Herr Bernhardt's conversation with Under Secretary Fernández Cuevas in the presence of the undersigned.[4]

At the outset Herr Bernhardt called the Under Secretary's attention to the fact that during his last trip to Germany he had again succeeded in having war matériel and extensive military aid made available. The situation was considered very serious by German circles, because they were obliged to recognize that the factors necessary for a successful conclusion of the war were not all working together as well as was necessary; i.e. the closest possible cooperation between the military, cultural, and economic factors for the purpose of achieving victory by means of a combined total effort was lacking. In particular Herr Bernhardt had felt during his visit to the front that the impres-

----

[1] The document is on a letterhead of Hisma, Ltda.
[2] Of the Ministry of Commerce and Industry.
[3] Marginal note: "1. Herr Masche has just told me that Herr Bernhardt came through San Sebastián today and immediately went on to Berlin. Because of lack of time it was impossible for him to call at the Embassy. He merely wanted it conveyed that the note regarding the question of capital was not to be sent yet, since the matter was to be discussed once more in Berlin. 2. To Herr Stille for consultation. H[eberlein] Sept. 2."
[4] The copy found is unsigned.

sion was prevalent there that the rear echelons were deluding themselves with irresponsible optimism. On the other hand, people in Germany did not understand how under present conditions week after week went by without the question of the mines being definitely settled. For Germany, as had been repeatedly stressed, the settlement of the mining question was a measure of the desire for German-Spanish cooperation. Germany had to solve her raw-materials question at all costs. She honestly desired to obtain these raw materials principally from friendly countries such as Spain, but, if no understanding in this matter could be obtained from the Spaniards, Germany would be forced against her will to seek and find a solution of the raw-materials question in other ways. When Fernández Cuevas tried to justify the delay by the Minister's illness, Herr Bernhardt pointed out that the Minister certainly must be well on the way to recovery, because he was already receiving certain people at his home. The Under Secretary said that only acquaintances of Señor Suances were involved, whereupon Herr Bernhardt most emphatically explained how collaboration between Germany and Spain should really look and that if the Minister received friends he certainly should, in view of the present situation, number among them such persons as Herr Bernhardt. Unless cooperation between the two countries were carried on in a spirit of confidence and without legalistic and bureaucratic objections, everything would go for nought in the long run. If difficulties arose they should be discussed openly, and certainly a solution would be found in every case. On the other hand, mistrust and reserve led to a situation which could in no case be understood or approved by Germany. Germany did not wish to exert pressure on Spain and would never do so but would merely draw her own conclusions, and she would regret it very much if Spain failed to utilize the present historic moment to establish her position in the world and to give it a decisive long-range orientation. The world struggle in regard to the democratic, Jewish, and Bolshevist ideology would continue, and Spain could exert a great influence on developments in North Africa and South America if she consistently carried out a decisive and clear policy. These countries, too, would sooner or later be faced with a decision and would regard Spain's good example a model for their own national movements. The delay in the problem of mines and the attitude of the Ministry of Labor toward our colleague in Galicia, mining engineer Kegel, were incomprehensible and in no way compatible with the spirit of cooperation. Germany wished to give Spanish engineers, students, and workers an opportunity for training and expected that young people eager to work would be sent to receive training there. In contrast with this, a deserving man, an expert who could not be replaced in Spain, was denied opportunity to carry on his work in the interest of Spain. This condition implied a frame of mind which was unworthy of Germany's unselfish and voluntary cooperation in making available men and equipment. In Germany Herr Bernhardt had continually sought to allay any rising doubts, but there was now imminent danger that people would hereafter receive his defense of the Spanish attitude with deprecatory smiles. Fernández Cuevas then remarked that he could not understand how, in view of the importance of the great questions which had been raised in connection with the Spanish struggle for freedom, the matter of the mines should be accorded such importance by Germany that the assistance given Spain might even be withdrawn if the mining question was not settled in accordance with German wishes. Herr Bernhardt then expressly emphasized that Germany would never seek to exert pressure of that kind, since she had a much higher conception of the friendship between the two people than to use means of pressure. If Spain did not act willingly and from conviction, then forced promises were of no value. Germany regarded the matter of the mines as the focal point in German-Spanish cooperation and a scale for measuring whether and to what extent the cooperation which Germany had proffered freely and openly had found an echo in Spain. Our situation in Germany required a clear picture of things so that we could judge correctly the value or the worthlessness of Spanish friendship. If the Ministry had any fault whatsoever to find with our proposal, it should state so openly and make frank counterproposals. There would always be a way to arrive at an understanding, if there was a real and earnest desire to cooperate. Herr Bernhardt added that, if Spain really was not able to rid herself of centuries-old mistrust even in this present case, then, for example, the Spanish coworkers in the Montana mine should be summoned before the Ministry and it should be made clear to them that it was their duty to cooperate with us only as true Spaniards and to act in accordance with their conscience. It would then probably become perfectly apparent that not a single one of these people would have to deviate in the slightest from his current attitude in cooperating with us. For example, the paragraph pertaining to the *Interventor General* in the by laws did not originate with us but, on the contrary, with two Spanish jurists who were convinced, first, that they were staying within the law and, second, that they were doing the right thing morally.

Fernández Cuevas promised to inform Señor Suances in detail of the conversation with Herr Bernhardt. He inquired when Herr Bernhardt would return to Bilbao. The time was tentatively given as next Monday or Tuesday, prior to Herr Bernhardt's departure for Berlin, which is scheduled for Wednesday of next week.

No. 656

2129/463916

The Chargé d'Affaires in Spain to the Foreign Ministry

No. 258 of September 8   San Sebastián, September 8, 1938.
                                               Pol. I 2100 g.

The liaison officer of the Condor Legion at Spanish headquarters sends the following report:

Franco is once again very much concerned about the situation in Czechoslovakia. He attaches unfavorable significance to the presence of Cot [1] in Prague. He is sending 10,000 prisoners to work on fortifications at the border between Spanish and French Morocco and has requested available maps of the frontier there. At the same time he is sending 10,000 prisoners to work on fortifications at the Pyrenees border. End of report.

HEBERLEIN

---

[1] Pierre Cot, former French Air Minister and Minister of Commerce.

No. 657

4446/E086680–81

The Chargé d'Affaires in Spain to the Foreign Ministry

SECRET   SAN SEBASTIÁN, September 12, 1938.
No. 536 g   Pol. III 3221.
POLITICAL REPORT

Subject: Spain and the Central European crisis.

The development of the Central European crisis is naturally being followed with the greatest tension also in Nationalist Spain, all the more since it is clearly realized here that the outbreak of a European conflict would be bound to have very serious consequences for the outcome of the Spanish Civil War. To be sure, thus far the predominant conviction, based on confidence in the Führer's unswerving policy of peace, is that war will be avoided. So far I have not been approached by any Spanish official in regard to this question. Insofar as the matter has been discussed among the Spaniards here, the opinion expressed is rather unanimous to the effect that the outbreak of a European war would endanger in the extreme the victory of the Spanish Nationalist cause. It is believed that Red Spain would immediately array herself on the side of France and her allies and possibly also confirm this stand by an open declaration of war against Germany. Red Spain could then expect extensive military support from France, Russia, and possibly also from England, whereby Franco's military situation, which is not favorable now anyway, would soon become untenable. Moreover, Franco would then be more or less cut off from German and Italian help. In order to prevent a complete military defeat Franco might then be forced to make an unfavorable compromise with Red Spain or retire and leave such a liquidation of the Civil War to some more "moderate" person. This, however, would mean the return to Spain of a democratic, if not even of a Bolshevist regime.

I am passing on the above explanations—which, as I have said, are not based on any statements from responsible Spanish officials—with all due reservations and merely to describe the fears arising in various circles here. A professional German newspaperman who just returned from Paris informed me that he had heard similar ideas expressed in France, too.

HEBERLEIN

No. 658

139/126089

The Ambassador in Spain to the Foreign Ministry [1]

Telegram

SAN SEBASTIÁN, September 16, 1938—10:30 p.m.

No. 264 of September 16   Received September 17—12:45 a.m.

The Spanish Foreign Minister asked me to call on him immediately after my return from Germany; during my visit in Burgos today Jordana appeared extremely worried about the consequences which could result for Nationalist Spain from a warlike settlement of the Czech question and French intervention in the conflict. The French Foreign Minister had informed him that the French General Staff contemplated as one of its first measures an invasion of Catalonia and the seizure of the harbors of the Red zone in southern Spain. In addition, he knew from another source that France was preparing an attack on the Spanish zone in Morocco. Bonnet's communication might perhaps merely have been a threat, but it was certain that the cause of the Spanish Nationalist revolution would be greatly endangered at the present moment by warlike developments in Central Europe. He had instructed the Spanish Ambassador in Berlin to call the attention of the German Government to these grave misgivings. The Foreign Minister expressly termed false the report circulating here to the effect that France was trying to secure Franco's neutrality in the European conflict. The German liaison officer at headquarters reports that a very depressed state of mind and ill-concealed dissatisfaction with us are prevalent there with reference to Central European events, because in choosing the time for settling the Sudeten question we did not seem to give any consideration to the cause of Nationalist Spain for which we ourselves, after all, had done so much.

STOHRER

---

[1] Another translation of this telegram was printed in vol. II as document No. 504, p. 814.

No. 659

1606/385773–74

Memorandum by the Under State Secretary [1]

BERLIN, September 19, 1938.
zu Pol. I g 2190.

The Spanish Ambassador called on me today and asked me whether the report was correct that the Führer and Chamberlain had dis-

---

[1] An account of this interview was sent to the Embassy in Spain by telegram on Sept. 21 (2129/463923).

cussed the Spanish question at Obersalzberg. I told the Ambassador this had not been the case. Marqués de Magaz then once more reverted to the apprehensions entertained by Spain in the event of a European conflict. I told him quite plainly that the statements he was making to me here, which had also been made to our Ambassador in Spain, sounded somewhat as if we wanted to precipitate a war and as if Spain wished to make us responsible for it. Spanish fears were concerned of course with French intervention. The Ambassador knew very well that we did not believe in this at all. Señor de Magaz thereupon said that the Spanish statements were not to be understood in this sense.

I then reverted to a question that the Ambassador had asked on the occasion of his last visit, namely, what would become of the German equipment and personnel in the event of a European war. In agreement with the Supreme Command of the Wehrmacht, I informed the Ambassador that no changes were contemplated with respect to either men or equipment. What would happen in the event of a long war could not, of course, be foreseen. The Ambassador said that in that case active collaboration would no doubt be considered and thus, possibly, reinforcement of the German contingents. I again said that this eventuality was certainly not at all apparent at the moment.

WOERMANN

No. 660

1606/385789–96

The Ambassador in Spain to the Foreign Ministry

STRICTLY CONFIDENTIAL   SAN SEBASTIÁN, September 19, 1938.
No. 553 g   Pol. I 2239 g III.
With reference to our report No. 495 g of August 19 of this year.[1]
Subject: Internal situation in Nationalist Spain.

*Failure of the Nationalist counteroffensive at the Ebro bend.
Reasons:*

Contrary to expectation, the Nationalist offensive against the Reds who had advanced beyond the Ebro to a point near Gandesa has so far been unsuccessful. The envelopment tried at first failed completely, while the frontal attacks which then took place gained but very little territory. The reasons for this failure, as reported by the German and Italian military officials, are that cooperation among the various arms was inadequate and that Franco's troops showed little fighting spirit, while the Red side demonstrated superior leadership— undoubtedly exercised by foreign officers—and, above all, superior

---
[1] Not printed (3366/E010466–74).

command of the Red artillery. The losses on Franco's side are said to be great.

Offensive against Almadén likewise ended by strong Red counter-action.

The advance upon Almadén in Estremadura, begun simultaneously with the Valencia offensive, has been brought to a halt by the Red troops mentioned in the previous report, who were sent there after being released before Valencia. At one spot the Reds even succeeded in regaining a considerable portion of the lost territory by means of a counteroffensive.

Military situation very unsatisfactory but not dangerous.

The military situation must therefore be termed very unsatisfactory at present. It is not yet dangerous, however. But the equilibrium brought about between the forces—greater even than at Teruel—gives no indication as to whether, when, and how Franco will again succeed in taking the initiative. Morale at headquarters is therefore low. Violent scenes between Franco and his generals, who do not carry out attack orders correctly, are multiplying. The threatening international situation adds to the general dejection.

Because of equilibrium of forces, a military settlement of the war is improbable.

On the other hand, however, it is not to be assumed that the Reds will succeed, in case of new thrusts, in achieving more than local successes. From the military standpoint, therefore, it is not possible to predict how much longer the war will last. A military decision seems likely within the near future only if one or the other combatant receives "substantial" support from abroad.

Internal situation in Nationalist Spain continues tense. All sorts of rumors. Position of Suñer.

The internal situation in Nationalist Spain has undergone little change since my last report. It remains in the same state of tension. As a result of the unfavorable military situation and the clouds threatening on the international horizon, however, dissension within the Government is dormant at present. Nevertheless, the atmosphere remains replete with rumors regarding a reorganization of the Cabinet, a military dictatorship, the appointment of the Generalissimo's brother-in-law, Serrano Suñer, as Prime Minister, etc. Presumably all these reports concern deliberations which are actually taking place in leading circles but which will, in the interest of the common cause, probably have no further consequences, at least at present. That differences between the Minister of the Interior, Serrano Suñer, and the other members of the Cabinet continue, and also that there is considerable annoyance with him in wide circles, particularly in military circles, is borne out by a strictly confidential circular that Franco recently addressed to the highest military authorities, refuting the charges being made against his brother-in-law.

Ending of the trial of the Falangists.

As has already been reported, the trial of the Falangists Vélez and Aznar ended with the sentencing of each of them to 5½ years of compulsory labor. Since the serious charges originally brought against these men were wisely dropped, this did not arouse any special feeling.

New civil governors, who are monarchists.

A number of changes were recently made in the administration of the provinces. Thus five civil governors were removed for reasons of various kinds; in monarchist circles it is stated that the newly appointed governors are all enthusiastic monarchists, which is not very surprising, to be sure, since the particular provinces involved are in the north of the country.

General war weariness grows.

War weariness is increasing everywhere. It seems to a certain extent even to be invading the front. So far there is no evidence anywhere of the measures for mobilization of all forces demanded by the military and other circles.

Spanish Reds active in the Nationalist zone.

Propaganda in the Nationalist zone by Spanish Reds continues. Recently transports of arms for the Basque provinces are even supposed to have been discovered.

In Red Spain, too, there is no optimism of any kind. Shortage of food and money.

Although the situation is at present unfavorable for Franco, there is by no means excessive optimism among the leaders in Red Spain. The food shortage seems to be increasing again, and it is feared that gold for the payment of purchases of war matériel and foods will gradually become scarce. Negrín is said to have stated in a circle of friends that it would be difficult to hold out a third winter.

Internal situation also very tense on the Red side. Influence of the Czech crisis upon Red Spanish internal conditions?

The internal situation on the Red side shows signs of growing tension. The more moderate politicians—Prieto and his friends—

are still in the background, although opposition to those in power, Negrín and Alvarez del Vayo, who are entirely under Russian influence, seems to be increasing. A peaceful or at least local settlement of the Czech conflict in the German sense, which would also bring with it a decided weakening of Russian prestige, might exert a certain influence on internal conditions in the Red Spanish zone.

The question of armistice and intervention. Reds demand amnesty above all. Franco unreceptive.

Prieto is said to be still in touch with England and to hope for intervention from that quarter after the Czech question is settled. Among the conditions that the Reds wish to impose for an armistice, the demand for a general amnesty is supposed to be foremost. In this respect, however, Franco has thus far not shown himself to be very receptive. As Foreign Minister Jordana told me a few days ago, he refused in the case of military and civil prisoners in his custody to make even small concessions of the same sort proposed to him by the Reds through the exchange commission of British Field Marshal Chetwode.[2]

No further mention of the Non-Intervention Committee. Hemming's trip to Spain unlikely. Intervention? Compromise peace?

The reply of the Spanish Nationalist Government to the Non-Intervention Committee was published in Spain a few days after dispatch of the preliminary report and was extensively commented upon by the press here. Since then there has been no talk about the matter here. Even the dispatch of Hemming, Secretary General of the Non-Intervention Committee, to Spain, which Franco finally agreed to in principle, seems to have come to nought. As General Jordana tells me, after the Russian objections he is no longer expecting Hemming's visit.[3] It almost looks as if the effectiveness and potentialities of the Non-Intervention Committee, so often assailed and ridiculed, had come to an end. In view of the balance of forces prevailing at present on the battlefield, what has up to now been a mere possibility of ending the war through intervention and agreement of the powers is gaining in probability. Since in England, too, the realization is growing that Russian influence must be forced out of Europe, a compromise peace would not necessarily be to Franco's disadvantage, in spite of the great anxieties the latter entertains on this score.

STOHRER

---

[2] A commission under the leadership of Field Marshal Sir Philip Chetwode to arrange the exchange of civilian prisoners had been accepted by both sides at the end of August. The commission remained in Spain from September 1938 until April 1939 but was able to accomplish little.

[3] Marginal note: "Superseded."

No. 661

632/252519

The Ambassador in Spain to the Foreign Ministry

Telegram

SAN SEBASTIÁN, September 21, 1938—8 : 30 p.m.
No. 271 of September 21   Received September 21—10 : 35 p.m.

I have it on excellent authority from headquarters that in yesterday's meeting of the Council of Ministers Franco expressed grave fears that a speedy and peaceful solution of the Sudeten question might be accomplished at the expense of Spain, i.e. through undesirable and unfavorable intervention by the powers. Franco has summoned the Ambassadors from Berlin and Rome for oral consultation.

STOHRER

No. 662

2129/463921

The Ambassador in Spain to the Foreign Ministry

Telegram

SECRET   SAN SEBASTIÁN, September 22, 1938.
No. 277 of September 22   Pol. I 2226.

The Italian Embassy informed me that Italy intended to ship home from Spain one division (about 10,000 men) after conclusion of the present operation at the Ebro bend.   Reason: illness, family matters, etc., of the volunteers in question.   Purpose: a gesture of good will vis-à-vis the Non-Intervention Committee.

STOHRER

No. 663

2946/576317

Memorandum by the Ambassador in Spain

SAN SEBASTIÁN, September 23, 1938.

In yesterday's consultation with Herr Bernhardt after the latter's return from Germany, I informed him that, in accordance with the request he had made of me at Nuremberg, the Spanish Government for the time being had merely been informed by *note verbale* that Herr Bernhardt was authorized by the Reich Government to accept the peseta equivalent of 15 million RM which come from the special deliveries of the German Government to the Nationalist Government and are to be used for financing the Montana companies.   On the other hand, the second portion of the note completed before my departure, containing a request that the Spanish Government permit German capital a share greater than 40 percent in the Montana companies, had not yet been delivered to the Foreign Ministry.

When I asked whether the Embassy should now also submit this request concerning capital participation, Herr Bernhardt asked that we refrain from this for the present.

STOHRER

No. 664

2129/463925

The Ambassador in Spain to the Foreign Ministry

Telegram

SAN SEBASTIÁN, September 25, 1938—11:30 p.m.
Received September 26—1:00 a.m.

No. 282 of September 25   Pol. III 3303.

The German liaison officer at Spanish headquarters advises as follows:

"Franco wonders why Berlin maintains no contact with him at all. He said he knew nothing about the political and military intentions of Germany in the event of a European war or a war confined to Czechoslovakia; that, even if Nationalist Spain was not at present a great power, she was nevertheless in a position, as a friendly power, to help us in some way or other; he asked what Germany intended to do with her fleet, and whether Spanish ports were desired for supply purposes; in that case preparations could be made. What will happen to the Condor Legion? The warship *Deutschland* had entered the port of Vigo with a large tanker, surely with intentions of some kind that were unknown to him. He had always hoped to receive requests and questions from Berlin—but in vain. Franco seems somewhat hurt. The persons around him speak of Nationalist Spain being ignored."

Upon my return from Germany I informed the Foreign Minister in accordance with the statements of the Reich Foreign Minister at Nuremberg and the conference with the State Secretary on the last evening of the Party Rally and I have now . . . (apparently the group "transmitted" is missing) to him the contents of telegram No. 376 of September 24 [1] containing information regarding the Godesberg conferences.

If it is possible to give the Franco Government further information, please send me instruction.

STOHRER

---

[1] Vol. II, document No. 597, p. 925.

No. 665

2685/528870

The Director of Hisma to the Ambassador in Spain

SECRET   SALAMANCA, September 26, 1938.

MY DEAR AMBASSADOR: Yesterday I had an exhaustive conversation with the Generalissimo. He is especially concerned:

1. About the cessation of deliveries. The problem is beginning to have extremely grave consequences in some areas. Above all, powder is lacking.

2. About the possibility of a French attack in Morocco (to secure their colonial line). He has sent troops there which, however, will not be adequate in an emergency.

3. About the unprotected border at Irún, which would be difficult for him to defend in case of a French invasion.

Franco expects French intervention in case of a war in Central Europe. He views the situation with a clear head but undoubtedly also with very great concern, and he regrets that he is relatively little informed and consulted.

I stated that in the tide of events little information was coming out of Germany anyway and that the greatest reserve was being exercised. He was not to take this amiss in any way. Franco understands this.

He finds the internal situation satisfactory despite many occurrences. There has been no change in his views.

I have been informed of Captain Wilhelmi's telegram.[1]

Heil Hitler!

Very sincerely,

BERNHARDT

---

[1] The telegram mentioned here has not been identified. Captain Wilhelmi was German liaison officer at Nationalist headquarters. For a report from him concerning General Franco's views see the preceding document.

[EDITORS' NOTE. For accounts of an interview between the Under State Secretary and the Spanish Ambassador on September 26 and an interview between the State Secretary and the Italian Ambassador on the same day, see volume II, documents Nos. 622 and 624, pp. 950 and 952. A minute of a further interview between the Under State Secretary and the Spanish Ambassador is printed as document No. 638, p. 969. A report of September 27 from Ambassador Mackensen in Rome on the Spanish question is printed as document No. 641, p. 972, and the Under State Secretary's further memorandum on the subject as document No. 659, p. 991.]

No. 666

5194/E307467–69

The Ambassador in Spain to the Foreign Ministry

Telegram

SAN SEBASTIÁN, September 28, 1938—9 : 30 p.m.

No. 292 of September 28

With reference to our telegraphic report No. 291 of September 27.[1] Even before I asked the question contemplated, the Foreign Minister declared today that France and England had addressed an inquiry to the Generalissimo as to what he contemplated doing in the event of a European war. This question had been put to Quiñones de León, as well as to Alba. The latter, in particular, had been told in the Foreign Office, with reference to the conference that had taken place in London on that day with the French Ministers and General Gamelin, that the French General Staff was prepared to take no action against Nationalist Spain if Franco declared himself neutral. Otherwise they would attack immediately at the Pyrenees and in Morocco. Spain's situation was very difficult. She could presumably count on no substantial military assistance from Germany and Italy and was therefore not capable of continuing her war against the Red Army and defending herself against the French besides. The Generalissimo regretted that Spain was not yet strong enough to range herself on our side. At the time, therefore, he unfortunately saw little prospect of any solution other than to declare Spain's neutrality, which was perhaps also the best solution for us and Italy, since Red rule in Spain would be prevented and for us their neutrality would naturally be of an entirely benevolent nature. In reply to my question as to what would happen to the Condor Legion in such a case, the Minister stated that the German and Italian volunteers were members of the Spanish Nationalist Army and would remain so. The question of their dismissal had not even been raised. Moreover, this matter belonged within the jurisdiction of the Non-Intervention Committee.

To an objection by me, the Minister said that it would naturally be difficult to bring up supplies for the German volunteers, but that the most important supplies could, after all, be brought by neutral ships, submarines, and airplanes. In the course of the conversation, the Minister also stated that in return for neutrality Nationalist Spain would naturally demand that the French, etc., cease giving Red Spain any further support.

The Minister requested me to report these views to my Government, to explain to it the difficulty of finding another solution, and to try to

---

[1] Not printed (140/75550). In this telegram Stohrer forwarded information that Franco had himself told the French that Spain would remain neutral. Stohrer said he would speak to Jordana on the subject the next day.

bring about understanding of Spanish intentions, which I promised to do. The Minister added in confidence at this point that the Generalissimo intended to address a private letter to the Führer on this question, if this should be necessary.

Finally Jordana declared that the Spanish Government would be very much relieved to learn that the friendly German Government approved its intention. The Spanish Ambassador in Berlin seems to have received instructions to this effect.

I have the impression that Franco has already committed himself rather extensively to neutrality.

Shortly after receiving me, the Minister made a similar *démarche* with the Italian Ambassador, whom I informed beforehand of the course of my interview.

General Veith has been informed.

STOHRER

No. 667

3364/E010269

The Head of Political Division IIIa to the Embassy in Great Britain

Telegram

No. 321 of September 28   BERLIN, September 28, 1938.
                                              zu Pol. III 3295 I.

The Spanish Nationalist Government has requested that, if the matter should come up for discussion in the Non-Intervention Committee, we reject intervention by the League of Nations in the combing-out of volunteers, as proposed in Geneva by Negrín.[1] If the occasion should arise, please act accordingly.

SCHWENDEMANN

---

[1] On Sept. 21 at the session of the League Assembly, Negrín had announced the decision of the Spanish Republican Government to release immediately all non-Spanish nationals serving in the Republican forces. He had asked that the League Council appoint a commission to supervise the evacuation.

No. 668

2129/463934-35

The Consul at Tetuán to the Foreign Ministry

SECRET

No. 1816/Pol. VIII

TETUÁN, September 28, 1938.

Pol. III 3364.

Subject: The military situation in Morocco.

High Commissioner Beigbeder expressed himself as follows regarding the military situation in Morocco in a conversation with me today:

Along the French border of the Protectorate some 80,000 French troops were concentrated, half of whom were ready to attack in the first line with excellent equipment, heavy artillery, assault tanks, and airplanes. In view of this menacing concentration of troops, Señor Beigbeder had found himself compelled to take effective countermeasures. He had had 40,000 guns distributed among the Riffs, who stood ready for an incursion into the French zone; they would receive an additional 40,000 guns for distribution among the natives in French Morocco if matters became serious and an advance were ordered for the purpose of supporting an armed rebellion against the French troops. Moreover, 18 battalions and sufficiently strong air forces stood ready in Spanish Morocco to oppose a possible French invasion. The High Commissioner takes an entirely confident view of the military situation in Spanish Morocco and believes that with the defense forces at his disposal he would surely be able to repel a French invasion. The French were very disturbed by the preparation of an armed insurrection of the natives. The French Military Attaché at Tangier had already called on the High Commissioner four times recently. Moreover, 2 days ago Señor Beigbeder had also received a visit from the French Minister at Tangier. These visits had presumably taken place at the instance of Resident General Noguès in Rabat. The French envoys in their conversations with the High Commissioner had denied any intention on the part of France to attack Spanish Morocco and had requested Señor Beigbeder to explain his military measures in the Spanish zone. The High Commissioner had declared that his measures were of a defensive character and had been justified by the French troop concentration along the border of the Protectorate.

Finally, the High Commissioner also told me that it was very difficult for him to restrain the Riffs he had armed from making attacks on the French zone, in view of the great hatred the natives entertained for France.

The German Embassy at San Sebastián has received a copy of the report.

BROSCH

No. 669

1606/385816–17

The Under State Secretary to the Embassy in Spain

Telegram

No. 391   BERLIN, September 28, 1938.
                              Sent September 29—7: 30 p.m.
                                        Pol. I 2294 g.

With reference to your telegram 291.[1]

The Spanish Ambassador informed me on September 26,[2] on instructions, that the Spanish Government intended to remain neutral in the event of a European conflict and wished to enter into negotiations with the British and French Governments regarding this. The reason he gave for this step was that Spain would not be in a position as long as the Civil War lasted to intervene actively on the side of friendly powers.

The Spanish Ambassador today informed me further that France had meanwhile inquired of the Spanish Nationalist Government how the latter would act in the event of a war and the Nationalist Government had replied that it would remain neutral. After prior consultation with Rome, I told the Spanish Ambassador today, as instructed, that we could understand it if Spain remained neutral in the event of a European conflict, which we did not believe would occur. But we expected that Spain would not negotiate with England and France in this regard and that it would exercise neutrality in a way entirely benevolent to Germany and Italy—which could still be discussed in detail if the occasion arises. If it can be ascertained whether the initiative actually came from France or whether it was from Spain, please report by wire.[3]

                                        WOERMANN

---

[1] Not printed; see document No. 666, footnote 1.
[2] See Editors' Note, p. 748.
[3] The text of this telegram was communicated to the German Embassies in France (as No. 459), Great Britain (as No. 329), and Italy (as No. 344). The telegram to Rome included the following additional paragraph: "The Spanish Ambassador stated that Germany's reaction to Spanish neutrality had been more cordial than that of Rome. I replied to him that according to my information the Italian Government had expressed itself to the Spanish Ambassador in Rome in similar fashion."

No. 670

2685/528905

The Ambassador in Spain to the Foreign Ministry

Telegram

SAN SEBASTIÁN, September 30, 1938—6 : 00 p.m.

No. 297 of September 30

With reference to your telegraphic instruction No. 391 of September 29, last paragraph.

Jordana told me expressly during the conversation of September 28 [1] that the initiative in the neutrality question had come from France and England and not from Spain.

STOHRER

---

[1] See document No. 666, p. 749.

No. 671

2685/528874

The Ambassador in Spain to the Foreign Ministry

Telegram

SAN SEBASTIÁN, September 30, 1938—5 : 45 p.m.

No. 298 of September 30

I suggest that after settlement of the Czech question we consider whether we should not take rapid and extensive action on the wishes expressed by Franco for deliveries of matériel and arms, which we could not fulfill heretofore, in order to place him in a better military position—especially in the event of a compromise in the Spanish Civil War. Such a spontaneous declaration on our part would surely be very gratefully acknowledged by Franco.

STOHRER

No. 672

442/221382–86

The Ambassador in Spain to the State Secretary

SECRET   SAN SEBASTIÁN, October 2, 1938.

DEAR WEIZSÄCKER : I do not know whether the newspaper reports are accurate, according to which other acute European problems and in particular the Spanish question have already been discussed in Munich. But there is probably no doubt that after the settlement of the Czech crisis certain preconditions for a promising attempt to end the Spanish Civil War by other than military means might be considered as indicated.

From my oral and written reports you know that I have stated with increasing emphasis that it is unlikely the Spanish war can be concluded by military means and that at different times I thought I saw indications that England was merely waiting for a suitable moment in order to intervene politically in Spain. According to reliable reports, Sir Robert Hodgson, the British agent here, stated recently in a circle of intimate friends that after the peaceful settlement of the Czech question England would attack the Spanish problem energetically.

If one examines the Spanish question from *here*—which is naturally all I can do—one must come to the conclusion that conditions now exist here too that might induce both sides to come to an agreement.

As I have been reporting up to the present time, there is, to be sure, in Spanish Nationalist Government circles no tendency whatever toward a compromise; on the contrary, any such plan is rejected with positively nervous intensity. But this attitude is by no means uniform. War-weariness in the Spanish Nationalist zone—behind the front as well as at the front—is doubtless increasing, which, moreover, is not to be wondered at in view of the long-drawn-out war, the not very energetic conduct of the war, and the failure of the planned "mobilization of all forces" to materialize. In the opinion of German and Italian military authorities—and that of the former is necessarily decisive for me in military matters—it is inconceivable that the war can be won by Franco militarily in the foreseeable future, unless Germany and Italy should decide once again to make new, great sacrifices in materials and personnel to Spain. From my reports the Foreign Ministry also knows that, quite apart from the military developments, the situation otherwise in the Nationalist zone can in no wise be described as altogether satisfactory. Even if during the anxious hours of international tension the hatchet was buried within government circles, domestic differences have by no means been settled. How the domestic situation is to be judged was shown during the days of political crisis, when the possibility, not to mention the probability, of Red coups and uprisings in the Nationalist zone was spoken of at Franco's headquarters with almost the same anxiety as the danger of an invasion by France over the Pyrenees and in the Spanish zone of Morocco. This latter fact also explains the sigh of relief in Spanish Nationalist Government circles when France and England made the proposal to Franco that in case of a European war he remain neutral. In view of this general situation on the part of the Whites it is probably not wrong to say that it is perhaps even in the interest of Franco himself no longer to reject the possibility of a compromise completely.

Among the Reds—and that is gratifying—the outlook is no better. For a long time none of the men in power there has believed in a military victory any more, as I have often reported. On the contrary, it is to be assumed that the speculations concerning a European war, which have now turned out to be wrong, and the severe defeat of Moscow at Munich will have a very depressing effect in the Red zone. In this connection, the Generalissimo told me yesterday that in the last two days Red units at different places on the front had deserted after hoisting white flags and, upon being questioned, had stated that after the settlement of the Czech crisis there was really no more hope for the Reds. The shortage of foodstuffs, very noticeably mounting again in the Red zone, and the approaching winter, which may confront the Reds with insurmountable difficulties in other respects also, should likewise really promote the idea there of yielding. Whether— as is assumed here in Government circles—the well-known proposal by Negrín in the League of Nations (see report No. 4548/38 of September 29 [1]) really is to be interpreted as a sign of weakness and a search for a compromise, I shall not decide. But it doubtless means a feeler in the direction of a negotiated peace. This appears to me to be evident from the very fact that the British Government—as I hear—was previously informed of Negrín's plan to announce in Geneva the withdrawal of all Red volunteers.

It is deplorable that Franco's troops are right now being bled white and are digging in at the bend of the Ebro. If it were possible for Franco at this moment to strike an important blow against the Reds, even with only local results, a compromise might perhaps be brought about, which would not appear to be very different from the "unconditional surrender" of the Reds demanded by Franco. In order to help Franco in this matter, I urged, in telegram No. 298 of September 30, that the shipments of materials which are already in principle intended for him but have been withheld because of the critical situation in Central Europe be placed at his disposal at the earliest possible moment.

If Franco does not succeed in the near future in softening up the Reds by military pressure, there will not be much else to do—always presupposing that we and Italy do not again wish to make a great effort—than to let things take their course, or for the powers to intervene. In the first case, we run the risk that the present regime in

---

[1] Not printed (5153/E303684–86).

Nationalist Spain will sooner or later disintegrate—which would necessarily result in new convulsions. On the other hand, if Franco, in case of intervention by the powers, does not show himself to be too intransigent, he should even now—for other reasons than the ones already mentioned—not come off so badly at all, as he certainly is somewhat in favor with France and England, since he pledged himself to neutrality in these countries' hours of anxiety during the last few weeks. This fact might, especially in England, weigh favorably in the scale against the other fact, likewise confirmed recently by Sir Robert Hodgson, that the prestige of the Generalissimo has suffered very much in England and that people there are beginning to doubt his ability to master the difficulties which are arising.

For our interests also—always viewed from the local standpoint here—I consider a quick settlement of the Civil War, naturally by a compromise altogether favorable to Franco, to be desirable. If the war continues, we face an uncertain future. If it is ended now in a manner that could be considered somewhat conciliatory—e.g. by magnanimous concessions on the part of Franco, and not by acceptance of the conditions of the Reds—the hatred against Germany and Italy nursed by the very strong Red element would decrease and this would affect us advantageously. At any rate we shall have to guard very much against playing a leading role in case of intervention or in connection with any pressure on Franco; we must rather take care that the political, and especially the military circles, which will presumably continue to be in power in the future, cannot reproach us with having betrayed the Nationalist revolution at the last moment. I have already reported that the Generalissimo has already given indications of a certain distrust in this regard, and that he fears that the peaceful settlement of the Czech crisis was effected at the expense of Spain. Yesterday, when I sat next to Franco for an hour and a half at a dinner, he expressed himself enthusiastically about the triumph of the Führer at Munich, but, when I remarked that the method of the successful solution of the Czech crisis could become a model for subsequent international conflicts, he avoided relating this in any way to the Spanish crisis and did not pursue the subject further.

Perhaps all the above-mentioned considerations are pointless because of decisions already made or plans formed there. If, however, developments should take the course I have set forth above, I wish to make the important request that I be kept currently informed regarding their implementation in order that, by suggesting details of procedure, I may on the basis of my knowledge of conditions here do my best to prevent a possible support of intervention from becoming politically disadvantageous to us here.

My Italian colleague shares the views developed above. Perhaps it would be useful, in case intervention is undertaken by someone else, even now to come to an understanding with Rome concerning the attitude to be taken by Germany and Italy.

With cordial greetings and Heil Hitler!

Sincerely yours,
STOHRER

No. 673

1606/385833–34

Memorandum by the Under State Secretary

BERLIN, October 3, 1938.
Pol. I 2325 g.

The Spanish Ambassador called on me today and requested me to convey to the Foreign Minister his congratulations on the settlement of the Sudeten German question.

The Ambassador claimed to have learned from Munich [1] that the Führer and Mussolini had discussed the Spanish problem and that Daladier, too, upon his departure, had expressed himself to the effect that the question would now have to be settled. I told him that I knew nothing about Daladier's statements; according to my information the word "Spain" had been mentioned between the Führer and Mussolini, to be sure, but nothing definite had been discussed. The Ambassador expressed the desire that the powers should make no decision about Spain without the participation of the Nationalist Government. I said this went without saying.

The Marqués de Magaz then again reverted to the subject of the Spanish declaration of neutrality and expressed his satisfaction at the fact that we had shown understanding for it. I told the Ambassador that we had indeed understood that Spain could not have waged war actively on our side as long as the Civil War lasted, if this question had come up at all. Nevertheless I had to tell him that in Berlin and, according to my information, also in Rome the handling of the question of neutrality had left somewhat of a nasty taste. In particular, we had considered it entirely unnecessary for Salamanca to publish the declaration of neutrality so prematurely. After all, there would have been plenty of time for that after a war had actually broken out.

WOERMANN

---

[1] For the discussions which took place at Munich see vol. II, documents Nos. 670 and 674, pp. 1003 and 1011.

No. 674

1606/385824–27

Memorandum by the Head of Political Division IIIa

BERLIN, October 5, 1938.
zu W W958 g.
e.o. Pol. I 2310 g.

The question of further deliveries to Franco, which was raised by telegram No. 298 (W958 g) of September 30 from San Sebastián, should be resolved only in connection with the question of the future policy of the Rome-Berlin Axis with respect to the Spanish problem. We have given Franco spontaneous assistance often enough, and the disproportion between our services and Franco's services in return, as well as the question how this disproportion could be remedied in our favor, has therefore had to be weighed repeatedly.

It therefore seems more nearly correct to consider the question of our further deliveries partly in connection with our desire to alter this disproportion in our favor. The first condition for further deliveries would be to demand that Franco acknowledge fully the deliveries made in the past (cf. memorandum W 909 g Rs.[1]).

Although the bogging down of the Spanish Nationalist advance and the apparent equilibrium of the military forces between White and Red Spain have recently again revived the idea of a compromise peace, nevertheless after the settlement of the Czech crisis the prospects for such a compromise probably have greatly diminished. A European war was *the* great hope of the Spanish Reds. Their readiness, recently expressed at Geneva, to evacuate the foreign volunteers under the supervision of a League of Nations commission may be explained by the fact that by this step, principally by getting rid of the Russians, they desire with the help of France and England to open the path to a compromise. The food situation in Red Spain is constantly deteriorating. There is probably no longer any possibility at all of victory for Red Spain. In view of Franco's superiority with regard to food supplies, raw materials, men, and leadership, the Reds must realize that a war of attrition could only result in their defeat.

On the other hand, Franco only recently rejected any compromise peace with the Reds and has always demanded unconditional surrender. It is hard to see why he should be inclined to a compromise now that the danger of a European war is over. At the same time it is hard to see how such a compromise could be forced on him from the outside without the assistance of the Rome-Berlin Axis.

---

[1] Not found.

Thus everything hinges on the question what we and Italy intend to do. The negative aim of preventing a victory of Bolshevism in Spain remains as before. This could also be achieved through a compromise peace. It would probably also be possible to preserve our economic interests in such a compromise peace. Beyond this, however, our interest lies in a strong Spain that leans toward the Rome-Berlin Axis. A strong Spain would have less in common with England and France than with us. It is obvious how much more favorable our situation would be in the event of a European conflict with a militarily and economically strong Spain on our side. A Spain that emerged from a compromise peace between the Whites and the Reds would not be a strong Spain, however, and it is precisely for this reason that England and France desire this compromise. A victorious Nationalist Spain with an authoritarian government of a military cast would, however—and Franco has expressed himself confidentially to this effect—desire above all to be strong in a military and economic respect. The ideology of Nationalist Spain clearly expresses this.

Our interest, therefore, is in a total victory for Franco. Italy's interest is probably the same. The Rome-Berlin Axis should therefore aim at a speedy and victorious ending of the Spanish Civil War as soon as possible.

We would not, however, as previous experience has shown, be able to attain this goal most rapidly by complying unconditionally with Franco's requests or by pressing assistance upon him, so to speak, as on earlier occasions, but rather by first conferring with him on the question how the war can most speedily be brought to a victorious conclusion and by jointly adopting a plan which will then be jointly carried out. We should not help without receiving in return guaranties for our future interests in Spain and without having something to say about the use to which our assistance is put, since otherwise we have no guaranty that this assistance would have the effect that we expect of it.

We therefore make the following proposals:

1. To approve no further shipments to Franco until agreement is reached between Rome and Berlin regarding the further handling of the Spanish question.

2. After this agreement is obtained, to negotiate with Franco regarding his intentions, based on the common desire of the Rome-Berlin Axis and Nationalist Spain to bring the war to a victorious end with all possible speed.

3. To determine what assistance is still necessary to effect this speedy, victorious ending and adopt a military plan for the effective employment of these means.

4. In the course of the plan outlined under 1–3, to clarify the obligations that Franco is willing to assume in return for the assistance granted and to commit him to these obligations.

Herewith submitted to Under State Secretary Woermann through the Deputy Director of the Political Department.

SCHWENDEMANN

No. 675

2661/527795–97

The Ambassador in Spain to the Foreign Ministry

STRICTLY CONFIDENTIAL   SAN SEBASTIÁN, October 6, 1938.
No. 570 g   Pol. III 3454.

Subject: The Foreign Minister on the present political situation in Spain.

I had a long conversation yesterday with Foreign Minister General Jordana on the general effects of the Munich agreement and the special consequences presumably resulting for Spain.

General Jordana fully shared the general view that the peaceful solution of the Czech conflict by the four great European powers without Russia, which had been entirely in accordance with German demands, meant a severe defeat for Moscow and that now the path had been smoothed for a pacification of Europe for a long time to come.

With respect to the Spanish Civil War, he immediately asked what would now happen. He answered this himself by stating that the war would now have to be prosecuted by Nationalist Spain with redoubled energy in order to bring about the capitulation of the Reds. The time was now particularly favorable, since Munich has destroyed the hopes of Red Spain for involving all of Europe. With evident anxiety, Jordana expressed the hope that the two great allied powers would not now at the last moment withdraw their aid from the Generalissimo. He asked particularly that the deliveries of war matériel from Germany—particularly powder—which had been held back for the time being because of the European crisis, be dispatched to Spain with all possible speed (cf. telegram No. 307 of October 6 [1]).

When I pointed out that in the whole foreign press there was so much talk of intervention and a compromise settlement of the Civil War, Jordana told me that no feelers had been put out in this direction from any quarter thus far. If the Civil War ended with a compromise, then the whole Nationalist effort would have been in vain. The

---

[1] Not printed (2685/528893).

Reds must absolutely be forced to capitulate. He very much hoped that the negotiations concerning Mediterranean questions, apparently already begun between England and Italy, would not turn out unsatisfactorily for Nationalist Spain.

To my question as to how he judged the situation of the Reds and what he thought of the speeches of Negrín and Vayo at the League of Nations and of other reports regarding the peace efforts of the Reds, the Foreign Minister replied that Negrín's proposal to withdraw the volunteers from the Red side was surely a tricky maneuver calculated to induce Franco to take a similar step. Moreover, Negrín's procedure surely indicated a certain weakness and need for peace on the Red side, which was also brought out clearly by the fact that Red politicians were in touch with Paris and London. At present, to be sure, the situation on the Red side, despite food and money shortages, did not seem to him bad enough as yet to make capitulation appear possible without further military successes by the Nationalist Army or heavy pressure from abroad. It was to be hoped, however, that after the Munich decisions France's support of the Reds would diminish.

In the course of the conversation, I called the Foreign Minister's attention to the remark made by the Generalissimo at the end of his recent radio speech to the effect that all those who had committed no crimes against the common law and sincerely wished to support the cause of Spain had nothing to fear (see report No. 4550/38 of October 3 [2]). This was surely good propaganda against the Reds, whose leaders were still saying that in case of a defeat or capitulation just about everyone would be executed by the victorious Nationalists.

In reply to a remark of mine, Jordana admitted that, on the other hand, an interminable protraction of the war without a decisive victory would entail other dangers for Nationalist Spain.

STOHRER

---

[2] Not printed (5158/E303729–31).

No. 676

650/255753–57

Memorandum by the Head of Political Division IIIa [1]

BERLIN, October 7, 1938.
e.o. Pol. III 3402.

Since the Spanish question is again apparently becoming acute and is perhaps entering the decisive stage, an inquiry into the state of our

---

[1] A memorandum similar to and in large part identical with this appears in the files of the Reich Chancellery under date of Oct. 26 (1534/374429–32).

interests there and the prospects for the realization of our interests seems to be in order. The following points appear noteworthy:

1. From observation of the Spanish Civil War, first in Red and then in White territory, the conclusion is drawn that the Spanish war raises fundamental issues and that new forces have appeared during its course which aim at a transformation of Spain. The Reds wanted to destroy traditional Spain in order to replace it with a Marxist-Communist or an Anarchist political and economic experiment. Nationalist Spain is fighting for the maintenance of tradition and simultaneously for the elimination of foreign influences directed against the spiritual traditions of Spain, and for the rebirth of Spain. The concept of the state in Nationalist Spain is directed toward a synthesis of Catholic tradition and the ideas of an authoritarian, socially minded government. The individualism in economy, domestic politics, and mode of life which was predominant in Spanish life heretofore is to be supplanted by the principles of the common weal, the supremacy of the state, and work. As regards foreign policy, they wish to arrest the decline in power which has been going on for centuries and, in the spirit of the old tradition, to reestablish a strong and even an imperial Spain, ready to take her place in the councils of Europe.

If the war had ended in a few months with a victory by Franco, its outcome would scarcely have been more than mere reaction. The long duration of the war has increasingly aroused the entire Spanish people and has made them receptive to new ideas. Widest groups of the population are aware today that after the victorious end of the war something entirely different from the Spain of before the Civil War or even before the fall of the monarchy must be brought about. What is in preparation in Nationalist Spain has its parallel in the change which took place in Italy under Mussolini's leadership. It means a very conscious turn toward a new period in Spanish history, actuated by the desire to put an end to the period of decadence and historical disintegration.

2. It is obvious that such intentions cannot be to the liking of France and England. These two nations have really been the ones that have benefited from the Spanish decline, without which their position in Africa and in the Mediterranean would have been impossible. They fear that a rejuvenated Spain will endanger their historical position in the Mediterranean and in Africa. Anyone who has lived among Spaniards in Nationalist Spain can understand this anxiety. The aims of Nationalist Spain are in the last analysis directed against France and England. This accounts for the desire on the part of England and France to prevent a victory by Franco.

3. It hardly needs to be stated that the above-mentioned aims of Nationalist Spain are entirely in the interest of ourselves and Italy.

The filling of the military and political vacuum on the Iberian peninsula, which has already been completed to a considerable extent, means a fundamental change in the position of France—before the war there were thirty to forty thousand soldiers worthy of the name in Spanish territory, and these were in Morocco; today, counting both the Whites and the Reds, there are one and a quarter million. Mazarin's words after the conclusion of the Peace of the Pyrenees in 1659, that the Pyrenees no longer existed, i.e. that France's rear was secure from attack by way of the Pyrenees, would lose their reality. France's connections with her colonial empire would be problematical. Gibraltar would be worthless, and the freedom of movement of the British fleet through the Straits would depend on Spain, not to mention the possibility of having submarines and light naval forces as well as the air force operating from the Iberian peninsula in all directions of the compass. A European conflict in which the Rome-Berlin Axis was alined against England and France would take on an entirely different aspect if a strong Spain joined the Rome-Berlin Axis.

4. The prerequisites for making Spain a strong military nation definitely exist. The people have displayed remarkable soldierly qualities in this war—for that matter, merely a reiteration of the fact that in the sixteenth and seventeenth centuries the Spanish infantry was the finest in Europe. The country has room for a much more numerous population. It has all the possibilities of being economically self-sufficient, particularly in regard to natural resources. An authoritarian government could make something very important out of this country in a few years, in spite of the losses and destruction caused by the Civil War.

5. From the above statements it is obvious that our Spanish policy, that is, the policy of the Rome-Berlin Axis, should do everything possible to enable Franco to achieve a quick victory, to promote the reconstruction of Spain, and to seek to bring about the close dependence of Spain upon the Rome-Berlin Axis.

6. Thus the following are necessary: further military and diplomatic support of Franco till final victory is won; frustration of all French and British efforts to prevent a victory by Franco or bring about a compromise between the Whites and the Reds by means of non-intervention or in any other way. As far as a compromise is concerned, in Nationalist Spain all the Red leaders are considered criminals with whom no agreement will be made, and quite correctly, for they are responsible for the murder of hundreds of thousands of Spaniards with Rightist sympathies.

It would be wrong to reproach Franco for his attitude on the neutrality question or to conclude that he is unreliable. The position of

Nationalist Spain in a European war would have been quite desperate. It must be remembered that it would not have been merely a question of victory or defeat but rather of the very existence of all men in Nationalist Spain who occupied any position of importance, along with their families; for the victorious Reds would have massacred as many of them as they could have laid hands on, as they had done with their relatives and friends in Red territory.

SCHWENDEMANN

No. 677

2650/527287–88

The Ambassador in Spain to the Foreign Ministry

No. 4650   SAN SEBASTIÁN, October 10, 1938.

POLITICAL REPORT

Subject: Withdrawal of Italian volunteers.   Rejection of the idea of mediation.

After the Spanish Nationalist Government yesterday officially announced the immediate withdrawal of all Italian volunteers who have been taking part in the fighting in Spain for more than 18 months, the press here has been at pains to counteract the impression that this measure is to be attributed in any way to a yielding disposition or an inclination on the part of the Franco Government to negotiate. In today's newspapers, obviously on instructions from higher up, all thought of a settlement with the Red Spanish Government and any mediation by third parties to this end are rejected most emphatically and in a variety of ways. Today's papers publish statements to this effect by General Jordana, the Vice President of the Government and Foreign Minister; General Queipo de Llano, the Commander of the Southern Army; General Kindelan, the head of the Spanish Air Force; and others. Although the possibility of negotiation with Red Spain is definitely rejected in these statements, still they contain certain expressions which indicate that this rejection is not to be taken quite so seriously; that is the case when General Jordana says that "harmony could be restored only if the opponents completely acknowledged and repented their mistake," or when it is stated in General Kindelan's declaration that "no negotiations can be entered into with the present Red rulers of Spain, but those who, weapon in hand, have engaged in an open and honorable fight on the other side will be received with a fraternal embrace."

These remarks and the entire somewhat exaggerated tone of the rejection of any mediation suggest the possibility that this emphatically unyielding attitude is a tactical move, which is understandable under the present circumstances, and that at the decisive moment the Burgos Government will agree to a compromise, after all, by which it will at least be able to preserve the appearance of success instead of complete victory.

For the Ambassador:
HEBERLEIN

No. 678

2129/463941–43

The Foreign Ministry to the Embassies in Spain, Italy, Great Britain, France, the Soviet Union, and the United States, the Legation in Portugal, and the Consulate at Geneva

TOP SECRET   BERLIN, October 12, 1938.
Pol. I 1177 g Rs.

On October 11 the Counselor of the Italian Embassy here gave the Under State Secretary a detailed presentation of the question of the withdrawal of Italian troops. From Count Magistrati's statements it was apparent that Mussolini was very much displeased because the international press had represented the withdrawal as a concession to England. He said that Propaganda Minister Alfieri had immediately communicated with Minister Goebbels.

Specifically, Count Magistrati, on the basis of a telegraphic instruction, gave the following explanation:

In August of this year Mussolini had summoned to Rome the commander of the Italian troops in Spain, General Berti, in order to discuss with him the question of the Italian contingents in Spain. The question had become urgent because the forces had greatly diminished. The Italian troops had suffered the following losses in the course of the 20 months of war:

Dead	2, 352
Wounded	8, 635
Missing	196
Prisoners	369
Total	11, 552

Mussolini's point of departure had been that Franco would have to be permitted to keep as many troops as he needed to win victory. Finally, General Berti on August 20, at Mussolini's instruction, gave Franco the choice of three proposals:

1. The dispatch of two or three more divisions;
2. The dispatch of 10,000 more men to compensate for the losses in the two divisions that were already in Spain;
3. Partial or complete withdrawal of the Italians.

On August 23 Franco had replied that he was against the first proposal, since he expected it to be followed by an invasion of French troops over the Pyrenees. He did not directly oppose the second proposal but did point out that the dispatch of 10,000 men could not be kept secret. On the other hand, he had stated that he agreed with the third proposal in that a partial withdrawal of the infantry might take place, but the special troops and the air force should be reinforced. After some negotiating back and forth the question of withdrawing all of the infantry was discussed at the beginning of September. At first Franco had requested a delay but had then, even though reluctantly, agreed in principle. Then the Duce had sent a telegram to Berti that he wished to avoid a complete withdrawal, since Franco had agreed to it only reluctantly. The exact wording of the telegram was as follows: "It is my custom to stand by my comrade to the end." Meanwhile came the well-known understanding with the Non-Intervention Committee, and General Berti and Franco had arrived at an agreement to the effect that the special troops (aviators, tank corps, engineers, and artillery) would remain there and the two infantry regiments would be merged into one division of picked men. This division was to consist of seven battalions at the front and two reserve battalions. From 10,000 to 12,000 men would thereby be released. At the end of September the withdrawal had again been postponed in view of the general political situation. The final agreement had been made on October 1. On October 16 the troops would embark at Cádiz and disembark in Naples and would be received with full military honors. The following troops would now remain in Spain:

1. The Littoria Division (nine battalions—12,000 men) ;
2. The aviators, tank corps, artillery, and special troops;
3. Cadres (officers and non-commissioned officers) for four mixed divisions.

The Under State Secretary told Count Magistrati that accordingly there was, to be sure, no immediate connection with the present negotiations with England, but the withdrawal of 10,000 to 12,000 men did at the same time result in fulfilling the British desires and would consequently enable the Anglo-Italian pact to go into effect. Magistrati shared this opinion.

Finally, Magistrati confirmed the Under State Secretary's opinion that the whole explanation brought out the fact that there had been no change at all in Mussolini's policy toward Spain and that Italy still desired, as before, to help Franco obtain victory. Count Magistrati also confirmed this.

By direction:
SCHWENDEMANN

No. 679

2662/527828–29

The Ambassador in Spain to the Foreign Ministry

Telegram

No. 322 of October 14 SAN SEBASTIÁN, October 14, 1938.
Received October 14—4 : 40 p.m.

With reference to our telegram No. 320 of October 13.[1]

If we are prepared to agree to Franco's wishes with regard to the delivery of new war matériel, I consider it desirable to ship it as soon as possible for the reasons stated in telegram No. 298 of September 30 and on page 4 of the personal letter to the State Secretary on October 2.[2]

In case we wish to fulfill even a considerable part of Franco's rather far-reaching demands, the question again comes up whether we should make these new sacrifices of ours contingent on counterclaims.

If we do not wish to utilize this occasion for a more energetic course of action and possibly require that Franco first commit himself more explicitly for the future (a political treaty or something similar), then the present moment appears to me unfavorable for making definite counterclaims—a thing which we have so far avoided in similar cases. In view of the rumors being circulated everywhere regarding mediation and the ending of the Civil War by compromise, Franco is anxiously watching the attitude of friendly powers, and we should under no circumstances create the impression that we are looking for a pretext to leave Franco in the lurch at the last minute. On the other hand, however, this time it might be advantageous, *before* granting the new demands by the Nationalist Spanish Government, to call attention emphatically to the extent of these sacrifices and to the balance in German-Spanish relations, which is constantly shifting more in our disfavor. Perhaps I could do this, stressing the fact that I was speaking without instructions and only for myself, and explain that Spain had given us a series of disappointments in the past and was still doing so (Spain's evasive attitude in regard to the offer of a political treaty; the slight enthusiasm in regard to the conclusion of a cultural agreement; the very slight spirit of accommodation as regards the Montana affair; difficulties in the exchange of prisoners; difficulties in the granting of visas and work cards, etc.). Then in whatever manner suggested itself in the course of this conversation I could point out the necessity or the advisability of Spain's exhibiting a very decided spirit of accommodation in these matters of

---

[1] Not printed (1606/385841).
[2] Document No. 672, pp. 755–756.

her own accord, thus acknowledging our attitude, which heretofore had avoided any sort of trade and barter.

The prerequisite for such a *démarche* would naturally be the readiness to agree to Franco's new desires, at least in principle. I should be grateful to receive instructions as soon as possible after the clarification of this preliminary question. I shall see the Foreign Minister next Monday.

STOHRER

No. 680

2666/527992

The Under State Secretary to the Embassy in Spain

Telegram

No. 422   BERLIN, October 15, 1938.

With reference to your No. 322 of October 14.

We do not yet know anything regarding new demands by Franco for the delivery of war matériel. We assume that Lieutenant Colonel von Funck, who will arrive here Monday, will bring this information with him. It will not be possible to make any decision before these requests have been received and the Italian Government has been consulted. For this reason, please delay the *démarche* which you suggested until the matériel question has been clarified. For your own information I may state that we have arrived at an understanding with the Italians for the time being to restore the German and Italian troop units which are in Spain to full combat strength by sending the necessary supplies and matériel. As you already know, Admiral Canaris, together with Counselor of Legation von der Heyden-Rynsch, will arrive there some time next week.

WOERMANN

No. 681

54/36324

Memorandum by the State Secretary

BERLIN, October 15, 1938.

Admiral Canaris told me today that the Wehrmacht was inclined to comply with Franco's desires with regard to matériel. I told Canaris once again that in accordance with the Führer's general instructions we considered it important to keep to the Italian line. That meant that we would maintain the Condor Legion at its present strength until the beginning of November and equip it sufficiently to keep it at its normal strength. In regard to further deliveries of matériel to Franco, however—following the example of Italy—no decision would be made before the beginning of November.

WEIZSÄCKER

No. 682

2946/576319–22

The Economics Minister to the Foreign Ministry

TOP SECRET   BERLIN, October 18, 1938.
V So. 809 g Rs.   W 1055 g Rs.

Subject: New demands for matériel by the Spanish Nationalist Government.

Attention Geheimrat Sabath.

The question of the delivery of new and increased amounts of matériel to Nationalist Spain is now being considered. In this connection I am calling attention to the following questions, which are still undecided at the present time and which need to be definitely cleared up in the near future:

1. Definitive guaranty of German mining rights in Nationalist Spain.

According to the assurances given both by the Spanish Chief of State, General Franco, and by the Foreign Minister, General Jordana, the Spanish Nationalist Government intends to guarantee decisive German influence in that complex of mining rights included under the name "Montana." This will require a decision by the Council of Ministers, recognizing that the German shares come under the exceptions provided for in the Spanish mining law .

Meanwhile, the following companies have been set up for the practical development of the mining rights in Nationalist Spain included under the name Montana:

Aralar, Compañía Explotadora de Minas S.A., Tolosa, capital stock 25,000,000 pesetas;
Cía. Minera Santa Tecla S.A., Vigo, capital stock 12,000,000 pesetas;
Montes de Galicia, Compañía Explotadora de Minas S.A., Orense, capital stock 16,000,000 pesetas;
Sierra de Gredos, Compañía Explotadora de Minas S.A., Salamanca, capital stock 8,000,000 pesetas;
Montañas del Sur, Compañía Explotadora de Minas S. A., Seville, capital stock 20,000,000 pesetas.

According to the provisions of the Spanish Nationalist mining law, foreigners are permitted a maximum participation of only 40 percent in the capital of Spanish mining development companies. Accordingly, 40 percent of the capital stock of the above-named companies was subscribed and paid in by the Rowak-Sofindus concern.

In order to guarantee predominant German influence, it is planned to have Rowak-Sofindus, i.e. Germany, take over an additional 25–30 percent of the capital stock. The remaining 35 or 25 percent would be reserved for Spanish Nationalist shareholders. Those institutions and persons designated by the Spanish Government as desirable would be given particular consideration.

This definitive guaranty of predominant German influence in Spanish Nationalist ore deposits which are developed by the above mining companies, including predominant capital participation in them, is an urgent necessity and will not brook further delay.

In order to avoid further delays and to obtain the desired decision by the Council of Ministers immediately, I consider it necessary that favorable consideration by Germany of Nationalist Spain's large-scale requests for matériel be made dependent upon the prior guaranty of predominant German influence in the above-named mining development companies.

Please have the German Embassy in Salamanca call the attention of the Spanish Nationalist Government immediately to the German wishes and point out the urgency of the matter. It might be advisable for the German Ambassador in Nationalist Spain to discuss the details of the matter in advance with Herr Bernhardt, the director of Hisma, Ltd. Herr Bernhardt will return to Spain around October 20 or 21.

In Spanish Morocco, moreover, there has been established the Compañía Mauretania de Minas, Tetuán, with a capital stock of 10,-000,000 pesetas. The Spanish Nationalist mining law, with which you are familiar, does not apply to Spanish Morocco at the present time. It is not impossible, however, that this law might be extended later to include Spanish Morocco, too. I therefore consider it advisable to call the attention of the Spanish Nationalist Government even now to the fact that this enterprise is 100 percent under the control of Rowak, that is, the German Reich.

Montana S.A., which was established with a capital stock of 5,000,000 pesetas and in which all of the German mining rights in Spain have up to now been concentrated, will be operated purely as a study and research organization in the future and as such will not be subject to the restrictions on mining development corporations under the Spanish mining law. I suggest that this also be called to the attention of the Spanish Nationalist Government.

2. Recognition of Germany's total present claims against Nationalist Spain.

The Wehrmacht has reserved to itself approval of the accounting of the large-scale credit granted the Spanish Nationalist Government. I have instructed the chief of Hisma, Ltd., Herr Johannes Bernhardt, to support the appropriate Wehrmacht authorities in Nationalist Spain in taking the measures necessary for bringing about recognition of Germany's claims. Herr Bernhardt will make available suitable people from Hisma who are familiar with the subject matter and ac-

customed to dealing with Spanish Nationalist officials. The Wehrmacht is in charge of this whole problem and is authorized to negotiate with the Spanish Nationalist Government.

From his knowledge of the Spanish Nationalist attitude Herr Bernhardt told me he did not consider it advisable to include in the Wehrmacht accounts the entire sum of the hazard bonuses [*Gefahrenzu-
lagen*], which were very high from the Spanish point of view. Herr
Bernhardt proposes that only 50 percent of these hazard bonuses be
entered in the accounts. The other 50 percent should be included in
the prices charged for deliveries of matériel. I am passing on this
opinion of Herr Bernhardt's to you with the request that you do whatever may be necessary.

By direction:

SCHLOTTERER

No. 683

2946/576318

Memorandum by the Ambassador in Spain

SAN SEBASTIÁN, October 19, 1938.

Yesterday I again spoke to the Foreign Minister regarding the approval requested of the Spanish Government for paying Herr Bernhardt the sums required for Montana from account I. Jordana stated
that the Cabinet had approved our request but that the document had
not been signed, since the Minister concerned (Suñer, I believe) had
not been present at the last meeting of the Council of Ministers.

The money would be paid out gradually as needed for the
investments.

ST[OHRER]

No. 684

1606/385856–63

The Ambassador in Spain to the Foreign Ministry

SECRET   SAN SEBASTIÁN, October 19, 1938.
No. 607 g   Pol. I 2499 g III.
Subject: The political situation in Spain.

With reference to my report No. 553 g of September 19.

*Military situation unchanged. No battles of importance. Dissatis-
faction in the Army.*

The military situation has not changed since my last monthly report.[1] The small, laborious advances made by the Spanish Nationalist

---

[1] See document No. 660, p. 742.

troops in the Ebro River bend are of no real importance. In the last few days all attacks have been discontinued there. According to what one of the Wehrmacht attachés told me after making a tour, many generals have expressed very great dissatisfaction with the conduct of the war.

A military decision unlikely in the foreseeable future. Also, a Red collapse not yet imminent.

The present withdrawal of 11,000 Italian ground troops probably has no important effect on the comparative strength of the two opponents. The same may be true with regard to the international volunteers withdrawn by the Reds, about whose number, moreover, nothing at all has as yet become known. By way of summary, therefore, there is nothing more to be said than was stated in my last report, namely, that at the present time "a military decision is possible in the foreseeable future only if either of the two opponents obtains substantial support from the outside." Judging from previous experience, an early Red collapse on account of the critical food situation is not very likely, though not entirely impossible.

The question of ending the Civil War by mediation. Violent Spanish Nationalist propaganda against mediation and compromise. Political circles explain that there are various forms of mediation and compromise, not all of which ought to be rejected. Unanimity that compromise in regard to the new form of government is impossible. In other respects, however, compromise is possible. Pressure on the Reds to recognize Franco's victory. Promotion of a magnanimous act of conciliation on the part of Franco.

Since the settlement of the Czech crisis by the Munich agreement, the idea of ending the Spanish Civil War through intervention of the powers has come to the fore. Continuing its previous policy of rejecting all compromise, the Spanish Nationalist Government has, therefore, launched a propaganda campaign against intervention, mediation, and compromise, which surpasses in violence all previous press campaigns undertaken here. I have sent separate reports on this (cf. report No. 4650 of October 10 and No. 4745 of October 17[2]). This propaganda is not generally approved here. It is also in fact somewhat forced, and an example which came to my attention shows that not all political figures who expressed themselves against intervention in accordance with the Government did so voluntarily and with complete conviction. It is explained in political circles that there are various kinds of intervention, mediation, and compromise; this idea, in fact, was expressly emphasized in the statement by Saínz

---

[2] Latter not printed (2650/527290–91).

Rodríguez, the Minister of Public Instruction, mentioned in the latter of the two reports referred to above. However, opposition to mediation and compromise is fully approved by all supporters of the new regime, insofar as it most emphatically rejects any attack on the system of the new authoritarian state and the reintroduction of a liberal form of government. Actually, any mediation between the two antagonistic ideologies is indeed useless. Still, diplomatic intervention and compromise are quite conceivable, in particular in the form of pressure on the Reds for the purpose of strengthening the more moderate elements, which are more inclined to lay down their arms, and promotion of the idea of an act of conciliation (amnesty) on the part of Franco. As I explained in report No. 553 g of September 19, such an act appears to be the principal demand of these more moderate political circles which are struggling for control on the Red side.

Results of the campaign against intervention at home and abroad. Opinion of the British agent. Foreign Minister Jordana's opinion.

The campaign against a compromise peace, as previously reported (report No. 4745 of October 17), has had the result that a more realistic attitude on the part of the people has gained ground as compared to the quite understandable desire for a quick end of the war. But the definite rejection of compromise by the Government does not appear to have been without effect abroad either. Thus, at any rate, the British agent here, Sir Robert Hodgson, told me during a rather lengthy conversation a few days ago that after this campaign any attempt by England or any other party to get Franco, so to speak, to sit down at the conference table with the Reds would be entirely hopeless and actually ridiculous. Otherwise, however, Sir Robert's ideas regarding intervention by the powers with the Reds and promotion of a gesture of conciliation on the part of Franco were entirely in line with what has been stated above. From statements made by Foreign Minister Jordana, moreover, I assume that he, too, would definitely welcome such a turn of events. Of course, it remains an open question—which cannot be decided here—whether England and France can be won over to such a course of action.

Spanish-French exchange of ideas regarding similar questions.

That the Spanish Nationalist Government does not rely exclusively on military victory is apparent from an exchange of views which has recently been carried on through intermediaries between the Burgos Government and the French Government. From two reliable but completely different sources I hear that in these discussions the Franco

Government is attempting to influence the French to take no further interest in the Reds and to guarantee Franco's complete victory by appropriate measures, in return for which Spain would agree to establish relations as demanded by wide circles in France and make promises concerning the future commercial activity of France in Spain.   I spoke to Foreign Minister General Jordana very cautiously about these rumors, and from his answer I received the impression that actually these reports were not sheer invention.   I shall attempt to pursue the matter further.

Franco's prospects would be very materially improved by a big military victory.   Alone he would scarcely be able to achieve this.   Perhaps with additional German and Italian help (war matériel).   Even these deliveries will, however, not bring about an immediate decision in the war.   Political action would still have to be taken if the war is not to be dangerously prolonged.

In view of this situation it is clear that Franco's prospects—as I have stressed on various occasions by telegrams and letter—would be materially and perhaps even decisively improved if he could succeed in winning a sizable military victory.   German and Italian military authorities insist that he cannot do this without additional support from Germany and Italy.   It is maintained, rather, that for this purpose a substantial increase in war matériel would be necessary; this would enable Nationalist Spain to organize the new divisions planned, and is now being requested by Franco on that account.   However, I would not venture to say whether the support now requested by Franco from us and Italy would actually suffice to bring the war to a quick military end, as Foreign Minister Jordana expects (telegram No. 328 of October 18 [3]).   In the judgment of the German military authorities this cannot be expected, particularly if no influence can be exerted regarding the use made of the new matériel.   I believe, therefore, that, even if the requests now made by Franco of us and Italy were completely fulfilled, diplomatic intervention would still be necessary if one wished to avoid a long war of attrition with all its attendant dangers or the giving of still more aid to Spain.

I have elsewhere expressed my opinion on the question of the services which we might possibly demand in return for the sacrifices again expected of us.

The question of the monarchy.

In the course of the campaign being waged against compromise and intervention the question of the monarchy was also taken up.   In a widely noted article in a paper called *Voz de España*, published in San

---

[3] Not printed (1606/385844).

Sebastián, the ranking party official [*Gauleiter*] of the province clearly served notice on England that any attempt from the outside to force a liberal monarchy on the new Spain would also be very sharply rejected. One of the leaders of the Spanish monarchists, the former Minister Goicoechea, thereupon stated in a political speech that no prince would lend himself to such infamy and that no monarchist would render allegiance to such a monarchy.

The question of the granting of belligerent rights.

In connection with the press campaign against intervention, the Spanish Nationalist press now demands with much ado—obviously in response to a *mot d'ordre* of the Government—the granting of belligerent rights, which ought not to be withheld from Spain any longer after the evacuation of half the Italian volunteers. This question forms an important part of the discussions which are at the present time being carried on in Burgos between the Spanish Nationalist Government and the Secretary General of the Non-Intervention Committee, Hemming (whose trip here—as reported in No. 4743 of October 15 [4]—was arranged for after all). I shall send a further report on this matter separately.

It is, furthermore, a great satisfaction to note that the domestic situation continues to appear calm.

STOHRER

Postscript: SAN SEBASTIÁN, October 22, 1938.

The Italian Ambassador just told me that Foreign Minister Jordana had indicated to him also that he considered it desirable for the friendly powers to make a political *démarche* with France and England in the sense of discontinuing further aid to the Reds.

STOHRER

---

[4] Not printed (5154/E303690–91). Stohrer reported further on Hemming's mission in his dispatch No. 4829 of Oct. 24 (667/257408–11), in which he mentioned a meeting between himself and Hemming.

No. 685

632/252556–57

Memorandum by the Head of Political Division IIIa

IMMEDIATE BERLIN, October 20, 1938.
e.o. Pol. I 2421 g.

The German Military Attaché in San Sebastián, Lieutenant Colonel Baron von Funck, who paid me a short visit yesterday, told me the following in regard to the order he received from Franco:

1. Franco had explained to him in detail that he had never had an army reserve and consequently was forced by any sizable Red attack occurring during an offensive to stop his own offensive for a time in order to meet the Red attack. His lack of an army reserve was not owing to any shortage of manpower. He had called up only 13 age classes so far and could call up other age classes at any time. He had not done this before because he lacked the armament needed for organizing more troop units.

2. He requested the delivery of

> 50,000 rifles,
> 1,500 light and
> 500 heavy machine guns, as well as
> 100 75-mm. guns.

Lieutenant Colonel von Funck has already spoken to the War Ministry about this request by Franco. The delivery of rifles and guns had already been approved. The delivery of the machine guns was occasioning some difficulty.

I told Herr von Funck that the Foreign Ministry was considering linking approval of this arms shipment to Franco with certain counterdemands, e.g. that he acknowledge all previous German deliveries to Nationalist Spain.

3. As far as the general military situation was concerned, Herr von Funck thought that the White and Red military forces were at present evenly matched and that Franco could not win final victory in the foreseeable future unless he once more received substantial support.

I told Herr von Funck that the decision regarding the question of further aid to Franco by us and the Italians was still pending.

4. Herr von Funck also expressed the desire to be received by the State Secretary and asked to be informed when he could come to the Foreign Ministry for an official conference.[1]

Herewith submitted to the Deputy Director of the Political Department, the Under State Secretary, and the State Secretary.

SCHWENDEMANN

---

[1] Marginal notes: "Herr Siegfried. I am ready to see Herr von Funck but preferably at the beginning of November after the Italian position is clearer. W[eizsäcker]."

"Lieutenant Colonel von Funck was received by the State Secretary today. Si[egfried]. Nov. 2."

No. 686

632/252558–60

Memorandum by the Under State Secretary

BERLIN, October 22, 1938.

DELIVERIES OF WAR MATÉRIEL TO SPAIN

1) Having withdrawn about 12,000 men from Spain the Italian Government is negotiating with the British Government as to whether this is sufficient to put the Anglo-Italian agreement of Easter [1] into force. The entry into force of this agreement was, as is well known, made conditional upon a "substantial withdrawal." [2] No decision in this matter can be made by the British until the beginning of November, since Chamberlain promised not to take any action without previously consulting the Commons, which does not meet again until the beginning of November.

2) In view of this situation we have agreed with the Italian Government that in any event we will for the time being merely maintain our present supplies of matériel in Spain at the present level. This means that the Condor Legion's supply of matériel will now have to be replenished again after the usual period of a few months. This is being ordered.

3) Beyond that, Franco is requesting further war matériel intended not for the Condor Legion but for the Spanish troops; specifically, he is requesting, in addition to a delivery of powder which is now being made, the delivery of 50,000 rifles, 1,500 light and 500 heavy machine guns, and 100 75-mm. guns.

In order to further the matter here, the German Military Attaché in San Sebastián, Lieutenant Colonel Baron von Funck, returned to Berlin. He presented Franco's wishes to the Commander in Chief of the Army and to the Supreme Command of the Wehrmacht. *He says that Colonel General von Brauchitsch will report to the Führer on the matter on Monday, October 24.*

The view of the Supreme Command of the Wehrmacht is that delivery of the rifles and the guns involves no special difficulties. On the other hand, the delivery of the machine guns constitutes about a month's production by Germany. It would therefore cause a month's delay in the further equipment of the German Army with machine

---

[1] The text of the Anglo-Italian agreement of Apr. 16, 1938, and accompanying documents are printed in the British White Paper, Cmd. 5726; also in *Documents on International Affairs, 1938*, vol. II, pp. 141–156. A detailed analysis of the agreement, prepared in the German Foreign Ministry on Apr. 27, 1938, is printed in vol. I of this series as document No. 755, p. 1097. On Nov. 2 the Commons voted to empower the Government to bring the agreement with Italy into force immediately.

[2] This phrase is in English in the original.

guns.   Whether this is something that has to be accepted should be determined from a political point of view, which it is not for the Wehrmacht to decide.

4) Franco told Lieutenant Colonel von Funck in justification of his requests that he did not lack men.   Rather, he had thus far refrained from calling up additional classes only because he could not arm them.   This circumstance had also had the effect that he had no army reserve at his disposal—which had shown itself to be highly disadvantageous.

5) The political problem therefore poses itself as follows:

(*a*) Are we willing to try to help Franco achieve a complete military success?   If so, he will require strong military assistance; the assistance now requested would surely not suffice.

(*b*) If, on the other hand, our aim is only to make Franco at least a match for the Reds, he will likewise need our support; for such support, as far as Germany is concerned, the matériel now requested would be of importance.

(*c*) If we give Franco no further help aside from the Condor Legion, no other prospect for Franco can be envisioned than some sort of compromise with the Reds.

6) Under these circumstances it would be advisable to let Franco have the matériel.   But he should not be informed of this until we have conferred again with the Italians.   It has been made certain that the Supreme Command of the Wehrmacht will not take any action independently of us.

7) If we deliver the matériel, the question again arises whether we are to make delivery contingent upon compensation.

To be considered here are:

(*a*) Renewed negotiation of a political treaty with Franco.

The position we have taken thus far should perhaps be maintained: that the time is hardly ripe at present for a decision on an important political treaty with Franco going beyond the existing secret protocol, since Franco has adopted a pronounced attitude of waiting.

(*b*) Recognition of our considerable credit balances [*Saldos*] for deliveries made thus far, including the new deliveries.

The Ambassador might be instructed to bring up this question again with Franco at the same time that he informs Franco of our willingness to render further assistance.   Negotiations on details could then be conducted through other channels.

(*c*) Lieutenant Colonel von Funck has personally brought up the idea here that our help could also be made contingent upon our obtaining a greater influence in the conduct of military operations.

He pointed out that Franco's organization is extremely inadequate from the point of view of a German General Staff officer. Such a request, which also could only be made in consultation with the Italians, who would then have to be granted the same influence, should probably not be made at present.

Herewith presented to the Foreign Minister through the State Secretary.

WOERMANN

No. 687

1606/385872–73

The Ambassador in Spain to the Foreign Ministry

Telegram

VERY URGENT   SAN SEBASTIÁN, October 27, 1938—5 : 00 p.m.
No. 339 of October 27   Received October 27—7 : 00 p.m.

For the Chief of the Supreme Command of the Wehrmacht and State Secretary Baron von Weizsäcker.

1. Franco describes the military situation to me as follows:

By shortening the front and by measures of reorganization he intends first of all to provide himself with the necessary reserves so as to be able in the very near future to resume the offensive. For this purpose Franco is planning first of all to make an attack at the bend of the Ebro, with the southeast as the general direction of the attack. Two larger offensive operations are at present being considered. One would be directed toward Catalonia, the other toward the Levant. So far no decision has been made as to which operation is to be carried out. For carrying out the operation, Franco needs, by all means, the war matériel requested from Germany and Italy but, according to his own statement, no additional personnel. Franco declared that he would then be able to carry the war to a victorious conclusion, especially since he considers that the fighting power of the Reds has been substantially weakened as a result of the apparent lack of trained reserves and the mounting food and financial difficulties. Franco therefore continues to reject any compromise with the Reds in the form of a negotiated peace.

I consider Franco's view of his military prospects—even in the event that all the new war matériel requested of us is delivered—as well as his appraisal of conditions among the Reds as too optimistic. A speedy and victorious conclusion of the war through purely military means is not probable. Nevertheless it seems to me extremely important that the war matériel requested by Franco be delivered as quickly and as completely as possible in order to enable him to win a

greater military victory and thereby convince the Reds of the useless-
ness of continuing the war.   If this solution is not brought about, a
war of attrition is inevitable.   Such a war would certainly not be hopeless for Franco, but it involves dangers in view of the internal situation among the Whites and the steady support which the Reds will receive in food and probably also in arms.

After new military successes by Franco, political action by the powers in the form of pressure on the Reds . . .   (group garbled)[1]
resistance and influence on Franco to proclaim a generous amnesty
would presumably not be without prospect of success.

The reorganization of the Italians, already announced, is probably
an indication that they, too, do not absolutely count on a military victory and are desirous of preparing the way for political action.   (Cf.
my telegram of October 26.[2])

2. Franco wants to have a discussion with the High Commissioner
of Morocco about events in North Africa during the last crisis and
about future cooperation.   A meeting with Beigbeder has been arranged for October 30 in Tetuán.

This telegram has been drafted with the approval of the Ambassador.

GUILLERMO [3]
STOHRER

---

[1] Probably "to cease."
[2] Probably a reference to Admiral Canaris' telegram to the Foreign Department
of the OKW (F20/123) in which he reported forthcoming changes in the Italian
command in Spain.   Both that telegram and the one here printed were forwarded to the Foreign Minister, who was then in Rome.   For documents concerning the visit of Ribbentrop to Rome see vol. IV.
[3] Admiral Canaris.

No. 688

650/255760–61

Memorandum by the State Secretary

BERLIN, November 2, 1938.
Pol. III 3704.

The Spanish Ambassador informed me today that Mr. Hemming
of the Non-Intervention Committee had employed an inappropriate,
almost threatening, tone in Spain but as a result had achieved nothing
with the Spanish Government.   The Spanish Government was adhering to its written reply to the British plan.   It objected, moreover, to
the fact that the well-known League of Nations commission [1] was
active in Red Spain and, in contradiction to the British plan, had

---

[1] In October a League of Nations commission under the Finnish General
Jalander visited Republican territory and drew up a plan for the evacuation of
volunteers

there taken over the function of controlling the so-called evacuation of the Red volunteers. Actually not a single Red volunteer had been evacuated as yet, in spite of all the talk about it. Only the wounded Frenchmen had been taken over by France. On the other hand, there was the fact of the evacuation of 10,000 Italians, which Hemming would certainly have noted. The Spanish Government put no value whatsoever on a continuation of the sessions of the Non-Intervention Committee; if the latter should meet, however, the Spanish Government would have to demand recognition of full belligerent rights.

The Ambassador then asked me about the approval of Spanish demands for war matériel. I told him we were just on the point of making definitive decisions on this subject and I could inform him that I considered the prospects for delivery of further war matériel favorable. At the same time, however, we expected that certain economic concessions to Germany which the Spanish Government had kept postponing would now reach a definite settlement.

When Señor Magaz put in a word about the consistency of Spanish policy, I remarked that we had really been somewhat surprised at the haste with which Spain had given the French Government a promise of neutrality during the critical days in September. The Ambassador attempted to excuse his Government on the grounds of the exceedingly critical situation of White Spain at that time. I did not accept this excuse, however.

WEIZSÄCKER

No. 689

2946/576327

The Director of Hisma to the Ambassador in Spain

SECRET   SALAMANCA, November 2, 1938.

Subject: The Mauritania S. A. Mining Company in Morocco.

MY DEAR AMBASSADOR: We are engaged in organizing a mining company in Morocco. It is to be called the Mauritania S.A. and will be supplied with 10 million pesetas. While there are at present no limitations of any kind in regard to the participation of foreign capital, we have reason to assume that the Spanish Government is engaged in formulating new laws of a prohibitive or at least a restrictive nature. Herr Pasch will send you a short special report regarding this.

I consider it important to call your attention to these tendencies and request that even now protests be entered against any such new restrictions. I am of the opinion that the recent plans of the Spanish Government run counter to the Act of Algeciras.

Heil Hitler!

J. BERNHARDT

No. 690

136/73642–45

Memorandum by the Ambassador in Spain

STRICTLY CONFIDENTIAL　　　　　　SAN SEBASTIÁN, November 3, 1938.

When I told the Spanish Foreign Minister yesterday that I had been called to Berlin for a short time, he asked me at once to use my influence again at this opportunity for fulfillment of the wishes expressed by the Generalissimo concerning further deliveries of war matériel, and I promised to do so.

I used this opportunity to explain at length to Jordana that, as he knew, I had always worked for the interests of Nationalist Spain in Berlin both now and in the past, and I believed that in this manner I had proved useful to the Generalissimo. On the other hand, however, as I had to state quite frankly, my efforts here in Spain to do something for German interests had not always found the proper response. He knew only too well that I had often had to leave with empty hands, since I had not always found the Spanish authorities as obliging as we believed we had a right to expect, considering our support of the Nationalist movement! Spain was by no means in a hurry to fulfill our wishes in a wide variety of fields. I reminded the Minister in this connection of the Montana project and the matter of the mining law relating to it, also of the many difficulties which were put in the way of German citizens in the issuing of visas and work permits, also of the little interest which Spain had shown—after taking a different position at the beginning—in concluding a political treaty with us. I also pointed out that Spain was not showing any very great interest in an early conclusion of the cultural agreement which the Generalissimo and he—Jordana—had been so enthusiastic about at first; then I related to the Minister several individual cases in which private German interests had not found the response from Spanish authorities which we could have expected. I was of the opinion that Spain, too, might also make some effort on occasion. The situation was by no means very pleasant for me either. In Berlin I constantly upheld Spanish interests, but in upholding German interests here I found only slight response.

Jordana sought to contradict me by referring to the success which we had after all achieved in the formulation of the new mining law; then he admitted, however, that, seen in the proper light, the balance in our favor was rather small. I used the opportunity to inform the Minister that we would probably make specific requests of the Spanish Government in the near future with reference to the Montana project, asking more than 40 percent capital participation in some of the mining companies now being formed. I emphasized that I hoped we would be accommodated in this matter. I also hoped that we would conclude the cultural agreement in the near future, and that also in the question of the work permits a way would be found which would satisfy our rightful demands.

Finally, in the course of these statements I also made it apparent that my own efforts in Berlin in behalf of the Generalissimo's recent wishes would be considerably facilitated if I could take the impression with me to Berlin that Spain was now also going to do something for us.

General Jordana answered in great detail that it went without saying that we would find every accommodation here. In the Council of Ministers, for instance, which was the deciding authority for the Montana project, an attitude very favorable to us prevailed. Naturally our requests had to be investigated. He believed he could say, however, that they would find very good prospects of fulfillment. With regard to the cultural agreement, he would do everything to hasten its conclusion. As for the question of the work cards, he had already spoken repeatedly with the Minister of Labor Organizations, who was competent on this question. He was entirely in favor of being accommodating. He would likewise have steps taken with regard to the individual cases which I had mentioned.

I emphasized during the whole conversation that I was acting without any instructions and entirely on my own initiative and was speaking in this frank manner as an old and, as I thought, proved friend of Spain. I emphasized this in particular in making a remark concerning the policy which Spain should follow in the future. In this matter I explained to the Minister that I had the impression that Spain was nervously trying to keep for herself full freedom of action for the postwar period and that it was for this reason that she was according our wishes so little attention; this was all very well and good but not very attractive to us. I could imagine that Berlin would appreciate it if Spain would define somewhat more precisely her future attitude toward us. After all—quite aside from the great gratitude which he had just stressed—Spain could not be entirely disinterested in having the support of the powerful German Reich.

Jordana fully admitted this and assured me it went without saying that Spain would go along with us entirely, even after the war.

It seemed to me that my statements had not been entirely without effect on Jordana and that he became thoughtful. In my opinion, however, it remains to be seen to what extent we will really find compliance in the matters which interest us—in particular, the Montana project. There is no doubt that the Spanish Government, or at least

Jordana, firmly intends to make as few commitments as possible and to retain political freedom of action for later. If we wish to effect an improvement in the unfavorable balance in German-Spanish relations, we will have to exert pressure in one way or another.

STOHRER

No. 691

2946/576343–48

The State Secretary to the Embassy in Spain

TOP SECRET BERLIN, November 7, 1938.
Pol. I 1274 g Rs.

With reference to instruction W 1055 g Rs. of October 20.[1]

General Franco's wishes for delivery of more war matériel, which you support and which are seconded here by the Military Attaché, Lieutenant Colonel von Funck, and by Herr Bernhardt, have undergone detailed investigation. Although it is by no means easy for us to relinquish the desired matériel, the Reich Government has decided after all to fulfill the wishes of the Spanish Generalissimo.

However, we cannot agree to this new service to Nationalist Spain without reservation. Considering the extent of our deliveries thus far and our own present economic situation, we feel impelled to set conditions.

Therefore, please inform Foreign Minister General Jordana as soon as you return to Spain that the requested war matériel will be made ready, but that for this new service, which is particularly difficult at the present moment, we have to impose conditions on Spain.

In the first place, considering the constantly increasing debt, it appears necessary to us to bring about clarity as to its payment. We are therefore asking the Spanish Nationalist Government to acknowledge in figures the past deliveries of war matériel and the expenses connected therewith, insofar as this has not already been done. This is exclusively a matter of the costs of the Condor Legion, since the bills for other deliveries have already been acknowledged or will be acknowledged. In delivering the appended list, please emphasize that, without prejudice to the self-evident right of checking the separate items later, we at least had to insist on acknowledgment in principle of the claims. Please point out that the bill had been made out in a very accommodating fashion, since none of the expenses

---

[1] Not printed (5156/E303704–09). In this instruction, Stohrer was told not to undertake any further step until it had been decided in principle whether or not additional deliveries of war matériel to Spain were to be made conditional on Spanish fulfillment of German requirements regarding mining rights.

for personnel, amounting to the considerable sum of 75 million RM, were included.

Furthermore, please point out to the Foreign Minister once more that we have still not received any definite promise with regard to the mining rights. Please bring forward the various wishes for recognition of German capital participation which are mentioned in the instruction of October 20, W 1055 g Rs., and are explained in more detail in the statement given you by Herr Bernhardt. By including article 3 in the new mining law of June 7, 1938, the Spanish Government left this possibility open and at the time also expressly promised you this. According to the above-mentioned law a decision by the Council of Ministers is necessary for permitting more than 40 percent foreign capital participation in a Spanish mining company. Please request the Spanish Government to make such a decision immediately; it is naturally its own affair whether it wishes to treat this decision as secret, as Herr Bernhardt was evidently told would be desirable, according to telegraphic report No. 350 of November 4,[2] from the Embassy.

As you know, Montana is now on the point of founding a mining company in Spanish Morocco, too. Since there seem to be no limitations up to now on foreign capital participation in mining companies in Spanish Morocco, Hisma intends to take over 100 percent of the capital of the undertaking in question for itself. According to recent reports, the Spanish Nationalist Government seems to be considering changing the legal situation in Spanish Morocco and possibly introducing there the new mining law of June 7, 1938. Therefore please point out at the same time to the Spanish Nationalist Government that we expected that it would not at the last minute frustrate the above-mentioned intentions of Hisma by new legal measures. Recognition of our participation in those mines has become all the more necessary, since our new deliveries of war matériel again involve a considerable burden on our own reserves in ores and other raw materials necessary for armament production, so that it is actually our duty toward our economy to secure an increased delivery of such ores, etc., from Spain.

I leave to your discretion how far and in what manner you wish to indicate that the deliveries of war matériel requested by General Franco depend upon compliance by the Spanish Nationalist Government with our wishes as explained above. Although we might possibly agree, on account of the need for haste in this matter, to ship a small part of the desired war matériel even before our counterdemands have been formally accepted, nevertheless delivery of the whole

---

[2] Not printed (2946/576325–26).

amount before we have been given the required promises is out of the question.

I also leave it to your discretion to point out to the Spanish Government, as you already have in your conversation with General Jordana on November 2 (your memorandum of November 3), that in general we should like to see a somewhat clearer position with regard to us, so that we may be able to judge the future intentions of the Spanish Government with regard to its relations with Germany.

Since General Franco asked the Military Attaché, Lieutenant Colonel von Funck, personally to support his wishes in Berlin, will you please, in company with Funck and independently of your *démarche* with the Foreign Minister, speak with the Generalissimo, too, in the same manner.

I am expecting a report concerning the result of your steps.

VON WEIZSÄCKER

[Enclosure]

TOP SECRET   BERLIN, November 7, 1938.

W 1146 g Rs.

STATEMENT CONCERNING EXPENDITURES FOR THE CONDOR LEGION (*Übung Rügen*)[3] FOR THE PERIOD FROM NOVEMBER 7, 1936, TO OCTOBER 31, 1938

A. *Expenditures for matériel*

I. Weapons (artillery, machine guns, rifles, bayonets)	6, 284, 356. 37 RM
II. Ammunition (bombs, antiaircraft and infantry ammunition)	44, 135, 235. 32
III. Equipment (airplanes, signal and motor equipment)	111, 069, 475. 63
IV. Transportation 16, 388, 677. 46 RM costs. 174, 794. 32 RM	16, 563, 471. 78
V. Fuel	1, 988, 603. 35
VI. Other (miscellaneous expenditures) . .	6, 819, 978. 63
	186, 861, 121. 08 RM

B. *Expenditures for personnel*

I. Insurance.	2, 430, 741. 44 RM
II. Travel expenses	851, 381. 87
III. Clothing allowance.	142, 117. 50
IV. Other (miscellaneous expenditures). .	55, 727. 92
V. Cash advances.	36, 800. 42
Total	190, 377, 890. 23 RM

[3] Code name.

1. No vouchers are attached. Detailed statements (account books and vouchers) are available at any time in Germany for examination by representatives of the Nationalist Government.

2. It is certified that the above statement includes only the expenses of the Condor Legion itself. Deliveries which have already been paid for (e.g. commercial deliveries to the Spaniards) or statements already acknowledged (for the period before November 7, 1936, etc.) are not included.

(Signature)

No. 692

136/73648–49

The Ambassador in Spain to the Foreign Ministry

Telegram

No. 362 of November 11   SAN SEBASTIÁN, November 11, 1938.
Received November 12—3 : 00 a.m.

With reference to instruction Pol. I 1274 g Rs. of November 7.

I carried out the instruction in question by appointment yesterday with the Foreign Minister and today, together with the Military Attaché, with the Generalissimo.

The Foreign Minister was very pleased and grateful for the deliveries promised, and after the fairly long explanation and justification of our own wishes he declared that he would explain them in broad outline at once to the Council of Ministers, which was just about to convene, and would recommend them very warmly. The Military Attaché reported to the Generalissimo the results of his mission to Berlin. Franco thanked him heartily and expressed the hope that with the help of the new matériel the war would be ended very soon. After my detailed explanation of the reasons for the return services which we were asking, the Generalissimo indicated first that he considered the question of the expense statement for Condor as a matter of form, which would cause no difficulties. With regard to our mining interests he then explained at some length that he had the firm intention of orienting Spain's commercial relations after the war toward the countries friendly to her, and particularly toward Germany; at the present time, however, this intention should not appear openly, since until the end of the war he had to take England into account. In the further course of the conversation, however, the Generalissimo promised that our demands for Montana would be granted—possibly by means of a secret decision by the Council of Ministers.

As arranged, I stated frankly both to the Foreign Minister and in particular to Franco that we had a number of criticisms concerning the Spanish attitude toward us and were especially dissatisfied on account of the bureaucratic delaying of a number of our wishes. At my request Franco promised to give the necessary instructions so that the various matters that were pending would now be treated with greater interest and speed.

The total impression was not unfavorable. I shall follow up the matter very vigorously. If possible, please have the first—not too extensive—shipment of matériel sent off, but keep back further shipments until matters have developed here according to our wishes.

I gather from the statements of the Foreign Minister that there are still considerable difficulties with regard to Italian deliveries.

A report follows.

STOHRER

No. 693

2946/576356–61

The Ambassador in Spain to the Foreign Ministry

SECRET   SAN SEBASTIÁN, November 12, 1938.
No. 617 g

With reference to your instruction of November 7, Pol. I 1274 g Rs., and to our other reports.

Subject: Deliveries of matériel and the Montana project.

In carrying out the instruction referred to above and in connection with the statement of our readiness to make further deliveries of matériel, I gave the Spanish Foreign Minister three memoranda which have to do with the return services that we expect. The German text of these memoranda is appended.[1]

My other statements were in accord with the ideas expressed in my strictly confidential memorandum of November 3, 1938, which is in your possession.

v. STOHRER

[Enclosure 1]

MEMORANDUM

SAN SEBASTIÁN, NOVEMBER 10, 1938.

As was already stated in this Embassy's memorandum of August 3, 1938,[2] the mining rights acquired at the time by Hisma, Ltda. or its

---

[1] The texts of only two of these memoranda accompany the file copy of this document. It is probable that the third memorandum was based on the enclosure to the instruction of Nov. 7, document No. 691, p. 786.
[2] Not printed (2946/576296–97).

representatives are to be gathered into five companies. These companies have the following names:

Compañía de Explotaciones Mineras "Aralar S.A.", Tolosa;
"Montes de Galicia", Compañía Explotadora de Minas S.A., Orense;
Sociedad Anónima de Estudios y Explotaciones Mineras "Santa Tecla", Vigo;
Compañía de Minas "Sierra de Gredos" S.A., Salamanca;
Compañía Minera "Montañas del Sur" S.A., Seville.

The statutes of these companies have already been drawn up and recorded before a Spanish notary. Thus the companies have been established. During the last few days the companies have submitted requests to the competent Jefaturas de Minas asking for approval of the acquisition of mining rights by Hisma representatives, which was declared invalid by article 9 of the law of June 7, 1938, and also for approval of the transfer of these mining rights to the companies. The German Embassy has the honor to request the Ministerio de Asuntos Exteriores to urge the appropriate Spanish authorities to give their approval in the near future.

In consideration of the capital needed to finance these firms and the stipulation in article 3 of the law of June 7, 1938, according to which at least 60 percent of the shares of mining companies must be in the hands of Spaniards or Spanish firms, the capital is distributed as follows:

Company	Capital stock in pesetas	German participation 40%	Spanish participation 60%
Aralar	25, 000, 000	10, 000, 000	15, 000, 000
Galicia	16, 000, 000	6, 400, 000	9, 600, 000
Tecla	12, 000, 000	4, 800, 000	7, 200, 000
Gredos	8, 000, 000	3, 200, 000	4, 800, 000
Sur	20, 000, 000	8, 000, 000	12, 000, 000
Total	81, 000, 000	32, 400, 000	48, 600, 000

In article 3 of the protocol of July 16, 1937, the Spanish Nationalist Government declared itself ready to facilitate as far as possible the establishment of Spanish firms for the development and economic exploitation of mineral resources as compatible with the general stipulations of Spanish law.

Article 3 of the law of June 7, 1938, provides that, in special cases in which Spanish nationals are unable to raise Spanish capital for the exploitation of mining concessions in the ratio required by article 3 of the law, the Minister for Industry and Commerce, on the basis of a decision by the Council of Ministers, can grant a reduction in the Spanish participation in mining companies. Taking account of the fact that at the present time there is not sufficient capital for financing the above-mentioned five companies in the hands of trustworthy Spanish persons whose character would guarantee the successful German-Spanish work of reconstruction, this Embassy has the honor to ask the Ministry of Foreign Affairs, in consideration of the special relations between Nationalist Spain and Germany, to agree that the Minister for Industry and Commerce, on the basis of a decision by the Council of Ministers, permit the following increase in the German participation in the mining companies:

Aralar	up 35%	or	8,750,000 pesetas
Galicia	up 35%	or	5,600,000 pesetas
Tecla	...		...
Gredos	up 20%	or	1,600,000 pesetas
Sur	up 35%	or	7,000,000 pesetas

The increased German quota of participation has been calculated in the effort to take account of Spanish interests, too.

The payment for the German shares in the five companies will be made from the peseta equivalent of the 15 million RM which this Embassy, in its memorandum of August 3, 1938, asked to have provided, to which the Spanish Nationalist Government agreed in the *note verbale* of October 29, 1938, No. 607,[3] from the Ministry of Foreign Affairs. Herr Johannes Bernhardt will therefore accept the peseta equivalent of 15 million RM and will give the Spanish Government a receipt for this amount. The German Embassy would therefore be grateful if the full payment were made, if possible at once, to the representative of the German Government, Herr Johannes Bernhardt. Herr Johannes Bernhardt, as the authorized trustee of the German Government, will also accept the shares of the five companies which accrue to Germany.

On October 21, 1938, the German citizens Wilhelm Pasch and Hermann Paege, together with the Spanish citizens Luis Saco and Rafael Benet, applied to the Spanish Vice Consul in Tetuán, in his capacity as notary, for certification of the articles of incorporation of the mining company Mauritania A.G., which, supplied with a capital of 10 million pesetas, intends to devote itself to the exploitation of mines in the Spanish protectorate zone of Morocco.

On October 22, 1938, the Spanish Vice Consul thereupon requested His Excellency the High Commissioner in Morocco for permission to execute the document. The Secretariat General of the High Commissioner answered on the same day that the requested permission would be issued on condition that the decrees issued by the Spanish

---

[3] Not printed (2946/576340–41).

Government on November 23, 1927, and on September 13, 1935, would be observed.

The German Embassy has the honor to point out that these provisions apply only to companies which are established on the basis of Spanish laws and are situated in Spain but conduct their business mainly in the Spanish protectorate zone of Morocco. Since the above-mentioned Mauritania company is to be established in Tetuán, however, and is also to have its seat in the protectorate, this Embassy has the honor to ask the Ministry of Foreign Affairs to instruct the High Commissioner in Morocco to grant permission for the establishment of the Mauritania company according to the document made out by the Spanish Vice Consul.

In closing, the German Embassy has the honor, on instructions from the Reich Government, to point out that permission for the German mining participation mentioned in this memorandum and recognition of the German interests have become all the more necessary since the new large deliveries of war matériel which had been requested have again involved a considerable burden on the German reserves of ores and other raw materials necessary for the production of armaments, so that it is, so to speak, the duty of the German economy to secure increased delivery of ores from Spain.

For this reason it seems necessary to have the requested new deliveries covered primarily by additional exports of raw materials and by payments in foreign exchange in accordance with an agreement to be concluded by Hisma with the competent Spanish authority.

[Enclosure 2]

PRO MEMORIA

SAN SEBASTIÁN, November 9, 1938.

The German Government has made available a credit of 5 million RM for the immediate restoration and reconstruction of the mining companies established with German capital participation; these funds are to be used to pay for machines in Germany, which must be shipped to Spain at once in order to reach the desired objective, since the machines and equipment in question are either not being produced at all in liberated Spain or not being produced on short order. Therefore the German Embassy has the honor to ask the Spanish Nationalist Government to approve a sum up to 5 million RM for the import of machines and other equipment for the five mining companies established with German capital participation.

The repayment of the credit is intended in such a manner that within a period of 5 years a corresponding amount of the ores extracted from the mines of these five companies will be shipped to Germany and the amount realized from the sale of these ores in Germany will be used for repaying the credit.

The German Embassy therefore has the honor to request the Spanish Nationalist Government to release a corresponding statement to the effect that within a period of 5 years at the most the necessary permission will be issued for exporting the required amounts of ore to Germany in order to repay the credit of 5 million RM in the above manner.

No. 694

2646/527164–65

The Consul at Geneva to the Foreign Ministry

No. 1776   GENEVA, November 12, 1938.
                                              Pol. III 3850.

Subject: Report of the League of Nations commission on the food supply of the refugees in Red Spain.

As is known, the League of Nations Council decided during its last session to send a commission to Red Spain to investigate the question whether the situation of the refugees in Red Spain was such that the League of Nations should undertake a relief project. This report has now been distributed to the members of the League of Nations as document C. 416.M.261.1938.VII. and is already available there.

It hardly needs to be emphasized that this report recommends assistance by the League of Nations. In the interest of promoting such action it pictures the distress in such a way that this report can be used as propaganda against the Red Spanish Government. In addition, I refer you particularly to annex II of the report, in which the Red Spanish Government asks for no less than £476,000 a month.

The funds for this assistance are probably supposed to be raised mainly by contributions from the Governments. In case such a resolution is not taken during the meeting of the Council in January 1939, the Red Spanish Government, significantly, intends to suggest a loan.

There can be no doubt that, if this relief action is undertaken by the League of Nations, it must be considered new evidence of one-sided espousal of the cause of Red Spain. As I have learned confidentially, this feeling has moved the Secretary General to ask Señor Barcenas, the representative of the Franco Government in Switzerland, to call on him in order to assure the latter that such action by no means constitutes a political stand but is a purely humanitarian matter, meant to benefit all Spaniards who are in distress as a result of the Civil War.

This attitude of the Secretary General is very significant for the efforts which he is making at the desire of England and France to prepare the way for Spain's return to the League of Nations after a victory by the Franco Government. According to my informant, these efforts are falling on such fertile ground in the case of a number of the diplomatic representatives of the Franco Government—for example, Quiñones de León, the Duke of Alba, and Señor Barcenas—that it is perhaps in the interest of Germany to take steps against these endeavors even now.[1]

KRAUEL

---

[1] Ambassador Stohrer, in a memorandum written on Dec. 22, 1938, while he was temporarily in Berlin (2649/527212), noted that he had discussed with Foreign Minister Jordana the question of the reportedly favorable attitude toward the League of Nations on the part of several diplomatic representatives of the Franco Government. General Jordana had categorically denied the existence of any such friendliness toward the League and had stated that Spain's attitude toward the League, as in other matters, would be governed after the war by that of Germany and Italy, and that concerning their attitude toward the League there was certainly no doubt.

No. 695

168/132575

Memorandum by the Under State Secretary

BERLIN, November 13, 1938.

General von Richthofen told me during his recent visit that he had informed Field Marshal Göring that a decision in Spain could be obtained only if the Condor Legion were tripled and then employed as a closed unit of German formations. Also, he considered German artillery necessary for Spain. With such a commitment the war in Spain would possibly be won, even if not by 100 percent. Considering the present state of the German Air Force such a shipment was quite possible and even useful from the standpoint of German rearmament, for reasons which he explained to me in detail.

Herr von Richthofen will attempt to take with him a decision on this point when he leaves about November 20.

A conference with the Foreign Minister is necessary very soon. However, please find out the opinion of General Keitel beforehand. As Herr von Richthofen told me, he has also spoken of this matter with General Keitel. Apparently the latter did not wish to anticipate the decision of the Field Marshal.

WOERMANN

No. 696

667/257422

The Ambassador in Great Britain to the Foreign Ministry

Telegram

No. 503 of November 14　　LONDON, November 14, 1938—10 : 45 p.m.

Received November 15—3 : 00 a.m.

Pol. III 3845.

A member of the Embassy spoke with Hemming, Secretary General of the Non-Intervention Committee, in Paris before his return to San Sebastián. He stated the following on this occasion concerning his conclusions from the impressions he had gained during his stay in Nationalist Spain:

1. Since 10,000 Italians on Franco's side and about 3,500 members of the international troops on the side of Red Spain had already been withdrawn, the withdrawal plan was not feasible in its present form. A new plan would have to be drawn up; a new combing-out plan could have prospects of success only if Franco were granted belligerent rights from the very start.

3.[1] The new plan need not provide for evacuation camps as heretofore; it was only necessary to have commissions which would count the withdrawn volunteers at the ports and check on the withdrawal as a whole after completion.

4. The new plan could work only if the Pyrenees frontier remained closed; the French would agree to this, however, only after reinforced naval patrols were instituted.

Hemming's report, which will be made after his final return to London to the . . . (groups missing) who authorized his mission, has been submitted in draft form to the Spanish Nationalist Government. In case that Government has no objections to the contents of the report, Hemming intends to conclude the conferences in Nationalist Spain as soon as possible and, after a short stay in London, to go to Red Spain. Hemming believes that the Non-Intervention Committee should not concern itself with the new plan until the five powers who are interested in his mission have reached fundamental agreement on the plan.

DIRKSEN

---

[1] Marginal note: "2. missing."

No. 697

F19/150

Minute by the Head of Political Division IIIa

TOP SECRET BERLIN, November 18, 1938.
zu Pol. I 1311 g Rs.

Counselor of Legation von der Heyden-Rynsch has just reported by telephone that the Führer and Chancellor has decided that General von Richthofen's suggestions with regard to sending further units to Spain [1] are not to be complied with.

SCHWENDEMANN

---

[1] See document No. 695, p. 793.

No. 698

136/73650–51

The Ambassador in Spain to the Foreign Ministry

Telegram

No. 377 of November 18 SAN SEBASTIÁN, November 19, 1938.
Received November 19—3 : 00 p.m.

With reference to my telegram No. 362 of November 11.

The Foreign Minister told me today that the Spanish Government had decided to fulfill the demands made by us according to instruction Pol. I 1274 g Rs. of November 7 as follows:

1. German capital participation in the mining companies established by Hisma to the extent desired by us (see report 617 g of November 12).

2. Establishment of a mining company in Spanish Morocco with 100 percent German capital. However, the Spanish Government would welcome the participation of some Spanish capital in this company, as we have already promised.

3. Duty-free import of mining machinery, etc., to the value of 5 million RM and repayment of this amount by deliveries from the mines.

The Minister asked that these concessions, particularly those in paragraph 1, be treated as confidential.

The Minister declared, as the Generalissimo had also done, that acknowledgement of the expense account for the Condor Legion which we had submitted was merely a matter of form which would cause no difficulty.

A corresponding written reply is to be made to the three memoranda known to you from the report referred to above.

The Foreign Minister added to this information a lengthy statement concerning the firm intention of Nationalist Spain to continue to orient itself toward Germany politically and economically after the end of the war.

Please inform Director Bernhardt, who is in Berlin at the moment, to this effect.

STOHRER

No. 699

1606/385910–20

The Ambassador in Spain to the Foreign Ministry

SECRET   SAN SEBASTIÁN, November 19, 1938.
No. 633 g   Pol. III 2747 g.

With reference to report No. 607 g of October 19.

Subject: Political situation in Spain.

Franco's military situation improved. The results of the Ebro victory; losses on both sides.

The military situation has considerably improved for the Nationalists since the last report.[1] Franco has succeeded, by means of an offensive in a direction not expected by the Reds, first in winning back the southeastern part of the bend of the Ebro River which was held by the Reds, and then, turning to the north, in mopping up the rest of the bend. However, he needed almost 3 months to win back the terrain which the Reds occupied in about 2 days by means of the attack across the Ebro. This effort, according to a confidential report from headquarters, cost him 33,000 men. I enclose a clipping of the official Nationalist Army report from the *Unidad* of November 17, in which the enemy's losses in men and equipment are listed. German military sources, however, term the statement that the Reds are supposed to have lost 75,000 men as too high.

Fruitless Red relief offensives. The balance of forces continues, however.

It is also gratifying that the relief offensives launched by the Reds against the Segre River have brought them only a small gain in terrain, and an attack made by them from the south against the Mediterranean corridor has collapsed without results. Nevertheless, the balance of forces between White and Red continues.

There is still no definite information concerning Franco's further military plans.

---

[1] See document No. 684, p. 771.

Morale in the Nationalist Army has improved. In the rear areas, however, increased unrest.

Because of these successes, morale in the Army has considerably improved once more. On the other hand, in the zone of communications and in the rear area of the Nationalist zone the unrest has increased again of late as a result of Red agitation. There have been cases where Reds, disguised in uniforms of the Nationalist Army and of the police, have carried out assassinations and endangered communications. In Burgos, as I have already reported (telegram No. 371 of November 17 [2]), a plot was discovered which seems to have had rather serious significance, even though it is said not to be true that assassination of the Generalissimo was planned. These incidents have resulted in innumerable additional arrests. The prisons are overflowing as never before. In the prison here, which is intended for 40 persons, there are supposed to be about 1,800 prisoners at the present time.

Political tension within the country continues.

Political tension in Government circles likewise continues. In the Cabinet there continues to be strong dissatisfaction with the policy and the dictatorial methods of Minister of the Interior Serrano Suñer. In Seville during the big demonstration of the Falangist Youth 2 weeks ago there was a fight between the Falange and the clergy, which they are trying to hush up.

Feeling inimical to foreigners.

Both from the south and from the north of the country I am informed that the feeling against foreigners continues to grow. I shall transmit under separate cover the reports promised on this subject by the Consulates concerned.

The military situation from the standpoint of the Reds. The discipline of the Red Army is still unbroken. Lack of ammunition and desire for reinforcement of heavy artillery.

Red Army reports state that the Army command withdrew its troops voluntarily from the bend in the Ebro River; since they actually did succeed in withdrawing the bulk of their troops from the encirclement and in bringing the main part of their matériel back across the Ebro, and since they were also in a position to publish victorious reports on their Segre offensive, Franco's Ebro victory will probably not have any permanent or decisive influence on the discipline of the Red Army, which is still good. From all reports, the

---

[2] Not printed (2646/527167).

Red Army is still well provided with matériel, although a certain scarcity of ammunition is making itself felt. During his recent stay in Paris, therefore, Negrín is supposed to have negotiated mainly for deliveries of heavy artillery.

Anxiety in Red Spanish Government circles concerning the attitude of France and England.

In Red Spanish Government circles there continues to be very strong dissatisfaction with France and England, since it is feared that the Spanish question might be settled, in the manner of Munich, by a decision of the four powers or by negotiations between the chancelleries of these powers.

The internal political evolution of the Reds is continuing. Change in propaganda slogans (fatherland, national honor).

The internal political evolution of the Reds is continuing. In order to resist the attack of the moderate elements, the present rulers have given their propaganda another form. They are now working not only with the slogan of Spanish independence, which must be defended against the foreign intruders, but also to a great extent with the slogans of fatherland and national honor. Prieto attacks Negrín more and more strongly. In this feud the argument has now appeared that a change in government on the Red side would certainly also result in a change on the White side and therewith would increase the prospect for the conclusion of an armistice. Franco is therefore more and more under attack; they declare that his prestige is disappearing, that he is not following any clear internal political aim, that he proceeds now against the Falange, now against the monarchists, and thus is losing in popularity everywhere.

Revival of the propaganda for autonomy in Catalonia.

On the other hand, a new development is the revival of the propaganda for autonomy in Catalonia. Supporters of this development also attack Negrín. For instance, the former president of the Catalonian Parliament, Casanova, published a proclamation a short time ago in which he demands a plebiscite for Catalonia and advocates having Catalonia secede from the remainder of Red Spain and conclude an independent peace. This man has supposedly gone so far as to offer French authorities in Paris an armistice by Catalonia in return for putting through Catalonian autonomy. It remains to be seen whether this propaganda will spread and take on a separatist tendency. There is no lack of certain signs of such a development: thus, for instance, the *Sunday Times* [3] pointed out a short time ago

---

[3] Of London.

that there were really four different Spains (Catalonia, the Basque country, Galicia, and "the rest"), which were entirely different from one another.

Red propaganda favorable to the Church.

In order to win over the Vatican, the Red Spanish Government more and more is permitting the reopening of churches, church marriages, etc. By means of a funeral of several well-known fliers, conducted with great churchly pomp, the propaganda of the Reds called the attention of foreign countries to this change in attitude. For instance, the *Temps*—which, by the way, is accused by the Spanish Nationalists of having accepted bribes from Red Spain—commented on this church funeral in a very friendly way in a detailed article and concluded that the earlier extremism had vanished in Red Spain. The familiar Basque propaganda, too, is now particularly concerned with religious matters. It is agitating against Cardinal Goma of Toledo, who is supposed to be entirely Franco's man, and demands his removal, whereas on the other hand it is attempting to promote relations between the Vatican and the Reds. For this purpose, too, Salvadores, the apostolic administrator of Lérida, is said to have been sent to Rome recently by the Red Spanish Government, armed with a Red Spanish diplomatic passport.

Food supplies have improved on the Red side. On the other hand, a shortage of money is feared.

All reports coming from the Red zone, as well as the press and radio there, agree that the food supply has improved of late. I have reported separately (cf. report No. 5094/38 of November 17 [4]) concerning Prieto's efforts in Geneva to organize a food drive among the League of Nations countries for the Red Spanish civilian population and particularly for the so-called refugees (who are nothing but persons forced to leave the White zone). On the other hand, according to reliable reports, the question of the further financing of the war is beginning to cause the Red leaders anxiety.

The French-Spanish special conferences are deadlocked.

There is nothing new about the French-Spanish conferences which I mentioned in my previous reports and which were supposed to bring about pressure by France on the Reds in return for which France was supposed to receive certain political and economic concessions; evidently the conferences are deadlocked, particularly in expectation of the result of Chamberlain's visit to Paris,[5] which is supposed to take place next week. That the Spanish question will be discussed

---

[4] Not printed (5159/E303741–42).
[5] Chamberlain and Halifax made an official visit to Paris Nov. 23–26.

on this occasion is evident also from Mr. Hemming's statement reported through other channels to the effect that he had to finish his report on his impressions in Nationalist Spain in time for it to be submitted to the British Prime Minister before his departure for France.

How will the Civil War end? [6]

As far as the question of an end of the Spanish Civil War is concerned, this naturally depends mainly on further developments in the military situation. We must first see what Franco is able to achieve under his own power or after receiving the new deliveries of war matériel sent by us and Italy. The decision on granting belligerent rights to Franco would probably also play an important part in this, and it is therefore impatiently awaited in Nationalist Spain.

What are the main obstacles in the way of conclusion of peace? It is not so much differences in the objectives of the Whites and the Reds which stand in the way of peace as. . . .

Apart from military developments, the intellectual developments in the two zones are worthy of special interest today. In observing them one comes to the surprising conclusion that the fundamental objectives set up by the opposing parties, both of which want to guarantee a new strong Spain—particularly with regard to the social and economic reforms considered necessary—are hardly so different from one another any longer as to justify a continuation of this fratricidal war. If the Falange program and the many statements of the Spanish Nationalist politicians are compared with the 13 points listed by Negrín some months ago, to which the Red leaders like to point of late in their speeches, it must be concluded that basically there is disagreement only concerning the future form of government and the manner in which this is to be attained (plebiscite). Although these points are certainly of great significance, nevertheless developments among the Reds (cf. report No. 631 g of November 11 [7]) show that among the more moderate elements, which are increasing in strength, there exists a definite will toward accommodation in these ideological questions.

. . . mistrust, fear, and hatred.

There is therefore no doubt that the main factors which still separate the belligerent parties are mistrust, fear, and hatred. The first of these exists especially among the Whites, the second among

---

[6] This and the next topical heading have been deleted and replaced by: "Belligerent rights decisive for a Franco victory."

[7] Not printed (1606/385905–08).

the Reds, while hatred and desire for revenge are present on both sides in almost the same degree.

Threats by Franco concerning later persecution of political opponents in present-day Red Spain.

In this connection it is interesting that Franco is supposed to have said recently to an American news agency, in a statement which was reproduced by the entire world press, that he had a list of 2 million (according to other reports even 2½ million) names of Spanish Reds who had been guilty of some crime or other and who would receive their punishment. When I asked Foreign Minister Jordana yesterday whether this statement had really been made, he answered evasively that he did not know whether the Generalissimo had made such a statement; it was a fact, however, that they had a long list of Red criminals who had to be given their just punishment.

On the Red side the desire for revenge—even though it is certainly not justified to the same extent—is no less strong; it was particularly aroused by the air raids. Most of all, however, the fear of punishment and of cruel reprisals, which is skillfully fanned by the Red propaganda, strengthens the determination to continue the war.

Our role in a possible compromise peace.

Perhaps Franco's threat—which has not yet been denied—is rather useful in that, in case a military decision is not reached and the way is opened for a negotiated peace, it will be absolutely necessary to exert pressure not only on the Reds to break off the useless war but also on Franco to make a conciliatory gesture, and thus a real compromise—concessions on both sides—will be brought about, which, however, will not force Franco to make political concessions. I already stated in Berlin recently that in such a case we should exert our influence on Franco in the sense of an extensive amnesty for the pacification of Spain, in order to neutralize as far as possible the feeling of hatred against us which will surely be retained by the Red element all over Spain after the war.

The opportunity for a compromise solution can arise very suddenly; therefore we shall have to decide in time whether and in what manner we wish to intervene.

Probably—always in case a military decision is not reached—the opportunity for such a compromise solution will arise very suddenly. We shall therefore have to follow with the greatest attention the further developments here in Spain with regard to the military and economic situation, the frame of mind in the two zones, and the international alinements, and we shall have to decide in time whether and in what manner we wish to intervene.

STOHRER

No. 700

136/73653

Memorandum by the Under State Secretary

BERLIN, November 21, 1938.

The Spanish Ambassador called on me today and gave me the *pro memoria* in the Spanish language, which I enclose for Pol. III, according to which the Spanish Government has complied to a large extent with the German wishes for capital participation in mining companies. Contrary to the Spanish laws, the Nationalist Government had agreed to 75 percent German participation in three companies, and 60 percent in two companies. In addition, it had agreed that the Mauritania mining company in Tetuán be entirely released from the provisions of Spanish law concerning capital participation. It had also granted the other concessions apparent in the *pro memoria*.

The Ambassador forgot to mention the fact that this is a return service for the German deliveries to Spain, and I reminded him of it. He replied that the new German deliveries had not yet been started and asked whether any difficulties had arisen. I replied in the negative and said that the deliveries would now get under way very soon.

WOERMANN

2666/527993 [Enclosure]

PRO MEMORIA

No. 215 BERLIN, November 21, 1938.

The Spanish Nationalist Government, in fulfillment of the wishes presented by the German Embassy, has granted an increase in German capital to 75 percent in three of the five mining companies which have been established, and to 60 percent in the other two. Furthermore, the Nationalist Government has agreed to the establishment of the Mauritania mining company in Tetuán, releasing it from the requirements of the present Spanish laws. The Spanish Nationalist Government also permits the import of machinery up to an amount of 5 million RM for the five companies with German participation and agrees to the export of ores from the mines for the period of 5 years, so that the equivalent of said ore may be used for repayment of the credit which the German Government now opens for the delivery of the above-mentioned machinery.

No. 701

1606/385936–38

Memorandum by the Head of Political Division IIIa

BERLIN, December 3, 1938.

e.o. Pol. III 2831 g.

The goal of our policy in Spain must be victory by Franco as the prerequisite for establishing an authoritarian Spain which is militarily and economically strong and will adhere to the Rome-Berlin Axis.

A victory by Franco requires that the volunteer units fighting for him in Nationalist Spain be retained, that their fighting power be preserved by means of regular reinforcements, and that Franco be supported with war matériel.

A development of the non-intervention policy which would endanger these goals is consequently not acceptable to us.

The London plan of July 5, 1938, for combing out the volunteers, the implementation of which could have endangered these goals, is dead because of Franco's opposition, as Lord Plymouth stated to Ambassador von Dirksen. Nevertheless, we ought not to permit the Non-Intervention Committee to dissolve; it might be that Belgium's withdrawal and the estrangement of Sweden mark a beginning. We must rather attempt to retain the committee as an instrument for providing Franco with diplomatic support and tying down French and British policy in regard to Spain.

The Non-Intervention Committee is now confronted with the question as to what is to be done after the failure of the London plan. Lord Plymouth has asked the countries most directly affected (Germany, Italy, France, and Portugal) to express their opinions on this score. We must above all insist on the granting of belligerent rights to Franco as the basis for any further activity by the Non-Intervention Committee, pointing out that Franco, as the head of an ordered state comprising two-thirds of Spain, which has already been accorded *de jure* or *de facto* recognition by most countries, is fully entitled to this on account of his military successes and after the release of 10,000 Italian volunteers. The granting of belligerent rights is also in the interest of Europe, since this would hasten the inevitable final victory of Franco and thereby promote a just and sensible settlement of the Spanish question, as well as the final elimination of the Communist danger on the Iberian Peninsula. Hemming's recently published report [1] on his investigation trip in Nationalist Spain—surely with the approval of the British Government—also terms the uncon-

---

[1] Of Nov. 17, 1938; not printed (5180/E307048–106).

ditional granting of belligerent rights to Franco as prerequisite for all further progress of the non-intervention policy.

The further activity of the Non-Intervention Committee thus ought to be directed toward thoroughly revising the London plan of July 5 on the basis of the immediate granting of belligerent rights to Franco.

Lord Plymouth told Ambassador von Dirksen that the granting of belligerent rights to Franco was not possible at present. This is obviously the result of the discussions of Chamberlain and Halifax in Paris. The negative attitude of the French Government is probably for the most part caused by uneasiness on account of Communist and Marxist agitation, since the granting of belligerent rights to Franco is *the* great concern of the Barcelona regime and its friends and in particular is also very bitterly opposed by Moscow.

We, as supporters of the anti-Comintern policy, should insist all the more on the granting of belligerent rights.

This question will also surely be one of the subjects discussed during Chamberlain's conversations in Rome in January. It is to be expected that Mussolini will also insist on the granting of belligerent rights to Franco. Franco's great offensive, which is now on the point of being launched, will perhaps have shifted the military situation still more in Franco's favor by the time the discussions are held in Rome.

Herewith submitted to the Foreign Minister through the Deputy Director of the Political Department and the Under State Secretary.[2]

SCHWENDEMANN

---

[2] The points of view appearing in this memorandum were communicated to the German Embassy in Great Britain in an instruction of Dec. 7 (2651/527313–15).

No. 702

1573/381039–45

Memorandum by the Ambassador in Spain

STRICTLY CONFIDENTIAL   SAN SEBASTIÁN, December 18, 1938.
No. 667 g

POINTERS FOR A REPORT IN BERLIN ON THE DEVELOPMENT OF GERMAN-SPANISH RELATIONS [1]

In my memorandum of February 1938 on "The Status of our *de facto* and *de jure* Relations with Nationalist Spain" [2] I advised against using ultimatums or interfering in Spanish domestic affairs in order

---

[1] Notation in handwriting: "(Not the final form)." However, another copy (136/73665–71) found in the files of the State Secretary shows that the document was submitted to him without modification.

[2] Document No. 529, p. 590.

to carry out our demands and wishes. On the contrary, I proposed attempting to achieve our ends by way of negotiation, thus improving our balance with relation to Spain.

The Foreign Ministry agreed with this view. Accordingly, in the last few months a number of negotiations and discussions have been held with the Spanish Government, most of which it was possible to bring to a satisfactory conclusion.

Of the nine wishes or demands set forth in my above-mentioned memorandum of February (pages 3, 4, and 17 [3]) we have put through or are about to put through five, some of them in a manner greatly exceeding the expectations voiced at that time. They are as follows:

1. The conclusion of a cultural agreement;

2. Guaranties regarding freedom of sojourn, settlement, and work for German nationals in Spain (work permit agreement ready to be signed);

3. Guaranties for our mining interests in Spain;

4. Police agreement. (Since this question was not handled by the Embassy, I do not definitely know whether the agreement, the contents of which were decided upon quite a while ago, has actually already been signed);

5. With regard to the desired "greater influence upon the training, development, etc., of the Spanish Army," it has been possible to get a German naval commission invited.

In addition to this, Hisma has put through continually increasing shipments of ores and other raw materials to Germany and has brought about partial payment for the credits granted to the Spanish Government for certain deliveries by means of supplementary deliveries of minerals, etc.

In other matters of lesser importance we have also found the Spanish Government to be accommodating in negotiations of late, as, for example, in the question of compensation for German citizens who have been injured by Spanish Nationalist war measures.

The other four points in my February memorandum on the privileges we could ask of Spain, about which no negotiations have been held as yet, are the following:

1. Expansion of the clauses on benevolent neutrality (articles 3 and 4 of the protocol of March 20, 1937);

2. Accession of Spain to the Anti-Comintern Pact;

3. Spanish support for our colonial claims and interests in Tangier;

4. Privileges for German commercial shipping and the like.

We should now examine the question whether we should try to clear up the above points, using the method of negotiation which has proved successful in the past, or whether possibly we should try to put through additional demands and wishes.

[3] See pp. 591, 592, and 598.

Re 1:

Franco's declaration of neutrality during the Czech crisis has shown that the question is important. I do not believe, however, that we can accomplish anything in regard to this question at the present time, since it would scarcely be possible to single it out from the whole complex of questions on German-Spanish political relations and since Spain has refused to conclude an official treaty with us on this point at the present time.

Re 2:

I have just discussed this question once more with the Foreign Minister, who did not seem to object to the idea *a limine*.

Re 3:

As far as support for our colonial claims and interests in Tangier is concerned, we can be virtually certain of complete support. If we wish to reestablish our rights in Tangier on the basis of the French-German agreement recently concluded in Paris by the Reich Foreign Minister [4] and should need the help of Spain to do so, this would surely be obtainable and commitments for it could be effected when indicated. The question of our colonial claims might perhaps be aired even now if the situation arises; it might be better after all, however, to reserve it for a later political treaty.

Re 4:

As regards privileges for German commercial shipping and the like, we need first of all to have the responsible German authorities formulate possible wishes in this field.

A list of the eight wishes which we formulated at the time for the conclusion of a political treaty is enclosed.

Point 7 has been carried out.

Point 6 is well under way.

Point 8 is probably not yet ripe for discussion.

Points 1 to 5 were in their essentials incorporated into the protocol of March 20, 1937. To formulate them anew and emphasize them would be of value to us only if this were done in a political treaty, which the Spaniards still hesitate to conclude at the present time.

In the relationship between Germany and Spain, however, the following points seem to me still more important than those mentioned above which have not yet been clarified by negotiations:

(*a*) Further guaranty of trade relations in the postwar period, i. e., in particular, a long-term guaranty of our ore imports from Spain;

(*b*) German participation in the economic reconstruction of the country.

---

[4] For Ribbentrop's visit to Paris and the agreement of Dec. 6, 1938, see vol. **IV**.

Re (*a*):

An immediate generous settlement of the Spanish debt problem at the end of the war still appears to me the best way to do this. (Cf. my personal letter of March 31, 1938, to State Secretary von Weizsäcker on this question.[5]) I consider the present prospects of reaching an agreement advantageous for both parties to be very good. It is extremely important to reach a settlement, if only because of the burning question of compensation for the Germans in Spain.

Re (*b*):

At the present time conditions are also favorable for this. In my report No. 5429/38 of December 14,[6] regarding Areilza's proposal, I wrote of a suggestion for close postwar industrial cooperation between Germany and Spain, emanating from an authoritative government source.

I shall work out proposals for the further strengthening of our political and economic position in Spain as soon as I have received basic instructions for the future treatment of the entire matter.

STOHRER

[Enclosure]

1. Constant liaison and, in case of danger, mutual consultation on questions of international policy affecting the common interests of both countries (in accordance with article 2 of the protocol of March 20, 1937).

2. Continued discussions about measures to combat Communism (as provided in article 1 of the above-mentioned protocol).

3. Diplomatic support in case of external danger affecting the security or vital interests of either of the two countries.

4. An agreement on non-participation in treaties and conventions directed against the other country (in corroboration of article 3 of the above-mentioned protocol). Mutual notification of treaties concluded, etc.

5. Benevolent neutrality in the event of warlike complications with a third power (in line with article 4 of the above-mentioned protocol).

6. Appropriate measures to foster comradeship between the two armies and exchange of experiences and information, regarding which special agreements are to be concluded.

7. Stabilization and promotion of cultural relations by means of a separate agreement (as provided in article 6 of the protocol of March 20, 1937).

8. Consolidation and extension of economic relations on the basis of a special agreement (in line with article 5 of the above-mentioned protocol).

---

[5] Not printed (5178/E307023–26).
[6] Not printed (5176/E307010–14).

No. 703

2946/576370–71

The Spanish Foreign Ministry to the Embassy in Spain

TOP SECRET   BURGOS, December 19, 1938.
No. 754

NOTE VERBALE [1]

The Ministry of Foreign Affairs presents its compliments to the German Embassy and, with reference to the German Embassy's *pro memorias* of November 9 and 10, 1938,[2] has the honor to inform the Embassy that, having considered in a spirit of the greatest cooperation the wishes of the German Government expressed in the above-mentioned documents and with the intention of furnishing new proof of its friendly sentiments for Germany, the Spanish Government has made the following decision:

(*a*) That in accordance with the proposal of the Embassy the percentage of German participation in the capital of the designated mining companies be increased as follows:

> Aralar S.A.—Tolosa. 75 percent
> Montes de Galicia S.A.—Orense. 75 percent
> Sierra de Gredos—Salamanca. 60 percent
> Montañas del Sur—Seville. 75 percent

The German participation in the capital of the "Mina Santa Tecla" company in Vigo remains unchanged and will not exceed 40 percent.

The capital increases are granted with the understanding that in carrying out the decisions of the Government the companies named will otherwise adhere to the existing Spanish legislation on the formalities of organization and management.

The Nationalist Government willingly approves the proposed method of payment of the increased German capital participation hereby granted.

(*b*) Desiring to accommodate the Reich Government, the Spanish Nationalist Government also approves the Embassy's proposal that the company called Sociedad Anónima Mauritania be established in conformity with the charter drawn up by the Spanish Vice Consul in Tetuán, bearing in mind that the above-named company not only is being established in the above-named city of the Spanish protectorate, but also is to have its seat in the Spanish protectorate of Morocco and carry on its activities there.

---

[1] The copy used is a German text in the files of the Embassy in Spain.
[2] See document No. 693, p. 788.

(c) The Spanish Nationalist Government likewise grants the Embassy's request that machinery and materials to the value of 5 million RM be imported for the five mining companies with German capital participation; furthermore, it agrees that ores from these mines shall be exported to Germany over a period of 5 years, to be used to cover the credit now being provided by the German Government for the above-mentioned deliveries of machinery.

With respect to:

(d) The general acknowledgement of the amounts entered in the bill covering the expenditures of the Condor Legion from November 7, 1936, to October 31, 1938, and

(e) The payment for the new deliveries requested by the Nationalist Government by means of an agreement between Hisma, Ltda. and the appropriate Spanish authorities, particularly on the subject of the supplementary export of raw materials and payments in foreign exchange, the Spanish Nationalist Government has the honor to inform the Embassy that it would like to examine these last two points in somewhat greater detail and make them the subject of separate negotiations.

No. 704

136/73672–73

Memorandum by the Ambassador in Spain

SECRET   SAN SEBASTIÁN, December 19, 1938.
No. 665 g

In Berlin the dissatisfaction with Generalissimo Franco appears to be continuing. It is founded less on the fact that during the Czech crisis Franco assured France and England of his neutrality in case of a European war than that he informed us belatedly of his negotiations with the above-mentioned powers and allegedly even promised them that the Condor Legion would be interned as proof of his good will.

To begin with, as far as the belated notification of the neutrality discussions with Paris and London is concerned, Franco really is somewhat to blame, even though it is true that he did not inform the press of his intention to maintain neutrality until after notifying us. (Cf. report No. 4757 of October 19, 1938.[1])

As regards the alleged intention or promise to intern the Condor Legion, the sources for this report circulating in Berlin are unknown to me. I knew nothing about any such intention. On the contrary,

---

[1] Not printed (2685/528902–04).

in answer to my question of what would happen to the German volunteers in case of neutrality, Foreign Minister Jordana answered immediately without hesitation that they as well as the Italians were part of the Generalissimo's army and that therefore this question had not been discussed during the neutrality negotiations with France and England.

It will not be possible to get to the bottom of this question, which is perhaps decisive for the dissatisfaction in Berlin, until the source of the information is known. Is this source known to the Foreign Ministry?

It seems necessary to me to eliminate the existing dissatisfaction in order to free German-Spanish postwar relations from a severe handicap. How can this be done? The following has been proposed:

1. The sending of an important Spanish Nationalist political figure for personal consultation with the highest Government and Party officials in Germany.

2. Having the Generalissimo send a personal letter to the Führer or the Field Marshal.[2] (Both measures for the purpose of explaining once again the attitude of the Spanish Nationalist Government during the Czech crisis and of giving assurances for the future.)

Perhaps we might also consider utilizing the situation described (the bad conscience of the Spaniards) in order to demand promises from Spain in regard to closer relations with us later.

I reserve further proposals.

December 20, 1938.

The Foreign Minister informed me that Franco intended to write a letter to the Führer; the Minister knew about the dissatisfaction in Berlin and deplored it. In answer to my question he declared categorically that an internment of the Condor Legion had *never* been considered.[3]

STOHRER

---

[2] i.e. Göring.
[3] The final paragraph was added in Stohrer's handwriting.

CHAPTER VII

THE CATALONIAN CAMPAIGN AND THE END OF THE WAR
DECEMBER 23, 1938–MARCH 31, 1939

No. 705

136/73658

Memorandum by the State Secretary

BERLIN, December 23, 1938.

Today the Spanish Ambassador brought me the communication, which had already been announced by Herr von Stohrer,[1] that a letter from the Generalissimo to the Führer was in preparation, for the purpose of dispelling any remaining misunderstanding or dissatisfaction with regard to Nationalist Spain stemming from the time of the September crisis.

In this connection I mentioned to Magaz the rumor that France had at that time suggested to the Spanish Government that in case of war it should intern the German and Italian volunteers. Magaz stated that this report was an invention, as, for that matter, Herr von Stohrer had already said earlier.

The Ambassador then went on to say that he had another important and pleasant message to convey: As was known, in the course of the past year we had come to a standstill in our conversations regarding a possible political treaty going beyond the protocol of March 20, 1937. He was authorized to inform us that, if we so desired, the Spanish Government was prepared to proceed to the conclusion of such a treaty on the basis of the treaty draft discussed by Herr von Stohrer.

WEIZSÄCKER

---

[1] Ambassador Stohrer was temporarily in Berlin.

No. 706

136/73662–64

Memorandum by the Head of Political Division IIIa

BERLIN, December 29, 1938.
e.o. Pol. III 3063 g.

The draft of a German-Spanish treaty of friendship, sent to the Embassy at San Sebastián on April 8, 1938,[1] was favorably received

---

[1] See document No. 558, enclosure, p. 632.

by Franco and Foreign Minister Jordana at first.   On May 19, however, Foreign Minister Jordana expressed doubts regarding the conclusion of the treaty,[2] for one reason because a solemnly concluded political treaty would become known to a large group of people and consequently could not really be kept secret.   Furthermore, he pointed out that the Spanish Nationalist Government had received reports that England wished a *rapprochement* and that there was a possibility that England would induce France to close the Pyrenees frontier effectively, which would enable Franco to end the war victoriously in a few months.

Ambassador von Stohrer then received telegraphic instructions on May 31 [3] that he should not urge matters further, and at the beginning of July he told General Franco that we had no intention whatever of pressing Spain to conclude this treaty.

The draft of the German-Spanish treaty of friendship in its content still suits the status of German-Spanish relations.   If the Spanish Nationalist Government now declares that it is prepared to conclude the treaty, we ought to do so without trying to extend its scope. Such an extension is conceivable in regard to article 2 (joint defense against Communism), in the form of accession by Nationalist Spain to the Anti-Comintern Pact.   The Spanish Government probably does not desire this, however, as long as it has not brought the war to a victorious conclusion.

In the light of our experiences during the Czech crisis, article 6 might be amplified in the sense of a stipulation of benevolent neutrality.   But that would be precisely what we blamed the Spaniards for during the Czech crisis.

Article 7 on military cooperation might also be expanded.   This matter, however, has developed so favorably by itself that it does not appear necessary to try to obtain any further agreements on this score for the duration of the war.   An amplification of article 7 would not be opportune if only in view of the apprehensions of the French and the British, and for this reason Franco also would probably not desire it.

With regard to the economic relations mentioned in article 8 considerable progress has been made in the Montana affair recently. Other special agreements in this field might develop in the course of events, without necessitating any change in the text of article 8.

It therefore seems advisable, with reference to the *démarche* by the Marquis de Magaz, to instruct Ambassador von Stohrer to try to bring about the conclusion of the treaty in Burgos in its present form.

The fact that the Spanish Nationalist Government is now offering

[2] See document No. 587, p. 664.
[3] Document No. 590, p. 668.

of its own accord to conclude the treaty might be explained from its experiences with England and France after the negative attitude shown in May of this year. Franco has repeatedly declared, to be sure, that he intended to have a close association with the Rome-Berlin Axis after the end of the Civil War, but he evidently desired to avoid a one-sided commitment as long as the war lasted and his position was so precarious. The tremendous political successes of the Rome-Berlin Axis during this year and the French and British opposition, both covert and overt, to vital Spanish Nationalist interests now appear to have brought about a certain change among the political leaders of Nationalist Spain. Evidently they now acknowledge the correctness of the principle that it is possible to develop a strong Spain only in opposition to, or at any rate in spite of, England and France, i.e. only in close association with the Rome-Berlin Axis.

Herewith submitted to the State Secretary through the Deputy Director of the Political Department.

SCHWENDEMANN

No. 707

136/73660–61

Memorandum by the Head of Political Division IIIa

BERLIN, December 29, 1938.

MINUTE ON THE "POINTERS FOR A REPORT IN BERLIN ON THE DEVELOPMENT OF GERMAN-SPANISH RELATIONS"[1]

The basis on which Herr von Stohrer proceeded in formulating the "Pointers" has been changed considerably by the Marquis de Magaz' declaration to the State Secretary on December 23, at the direction of his Government, that it was now willing to conclude the political treaty. The eight points listed in the annex to the "Pointers" exactly correspond in content to the articles in the treaty draft. In regard to the other problems mentioned in the "Pointers," reference can be made to the memorandum (Pol. III 3063 g[2]) on the Anti-Comintern Pact, benevolent neutrality, and military cooperation.

The following questions still remain:

(*a*) Spanish support for our colonial claims and interests in Tangier;

(*b*) Privileges for German commercial shipping and the like;

(*c*) Further guaranty of economic and trade relations;

(*d*) In particular, a long-term guaranty of our ore imports from Spain after the war;

[1] Document No. 702, p. 804.
[2] Document No. 706, *supra*.

(e) German participation in the economic reconstruction of the country.

As regards Tangier, it is doubtful whether the present moment is opportune for pressing our claims, since the French are perhaps already nervous enough about North Africa.

Regarding the interests of our maritime shipping, the proper authorities should first be consulted in order to learn their wishes.

The same is true of the other economic questions, concerning which Department W [3] should first express an opinion. It would naturally be desirable for political reasons also to obtain long-term agreements on the import of raw materials from Spain and on our participation in the economic reconstruction of the country.

Herewith submitted to the State Secretary through the Deputy Director of the Political Department.

SCHWENDEMANN

---

[3] The Economic Policy Department.

No. 708

136/73682–83

Memorandum by the Under State Secretary

BERLIN, January 4, 1939.

During a conference with the State Secretary, in which Ambassador von Stohrer, Ministerialdirektor Wiehl, and I participated, Ambassador von Stohrer was given the following instructions:

1. He is authorized to resume negotiations with the Spanish Nationalist Government on the drafting of a German-Spanish treaty of friendship.

2. The present draft text is to form the basis of the negotiations without change. Since there is a question whether the text presented by the Embassy in San Sebastián coincides in all details with the text in Berlin, Ambassador von Stohrer will attend to the early presentation of the latest text.

3. If an article concerning the cultural agreement is included in the text transmitted to the Spanish Nationalist Government, this article is to be deleted in conformity with the Berlin draft, since the matter has been settled.

4. During the discussion of article 2 Ambassador von Stohrer is to sound out the Spanish Nationalist Government privately and cautiously on whether it is inclined to join the Anti-Comintern Pact.

5. Spain is not yet to be approached in the Tangier question, since the result of the Paris conferences between the Reich Foreign Minister

and the French Foreign Minister should first be awaited and Spanish support in this question seems certain in any case.

6. The Italian Government is not to be given additional information until later, and then it should be with reference to that given by the Reich Foreign Minister on May 7, 1938, when he was in Rome. The time for this will have come when an agreement in principle has been reached on the conclusion of the treaty with the Spanish Nationalist Government.

7. The economic questions, including possible advantages for German merchant shipping, are first to be clarified further within the Ministry. Ministerialdirektor Wiehl will discuss the particulars with Ambassador von Stohrer.

WOERMANN

No. 709

168/132511–12

Minute by the Head of Political Division IIIa

TOP SECRET   BERLIN, January 6, 1939.
                                             e.o. Pol. III 20 g Rs.

The Commander of the Condor Legion has reported that he could send 800 to 1,000 men back to Germany without weakening the combat strength of the Legion. The Supreme Headquarters of the Wehrmacht inquired whether there were political objections to sending them home. In accordance with the State Secretary's decision I informed Captain [*Kapitän*] Bürkner yesterday that the Foreign Ministry at the present time had doubts about sending the 1,000 men back home, first, because of the offensive in progress, during which it would probably be difficult for the Spaniards to understand the withdrawal of German forces, and, second, in consideration of the pending Anglo-Italian negotiations in Rome and the Non-Intervention Committee. We might soon find ourselves in a situation in which we could use such a substantial withdrawal to good advantage within the framework of the non-intervention policy and should not deprive ourselves of this possibility at this time.

We were informed yesterday that Colonel General Keitel suggested to the Führer that 1,000 men be withdrawn but called attention to the doubts of the Foreign Ministry. According to the information just telephoned to Herr von Kamphoevener [1] by the Supreme Headquarters of the Wehrmacht, the Führer decided against withdrawing the 1,000 men at the present moment and instructed Colonel General Keitel to

---

[1] An official of Political Division I.

keep in contact with the Foreign Minister concerning withdrawal at a later time.

Herewith submitted to the State Secretary through the Deputy Director of the Political Department and the Under State Secretary.

SCHWENDEMANN

No. 710

136/73684–85

Memorandum by the Director of the Economic Policy Department

BERLIN, January 10, 1939.

Subject: German economic interests in Spain.

In accordance with the suggestion made in Ambassador von Stohrer's reports, I discussed with the bureaus concerned what else might be done to safeguard our economic interests in Spain during the postwar period following victory by Franco. The conference took place yesterday in the presence of Ambassador von Stohrer. It was decided to take up a number of preparatory measures at once (continued efforts to get the bills for what we have supplied acknowledged by the Spanish, compilation of a statement of the entire debt together with interest as of the end of 1938). It was agreed that the present large ore deliveries from Spain should also be guaranteed in peacetime insofar as possible and that Germany should if possible make sure of having first option on the investments necessary for Spain's reconstruction.

Ambassador von Stohrer suggested that the Spaniards who would probably decide this question should be invited to visit Germany; these would include the Spanish Minister of Commerce, the Director of Trade and Industry in the Ministry of Commerce, the Director in the Finance Ministry, and a member of the Foreign Ministry. The visit should take place around February and should be used to discuss all the questions with the Spaniards in greater detail and to give them a picture of German industrial capacity. All bureaus concerned welcomed this suggestion.

To be submitted to the Foreign Minister through the State Secretary with the request for approval that Herr von Stohrer be instructed to extend the invitation for this visit to the representatives of the Spanish Government and also that the Reich Economics Minister be approached in the matter; it would probably be best to have him issue the invitation, since the Spanish Minister of Commerce is involved.[1]

WIEHL

---

[1] Marginal note: "I am in favor of this suggestion, which Stohrer has been making for some time. v. Weizsäcker."

No. 711

650/255767

The Ambassador in Spain to the Foreign Ministry

Telegram

No. 21 of January 14   SAN SEBASTIÁN, January 14, 1939—3 : 00 p.m.
Received January 14—4 : 30 p.m.
Pol. III 219.

Because of the demands made on Franco at the front, the completion of the letter he intended for the Führer[1] was delayed. The Foreign Minister told me, however, that it was signed yesterday. The communication will be sent at once.

STOHRER

---

[1] See document No. 705, p. 811.

No. 712

109/115081

The Ambassador in Italy to the Foreign Ministry

Telegram

URGENT   ROME, January 14, 1939—1 : 00 p.m.
SECRET   Received January 14—3 : 00 p.m.
No. 23 of January 14

The Duce, with whom I spoke at the British Ambassador's reception yesterday evening, indicated to me that Chamberlain's visit,[1] as he had expected, had had pitifully meager results, also in relation to further concrete developments. For the rest, the Duce twice emphasized strongly how much he had felt himself in the role of advocate and how he had spoken as such. He probably had in mind his statements on the subject of our armaments and Chamberlain's concern regarding our future plans. He spoke sharply about France and emphasized his firm determination to take drastic measures at once in reply to any action in favor of the Reds. He is satisfied with radio reports about the Spanish offensive, although he did not seem to be totally unskeptical as to its decisive character. It was highly important for Franco that the Reds now had to fight with their backs to the sea, which, as history demonstrated, was very hard on the morale of the troops. Finally, he confirmed the great losses suffered by the Italian volunteers in the present offensive, of whom, counting officers alone, 27 had been killed and more than 200 wounded, among them the commanding officer.

MACKENSEN

---

[1] Chamberlain and Halifax visited Rome Jan. 11–14, 1939.

No. 713

168/132496–97

*Memorandum by the Deputy Director of the Cultural Policy
Department*

BERLIN, January 20, 1939.
zu Kult. Gen. 58 V.

According to a telegraphic report from the German Embassy in San Sebastián, the German-Spanish cultural agreement is on the point of being signed.

The agreement is similar in its principal features to the German-Italian cultural agreement; it is not, however, so extensive as the latter. The negotiations, which were carried on in San Sebastián on the basis of a German draft, proceeded smoothly on the whole. Only in the technical question of recognition of diplomas from the German schools in Spain (article 11) was some effort required in order to find a solution that would do justice to German interests.

For the position of the German language in the Spanish curriculum (article 12) a settlement favorable to us was achieved by granting reciprocity in principle.

As in German-Italian cultural relations, in relations with Spain, too, considerable significance will be accorded the cultural committee provided for in the agreement (article 21). Suggestions concerning the composition of the cultural committee will be submitted to the Foreign Minister after the agreement has been signed.

Since it is to be expected, to judge from the cultural reports from the Embassy in San Sebastián, that clerical circles will continue to gain ground in Spain, it is particularly fortunate that it was still possible to conclude the agreement at the present time.

Herewith submitted through Pol. III, the Under State Secretary, and the State Secretary (copies of the memorandum and the agreement attached) to the Foreign Minister for information.

v. TWARDOWSKI

No. 714

1573/381066–67

Memorandum by the Head of Political Division IIIa

BERLIN, January 23, 1939.
e.o. Pol. III 184 g.

Major General Baron von Richthofen, the Commander of the Condor Legion, told me the following about a conversation which he had with General Franco recently:

Herr von Richthofen had emphasized to Franco the great dissatisfaction aroused in leading circles in Germany by the Spanish Nationalist Government's neutrality declaration during the Sudeten crisis. Franco had thereupon spoken in detail of the reasons which had forced him into neutrality at the time, and according to Herr von Richthofen he had done so in a thoroughly convincing manner.

At the same time Franco had pointed out that during the entire course of the Czech crisis he had received no information from Germany and had been obliged to draw the conclusion that the intention was to exclude the Spanish ally completely. He had also emphasized that benevolent neutrality would have been more useful for Germany than active intervention, which for the most varied reasons would have endangered Nationalist Spain directly.

With reference to the future policy of Nationalist Spain, Franco stressed that the fear evidently existing in Germany that he would turn to France and England after the victory was entirely unfounded. He would not think of doing so, since England and France had antiquated political and economic convictions and were declining powers whose methods were not suited to a rising Spain. Germany could supply him with everything he needed and could receive raw materials and food in return.

Concerning Italy, Franco expressed himself rather unfavorably. Italy's industry was no better than Spain's. In exports Spain and Italy were rivals throughout the world, since they had the same export products.

Franco stated further that he did not understand why German policy always approached him via Rome. He would prefer to deal with Germany directly.

Franco's statements quoted above are quite noteworthy. They at least prove that Franco is giving thought to a number of important problems and seems to be endeavoring to recognize quite soberly his country's interests with reference to its reconstruction and its orientation in foreign policy.

Herewith submitted to the Director of the Political Department,[1] the Under State Secretary, and the State Secretary.

SCHWENDEMANN

---

[1] Probably should read "Deputy Director of the Political Department."

No. 715

136/73689–90

The Ambassador in Spain to the Foreign Ministry

Telegram

URGENT   SAN SEBASTIÁN, January 23, 1939—3 : 00 p.m.
No. 41 of January 23   Received January 23—4 : 30 p.m.

While the Spanish Government has recently exhibited remarkable cooperation with us, the sentiment among the broad masses is developing less satisfactorily, especially under the influence of Red propaganda, as I have reported on several occasions (cf. for example report No. 644 g of December 2, 1938 [1]).

In order to counteract this development, which can create an atmosphere very prejudicial to German-Spanish relations after the war, the idea was discussed during my last stay in Berlin that we take the humanitarian initiative in the question of the exchange of prisoners, persons seeking asylum, and so forth. The prerequisite for this was the . . . (group incomprehensible) expected failure of the British exchange commission [2] which was working here at the time for the same purpose (cf. report No. 5181 of November 25, 1938 [3]). According to present information, however, the British commission has lately been functioning successfully again, so that the plan cannot be carried out at the present time.

Yesterday's appeal by the Spanish Foreign Minister to the entire Spanish people and their Spanish brothers overseas to donate bread grains, milk, coffee, and rice for the starving population of Catalonia, which has now been liberated, suggests the idea of showing our friendly attitude toward the Spanish people for the above purpose and underscoring our desire to alleviate their suffering by spontaneously sending from Germany a shipload of flour, etc., and especially nourishing foods for the children of Barcelona and Catalonia, who are suffering from malnutrition. Such a gesture could be very effective as propaganda if skillfully exploited.

To begin with I request immediate consideration and telegraphic instructions as to whether you think such aid is desirable and feasible, so that the approval of the Government, which the sensitivity of the Spaniards makes necessary, can then be obtained beforehand and suggestions can be made concerning the form and execution of the aid to be given and its propagandistic exploitation.

This step of ours would have to be announced when Barcelona is captured, at the latest, and then be started at once; in making the

---

[1] Not printed (1606/385941–51).
[2] See document No. 660, p. 745.
[3] Not printed (5174/E306998–99).

decision we should keep in mind that we may have to repeat the gesture when Madrid is taken.

STOHRER

No. 716

5205/E307745–74

Agreement Between the German Reich and Spain for Intellectual and Cultural Cooperation, Signed at Burgos January 24, 1939

The Chancellor of the German Reich and the Chief of the Spanish Nationalist Government, convinced that in order to deepen the friendly relationship existing between the two countries it is desirable to expand the mutual intellectual and cultural relations and in connection therewith to promote a reciprocal knowledge of the culture and the intellectual life of the two peoples, have decided to conclude an agreement on intellectual and cultural cooperation between the two states and have for this purpose appointed as their plenipotentiaries:

THE CHANCELLOR OF THE GERMAN REICH

The Ambassador Extraordinary and Plenipotentiary to the Spanish Nationalist Government,

Eberhard von Stohrer, Dr. rer. pol., Dr. jur.

THE CHIEF OF THE SPANISH NATIONALIST GOVERNMENT

The Vice President and Foreign Minister of the Nationalist Government,

Lieutenant General Don Francisco Gómez Jordana y Sousa, Count of Jordana,

who, having communicated to each other their full powers, found to be in good and due form, have agreed on the following:

Article 1

The High Contracting Parties declare that they are prepared to lend their special support and their protection to the maintenance or establishment of cultural and scientific institutions whose aim it is to spread and perfect the knowledge of the culture of either of the two countries in the territory of the friendly state.

In order to establish reciprocity with the institutions in Germany dedicated to the study of Spanish culture, the Spanish Government will strive to create corresponding institutions in Spain for the study of German culture.

Article 2

The High Contracting Parties will make arrangements for the establishment of a German House in Spain by the German Government and for the establishment of a Spanish House in Germany by the Spanish Government.

Article 3

The High Contracting Parties will jointly, and in accordance with the principle of reciprocity, examine the possibilities of financial benefits which may be granted to the cultural institutions of the two countries for the promotion of their intellectual task.

Article 4

The High Contracting Parties will also promote the study of the language and culture of the other country within the framework of university institutions.

Article 5

In order to promote the teaching of the language of the other country the High Contracting Parties will strive to maintain lectureships at universities and other schools of higher learning.

In filling the lectureships preference will be given to candidates who are Spanish or German nationals. The High Contracting Parties obligate themselves to appoint candidates who are nationals of the other state only if these candidates have been declared by that state to be suitable for the lectureships.

The High Contracting Parties will, in mutual agreement, give special attention to the selection of the books to be used for instruction in the universities and schools of higher learning.

Article 6

The High Contracting Parties will promote courses and lectures at their universities and schools of higher learning by visiting scholars and scientists of the other country and will also, when the opportunity presents itself, effect an exchange of university professors and, from time to time, of assistants.

Invitations to university teachers and scholars of the other country to give courses and lectures and appointments to permanent academic chairs will be undertaken only in consultation with the other Government.

Positions will be made available in research institutes for the support of scholarly research. The specific details will be arranged by the German-Spanish Cultural Committee provided for in article 21 of this agreement.

Article 7

A regular student exchange between the German Reich and Spain shall be established. The implementation of the student exchange shall, on the German side, be the responsibility of the German Academic Exchange Service, Inc. [*Deutscher Akademischer Austauschdienst e. V.*] and, on the Spanish side, the corresponding division of the Ministry of National Education.

Article 8

The Alexander von Humboldt Foundation intends to grant several stipends each year to Spanish applicants in accordance with the usual conditions of the said foundation. In the event that a similar Spanish institution is created, Spain, in accordance with the principle of reciprocity, will likewise grant stipends to German students.

Article 9

The High Contracting Parties will promote participation by students in the summer courses organized at the universities and schools of higher learning of the other country.

Article 10

The High Contracting Parties will, observing the principle of reciprocity, promote closer contact between German and Spanish youth by an exchange of students between German and Spanish schools and by the organization of educational trips and fellowship hostels.

In order to promote the training of teachers and their knowledge of the other country, special attention shall be given to the exchange of teachers of the German and Spanish languages and literatures.

Article 11

The High Contracting Parties will give special protection to the schools of the other country that are established or are to be established on their territory.

The German schools in Spain shall be authorized to teach according to the German system of instruction. The diploma of graduation given by the German schools in Spain will be regarded in Spain as equivalent to the diploma of graduation given by German schools of higher learning in Germany, but possession of it shall not exempt the Spanish students of these schools from taking the state examination prescribed by the school laws of Spain.

The German schools in Spain shall be authorized to prepare their Spanish students for the Spanish *bachillerato* by supplementary courses, the details of which shall be determined by mutual agreement.

The Spanish schools that may be founded in Germany shall be treated correspondingly.

Article 3 shall be applied duly to these schools.

Article 12

The High Contracting Parties will foster the teaching of the language of the other country in the secondary schools of their own country, observing as far as possible the principle of reciprocity.

Article 13

The High Contracting Parties will, in all questions related to the circulation of books, grant each other the facilities possible within the framework of the regulations in force.

They propose making arrangements for promoting the circulation of books and periodicals of the two countries by book exhibits, bibliographical publications, and facilities and favored treatment for their importation and exportation, as well as for facilitating journalistic exchanges.

Article 14

In order to provide the German and Spanish libraries with the most important works of the other country in science, literature, and contemporary history, an exchange of publications between the Exchange Service for German and Foreign Books [*Deutsch-Ausländischer Buchtausch*] and the Division of Libraries, Archives, and Museums of the Ministry of National Education will be effected.

Article 15

The High Contracting Parties will promote the translation of suitable German books into Spanish and of suitable Spanish books into German. Private arrangements between German and Spanish publishing houses will not thereby be excluded.

The High Contracting Parties obligate themselves to make provision for the publication of a certain number of translations of such works as are important for a knowledge of the other country. They will send each other every 6 months a list of works especially suited for this purpose, on the basis of which the selection will be made by the other party. The works selected for translation from these Government lists shall be published by reputable and well-known publishing houses, after the translations have been examined officially in order to prevent a rendering that distorts the sense. At the sessions of the German-Spanish Cultural Committee provided for in article 21 of this agreement reports will be made on the progress of these officially sponsored works of translation.

The High Contracting Parties will, within the framework of the regulations in force, prevent the publication of translations of works by political émigrés of the other country.

Article 16

The High Contracting Parties will not permit the sale in the book trade, or the circulation through public libraries, of works which, falsifying historical truth, are directed against the other country, its form of government, or its leading personalities.

Article 17

The High Contracting Parties will, observing the principle of reciprocity, organize and promote cultural and scientific exhibits suitable for deepening the understanding of the culture of the other country.

Objects which shall be imported for such exhibits will, on condition that they are reexported, be exempt from customs.

Article 18

The High Contracting Parties will make the necessary arrangements to assure an effective exchange between the two countries in the fields of music and the theater.

Article 19

The High Contracting Parties will also strive to promote mutual understanding in the fields of film and radio. They will make arrangements for facilitating the importation of films, especially cultural and educational films, from the other country. In the preparation of radio programs, proper consideration shall be given to such broadcasts as are suitable for promoting general acquaintance with the culture of the friendly country.

Article 20

The High Contracting Parties will make special arrangements in order to prevent foreign-exchange difficulties from arising in the implementation of the agreement.

Article 21

For the implementation of this agreement a German-Spanish Cultural Committee shall be formed. Its composition shall be determined after previous agreement by the two Governments.

It shall be the duty of this committee to insure the execution of the measures stipulated in this agreement and discuss and point out further possibilities for the development of German-Spanish cultural relations.

This committee shall, if possible, meet once a year by previous arrangement, alternately in Germany and Spain.

Article 22

This agreement shall be ratified.

The instruments of ratification shall be exchanged in Berlin as soon as possible.

This agreement shall enter into force 30 days after the exchange of the instruments of ratification.[1]

This agreement is concluded for an indefinite period. It may be terminated by either of the High Contracting Parties by notice one year in advance.

In witness whereof the plenipotentiaries have signed the agreement and affixed their seals.

Done in duplicate, in the German and Spanish languages, the two texts being equally authentic, in Burgos, on the twenty-fourth day of January, nineteen hundred and thirty-nine.

EBERHARD VON STOHRER   JORDANA
[SEAL]   [SEAL]

---

[1] The agreement was never ratified. On Feb. 16, 1939, the Vatican protested to Franco's government that it was contrary to the Concordat of 1851 (see document No. 739, p. 843), and on Sept. 25 Colonel Beigbeder, then Spanish Foreign Minister, informed Stohrer that the Spanish Government must delay ratification because of further difficulties with the Vatican, the Spanish clergy, and the Traditionalists (telegram No. 1256, Stohrer to the Foreign Ministry, 136/73882–83). Postponements continued, and the matter finally lapsed.

No. 717

2130/464997

The Foreign Ministry to the Embassies in Italy, Spain, Japan, and the Soviet Union, and the Legation in Hungary

SECRET   BERLIN, January 25, 1939.
Pol. III g 188 I.

The Italian Ambassador here told the Reich Foreign Minister on January 23 during a conversation concerning the inclusion of Spain in the Anti-Comintern Pact that Count Ciano was of the opinion that it was better to postpone this problem until the conquest of Catalonia was completed. The State Secretary told Signor Attolico that Ambassador von Stohrer had in the course of conversation and on his own initiative mentioned to the Spanish Foreign Minister last week Spain's relation to the Anti-Comintern Pact, and his words had fallen on fertile soil. The Spanish Foreign Minister intended soon to speak with Herr von Stohrer about the matter again.

The Japanese Ambassador told the State Secretary on January 24 that he believed it very desirable for the Spanish Nationalist Government to join the Anti-Comintern Pact as soon as possible, perhaps after the fall of Barcelona. After the establishment of peace it was to be feared that England, especially because of her predominant financial position, would gain such strong influence over the Spanish Government that the latter would be little inclined to join. The Under State Secretary [*sic*] remained noncommittal and especially did not mention to the Japanese Ambassador the exchange of ideas on this question between Ambassador von Stohrer and the Spanish Foreign Minister.

By direction:
SCHWENDEMANN

No. 718

168/132489

The Ambassador in Spain to the Foreign Ministry

Telegram

No. 48 of January 25

SAN SEBASTIÁN, January 25, 1939.
Received January 26—12:10 a.m.

During yesterday's second conference on the conclusion of the treaty of friendship, the Foreign Minister gave me a new draft, which, however, contains no important changes as compared to the draft which we suggested some time ago. Difficulties could only be caused by the question as to when the treaty would be made public. The Minister believes the present moment to be inopportune and wishes to withhold it pending a later agreement by the two Governments. The Spanish counterproposal, together with a detailed report (also regarding Spain's position on the question of the Anti-Comintern Pact)[1] is leaving by special courier and will arrive Monday morning.

STOHRER

---

[1] Not found.

No. 719

136/73696

Memorandum by the State Secretary

CONFIDENTIAL

BERLIN, January 28, 1939.

St. S. No. 76

The Italian Ambassador asked me today how we planned to handle, vis-à-vis the public, the treaty of friendship to be concluded between us and the Spaniards. I answered Attolico as follows: In principle we were thinking of publishing it, but the question of the date of publication was still open, since the negotiations in general were still in the beginning stages. I promised Attolico to inform him of the date prior to publication.

WEIZSÄCKER

No. 720

136/73697–99

The Ambassador in Spain to the State Secretary

SECRET   SAN SEBASTIÁN, January 28, 1939.

DEAR WEIZSÄCKER: I wish to add the following confidential information to my report concerning my last conference with Foreign Minister Jordana on the treaty of friendship to be concluded with Spain.

The Minister is obviously trying to avoid publishing the treaty. In this connection he pointed out that there were, after all, such things as secret treaties. For example, the treaty which was the basis of the Berlin-Rome Axis had not been published. I told him that as far as I knew no such secret treaty existed and that we were of the opinion that the intended German-Spanish treaty did not contain anything that could not be made public. I rather assume that we will finally get the Spaniards to agree to make the treaty public at the proper time; however, they will hardly agree to immediate publication.

Since my return from Berlin I have not reported on the development of the political situation here, since it naturally depends entirely on the onrush of military events. The Catalonian campaign developed much more favorably and rapidly than the military experts ever expected. After the first break-through, Red resistance decreased steadily and finally collapsed at Barcelona. The capture of Barcelona cost the Nationalist troops only a single life. It is still impossible at the present time to tell whether the Reds are still in a position to offer considerable resistance anywhere in Catalonia and to continue the war in the southern zone. At any rate, the Government is expecting the latter possibility.

As a result of Franco's great military victories the internal unrest in the Nationalist zone, which gave rise to some concern even in December, has quieted down. Instead, there is more and more talk about Franco's intention to make changes in his Cabinet. In particular, it is assumed that the vice-presidency is to be transferred from Foreign Minister Jordana to the Generalissimo's brother-in-law, who is Minister of the Interior. In that case it appears very questionable whether Jordana will remain Foreign Minister. For this reason it might be useful to conclude the treaty of friendship as quickly as possible, since one can never tell whether Jordana's successor would be as cooperative as Jordana himself is now. I should therefore be very grateful if I were provided as quickly as possible with telegraphic instructions concerning the further handling of the treaty of friendship.

With cordial greetings and Heil Hitler,

As ever,

STOHRER

No. 721

462/225465

The Ambassador in Spain to the Foreign Ministry

Telegram

No. 70 of January 31   SAN SEBASTIÁN, January 31, 1939—9 : 00 p.m.

With reference to instruction No. Pol. III g 188 I of January 25.

My Italian colleague informs me that he has received instructions to the effect that after coming to an understanding with me he is to see the Foreign Minister with regard to Spain's accession to the Anti-Comintern Pact. He will do this in the next few days. Please send new instructions if necessary.

If we desire Spain's accession, a German-Italian step might possibly be supported by the Japanese Minister [1] and the Hungarian Chargé d'Affaires here.

STOHRER

---

[1] Makoto Yano.

No. 722

462/225466–67

The Ambassador in Spain to the Foreign Ministry

Telegram

SECRET   SAN SEBASTIÁN, February 1, 1939—11 : 50 a.m.

No. 73 of February 1

With reference to our telegram No. 70 of January 31.

The Japanese Minister called on me today after returning from a lengthy vacation, part of which he spent in Berlin. In the course of the conversation he asked me whether I had not already discussed with the Spanish Government the question of Spain's accession to the Anti-Comintern Pact.

Since the Minister had just called on the Italian Ambassador and I did not know what had been discussed, I did not think it right to reply in the negative, in spite of the statement in paragraph 2 of instruction Pol. III g 188 of January 25. I stated that I had recently broached the question to the Foreign Minister on my own initiative and he had shown interest but had proposed dilatory treatment.

The Japanese Minister opposed to this the view expressed by the Japanese Ambassador in Berlin on January 24, that it was desirable for Spain to join as soon as possible. He said that he would ask his Government for instructions and wished to remain in close contact with me in the further treatment of the question.

The Minister asked the Italian Ambassador the same question and expressed himself in the same way to him.

STOHRER

No. 723

632/252635

The State Secretary to the Embassy in Spain

Telegram

No. 51   BERLIN, February 1, 1939.

With reference to your report of January 27.[1]

In cooperation with the Italian Ambassador, who is receiving identical instructions, and if possible on February 2, please at once officially invite the Government to which you are accredited to join the Anti-Comintern Pact. Please add that we had reason to believe that a similar step would soon be taken by Japan and inform your Japanese colleague to this effect.

WEIZSÄCKER

---

[1] Not found.

No. 724

462/225469

The State Secretary to the Embassy in Spain

Telegram

URGENT   BERLIN, February 1, 1939.

No. 53 of February 1

With reference to my telegram No. 51 of February 1.

If additional countries join the Anti-Comintern Pact, we are interested in having Germany, Italy, and Japan the only powers to issue the invitations. The support of the Hungarian Chargé d'Affaires suggested in telegram No. 70 [1] is therefore not desirable.

WEIZSÄCKER

---

[1] Document No. 721, p. 829.

No. 725

168/132483

The Ambassador in Spain to the Foreign Ministry

Telegram

No. 75 of February 1   SAN SEBASTIÁN, February 2, 1939—12 : 17 a.m.
                                      Received February 2—12 : 50 a.m.

With reference to your telegram No. 49 of January 31 [1] and our telegram No. 61 of January 29.[2]

I informed the Foreign Minister that the Italians did not know of the protocols of July 1937 and that it would therefore perhaps be bet-

---

[1] Not printed (3882/E047482).
[2] Not found.

ter to avoid mentioning them in the treaty of friendship. The Minister understood this and proposed deleting the sentence in question; the protocols remained in force in any case, so long as they were not expressly terminated.

STOHRER

No. 726

2130/465002

The Ambassador in Spain to the Foreign Ministry

Telegram

SECRET   SAN SEBASTIÁN, February 5, 1939—12:01 a.m.
No. 89 of February 4   Received February 5—2:00 a.m.

With reference to my telegram No. 80 of February 2.[1]

Today, together with the Italian Ambassador, I gave the Foreign Minister the official invitation to the Spanish Government to join the Anti-Comintern Pact. Jordana, after having been informed by telephone of our proposed step, had already discussed the question in broad outline with the Generalissimo. He now replied that both Franco and he himself had strong objections to joining at the present moment. England and particularly France might suspect that this accession to the pact involved more extensive commitments and might feel themselves menaced. They might then possibly try to prevent a victorious ending of the war, now well under way, by renewed support of the Reds. The Minister referred, among other things, to the fact that the money deposited in France was still in danger, and, above all, to the ticklish situation now in the offing when the French border was reached.

The Minister showed understanding for our counterargument, to be sure, but persisted in his misgivings.

Jordana's statements do not represent a final stand; this is reserved for the Generalissimo. The conversation had more the nature of a preliminary exchange of ideas, for the continuation of which the Minister will obtain an audience for us with Franco.

The Italian Ambassador and I said that we would meanwhile continue to try indirectly to influence the Generalissimo and the Foreign Minister to accept our invitation. I have the impression that after the end of the Catalonian campaign, which Jordana expects in about 2 weeks, there will be fewer hesitations; perhaps they can be entirely eliminated.

I am keeping the Japanese Minister informed. He still has no instructions.

STOHRER

---

[1] Not printed (462/225470).

No. 727

136/73701–03

Memorandum by an Official of Political Division IIIa

BERLIN, February 6, 1939.
e.o. Pol. 485.

Drafting Officer: Counselor of Legation Count Du Moulin.

INTERMINISTERIAL CONFERENCE ON FEBRUARY 6, 1939, REGARDING RELIEF TO BARCELONA

Participants

Foreign Ministry:	Deputy Director of the Political Department, Minister Prince Bismarck
	Counselor of Legation Heinburg
	Counselor of Legation Sabath
	Counselor of Legation Schellert
	Counselor of Legation Count Du Moulin
	Secretary of Legation Stahlberg
Supreme Command of the Wehrmacht:	
Foreign Department	Commander Müller
Special Staff W	Major von Lossberg
Ministry of Economics:	Ministerial Counselor Seeliger
Food Ministry:	Ministerial Counselor Ebner
Ministry of Transportation:	Oberregierungsrat Langguth

The Deputy Director of the Political Department stated that the Foreign Minister had given his consent to the relief program contemplated, and he emphasized that speed was advisable, if only because of the arrival of an Italian food ship in Barcelona. Preparations would have to be completed insofar as possible by the time the Ministry of Finance had given final approval of the necessary funds.

The representative of the Food Ministry stated that wheat was available. The Reich Grain Office could be given the necessary instructions at any time. Upon his statement that sugar was also available, it was proposed to ask the Embassy at San Sebastián to determine the wishes of the Spanish Government in this respect. It was agreed that the equivalent of the sum of 1,027,000 RM requested of the German Ministry of Finance should not be exceeded.

In reply to a question by the Deputy Director of the Political Department, Ministerial Counselor Ebner remarked that there was no reason to fear an unfavorable reaction by German public opinion at the giving away of food. An announcement to this effect was also quite unobjectionable.

The representative of the Ministry of Transportation stated that the Neptun and Sloman steamship companies were willing to take over the transportation at 9 RM per ton. Storage space was available. The sea voyage took about 10 days. The Reich Grain Office had only to get in touch with the steamship companies.

The representative of Special Staff W stated that 4,000 to 5,000 civilian suits and overcoats of the Condor Legion were already available in Burgos. At the request of the Foreign Ministry they were to be sent to Barcelona and stored there so that they could appear as a shipment from Germany. He considered military protection for the vessel unnecessary. The representative of the Supreme Command of the Wehrmacht (Foreign Department) agreed.

At the suggestion of the Deputy Director of the Political Department, it was declared expedient to ask the NSV [*Nationalsozialistische Volkswohlfahrt*] to lend its support in carrying out the project and to consent to appear as the bearer of the gift so that at the proper time Ambassador von Stohrer could tell Franco that the NSV, in cooperation with the Reich Government, had made the shipment available to the Generalissimo for Barcelona.

The following conclusions were reached:

It was decided to undertake the following immediately:

1. To expedite approval of the funds by the Ministry of Finance (Personnel Department).

2. To consult with the NSV in order to request their cooperation (also the question of packing and labeling "Auxilio Alemán").

3. To instruct San Sebastián to ascertain whether sugar was desired, to report whether suits should be distributed even before the arrival of the flour ships, and to propose effective measures for guaranteeing the desired propaganda effect (sent February 6).

After obtaining the approval of the Ministry of Finance:

1. To instruct the Embassy in San Sebastián to make formal inquiries of the Spanish Government.

2. To inform the Food Ministry, the Ministry of Transportation, and the NSV and then to have the ships loaded and dispatched at once.

3. To inform the Propaganda Ministry.

No. 728

485/231619

Memorandum by the State Secretary

St. S. No. 111   BERLIN, February 9, 1939.

While calling on me today the Spanish Ambassador reverted to a conversation the Foreign Minister had had with him regarding the Anti-Comintern Pact. He said that his Government felt that, weapon in hand, it was doing more than any other in the spirit of the Anti-Comintern Pact (a remark which I answered by saying that we and other countries had previously taken the necessary steps against Bolshevism). Magaz then continued that his Government was naturally entirely in favor of joining the Anti-Comintern Pact in principle but thought that a better time for it would be after the end of the Civil War.

I again gave the Ambassador to understand how much importance we attach to having Spain accede as soon as possible, and I also told him that his instructions were probably already superseded, for meanwhile, to my knowledge, not only the German but also the Italian and Japanese Ambassadors had made new *démarches* with his Government in this matter.

WEIZSÄCKER

No. 729

136/73711

Memorandum by the State Secretary

St. S. No. 117   BERLIN, February 9, 1939.

Today the Italian Ambassador read me a laconic personal telegraphic instruction from Ciano to Attolico to the effect that the Italian Government viewed with sympathy the conclusion of the German-Spanish treaty of friendship now in process of negotiation and hoped that it would soon materialize. No reason for this step was given in the communication.

I replied to Attolico that Herr von Stohrer was provided with instructions for continuing the negotiations and was authorized to work both for the treaty and at the same time for Spain's accession to the Anti-Comintern Pact, but in such a way as not to be detrimental to the latter, which was particularly close to the heart of the Foreign Minister.[1]

WEIZSÄCKER

---

[1] An account of this interview was communicated to the Embassy in Spain in an instruction of Feb. 15 (2130/465286).

No. 730

2442/514684

The Foreign Ministry to the Embassy in Spain

Telegram

No. 70 of February 9   BERLIN, February 9, 1939.
                                                                    e.o. Pol. III 534.

Drafting Officer: Counselor of Legation Count Du Moulin.

According to reports in the British and French press, the British Government allegedly collaborated in the negotiations regarding the surrender of Minorca, bringing the Spanish Nationalist negotiators to Minorca on the cruiser *Devonshire* and also expressing willingness to transfer the Nationalist Governor and his staff to Minorca after the surrender. Franco supposedly intends to promise to occupy the island with exclusively Spanish troops.

The British Government is also alleged to have stated its readiness to act as mediator in negotiations between the Spanish parties. There are also quite a few unverifiable reports regarding Bérard's visit.[1]

Therefore please send me a telegraphic report at once about any Anglo-French attempts at mediation and any negotiations relating to Minorca.

HEINBURG

---

[1] Léon Bérard, French Senator and former Minister, had returned to Paris on Feb. 8 from a mission on which he had gone as an unofficial envoy to Nationalist Spain.

No. 731

2442/514686–87

The Ambassador in Spain to the Foreign Ministry

Telegram

No. 113 of February 10   SAN SEBASTIÁN, February 10, 1939.
                                                Received February 10—6: 00 p.m.
                                                                    Pol. III 578.

With reference to your telegram No. 70 of February 9.

According to reports so far, the British cruiser *Devonshire* brought the Spanish Nationalist negotiators from Majorca to Minorca in order to conduct the negotiations for surrender of the island, which had apparently been in progress privately for some time.

The negotiations were successful, as reported yesterday (telegram No. 111[1]). The British cruiser then brought several hundred Red

---

[1] Not printed (5175/E307003).

leaders from the island to safety in the direction of France; British radio reports state that the ship took this action independently but in harmony with the British Government.

The military occupation of the island with Spanish infantry and artillery has been carried out in its entirety by Spanish ships. So far nothing is known of Franco's promise to occupy the island with exclusively Spanish troops.

As reported in today's telegram No. 112 [2] and again ascertained in Burgos, a general mediation proposal by the British has not yet been received and is no longer expected by the Spanish Government.

As reported by telegram 101 of February 8,[3] the Foreign Minister insisted sharply to Léon Bérard on *de jure* recognition by France before the French representative would be received in Spain. Besides refugee questions, the matter of the restitution of Spanish art treasures carried off to France, as well as Spanish money and utilization of the arms taken from the Red Militia, was also discussed with Bérard. Thus, in negotiating on *de jure* recognition, Spain apparently intends to include conditions with regard to restitution of the properties in question. The Foreign Ministry therefore expects that there will still be difficult negotiations on this score.

Spain has also pressed insistently for *de jure* recognition by England, according to the Foreign Ministry. As I hear from a private British source, the British agent, Hodgson, whom the newspapers report to be en route from London to Burgos, is said already to be bringing communications regarding *de jure* recognition. Charles Michael Palairet, who was Minister in Stockholm until 1937 and who is married to Chamberlain's sister, is already being spoken of as England's future representative.

STOHRER

---

[2] Not found.
[3] Not printed (454/223630).

No. 732

2442/514689–90

The Ambassador in Spain to the Foreign Ministry

[Telegram]

URGENT   SAN SEBASTIÁN, February 12, 1939.

No. 128 of February 12

With reference to my report No. 529 of February 10.[1]

Yesterday I told the Foreign Minister, who had returned from a short trip, that the attitude of the Spanish authorities toward the

---

[1] Not printed (454/223632–33).

numerous French visitors and the reports on intervention in the evacuations during the surrender of Minorca might give the impression that Spain was approaching its former foes with open arms. The Minister protests against such an interpretation; he replied as follows to the separate points which I raised:

1. The commission of French officers to tour the Pryenees frontier had been invited a long time ago, particularly in order to put an end to attacks upon us for alleged German activity there. Moreover, he had declined to receive the officers or

2. The Deputies who were touring Spain and who were there in an entirely private capacity.

3. In the negotiations with Bérard he had been very energetic and had made any resumption of relations dependent upon *de jure* recognition and the familiar conditions (cf. telegram of February 11[2]), including return of the Red ships which had fled to France; he had even refused resumption of railway communications between Catalonia and France until that time.

4. He had also refused to contribute to the expense of maintaining the refugees in France.

5. All newspaper reports on arrangements having to do with *de jure* recognition by France and England were incorrect. The Spanish Government did not know what France and England would do; this question had not yet even been discussed with England, nor did the Spanish Government know any reason for the two countries to send representatives here. Reports on a mission by Marshal Pétain were incorrect.

6. British intervention at Minorca was confined to . . . (group missing) and Spanish consent was given . . . (group missing) a trip there from Majorca by the negotiators for the purpose of studying the situation and removing the Red leaders on a British cruiser, thus avoiding bloodshed. A proof of the lack of any sort of Anglo-Spanish agreement was the fact that the British mission here had asked the Foreign Ministry whether the newspaper reports regarding intervention by the cruiser were accurate. No other act of mediation had been undertaken by England either. However, the Minister stressed the great importance of the earliest possible *de jure* recognition by France and England, since further Red resistance would then be hopeless and the southern zone would probably capitulate.

STOHRER

---

[2] No. 121, not printed (649/255569).

No. 733

136/73713

The Ambassador in Spain to the Foreign Ministry

Telegram

SECRET   SAN SEBASTIÁN, February 13, 1939—1:00 p.m.
No. 131 of February 13   Received February 13—3:45 p.m.

With reference to our telegram No. 115 of February 10.[1]

During yesterday's conversation regarding the treaty of friendship, the Foreign Minister again referred to the question of Spain's accession to the Anti-Comintern Pact and explained that as long as the difficult negotiations on *de jure* recognition by France and England were in progress (see last paragraph of today's telegram No. 125 [2]), he had strenuous objections to accession.

The Minister added that the Generalissimo, who was usually at the front at the present time, would not yet receive the Italian Ambassador and me.   STOHRER

---

[1] Not printed (2442/514685).
[2] Not found.

No. 734

136/73714

The State Secretary to the Embassy in Spain

Telegram

No. 86   BERLIN, February 15, 1939.

With reference to your telegraphic reports Nos. 126 [1] and 131,[2] regarding signing of the treaty of friendship.

Further instructions will follow after receipt of your report on the new text of the treaty.

In the meantime please continue to work persistently for Spanish accession to the Anti-Comintern Pact. We are in agreement with the Italian Government regarding the importance of this accession. The Anti-Comintern Pact should by no means be allowed to suffer through parallel discussion of the treaty of friendship.[3]

                                       WEIZSÄCKER

---

[1] Not printed (136/73712).
[2] Not printed (136/73713).
[3] Typed marginal note: "N.B. At the special direction of the Foreign Minister."

No. 735

1573/381135

Memorandum by the State Secretary

IMMEDIATE BERLIN, February 16, 1939.
St. S. No. 139 Pol. III 359 g.

The Spanish Ambassador today gave me the memoranda of the conversations that took place recently between the Spanish Foreign Minister and M. Léon Bérard. The Spanish Ambassador described the contents of the memoranda as quite worth reading. He told me that he had not been instructed to give them to us but, in view of our close relations, saw no objection to doing so.

I expressed my thanks to the Ambassador for the information.

Since the memoranda are in Spanish, please have them translated into German and resubmitted to me at once. Herewith to Counselor of Legation Schwendemann or deputy.[1]

WEIZSÄCKER

---

[1] Marginal note: "Resubmitted to the State Secretary with a German translation. Schw[endemann] February 17." The memoranda (1573/381098–110), consisting of summaries of conversations between Bérard and Jordana on Feb. 4 and 6, are not printed here.

No. 736

650/255778–79

Memorandum by the State Secretary

St. S. No. 140 BERLIN, February 16, 1939.
e.o. Pol. III 725.

The Spanish Ambassador asked me today for my personal advice in the following matter:

As we knew, he had had a letter from the Generalissimo to deliver to the Führer. The delivery of this letter had been somewhat delayed, through certain circumstances which he fully appreciated, before the audience with the Führer materialized. In order that the letter might not lose its timeliness, he, Magaz, had finally offered the original of the letter to Minister Meissner[1] for delivery to the Führer. Herr Meissner had then requested a copy of the letter for himself. A few days later he had been formally received. The Ambassador spoke with deep gratitude of what had transpired at this audience. The Chief of Protocol had subsequently summoned him, Magaz, in order

---

[1] Head of the Presidential Chancellery (*Präsidialkanzlei*). No copy of this letter has been found in the files of the Foreign Ministry.

to tell him by direction of the Foreign Minister that he had made an error of protocol by giving Franco's letter directly to Meissner and not to the Foreign Ministry.

The Ambassador made the following explanation of this matter:

He had not been aware of having committed an error of protocol. He was not familiar in such detail with matters of jurisdiction between the Foreign Ministry and the Chief of the Presidential Chancellery. Herr Meissner was probably better acquainted with these questions and could have put him on the right track insofar as he had erred in the matter of protocol. He, Magaz, was very ready to offer the Foreign Minister every kind of apology for any mistake he may actually have made. What struck him as embarrassing, however, was the fact that he, as an Ambassador, had been summoned to the Protocol Department and taken to task by the Chief of Protocol—a procedure that seemed to him for his part contrary to protocol. Magaz then continued that he would like me to tell him sincerely whether he was *persona non grata*. He had no other ambition than to do his best for his country. If his person interfered in any way with the necessary intimate and cordial relations with Germany, he would not for a moment hesitate to resign.

My reply to Magaz was, briefly, somewhat as follows:

If he had asked me for advice beforehand, I, too, should have told him he should submit Franco's letter to the Führer only through the Foreign Ministry. His suspicion that there might be some objection to his, Magaz's, person, was entirely unfounded. Since, as Magaz said, the Foreign Minister was going to receive him before the end of the week, I could only advise him to present the facts of the case to Herr von Ribbentrop in the same confidential manner as he had done to me.

WEIZSÄCKER

No. 737

2442/514702

The Ambassador in Great Britain to the Foreign Ministry

Airgram

No. 41 of February 16   LONDON, February 16, 1939.
                                    Received February 17—4: 50 p.m.
                                                    Pol. III 703.

The British Government intends to let the French take the lead in the question of recognizing Franco. This is to be done out of consideration for American public opinion, which the British feel will not be so much aroused if the French have recognized Franco first. The French are said to have indicated plainly here that they are indifferent to American sensitivity in this question which is of vital importance to France.

According to reliable reports, General Jordana has again assured Senator Bérard[1] that the foreign volunteers will be sent home immediately after the last remnant of Red Spain is subdued. Bérard had received instructions to try to influence Jordana to make this a definite commitment.

Bérard is also instructed to obtain from Franco a precise statement of his attitude on the question of an amnesty. With this concession the French Government intends to bring about the surrender of Negrín. Should Negrín even then continue to offer resistance, France would recall its diplomatic mission from Red Spain and recognize Franco's as the only legal government in Spain.

Dirksen

---

[1] On Feb. 14 the French Council of Ministers decided to send Bérard back to Spain, this time as official representative to continue negotiations and pave the way for establishment of normal diplomatic relations.

No. 738

472/228775–78

The Ambassador in Spain to the State Secretary

SECRET   SAN SEBASTIÁN, February 17, 1939.

DEAR WEIZSÄCKER: In reply to your telegram No. 86 of the 15th regarding the anti-Comintern agreement and the German-Spanish treaty of friendship, I should like to inform you of the following. Since—as reported—the Italian Ambassador together with me, and the Japanese Minister independently of us, extended an invitation to the Spanish Foreign Minister, General Jordana, for Spain to join the Anti-Comintern Pact, Count Viola and I have at various times and independently of each other made great efforts to further the matter with Jordana. In doing so we have come to believe that the Spanish Foreign Minister at the present moment is quite decidedly against Spain's accession to the Anti-Comintern Pact because, as long as the negotiations with France and England regarding *de jure* recognition are not concluded, he considers such action to be highly questionable.

For this reason my Italian colleague and I asked to see the Generalissimo, although it is hardly to be assumed that the latter will decide differently in the matter than his Foreign Minister. Continual inquiries from both of us and also an inquiry by the Japanese Minister, who intends to join in the *démarche* with Franco, have thus far always been answered most courteously with the explanation that the Generalissimo was extremely busy and his presence was needed at the front.

But there is no doubt that this is not the reason for the delay—at least not the only one. Although Franco did not, to be sure, appear yesterday at the solemn requiem in Burgos for the late Pope, he would surely have been able to find the time to see us at headquarters or anywhere at the front, especially since we had, of course, offered to call on him anywhere at all. The principal reason for the dilatory treatment of the question is surely Franco's aversion to giving a negative reply—even if only a temporary one—to the two representatives of the powers especially friendly to Spain. This is entirely in keeping with the Spanish mentality. He is trying instead to postpone the reply in the hope that the events which have recently been occurring in rapid succession will perhaps soon make possible a more favorable decision or at least the setting of a definite date for Spain's accession to the pact. To hold a pistol at Franco's breast in the matter of the audience is thus perhaps to use a two-edged sword [*Es ist daher vielleicht ein zweischneidiges Schwert, Franco hinsichtlich des Empfangs die Pistole auf die Brust zu setzen*]. After detailed discussions with Count Viola and without relaxing my demand for an early conference with Franco, I intended to speak to Jordana once more on Monday, or as soon as he returns from his latest trip to the front, and point out to him again amicably and in private the great importance the German Government attaches to the matter. In view of the great concessions that we have obtained from the Spaniards in the past 2 or 3 months and also the fine spirit of cooperation that Jordana, particularly, has shown in the matter of the treaty of friendship, I would naturally like to avoid *too* energetic a stand in the matter of the pact. Moreover, such a stand would probably produce the opposite result in view of the Spanish character, and Jordana's in particular.

From the instructions which Count Viola received yesterday from Count Ciano parallel to and at the same time as mine, it appears that the Italian Foreign Minister again spoke with the Spanish Ambassador at Rome in the sense of Italian and German wishes. I therefore assume that the matter has also been discussed with Magaz in Berlin, although Jordana has told me nothing about it. It was my experience in a previous case, when parallel action was taken through me and the Spanish Ambassador in Berlin, that the latter did nothing at all about it or only after considerable delay. Conceivably, therefore, pressure on him might further the entire action and at any rate avoid giving the impression here that I alone, on my own initiative, am pressing the matter.

With cordial greetings, and Heil Hitler!

As ever,

STOHRER

No. 739

1819/416480

The Foreign Ministry to the Embassies in Italy, France, and Spain and at the Holy See

BERLIN, February 18, 1939.
Pol. III 720.

The Spanish Ambassador here informed the State Secretary on February 16 that the Vatican had protested to the Spanish Government with regard to the German-Spanish cultural agreement. This agreement could not be reconciled with the Concordat. The Ambassador added that he himself did not know what this had to do with the Concordat. He also launched forth into reflections on the rigid and faulty policy of Pius XI.

By direction:
SCHWENDEMANN

No. 740

1573/381142–58

The Ambassador in Spain to the Foreign Ministry

SECRET
No. 755 g

SAN SEBASTIÁN, February 19, 1939.
Pol. III 452 g.

With reference to my report No. 633 g of November 19 and to report No. 664 g of December 19, 1938,[1] on pointers for a report in Berlin on the political situation in Spain.

Subject: The political situation in Spain.

The big Catalonian offensive. 1. Delay and beginning.

The last 2 months were completely dominated by the military events, which followed each other in rapid succession. The large-scale offensive against Catalonia, which the German and Italian military had long since characterized to Generalissimo Franco as the only one which could decide the war, began on December 23 after it had been necessary to postpone it for 2 weeks because of bad weather and difficulties of deployment. The order to attack was given in spite of the fact that Christmas was imminent; the Nuncio had vainly requested a truce in the name of the Pope.

---

[1] Not printed (1573/381046–51). In this memorandum Ambassador Stohrer summed up the military situation in Spain and the internal political situation of the two warring factions.

2. *Sequence of events. Occupation of Barcelona. Occupation of all of Catalonia. End of the Catalonian campaign.*

The Catalonian campaign developed into an irresistible advance by the Nationalist troops that was much faster than had been expected. These troops, partly carried along by the Italians, who pushed ahead sharply, were able to occupy Barcelona only 1 month later—on January 26—almost without firing a shot. The occupation of the rest of Catalonia then automatically followed without much resistance on the part of the defeated Red Army, so that there was nothing left during that time for the remainder of the Red troops—insofar as they had not been captured—but to flee across the French frontier and be disarmed in France. Innumerable civilian refugees followed them on this road of suffering. Diversionary maneuvers by the Red troops assembled in the Red zone to the south—especially near Córdoba—had been unable to prevent or even delay the course of the tragedy.

Causes of the Red defeat.

The explanation for Franco's decisive victory, the scope of which had been considered unlikely by the German and Italian military experts—as reported on a number of occasions (report No. 607 of October 19, 1938)—lies in the better morale of the troops fighting for the Nationalist cause as well as in their great superiority in the air, and better artillery and other war matériel, which the Reds, still shaken by the fighting in the Ebro bend and in part greatly hampered by ammunition shortage and difficulties of food supply, were unable to resist.

Flight of the Red government to France. Its return to Madrid.

After long hesitation the Red "government," which had also fled to France, decided to return to the Red zone in the south and to try there to organize a last resistance. In this, Negrín and Alvarez del Vayo— the tools of Russia—showed themselves to be the driving forces, as in the past, whereas President Azaña had long since advocated yielding and was obviously loath to lend his name, from the Spanish Embassy in Paris, to the decree transferring the seat of the government back to Madrid. Azaña himself, however, does not seem inclined to leave France.

Organization of last resistance. Hopes of the Reds. Franco will accept only surrender.

It is generally agreed that successful resistance by the remainder of the Red Army in central Spain is unthinkable. Therefore the opinion is frequently expressed, also in Spanish Government circles, that the measures taken by the Reds for continuing the war are only a sham maneuver for the purpose of pushing through at least some of Negrín's

13 points—long since reduced to 3 demands (see report No. 633 g of November 19, 1938). However, under the given circumstances even this hope appears to be a great misconception of the actual situation. As is known, Franco has always declared that he would accept only an unconditional surrender. The victor in the Catalonian campaign will therefore be less inclined than ever before to grant a general amnesty and a plebiscite concerning the future regime. The third point demanded by Negrín—withdrawal of all foreign troops from Spain after the war—is a foregone conclusion and does not need to be made the subject of conditions or concessions.

Even the next few days may clarify whether the war will continue . . . and what attitude France and England will adopt.

The next few days will probably clarify whether no more than a feint by the Reds is involved or whether it is actually intended to continue the war. Likewise it will then become clearer what attitude England and France are planning to adopt vis-à-vis Nationalist Spain, i.e. whether they will definitely break with their previous policy and accord Franco *de jure* recognition or whether, forced by their Leftist parties, they again wish to confine themselves to waiting.

For the eventuality the war should continue . . . Franco is already assembling troops against central Spain. Probable offensive against Madrid.

Although it is unlikely, nevertheless the possibility that the war may continue must at the present time be taken into consideration—regrettable as the further futile shedding of blood in this civil war may be— a fact which Franco has already taken into account by concentrating troops against the south. Nothing definite has so far been heard about Franco's military intentions. Thus it is not yet certain whether the Generalissimo is still planning to continue the offensive against Valencia, which was stopped in September by the Red penetration across the Ebro, or whether, as certain things now indicate, he first wishes to put through the attack on Madrid.

Negotiations with France concerning de jure *recognition. British attitude not clarified.*

I have made frequent telegraphic reports on the demands made by Spain to the French intermediary Léon Bérard concerning the resumption of relations with France; likewise I have reported on the fact, confirmed by the Foreign Ministry as late as February 14, that no exchange of ideas of any kind has occurred on this question between Spain and England.

The meaning of full recognition of Franco by France and England.

It is understandable that the Spanish Government attaches the greatest importance to the stand taken by France and England, since after *de jure* recognition of Franco by these two powers further Red resistance could hardly be expected—in the opinion of Foreign Minister Jordana.

Does England want to assume the role of mediator after all?

Unclear as the attitude of England and France is, in spite of all the reports in the press concerning the imminence of *de jure* recognition, it appears equally uncertain whether England will try after all to assume the role of mediator in order to prevent bloodshed or to strengthen her own position in Spain. There are certain indications that England is not loath to repeat the unofficial intervention which led to the subjugation of the Island of Minorca.

Development of the internal situation in the Nationalist zone. General pacification.

The development of the internal situation in Nationalist Spain in the last 2 months has, of course, been determined completely by the victorious Catalonian campaign. Penetration by disguised Red militia, which occurred in the Nationalist zone as late as December, has stopped and nothing further is heard about assassinations and plots. The generally joyful, or fearful, tension with which the entire population followed events in Catalonia has, understandably enough, caused a change of sentiment. The Nationalist elements and those in favor of Franco's regime have shaken off their pessimism in anticipation of an early final victory and have stopped their criticism, which was frequently severe, of the Government's military and political measures; those parts of the population which are Reds or regional nationalists, on the other hand, maintain a cautious silence and scarcely dare to continue surreptitiously their agitation against the Government.

Franco's prestige has risen tremendously.

Accordingly Franco's prestige, which had suffered somewhat even in the Army at the time of the Ebro operations, has again risen very much, and the influence of the victorious Army has become a new or at least a greater factor.

Food difficulties in the Nationalist zone. Hostility against foreigners is less apparent.

Under these circumstances the food shortage, which became really apparent for the first time in the Nationalist zone after the conquest of Catalonia—until then there were only scattered instances of food shortages or price increases—is so far being accepted without complaint. At the same time manifestations of hostility against foreigners—including Germans and Italians—which I have had to report previously, appear to have become less frequent.

Internal conflicts have abated.

In these weeks of victory, which by its nature adjusts existing antagonisms, there can hardly be any talk of conflict within the Falange or disagreement between it and the military or the Church. Latently, however, the antagonisms persist. The effect which they will have and the scope they will assume will not become evident until the end of the war when the soldiers returning home from the front will assume their political attitudes.

The influence of the original Falange has decreased. What direction will the Falange take after the war?

As far as the Falange itself is concerned, its influence has probably declined vis-à-vis the victorious Army, and within the Falange proper the power of the original Falange has doubtless been considerably diminished by the skillful political measures of the Caudillo against the extreme Leftist (as well as Rightist) elements and by the lack of real leaders that has frequently been mentioned in the past. This goes so far that there is talk that some of the original Falangists who occupy the most important party and governmental positions, especially the Secretary General of the Party, Minister of Agriculture Fernández Cuesta, are supposedly attempting to retire to diplomatic posts abroad. It remains to be seen whether the "Camisas viejas" still at the front will be in a position to imbue the original Falange with new life at the end of the war. I consider it entirely possible. In that case, however, this will probably take the direction of making the objectives of the Falange more radical, as I have repeatedly stated in the past. Such a development would carry in it the seeds of new difficulties leading to increased antagonism not only toward the Rightist elements of the Unity Party but also toward the military. The latter were never especially favorably inclined toward the Falange— particularly the original Falange—and will demand a position of greater power after the victorious conclusion of the war, as well as toward the Church, which has in the meantime again assumed great power.

New problems after the war. The importance of Minister of the Interior Serrano Suñer. His Church policy.

Thus it is possible not only that a number of problems which have now been relegated to the background by the final efforts and the victory will again become more acute but that new ones will appear as well. It will require great skill on the part of Franco and his Government to overcome them. The manner in which these tasks will be tackled is likely to depend primarily on the Generalissimo's brother-in-law, the present Minister of the Interior, Serrano Suñer, who today is indisputably the leading and most important adviser of the Chief of State and Generalissimo. I have repeatedly made reference to the importance of Serrano Suñer in my reports in the past. The Generalissimo's brother-in-law is undoubtedly the most outstanding person in the present Cabinet. But he is a fanatic who inclines toward mysticism and whose actions it will be difficult to predict. Although, or perhaps precisely because, he always emphasized his great sympathy for Germany in his meetings with me and tries to prove it by examples, I am inclined to believe, as I always have, that he is no friend of ours. He is Jesuit-trained and has strong Church leanings. This permits the assumption that he is open to suggestions from the Vatican, although—as I explained in my report No. 452 g of July 19, 1938 [2]—he seems so far nevertheless to have preserved a somewhat independent conception of future Spanish policy with reference to the Church. However, the decree revoking the separation of Church and State, which was issued not long ago (report No. 600 of February 13 [3]) and was certainly proclaimed with Suñer's consent if not even at his instigation, is another relapse into the former subjugation of the State to the Church, which is now, at the end of the war, at least as strong as prior to the proclamation of the Republic.

The most important question: social reform.

The antagonism between Serrano Suñer and the other Ministers continues; the death of Martínez Anido, the Minister for Public Security, however, has eliminated the principal enemy of the Minister of the Interior, who has now also taken over the tasks of the former Police Minister.

The future treatment of social questions and reforms, however, will be even more important for the existence of the new Spain and its further development than the Church problem, as I have emphasized again and again. A memorandum of considerable length (report No. 277 of January 23 [4]) shows in detail that there are promising beginnings in this direction. However, the numerous enemies of the new regime can be converted only by means of further energetic developments in this direction, and only in this manner will it be possible to prevent everything from remaining as it used to be. A German who has been active in Spain for decades recently answered the question: "How do you find the new Spain?" by saying: "When I find it I shall tell you about it." I believe that this view is too pessimistic, but there is doubtless some truth in it.

---

[2] Not found.
[3] Not printed (5177/E307018–19).
[4] Not found.

The internal situation of the Reds. The morale of the Red troops.

The present situation of the Reds is affected by the crushing defeat in Catalonia. Consequently the Red troops still stationed in the southern Red zone can no longer be expected to have much spirit for offensive operations, and on the defensive—although the accomplishments of the Spanish soldiers are especially outstanding in this respect—they will presumably also fail because of the shortage of war matériel and the superiority of Franco's troops confronting them, who are accustomed to victory.

Intentions of the Red leaders still unclarified. New wave of terror in Red Spain.

The situation of the Red Government itself is still entirely unclear. Day after day the newspapers report that Azaña has resigned; then again he has issued proclamations which call for surrender or, on the other hand, for ruthless resistance, or even express complete confidence in victory. Concerning Miaja, the commander in chief of the southern zone, it was also reported that he wanted to surrender, that he had fled, etc. Even the Foreign Ministry of the Spanish Nationalists is at present completely uninformed on the true situation in the Red camp, as the Foreign Minister told me only a few days ago. Only one thing seems to be certain; namely, that the Russian hirelings Negrín and Alvarez del Vayo want to lead the remainder of their unfortunate troops to slaughter once more. It may be taken for granted that they have not only assured their own retreat but prepared a very comfortable future for themselves. Under their Russian reign of terror, however, a new wave of bloodshed is at present inundating the hapless country still under their subjugation.

The question of restoring the monarchy. Opinion of the Falange and . . . of the military. The decision lies with Franco.

Next to the Church question and the social question mentioned above, of all Spanish problems that of the monarchy is probably of particular importance for future developments. As I reported orally in Berlin, the movement for the restoration of the monarchy has shown further progress during recent months. It was peculiar that even in circles of the original Falange the restoration of the monarchy has been discussed with less opposition than before. The reason is said to be that the Falange assumes that the military will push it aside, especially in the event of an overwhelming victory, and hopes to find backing in the monarchy, which the Spaniards call *poder moderador*, or moderating power. On the other hand, however, it can by no means be said that the influential military leaders, Franco's generals, advocate a restoration. A number of important generals, such as the "social" General Queipo de Llano, the commander of the southern army, and Yagüe, the so-called Falange general, are considered opponents of the monarchy.   They are probably opposed by the majority of the other military leaders, among them the Commander in Chief of the Air Force, General Kindelan, the Chief of Staff, General Vigon, who was formerly King Alfonso's aide-de-camp, and others.   Under these circumstances what I said about the question of restoration in one of my first reports probably still holds true; namely, that in case of a victorious conclusion of the campaign the decision about the restoration of the monarchy will depend almost exclusively on Franco.   Should he decide for the restoration, probably the only person to be considered is the third son of the former King Alfonso XIII, Infante Don Juan, who now lives in Rome.

The date of a possible restoration is uncertain.   Reasons which may cause postponement of a possible restoration.

Opinions on the date of a possible restoration of the monarchist regime are even more divided than on the question of the restoration itself.   Franco once told me that there could be no question at all of a return to the monarchy until after the end of the war and the restoration of peace and order in Spain.   I therefore consider it altogether possible that more time will pass before the question becomes acute; I even believe that the great Catalonian victory, especially if crowned by an early final victory, may tend to give the ideas of the two leading Spanish personalities, i.e. the Generalissimo and his brother-in-law, a somewhat different direction than in times of uncertainty and distress; perhaps the victory will reawaken the hope doubtless entertained earlier by the highly ambitious Serrano Suñer of establishing a permanent regime with Franco as Chief of State and himself as the all-powerful Prime Minister.

However that may be, in spite of information to the contrary (cf. instruction Pol. III 252 g of February 7 [5]), I nevertheless believe that a restoration of the monarchy in Spain is more probable than its permanent abolition.   This opinion is shared by the Italian Ambassador, who even told me a short while ago that according to his information the Infante Don Juan had been given to understand from here that he should hold himself in readiness.   My Portuguese colleague, too, believes in the restoration.

Our stand on the monarchist problem.

In the light of future German-Spanish relations it would be better—as I have always emphasized—if the restoration of the monarchist regime did not come about, since there is reason to fear that a Spanish monarch from the former royal family will fall under the influence of the British and above all of the Vatican.

---

[5] Not printed (1573/381080-81).

Welcome development in German-Spanish relations. Favorable prospects.

A considerable improvement in mutual relations can be noted in dealings between Germany and Spain during the last 4 months. Whereas we used to meet with very little sympathy as late as this summer when we presented our wishes, even unimportant ones, this situation has now changed considerably. In all dealings between the official agencies of the two countries a much friendlier and above all a much more sincere atmosphere has been created, which opens up favorable prospects for the future, especially if we now succeed, after concluding the cultural agreement and other less important agreements, in cementing the relations between the two countries in a treaty forming the basis for future intercourse.

Spanish public opinion and Germany.

It is hoped that we will also succeed in again winning for ourselves a stronger position in the public opinion of the country. Although the Germans are the least disliked foreigners in Spain even today, we have nevertheless lost in popularity and favor as compared to the first year of the war, because of the Spanish nature (which is opposed to foreign intervention of any kind), the length and hardships of the war, and the propaganda of the Reds (especially of the Red Basques). Skillfully exploited relief measures for the needy population of the liberated territory and for the refugees returning to Nationalist Spain, etc., would be likely to improve the atmosphere.

Conclusions.

If we accomplish this and if we succeed in finding a sound basis for cooperation with Spain in economic matters, too, then—in addition to accomplishing the main goal of our Spanish policy in recent years, i.e. preventing the establishment of a Bolshevist regime in Spain—we will have prospects of obtaining a certain compensation for the sacrifices in life and property that we have made here.

Franco's military victory, which is now assured insofar as it is humanly possible to judge, has delivered us from the politically very awkward intervention I have often mentioned in my reports as a matter of precaution, which would probably have become necessary in case of a compromise; and thus our position vis-à-vis the new Spanish regime has fortunately not been prejudiced.

v. Stohrer

No. 741

462/225486

The Ambassador in Spain to the Foreign Ministry

Telegram

STRICTLY SECRET   BARCELONA, February 20, 1939.
Unnumbered

1. The Council of Ministers, presided over by Franco, has decided to accede to the Anti-Comintern Pact. The Spanish Government is prepared to sign at any time but urgently requests that the accession itself be treated with strict secrecy until the end of the war.

2. The Generalissimo has approved the new text of the German-Spanish treaty of friendship. The signing may take place at any time, subject to a review from the standpoint of language and style.

Please send telegraphic instructions with regard to the signing of 1 and 2.

STOHRER

No. 742

472/228521

The State Secretary to the Ambassador in Italy

BERLIN, February 22, 1939.
By courier on February 22.

DEAR FRIEND: I hope that we shall be able to send you a telegram of information today regarding the handling of Spain's accession to the anti-Comintern agreement. You know that on the part of Herr von Ribbentrop this matter was dealt with energetically, but until recently no further result had been obtained than a promise in principle by the Spanish Government to join at the end of the war. The day before yesterday Ciano again took up the matter urgently in several direct telephone conversations with Herr von Ribbentrop. It was due to this initiative that urgent instructions to Stohrer were drawn up, but they were finally not sent after all, because meanwhile the Spanish Council of Ministers had anticipated us. It is not quite clear to me what motives induced the Italian Government to revert so insistently to the matter. The Italian Government is surely not jealous of the German-Spanish friendship agreement which we have also prepared and with whose history you are, of course, familiar. We have now made fairly good progress in the matter, and I think that we will be able to conclude it in the not too distant future.

Cordial greetings and Heil Hitler!

Yours sincerely,
WEIZSÄCKER

No. 743

462/225493-94

The State Secretary to the Embassy in Spain

Telegram

No. 102 of February 23   BERLIN, February 23, 1939.
                                        Received February 23—7: 30 p.m.

Please transmit the following to the Ambassador at once:

"Following receipt of your communication via the radio of Special Staff W concerning Spain's readiness to sign the anti-Comintern agreement at any time,[1] it was agreed with the Italian Government that this offer was to be accepted and implemented at once. The approval of the Japanese Government, which was also consulted, is likewise to be expected shortly.

"I therefore request that you call on Franco within the course of the present week together with your Italian and Japanese colleagues and tell him the following (you may give precedence to Count Viola on this occasion) : Our respective Governments gratefully welcomed the decision of the Generalissimo to accede to the anti-Comintern agreement. You were authorized to arrange the formalities with the Spanish Government and to undertake the signing within the shortest possible time. We agreed to postponing publication of the accession, but publication could probably be contemplated as soon as the first great victory was achieved in the remaining theater of war, since such a victory was practically equivalent to the end of the war.

"You may also mention, as far as the importance of Spain's accession is concerned, that both the Führer and the Duce attribute to the act eminent significance for the future development of our relations with Spain. We also believed that, once the Spanish decision became known, it would not restrain the French and British Governments from according *de jure* recognition to Nationalist Spain but, on the contrary, would urge them to do so. You might also emphasize what importance this step on the part of Spain, as the dominant power in the Ibero-American world, has for the question of fighting Communism in the Latin American countries. Should your Japanese colleague not receive similar instructions by Friday noon, please send me a telegraphic report at once.

"The details for the accession of new countries to the anti-Comintern agreement have been discussed and established here with Italy and Japan on the occasion of the accession of Hungary and Manchukuo, so that the formalities of signing can be concluded in Spain within a short time."[2]

WEIZSÄCKER

---

[1] Document No. 741, p. 852.
[2] Marginal note: "Obviously drafted before the Foreign Ministry received my telegram from Saragossa and, of course, my telegraphic report of today concerning the Japanese Minister's instructions. St[ohrer]." The telegram from Saragossa has not been found. The telegram of the 23d regarding the Japanese Minister's instructions (462/225492) stated that the Japanese Minister had been instructed to express, along with his German and Italian colleagues, their satisfaction at Franco's decision regarding the Anti-Comintern Pact.

No. 744

2130/465011–13

The Ambassador in Italy to the Foreign Ministry

CONFIDENTIAL   ROME, February 24, 1939.
No. 1510

Subject: Memoranda regarding developments in Spain.

I have the honor to submit herewith copies of two memoranda of February 22 and 24 from a reliable informant, which contain comments on the attitude of the Palazzo Chigi on developments in domestic and foreign policy in Spain.

For the Ambassador:
PLESSEN

[Enclosure 1]

MEMORANDUM

ROME, February 22, 1939.

The Palazzo Chigi is well satisfied with the development of Franco's political stand and his personality. As the result of the line now adopted, it is believed here that Franco is on the way to acquiring the importance of a leader with respect to both his own people and foreign countries. If he persists in this course, the further inevitable developments of the revolution and the modern army which he now commands will finally make him the actual master of Spain even in the sense of his status as Chief of State. To be sure, these things are only in the making at present, and the question, for instance, of forming a new Spanish government with Suñer as Prime Minister is not yet ripe for decision. As opposed to the British wishes for restoration of the monarchy, Italy gives decided preference to the solution with Franco as Chief of State. The Palazzo Chigi is fairly confident that it will be possible to encourage and establish Spain and Franco in this way by degrees, since, as they believe here, a reversion to the old Spain of before the Civil War days is no longer possible and the prodigious event of the Civil War will necessarily result in the creation of a Spain which is entirely new politically and socially. With this expected development, the Palazzo Chigi also sees the possibility of bringing Spain permanently into the sphere of the Rome-Berlin Axis, which would also make itself distinctly felt from a strategic point of view. Italy's aversion to the monarchistic solution is explained principally by the very close relations of the Spanish aristocracy and monarchy with England.

[Enclosure 2]

MEMORANDUM

ROME, February 24, 1939.

Developments in the Spanish question have aroused the greatest satisfaction in the Palazzo Chigi, a feeling which Count Ciano has expressed in a very definite manner in confidential talks. He is not only certain that Spain will accede to the Anti-Comintern Pact very shortly but is already negotiating with Franco regarding the conclusion of a political and military alliance. He considers the conclusion of this alliance a certainty. "The Spanish affair is going magnificently."[1] By this development Italy was at one stroke obtaining breathing space and access to the Atlantic Ocean; Gibraltar's importance was reduced and France's overland route to Africa cut. "We are establishing a strong system whose skeleton is the Rome-Berlin Axis and the Rome-Berlin-Tokyo triangle, a system which is being perfected by the alliance with Spain and the adherence of other states: Manchukuo and Hungary."[1] This system would in the course of time make its effect felt on other countries which are at present irresolute and uncertain, such as Poland and Yugoslavia. As far as the triangle of Italy-Japan-Germany was concerned, in Ciano's opinion the common interests of Germany and Japan against Soviet Russia would finally prevail and result in additional ties between these three countries.

[1] The quoted passages are in Italian in the original.

No. 745

2655/527403

The Ambassador in Spain to the Foreign Ministry

Telegram

URGENT   SAN SEBASTIÁN, February 26, 1939—10:00 p.m.
No. 173 of February 26   Received February 26—11:00 p.m.

The Foreign Minister has informed me that negotiations with Léon Bérard were concluded with complete success for Spain. Tomorrow, Monday, the statement about the result would be published. France had accepted all Spanish demands with respect to *de jure* recognition, dispatching of an ambassador (but probably *not* Bérard), the return of the Spanish gold, art treasures, ships, and arms. The preamble expressed the desire for good neighborliness between the two countries. In this connection Spain seems to have expressed a determination to preserve her unlimited sovereignty. On the other hand, the Minister emphasized that—as he had always said—Spain had rejected any commitments or acceptance of conditions.

Jordana added that now everything depended, of course, on how France would live up to her promises. The refugee question, too, remained a difficult problem.

With regard to *de facto* recognition on the part of France and England, the Minister explained that he knew only what was in the newspapers; but he believed that reports about an imminent decision were correct.

STOHRER

No. 746

472/228779–80

The Ambassador in Spain to the State Secretary

SECRET   SAN SEBASTIÁN, February 26, 1939.

DEAR WEIZSÄCKER: 1. In continuation of my private letter of the 17th [1] and the official communications I have meanwhile sent on the question of Spain's accession to the Anti-Comintern Pact, I should like to give you the following further information:

The Generalissimo told me at the luncheon following the big parade in Barcelona that his decision to join the Anti-Comintern Pact had been a foregone conclusion, in view of his previous stand on Communism, and came "from the heart." It had only been a matter of choosing the right moment.

The assumption expressed in my last private letter, to the effect that the Generalissimo had hesitated to receive the Italian Ambassador and me as long as he could not give us a positive reply, thus seems to have been correct. Further, however, Count Viola and I gather from Franco's words which I have quoted, and which Franco repeated almost word for word to the Italian Ambassador in Barcelona, that the principal opponent of Spain's immediate accession to the Anti-Comintern Pact was Foreign Minister Jordana, who feared that his negotiations with France and England might meet with difficulties if the accession became known. It was therefore probably correct to try to influence him particularly.

If this assumption with regard to Jordana proves right, it may be hoped that when the Generalissimo receives us within the next few days he will not make any great difficulties with regard to our desire of advancing the date of publication to coincide with the next great military victory in the remaining theater of war. For the rest, it

---

[1] Document No. 738, p. 841.

looks again today as if there would be no further important military operations at all. But one cannot prophesy in this respect.

2. By the last courier I was informed of the contents of the Generalissimo's letter to the Führer of the beginning of January. I do not know whether the Führer intends to reply to it. Should this be the case, it might be possible to wait until the German-Spanish treaty of friendship is concluded and Spain has signed the Anti-Comintern Pact, for then an important chapter in the development of German-Spanish relations will have been concluded. This fact could then serve as an occasion for expressing in general terms or with respect to points of particular interest to us our hopes and wishes regarding the further development of these relations.

With cordial greetings and Heil Hitler!

As ever,
STOHRER

No. 747

168/132441

The State Secretary to the Embassy in Spain

Draft Telegram

BERLIN, March 1, 1939.

For your information:

According to the Supreme Headquarters of the Wehrmacht, General von Richthofen has been instructed to anticipate a suitable date for withdrawing the Condor Legion and to consult you in this question. For a final decision on this question, naturally, in addition to Franco's agreement, that of the Italian Government would first have to be obtained from here.

WEIZSÄCKER

No. 748

462/225506—07

The Ambassador in Spain to the Foreign Ministry

Telegram

VERY SECRET   SAN SEBASTIÁN, March 1, 1939.

No. 186 of March 1

With reference to my telegraphic report No. 181 of February 27.[1]

Together with the Italian Ambassador and the Japanese Minister, I made the *démarche* with the Generalissimo today on Spain's acces-

---

[1] Not printed (462/225505).

sion to the Anti-Comintern Pact; the Foreign Minister was also present. In accordance with instructions, Count Viola acted as spokesman. Franco answered that, considering Spain's hard fight against Bolshevism for the last 2 years, her accession to the pact was a matter of course and entirely sincere. When the time for announcing this was mentioned, however, Franco explained in detail that an announcement before the end of the war appeared very dangerous for Spain. He adhered to this opinion in spite of numerous objections by me and the Japanese Minister, who had yesterday evening received the awaited instructions requiring him to press vigorously for both announcement and signature at the same time. Franco's main arguments were the following: Even after recognition France and England could still do Spain great injury, for instance, by giving further support to the Reds, making difficulties in carrying out the stipulations for return of Spanish property, war matériel, etc., as accepted by France, or even bribing of Red naval commanders to sink warships at the last minute instead of delivering them up. An announcement of Spain's accession to the Anti-Comintern Pact at the present moment would arouse serious anxiety in France and England on the score of the policy of continued close cooperation with the friendly powers which Franco was resolved to follow, and this could be inconvenient both for Spain and for us at the present time.

The Foreign Minister finally interceded with the remark that we could very well trust the Generalissimo, who would know how to reconcile the views we had expressed with the interests of Spain as regards the choice of the time for publication.

It came out during the conversation, incidentally, that the Generalissimo is now, after all, counting for certain on further resistance by the Reds and on new battles. He wishes, however, to eliminate as far as possible any interference by French and British policy in the final phase of the struggle.

v. STOHRER

No. 749

1819/416481

The Ambassador in Spain to the Foreign Ministry

STRICTLY CONFIDENTIAL   SAN SEBASTIÁN, March 1, 1939.
No. 917   Pol. III 1065.
Subject: Personal letter from the Generalissimo to Mr. Chamberlain.

I was told by a reliable informant several days ago that the Generalissimo had sent a personal letter to Mr. Chamberlain around February 20, which was taken by Foreign Minister General Jordana from

Barcelona to Burgos and delivered to the British representative (the present Chargé d'Affaires), Sir Robert Hodgson, there. The questions of neutrality, the withdrawal of the foreign volunteers, and the reprisals against the Reds were allegedly discussed in this letter in a manner calculated to cause satisfaction and the feeling of security in England.

Since a confirmation of this report could not be obtained by other means, I spoke to the Foreign Minister of this letter in a plausible connection yesterday as though it were an accepted fact and received from him confirmation of the truth of the report.

However, General Jordana told me that the letter had no particular importance. It had been caused by a British attempt to bring about an armistice. The Minister did not say any more about it, and I felt it was not right to insist.

Since the report is thus accurate, probably the account of the contents was also approximately correct. I do not believe, however, that Franco jeopardized his later freedom of action in any way in the letter.

The existence of such a letter, moreover, was also not improbable on the basis of Chamberlain's statements in the House of Commons concerning the recognition of Franco's Government.[1] The French press also made this point.

v. STOHRER

---

[1] On Feb. 27 Chamberlain announced that *de jure* recognition had been accorded to the Nationalists that day.

No. 750

168/132440

Memorandum by the State Secretary

St. S. No. 195   BERLIN, March 2, 1939.

I informed the Italian Ambassador of the status of our negotiations with Spain regarding a treaty of friendship and promised Attolico to inform him once more before the date for publication, which as yet has not been determined. I added that the German-Spanish treaty of friendship would not be signed until after the signing of the protocol on Spain's accession to the Anti-Comintern Pact.

To my question during this conversation as to whether the Italians for their part were also still carrying on negotiations with the Spaniards, Attolico answered with an unequivocal "no."

WEIZSÄCKER

No. 751

462/225511–13

The State Secretary to the Embassy in Spain

SECRET   BERLIN, March 2, 1939.
No. 778 g   Pol. III 459 g.

Since the Government to which you are accredited has declared its basic willingness to join the pact against the Communist International, a draft protocol for this accession is enclosed.[1]

The documents of November 25, 1936,[2] and November 6, 1937,[3] (*Reichsgesetzblatt* 1937 part II No. 4 and *Reichsgesetzblatt* 1938 part II No. 4), which are mentioned in the draft protocol, are enclosed in duplicate.

The text of the draft protocol for Spain's accession corresponds in its wording to the protocols with which Hungary and Manchukuo acceded to the Anti-Comintern Pact.[4] We, along with Italy and Japan, attach importance to having this text adopted without change for all future declarations of accession.

In paragraph (*c*) of the supplementary protocol to the pact against the Communist International of November 25, 1936 (*Reichsgesetzblatt* 1937 part II, page 30), provision is made for the establishment of a permanent commission for the cooperation of the proper authorities in the fight against Communism. When Hungary and Manchukuo joined the Anti-Comintern Pact, we agreed with the Italians and the Japanese that the two new member states should not necessarily become members of the commission provided for in section (*c*) of the supplementary protocol of November 25, 1936, so that a certain difference is made between the original signers of the pact and the countries joining later.

Please do not bring up this question with the Spanish Government, however. If it should bring it up itself, please say approximately the following:

The commission has not yet been formally constituted; it has no permanent seat and no agenda. By broadening the circle of the member states the difficulties which already face the formation of the

---

[1] Not enclosed with file copy of this document.
[2] The German-Japanese Anti-Comintern Pact, signed in Berlin on Nov. 25, 1936. It provided for measures toward a common defense against the activities of the Communist International and for inviting third powers to join. An English translation of this published part of the pact will be found in *Documents on International Affairs, 1936*, pp. 297–299. Added to the published part, however, was a secret supplementary agreement (for the text, see vol. I, p. 734, footnote 2a).
[3] The accession of Italy to the Anti-Comintern Pact. For this document, see vol. I, document No. 17, p. 26.
[4] Concerning the accession of Manchukuo and Hungary to the Anti-Comintern Pact, see vols. IV and V respectively.

commission will be still further increased. We therefore consider it expedient not to undertake until a suitable later time deliberations on what form the participating governments should choose for facilitating cooperation, as provided in the supplementary protocol. Moreover, practical cooperation in police matters is already under way.

As was done at the accession of Hungary and Manchukuo, please consult with the Italian and Japanese representatives at once in order to obtain, together with them, the agreement of the Spanish Government to the draft protocol concerning the accession.

It is assumed that the text will be printed there. Four copies will be signed in each of the four languages involved, that is, a total of 16 copies. The only annexes which are necessary for the copies designed for us are in each case one German copy of the text, one of the supplementary protocol of November 25, 1936, and one of the protocol of November 6, 1937. There will be annexed to the protocol in the Spanish language the pact and the supplementary protocol of November 25, 1936, in German and Japanese, and the protocol of November 6, 1937, in German, Japanese, and Italian.

Please check on the Spanish text of the protocol concerning Spain's accession as submitted by the Spanish Government and then send it here at once.

The necessary full powers will be sent as soon as possible. We reserve a further directive on the time for the signature.

WEIZSÄCKER

No. 752

F8/0084–83

Memorandum by the Foreign Minister

TELEPHONE CONVERSATION BETWEEN THE FOREIGN MINISTER AND COUNT CIANO ON MARCH 4, 1939

SECRET   BERLIN, March 4, 1939.
RM No. 16

(For the Foreign Minister only.)

Count Ciano called me this morning and informed me that the Japanese Ambassador [*sic*] in Spain had evidently insisted that the Anti-Comintern Pact not only be signed now but also be made public. Difficulties had resulted therefrom and the circles in Spain which wished to prevent Spain's accession to the pact were making renewed efforts.

I arranged with Count Ciano that we would telegraph to Tokyo that the Japanese Ambassador should receive new instructions at once according to which the pact should be signed immediately, but the date of publication should be left for Franco to set after his victory.[1]

Count Ciano also asked about the tripartite negotiations.[2] If the negotiations had come to no concrete results by the end of the month, he suggested bilateral negotiations between Germany and Italy. I told him that I hoped we would reach final results in the course of this month.

R[IBBENTROP]

---

[1] Such a telegram was sent on Mar. 4, and new instructions for the Japanese Minister in Spain were promised. The German Embassy in Spain was informed accordingly (462/225514, 225521).

[2] Negotiations for converting the German-Italian-Japanese Anti-Comintern Pact into a military alliance, which are treated in vol. IV.

No. 753

1573/381173–74

Memorandum by the Head of Political Division IIIa

BERLIN, March 11, 1939.

e.o. Pol. III 599 g.

According to press reports the French Government intends to send a commercial delegation to Burgos in the near future in order to conclude a commercial treaty with the Spanish Government. It should be remembered in this connection that in the secret protocol concluded on July 12, 1937, between us and the Spanish Nationalist Government it was agreed as follows: The two Governments are postponing until a later, more suitable time a comprehensive settlement of the economic relations between their countries but nevertheless declare their intention to place economic cooperation between their countries on a firm basis now and also for the future. "From this standpoint, the Spanish Nationalist Government declares that it is prepared," the protocol goes on to say, "to conclude with Germany its first general trade agreement with any country. Accordingly, if it intends to enter upon international economic negotiations, it will inform the German Government in good time, in order to give the German Government the possibility of previously concluding an economic treaty. If for special reasons the Spanish Nationalist Government should feel impelled to take up comprehensive economic negotiations with a third country before doing so with Germany, it will inform the German Government concerning such negotiations, insofar as they could be of interest to Germany, in order to give it the possibility of expressing its wishes in time. The carrying through of such negotiations shall not be affected thereby."

Thus we are entitled to be the first to conclude a new commercial treaty with the Spanish Government. For its part, the Spanish Government is entitled to negotiate with other governments before doing so with us, but it must inform us.

Since the end of the Civil War, and therewith the restoration of a unified Spanish economic area, is imminent, it seems expedient to provide for initiating commercial negotiations with the Spanish Government immediately after the end of the Civil War, so that other countries cannot anticipate us. It seems advisable to approach the Spanish Government on this point as soon as the Anti-Comintern Pact and the treaty of friendship have been signed. Since this will probably be done on March 23 or shortly thereafter, we might plan to approach the Spanish Nationalist Government for the first time on starting negotiations for the conclusion of a commercial treaty at the end of March or beginning of April.

Herewith submitted to the Under State Secretary through the Deputy Director of the Political Department.

SCHW[ENDEMANN]
Mar. 13

No. 754

322/193582–85

The Ambassador in Spain to the Director of the Economic Policy Department

PERSONAL   SAN SEBASTIÁN, March 11, 1939.
STRICTLY CONFIDENTIAL

DEAR WIEHL: With today's courier you will receive a double report, that is, the report requested on future Spanish economic policy (insofar as one can express an opinion on this subject today) and a report on the expediency of starting negotiations with Spain soon with regard to a settlement of the war debt including the important problem of indemnification. The reports bear numbers 1055/39 [1] and 1054/39 [2] and are both dated March 11. I should like to discuss two delicate points here quite confidentially and personally:

1. On page 5 of the latter report I termed it desirable for us to make an immediate decision on the question of a possible reduction of the debt, so as to "work out proposals which could be submitted at

---

[1] Not printed (322/193586–600).
[2] Not printed (322/193601–09). In these two long and detailed reports Stohrer discusses the possibility of German economic assistance to Spain, with particular reference to the increasing competition of England, France, and the United States. He foresaw, among other things, that Hisma-Rowak would no longer be able to maintain its monopoly in handling German-Spanish trade and that a new payments agreement would have to be negotiated. He urged that Germany take the initiative in opening these negotiations.

the proper moment to the persons who can make the decisions." I did not want to express myself differently in the official report but was alluding to a statement by Field Marshal Göring that Herr Bernhardt told me of at the time, according to which the former had evidently expressed resentment at the fact that the bureaus concerned seemed to be discussing the question of a reduction of the Spanish debt without asking him in advance. The Field Marshal is supposed to have added, "I shall decide this question myself at the proper time."

2. As regards the report on future Spanish economic policy and the future form of our commercial relations with Spain, in my opinion this question, as well as the questions as to whether we should take the initiative ourselves in starting economic negotiations with Spain and what aims we should follow in such negotiations, is inextricably connected with the question whether the Hisma organization and the Hisma-Rowak clearing system should be maintained, and if so in what form. Herr Bernhardt should first declare himself on this question and clearly define what his plans are with regard to the future of Hisma; then a final decision with regard to the future of Hisma and the Hisma clearing system should be made by Herr Bernhardt's superiors in the Economics Ministry and the Four Year Plan. In this matter it would probably be well if Herr Bernhardt were not the only one to inform the two above-mentioned agencies with regard to conditions here. Only after such a decision will it be possible to draft a program for more extensive German-Spanish economic negotiations and to approach the Spaniards with this program. Otherwise we might first have to argue among ourselves during the negotiations about the question of the continuation of Hisma. Perhaps for this reason, too, it would be well to send several German businessmen here, as I recommend in my report on "Future Spanish Economic Policy."

3. With regard to both reports, which overlap in many respects, I should like to remark briefly that they were discussed with Herr Bernhardt and that in the reports I have taken up at some length the point of view which he advocates. Nevertheless I have given Herr Bernhardt copies of the economic report and the part of the second report which refers to debt settlement, suggesting that he might himself perhaps comment on the reports. However, I told him distinctly that I expected his comment to be dispassionate and objective and not personal, as was unfortunately often the case with him! Herr Bernhardt promised me this.

Please treat this letter as a *purely personal* one for you and Herr Sabath.

With best greetings and Heil Hitler!

As ever,

STOHRER

No. 755

2655/527426–27

The Ambassador in Spain to the Foreign Ministry

No. 782 g SAN SEBASTIÁN, March 13, 1939.
Pol. III 1243.

With reference to telegraphic report No. 223 of March 10.[1]

Subject: Statements by Generalissimo Franco to the Italian General Gambara.

A few days ago, after his return from Rome, General Gambara, the commander of the Italian troops here, was received by Franco and gave him the Duce's message reported in the above-mentioned telegram. Shortly thereafter General Gambara informed Military Attaché Colonel von Funck in general outline of his conversation with the Generalissimo and on March 11 sent a detailed report on it to his Ambassador, who read it to me today.

In addition to a discussion of the military preparations for the new offensive and of the dispute in what is left of the Red zone between the so-called Defense Council formed in Madrid and the Communists, which questions were naturally in the foreground, the following themes were treated in particular:

1. *Spain's attitude in a possible European conflict.*

Franco informed the Italian General on this point that after the end of the Civil War Spain would absolutely have to have a period of quiet in order to recover from the effects of the war and to build up a strong defense force. If an armed conflict should develop in Europe in the foreseeable future, Spain would have to remain neutral.

2. *Support of Spain in building up a strong military establishment.*

According to General Gambara, the Generalissimo stated on this point that after the war he would unquestionably have need of the support of the two friendly powers, Germany and Italy, in building up a strong defense force. In order to eliminate competition between these two countries he considered it expedient for the German and Italian Governments to come to an agreement between themselves concerning the manner and the distribution of this assistance.

3. *The question of a restoration of the monarchy.*

The Generalissimo stated that England, in particular, but also France, were trying to promote a restoration. He was observing these intrigues carefully. They had only the result of discrediting

---

[1] Not found.

the monarchical system. There was no question of a restoration of the monarchy for the next few years. (Gambara told Colonel von Funck that Franco had spoken of "about five years".)

v. STOHRER

No. 756

336/196959

The Ambassador in Spain to the Foreign Ministry

Telegram

No. 241 of March 15   SAN SEBASTIÁN, March 15, 1939—5 : 10 p.m.
                                            Received March 15—5 : 30 p.m.

With reference to report No. 1055 of March 11.[1]

The Minister of Commerce, in the course of a detailed conference on future German-Spanish economic relations, suggested immediate discussion with us for the purpose of arranging the bases for cooperation in the fields of debt settlement, general exchange of goods, and German participation in the Spanish reconstruction.

The Minister's wish: Through discussion with the friendly powers, Germany and Italy, to determine in principle what these countries can do for Spain or what they desire of Spain, so that agreements can then be made with other countries with regard to remaining Spanish requirements and utilization of surplus exports.

In particular the Minister is giving intensive consideration to the plans developed in Areilza's memorandum,[2] which is known there, and he asks agreement in principle in advance.

The Minister and other responsible persons are not able to leave Spain at the moment. Therefore the Minister suggested that one or two representatives of the German Government be sent at once and be empowered to negotiate on the principles of future cooperation. The Minister warns us, however, not to send a large commission which might attract notice. Particular questions could be settled by commissions to be sent by Germany later. I most heartily recommend that this wish be fulfilled.

A detailed report follows at the next safe opportunity.

STOHRER

---

[1] Not printed (322/193586–600).
[2] See document 757, *infra*.

No. 757

322/193578–81

The Ambassador in Spain to the Foreign Ministry

No. 1104   SAN SEBASTIÁN, March 15, 1939.
                                                           W II 1729.

With reference to my report No. 1055 of March 11 [1] and telegram
No. 241 of March 15.

Subject: The Spanish Minister of Commerce on the problem of future
German-Spanish commercial relations.

Yesterday I was finally able to have a detailed conversation in Bilbao with the Spanish Minister of Economics, who has constantly been
out of town recently, on the problem which interests us of future German-Spanish commercial relations. Señor Suances began his statements with a description of the enormous losses which the Spanish
economy had suffered as a result of the Civil War and the resulting
colossal requirements after the war. He then continued in detail:

I. *Basic questions:*

In order to cover these tremendously increased requirements we
must approach foreign countries on a very wide range. As little as
I like the idea, nevertheless I believe that we will need credits of all
kinds from foreign countries, including credit in foreign exchange.
(The Minister adhered to this opinion in spite of my objections; it
should be remembered, however, that the Minister of Finance has the
main jurisdiction in this question.) Certain countries, in particular
England, France, and the United States of America, will certainly offer us very extensive deliveries on credit. Even now their businessmen
are trying to urge us along this course. I consider it incorrect, however, not only from a feeling of natural gratitude but also for considerations of political expediency, to respond to these offers before we
have ascertained what Germany and Italy, the powers friendly to
us, can deliver and how they are able and willing to aid us. I wish
to eliminate from the very beginning any competition between the
friendly powers and the other countries interested in the Spanish
economy. In addition, however, I should also like to avoid having
Germany and Italy appear as competitors here in Spain in one field
or another. Therefore it should still be investigated to what extent
negotiations should be instituted between Spain and Germany, or
Spain and Italy, or all three countries on the question of German
and Italian participation in Spanish commerce and in Spanish
reconstruction.

---

[1] Not printed (322/193586–600).

In the first place I wish to emphasize that at the present time I consider it premature and therefore incorrect to go into any sort of particulars, detailed industrialization plans, etc. The basic questions must be clarified first. There are three distinct fields:

1. Debt settlement,
2. General exchange of goods,
3. Participation in the reconstruction of Spain.

In order to clarify these fundamental questions, in my opinion it is necessary to bring about contact at once between Germany and ourselves on the one hand and between Spain and Italy on the other. As is known, to a certain extent we are already in the stage of negotiation with Italy, although we have met with great difficulties due to a combining of the three above-named fields (cf. report No. 1048/39 of today[2]). It will be much easier to regulate future German-Spanish economic relations, since it is well known that our countries supplement each other economically in such a fortunate way.

In order to clarify the basic questions mentioned above, in my opinion consultations should be held between Spain and Germany at once. (To an objection from me:) Unfortunately at the present time it is impossible either for me or for any other responsible Spanish person to go to Germany for this purpose. I should therefore be very happy if Germany would oblige us by sending one or two responsible representatives of the German Government here for consultation on these questions. So as not to attract attention it might be well to refrain from sending a large commission. When we are clear about the basic questions, in particular about the question of Germany's participation in the reconstruction of Spain, then commissions of experts for the various fields can go to Germany or be sent here from Germany.

(In reply to a question from me:) In a number of fields we must strive for the construction of our own industries in Spain, in particular for the production of:

1. Nitrogen,
2. Synthetic methane,
3. Certain types of automobiles,
4. Simple machinery,
5. Certain of the more simple chemical and pharmaceutical products,
6. Petroleum.

A comparison with the memorandum by Areilza, Chief of the Industrial Department of the Spanish Ministry of Commerce, which is

---

[2] Not found.

known in Berlin—report No. 5429 of December 14, 1938 [3]—shows that the Minister evidently desires to produce all of the items mentioned by Areilza except two: heavy-oil motors and electrical equipment; on the other hand, unlike Señor Areilza, he also mentioned the construction of certain types of automobiles.

During the further course of the conversation the Minister touched on the following questions:

II. *Currency:*

As far as the Spanish currency is concerned, I advocate very strongly the view that a devaluation of the peseta must be avoided. I hope it will be possible to keep the peseta at its present level. Experiences of other countries show that it is too difficult to undertake a moderate devaluation within certain limits without making the whole currency structure slide.

III. *Hisma:*

As far as Hisma is concerned, it seems necessary to me to replace it with another type of organization (*otro tipo de organización*). During the war Hisma did us excellent service; in normal times, however, instead of a private enterprise, which Hisma is, after all, an organization must step in which, while utilizing the valuable experiences gained by Hisma, serves the purpose of once more strengthening the private connections between exporters and importers. Details must naturally be studied when the time for the change-over has arrived.

It was very clear that prestige questions play a not unimportant role in this demand.

Following the conference I gave a luncheon for the Minister and his chief colleagues in the Ministry of Commerce, at which Herr Bernhardt and representatives of Hisma were also present. After the luncheon the Minister expressed himself in the same manner to Herr Bernhardt.

In a subsequent conversation continued by the three of us, it was evident that our views largely coincide. Under these circumstances I should like expressly to confirm once again my advocacy, which I have already telegraphed, of the desire voiced by Señor Suances. Herr Bernhardt, who leaves for Germany today and with whom this report was discussed, said that he intends to make the same recommendation.

v. STOHRER

---

[3] Not printed (5176/E307010–14).

No. 758

F19/148–49

Memorandum by the Head of Political Division IIIa

TOP SECRET   BERLIN, March 17, 1939.
                                         e.o. Pol. III . . . g Rs.

With regard to Spain's accession to the Anti-Comintern Pact, the Japanese Government at first took the position that Spain's accession should be announced at the same time as the signing of the protocol. However, when the Spanish Government refused to do this, for excellent reasons, and the German and Italian Governments supported the Spanish desire to delay publication until a later time (the end of the Civil War or further important military successes by Franco), the Japanese Government stated that it agreed to later publication.

When Hungary and Manchukuo joined the pact, the original signers agreed that the protocol drawn up for the accession of these two states should also be used without change when other countries joined. The Japanese Ambassador here then suggested on March 9 that the following be inserted in article 1 of this protocol:

"and to which Manchukuo and Hungary acceded on February 25, 1939."

Earlier the Japanese Embassy had taken the view that Manchukuo and Hungary should participate in inviting Spain to join the pact, whereas we, in agreement with the Italians, insisted that only the original signatories of the Anti-Comintern Pact should issue the invitation and it was entirely up to them to decide when they wished to include the later signatories. The Minister of Manchukuo in Rome nevertheless invited the Spanish Ambassador in Rome to join. The Japanese also brought up the question as to what legal relation the later signatories of the Anti-Comintern Pact would have with the new member, Spain. We emphasized in this connection that this question was of no importance.

The Spanish Government rejected the Japanese insertion in article 1 of the protocol, as Ambassador von Stohrer reports, evidently because it did not wish to be put on the same footing with powers like Manchukuo and Hungary. Ambassador von Stohrer pointed out the justification of the Spanish view, particularly considering the sacrifices which Spain had made in the fight against Communism.

The Japanese Embassy here was asked yesterday to urge its Government to give up the desired insertion in article 1 of the protocol. Ambassador Ott in Tokyo was instructed yesterday in the same sense. Ambassador von Stohrer was also instructed yesterday to inform the

Japanese Minister accordingly. The Japanese Embassy states today that it has received no instructions from Tokyo as yet to give up the insertion.

Herewith submitted to the Foreign Minister through the Deputy Director of the Political Department, the Under State Secretary, and the State Secretary.

SCHWENDEMANN

Addendum: The signing of the protocol on Spain's accession to the Anti-Comintern Pact has so far been set for March 23. The texts have been prepared in Burgos except for the Japanese text; the Japanese Embassy prepared the printing of this text in such a manner that, after notification that the Japanese Government will give up the insertion to article 1, the Japanese texts can still be brought to Burgos in time by a special plane courier. Mr. Takeuchi of the Japanese Embassy has promised this.

No. 759

836/196964

The Director of the Economic Policy Department to the Embassy in Spain

Telegram

[No. 172 of March 18]   BERLIN, March 18, 1939.
W II 1658.

With reference to your No. 241 of March 15.

The Economics Ministry is afraid that, even if negotiations are limited to principles, there might be a change for the worse in commercial relations, which have been satisfactory in the past, and therefore recommends dilatory treatment of the proposal to send representatives; this could be explained by recent international events and the resulting necessity of checking our own economic possibilities. The Ministry also believes that there need be no hurry in sending the representatives for the reason that considerable time will probably still elapse before the Civil War is ended.

Please send your opinion by wire and particularly on

1) Whether the suggestion by the Minister of Commerce should be regarded as a personal opinion or as an official invitation by the Spanish Government in the sense of the protocol of July 12, 1937,

2) Whether if we delay there is danger that Spain might enter into negotiations with other countries before us.

WIEHL

No. 760

462/225555

The Under State Secretary to the Embassy in Spain

Telegram

No. 174 of March 18   BERLIN, March 18, 1939—10 : 00 p.m.
                                       Received March 18—10 : 15 p.m.

In answer to the representations of the German Ambassador in Tokyo with regard to eliminating in the protocol on the Anti-Comintern Pact the insertion regarding the accession of Manchukuo and Hungary, the Deputy Foreign Minister declared that the protocol would be submitted to the Privy Council without the insertion and that signature is expected on March 23.

Please report by wire whether the Japanese Ambassador [*sic*] in San Sebastián has instructions to that effect and whether signature on March 23 is now assured.

WOERMANN

No. 761

462/225556–57

The Ambassador in Spain to the Foreign Ministry

Telegram

No. 263 of March 19   SAN SEBASTIÁN, March 19, 1930—7 : 30 p.m.

With reference to your telegram No. 174 of March 18.

The Japanese Minister, who tried without success yesterday to obtain the approval of the Foreign Minister to the addition to article 1 of the protocol on the Anti-Comintern Pact, received instructions from his Government today to abandon the addition; he will inform Burgos today. Thus the matter is settled in principle.

The Japanese Minister will ask his Government today for permission to formulate the Japanese text of the protocol here.

Then the only things lacking before signing the pact will be Italian and Japanese (telegraphic) full powers, which have still not arrived, and notification of the consent of the Japanese Privy Council, which meets on March 22.

To judge from past experience, it is improbable that this will have arrived here by March 23, in spite of the difference in time. Furthermore, four copies of each of the four texts have to be made, and they must be compared, which the Spaniards do very painstakingly. By means of personal representations, however, the three missions will try to accelerate the formalities as much as possible, so that the signing can be done immediately after receipt of the approval of the Japanese Privy Council.

Please send instructions with regard to the sequence of the signatures on the four different texts.

STOHRER

No. 762

336/196965

The Ambassador in Spain to the Foreign Ministry

Telegram

No. 269 of March 20

SAN SEBASTIÁN, March 20, 1939.
Received March 21—12:30 a.m.

With reference to your telegram No. 172 (W II 1658) of March 18.[1]

The suggestion of the Minister of Commerce was his personal opinion, although certainly in agreement with the Cabinet.

Dilatory treatment of the sending of a representative is possible without further discussion.

It is not immediately clear why a systematic exchange of views concerning the postwar treatment of economic problems, particularly Spanish reconstruction, should bring about a deterioration in the present trade situation, since we can still postpone any participation in negotiations or agreements inconvenient to us.

If we refuse to resume contact, this involves the danger that Spain, urged by other countries, in particular France and England, will begin comprehensive negotiations—which could be inconvenient for us under certain circumstances. After all, paragraph 3 of the protocol of July 12, 1937, provides expressly that economic negotiations with third countries are not to be affected by the precedence accorded to Germany.

I should like to think that my report No. 1104 of March 15, which arrived in Berlin yesterday, and a report[2] by Bernhardt, who was entirely in agreement with the suggestion of the Minister of Commerce, have already to a large extent dispelled the fears of the Economics Ministry.

STOHRER

---

[1] Apparently a reference to document No. 759, p. 871, as sent.
[2] The German text has *Vertrag,* apparently a typographical error for *Vortrag.*

No. 763

1573/381195–98

The Ambassador in Spain to the Foreign Ministry

SECRET   SAN SEBASTIÁN, March 20, 1939.
                                                              Pol. III 730 g.

Subject: Future German-Spanish relations in military matters.

In case the military authorities there do not at once send on the communication to the Foreign Ministry, I enclose a copy of a memorandum by Colonel von Funck, Military Attaché of the Embassy, on the question of future cooperation with Spain in developing and training the Spanish peacetime army and building up a Spanish armament industry.

It appears from this memorandum that the Italians also are already very much concerned with these questions but that evidently the Spaniards are still not very clear about the steps to be taken after the war in the above-mentioned questions.

                                                              STOHRER

[Enclosure]

NOTES ON THE CONFERENCE WITH ITALIAN GENERAL GAMBARA IN LOGROÑO ON MARCH 15

SECRET   March 16, 1939.

The conversation took place at the express wish of General Gambara, who had also pressed for an early date. It was a continuation and expansion of the conversation on March 10.[1]

G[ambara] stated that after the war the Spaniards would need support:

(*a*) In developing and training the peacetime army.
(*b*) In building up their armament industry.

In both questions, Italy and Germany would have to inject themselves promptly, before other powers achieved results here. He pointed with some concern to the strong military stamp of the new French Embassy, which, in its composition, already looked almost like a military mission.

G[ambara] was obviously trying to find out what *our* intentions were for the future and in what fields we were particularly interested. For his part, he gave me to understand that Franco had spoken with him about an exchange of officers. He believed, however, that he could discern more far-reaching wishes. Fr[anco] would find himself forced for reasons of both foreign and domestic policy to build up a strong army rapidly right after the end of the war, in order to

_____
[1] See document No. 755, p. 865.

secure his position and to provide satisfactorily for numerous persons (officers and soldiers) who were used to war and estranged from their civilian occupations. He would not be able to carry through this program in modern style as regards either personnel or matériel. Fr[anco] had too much common sense not to recognize the inadequacies in his own camp, in spite of all his success. For instance, the old Spanish instructors, unacquainted with modern requirements, would no longer be able to make a useful contribution in the military and general staff schools; the most modern (that is, foreign) instructors would have to be obtained. Similarly, the mosaic-like picture presented by the present armament situation and the small capacity of the Spanish armament industry would probably be a forcible inducement for making quick use of foreign assistance.

I tried to direct the conversation in such a manner that G[ambara] did most of the talking, and I for my part contributed only the following points:

1. It appeared to me necessary for the Spaniards themselves to express their wishes in a binding form. (I did not mention the talk with the Generalissimo on February 29! [sic]) I had the impression that at the moment—because of the pressure of present events—the responsible Spanish authorities had not yet given thorough consideration to the problems of the future. It was all the more desirable, to be sure, to stimulate their initiative in this direction.

2. The decision on any assistance in development and training was, after all, mainly dependent on political considerations. I did not know at the moment whether they had already made any decisions on this question at home (in Berlin *and* Rome) and what they might be. I would thus all the more quickly inform the German authorities of the conversation which had taken place.

Gambara agreed with this attitude and asked, as always in a cordial and comradely way, that contact be maintained.

He stressed once more that he considered the matter urgent, for we had to strike the iron now, before foreign competition could become active.

At the subsequent dinner the German successes in Czechoslovakia were toasted in a rather ceremonious and very friendly way.

It is very probable that the Italians are continuing to hope for military influence in Spain and a large share in supplying Spanish armaments after the war. General G[ambara] obviously has instructions (having just returned from Rome) to take preparatory steps to clarify the situation.

Postscript on March 17.

During a visit I just paid to the War Minister, General Dávila, I received the definite impression that leading Spanish authorities actually are extraordinarily uncertain concerning plans for the future. General Dávila answered my direct question with: "I have not yet received any directives from the Generalissimo."

With regard to armament in the future he said: "We shall certainly depend to a great extent on the calibers used by our allies in the present war."

BARON V. FUNCK

No. 764

322/193572–73

The Ambassador in Spain to the Director of the Economic Policy Department

SECRET SAN SEBASTIÁN, March 22, 1939.

DEAR WIEHL: I do not know to what extent you are aware that the German aircraft industry, through the Condor Legion or the Air Attaché, has approached Spanish authorities about setting up factories here after the war. I am not informed about the details, since the matter is being handled exclusively by the military authorities here.

The commander of the Condor Legion told me yesterday that in his opinion it was quite possible that the Army would take similar steps informally with regard to war matériel industries in order to make relations with Spain in this field as close as possible. General von Richthofen said quite correctly that these matters really should be centralized somehow or somewhere, since otherwise less important projects might be agreed upon or organized first, leaving no money for more important things later. Moreover, it could happen that when the Spaniards noticed that there was no unified procedure they might try to play the one against the other.

I inform you of this at once since, after all, all of us surely feel that it is well first to reach agreement with the Spaniards on the bases of any future participation by us in the reconstruction. In any case it was resolved unanimously during the departmental conference at your office on January 9 that we should avoid undertaking separate projects. Although I freely admit that the projects in question are of particular importance, it is nevertheless necessary that they be included in the general economic program for Spain.

I should like to add that according to the General the suggestions with regard to preparatory discussions on setting up an aircraft industry in Spain originated with the Spaniards.

With cordial greetings and Heil Hitler!

Yours,

STOHRER

No. 765

2666/527994

Memorandum by the Director of the Economic Policy Department

BERLIN, March 23, 1939.

The initiation of commercial negotiations with Spain for the purpose of regulating economic relations between the two countries after the end of the Civil War is urgent in view of today's telegraphic report of negotiations for the unconditional surrender of the Red Army. In accordance with the proposal of the Spanish Minister of Commerce, one or two German representatives are first to be sent to Spain in order to negotiate regarding the outlines of an arrangement. The details are to be settled later by negotiations between delegations.

To conduct the first general discussions, which probably will not last very long, the Foreign Ministry is considering Minister Eisenlohr, who because of his position and because of his familiarity with economic questions is particularly well qualified. His present duties as representative of the Foreign Ministry with the army group in Brünn will presumably be concluded in a few days when the Protector takes over the duties of his office, whereupon Herr Eisenlohr would be free for the new task.

To be submitted to the Foreign Minister through the State Secretary, with the request for permission to propose to the other agencies in the Economic Policy Committee that Minister Eisenlohr conduct the negotiations.

WIEHL

No. 766

2937/569659–60

The Ambassador in Spain to the Foreign Ministry

No. 2043   SAN SEBASTIÁN, March 23, 1939.
                                            Pol. III 1441.

Subject: Spanish-French relations and Marshal Pétain.

Spanish Nationalist relations with France, in spite of the *de jure* recognition meanwhile accorded Franco's Government and the sending of Marshal Pétain as Ambassador, must still be considered very tense. This tension is clearly expressed in the commentaries published in the Spanish Nationalist press regarding certain details of the French attitude. I enclose several samples in the attached newspaper clippings. With astonishment and bitterness it is stated therein that the French Government—contrary to its promises prior to the *de jure* recognition—is not returning the Spanish cattle which were driven over the boundary by the Reds but is selling them for its own account; that the French military authorities are appropriating the trucks of the Red Army units which crossed the border; that the Red Spanish refugees in the concentration camps in France are being victimized in every possible manner, worked on by Communist agitators, and recruited for the French Foreign Legion. There is particularly strong resentment—as reported in my telegram No. 262 of March 19, 1939 [1]—that the French Government has thus far refused to hand over to the Spanish Government the Red Spanish warships which took refuge in the harbor of Bizerta and were interned there. There is even a report from Orán that the French authorities had returned Russian tank trucks destined for Red Spain to Russia instead of forwarding them to Nationalist Spain, as agreed.

The *Diario Vasco* of March 22, 1939, expresses its indignation in a long article over the fact that a French Minister (the name is not given) called the Red Spanish refugees "honorable Spaniards" who would never be able to return to their homeland. Surely the French must meanwhile themselves have learned the lesson—well deserved, for that matter—that a large part of these refugees were common criminals. The article closes with the remark that the French Government's conduct thus far is not calculated to permit Spain to forget very soon the damages which the French Popular Front has inflicted upon it during the 3 years of war.

The Nationalist radio attacks France even more violently.

The Foreign Minister himself complained to me bitterly a few days ago about the attitude of the French, who were keeping scarcely any of their promises. General Jordana gave me to understand that the reception of Marshal Pétain by the Generalissimo had in fact been delayed in order to exert pressure on France toward handing over the Red fleet and that he hoped to be able to hold out in this matter.

The position of the new French Ambassador, who arrived here a week ago, has become rather awkward because of these polemics and the attitude of the Spanish Government. It appears that the Marshal expected to be received by Franco immediately and that for this reason he considered superfluous the personal consultation with the Foreign Minister which is otherwise customary. The fact is that he did not—as announced—immediately go to Burgos but on the contrary is com-

---

[1] Not printed (632/252679).

pletely isolated here, since the local authorities in Burgos have received instructions to avoid having any dealings with him as yet. The Marshal has so far been able to see only a few personal Spanish acquaintances, to whom he is said to have expressed himself about this state of affairs in no uncertain terms.

It is characteristic that the French newspapers blame the delay in the Ambassador's reception by Franco on the weather, stating that communications between here and Burgos had been interrupted, which is not by any means the case.

v. STOHRER

SAN SEBASTIÁN, March 25, 1939.

As I have meanwhile reported by wire, Marshal Pétain was yesterday formally received at last by the Generalissimo in Burgos for the purpose of presenting his credentials. I am told by the Embassy's representative in Burgos that all the streets between the hotel and the Capitanía General, in which the reception took place, were completely blocked off, so that there could be no demonstrations of disapproval. Consequently the population displayed no interest whatsoever in the entire proceedings. According to reports from another source, balconies and windows in the houses along the route followed also remained closed and unoccupied, quite contrary to the usual Spanish custom.

I enclose a clipping from *La Petite Gironde* of March 25, 1939,[2] which gives the remarks exchanged between the new French Ambassador and the Spanish Chief of State. In the Generalissimo's reply that passage is noteworthy in which, plainly referring to the hostile attitude previously displayed by France toward Nationalist Spain, he states that friendship between nations is no capricious fact which can be directed but is a true picture of the past and of the mutual regard which develops in the course of years.

From circles in the Foreign Ministry I hear that the pressure exerted on France through the delay in the reception of Pétain was successful and that the handing over of the Red fleet interned in Bizerta will take place during the next few days, now that England has also declared herself prepared to return the well-known Red Spanish destroyer *José Luis Díaz*, which on various occasions sailed into Gibraltar. I have just been told by the Naval Attaché that the return of this destroyer may be expected tomorrow morning.

---

[2] Not reprinted.

No. 767

2130/465082–83

The Ambassador in Spain to the Foreign Ministry

No. 804 g   SAN SEBASTIÁN, March 27, 1939.
                                                      Pol. III 768 g.

With reference to my telegram No. 295 of March 25.[1]

Subject: Accession of Spain to the Anti-Comintern Pact.

The accession of Spain to the Anti-Comintern Pact was carried out yesterday afternoon. After the completion of the protocol, done in four languages, and the annexes, the signing by the Spanish Foreign Minister, General Jordana, the Italian Ambassador, Count Viola, the Japanese Minister, Makoto Yano, and myself took place this afternoon in the Foreign Ministry in Burgos. The signing was accomplished without the usual outward pomp customary in such cases, since at the request of the Spanish Government the fact of the accession of Spain to the Anti-Comintern Pact is to be kept secret for the time being.

The signing of the anti-Comintern protocol took place later than was to be expected from the negotiations with the Spanish Government, which went quite smoothly at the end. The principal reason was that the Japanese Government at first urged that Spain's accession be made public immediately and then proposed an amendment (reference in article 1 of the protocol to Manchukuo and Hungary) which the Spanish Government did not wish to accept and finally did not accept. Fortunately this latter Japanese request did not induce the Spaniards on their part to demand that in view of their particularly bloody struggle against Bolshevism they be formally placed on the same footing as the three Great Powers, Germany, Japan, and Italy, of which there was undoubtedly some danger in view of certain remarks made in the Spanish Foreign Ministry. Furthermore, the often belated and incomplete instructions received by the Japanese Legation and also the Italian Embassy here were an obstructing influence on the course of the negotiations. But as a result of the information and instructions which I received so very expeditiously from the Foreign Ministry and for which I am grateful, it was possible for the Embassy, so to speak, to carry on negotiations for the other two missions in Burgos and thus to press the matter forward.

The original texts will be transmitted at the next safe opportunity.

STOHRER

---

[1] Not printed (462/225567).

No. 768

2871/564736-37

Protocol Signed at Burgos on March 27, 1939

THE GOVERNMENT OF THE GERMAN REICH,
THE ITALIAN GOVERNMENT,
THE IMPERIAL JAPANESE GOVERNMENT
on the one hand
and
THE SPANISH GOVERNMENT
on the other

declare the following through their undersigned plenipotentiaries:

Article I

Spain adheres to the pact against the Communist International which is formed by the agreement and the supplementary protocol of November 25, 1936, and the protocol of November 6, 1937.

Article II

The form of the facilitation of cooperation between the proper authorities of the participating states envisaged in the supplementary protocol shall be the subject of a future agreement between these authorities.

Article III

The texts of the agreement and the supplementary protocol of November 25, 1936, as well as the protocol of November 6, 1937, are attached to this protocol as annexes.

The present protocol is drawn up in the German, Italian, Japanese, and Spanish languages, of which each text is equally authentic. It shall enter into force on the day it is signed.

In witness whereof the undersigned, being fully and properly empowered by their respective Governments, have provided this protocol with their signatures and seals.

Done in quadruplicate at Burgos, on March 27, 1939, in the XVIIth year of the Fascist Era, which is March 27 of the XIVth year of the Showa period, which is March 27 of the IIId Year of Triumph of the new Spanish state.

EBERHARD VON STOHRER
VIOLA DI CAMPALTO   GÓMEZ JORDANA
M. YANO

No. 769

136/73736

The Ambassador in Spain to the Foreign Ministry

Telegram

No. 306 of March 28   SAN SEBASTIÁN, March 28, 1939—5 : 00 p.m.
Received March 28—3 : 50 p.m. [*sic*]

With reference to your telegram No. 194 of March 27.[1]

The signing of the treaty of friendship has been set for Friday,
March 31.   The Foreign Minister communicated the contents to the
Italian Ambassador yesterday.

STOHRER

---

[1] Not found.

No. 770

462/225584

The State Secretary to the Embassy in Spain

Telegram [1]

VERY URGENT   BERLIN, March 29, 1939—9 : 15 p.m.
No. 199 of March 29   Received March 29—9 : 20 p.m.

For the Ambassador.

Now that the fall of Madrid has produced that decisive victory in
the remaining theater of war upon which publication of the accession
of Spain to the Anti-Comintern Pact was made dependent, we are
very anxious to have it made public at the end of this week, around
March 31 or April 1.   The announcement should be made simultaneously and with great ceremony in Spain itself, in Berlin, in Rome,
and in Tokyo, as well as in Budapest and Hsingking.   You are therefore requested in agreement with your Italian and Japanese colleagues
immediately to obtain the consent of the Spanish Government and
to wire us the date.

Rome and Tokyo have been informed.

WEIZSÄCKER

---

[1] This instruction was received in Spain both as a telegram (frame 225584)
and a radiogram (frame 225585).   The parts underscored were contained in the
radiogram but not in the telegram.   A marginal note in handwriting on the
radiogram reads: "Herr Heberlein.   I request that you immediately make representations at the Foreign Ministry accordingly.   I attach great importance
to the signing of the treaty of friendship taking place Friday—if possible at
1 p.m.   Stohrer."

No. 771

632/252687

The State Secretary to the Embassy in Italy

Telegram

No. 149   BERLIN, March 30, 1939.
                                           Pol. III 340 g Rs.

It is the intention of the military authorities, subject to the decision of the Führer, to withdraw the Condor Legion as soon as possible now that the Spanish Civil War is ended. Since there has been considerable discussion of undertaking a joint withdrawal of volunteers by mutual agreement, you are requested to get in touch with the Italian Government immediately and inquire regarding Italian intentions. Report by wire.

                                           WEIZSÄCKER

No. 772

462/225593

The Ambassador in Spain to the Foreign Ministry

Telegram

No. 322 of March 31   SAN SEBASTIÁN, March 31, 1939—10 : 50 p.m.

With reference to my telegram No. 317 of March 31.[1]

The Foreign Minister expressed the objections already made known against immediate publication of the accession to the A[nti-Comintern] Pact and in answer to my own arguments declared that he would try to bring about a decision by the Generalissimo as soon as possible. Franco has meanwhile been ill with the grippe for several days.

I have asked Vice Admiral Canaris, who will see the Foreign Minister this evening and hopes to gain access to Franco tomorrow, to support my *démarche*.

                                           STOHRER

---

[1] Not printed (168/132419).

No. 773

2871/564100–105

*German-Spanish Treaty of Friendship Signed at Burgos
on March 31, 1939*

The German Chancellor

and

The Chief of the Spanish Government,

In view of the community of interests of their Governments, the affinity of their political views, and the bonds of lively sympathy existing between their peoples,

filled with deep satisfaction over the fact that their friendly association has thus far proved so successful,

and convinced that the development and consolidation of their mutual relations will serve the welfare of both peoples and, in addition, will constitute an important factor in the preservation of high spiritual values and the maintenance of the peace,

are agreed in their desire to affirm their common purposes through the conclusion of a treaty and have for this purpose appointed as their plenipotentiaries:

THE GERMAN CHANCELLOR:

Eberhard von Stohrer, Dr. rer. pol., Dr. jur., Ambassador Extraordinary and Plenipotentiary.

THE CHIEF OF THE SPANISH GOVERNMENT:

Lieutenant General Don Francisco Gómez Jordana y Sousa, Count of Jordana, Vice President of the Government and Minister of Foreign Affairs

who, having communicated to each other their full powers, found to be in good and due form, have agreed upon the following provisions:

Article 1

The High Contracting Parties will constantly maintain contact with each other in order to inform each other concerning questions of international policy affecting their common interests.

Should their common interests be jeopardized by international events of any kind, they will enter into consultation without delay regarding the measures to be taken to safeguard these interests.

Article 2

The High Contracting Parties are aware of the dangers facing their countries through the aspirations of the Communist International and will consult constantly as to measures that seem appropriate for combating them.

Article 3

In the event that the security or other vital interests of one of the High Contracting Parties should be externally threatened, the other High Contracting Party will grant the threatened party its diplomatic support in order to contribute to the best of its ability toward eliminating this threat.

Article 4

In view of the close friendship in which Germany as well as Spain is bound with Italy, both the High Contracting Parties will be mindful in the execution of the agreements made in articles 1 to 3 above of assuring also the collaboration of the Royal Italian Government.

Article 5

Neither of the High Contracting Parties will enter into treaties or other agreements of any kind with third powers which are aimed directly or indirectly against the other High Contracting Party.

The High Contracting Parties agree to inform each other regarding treaties and agreements affecting their common interests which they have previously concluded or will in the future conclude with third countries.

Article 6

In case one of the High Contracting Parties should become involved in warlike complications with a third power, the other High Contracting Party will avoid anything in the political, military, and economic fields that might be disadvantageous to its treaty partner or of advantage to its opponent.

Article 7

The High Contracting Parties will in special agreements arrange for measures which are calculated to promote the fostering of comradely relations and the exchange of practical military experience between their armed forces.

Article 8

Both High Contracting Parties shall make it their special concern to extend and promote their cultural relations. The implementation of this principle is reserved for special agreements.

Article 9

The High Contracting Parties are agreed in their desire to intensify economic relations between their countries as much as possible and affirm their intention of having Germany and Spain supplement each other and cooperate in economic matters in every way.

The implementation of these principles shall be reserved for special agreements.

Article 10

This treaty shall be ratified and the instruments of ratification shall be exchanged at Berlin as soon as possible.

The treaty shall remain in full force for a period of 5 years from the date of exchange of the instruments of ratification.

If 6 months before the expiration of the aforesaid period no notice of termination has been given, the treaty shall remain in force for 5 more years and in a like manner continue in the following periods of time.

In witness whereof the plenipotentiaries have signed this treaty.

Done in duplicate in the German and Spanish languages at Burgos on March thirty-first, nineteen hundred and thirty-nine.

EBERHARD VON STOHRER
GÓMEZ JORDANA

CHAPTER VIII

GERMAN WITHDRAWAL FROM SPAIN
APRIL 2–JULY 8, 1939

No. 774

2130/465072

The Ambassador in Italy to the Foreign Ministry

Telegram

No. 115 of April 2   ROME, April 2, 1939—10 : 00 p.m.

With reference to your telegram No. 149 of March 30 and to my telegram No. 111 of March 31.[1]

Ciano, to whom in the course of today's conversation I mentioned the question of the time for withdrawing the volunteers of both our countries, replied that in this regard Italy was in no hurry, in fact at the present moment did not deem it disadvantageous if the volunteers remained there a little while longer (not because we are thinking in terms of Spain but of "others"). At the present time they were concentrated in certain centers to recuperate. It was certainly not intended to leave them in Spain too long, but it had not yet been decided whether they would be removed in 2 weeks, 4 weeks, or even later. In reply to my question he confirmed the fact that Italy had no objections whatsoever if for some reason of other we wished to withdraw our volunteers earlier.

MACKENSEN

---

[1] Not printed (168/132423).

No. 775

462/225600–02

The Foreign Minister to the Embassy in Spain

Telegram

URGENT   BERLIN, April 3, 1939—8 : 00 p.m.
No. 210 of April 3   Received April 3—8 : 00 p.m.

For the Ambassador.

With reference to your telegram No. 322.[1]

We fail to understand how the Spanish Foreign Minister can raise any new objection to the announcement of Spain's accession to the Anti-Comintern Pact. The precondition for the announcement, as has already been explained in telegraphic instruction No. 199,[2] was

---

[1] Document No. 772, p. 883.
[2] Document No. 770, p. 882.

887

created by the fall of Madrid. General Franco declared on April 1 that the Red Army had been captured and disarmed, the last military objective achieved, and the war ended. Thus, if objections to the announcement are again raised on the part of the Spaniards, this cannot be regarded as anything but an attempt on the part of certain elements in the Spanish Government to disregard previous agreements and to evade the treaty pledge to acknowledge Spain's accession to the anti-Comintern circle.

Both in view of the hitherto compelling circumstances and in consideration of the requirements of our highly tense general political situation, the announcement of the treaty cannot be put off any longer. Therefore, if by the time you receive this telegraphic instruction you are not in possession of Spanish approval for making the announcement, please call immediately on the Foreign Minister there or the Generalissimo himself, together with your Italian and Japanese colleagues, whose Governments share our view and, as you know, last week issued similar instructions to them, and demand immediate publication. You may add that the international press has already become aware of and has reported on Spanish accession and that concealment of this fact, already internationally known, would be interpreted as a sign of weakness of the anti-Comintern powers. This is undesirable.

In my name, please propose to the Spanish Foreign Minister publication in Wednesday morning's newspapers.

RIBBENTROP

No. 776

462/225597

The Ambassador in Spain to the Foreign Ministry

Telegram

URGENT SAN SEBASTIÁN, April 3, 1939—7:45 p.m.

No. 335 of April 3

With reference to my telegram No. 329 of April 1.[1]

The Foreign Minister told me that the Generalissimo shared his objections to an immediate announcement of Spain's accession to the Anti-Comintern Pact and requested us to have patience a while longer.

The result of the *démarches* made by my Italian and Japanese colleagues, who at the present time cannot be reached, is not yet known. It could hardly be different.

---

[1] Not printed (462/225596).

Admiral Canaris did not see the Generalissimo because of [the latter's] illness but has conferred with Jordana twice. The result is as yet unknown.

STOHRER

No. 777

462/225598

The Ambassador in Spain to the Foreign Ministry

Telegram

No. 337 of April 3   SAN SEBASTIÁN, April 3, 1939—8 : 10 p.m.

With reference to my telegram No. 335 of April 3.

The Generalissimo told Vice Admiral Canaris through the Foreign Minister that he requested 2 or 3 weeks more before announcing the accession to the Anti-Comintern Pact so that France might meanwhile hand over the Red war matériel, Spanish merchant vessels, etc.

STOHRER

No. 778

462/225605

The Ambassador in Spain to the Foreign Ministry

Telegram

VERY URGENT   SAN SEBASTIÁN, April 4, 1939—1 : 55 p.m.
SECRET

No. 341 of April 4

With reference to your telegrams Nos. 210,[1] 213,[2] 216 [3] of April 3 and 4 (all of which arrived here only early this morning).

The reasons for Spanish objections to the immediate announcement of accession to the Anti-Comintern Pact are indicated in telegram No. 337 of yesterday and preceding reports. There is no cause to fear any attempt to evade treaty commitments.

After the Generalissimo, as reported, rejected the immediate announcement of the accession, in spite of the support given my *démarche* by the Italian Ambassador and Vice Admiral Canaris, the success of a new *démarche* is very doubtful. I shall nevertheless try to do what I can. I am leaving immediately for Burgos for a conference with the Foreign Minister this evening. The Generalissimo

---

[1] Document No. 775, p. 887.
[2] Not printed (462/225603).
[3] Not printed (462/225604).

is still ill. It will in no event be possible to make the announcement tomorrow.

The Italian Ambassador will support the *démarche* although he has received no instructions as yet. The Japanese Minister cannot be reached.

STOHRER

No. 779

462/225606

The State Secretary to the Embassy in Spain

Telegram

No. 218 of April 4   BERLIN, April 4, 1939.
                          Received April 4—7 : 30 p.m.

With reference to your telegram No. 337 of April 3.

The reasons given by you for the delay in announcing Spain's accession to the Anti-Comintern Pact cannot be considered valid. In our opinion France will be much more ready to hand over the Red war matériel and the Spanish merchant vessels if Franco takes a clear and definite position. The Spanish Ambassador here, with whom the Reich Foreign Minister has just discussed the situation, shares the view that any further delay is now out of place. Since Spain's accession has already been reported by the foreign press in any case, withholding of the official announcement would tend to create a situation which would cause surprise in foreign countries and give rise to comment.

You are therefore requested to make very energetic representations in line with yesterday's instructions; you should reach an agreement on the date on which Spain's accession is to be announced and the manner in which this is to be done—if not tomorrow then at least in the course of the week—and inform us of further developments by telegram.

WEIZSÄCKER

No. 780

F19/141

Memorandum by an Official of Political Division I [1]

BERLIN, April 4, 1939.

The Supreme Command of the Wehrmacht still desires the Condor Legion to be withdrawn as soon as possible, since it is not supposed to

---

[1] On receipt of telegram No. 115 from Rome (document No. 774) Ribbentrop instructed the State Secretary to invite the OKW to state its views on the evacuation of the German units in Spain (F19/142).

take part in any policing and consequently has nothing to do at the present time. Since it is primarily a matter of Luftwaffe personnel, Field Marshal Göring has reserved to himself the decision regarding the date of the withdrawal.

For the following reasons it is unlikely that the withdrawal will take place before the middle of April:

1. Franco wishes the Condor Legion to take part in the parade which will be held in Madrid about April 12. In all probability this wish will be granted.

2. It has not been made clear whether all war matériel or only a part of it will be sold to the Spaniards and thus left behind. If no war matériel is taken along, the withdrawal will be carried out more rapidly.

3. The Führer has ordered a parade of the Condor Legion to be held in Berlin. The preparations for this will take a little time, since all former members of the legion are also to take part, and these are scattered throughout the Reich.

The evacuation—up to the time of arrival in a German harbor—will require approximately 3 weeks.

Herewith submitted to the Secretariat of the Foreign Minister through the Under State Secretary and the State Secretary.

NOSTITZ

No. 781

462/225607–08

The Ambassador in Spain to the Foreign Ministry

Telegram

SECRET   SAN SEBASTIÁN, April 4, 1939.
No. 342 of April 4   Sent April 5—1:40 a.m.

With reference to my telegram No. 341 of today's date.

In a long conversation with the Foreign Minister I have just developed in great detail and most emphatically the arguments sent me in telegrams No. 210 ff.,[1] as well as other arguments setting forth the necessity for an immediate announcement of Spain's accession to the Anti-Comintern Pact.

The Minister admitted that some of my statements were correct but nevertheless persisted in his objections; he emphasized the fact that the war had ended sooner than expected and for this reason several delicate questions were still pending, such as the return of the gold, the fishing fleet, and the entire armament of the Reds, including 100

---

[1] Document No. 755, p. 887. See also those cited in footnotes 2 and 3, p. 889.

airplanes which would be endangered by a public announcement of Spain's accession to the pact; countries friendly to Spain were surely interested in shielding her from difficulties at a moment when she was beginning to recuperate.

Finally the Minister promised to lay the matter before the Council of Ministers, which is meeting tomorrow evening, and then once more before the Generalissimo, and to present my ideas in an objective manner.

I am to receive a reply concerning the decision Thursday morning.

STOHRER

No. 782

462/225614

The Under State Secretary to the Embassy in Spain

Telegram

No. 226 of April 5   BERLIN, April 5, 1939.
                                    Received April 6—9 : 00 a.m.

Reports regarding Spain's accession to the Anti-Comintern Pact have already appeared in the foreign press on several occasions. The *Evening Standard* of April 4 has now reported that General Franco signed the pact on March 27, the day before his troops entered Madrid, but on the condition that the accession be kept secret for the time being. The fact that Spain acceded is therefore already known to the public. Please make use of this when dealing with the Government there in connection with our efforts regarding announcement of the accession.[1]

WOERMANN

---

[1] At 1 : 50 a.m. on Apr. 5 the Trans-Ocean news agency distributed a report that "it is learned from informed circles that an official announcement of Spain's adherence to the Anti-Comintern Pact is about to be made." Stohrer reported that on the evening of Apr. 5 the Spanish Council of Ministers decided upon immediate announcement of Spain's adherence to the pact but added that he did not think Trans-Ocean's report had been noticed in Spain (telegram No. 350 of Apr. 6, 462/225616). The announcement appeared in the German and Italian press on Apr. 7 (462/225643).

No. 783

322/193561-63

Memorandum by an Official of the Economic Policy Department

[Undated]
zu W 244 III g Rs.

Drafting Officer : Counselor of Legation Sabath.

The final figures for our total expenditures in Spain are close to 500,000,000 RM.

Deducting 88,000,000 RM for reimbursement of expenditures and salaries (but including 5,000,000 RM for other personal expenditures such as insurance and traveling expenses), the total amount is 412,000,000 RM.

Approximately 20 million RM in interest and compound interest have not yet been taken into account.

Franco has expended approximately 200,000,000 pesetas of his own resources for the material and personal support of the troops.

I. In round numbers the figures appear as follows:

A. Direct Deliveries to Spain

	Acknowledged	Paid	Unpaid balance	Remarks
163,000,000	65,200,000	58,300,000	104,700,000	
19,000,000	19,000,000		19,000,000	
182,000,000	84,200,000	58,300,000	123,700,000	

B. To the Condor Legion

232,500,000	11,400,000	2,500,000	230,000,000	
414,500,000	95,600,000	60,800,000	353,700,000	

In addition to the above-mentioned payments by the Spaniards, there are 15 million RM in pesetas, which were paid to Herr Bernhardt chargeable to the credit granted. This amount will have to be included in the earliest acknowledged accounts. Thus, the figure 58.3 under A is increased to 73.3 so that the unpaid balance under A will come to 108.7 million RM. Since no other payments worthy of mention are to be expected, this sum can be considered unchanged for group A.

The figure 232.5 million RM in group B (Condor) includes 10.3 million RM for materials which the Legion handed over to the Spaniards. This figure represents the value of the materials at the time of the transfer. In other words the original value, and thus the expenditure for the Condor Legion, was higher. It is, however, hardly possible subsequently to demand payment for depreciation in order to arrive at a figure equal to the original value; this would mean, actually, that the Spaniards would subsequently have to pay the original value. The amount of 230 million RM under Condor can therefore be retained as a starting point.

Among the 228 million RM worth of materials delivered to the Condor Legion (232.5 minus 4.5 for personnel expenditures) equipment is included which for reasons of security will be taken back to Germany. The value of this equipment is tentatively estimated at 30 million RM; exact figures are still being determined. Since this equipment has scarcely been used, there is no point in calculating depreciation. It should therefore be deducted from the Condor Legion's expenditures for materials, so that the resulting claim for money spent for materials amounts to:

$$228 - (30 + 2.5) = 195.5 \text{ million RM}$$

II. The matériel which is to be left in Spain permanently is, in accordance with the Field Marshal's decision, to be handed over to the Spaniards. It is of importance for the settlement with the Spaniards whether this matériel is to be turned over to them at its original or its depreciated value. The Supreme Command of the Wehrmacht wants to turn the matériel over at its depreciated value. We should agree to this because:

(a) Some equipment has already been transferred to the Spanish troops by the Legion at its depreciated value, i.e. there is a precedent;

(b) It is to be feared that Franco will refuse to accept the equipment at its original value. The Supreme Command of the Wehrmacht, however, has considerable interest in having Franco take over the equipment.

If the depreciated value alone is taken into consideration, the following calculation results:

The value of the matériel in Spain at the present time is estimated at 100 million RM. After withdrawal of the modern equipment, there would still remain in Spain the equivalent of 70 million RM. The average decrease in value due to depreciation being 30 percent, the resulting claim against Franco would amount to approximately 50 million RM.

If we further entirely forego compensation for equipment that has been used up, the amount involved would be:

$$225.5 - 30 = 195.5 - 70 = 125.5 \text{ million RM}$$

According to previous calculations, our claim will amount at the very most to $353.7 - (15 + 30) = 308.7$, and $108.7 + 50 = 158.7 + 4.5$ million RM $= 163.1$ million RM.

III. As a third solution the following might be considered:

The available equipment is handed over for 50 million RM in accordance with the above calculation. The equipment used up for Spain will, however, be calculated at its original value. Since this equipment was worth 125.5 million RM, the claim for Condor would be

125.5 + 50 = 175.5 million RM for materials
4.5 million RM for personnel expenditure
———
180.0 million RM for Condor
108.7 million RM for group A

Total claim . . 288.7 million RM

No. 784

1573/381175-76

Memorandum by an Official of the Economic Policy Department

SECRET   BERLIN, April 6, 1939.
W 513 g   Pol. III 199 g.

Subject: Spain.

The Foreign Minister has agreed to having Ministerialdirektor Wohlthat direct the German-Spanish negotiations.

For the preliminary negotiations the following persons will accompany him:

Counselor of Legation Sabath from the Foreign Ministry,

Herr Bethke from the Economics Ministry,

Oberregierungsrat Könning from the Finance Ministry.

The latter is participating in spite of the protest of the Foreign Ministry, which regards his participation as unnecessary at the present moment and does not wish to approve it unless Herr Könning can combine with his trip to Spain a trip to Lisbon for negotiations regarding transfer of capital [*Kapitalverkehr*].

Herr Wohlthat does not want to leave before April 24, because he wishes first to obtain instructions from the Field Marshal in addition to those which he has already received from the Foreign Minister.

The Embassy in San Sebastián has been requested by wire to state whether it considers postponement of the time of departure acceptable; if not, Ministerialdirektor Wohlthat is to leave on April 17.

The Foreign Minister has issued the following special instructions and made it the particular duty of the representative of the Foreign Ministry to observe them:

1. The Spaniards are to be treated chivalrously and are not to be given the feeling that we are demanding payment for the shedding of German blood.

2. The personnel expenditures may be mentioned to the Spaniards, but compensation for them is not to be demanded.

The figures on our expenditures are to be submitted to the Foreign Minister.

3. The Italians are not to be offended. Any pointed rivalry with them is to be avoided, even if it should be at our expense. The Italians are to be regarded as partners and not as competitors.

SABATH

No. 785

632/252693

Memorandum by the Under State Secretary

BERLIN, April 12, 1939.

General [*General der Flieger*] Schweickardt reported by telephone that the Führer had now decided that the reception of the Condor Legion should take place in Hamburg on June 2 and in Berlin on June 5. The departure from Spain would be timed accordingly and would not begin earlier than May 25 in any case.

WOERMANN

No. 786

136/73739–48

Memorandum by the Ambassador in Spain

PRO MEMORIA CONCERNING THE "PRESENT STATUS OF OUR RELATIONS WITH SPAIN"

PARTLY SECRET   SAN SEBASTIÁN, April 14, 1939.

References:

A. Memorandum concerning the "Status of our *de facto* and *de jure* relations with Spain," dated the middle of February 1938.[1]

B. "Pointers for a report in Berlin on the development of German-Spanish relations," dated December 18, 1938.[2]

C. Memorandum of January 4, 1939, on the above-mentioned "Pointers for a report. . . ."[3]

I.

The demands set forth in the memorandum mentioned above under A, insofar as they are still pertinent, have all been fulfilled through the negotiations carried on with Spain during the past few months, by:

1. Settlement of the Montana affair (Spanish mining concessions for Hisma). Simultaneously the founding of a German mining company, the Mauritania, in Spanish Morocco was guaranteed, as well as the procurement of German mining machinery in return for payment in additional ore deliveries.

2. A police treaty. The conclusion of this treaty was obtained without the mediation of the Embassy. According to information which I have just received, it was signed as early as July 31, 1938.

---

[1] Document No. 529, p. 590.
[2] Document No. 702, p. 804.
[3] Document No. 708, p. 814.

3. The cultural agreement of January 24, 1939.[4]

4. The labor-permit agreement of January 29, 1939 (preferential treatment for Germans returning to Spain).

5. Spain's accession to the Anti-Comintern Pact, March 27, 1939.[5]

6. The German-Spanish treaty of friendship of March 31, 1939.[6] (This restated and solemnly confirmed the political assurances which were mentioned in the "Pointers for a report . . ." referred to under B above and which were already included in the political protocols of March 20, 1937.)

The question of "Spanish support of our colonial demands and of our interests in the Tangier Zone," which was another demand mentioned in the memorandum of the middle of February 1938, is not pertinent at the present time, while the question of "Advantages for German merchant shipping and the like," according to a decision made in a departmental conference in the Foreign Ministry on January 9, 1939, is to be reserved for later economic negotiations.

II.

The German-Spanish treaty of friendship concluded on March 31, 1939, now forms the basis of further development of German-Spanish relations. Together with it, however, the protocol of March 20, 1937, as well as the protocols of July 1937, remains fully effective, and this is of significance for our economic relations.

After the conclusion of the cultural treaty in January and Spain's accession to the Anti-Comintern Pact, the treaty of friendship leaves only two questions pending, or rather reserves them for a later, more detailed settlement:

1. the relations between the armed forces of the two countries, and

2. economic relations.

As far as the question of the development of relations between the German and Spanish armed forces is concerned, I purposely mentioned this point only in passing in my previous reports, since during the Spanish Civil War it was best to leave the cultivation of these relations primarily to our military authorities. Now, however, in view of the impending departure of the Condor Legion, this question comes into the foreground of political interest, since the development of military relations and—as stated in the treaty of friendship—such "measures" to be agreed upon by the two treaty partners as are "calculated to promote fostering of comradely relations and the exchange of practical military experience between their armed forces" will have the greatest possible effect on general German-Spanish relations.

---

[4] Document No. 716, p. 821.
[5] Document No. 768, p. 881.
[6] Document No. 773, p. 884.

According to official statements so far available from German and Spanish authorities, the further development of relations between the two armies might, in particular, take the form of an exchange of officers. A certain part will be played also by the question of the standardization of armaments and a question affecting the economic situation, namely, that of establishing factories for war matériel (including airplanes) with German aid. General Franco showed very lively interest in this question a few days ago during a conference concerning future military cooperation by the two countries. He told me that in case we agreed he intended to form a military commission and send it to Germany in order to study all these military questions there and to work out suggestions.

With reference to economic relations, my report No. 1104/39 of March 15, 1939, concerning "The Spanish Minister of Commerce on the problem of future German-Spanish commercial relations" pointed out that in the opinion of Señor Suances three aspects would have to be sharply differentiated during the prospective economic conferences:

1. Settlement of debts,
2. General exchange of goods,
3. Participation in the reconstruction of Spain.

As I have reported in the meantime by telegram (telegram No. 392 of April 13),[7] the Foreign Minister shares the opinion of the Economics Minister concerning the expediency of an early exchange of views on these problems. The Generalissimo, too, showed the greatest interest in this matter; he told me that he had quite recently discussed these questions on a number of occasions with the Foreign Minister and the Minister of Commerce.

III.

In summary it might therefore be stated that from now on we must turn our attention primarily to our military and economic relations with Spain. In dealing with these two questions, however, we must not, in my opinion, for psychological reasons, disregard the following: In recent months the Franco Government has shown the best intention of making valuable concessions to us on a most extensive scale for the great and decisive aid given to it during the war—concessions in the political as well as the economic field. In the negotiations carried on with Spain for this purpose we have had our way for the most part, even down to details. I refer especially to the Montana affair, the drafting of the treaty of friendship, the difficult negotiations concerning Spain's accession to the Anti-Comintern Pact, as well as the question of making this accession public. I do not know in what spirit and with what success the Italo-Spanish economic negotiations which began in Rome and which evidently have not yet been concluded have

---

[7] Not printed (3868/E045775).

been carried on. I would assume, however, that by these negotiations Italy has not come close to achieving so much as we. Also with reference to political commitments and the settlement of cultural relations, we have obtained more from Spain than Italy has. The negotiations concerning Spain's accession to the Anti-Comintern Pact and its publication were in the main carried on by us, because of the great speed with which instructions always arrived from Berlin. The result is that the Spanish Government, with some justification, is at the present time doubtless under the impression that it has been especially cooperative with us recently—even as compared with Italy—and that it has made very special concessions to us. I do not believe it wise to bend the bow too far and to exert too much pressure in the questions still pending—the military as well as the economic ones. The Spanish character being what it is, we should thereby probably achieve only the opposite. Although I am still of the opinion that we should retain the initiative in the further development of our relations with Spain, I should nevertheless like to ask that in the matter of further requests to be made of Spain the tempo be slackened for a while.

This in no way precludes initiating an exchange of views concerning future economic relations (settlement of debts, future trade, and participation in reconstruction), which is entirely in place at the present time (question of indemnities!) and, as has been reported, is also desired by Spain. I should like to recommend, however, that in these conferences we place more emphasis on our readiness to agree to the most convenient possible debt settlement for Spain and in the form of amicable cooperation to participate to the greatest possible extent in the reconstruction of Spain, instead of making new demands on Spain from the outset or demanding commitments of an extensive nature. I am convinced that these tactics would make it possible for us to prevent Spain from entering into any commitments inconvenient for us with other countries, especially with France and England, and still gradually to put through our wishes.

Among the measures which might at first appear to be of secondary importance but which would certainly greatly further our aims would be a generous attitude in the question of giving German decorations to Spanish military and civilian personnel. I therefore would like to request that in this respect, too, the mentality of the Spaniards be taken into account for political reasons.

Measures facilitating travel could also contribute considerably to furthering friendly relations between Germany and Spain. Perhaps provisions of this kind could be included in the economic agreements.

I have repeatedly emphasized lately that by means of suitable relief projects—food shipments, assistance in solving the transportation problem, shipments of medicine, etc.—we should in addition strive as far as possible to alleviate the grave wounds which the Spanish Civil

War has inflicted on the population. Although a Spanish Government favorably inclined toward us is, of course, the main factor in the further satisfactory development of German-Spanish relations and the achievement of our goals in Spain, we nevertheless cannot disregard the opinion of the Spanish people, the greater part of whom even now secretly favors the Reds. We should be able to achieve a good deal with the people by such humanitarian measures, skillfully exploited for propaganda purposes.

Friendly gestures of other kinds should not be neglected either, since they would serve to keep alive the interest of the two peoples in each other; Spanish exhibitions in Germany and German exhibitions in Spain should be encouraged; we might consider naming streets in German cities after important Spanish localities and persons, just as in a number of Spanish cities large streets were given such names as *Avenida de Alemania,* as a sign of gratitude. A monument to the Condor Legion in Spain would emphasize German-Spanish brotherhood in arms for a long time to come; perhaps donation of some other monument or fountain to replace a work of art destroyed by the Reds in Madrid or Barcelona or elsewhere might be considered; similarly, large German cities might sponsor small Spanish towns that were especially devastated, and, finally, German Catholics might even reconstruct some destroyed church or shrine with the approval of the German Government. The cultural agreement gives still further suggestions for the cultivation of amicable relations—not really of a political nature—between the two countries. The time and the manner in which such measures are to be carried out must, of course, be exactly adapted to the Spanish mentality.

STOHRER

[EDITORS' NOTE. At the conference between Göring, Mussolini, and Ciano in Rome on April 16 the possibility of securing naval and air bases in the Balearics and elsewhere in Spanish territory in case of a general war was discussed. A memorandum of this conference appears in volume VI.]

No. 787

472/228781–83

The Ambassador in Spain to the State Secretary

STRICTLY PERSONAL   SAN SEBASTIÁN, April 27, 1939.

DEAR WEIZSÄCKER: Upon my return here I learned that the intrigues of the Köhn "Special Staff"[1] against the Embassy are again

---

[1] This special staff under the leadership of Willi Köhn was a group of representatives of the German Ministry of Propaganda operating in Spain.

in full swing. I shall spare you the details, but the refrain in the agitation is the following: The Ambassador, who in other respects is perhaps not so bad, is entirely unsuited to represent the Third Reich in Nationalist-Syndicalist Spain; his views regarding propaganda and press policy also show that his orientation is wrong and entirely of the old school! *Who*, in the opinion of these gentlemen, would be the proper representative of the Reich here remains unexpressed, but it is sufficiently evident that Herr Köhn is considered to be the right man!

It is strange that the military (General von Richthofen) is supposed to be not entirely unsympathetic to these ideas. I have just now heard that Herr von Richthofen is allegedly striving to become the chief of a permanent military mission here; for this reason he is said to be trying to influence Berlin to recall the present air attaché, Lieutenant Colonel von Scheele (in my opinion a very capable person, whom he reproached, by the way, for having "cooperated too closely with the Embassy"). It is also said that he then wants the other military attachés subordinated to him.

Since these intrigues are unfortunately beginning to be known in broader German circles, I urgently request that the "Special Staff" be dissolved and Herr Köhn recalled as quickly as possible. After our discussion in Berlin I hardly need emphasize that for me, or rather my further activity—if it is to be at all useful—any compromise in this question is impossible.

As far as Herr von Richthofen's plans are concerned, I should be grateful if you would examine the question of their political expediency [2] but would *not* mention my name as the source of this information. I might add that during the festivities in the Kaiserhof recently General Milch made a remark—which is comprehensible to me only now, after receipt of the above information—according to which he did not seem to be in favor of a permanent military mission here. Subordination of the military attachés to the chief of such a mission or continuation of their present undetermined status, which causes all sorts of difficulties, would however not be acceptable to the Foreign Ministry or the Embassy in any case.

I should appreciate it very much if you would continue your efforts to create a normal situation here with regard to the Special Staff as well as the military attachés. However, please treat the above information, especially the delicate subject mentioned last, as strictly confidential.

With cordial greetings and Heil Hitler,

As ever,

STOHRER

---

[2] Footnote in the original: "The Italians would then certainly demand the same thing."

No. 788

2929/566890–91

The State Secretary to the Embassy in Spain

Telegram

VERY URGENT　　　　　　　　　　　　　BERLIN, May 2, 1939.
No. 292 of May 2　　　　　　　　　　　　　　　　Partei 16 g.
[Drafting Officer:] Counselor of Legation Luther.

For the Ambassador personally.

Field Marshal Göring is considering the idea of arriving in Spain from San Remo about May 13 and participating in the parade if an invitation is extended by General Franco.

Please intervene at once and establish contact with Bernhardt of Hisma, who is supposed to be handling the matter. Any invitation would have to go through you to the Foreign Ministry for transmittal to Field Marshal Göring. Since the trip has not been definitely decided upon as yet, please handle the matter accordingly as confidential.

WEIZSÄCKER

No. 789

2929/566892

The State Secretary to the Embassy in Spain

Telegram

VERY URGENT　　　　　　　　　　　　　BERLIN, May 2, 1939.
SECRET　　　　　　　　　　　　　　　　　　Partei 14 g.
No. 295

With reference to my telegram No. 292.[1]

For the Ambassador personally.

According to reports the Spaniards are said to have expressed certain objections already, since they believe that they cannot assume responsibility for the safety of the Field Marshal on his trip through Spain and also fear that the Italians might feel slighted. Consequently the idea of having a meeting with Franco take place aboard ship seems to be under consideration. Please keep this in mind in your procedure. Communication with the commander of the Condor Legion appears expedient.

WEIZSÄCKER

---

[1] Document No. 788, *supra*.

No. 790

2929/566894–95

The State Secretary to the Embassy in Spain

Telegram

URGENT   BERLIN, May 5, 1939.
SECRET   zu Partei 19 g.
No. 305

For the Ambassador personally.

With reference to telegram No. 458 of May 3.[1]

Field Marshal Göring will presumably meet Generalissimo Franco after May 8 on a German steamer off the Spanish coast. Strictest secrecy should be observed in this matter. In case Generalissimo Franco should nevertheless invite the Field Marshal to visit Spain and participate in the parade, which is unlikely according to your telegram, the Field Marshal will ask you either directly, or via the Foreign Ministry or Ambassador von Mackensen, who was also informed today, to take over official preparations for the visit. In that case please take the necessary steps at once to carry out this request. Also, please report immediately by telegram as soon as you learn any further details.

WEIZSÄCKER

---

[1] Not printed (2929/566893).

No. 791

614/249733–35

The Ambassador in Spain to the State Secretary

STRICTLY PERSONAL   SAN SEBASTIÁN, May 5, 1939.

DEAR WEIZSÄCKER: I should like to add the following strictly confidential information to my telegram[1] concerning a possible meeting between Field Marshal Göring and Generalissimo Franco at the parade in Madrid or in the Mediterranean:

Herr Bernhardt seems to have been in communication with Franco on this question for some time. My informant told me that Herr Bernhardt stated on one occasion that "the Ambassador, however, should in no case be permitted to know anything about this matter"! I do not know whether this conforms to the Field Marshal's wishes or whether it represents one of the friendly gestures of Herr Bernhardt toward me which I have gradually become accustomed to expect.

---

[1] Probably a reference to telegram No. 458 of May 3 (2929/566893), not printed.

I am telling you this only as a side light on the present situation here, where: (1) the press staff under the Ministry of Propaganda pursues its own policy, which is, of course, directed against the Embassy; (2) Herr Bernhardt uses every opportunity to entrench himself behind direct instructions of the Four Year Plan and plays off this position of his against the Embassy; and (3) recently the commander of the Condor Legion, too, in his independent military position—which he is evidently trying to safeguard for himself for the future—is also going his own way, which is not very friendly to the Embassy.

You told me recently in Berlin that I would have the full support of the Foreign Ministry in my demand, based on purely objective considerations, for a normalization of conditions here and a strengthening of the authority of the Ambassador and thus of the Foreign Ministry. I believe that it has now become necessary to assert this support with all emphasis. I should like to repeat that the present conditions, which I tolerated patiently during the Civil War out of consideration for peace in the German colony here and unity of the German effort in Spain, must end if the intention is to leave me here any longer. If the conditions described continue, it would be impossible for me any longer to bear the responsibility for successfully carrying out in Spain the policies ordered by the Foreign Ministry.

Please consider this conclusion for the time being merely as a statement made to you personally but one which has been carefully weighed in the light of considerations fully approved by you previously.

With cordial greetings and Heil Hitler,

As ever,

STOHRER

No. 792

472/228784

The State Secretary to the Ambassador in Spain

BERLIN, May 6, 1939.

DEAR STOHRER: On the basis of your letter of April 27 I have spoken once more with State Secretary Hanke[1] and requested him to speed up the recall of the Special Staff. Apparently the intention was to leave the Special Staff in Spain until the departure of the Condor Legion. Hanke promised me, however, to give orders for its early recall and return.

---

[1] Of the Propaganda Ministry.

I did not further explain to Hanke the reasons for my request, but he probably sensed them.

Let us hope for the best!

Cordial greetings and Heil Hitler,

As ever,

WEIZSÄCKER

No. 793

168/132411–12

The Ambassador in Spain to the Foreign Ministry

Telegram

VERY SECRET   SAN SEBASTIÁN, May 8, 1939.

No. 475 of May 8   Received May 8—5 : 45 p.m.

For the State Secretary.

With reference to my telegram No. 468 of May 6.[1]

I have just been informed through General von Richthofen that Bernhardt had been carrying on negotiations here with Franco and Jordana concerning a meeting between Field Marshal Göring and the Generalissimo. After agreeing at first, the Spaniards had raised objections, as was reported to the Field Marshal in Berlin approximately a week ago by both Bernhardt and von Richthofen himself; the Field Marshal had nevertheless insisted on arranging an early personal conference with Franco, especially since he had already received the Führer's approval and had notified Mussolini.

Upon his return here, Bernhardt had continued negotiations but had received another refusal. Thereupon he—General Richthofen—at Bernhardt's request, had personally interceded with Franco concerning the meeting in order to prevent ill feeling and had received an affirmative answer last night, Saturday. Franco wished the meeting to take place at a Spanish country estate. The suggested date seems to be May 11 or 13. Only Bernhardt and Rocamora, the Spanish Military Attaché in Berlin, would participate in the meeting.

I have also been informed through General Richthofen that Franco had expressed surprise that the Ambassador had not been entrusted with the matter.

In addition I learned from a reliable source that the whole matter was brought about at Bernhardt's initiative; quite some time ago he had called Field Marshal Göring's attention to the expediency of an early visit to Spain and a meeting with Franco. The Field Marshal had agreed to the idea, and Bernhardt had at first obtained the approval of Franco and Jordana. After later conferences on the details,

---

[1] Not printed (614/249739).

however, Jordana had informed Bernhardt on April 29 at the Generalissimo's order that the time was unfavorable, for the reasons mentioned in your telegram No. 295 [2] and my telegram No. 458,[3] with special emphasis on the fact that the Italians would feel slighted. Bernhardt had therefore been requested to take the matter up in Berlin with the Field Marshal in this sense, whereupon he had gone to Germany again.

Bernhardt had stated repeatedly that no one, not even the Embassy, should be informed.

I shall see the Foreign Minister and General von Richthofen at Burgos tomorrow.

If possible, please send immediate instructions for my further conduct, also vis-à-vis my Italian colleague, who the day before yesterday asked whether press reports to the effect that the Field Marshal would extend his trip to Spain were correct.

STOHRER

---

[2] Document No. 789, p. 902.
[3] Not printed (2929/566893).

No. 794

2929/566896

The State Secretary to the Embassy in Spain

Telegram

VERY URGENT   BERLIN, May 8, 1939.
No. 316   Partei . . . g.

For the Ambassador personally.

By order of the Foreign Minister I request that you do the following:

1. Ask General Richthofen and Herr Bernhardt to come to the Embassy at once and explain to them most distinctly that the conduct of negotiations with the Spanish Government is the business of the Ambassador alone and therefore your business.

2. Officially inform the Spanish Government at once that you yourself, in your official capacity, are now taking over all arrangements for the Field Marshal's visit.

Moreover, it might be expected of the Spanish Government that concerning so important an event as the Field Marshal's visit it would negotiate only with the German Ambassador and not with other agencies.

The Italians are informed about the trip in general outline. Therefore there is no objection to your informing your Italian colleague.

WEIZSÄCKER

No. 795

2929/566897–98

The State Secretary to the Embassy in Spain

Telegram

No. 319   BERLIN, May 9, 1939.

For the Ambassador personally.

With reference to my telegram No. 316.[1] By order of the Foreign Minister.

As you mentioned in your telegraphic report No. 475 [2]—and nothing else could be expected—the circumvention of the official representative in Spain during the preparations for Field Marshal Göring's trip could not but arouse surprise among the Spaniards. Actually such lack of discipline can create no other impression than one of complete confusion on the German side, which in the final analysis even touches on the authority of the Führer himself, whose Ambassador you are. The prestige of the Field Marshal must suffer, too, especially when such evidence of tactlessness as you describe is involved.

It is therefore in the interest of our general prestige and our political relations with Spain if you most distinctly forbid Herr Bernhardt any further activity of this kind and call his attention to the fact that any contravention would have very serious consequences for him.

After the Field Marshal's visit, in which you are to take full part as instructed, please send a detailed telegraphic report on what happened, so that further steps may be taken here in order to establish the unity of German representation in Spain, without which no consistent policy is possible there.

WEIZSÄCKER

---

[1] Document No. 794, *supra*.
[2] Document No. 793, p. 905.

No. 796

2929/566899

The Ambassador in Spain to the Foreign Ministry

Telegram

URGENT   SAN SEBASTIÁN, May 9, 1939.
VERY SECRET   Received May 10—3 : 45 a.m.

No. 481 of May 9

For the State Secretary.

The instructions in telegram No. 316 of May 8 were at once carried out most emphatically.

There is great dissatisfaction in Burgos about the whole matter.

Although Franco definitely refused at first to agree to a new date for the meeting, I nevertheless succeeded after several hours of negotiation in persuading him again to change his program for the next few days and to be at the disposal of the Field Marshal on the morning of May 11 in the former headquarters near Saragossa.

A meeting in one of the harbors in eastern or northern Spain was rejected because of the distance and presumably for reasons of security.

The Field Marshal, who is already aboard ship, was informed via the radio of the Condor Legion.

STOHRER

No. 797

2929/566900

The Ambassador in Spain to the Foreign Ministry

Telegram

URGENT   SAN SEBASTIÁN, May 10, 1939—time not indicated.
VERY SECRET   Received May 10—3 : 30 p.m.
No. 482 of May 10

For the State Secretary.

Preparations for the meeting between the Field Marshal and the Generalissimo are now entirely in my hands. The Foreign Minister has already refused to continue to receive Bernhardt.

Should the meeting still come about, I nevertheless do not plan to attend:

1. The Spaniards desire only a conversation between the two statesmen with two interpreters and as little publicity as possible.

2. The Field Marshal has therefore given up the idea of bringing his personal staff.

3. The Field Marshal has designated Bernhardt as interpreter on his side.

The result would be that Bernhardt, but not I, would be present at the conference, which is probably undesirable in view of past events.

It would be impossible for me to receive the Field Marshal on the coast in any case, because of the distance (San Sebastián has no airfield). As soon as the meeting is certain, however, I shall send the Field Marshal a telegram and request his orders.

In case you wish me to proceed differently, please send immediate instructions, since I shall otherwise, in accordance with your telegram No. 317 of May 9,[1] leave tomorrow morning for the parade at Madrid.

STOHRER

---

[1] Not found.

No. 798

614/249738-41

The Ambassador in Spain to the Foreign Ministry

Telegram

No. 484 of May 10   SAN SEBASTIÁN, May 10, 1939.
                                     Received May 10—7 : 45 p.m.

For the State Secretary.

Supplementary to my telegram No. 481 of May 9.

After informing the Foreign Minister yesterday that I was the only one on the German side authorized to carry on further negotiations with regard to the meeting with the Field Marshal, I reproached him emphatically for bearing much of the blame in the matter which he termed "mismanaged from the very beginning," because he had not consulted me.   The Minister was embarrassed and tried to excuse himself by saying that Herr Bernhardt, in the Field Marshal's name, and also the Spanish Government had desired that the meeting be kept strictly secret, a statement which I rejected emphatically.   The Minister finally admitted that departure from the normal channels of negotiation was undesirable and that this was responsible for the difficult situation.

In a conversation lasting more than an hour I demanded that Bernhardt and General von Richthofen be excluded in this matter and that the meeting take place.   With reference to the meeting, General Franco on Saturday evening designated General Richthofen's former headquarters at a country estate near Saragossa and the date of May 10 but refused a meeting at the coast because of the distance. On this point the Foreign Minister further emphasized the impossibility of the Chief of State's agreeing to a meeting aboard ship, since he could not leave the country at the present time.

General von Richthofen actually flew to San Remo with this answer early Monday morning (cf. telegram No. 476 of May 8 [1]).   The Field Marshal rejected the proposed time and place, since his ship could not arrive at Castellón until the afternoon of May 10 and the Führer had asked him to refrain from visiting the interior of the country; he had also informed the Italians to this effect.   During the conversation General von Richthofen obtained the Field Marshal's permission to inform me about the matter at this time.

After leaving the Minister, I encountered in the Ministry General von Richthofen, who had just returned from San Remo and who was to transmit this refusal to Jordana.   I undertook this task without

---

[1] Not printed (168/132410).

the General being present, whereupon the Foreign Minister appeared even more annoyed than before. Jordana rejected all sorts of other solutions which I proposed, especially the landing at Santander on May 14 which was considered by the Field Marshal. He said that Saragossa was the only possible meeting place in view of Franco's schedule, which was completely filled with public functions. At my insistence, however, the Foreign Minister promised to obtain new instructions from the Generalissimo.

In the afternoon I once more called on the Foreign Minister; he told me that he had refused to receive Bernhardt, who had returned from Saragossa in the meantime. In a further conference lasting over an hour I insisted that the meeting take place, especially in view of the very unpleasant situation in which the Field Marshal would be placed; he had already gone aboard ship this morning and was sailing right around Spain on his way back to Germany. I declared that I was prepared in his presence to explain at once to the Generalissimo about the state of affairs. The Minister said that the Generalissimo was occupied all afternoon and evening but that he would ask for a new decision. He did this by telephone several times in the course of our conversation but evidently received rather sharp refusals. I left the Minister with the statement that I could under no circumstances accept such a refusal, asking him to think the matter over once more and if necessary talk with the Generalissimo again.

Two hours later I called once more on the Minister, who claimed to have received another refusal. Following my renewed insistence that the matter could not possibly end in this manner, Jordana finally succeeded in having the Generalissimo, in spite of his completely filled schedule, set a new date, the morning of May 11 at Saragossa. A city on the east coast was rejected because of the distance, and likewise Santander, whereby it was evident that if the meeting were held today fears concerning security played a considerable part.

I informed General von Richthofen of the outcome at once. Together with him I drafted a telegram to the Field Marshal, stating the number of hours from Castellón to Saragossa by car and by plane. The answer is still pending today at 12 o'clock noon.

In the afternoon Bernhardt, whom I had asked to come, arrived from Saragossa, and I explained matters to him according to instructions as I had done with General von Richthofen in the morning.

In the meantime I found out that Bernhardt initiated negotiations concerning the visit as early as the beginning of April. In a letter of April 15 he had informed the Field Marshal that Franco had agreed to a meeting in the harbor of Sitges near Barcelona on May 6. Thereupon the Field Marshal had made his preparations. Later, as reported in telegram No. 475 of May 2[8], the Spaniards wished to postpone the meeting to a later date. On this score the Foreign Minister told me that a definite agreement had by no means been reached for meeting on May 6, a statement which Bernhardt violently contests. The main responsibility for the completely impossible situation at the present time therefore rests upon Bernhardt, who took the initiative in a purely political matter by suggesting a visit to Spain by the Field Marshal, stating that Franco wished to see the Field Marshal as soon as possible. The Foreign Minister is also to blame, however, since he later wished to retract apparently far-reaching promises which he had made at the beginning and which he now claims were not meant. I bluntly said as much to both Bernhardt and the Foreign Minister. Bernhardt did not negotiate with Franco himself at all about the affair. According to General von Richthofen, Franco told him Saturday evening that the whole matter was very embarrassing to him, especially with reference to me, since he had been unable to inform me because of the promise to keep the matter completely secret.

With reference to the closing sentence of your telegram No. 319 of May 9,[2] please for the time being refer to my telegram No. 442 of April 28 [3] and private letters of April 27 [4] and May 5 [5] to the State Secretary.

STOHRER

---

[2] Document No. 795, p. 907.
[3] Not printed (614/249731).
[4] Document No. 787, p. 900.
[5] Document No. 791, p. 903.

No. 799

168/132407

The Ambassador in Spain to the Foreign Ministry

Telegram

VERY SECRET   SAN SEBASTIÁN, May 10, 1939—time not indicated.
No. 485 of May 10   Received May 10—4 : 50 p.m.

For the State Secretary.

With reference to my telegram No. 482 of May 10.

The Field Marshal's answer from aboard ship just arrived. The Field Marshal regrets that he cannot accept the suggestion of May 11 at Saragossa, since the Führer desired only an informal meeting at the coast but not a visit in the interior. The Field Marshal countered with a suggestion for a meeting on the coast on May 13 or 14, until which time he would be cruising off the Spanish east coast.

The Foreign Minister just telephoned me in a state of complete perplexity, since he considers it impossible for Franco to agree to a meeting at the coast for the reasons reported. I insisted most emphatically and stated that in the present situation I would have to decline any responsibility if the meeting failed to take place, adding that above all an immediate decision was required, since it was completely preposterous for the Field Marshal to cruise off the Spanish coast unless a meeting finally took place.

The Field Marshal ordered Bernhardt to proceed to Castellón at once and to come aboard ship. Through General von Richthofen I warned Bernhardt very sharply against continuing his agitation against the Embassy with the Field Marshal since otherwise drastic measures were to be expected. Nevertheless I fear that he will do the opposite. I further authorized Bernhardt to tell the Field Marshal that I was expecting his orders, since I myself have no radio contact. Cf. telegram No. 481 of yesterday.[1]

STOHRER

---

[1] Document No. 796, p. 907.

No. 800

614/249743

The Ambassador in Spain to the Foreign Ministry

Telegram

URGENT   SAN SEBASTIÁN, May 10, 1939—3 : 30 p.m.
VERY SECRET   Received May 10—4 : 40 p.m.
No. 486 of May 10

For the State Secretary.

With reference to my telegram No. 485 of May 10.

Foreign Minister Jordana, after having previously requested my approval by telephone, has just received General von Richthofen once more. The latter called me from the office of the Minister, who for security reasons did not wish to have Spanish spoken, to inform me that Franco had rejected the Field Marshal's new proposal. Reasons:

1. In view of official obligations, the Generalissimo was unable to leave at the time suggested.

2. Since the entire European press was talking about the impending visit of the Field Marshal, the visit, which had been intended as a friendly private meeting, had assumed the far-reaching significance of a political action, which was undesirable to Spain at the present time.

3. Under these circumstances the Italians would also have to be consulted about the visit ahead of time.

4. If the Field Marshal paid an official visit to Spain, it would have to be prepared and carried out in accordance with his high position.

As a last resort, in order to alleviate the unpleasantness of the situation at least to some extent, I urged the Foreign Minister to persuade Franco to initiate a friendly and public exchange of telegrams.[1]

STOHRER

[1] This in fact was agreed to, and the greetings between Göring and Franco were exchanged on May 11 (5179/E307040–41).

No. 801

1588/383359

The Ambassador in Spain to the Foreign Ministry

Telegram

No. 488 of May 10   SAN SEBASTIÁN, May 10, 1939.
Received May 11—1:30 a.m.
Pol. III 1111 g.

With reference to your telegram No. 321 of May 9.[1]

During my last stay in Berlin I raised the question orally whether the Spaniards should be invited to the ceremony of the Legion's entry into Berlin. At that time nothing was known as yet. Since then I learned only through a private letter from Du Moulin of the intention to extend such an invitation, to which I replied [2] that I would not suggest civilians.

General von Richthofen did not consult me in the matter.

However, along with your telegram referred to above, I received a report from the Consul at Seville, stating that according to information from the Chief of Staff of the well-known General Queipo de Llano, Herr Bernhardt had recently transmitted an invitation to the General to be present when the Condor Legion enters Berlin!

Since Bernhardt has been summoned to the Field Marshal, I shall not be able to call him to account for this intervention and telegraph the particulars until after his return.

STOHRER

[1] Not printed (1588/383326–27).
[2] Unsigned marginal note: "Not received."

No. 802

2929/566901–04

The Foreign Minister to Field Marshal Göring (Draft Letter)[1]

[Undated, ca. May 16, 1939.]

The events connected with the visit with General Franco which you recently planned and then abandoned impel me to make the following statements:

[1] Unsigned marginal note: "Not sent. See the Foreign Minister's letter of May 16, 1939." This letter has not been found.

A private person not authorized to carry on such negotiations with the Spanish Government initiated your visit with Franco. After it became apparent that the visit was not acceptable to the General and the Spanish Government for political reasons, the agent nevertheless insisted on the plan. He pressed it without any consideration for international usage and did so with such emphasis that the failure of the plan became a question of prestige for you and for the Reich. The German Ambassador, from whom the discussions had purposely been keep secret until that time, therefore tried to save the planned visit when he finally was able to step in. He did this all the more energetically since the foreign press had in the meantime taken up the visit. His efforts, however, came too late. The Spaniards finally insisted on a schedule that was unacceptable to you, so that the visit had to be given up entirely.

It is regrettable that you, who did General Franco's cause such extraordinary and perhaps decisive service during the Civil War, both personally and through the commitment of your units, should now be accorded such negative treatment at the hands of the Generalissimo. Because of the failure of the plan, the rest of the world must conclude that there is ill feeling between Germany and Spain. As a matter of fact, the Spanish Government and Franco himself are greatly surprised and annoyed with the manner in which this plan was handled and was to be carried out. Not only your personal prestige suffered, however. The fact that an agent, allegedly at your instruction, told the Spanish Government that the German Ambassador, i.e. the only authorized representative of the Reich, should be told nothing about the negotiations, affects the prestige of the Führer himself. Whereas Germany's strength vis-à-vis the outside world must be based especially on absolute unity and solidarity of action and appearance, as a result of this incident an impression of confusion, disorder, and lack of discipline has been created in Spain, a picture which seriously impairs our political position.

All this would have been avoided if:

(1) the plan of your trip and your visit had been communicated to the Foreign Ministry beforehand for the necessary approval in accordance with the Führer's well-known directive (letter No. 3657/38A of the Reich Minister and Chief of the German Chancellery, March 6, 1939), and

(2) the German Ambassador, who was appointed by the Führer for this purpose and who is familiar with international usage, had carried on the negotiations.

In order to keep the damage done from becoming even greater, it is necessary to take remedial steps at once. In the interest of our prestige in Spain I must request that the guilty person there, the director of Hisma, Herr Bernhardt, leave his post at once and be definitely recalled. Please let me know when you have taken suitable measures and inform me when Bernhardt will depart.

I may assume that it is understood that the general regulations issued by the Führer for trips abroad by leading personalities of the Reich will be observed in your future travel plans.

RAM

No. 803

136/73765

The Ambassador in Spain to the Foreign Ministry

Telegram

No. 541 of May 22   SAN SEBASTIÁN, May 22, 1939.
Received May 23—12:40 a.m.

Telephoned from Burgos:

The farewell parade of the Condor Legion in León went off splendidly; among those present were Franco, all of the Spanish generals, including General Kindelan, the Italian Ambassador, the Italian Commander, the Italian General of the Air Forces.

After reviewing the troops, Franco made them a brilliant speech; General Baron von Richthofen answered in Spanish. Next, Baron von Richthofen announced a large donation by the Condor Legion to the families of the men killed in the Spanish Air Force, amounting to one million pesetas. Then came the parade, with both the troops and the instructors making an excellent impression.

Next there was a joint luncheon in a cordial, comradely spirit; there were expressions of friendship between the Spanish, Italian, and German comrades at arms. I proposed a toast to Franco.

Details are being published by DNB, which will also report, according to instructions, on the announcement of Reichsleiter Ley's large gift to Franco (your telegram of May 20, No. 347 [1]). Publication in the Spanish press has been arranged.

STOHRER

---

[1] Not found.

No. 804

1588/383390

The Ambassador in Spain to the Foreign Ministry

Telegram

URGENT   SAN SEBASTIÁN, June 2, 1939.
SECRET   Received June 2—2:10 a.m.
No. 577 of June 1   Pol. III 1275 g.

For the State Secretary.

The Chief of the Special Staff in Salamanca sent me the following message dated May 30:

"On the basis of my proposal the Reich Minister for Public Enlightenment and Propaganda has ordered the liquidation of the Special Staff in its present form on July 1, 1939. The Attaché of the Reich Ministry for Public Enlightenment and Propaganda, Hans Kroeger, will remain in Spain with the necessary assistants and will have his headquarters in Madrid."

This arrangement would mean retention of the present state of affairs. It does not accord either with the request of the Foreign Ministry or with the Propaganda Ministry's promise. It is also intolerable with respect to Kroeger personally.

It is said privately that Köhn instead of Hasenöhrl is to take over the Spanish section, etc., in the Propaganda Ministry.[1]

STOHRER

---

[1] Marginal note: "Settled by oral negotiations by Herr von Stohrer in the Foreign Ministry during his last visit. Schw [endemann] June 17."

No. 805

100/64498–501

The Ambassador in Italy to the State Secretary

ROME, June 9, 1939.

DEAR FRIEND: I am sending you as enclosure No. 4 [1] three documents which Ciano pressed upon me during our conversation yesterday. I believe I can take the responsibility for sending them by the regularly scheduled courier, since in my opinion the contents are interesting, to be sure, but not so urgent as to justify the cost of a telegram or a special courier.

---

[1] There are no enclosures with the file copy of this letter.

The rest of the conversation with Ciano was concerned mainly with the question in regard to which I had been instructed to visit him and concerning which I reported by wire to Counselor of Legation Schmidt immediately afterward.[2]

For the rest, Ciano confirmed to me what the Duce had told me the previous evening concerning his impressions of Serrano Suñer and added that as far as his attitude toward England and France was concerned Suñer was actually an extremist going far beyond his own, Ciano's, attitude and that of Herr von Ribbentrop in his rejection of these two Western democracies. His Francophobia came in fact close to being pathological. He had made no secret of the fact that Gibraltar must under all circumstances be among Spain's objectives once she had regained her strength.

At the gala dinner in the Palazzo Venezia, unfortunately one distinctly jarring note crept in. The Duce, who was very cordial that evening to us Germans, including the 10 German Air Force officers whom he had invited, and who kept me at his side as he received the guests, expressly mentioned the German-Italian comradeship in arms on Spanish soil in making his toast. In his answer, however, the Spanish Minister of the Interior, although he gave in broad outline a picture of the development of the Civil War, did not say a word about the German companions in arms. I noticed this during his speech but have now made sure of it on the basis of the official text of the toasts. I shall limit myself here to saying a few words on the subject to the Spanish Ambassador, at whose house I shall attend a dinner tomorrow evening being given in honor of Suñer, but also as an anti-Comintern affair. I wish to call the matter to your attention, however, so that in any case you have the opportunity, if you think it advisable, also to point out to Franco, via Stohrer, this slip of his brother-in-law. Not only the Italians, but, as it appears from his urgent invitation to me for tomorrow evening, the Spaniard too lays very great value on our participation in the Spanish-Italian fraternization; thus it is naturally doubly noticeable when not a word is said in Suñer's review of the events of the last 2½ years of what we have contributed to making it possible to celebrate a victory today at all.

With cordial greetings and Heil Hitler!

As ever,

v. MACKENSEN

Enclosure: *Corriere della Sera* of June 8 with both toasts.

---

[2] For other documents dealing with relations with Italy at the time and with the visit of Serrano Suñer to Rome, see vol. VI.

No. 806

137/73781–82

The State Secretary to State Secretary Hanke of the Propaganda Ministry

No. Pv. 568   BERLIN, June 16, 1939.

MY DEAR STATE SECRETARY: I wish to inform you that the director of the Special Staff in Salamanca communicated the following to the German Ambassador in Spain:

"On the basis of my proposal the Reich Minister for Public Enlightenment and Propaganda has ordered the liquidation of the Special Staff in its present form on July 1, 1939. The attaché of the Reich Ministry for Public Enlightenment and Propaganda, Hans Kroeger, will remain in Spain with the necessary assistants and will have his headquarters in Madrid."

Such arrangements do not conform to our agreement. I therefore assume that an error is involved and request that you take the necessary steps to have the *entire* Special Staff liquidated by July 1, 1939.

The technical equipment (teletype receivers, high-powered radio receivers, printing presses, photostat equipment, sound film projectors, etc.) can, however, continue to be used to good advantage in Spain in Germany's interest, so that it would be advisable not to ship it back to Germany.

I should be grateful if you would inform me as soon as possible about further arrangements you make with reference to the Special Staff and the technical equipment. I shall then send instructions to the Embassy in Madrid for taking over the latter.

With best regards and Heil Hitler,

Sincerely yours,
WEIZSÄCKER

No. 807

136/73787

The Ambassador in Spain to the Foreign Ministry

Telegram

No. 624 of June 22   SAN SEBASTIÁN, June 22, 1939.
                                            Received June 22—11: 00 p.m.

For the State Secretary.

I have heard that Consul General Köhn will take with him to Germany on July 1 almost all of his former co-workers, most of whom are German, and a number of Spanish employees of the Special Staff in order to continue to carry on press and propaganda work for Spain and South America from there. This would again jeopardize the uniformity of our Spanish policy.

STOHRER

No. 808

136/73790

The Ambassador in Spain to the Foreign Ministry

Telegram

SECRET   SAN SEBASTIÁN, July 2, 1939.
No. 642 of July 2   Received July 3—11 : 00 p.m.

With reference to your telegram No. 424 of June 21.[1]

For the State Secretary.

Attaché Kroeger of the Special Staff in Salamanca reported under date of June 27 that after the liquidation of the Staff he had, as the attaché of the Propaganda Ministry, taken over the archives and furniture necessary for his future work, "as ordered," and would move to Madrid in the near future with his staff.

This information conflicts anew with the clear promise which the Propaganda Ministry made to the Foreign Ministry.

In accordance with a personal directive by the Reich Foreign Minister I have taken the measures announced in report No. 899 g of June 13.[2] In order to prevent these disagreements among Germans from becoming noticeable to the Spaniards, Kroeger's immediate recall is necessary. This I have already announced, as instructed, to the responsible Minister of the Interior. Lazar must be appointed Press Attaché.

The small number of associates left to Kroeger, which is entirely inadequate for continuing the press and propaganda work, shows that the main work with regard to Spain is to be done in the future through Köhn in Berlin. This whole arrangement is intolerable.

STOHRER

---

[1] Not printed (136/73783).
[2] Not found.

No. 809

322/193543–60

Memorandum by an Official of the Economics Ministry

W XXII/247   [Undated]

REPORT ON THE NEGOTIATIONS WITH THE SPANISH GOVERNMENT ON ECONOMIC AND FINANCIAL QUESTIONS FROM JUNE 12 TO JULY 5, 1939, IN BURGOS AND THE INSPECTION OF FIRMS OF THE HISMA-SOFINDUS GROUP IN SEVILLE, SALAMANCA, AND BILBAO

I.

The delegation was composed of Staatsrat Wohlthat, Counselor of Legation Sabath, Director Bethke, Oberregierungsrat Dr. Könning.

After conferences on June 12 and 13 in the Embassy at San Sebastián, the delegation left on June 14 for Burgos, then the seat of the Spanish Government. There were detailed discussions with the Foreign Minister, General Jordana; Minister of Finance Amado; Minister of Agriculture Fernández Cuesta, who is also the leader of the Falange; and, on the following day, with the Minister of Commerce and Industry, Suances. Common to all the visits was the expression of the desire for mutual cooperation and the repeatedly stressed gratitude which Spain feels for the military accomplishments of the German volunteers and the additional support provided by Germany.

The visits had the purpose of making the delegation acquainted with the responsible Ministers and their immediate associates and of establishing connections with the main departments participating in the economic and financial negotiations with Germany. From these visits it became evident that the Spanish Ministers still had no idea of what form the German-Spanish economic and financial relations should take in the future. This can be explained from the fact that the Spanish administration has been in a state of demobilization since the end of the war, and thus everything has been concentrated on reintegrating the discharged soldiers into the economic life and reconverting industry, which has heretofore been exclusively geared to the war economy. Furthermore, a large number of the higher officials were either executed by the Reds or are missing for other reasons, so that many new persons have moved into key positions, some of them where they have to deal for the first time with international economic and financial negotiations of the scope of those being carried on between Germany and Spain. In particular, the Foreign Minister showed a certain unsureness and reserve in his opinions. The Minister of Finance, who is considered a seasoned administrator of the tax and customs apparatus, was also very reserved with regard to the far-reaching financial, transfer, economic, and organizational problems arising between Germany and Spain. On the other hand, Minister Suances, who used to be a naval engineer, revealed himself as a resourceful, energetic man, receptive to new ideas. While recognizing the services of Hisma under the special war conditoons, he also expressed the desire of the Spanish Government to replace the present Rowak-Hisma system with a clearing system between German and Spanish Government agencies. The slogan used by all the Ministers was "normalization" of trade and payments.

The following noteworthy points also emerged from the conversation with Suances:

Contrary to all rumors of the devaluation of the Spanish peseta, as propagated especially by Juan March, Suances declared himself in favor of keeping the peseta stable. As regards the disparity in the rate of exchange between the reichsmark and the peseta in relation to the pound sterling, he was willing to make an adjustment. He complained that, because of the effects of the war and also purchases by Hisma, prices in Spain had been forced to such a high level that they are now about 40 percent above the world market. He was trying to bring the Spanish price level down to normal. The Spanish stocks of raw materials were exhausted, and much of the machinery had been overworked as a result of the great demands made on it during the war. Therefore Spain urgently needed fresh capital for the replacement of her production apparatus and the replenishment of her stocks.

With regard to Spain's war debt to Germany he stated that, in recognition of the assistance given by Germany, Spain would fulfill her obligations. He objected, however, to the idea of making new investments in Spain with the proceeds of German claims which had fallen due and could not be transmitted to Germany because of transfer difficulties, since he evidently feared that German interests might pervade the Spanish economy to too great an extent.

During the conference with Foreign Minister Jordana, he asked that he be given a German memorandum outlining our ideas with regard to future German-Spanish cooperation, Germany's participation in the reconstruction of Spain, and debt settlement. This German memorandum was transmitted, with a Spanish translation, on June 19. During the time available before June 26 the Hisma plants in Spain were inspected.

On the afternoon of June 26 the conferences with the Spanish delegation began in Burgos. The chairman was General Barbero, chief of the Spanish Army's acceptance unit for war deliveries from Germany and Italy. General Barbero took the position that Spain's war debt to Germany should be determined before the start of the conferences on commercial and economic questions. Insofar as Spain had acknowledged the debt, she would fulfill her obligations "to the last céntimo." Of course, the counterclaims arising from Spanish services would also have to be taken into consideration; he assumed that in this settlement Spain would probably remain the debtor. He suggested that a subcommittee be appointed to determine the amount of the debt.

In contrast to Barbero's attitude, a striving for the complete normalization of German-Spanish economic relations was noted during the consultation with the Spanish ministries. Therefore, from the very beginning the German side put greater emphasis on agreement with regard to the question of the rate of exchange and also on the question as to what clearing system should be used until a new arrangement is made. Barbero had cut off rather brusquely every attempt to direct the negotiations to other fields than the debt question. He showed the same attitude when the negotiations were continued on June 27. However, since Señor Huete, the representative of the Spanish National Bank, had arrived in the meantime and Barbero had to go to Madrid, it was possible to open negotiations simultaneously with the Bank of Spain on the question of the rate of exchange and within the subcommittee on the determination of the debt.

Oberregierungsrat Dr. Könning, Director Bethke, and Secretary of Legation Dr. Stille were appointed on the part of the Germans to the subcommittee for determination of the debt. The enclosed list of delegates gives the composition of the Spanish delegation and the subcommittee.

The first session of the subcommittee was held on June 27.

The Spanish representatives stated that the Spanish Government would honor all claims which it had acknowledged.

It was agreed that the amount of the debt would be determined as of a stipulated date; June 1, 1939, was chosen (the Condor Legion left on May 26, 1939).

It was pointed out by the Germans that in determining the debt consideration should be given to the evaluation made by the mixed German-Spanish commission of the matériel left behind and turned over to the Spanish Government—the amount being left open.

The equipment which the Condor Legion took back to Germany will be deducted from the German claim, taking into account the depreciation.

The Germans claimed about 18 million RM as interest for unpaid debts.

The personnel expenses of the Condor Legion in reichsmarks were claimed, but the amount, which is not yet known, was left open.

Charges for survivors' pensions and disability pensions for killed and wounded in the Condor Legion were claimed; the amount was reserved.

The sums spent in Spain for the maintenance of the Condor Legion have already been made available by the Spanish Government to the total amount of about 77,400,000 RM and can be ignored in drawing up the account.

An attempt to make an official record of the details discussed in the session of the committee failed as a result of the fear of the Spanish negotiators and Foreign Minister Jordana that they would thereby commit themselves to too great an extent. The German draft protocol was sent to the different departments with the annexes enclosed in letter W XXII/203 of July 13, 1939.[1]   It was agreed that the German Government would submit the final account to the Spanish Government within a very short time, and the Spanish Government would thereupon proceed to acknowledge it; if the Spanish Government agreed to this proposal of the German Government, the subcommittee was then to convene in Berlin for its concluding session in order to determine the final amount.

At first there were also separate discussions with the members of the Spanish delegation.   In order to make it easier for the Spaniards to understand the proposals which the German delegation made in the memorandum of June 17, 1939,[2] they were given papers elaborating on the important points of this memorandum, which had already been sent to the various departments along with letters W XXII/203 of July 13, 1939 :

Plan for the German-Spanish balance of payments (June 30, 1939)

This survey was drawn up in order to make clear to the Spaniards the manner in which the annuity for the repayment of the war and reconstruction debt is included in the German-Spanish balance of payments.   It is made evident therein that Germany is counting on yearly imports from Spain amounting to 200 million RM and expects them gradually to increase to 250 million RM and more.   The survey shows that German exports to Spain, insofar as they are not covered by the reconstruction credit, can increase from about 150 million to 200 million RM, and thus the necessary surpluses could be provided for transferring the annuities.

A proposal for quotas of goods in the sense of the secret protocols of July 1937 (June 30, 1939)

The German want list is fixed at 250 million RM, of which about 129,300,000 RM is in commodities specified as wanted by Germany, thus leaving it up to Spain to propose almost 50 percent of the yearly imports.

Statistical data on German-Spanish commercial relations, with three annexes (July 1, 1939)

Since the Spaniards are accustomed to judge according to the very inadequate Spanish statistics, it was necessary to explain the sources of error in those statistics and to present the German statistical data.

Provision and utilization of funds for economic purposes in Spain (July 3, 1939)

The statement is meant to give the Spaniards a view of the activity of the Sofindus concern in Spain and to announce the requirements

---

[1] Not found.
[2] Not printed (4366/E082345–50).

for further investments in Spain. The Spanish Government is to provide the funds for these investments, and their equivalent value will be deducted from the principal amount of the war debt.

Account of the situation with respect to a treaty on German-Spanish trade and payments (July 3, 1939)

The above papers, which were also submitted in Spanish translation, evidently facilitated an understanding of the entire German plan on the part of the Spaniards.

On July 3 the final plenary session of the delegations was held. Not General Barbero but Vice President Pan de Soraluce presided on the Spanish side, and he endeavored to advance the negotiations in a practical way. He laid great value on finding a *modus vivendi* as soon as possible, which would make it possible to put into operation normal trade and payments with Germany. For this purpose it was resolved to establish further subcommittees, one to be concerned with trade and payments and the other with the credit agreement. The Spaniards now wished to enter into negotiations at once.

Staatsrat Wohlthat objected that the German delegation present did not have sufficient members to be able to take up the quota negotiations suggested by the Spaniards. The German delegation had come to Spain in order to learn the general ideas of the Spanish Government concerning future cooperation. At the question as to how the Spaniards pictured the German-Spanish exchange of goods in the future and what the counterproposals were which they had promised us in answer to the German list of goods desired, the Spanish Vice President presented a quota list which, as he expressly remarked, is only meant for a transitional period. The list amounts to a total sum of 216.8 million RM in exports, of which 66.8 million RM consists of goods in which Germany is interested and 150 million RM of goods in which Spain is interested, including 70 million RM for oranges. Although the wishes of the Spaniards as regards quotas still differ considerably from our wishes, still their proposals do recognize in principle that they are prepared to make deliveries to Germany up to the amount of 216.8 million RM. This would provide a not unfavorable point of departure for Spain to transfer the war-debt annuity to be paid to Germany.

The Spanish delegation said that they would be ready from July 26 on to resume the negotiations in Spain.

Staatsrat Wohlthat reserved a statement of the German position until he returned to Berlin. The subcommittee for determining the debt question was to continue its work in the manner arranged. He asked for an early statement of position by the Spanish Government on the question of setting the rate of exchange for the peseta in relation to the reichsmark (1 reichsmark=3.63 pesetas). On the question of balancing the old accounts the Spanish representatives asked for copies of abstracts of clearinghouse accounts, etc., since they have no records, and they reserved the right to give notification of the date after which they would need these records.

There were a number of conferences between the representatives of the finance departments and with the Comité de Moneda (Bank of Spain) on the German proposal for settling the Spanish portion of the Austrian conversion loan of 1934–39. The Spanish Government promised an immediate written statement of position on this matter.

The drafting of a joint press report on the status and the intended continuation of the negotiations met with unexpected difficulties; the draft prepared by the German side was not published, since the Generalissimo considered this undesirable at the present time. Evidently the Spaniards wished to be particularly considerate of their Italian treaty partners, since the debt negotiations in Rome were not mentioned either in the Spanish or in the Italian press.

List of Spanish delegation

Chairman: General Don Abilio Barbero

Deputy: Don José Pan de Soraluce (Chief of the European Section of the Ministry of Foreign Affairs)

Don Emilio Navascués y Ruiz de Velasco, Chief of the National Service of Commerce and Customs Policy

Don Manuel Goitia Angulo, Chief of the National Wheat Service (Agriculture)

Don Blas Huete Carraso, Director of the Foreign Currency Committee

Don Manuel Arburrua, Assistant Director of the Foreign Currency Committee

Don Manuel Vila Garriz, Assistant Director of the Foreign Currency Committee

Don Gustavo Navarro (Customs, Treasury)

Don José Ma. Aguirre y Gonzalo, Commercial Attaché (Industry and Commerce)

Don Mariano Iturbalde y Orbegozo, Inspector of Foreign Commerce (Industry and Commerce)

Don Luis García Llera, Commercial Attaché (Industry and Commerce)

Don Julio Carlos Suárez y Sánchez, Commercial Attaché (Industry and Commerce)

Don Manuel Sierra Pomares, State's Attorney (Treasury)

Don Enrique Valera y Ramírez de Saavedra, Chief of Section of the Ministry of Foreign Affairs

Don Ramón Martín Herrero, Secretary of Embassy (Ministry of Foreign Affairs)

Subcommittee for the determination of debts

Chairman: Don Abilio Barbero Saldaña, National Chief of the Supply Service

Don Antonio Ma. Aguirre y Gonzalo, Commercial Attaché in Berlin
Don Manuel Arburrua, Finance Committee
Don Arturo Génova, Naval Commander
Don Rafael Calvo, Air Force Commander
Don Miguel López Uriante, Artillery Commander
Don Juan Roca de Togores, Military Attaché in Berlin
Don Manuel Sierra Pomares, State's Attorney

II

Before the start of the negotiations with a Spanish delegation there were several days left for an inspection of the most important firms of the Hisma-Sofindus group.

On June 19, 1939, the central office of Hisma in Seville was visited; it is housed in a building of its own and regulates the entire clearing traffic, insofar as this is concerned with war deliveries. The Hisma office is organized in a modern way and employs about 260 persons. About half of these are Spaniards. Under the method of payment used thus far by Rowak-Hisma, Spanish exporters, on presentation of the shipping papers, receive, as a rule, 100 percent of the amount of the invoice. With goods which are subject to certain changes caused by transshipment or climate during the journey, immediate payment is limited to about 75 percent of the amount of the invoice, since it is usual in commercial dealings not to determine the final value of the goods until they have arrived in Germany. In the same way, the German exporters have thus far, on presentation of the proper shipping papers, been receiving from Rowak, via the Reichs-Kredit-Gesellschaft, the amount of the invoice due them for the goods delivered. The fees charged by Hisma and Rowak are supposed to be from 3 to 4 percent of the amount of the invoice.

On June 20, 1939, the farms of the Agro S.A., Seville, which are located south and southwest of Seville, were visited.

Jaime Pérez farm—Professor Guyot's experiments in raising agricultural products

Professor Guyot is engaged in growing seeds for soybeans, corn, Capelli wheat, fodder plants (lucerne), China grass, cotton, castor oil plants, and medicinal herbs. The experiments are carried out both on artificially irrigated soil, which makes up a large part of the farming area in Spain, and on unirrigated soil and are directed toward raising the plant types which are best adapted to each manner of cultivation. Professor Guyot was hopeful with regard to his work.

The advantages to be obtained from the use of proper seeds were evident from two adjacent fields of corn, one planted with the usual Spanish corn and the other with specially raised seeds. Spanish agriculture, in which extensive cultivation is generally employed, uses very little specially raised seed. A number of crops raised in Spain, such as wheat and corn, therefore show very pronounced signs of degeneration.

The Jaime Pérez farm, which belongs to the Agro and consists of about 200 hectares, is administered by a farmer from Bavaria, who had previously had a farm in Mexico. While Professor Guyot's plant experiments require subsidies, the farm makes a profit, obtained particularly from the sale of seed potatoes, which are marketed at a good price. Soybeans are also raised in considerable amounts on this farm with good results, and the newest machinery is employed. The plant residue is fed to milk cattle. The methods of cultivation and the special German machinery used on this farm are observed with interest by the Spanish landowners and serve to advertise German agricultural machinery.

The large Boyal farm

This is 1,200 hectares in size and has been leased for 20 years. The farm is managed by a German farmer who used to work in East Africa. Wheat, barley, and soybeans are the main crops. In addition, experiments are made in breeding cattle and hogs. The farm still needs to be subsidized for the present, but they count on being able to make a profit after the necessary investments have been made.

The Agro firm is also supposed to conclude cultivation contracts under the program for raising cotton for the Spanish textile industry. The Agro expects to be able to develop these two farms into entirely profitable undertakings, which should also be able to cover the expenses of the agricultural experiments from their surpluses.

On June 21, 1939, a visit was made to the cork factory of the firm Corchos zum Hingste S.A. in Fregenal, which is located in the middle of the main Spanish cork-producing area on the railroad to Huelva on the Atlantic Coast. The factory, which was closed down by its former owner, was bought by Sofindus, which possesses 90 percent of the shares. The corporate capital amounts to 3 million pesetas. The factory, which is concerned mainly with processing and sorting cork bark, has a storehouse of considerable size. The factory is under the management of a Spanish expert who speaks German. The commercial section is located in Seville. There seem to be considerable reserves in the inventory of the firm.

In the immediate vicinity of the cork factory are the loading platform and terminal station of the 14-kilometer-long cable railroad of the Nertobriga mines, which produce pyrites. The ore is loaded on railroad cars at the loading platform and sent by rail to Huelva. In the opinion of an expert, Engineer Wiese, this mine is a marginal undertaking because of these difficulties in transportation.

During the return trip to Seville through the Rio Tinto mining area, mining engineer Wiese gave a long report on the present situation of the Rio Tinto mines, which are in the hands of the London and Paris Rothschilds. The Rio Tinto mines are administered in London. Rio Tinto receives only 1 shilling per ton of the ore exports in foreign exchange; the remainder is paid for in pesetas, for which there is no possibility of transfer. The amounts frozen are said to have reached 25 million pesetas at the present time. Since the staff of experts working in Spain is paid in pounds sterling, and the expenses in pounds incurred in Spain, in addition to the sums necessary for the London administration, are larger than the proceeds in foreign exchange received from the exports, the interest of the Rothschilds in the mine has greatly declined. According to what a representative of the Spanish Government told me confidentially during the later negotiations, the Spanish Government has found that the flight of capital has been carried on by means of incorrect accounts in the exports of ores from the Rio Tinto mines. The Spanish Government was now considering whether and in what manner it can proceed against the Rio Tinto mines.

Wiese also spoke of the mercury mine at Almadén. The waste heaps there are still supposed to contain up to 40 percent mercury, in the opinion of experts. By means of the German method used in Wiesbaden, ore could be extracted from these remnants without danger to the workers, and a considerable increase in the total Spanish mercury production could thus be attained. This question was mentioned in the later negotiations with the Spanish delegation, and it was suggested that an investigation be made of whether, in spite of the cartelization of mercury production, it would not be possible to make use of the waste by means of the German method of extraction.

On June 23 the business office of Sofindus in Salamanca was visited and the extensive bookkeeping and statistical material there was studied. The chiefs of several of Sofindus' affiliates took part in the conference, so that it was possible to get direct information. There was particular discussion of the field of activity of the Nova S.A. Salamanca, which is conceived as a liaison office of German industrial groups with the planning office for the reconstruction of the Spanish economy as set up by Suances in the Ministry for Industry.

The following fields in particular are intended for the preparatory and intermediary activity of Nova, which is not to carry on transactions of its own:

1. Air armament
2. Army equipment
3. Communications system
4. Military economy duties
5. Increase of Spanish export to Germany
6. Investments and deliveries of machinery to Spain.

Among other things, Nova has carried on special negotiations with the Spanish Government on the setting up of a telephone network, police radio, and coastal radio. For this purpose the Reich Postal Ministry has sent Oberpostrat Frahm to Salamanca. The following information was obtained during a talk with Oberpostrat Frahm:

For the purpose of building up the Spanish radio network, it is intended to have four transmitters, which the German Reichspost agreed to deliver after Director Pflanze's visit to Spain. The project was submitted to the responsible Spanish ministries and it was resolved in advance to send two transmitters (Madrid transmitter and short-wave transmitter). As the delivery of the short-wave transmitter was said to be particularly urgent, one was dismounted at the Zeesen station last year but has still not been unpacked in Spain. Director Pflanze's second visit to Spain was made in September 1938, at which time it was decided to send two additional transmitters. They are to be paid for, according to negotiations with the Minister of the Interior (Serrano Suñer), who is entrusted with these questions, over a period of 20 years, with 4½ percent interest and a 1-percent, lump-sum bank commission for the credit. At the present time the credit is supposed to have been used to the extent of 1.4 million RM. The scope of the whole project was given by Sofindus as involving about 100 million RM. A mobile transmitter (value, 700,000 RM), which is still in Spain at the present time, is to be brought back to Germany, according to the representative of the Postal Ministry. According to Sofindus, a decision is supposed to have been made by German officials to the effect that the transmitter may, if necessary, be donated to the Spanish Government.

The firms under Sofindus are mainly concerned with obtaining raw materials for Germany, namely, wool, skins and hides, ores and metals, resin products, agricultural products, canned fish, etc. These firms have taken the place of the Spanish dealers and German firms which formerly arranged the purchases. These firms also represent most of the German business interests and act on instructions from the German supervisory offices which they advise.

The following firms were visited:

Compañía General de Lanas

(Corporate capital 2,100,000 pesetas, 90 percent of this with Sofindus) According to information from the manager, a considerable increase in Spanish production and Spanish exports to Germany is quite feasible. Considering the needs of Spanish industry, however, the prospects are uncertain. Although the prices are officially fixed, price conditions are extremely bad, since it is very common to evade price ceilings by means of differences in quality or quantity. The item entitled "inventory" in the balance sheet contains a considerable secret reserve.

Soc. Exportadora de Pieles

(Corporate capital 2,100,000 pesetas, 90 percent of this with Sofindus)

The manager of the company was of the opinion that it is possible for Germany to make more purchases of skins and hides in Spain than in the past.

It is noteworthy that the Italians have competed in the purchase of hides and that they have bought lots intended for purchase by Germany by bidding higher and have tried to unload these lots later on the world market in return for foreign exchange. After this was unsuccessful, they are supposed to have offered these lots on the Spanish market again. There are large reserves in the balance sheet.

Marion Transport Company

(Corporate capital 2,100,000 pesetas, 90 percent of this with Sofindus)

This company mainly serves to provide the necessary transportation within the Sofindus concern. It possesses 30 large trucks with a loading capacity of about 260 tons, which, however, because of a general Spanish prohibition, may not be driven with trailers; it also has about 33 private automobiles, part of them taken over from the stocks of the Condor Legion. Freight expenses of the Marion firm amount to about 24 or 25 pesetas, that is, 7.25 RM per ton-kilometer, and thus, according to the data of the firm itself, are 10 to 20 percent above the railroad charges. The manager of the company believes that the undertaking will also make profits in the future.

During the stay in Salamanca the remaining equipment of the Condor Legion was also inspected; this has been taken over for sale by Hisma, as trustee, and consists mainly of private automobiles and trucks—part of which, to judge from their appearance, still seem to be in rather good condition—as well as of equipment from army workshops and supplies from canteens. The trucks will be purchased by the Marion Company, whereas the private cars are partly to be sold in Spain and partly to be used by the Embassy, at its request.

On June 26 the Minerales (company dealing in ores) and the Montana (research company) in Bilbao were visited. In the opinion of the management of Montana, ore and metal production in Spain is definitely capable of development. The various mines, etc., are discussed in the expert opinion of Ministerial Counselor Arlt of the Mining Section of the Reich Economics Ministry.

The total impression of the Hisma and Sofindus organizations can be summarized to the effect that, with increased production, most of the affiliated firms can operate at a profit, insofar as Spanish exports to Germany can be expanded to the necessary degree. The fees charged by Hisma, which constitute an important source of its income, will be lost in the future, however, as the present clearing system of Rowak-Hisma is to be replaced, at the desire of the Spanish Government in particular, by a clearing system between German and Spanish Government offices. It should also be considered that competition with other foreign firms on the Spanish market will be more noticeable than before, so that for this reason also exact calculations and a decrease in overhead expenses will be necessary. Up to now about 25 million RM have been invested in the Sofindus firms. In the next three to four years it is planned, under the Sofindus program, to invest an additional sum of about 35 million RM. These new investments are to be made from the pesetas which the Spanish Government is to be induced to provide in the form of debt settlement over and above that now planned.

Under the conditions explained above most of the undertakings belonging to the Sofindus concern will probably be able to work successfully within the framework of normal German-Spanish commercial relations guided by Government committees.

WOHLTHAT

No. 810

136/73793

The Ambassador in Spain to the Foreign Ministry

Telegram

No. 657 of July 7   SAN SEBASTIÁN, July 7, 1939.
                                     Received July 7—10:15 p.m.

With reference to my telegram No. 642 of July 2.

For the State Secretary.

Attaché Kroeger called on me today in order to inform me that he has taken over the affairs of what was left of the Special Staff. He did not know of the agreement with the Propaganda Ministry mentioned in your telegram No. 424 of June 21 [1] and thought that he could remain here indefinitely. I have enlightened him.

I should appreciate your having the Propaganda Ministry send him instructions as soon as possible.

STOHRER

_____

[1] Not printed (136/73783).

No. 811

2946/576384

The Ambassador in Spain to the Foreign Ministry

TOP SECRET   SAN SEBASTIÁN, July 8, 1939
No. 926 g

With reference to instruction No. W 68 g Rs of January 20, 1939.[1]

Subject: Extension of the 5 million RM credit to include the Mauritania Mining Company in Tetuán.

Attention Counselor of Legation Sabath or his deputy.

After repeated oral and written representations to the Spanish Foreign Ministry, the latter has now informed the Embassy that the Spanish Government had agreed to permit the Mauritania Company in Tetuán to be supplied with machinery and materials up to 5 million RM in value under the same conditions as were earlier agreed on for deliveries to the five mining companies operating on the mainland. However, the Spanish Foreign Ministry points out explicitly that the granting of this extension cannot be utilized to increase deliveries to all six companies in excess of a total of five million RM, or to increase exports in order to pay for these deliveries.[2]

By direction:
S[TILLE?]

---

[1] Not printed (2946/576376–79).

[2] Unsigned marginal note: "Copy to Sociedad Financiera Industrial S. A., Salamanca."

[EDITORS' NOTE. In a discussion with Ciano on September 28, 1940 (F6/0404–09), of a possible role for Spain in the European war, Hitler delivered the following judgment on Germany's intervention in the Spanish Civil War:

"When the Civil War broke out in Spain, Germany supported Franco on what was for her situation at the time a very extensive scale. This support, moreover, had not been without risk. It had not been confined merely to the delivery of matériel, but volunteers had also been provided and many Germans and Italians had fallen in Spain. He did not wish to reckon this sacrifice of blood in economic terms but regarded it as an absolute gift to Spain.

"Economically, Germany had expended many hundreds of millions for Spain. He (the Führer) had taken the position at the time that the repayment of this debt should not be discussed during the war but must be taken up after Franco's victory. When Germany now requested payment of the 400 million Spanish Civil War debt, this was often represented by the Spaniards as a tactless mixing of economic and ideal considerations; as a German one found oneself appearing to the Spaniards almost like a Jew who wished to do business in the most sacred human values. Therefore, in all agreements with the Spaniards the position must be made clear in advance; if Germany was to provide grain, the question of compensation must be clarified at once.

"Italy and Germany had done a great deal for Spain in 1936. Italy had just been through her Abyssinian enterprise, and Germany was in the middle of her rearmament. Without the help of both countries there would be no Franco today."

Ciano replied that Mussolini shared Hitler's reservations about Spanish participation in the European war and added:

"Italy had not forgotten the experiences of the Spanish Civil War either. Franco had declared at that time that, if he received 12 transport or bombing planes, he would win the war in a few days. These 12 planes had grown into more than 1,000 planes, 6,000 dead, and 14 billion lire. With all their sympathy for Spain this had nevertheless given them pause, and the Duce feared that now also great sacrifices would be demanded of Germany and Italy without compensation. In addition it was to be feared that, after the pattern of the Spanish Civil War, the demands now put forward by Spain would be constantly increased in the further course of events. Therefore, caution was indicated. . . ."

The whole of the memorandum from which the above quotations are taken will be published in volume IX of this series.]

APPENDICES

APPENDICES

Appendix I

ORGANIZATION OF THE GERMAN FOREIGN MINISTRY SEPTEMBER 1936 [1]

THE REICH FOREIGN MINISTER

Baron von Neurath

THE STATE SECRETARY OF THE FOREIGN MINISTRY

Acting: Ministerialdirektor Dr. Dieckhoff

Protocol Department

Diplomatic corps in Berlin, foreign consuls in the German Reich, audiences with the Führer and Reich Chancellor, ceremonial, decorations:	Counselor of Legation Minister von Bülow-Schwante.
Internal German affairs (German Section):	Counselor of Legation Minister von Bülow-Schwante.

PERSONNEL AND BUDGET DEPARTMENT (PERS.)

Director of Department:	Ministerialdirektor Dr. Prüfer.
Deputy Director of Department:	Counselor of Legation Dr. Dienstmann.
Head of budget and financial affairs:	Counselor of Legation Schellert.
Special duties:	Counselor of Legation (unassigned) Schroetter.
Pers. H	Organization of the foreign service, training for the foreign service, personal data of higher officials, of honorary consuls, experts, etc., information center:	Counselor of Legation Dr. Mayr.
Pers. M	Personal data on other officials and employees, organization and efficiency of the working of the Ministry:	Counselor of Legation Dr. Schmidt-Rolke.
Pers. R	Preparation and general administration of the budget, and general questions relating thereto:	Counselor of Legation Kammler.
Pers. B	Salaries and wages, welfare and maintenance, travel and removal expenses of officials and employees of the foreign service and other persons:	Counselor of Legation Dr. Bischof.
Pers. D	Administration of funds for official requirements:	Counselor of Legation Dr. Hempel.

[1] This organization plan has been translated and condensed from a German Foreign Ministry organization circular of September 1936, filmed as serial 1780, frames 406764–78. A similar table of organization for Dec. 1, 1937, is printed in vol. I; for June 1, 1938, in vol. II; and for Feb. 15, 1939, in vol. IV.

Library: Dr. Holleck-Weithmann.
Political archives, historical section: Dr. Frauendienst.
Cipher and communications: Counselor Selchow.
Language services: Counselor Gautier.

POLITICAL DEPARTMENT (POL.)

Director of Department: Acting: Minister Baron von Weizsäcker.

A. European Section
Head: Minister Dr. Woermann

Pol. I	League of Nations, military questions, armaments, aviation, defense:	Counselor of Legation von Kamphoevener.
Pol. II	Western Europe (Great Britain, Ireland, British possessions—unless dealt with elsewhere—France—North Africa, Morocco, Tunis—Belgium, Netherlands, Switzerland, Luxembourg):	Counselor of Legation von Rintelen.
Pol. III	Southern Europe (Spain, Portugal, Vatican):	Counselor of Legation Dr. Dumont.
Pol. IV	Southeast Europe (Albania, Bulgaria, Greece, Italy, Libya, Yugoslavia, Austria, Rumania, Czechoslovakia, Hungary):	Counselor of Legation Dr. Heinburg.
Pol. V	Eastern Europe	
	(a) Poland, Danzig:	Counselor of Legation von Lieres und Wilkau.
	(b) Soviet Union:	Counselor of Legation Dr. Schliep.
Pol. VI	Scandinavia and bordering states (Denmark, Sweden, Norway, Iceland, Finland, Estonia, Latvia, Lithuania—Memel Territory):	Counselor of Legation Dr. von Grundherr.

B. Extra-European Section
Head: Minister Dr. von Erdmannsdorff

Pol. VII	Near and Middle East (Egypt, Ethiopia, Afghanistan, Arabia, Ceylon, Cyprus, Palestine, South Africa, Syria, Turkey, India, Iraq, Iran, Sudan):	Counselor of Legation Pilger.
Pol. VIII	East Asia and Australia (Japan, Japanese mandated territories, China, Manchukuo, Mongolia, French Indochina, Siam, Straits Settlements, Malay States, Netherlands East Indies, Philippines, Australia, New Zealand, South Sea territories):	Counselor of Legation Dr. Rohde.

Pol. IX	America	
	(a) North America (United States with possessions—except Philippines; Canada):	Counselor of Legation Leitner.
	(b) Central and South America, Cuba, Haiti, Dominican Republic:	Counselor of Legation Dr. Poensgen.
Pol. X	Colonial questions; Africa, except Union of South Africa; colonial policy:	Counselor of Legation Gunzert.

ECONOMIC POLICY DEPARTMENT (W)

Director of Department:	Ministerialdirektor Dr. Ritter.
Deputy Director of Department:	Counselor of Legation Benzler.
Directly subordinate to Director of Department:	
Leader of delegation for negotiation of commercial treaties:	Counselor of Embassy Dr. Hemmen.
W I General section for questions concerning economics and finance:	Counselor of Legation Dr. Knoll.
W II Western and Southern Europe—except Great Britain and Italy—	
France, including colonies, protectorates, and mandated territories, Portugal, including colonies, Spain, including colonies:	Counselor of Legation Sabath.
Belgium, including colonies and mandated territories, Luxembourg, Netherlands, including colonies, Switzerland:	Counselor of Legation Dr. Wingen.
W III Southeast Europe with Italy and Near East (Albania, Bulgaria, Greece, Italy with colonies, Yugoslavia, Austria, Rumania, Czechoslovakia, Hungary, Afghanistan, Egypt, Arabia, Ethiopia, Cyprus, Iraq, Iran, Palestine, Sudan, Turkey):	Counselor of Legation Dr. Clodius.
W IV Eastern Europe (Danzig, Estonia, Latvia, Lithuania, Memel, Poland, Soviet Russia):	Counselor of Legation Dr. Schnurre.
W V Northern Europe (Denmark, Finland, Iceland, Norway, Sweden); monopolies:	Counselor of Legation Dr. van Scherpenberg.
W VI Great Britain, Dominions and British possessions except Canada (Australia, Ceylon, Great Britain, British India, Ireland, New Zealand, South Africa):	Counselor of Legation Rüter.
W VII East Asia (China, Japan, Manchukuo, Siam):	Counselor of Legation Dr. Voss.

W VIII	America	
	(a) North America including Canada and Mexico (Canada, Cuba, Dominican Republic, Haiti, Liberia, Mexico, United States, also trade promotion):	Counselor of Legation Dr. Davidsen.
	(b) South America including Central America (Argentina, Bolivia, Brazil, Chile, Colombia, Costa Rica, Ecuador, Guatemala, Honduras, Nicaragua, Panama, Paraguay, Peru, Salvador, Uruguay, Venezuela):	Counselor of Legation Fricke.
W IX	Shipping:	Counselor of Legation Bleyert.
W X	Reich Office for Foreign Trade (economic news and information service; chambers of commerce abroad):	Counselor of Legation Dr. Bozenick.

LEGAL DEPARTMENT (R)

Director of Department:		Ministerialdirektor Dr. Gaus.
Deputy Director of Department:		Counselor of Legation Dr. Barandon.
R I	International law, cooperation in conclusion of treaties:	Counselor of Legation Albrecht.
R II	Trade treaties and concessions. International traffic law except international motor vehicle traffic. Extraterritorial rights. Customs matters affecting German and foreign diplomats. Taxation laws:	Counselor of Legation Busch.
R III	Nationality. Constitutional and administrative law. Ecclesiastical law. Penal law:	Counselor of Legation Siedler.
R IV	Compulsory military service. Compulsory labor service:	Consul (unassigned) Dr. Sethe.
R V	Labor law. International aspects of German Labor Front and the Strength through Joy organization. International Labor Office:	Counselor of Legation Rödiger.
R VI	Consular jurisdiction in matters of civil law and lawsuits. International legal protection and legal aid in civil matters. International private law:	Secretary of Legation von Haeften.

CULTURAL POLICY DEPARTMENT (KULT.)

Director of Department:		Minister Dr. Stieve.
Deputy Director of Department:		Counselor of Legation Dr. von Twardowski.
Kult. A	Position of German racial groups abroad and of minorities in the Reich:	Counselor of Legation Langmann.

Kult. B	Economic questions relating to Germanization:	Counselor of Legation Dr. Schwager.
Kult. E	Emigration and repatriation. Settling abroad. Germanism in Russia. Inquiries abroad about Reich Germans and foreign nationals:	Counselor of Legation Dr. Kundt.
Kult. W	General cultural policy. Scientific relations with foreign countries:	Counselor of Legation Dr. Roth.
Kult. S	German educational system abroad. Youth movement:	Counselor of Legation Dr. Böhme.
Kult. H	Administration of funds of department:	Counselor of Legation Dr. Roth.

PRESS DEPARTMENT (P)

Director of Department:	Minister Aschmann.
Deputy Director of Department:	Counselor of Legation Wolf.
Southeast Europe (Albania, Bulgaria, Greece, Yugoslavia, Austria, Rumania, Czechoslovakia, Hungary); German minorities:	Counselor of Legation Wolf.
Western Europe—except Netherlands and Switzerland (Belgium and colonies, France and colonies, Italy, Luxembourg, Morocco, Vatican, League of Nations), also *Deutsche diplomatisch-politische Korrespondenz:*	Counselor of Legation Braun von Stumm.
East and Near East (Baltic States—Estonia, Latvia, Lithuania—Danzig, Poland, Soviet Russia, Egypt, Ethiopia, Afghanistan, Iraq, Iran, Palestine, Syria, Turkey):	Consul (unassigned) Dr. Schönberg.
England with Dominions, protectorates and colonies, Portugal, Spain, United States of America, Central and South America:	Secretary of Legation von Strempel.
Scandinavia (Denmark, Iceland, Norway, Sweden, Finland):	Secretary of Legation Dr. Schlemann.
Far East, also Netherlands and Switzerland (China, Japan, Siam, India, Netherlands Indies, Netherlands, Switzerland); currency matters:	Counselor of Legation (unassigned) Dr. Katzenberger.
Reporting on the press:	Dr. Schacht.

Appendix II

LIST OF GERMAN FILES USED

The following table identifies the German file from which each document has been derived. The documents of the Foreign Ministry were bound into volumes by the Germans. The documents in these volumes have been microfilmed, and each film of a file has been identified by a film serial number, while each page of the documents has been identified by a frame number stamped on the original at the time of filming. The documents published in this collection are identified by the film serial number and frame numbers in the upper left-hand corner of each document. By reference to the following table of film serial numbers the location in the German Foreign Ministry archives of the copy of the document used in this publication may be determined.

Film Serial Numbers	German Title of File
33	Reich Foreign Minister: Memoranda on Visits of Foreign Statesmen.
43	*Dienststelle Ribbentrop:* Confidential Reports.
47	*Pol. geheim:* Spain.
54	State Secretary: Memoranda on Visits of Non-Diplomatic Personages.
100	German Embassy in Italy: Mackensen's Papers.
109	State Secretary: Anglo-Italian Relations.
136	State Secretary: German-Spanish Relations.
137	Under State Secretary: Spain.
139	State Secretary: Czechoslovakia.
168	Under State Secretary: Spain.
307	Under State Secretary: Non-Intervention.
309	Under State Secretary: Non-Intervention.
322	Economic Policy Department: Wiehl, Spain.
332	Economic Policy Department: Clodius, Spain.
336	Economic Policy Department: Clodius, Spain.
395	State Secretary: Memoranda on Visits of Diplomats.
424	State Secretary: Non-Intervention Committee.
428	State Secretary: Non-Intervention Committee.
435	State Secretary: Non-Intervention Committee.
442	State Secretary: Correspondence of State Secretary with German Diplomatic Representatives Abroad.
462	German Embassy in Spain: Secret Papers on Anti-Comintern Pact.
472	State Secretary: Correspondence of State Secretary with German Diplomatic Representatives Abroad.
485	State Secretary: Memoranda on Visits of Diplomats.
586	State Secretary: Non-Intervention Committee.
614	State Secretary: Visit of Göring to Spain, April–May 1939.
629	*Pol. III:* Spain, Political Relations of Spain with Germany.
630	*Pol. III:* Spain, Political Relations of Spain with Germany.
632	State Secretary: Non-Intervention Committee.
643	*Pol. III:* Spain, Political Relations of Spain with Germany.

Film Serial Numbers	German Title of File
650	*Pol. III:* Spain, Political Relations of Spain with Germany.
654	*Pol. III:* Spain, Internal Politics, Parliament and Parties.
660	*Pol. III:* Spain, Internal Politics, Parliament and Parties.
665	*Pol. III:* Spain, Internal Politics, Parliament and Parties.
666	*Pol. III:* Spain, Internal Politics, Parliament and Parties.
667	*Pol. III:* Spain, Control Plan, Non-Intervention Agreement, Arms Embargo.
682	*Pol. III:* Spain, Internal Politics, Parliament and Parties.
690	*Pol. III:* Spain, Internal Politics, Parliament and Parties.
696	*Pol. III:* Spain, German Diplomatic and Consular Representation in Spain.
701	German Embassy in Italy: Secret Papers.
860	State Secretary: German Foreign Minister's Visit to London.
1534	Reich Chancellery: Spain, 1935–1939.
1547	*Pol. IV:* Italy, Political Relations of Italy with Spain.
1557	*Pol. geheim:* Spain.
1568	*Pol. geheim:* Spain.
1573	*Pol. geheim:* Spain.
1588	*Pol. geheim:* Spain.
1606	*Pol. geheim:* Spain.
1629	*Pol. III:* Spanish Morocco, Internal Politics.
1758	*Pol. III:* Spain, Non-Intervention Agreement, Arms Embargo.
1759	*Pol. III:* Spain, Non-Intervention Agreement, Arms Embargo.
1810	German Embassy in the Soviet Union: Spain, Political Relations of Spain with the Soviet Union.
1819	German Embassy in France: Spain.
1877	State Secretary: Shelling of Cruiser *Leipzig.*
2128	German Embassy in Italy: Secret Papers.
2129	German Embassy in Italy: Secret Papers.
2130	German Embassy in Italy: Secret Papers.
2134	State Secretary: Memoranda on Visits of Diplomats.
2442	*Pol. II:* England, Political Relations of England with Spain.
2646	*Pol. III:* Spain, Internal Politics, Parliament and Parties.
2650	*Pol. III:* Spain, Non-Intervention Agreement, Arms Embargo, New Control Plan.
2655	German Embassy in France: Spain.
2661	*Pol. III:* Spain, Non-Intervention Agreement, Arms Embargo.
2662	Economic Policy Department: Clodius, Spain.
2666	Economic Policy Department: Wiehl, Spain.
2685	German Embassy in Spain: Secret Papers on Sudeten German Question and Central European Crisis.
2871	Political Department: Treaties, 1936–1944.
2929	State Secretary: Göring's Trip to Spain.
2937	German Legation in Portugal: Spain and the Spanish Civil War.
2938	Economic Policy Department: Spain, Industry, Mining.
2946	German Embassy in Spain: Secret Papers, Montana.
2948	German Embassy in Spain: Secret Papers, Condor Legion.
3162	*Pol. III:* Spain, Internal Politics, Parliament and Parties.
3174	*Pol. III:* Spain, Non-Intervention Agreement, Arms Embargo.
3176	Economic Policy Department: Clodius, Spain.
3204	Economic Policy Department: Wiehl, Spain.

*Film Serial
Numbers*   *German Title of File*

3205   Economic Policy Department: Treaties, Spain.
3206   German Embassy in France: Spain.
3207   German Embassy in Spain: Nationalist Uprising.
3242   Secretariat of the Foreign Minister: Spanish Non-Intervention Question up to the Case of the *Leipzig.*
3253   *Pol. III:* Spain, Non-Intervention Agreement, Arms Embargo.
3357   *Pol. III:* Spain, Non-Intervention Agreement, Arms Embargo.
3359   *Pol. II:* England, Political Relations of England with Spain.
3360   *Pol. III:* Spain, Non-Intervention Agreement, Arms Embargo, New Control Plan.
3361   *Pol. III:* Spain, Non-Intervention Agreement, Arms Embargo, New Control Plan.
3362   *Pol. III:* Spain, Non-Intervention Agreement, Arms Embargo, New Control Plan.
3363   *Pol. III:* Spain, Non-Intervention Agreement, Arms Embargo, New Control Plan.
3364   *Pol. III:* Spain, Non-Intervention Agreement, Arms Embargo, New Control Plan.
3366   *Pol. III:* Spain, Internal Politics, Parliament and Parties.
3367   Economic Policy Department: Spain, Industry, Mining.
3368   *Pol. IV:* Mediterranean (Nyon) Agreement.
3369   German Legation in Portugal: Non-Intervention Agreement, Arms Embargo.
3370   Economic Policy Department: Wiehl, Spain.
3371   German Legation in Portugal: Delivery of Arms to Spain.
3372   German Embassy in Spain: Non-Intervention Policy.
3373   *Pol. III:* Spain, Non-Intervention Agreement, Arms Embargo.
3374   *Pol. III:* Spain, Non-Intervention Agreement, Arms Embargo.
3376   German Embassy in Spain: Morocco.
3406   *Pol. II:* France, Political Relations of France with Germany.
3414   *Pol. III:* Spain, Internal Politics, Parliament and Parties.
3416   *Pol. III:* Spain, Non-Intervention Agreement, Arms Embargo.
4078   *Pol. III:* Holy See, Relations of the Holy See with Spain.
4445   German Embassy in Spain: Papers on Montana.
4446   *Pol. III:* Spain, Internal Politics, Parliament and Parties.
4793   *Ha. Pol. geheim:* Trade in War Matériel: Europe.
5194   German Embassy in Spain: Secret Papers.
5205   Cultural Policy Department: Treaties.
F 3, 6,   German Foreign Ministry Film of Files of the Reich Foreign Minister's Secretariat.
8, 14, 19

Appendix III

LIST OF PERSONS [1]

ALBA AND BERWICK, Duke of, Jacobo María del Pilar Carlos Manuel Fitz-James Stuart, agent of General Franco's government in Great Britain, 1937; Ambassador in Great Britain, 1939.

ALVAREZ DEL VAYO, Julio, Spanish Socialist leader and journalist; chief political commissioner of Republican Army, 1937; Foreign Minister, 1936–1937, 1938.

ASCHMANN, Dr. Gottfried, Minister, Director of the Press Department of the German Foreign Ministry, 1933–1939.

ATTLEE, Clement Richard, British Labor M.P. since 1922; Leader of the Labor Party since 1935; Leader of the Opposition, 1935–1939.

ATTOLICO, Dr. Bernardo, Italian Ambassador in Germany, 1935–1940.

AZAÑA DÍAZ, Manuel, Spanish Republican leader; President of the Council of Ministers, February–May 1936; President of the Republic, May 1936.

BALDWIN, Stanley, Earl Baldwin of Bewdley, British Prime Minister, 1935–1937.

BASTIANINI, Giuseppe, Italian Under Secretary of State in the Italian Foreign Office, 1936–1943.

BENZLER, Felix, Counselor of Legation, Deputy Director of the Economic Policy Department of the German Foreign Ministry; Consul General at Amsterdam, 1937–1940.

BERNHARDT, Johannes, German merchant in the Spanish zone of Morocco; organizer and director of Hisma (*see* Editors' Note, pp. 1 ff.).

BETHKE, Friedrich, department head in the German Economics Ministry; director of Rowak (*see* Editors' Note, pp. 1 ff.).

BISMARCK, Otto Christian, Prince von, Counselor of the German Embassy in Great Britain, 1928–1936; Deputy Director of the Political Department of the Foreign Ministry, 1936–1939.

BLOMBERG, Werner von, Field Marshal, German War Minister and Commander in Chief of the Wehrmacht, 1935–1938.

BLUM, Léon, President of the French Socialist Party, President of the Council of Ministers, June 1936–June 1937; Vice President of the Cabinet, June 1937–January 1938; President of the Council, March–April 1938.

BOHLE, Ernst Wilhelm, Gauleiter and Head of the Auslandsorganisation of the Nazi Party, 1933–1945; also State Secretary in the German Foreign Ministry, 1937–1941.

CABANELLAS, San Miguel, Spanish General, member and for a time president of original Junta of National Defense set up at Burgos, July 25, 1936.

CADOGAN, Sir Alexander, Deputy Under Secretary of State in the British Foreign Office, 1936; Permanent Under Secretary of State for Foreign Affairs, 1938–1946.

CANARIS, Wilhelm, German Admiral, in the Secret Intelligence Branch of the Reichswehr, 1934; later head of the Intelligence Service of the OKW.

CARLS, Rolf, Rear Admiral, Commander of German fleet off Spanish coast, 1936.

---

[1] The biographical details given relate principally to the period and subjects covered by the documents in this volume.

945

CHAMBERLAIN, Neville, British Conservative M.P., 1918–1940; leader of the Conservative Party; Prime Minister, 1937–1940.

CHAUTEMPS, Camille, President of Radical Socialist Group of the French Chamber; Minister of State in Blum cabinet, 1936–1937; President of the Council of Ministers, June 22, 1937–January 15, 1938, and January 18–March 10, 1938; Vice President of Council of Ministers and Minister of Coordination in Daladier cabinet, 1938–1939; Minister of State, 1939–1940.

CHILSTON, Viscount, Aretas Akers-Douglas, British Ambassador in the Soviet Union, 1933–1938.

CHILTON, Sir Henry Getty, British Ambassador in Spain, 1935–1938.

CHURCHILL, Winston Spencer, British Liberal and Conservative M.P. since 1900.

CIANO DI CORTELLAZZO, Count Galeazzo, son-in-law of Mussolini; Italian Foreign Minister, 1936–1943.

COMPANYS, Luis, Spanish Republican, leader of Catalonian Left, President of Catalonian Government (Generalidad), 1936–1939.

CORBIN, Charles, French Ambassador in Great Britain, 1933–1940.

COT, Pierre, French Radical Socialist Deputy from 1928; Minister for Air in Blum cabinet, 1936–1937, and in Chautemps cabinet, 1937–1938; Minister of Commerce, January–April 1938.

CRANBORNE, Viscount, Robert Arthur James Cecil, Parliamentary Under Secretary of State for Foreign Affairs in the British Foreign Office, 1935–1938.

DALADIER, Édouard, French Radical Socialist Deputy since 1919; Minister of National Defense, 1936–1938; President of the Council of Ministers and Minister of National Defense, April 1938–March 1940.

DELBOS, Yvon, French Radical Socialist Deputy since 1924; Foreign Minister in Blum cabinet, 1936–1937, and in two Chautemps cabinets, 1937–1938.

DIECKHOFF, Dr. Hans Heinrich, Director of the Political Department of the German Foreign Ministry, April–August 1936; Acting State Secretary, August 1936–April 1937; Ambassador in the United States, May 1937; was recalled to Berlin for consultation November 1938 and did not return to his post.

DIRKSEN, Dr. Herbert von, German Ambassador in Japan, 1933–1938, and in Great Britain, May 1938–August 1939.

DÖRNBERG, Alexander von, Secretary of Legation in Political Division I of the German Foreign Ministry, 1936; in the Embassy in Great Britain, 1937; in the Protocol Department of the Foreign Ministry, 1938; Counselor of Legation, 1938; Minister, 1939.

DUMONT, Dr. Karl, Counselor of Legation, head of Political Division III of the German Foreign Ministry, 1936–1937.

DU MOULIN-ECKART, Count, Counselor of the German Legation in Portugal; later in Political Division III of the Foreign Ministry.

EDEN, Anthony, British Conservative M.P. since 1923; Secretary of State for Foreign Affairs, 1935–1938.

ERDMANNSDORFF, Otto von, head of the Extra-European Section of the Political Department of the German Foreign Ministry, 1936–1937; Minister in Hungary, May 1937–July 1941.

FAUPEL, Wilhelm, Lieutenant General (Ret.), head of Ibero-Amerikanisches Institut; German Chargé d' Affaires in Spain, November 1936–February 1937; Ambassador to the Spanish Nationalist Government, February–September 1937.

FORSTER, Dr. D., Counselor of the German Embassy in France, 1936–1938.

FRANCO Y BAHAMONDE, Francisco, Spanish General, Chief of the General Staff, 1935; Chief of State, October 1, 1936.

FRANCO, Nicolás, brother of General Franco, at head of General State Secretariat (political department) of the Spanish Nationalist Government; later Ambassador in Portugal.

FRANÇOIS-PONCET, André, French Ambassador in Germany, 1931–1938; Ambassador in Italy, 1938–1940.

FUNCK, Baron von, Colonel (General Staff), Military Attaché of the German Embassy in Spain.

GAUS, Dr. Friedrich, Ministerialdirektor, Director of the Legal Department of the German Foreign Ministry.

GOEBBELS, Dr. Josef, German Minister of Propaganda, 1933–1945; Gauleiter of Berlin.

GÖRING, Hermann Wilhelm, Field Marshal, National Socialist member of the German Reichstag from 1928; President of the Reichstag from 1932; Minister President of Prussia and Reich Minister for Air from 1933; Commander in Chief of the Luftwaffe from 1935; Commissioner for the Four Year Plan, 1936.

GRANDI, Count Dino, Italian Ambassador in Great Britain, 1933–1939.

HALIFAX, Viscount, Edward Wood, British statesman; Lord Privy Seal, 1935–1937; Lord President of the Council, 1937–38; Secretary of State for Foreign Affairs, 1938–1940.

HASSELL, Ulrich von, German Ambassador in Italy, November 1932–February 1938.

HEBERLEIN, Dr. Erich, Counselor of the German Embassy to the Spanish Nationalist Government.

HEMMING, Francis, British official; secretary of the Economic Advisory Council; secretary of the Non-Intervention Committee.

HENDERSON, Sir Nevile, British Ambassador in Germany, 1937–1939.

HESS, Rudolf, German National Socialist leader, member of the Nazi Party from 1920; chairman of the Central Committee of the Party from 1932; Hitler's Deputy, 1933–1941; member of the Reichstag; Minister without Portfolio, 1933–1941; member of the Secret Cabinet Council, 1938–1941.

HESSE, Prince Philip of, German nobleman, son-in-law of the King of Italy, employed as a special envoy between Hitler and Mussolini.

HEYDEN-RYNSCH, Dr. Bernd Otto, Baron von der, Counselor of Legation, official in Political Division I of the German Foreign Ministry.

HITLER, Adolf, German National Socialist leader, Führer and Chancellor of the German Reich, 1933–1945.

HODGSON, Sir Robert, British diplomat, appointed agent to the Spanish Nationalist Government, November 1937.

HOYNINGEN-HUENE, Dr. Oswald, Baron von, German Minister in Portugal, 1934–1944.

HULL, Cordell, United States Secretary of State, 1933–1944.

JAGWITZ, Eberhard von, official of the Auslandsorganisation; leading figure in the organization of Rowak; Under State Secretary in the German Economics Ministry.

JORDANA, Count Francisco Gómez, General, President of the Junta Técnica, 1938; Vice President and Foreign Minister of the Spanish Nationalist Government, 1938–1939.

KEITEL, Wilhelm, General, Chief of the Wehrmachtsamt in the Reich War Ministry, 1935–1938; Chief of the OKW, 1938–1945.

KINDELAN DUANY, Alfredo, Lieutenant General, Commander of Spanish Nationalist Air Force in the Civil War; Minister for Air in the Nationalist Government of January 30, 1938.

KÖCHER, Dr. Otto Carl Albrecht, German Minister in Switzerland, 1937–1945.

KORDT, Dr. Erich, First Secretary of the German Embassy in Great Britain, 1936–1938; head of Ribbentrop's Secretariat (Büro RAM), 1938–1941.

KOTZE, Herr, Counselor of Legation on the staff of German Foreign Minister von Neurath.

KRAUEL, Dr. Wolfgang, German Consul at Geneva.

LAMMERS, Dr. Hans, State Secretary and Chief of the Reich Chancellery, 1934–1937; Reich Minister and Chief of the Reich Chancellery, 1937–1945; member and Executive Secretary of the Secret Cabinet Council, 1938–1945.

LANGENHEIM, Adolf P., German National Socialist Ortsgruppenleiter of Tetuán area of Spanish Morocco; a leading figure in early negotiations for German assistance to Franco (*see* Editors' Note, pp. 1 ff.).

LARGO CABALLERO, Francisco, Spanish Socialist and trade-union leader; President of the Council of Ministers, 1936–1937.

LAVAL, Pierre, French statesman, Senator, 1926–1940.

LEBRUN, Albert, President of the French Republic, 1932–1940.

LITVINOV, Maxim Maximovich, People's Commissar for Foreign Affairs of the Soviet Union, 1930–1939.

MACKENSEN, Hans Georg von, son of Field Marshal von Mackensen; German Minister in Hungary, 1933–1937; State Secretary in the Foreign Ministry, Berlin, 1937–1938; Ambassador in Italy, April 1938–September 1943.

MAGAZ Y PERS, Antonio, Marquis de, Spanish Nationalist Ambassador in Berlin 1937–1940.

MAGISTRATI, Count Massimo, Counselor of the Italian Embassy in Germany.

MAISKY, Ivan Mikhailovich, Soviet Ambassador in Great Britain, 1932–1943.

MARCH ORDINAS, Juan, Spanish industrialist with interests in many fields of the Spanish economy; deputy in the Cortes during the Republican period; supporter and large contributor to Franco's Nationalist movement.

MIAJA, José, Spanish General in charge of defense of Madrid, October 1936; Commander in Chief of Loyalist forces; participated in *coup d'état* of March 1939, which overthrew Negrín government and prepared capitulation.

MILCH, Erhard, General, German Secretary of State for Air, 1933–1945.

MOLA Y VIDAL, Emilio, Spanish Nationalist General; one of original members of Junta of National Defense; Commander of Nationalist northern armies; killed in airplane accident, June 3, 1937.

MOLOTOV, Vyacheslav Mikhailovich, chairman of the Council of People's Commissars of the Soviet Union, 1930–1941.

MORRISON, William Shepherd, British Conversative M.P.; Minister of Agriculture and Fisheries, 1936–1939; first chairman of the Non-Intervention Committee, September 1936.

MUSSOLINI, Benito, founder of the Italian Fascist Party; Head of the Government and Prime Minister, 1922; Commander of the Armed Forces, 1938.

NEGRÍN, Dr. Juan, Spanish Socialist leader; Minister of Finance, 1936; President of the Council of Ministers, 1937–1939; Minister of National Defense, 1938–1939.

NEURATH, Constantin, Baron von, German Foreign Minister, June 2, 1932–February 4, 1938; Reich Minister and President of the Secret Cabinet Council, 1938–1945.

NEWTON, Basil, Minister in British Embassy in Germany, 1935–1937; Minister in Czechoslovakia, 1937–1939.

OLIVEIRA SALAZAR, Antonio de, President of the Portuguese Council of Ministers since 1932; also Minister of Foreign Affairs and of War, 1936.

PERTH, Earl of, Sir Eric Drummond, British Ambassador in Italy, 1933–1939.

PÉTAIN, Henri Philippe, Marshal of France; Ambassador in Spain, 1939–1940.

PHIPPS, Sir Eric, British Ambassador in Germany, 1933–1937; in France, 1937–1939.

PLESSEN, Dr. Johann, Baron von, Counselor of the German Embassy in Italy.

PLYMOUTH, Earl of, Ivor Miles Windsor-Clive, British Parliamentary Under Secretary of State for Foreign Affairs, 1936–1939; chairman of the Non-Intervention Committee.

PRIETO, Indalecio, Spanish Socialist leader; Minister of Marine and Air in Largo Caballero cabinet, 1936–1937; Minister of National Defense in Negrín cabinet, 1937–1938.

PRIMO DE RIVERA, José Antonio, Spanish Rightist leader, son of General Miguel Primo de Rivera (Dictator of Spain 1923–1930); founder of Falange, 1932; in prison at Alicante at outbreak of Civil War; executed by Loyalists, November 20, 1936.

QUEIPO DE LLANO, Gonzalo, Spanish General; Inspector General of Carabineers at beginning of Civil War; occupied Seville for Nationalists; in charge of operations in Andalusia.

QUIÑONES DE LEÓN, José María, Spanish Ambassador in France during last years of monarchy; agent of Nationalist Government.

RAEDER, Erich, Admiral, Commander in Chief of German Navy, 1935–1943.

RIBBENTROP, Joachim von, German National Socialist leader; Ambassador-at-large, 1935–1938; Ambassador in Great Britain, 1936–1938; Reich Foreign Minister, February 4, 1938–1945.

RICHTHOFEN, Baron von, German General, Chief of Staff, Condor Legion, January 1937–October 1938; Commander, Condor Legion, November 1, 1938.

RINTELEN, Emil von, Counselor of Legation, Head of Political Division II in the German Foreign Ministry.

RÍOS, Fernando de los, Spanish Republican leader; Ambassador in the United States, 1936–1939.

RIPKEN, Dr., Secretary of Legation; official of the Economic Policy Department of the German Foreign Ministry.

RITTER, Dr. Karl, Ministerialdirektor in the German Foreign Ministry, 1924–1937; Ambassador in Brazil, 1937–1938; Ambassador on special assignment in the Foreign Ministry, 1938–1945.

ROOSEVELT, Franklin Delano, President of the United States, March 4, 1933–April 12, 1945.

SABATH, Hermann Friedrich, Counselor of Legation, an official of the Economic Policy Department of the German Foreign Ministry.

SANGRONIZ Y CASTRO, José Antonio de, Marquis de Desio, Chef de Cabinet in the Spanish Nationalist Ministry of Foreign Affairs; later Ambassador in France and in Italy.

SCHACHT, Dr. Hjalmar, President of the German Reichsbank, 1933–1939; Minister of Economics, 1934–1937.

SCHMIDT, Dr. Paul, Director of the Press Department of the German Foreign Ministry, 1939–1945.

SCHWENDEMANN, Dr. Karl, Counselor in the German Embassy in Spain at outbreak of Civil War; later head of Political Division IIIa (Spain and Portugal) in the Foreign Ministry.

SELZAM, Dr. Eduard von, Secretary of Legation and Press Attaché in the German Embassy in Great Britain.

SCHULENBURG, Friedrich Werner, Count von der, German Ambassador in the Soviet Union, October 1934–June 1941.

SERRANO, SUÑER, Ramôn, brother-in-law of General Franco, lawyer; Minister of Interior, Press, and Propaganda in the Spanish Nationalist Government of January 30, 1938.

SPERRLE, Hugo, German General of Aviation, Commander of the Condor Legion, November 6, 1936–October 31, 1937.

STALIN, Josef Vissarionovich, General Secretary of the Central Committee of the Communist Party of the Soviet Union, member of the Politburo and Orgburo since 1922.

STOHRER, Dr. Eberhard von, German Ambassador in Spain, September 1937–January 1943.

SUANCES Y FERNÁNDEZ, Juan, Minister of Industry and Commerce in the Spanish Nationalist Government.

VEITH, General, in command of the German air force in Spain.

VIOLA DI CAMPALTO, Count Guido, Italian Ambassador to the Spanish Nationalist Government, 1937–1939.

VOELCKERS, Hans Hermann, Counselor of the German Embassy in Spain, 1933–1936, and Chargé d'Affaires, April–November 1936.

VOLKMANN, Hellmuth, German General of Aviation, Commander of the Condor Legion, November 1, 1937–November 1, 1938.

WARLIMONT, Walter, German General, on special mission in Spain, July–December 1936; later Deputy Chief of the Operations Staff in the War Ministry and Supreme Headquarters of the Wehrmacht.

WEIZSÄCKER, Ernst, Baron von, Director of the Political Department of the German Foreign Ministry, 1936–1938; State Secretary, 1938–1943.

WELCZECK, Johannes, Count von, German Ambassador in Spain, 1926–1936; Ambassador in France, April 1936–September 1939.

WIEHL, Emil Karl Josef, Director of the Economic Policy Department of the German Foreign Ministry, 1937.

WILBERG, Hellmuth, German General of Aviation, head of Sonderstab W in the War Ministry and in the Supreme Headquarters of the Wehrmacht.

WOERMANN, Dr. Ernst, official in the German Foreign Ministry, 1933–1936; Counselor of Embassy in Great Britain with the rank of Minister, 1936–1938; Ministerialdirektor and Director of the Political Department of the Foreign Ministry with the title of Under State Secretary, 1938–1943.

WOHLTHAT, Helmut, official of the German Economics Ministry; appointed by Göring to collaborate in the Four Year Plan, 1938; on economic mission in Spain, 1939.

WUCHER, Dr. Theodor, Ministerialdirektor in the German Ministry of Finance.

Appendix IV

LIST OF GERMAN ABBREVIATIONS[1]

AA, Auswärtiges Amt, German Foreign Ministry

AGK, Ausfuhrgemeinschaft für Kriegsgerät, Export Cartel for War Matériel

AO, Auslandsorganisation, Foreign Organization of the Nazi Party concerned with German nationals living abroad

DNB, Deutsches Nachrichtenbüro, German News Agency, owned by the Ministry of Propaganda

e.o., ex officio; where this precedes the file number, it indicates a draft for which there are no preceding papers (*see* **zu**)

g, geheim, secret

g Rs, geheime Reichssache, top secret

Ha Pol, Handelspolitik, Handelspolitische Abteilung, Economic Policy Department of the Foreign Ministry; renamed Wirtschaftspolitische Abteilung between March and June 1938

Kult., Kulturpolitische Abteilung, Cultural Policy Department of the Foreign Ministry

NSDAP, Nationalsozialistische Deutsche Arbeiterpartei, National Socialist German Workers' Party, the full title of the Nazi Party

OKH, Oberkommando des Heeres, High Command of the Army; Supreme Headquarters of the Army

OKM, Oberkommando der Kriegsmarine, Supreme Command of the Navy

OKW, Oberkommando der Wehrmacht, Supreme Command of the Wehrmacht; Supreme Headquarters of the Wehrmacht

Pol., Politische Abteilung, Political Department of the Foreign Ministry; subdivided according to geographical areas, each designated by a Roman numeral, e. g. Pol. IV (*see* appendix I)

Qu, Quirinal; thus "Rom (Qu)" in addresses to distinguish the German Embassy to the Kingdom of Italy from that to the Holy See

RAM, Reichsaussenminister, Reich Foreign Minister

RM, Reichsminister, Reich Minister; any member of the Reich Cabinet but in Foreign Ministry documents usually the Reich Foreign Minister; reichsmark

St.S., Staatssekretär, State Secretary; the Permanent Head of a Reich Ministry

U.St.S., Unterstaatssekretär, Under State Secretary

v., von

W, Wirtschaftspolitische Abteilung, Economic Policy Department of the Foreign Ministry

zu, to, in connection with; where this precedes the file number, it indicates that the previous papers on the subject have this file number.

---

[1] This list includes such German abbreviations as are found in the text of documents appearing in this volume. For an explanation of a number of other terms appearing in Foreign Ministry documents see vol. I, pp. 1215–1220, and vol. II, pp. 1061–1070.

951